FILM
WRITERS
GUIDE

Fifth Edition

COMPILED AND EDITED SUSAN AVALLONE

(FIRST EDITION BY KATE BALES)

LONE EAGLE PUBLISHING CO.
Los Angeles, California

FILM WRITERS GUIDE   Fifth Edition
Copyright © 1995 by Susan Avallone

LONE EAGLE PUBLISHING CO.
2337 Roscomare Road, Suite Nine
Los Angeles, CA 90077-1851
310/471-8066

Printed in the United States of America

Cover design by Heidi Frieder
Logo Art by Liz and Frank Ridenour

This book was entirely typeset using an Apple Quadra 950, New Gen Turbo
Printer, Microsoft Word and Aldus Pagemaker.

Printed by McNaughton & Gunn, Saline, Michigan 48176
Printed entirely on recycled paper.

ISBN: 0-943728-68-1
ISSN 0894-864X

NOTE: We have made every reasonable effort to ensure that the information
contained herein is as accurate as possible. However, errors and omissions are sure
to occur and are unintentional. We would appreciate your notifying us of any
which you may find.

Lone Eagle Publishing is a division of Lone Eagle Productions, Inc.

LONE EAGLE PUBLISHING STAFF

Publishers	Joan V. Singleton
	Ralph S. Singleton
VP - Editorial	Bethann Wetzel
Customer Service	Douglas Deacon
Art Director	Heidi Frieder
Computer Consultant	Clive McKay

LETTER FROM THE PUBLISHERS

In a perfect world, a producer looking for that next big hit would simply contract the writer of last year's big hit, provide him or her a cushy working environment and wait for the "hits" to keep on rolling out. Well, as we all know, it's simply not that easy. Many writers have dry spells between hits; some have only one hit, and a lot of near-misses; and for some, that hit is the first one hot off the laserprinter.

So, how do producers "pick-a-hit" in the sea of screenplays that are offered to them by everyone from the waiter at their favorite restaurant to the best-known agents in town? Well, to paraphrase the late John Houseman in that oft-quoted commercial, "They do it the old-fashioned way . . . they *research* it." And, we are bold enough to suggest that one of the first places those savvy producers turn to is our FILM WRITERS GUIDE.

Editor Susan Avallone has made the trip through the treacherous jungle of "finding the next hit" that much more navigable by doing the research for you. She has listed the unproduced screenplays—now all you have to do is read them (and option them and produce them and hope they make money). Still a tough task, but if it were that easy, everybody would be a film producer (No, we mean *everybody*—not just everybody in L.A.)

Not to overlook the other important features of this book that, by now you have come to expect—FILM WRITERS GUIDE still earns its marks for impeccable research, credits for cable features, cable miniseries, feature-length documentaries, animated features, stageplays as well as, of course, feature films. Browsing through the new "Notable Writers of the Past" section may evoke a tear or two as we remember some of the late greats.

Now in its Fifth Edition, FILM WRITERS GUIDE has earned its place among the treasured research books of our industry. Our thanks to you for letting us know what you need and want in terms of research on screenwriters.

For all of you who are convinced that in the beginning there was "the word", take heart and enjoy browsing through these pages. Then start reading some screenplays. Who knows what might happen. Let us know. We love hearing success stories.

Happy reading!

Joan V. Singleton and Ralph S. Singleton
Publishers

TABLE OF CONTENTS

INTRODUCTION

Each year seems to bring a big change for the book. This time we've finally added the NOTABLE WRITERS OF THE PAST section; the number of writers who have died since the first edition of the book was sadly becoming so great that we needed to put back in all that information. Further research will make this a more comprehensive section in future editions. It took on a personal meaning this year, and I'd like to dedicate this section to my dear family friend and a great writer, Robert Bloch.

The other big change, for me at least, is my own listing being added. I've been writing forever, but felt I couldn't join the ranks until I got an agent and a writing job. A Hollywood "thank you, you're a beautiful human being" (but I really mean it) to Lisa Helsing for taking me on, and Adeena Karseboom and Raffaella DeLaurentis for giving me a shot. Additional thanks to Cari-Esta Albert for being a fan and a friend, when both are greatly needed.

As always, a big thanks to all my development buddies who helped me ferret out information on projects and writers. I will continue to bug you, until the end of time, or the run of this book, whichever comes first. The agency information, unfortunately, continues to be hit or miss, no matter how hard we try. Some agencies have extremely helpful and hard-working assistants whom we're sure will go on to successful careers and then there are others . . . well, we don't want to talk about them. We do a little better each year as people get more accustomed to seeing the book around the office, but we will continue to urge writers to contact us directly to make sure we've got you covered.

Many thanks to my compelling interview subjects, the reason I take on the mountain of work that is the rest of the book (it's cheaper and more fun than paying for a screenwriting course): Scott Alexander and Larry Karaszewski, Jane Anderson, George Gallo and Robin Swicord. And thanks as well to those who helped me reach them: Dan Jinks, Mike Petzold, and Jonathan Westover. Much appreciation to my brother David for spending countless hours transcribing countless hours.

It was great to get up-to-the-minute information on British writers from Jack Lechner, but it's even better to have him return triumphant to the states—welcome back and congratulations, you're now the New York correspondent! (If anyone is thinking of moving to the U.K. and would like to be my new supplier, just let me know.) Thanks to Joan Singleton for appreciating the difference between a book and a good book; and to Bethann Wetzel for making this easier every year. Super thanks to Cristi Limm for holding down the fort, a shoulder to cry on, and countless other cliches that apply.

And of course, a super-enormous smooch to my husband Carr D'Angelo for numerous years of riding the emotional rollercoaster otherwise known as being married to a writer. Maybe next year in your honor I'll start a section on "writer support" for all those persons-behind-the-person that none of us could do a draft (or twenty) without. Better yet, can I take you to a movie?

Susan Avallone

Susan Avallone

KEY TO ABBREVIATIONS

(CTF) = **CABLE TELEFEATURE**
Motion pictures made for cable television with an on-air running time of 1 to 4 hours.

(CMS) = **CABLE MINISERIES**
Motion pictures made for cable television with an on-air running time of 4 hours or more.

(FD) = **FEATURE DOCUMENTARY**
Documentary films made for theatrical distribution of feature length (1 or more hours).

(CTD) = **CABLE TELEVISION DOCUMENTARY**
Documentary films made for cable television of feature length (1 or more hours).

(SHORT) = **SHORT FILM**
Films under 1 hour that were released theatrically, aired on cable television, or screened at a festival.

(AF) = **ANIMATED FEATURE**

(P) = **STAGEPLAY**

KEY TO SYMBOLS

* = denotes membership in the Writers Guild of America

★ = after a film title denotes an Academy Award nomination

★★ = after a film title denotes an Academy Award win

† = (in Index listing only) denotes deceased writer

S = (in Index listing only) denotes unproduced screenplay

HOW TO USE THIS BOOK

The main purpose of this book is to provide an easy, practical and comprehensive reference to screenwriters and their work. While we do not editorialize in the listings, we continue to emphasize professionals who are currently active in the industry (i.e. have movies in production or development, have material optioned, have been produced in other areas such as television or stageplays.)

Among our features are:

* An alphabetical listing of writers by name and a rundown of their credits by year, followed by their unproduced screenplays that are known to us or have been chosen by the writer or agent.

* *DIALOGUE*, a special section highlighting screenwriters, representing a cross-section of writers with different specialities and experiences. These interviews are conducted by the editor especially for this book.

* *NOTABLE WRITERS OF THE PAST*, an alphabetical listing of deceased writers by name and a rundown of their credits by year. This is not a comprehensive list, it mostly covers writers who appeared in previous editions of this book, and will be expanded in future editions.

* A cross-referenced index to film titles in alphabetical order followed by the names of their writers.

* Academy Award nominees and winners are listed among the writers as well as in a separate index by year.

Here are some tips on how to make your way through this treasure trove of information:

WRITERS: Included are feature film titles produced and unproduced, cable features and miniseries, stageplays and short films. As the focus of this directory is the feature film world, network television credits are not listed, though there is a sampling of cable television credits, as some of those films are distributed theatrically in the U.S. and abroad. Lone Eagle also publishes **TELEVISION WRITERS GUIDE**, edited by Lynne Naylor, which contains *only television credits*. That book can be used in conjunction with **FILM WRITERS GUIDE** to provide more comprehensive information on a working writer.

Our focus is on English-language writers, though there are some foreign writers included, particularly if they've won an Academy Award, or have worked or are working on English-language films. Many foreign writers are also directors and are more often hired to direct than to write English-language features, therefore we advise looking for those individuals in Michael Singer's **FILM DIRECTORS GUIDE** [Lone Eagle.]

When a writer has both scripted and directed a project, it is so indicated. Short films are included because for many beginning writers their short film is their calling card and occasionally these become feature-length scripts. Likewise, a selection of stageplays are listed as they too are often submitted to producers and studios as writing samples or are optioned for features or television. When the play is a musical, its inclusion indicates that the writer is the one responsible for the book. If the play also exists as a screenplay by the playwright, that is indicated.

PSEUDONYMS: Pseudonyms are a researcher's nightmare, and we try to catch them all, but certainly some clever ones slip through. If a writer's pseudonym was deciphered, we'll direct you from the pseudonym to the writer, as well as list under that writer the name used for that credit. It's a sticky business, and though we'd like to provide the true writer's name for each feature, we have honored some writers' personal requests to keep a credit off their list—but only if they took a pseudonym for that credit.

CONTACT INFORMATION: This is surely the most difficult aspect of this book, as the information changes on a daily basis. We've provided as many contacts for the writers listed as we could find, whether that is an agent or manager, or a home address and phone number. Those that are Writers Guild of America members are noted (an asterisk follows a guild member's name). If WGA is listed as the contact, that means that at the time we went to press either the WGA had no contact information or the writer had left the agency that WGA had listed for them. You can contact writers by writing to them care of the WGA (the address is in the back of this book). We've also noted Directors Guild or Screen Actors Guild members as an alternate route to contact a director or actor who has written for the screen.

When an agency is listed, we do not include a particular agent's name because many agencies expressed their policy that each writer is really a client of all the agents at that agency. The people who answer the phone at any agency should be able to direct you to the proper contact person.

CREDITS: Both Story and Adaptation credits are included, however, for the sake of brevity, the story credit is not indicated if the writer also has screenplay credit. A typical example: Michael Mahern has shared screenplay credit on *MOBSTERS* with Nicholas Kazan, but his sole story credit is not indicated. If you come across a writer with sole story credit and want to discover who got screenplay credit, please consult the index for the other writers.

The potential mess of including *uncredited* work is more than we are willing to bear. It's common knowledge that often a legion of unnamed writers have worked on any given film release, but we have adopted the policy of only listing those writers that are credited on the film. Agents and writers will certainly talk about who *really* wrote what, but we must leave that to them.

SCREENPLAYS: This section means different things for different titles: the listings include screenplays that are available, in development, or actually in production or post-production. Since writing credits during production are unofficial, many movies that were not released by the time we went to press are listed as screenplays. For projects that several writers have worked on, the title may appear as a screenplay under each of them, but without referencing each other since they usually work independently. When the movie is released, the credit will go only to the writer(s) who receives screen credit and any other listings will be removed. We try to make the list of screenplays comprehensive, but in this section titles are removed or added at the individual writer's request.

The production companies or studios that have optioned screenplays are not featured, as this would be impossible to keep up-to-date, with projects constantly going into turnaround and changing hands. If a company appears in parentheses after a title, this means that the project is either in pre-production, production, or post-production; it can also mean that the film is completed but we are not sure who will be receiving screen credit.

INDEX: It should be noted that there are many films from different years with the same title. Wherever these examples were found, the year has been added in parentheses to distinguish the films; it is also indicated if a screenplay with the same title as a released film is a remake of that film. The same codes are used as in the body of the book (P for stageplay, etc.) When a film was written by a deceased writer, that writer's name is followed by a "†."

★★★

DIALOGUE

Lynn Houston

JANE ANDERSON

J ANE ANDERSON IS NO LONGER ACTING IN OTHER PEOPLE'S PLAYS, BUT IS still writing her own, while maintaining a rising career as a screen-writer. For her outrageous satire on the media, THE POSITIVELY TRUE ADVENTURES OF THE ALLEGED TEXAS CHEERLEADER-MURDERING MOM, she received an Emmy and the Writers Guild award for best television movie. And her sweet romantic comedy, IT COULD HAPPEN TO YOU, was greatly enjoyed by audiences and critics, except for the title, a late substitute for Anderson's better, "Cop Gives Waitress $2 Million Tip." Due out in 1995 is her adaptation of the best-seller, HOW TO MAKE AN AMERICAN QUILT by Whitney Otto. Anderson specializes in finding the drama and point of view in a true story, and we can expect that from her next project about an Avon lady in the Amazon.

SUSAN AVALLONE: It seems you're doing an equal amount of movie and theater writing these days. How do these compare?

JANE ANDERSON: When a play is bad, the experience is insufferable. When a movie is bad, there's always something to keep you entertained—you can check out the scenery or the special effects or the actor's biceps, or stroll up the aisle to go fetch yourself another bag of popcorn. Theater is like going out on a date—it's one-on-one, you can't walk out. You have an obligation to give something back to the actors. When you watch a movie, the experience is more passive, unless it's a brilliant film; then, you're right there.

Some plays are getting more visual, more imaginative in their staging, maybe for that reason.

Maybe, but there's a danger now of writers and directors trying to make plays resemble movies with lots of quick-cut scenes that keep the poor backstage crew running around like crazed chickens. The elegance of theater is that the language more than the pictures take us on the journey. Shakespeare would throw a character out on the stage who could paint a whole world with a few gorgeous stanzas. I love going back to play writing after I've written a film. It's a great luxury to play with words, let my characters go blah, blah, blah. But then I love making the switch back to screenwriting where I can become a picture-painter. They're both valid art forms. Some people consider screenwriting and television writing "unliterary." There's this false ranking of who's the worthiest kind of writer. I guess that poets would be at the top of the pyramid, then novelists, then playwrights, then film writers, and of course, the lowest of the low, staff writers for sitcoms—or is it the monologue writers for late-night? This is ridiculous, of course. All these writers have a special discipline; all of them still sweat blood.

How did you feel about the title change for IT COULD HAPPEN TO YOU from "Cop Gives Waitress $2 Million Tip," a much better title?

It killed me the way it was revealed to me, I found out on Easter Sunday when I opened the *L.A. Times Calendar* section. If they had found another title with just as much personality in it I would have been happy, but IT COULD HAPPEN TO YOU? What's that? Even the people who've seen the movie can't remember what it's called. But I did get some rather sweet revenge when Siskel & Ebert devoted half their review to scolding the studio for changing the title. Almost all the critics did. What a hoot.

On HOW TO MAKE AN AMERICAN QUILT, the marketing department was thinking about changing the title before we even got a cast. Apparently they went out on the street and said to people, "Here's a title, what does it mean to you?" And some people said, "Oh, is

> *"The joy of writing for me is that I get to be anybody in the world. I get to learn things I never knew before. I get out of myself."*
> —*Jane Anderson*

that about the AIDS quilt?" So of course, the marketing people freaked out. It's ridiculous. What if, a year ago, marketing did a poll, asked people, "What does FORREST GUMP say to you?" What are people supposed to say, "I dunno, a weird group of trees?" The problem is that a lot of marketing people never see films the way regular folk do. They go to special screenings and they forget that the rest of us sit in movie theaters and watch previews. It's not the title that clues you into a film, it's what you see in the trailer.

"How to Make an American Quilt" is such a beloved book. Do you feel there are some books that should be left alone?

Absolutely. Certain books should stay books because their brilliance is in the prose, not the story. What surprises me is that a lot of established authors don't feel their book is a success until it's been turned into a movie. I talked about that pyramid before—poet, novelist, etc.,—well this is the reverse of that. First you write the book, then it becomes a movie, then a TV series . . . then what, the cartoon?

My mother had given me "How to Make an American Quilt" to read one summer. She has great taste in writing. I read the book while I was rehearsing a play and when I came back I got a call from Amblin about adapting it and I jumped at it. I had no idea how I'd make it into a movie, but I so loved what the book had to say that I took the job on a wing and a prayer and hoped that somehow I could solve it. It took me several weeks to get over my awe of Whitney Otto's writing, and to get into the business of my own writing.

Adapting a book is almost like an acting exercise. You start living with the other writer's voice and characters until they're a part of your own. It got to be that I'd call Whitney up and say, "I need to add this new scene for one of your characters, does this sound right?" And she'd say, "Yeah, as a matter of fact I once thought about writing that but the novel was getting too long." We'd have long talks about the characters as if they were people we both had known for years, "Oh yeah, Glady Joe was always a little bit odd." It's been a treat schmoozing with the novelist. It's been a collaboration of great respect.

Tell me about your background. Many playwrights start in college.

Well, I dropped out of college. I went to Emerson in Boston, and Ohio University, but I went in the very early seventies when all that lousy alternative education was going on. I went to New York to become an actress, so I consider New York my finishing school. I was in David Mamet's first big hit in New York, SEXUAL PERVERSITY IN CHICAGO, with F. Murray Abraham and Peter Reigert. I was really green, I was 23. A year ago I saw an article in the *New York Times* about Mamet's women and I finally realized why he cast me. It was because when I was 23 I was completely and utterly cut off from my emotions!

3

I learned how to write by being in that play, and I owe a lot to that experience and to his writing. The play had been done in Chicago but it was still a very obscure piece, so there was no style set for it. It had never really been "solved" before. The process of rehearsing and decoding Mamet's words and what's underneath them was my greatest training for what goes into playwriting—how playwrights serve actors and actors serve the writer. I didn't know it at the time, but that's when I started learning how to write.

Did you start writing soon after that?

No. I knocked around as an actress for several years and then I became a comedienne. That's when I started writing my own material. I did Lily Tomlin types of characters, everything from a 500-pound woman named Miss Peggy to a male sperm donor, to an alcoholic 80-year-old Russian ballet teacher. I started to get some success and was brought out to Los Angeles to be in the BILLY CRYSTAL COMEDY HOUR, which only lasted a few weeks. I stayed and got a small acting part on THE FACTS OF LIFE. I'd already written a spec script for NIGHT COURT, and I said to the producers, "I want to write for your show." They said, "Give us a script," and then hired me a week later. What I learned was they had just fired four writers that week so it was all serendipity. I lasted about a year and a half and then I had to leave. I'm not fit to be a TV writer. It's a very specific discipline and I respect people who are in it, but it's not my kind of writing.

What finally led you to write a play?

I've always loved space travel, and while I was getting ready to go to work on FACTS OF LIFE, I turned the on TV and watched the Challenger blow up in front of my eyes. Live. I was so deeply disturbed, profoundly changed, by watching that and it made me question my mortality. The fact that anything can happen to a good person. Christa McAuliffe so touched me, I started writing another one-woman show around that, and then I realized it was too large a subject to make into a personal showcase, so it became my first play, DEFYING GRAVITY.

It seems like you have a history of being influenced by true stories.

I'm a voyeur. I think there are two kinds of writers. I think there are writers who report what's internal, like Eugene O'Neil. Biographical writers. Writers who go deeper and deeper into themselves and pull stories out of their psyche, or their family life. And then there's the other kind of writer—which I am—which has a fascination with the world around them. I call it "tourist-writing." The joy of writing for me is that I get to be anybody in the world. I get to learn things I never knew before. I get out of myself. Real stories are out there and I get attracted to what they are saying, but I don't consider myself a documentarian or a "movie of the week" writer.

The trick to writing real events is to find an artful spin on them. The trap of writing a real event is reporting, and falling in love with your research, so that your research gives the structure rather than what you want to say. With all the real-life stories I try to figure out: what do I want the audience to feel by the time the movie's done and they get up from their seats? What is it about? So I find the abstract concept and form the story around that. For THE POSITIVELY TRUE ADVENTURES OF THE ALLEGED TEXAS CHEERLEADER-MURDERING MOM it was "the media creates a monster." The "Challenger" play is about learning how to fly again. I'm a painter too, and my favorite way to paint is to go out with my journal and paint whatever I see. I need something out there to feed me.

With the CHEERLEADER movie you didn't get rights to the story—what was the reaction from those people?

They complained, but they still showed up at the opening and ate all the food. The thing that made it easy for me to write CHEERLEADER was that, except for the poor kids, everyone I wrote about were such heinous, sleazy people that I didn't much care what they thought. My only responsibility was to keep HBO from being sued.

In contrast to that, I feel very different about the subject of a script I've just finished, "Lady Icarus." It's about a woman pilot who's still alive. I met her and fell in love with who she is, and I felt deeply obligated to be respectful to her wishes for the script and to do her story justice. I worked like a dog on the script and when I finally sent it to her, she *hated* it! I had even sent a letter with the script, a kind of "How To Read a Screenplay That's Based on Your Life" instruction sheet. I tried to explain about dramatic license and the demands of structure and pace, but I think I overestimated her ability to be objective. She wrote back saying, "I wish the movie was like JONATHAN LIVINGSTON SEAGULL." I talked to another writer, and she said it's impossible to make friends with your subject and then write the script you want to write, because you have to put your personal stamp on it. You can rarely expect a good reaction, unless this person is very sophisticated. I was really naïve when I sent the script. Now I know.

Do you still go back and forth between plays and scripts? Does writing in one medium affect your writing in the other?

I slide back and forth. It's kind of like having two lovers. When one lover's giving you a lot of trouble and, you know, burps and starts to get on your nerves, you can go on to the other one.

> "*Theater is like going out on a date—it's one-on-one, you can't walk out. When you watch a movie, the experience is more passive, unless it's a brilliant film; then, you're right there.*"
> —*Jane Anderson*

Then when that one gives you problems and breaks your heart you can go to the other. Both media break your heart. Both break your back. Both are marvelous. I find it a healthy way to keep balance. That way if I have disappointments in either one I don't take it too seriously because I go to the next. It's also like visual artists. It used to be that artists would work in oil, watercolor and sculpture. Matisse, Picasso, Michaelangelo, they all worked in all mediums, and I think it's only now that people feel they have to have artists only do one thing and that's it. Working in different mediums keeps you loose. One only improves the craft of the other.

Do you do rewrite work as well?

I get offered a lot of rewrite work but I turn it all down. It's a personal policy. Too many good scripts are being thrown into the rewrite mill when the original writers are perfectly capable of doing the next drafts. I don't want to be a part of that process. That's not to say that there aren't some really rotten scripts floating around that need big help. But I still fault the studio for buying bad material from writers who haven't developed their craft yet and then expecting someone else to figure out how to make it work. Would you buy plans from one architect and then hire five more to change everything around? Would anyone want to live in a house built like that? Studios get into the bad habit of firing and hiring writers as a matter of course. With COP GIVES WAITRESS . . ., which I sold to TriStar as a spec script, they had me do one rewrite then dumped me from the project. Stephen Metcalfe was then hired on. He said to them, "Why did you fire this writer?" He stood up for my work and I owe him a lot because in his rewrite he honored what I did.

Were you happy with the final product?

Yeah. I think they did a lovely job.

There must be moments when a character is about to speak and you think they're going to say something different.

When I went to my first screening of IT COULD HAPPEN TO YOU, the first half of it, my stomach was in knots. I was torturing myself with, what was mine and what was theirs. But then when I heard the audience laughing, or saw people wiping their eyes, I relaxed. In the end, you can't make yourself crazy with the details. All you can really look at is: does the movie say what I wanted it to say? We write movies for the audience. When the lights go up and that audience walks out, are they affected the way you hoped they would be when you first conceived this crazy film?

Some people told me that after they saw IT COULD HAPPEN TO YOU they gave a couple of bucks to a guy out on the street. That's why I wrote the movie. I'm not going to do a line-count and worry how many of my *bon mots* are left. It's a miracle that this script in your computer even finds a life. You have to put your ego aside, which is very hard. Everyone is kicked off their own movie at some point in their career. Let it go, forget about it. Life is short.

How did you feel about all the Frank Capra comparisons? Do you have a particular affection for that style of storytelling?

I love all styles. Every movie, or play I write is different and the subject demands a different style. FOR COP GIVES WAITRESS . . . I knew I wanted it to be a fable, and I'm very glad that Andrew Bergman picked up on that. I wanted to see if I could carry off a script in which the hero is a hero because he's just plain good. It's hard to get a modern audience to buy that. We're used to our heroes being fairly tortured and complex. I love hard-edged films, don't get me wrong. But I wrote this story in honor of my dad who was a truly good man, one of those Jimmy Stewart-type guys. He taught me to be generous. I just wanted to see if I could get that out there, into the consciousness. Maybe people are ready for that right now.

Kerry Hayes

GEORGE GALLO

T HOUGH GEORGE GALLO DECRIBES HIMSELF AS A BOHEMIAN ARTIST, whose paintings still hang in a gallery in New York, he's also carved out a successful career in Hollywood. His first screenplay to be produced, WISE GUYS, brought him out to L.A., and he followed that with the hilarious and highly-regarded buddy comedy, MIDNIGHT RUN, which has since spawned a series of television movies. Then in 1991, he finally realized his dream of directing, with the warm-hearted comedy 29TH STREET. Gallo's latest film as a writer/director, TRAPPED IN PARADISE, is a sentimental Christmas story featuring his usual streetwise dialogue. When he's not writing or directing, Gallo's painting or playing the guitar or spending time with his fiancée Julie Lott.

SUSAN AVALLONE: I heard you had your first meeting at nineteen. How did that come about?

GEORGE GALLO: I didn't go to film school; I didn't get accepted, as a matter of fact. I went to art school. I wanted to be a real Bohemian artist—a painter, yelling and screaming out the window, models over the house—I had it all figured out. But I wrote a screenplay over the summer my second year of college. Just to try doing it. And I sent it to Marty Bregman, because he was the only producer I knew of in New York.

At the meeting, I had a tape recorder. I was trying to explain the movie, and I played music in the background. I was nineteen years old. I didn't know any better. Then I didn't have cab fare to get home. I was really living hand-to-mouth. I asked Marty to borrow twenty bucks so I could get home. He started cracking up. He optioned the script. I think he liked me, or something. It was pretty amazing. The movie never got made, though.

Were you self-taught, from watching a lot of movies? How did you know the format?

The format I got from books, but in terms of structure—see, there's no such thing as being self-taught. You can learn from an instructor, but it's always right there in front of you. I had the best teachers in the world, like Preston Sturges, Frank Capra, William Goldman; those were my teachers. I just watched movies constantly. I tried to take them in as much as I could. Why does one work, why does one not work? How can two minutes of film be incredibly interesting and ten seconds be incredibly boring? Those are the kinds of questions I would ask myself.

And once you sold the script you just kept going, never looked back?

I didn't complete my college education. I just started trying to write for a living. I didn't move out here until I was 27 or 28, when I sold WISEGUYS. That was my first script to get made, so the second I knew it was going into preproduction, I came to L.A. I had enough money to get a place and start writing here. Then I wrote MIDNIGHT RUN and my life just changed. Marty

Brest had an idea for a movie he wanted to meet with me about. We were in the middle of working on the story and I said to him, "Look, I've got this other idea and I can't help myself; I've gotta tell you about it. It's about a bounty hunter." I started explaining the story to him and he said, "You know, that's a better idea. Why don't you write that?" That was MIDNIGHT RUN.

Is it true that you wrote the script at a deli counter?

Yes. At Jerry's Deli in Studio City. There's a plaque there, on the wall. I wrote at the first seat at the counter. I used to sit there late at night. Writing longhand on stacks of legal pads I used to bring with me everywhere. I can't seem to sit at a word processor, so I'll just go someplace with a pad and a pen. Maybe it's because I like to draw and paint still. It's a tactile thing, touching the paper, my excitement when I'm writing fast . . . Sometimes if I get stuck in a place I'll move to another location. I'll be sitting in some restaurant, and then I'll go out to the park, I'll go here and there, until I get it all together. If I get lucky, if I get on a roll in one place, I'll start going there a lot. That happened at Jerry's.

I know a lot of people, when they write, they're thinking "I'm gonna get so-and-so . . . " Did you imagine Robert DeNiro for it?

I never did. My mind never went there for a minute. I knew it was a tough-guy character, but that Robert DeNiro read it and said he wanted to do it . . . I remember the day I heard that. I was running down the street, screaming, happy. I couldn't believe it. First, he'd never done a film like that, I don't think he'd ever done a comedy until then. And DeNiro and Marty Scorsese—those guys are like icons, they're my heroes. I saw MEAN STREETS in 1974, I was a senior in high school. When I saw that film, that was the final clincher: "All right, I gotta be a writer-director." In fact, I didn't even want to be a writer at first, I wanted to be a director. I thought directors wrote, I really didn't know. The more I started to figure out how movies were made, I wanted to tell the story from both ends. Verbally and visually.

Having done both, would you say directing is more difficult than writing?

I think the pressure of directing is harder than writing. Writing is ultimately more difficult because you're starting from nothing. At least a director's got characters and stage direction, he's got something to start with. The thing that's exhausting about directing is the pressure, especially if you're starting out. I'm only doing my second film. I say, "Trust me, this is going to be funny," or "This is not where the joke should be." But I don't have a body of work as a director yet. I mean, they know I wrote MIDNIGHT RUN, and that people liked it, but as a director I'm not trusted yet, even though 29TH STREET turned out very well. I'm especially proud that we shot it in less than 40 days and never set foot in New York City. We shot it all on a backlot in North Carolina, so I know how good that film is, especially given the limitations of what I had to make it. DeNiro called to tell me how much he liked 29TH STREET, which meant a lot to me. And other directors have told me that they know what I pulled off in that picture.

It's a difficult tone, like TRAPPED IN PARADISE. That isn't a common mix, an uplifting drama mixed with a caper-comedy.

It's not easy, because there's not a lot of other films like it. There's elements of other films, but to put the two together is really a tough tapdance. I don't like straight-ahead pictures. I always try to run opposites when I'm telling a story. With TRAPPED IN PARADISE, I knew it was going to be about a bank robbery. So: when's the oddest time to commit a bank robbery, which is essentially a violent act? How about Christmas Eve? Then you've got some friction going in your story. The entire movie is basically these guys want to get out of town, so they get hit with the worst blizzard in twenty years, they're stuck.

And in MIDNIGHT RUN, DeNiro and Charles Grodin are complete opposites. The fact that DeNiro is a completely impatient human being, and you stick him with Grodin and then you add that he won't fly—it's all right there. It's an action film, yet it really was a very warm story in a lot of ways. I love taking those opposites and mixing them up. It gives you a headache during the process, when you're figuring it out, but when you get there you really feel like you did something.

Do you think you could have written in the old studio system? Like in BARTON FINK, "This week you're doing a Wallace Beery wrestling picture."

I guess maybe I could have. The thing is, I can write anything if I see the humor in it. But no, I don't think I'd be good at that sort of "writer-for-hire" thing. Plus, I'm a little lazy and I like being on my own time too much. I certainly could have produced more work than I have, but I'm also a painter and musician. I dabble in a lot of other things. When I'm done with a movie, the last thing I want to do is think about a character saying something. I'm gonna go play my guitar or paint some pictures or do something to forget about the film business for a while. Then one day, in the middle of whatever I'm doing, somebody will say something and I'll go, "You know, that would be an interesting movie," and then BANG—I'll be sucked right back into it.

For you the writing is all-encompassing or nothing. No rewrites, no polishes . . .

No, I'd rather not. I just bought a house, though, so maybe I'll be doing some of that, against my better judgment. I've been asked a lot, but I'll read it and go, "Ahhhhh . . . . I've got a finite number of heartbeats. Why am I going to waste it on this?" I'd rather just lay in the shade for a while and wait until the bill collector's knocking on the door. I'm in love. I've been with my girlfriend Julie for 11 years, and we're getting married. I just like spending time with her. You know, I do this—writing, directing—because I love it. I enjoy doing it, I love having done it. There's nothing like it. I get the laserdisc out of 29TH STREET and look at it—man, I wrote and directed this! I can't believe it. Look at all my ideas up there! And that's an amazing feeling. That's like a dream come true, far beyond what I ever hoped.

Why turn it into something else? Why turn it into torture? The only reason

I got involved with films was because I wanted it to be special, and I wanted to enjoy doing this. If it starts turning into a grind, then I might as well have not bothered. I should just have done one of those jobs that *are* a grind. I don't ever want to turn it into that. I wouldn't want to do that to myself. The biggest thing was I never got myself finacially strung out. We had a little condo we lived in forever, and people said, "What are you living in this condo for?" and I said, "Hey, Jack, I am free! I'm not a slave to some thing, you know?" I'm still driving an '87 Jeep. It's okay. The Jeep gets me where I got to go. I'm not going to buy some ludicrous car. I don't need any of that. I'd rather take the bus and be free, if that makes any sense at all . . .

> *"The more you start relying on a sixth sense, I think the better you get . . . Otherwise you're just a machine, and I've seen perfectly crafted screenplays that had no soul.*
>
> —George Gallo

It makes a lot of sense. You want to be a writer and get into this so that you can have a life . . .

To have free time. That was the whole point of it for me. I used to sell stereos; it wasn't that bad. I'm not saying I want to go back there, but if I had to I know I could make it. I really mean that. I'm not living in fear of it going away every ten seconds. If it goes away it goes away, what can I do about that? As long as I don't worry about that the work will stay clear, and then it won't go away.

You know, I've got my gripes. I'm miserable about certain things, but essentially, everything I've ever written about was about optimism, and I am an optimistic guy. I'd have to be, because I came from a working-class neighborhood in New York, and I came out to Los Angeles and I fought very, very hard over the years, but look where I landed. How can you not be an optimist? I can't say "mankind sucks" while I live in a house writing movies and directing them. That would be a lie. Things are pretty damn good, actually.

In your movies, bad things happen to people, but human nature is essentially good. Is that how you see the world?

I do believe in human nature. I also think that artists should be more responsible in what they put out there. I'm interested in the people that defy the odds and win. The scumbags and the losers don't interest me that much. If a guy walks around with a gun killing people, I'm sorry for him, and he should be under psychiatric care. I think it's irresponsible to constantly put that in people's minds. I don't believe in censorship, but I'm not a believer in when people say: "Well, that stuff doesn't affect you."

I know I'm a better person because I've seen Monet's "Lilypads" and I know that it's enriched my life. So, I know some of these negative images that I've seen must have made an impact on my life, too. Every once in a while I do think about them and I'm like . . . why is that in my subconscious? Why did I have to get subjected to that nonsense? I know it's out there. I know it's important to recognize it. I'm not saying, "Live your life pretending that these things don't exist." But I think we have a tendency to help perpetuate it by making such an issue out of it, even more in the media than possibly movies. This constant barrage of stuff that people are basically no good, and that the streets are unsafe, and everybody's out to kill everybody . . . This wholesale slaughter of people onscreen is pointless and it dirties the well of your brain and your conscience.

But it's great when you can look at this summer and see FORREST GUMP made more money than TRUE LIES.

I agree. I'm tired of seeing people blown up. I mean, I just don't care about it any more. I hope that change is confirmed with my movie, because these are the kinds of movies I want to make. I want to show that people can beat the odds and change. The idea of TRAPPED IN PARADISE came when I was painting in rural Pennsylvania years ago. I was walking down the road and had an easel with me and this guy pulled over and said, "Do you need a lift?" The first thing that went off in my mind was "serial killer." Then I walked down the road a bit more and I saw the guy driving with his family, so he'd just gone further down the road. I'm thinking to myself, "You know, I'm out in the country here, and these people are okay." I've got an urban mentality that everybody wants something, they're going to cut my throat, throw me in the river, you know. That always stuck with me.

There are good people out there who really don't have an agenda, except they'd like to help you. I know this sounds like pie-in-the-sky, but if you leave yourself open, you'll see it out there. I'm not saying be vulnerable to the point of stupidity, but goodness is out there. I'm sure that I've lost certain chances because I was acting out of fear and paranoia that I didn't let certain good people into my life. To me, this movie's about three cynical guys who don't trust in anyone, who figure, "Let's get them before they get us," and then realize that's not the way to go.

How do you switch from the isolation of writing to directing, which has been compared to being a general?

A director who I wrote for (there are only two of them, but I don't want to say who it is) said, "Making a movie's like going to war." And I always thought making a movie was like going to a party. Where else can you get to shut down streets, hang out with great actors, crew people, eat for free? You laugh all day long. I'm a real Bohemian type anyway, I love keeping odd hours. You get paid a lot of money. How is that a war? Man, that just never sounds like a war to me. War is about killing, maiming, shooting. Making a movie is a party.

I don't understand why a director would run around yelling at everybody. A crewperson can make you or break you. They're all there to help you. Some people want to turn it into a war, but I don't see it. Sure, I like the leverage of protecting what I wrote. Plus, I come from this painting background, and I love visuals. The idea of turning a two-dimensional thing into a three-dimensional thing.

Do you visualize it when you're writing?

Absolutely. I see every shadow and I see the cuts. I hear the music cues. I hear it from the beginning. Fade in: Street sounds, traffic, whatever . . . .

When you see the finished product does it come close to what you imagined?

It's pretty mind-boggling. The best way to explain it is: you have what you perceive to be a great idea, you're enormously excited about it, and it never quite gets back to that original thing until you're at the very end of it, which can be years later. First, you have a sort of feeling about what you're trying to do. You see it. Then it becomes real, which is always frightening and shocking. And somehow, you lose it along the way as you're putting it all together. You forget why you ever wanted to do it and start to not even care. Then somewhere near the end, that original thought or feeling starts to come back, and you get to that point where you first visualized it.

Action-comedies like MIDNIGHT RUN work best when the characters are completely unique, yet the action must also be compelling. How do you get that combination?

What I do, for what it's worth—it's the best when it's the most organic, when it somehow comes from the material. Here's what I'm saying: if you have a guy who has a fear of heights, you have to stick him at the top of a skyscraper. You just must. If you're looking for a joke, like irony, if he's getting shot at by helicopters, his job was that he used to manufacture those helicopters. Then the stuff suddenly takes on some sort meaning. It's the only way it's interesting. Like in MIDNIGHT RUN, the entire movie is about time. Everything was about being up against a clock—that's why I made a watch the thing that meant the most to DeNiro's character. It could have been something else. I thought with a watch, it all goes back to what the movie's about. It could have been a hat, but it wouldn't have meant anything—the story was about time.

Does that kind of stuff usually come to you in your first draft of the story?

Yeah, absolutely. I don't think my stuff to death like a lot of people do. If

something just feels right I'll go with it. The more you start relying on a sixth sense, I think the better you get. At anything. "Feel" is really . . . you can't buy that. Otherwise you're just a machine, and I've seen perfectly crafted screenplays that had no soul. Everything lands in the right place and nobody gives a shit. Yet there's those lumpy ones that have so much heart you don't care. You go right with it.

29TH STREET was a lot less of a structured story. I broke screenwriting rule number one—and I knew when I was doing it—that every character has an objective. This guy had no objective on earth. He didn't have any goals. He doesn't want to work, he doesn't even care about marrying his girl. He just floats through life. Stuff happens to him as opposed to him generating the action. He's kind of a lox of a character, and then finally he wins the lottery. I thought it would be kind of challenging, to do a movie about a guy who basically had zero ambition.

How do you get started, once you have the idea? Do you do many drafts?

I'll do an outline of some kind, but I've written enough to know that I'm gonna somehow get to the other end. I trust that I'll arrive at a decent place. I'll work out a basic outline and just go for it. Sometimes I'll change two pages and it's a new draft. With TRAPPED IN PARADISE, I know that 53 drafts came out of the computer but I would say I rewrote this thing solidly 20 times to get it right. MIDNIGHT RUN and this last script, there'd have to be a tie-breaker.

Do you find that your structure keeps changing or is it mostly dialogue?

Mostly structure, because I write pretty complicated stories, they're kinda dense. I write a lot of characters. MIDNIGHT RUN had a whole bunch of characters, and TRAPPED IN PARADISE has a lot. They're all in there for a reason and they all meet at the end. I love stuff like that. The average day in your life you run into how many people? . . . I can't put enough people in my scripts. If you've got three characters in a movie they'd better be pretty interesting if you're going to hang on them for two hours.

LARRY KARASZEWSKI
AND
SCOTT ALEXANDER

SCOTT ALEXANDER AND LARRY KARASZEWSKI BOTH STARTED MAKING Super 8 films when they were kids, though not as a team; Scott was growing up in L.A.—Larry in South Bend, Indiana. They met at USC freshman year, wrote a script together their senior year, and were pleasantly surprised when it sold two weeks after they graduated. Since then they have continued to write together, seeing their first produced screenplay become a big success, PROBLEM CHILD, followed by its sequel. They've recently enjoyed success of a different kind as their movie ED WOOD, directed by Tim Burton, got rave reviews and Oscar talk. Right now they're working on a script about *Hustler* publisher Larry Flynt, though they swear they're not in the biopic business.

SUSAN AVALLONE: Tell me about that first script you sold, right after film school.

SCOTT ALEXANDER: "Homewreckers." It was a big spec sale before there was such a thing, and it was a classic introduction to Hollywood, in that everything good and everything bad that can happen to a project happened to it, and it never got made. It was a comedy about a thief who's robbing a house and injures himself, falls through a skylight. He hooks up with a shady lawyer and sues the homeowner for negligence. It goes to trial, and the homeowner makes a stink in the courtroom and loses the case, can't pay the settlement and the thief takes over all his belongings. It was a parody about all of the faults of the legal system. A year and a half of development at the studio, and then other writers worked on it, and it never got made.

LARRY KARASZEWSKI: Someone in one of my classes was working in the mailroom at ICM. And they said, "Who're the hot new people at USC?" We sent a young ICM agent a copy of the script, and she really liked it, and literally two weeks after we graduated from college, it sold. It's such a strange thing, because you assume that you're going to be struggling for so many years.

S. A: I was actually set to be production coordinator on a low-budget feature.

L. K: I think I was applying at record shops, just to get a job somewhere. What's so funny is that, coming from Indiana, my family always supported my decision to make movies but they always were like, "Well, when you graduate what's gonna happen?" And I would say, "Maybe I'll write a script and sell it, or direct something . . ." It was all kind of pie-in-the-sky, but sure enough, two weeks after graduation I sold a script. So my mom just assumed that this is what happens.

What happened with "Homewreckers"?

S. A: We always like to write with actors in mind, and we were writing this script for Albert Brooks and Morris Day. This was our dream cast.

L. K: PURPLE RAIN had come out the summer before, and we thought, "Wouldn't Morris Day be funny?"

S. A: So we finished the script and said, "Okay, we have to get it to Morris Day now." We looked at the back of a record and called his management and they connected us to someone, and they said, "You wrote a script for Morris Day? Really? Sure, we'll take a look at it, no one else has ever called us." When it got sold the studio said, "You got it to Morris Day? Well, you better get it back! It's not available now!" Instant, typical Hollywood paranoia.

So what's the current status of it?

S. A: Dead in the water. Lots of money against it, years and years of overhead and producer's fees and writers. It's a really good script, but it's a very simple movie, and with all the money against it now, it's hard to get people interested in it.

L. K: Although surprisingly enough, every couple of years we get a phone call from somebody saying, "What's this script 'Homewreckers'?" It has a life of its own. People send it around and every once in a while it'll go to an executive and he'll say, "That was one of the first scripts I read, and I always thought it would be a movie I would make someday."

S. A: We don't believe in letting scripts die, much to the chagrin of our agent. Every couple of years when we have some free time we'll pull out one of our old scripts and spiff it back up. Make it more contemporary, make the black character white this time, or what have you, and we'll send it back out, "Homewreckers 92"! Our agent is like, "just let these things die, please! Move on with your lives!"

L. K: You change the Reagan references to Clinton references . . . it doesn't smell as moldy as it did.

I remember hearing differing stories about how PROBLEM CHILD came about; there was a serious piece in People magazine . . .

L. K: There was a story floating around about parents who were suing an adoption agency because they got a kid who was awful. There was nothing funny about it. The kid burned down their house, he would draw Devil signs in his own feces on the wall; he was just a bad, bad, kid. I think a bunch of people in town saw these stories and thought,

"This is the next OMEN, the next EXORCIST." A couple of people were out there pitching it as a horror movie.

S. A: Someone was pitching it as "Fetal Attraction."

L. K: Scott and I looked at it and said, "No... this is funny." It could be a very dark version of "Dennis the Menace." We pitched it as a dark comedy, with the kid sawing a kid in half . . .

S. A: That was the big comic setpiece—he saws the girl in half.

L. K: Literally.

S. A: They actually shot it, but it got cut out of the movie.

At what point did you realize the movie was being done with a much different tone than you intended?

S. A: After we got fired.

L. K: We wrote a first draft, and turned it into the studio. The producer, Bob Simonds, said, "I've got good news and bad news. The good news is they're making the movie. The bad news is you're fired."

S. A: We couldn't understand why if you greenlight literally a first draft you would want to fire the writers. Clearly the writers had done something right. It turned out, in terms of the studio politics, that one of the executives didn't like the script at all, but Tom Pollock loved it. So the concession to the other executive was let's bring in some writers he's friends with, make him happy. That started a whole string of writers that went on for another year.

L. K: There were about ten or fifteen writers on this thing at some point. It went from an adult black comedy to a dumb kids film. But surprisingly enough, the structure always stayed very close to what we did.

S. A: But the movie's a mess, because that's what happens when you throw so many cooks in the project. Things get sloppy. Phil Alden Robinson once said, "Screenwriting is a series of Bandaids, and when you're writing it you're layering lots of little pieces in and only you know where the Bandaids are." If you suddenly realize, "Oh, we need to set up this one subsidiary character. Well, I'll find a place on page 20, page 42 and page 72. Keep him in the movie." When the next guy comes in to rewrite you, he doesn't know any of this. He's just gonna

11

start hacking out— "The executive didn't like this section, the executive doesn't like this subplot." He doesn't know where the Bandaids are. The movie starts to disintegrate into chaos, and it becomes a sloppy mess by the end of the day. We were actually brought back on, a week before shooting, even though we had been fired and weren't extraordinarily popular at the studio. But when it's that late you can't do a lot.

After all that, how did you feel watching the movie?

S. A: When I went to the cast and crew screening I was almost crying afterwards: I was so ashamed of the final result. It was one of the most dramatic nights of my life. The people around me were laughing. I was close to tears. My Grandmother had laughed her head off. She thought it was such a great movie.

L. K: I wasn't as badly affected by it as Scott was. The movie is a mess. But it does have a lot of laughs. So many movies I go to that are comedies, particularly comedies from that time period—the late eighties, even still today— you go to see those movies that are billed as comedies and there are no jokes in them. It's not like the jokes are failing. There are not even jokes in them.

We like to say that what makes something funny, what makes something a joke, is a break in normality, a break in logic, of some kind. That's why, usually, you can't remember a punch line, because it really doesn't connect to the set-up until after you hear it. So when you're in a room with executives and producers, it's very easy for them to say, "This joke doesn't work for me," or "Why would he say this?" So you say fine, whatever, I'm not going to argue about one joke and you circle that. And then the other guy says that about another joke, and another guy says that about another joke, and before you know it you've taken fifty percent of the jokes out of the script. That's one of the reasons why ACE VENTURA was such a hit . . .

S. A: It wasn't ashamed to be funny. Critics have had their day with PROBLEM CHILD and rightfully so, but it makes people laugh, and that's the reason why it was successful. It wasn't afraid to be funny.

Despite how you felt about that, though, you went on and did the second one.

S. A: That's hard to explain in retrospect. They wanted that sucker out less than a year after the first movie. Which is really fast. And I believe we set the all-time record. I think the film was finished nine months after the first film's release date. Something astonishing. They needed to rush it, so the obvious thing is, "Let's go to the original writers because they know the material better than anyone else." We passed. Then the money got high enough that we caved in; we sold out.

L. K: What's really intriguing was that, we couldn't go and write a sequel to the movie we wrote, we had to write a sequel to the movie that came out. So, it was a strange kind of thing to deal with. The director, Brian Levant, was really terrific to us. I think the second movie is funny, also. Our secret goal was to write a John Waters movie for ten-year-olds.

S. A: The studio didn't know this. As long as someone is going to pay us to write something called "Problem Child Two" let's at least get something on screen that no one's ever seen before. It's "Salo" for kids. It's John Waters for kids. It's Pasolini for children. No one's ever seen anything like this.

L. K: And the film actually got rated "R" on the first pass.

S. A: Uh-oh! Larry just blew the big secret. No one was ever supposed to know that.

L. K: Universal blew their lid. They were like, "Oh my god, our kiddie franchise is rated R!" Not even PG-13. They were just freaked, because there was so much piss and vomit and language, it was out of control.

So you tried to appeal to the lowest common denominator . . .

L. K: And succeeded. I remember one critic actually hit the nail on the head. He was reviewing PROBLEM CHILD 2 and he said, "It was like the writers read the reviews of the original movie and said, 'Bad taste? I'll show you bad taste!'"

S. A: We might have gotten caught up in our own delusions during that six-month period, and kind of got carried away with that sentiment. Looking back

on it, maybe we could have come up with a bit of a classier film, but that's life, you know . . . . You're writing whatever you're feeling at that time, and at that time we were smarting from all the mean reviews. "Well fine, we'll show you! You ain't never seen nothing like this!" Of course, we got it out of our system and now we can move on to classier material. You're not going to catch us writing any more of these movies.

What do you mean by "these movies"?

S. A: Crappy kids films. We have now spent the last two years passing on a lot of these movies. Even when we couldn't get a job, we were still passing on these rewrites, assignments, production polishes . . .

L. K: All our scripts are very different, and when the PROBLEM CHILD movies came out and were so successful, Hollywood in general said, "Oh, these guys write kids movies." Which was never our intention at all. So basically the only jobs we were being offered were to rewrite these other kids movies. This was the time when all those franchise things started happening, where every time it would be a phonecall saying, "Remake this old kids TV show." We started turning everything down, and there was a whole year where we just didn't get a job.

S. A: We didn't work in '92. This is less than a year after these movies made all this money, and we couldn't get a job. Finally, it came down to the only job we could get was COP AND A HALF and we said no. It was very disillusioning and upsetting, and meanwhile we had written a lot of other scripts around town for different studios, that we thought were so much better than PROBLEM CHILD, but they hadn't gotten made. People know you from what they've seen up on screen.

L. K: We'd go out on pitches with new ideas and literally it would be like, "Well, you know, I don't know if you guys really can write this, because you write kids movies."

S. A: "We don't know if you're right for it." People were telling us we're not right for our own ideas.

L. K: It would freak us out entirely. ED WOOD was an idea that we had talked about since we were in college, it was always a dream project that we wanted to do, but we figured no one in their right mind would want to make this movie. But since no one in their right mind was making anything else we were coming up with, no matter how commercial we thought it was, we said, "Well, fine. If we're not getting a job writing these other things . . ."

S. A: These other things were commercial. It should not be construed that ED WOOD is typical of our scripts. Our taste is commercial, as a rule. Not because we're pandering—we just like

> "Being torn apart by the press for the PROBLEM CHILD movies really brought a sense of identifying with the man Ed Wood. We really grabbed this concept: it takes just as much passion and hard work to make a movie that turns out bad than it does to make something good."
> —Larry Karaszewski

movies. But our good, smart commercial ideas had not gotten made and we couldn't sell them, and so the hell with it, let's go show these people, and write the most obscure thing of all time, just to please ourselves. If we don't get paid for it, fine, but it's something we want to do.

L. K: And also, being torn apart by the press for the PROBLEM CHILD movies really brought a sense of identifying with the man Ed Wood. We really grabbed this concept: it takes just as much passion and hard work to make a movie that turns out bad than it does to make something good.

S. A: We had to live with reviews saying the writers should be run out of town. So we could identify with Ed. We were feeling at a low point in our lives so we thought, let's go do something right from the heart.

At what point did Tim Burton become involved?

S. A: We wrote a treatment, and we gave it to a friend of ours, Michael

Lehmann, who was in a funny mood himself at that time because he'd just come off HUDSON HAWK. It was like, this is funny, the writers of PROBLEM CHILD and the director of HUDSON HAWK make a movie about the worst filmmaker of all time. How apropos! We were all in agreement—let's try and get this made as a $2 million movie, a little independent film. So we wrote a treatment and Michael gave it to Tim Burton and Denise Di Novi to produce.

L. K: The material was weird enough that even thinking about it on that small a scale, we knew we would need somebody with clout to shepherd us through it. Tim read the treatment and kind of flipped out over it. Apparently it had been something he'd been thinking about too. He and Michael had a long conversation and agreed to swap positions: Michael became one of the producers and Tim would direct, he'd make it his next movie. So he came to us and said, "Where's the script?" At that point we just had a treatment, so we literally took off and wrote the script in six weeks.

It flowed straight out. It was something we'd been talking about writing for so long and it was such an easy thing to write, such a pleasure, that it wound up being very long, 150 pages. We usually never turn in a draft that long, but we were afraid about pruning it because Tim had responded so well to the treatment and we didn't want to take out scenes that he might be into.

S. A: Also, rewriting takes time. It was a spec script, being written for a marketplace of one. And there was a timeclock ticking down because Tim was supposed to start another movie. He had read the treatment and said, "I'd love to see a script." That's all we had. We knew we were writing such a weird piece of material, that if Tim Burton

didn't like it, it's not like we could try to sell it. It's not like we could shop it around town; people would think we were out of our minds. So, we had this window and we didn't want to let it go away. If Tim liked it, then maybe something would happen. If he didn't like it we would stick it in a drawer.

So you gave Tim Burton a 150-page script . . .

S. A: We gave it to him on a Friday and on Sunday night he called and said, "I want it to be my next film. And I don't want to change a word." Literally. He did not have one note.

L. K: He shot our first draft. The only changes were for production reasons: scheduling and budget.

S. A: Tim, God bless him, had the confidence in the material that he didn't want to change a word.

L. K: He also didn't want to get into any kind of development, where he felt like he would be in a room hearing, "Does Ed Wood have to be such a bad filmmaker?"

S. A: Tim used his clout to make it, essentially, as an independent movie—"Who will give me $19 million to make this movie as is, and I will deliver you an answer print next year? Your input is you get to write the check." That's it. And it was a dream experience.

L. K: We were on the set every day, we were at dailies, Tim showed us rough cuts. We were sitting in on all sorts of meetings, so it wound up being a terrific experience.

How do you go from biopic to biopic? Was Larry Flynt also a story you always wanted to tell?

S. A: With ED WOOD we had a good time doing the research; taking all this factual material and shaping it into a movie was really satisfying. So we started thinking, what are some other good, freaky stories that haven't been told? "Flynt" is really off-the-wall again, and yet it was a way for us to exploit the success of ED WOOD, to go set up a weird project and be paid to write it this time. We did vow we would not write another biopic on spec, because it's such a crapshoot. There's so much research involved, ten times more than ED WOOD, because Flynt was such a public personality. There was so much material to wade through. It took us six months just to sift through the material.

L. K: Six terrible months of looking at every single issue of "Hustler" magazine. "Honey, it's research!"

S. A: And "Flynt" was the right kind of biopic to write. We did come up with a whole theory of biography, which is: everyone does it wrong except us. People make biopics about great human beings with wonderful successes, who are role models, and this is stupid. Who wants to watch someone so terrific for three hours? Who needs that? We believe in dramatizing people with screwed-up lives, who pissed off a lot of people and made a lot of enemies. It's nothing but conflict. It's nothing but juicy scenes, because all they're doing is alienating everybody.

L. K: So we have this concept of writing biopics for people . . .

S. A: . . . who don't deserve them.

L. A: Normally, why would you want to write a biopic about the worst director of all time? Why would you want to write a biopic about the biggest porn king in the world? Our goal is not to whitewash these people—we don't try to do that at all—but to find something in there that you can kind of identify with, so you're actually saying, "Oh, maybe with Ed Wood it's the passion, the fact that he loves these movies and really wants to make them." With Larry Flynt we're trying to deal with the integrity of the First Amendment. The script is going to be less about the porno industry and more about his troubles in the political arena and the courtroom.

S. A: So what's fascinating is, you've got a guy who most people think is a disgusting monster, and our goal is that by the third act you're rooting for him to beat Jerry Falwell in court. That is the trick. That is what we're trying to pull off. So we wrote a three-page treatment to turn into a pitch. We said, "Well, you need a warm-up pitch. Pitches are hard to pull off. So let's do a practice one. Let's see. Where would be the one place that nobody would ever want to buy this, so we can just do a dress rehearsal without them knowing it? Oh,

Columbia! Columbia hates us because they wouldn't make ED WOOD. What a perfect place to use as a run-through audience and they don't know it." They got a couple of executives in the room, we pitched it, and they were blown away. They really responded. Then we took our treatment and mailed it to Oliver Stone—didn't even know the man—just saying, "You might be interested in this." He read it, called Columbia, and said, "I want in."

L. K: It's to Columbia's benefit . . . they actually were very intrigued even before Oliver Stone got involved. They really responded to the pitch.

S. A: Now we're getting offered other biopics. Our agent just had us pass on Timothy Leary. "You don't want to get typecast, boys . . ." We do have another great person out there I think we should do. Larry knows who I'm talking about.

But you don't want to say who

it is?

S. A: No way. It's so beautiful. It's such a great story. It's right out there and people don't even see it. Because this person is so ridiculous.

L. A: The reason they don't see it, is because it's another one of these losers we like to glorify.

S. A: We love writing about losers. Look at the ten scripts we've written—they're about nothing but losers. We think losers are funny.

L. K: When we were first starting out Albert Brooks was a real hero to us, because his characters in all of his movies are, on the surface, so unlikable. So stubborn, so wrong-headed, but they're

funny and they crack you up. I find myself getting so hooked into those movies and seeing them over and over, because of that.

S. A: He's probably been more influential on us than anyone else in our writing. Just in terms of set-pieces about someone who's out of line, and they won't back off.

L. K: You're laughing and cringing at the same time.

S. A: You're covering your face while you're laughing because you are so embarrassed by what you are seeing. It's a beautiful school of comedy.

L. K: The cringe and laughing factor, the perfect example is ED WOOD, which is where this guy is trying so hard, and he's so wrong about what he's doing, and you like him, and you wish he would succeed, but you wish . . .

S. A: You wish he would get a clue. You laugh and you feel bad that you're laughing.

"ED WOOD is an amazing example of writing straight from the heart. Not trying to pander to the marketplace. It's a miracle, it's certainly not going to happen every day, but we wrote something completely insane and it got made. We weren't trying to please anybody but ourselves."
—*Scott Alexander*

Since you're a team, I have to ask the obvious question: how do you write together?

L. K: We write in the same room, together, all the time. Scott is a three hundred times better typist than I am, and so he always sits behind the console, and I kind of pace around or lay on the couch.

S. A: I don't think Larry sees a word until there's a printout.

L. K: I often will come around and look, but we'll work on the dialogue and say, "What happens next?" and things like that. I know some writing teams who say, "You take the first act and I'll take the second act and I'll see you in two months." If I'm writing the first act by myself, I probably can write the second act by myself. We're not a team for speed purposes, or anything like that. We're a team because we both bring something different to the table, and when we agree on something generally it's pretty good and it'll make the page. But it makes us, actually, kinda slow, because we argue out every little part.

S. A: We spend as much time outlining as we do writing the script. Some movies we write a treatment, some movies we just do cards. We've been anti-treatment all these years because treatments are lifeless. They can't capture the tone and the spirit of the piece because they're only a few pages long. So we always avoided doing them when we were asked to. And yet, "Flynt" and ED WOOD both got started because of treatments.

I think it's a good way to "see" the movie. . .

S. A: Usually you don't, though. You can't get your tone in it, it's so difficult. All you end up with is structure.

L. K: Well, the reason we tended to not give treatments, at least in the first part of our career . . .

S. A: Pre-biopic . . .

L. K: . . . was that we're also very good at the pitch. We found that if you pitch an idea, and you get people laughing in the room—when you leave, all they remember was that great pitch. But then they go home at night and look at it written up on three sheets of paper. And they look over it, and they're like, "That's really not that good. That made me laugh before, but that doesn't really work."

S. A: Actually, that cost us a job. We had the most amazing experience pitching something to TriStar. We did this ferociously funny pitch for this really convoluted farce, with just a lot of stuff going on: switcheroos and back and forths. The executives were laughing their heads off. Two hours later, our agent called and said they've made a deal. A couple of days later the executive calls up and says, "The head of production signed off on it. We have a deal. But I'd love Medavoy to able to understand what it is we bought. And it's so complicated I can't remember everything." So we write out our treatment, give it to the executive, he gives it to Medavoy. They called us back and said they don't want to do the deal. So then we just turned around and did the same pitch at Disney and they bought it. It worked out. But that was an example of how treatments blow up in your face.

L. K: I think it works better with the biopics, because they're not as dependent on the comedy. You're definitely seeing someone's life in a couple of pages. This particular pitch was all chaos, so when you typed out a treatment, it was basically the outline with none of the jokes. None of the real humor to it.

S. A: Also, just in terms of the biopics, I think one of our key strengths is our structure. We're very good structuralists. We're good at looking at someone's life and putting it into three acts, giving it some order, an arc and a sense of completion. The biopics work well in treatment form, because you can see how someone's life has been distilled down to a story with a beginning, middle and end. So they're quite clean.

When we gave Tim Burton the treatment for ED WOOD, he said what he loved about the story is, "It's funny and sad at the same time. If the script is that way I want to make this movie." ED WOOD is an amazing example of writing straight from the heart. Not trying to pander to the marketplace. It's a miracle, it's certainly not going to happen every day, but we wrote something completely insane and it got made. We weren't trying to please anybody but ourselves.

Patricia Williams

ROBIN SWICORD

NINETEEN NINETY-FOUR IS A GOOD YEAR FOR ROBIN SWICORD. SHE finally achieved her goal to direct, a short film she wrote about her grandmother called THE RED COAT. And two of her screenplay adaptations, THE PEREZ FAMILY and the classic LITTLE WOMEN, will be released at the end of this year. It's been a long road, from producing/writing/directing educational short films in the South, to playwrighting in New York, to her first produced feature credit, a rewrite of SHAG. Now Swicord is a highly sought-after screenwriter, and hopes to turn her newfound success into a shot at directing a feature. She and writer/director husband Nicholas Kazan have recently completed an adaptation of Roald Dahl's MATILDA for Universal Pictures. They have two children.

SUSAN AVALLONE: How did you get started writing? What did you do before?

ROBIN SWICORD: The short answer is that I've always been a writer, since I could pick up a pencil, and it was just finding the thing that I wanted to write. I went to school in Florida State University where they did not have a writing program, so I took a double major in theater and English with the intention of writing for film. To support myself I worked as a journalist and a photographer for a number of years. At some point I got a job to write and produce educational films, but I quickly broke away from that company and started writing and producing my own educational films. I was hoping that somehow I would parlay this into finally making feature films. I thought, "Well, first you do them little and then you do them big." I didn't really understand, because I'd never been anywhere in my life, what the drill was for getting a movie made. I got offered a job in advertising in New York, which got me out of the South. There I tried to meet independent film-makers, and everyone told me the same things, like, "You should be a script girl, because there aren't any filmmakers who are women."

I wrote a play, because at that time in New York, around 1978-79, there was a fairly booming off-off-Broadway showcase world. I got together with some people I did not know previously who had also come through FSU's Theater Department, and they were trying to put on plays. I wrote a play, and we put it on together, and it moved to off-Broadway. I got an agent, and I was suddenly considered a playwright. Then I wrote a screenplay, the very next logical step, because what I really wanted to do was to make movies. My agent, Merrily Kane, who had seen my play "Last Days At The Dixie Girl Cafe," sold that screenplay, "Stock Cars For Christ," the week I finished it. It brought me out to California and I started meeting movie people. I just kept saying, "I want to make movies!" I never could have imagined that I would spend ten years or so not making movies, but writing screenplays that people bought and then did not make into films. So what's happening now is so astonishing to me, because it's turn-

ing out the way I thought it was gonna go when I was 25 years old and had my play on in New York. Now I'll be an overnight success.

Now that you finally have directed your short film THE RED COAT, was it what you expected?

When I was directing, I realized that all of the things I had done all of my life to amuse myself were exactly the things preparing me to direct. Everything—from an interest in clothes, drawing pictures of houses, walking into rooms and imagining what they would look like if they were decorated completely differently, playing with paper dolls, the administrative things of working with people in a newsroom, trying to make everybody be on the same team. Everything I had ever done made sense when I was making this short film. It was the thing that I had come here to do.

I would imagine being a mother is also good preparation, since that's about getting people to do things they don't want to do!

Absolutely! I would never have been able to do what I did on THE RED COAT in such a short amount of time if I had not had two children for ten years first. You learn how to get people on your program.

For me one of the hard things was separating the writing from directing. In fact, the first thing I ever heard about "Stock Cars For Christ" was the producer saying, "We want to be able to show this to directors so you're going to have to take out all these things saying that the camera's overhead and where they move and what color their clothes are." He basically wanted me to take out everything that made a film image, because he didn't want a director to look at it and say, " There's no room for me." On my second screenplay I took the guy's advice because I thought, "I want to succeed, I want my movies to get made. I won't write that way." And I felt as though someone had put a bag over my head—I never did it again. I write as vividly as I can. I describe everything I see, in as short a way as possible. As a writer, I feel that I am the architect; and the director, if it's not me, is the contractor. My father's a contractor, that's not a

put-down. There are great contractors who come in and say, "You've made a mistake here in your plan." Architects write along the margin, "verify in the field"—they need someone who's an expert to carry out the building they have imagined. I don't think that my job is to make something that's a very rough version, that somebody can then embroider enormously and add on sun-rooms and second floors. I don't see myself as that kind of a writer.

Did "The Red Coat" just evolve into a short film, or was writing in that format something you had planned?

I think that a story is exactly as long as a piece of string. I could have made a film about my grandmother's whole life, which I'd be tempted to do, but there was an adventure that had happened to us together, and that particular piece of string happened to be about the size of a short story. I wrote it as a short story first, so that I wouldn't lose it, because I knew it was something I wanted to return to. I made the film because I'm ready to direct the screenplays that I write. I have had some good experiences and some bad, and at this point I just feel—what am I waiting for? I am supposed to be making my own movies. And the only way that I could get there would be to make a directing sample. So, I wrote THE RED COAT as a directing sample, and I knew that it was going to be about a thirty-minute film.

I think people are starting to make more short films again, because at a storytelling level there was disappointment in some directors who came out of film school. I don't think anybody faults film school directors for their technical expertise, but storytellers are not always drawn to a highly technical school. So there's been a feeling among a number of executives that they would give writers a chance to direct if they had a sample of what they'd be getting beforehand.

I went to the Aspen Film Festival with my film, shown out of competition, and I saw so many wonderful movies, very personal work. It was interesting to see how many short films were made from a kind of pure level. My film was not completely pure, because I knew that when it was done, if nothing else ever happened, I could show it when I wanted to direct. But at an emotional level, I had to make it before my grandmother died. I wanted to show it to her, as a kind of "thank you."

When you tackle an adaptation, are you able to get involved emotionally in a story that isn't your own?

Every adaptation I've done I have considered to be a personal work, I had a strong personal reason for taking on the book. With LITTLE WOMEN it's very personal, in terms of my attachment to the book, in my feeling a gratitude to it. The character of Jo was my female role model as a child. I didn't know any writers, and I certainly didn't know any women writers, until I had left the South. Jo expressed me, and was like a little light that I followed. To grow up and be able to adapt that, and make this movie to show my two little girls, was about as personal as I can get without actually telling a story that happened to me. Material that I feel a really strong connection to is the material that I take on. I don't think that I write very well on material that I have to approach purely at a level of craft, because I get bored. For me that's what film is, an expression of emotions, and that's what I look for when I go to the movies.

I think that it's very hard for people to get their own personal story told unless it happens to coincide at a strong thematic level with the personal stories of the studio executives. Nick and I have often joked about how if we could only have a complete psychological dossier of every person we ever work with that we would have no trouble getting movies made. Someone asks you to come in and tell them the story, and they say, "Yes, but can't she be from Long Island, and can't it be a guy, and can't his father have been a tailor?" and you realize they're attracted to this, whatever, coming-of-age story, they just want it to be *their* coming-of-age story.

I think that's because, like writers, executives drawn to the movie business want to tell stories, and development is their way.

I think you're exactly right. They have come here, to this job, because they are attracted to storytelling and they want to express themselves, and not having the gift for writing, they find themselves

in this kind of very funny thing of trying to tell their story through other people, very circuitously. The first eight or so screenplays that I wrote went into turnaround almost as soon as I turned them in because the executives who had developed them were fired. I could not figure out, for the life of me, what these people were doing developing screenplays— for tons of money— then throwing all that work out. It's still work. It shouldn't be dependent upon somebody's idiosyncratic take on it. It should be able to stand on its own. There isn't any objective standard. The next person comes in with their own subjective needs to tell a certain story, and they want to develop completely different stuff. Or if they happen to respond to the thing that's already there, they are afraid somebody else will get the credit, it won't seem like their story.

Another factor to deal with these days is "political correctness," not offending anyone in the movies. Have you noticed a new "careful" attitude?

My experience in the development situation, along these lines, is not that there's any kind of P.C. thing happening, but instead it's actually the reverse. I find myself in rooms, having to explain to usually male executives, or male producers sometimes, why a woman would not behave in a certain way. I wrote this project about Dick Rutan and Jeana Yeager called "Voyager," which I loved very much, and I sat in a room with people who said, "Why does she have to be a rocket scientist? Why can't she be a housewife? Why do they have to fight over who's gonna fly the plane? Why can't they fight over who's gonna have

to do the dishes? Why do they have to break up because she needs to be independent? Why can't they break up because she has an affair with his best friend?" And I would have to say, "These are living people who have sold you the rights of their heroic story. They're not felons. You can't say whatever you want to about them." I finally had to leave the project, which for me was like leaving a child. I almost didn't recover from that. The only happy coda is that years later that company went bankrupt and Goldwyn bought "Voyager" and has resurrected it. But at that time, I just felt, "I can't do this. I can't demean Jeana Yeager by making her some sort of slutty, unhappy housewife."

The same thing with Dottie in THE PEREZ FAMILY. The book is very direct in saying that she was not a prostitute, that things happened to her, that her autonomy was taken away, and that eventually she found herself trading sex for things like not being beaten or raped. The author, Christine Bell, did a lot of research before she came up with Dottie as a character. One of the things that I did was make it amply clear that Dottie wasn't a prostitute. She was a person who was sexual, she had control over her own body, and for her, keeping control was an issue. One of the things that kept coming up in story meetings was, "The character of Dottie—is she a prostitute or isn't she?" I said, "She's not a prostitute." "Well, then, why is she sexual and why is she so sensitive about being mistaken for a prostitute?" And I said, "Well, when she was in Cuba she was used as a prostitute, but in this country she's not a prostitute because she says she is not one." And they said, "Well, we've got to make it more clear that she was a prostitute." And I just dug in like a mule, because in this culture, when a woman is in a movie, and she's kind of flirtatious, something bad happens to her. Or she's typed, she's the slut. It's in every goddamn movie—even BULL DURHAM, which is a movie I liked, with an actress that I'm crazy about. If they

> *"Men do have a greater chance of going to a movie and seeing somebody who resembles a male who might actually live and breathe in real life . . . It's not about creating characters who are 'role models, it's just that it would be nice to go to a movie and feel, 'That could have been me.' "*
>
> —*Robin Swicord*

hadn't had Susan Sarandon bringing an enormous amount of humanity to this character, it would just be another kooky broad who likes to have sex. Movies don't even begin to address what our real lives as women are like. When this whole thing broke about Heidi Fleiss and there was such a strong movie business connection to her, I turned to my husband and said, "Well, no wonder there's so many hooker movies! These are the only women these guys know! No wonder they think it's so kinky and fun, and anybody who's in business for herself must really be sleeping around for money." It's totally a fantasy.

So despite the cries of the business being taken over by P.C., you say things *haven't* changed, at least the attitude about women.

I want to write real people. Not just real women, but also real men, because men get the short shrift in these movies too. Men do have a greater chance of going to a movie and seeing somebody who resembles a male who might actually live and breathe in real life. But in so many movies men can't show their emotions without it being one of those movies that's *about* showing their emotions, like KRAMER VS. KRAMER. It's not about creating characters who are "role models," it's just that it would be nice to go to a movie and feel, "That could have been me."

That was actually my impulse on SHAG. That was somebody else's screenplay; it's one of the few things that I've ever rewritten. The writers had a movie that was a little bit more like PORKY'S, it was about finding moonshine liquor. That was the plot: "Can we get drunk?" My version of it was like a summer weekend that I spent with my girlfriends in a town very much like Myrtle Beach. I grew up in Panama City Beach, Florida, and I felt that in SHAG I had accomplished making Southern girls who were not ridiculous and simpering. We knew that they were comic characters, but we also knew that they were real. Each one of them wanted something real. They had a real friendship, with all the little betrayals that happen in female friendships, and also all the good closeness of company.

SHAG was in development forever at several different places. At one point,

an executive said, "Whitney Houston won five Grammys last night, and we want you to make one of these girls black." I said, "Well, I just don't see how we can possibly do that in 1963 in the South. It would be extremely unusual for three upperclass white girls to be such good friends with a black girl, that they would all go away together for a weekend. The schools were not integrated yet. How would they even have met?" And the guy said, "Maybe she's the daughter of the maid." For him it was just about exploiting Whitney Houston, but I can imagine the response if we had blithely made one of these characters black, without acknowledging the whole context. As a writer, you can't have a character who's doing something that is just patently untruthful. You can't make it work.

Do you feel you have to take an even stronger position regarding the "truth" about women because so little truth is being told through movies?

Yes. We become fantasy objects, and that harms us. I'll speak for myself: I grew up in a family of boys. For many years, it never occurred to me that I was any different from my brothers. I was certainly treated exactly the same. I was punished in the same way that they were punished and I was rewarded in the same way that they were rewarded. We were raised with a certain amount of equality. At one point in my life, I began having to do a lot more housework than they did, which really bothered me. All of a sudden, lines were being drawn. Then I had a tremendous shock when I was twelve. I was a skinny, little girl—I didn't look like any kind of teenage bombshell—and someone drove by in a car and screamed at me, along the lines of, "Hey baby, come get in my car." Then they threw a can of beer at me, which for me completely summed up the enormous ambivalence that many men in this culture have toward women: they want to love them, they want to hurt them. I don't understand that, and I feel like I have a lot of thinking and writing to do about that, because I think it is a core experience for young women. It's one of the big shocks: I'm not a boy, I'm this other thing. I thought I was a person, but it turns out I'm this other thing.

Boys grow up in a world in which

they never have that experience. They have a lot of other experiences, many of them not all that wonderful. One of the interesting things that they get that we don't get is constant references to men having formed the world. They read history and it's all men. When we grew up they hadn't *P.C.ed* the language yet, so it was always "men of science," "men of medicine," "mankind." The only female models that we ever got were like Clara Barton, she was a nurse, and Betsy Ross, she sewed a flag. It was pitiful to even have that be included, because the full stories of countless other women weren't told. Catherine Littlefield Greene invented the cotton gin—but women couldn't hold patents then, so her friend Eli Whitney ended up with the credit. This is all by way of saying that you go into these story meetings with men who have never had to project themselves into the female one time—except maybe to try to understand their girlfriend's point of view when they're quarreling.

Girls have to grow up projecting themselves into the male, all the time, just to be included in the dominant culture. I go to the movies and see Mel Gibson jumping out of a car, and running heroically down the street, and jumping back in the car, and saying a wonderful wisecrack to Danny Glover, and *I'm* Mel Gibson. I have no problem putting myself in that character and being him. I'm on the ride. Give me a guy who's funny and cute and is doing something active and I'll be him. We are trained to do that. We've been doing it all of our lives. But if you have the same thing of a girl doing all that, there's a great distance that a male executive has to cross before he can understand that he is Geena Davis or Jodie Foster.

A big breakthrough was Denzel Washington being cast in MUCH ADO ABOUT NOTHING, where he's got a white brother. There he is: he's an actor, not a "black actor." It's kind of insisting on representing the universal, not some eccentric thing off to the side that can be dismissed. It's not just about creating reality for women, but for an entire audience. As writers and as filmmakers what we have to do is take down these barriers that have been up for so long.

★ ★ ★

FILM WRITERS

A

PAUL AARON*
Agent: CAA - Beverly Hills, 310/288-4545

THE OCTAGON   American Cinema, 1980, Story w/Leigh Chapman
LAUREL AVENUE (CMS)   HBO Independent Productions, 1993,
    Story w/Michael Henry Brown

SHEPARD ABBOTT*
Contact: WGA - New York, 212/245-6180

C.H.U.D.   New World, 1984, Story

LEWIS ABERNATHY
DEEPSTAR SIX   Tri-Star, 1989, w/Geof Miller

JIM ABRAHAMS*
Agent: United Talent Agency - Beverly Hills, 310/273-6700

THE KENTUCKY FRIED MOVIE   United Film Distribution, 1977,
    w/David Zucker & Jerry Zucker
AIRPLANE!   Paramount, 1980, w/David Zucker &
    Jerry Zucker, co-directed
TOP SECRET!   Paramount, 1984, w/Martyn Burke, David Zucker &
    Jerry Zucker, co-directed
THE NAKED GUN: FROM THE FILES OF POLICE SQUAD!
    Paramount, 1988, w/Pat Proft, David Zucker & Jerry Zucker
HOT SHOTS!   20th Century Fox, 1991, w/Pat Proft, directed
HOT SHOTS! PART DEUX   20th Century Fox, 1993,
    w/Pat Proft, directed

JERRY ABRAHAMSON
WAGONS EAST!   TriStar, 1994 Story

JACK ABRAMOFF
RED SCORPION   Shapiro Glickenhaus, 1989,
    Story w/Robert Abramoff & Arne Olsen

ROBERT ABRAMOFF
RED SCORPION   Shapiro Glickenhaus, 1989,
    Story w/Jack Abramoff & Arne Olsen

CELIA ABRAMS
EASY WHEELS   Fries Entertainment, 1989, w/David O'Malley &
    Ivan Raimi

IAN ABRAMS*
Agent: CAA - Beverly Hills, 310/288-4545
Manager: Jonathan Baruch/PRO Management - Los Angeles,
    310/478-5159

UNDERCOVER BLUES   MGM, 1993

Screenplays:
THE CLASS OF MONTE CRISTO
HOUSE-A-MATIC
THEATER OF LIFE
PRESUMED IMPOTENT
THE DUST DEVIL
JOY
MR. WONDERFUL
THE WIZARD OF SANTA MONICA

JEFFREY (J.J.) ABRAMS*
Agent: CAA - Beverly Hills, 310/288-4545

TAKING CARE OF BUSINESS   Buena Vista, 1990, w/Jill Mazursky
REGARDING HENRY   Paramount, 1991
FOREVER YOUNG   Warner Bros., 1992

Screenplays:
SHELTER w/David Klass
UNDER THE GUN w/Jill Mazursky
GONE FISHIN' w/Jill Mazursky

JON ACEVSKI
Contact: Hollywood Road - London, 071/352-4517

FREDDIE AS F.R.0.7. (AF)   Miramax, 1992,
    w/David Ashton, directed

HAL L. ACKERMAN*
Office: 6010 Wilshire Blvd., Los Angeles, 213/936-2446

SECOND WIND   Health and Entertainment Corporation of
    America, 1976

Screenplays:
HOLMEYER'S BRIDGE
BENJAMIN'S BABIES
I'LL GET THERE, IT BETTER BE WORTH THE TRIP

ALLEN ACTOR
THE DUNGEONMASTER   Empire Pictures, 1985

CATLIN ADAMS*
Contact: WGA - Los Angeles, 310/550-1000

STICKY FINGERS   Spectrafilm, 1988, w/Melanie Mayron, directed

Screenplays:
SERENADING LOUIE w/Lee Grant

DANIEL ADAMS
PRIMARY MOTIVE   Fox Video/Blossom Pictures, 1992,
    w/William Snowden, directed

MIKHAILA MAX ADAMS
Agent: CAA - Beverly Hills, 310/288-4545

Screenplays:
EXCESS BAGGAGE
MY BACKYARD

RICHARD D. ADAMS*
Contact: WGA - Los Angeles, 310/550-1000

Screenplays:
WHAT THE HEART WANTS
REEF
COVER OF DARKNESS
JOURNEY BEYOND THE SUN
THE DAMNED
CALIFORNIA ZEPHYR

RICHARD ADCOCK*
Contact: WGA - New York, 212/245-6180

HYPER SAPIEN   Tri-Star, 1986, w/Christopher Blue & Marnie Paige

VAL PENN ADDAMS*
Contact: WGA - Los Angeles, 310/550-1000

Screenplays:
RECOVERING MARTY w/Jake Messer
JUST DESERTS

**F
I
L
M**

**W
R
I
T
E
R
S**

ALAN J. ADLER*
Contact: Mark Temple, 310/444-8337

PARASITE   Embassy, 1982, w/Frank Levering & Michael Shoob
THE CONCRETE JUNGLE   Pentagon/Aquarius, 1982
METALSTORM: THE DESTRUCTION OF JARED-SYN
   Universal, 1983
THE ALCHEMIST   Empire Pictures, 1986

EDWARD ADLER*
Agent: The Artists Agency - Los Angeles, 310/277-7779

Screenplays:
FAMILY VALUES
THE GARLAND BUNTING STORY
DOLLAR COVENANT
JENNIFER'S HUSBAND
FLYING COLORS
SOMEBODY OWES ME MONEY
THE PROXY
THE BRAVE w/Alfred Boretz
BULLETPROOF
CELLS w/Buck Henry
SHOOT IT

GILBERT ADLER*
Manager: Allan Kassirer - 818/340-9800

CHILDREN OF THE CORN II: THE FINAL SACRAFICE
   Dimension Entertainment, 1993, w/A.L. Katz

Screenplays:
FAT TUESDAY w/A.L. Katz & J.P. Kelly (Universal)

WARREN ADLER*
Contact: WGA - Los Angeles, 310/550-1000

THE SUNSET GANG (P)

Screenplays:
CRIES OF LAUGHTER
PRIVATE LIES
HOUSEWIFE BLUES
REGRETS ONLY
SILVER LINING

ELEONORE ADLON
Contact: German Film & TV Academy, Pommernallee 1,
   1 Berlin 19, 0311/302-6096

BAGDAD CAFE   Island Pictures, 1987, w/Percy Adlon
ROSALIE GOES SHOPPING   Four Seasons Entertainment, 1990,
   w/Percy Adlon & Christopher Doherty

FELIX ADLON
Contact: German Film & TV Academy, Pommernallee 1, 1 Berlin 19,
   0311/302-6096

SALMONBERRIES   Weltvertrieb/Pelemele Film, 1991,
   w/Percy Adlon
YOUNGER AND YOUNGER   Academy Entertainment, 1993,
   w/Percy Adlon

PERCY ADLON
Agent: William Morris Agency - Beverly Hills, 310/274-7451

CELESTE   New Yorker, 1981, directed
SUGARBABY   Kino International, 1985, directed
BAGDAD CAFE   Island Pictures, 1987, w/Eleonore Adlon, directed
ROSALIE GOES SHOPPING   Four Seasons Entertainment, 1990,
   w/Eleonore Adlon & Christopher Doherty, directed
SALMONBERRIES   Weltvertrieb/Pelemele Film, 1991,
   w/Felix Adlon, directed
YOUNGER AND YOUNGER   Academy Entertainment, 1993,
   w/Felix Adlon, directed

GILLES ADRIEN
DELICATESSEN   Miramax, 1992

MARTIN L. AGUILAR
MOONDANCE   Ziggurat Film Releasing, 1994, directed

KAMAL AHMED
(w/John G. Brennan: The Jerky Boys)
THE JERKY BOYS   Buena Vista, 1995, w/John G. Brennan,
   James Melkonian & Rich Wilkes

JULIET AIRES
Agent: Innovative Artists - Los Angeles, 310/553-5200
Manager: Jonathan Baruch, PRO Management - Los Angeles,
   310/478-5159

Screenplays:
THE BROADWAY BRAWLER w/Keith Giglio
WELCOME TO THE FAMILY w/Keith Giglio
VERONA w/Keith Giglio
THE SENTINEL w/Keith Giglio

WILLIAM K. AKERS*
Business Manager: Cooper, Epstein, Hurewitz - Beverly Hills,
   310/278-1111

ERNEST RIDES AGAIN   Emshell Producers Group, 1993,
   w/John Cherry

JOHN AKOMFRAH
Contact: Black Audio Film Collective, 7-12 Greenland Street, London
   NW1 0ND, 071/267-0846, fax 267-0845

WHO NEEDS A HEART   Black Audio Film Collective/Channel
   Four/ZDF, 1991, w/Eddie George, directed

NORMAN ALADJEM
FIREWALKER   Cannon, 1986, Story w/Robert Gosnell &
   Jeffrey Rosenbaum

REZA ALAMEHZADEH
THE GUESTS OF HOTEL ASTORIA   Melior Films, 1989, directed

JORDAN ALAN
TERMINAL BLISS   Cannon, 1992, directed

Screenplays:
CAT'S CRADLE (directing)

TIMOTHY T. ALBAUGH
Agent: Renaissance-H.N. Swanson - Los Angeles, 310/246-6000

Screenplays:
DO ME A FAVOR

EDWARD ALBEE*
Agent: William Morris Agency - New York, 212/586-5100

WHO'S AFRAID OF VIRGINIA WOOLF? (P)
SEASCAPE (P)
THREE TALL WOMEN (P)
A DELICATE BALANCE   American Film Theatre, 1975,
   from his play

JEFF ALBERT
NEVER SAY DIE   Nu-Image, 1994, w/Danny Lerner & Yossi Wein
CYBORG COP III   Nu-Image, 1994
HUMAN TIMEBOMB   Nu Image, 1994

ALAN ALDA*
Agent: United Talent Agency - Beverly Hills, 310/273-6700

THE SEDUCTION OF JOE TYNAN   Universal, 1979
THE FOUR SEASONS   Universal, 1981, directed
SWEET LIBERTY   Universal, 1986, directed
A NEW LIFE   Paramount, 1988, directed
BETSY'S WEDDING   Buena Vista, 1990, directed

JEROME ALDEN*
Agent: Preferred Artists - Encino, 818/990-0305

A PROGRAM FOR TWO PLAYERS (P)
TEDDY AND ALICE (P)
SAM (P)
BULLY (P)   also screenplay
THESE ARE NOT CHILDREN (P)
LILLIAN HELLMAN (P)

Screenplays:
THE MAN WHO STOLE THE MONA LISA
ESCAPE TO CHINA

JOAN FREEMAN ALDEN*
Contact: WGA - Los Angeles, 310/550-1000

STREETWALKIN'   Concorde/Cinema Group, 1985,
   w/Robert Alden & Diane Gonciarz, directed
UNCAGED *ANGEL IN RED*   Califilm, 1992, Story w/Robert Alden

ROBERT ALDEN*
Contact: WGA - Los Angeles, 310/550-1000

STREETWALKIN   Concorde/Cinema Group, 1985,
   w/Joan Freeman & Diane Gonciarz
UNCAGED *ANGEL IN RED*   Califilm, 1992,
   Story w/Joan Freeman Alden

STEVE ALDEN
Agent: United Talent Agency - Beverly Hills, 310/273-6700

Screenplays:
FALL TIME w/Paul Skemp

ROSEMARY ALDERETE*
Agent: Susan Smith & Associates - Beverly Hills, 213/852-4777

Screenplays:
SPURS
ANGEL BABY
FOR ONE SHINING MOMENT
LILY & EDDIE

PHILLIP ALDERTON
Agent: The Artists Group - Los Angeles, 310/552-1100

THE EXPENDABLES   Concorde, 1989
THE FACE OF THE ENEMY   Tri-Culture Pictures, 1990

WILL ALDIS*
(Will Porter)
Agent: William Morris Agency - Beverly Hills, 310/274-7451

BACK TO SCHOOL   Orion, 1986, w/Steven W. Kampmann,
   Harold Ramis & Peter Torokvei
THE COUCH TRIP   Orion, 1988, w/Steven W. Kampmann &
   Sean Stein
STEALING HOME   Warner Bros., 1988,
   w/Steven W. Kampmann, co-directed
CLIFFORD   Orion, 1994, w/Steven W. Kampmann as
   "Bobby Von Hayes & Jay Dee Rock"

Screenplays:
DID SHE LEAVE ME ANY MONEY?
YOUNG MEN WITH UNLIMITED CAPITAL
RECRUITING VIOLATIONS

DAVID ALEXANDER
Agent: The Parness Agency - Santa Monica, 310/319-1664

Screenplays:
VICTORY CITY

JESSE ALEXANDER
Agent: Broder-Kurland-Webb-Uffner - Beverly Hills, 310/281-3400

Screenplays:
SPRINT

LAWRENCE ALEXANDER*
Manager: The Anthony Elliot Company - Los Angeles, 310/284-6804

Screenplays:
TWISTER w/David Gordon

SCOTT LAWRENCE ALEXANDER*
Contact: WGA - Los Angeles, 310/550-1000

SPACED INVADERS   Buena Vista, 1990, w/Patrick Read Johnson

SCOTT M. ALEXANDER*
Agent: ICM - Beverly Hills, 310/550-4000

PROBLEM CHILD   Universal, 1990, w/Larry Karaszewski
PROBLEM CHILD 2   Universal, 1991, w/Larry Karaszewski
ED WOOD   Buena Vista, 1994, w/Larry Karaszewski

Screenplays:
LARRY FLYNT w/Larry Karaszewski
THAT DARN CAT   (remake) w/Larry Karaszewski
LITTLE DEMONS w/Larry Karaszewski
SLUSHY (Story) w/Larry Karaszewski
JUPITER NEEDS PARKING w/Larry Karaszewski
BLACKBALLED w/Larry Karaszewski
HOMEWRECKERS w/Larry Karaszewski
SEVEN DEADLY TIMS w/Larry Karaszewski

DANIELLE ALEXANDRA
Contact: Peter Dekom, Bloom, Dekom, Hergott & Cook - Los Angeles,
   310/278-8622

Screenplays:
UNDISCLOSED
THE DIARY OF A MADMAN
HIT ME WITH YOUR BEST SHOT
GQ
HOW TO HOST A MURDER (CTF)

RICHARD ALFIERI*
Manager: Creative Alliance Management - Los Angeles,
   213/962-6090

CHILDREN OF RAGE   LSF Productions, 1975
ECHOES   Entertainment Professionals, 1983

Screenplays:
MOONLIGHT BLONDE

DANIEL ALGRANT*
Agent: CAA - Beverly Hills, 310/288-4545

NAKED IN NEW YORK   Fine Line Features, 1993, directed

Screenplays:
THE NOVICE
CALL MY BROTHER BACK
DUET

TED ALLAN*
Agent: Mike Zimring Agency - Los Angeles, 310/278-8240

LIES MY FATHER TOLD ME ★   Columbia, 1975
FALLING IN LOVE AGAIN   International Picture Show Company,
    1980, w/Steven Paul & Susannah York
LOVE STREAMS   Cannon, 1984, w/John Cassavetes,
    from his play
DR. BETHUNE   Tara Releasing, 1993

Screenplays:
WEDDING BAND (from his play "The Third Day Comes"
    w/John Cassavetes)

ERIC ALLARD
Agent: Wallerstein-Kappelman Agency - Los Angeles, 213/782-0225
Contact: All Effects, 10845 Vanowen St. - Unit D, North Hollywood,
    CA 91605, 818/769-7300

Screenplays:
ROBONANNY

CANDACE ALLEN
Agent: CAA - Beverly Hills, 310/288-4545

Screenplays:
BOOKER T. WASHINGTON BRIGGS

CARLO ALLEN
Agent: Leslie Kallen Agency - Sherman Oaks, 818/906-2785

Screenplays:
ZEPATA M.D.
JUANITA'S GOLD
TIERRA

CHRIS ALLEN
THE LAST REMAKE OF BEAU GESTE   Universal, 1977,
    w/Marty Feldman
IN GOD WE TRUST   Universal, 1980, w/Marty Feldman

COREY ALLEN*
Agent: The Irv Schechter Company - Beverly Hills, 310/278-8070

AVALANCHE   New World, 1979, w/Claude Pola, directed

CURTIS ALLEN
WALKING THE EDGE   Empire Pictures, 1985
HARRY'S MACHINE   Cannon, 1986
BLOODSTONE   Omega Pictures, 1989, w/Nico Mastorakis
BLIND VENGEANCE (CTF)   Spanish Trail Productions, 1990,
    w/Henri Simoun
ALLIGATOR II: THE MUTATION   New Line Home Video/
    Group 1 Films, 1992

JAMES ALLEN*
Contact: WGA - Los Angeles, 310/550-1000

HIDDEN AGENDA   Hemdale, 1990
RAINING STONES   Northern Arts Entertainment, 1994

JANIS ALLEN
MEATBALLS   Paramount, 1979, w/Len Blum & Dan Goldberg
DOUBLE NEGATIVE   Best Film and Video, 1980,
    w/Thomas Hedley Jr. & Charles Dennis

JAY PRESSON ALLEN*
Agent: ICM - New York, 212/556-5600

THE FIRST WIFE (P)
A LITTLE FAMILY BUSINESS (P)
TRU (P)
THE BIG LOVE (P) w/Brooke Allen
MARNIE   Universal, 1964
THE PRIME OF MISS JEAN BRODIE   20th Century-Fox, 1969

CABARET ★   Allied Artists, 1972
TRAVELS WITH MY AUNT   MGM, 1972, w/Hugh Wheeler
FUNNY LADY   Columbia, 1975, w/Arnold Schulman
JUST TELL ME WHAT YOU WANT   Warner Bros., 1980
PRINCE OF THE CITY ★   Orion/Warner Bros., 1981,
    w/Sidney Lumet
DEATHTRAP   Warner Bros., 1982

Screenplays:
THE DOUBT
THE AMERICAN FLAG
STONE w/J. Calley

J.T. ALLEN*
Agent: Broder-Kurland-Webb-Uffner - Beverly Hills, 310/281-3400

GERONIMO (CTF)   Turner Pictures, 1993
THE GOOD OLD BOYS (CTF)   Turner Pictures, 1994,
    w/Tommy Lee Jones

Screenplays:
MRS. WRIGHT
PRINCESS OF PLUTO
LIKE ANGELS
CLUB TABOO

KAREN ALLEN
Agent: The Gersh Agency - Beverly Hills, 310/274-6611

Screenplays:
SECOND COMING

STEPHANIE ALLEN*
Agent: Susan Smith & Associates - Beverly Hills, 213/852-4777

Screenplays:
MONTANA

WOODY ALLEN*
(Allen Stewart Konigsberg)
Agent: ICM - New York, 212/556-5600
Business Manager: Jack Rollins/Charles Joffe, 212/582-1940

DON'T DRINK THE WATER (P)   also teleplay
THE FLOATING LIGHT BULB (P)
WHAT'S NEW PUSSYCAT?   United Artists, 1965
TAKE THE MONEY AND RUN   Cinerama Releasing Corporation,
    1969, w/Mickey Rose, directed
BANANAS   United Artists, 1971, w/Mickey Rose, directed
PLAY IT AGAIN, SAM   Paramount, 1972, from his play
EVERYTHING YOU ALWAYS WANTED TO KNOW ABOUT SEX*
    (*BUT WERE AFRAID TO ASK)   United Artists, 1972, directed
SLEEPER   United Artists, 1973, w/Marshall Brickman, directed
LOVE AND DEATH   United Artists, 1975, directed
ANNIE HALL ★★   United Artists, 1977,
    w/Marshall Brickman, directed
INTERIORS ★   United Artists, 1978, directed
MANHATTAN ★   United Artists, 1979, w/Marshall Brickman, directed
STARDUST MEMORIES   United Artists, 1980, directed
A MIDSUMMER NIGHT'S SEX COMEDY   Orion/Warner Bros.,
    1982, directed
ZELIG   Orion/Warner Bros., 1983, directed
BROADWAY DANNY ROSE ★   Orion, 1984, directed
THE PURPLE ROSE OF CAIRO ★   Orion, 1985, directed
HANNAH AND HER SISTERS ★★   Orion, 1986, directed
RADIO DAYS ★   Orion, 1987, directed
SEPTEMBER   Orion, 1987, directed
ANOTHER WOMAN   Orion, 1988, directed
NEW YORK STORIES   Buena Vista, 1989,
    "Oedipus Wrecks," directed
CRIMES AND MISDEMEANORS ★   Orion, 1989, directed
ALICE ★   Orion, 1990, directed
SHADOWS AND FOG   Orion, 1992, directed
HUSBANDS AND WIVES ★   TriStar, 1993, directed
MANHATTAN MURDER MYSTERY   TriStar, 1993,
    w/Marshall Brickman, directed
BULLETS OVER BROADWAY   Miramax, 1994,
    w/Doug McGrath, directed

KIRSTIE ALLEY
Agent: Metropolitan Talent Agency - Los Angeles, 213/857-4500

Screenplays:
HOLD ON TIGHT

MICHAEL ALMEREYDA*
Contact: WGA - New York, 212/245-6180

CHERRY 2000   Orion, 1988
TWISTER   Vestron, 1989, directed
ANOTHER GIRL, ANOTHER PLANET   1993, directed
SEARCH AND DESTROY   October Films, 1994
NADJA   Kino Link Co., 1994, directed

Screenplays:
HAPPY HERE AND NOW
THE FUTURE
TESLA
THE RED HANDS
MANDRAKE THE MAGICIAN

PEDRO ALMODOVAR
Business: El Deseo, Ruiz Perello 15, Madrid 28028, Spain, 255-0285

PEPI, LUCI & BOM   Figaro, 1981, directed (rereleased 1989)
LABYRINTH OF PASSION   Cinevista, 1982, directed
DARK HABITS   Cinevista, 1984, directed
WHAT HAVE I DONE TO DESERVE THIS?   Cinevista,
   1985, directed
MATADOR   Cinevista, 1986, directed
LAW OF DESIRE   Cinevista/Promovision International,
   1987, directed
WOMEN ON THE VERGE OF A NERVOUS BREAKDOWN
   Orion Classics, 1988, directed
TIE ME UP! TIE ME DOWN!   *ATAME!*   Miramax, 1990, directed
HIGH HEELS   Miramax, 1991, directed
KIKA   October Films, 1994, directed

Screenplays:
THE KILLER'S TOENAILS (directing)

ARTHUR ALSBERG*
Contact: WGA - Los Angeles, 310/550-1000

NO DEPOSIT, NO RETURN   Buena Vista, 1976,
   w/Donald R. Nelson
GUS   Buena Vista, 1976, w/Donald R. Nelson
HERBIE GOES TO MONTE CARLO   Buena Vista, 1977,
   w/Donald R. Nelson
HOT LEAD AND COLD FEET   Buena Vista, 1978,
   w/Donald R. Nelson & Joe McEveety

JOHN ALSOP
BRIDES OF CHRIST (CMS)   Roadshow, Coote & Carroll, 1993,
   w/Sue Smith

EMMETT ALSTON
NEW YEAR'S EVIL   Cannon, 1981,
   Story w/Leonard Neubauer, directed
NINE DEATHS OF THE NINJA   Crown International, 1985, directed
HUNTER'S BLOOD   Concorde, 1987

Screenplays:
DEATH AMONG STRANGERS   w/Andrew Chiaramonte

GREG ALT
ZORRO, THE GAY BLADE   20th Century-Fox, 1981,
   Story w/Hal Dresner, Don Moriarty & Bob Randall

RICHARD ALTABEF
THE KISSING PLACE (CTF)   Wilshire Court Productions, 1990,
   w/Cynthia A. Cherbak & Michael Wing

ERIC ALTER
HARDBODIES   Columbia, 1984, w/Steven Greene & Mark Griffiths
HARDBODIES 2   CineTel Films, 1986, as "Curtis Wilmot,"
   w/Mark Griffiths
THE EXPERTS   Paramount, 1988, w/Steven Greene & Nick Thiel

Screenplays:
MARRYING UP   w/Steven Greene

SERGIO D. ALTIERI
Agent: Susan Smith & Associates - Beverly Hills, 213/852-4777

BLIND FEAR   Image Organization, 1989
HIDDEN LENS   Taitanus Distrubuzione International, 1992,
   w/Massimo Mazzucco
LITTLE SISTER   Video 80 Productions, 1992, w/Franco Ferrini,
   Carlo Vanzina & Enrico Vanzina

Screenplays:
GROUND ZERO   w/Martin Zurla
DARK RAIN
IRONHORSE 1
FIRESTORM   w/John Eckenrod
THE ARMAGEDDON MACHINE
EDGE OF THE LABYRINTH   w/Richard Friedman
PANAMA RED   w/Barry Roberts
AFTERBURNER
TANKER HILL
THE ALGONQUIN GOOD-BYE
DEADLY VISION
DIE, YUPPIE SCUM!
NEMESIS   w/Steven Iyama
KATANGA

ROBERT ALTMAN*
Agent: William Morris Agency - Beverly Hills, 310/274-7451
Business: Sandcastle 5 Productions, 502 Park Avenue - Suite 156,
   New York, NY 10022, 212/826-6641

McCABE & MRS. MILLER   Warner Bros., 1971,
   w/Brian McKay, directed
IMAGES   Columbia, 1972, directed
THIEVES LIKE US   United Artists, 1974, w/Joan Tewkesbury &
   Calder Willingham, directed
BUFFALO BILL AND THE INDIANS or SITTING BULL'S HISTORY
   LESSON   United Artists, 1976, w/Alan Rudolph, directed
3 WOMEN   20th Century-Fox, 1977, directed
A WEDDING   20th Century-Fox, 1978, w/John Considine,
   Allan Nicholls & Patricia Resnick, directed
QUINTET   20th Century-Fox, 1979, w/Frank Barhydt &
   Patricia Resnick, directed
A PERFECT COUPLE   20th Century-Fox, 1979,
   w/Allan Nicholls, directed
HEALTH   20th Century-Fox, 1980, w/Frank Barhydt & Paul Dooley
BEYOND THERAPY   New World, 1987,
   w/Christopher Durang, directed
SHORT CUTS   Fine Line Features, 1993,
   w/Frank Barhydt, directed
READY TO WEAR (PRET-A-PORTER)   Miramax, 1994,
   w/Barbara Shulgasser, directed

Screenplays:
KANSAS CITY   w/Frank Barhydt

SHELLY ALTMAN*
Agent: The Gersh Agency - New York, 212/997-1818

SWEET LORRAINE   Angelika Films, 1987, w/Michael Zettler

JOHN ALTSCHULER*
Agent: ICM - Beverly Hills, 310/550-4000

Screenplays:
HEADHUNTERS   w/David Krinsky
BRAINMAN   w/David Krinsky & David Palmer
DOUBLE HITCH   w/David Krinsky & David Palmer

DAVID AMANN*
Agent: Sanford-Gross & Associates - Los Angeles, 310/208-2100

DEAD AIR (CTF)   MCA Television Entertainment, 1994

MARINO AMARUSO
BEACH HOUSE   New Line Cinema, 1982, w/John Gallagher

ROD AMATEAU*
Agent: CAA - Beverly Hills, 310/288-4545

HOOK, LINE AND SINKER   Columbia, 1968
WHERE DOES IT HURT?   American International, 1972, directed
THE WILBY CONSPIRACY   United Artists, 1975,
    w/Harold Nebenzal
THE GARBAGE PAIL KIDS MOVIE   Atlantic Releasing Corporation,
    1987, w/Melinda Palmer, directed
SUNSET   Tri-Star, 1988, Story

Screenplays:
PURSUIT MANUMIT w/Harold Nebenzal

STEVEN AMBLIN
Contact: British Academy of Film & Television Arts, 195 Piccadilly,
    London W1, England, 01/734-0022

Screenplays:
FIRST (BBC Productions/British Screen)

DAVID AMBROSE*
Agent: William Morris Agency - Beverly Hills, 310/274-7451

BATTLE FOR ROME   CCC Filmkunst, 1969
THE 5TH MUSKETEER   Columbia, 1979
THE FINAL COUNTDOWN   United Artists, 1980, w/Gerry Davis,
    Thomas Hunter & Peter Powell
THE SURVIVOR   Hemdale, 1981
A DANGEROUS SUMMER   Filmco Ltd., 1982
AMITYVILLE 3-D   Orion, 1983, as "William Wales"
D.A.R.Y.L.   Paramount, 1985, w/Jeffrey Ellis & Allan Scott
BLACKOUT (CTF)   1985
TAFFIN   MGM/UA, 1988
THE FRENCH REVOLUTION   Films Ariane/Films A2/Laura Films/
    Antea, 1989
YEAR OF THE GUN   Triumph Releasing, 1991

Screenplays:
TREASURE HUNT
THE LIARS
THE RESCUE OF GENERAL DOZIER (CTF)
SPECTER
TREACHEROUS
INSIDE OUT
KISS OR KILL (CTF)
THE SEDUCTRESS
THE BOOKBINDER
QUEEN CHRISTINA
GOOD MORNING, HE LIED

DEBORAH L. AMELON*
Agent: Jim Preminger Agency - Los Angeles, 310/475-9491

THE LAST SHOT (Short)   1993, directed
EXIT TO EDEN   Savoy, 1994, w/Bob Brunner

Screenplays:
AN AMERICAN TRAGEDY: THE TONYA HARDING STORY
    (directing)
TRICKS
ROPE DANCING
MY SENIOR YEAR
TRAVELLING SALESLADY

CHRISTOPHER AMES*
Agent: Richland/Wunsch/Hohman Agency - Los Angeles,
    310/278-1955
Business: North Beach Productions, 818/591-2222

CLASS ACTION   20th Century Fox, 1991, w/Carolyn Shelby &
    Samantha Shad

Screenplays:
LEADER OF THE PACK w/Carolyn Shelby
IT'S NOT THE MONEY w/Carolyn Shelby
BLACK AND BLUE w/Carolyn Shelby
CHAPEL OF LOVE w/Carolyn Shelby
THE MAGIC COTTAGE w/Carolyn Shelby

TAYLOR AMES*
Agent: The Partos Company - Los Angeles, 213/876-5500

HE'S MY GIRL   Scotti Bros., 1987, w/Charles F. Bohl

STEVE AMICK
Agent: Writers & Artists Agency - Los Angeles, 310/824-6300

Screenplays:
BARNABY'S ARMY

GIDEON AMIR*
Contact: Action Plus Pictures - Los Angeles, 310/271-8596

AMERICAN NINJA   Cannon, 1985, Story w/Avi Kleinberger
P.O.W. THE ESCAPE   Cannon, 1986,
    Story w/Avi Kleinberger, directed

MARTIN AMIS
Agent: Peters, Fraser & Dunlop - London, 071/376-7676

SATURN 3   AFD, 1980

FRANCO AMURRI*
Agent: The Gersh Agency - Beverly Hills, 310/274-6611
Business Manager: Armstrong, Hirsch, Jackoway, Tyerman &
    Wertheimer - Los Angeles, 310/553-0305

MONKEY TROUBLE   New Line Cinema, 1994,
    w/Stu Krieger, directed

ALLISON ANDERS*
Agent: Broder-Kurland-Webb-Uffner - Beverly Hills, 310/281-3400

BORDER RADIO   International Film Marketing, 1988,
    w/Dean Lent & Kurt Voss
GAS, FOOD, LODGING   I.R.S. Releasing, 1992, directed
MI VADA LOCA   Sony Pictures Classics, 1994, directed
FOUR ROOMS   Miramax, 1995, "Strange Brew," directed

Screenplays:
GRACE OF MY HEART (directing)
PAUL IS DEAD
THE LOST HIGHWAY

ANDY ANDERSON
Business: 817/461-1228

POSITIVE I.D.   Universal, 1987, directed

ELIZABETH ANDERSON*
Agent: Sanford-Gross & Associates - Los Angeles, 310/208-2100

LASSIE   Paramount, 1994, w/Matthew Jacobs & Gary Ross

Screenplays:
THREE WISHES (Rysher Entertainment)

ELLIOTT ANDERSON*
Agent: Ken Sherman & Associates -213/273-8840

Screenplays:
KIT BRANDON w/Adrianne Fincham
MINUS ONE w/Adrianne Fincham
FREE JOANN LITTLE
BOOKER
SALSA
MAGICIAN
RIDEOUT

GERRY ANDERSON
THUNDERBIRD SIX   United Artists, 1968, w/Sylvia Anderson
JOURNEY TO THE FAR SIDE OF THE SUN   Universal, 1969,
    w/Sylvia Anderson & Donald James

HESPER ANDERSON*
Agent: United Talent Agency - Beverly Hills, 310/273-6700

L.A. WOMAN (P)
BILLIE BOY (P)
TOUCHED BY LOVE   Columbia, 1980
CHILDREN OF A LESSER GOD ★   Paramount, 1986,
    w/Mark Medoff
GRANDE ISLE (CTF)   Turner Pictures, 1991

Screenplays:
PEKING STORY
WYATT'S PARADISE
GOING HOME
BECOMING THE BUTLERS
COLOR OF EVENING
LEADER OF THE PACK
LOVE, HONOR, THE U.S. ARMY
THE WOMEN WHO RODE AWAY
MORNING, WINTER AND NIGHT

HOWARD L. ANDERSON*
Contact: WGA - Los Angeles, 310/550-1000

Screenplays:
F AS IN PHILADELPHIA
SAGITTARIUS PART I — DUBLINERS
ANNIE II

JANE ANDERSON*
Agent: The Gage Group - Los Angeles, 310/859-8777

THE BABY DANCE (P)
THE PINK STUDIO (P)
HOTEL OUBLIETTE (P)
FODD AND SHELTER (P)
DEFYING GRAVITY (P)
LYNETTE AT 3 A.M. (P)
THE POSITIVELY TRUE ADVENTURES OF THE ALLEGED TEXAS
    CHEERLEADER-MURDERING MOM (CTF)   HBO Pictures, 1993
IT COULD HAPPEN TO YOU   TriStar, 1994
HOW TO MAKE AN AMERICAN QUILT   Universal, 1995

Screenplays:
PEACE OF MIND (CTF)
LADY ICARUS

KATHLEEN MCGHEE - ANDERSON
(See Kathleen McGHEE-Anderson)

KENT ANDERSON
MOTORCYCLE GANG (CTF)   Showtime/Drive-In Classic Cinema,
    1994, w/Laurie McQuillan

PAUL ANDERSON
Manager: Carlyle Management - Los Angeles, 213/469-3086

SHOPPING   Film Four, 1994, directed

Screenplays:
THE COMMANDER
PROVIDENCE

ROBERT ANDERSON*
Agent: ICM - Beverly Hills, 310/550-4000

THE LAST ACT IS A SOLO (P)
TEA AND SYMPATHY   MGM, 1956, from his play
UNTIL THEY SAIL   MGM, 1957
THE NUN'S STORY ★   Warner Bros., 1959
THE SAND PEBBLES   20th Century-Fox, 1966
I NEVER SANG FOR MY FATHER ★   Columbia, 1969,
    from his play

STERLING ANDERSON
Agent: APA - Los Angeles, 310/273-0744

Screenplays:
PHOENIX

STEVE ANDERSON*
Agent: The Gersh Agency - Beverly Hills, 310/274-6611

HEARTS OF STONE (Short)   1991, w/Jana Sue Memel &
    Tee Rodgers, directed
SOUTH CENTRAL   Warner Bros., 1992, directed

Screenplays:
BLUE, BLUE MONEY
BABY INSANE AND THE BUDDHA

WES ANDERSON
Agent: United Talent Agency - Beverly Hills, 310/273-6700

BOTTLE ROCKET   Columbia, 1995, w/Owen Wilson, directed,
    from their short film

WILLIAM C. ANDERSON*
Contact: 208/853-4812

BAT-21   Tri-Star, 1988, w/Marc Norman

MARIO ANDREACCHIO
NAPOLEON   Samuel Goldwyn Company, 1995,
    w/Michael Bourchier, directed

GUY ANDREWS
Agent: Curtis Brown - London, 071/872-0331

LIE DOWN WITH LIONS (CMS)   Hannibal Productions, 1994,
    w/Julian Bond

PETER ANTHONY ANDREWS
THE IMPORTANCE OF BEING EARNEST   Eclectic/Paco Globall
    Productions, 1991, Adaptation, w/Kurt Baker

TINA ANDREWS*
Agent: William Morris Agency - Beverly Hills, 310/274-7451

Screenplays:
MISTRESS OF MONTICELLO
FRANKIE: THE FRANKIE LYMON STORY
IN SEARCH OF DOROTHY
THE POWER OF NO

An

FILM
WRITERS
GUIDE

F
I
L
M

W
R
I
T
E
R
S

JAMES ANDRONICA
Contact: Herb Nanas, MNS Entertainment, 310/820-9897

NUNZIO   Universal, 1978
THE NOVEMBER MEN   Arrow Releasing, 1993

DAVID H. ANDRUS*
Contact: WGA - Los Angeles, 310/550-1000

Screenplays:
THE MAN WITH NO SOUL
BOLT UPRIGHT
HARRY
GHOST BOY
PILGRIM

MARK ANDRUS*
Agent: Richland/Wunsch/Hohman Agency - Los Angeles,
   310/278-1955

LATE FOR DINNER   Columbia, 1991

Screenplays:
OLD FRIENDS
BE TRUE TO YOUR SCHOOL
THE M WORD
QUARTERTIME
HARDCOVER DREAMS
JUMP
THE BORRIBLES
ACTING ITALIAN

DAN ANGEL*
Contact: Bob Wyman, 310/277-2001 or Evan Corday, 818/972-4330

JOHN CARPENTER'S BODY BAGS (CTF)   Showtime, 1993,
   w/Billy Brown

Screenplays:
THE MIGHTY MORPHIN POWER RANGERS MOVIE w/Billy Brown
DYSFUNCTIONALLY YOURS w/Billy Brown
BOX OFFICE GROSS w/Billy Brown
RUDE WARRIORS w/Billy Brown
SHOCK TREATMENT w/Billy Brown

MIKEL ANGEL
EVIL SPIRITS   Prism Entertainment, 1991

MICHAEL ANGELI
Agent: William Morris Agency - Beverly Hills, 310/274-7451

SKETCH ARTIST (CTF)   Motion Picture Corporation of
   America, 1992

Screenplays:
MOTION'S BIBLE
THE RED RIVER GANG
THE LEGEND OF GALGAMETH

EDWARD ANHALT*
Contact: WGA - Los Angeles, 310/550-1000

PANIC IN THE STREETS ★   20th Century-Fox, 1950,
   w/Edna Anhalt & Richard Murphy
THE SNIPER ★   Columbia, 1952, w/Edna Anhalt
A GIRL NAMED TAMIKO   Paramount, 1952
THE MEMBER OF THE WEDDING   Columbia, 1953, w/Edna Anhalt
NOT AS A STRANGER   United Artists, 1955, w/Edna Anhalt
THE PRIDE AND THE PASSION   United Artists, 1957,
   w/Edna Anhalt
IN LOVE AND WAR   20th Century-Fox, 1958
THE YOUNG LIONS   20th Century-Fox, 1958
THE RESTLESS YEARS   Universal-International, 1959
THE SINS OF RACHEL CADE   Warner Bros., 1960
THE YOUNG SAVAGES   United Artists, 1961, w/J.P. Miller
GIRLS, GIRLS, GIRLS   Wallis-Hazen, 1962, w/Allan Weiss

WIVES AND LOVERS   Paramount, 1963
BECKET ★★   Paramount, 1964
BOEING-BOEING   Paramount, 1965
THE SATAN BUG   United Artists, 1965, w/James Clavell
HOUR OF THE GUN   United Artists, 1967
IN ENEMY COUNTRY   Universal, 1968
THE BOSTON STRANGLER   20th Century-Fox, 1968
THE MADWOMAN OF CHAILLOT   Warner Bros., 1969
JEREMIAH JOHNSON   Warner Bros., 1972, w/John Milius
LUTHER   American Express, 1973
THE MAN IN THE GLASS BOOTH   American FilmTheatre, 1975
ESCAPE TO ATHENA   AFD, 1979, w/Richard S. Lochte
GREEN ICE   Universal/AFD, 1981, w/others
THE HOLCROFT COVENANT   Universal, 1985,
   w/George Axelrod & John Hopkins

KEN ANNAKIN*
Business Manager: Stephany Hurkos - 818/763-6601

THOSE MAGNIFICENT MEN IN THEIR FLYING MACHINES ★
   20th Century-Fox, 1965, w/Jack Davies, directed
THOSE DARING YOUNG MEN IN THEIR JAUNTY JALOPIES
   Paramount, 1969, w/Jack Davies, directed
THE NEW ADVENTURES OF PIPPI LONGSTOCKING   Columbia,
   1988, directed

JEAN-JACQUES ANNAUD
Agent: ICM - Beverly Hills, 310/550-4000

BLACK AND WHITE IN COLOR   *LA VICTOIRE EN CHANTANT*
   Allied Artists, 1978, w/Georges Conchon, directed
THE LOVER   MGM, 1992, w/Gerard Brach, directed
WINGS OF COURAGE   TriStar, 1994, directed

JOSEPH ANSOLABEHERE*
Contact: WGA - Los Angeles, 310/550-1000

Screenplays:
SURFIN' CIA w/Stephen Viksten
EXTERMINATORS w/Stephen Viksten

BRIAN ANTHONY
VICTOR'S BIG SCORE   Mushikuki Productions, 1992, directed

RICHARD J. ANTHONY
ECHOES   Continental, 1983

STEVE ANTIN
Agent: ICM - Beverly Hills, 310/550-4000

INSIDE MONKEY ZETTERLAND   Coast Entertainment, 1992

Screenplays:
FROM THIS DAY FORWARD

MICHELANGELO ANTONIONI
CACCIA TRAGICA (THE TRAGIC PURSUIT)   Lux, 1947, w/others
IL GRIDO (THE CRY)   Astor, 1957, w/Elio Bartolini &
   Ennio de Concini, directed
L'AVVENTURA   Janus, 1961, w/Tonino Guerra &
   Elio Bartolini, directed
LA NOTTE   Lopert, 1961, w/Ennio Flaiano &
   Tonino Guerra, directed
L'ECLISSE   Times, 1962, w/others, directed
RED DESERT   Rizzoli, 1965, w/Tonino Guerra, directed
BLOW-UP ★   Premier, 1966, w/Tonino Guerra &
   Edward Bond, directed
ZABRISKIE POINT   MGM, 1970, w/Fred Gardner, Tonino Guerra,
   Clare Peploe & Sam Shepard, directed
THE PASSENGER *PROFESSIONE: REPORTER*   MGM/United
   Artists, 1975, w/Mark Peploe & Peter Wollen, directed

Screenplays:
THE CREW w/Mark Peploe (directing)

30

GREG ANTONACCI*
Agent: The Irv Schechter Company - Beverly Hills, 310/278-8070

Screenplays:
TIL DEATH DO US PART

BILL APABLASA
Agent: Maggie Field Agency - Studio City, 818/980-2001

AIRBORNE   Warner Bros., 1993

JUDD APATOW*
Agent: United Talent Agency - Beverly Hills, 310/273-6700

HEAVYWEIGHTS   Buena Vista, 1995, w/Steven Brill

Screenplays:
CELTIC PRIDE

LEAH APPET*
Agent: David Shapira & Associates - Sherman Oaks, 818/906-0322

EVERY TIME WE SAY GOODBYE   Tri-Star, 1986,
   w/Rachel Fabien & Moshe Mizrahi

Screenplays:
THE WAY WE ARE
VALENTINE
UNFINISHED BUSINESS
THE BLUE VEIL

MAX APPLE*
Agent: ICM - Beverly Hills, 310/550-4000

SMOKEY BITES THE DUST   New World, 1981
THE AIR UP THERE   Buena Vista, 1994
ROOMMATES   Buena Vista, 1994, w/Stephen Metcalfe

DANIEL APPLEBY
BOUND AND GAGGED: A LOVE STORY   G.E.L., 1993, directed

GREGG ARAKI
THREE BEWILDERED PEOPLE IN THE NIGHT
   Desperate Pictures Ltd., directed
THE LONG WEEKEND (O'DESPAIR)   Desperate Pictures Ltd.,
   1989, directed
THE LIVING END   Strand Releasing, 1992, directed
TOTALLY F***ED UP   Strand Releasing, 1994, directed

SHIMON ARAMA
Business: Arama Entertainment, 4614 Monarca Dr., Tarzana, CA
   91356, 818/344-4477

TRIUMPH OF THE SPIRIT   Nova International Films, 1989,
   Story w/Zion Haen

DAVID ARATA*
Agent: Innovative Artists - Los Angeles, 310/553-5200

Screenplays:
NOCTURNE w/Alex Sokoloff
DOUBLE FAULT w/Alex Sokoloff

PAUL ARATOW*
Contact: WGA - Los Angeles, 310/550-1000

PURGATORY   New Star Entertainment, 1989, w/Felix Kroll

ALFONSO ARAU
Agent: CAA - Beverly Hills, 310/288-4545

Screenplays:
REGINA w/Laura Esquivel

DENYS ARCAND
Agent: CAA - Beverly Hills, 310/288-4545
Address: 3365 Ridgewood - Suite 1, Montreal, Quebec H3V 1B4,
   Canada, 514/341-6139

THE DECLINE OF THE AMERICAN EMPIRE   Cineplex Odeon,
   1986, directed
JESUS OF MONTREAL   Orion Classics, 1990, directed

Screenplays:
THE LAST SHOT (directing)

MANUEL ARCE*
Contact: WGA - New York, 212/245-6180

EL SUPER   Columbia, 1979, w/Leon Ichaso
CROSSOVER DREAMS   Miramax, 1985, w/Leon Ichaso &
   Ruben Blades

JEFFREY ARCH*
Agent: William Morris Agency - Beverly Hills, 310/274-7451

FOR SALE (P)
SLEEPLESS IN SEATTLE ★   TriStar, 1993, w/Nora Ephron &
   David S. Ward
IRON WILL   Buena Vista, 1994, w/John Michael Hayes &
   Djordje Milicevic

Screenplays:
LONGFELLOW BRIDGE
PEOPLE WATCHERS
PERFECT TIMING
BLUE MOON
THE DIEGO AFFAIR
THE GEORGIA WALTZ
SPECIAL DELIVERY
DESPERATE MEASURES
EXIT THE RAINMAKER
FRENCH TOAST
FREE AGENTS
THE BELL TOWER

VICTORIA ARCH
Agent: Warden, White & Kane - Beverly Hills, 213/852-1028

Screenplays:
A TERRIBLE BEAUTY
CARDANO
QUEENSLAND
ENGAGED

EVAN P. ARCHERD
AMERICAN ANTHEM   Columbia, 1986, w/Jeff Benjamin

DARIO ARGENTO
Agent: United Talent Agency - Beverly Hills, 310/273-6700

THE BIRD WITH THE CRYSTAL PLUMMAGE   UMC, 1970, directed
CAT O'NINE TAILS   National General, 1971, directed
SUSPIRIA   International Classics, 1977, w/Dario Nicolodi, directed
UNSANE *TENEBRAE*   Bedford Entertainment/FilmGallery,
   1982, directed
CREEPERS *PHENOMENA*   New Line Cinema, 1985, directed
INFERNO   20th Century Fox, 1986, directed
TWO EVIL EYES   Taurus Entertainment, 1993, "The Black Cat"
   w/Franco Ferrini, directed

KEVIN ARKADIE*
Agent: United Talent Agency - Beverly Hills, 310/273-6700

UP THE MOUNTAIN (P)
A LIFE LIKE THE REST (P)

Screenplays:
ALMA'S
FIRE IN THE HOLE
TOTAL ECLIPSE

ADAM ARKIN
Agent: Susan Smith & Associates - Beverly Hills, 213/852-4777

IMPROPER CHANNELS   Crown International, 1981,
   w/Morrie Rubinsky & Ian Sutherland

ALICE ARLEN*
Agent: ICM - New York, 212/556-5600

SILKWOOD ★   20th Century-Fox, 1983, w/Nora Ephron
ALAMO BAY   Tri-Star, 1985
COOKIE   Warner Bros., 1989, w/Nora Ephron

Screenplays:
STRANGE JUSTICE: THE SELLING OF CLARENCE THOMAS (CTF)
   w/Jamal Joseph
HIGGINS & BEECH w/Nora Ephron
MODERN BRIDE w/Nora Ephron & Joan Taylor
OH BABY
THEN SHE FOUND ME
I THOUGHT I SAW YOU
SKINNER
DEMOCRACY
TROUBLESHOOTER

ANDY ARMITAGE
FRANKIE'S HOUSE (CMS)   Roadshow, Coote & Carroll/A&E, 1993

Screenplays:
FEMME FATALE

FRANK ARMITAGE
(See John Carpenter)

GEORGE B. ARMITAGE*
Agent: ICM - Beverly Hills, 310/550-4000

GAS-S-S-S!...OR HOW IT BECAME NECESSARY TO
   DESTROY THE WORLD IN ORDER TO SAVE IT!
   American International, 1970
HIT MAN   MGM, 1972, directed
PRIVATE DUTY NURSES   New World, 1972, directed
NIGHT CALL NURSES   New World, 1974
DARK TOWN STRUTTERS   New World, 1975
VIGILANTE FORCE   United Artists, 1976, directed
THE LAST OF THE FINEST   Orion, 1990, w/Jere Cunningham &
   Thomas Lee Wright
MIAMI BLUES   Orion, 1990, directed

Screenplays:
THE LATE SHIFT (CTF, directing)
RADIANT CURSOR
DANCING IN THE STREET
HYPE
CAPISTRANO

CURTIS ARMSTRONG*
Contact: WGA - Los Angeles, 310/550-1000

Screenplays:
HOLLYWOOD SCANDAL w/John Doolittle

MICHAEL ARMSTRONG
Agent: William Morris Agency - Beverly Hills, 310/274-7451

Screenplays:
TWO IF BY SEA w/Denis Leary
NOOSE w/Denis Leary

MICHAEL ARMSTRONG
Home: 114 N. Doheny Drive, Los Angeles, CA 90048

HORROR HOUSE   *THE HAUNTED HOUSE OF HORROR*
   American International, 1970, w/Peter Marcus, directed
THE BLACK PANTHER   Impics, 1977
HOUSE OF THE LONG SHADOWS   Cannon, 1984

EDDIE ARNO
Agent: William Morris Agency - Beverly Hills, 310/274-7451

MURDER STORY   Contracts International/Elsevier-Vendex Film,
   1989, w/Markus Innocenti, co-directed

DANNY ARNOLD*
Contact: WGA - Los Angeles, 310/550-1000

THE CADDY   Paramount, 1953, w/Edmund Hartmann
THE LADY TAKES A FLYER   Universal International, 1958

FRANK ARNOLD
HUMANOIDS FROM THE DEEP   New World, 1980,
   Story w/Martin B. Cohan

DAVID ARNOTT*
Agent: ICM - Beverly Hills, 310/550-4000

THE ADVENTURES OF FORD FAIRLANE   20th Century Fox, 1990,
   w/James Cappe & Daniel Waters
LAST ACTION HERO   Columbia, 1992, w/Shane Black

Screenplays:
MR. COOL w/Fred Dekker

LARRY ARNSTEIN*
Agent: United Talent Agency - Beverly Hills, 310/273-6700

Screenplays:
MULTIPLE CHOICES w/David Hurwitz
ATOLL

BRUCE ARTHURS
Agent: Berzon Agency - Glendale, 818/548-1560

Screenplays:
JUNKER TOMMY

MORRIS ASGAR
PROJECT ELIMINATOR   South Gate Entertainment, 1991,
   Story w/H. Kaye Dyal

WILLIAM ASHER*
Agent: The Cooper Agency - Los Angeles, 310/277-8422

MUSCLE BEACH PARTY   American International, 1963, directed
BIKINI BEACH   American International, 1964, w/Robert Diller &
   Leo Townsend, directed
BEACH BLANKET BINGO   American International, 1965, directed
HOW TO STUFF A WILD BIKINI   American International,
   1965, directed
FIREBALL 500   American International, 1966, directed

MICHAEL ASHLEY*
Manager: Rix-Ubell Management - Los Angeles, 310/859-9733

Screenplays:
MURRAY

AL ASHTON
SAFE   BBC, 1993

PIERS ASHWORTH
NOSTRADAMUS   Orion Classics, 1994, w/Knut Boeser

Screenplays:
WAGES OF SIN
THE BARTENDER
FAMILY DIES
THE FRUIT PALACE

DYANNE ASIMOW*
(Dyanne A. Simon)
Agent: Broder-Kurland-Webb-Uffner - Beverly Hills, 310/281-3400

Screenplays:
RETURN TO TWO MOON JUNCTION
SIGHTSEER
GOLDEN GATE w/Roger Simon
A WILD SANCTUARY w/Roger Simon
PERSONAL LEAVE
MADCAP
PANAMA
TAKING CHARGE
THE BELA LUGOSI STORY
HARD FEELING

PETER ASKIN*
Agent: ICM - New York, 212/556-5600

SMITHEREENS   New Line Cinema, 1982, w/Ron Nyswaner

SAMSON ASLANIAN
TORMENT   New World, 1986, w/John Hopkins, co-directed

DAVID ASSAEL*
Agent: Wile Enterprises - Santa Monica, 310/828-9768

Screenplays:
CHAMPIONS OF THE HEART w/Sam Kute

PATTI ASTOR
ASSAULT OF THE KILLER BIMBOS   Empire, 1988,
    Story w/Ted Nicolau & Anita Rosenberg

JEFF ASTROF
Agent: Paradigm - Los Angeles, 310/277-4400

Screenplays:
THE CRUISE w/Mike Sikowitz

J.D. ATHENS
(See J. F. Lawton)

DAVID ATKINS
Agent: ICM - Beverly Hills, 310/550-4000

ARIZONA DREAM   UGC, 1993

Screenplays:
HOTEL CUCURACHA w/Ethan Cohen-Sitt

PETER ATKINS
Agent: William Morris Agency - Beverly Hills, 310/274-7451

HELLBOUND: HELLRAISER 2   New World, 1989
HELLRAISER III: HELL ON EARTH   Dimension Pictures, 1992

LARRY ATLAS*
Agent: William Morris Agency - New York, 212/586-5100

TOTAL ABANDON (P)

Screenplays:
BLUE HORIZON
TELL ME TRUE

PAUL ATTANASIO*
Agent: CAA - Beverly Hills, 310/288-4545

QUIZ SHOW   Buena Vista, 1994
DISCLOSURE   Warner Bros., 1994

Screenplays:
CAMPAIGN w/Andy Wolk
MOVING TARGET

THE BOBBY DARIN STORY
DONNIE BRASCO (directing)
SLOW BURN
STRANGERS IN THE NIGHT

DAVE AUBURN
Agent: CAA - Beverly Hills, 310/288-4545

Screenplays:
LAKE SHORE DRIVE

JOHN P. AUERBACH*
Agent: ICM - Beverly Hills, 310/550-4000

STEPFATHER II   Millimeter Films, 1989

MICHAEL J. AUERBACH*
Manager: Jon Brown, The Brown Group - Burbank, 818/955-7040

CITY OF GOD (P)
THE TIE THAT BINDS   Buena Vista, 1995

Screenplays:
WEB
DOUBLE HELIX
GOLDEN EAGLE
DETONATOR
PIROUETTE w/Daniel Faraldo
TERMINAL STATION
THE SEERSUCKER WHIPSAW
UNDERWORLD
EL DORADO
ALWAYS REMEMBERED
THE DEATH-SHIP
KABYLIA
LINE OF FIRE

BILLE AUGUST
Agent: CAA - Beverly Hills, 310/288-4545

TWIST AND SHOUT   Miramax, 1984, w/BjarneReuter, directed
PELLE THE CONQUEROR   Miramax, 1988, directed
THE HOUSE OF THE SPIRITS   Miramax, 1993, directed

JOHN AUGUST
Agent: Sanford-Gross & Associates - Los Angeles, 310/208-2100

Screenplays:
NOW AND THEN

JOE AUGUSTYN
Business: Paragon Arts International, 6777 Hollywood Blvd. -
    Suite 700, Hollywood, CA 90028, 213/465-5355

NIGHT OF THE DEMONS   International Film Marketing, 1988
NIGHT ANGEL   Fries Entertainment, 1990, w/Walter Josten
NIGHT OF THE DEMONS 2   Republic Pictures, 1994

PAUL AUSTER
Agent: William Morris Agency - Beverly Hills, 310/274-7451

SMOKE   Miramax, 1995

SAM AUSTER
Agent: Renaissance-H.N. Swanson - Los Angeles, 310/246-6000

SCREEN TEST   CineTel Films, 1986, w/Laura Auster, directed
BOUNTY HUNTER 20002   Westside Pictures, 1994

AL AUSTIN*
Agent: Camden-ITG - Los Angeles, 310/289-2700

Screenplays:
THE FIFTH STEP
HIDE YOUR LOVE AWAY
SAFE

CARL AUSTIN
IMPROPER CONDUCT   Everest Pictures, 1994

Screenplays:
THE KIDNAPPING w/J. Pepper Berry (directing)

IRVING AUSTIN
WARLORDS OF THE 21ST CENTURY   New World, 1982,
    w/John Beech & Harley Cokliss

MICHAEL AUSTIN*
Agent: ICM - Beverly Hills, 310/550-4000

THE SHOUT   Films Inc., 1979, w/Jerzy Skolimowski
FIVE DAYS ONE SUMMER   The Ladd Company/
    Warner Bros., 1982
GREYSTOKE: THE LEGEND OF TARZAN, LORD OF THE APES ★
    Warner Bros., 1984, w/P.H. Vazak
KILLING DAD   Scottish Television Film Enterprises, 1989, directed
PRINCESS CARABOO   TriStar, 1994, w/John Wells, directed

Screenplays:
WILD BILLY
MADNESS OF A SEDUCED WOMAN
TIMOTHY GEDGE
BARRICADE
SAINT HARRY
COSMIC CHARLIE

RAYMOND AUSTIN*
Agent: The Chasin Agency - Los Angeles, 310/278-7505

Screenplays:
THE GAME CONTINUES
SECRETS
THE BANKER
GHOST OF A CHANCE
FIND ME A SPY

RONALD AUSTIN*
Business Manager: Jon Vein, Dern & Vein, 310/557-2244

THE HAPPENING   Columbia, 1967, w/James D. Buchanan &
    Frank R. Pierson
HARRY IN YOUR POCKET   United Artists, 1973,
    w/James Buchanan

PHIL AVALON
Contact: Australian Film Commission, 8 West St., North Sydney,
    NSW 2026, Australia, tel.: 2/925-7333

EXCHANGE LIFEGUARDS   Beyond Films, 1993

DAVID AVALLONE
Manager: Melanie Luciano, Global Entertainment Network -
    Los Angeles, 213/848-4380

WHEN THE SKY WAS FALLING (Short) 1987, directed

Screenplays:
HELLEVATOR
CONJUGAL SON w/Susan Avallone
GRAND SAND WINDMASTER "T"
MAX RENEGADE
HIGH NOON AT MIDNIGHT
INTERSTATE JAKE

SUSAN AVALLONE
Agent: Susan Smith & Associates - Beverly Hills, 213/852-4777

Screenplays:
HOW TO BE A WOMAN AND NOT DIE IN THE ATTEMPT (remake)
CONJUGAL SON w/David Avallone
GROOM IS NONPRO   FIRST COMES MARRIAGE
AND SHE WAS

ROGER AVARY
Agent: William Morris Agency - Beverly Hills, 310/274-7451

KILLING ZOE   October Films, 1994, directed
PULP FICTION   Miramax, 1994, Story w/Quentin Tarantino

Screenplays:
STITCH (directing)
99 DAYS
MAFIA COP

HOWARD (HIKMET) AVEDIS*
Contact: Jerome E. Weinstein, Weinstein & Hart, 433 N. Camden Dr. -
    Suite 600, Beverly Hills, CA 90210, 310/274-7157

SCORCHY   American International, 1976, directed
THE FIFTH FLOOR   Film Ventures International, 1980,
    Story w/Marlene Schmidt, directed
MORTUARY   Artists Releasing Corporation/FilmVentures
    International, 1983, w/Marlene Schmidt, directed
THEY'RE PLAYING WITH FIRE   New World, 1984,
    w/Marlene Schmidt, directed
KIDNAPPED   Virgin Vision, 1987, directed

RUTH AVERGON
NIGHT SCHOOL   Paramount/Lorimar, 1981

CARLOS AVILA
LA CARPA   American Playhouse, 1993, w/Edit Villareal, directed

ROBERT J. AVRECH*
Agent: CAA - Beverly Hills, 310/288-4545

BODY DOUBLE   Columbia, 1984, w/Brian De Palma
DARK TOWER   Spectrafilm, 1989, w/Ken Weiderhorn &
    Ken Blackwell
A STRANGER AMONG US   Buena Vista, 1992

Screenplays:
THE CONSPIRACY w/William Bairn
LEDA AND SWAN
THE LADY KILLER
THE GAITS OF THE FOREST
BEAST
HOUR OF THE ANGEL
MAIDEN RUN
MABEL
HORSEMEN OF THE SILVER WALL

GEORGE AXELROD*
Manager: Krost/Chapin Management - Los Angeles, 310/281-3585

WILL SUCCESS SPOIL ROCK HUNTER (P)
GOODBYE CHARLIE (P)
PHFFFT   Columbia, 1954
THE SEVEN YEAR ITCH   20th Century-Fox, 1955, w/Billy Wilder,
    from his play
BUS STOP   20th Century-Fox, 1956
BREAKFAST AT TIFFANYS ★   Paramount, 1961
THE MANCHURIAN CANDIDATE   United Artists, 1962
HOW TO MURDER YOUR WIFE   United Artists, 1964
PARIS WHEN IT SIZZLES   Paramount, 1964
LORD LOVE A DUCK   United Artists, 1966,
    w/Larry H. Johnson, directed
THE SECRET LIFE OF AN AMERICAN WIFE   20th Century-Fox,
    1968, directed
THE LADY VANISHES   Rank, 1979
THE HOLCROFT COVENANT   Universal, 1985, w/Edward Anhalt &
    John Hopkins
THE FOURTH PROTOCOL   Lorimar, 1987, Story

M.R. AXELROD
Agent: Barry Perelman Agency - Los Angeles, 310/274-5999

TI AMO LUCIO OLIVETTI (P)
HUNGER (P) Adaptation
AN AUTHOR'S MOTHER (Short) Strawberry Mansion Films/
   Sagebrush Productions, 1990

Screenplays:
AND FOR THE GLORY OF SPORT
NAPOLEON AWAKENING
CHICAGO BARES
THE SHAKESPEARE CONSPIRACY
PARIS MATCH
FULL COURT PRESS
AUTUMN OF EVENING THUNDER
AFTER DORIS
THE FRAT
THE SEPHIROS PROJECT
THE AUGUST SPRINTER

DAVID AXLEROD*
Agent: ICM - New York, 212/556-5600

CHARLIE CHAN AND THE CURSE OF THE DRAGON QUEEN
   American Cinema, 1981, w/Stan Burns

ALAN AYCKBOURN
Agent: The Casarotto Company - London, 071/287-4450

ABSENT FRIENDS (P)
WOMAN IN MIND (P)
THE NORMAN CONQUESTS (P)
RELATIVELY SPEAKING (P)
MAN OF THE MOMENT (P)
HENCEFORWARD... (P)
TAKING STEPS (P)
ABSURD PERSON SINGULAR (P)
A SMALL FAMILY BUSINESS (P)
INTIMATE EXCHANGES (P)
WILDEST DREAMS (P)
MR. A'S AMAZING MAZE PLAYS (P)
A CHORUS OF DISAPPROVAL South Gate Entertainment, 1989,
   w/Michael Winner, from his play

DAN AYKROYD
Agent: CAA - Beverly Hills, 310/288-4545

THE BLUES BROTHERS Universal, 1980, w/John Landis
GHOSTBUSTERS Columbia, 1984, w/Harold Ramis
SPIES LIKE US Warner Bros., 1985, w/Lowell Ganz &
   Babaloo Mandel
DRAGNET Universal, 1987, w/Tom Mankiewicz & Alan Zweibel
GHOSTBUSTERS II Columbia, 1989, w/Harold Ramis
NOTHING BUT TROUBLE Warner Bros., 1991, directed
CONEHEADS Paramount, 1993, w/Tom Davis, Bonnie Turner &
   Terry Turner

Screenplays:
LAW OF THE YUKON

PETER J. AYKROYD*
Contact: Cooper, Epstein & Hurewitz - Beverly Hills, 310/278-1111

NOTHING BUT TROUBLE Warner Bros., 1991, Story

ALAN AYLWARD
CHAINDANCE Festival Films, 1991, w/Michael Ironside

JON AYRE
SURF NAZIS MUST DIE Troma, 1987

ALEX AYRES*
Agent: Preferred Artists - Encino, 818/990-0305

Screenplays:
MARLOWE
THE DEVIL'S ADVOCATE
FREE AT LAST

GERALD AYRES*
Agent: Paradigm - Los Angeles, 310/277-4400

FOXES United Artists, 1980
RICH AND FAMOUS MGM, 1981
CRAZY IN LOVE (CTF) Turner Pictures, 1992

Screenplays:
CHANGE OF HEART w/J.P. Miller
STEPPING
SMALL HOTEL
LADY FINGERS

RAFAEL AZCONA
AY, CARMELA! Prestige Films, 1991
BELLE EPOQUE Sony Classics, 1993

B

BETH B
Business: B Movies, Inc., 45 Crosby St., New York, NY 10012

VORTEX B Movies, 1982, w/Scott B, co-directed
SALVATION! Circle Films, 1987, w/Tom Robinson, directed
TWO SMALL BODIES Castle Hill, 1994, w/Neal Bell, directed

SCOTT B
Agent: The Tantleff Office - New York, 212/941-3939

VORTEX B Movies, 1982, w/Beth B, co-directed

THOM BABBES*
Agent: Renaissance-H.N. Swanson - Los Angeles, 310/246-6000

JUDGEMENT IN JERUSALEM (P)
ACROSS THE RIVER (P)
DEADLY DREAMS Concorde, 1989
BODY CHEMISTRY Concorde, 1990

Screenplays:
INSURRECTION
BLEEDING, WRITING & ARITHMETIC
THE SUBSTITUTE
ISLAND OF LONELY MEN

THOMAS BABE*
Agent: The Marion Rosenberg Office - Los Angeles, 213/653-7383

REBEL WOMEN (P)
KID CHAMPION (P)
A PRAYER FOR MY DAUGHTER (P)
FATHERS AND SONS (P)
TAKEN IN MARRIAGE (P)
SALT LAKE CITY SKYLINE (P)
BORN EVERY MINUTE (P)
BILLY IRISH (P)
BURIED INSIDE EXTRA (P)
MURDER IN THE DESERT (P)

Ba

**FILM
WRITERS**
GUIDE

F
I
L
M

W
R
I
T
E
R
S

GREAT SOLO TOWN (P)
HOME AGAIN, KATHLEEN (P)
WHEN WE WERE VERY YOUNG (P)
GREAT DAY IN THE MORNING (P)

Screenplays:
GRAD WEEK
DEATH IN THE DESERT
PHOTO

HECTOR BABENCO
Agent: ICM - Beverly Hills, 310/550-4000

LUCIO FLAVIO   Unifilm/Embrafilme, 1978, directed
PIXOTE   Unifilm/Embrafilme, 1981, directed
AT PLAY IN THE FIELDS OF THE LORD   Universal, 1991,
   w/Jean-Claude Carriere, directed

JIMMY SANTIAGO BACA*
Agent: Reid Boates Agency - 908/730-8523

BOUND BY HONOR   Buena Vista, 1993, w/Jeremy Iacone &
   Floyd Mutrux

DANIEL F. BACANER
Business: Fremont II, 8489 W. 3rd St., Los Angeles, CA 90048

SCARED STIFF   International Film Marketing, 1987,
   w/Richard Friedman & Mark Frost

DANILO BACH*
Agent: ICM - Beverly Hills, 310/550-4000

BEVERLY HILLS COP ★   Paramount, 1984,
   Story w/Daniel Petrie, Jr.
APRIL FOOL'S DAY   Paramount, 1986

Screenplays:
BOSS OF BOSSES
BEVERLY DRIVE
THE TRACE
FOXBAT
ACTUARY
EL SALVADOR
ENDANGERED
HORSE OPERA
TRIALS & TRIBULATION

MICHAEL BACKES*
Agent: The Brandt Company - Sherman Oaks, 818/783-7747

RISING SUN   20th Century Fox, 1993, w/Michael Crichton &
   Philip Kaufman

Screenplays:
THE STARS MY DESTINATION

TOM BADAL*
Contact: WGA - Los Angeles, 310/550-1000

OUT ON BAIL   Trans World Entertainment, 1989, w/Jason Booth &
   Michael D. Sonye
VIETNAM, TEXAS   Epic Productions, 1990, w/C. Courtney Joyner

R.M. (RANDALL) BADAT*
Agent: Paradigm - Los Angeles, 310/277-4400

SURF II   Arista, 1983, directed
HEAR NO EVIL   20th Century Fox, 1993, w/Kathleen Rowell

Screenplays:
SWEETHEART
FOREVER 17
THE DEVILS EYE
THE CUTTING EDGE
CHINESE HANDCUFFS

MEREDITH BAER*
Agent: The Gersh Agency - Beverly Hills, 310/274-6611

PRISONERS   20th Century Fox, 1984, w/H. Hincken
UN-BECOMING AGE   Castle Hill, 1993, w/Geoff Prysirv

Screenplays:
NOTHING BUT THE TRUTH
ROSES ARE RED   w/Gary Goldman
LOST AND FOUND
THE CONSULTANT
AT ANY COST

GEOFFREY BAERE*
Agent: Peter Turner Agency - Santa Monica, 310/315-4772

SCHOOL SPIRIT   Concorde/Cinema Group, 1985
CAMPUS MAN   Paramount, 1987, w/Matt Dorff & Alex Horvat
CORPORATE AFFAIRS   Concorde, 1990, w/Terence H. Winkless

Screenplays:
TEETH'N'SMILES
DATELINE: PARIS

RANDY C. BAER
BETTER OFF DEAD (CTF)   Viacom Productions, 1993, Story

TED BAFALOUKAS*
Contact: Keller & Vandernoth - New York, 212/741-0202

ROCKERS   New Yorker, 1979, directed

Screenplays:
SOUTH OF HEAVEN

MILTON BAGBY JR.
REBEL LOVE   Troma, 1985, directed

ROSS BAGDASARIAN
Business: Bagdasarian Productions, 4400 Coldwater Canyon -
   Suite 315, Studio City, CA 91604, 818/769-3210

THE CHIPMUNK ADVENTURE (AF)   Samuel Goldwyn Company,
   1986, w/Janice Karman

FAX BAHR*
Agent: United Talent Agency - Beverly Hills, 310/273-6700

HEARTS OF DARKNESS: A FILMMAKER'S APOCALYPSE (FD)
   Triton, 1992, w/George Hickenlooper, co-directed
SON-IN-LAW   Buena Vista, 1993, w/Adam Small & Shawn Schepps
IN THE ARMY NOW   Buena Vista, 1994, w/Adam Small,
   Ken Kaufman, Stu Krieger & Daniel Petrie Jr.
JURY DUTY   Buena Vista, 1995, w/Adam Small & Neil Tolkin

Screenplays:
SHOCKED   w/Adam Small (Savoy)
SHACKLED   w/Adam Small
CRAVINGS   w/Adam Small
CHAMELEON STREET   w/Adam Small
ERNEST/VOODOO

STEVEN BAIGELMAN*
Agent: William Morris Agency - Beverly Hills, 310/274-7451

Screenplays:
FEELING MINNESOTA   (directing)
THE YEAR OF THE ZINC PENNY

FREDERICK BAILEY
DESERT WARRIOR   Concorde/Cinema Group, 1985

Screenplays:
QUICK
KENTUCKY BLUE

PATRICK BAILEY
SPACECAMP   20th Century Fox, 1986, Story w/Larry B. Williams

ROBERT BAILEY*
Contact: Brandywine Communication Company, 3000 W. Olympic
   Blvd., Santa Monica, CA

YOR, THE HUNTER FROM THE FUTURE   Columbia, 1983,
   w/Anthony M. Dawson

SANDRA K. BAILEY*
Contact: Anne McDermott, Michael D. Robins & Associations -
   818/343-1755

HAMBONE AND HILLIE   New World, 1984, w/Michael Murphey &
   Joel Soisson
KGB: THE SECRET WAR   *LETHAL*   Cinema Group, 1986
PRETTYKILL   Spectrafilm, 1987
FALSE IDENTITY   RKO Pictures, 1990

GARY L. BAIN
ICE CASTLES   Columbia, 1978, w/Donald Wrye

BERYL BAINBRIDGE
SWEET WILLIAM   World Northal, 1982

HARWANT BAINS
Agent: A.P. Watt - London, 071/405-6774

BLOOD (P)
WILD WEST   Samuel Goldwyn Company, 1993

JON ROBIN BAITZ*
Agent: William Morris Agency - New York, 212/586-5100

POLLOCK (P)
MIZLANSKY/ZILINSKY (P)
THE FILM SOCIETY (P)
DUTCH LANDSCAPE (P)
THREE HOTELS (P)
THE SUBSTANCE OF FIRE (P)
THE END OF THE DAY (P)
IT CHANGES EVERY YEAR (P)

Screenplays:
THE MUSIC ROOM
DODSWORTH
JACK & JILL
FINALE

DORIS BAIZLEY*
Agent: The Gage Group - Los Angeles, 310/859-8777

CATHOLIC GIRLS (P)
MRS. CALIFORNIA (P)   also screenplay
HEARTS ON FIRE (P)
TEARS OF RAGE (P)

Screenplays:
WIVES
MR. RIGHT

AMY BROOKE BAKER*
Agent: United Talent Agency - Beverly Hills, 310/273-6700

Screenplays:
COUNTERMEASURE w/Peter Osterlund
SPIN w/Peter Osterlund
THE CANTOR'S DILEMMA w/Peter Osterlund
SYCAMORE DRIVE w/Peter Osterlund
MEMORY BOY w/Peter Osterlund

BART BAKER*
Agent: APA - Los Angeles, 310/273-0744

RELAY (P)   also screenplay
LIVE WIRE   New Line Cinema, 1992

Screenplays:
TAKE IT BACK
THE ID
THE QUEEN OF SPADES w/Glenn Rabney

EDWARD ALLEN BAKER
Agent: The Gersh Agency - New York, 212/997-1818

PRAIRIE AVENUE (P)   also screenplay
NORTH OF PROVIDENCE (P)
THE BUFFER (P)   also screenplay
A PUBLIC STREET MARRIAGE (P)
THE BRIDE OF OLNEYVILLE SQUARE (P)
FACE DIVIDED (P)
LADY OF FADIMA (P)
27 BENEDICT STREET (P)
IN THE SPIRIT (P)
DOLORES (Short)   from his play, also screenplay

Screenplays:
ONE TRACK MIND
COASTAL FRAMES
WELCOME TA BROOKLYN

EDWIN BAKER
Agent: APA - Los Angeles, 310/273-0744

COMBINATION PLATTER   Arrow Releasing, 1993, w/Tony Chan

KURT BAKER
Business: Eclectic Concepts Ltd. - Los Angeles, 213/476-7095

THE IMPORTANCE OF BEING EARNEST   Eclectic/Paco
   Globall Productions, 1991, Adaptation,
   w/Peter Anthony Andrews, directed

KYLE BAKER*
Agent: Sanford-Gross & Associates - Los Angeles, 310/208-2100

Screenplays:
THE EARTH MOVED

MARK H. BAKER
Agent: Candace Lake - Beverly Hills, 310/289-0600

FLIGHT OF THE NAVIGATOR   Buena Vista, 1986, Story

Screenplays:
AUTOMATION
THE EYE OF LUNA

MICHAEL BAKER
DEAD AHEAD: THE EXXON VALDEZ DISASTER (CTF)
   HBO Showcase/BBC Productions, 1993

RALPH BAKSHI*
Agent: United Talent Agency - Beverly Hills, 310/273-6700
Business: Ralph Bakshi Productions, 8125 Lankershim Blvd.,
   North Hollywood, CA 91605, 818/985-4463

FRITZ THE CAT (AF)   American International, 1972, directed
HEAVY TRAFFIC (AF)   American International, 1973, directed
COONSKIN STREETFIGHT (AF)   Bryanston, 1974, directed
WIZARDS (AF)   20th Century-Fox, 1977, directed
HEY GOOD LOOKIN' (AF)   Warner Bros., 1982, directed
FIRE AND ICE (AF)   20th Century-Fox, 1983, directed
COOL AND THE CRAZY (CTF)   Showtime/Drive-In Classic Cinema,
   1994, directed

Screenplays:
3 DAYS, 4 NIGHTS

BOB BALABAN*
Business Manager: Gelfand, Rennert & Feldman - 212/682-0234

THE LAST GOOD TIME   Samuel Goldwyn Company, 1994,
   w/John McLaughlin, directed

RENE BALCER*
Agent: ICM - Beverly Hills, 310/550-4000

Screenplays:
ARMED RESPONSE w/Steve Gaydos
DARK PASSION
I FOUGHT THE LAW
BURDEN OF PROOF
WARHEAD
MONIMBO
NUTS & BOLTS
PROJECTIONS

DAVID BALKAN*
Agent: Dytman & Schwartz - Los Angeles, 310/274-8844

Screenplays:
PANCHO'S WAR (Story w/Marcel Montecino)
SERPENT'S ROUTE

DAVID BALL
HARD ROCK ZOMBIES   Cannon, 1985, w/Krischna Shas

NICK BALLO
Agent: William Morris Agency - Beverly Hills, 310/274-7451

Screenplays:
LUCKY CHARM

PETER I. BALOFF*
Agent: Broder-Kurland-Webb-Uffner - Beverly Hills, 310/281-3400

QUICKSAND: NO ESCAPE (CTF)   Finnegan Pinchuk/
   MCA Television Entertainment, 1992, w/Dave Wollert
NEAR MISSES   Media Home Entertainment, 1992,
   w/Dave Wollert

ANNE BANCROFT*
Business: Brooksfilms Limited, 20th Century Fox, P.O. Box 900,
   Beverly Hills, CA 90213, 310/203-1375
Business Manager: Bernstein, Fox & Goldberg - 310/277-3373

FATSO   20th Century-Fox, 1980, directed

CHARLES BAND
Business: Fullmoon Entertainment, 3030 Andrita St., Los Angeles,
   CA 90065, 213/341-5959

PUPPET MASTER   Fullmoon, 1989, Story w/Kenneth J. Hall
DOCTOR MORDRID   Fullmoon, 1992, Idea, directed
SHRUNKEN HEADS   Fullmoon, 1994, Idea

ARNOLD BANKS
WADECK'S MOTHER'S FRIEND'S SON   Accordion Films, 1992,
   based on his short, directed

STEVEN BANKS*
Agent: APA - Los Angeles, 310/273-0744

HOME ENTERTAINMENT CENTER (P)
SID & ERNIE (P)
SPLIT PERSONALITIES (P)

Screenplays:
ROCK & ROLL FANTASY CAMP

WALTER BANNERT
THE INHERITORS   Island Alive, 1985, w/Eric A. Richter, directed

ILANA BAR-DIN*
Agent: United Talent Agency - Beverly Hills, 310/273-6700

THE JAMIE FORT STORY (Short)   directed

Screenplays:
FRIDA AND DIEGO
LOST IN TRANSLATION (Shared)

JACK BARAN*
Agent: The Daniel Ostroff Agency - Los Angeles, 310/278-2020

ROOMMATES   Pantages, 1971, directed
BAND OF THE HAND   Tri-Star, 1986, w/Leo Garen
GREAT BALLS OF FIRE   Orion, 1989, w/Jim McBride
UNCOVERED   CIBY 2000, 1994, w/Jim McBride & Michael Hirst

STEVE BARANCIK
Agent: Sanford-Gross & Associates - Los Angeles, 310/208-2100

THE LAST SEDUCTION   October Films, 1994

Screenplays:
FEMALE SUPERIOR

JEAN BARASH*
Contact: WGA - Los Angeles, 310/550-1000

Screenplays:
THE SPRAY w/Ellen Erwin
THE IMMORTALIST w/Ellen Erwin

DANA BARATTA
Agent: Premiere Artists - Los Angeles, 310/271-1414

ANDRE   Paramount, 1994

Screenplays:
THE MAGIC FOREST

BENNY BARBASH
BEYOND THE WALLS   Warner Bros., 1985, w/Eran Pries
ONE OF US   Israfilm, 1990
REAL TIME   Sunrise Films, 1991

LARRY BARBER*
Agent: CAA - Beverly Hills, 310/288-4545

Screenplays:
HOOVER w/Paul Barber

PAUL BARBER*
Agent: CAA - Beverly Hills, 310/288-4545

Screenplays:
HOOVER w/Larry Barber

JOSEPH BARBERA
Business: Hanna-Barbera Productions, Inc., 3400 Lankershim Blvd.
   West, Los Angeles, CA 90068, 213/851-5000

HEIDI'S SONG (AF)   Paramount, 1982, w/Jameson Brewer &
   Robert Taylor, directed

NEAL BARBERA*
Contact: WGA - Los Angeles, 310/550-1000

THE PROWLER   Sandhurst Corporation, 1982, w/Glenn Leopold
TOO SCARED TO SCREAM   Moviestore Entertainment, 1985,
   w/Glenn Leopold
P.K. AND THE KID   Castle Hill Productions, 1987

MALCOLM BARBOUR
Contact: Browning, Jacobson & Klein - Beverly Hills, 310/247-8777

P.O.W. THE ESCAPE   Cannon, 1986, w/James Bruner,
   Jeremy Lipp & John Langley

Screenplays:
VESPERS w/John Langley

JERI BARCHILON*
Contact: WGA - Los Angeles, 310/550-1000

Screenplays:
BOARDWALK QUEENS

PARIS BARCLAY*
Agent: William Morris Agency - Beverly Hills, 310/274-7451

Screenplays:
THE NEXT HOT NEGRO
TALK FAST

ANN LOUISE BARDACH*
Agent: Sanford-Gross & Associates - Los Angeles, 310/208-2100

BACKTRACK (CTF)   Dick Clark Cinema Productions/Vestron,
   1992, w/Rachel Kronstadt Mann

Screenplays:
JOHNNY DESOTO
COMPOSURE
THE CANVAS
RECLAIMED

JAMES H. BARDEN
THE JUDAS PROJECT   RS Entertainment, 1994, directed

RONDA BARENDSE
Agent: Warden, White & Kane - Beverly Hills, 213/852-1028

BODILY HARM   Rysher Entertainment, 1994, w/James Lemmo &
   Joseph Whaley

Screenplays:
THE PROMISE w/Joseph Whaley

FRANK BARHYDT*
Agent: William Morris Agency - Beverly Hills, 310/274-7451

QUINTET   20th Century-Fox, 1979, w/Robert Altman &
   Patricia Resnick
HEALTH   20th Century-Fox, 1980, w/Robert Altman & Paul Dooley
SHORT CUTS   Fine Line Features, 1993, w/Robert Altman

Screenplays:
KANSAS CITY w/Robert Altman

LEORA BARISH*
Agent: William Morris Agency - Beverly Hills, 310/274-7451

DESPERATELY SEEKING SUSAN   Orion, 1985

Screenplays:
DESIRE w/Henry Bean & Frederic Raphael
LABYRINTH 9 w/Henry Bean
EL DORADO w/Henry Bean
RINGOLEVIO w/Henry Bean
A STAR IS BORN (remake)
COUNT FROM ONE TO TEN
DAYLIGHTING

CLIVE BARKER*
Agent: CAA - Beverly Hills, 310/288-4545

UNDERWORLD   Limehouse, 1985, w/James Caplin
RAWHEAD REX   Empire Pictures, 1987
HELLRAISER   New World, 1987, directed
NIGHT BREED   20th Century Fox, 1990, directed
LORD OF ILLUSIONS   MGM/UA, 1995, directed

Screenplays:
PRIMAL
THE GREAT UNKNOWN
THE BIG NOWHERE

LYNN BARKER
Contact: 818/763-0046

Screenplays:
RESURRECTIONS w/Bob Skotak
ACES
HEROES

EDWARD S. BARKIN
RIFT   (No Distributor), 1993, from his play, directed

MICHAEL BARLOW*
Agent: Jim Preminger Agency - Los Angeles, 310/475-9491

Screenplays:
BRIGHT DANGER
TRUE CRIME
KIDNAPPED

IRA BARMAK*
Contact: Marvin Meyer, Esq. - 310/858-7700

HOTEL COLONIAL   Columbia, 1987, w/Enzo Monteleone,
   Cinzia Torrini & Robert Katz

JOSLYN BARNES
TOUCH OF A STRANGER   Raven-Star Pictures, 1990,
   w/Brad Gilbert

PETER BARNES
Agent: William Morris Agency - Beverly Hills, 310/274-7451 &The
   Casarotto Company - London, 71/287-4450

OFFBEAT   British Lion, 1960
RING OF TREASON   *RING OF SPIES*   British Lion, 1963,
   w/Frank Launder
NOT WITH MY WIFE YOU DON'T   Warner Bros., 1966,
   w/Larry Gelbart & Norman Panama
THE RULING CLASS   Avco Embassy, 1972, from his play
ENCHANTED APRIL ★   Miramax, 1992
VOICES FROM A LOCKED ROOM   Columbia, 1995

Screenplays:
MOI GOES TO WASHINGTON
JUST THE THREE OF US
THE WITZARD OF ID
LOST IN THE CITY OF LIGHTS
PLUNKITT MACLEANE

STEVEN BARNES
Agent: The Gage Group - Los Angeles, 310/859-8777

Screenplays:
THE SOULSTAR COMMISSION
GATEWAY

RICHARD BARNETT
Contact: Australian Film Commission, 8 West St., North Sydney,
   NSW 2026, Australia, tel.: 2/925-7333

THE HEARTBREAK KID   Roadshow Pictures, 1993,
   w/Michael Jenkins, from his play

M. NEEMA BARNETTE
Agent: CAA - Beverly Hills, 310/288-4545
Business: Harlem Lite Inc., 4219 Olive St. - Suite 119, Burbank, CA
  91505, 213/669-1050

SKY CAPTAIN (Short)   1984, directed

Screenplays:
THE GUIDE w/Reed "Live" McCants (directing)

BEVERLY BAROFF
Agent: Jon Klane Agency - Beverly Hills, 310/278-0178

Screenplays:
ICE
LET THE COWGIRLS RIDE
THE HUNCHBACK OF NOTRE DAME
ANT DANCE
DIRTY POOL

DANNIEL BARON*
Agent: United Talent Agency - Beverly Hills, 310/273-6700

HANG 'EM REALLY HIGH (Short)   1989, w/Chris Faber, directed

Screenplays:
ASSAULT ON EMPIRE STATE MOUNTAIN (CTF) w/Chris Faber
  (directing)
MUCKRAKER w/Chris Faber
FAT CHANCE w/Chris Faber
JACKPOT w/Chris Faber
THE BIG PLUNGE w/Chris Faber

DEBORAH R. BARON*
Agent: Maggie Field Agency - Studio City, 818/980-2001

Screenplays:
FOREVER YOUNG
JUST BETWEEN US
STILL FRIENDS
STEAM HEAT
NO FREE LUNCH
INSIDE OUT
GIZMO
SECOND THOUGHTS
SUMMERSTOCK

JEFF BARON*
Contact: Attorney Susan H. Bodine - 212/888-1777

Screenplays:
HOUSE SWAP
MAID OF HONOR
JERSEY GIRL

JESSICA BARONDES
Agent: The Irv Schechter Company - Beverly Hills, 310/278-8070

Screenplays:
WISH UPON A STAR
THE SECRET KEEPER

DOUGLAS BARR*
Agent: Broder-Kurland-Webb-Uffner - Beverly Hills, 310/281-3400

FADE TO BLACK (CTF)   Wilshire Court, 1993
THE COVER GIRL MURDERS (CTF)   River Enterprises/
  Wilshire Court, 1993, w/Bernard Maybeck

Screenplays:
DEAD BADGE
CONUNDRUM
EVERYBODY'S SOMEBODY'S FOOL
THE HIT w/William Link

JACKSON BARR
BODY CHEMISTRY   Concorde, 1990
JULES VERNE'S 800 LEAGUES DOWN THE AMAZON   Concorde,
  1993, w/Laura Schiff

Screenplays:
BODY CHEMISTRY III (New Horizons)
TRANCERS II
VOICE OF A STRANGER w/Christopher Wooden

MATTHEW F. BARR*
Contact: WGA - Los Angeles, 310/550-1000

DEADLY BLESSING   United Artists/Polygram, 1981,
  w/Glenn M. Benest & Wes Craven

EARL BARRET*
Business Manager: Jamner, Pariser & Meschures - Los Angeles,
  310/652-0222

SEE NO EVIL, HEAR NO EVIL   Tri-Star, 1989, w/Andrew Kurtzman,
  Arne Sultan, Eliot Wald & Gene Wilder

BRUNO BARRETO
Business: Producoes Cinematograficas L.C. Barreto Ltda.,
  Rua Visconde De Caravelas, 28-Botafogos, Rio de Janeiro, Brazil,
  021/286-7186

DONA FLOR AND HER TWO HUSBANDS   New Yorker,
  1977, directed
GABRIELA   MGM/UA Classics, 1983,
  w/Leopoldo Sarran, directed

LEZLI-AN BARRETT
Agent: Casarotto Ramsay - London, 071/287-4450

BUSINESS AS USUAL   Cannon, 1987, directed

MICHAEL BARRIE*
Agent: Broder-Kurland-Webb-Uffner - Beverly Hills, 310/281-3400

THE RATINGS GAME (CTF)   Imagination-New Street Productions,
  1984, w/Jim Mulholland
AMAZON WOMEN ON THE MOON   Universal, 1987,
  w/Jim Mulholland
OSCAR   Buena Vista, 1991, w/Jim Mulholland

CHUCK BARRIS*
Contact: WGA - Los Angeles, 310/550-1000

THE GONG SHOW MOVIE   Universal, 1980,
  w/Robert Downey, directed

ARTHUR S. BARRON*
Contact: Bloom, Dekom, Hergott & Cook - Los Angeles,
  310/278-8622

JEREMY   United Artists, 1973, directed

FRED BARRON*
Agent: CAA - Beverly Hills, 310/288-4545

BETWEEN THE LINES   Midwest Film Productions, 1977
SOMETHING SHORT OF PARADISE
  American International, 1979
GOING ALL THE WAY   Paramount, 1980

Screenplays:
FUN WHILE IT LASTED w/Joan Micklin Silver

ZELDA BARRON
Agent: The Artists Agency - Los Angeles, 310/277-7779
Business: Limelight Films, 1724 Whitley Ave., Los Angeles, CA
   90028, 213/464-5808; London, 071/255-3939

VIVIEN...A LASS UNPARALLEL'D (P)
SECRET PLACES   TLC Films/20th Century-Fox, 1984, directed

Screenplays:
HEROD'S GATE
SHATTERED SILENCE
LISTEN, RUBEN FONTANEZ
DIGGER
THE GHOST
TWO CRIMES

JoANNA BARRY
Agent: Sanford-Gross & Associates - Los Angeles, 310/208-2100

Screenplays:
BACHELOR GIRLS

JULIAN BARRY*
Agent: United Talent Agency - Beverly Hills, 310/273-6700

THE MATTER OF THE OFFICERS (P)
SITCOM (P)
BORN AGAIN (P)
JEAN SEBERG (P)   also teleplay
RHINOCEROS   American Film Theatre, 1974,
   from the play by Ionesco
LENNY ★   United Artists, 1974, from his play
THE RIVER   Universal, 1984, w/Robert Dillon
A MARRIAGE: GEORGIA O'KEEFFE AND ALFRED STIEGLITZ ✓
   American Playhouse, 1992
ME, MYSELF AND I   I.R.S. Releasing, 1993

Screenplays:
THE PROMISED LAND
I GOT A NAME
THE CALLING
MR. POTATOHEAD
FIDEL IN HOLLYWOOD
APPASSIONATA
A PLACE TO COME TO
DEAD BEAUTY

LYNDA BARRY
Contact: WGA - New York, 212/245-6180

THE GOOD TIMES ARE KILLING ME (P), also screenplay

PETER BARSOCCHINI*
Office: 213/460-2235

DROP ZONE   Paramount, 1994, w/John Bishop

PAUL BARTEL*
Agent: ICM - Beverly Hills, 310/550-4000

EATING RAOUL (P)
CANNONBALL   New World, 1976, w/Donald C. Simpson, directed
EATING RAOUL   20th Century Fox International Classics, 1982,
   w/Richard Blackburn, directed
NOT FOR PUBLICATION   Samuel Goldwyn Company, 1984,
   w/John Meyer, directed

Screenplays:
BLAND AMBITION w/Richard Blackburn
FRANKENCAR w/Richard Blackburn

KEVIN BARTELME
INSIDE OUT   Hemdale, 1986, w/Roy Teicher

WILLIAM S. BARTMAN
Agent: Tom Klassen, 73 Market Street, Venice, CA 90291,
   310/396-5937

O'HARA'S WIFE   Davis-Panzer Productions, 1982,
   w/James Nasalla, directed

DANIEL BARTOLINI*
Agent: United Talent Agency - Beverly Hills, 310/273-6700

Screenplays:
MAN'S FATE
IF I SHOULD DIE IN NO MAN'S LAND
THE LAST ILLUSION
HEATLIGHTNING

JAMES BARTON
Agent: United Talent Agency - Beverly Hills, 310/273-6700

Screenplays:
DARK BLOOD
THE JAM FACTORY
THAT EYE IN THE SKY
ONLY YOU
A LITTLE PERESTROIKA
ESKIMOS DO IT

HAL BARWOOD*
Agent: ICM - Beverly Hills, 310/550-4000

THE SUGARLAND EXPRESS   Universal, 1974,
   w/Matthew Robbins & Steven Spielberg
THE BINGO LONG TRAVELING ALL-STARS & MOTOR KINGS
   Universal, 1976, w/Matthew Robbins
MACARTHUR   Universal, 1977, w/Matthew Robbins
CORVETTE SUMMER   MGM/United Artists, 1978,
   w/Matthew Robbins
DRAGONSLAYER   Paramount, 1981, w/Matthew Robbins
WARNING SIGN   20th Century Fox, 1985,
   w/Matthew Robbins, directed

Screenplays:
THE GRID w/Matthew Robbins
NEWSREEL w/Matthew Robbins
WITNESSES w/Matthew Robbins
HOME FREE w/Matthew Robbins
NIGHT SHADE w/Matthew Robbins
OTHERWHERE

LULI BARZMAN
Business: Barman/Ziolkowski, 2 rue de la Pierre Levee, 75011,
   Paris, France

CHICAGO BLACK AND WHITE (Short)   1990,
   w/Fabrice Ziolkowski, co-directed
CACAPHONIE D'AMOUR (Short)   1991,
   w/Fabrice Ziolkowski, co-directed

Screenplays:
SANDGRASS PEOPLE w/Fabrice Ziolkowski
CIRCLES IN A FOREST w/Fabrice Ziolkowski
DOUBLE BIND w/Fabrice Ziolkowski

RON BASE
HEAVENLY BODIES   MGM/UA, 1985, w/Lawrence Dane

SUSAN BASKIN*
Agent: Broder-Kurland-Webb-Uffner - Beverly Hills, 310/281-3400

VIOLET (Short) ★

Screenplays:
MAKE IT PARADISE
YOURS 'TILL NIAGARA FALLS
MIRACLES

KIM BASS*
Contact: Bass Entertainment - 213/876-7946

Screenplays:
ICE CREAM MAN w/Michael Kane *(Capella International)*

RONALD BASS*
Agent: CAA - Beverly Hills, 310/288-4545
Manager: Melinda Jason - Beverly Hills, 310/289-6134

CODE NAME: EMERALD   MGM/UA, 1985
BLACK WIDOW   20th Century Fox, 1987
GARDENS OF STONE   Tri-Star, 1987
RAIN MAN ★★   MGM/UA, 1988, w/Barry Morrow
SLEEPING WITH THE ENEMY   20th Century Fox, 1991
THE JOY LUCK CLUB   Buena Vista, 1993, w/Amy Tan
WHEN A MAN LOVES A WOMAN   Buena Vista, 1994, w/Al Franken
THE ENEMY WITHIN (CTF)   Vincent Pictures/HBO Pictures, 1994,
   w/Darryl Ponicsan
MY POSSE DON'T DO HOMEWORK   Buena Vista, 1995

Screenplays:
TEARS OF THE SUN w/Joel Gross
THE KITCHEN GOD'S WIFE w/Amy Tan
WAITING TO EXHALE w/Terry McMillan
TO FORGIVE, DIVINE
MARTINE
ARTURO
MANHATTAN GHOST STORY
PASSION OF MIND
STAR SAILOR w/Patrick Read Johnson
THE BUM
NO FURTHER QUESTIONS
SWING VOTE
THE HUNTING CLUB
HOSTILE WITNESS
BLAKE
LIME'S CRISIS w/David Field
TARGET w/Ulu Grosbard
REUNION
SECOND SON
THE PRESIDENT ELOPES
WINDWARD PASSAGE
THE DIVE
TRADEOFF

SETH BASS*
Agent: William Morris Agency - Beverly Hills, 310/274-7451

Screenplays:
THE VESTAL VIRGIN ROOM w/Jonathan Tolins
GOING PUBLIC w/Jonathan Tolins
THE TWILIGHT OF THE GOLDS w/Jonathan Tolins
REDEMPTION w/Jonathan Tolins
KUMBAYA w/Jonathan Tolins

LAWRENCE BASSOFF
Business: Dauntless Director, 228 Main Street -Suite D, Venice,
   CA 90291, 310/553-5380

WEEKEND PASS   Crown International, 1984, directed
HUNK   Crown International, 1987, directed

WILLIAM E. BAST*
Agent: Major Clients Agency - Los Angeles, 310/284-6400

HAMMERHEAD   Columbia, 1968, w/Herbert Baker
THE VALLEY OF GWANGI   Warner Bros., 1969
THE BETSY   Allied Artists, 1978, w/Walter Bernstein

JANET SCOTT BATCHLER*
Agent: William Morris Agency - Beverly Hills, 310/274-7451

BATMAN FOREVER   w/Lee Batchler & Akiva Goldsman
   Warner Bros., 1995

Screenplays:
SMOKE AND MIRRORS w/Lee Batchler

LEE BATCHLER*
Agent: William Morris Agency - Beverly Hills, 310/274-7451

BATMAN FOREVER   w/Janet Scott Batchler & Akiva Goldsman
   Warner Bros., 1995

Screenplays:
SMOKE AND MIRRORS w/Janet Scott Batchler

KENT BATEMAN
Contact: Directors Guild of America - Los Angeles, 310/289-2000

THE LAND OF NO RETURN   International PictureShow, 1981,
   w/Frank Ray Perilli
THE HEADLESS EYES   J.E.R. Pictures, 1983, directed

CARY BATES*
Agent: Peter Lampack, 551 Fifth Ave., New York, NY 10017

CHRISTOPHER COLUMBUS: THE DISCOVERY   Warner Bros.,
   1992, w/John Briley & Mario Puzo

Screenplays:
SUPERMAN: THE NEW MOVIE

JOE BATTEER*
Agent: William Morris Agency - Beverly Hills, 310/274-7451

CURIOSITY KILLS (CTF)   MCA Television Entertainment, 1990,
   w/John Rice
CHASERS   Warner Bros., 1994, w/John Rice & Dan Gilroy
BLOWN AWAY   MGM/UA, 1994, w/John Rice

BRADLEY BATTERSBY*
Agent: Paradigm - Los Angeles, 310/277-4400

BLUE DESERT   Neo Motion Pictures, 1991,
   w/Arthur Collis, directed

LLOYD BATTISTA
COMIN' AT YA!   Filmways, 1981, w/Wolf Lowenthal & Gene Quintano
TREASURE OF THE FOUR CROWNS   Cannon, 1983,
   w/Jim Bryce & Jerry Lazarus

FRED BAUER
UNDER THE RAINBOW   Orion/Warner Bros., 1981,
   w/Pat McCormick, Harry Hurwitz, Martin Smith & Pat Bradley

HANS BAUER
Agent: William Morris Agency - Beverly Hills, 310/274-7451

Screenplays:
ANACONDA

DAVID BAUGHN
BEYOND EVIL   IFI-Scope III, 1980, Story
GRADUATION DAY   IFI-Scope III, 1981, Story

THOMAS BAUM*
Agent: The Artists Agency - Los Angeles, 310/277-7779

HUGO THE HIPPO (AF)   1975
CARNY   United Artists, 1980
SIMON   Orion/Warner Bros., 1980, Story w/Marshall Brickman
THE SENDER   Paramount, 1982
THE MANHATTAN PROJECT   20th Century Fox, 1986,
   w/Marshall Brickman
DROP DEAD GORGEOUS (CTF)   Power Pictures Corp., 1992,
   w/Mimi Shapiro & Bill Wells

Screenplays:
UNRAVELLED
LOUIE, LOUIE
CADAVERS
ACTS OF GOD
SHARUN

WILL BAUM
Agent: United Talent Agency - Beverly Hills, 310/273-6700

Screenplays:
THE WRONG ONES

NOEL BAUMBACH
Contact: Fifth Year Productions, 1639 11th Street, Santa Monica,
   CA 90403

Screenplays:
KICKING AND SCREAMING (Trimark, directing)

GEORGE L. BAXT*
Contact: Sam Gelfman, B.D.P. Associates - 818/506-7165

CIRCUS OF HORRORS   Anglo Amalgamated, 1960
CITY OF THE DEAD HORROR HOTEL   Vulcan, 1960

KHRIS BAXTER*
Agent: Candace Lake - Beverly Hills, 310/289-0600

VOYAGE (CTF)   Davis Entertainment/Quinta/USA Network, 1993,
   Story w/Mark Montgomery

WAYNE BEACH*
Agent: Writers & Artists Agency - Los Angeles, 310/824-6300
Manager: Creative Alliance Management - Los Angeles,
   213/962-6090

Screenplays:
EXECUTIVE PRIVILEGE w/David Hodgin
EX w/David Hodgin

PETER S. BEAGLE*
Agent: Maggie Field Agency - Studio City, 818/980-2001

THE DOVE   Paramount, 1974, w/Adam Kennedy
THE LORD OF THE RINGS (AF)   United Artists, 1978,
   w/Chris Conkling
THE LAST UNICORN   Jensen Farley Pictures, 1982

Screenplays:
GNOME
PUSS N' BOOTS
LILA: A LOVE STORY

DAVID BEAIRD*
Agent: William Morris Agency - Beverly Hills, 310/274-7451

900 ONEONTA (P)
OCTAVIA   International Film Marketing, 1984, directed
THE PARTY ANIMAL   International Film Marketing, 1985, directed
MY CHAUFFEUR   Crown International, 1985, directed
SCORCHERS   Goldcrest Films, 1992, from his play, directed

Screenplays:
WASTED GRACE (directing)

HENRY S. BEAN*
Agent: William Morris Agency - Beverly Hills, 310/274-7451

RUNNING BRAVE   Buena Vista, 1983, w/Shirl Henryx
INTERNAL AFFAIRS   Paramount, 1990
DEEP COVER   New Line Cinema, 1992, w/Michael Tolkin

Screenplays:
MULHOLLAND FALLS (MGM/UA)
THE DAY AFTER TOMORROW
THE DONNER PARTY w/Mark Jacobson
YOJIMBO
RINGOLEVIO w/Leora Barish
DESIRE w/Leora Barish & Frederic Raphael
EL DORADO w/Leora Barish
LABYRINTH 9 w/Leora Barish

CAR THIEVES
WHO YOU KNOW
THE BIG U
THE EDNA BUCHANAN STORY

DOUGLAS CARTER BEANE
Agent: William Morris Agency - Beverly Hills, 310/274-7451

ADVICE FROM A CATERPILLAR (P)
TO WONG FOO, THANKS FOR EVERYTHING, JULIE NEWMAR
   Universal, 1994

Screenplays:
QUEEN OF THE BOILER ROOM

NICHOLAS BEARDSLY
SAVAGE ISLAND   Empire Pictures, 1985,
   w/Michelle Tomski, directed

RICHARD BEATTIE
COLD SWEAT (CTF)   Norstar Entertainment, 1994

ANNE BEATTS*
Agent: Broder-Kurland-Webb-Uffner - Beverly Hills, 310/281-3400

GILDA LIVE (FD)   Warner Bros., 1980, w/others

Screenplays:
THE WOMEN
WHERE THE GIRLS WERE
CARIBBEAN WOMAN
COMMUNITY PROPERTY

BRIAN BEATTY
Agent: Berzon Agency - Glendale, 818/548-1560

Screenplays:
SHADOWS OF MOUNTAINS

WARREN BEATTY*
Agent: CAA - Beverly Hills, 310/288-4545

SHAMPOO ★   Columbia, 1975, w/Robert Towne
HEAVEN CAN WAIT ★   Paramount, 1978, w/Elaine May, directed
REDS ★   Paramount, 1981, w/Trevor Griffiths, directed
LOVE AFFAIR   Warner Bros., 1994, w/Robert Towne

JEAN BEAUDIN
Contact: Academy of Canadian Cinema & Television, 753 Yonge St. -
   2nd Floor, Toronto M4Y 1Z9, Canada, 416/967-0315

BEING AT HOME WITH CLAUDE   Strand Releasing, 1994, directed

PHILIP E. BEAUMAN*
Contact: WGA - Los Angeles, 310/550-1000

Screenplays:
DON'T BE MENACE IN SOUTH CENTRAL WHILE DRINKING YOUR
*   JUICE IN THE HOOD w/Marlon Wayans & Shawn Wayans*

DAVID PATRICK BEAVERS
Agent: Berzon Agency - Glendale, 818/548-1560

BURIED TRUTHS (P)
IN THE DARK...ALONG THE WAY (P)
SISTERS (P)

Screenplays:
PINK LADIES
OUT THERE, SOMEWHERE
A COMMON PAIR
HIDES
HOME FIRE'S BURNING

GORMAN BECHARD*
Business: Generic Films, Inc., P.O. Box 2715, Waterbury, CT 06723,
203/756-3017

CEMETARY HIGH   Titan Productions, 1989,
w/Carmine Capobianco, directed

JOSH BECKER
LUNATICS: A LOVE STORY   Renaissance Pictures, 1992, directed

Screenplays:
CYCLES w/Dario Scardapane

BARRY BECKERMAN*
Agent: William Morris Agency - Beverly Hills, 310/274-7451

SHAMUS   Columbia, 1972
ST. IVES   Warner Bros., 1976

Screenplays:
HALLIBURTON
BATTLE OF THE PHILLIPINE SEA
RHYTHM & BLUES

GEORGE BECKERMAN*
Agent: United Talent Agency - Beverly Hills, 310/273-6700

Screenplays:
IN DEEP
THE WITCHES REVENGE

MICHAEL FROST BECKNER*
Agent: ICM - Beverly Hills, 310/550-4000

SNIPER   TriStar, 1993, w/Crash Leyland

Screenplays:
CUTTHROAT ISLAND Story w/Jim Gorman (MGM/UA)
THE HUNCHBACK OF NOTRE-DAME
HOGAN'S HEROES
TEXAS LEAD AND GOLD w/Jim Gorman
HOSTLIE TAKEOVER w/Jim Gorman
PRINCE VALIANT
THE WESTERN FRONT
STORMING INTREPID
SADDLE SORE

DICK BEEBE*
Agent: CAA - Beverly Hills, 310/288-4545

BAYOU CONFIDENTIAL (P)
THE RAPTURE TWO-STEP (P) also screenplay
HEAVENZAPOPPIN' (P)
VAMPIRES IN KODACHROME (P)
ANDROSCOGGIN FUGUE (P)
THE GUITEAU BURLESQUE (P)
OH, CLORIS! (P)
NAKED CHAMBERS (P)
ANAPEST DESTINY (P)
PRISON STORIES: WOMEN ON THE INSIDE (CTF)
    Francine LeFrak Productions/HBO Showcase, 1991,
    "New Chicks" w/Martin Jones & Jule Selbo
INTO THE BADLANDS (CTF) Ogiens/Kane Productions, 1992,
    w/Marjorie David & Gordon Dawson

Screenplays:
THE NET
A THIEF OF TIME
EXIT WOUNDS
CITIZEN SICK
BIJOU DREAMS: BUSTER KEATON GOES TO HOLLYWOOD (CTF)
ONLY THE LONELY: HOW THE SONG DIDN'T ALMOST NEVER
    COME TO BE (CTF)
THE LAST PELT (CTF)
JACK AMERICA

THE DARK HORSE w/Wesley Strick
JAN KEMP
LOUIE LOUIE w/Anna Cascio

JOHN BEECH
WARLORDS OF THE 21ST CENTURY   New World, 1982,
w/Irving Austin & Harley Coklis

GREG BEEMAN*
Manager: International Arts Entertainment - Los Angeles,
310/551-0014

TALES OF THE UNKNOWN   AIP Home Video, 1990,
"The Big Garage," directed

JEFF BEGUN
SATURDAY THE 14TH   New World, 1981, Story

Screenplays:
STAR LEGION w/Peter Jobin (Blue Ridge Entertainment)

MARC BEHM
HELP!   United Artists, 1965, w/Charles Wood
THE PARTY'S OVER   Allied Artists, 1966
THE BLONDE FROM PEKING   Paramount, 1968,
    w/Nicholas Gessner
THE MAD BOMBER   Cinemation, 1973, Story
HOSPITAL MASSACRE   Cannon, 1982
NANA   Cannon, 1983

EDWARD BEHR
HALF MOON STREET   20th Century Fox, 1986, w/Bob Swaim

IRA STEVEN BEHR*
Agent: William Morris Agency - Beverly Hills, 310/274-7451

Screenplays:
HICKOCK AND CODY
WAR BOYS

JACK BEHR*
Contact: WGA - Los Angeles, 310/550-1000

BIRDY   Tri-Star, 1984, w/Sandy Kroopf

Screenplays:
LOOSE WOMEN
MICKEY FINN
THIN ICE
ENDANGERED
EASY STREET
B STREET w/Sandy Kroopf
PUBLIC SECRETS w/Sandy Kroopf
MATINEE w/Sandy Kroopf
RUNAWAY w/Sandy Kroopf
ALIAS EDDIE SHERBERT w/Sandy Kroopf
WITNESS TO WAR w/Sandy Kroopf
BOOK OF EPPE w/Sandy Kroopf
THE MONKEY WRENCH GANG w/Sandy Kroopf
PERFECT COUNTERFEIT w/Sandy Kroopf
SPEECHLESS w/Sandy Kroopf
SERIOUS LIVING w/Sandy Kroopf

PETER BEHRENS*
Agent: Sterling Lord Literistic - New York, 212/696-2800

Screenplays:
CADILLAC GIRLS (Saban Pictures)

JEAN-JACQUES BEINEIX
Contact: French Film Office, 745 Fifth Ave., New York, NY 10151,
212/832-8860

DIVA   United Artists Classics, 1982, w/Jean Van Hamme, directed
THE MOON IN THE GUTTER   Triumph/Columbia, 1983, directed

BETTY BLUE *37.2 DEGREES LE MATIN*   Alive Films,
   1986, directed
I.P.5: THE ISLAND OF PACHYDERMES   Gaumont, 1992,
   w/Jacques Forgeas, directed

Screenplays:
ICE MAIDENS

WILLIAM BEKKALA*
Contact: WGA - Los Angeles, 310/550-1000

SILENT MOTIVE (CTF)   Viacom Productions, 1991

Screenplays:
BLOOD AND FLAMES
RECRIMINATIONS

ADAM BELANOFF*
Agent: Kaplan-Stahler - Beverly Hills, 213/653-4483

Screenplays:
BALONEY BOY
CASEY SPEAKS w/P.J. Pesce

IRVING BELATECHE*
Agent: ICM - Beverly Hills, 310/550-4000

SAVING SOULS (Short)   1994, directed

Screenplays:
SHORT CIRCUIT III w/Larry Guterman
JACK SPRINGER w/Larry Guterman

ELISA BELL *
Agent: APA - Los Angeles, 310/273-0744

WRITER'S BLOCK (CTF)   USA Network/Wilshire Court Productions,
   1991, from her Short Film
TREACHEROUS CROSSING (CTF)   Wilshire Court
   Productions, 1992
DANCING WITH DANGER (CTF)   Fast Track Films/Wilshire Court
   Productions, 1994

Screenplays:
30 WISHES
THE BOX
THE UMP
SLOW BURN
VIRTUE
THE GHOST AND MRS. MUIR
BLONDIE

JEFFREY BELL*
Agent: Jim Preminger Agency - Los Angeles, 310/475-9491

RADIO INSIDE   Capitol Films, 1993,
   based on his Short Film, directed

Screenplays:
LOST SOUL w/Stephen Volk
HYMN TIME IN THE LAND OF ABANDON (directing)
UNRAVELED

MARTIN BELL
AMERICAN HEART   Triton Pictures, 1993,
   Story w/Mary Ellen Mark & Peter Silverman, directed

NEAL BELL*
Agent: William Morris Agency - New York, 212/586-5100

COLD SWEAT (P)
READY FOR THE RIVER (P)
ON THE BUM, OR THE NEXT TRAIN THROUGH (P)
THERESE RAQUIN (P)
TERMINAL CHOICE   Almi Pictures, 1985
TWO SMALL BODIES   Castle Hill, 1994, w/Beth B, from his play

ROBERT BELL
FREE RIDE   Galaxy International, 1986, w/Lee Fulkerson &
   Ronald Zwang

ROSS BELL
Business: Rastar Productions, 335 N. Maple Dr. - Suite 356,
   Beverly Hills, CA 90210, 310/247-0130

CRACKDOWN   Concorde, 1990, w/Daryl Haney
TO DIE STANDING   Califilm, 1992

BRUCE BELLAND*
Contact: WGA - Los Angeles, 310/550-1000

WEEKEND WARRIORS   The Movie Store, 1986, w/Roy M. Rogosin

DONALD P. BELLISARIO*
Agent: Broder-Kurland-Webb-Uffner - Beverly Hills, 310/281-3400

LAST RITES   MGM/UA, 1988, directed

JOSEPH B. BELLISSIMO
Agent: Renaissance-H.N. Swanson - Los Angeles, 310/246-6000

Screenplays:
WHITE HOUSE PARTY w/Jeffrey J. LoGrosso

STEPHEN F. BELLO*
Agent: The Gersh Agency - Beverly Hills, 310/274-6611

CIRCLE OF POWER *MYSTIQUE/BRAINWASH/THE NAKED
   WEEKEND*   Televicine, 1983, w/Beth Sullivan

MARCO BELLOCCHIO
Address: Viale Angelico 36/B, Rome, Italy

FIST IN HIS POCKET   Peppercorn-Wormser, 1965, directed
CHINA IS NEAR   Royal Films International, 1967, directed
LEAP INTO THE VOID   Summit Features, 1979, directed
THE EYES, THE MOUTH   Triumph/Columbia, 1983, directed
HENRY IV   Orion Classics, 1985, w/Tonino Guerra, directed
DEVIL IN THE FLESH   Orion Classics, 1987,
   w/Enrico Palandri, directed

PETER BELLWOOD*
Agent: The Agency - Los Angeles, 310/551-3000

PHOBIA   Paramount, 1981, w/Lew Lehman, James Sangster,
   Gary A. Sherman & Ronald Shusett
ST. HELENS   Davis-Panzer Productions, 1981, w/Larry Ferguson
HIGHLANDER   20th Century Fox, 1986, w/Larry Ferguson &
   Gregory Widen
HIGHLANDER 2: THE QUICKENING   InterStar Releasing, 1991

Screenplays:
THE DOCTOR AND THE DRAGON LADY w/Dennis Shryack
GORILLAS w/Dennis Shryack
THE KILLING SEED w/Dennis Shryack
WEAVEWORLD (CMS) w/Dennis Shryack
THE MIST THAT THUNDERS
THE LAST LAUGH w/Larry Ferguson
MALACHI w/Larry Ferguson

VERA BELMONT
Contact: French Film Office, 745 Fifth Ave., New York, NY 10151,
   212/832-8860

ROUGE BAISER *RED KISS*   Circle Releasing Corporation, 1986,
   w/Guy Konopnicki, directed

PAUL BELOUS*
Agent: Paul Kohner, Inc. - Beverly Hills, 310/550-1060

Screenplays:
NIGHT OF THE LONG KNIVES

F
I
L
M

W
R
I
T
E
R
S

JERRY BELSON*
Agent: ICM - Beverly Hills, 310/550-4000

HOW SWEET IT IS   National General, 1968, w/Garry Marshall
THE GRASSHOPPER   National General, 1969, as "Gary Belsen,"
    w/Garry Marhsall
SMILE   United Artists, 1975
FUN WITH DICK AND JANE   Columbia, 1977, w/David Giler &
    Mordecai Richler
THE END   United Artists, 1978
SMOKEY AND THE BANDIT - PART II   Universal, 1980,
    w/Brock Yates
JEKYLL AND HYDE...TOGETHER AGAIN   Paramount, 1982,
    w/Monica Johnson, Michael Leeson & Harvey Miller, directed
SURRENDER   Warner Bros., 1987, directed
ALWAYS   Universal, 1989

Screenplays:
THE PITCH
LOVE, ROGER w/Garry Marshall
KIDS
CAPTAIN YAWK & THE SILVER STREAK
CARS
THE GREAT CAPE GIRARDEAU LEAP

JAMES A. BELUSHI*
Contact: Whitehorse Productions, 8033 Sunset Blvd. - Suite 88,
    Los Angeles, CA 90046, 818/362-1181

NUMBER ONE WITH A BULLET   Cannon, 1987, w/Gail Morgan
    Hickman, Andrew Kurtzman & Rob Riley

MARIA LUISA BEMBERG
Business: GEA Cinematoprafica SA, Pacheco de Melo 2141, 1126
    Buenos Aires, Argentine, tel.: 803-7779

MISS MARY   New World, 1986, w/Jorge Goldenberg, directed
I, THE WORST OF ALL   GEA Cinematografica, 1990,
    w/Antonio Larreta, directed
I DON'T WANT TO TALK ABOUT IT   Sony Pictures Classics, 1994,
    w/Jorge Goldberg, directed

JONATHAN BENAIR*
Agent: The Artists Agency - Los Angeles, 310/277-7779

Screenplays:
TROLLOPS w/Meredith Brody
BEETHOVEN'S TENTH
JAGGED EDGE 2

PETER BENCHLEY*
Agent: ICM - Beverly Hills, 310/550-4000

JAWS   Universal, 1975, w/Carl Gottlieb
THE DEEP   Columbia, 1977, w/Tracy Keenan Wynn
THE ISLAND   Universal, 1980

Screenplays:
AMAZON RUN
WHITE SHARK

LAWRENCE BENDER
Agent: William Morris Agency - Beverly Hills, 310/274-7451
Business: A Band Apart Productions, 6525 Sunset Blvd. -
    Garden Suite 12, Los Angeles, CA 90028, 213/468-2555

INTRUDER   Phantom Productions, 1989, w/Scott Spiegel

BARBARA BENEDEK*
Agent: United Talent Agency - Beverly Hills, 310/273-6700

THE BIG CHILL ★   Columbia, 1983, w/Lawrence Kasdan
IMMEDIATE FAMILY   Columbia, 1989
MEN DON'T LEAVE   The Geffen Company/Warner Bros., 1990,
    w/Paul Brickman

Screenplays:
SABRINA (remake)
TURTLE MOON
MAN IN THE WINDOW
BEGINNERS w/Harriet Frank Jr. & Irving Ravetch

TOM BENEDEK*
Agent: United Talent Agency - Beverly Hills, 310/273-6700

COCOON   20th Century Fox, 1985

Screenplays:
ZEUS AND ROXANE
LOVE IN THE AFTERNOON
BEYOND LOVE
MONSOON
SPELLS w/Abbie Bernstein
HALFWAY HOUSE
SHATTERED SILENCE
ORANGE COUNTY RED
ROLLING NOWHERE
RED ROOSTER

ROBERT BENEDETTO*
Contact: WGA - Los Angeles, 310/550-1000

ALOHA SUMMER   Spectrafilm, 1988, w/Mike Greco

GLENN M. BENEST*
Agent: The Irv Schechter Company - Beverly Hills, 310/278-8070

DEADLY BLESSING   United Artists/Polygram, 1981,
    w/Matthew Barr & Wes Craven

ROBERTO BENIGNI
Address: via Sant-Anselmo 29, Rome, Italy, tel: 06/575-8856

JOHHNY STECCHINO   New Line Cinema, 1992,
    w/Vincenzo Cerami, directed

TOMAS BENITEZ
SALSA   Cannon, 1988, w/Boaz Davidson & Shepard Goldman

JEFF BENJAMIN*
Contact: WGA - Los Angeles, 310/550-1000

AMERICAN ANTHEM   Columbia, 1986, w/Evan Archerd
WIND   TriStar, 1992, Story w/Kimball Livingston & Roger Vaughn

ALAN BENNETT
Agent: Peters, Fraser & Dunlop - London, 071/376-7676

THE WIND IN THE WILLOWS (P)
HABEAS CORPUS (P)
A PRIVATE FUNCTION   Island Alive, 1985
PRICK UP YOUR EARS   Samuel Goldwyn Company, 1987
A QUESTION OF ATTRIBUTION   BBC Enterprises, 1992,
    from his play
THE MADNESS OF GEORGE III   Samuel Goldwyn Company, 1994,
    from his play

BILL BENNETT*
(William Regis Bennett)
Contact: WGA - New York, 212/245-6180

BACKLASH   Samuel Goldwyn Company, 1987, directed
SPIDER AND ROSE   Australian Film Finance Corp. 1994, directed

CHARLES BENNETT*
Agent: Renaissance-H.N. Swanson - Los Angeles, 310/246-6000

PAGE FROM A DIARY (P)
AFTER MIDNIGHT (P)
DANGER LINE (P)

THE LAST HOUR (P)
THE RETURN (P)
SENSATION (P)
BIG BUSINESS (P)
BLACKMAIL   British International Pictures, 1929,
   w/Alfred Hitchcock & Benn W. Levy, from his play
THE CLAIRVOYANT   Gainsborough, 1934, w/Robert Edmunds &
   Bryan E. Wallace
THE MAN WHO KNEW TOO MUCH   Gaumont-British, 1934,
   w/A.R. Rawlinson, D.B. Wyndham Lewis, Edwin Greenwood &
   Emlyn Williams
THE THIRTY-NINE STEPS   Gaumont-British, 1935, w/Alma Reville
KING OF THE DAMNED   Gaumont, 1935, w/Sidney Gilliat &
   Noel Langley
SABOTAGE A WOMAN ALONE Gaumont, 1936, w/others
THE SECRET AGENT Gaumont, 1936
THE YOUNG IN HEART   Selznick, 1938, w/Paul Osborn
FOREIGN CORRESPONDENT   United Artists, 1940,
   w/Joan Harrison, James Hilton & Robert Benchley
THEY DARE NOT LOVE   Columbia, 1941, w/Ernest Vajda
JOAN OF PARIS   20th Century-Fox, 1942, w/Ellis St. Joseph
FOREVER AND A DAY   RKO, 1943, w/others
THE STORY OF DR. WASSELL   Paramount, 1944, w/Alan le May
UNCONQUERED   Paramount, 1947, w/Frederic M. Frank &
   Jesse Lasky Jr.
IVY   Universal, 1947
THE SIGN OF THE RAM   Columbia, 1948
BLACK MAGIC   United Artists, 1949
MADNESS OF THE HEART   GFD, 1949, directed
WHERE DANGER LIVES   RKO, 1950
KIND LADY   MGM, 1951, w/Edward Chodorov & Jerry Davis
THE GREEN GLOVE   United Artists, 1952
NO ESCAPE CITY ON A HUNT 1953, directed
DANGEROUS MISSION   RKO, 1954, w/W.R. Burnett,
   James Edmiston & Horace McCoy
NIGHT OF THE DEMON CURSE OF THE DEMON Columbia,
   1957, w/Hal E. Chester
THE STORY OF MANKIND   Warner Bros., 1957, w/Irwin Allen
THE BIG CIRCUS   Allied Artists, 1959, w/Irwin Allen &
   Irving Wallace
THE LOST WORLD   20th Century-Fox, 1960, w/Irwin Allen
VOYAGE TO THE BOTTOM OF THE SEA   20th Century-Fox, 1961,
   w/Irwin Allen
FIVE WEEKS IN A BALLOON   20th Century-Fox, 1962,
   w/Irwin Allen & Albert Gail
WAR-GODS OF THE DEEP THE CITY UNDER THE SEA
   American International, 1965, w/Louis M. Heyward

Screenplays:
BLACKMAIL w/Stuart Birnbaum (remake)

GARY BENNETT
RAIN WITHOUT THUNDER   Orion, 1993, directed

HARVE BENNETT*
Business Manager: Barry Greenfeld, Atlman, Greenfield & Selvaggi,
   310/444-9044
Contact: Harve Bennett Productions, Warner Bros. TV - 818/954-2079

STAR TREK II: THE WRATH OF KHAN   Paramount, 1982, Story
STAR TREK III: THE SEARCH FOR SPOCK   Paramount, 1984
STAR TREK IV: THE VOYAGE HOME   Paramount, 1986,
   w/Peter Krikes, Steve Meerson & Nicholas Meyer
STAR TREK V: THE FINAL FRONTIER   Paramount, 1989,
   Story w/David Loughery & William Shatner

PARKER BENNETT*
Agent: William Morris Agency - Beverly Hills, 310/274-7451

MYSTERY DATE   Orion, 1991, w/Terry Runte
SUPER MARIO BROS.   Buena Vista, 1993, w/Terry Runte &
   Ed Solomon

RICHARD BENNETT
(See Bert I. Gordon)

VALERIE BENNETT
Agent: APA - Los Angeles, 310/273-0744

THE COMPANION (CTF)   USA/Michael Phillips Productions, 1994,
   w/Ian Seeberg

Screenplays:
MYSTERY BENEATH w/Ian Seeberg
WAKE UP CALL w/Ian Seeberg
TIMERS w/Ian Seeberg
HIGHER GROUND TEMPTATION w/Ian Seeberg
MORT w/Ian Seeberg
CAT & MOUSE w/Ian Seeberg

WALLACE BENNETT*
Agent: Harold R. Greene Inc. - Marina del Rey, 310/823-5393
Business: 5598 South Rim St., Westlake Village, CA 91362

SILENT SCREAM   American Cinema, 1980, w/Jim Wheat &
   Ken Wheat
THE PHILADELPHIA EXPERIMENT   New World, 1984,
   Story w/Don Jakoby
RAGE OF HONOR   Trans World Entertainment, 1987,
   w/Robert Short

TYLER BENSINGER*
Agent: United Talent Agency - Beverly Hills, 310/273-6700

Screenplays:
HOME
SPADE & GRAVE
THE PILLERS
JUST LOOKING

BEAU BENSINK*
Agent: ICM - Beverly Hills, 310/550-4000

Screenplays:
THE AGENDA
MISTER SANDMAN
BLIND SPOT

ROBBY BENSON*
(Robby Segal)
Agent: The Rothman Agency - Beverly Hills, 213/655-2020
Manager: Krost/Chapin Management - Los Angeles, 310/281-3585

ONE ON ONE   Warner Bros., 1977, w/Jerry Segal
THE MILER   Warner Bros., 1978, Shared
DIE LAUGHING   Orion/Warner Bros., 1980, w/Jerry Segal &
   Scott Parker
WHITE HOT CRACK IN THE MIRROR Triax Entertainment Group,
   1988, as "Robert Modero," directed
MODERN LOVE   Skouras Pictures, 1990, directed
BETRAYAL OF THE DOVE   I.T.C. Entertainment, 1993

ROBERT BENSON
SEXBOMB   Phillips & Mora Entertainment, 1989

TREVOR BENTHAM
A MONTH BY THE LAKE   Miramax, 1994

ERIC BENTLEY
Agent: The Tantleff Office - New York, 212/941-3939

Screenplays:
ARE YOU NOW OR HAVE YOU EVER BEEN (CTF, from his play)

ROBERT BENTLEY*
Agent: The Mitchell J. Hamilburg Agency - Los Angeles,
   310/657-1501

SHANGHAI SURPRISE   MGM/UA, 1986, w/John Kohn

ROBERT BENTON*
Agent: ICM - New York, 212/556-5600

BONNIE AND CLYDE ★ Warner Bros., 1967, w/David Newman
THERE WAS A CROOKED MAN... United Artists, 1970,
   w/David Newman
WHAT'S UP DOC? Warner Bros., 1972, w/Buck Henry &
   David Newman
BAD COMPANY Paramount, 1972, w/David Newman
THE LATE SHOW ★ Warner Bros., 1977, directed
SUPERMAN Warner Bros., 1978, w/David Newman,
   Leslie Newman & Mario Puzo
KRAMER VS. KRAMER ★★ Columbia, 1979, directed
STILL OF THE NIGHT MGM/UA, 1982, directed
PLACES IN THE HEART ★★ Tri-Star, 1984, directed
NADINE Tri-Star, 1987, directed
NOBODY'S FOOL Paramount, 1994, directed

LEO BENVENUTI*
Agent: United Talent Agency - Beverly Hills, 310/273-6700

THE SANTA CLAUSE Buena Vista, 1994, w/Steve Rudnick

Screenplays:
LEGAL MISFITS w/Steve Rudnick

ERIC BERCOVICI*
Agent: CAA - Beverly Hills, 310/288-4545

THE DAY OF THE EVIL GUN MGM, 1968,
   w/Charles Marquis Warren
CHANGE OF HABIT Universal, 1969, w/James Lee &
   Lewis Meltzer
HELL IN THE PACIFIC Cinerama Releasing Corporation, 1969,
   w/Alexander Jacobs
THE CULPEPPER CATTLE CO. 20th Century-Fox, 1972,
   w/Gregory Prentiss

Screenplays:
DUNN'S CONUNDRUM
TRACKS END

KAREN BERCOVICI*
Agent: Richland/Wunsch/Hohman Agency - Los Angeles,
   310/278-1955

Screenplays:
THE CHEERLEADER
THE WIDOWS CLUB
GEE WHIZ
HELLER

LUCA BERCOVICI*
Business Manager: Cindy S. Matyas, The Business Management
   Office, 818/509-1811

GHOULIES Empire Pictures, 1986, w/Jefery Levy, directed
ROCKULA Cannon, 1989, w/Jefery Levy &
   Christopher Verweil, directed

GLENN BERENBEIM*
Agent: The Irv Schechter Company - Beverly Hills, 310/278-8070

THE HEART IS A LONELY HUNTER (P), Adaptation
MAD SCENES (P)
BIRTHDAY SUIT (P)

TOM BERENGER
Agent: CAA - Beverly Hills, 310/288-4545

Screenplays:
ON THE RUN

BRUCE BERESFORD
Agent: William Morris Agency - Beverly Hills, 310/274-7451

THE ADVENTURES OF BARRY McKENZIE Double Head
   Productions, 1972, w/Barry Humphries, directed
BARRY McKENZIE HOLDS HIS OWN Satori, 1974,
   w/Barry Humphries, directed
MONEY MOVERS South Australian Film Corporation,
   1978, directed
BREAKER MORANT ★ New World/Quartet, 1980,
   w/Jonathan Hardy & David Stevens, directed
THE FRINGE DWELLERS Atlantic Releasing Corporation, 1986,
   w/Phoison Beresford, directed
THE CURSE OF THE STARVING CLASS Trimark, 1994, directed

PHOISON BERESFORD
THE FRINGE DWELLERS Atlantic Releasing Corporation, 1986,
   w/Bruce Beresford

A. SCOTT BERG
MAKING LOVE 20th Century-Fox, 1982, Story

JAMES BERG*
Agent: ICM - Beverly Hills, 310/550-4000

Screenplays:
THE PRITCHARD EXHIBIT w/Stan Zimmerman

JUDITH BERG*
Contact: WGA - Los Angeles, 310/550-1000

ALMOST SUMMER Universal, 1978, w/Sandra Berg &
   Martin Davidson

RICHARD BERG*
Business: Stonehenge Productions, Viacom, 818/505-7566

SHOOT Avco Embassy, 1976

SANDRA BERG*
Contact: WGA - Los Angeles, 310/550-1000

ALMOST SUMMER Universal, 1978, w/Judith Berg &
   Martin Davidson

ALAN BERGER
Agent: Paradigm - Los Angeles, 310/277-4400

SAVE THE LAST DANCE FOR ME Swann American Pictures,
   1981, w/Kathy Gori

Screenplays:
LIFE RIGHTS (CTF) w/Kathy Gori
THE BUFF w/Kathy Gori
THE GOLD COAST w/Kathy Gori
MERCY GIRLS w/Kathy Gori
I'M NOT CHARLIE w/Kathy Gori
THE MAN SHE KNEW w/Kathy Gori
HER SAINTED HUSBAND w/Kathy Gori
GOODBYE FOREVER w/Kathy Gori
RICH LITTLE POOR GIRLS w/Kathy Gori & Joan Rivers
FOR BETTER OR FOR WORSE w/Kathy Gori
ROCKET MAN LIFE ON EARTH w/Kathy Gori
NATIONAL PARK w/Kathy Gori
LADIES DAY w/Kathy Gori
UNDER WRAPS w/Kathy Gori
SHAGGY w/Kathy Gori

PAMELA BERGER
THE IMPORTED BRIDEGROOM Lara Classics, 1990, directed

PHIL BERGER*
Agent: Innovative Artists - Los Angeles, 310/553-5200

Screenplays:
THE BOYS FROM NOWHERE

ROBERT BERGER
FINAL ANALYSIS   Warner Bros., 1992, w/Wesley Strick

STEPHEN BERGER
Agent: Susan Smith & Associates - Beverly Hills, 213/852-4777

Screenplays:
THE CONJURER w/Rand Ravich
MICROCOP
MONKEY MAN
THE PAW
UNDER THE LAW
THE COLD EQUATIONS
ROADFEVER

ANDREW BERGMAN*
Agent: CAA - Beverly Hills, 310/288-4545
Business: Lobell-Bergman Productions, 9336 W. Washington Blvd.,
   Culver City, CA 90230, 310/202-3362

SOCIAL SECURITY (P)
BLAZING SADDLES   Warner Bros., 1973, w/Mel Brooks,
   Richard Pryor, Norman Steinberg & Alan Uger
THE IN-LAWS   Warner Bros., 1979
SO FINE   Warner Bros., 1981, directed
OH GOD! YOU DEVIL   Warner Bros., 1984
FLETCH   Universal, 1985
BIG TROUBLE   Columbia, 1986, as "Warren Bogle"
THE FRESHMAN   Tri-Star, 1990, directed
SOAPDISH   Paramount, 1991, w/Robert Harling
HONEYMOON IN VEGAS   Columbia, 1992, directed
THE SCOUT   20th Century Fox, 1994, w/Albert Brooks &
   Monica Johnson

Screenplays:
STRIPTEASE
RHAPSODY IN CRIME
NIGHT OF THE TOY SOLDIERS THE SNATCH

ANDREW C.J. BERGMAN*
Contact: WGA - New York, 212/245-6180

Screenplays:
DOUBLES
MIRACLE AT MOOSEHEAD

INGMAR BERGMAN
Agent: Paul Kohner, Inc. - Beverly Hills, 310/550-1060

THE DEVIL'S WANTON   Terrafilm, 1949, directed
ILLICIT INTERLUDE *SOMMARLEK* Janus, 1951,
   w/Herbert Grevenius, directed
SECRETS OF WOMEN   Janus, 1952, directed
MONIKA   Janus, 1953, directed
SAWDUST AND TINSEL *THE NAKED NIGHT* Janus,
   1953, directed
A LESSON IN LOVE   Janus, 1954, directed
DREAMS   Janus, 1955, directed
SMILES OF A SUMMER NIGHT   Janus, 1955, directed
WILD STRAWBERRIES   Janus, 1957, directed
THE SEVENTH SEAL   Janus, 1957, directed
THE MAGICIAN   Janus, 1958, directed
THE DEVIL'S EYE   Janus, 1960, directed
THROUGH A GLASS DARKLY ★   Janus, 1962, directed ✓
WINTER LIGHT   Janus, 1962, directed
THE SILENCE   Janus, 1963, directed
ALL THESE WOMEN *NOW ABOUT THESE WOMEN...*
   Janus, 1964, directed
PERSONA   United Artists, 1966, directed
HOUR OF THE WOLF   United Artists, 1968, directed

SHAME   United Artists, 1968, directed
THE PASSION OF ANNA   United Artists, 1969, directed
THE TOUCH   Cinerama Releasing Corporation, 1971, directed
CRIES AND WHISPERS ★   New World, 1973, directed
SCENES FROM A MARRIAGE   Cinema 5, 1973, directed
FACE TO FACE   Paramount, 1976, directed
THE SERPENT'S EGG   Paramount, 1978, directed
AUTUMN SONATA ★   New World, 1978, directed
FROM THE LIFE OF THE MARIONETTES   Universal/AFD,
   1980, directed
FANNY AND ALEXANDER ★   Embassy, 1983, directed
AFTER THE REHEARSAL   Triumph/Columbia, 1983, directed
BEST INTENTIONS   Samuel Goldwyn Company, 1992
SUNDAY'S CHILDREN   (No Distributor), 1993

LINDA J. BERGMAN*
Agent: CAA - Beverly Hills, 310/288-4545

THE LOOKALIKE (CTF)   Gallo Entertainment, 1990,
   w/Martin Tahse
MATTERS OF THE HEART (CTF)   Tahse-Bergman/MCA, 1990,
   w/Martin Tahse

MARTIN BERGMAN*
Agent: ICM - Beverly Hills, 310/550-4000

PETER'S FRIENDS   Samuel Goldwyn Company, 1992,
   w/Rita Rudner

Screenplays:
GREEN ACRES w/Rita Rudner
WILD KINGDOM w/Rita Rudner

PETER BERGMAN*
Contact: WGA - Los Angeles, 310/550-1000

HE'S MY GIRL   Scotti Bros., 1987, Story w/Taylor Ames &
   Terence H. Winkless

ROBERT BERGMAN
Agent: The Artists Group - Los Angeles, 310/552-1100

SKULL: A NIGHT OF TERROR   Geonib Properties, 1989,
   w/Gerard Ciccoritti, directed
A WHISPER TO A SCREAM   Distant Horizon and Lighthouse
   Communications, 1989, w/Gerard Ciccoritti, directed

ERIC BERGREN*
Agent: William Morris Agency - Beverly Hills, 310/274-7451

THE ELEPHANT MAN ★   Paramount, 1980,
   w/Christopher DeVore & David Lynch
FRANCES   Universal/AFD, 1982, w/Christopher DeVore &
   Nicholas Kazan
THE DARK WIND   Le Studio Canal/7 Arts, 1993, w/Neal Jimenez

Screenplays:
THE BLACK DAHLIA
BIOSPHERE w/Patrick Read Johnson
A WRINKLE IN TIME w/Chris DeVore
CHRIS LUCAS STORY
EPIPHANY

ELEANOR BERGSTEIN*
Agent: CAA - Beverly Hills, 310/288-4545

IT'S MY TURN   Columbia, 1980   ✓
DIRTY DANCING   Vestron, 1987
LET IT BE ME   Savoy, 1995, directed

HOWARD BERK*
Agent: Barry Perelman Agency - Los Angeles, 310/274-5999

TARGET   Warner Bros., 1985, w/Don Peterson

**F
I
L
M

W
R
I
T
E
R
S**

STEVEN BERKOFF
Agent: The Gage Group - Los Angeles, 310/859-8777

EAST (P)
GREEKS (P)
KVETCH (P)
ACAPULCO (P)
ONE MAN (P)
DECADENCE   Mayfair Entertainment, 1994, from his play, directed

JEANNIE BERLIN
Contact: 212/888-0080

IN THE SPIRIT   Castle Hill Productions, 1990, w/Laurie Jones

MICHAEL BERLIN*
Agent: Paradigm - Los Angeles, 310/277-4400

Screenplays:
MIRROR IMAGE w/Eric Estrin (World Vision)
TAX MAN w/Eric Estrin
RED BIRD DOWN w/Eric Estrin

MICHAEL BERLLY
Manager: I.R.S./Harris Management - Culver City, 310/841-4169
Contact: Karl Austen, Armstrong, Hirsch, Jackoway, Tyerman &
   Wertheimer - Los Angeles, 310/553-0305

Screenplays:
SOFT KILL w/Craig Randelman
LITTLE NAPOLEON w/Craig Randelman
COUP D'ETAT w/Craig Randelman

BARRY BERMAN*
Agent: ICM - Beverly Hills, 310/550-4000

BENNY & JOON   MGM, 1993

Screenplays:
SPIDER AND THE PRINCE

JEFF BERMAN
Contact: ITB Cinegroup, 800 N. Seward, Los Angeles, CA 90038,
   213/469-7244 x18

Screenplays:
ON THE AIR w/Jerry Rapp
THE TOURISTS w/Jerry Rapp
STRAY KIDS w/Jerry Rapp
WISHING w/Jerry Rapp
TENANT OF THE LAND w/Tony Caballero
MS. ROMANCE

RICK BERMAN*
Contact: WGA - Los Angeles, 310/550-1000

STAR TREK: GENERATIONS   Paramount, 1994,
   Story w/Brannon Braga & Ron Moore

TED BERMAN
Contact: 818/956-2612

THE FOX AND THE HOUND (AF)   Buena Vista, 1981,
   Story w/others, directed
THE BLACK CAULDRON (AF)   Buena Vista, 1985,
   Story w/others, directed

CARLOS R. BERMUDEZ
Agent: The Artists Group - Los Angeles, 310/552-1100

Screenplays:
CHIPPER'S LEGACY
UNDENIABLE TRUTH
A DOLPHIN'S TALE
GENUINE DESIRE
DRACULA IN THE CARIBBEAN
THE DAY THE MUSIC DIED

JUDD BERNARD*
Contact: The Kettledrum Film Co. - 818/506-7525

THE MARSEILLE CONTRACT   Warner Bros., 1974
THE CLASS OF MISS MacMICHAEL   Brut Productions, 1978
ENTER THE NINJA   Cannon, 1981, w/Menaham Golan

SAM BERNARD
Contact: Tapestry Films, 9328 Civic Center Drive, Beverly Hills, CA
   90210, 310/275-1191

RAD   Tri-Star, 1986, w/Geoffrey Edwards
3:15   Dakota Entertainment, 1986, w/Michael Jacobs
WARLOCK: THE ARMAGEDDON   Trimark, 1993, w/Kevin Rock

PAUL BERNBAUM*
Agent: ICM - Beverly Hills, 310/550-4000

ROYCE (CTF)   Showtime Entertainment/Gerber/
   ITC Productions, 1994

EDWARD BERNDS*
Contact: WGA - Los Angeles, 310/550-1000

REFORM SCHOOL GIRLS (CTF)   Showtime/Drive-In Cinema,
   1994, Story

SANDRA BERNHARD*
Contact: WGA - Los Angeles, 310/550-1000

GIVING TIL IT HURTS (P)   w/John Boskovich
WITHOUT YOU I'M NOTHING   MCEG, 1990, from her play,
   w/John Boskovich

KEVIN BERNHARDT
Agent: CNA & Associates - Los Angeles, 310/556-4343

Screenplays:
THE PRODIGAL

GISELA BERNICE
PARALLEL LIVES (CTF)   Showtime, 1994

JEFFREY S. BERNINI
Contact: 818/986-7764

TAKE THIS JOB AND SHOVE IT   Avco Embassy, 1981,
   Story w/Barry Schneider

CORBIN BERNSEN*
Agent: ICM - Beverly Hills, 310/550-4000

Screenplays:
411

ABBIE BERNSTEIN*
Agent: Above the Line - West Hollywood, 310/859-6115

Screenplays:
SPELLS w/Tom Benedek
THE HITCHHIKERS GUIDE TO THE GALAXY
SHATTERED MOON
RAIN CRYSTALS
MEANT TO BE WILD
THE MUMMY
VERY OLD MONEY

ARMYAN BERNSTEIN*
Agent: CAA - Beverly Hills, 310/288-4545
Business: Beacon Pictures, Warner-Hollywood Studios -
   213/850-2651

THANK GOD IT'S FRIDAY   Columbia, 1978
ONE FROM THE HEART   Columbia, 1982, w/Francis Coppola

WINDY CITY   Warner Bros., 1984, directed
CROSS MY HEART   Universal, 1987, w/Gail Parent, directed

Screenplays:
HURRICANE CARTER
SHE'S GONE

JACK BERNSTEIN*
Agent: Douroux & Co. - Beverly Hills, 310/552-0900

ACE VENTURA, PET DETECTIVE   Warner Bros., 1994,
   w/Jim Carrey & Tom Shadyac

Screenplays:
WHAT'S UP WITH DAD?

JANE BERNSTEIN*
Agent: Shapiro/Lichtman - Los Angeles, 310/859-8877

SEVEN MINUTES IN HEAVEN   Warner Bros., 1986,
   w/Linda Feferman

JON BERNSTEIN
Agent: Renaissance-H.N. Swanson - Los Angeles, 310/246-6000

Screenplays:
MYSTERY MAN
WAVES
LOOKALIKE
TRAVELING WITHOUT BAGGAGE
ANONYMOUS

NAT BERNSTEIN*
Agent: CAA - Beverly Hills, 310/288-4545

OPPORTUNITY KNOCKS   Universal, 1990, w/Mitchel Katlin

Screenplays:
ON THE AIR w/Mitchel Katlin
WHEN THE WIFE'S AWAY w/Mitchel Katlin
LORD OF THE MANOR w/Mitchel Katlin

REED BERNSTEIN
Agent: Susan Smith & Associates - Beverly Hills, 213/852-4777

Screenplays:
LES SPLENDIDES w/James Mathers

WALTER BERNSTEIN*
Agent: ICM - New York, 212/556-5600
Address: 320 Central Park West, New York, NY 10025,
   212/724-1821

KISS THE BLOOD OFF MY HANDS   Universal, 1948
THAT KIND OF WOMAN   Paramount, 1959
HELLER IN PINK TIGHTS   1960, Paramount, w/Dudley Nichols
PARIS BLUES   United Artists, 1961, w/Irene Kamp & Jack Sher
FAIL SAFE   Columbia, 1964
THE TRAIN   United Artists, 1964, w/Franklin Coen & Frank Davis
THE MONEY TRAP   MGM, 1966
THE MOLLY MAGUIRES   Paramount, 1970
THE FRONT ★   Columbia, 1976   ✓
SEMI-TOUGH   United Artists, 1978
THE BETSY   Allied Artists, 1978, w/William Bast
AN ALMOST PERFECT AFFAIR   Paramount, 1979,
   w/Don Peterson
YANKS   Universal, 1979, w/Colin Welland
LITTLE MISS MARKER   Universal, 1980, directed
THE HOUSE ON CARROLL STREET   Orion, 1988
DOOMSDAY GUN (CTF)   Griffin Productions/HBO Showcase,
   1994, w/Lionel Chetwynd

Screenplays:
F.B.I. STING
HOMAGE TO CATALONIA
LOW DOWN

SPOOKWAFFE
STAR QUALITY

ERIC BERNT*
Agent: ICM - Beverly Hills, 310/550-4000

SURVIVING THE GAME   New Line Cinema, 1994

Screenplays:
VIRTUOSITY (Paramount)
WILD BLUE YONDER
OUR MAN SALLY
NOT FOR PUBLIC VIEWING
ROCK THE BOAT

CLAUDE BERRI
Agent: Artmedia, 10 Avenue Georges V, 75008 Paris, France,
   04/723-7860
Business: Renn Productions, 10 rue Lincoln, 75008 Paris, France,
   04/256-2590

ONE WILD MOMENT   Quartet/Films Incorporated, 1978, directed
JEAN DE FLORETTE   Orion Classics, 1987,
   w/Gerard Brach, directed
MANON OF THE SPRING   Orion Classics, 1987,
   w/Gerard Brach, directed
URANUS   Prestige Films, 1991, w/Arletta Langmann, directed
GERMINAL   Sony Classics, 1993, w/Arletta Langmann, directed

GINA BERRIAULT*
Agent: The Gersh Agency - Beverly Hills, 310/274-6611

THE STONE BOY   TLC Films/20th Century-Fox, 1984

DAVID BERRY
THE WHALES OF AUGUST   Alive Films, 1987, from his play

JULIAN BERRY
AFTER THE FALL OF NEW YORK   Almi Pictures, 1985,
   w/Martin Dolman & Gabriel Rossini

MICHAEL BERRY*
Agent: United Talent Agency - Beverly Hills, 310/273-6700

SHORT TIME   20th Century Fox, 1990, w/John Blumenthal

Screenplays:
BREAKFAST WITH SPAULDING w/John Blumenthal
TWILIGHT w/John Blumenthal
BLUE STREAK w/John Blumenthal
CHUMPS w/John Blumenthal
NIGHT WORK

TOM BERRY
CRAZY MOON   Miramax, 1987, w/Stefan Wodoslawsky

WILLIAM BERRY*
Contact: WGA - Los Angeles, 310/550-1000

Screenplays:
BLUE MURDER

ERIK BERTELLOTTI
Agent: Jon Klane Agency - Beverly Hills, 310/278-0178

Screenplays:
LAWS OF NATURE

BERNARDO BERTOLUCCI
Agent: ICM - Beverly Hills, 310/550-4000

BEFORE THE REVOLUTION   New Yorker, 1964, directed
THE SPIDER'S STRATAGEM   New Yorker, 1970, w/Eduardo de
   Gregorio & Marilu Parolini, directed

THE CONFORMIST ★   Paramount, 1971, directed
LAST TANGO IN PARIS   Universal, 1973,
   w/Franco Arcalli, directed
1900   Paramount, 1976, w/Franco Arcalli &
   Giuseppe Bertolucci, directed
LUNA   20th Century-Fox, 1979, w/Giuseppe Bertolucci &
   Clare Peploe, directed
TRAGEDY OF A RIDICULOUS MAN   The Ladd Company/Warner
   Bros., 1982, directed
THE LAST EMPEROR ★★   Columbia, 1987,
   w/Mark Peploe, directed
THE SHELTERING SKY   Warner Bros., 1990,
   w/Mark Peploe, directed
LITTLE BUDDHA   Miramax, 1994, Story, directed

DAN BESSIE
HARD TRAVELING   New World, 1986, directed

LUC BESSON
Agent: CAA - Beverly Hills, 310/288-4545

LE DERNIER COMBAT   Gaumont/Les Films du Loup/Constantin
   Alexandrof Productions, 1983
SUBWAY   Island Alive, 1985, w/Marc Perrier, directed
THE BIG BLUE   Columbia/WEG, 1988, w/Robert Garland, directed
LA FEMME NIKITA   Gaumont, 1991, directed
THE PROFESSIONAL   Columbia, 1994, directed

PETE BEST
ACCIDENTAL MEETING (CTF)   Fast Track Film/Wilshire Court
   Productions, 1994, w/Christopher Horner

KATHLEEN BETSKO-YALE*
Contact: WGA - Los Angeles, 310/550-1000

Screenplays:
STICHERS AND STARLIGHT TALKERS

GIL BETTMAN*
Agent: Rogers & Associates - North Hollywood, 818/509-1010
Business Manager: Alan Grodin, Cooper, Epstein, Hurewitz -
   Beverly Hills, 310//278-1111

NEVER TOO YOUNG TO DIE   Paul Releasing, 1986,
   w/Anton Fitz & Steven Paul, directed

JONATHAN BETUEL*
Agent: William Morris Agency - Beverly Hills, 310/274-7451

THE LAST STARFIGHTER   Universal, 1984
MY SCIENCE PROJECT   Buena Vista, 1985, directed
T. REX   New Line Cinema, 1995, directed

Screenplays:
INTERCEPTORS
THEODORE

RADHA BHARADWAJ*
Contact: Bill Skryzniarz, Esq. - 310/858-7700

CLOSET LAND   Universal, 1991, directed

GRACE CARY BICKLEY*
Agent: Sanford-Gross & Associates - Los Angeles, 310/208-2100

THE GUN IN BETTY LOU'S HANDBAG   Buena Vista, 1992

WILLIAM BICKLEY*
Agent: ICM - Beverly Hills, 310/550-4000
Contact: Ziffren, Brittenham & Branca - Beverly Hills, 310/552-3388

HAWMPS   Mulberry Square, 1976, w/Michael Warren

ANN BIDERMAN*
Agent: ICM - Beverly Hills, 310/550-4000

AMERICAN DREAMER   Warner Bros., 1984, Story

Screenplays:
COPYCAT
THE WOMEN
HEADING WEST
MIAMI STORY
THE CHELSEA
LIBERTY CITY
THE THREE "C"S

CHRISTIAN BIEGALSKI
TARGET OF SUSPICION (CTF)   USA Pictures, 1994,
   Story w/Benedicte Popper

PETER BIEGEN
Agent: Lisa Callamaro Literary Agency- Beverly Hills, 310/274-6783

CEREMONIES OF HORSEMEN (P)
CAT-KILLER (P)
SHERMAN (P)
THE FAILED TRAGEDY OF JAMES MONROE (P)
CHEAP STATIONS (P)

Screenplays:
HITSVILLE
LIKE DREAMERS DO
FAR CRY

KATHRYN BIGELOW*
Agent: CAA - Beverly Hills, 310/288-4545
Business: First Light, 20th Century Fox - 310/203-2112

THE LOVELESS   Atlantic Releasing Corporation, 1981,
   w/Monty Montgomery, co-directed
NEAR DARK   Warner Bros., 1987, w/Eric Red, directed
BLUE STEEL   MGM/UA, 1990, w/Eric Red, directed

Screenplays:
THE BLUNDERER
EVERY BREATH
NIGHT BY NIGHT
UNDERTOW w/Eric Red

WILLIAM BIGELOW
Agent: Broder-Kurland-Webb-Uffner - Beverly Hills, 310/281-3400

Screenplays:
THE LAST STRAW
THIEVES AND LOVERS
FOOLPROOF
A SEASON OF CHAMPIONS
WEB OF DECEIT

TONY BILL
Agent: ICM - Beverly Hills, 310/550-4000
Business: Barnstorm Films, 73 Market St., Venice, CA 90291,
   310/396-5937

Screenplays:
OCEAN OF STORMS w/Ben Mason

DANNY BILSON*
Agent: CAA - Beverly Hills, 310/288-4545
Business: Pet Fly Productions, Paramount TV - 213/956-8625

FUTURE COP   *TRANCERS*   Empire Pictures, 1985,
   w/Paul De Meo
ZONE TROOPERS   Empire Pictures, 1986,
   w/Paul De Meo, directed
ELMINATORS   Empire Pictures, 1986, w/Paul De Meo
THE WRONG GUYS   New World, 1988, w/Paul De Meo, directed
ARENA   Empire Pictures, 1988, w/Paul De Meo

PULSEPOUNDERS Empire Pictures, 1988, w/Paul De Meo
THE ROCKETEER Buena Vista, 1991, w/Paul De Meo

Screenplays:
EDWIN MULLHOUSE w/Paul De Meo
G-MEN w/Paul De Meo

CARL BINDER*
Agent: Annette Van Duren Agency - Los Angeles, 213/650-3643

Screenplays:
POCAHONTAS (AF) (Buena Vista)
A DAY IN THE AFTERLIFE
LIGHT BLACK
HOTEL DO

JOHN BINDER*
Agent: APA - Los Angeles, 310/273-0744

HONEYSUCKLE ROSE Warner Bros., 1980, w/Carol Sobieski &
    William Wittliff
ENDANGERED SPECIES   MGM/UA, 1982, w/Alan Rudolph
UFORIA Universal, 1984, directed

Screenplays:
THE REVOLUTION w/Michael Wadleigh

MIKE BINDER*
Agent: United Talent Agency - Beverly Hills, 310/273-6700
Business: Mike Binder Productions, Columbia Pictures - Los Angeles,
    310/280-6752

COUP DE VILLE Universal, 1990
CROSSING THE BRIDGE Buena Vista, 1992, directed
INDIAN SUMMER Buena Vista, 1993, directed

Screenplays:
FRIEND OF THE FAMILY (directing)
NORTHERN LIGHTS

WILLIAM BINDLEY*
Agent: William Morris Agency - Beverly Hills, 310/274-7451

JUDICIAL CONSENT Rysher, 1994, directed

Screenplays:
MY LOVE, YOUR HONOR
SNOW DAY w/Scott Bindley

STEVE BING*
Manager: Brillstein-Grey - Beverly Hills, 310/275-6135

MISSING IN ACTION 2: THE BEGINNING Cannon,1985,
    w/Arthur Silver & Larry Levinson
EVERY BREATH Motion Picture Corporation of America, 1993,
    w/Andrew Fleming & Judd Nelson

BRAD BIRD*
Agent: CAA - Beverly Hills, 310/288-4545

BATTERIES NOT INCLUDED Universal, 1986, w/Brent Maddock,
    Matthew Robbins & S.S. Wilson

Screenplays:
QUALITY TIME

BRIAN BIRD*
Agent: The Gersh Agency - Beverly Hills, 310/274-6611

BOPHA! Paramount, 1993, w/John Wierick

Screenplays:
THE MAGNOLIA PASSION w/John Wierick

SARAH BIRD
THE BOYFRIEND SCHOOL Hemdale, 1990

DAVID BIRKE*
Agent: CAA - Beverly Hills, 310/288-4545

THE FEAR INSIDE (CTF) Viacom Pictures, 1992

Screenplays:
BLACK BLOOD
MR. ADVENTURE
THE CROOKED TREE
THE POLICEMAN
NOCTURNUS
CAPTAIN JACK AND THE MUFFIN TWINS
HOMESICK
BORDER TOWN

ANDREW BIRKIN
Agent: William Morris Agency - Beverly Hills, 310/274-7451

THE PIED PIPER Paramount, 1972, w/Jacques Demy &
    Mark Peploe
FLAME Goodtime Entertainment, 1975
THE FINAL CONFLICT 20th Century-Fox, 1981
KING DAVID Paramount, 1985, w/James Costigan
THE NAME OF THE ROSE 20th Century Fox, 1986,
    w/Gerard Brach, Howard Franklin & Alain Godard
BURNING SECRET Vestron, 1988, directed
SALT ON OUR SKIN Warner Bros. Transatlantic, 1993,
    w/Bee Gilbert, directed
THE CEMENT GARDEN October Films, 1994, directed

Screenplays:
FIELDS OF HONOR w/Wolfgang Petersen
INSIDE THE THIRD REICH
LITTLE LORD FAUNTLEROY
THE GLORY & THE DREAM
PETER PAN
RUNAWAY

STUART BIRNBAUM*
Agent: The Brandt Company - Sherman Oaks, 818/783-7747

SMOKEY AND THE BANDIT PART 3 Universal, 1983,
    w/David Dashev
THE ZOO GANG New World, 1985, Story w/David Dashev,
    Pen Densham & John Watson
SUMMER SCHOOL Paramount, 1987, Story w/David Dashev &
    Jeff Franklin

Screenplays:
BLACKMAIL w/Charles Bennett (remake)
THE SILVER CROSS w/David Dashev
CHAMPAGNE FOR CAESAR CHANCE OF A LIFETIME
    w/David Dashev
SOME OF MY BEST FRIENDS w/David Dashev
THUNDERBOAT w/Dennis Hackin
LAST CHANCE TO DANCE
THE RESTLESS SWORDS OF SHERWOOD FOREST
PRANKSTER CHRONICLES
KING OF THE SHADOWS

LARRY J. BISCHOF*
Business Manager: Gold, Marks, Ring & Pepper - Los Angeles,
    310/277-1000
Contact: Bischof & Lowry Entertainment - 909/659-4949

DREAMER 20th Century-Fox, 1979, w/James Proctor

JOHN BISHOP*
Agent: CAA - Beverly Hills, 213/288-4545

BORDERLINES (P) also screenplay
EMPTY HEARTS (P)
KEEPIN AN EYE ON LOUIE (P)
THE PACKAGE Orion, 1989
THE DROP ZONE Paramount, 1994, w/Peter Barsocchini

Screenplays:
THE TRIP BACK DOWN
CHAPPIE

LARRY BISHOP*
Agent: The Coppage Company - North Hollywood, 818/980-1106

Screenplays:
GANGSTERS IN LOVE
BADMAN
THE DEBT
TRIGGER-HAPPY
FLYING BULLETS
UNDERWORLD
BLOWN AWAY
RED HARVEST (Adaptation)
SPEED
ROUGH STUFF

ROD BISHOP
Contact: Australian Film Commission, 8 West St., North Sydney,
    NSW 2026, Australia, tel.: 2/925-7333

BODY MELT   Dumb Films, 1993, w/Philip Brophy

LOUISA BURNS BISOGNO
Agent: William Morris Agency - Beverly Hills, 310/274-7451

MARY SILLIMAN'S WAR (CTF)   Heritage Films/Citadel Films,
    1994, w/Steven Schechter

SHEM BITTERMAN
THE RAMP (P)
IOWA BOYS (P)
TULSA (P)
BEIJING LEGENDS (P)
1 + 1 = 3 (P)
SELF STORAGE (P)   w/Tony Spiridakis
PEEPHOLE (P)
HALLOWEEN 5: THE RETURN OF MICHAEL MYERS
    Galaxy International, 1989, w/Michael Jacobs &
    Dominique Othenin-Girard

Screenplays:
IOWA BOYS
OUT OF THE RAIN (from his play 1 + 1 = 3)

EMERSON BIXBY
DISTURBED   Odyssey-Cinecom International, 1990,
    w/Charles Winkler
BIKINI ISLAND   Curb-Esquire Films, 1991

CAROL BLACK*
Business: The Black/Marlens Company, 17351 Sunset Blvd. -
    Suite 504, Pacific Palisades, CA 90272, 310/573-1717

SOUL MAN   New World, 1986

Screenplays:
THE JUMPING OFF POINT w/Neal Marlens

DAVID BLACK*
Agent: ICM - Beverly Hills, 310/550-4000

LEGACY OF LIES (CTF)   RAH Productions/MCA Television
    Entertainment, 1992

Screenplays:
FERTIG

DON BLACK
SUNSET BLVD. (P)   w/Christopher Hampton
GULLIVER'S TRAVELS   Sunn Classic, 1981

JOHN D.F. BLACK*
Contact: Mark Boykin - 818/986-7561

GUNFIGHT IN ABILENE   Universal, 1967
THE RIDE TO HANGMAN'S TREE   Universal, 1967

NOBODY'S PERFECT   Univeral, 1968
SHAFT   MGM, 1971, w/Ernest Tidyman
THE CAREY TREATMENT   MGM, 1972
TROUBLE MAN   20th Century-Fox, 1982

NOEL BLACK*
Agent: The Chasin Agency - Beverly Hills, 310/278-7505

MISCHIEF   20th Century Fox, 1985

SHANE BLACK*
Agent: ICM - Beverly Hills, 310/550-4000

LETHAL WEAPON   Warner Bros., 1987
THE MONSTER SQUAD   Tri-Star, 1987, w/Fred Dekker
LETHAL WEAPON 2   Warner Bros., 1989, Story w/Warren Murphy
THE LAST BOY SCOUT   Warner Bros., 1991
LAST ACTION HERO   Columbia, 1992, w/David Arnott

Screenplays:
THE LONG KISS GOODNIGHT
SHADOW COMPANY

SUSAN BLACK*
Agent: Becsey/Wisdom/Kalajian Agency - Los Angeles, 310/550-0535

STATE OF EMERGENCY (CTF)   Chestnut Hill, 1994,
    w/Lance Gentile

Screenplays:
BLACKBIRD MOON
ASPHYXIATION
CURRENT AFFAIRS
BROKEN TIME w/David Schwimmer

TERRY BLACK*
Contact: Coast To Coast - 818/762-6278

DEAD HEAT   New World, 1988

Screenplays:
FERRET

RICHARD C. BLACKBURN*
Agent: Paul Kohner, Inc. - Beverly Hills, 310/550-1060

EATING RAOUL   20th Century-Fox International Classics, 1982,
    w/Paul Bartel

Screenplays:
BLAND AMBITION w/Paul Bartel
FRANKENCAR w/Paul Bartel

WILLIAM BLACKBURN
CHALLENGE THE WIND   Sell Entertainment, 1990,
    w/Ken Howard & Marla Young, directed

KENNETH G. BLACKWELL*
Agent: Preferred Artists - Encino, 818/990-0305

DEADLY FORCE   Embassy, 1983, as "Ken Barnett,"
    w/Robert Vincent O'Neil & Barry Schneider
TRIUMPHS OF A MAN CALLED HORSE   Jensen Farley Pictures,
    1984, w/Carlos Aured & Jack DeWitt
DARK TOWER   Spectrafilm, 1989, w/Robert J. Avrech &
    Ken Weiderhorn

Screenplays:
RUN THROUGH THE JUNGLE
WINGS
BULLET AND THE ROSE
STONE BIRD
DOUBLE VISION
YEAR OF THE CANNIBAL
ANNABELLE, THE CHRISTMAS COW (AF)

CAROLYN MARKS BLACKWOOD
Agent: ICM - New York, 212/556-5600

Screenplays:
BARBETTE
THE KID GOES TO HOLLYWOOD

RICKY BLACKWOOD*
Agent: Richland/Wunsch/Hohman Agency - Los Angeles,
   310/278-1955

Screenplays:
PYRAMIDER w/Sam Denno
DEADLOCK
PLAISIR D'AMOUR
ST. JUDE

RUBEN BLADES
Agent: United Talent Agency - Beverly Hills, 310/273-6700

CROSSOVER DREAMS   Miramax, 1985, w/Manuel Arce &
   Leon Ichaso

DENNIS BLAIR*
Contact: WGA - New York, 212/245-6180

EASY MONEY   Orion, 1983, w/Rodney Dangerfield,
   Michael Endler & P.J. O'Rourke

JEANNE BLAKE*
Agent: United Talent Agency - Beverly Hills, 310/273-6700

Screenplays:
STEAL BIG, STEAL LITTLE w/Lee Blessing & Andrew Davis (Savoy)

MICHAEL BLAKE*
Agent: The Daniel Ostroff Agency - Los Angeles, 310/278-2020

STACY'S KNIGHTS   Crown International, 1983
DANCES WITH WOLVES ★★   Orion, 1990

TONY BLAKE*
Agent: Major Clients Agency - Los Angeles, 310/284-6400

Screenplays:
DEAD MATCH w/Paul Jackson

MICHAEL BLAKEMORE
Agent: The Lantz Office - New York, 212/586-0200

COUNTRY LIFE   Miramax, 1994, directed

BEVERLY BLAKENSHIP
SHAME   Skouras Pictures, 1988, w/Michael Brindley

KEN BLANCATO*
Contact: Weissmann, Wolff, Bergman, Coleman & Silverman -
   Beverly Hills, 310/858-7888

STEWARDESS SCHOOL   Columbia, 1987, directed

CARTER BLANCHARD
Agent: Candace Lake - Beverly Hills, 310/289-0600

Screenplays:
BLIND SPOT
HAZARDOUS WASTE

JOEL BLASBERG*
Agent: William Morris Agency - Beverly Hills, 310/274-7451

Screenplays:
THE COWARD COP
PAROLE OFFICER
AFTERBURNER w/Sergio Altieri

RICHARD BLASUCCI*
Contact: WGA - Los Angeles, 310/550-1000

Screenplays:
SIDEKICK w/Paul Flaherty

JERRY BLATT
DIVINE MADNESS   Warner Bros., 1980, w/Bette Midler &
   Bruce Vilanch

WILLIAM PETER BLATTY*
Contact: WGA - Los Angeles, 310/550-1000

THE MAN FROM THE DINERS CLUB   Columbia, 1963
A SHOT IN THE DARK   United Artists, 1964, w/Blake Edwards
JOHN GOLDFARB, PLEASE COME HOME   20th Century-Fox, 1965
PROMISE HER ANYTHING   Paramount, 1966
WHAT DID YOU DO IN THE WAR, DADDY?   United Artists, 1966,
   w/Blake Edwards
GUNN   Warner Bros., 1967, w/Blake Edwards
THE GREAT BANK ROBBERY   Warner Bros., 1969
DARLING LILI   Paramount, 1970, w/Blake Edwards
THE EXORCIST ★★   Warner Bros., 1973
THE NINTH CONFIGURATION   Warner Bros., 1979,
   rereleased under title TWINKLE, TWINKLE, KILLER KANE
   by United Film Distribution in 1980, directed
THE EXORCIST III   20th Century Fox, 1990, directed

Screenplays:
ELSEWHERE

BARRY BLAUSTEIN*
Agent: CAA - Beverly Hills, 310/288-4545

POLICE ACADEMY 2: THEIR FIRST ASSIGNMENT   Warner Bros.,
   1983, w/David Sheffield
COMING TO AMERICA   Paramount, 1988, w/David Sheffield
BOOMERANG   Paramount, 1992, w/David Sheffield

Screenplays:
THE NUTTY PROFESSOR w/David Sheffield (remake)
KNOCKOUT! w/David Sheffield
THE GELFAN w/David Sheffield
OPTIMUM w/David Sheffield
BUTTERSCOTCH KID w/David Sheffield
LAST HOLIDAY w/David Sheffield
BROTHERS KEEPERS w/David Sheffield
SAVIN A FACE

COREY BLECHMAN*
Agent: ICM - Beverly Hills, 310/550-4000

THE WHITE LIONS   Alan Landsberg Productions, 1979
DOMINICK & EUGENE   Orion, 1988, w/Alvin Sargent
MAX AND HELEN (CTF)   Citadel Entertainment, 1990
FREE WILLY   Warner Bros., 1993, w/Keith Walker
FREE WILLY 2   Warner Bros., 1995, w/Karen Janszen &
   John Mattson

ROBERT BLEES*
Business Manager: Joseph Miller, Bjerre & Miller - Los Angeles,
   310/556-2472

PAID IN FULL   Paramount, 1949, w/Charles Schnee
ALL I DESIRE   Universal-International, 1953, w/James Gunn
THE GLASS WEB   Universal-International, 1953, w/Leonard Lee
PLAYGIRL   Universal-International, 1954
CATTLE QUEEN OF MONTANA   RKO, 1954, w/Howard Estabrook
MAGNIFICENT OBSESSION   Universal, 1954
ONE DESIRE   Universal-International, 1955, w/Lawrence Roman
SLIGHTLY SCARLET   RKO, 1956
AUTUMN LEAVES   Columbia, 1956, w/Jack Levne & Lewis Meltzer
THE BLACK SCORPION   Warner Bros., 1957, w/David Duncan
SCREAMING MIMI   Columbia, 1958
FROM THE EARTH TO THE MOON   Waverly, 1958,
   w/James Leicester

FROGS   American International, 1972, w/Robert Hutchinson
WHO SLEW AUNTIE ROO?   American International, 1972,
    w/Jimmy Sangster
DR. PHIBES RISES AGAIN   American International, 1972,
    w/Robert Fuest
SAVAGE HARVEST   20th Century-Fox, 1981, w/Robert Collins

WILLIAM BLEICH*
Agent: CAA - Beverly Hills, 310/288-4545

THE HEARSE   Crown International, 1980

BERT BLESSING
(See Frank Gilroy)

LEE BLESSING*
Agent: United Talent Agency - Beverly Hills, 310/273-6700

COBB (P)
DOWN THE ROAD (P)
PATIENT A (P)
A WALK IN THE WOODS (P)
INDEPENDENCE (P)
RICHES (P)
ELEEMOSYNARY (P)
FORTINBRAS (P)
TWO ROOMS (P)
THE AUTHENTIC LIFE OF BILLY THE KID (P)
LAKE STREET EXTENSION (P)
OLD TIMERS GAME (P)
COOPERSTOWN (CTF)   Michael Brandman Productions/Amblin
    Entertainment, 1993

Screenplays:
*STEAL BIG, STEAL LITTLE w/Andrew Davis & Jeanne Blake
    (Savoy)*

TONE BLEVINS
BOOK OF DAYS   The Stutz Company, 1991, w/Meredith Monk

BERTRAND BLIER
Contact: French Film Office, 745 Fifth Avenue, New York,
    NY 10151, 212/832-8860

GOING PLACES   *LES VALSEUSES*   Cinema 5,
    1974, directed
FEMMES FATALES   *CALMOS*   New Line Cinema,
    1976, directed
GET OUT YOUR HANDKERCHIEFS   New Line Cinema,
    1978, directed
BUFFET FROID   Parafrance, 1979, directed
BEAU PERE   New Line Cinema, 1981, directed
MY BEST FRIEND'S GIRL   European International, 1983,
    w/Gerard Brach, directed
SEPARATE ROOMS   *NOTRE HISTOIRE*   Spectrafilm,
    1984, directed
MENAGE   *TENUE DE SOIREE*   Cinecom, 1986, directed
TOO BEAUTIFUL FOR YOU   *TROP BELLE POUR TOI*
    Orion Classics, 1990, directed
THANKS FOR LIFE   *MERCI LA VIE*   AMLF, 1991, directed

WILLIAM BLINN*
Contact: WGA - Los Angeles, 310/550-1000

PURPLE RAIN   Warner Bros., 1984, w/Albert Magnoli

JOEL BLOCK
NOBODY'S PERFECT   Moviestore Entertainment, 1990,
    w/Annie Korzen

LAWRENCE J. BLOCK*
Contact: WGA - Los Angeles, 310/550-1000

THE FUNHOUSE   Universal, 1981
CAPTAIN AMERICA   21st Century Releasing Corp., 1992, Story

Screenplays:
URIAH
SPOTTERS
FANTASTIC FOUR

MICHAEL BLODGETT*
Agent: The Agency - Los Angeles, 310/551-3000

RENT-A-COP   Kings Road, 1988, w/Dennis Shryack
HERO AND THE TERROR   Cannon, 1988, w/Dennis Shryack
TURNER & HOOCH   Buena Vista, 1989, w/Dennis Shryack,
    Daniel Petrie Jr., Jim Cash & Jack Epps
RUN   Buena Vista, 1991, w/Dennis Shryack

Screenplays:
TRIADS w/Ron Casden
THE WHITE RAVEN
THE HOUSE OF CHANG
CAPTAIN'S BLOOD
LUCIFER'S REEF
COBRA II
MAN OF HONOR

ERIC L. BLOOM*
Contact: WGA - Los Angeles, 310/550-1000

EYES OF A STRANGER   Warner Bros., 1981, w/Mark Jackson

GEORGE ARTHUR BLOOM*
Contact: 310/277-7782

THE LAST FLIGHT OF NOAH'S ARK   Buena Vista, 1980,
    w/Steve Carabatsos & Sandy Glass
MY LITTLE PONY (AF)   DEG, 1986
A KNIFE FOR THE LADIES   Spangler-Jolly Productions, 1972
MOONLIGHT FLIGHT (CTF)   Astral/Lorimar, 1989
SUNSET COURT (CTF)   Astral/Lorimar, 1989
MAN WHO GUARDS THE GREENHOUSE (CTF)
    Astral/Lorimar, 1989
EMERALD TEAR (CTF)   Astral/Lorimar, 1989

HAROLD JACK BLOOM*
Contact: WGA - Los Angeles, 310/550-1000

ARENA   MGM, 1953
LAND OF THE PHARAOHS   Warner Bros., 1955,
    w/William Faulkner & Harry Kurnitz
BEHIND THE HIGH WALL   Universal-International, 1956
A GUNFIGHT   Harvest, 1970

JEFFREY BLOOM*
Agent: The Coppage Company - North Hollywood, 818/980-1106

SNOW JOB   Warner Bros., 1972, w/Ken Kolb
DOGPOUND SHUFFLE   Paramount, 1974, directed
11 HARROWHOUSE   20th Century-Fox, 1974
SWASHBUCKLER   Universal, 1976
THE STICK UP   Trident-Barber, 1978, directed
BLOOD BEACH   Jerry Gross Organization, 1981, directed
NIGHTMARES   Universal, 1983, w/Christopher Crowe
FLOWERS IN THE ATTIC   New World, 1987, directed

MAX BLOOM*
Contact: WGA - Los Angeles, 310/550-1000

FISTFIGHTER   Taurus Entertainment, 1989

STEVEN L. BLOOM*
Agent: CAA - Beverly Hills, 310/288-4545

THE SURE THING   Embassy, 1985, w/Jonathan Roberts
LIKE FATHER LIKE SON   Tri-Star, 1987, w/Lorne Cameron
TALL TALE   Buena Vista, 1994, w/Robert Rodat

Screenplays:
DREAM DATE w/Jonathan Roberts
DEAD SLEEP (Story w/Scott Fields & John Stockwell)
AFTER ALL
ROGUES

PHILIPPE BLOT
THE ARROGANT   Cannon, 1989, directed

NOAH BLOUGH
CROSS FIRE   Silvertree Pictures, 1989, w/Anthony Maharaj

CHRISTOPHER BLUE
HYPER SAPIEN   Tri-Star, 1986, w/Richard Adcock & Marnie Paige

DEBORAH BLUM*
Contact: Lichter, Grossman & Nichols - Los Angeles, 310/205-6999

VIBES   Columbia, 1988, Story w/Lowell Ganz & Babaloo Mandel

EDWIN BLUM*
Contact: WGA - Los Angeles, 310/550-1000

THE CANTERVILLE GHOST   MGM, 1943
THE BOOGIE MAN WILL GET YOU   Columbia, 1944
DOWN TO EARTH   Columbia, 1947, w/Don Hartman
SOUTH SEA WOMAN   *PEARL OF THE SOUTH PACIFIC*
   United Artists, 1953
STALAG 17   Paramount, 1953, w/Billy Wilder
THE BAMBOO PRISON   Columbia, 1955, w/Jack deWitt
GUNG HO   Paramount, 1986, Story w/Lowell Ganz &
   Babaloo Mandel

HOWARD BLUM*
Agent: ICM - Beverly Hills, 310/550-4000

Screenplays:
CROSSFIRE
THE OCTOPUS

LEN BLUM*
Agent: CAA - Beverly Hills, 310/288-4545

MEATBALLS   Paramount, 1979, w/Janis Allen, Dan Goldberg &
   Harold Ramis
STRIPES   Columbia, 1981, w/Dan Goldberg & Harold Ramis
HEAVY METAL (AF)   Columbia, 1981, w/Dan Goldberg
SPACEHUNTER: ADVENTURES IN THE FORBIDDEN ZONE
   Columbia, 1983, w/Dan Goldberg, Edith Rey & David Preston
FEDS   Warner Bros., 1988, w/Dan Goldberg
BEETHOVEN'S 2ND   Universal, 1993

Screenplays:
RABBIT BOY w/Dan Goldberg
WIDOWS w/Dan Goldberg

JOHN BLUMENTHAL*
Agent: United Talent Agency - Beverly Hills, 310/273-6700

SHORT TIME   20th Century Fox, 1990, w/Michael Berry

Screenplays:
BREAKFAST WITH SPAULDING w/Michael Berry
TWILIGHT w/Michael Berry
BLUE STREAK w/Michael Berry
CHUMPS w/Michael Berry

DON BLUTH
Contact: Fox Animation Studios, 2747 E. Camelback Rd., Phoenix,
   AZ 86016, fax 602/224-0160

THE SECRET OF NIMH (AF)   MGM/UA, 1982, Story Adaptation
   w/Will Finn, John Pomeroy & Gary Goldman, directed
ALL DOGS GO TO HEAVEN (AF)   MGM/UA, 1989, Story w/others
HANS CHRISTIAN ANDERSON'S THUMBELINA (AF)   Warner Bros,
   1994, co-directed

MARK BLUTMAN
Agent: United Talent Agency - Beverly Hills, 310/273-6700

Screenplays:
FRIEND OF THE FAMILY (Story w/Mike Binder & Howard Busgang)

JEFFREY BOAM*
Agent: CAA - Beverly Hills, 310/288-4545

STRAIGHT TIME   Warner Bros., 1978, w/Edward Bunker &
   Alvin Sargent
THE DEAD ZONE   Paramount, 1983
INNERSPACE   Warner Bros., 1987, w/Chip Proser
THE LOST BOYS   Warner Bros., 1987, w/Janice Fischer &
   James Jeremias
FUNNY FARM   Warner Bros., 1988
INDIANA JONES AND THE LAST CRUSADE   Paramount, 1989
LETHAL WEAPON 2   Warner Bros., 1989
LETHAL WEAPON 3   Warner Bros., 1992 (Shared)

SAM BOBRICK*
Agent: Becsey/Wisdom/Kalajian Agency - Los Angeles, 310/550-0535

MURDER AT THE HOWARD JOHNSON'S (P) w/Ron Clark
NORMAN, IS THAT YOU?   MGM/United Artists, 1976,
   w/Ron Clark & George Schlatter, from his play w/Ron Clark
JIMMY THE KID   New World, 1982

STEVEN BOCHCO*
Contact: Attorney Frank Rohner - Los Angeles, 310/477-5001
Business: Bochco Productions, 10201 W. Pico Blvd., Los Angeles,
   CA 90035, 310/203-2400

SILENT RUNNING   Universal, 1971, w/Michael Cimino &
   Deric Washburn

ROBERT BOCK
Agent: Berzon Agency - Glendale, 818/548-1560

Screenplays:
THE ORACLE

SERGEI BODROV
SOMEBODY TO LOVE   Lumiere Pictures, 1994,
   w/Alexandre Rockwell

BILL BOESKY
Agent: Susan Smith & Associates - Beverly Hills, 213/852-4777

FALLEN ANGEL (P)   also screenplay

Screenplays:
IN SEARCH OF THE FAMOUS ORIGINAL

YUREK BOGAYEVICZ
Agent: The Gersh Agency - Beverly Hills, 310/274-6611

ANNA   Vestron, 1987, w/Agnieszka Holland, directed

JOSEF BOGDANOVICH
BOXOFFICE   Bee Movies, 1982

PETER BOGDANOVICH
Agent: CAA - Beverly Hills, 310/288-4545

THE WILD ANGELS   American International, 1966
TARGETS   Paramount, 1968, directed
THE LAST PICTURE SHOW ★   Columbia, 1971,
   w/Larry McMurtry, directed
AT LONG LAST LOVE   20th Century-Fox, 1975, directed
NICKELODEON   Columbia, 1976, w/W.D. Richter, directed
SAINT JACK   New World, 1979, w/Howard Sackler &
   Paul Theroux, directed
THEY ALL LAUGHED   United Artists Classics, 1982, directed
TEXASVILLE   Columbia, 1990, directed

Screenplays:
PROTECT AND DEFEND

MICHAEL BOGERT
DEAD END CITY   Action International, 1989, w/Peter Yuval

WARREN BOGLE
(See Andrew Bergman)

STEVEN BOGNAR
EMMA AND ELVIS   Northern Arts Entertainment, 1992,
   w/Martin M. Goldstein & Julia Reichert

NICHOLAS BOGNER*
Agent: Innovative Artists - Los Angeles, 310/553-5200

Screenplays:
NO STRINGS ATTACHED w/Michael Holden
MATING SEASON
QUEEN BEE
ZERO VISIBILITY
THE LITTLE DEATH

NORMAN BOGNER*
Agent: The Artists Agency - Los Angeles, 310/277-7779

Screenplays:
SNOWMAN
THE MADONNA COMPLEX

WILLY BOGNER
FIRE AND ICE   20th Century-Fox, 1983, directed

ERIC BOGOSIAN*
Agent: William Morris Agency - New York, 212/586-5100

DRINKING IN AMERICA (P)
FUN HOUSE (P)
SUBURBIA (P)   also screenplay
POUNDING NAILS IN THE FLOOR WITH MY FOREHEAD (P)
TALK RADIO   Universal, 1988, w/Oliver Stone,
   from his play (w/Tad Savinar)
SEX, DRUGS, ROCK & ROLL   Avenue Pictures, 1991, from his play

Screenplays:
BLUE SMOKE
STAND UP
MITTY

LESLIE BOHEM*
Agent: Peter Turner Agency - Santa Monica, 310/315-4772

A NIGHTMARE ON ELM STREET 5: THE DREAM CHILD
   New Line Cinema, 1989
HOUSE III: THE HORROR SHOW   MGM/UA, 1989, w/Allyn Warner
NOWHERE TO RUN   Columbia, 1993, w/Joe Eszterhas &
   Randy Feldman
TWENTY BUCKS   Triton Pictures, 1993, w/Endre Bohem

Screenplays:
BLACK AND WHITE (Warner Bros.)
DAYLIGHT

MIGHTY, MIGHTY
DAYDREAMS w/M. Robinson
ON THE LINE
BRICK DUST
VIDEO KILLED THE RADIO STAR
GUITAR
KID
CRYSTAL KNIGHTS
LIVE WIRE

CHARLES F. BOHL*
Agent: Broder-Kurland-Webb-Uffner - Beverly Hills, 310/281-3400

HE'S MY GIRL   Scotti Bros., 1987, w/Taylor Ames

Screenplays:
MY ILLEGAL ALIEN
TURN ON THE RADIO
PANTS

DON BOHLINGER*
Contact: WGA - Los Angeles, 310/550-1000

THE KILLING TIME   New World, 1987, w/Bruce Franklin Singer &
   James Nathan

Screenplays:
SMOKESCREEN w/James Nathan

JEROME BOIVIN
Contact: French Film Office, 745 Fifth Avenue, New York, NY 10151,
   212/832-8860

BAXTER   Backstreet Films, 1990, w/Jacques Audiard, directed
BARTO   Myriad Pictures, 1993, w/Jacques Audiard, directed

JOSEPH BOLOGNA*
Business Manager: Zipperstein & Kantor, 818/986-4640

LOVERS AND OTHER STRANGERS ★   Cinerama Releasing
   Corporation, 1970, w/Renee Taylor & David Z. Goodman
MADE FOR EACH OTHER   20th Century-Fox, 1971,
   w/Renee Taylor
MIXED COMPANY   United Artists, 1974, w/Renee Taylor
IT HAD TO BE YOU   Limelite Studios, 1989, w/Renee Taylor,
   from their play, directed
OH NO, NOT HER!   Cinema 7 Productions, 1994,
   w/Renee Taylor, directed

CRAIG BOLOTIN*
Agent: CAA - Beverly Hills, 310/288-4545

NO SMALL AFFAIR   Columbia, 1984, w/Michael Leeson,
   as "Charles Bolt"
BLACK RAIN   Paramount, 1989, w/Warren Lewis
SAPPHIRE MAN (Short)   1991, directed
STRAIGHT TALK   Buena Vista, 1992, w/Patricia Resnick
THAT NIGHT   Warner Bros., 1993

Screenplays:
COME WEST WITH ME
AMERICAN EXPRESS w/Richard Kletter
HEARTS
PRIVATE PICTURES

CHARLES BOLT
(See Craig BOLOTIN)

ROBERT BOLT
Agent: The Casarotto Company - London, 071/287-4450

LAWRENCE OF ARABIA ★   Columbia, 1962
DOCTOR ZHIVAGO ★★   MGM, 1965
A MAN FOR ALL SEASONS ★★   Columbia, 1966, from his play
RYAN'S DAUGHTER   MGM, 1970
LADY CAROLINE LAMB   United Artists, 1973, directed

THE BOUNTY   Orion, 1984
THE MISSION   Warner Bros., 1986
WITHOUT WARNING: THE JAMES BRADY STORY (CTF)
   Enigma Television Productions, 1991

Screenplays:
NOSTROMO w/Christopher Hampton
BUDDHA
PLUMED SERPENT
PITCAIRN ISLAND
THE LONG ARM
INTERNATIONAL BRIGADES

JAY R. BONANSINGA*
Agent: PMA Literary & Film Management - New York, 212/929-1222

Screenplays:
THE BLACK MARIAH

JAMES BOND III
Agent: Broder-Kurland-Webb-Uffner - Beverly Hills, 310/281-3400

DEF BY TEMPTATION   Troma, 1990, directed

JULIAN BOND*
Agent: Peters, Fraser & Dunlop - London, 071/376-7676

TRIAL BY COMBAT   *CHOICE OF WEAPONS*   Warner Bros.,
   1976, w/Steven Rossen & Mitchell Smith
THE SHOOTING PARTY   European Classics, 1984
THE WHISTLE BLOWER   Hemdale, 1987
A SEASON OF GIANTS (CTF)   TNT/RAI 1, 1991,
   w/Vincenzo Labella
LIE DOWN WITH LIONS (CMS)   Hannibal Films, 1994,
   w/Guy Andrews

Screenplays:
BURMESE DAYS w/Hugh Stoddart

TIMOTHY BOND
HAPPY BIRTHDAY TO ME   Columbia, 1981, w/John Saxton &
   Peter Jobin

MIKE BONIFER*
Contact: WGA - Los Angeles, 310/550-1000

THE LIPSTICK CAMERA   Triboro Entertainment, 1994, directed

JAMES P. BONNER
HOUSE OF CARDS   Universal, 1968
THE CAREY TREATMENT   MGM, 1972

BOB BONNEY
THE NIGHT THE LIGHTS WENT OUT IN GEORGIA
   Avco Embassy, 1981

JAMES P. BONNY*
Agent: Innovative Artists - Los Angeles, 310/553-5200

Screenplays:
VEXERS w/Richard Finney
EVOLUTION w/Richard Finney
MEN IN BLACK w/Richard Finney
PUPPET MASTERS w/Richard Finney

J.R. BOOKWALTER
Business: The Suburban Tempe Co., P.O. Box 6573, Akron,
   OH 44312, 216/628-1950

THE DEAD NEXT DOOR   Electro Video, 1989, directed
ROBOT NINJA   Cinema Home Video, 1989, directed
MAXIMUM IMPACT   Cinema Home Video, 1992,
   w/Thomas Brown, directed
HUMANOIDS FROM ATLANTIS   Cinema Home Video, 1992,
   w/Lloyd Taylor, directed

JOHN BOORMAN
Agent: ICM - Beverly Hills, 310/550-4000

LEO THE LAST   United Artists, 1970, w/William Stair, directed
ZARDOZ   20th Century-Fox, 1974, directed
EXCALIBUR   Orion/Warner Bros., 1981,
   w/Rospo Pallenberg, directed
HOPE AND GLORY ★   Columbia, 1987, directed
WHERE THE HEART IS   Buena Vista, 1990,
   w/Telsche Boorman, directed
I DREAMT I WOKE UP (FD)   Merlin Films, 1991, directed

Screenplays:
BROKEN DREAMS w/Neil Jordan (directing)

TELSCHE BOORMAN
WHERE THE HEART IS   Buena Vista, 1990, w/John Boorman

JON BOORSTIN*
Agent: Camden-ITG - Los Angeles, 310/289-2700

DREAM LOVER   MGM/UA, 1986

PAUL BOORSTIN*
Contact: WGA - Los Angeles, 310/550-1000

MOVING VIOLATIONS   20th Century Fox , 1985,
   Story w/Sharon Boorstin
FIRE WITH FIRE   *CAPTIVE HEARTS*   Paramount, 1986,
   w/Sharon Boorstin, Bill Phillips & Warren Skaaren

Screenplays:
PREGGERS w/Sharon Boorstin
NAKED REVERSE w/Sharon Boorstin
SAVAGE w/Sharon Boorstin
FAERIE TALE w/Sharon Boorstin
HOT MINUTE w/Sharon Boorstin

SHARON BOORSTIN*
Contact: WGA - Los Angeles, 310/550-1000

MOVING VIOLATIONS   20th Century Fox, 1985,
   Story w/Paul Boorstin
FIRE WITH FIRE   *CAPTIVE HEARTS*   Paramount, 1986,
   w/Paul Boorstin, Bill Phillips & Warren Skaaren

Screenplays:
PREGGERS w/Paul Boorstin
NAKED REVERSE w/Paul Boorstin
SAVAGE w/Paul Boorstin
FAERIE TALE w/Paul Boorstin
HOT MINUTE w/Paul Boorstin

JAMES BOOTH*
Agent: Stone Manners Agency - Los Angeles, 213/654-7575

SUNBURN   Paramount, 1979, w/John Daly & Stephen Oliver
PRAY FOR DEATH   American Distribution Group, 1985
AVENGING FORCE   Cannon, 1986
AMERICAN NINJA 2   Cannon, 1987, w/Gary Conway

JASON BOOTH
OUT ON BAIL   Trans World Entertainment, 1989, w/Tom Badal &
   Michael D. Sonye

JOSE LUIS BORAU
Business: El Iman S.A., Alberto Alcocer 42, Madrid 16, Spain,
   250-5534

ON THE LINE   Miramax, 1987, w/Barbara P. Solomon, directed

LIZZIE BORDEN
(Linda Elizabeth Borden)
BORN IN FLAMES   First Run Features, 1986, directed
WORKING GIRLS   Miramax, 1986, w/Sandra Kay, directed

ALVIN BORETZ*
Agent: Preferred Artists - Encino, 818/990-0305

MADE IN AMERICA (P)
I REMEMBER YOU (P)
BRASS TARGET   MGM/UA, 1978

Screenplays:
BAKER AND BERNSTEIN

DOUGLAS STEFEN BORGHI*
Agent: The Brandt Company - Sherman Oaks, 818/783-7747

WHO KILLED BABY JESUS   Northern Arts Entertainment,
   1993, directed

Screenplays:
TREASURE

ROBERT BORIS*
Agent: Innovative Artists - Los Angeles, 310/553-5200

ELECTRA GLIDE IN BLUE   United Artists, 1973
SOME KIND OF HERO   Paramount, 1982, w/James Kirkwood
DOCTOR DETROIT   Universal, 1983, w/Bruce Jay Friedman &
   Carl Gottlieb
OXFORD BLUES   MGM/UA, 1984, directed
STEELE JUSTICE   Atlantic Releasing Corporation, 1987, directed
EXTREME JUSTICE (CTF)   Trimark, 1993, w/Frank Sacks
FRANK AND JESSE   Trimark, 1995, directed

Screenplays:
ANASTASIA
THE ROOKIE
HOT MAN (CTF)
DUE PROCESS
AIR FORCE ONE
DECLARED DEAD

ARTHUR BORMAN
Agent: ICM - Beverly Hills, 310/550-4000

...AND GOD SPOKE   LIVE Entertainment, 1994,
   Story w/Mark Borman, directed

MARK BORMAN
...AND GOD SPOKE   LIVE Entertainment, 1994,
   Story w/Arthur Borman

ANDY BOROWITZ*
Agent: CAA - Beverly Hills, 310/288-4545

Screenplays:
CROSS THE LINE w/Susan Borowitz
YOUNG BUCKS
SCOUTMASTER
AMERICAN WIFE
NEVER SAY DIE
HOW TO MARRY A MILLIONAIRE
CLEVELAND ROCKS

SUSAN BOROWITZ*
Agent: CAA - Beverly Hills, 310/288-4545

Screenplays:
CROSS THE LINE w/Andy Borowitz

JIM BORRELLI*
Contact: WGA - Los Angeles, 310/550-1000

CAT CHASER   Vestron, 1990, w/Elmore Leonard & Alan Sharp

CLAY BORRIS
Agent: Great North Artists Management - Toronto, 416/925-2051

QUIET COOL   New Line Cinema, 1986,
   w/Susan Vercellino, directed

PHILLIP BORSOS
Agent: United Talent Agency - Beverly Hills, 310/273-6700

ONE MAGIC CHRISTMAS   Buena Vista, 1985,
   Story w/Barry Healey & Thomas Meehan, directed
FAR FROM HOME: THE ADVENTURES OF YELLOW DOG
   20th Century Fox, 1995, directed

TERRY BORST*
Manager: Jon Brown, The Brown Group - Burbank, 818/955-7040

PRIVATE WAR   Smart Egg Pictures, 1989, w/Frank DePalma &
   Bjorn Carlstrom
WING COMMANDER III: THE HEART OF THE TIGER
   Electronic Arts, 1994, w/Frank DePalma

Screenplays:
THE WAR TRAIN w/Frank DePalma
BOTH ENDS BURNING w/Frank DePalma
THE RULES OF GRAVITY w/Frank DePalma
BORDERLINE TANGO w/Frank DePalma
A PLACE ON EARTH w/Frank DePalma

CHRIS BORTHWICK
ANNIE'S COMING OUT   Film Australia, 1981, w/John Paterson
A TEST OF LOVE   Universal, 1985, w/John Paterson

MICHAEL BORTMAN*
Agent: United Talent Agency - Beverly Hills, 310/273-6700

THE GOOD MOTHER   Buena Vista, 1988
CROOKED HEARTS   MGM-Pathe, 1991, directed

Screenplays:
IMAGINING ARGENTINA
CHEEK TO CHEEK

AIDA BORTNIK*
Agent: William Morris Agency - Beverly Hills, 310/274-7451

THE OFFICIAL STORY ★   Historias Cinematograficas, 1985,
   w/Luis Puenzo
OLD GRINGO   Columbia, 1989, w/Luis Puenzo

Screenplays:
FADEOUT

ROSELYNE BOSCH
1492: CONQUEST OF PARADISE   Paramount, 1992

JOHN BOSKOVICH
Agent: ICM - Beverly Hills, 310/550-4000

GIVING TIL IT HURTS (P) w/Sandra Bernhard
WITHOUT YOU I'M NOTHING   MCEG, 1990,
   w/Sandra Bernhard, directed

JAMES BOSLEY
FUN   Neo Modern Entertainment, 1994, from his play

NANCY TRITES BOTKIN
RACE TO FREEDOM: THE UNDERGROUND RAILROAD (CTF)
   The Family Channel/BET, 1994, w/Diana Braithwaite &
   Peter Mohan

ROY BOULTING

Agent: John Redway and Associates Ltd., 5 Denmark St., London
   WC2H 8LP, England, 71/836-2001

HIGH TREASON   Rank, 1951, w/Frank Harvey, directed
JOSEPHINE AND MEN   Charter, 1955, w/Nigel Balchin &
   Frank Harvey, directed
HAPPY IS THE BRIDE   British Lion, 1957,
   w/Jeffrey Dell, directed
BROTHERS IN LAW   British Lion, 1957, w/Jeffrey Dell &
   Frank Harvey, directed
MAN IN A COCKED HAT   *CARLTON-BROWNE OF THE F.O.*
   Show Corporation, 1960, w/Jeffrey Dell, co-directed
A FRENCH MISTRESS   British Lion, 1960,
   w/Jeffrey Dell, co-directed
TWISTED NERVE   National General, 1969,
   w/Leo Marks, directed
UNDERCOVERS HERO   *SOFT BEDS AND HARD BATTLES*
   United Artists, 1975, w/Leo Marks, directed

MICHAEL BOURCHIER

NAPOLEON   Samuel Goldwyn Company, 1995,
   w/Mario Andreacchio

JOHN BOWEN

Agent: The Casarotto Company - London, 071/287-4450

TREVOR (P)

Screenplays:
BRIEF ENCOUNTER

DOUGLAS BOWIE

THE BOY IN BLUE   20th Century Fox, 1986

ANTHONY J. BOWMAN

Agent: The Artists Group - Los Angeles, 310/552-1100

RELATIVES   Archer Films, 1985, directed
CAPPUCCINO   Archer Films, 1989, directed

Screenplays:
ROMANTIC HERO

KENNETH BOWSER

Agent: Lucy Kroll Agency - New York, 212/877-0627

IN A SHALLOW GRAVE   Skouras Pictures, 1988, directed

DON BOYD

Agent: ICM - London, 071/636-6565

EAST OF ELEPHANT ROCK   Boyd's Company,
   1976, directed
TWENTY-ONE   Triton Pictures, 1991, w/Zoe Heller, directed
KLEPTOMANIA   Curb International, 1993, directed

WILLIAM BOYD*

Agent: Sanford-Gross & Associates - Los Angeles, 310/208-2100

STARS AND BARS   Columbia, 1988
TUNE IN TOMORROW...   Cinecom, 1990
MISTER JOHNSON   Avenue Pictures, 1991
CHAPLIN   TriStar, 1992, w/Bryan Forbes & William Goldman
A GOOD MAN IN AFRICA   Gramercy, 1994

RICHARD BOYLE*

Contact: WGA - Los Angeles, 310/550-1000

SALVADOR ★   Hemdale, 1986, w/Oliver Stone   ✓

BILL BOZZONE*

Agent: The Gersh Agency - New York, 212/997-1818

FULL MOON IN BLUE WATER   Trans World Entertainment, 1988
THE LAST ELEPHANT (CTF)   Ritti Entertainment Inc./Quintex
   Entertainment Inc., 1990, w/Richard Guttman

Screenplays:
ROSE COTTAGES

GÉRARD BRACH

DO YOU LIKE WOMEN?   Francoriz, 1964, w/RomanPolanski
REPULSION   Royal Films International, 1965, w/Roman Polanski
CUL-DE-SAC   Sigma III, 1966, w/Roman Polanski
SECRET WORLD   1966, w/J. Glagg
THE FEARLESS VAMPIRE KILLERS, OR PARDON ME BUT YOUR
   TEETH ARE IN MY NECK   *DANCE OF THE VAMPIRES*
   MGM, 1967, w/Roman Polanski
WHAT?   Avco Embassy, 1973, w/Roman Polanski
THE TENANT   Paramount, 1976, w/Roman Polanski
LE POINT DE MIRE   Warner Bros./Columbia, 1977
BYE BYE MONKEY   Fida, 1978
TESS   Columbia, 1980, w/John Brownjohn & Roman Polanski
I SENT A LETTER TO MY LOVE   *CHERE INCONNUE*
   Atlantic Releasing Corporation, 1981, w/Moshe Mizrahi
L'AFRICAIN   Renn Productions, 1982, w/Philippe de Broca
QUEST FOR FIRE   20th Century-Fox, 1982
MY BEST FRIEND'S GIRL   European International, 1983,
   w/Bertrand Blier
FAVORITES OF THE MOON   1984, w/Otar Iosseliani
MARIA'S LOVERS   Cannon, 1984, w/Marjorie David,
   Andrei Konchalovsky & Paul Zindel
THE NAME OF THE ROSE   20th Century Fox, 1986,
   w/Andrew Birkin, Howard Franklin & Alain Godard
PIRATES   Cannon, 1986, w/Roman Polanski
SHY PEOPLE   Cannon, 1987, w/Marjorie David &
   Andrei Konchalovsky
JEAN DE FLORETTE   Orion Classics, 1987, w/Claude Berri
MANON OF THE SPRING   Orion Classics, 1987, w/Claude Berri
FRANTIC   Warner Bros., 1988, w/Roman Polanski
THE BEAR   Tri-Star, 1989
THE LOVER   MGM, 1992, w/Jean-Jacques Annaud
BITTER MOON   Fine Line, 1993, w/John Brownjohn &
   Roman Polanski

Screenplays:
TRISTAN w/G.V. Hughes & R. Scott
SATAN & EVE
CRAZY & DAISY

JACOB BRACKMAN*

Agent: ICM - New York, 212/556-5600

THE KING OF MARVIN GARDENS   Columbia, 1972
TIMES SQUARE   AFD, 1980

MALCOLM BRADBURY

Agent: Curtis Brown Ltd. - London, 071/872-0331

THE GREEN MAN (CTF)   BBC-TV/A&E Network, 1991

RAY BRADBURY*

Contact: WGA - Los Angeles, 310/550-1000

NEXT IN LINE (P) w/Charles Rome Smith & S.L. Stebel
MOBY DICK   Warner Bros., 1956, w/John Huston
SOMETHING WICKED THIS WAY COMES   Buena Vista, 1983

Screenplays:
FARENHEIT 451

REB BRADDOCK

Agent: United Talent Agency - Beverly Hills, 310/273-6700

CURDLED (Short)   1994, w/John Maass, co-directed,
   also screenplay

**F
I
L
M

W
R
I
T
E
R
S**

SCOTT BRADFIELD
Agent: ICM - Beverly Hills, 310/550-4000

THE SECRET LIFE OF HOUSES   Rainbreaker Films, 1994,
   w/Adrian Velicescu

AL BRADLEY
IRON WARRIOR   Tri-Star, 1987, w/Steven Luotto

DAVID BRADLEY*
Agent: CAA - Beverly Hills, 310/288-4545

Screenplays:
OTIS

ELIZABETH BRADLEY*
Agent: Richland/Wunsch/Hohman Agency - Los Angeles,
   310/278-1955

COCOON: THE RETURN   20th Century Fox, 1988,
   Story w/Stephen McPherson

Screenplays:
DOCTOR GOODNIGHT   w/Steven McPherson
GOING HOME   w/Stephen McPherson
OUTWARD BOUND   w/Stephen McPherson
MAD DASH   w/Stephen McPherson
TO THE MANOR BORN   w/Stephen McPherson
THE GRAY GHOST   MIDNIGHT FLYER   w/Stephen McPherson

PAT BRADLEY
UNDER THE RAINBOW   Orion/Warner Bros., 1981,
   w/Pat McCormick, Harry Hurwitz, Martin Smith & Fred Bauer

JIM BRADY
BOY MEETS GIRL   Kino Eye, 1994, w/Jim Crosbie, directed

PAM BRADY
Agent: Maggie Field Agency - Studio City, 818/980-2001

Screenplays:
THE FRY GIRL   w/Matt Prager

BRANNON BRAGA
Agent: ICM - Beverly Hills, 310/550-4000

STAR TREK: GENERATIONS   Paramount, 1994, w/Ron Moore

MELVYN BRAGG
Business: The South Bank Show, London Weekend Television

THE HIRED MAN (P)
PLAY DIRTY   United Artists, 1969, w/Lotte Colin
ISADORA   *THE LIVES OF ISADORA*   Universal, 1969,
   w/Clive Exton
THE MUSIC LOVERS   United Artists, 1970
JESUS CHRIST SUPERSTAR   Universal, 1973, w/Norman Jewison

DIANA BRAITHWAITE
RACE TO FREEDOM: THE UNDERGROUND RAILROAD (CTF)
   The Family Channel/BET, 1994, w/Nancy Trites Botkin &
   Peter Mohan

MALCOLM BRALY
ON THE YARD   Midwest Film Productions, 1978

KENNETH BRANAGH
Agent: Paradigm - Los Angeles, 310/277-4400

PUBLIC ENEMY (P)
HENRY V   Renaissance Films, 1989, Adaptation, directed
MUCH ADO ABOUT NOTHING   Samuel Goldwyn Company, 1993,
   Adaptation, directed

CHRIS BRANCATO*
Agent: CAA - Beverly Hills, 310/288-4545

Screenplays:
SHOCKED   w/Dan Fesman   (Savoy)
THE FOURTH SHIP

JOHN BRANCATO*
Agent: United Talent Agency - Beverly Hills, 310/273-6700

WATCHERS II   Concorde, 1990,
   w/Michael Ferris as "Henry Domonic"
FLIGHT OF BLACK ANGEL (CTF)   Hess-Kallberg Productions,
   1991, w/Michael Ferris as "Henry Domonic"
THE UNBORN   Califilm, 1991, w/Michael Ferris as "Henry Domonic"
FEMME FATALE   Republic Pictures, 1991, w/Michael Ferris
INTO THE SUN   Trimark, 1992, w/Michael Ferris
INTERCEPTOR   Trimark, 1993, w/Michael Ferris

Screenplays:
PHASING   w/Michael Ferris
THE GAME   w/Michael Ferris
LOWLIFE   w/Michael Ferris
THE FLYING DUTCHMAN   w/Michael Ferris
THE NET   w/Michael Ferris
GUYS   w/Michael Ferris & Peter Gaffney

LARRY BRAND*
Agent: Preferred Artists - Encino, 818/990-0305

BACKFIRE   New Century/Vista, 1987, w/Rebecca Reynolds
THE DRIFTER   Concorde, 1988, directed
MASQUE OF THE RED DEATH   Concorde, 1989,
   w/Daryl Haney, directed
OVEREXPOSED   Concorde, 1990, w/Rebecca Reynolds, directed

DAVID BRANDES*
Manager: 3 Arts Entertainment - Los Angeles, 213/851-5700

THE DIRT BIKE KID   Concorde/Cinema Group, 1985,
   w/Lewis Colick
THE QUARREL   American Playhouse/Atlantis, 1992

RICHARD BRANDES
PARTY LINE   SVS Films, 1988
MARTIAL LAW   Image Organization, 1990

Screenplays:
THE CHILEAN PUZZLE

GARY BRANDNER*
Contact: WGA - Los Angeles, 310/550-1000

HOWLING II...YOUR SISTER IS A WEREWOLF   Thorn-EMI, 1986,
   w/Robert Sarno
CAMERON'S CLOSET   SVS Films, 1989

TIM BRANDOFF*
Agent: United Talent Agency - Beverly Hills, 310/273-6700

Screenplays:
G-MAN
THE CHELSEA PROJECTS
LOBBY
CITIZEN EDDIE
AFFIRMATIVE ACTION

CLARK BRANDON
FAST FOOD   Fries Entertainment, 1989, w/Lanny Horn

Screenplays:
SECOND UNIT   w/Lanny Horn
SKEETER   w/Lanny Horn

CHARLOTTE BRANDSTROM
Agent: ICM - Beverly Hills, 310/550-4000

STORMY SUMMER MGM-Pathe, 1991,
   w/Nicolas Bernheim, directed
A BUSINESS AFFAIR Capella International, 1994,
   Story w/William Stadiem, directed

MARCIA BRANDWYNNE
Business: Kalola Productions, CBS Entertainment - 213/852-4300

MADE IN AMERICA Warner Bros., 1993, Story w/Nadine Schiff &
   Holly Goldberg Sloan

CARLYON BRANSFORD
Agent: Renaissance-H.N. Swanson - Los Angeles, 310/246-6000
Contact: Attorney David Evans - Santa Monica, 310/395-0965

Screenplays:
DOGGONE
ROCK BOTTOM
THE KILLING ZONE

JOHN F. BRASCIA*
Contact: WGA - Los Angeles, 310/550-1000

THE BALTIMORE BULLET Avco Embassy, 1980,
   w/Robert Vincent O'Neill

JOE BRATCHER*
Agent: The Wright Concept - Burbank, 818/954-8943

Screenplays:
THE INVASION OF GARRETT PORTER w/Judy Farrell
CONNECTIONS w/Judy Farrell
SHADES OF GREY w/Judy Farrell

CALIOPE BRATTLESTREET*
Agent: The Agency - Los Angeles, 310/551-3000

SHOWDOWN IN LITTLE TOKYO Warner Bros., 1991,
   w/Stephen Glantz

Screenplays:
THE GOLDEN 13 w/Stephen Glantz
DANCING CROSS THE RIVER w/Stephen Glantz
JUNKYARD DOGS w/Stephen Glantz
MEN OF BRONZE w/Stephen Glantz
GROWING UP RICH w/Stephen Glantz
SKIPTRACER w/Stephen Glantz

FRED BRAUGHTON
ANOTHER 48 HRS. Paramount, 1990, Story

EDGAR MICHAEL BRAVO
I'LL LOVE YOU FOREVER...TONIGHT Headliner Productions,
   1993, directed

IRVING BRECHER*
Contact: WGA - Los Angeles, 310/550-1000

BEST FOOT FORWARD MGM, 1943, w/Fred Finkelhoffe
DUBARRY WAS A LADY MGM, 1943
CRY FOR HAPPY Columbia, 1961
BYE BYE BIRDIE Columbia, 1963

ANDREW BRECKMAN*
Manager: 3 Arts Entertainment - Los Angeles, 213/851-5700

MOVING Paramount, 1988
ARTHUR 2 ON THE ROCKS Warner Bros., 1988
TRUE IDENTITY Buena Vista, 1991
I.Q. Paramount, 1994, w/Michael Leeson

Screenplays:
SERGEANT BILKO
TODDLERS
MONEY
FRANK
KICK THE CAN

PHILIP M. BREEN
Business: Rolling Hills Productions, 204 S. Beverly Dr. - Suite 166,
   Beverly Hills, CA 90212, 310/454-3940

SWORD OF THE VALIANT Cannon, 1984, w/Howard C. Pen &
   Stephen Weeks

RICHARD BREEN JR.*
Contact: WGA - Los Angeles, 310/550-1000

Screenplays:
DARK PROMISE

EMILY BREER
THE GENIUS Fugitive Productions, 1993,
   w/Joe Gibbons, co-directed

GREGORY BREHM*
Contact: Bloom, Dekom, Hergott & Cook - Los Angeles, 310/278-8622

Screenplays:
JADE
AND THE HOME OF THE BRAVE

VALERIE BREIMAN*
Agent: The Coppage Company - North Hollywood, 818/980-1106

THE UNSINKABLE SCHECKY MOSKOWITZ TTI, 1990, directed

Screenplays:
THE MOST BEAUTIFUL GIRL IN THE WORLD
PIZZA U
TWICE SEDUCED
SHRINKING VIOLET

STEPHEN BREIMER
NIGHT WARNING ComWorld, 1983, w/Boom Collins & Alan Jay
   Glueckman

TIA BRELIS*
Agent: The Gersh Agency - Beverly Hills, 310/274-6611

TRADING MOM Trimark, 1994, directed

JOHN G. BRENNAN
(w/Kamal Ahmed: The Jerky Boys)
THE JERKY BOYS Buena Vista, 1995, w/Kamal Ahmed,
   James Melkonian & Rich Wilkes

TERENCE (TERRY) BRENNAN
ROOFTOPS New Century/Vista, 1989

Screenplays:
OUT OF THE DARKNESS
BLATNOY
THE SEARCH FOR TYPHOID MARY
WONDER WHEELS

RICHARD BRENNE
CLASS ACT Warner Bros., 1992, Story w/Wayne Rice &
   Michael Swerdlick

Screenplays:
CHANGING LABELS
HEADING HOME

ARTHUR J. BRESSON, JR.
BUDDIES   New Line Cinema, 1985, directed

ROBERT BRESSON
Contact: French Film Office, 745 Fifth Avenue, New York, NY 10151,
   212/832-8860

THE LADIES OF THE PARK   Brandon, 1945,
   w/Jean Cocteau, directed
DIARY OF A COUNTRY PRIEST   Brandon, 1950, directed
AU HASARD, BALTHAZAR   Cinema Ventures, 1966, directed
LE DIABLE PROBABLEMENT   Gaumont, 1977, directed
L'ARGENT (MONEY)   Cinecom, 1983, directed

MARTIN BREST*
Agent: CAA - Beverly Hills, 310/288-4545
Business: City Lights Films, 2110 Main St. - Suite 200, Santa Monica,
   CA 90405, 310/314-3500

HOT TOMORROWS   American Film Institute, 1977, directed
GOING IN STYLE   Warner Bros., 1979, directed

JASON BRETT*
Agent: Jon Klane Agency - Beverly Hills, 310/278-0178

Screenplays:
THE EXECUTIVE w/Thom Bishop
ROUTE 66 w/Thom Bishop
THE STREET WHERE YOU LIVE w/Thom Bishop
SILENT SERVICE
WILD CARD

JONATHAN BRETT*
Agent: Annette Van Duren Agency - Los Angeles, 213/650-3643

EROTIC TALES ★   Regina Ziegler Filmproduktion/Mercure
   Distribution, 1994, w/Susan Seidelman, "The Dutch Master"

Screenplays:
THAT LOVING FEELING
DYLAN
YESTERDAY

JAMESON BREWER*
Agent: Jerome S. Siegel Associates - Los Angeles, 213/850-1275

GHOST TOWN   United Artists, 1956
THE INCREDIBLE MR. LIMPET   Warner Bros., 1964,
   w/John C. Rose
TERROR IN THE WAX MUSEUM   Bing Crosby
   Productions, 1973
ARNOLD   Avco Embassy, 1973, w/John Fenton Murray
HEIDI'S SONG (AF)   Paramount, 1982, w/Joseph Barbera &
   Robert Taylor

E. KIM BREWSTER
FOOD OF THE GODS II   Concorde-Centaur, 1989,
   w/Richard Bennett

SALOME BREZINER
Agent: The Gersh Agency - Beverly Hills, 310/274-6611
Manager: 3 Arts Entertainment - Los Angeles, 213/851-5700

LIFT (Short)   Fujimo Productions, 1991,
   w/Herschel Weingrod, directed
TOLLBOOTH   Trans Atlantic Entertainment, 1994, directed

MARSHALL BRICKMAN*
Agent: ICM - Beverly Hills, 310/550-4000

SLEEPER   United Artists, 1973, w/Woody Allen
ANNIE HALL ★★   United Artists, 1977, w/Woody Allen
MANHATTAN ★   United Artists, 1978, w/Woody Allen
SIMON   Orion/Warner Bros., 1980, directed
LOVESICK   The Ladd Company/Warner Bros., 1983, directed

THE MANHATTAN PROJECT   20th Century Fox, 1986,
   w/Thomas Baum, directed
FOR THE BOYS   20th Century Fox, 1991, w/Neal Jimenez &
   Lindy Laub
MANHATTAN MURDER MYSTERY   TriStar, 1993, w/Woody Allen
INTERSECTION   Paramount, 1994, w/David Rayfiel

Screenplays:
ONE MORE TIME (directing)
THE OLD NEIGHBORHOOD
PINK VODKA BLUES
THE 730 CLUB
AFTER YOU'VE GONE
NORTH BY SOUTH

PAUL BRICKMAN*
Agent: CAA - Beverly Hills, 310/288-4545

THE BAD NEWS BEARS IN BREAKING TRAINING
   Paramount, 1977
CITIZEN'S BAND   *HANDLE WITH CARE*   Paramount, 1977
RISKY BUSINESS   The Geffen Company/Warner Bros.,
   1983, directed
DEAL OF THE CENTURY   Warner Bros., 1983
MEN DON'T LEAVE   The Geffen Company/Warner Bros., 1990,
   w/Barbara Benedek, directed

LESLIE BRICUSSE*
Contact: WGA - Los Angeles, 310/550-1000

ROAR OF THE GREASEPAINT, SMELL OF THE CROWD (P)
   w/Anthony Newley
OUT OF THE BLUE (P)
AN EVENING WITH BEATRICE LILLIE (P)
LADY AT THE WHEEL (P)
ONE SHINING MOMENT (P)
CHARLEY MOON   British Lion, 1956
BACHELOR OF HEARTS   Rank, 1958, w/Frederic Raphael
THE SWINGING MAIDEN   *THE IRON MAIDEN*
   Anglo Amalgamated, 1962, w/Vivian Cox
THREE HATS FOR LISA   Seven Hills, 1965, w/Talbot Rothwell
STOP THE WORLD - I WANT TO GET OFF   Warner Bros., 1966,
   w/Anthony Newley
DR. DOOLITTLE   20th Century-Fox, 1967
SCROOGE   National General, 1970, from his play
SUNDAY LOVERS   United Artists, 1981, w/Francis Veber &
   Gene Wilder
BULLSEYE!   21st Century Film Corporation, 1991,
   w/Maurice Gran & Laurence Marks

Screenplays:
CHARLIE MOON
EAST COAST, WEST COAST
MUSICAL CHAIRS
THE GREAT MUSIC CHASE

MATTHEW BRIGHT
FORBIDDEN ZONE   Sutton Marketing, 1980, w/Richard Elfman,
   Nick James & Nick L. Martinson
WILDFIRE   Cinema Group, 1986, w/Zalman King
GUNCRAZY   Academy Entertainment, 1992
SHRUNKEN HEADS   Fullmoon Entertainment, 1994

JOHN BRILEY*
Agent: ICM - Beverly Hills, 310/550-4000

INVASION QUARTET   MGM, 1961, w/Jack Trevor Story
POSTMAN'S KNOCK   MGM, 1961, w/Jack Trevor Story
CHILDREN OF THE DAMNED   MGM, 1964
POPE JOAN   Columbia, 1972
THAT LUCKY TOUCH   United Artists, 1975
THE MEDUSA TOUCH   Warner Bros., 1978, w/Jack Gold
EAGLE'S WING   International Picture Show, 1979
GANDHI ★★   Columbia, 1982
ENIGMA   Embassy, 1983
MARIE   MGM/UA, 1985

TAI-PAN   DEG, 1986, w/Stanley Mann
CRY FREEDOM   Universal, 1987
CHRISTOPHER COLUMBUS: THE DISCOVERY   Warner Bros.,
   1992, w/Cary Bates & Mario Puzo

Screenplays:
THE WARRIORS OF THE RAINBOW   w/David Williamson
WIND IN THE WILLOWS
GENGHIS KHAN
WEST WITH THE NIGHT
HENDERSON, THE RAIN KING
THE LOVES OF KAFKA
THE FOURTH SEASON
A FRAGILE LIFE
WHY DID I EVER LEAVE HORSES?   CAPTAIN BARNES,
   LIEUTENANT FARNUM
OFFERING
TO DIE A STRANGER
THE VEIL
THE GREAT BABY BLUE
HOW SLEEP THE BRAVE
MISTER GOD, THIS IS ANNA
THE BIG APPLE
THE DEADLY INHERITANCE

STEVEN BRILL*
Agent: CAA - Beverly Hills, 310/288-4545

THE MIGHTY DUCKS   Buena Vista, 1992
D2: THE MIGHTY DUCKS 2   Buena Vista, 1994
HEAVYWEIGHTS   Buena Vista, 1995, w/Judd Apatow, directed

Screenplays:
MEET YOUR MATCH

MAX BRINDLE
THE WHIPPING BOY (CTF)   Gemini Films/Jones Entertainment/
   Le Sabre Group, 1994

MICHAEL BRINDLEY
SHAME   Skouras Pictures, 1988, w/Beverly Blakenship

BO BRINKMAN
BAY HOUSE (P)
ICEHOUSE   Upfront Films, 1989, from his play
   "Ice House Heat Waves," directed

MORT BRISKIN*
Contact: WGA - Los Angeles, 310/550-1000

WALKING TALL   Bing Crosby Productions, 1973
FRAMED   Paramount, 1974

JEFF BROADSTREET
Agent: The Artists Group - Los Angeles, 310/552-1100

SEXBOMB   Phillips & Mora Entertainment, 1989,
   Story w/Robert Benson, directed

DEBORAH BROCK*
Agent: The Gersh Agency - Beverly Hills, 310/274-6611
Business: Fiat Lucre Productions, 11850 Wilshire Blvd. - Suite 200,
   Los Angeles, CA 90025

SLUMBER PARTY MASSACRE II   Concorde, 1987, directed
ROCK'N'ROLL HIGH SCHOOL FOREVER   Concorde,
   1991, directed

Screenplays:
SANDMAN
THE STRIP

ADAM LARSON BRODER*
Agent: APA - Los Angeles, 310/273-0744

EVERYBODY WORE HATS (Short)   1992, directed,
   also screenplay

Screenplays:
THE BRIDGE
THE GAME

JOHN BRODERICK
Agent: Associated Talent International - Beverly Hills, 310/271-4662

THE WARRIOR AND THE SORCERESS   New Horizons,
   1984, directed

PATRICIA BRODERICK
INFINITY   Neo Motion Pictures/First Look Pictures, 1995

OSCAR BRODNEY*
Contact: WGA - Los Angeles, 310/550-1000

SHE WROTE THE BOOK   Universal, 1946, w/Warren Wilson
ARE YOU WITH IT?   Universal-International, 1948
MEXICAN HAYRIDE   Universal, 1948, w/John Grant
SOUTH SEA SINNER   Universal-International, 1949,
   w/Joel Malone
YES SIR, THAT'S MY BABY   Universal-International, 1949
CURTAIN CALL AT CACTUS CREEK
   Universal-International, 1949
HARVEY   Universal-International, 1950, w/Mary Chase
FRENCHIE   Universal-International, 1950
COMANCHE TERRITORY   Universal-International, 1950,
   w/Louis Meltzer
DOUBLE CROSSBONES   Universal-International, 1950
LITTLE EGYPT   *CHICAGO MASQUERADE*   Universal-International,
   1951, w/Doris Gilbert
SCARLET ANGEL   Universal-International, 1952
WALKING MY BABY BACK HOME   Universal-International, 1953,
   w/Don McGuire
THE SIGN OF THE PAGAN   Universal-International, 1954,
   w/Barre Lyndon
THE BLACK SHIELD OF FALWORTH
   Universal-International, 1954
THE GLENN MILLER STORY   Universal-International, 1954,
   w/Valentine Davies
THE SPOILERS   Universal-International, 1955,
   w/Charles Hoffman
THE PURPLE MASK   Universal-International, 1955
LADY GODIVA   Universal International, 1955, w/Harry Ruskin
CAPTAIN LIGHTFOOT   Universal-International, 1955,
   w/W.R. Burnett
A DAY OF FURY   Universal, 1956, w/James Edmiston
TAMMY AND THE BACHELOR   Universal-International, 1957
BOBBIKINS   20th Century-Fox, 1959
TAMMY TELL ME TRUE   American-International, 1961
TAMMY AND THE DOCTOR   American-International, 1963
I'D RATHER BE RICH   Universal-International, 1964,
   w/Norman Krasna & Leo Townsend
THE BRASS BOTTLE   Universal-International, 1964
GHOST FEVER   Miramax, 1987, w/Ron Rich

HUGH BRODY
Contact: British Academy of Film & Television Arts, 195 Piccadilly,
   London W1, England, 071/734-0022

1919   Spectrafilm, 1985, directed

LARRY BRODY*
Contact: WGA - Los Angeles, 310/550-1000

BAD COMPANY   Moonstone Entertainment, 1993,
   w/Janice Hendler

**F
I
L
M
W
R
I
T
E
R
S**

HENRY BROMELL*
Agent: United Talent Agency - Beverly Hills, 310/273-6700

Screenplays:
CLARKSVILLE
REVOLVER
RESPECT
STARBRIGHT
AMERICAN BOYS
COLD WARRIORS

REX BROMFIELD
Business: BromFilms Productions 1988 Inc., 6395 Chatham St., West Vancouver, B.C. V7W 2E1 Canada, 604/921-9394

HOME IS WHERE THE HART IS   Atlantic Releasing Corporation, 1987, directed

VALRI BROMFIELD*
Agent: Major Clients Agency - Los Angeles, 310/284-6400

Screenplays:
HOUSEWIVES IN PRISON
LUCKY IN LOVE
THE KID WHO ATE HER PARENTS

DAN BRONSON*
Agent: The Irv Schechter Company - Beverly Hills, 310/278-8070

THE LAST INNOCENT MAN (CTF)   HBO Pictures/Maurice Singer Productions, 1987
A TASTE FOR KILLING (CTF)   Bodega Bay Productions, 1992

Screenplays:
JUGGERNAUT
MOVING TARGET
THE WIRE (CTF)
TRUANTS
SILENCER
DOUBLE EXPOSURE
IN A LONELY PLACE
MANHUNT
BLOOD MONEY
WHISPERS

PETER BROOK
Address: c/o C.I.R.T., 9 rue du Cirque, 75008 Paris, France, tel. 43-59-13-33

LORD OF THE FLIES   Continental, 1963, directed
SWANN IN LOVE   Gaumont, 1983, w/Jean-Claude Carriere & Marie-Helene Estienne

GREG BROOKER*
Agent: ICM - Beverly Hills, 310/550-4000

Screenplays:
THE FALL AND RISE OF GLEN
SPRING '61
MAX LAKEMAN AND THE BEAUTIFUL STRANGER
MY SUMMER, MY HONEYMOON

WILLIAM BROOKFIELD
ROUGH MAGIC   Savoy, 1995, w/Clare Peploe

ADAM BROOKS*
Agent: ICM - Beverly Hills, 310/550-4000

ALMOST YOU   20th Century-Fox, 1982, Story, directed
HEADS (CTF)   Atlantic Films/Evermore/Davis Entertainment, 1994, w/Jay Stapleton
PARIS MATCH   20th Century Fox, 1995

ALBERT BROOKS*
Agent: ICM - Beverly Hills, 310/550-4000

REAL LIFE   Paramount, 1979, w/Monica Johnson & Harry Shearer, directed
MODERN ROMANCE   Columbia, 1981, w/Monica Johnson, directed
LOST IN AMERICA   The Geffen Company/Warner Bros., 1985, w/Monica Johnson, directed
DEFENDING YOUR LIFE   The Geffen Company/Warner Bros., 1991, directed
THE SCOUT   20th Century Fox, 1994, w/Monica Johnson & Andrew Bergman

HALLE BROOKS
WHO SHOT PAT?   Castle Hill Productions, 1992, w/Robert Brooks

JAMES L. BROOKS*
Agent: ICM - Beverly Hills, 310/550-4000
Business: Gracie Films, Columbia Pictures, 310/280-4222

STARTING OVER   Paramount, 1979
TERMS OF ENDEARMENT ★★   Paramount, 1983, directed
BROADCAST NEWS ★   20th Century Fox, 1987, directed
I'LL DO ANYTHING   Columbia, 1994, directed

JOSEPH BROOKS*
Business: Chancery Lane Films, Inc., 41-A East 74th St., New York, NY 10021, 212/759-8720

YOU LIGHT UP MY LIFE   Columbia, 1977, directed
IF EVER I SEE YOU AGAIN   Columbia, 1978, w/Martin Davidson, directed
HEADIN' FOR BROADWAY   20th Century-Fox, 1980, w/Hilary Henkin & Larry Gross, directed

MEL BROOKS*
Business: Brooksfilms Limited, 20th Century Fox, P.O. Box 900, Beverly Hills, CA 90213, 310/203-1375

THE PRODUCERS ★★   Avco Embassy, 1967, directed
THE TWELVE CHAIRS   UMC, 1970, directed
BLAZING SADDLES   Warner Bros., 1973, w/Andrew Bergman, Richard Pryor, Norman Steinberg & Alan Uger, directed
TEN FROM YOUR SHOW OF SHOWS   1973, w/others
YOUNG FRANKENSTEIN ★   20th Century-Fox, 1974, w/Gene Wilder, directed
SILENT MOVIE   20th Century-Fox, 1976, w/Ron Clark, Rudy DeLuca & Barry Levinson, directed
HIGH ANXIETY   20th Century-Fox, 1977, w/Ron Clark, Rudy DeLuca & Barry Levinson, directed
HISTORY OF THE WORLD - PART 1   20th Century-Fox, 1981, directed
SPACEBALLS   MGM/UA, 1987, w/Ronny Graham & Thomas Meehan, directed
LIFE STINKS   MGM-Pathe, 1991, w/Rudy DeLuca & Steve Haberman, directed
ROBIN HOOD: MEN IN TIGHTS   20th Century Fox, 1993, w/Evan Chandler & J. David Shapiro, directed

Screenplays:
SHE STOOPS TO CONQUER

ROBERT BROOKS
WHO SHOT PAT?   Castle Hill Productions, 1992, w/Halle Brooks, directed

ROBERT BROOKS
TATTOO   20th Century-Fox, 1981, Story

RYAN BROOKS
Agent: CAA - Beverly Hills, 310/288-4545

Screenplays:
THEY FROZE MY MOTHER w/Todd Komarnicki

PHILIP BROPHY
Contact: Australian Film Commission, 8 West St., North Sydney,
   NSW 2026, Australia, tel.: 2/925-7333

BODY MELT   Dumb Films, 1993, w/Rod Bishop, directed

ALINE BROSH*
Agent: The Irv Schechter Company - Beverly Hills, 310/278-8070

INSIDE LOIS (P)

Screenplays:
BILLIONAIRES
JERSEY ANGEL
THROUGH TO LOVE

PETER BROSNAN
HIT LIST   New Line Cinema, 1989, w/John Goff

LARRY BROTHERS*
Agent: William Morris Agency - Beverly Hills, 310/274-7451

AN INNOCENT MAN   Buena Vista, 1989
FEVER (CTF)   Saban/Scherick, 1991

Screenplays:
THE LEGEND OF LIBERTY AVENUE
THE KILLING GAME

JOYCE BROTMAN
Agent: William Morris Agency - Beverly Hills, 310/274-7451

Screenplays:
STATE OF THE UNION w/Ellen Weston

TAMAR BROTT
Agent: Writers & Artists Agency - Los Angeles, 310/824-6300

THE LINGUINI INCIDENT   Academy Entertainment, 1992,
   w/Richard Shepard

Screenplays:
CAT'S CLAW
LITTLE DEMONS

WALTER BROUGH*
Contact: WGA - Los Angeles, 310/550-1000

THE DESPERADOS   Columbia, 1968

GIDEON BROWER*
Agent: Broder-Kurland-Webb-Uffner - Beverly Hills, 310/281-3400

Screenplays:
THE FISH BURGLARS

BARRY ALEXANDER BROWN
LONELY IN AMERICA   Arista Films, 1990,
   w/Satyajit Joy Palit, directed

BILLY BROWN*
Contact: WGA - Los Angeles, 310/550-1000

JOHN CARPENTER'S BODY BAGS (CTF)   Showtime, 1993,
   w/Dan Angel

Screenplays:
THE MIGHTY MORPHIN POWER RANGERS MOVIE w/Dan Angel
DYSFUNCTIONALLY YOURS w/Dan Angel
BOX OFFICE GROSS w/Dan Angel
RUDE WARRIORS w/Dan Angel
SHOCK TREATMENT w/Dan Angel

BRUCE BROWN
ENDLESS SUMMER (FD)   Cinema 5, 1966, directed
BRUCE BROWN'S ENDLESS SUMMER II (FD)   New Line Cinema,
   1994, w/Dana Brown, directed

BRYAN BROWN
Agent: CAA - Beverly Hills, 310/288-4545

SWEET TALKER   New Visions, 1991, Story w/Tony Morphett

CURTIS BROWN
THE GAME   Visual Perspectives, 1989, w/Julia Wilson, directed

DANA BROWN
BRUCE BROWN'S ENDLESS SUMMER II (FD)   New Line Cinema,
   1994, w/Bruce Brown

EDWIN SCOTT BROWN
THE PREY   New World, 1984, w/Summer Brown

GERARD BROWN*
Agent: Amsel, Eisenstadt & Frazier - Los Angeles, 310/939-1188

JONIN' (P)   also screenplay
JUICE   Paramount, 1992, w/Ernest Dickerson

Screenplays:
FUTURE CRIMES

JAMIE BROWN
Contact: 514/288-1638

TOBY MCTEAGUE   Spectrafilm, 1986, w/Djordje Milicevic &
   Jeff Maguire

JEFF BROWN
Agent: William Morris Agency - Beverly Hills, 310/274-7451

PONTIAC MOON   Paramount, 1994, w/Finn Taylor

JIM BROWN
Agent: ICM - Beverly Hills, 310/550-4000

Screenplays:
LUCKY TOWN

JULIE BROWN*
Contact: Screen Actors Guild - Los Angeles, 213/954-1600

EARTH GIRLS ARE EASY   Vestron, 1988, w/Charlie Coffey &
   Terrence E. McNally

LARRY BROWN
Agent: Pleshette & Green - Los Angeles, 213/465-0428

Screenplays:
JOE

LEIGH BROWN*
Contact: WGA - New York, 212/245-6180

A CHRISTMAS STORY   MGM/UA, 1983, w/Bob Clark &
   Jean Shepherd
IT RUNS IN THE FAMILY   MGM/UA, 1995, w/Bob Clark &
   Jean Shepherd

**F
I
L
M

W
R
I
T
E
R
S**

MICHAEL HENRY BROWN*
Agent: CAA - Beverly Hills, 310/288-4545

THE DAY THE BRONX DIED (P)
LAUREL AVENUE (CMS)   HBO Independent Productions, 1993
DEAD PRESIDENTS   Buena Vista, 1995

Screenplays:
JUMP
THE LAST SHOT

MITCH BROWN
IN DANGEROUS COMPANY   Manson International, 1988

PAUL BROWN*
Agent: CAA - Beverly Hills, 310/288-4545

THRASHIN'   Fries Entertainment, 1986, w/Alan Sacks

Screenplays:
BLUE TATTOO

PETER BROWN
Agent: United Talent Agency - Beverly Hills, 310/273-6700

Screenplays:
DRASTIC MEASURES
REPRESSED MEMORY THRILLER

RITA MAE BROWN*
Agent: Paradigm - Los Angeles, 310/277-4400

SLUMBER PARTY MASSACRE   Santa Fe, 1982

Screenplays:
TABLE DANCING

SAM O. BROWN
(See Blake Edwards)

STEVE BROWN*
Agent: David Shapira & Associates - Sherman Oaks, 818/906-0322

SECOND THOUGHTS   Universal, 1983

SUMMER BROWN
THE PREY   New World, 1984, w/Edwin Scott Brown

TONY BROWN
Business: Tony Brown Productions, Inc., 1501 Broadway -
    Suite 2014, New York, NY 10036, 212/575-0876

THE WHITE GIRL   Tony Brown Productions, 1990, directed

HOWARD BROWNE*
Contact: WGA - Los Angeles, 310/550-1000

CAPONE   20th Century-Fox, 1975

L. VIRGINIA BROWNE*
Agent: ICM - Beverly Hills, 310/550-4000
Manager: Rix-Ubell Management - Los Angeles, 310/859-9733

SIOUX CITY   I.R.S. Releasing, 1994

Screenplays:
CASTLE RISING
RUNDOWN
HEROES, GYPSIES AND RENEGADES

JANET BROWNELL*
Agent: CAA - Beverly Hills, 310/288-4545

SWEET REVENGE (CTF)   Turner Pictures/The Movie Group, 1990
CHRISTMAS IN CONNECTICUT (CTF)   Once Upon a Time/Turner
    Pictures, 1992

Screenplays:
THE YEAR OF FRANK SINATRA
HOW TO MURDER YOUR MOTHER-IN-LAW

MICHAEL BROWNING
Agent: Monteiro Rose Agency - Encino, 818/501-1177

Screenplays:
THE PORTAL
MORE DOGS THAN BONES
DEAD BOYS DON'T LIE
ASTRO ISLAND w/Hilary Hinkle

ROD BROWNING*
Contact: WGA - Los Angeles, 310/550-1000

OH HEAVENLY DOG   20th Century-Fox, 1980, w/Joe Camp

WILLIAM BROYLES JR.*
Agent: CAA - Beverly Hills, 310/288-4545

APOLLO 13   Universal, 1995, w/Al Reinhart

GLENN A. BRUCE
Attorney: Jay Kenoff, Kenoff & Machtinger - Los Angeles,
    310/552-0808
Address: P.O. Box 30501, Palm Beach Gardens, FL 33420,
    407/624-1446

KICKBOXER   Cannon, 1989
VICTOR ONE: THE STORY OF SGT. GEORGE AGUILAR
    Peacock Films, 1992
CYBORG COP   Nu-Image Releasing, 1993, Shared

Screenplays:
DEADLY RIVALS
INTO THE MOVIES
THE LAST GOOD FIGHT
ROAD HAZARD
BANANA REPUBLIC
JUSTICE CRUCIFIED: THE TRUE STORY OF SACCO
    AND VANZETTI
THE SWEET SPOT w/Colleen Creamer
BACK FROM THE DEAD

JAMES BRUCE
Agent: Renaissance-H.N. Swanson - Los Angeles, 310/246-6000

DIRTY MONEY (CTF)   Cinemax, 1994

PEGGY BRUEN
ALEXA   Platinum Pictures, 1989, w/Sean Delgado

JAMES BRUNER*
Contact: Attorney Craig Emanuel, Sinclair-Tennenbaum -
    Los Angeles, 310/285-6222

AN EYE FOR AN EYE   Avco Embassy, 1981, w/William Gray
MISSING IN ACTION   Cannon, 1984
INVASION U.S.A.   Cannon, 1985, w/Chuck Norris
SWORDS OF HEAVEN   Trans World Entertainment, 1985,
    w/Britt Lomond, William P. O'Hagan & Joseph Randazzo
THE DELTA FORCE   Cannon, 1986, w/Menahem Golan
P.O.W. THE ESCAPE   Cannon, 1986, w/Malcolm Barbour,
    John Langley & Jeremy Lipp
BRADDOCK: MISSING IN ACTION III   Cannon, 1988,
    w/Chuck Norris

MARK BRUNET*
Agent: Innovative Artists - Los Angeles, 310/553-5200

Screenplays:
MINNESOTA MOON
PEELER
STRAITS OF HELL
FIRST WORLD FLIGHT

BOB BRUNNER*
Agent: Dytman & Schwartz - Los Angeles, 310/274-8844

EXIT TO EDEN   Savoy, 1994, w/Deborah Amelon

BILL BRYAN*
Agent: William Morris Agency - Beverly Hills, 310/274-7451

Screenplays:
SEX AND VIOLENCE
HELL OF AN ANGEL

CHRIS BRYANT*
Agent: Candace Lake - Beverly Hills, 310/289-0600

THE MAN WHO HAD POWER OVER WOMEN   Avco Embassy,
   1971, w/Allan G. Scott
DON'T LOOK NOW   Paramount, 1974, w/Allan G. Scott
THE GIRL FROM PETROVKA   Universal, 1974, w/Allan G. Scott
THE SPIRAL STAIRCASE   Warner Bros., 1975, w/Allan G. Scott
JOSEPH ANDREWS   Paramount, 1977, w/Allan G. Scott
THE AWAKENING   Orion/Warner Bros., 1980, w/Clive Exton &
   Allan G. Scott
MARTIN'S DAY   MGM/UA, 1985, w/Allan G. Scott
LADY JANE   Paramount, 1986, Story
SWORD OF GIDEON (CTF)   Alliance Entertainment/Les Films
   Ariane/HBO Premiere Films/CTV/Telefilm Canada/Rogers
   Cablesystems/Radio-Canada, 1986
STEALING HEAVEN   FilmDallas, 1988
YOUNG CATHERINE (CTF)   Consolidate/Primedia/Lenfilm, 1991
FOREIGN AFFAIRS (CTF)   Interscope Communications, 1993

Screenplays:
NINE TIGER MAN w/Allan G. Scott
GOODBYE CALIFORNIA w/Allan G. Scott
ST. PETERSBURG/CANNES EXPRESS
WHISPERS
GEORGIA O'KEEFE A WAY OF SEEING
BLOOD MONEY
THE GRAY GHOST

JOHN BRYANT
Contact: Howard M. Frumes, Manatt, Phelps, Phillips & Kantor -
   Los Angeles, 310/312-4166
Business: 213/882-4104

TEEN ANGEL   Cannon, 1991, w/George Saunders
MISSION OF JUSTICE   Image/Westwind, 1992,
   w/George Saunders
MARTIAL OUTLAW   Republic, 1993, Story w/George Saunders
LITTLE NINJA MAN   Cannon, 1993, w/George Saunders
SCANNER COP   Image Organization, 1993, w/George Saunders

Screenplays:
BOMB SQUAD w/George Saunders
MAGIC BUS w/George Saunders
CUSTODY w/George Saunders
LONE JUSTICE w/George Saunders
THE FRAUD FIGHTERS
KUNG FU STU

JAMES BRYCE*
Agent: Heacock Literary Agency - Santa Monica, 310/393-6227

TREASURE OF THE FOUR CROWNS   Cannon, 1983,
   w/Lloyd Battista & Jerry Lazarus

BILL BRYDEN
THE LONG RIDERS   United Artists, 1980, w/James Keach,
   Stacy Keach & Steven Philip Smith

Screenplays:
A HANDSOME AND CHARMING MAN

JAMES DAVID BUCHANAN
Agent: CAA - Beverly Hills, 213/288-4545

THE HAPPENING   Columbia, 1967, w/Ronald Austin &
   Frank R. Pierson
MIDAS RUN   1969, w/Ronald Austin & Berne Giler
HARRY IN YOUR POCKET   United Artists, 1973, w/Ronald Austin
BRENDA STARR   Triumph, 1991, w/Delia Ephron & Noreen Stone
CURACAO (CTF)   Jones Entertainment Group, 1993

Screenplays:
THE MICK
FOOL'S GOLD
DIFFERENT RULES
MIDNIGHT SUN
THE NEW ROSE
RIOTOUS CONDUCT

SCOTT R. BUCK*
Agent: William Morris Agency - Beverly Hills, 310/274-7451

Screenplays:
EXIT NOW

KIM BUCKLEY*
Contact: WGA - Los Angeles, 310/550-1000

Screenplays:
CLIPPED w/James Gierman

PETER BUCKMAN
APPOINTMENT WITH DEATH   Cannon, 1988, w/Anthony Shaffer &
   Michael Winner

BRAD BUCKNER*
Agent: ICM - Beverly Hills, 310/550-4000
Business: B & E Enterprises - 818/954-1921

Screenplays:
ANNIE AND THE CASTLE OF TERROR w/Eugenie Ross-Leming
UFO w/Eugenie Ross-Leming
ROMANTIC FOOLS w/Eugenie Ross-Leming
SVENGALI w/Eugenie Ross-Leming
FOREIGNERS w/Eugenie Ross-Leming
CADETS w/Eugenie Ross-Leming
LOOSE WOMEN w/Eugenie Ross-Leming
LAMB OF GOD w/Eugenie Ross-Leming
THE KID w/Eugenie Ross-Leming
FORGET ME NOT w/Eugenie Ross-Leming

VICTOR BUELL*
Agent: Schiowitz/Clay/Rose - Los Angeles, 213/650-7300

SILHOUETTE (CTF)   MCA Television Network, 1990, w/Jay Wolf

Screenplays:
NOWHERE FAST w/Jay Wolf & Alan Beattie

TAKASHI A. BUFFORD
Agent: ICM - Beverly Hills, 310/550-4000
Manager: Addis-Wechsler - Los Angeles, 213/954-9000

HOUSE PARTY 3   New Line Cinema, 1994

Screenplays:
BLACK AND WHITE IN COLOR
BELLY OF THE BEAST
BUSTER AND TULLIP

SIREN'S SONG
SET IT OFF
X'S AND O'S
THE LOTTERY

JEFF BUHAI*
Agent: Broder-Kurland-Webb-Uffner - Beverly Hills, 310/281-3400

REVENGE OF THE NERDS   20th Century-Fox, 1984,
    w/Steve Zacharias
THE WHOOPEE BOYS   Paramount, 1986, w/Steve Zacharias &
    David Obst
LAST RESORT   Concorde/Cinema Group, 1986, w/Steve Zacharias
JOCKS   Crown International, 1987, w/David Obst &
    Steve Zacharias as "Mike Lanahan & David Oas"
JOHNNY BE GOOD   Orion, 1988, w/David Obst & Steve Zacharias
IN THE ARMY NOW   Buena Vista, 1994,
    Story w/Steve Zacharias & Robbie Fox

Screenplays:
EDDIE w/Steve Zacharias
NOUVEAU GUINEANS w/Steve Zacharias
BIKERS FROM HELL w/Steve Zacharias
DALLAS DEBS w/Steve Zacharias
GIRLS IN TROUBLE w/Steve Zacharias
DEEP COVER w/Steve Zacharias
HOPELESSNESS & DESPAIR w/Steve Zacharias
MR. VICE PRESIDENT w/Steve Zacharias & Robert Kears
THE TRUTH ABOUT SWEDES w/Steve Zacharias
LOVELINE w/Steve Zacharias
AFTERGLOW w/Steve Zacharias
HARRAD II w/Steve Zacharias
HOSPITAL w/Steve Zacharias
INSIDE THE INQUIRER w/Steve Zacharias
VULGARIANS w/Steve Zacharias
HEAVY METAL WEEKEND w/Steve Zacharias
REVENGE OF THE NUDES w/Steve Zacharias

BULL DOG E.
(Greg Howard)
Agent: ICM - Beverly Hills, 310/550-4000

Screenplays:
THE ADVENTURES OF SPIKE AND PANCAKE
THE WALLS CAME TUMBLING DOWN

HARVEY BULLOCH*
Agent: Preferred Artists - Encino, 818/990-0305

HONEYMOON HOTEL   MGM, 1964, w/R.S. Allen
GIRL HAPPY   MGM, 1965, w/R.S. Allen

VICANGELO BULLOCK*
Contact: Eric Weissman, Weissmann, Wolff, Bergman, Coleman &
    Silverman - Beverly Hills, 310/858-7888
Business: Vicangelo Films - 310/458-4470

OUT OF CONTROL   New World, 1985,
    w/Sandra Weintraub Rolland

ALAN BUNCE
BABAR: THE MOVIE (AF)   New Line Cinema, 1989,
    w/John De Klein, Raymond Jaffelice, Peter Sauder &
    J.D. Smith, directed

EDWARD BUNKER*
Agent: Martin Hurwitz - Beverly Hills, 310/274-0240

STRAIGHT TIME   Warner Bros., 1978, w/Jeffrey Boam &
    Alvin Sargent
RUNAWAY TRAIN   Cannon, 1985, w/Djordje Milicevic &
    Paul Zindel

Screenplays:
MARCUS TIMBERWOLF

MARK BUNTZMAN
Contact: 818/980-3007

EXTERMINATOR 2   Cannon, 1984, w/William Sachs, directed

JOYCE BUNUEL*
Agent: The Marion Rosenberg Office - Los Angeles, 213/653-7383

TATTOO   20th Century-Fox, 1981

JOHN BUNZEL*
Agent: Innovative Artists - Los Angeles, 310/553-5200

Screenplays:
KATIE w/John Gray & Paul Young
DEATH OF A BUICK (from his play)

CURTIS BURCH*
Contact: Castle Rock Entertainment - 310/285-2300

LADYBUGS   Paramount, 1992

Screenplays:
FOREVER ANNA

CONSTANCE BURGE*
Agent: The Agency - Los Angeles, 310/551-3000

Screenplays:
MR. AND MRS. SEVENTH GRADE

ROBERT BURGE
VASECTOMY, A DELICATE MATTER   Seymour Borde &
    Associates, 1986, w/Robert Hilliard, directed

NEAL R. BURGER*
Agent: APA - Los Angeles, 310/273-0744

Screenplays:
UP THE GARDEN PATH w/George E. Simpson
GHOSTBOAT w/George E. Simpson
DAN HAZARD AND THE LEGION OF EVIL w/George E. Simpson

JOHN BURGESS
SUNDOWN: THE VAMPIRE IN RETREAT   Vestron, 1989,
    w/Anthony Hickox

DAVID BURKE*
Agent: William Morris Agency - Beverly Hills, 310/274-7451

THE TAKING OF BEVERLY HILLS   Columbia, 1991,
    w/David Fuller & Rick Natkin

ERIK BURKE
LOSER   LTM, 1991, directed

MARTYN BURKE*
Agent: ICM - Beverly Hills, 310/550-4000

POWER PLAY   Magnum International Pictures/Cavry Film
    Productions, 1978, directed
TOP SECRET!   Paramount, 1984, w/Jim Abrahams, David Zucker &
    Jerry Zucker
THE LAST CHASE   Crown International, 1981,
    w/Christopher Crowe & Taylor Sutherland

Screenplays:
BIG BAND MUSIC
HOT FOOT
COUP D'ETAT
LAUGHING WAR

JEFF BURKHART*
Contact: WGA - Los Angeles, 310/550-1000

WHERE THE BOYS ARE   Tri-Star, 1984, w/Stu Krieger
DEFENSELESS   7 Arts/New Line Cinema, 1991,
   Story w/James Hicks

Screenplays:
AMERICAN TRAGEDY

STEVEN H. BURKOW*
Contact: WGA - Los Angeles, 310/550-1000

BODY SLAM   DEG, 1987, w/Shel Lytton

TOM BURMAN
MEET THE HOLLOWHEADS   Moviestore Entertainment, 1989,
   w/Lisa Morton, directed

ALAN BURNETT
DUCKTALES: THE MOVIE - THE TREASURE OF THE
   LOST LAMP (AF)   Buena Vista, 1990
BATMAN: MASK OF THE PHANTASM (AF)   Warner Bros., 1993,
   w/Paul Dini, Martin Pasco & Michael Reeves

ALLISON BURNETT*
Agent: Paradigm - Los Angeles, 310/277-4400
Manager: Robert Majeski - 213/469-0171

BLOODFIST III: FORCED TO FIGHT   Concorde, 1992,
   w/Charles Mattera
WHITE MAN'S BURDEN   1994

Screenplays:
THE ROLE OF A LIFETIME   FRECKLES
LAUGHTER IN THE DARK
SHOOTING LARGE   w/Charles Mattera
RED MEAT

CHARLES BURNETT*
Agent: Broder-Kurland-Webb-Uffner - Beverly Hills, 310/281-3400

SEVERAL FRIENDS   1969, directed
THE HORSE   1973, directed
KILLER OF SHEEP   1977, directed
BLESS THEIR LITTLE HEARTS   1982
MY BROTHER'S WEDDING   1984, directed
I FRESH   1987
TO SLEEP WITH ANGER   Samuel Goldwyn Company,
   1990, directed
THE GLASS SHIELD   Miramax, 1994, directed

Screenplays:
BLACKBIRD FLY

ROBERT BURNETT*
Agent: CAA - Beverly Hills, 310/288-4545

Screenplays:
THE REAL WORLD   w/Stephen Engel

ED BURNHAM*
Agent: The Artists Group - Los Angeles, 310/552-1100

Screenplays:
THE MARRIAGE THING   w/Elaine Newman

ALLAN BURNS*
Agent: CAA - Beverly Hills, 310/288-4545

BUTCH AND SUNDANCE: THE EARLY DAYS
   20th Century-Fox, 1979
A LITTLE ROMANCE ★   Orion/Warner Bros., 1979
JUST THE WAY YOU ARE   MGM/UA, 1984
JUST BETWEEN FRIENDS   Orion, 1986, directed

Screenplays:
HOLDING ON   DOUBLE FAULT   w/James L. Brooks
CHINA BLUES
PARENTAL GUIDANCE
HAPPY ALL THE TIME
HEARTS DESIRE

FRANCIS BURNS
(See Larry Gelbart)

JACK BURNS
Business Manager: Kaufman & Bernstein - Los Angeles,
   310/277-1900

THE MUPPET MOVIE   ITC, 1979, w/Jerry Juhl

MARK BURNS*
Agent: Broder-Kurland-Webb-Uffner - Beverly Hills, 310/281-3400

MARRIED TO THE MOB   Orion, 1988, w/Barry Strugatz
SHE-DEVIL   Orion, 1989, w/Barry Strugatz

Screenplays:
MY FAVORITE MARTIAN   w/Barry Strugatz
I OWE YOU MY LIFE   w/Barry Strugatz
ON THE LAM   w/Barry Strugatz

RICH BURNS
Agent: Writers & Artists Agency - Los Angeles, 310/824-6300

Screenplays:
A PRAIRIE TALE
HOUND DOGS

STANLEY BURNS*
Agent: Shapiro/Lichtman - Los Angeles, 310/859-8877

CHARLIE CHAN AND THE CURSE OF THE DRAGON QUEEN
   American Cinema, 1981, w/David Axelrod

TIMOTHY W. BURNS*
Agent: ICM - Beverly Hills, 310/550-4000

FREAKED   20th Century Fox, 1993, w/Tom Stern & Alex Winter

Screenplays:
COMING OF AGE
STORM CLOUDS

JIM BURNSTEIN*
Agent: Paradigm - Los Angeles, 310/277-4400

RENAISSANCE MAN   Buena Vista, 1994

Screenplays:
THE PATRICK DALY STORY

JEFF BURR
Agent: Paradigm - Los Angeles, 310/277-4400
Business: Conquest Entertainment, 9417 Wexford Drive, Tujunga,
   CA 91042, 818/352-4316

DIVIDED WE FALL   Conquest Entertainment/Pegasus Productions,
   1982, co-directed
THE OFFSPRING   FROM A WHISPER TO A SCREAM   TMS
   Pictures, 1987, w/C. Courtney Joyner & Darin Scott, co-directed

MARYEDITH BURRELL*
Contact: WGA - Los Angeles, 310/550-1000

Screenplays:
DOMINION (CTF)
BELLADONNA
MARMALADE
CHOCOLATE   w/Ginny Cerella

RICHARD BURRIDGE
Agent: Peters, Fraser & Dunlop - London, 071/376-7676

ABSOLUTE BEGINNERS   Orion, 1986, w/Don MacPherson &
   Christopher Wicking

Screenplays:
THE SCARLET PIMPERNEL
SUNDAY BEER

GEOFF BURROWES
Agent: ICM - Beverly Hills, 310/550-4000

RETURN TO SNOWY RIVER   Buena Vista, 1988,
   w/John Dixon, directed

GUY BURTON
Agent: Berzon Agency - Glendale, 818/548-1560

Screenplays:
LATENT BLOOD

MICHAEL BURTON*
Contact: Burton Films Ltd. - 213/656-6711

FLIGHT OF THE NAVIGATOR   Buena Vista, 1986,
   w/Matt MacManus
SHOOT TO KILL   Buena Vista, 1988, w/Daniel Petrie Jr. &
   Harv Zimmel

Screenplays:
THE BUSH PILOT
WHEN WORLDS COLLIDE

ROD BURTON*
Contact: WGA - Los Angeles, 310/550-1000

Screenplays:
ITALIAN BASKETBALL

TIM BURTON
Agent: CAA - Beverly Hills, 310/288-4545
Business: Tim Burton Productions, 1041 N. Formosa Ave.,
   West Hollywood, CA 90046, 213/850-2665

VINCENT (Short)   directed
FRANKENWEENIE (Short)   1984, Story, directed
EDWARD SCISSORHANDS   20th Century Fox, 1990,
   Story, directed
THE NIGHTMARE BEFORE CHRISTMAS (AF)   Buena Vista,
   1993, Story

SCOTT BUSBY*
Agent: Renaissance-H.N. Swanson - Los Angeles, 310/246-6000

Screenplays:
RANGER w/Martin Copeland
EARTH ANGEL
TROUBLED WATERS
THE RIG
CHANGE OF HEART
STRIP

STEVE BUSCEMI
Agent: Ambrosio/Mortimer - Beverly Hills, 310/274-4274

WHAT HAPPENED TO PETE (Short)   1993, directed

Screenplays:
TREES LOUNGE

CHARLES L. BUSCH*
Agent: Gold/Marshak - Burbank, 818/972-4300

PSYCHO BEACH PARTY (P)
VAMPIRE LESBIANS OF SODOM (P)
RED SCARE ON SUNSET (P)

Screenplays:
UNTITLED WITCHES PROJECT (AF)

HOWARD BUSGANG
Agent: United Talent Agency - Beverly Hills, 310/273-6700

Screenplays:
FRIEND OF THE FAMILY (Story w/Mike Binder & Mark Blutman)

KEN BUSH
Contact: 508/794-5489

Screenplays:
MY SISTER IS A STRANGER (directing)

JOHN BUSHELMAN
Contact: Directors Guild of America - Los Angeles, 310/289-2000
Address: 11972 Sunshine Terrace, Studio City, CA 91604,
   818/760-7575

THE IRON TRIANGLE   Scotti Bros., 1989, w/Larry Hilbrand &
   Eric Weston
VIOLENT ZONE   Arista Films, 1989, w/David Pritchard

AKOSUA BUSIA*
Agent: CAA - Beverly Hills, 310/288-4545

Screenplays:
SEASONS

DAVE BUSSAN
SECOND COUSIN, ONCE REMOVED   Intrepid Ventures Group,
   1994, w/Pete Ellis, John McColpin & John Shorney

OLIVER BUTCHER*
Agent: ICM - Beverly Hills, 310/550-4000

Screenplays:
REMOTE w/Tim John
A REAL MOTHER KEEPING MUM w/Tim John

DAVID BUTLER
Agent: Peters, Fraser & Dunlop - London, 071/376-7676

VOYAGE OF THE DAMNED ★   ITC, 1976, w/Steve Shagan
BEAR ISLAND   Taft International, 1980, w/Don Sharp &
   Murray Smith

MICHAEL BUTLER*
Agent: Jim Preminger Agency - Los Angeles, 310/475-9491

THE DON IS DEAD   Universal, 1973, w/Christopher Trumbo
BRANNIGAN   United Artists, 1975, w/William P. McGivern,
   William Norton & Christopher Trumbo
THE CAR   Universal, 1977, w/Dennis Shryack & Lane Slate
THE GAUNTLET   Warner Bros., 1977, w/Dennis Shryack
MURDER BY PHONE   New World, 1982, w/Dennis Shryack &
   John Kent Harrison
FLASHPOINT   Tri-Star, 1984, w/Dennis Shryack
PALE RIDER   Warner Bros., 1985, w/Dennis Shryack
CODE OF SILENCE   Orion, 1985, w/Dennis Shryack & Mike Gray
FIFTY FIFTY   Cannon, 1993, w/Dennis Shryack
WHITE MILE (CTF)   Stonehenge Productions/Viacom, 1994

Screenplays:
PRONTO
SUPER BARRIO
EMERALD CITY

THE WINDMILL MAN
ROSE & BRIAR
EXCESSIVE FORCE
THE NEGOTIATOR
PTICH POINTS
THE EXECUTIONER w/Dennis Shryack
METZGER'S DOG w/Dennis Shryack
SEIZURE w/Dennis Shryack
IRIS w/Dennis Shryack
TWO WEEKS WITH PAY w/Dennis Shryack
THE BULL w/Christopher Trumbo

ROBERT OLEN BUTLER*

Agent: Michael Siegel & Associates - Los Angeles, 310/274-5222

Screenplays:
A GOOD SCENT FROM A STRANGE MOUNTAIN

CATHERINE BUTTERFIELD

Agent: ICM - Beverly Hills, 310/550-4000

JOINED AT THE HEAD (P)

FLOYD BYARS*

Agent: Paradigm - Los Angeles, 310/277-4400

MAKING MR. RIGHT   Orion, 1987, w/Laurie Frank
MINDWALK   Triton Pictures, 1991, w/Fritjof Capra

Screenplays:
TATIANA w/Andrei Konchalovsky
SO SUE ME
BROKEN CIRCLE

DAVID BYRNE

Contact: Gary Kurfirst Management - New York, 212/957-0900

TRUE STORIES   Warner Bros., 1986, w/Beth Henley &
    Stephen Tobolowsky, directed

GABRIEL BYRNE

Agent: ICM - Beverly Hills, 310/550-4000
Business: Mirabillis Films, 40 W. 57th St., New York, NY 10019,
    212/556-5625

Screenplays:
THE LARK

JOHNNY BYRNE

Contact: British Academy of Film & Television Arts, 195 Piccadilly,
    London W1, England, 01/734-0022

TO DIE FOR   Victor Film Company, 1994

JOSEPH BYRNE*

Agent: Paul Kohner, Inc. - Beverly Hills, 310/550-1060

Screenplays:
FAST FRIENDS w/Jeb Rosebrook

JIM BYRNES*

Agent: David Shapira & Associates - Sherman Oaks, 818/906-0322

MIRACLE IN THE WILDERNESS (CTF)   Ruddy & Morgan
    Productions/Turner Pictures, 1991, w/Michael Michaelian
CONCRETE WAR   Promark Entertainment Group, 1991
DEAD MAN'S REVENGE (CTF)   MCA Television Entertainment,
    1994, w/David Chisolm

Screenplays:
YOU ONLY DIE ONCE (CTF) Story w/Matthew McDuffie
CLASH OF EAGLES
HIT MAN
BIG CITY, BIG SKY

JOHN BYRUM*

Agent: CAA - Beverly Hills, 310/288-4545

MAHOGANY   Paramount, 1975
INSERTS   United Artists, 1976, directed
HARRY AND WALTER GO TO NEW YORK   Columbia, 1976,
    w/Robert Kaufman
VALENTINO   United Artists, 1977, w/Ken Russell
HEART BEAT   Orion/Warner Bros., 1979, directed
SPHINX   Orion/Warner Bros., 1981
SCANDALOUS   Orion, 1984, w/Rob Cohen
THE RAZOR'S EDGE   Columbia, 1984, w/Bill Murray, directed

Screenplays:
THE RECOVERY w/Rob Cohen
YOUNG MEN WITH UNLIMITED CAPITAL
BUYOUT
THE CONFIDENCE MAN

C

DAN CAHILL

Agent: United Talent Agency - Beverly Hills, 310/273-6700

Screenplays:
THE SHADOW WAR w/Claude Kerven

GERARD M. CAHILL*

Contact: WGA - Los Angeles, 310/550-1000

SURVIVAL RUN   *SPREE*   Film Ventures, 1978, w/Frederic Shore &
    Larry Spiegel

BARRY CAILLIER

DAREDREAMER   Lensman Co., 1989, w/Pat Royce, directed

ALAN CAILOU*

Agent: Reece Halsey Agency - Los Angeles, 213/652-2409

CLARENCE THE CROSS-EYED LION   MGM, 1965, w/Art Arthur &
    Marshall Thompson
EVIL KNIEVAL   MGM, 1971, w/John Milius
KINGDOM OF THE SPIDERS   Dimension, 1977,
    w/Richard Robinson

CHRISTOPHER CAIN

Agent: ICM - Beverly Hills, 310/550-4000

SIXTH AND MAIN   National Cinema, 1977, directed

DEAN CAIN

Contact: Screen Actors Guild - Los Angeles, 213/954-1600

Screenplays:
LOVE KILLS

JEFFREY CAINE*

Agent: Shapiro/Lichtman - Los Angeles, 310/859-8877

Screenplays:
HEROIC MEASURES
BUDDY
VINTAGE MUSCATEL
THE COLTSVILLE COTTON MILLS

YULE CAISE*
Agent: CAA - Beverly Hills, 310/288-4545

Screenplays:
FREE OF EDEN

JOSEPH M. CALA
ANGEL   New World, 1984, w/Robert Vincent O'Neil
AVENGING ANGEL   New World, 1985, w/Robert Vincent O'Neil

PHILIPPE CALAND
BOXING HELENA   Orion, 1993, Story

WIL CALHOUN
Agent: ICM - Beverly Hills, 310/550-4000

THE BALCONY SCENE (P)
CALL IT CLOVER (P)

PETER CALLAHAN
Agent: Jon Klane Agency - Beverly Hills, 310/278-0178

Screenplays:
IN SPITE OF LOVE
GOOD INTENTIONS
BOSTON STORY

ANNE CAMERON
TICKET TO HEAVEN   United Artists Classics, 1981,
   w/R.L. Thomas

JAMES CAMERON*
Contact: Bert Fields, Greenberg, Glusker, Fields, Claman &
   Machtinger - Los Angeles, 310/553-3610
Business: Lightstorm Entertainment, 919 Santa Monica Blvd.,
   Santa Monica, CA 90401, 310/587-2500

THE TERMINATOR   Orion, 1984, w/Gale Anne Hurd, directed
RAMBO: FIRST BLOOD PART II   Tri-Star, 1985,
   w/Sylvester Stallone
ALIENS   20th Century Fox, 1986, directed
THE ABYSS   20th Century Fox, 1989, directed
TERMINATOR 2: JUDGMENT DAY   Tri-Star, 1991,
   w/William Wisher, directed
TRUE LIES   20th Century Fox, 1994, directed
STRANGE DAYS   20th Century Fox, 1995

Screenplays:
SPIDERMAN (Carolco, directing)

JULIA CAMERON
PUBLIC LIVES (P)
BLOOD LINES (P)
AMERICAN BOY (FD)   1978
GOD'S WILL   Power and Light Productions, 1989, directed

Screenplays:
THE BEST TABLE
NORMAL MURDER
LUDES
OZARK
THE WORKS
MILE STRAIGHT DOWN
TWINKLE

KEN CAMERON
Agent: Becsey/Wisdom/Kalajian Agency - Los Angeles, 310/550-0535
Business: Pavilion Films, 117 Blues Point Road, McMahons Point,
   NSW Australia 2060, 02/92-8358

MONKEY GRIP   Cinecom, 1982, w/Helen Garner, directed
FAST TALKING   Cinecom, 1986, directed

LORNE CAMERON*
Agent: The Rothman Agency - Beverly Hills, 213/655-2020

LIKE FATHER LIKE SON   Tri-Star, 1987, w/Steven Bloom
CLARENCE (CTF)   Atlantis Films/Northstar Entertainment/South
   Pacific Pictures, 1990, w/David Hoselton

Screenplays:
FIRST KNIGHT   w/David Hoselton (Columbia)
CUPID
COURTING

E.J. CAMFIELD
Agent: Metropolitan Talent Agency - Los Angeles, 213/857-4500

Screenplays:
BARRACUDA
NEPHITE

PAUL CAMINI
SILENT NIGHT, DEADLY NIGHT   Tri-Star, 1984, Story

CHINA CAMMELL
WHITE OF THE EYE   Palisades Entertainment, 1987,
   w/Donald Cammell

Screenplays:
THE WILDSIDE w/Donald Cammell (August Entertainment)

DONALD CAMMELL*
Agent: William Morris Agency - Beverly Hills, 310/274-7451

DUFFY   Columbia, 1968, w/Harry Joe Brown Jr.
PERFORMANCE   Warner Bros., 1970, co-directed
TILT   Warner Bros., 1979, w/Rudy Durand
WHITE OF THE EYE   Palisades Entertainment, 1987,
   w/China Cammell, directed
CENTRIFUGE   Vestron, 1990, w/J.C. Pollack

Screenplays:
THE WILDSIDE w/China Cammell (August Entertainment, directing)
ALAMO GORDO w/Ken Finkleman
THE LAST VIDEO
A COFFIN FOR DIMITRIOS

JOE CAMP*
Business: Mulberry Square Productions, 1407 Jackson Ave. - Suite 5,
   Pascagoulla, MS 39567, 601/769-1993

BENJI   Mulberry Square, 1974, directed
FOR THE LOVE OF BENJI   Mulberry Square, 1978, directed
OH, HEAVENLY DOG!   20th Century-Fox, 1980,
   w/Rod Browning, directed
BENJI: THE HUNTED   Buena Vista, 1987, directed

Screenplays:
BENJI-BENJI (Vision International, directing)

TOM CAMP*
Contact: WGA - Los Angeles, 310/550-1000

SHARK (P)

Screenplays:
HASENPFEFFER IN THE TORRID ZONE
DISCREET COMPANY
ANGEL PANGS
WEATHERCHILD

JUAN CAMPANELLA
Agent: William Morris Agency - Beverly Hills, 310/274-7451

Screenplays:
HOT WHISKEY & LEMON

BRUCE L. CAMPBELL*
Agent: APA - Los Angeles, 310/273-0744

Screenplays:
BRUCE CAMPBELL'S THE MAN WITH THE SCREAMING BRAIN
 (IRS, directing)
THE CLUMSY IDIOT w/Scott Spiegel & Ron Zwang

CLIFTON CAMPBELL*
Contact: WGA - Los Angeles, 310/550-1000

CHECKERS (P)
NATIVOS (P)
EMERALD TREE BOA (P)
THE FIGURE (P)
TETHER DISORDER (P)

Screenplays:
PUNTA GORDA
LOVING WIFE
THE ACCORD
POWDER BLUE
OF SOUND MIND AND BODY
A MENTION OF HER FORMER SELF
STROKE OF GENIUS
ACT OF ATTRITION

DARREL CAMPBELL*
Agent: United Talent Agency - Beverly Hills, 310/273-6700

THE PISTOL: BIRTH OF A LEGEND   Premier Pictures, 1991

Screenplays:
THE LAST BANDIT
THE BIRD'S CHRISTMAS CAROL

DOUG CAMPBELL
Agent: Carl Belfor Entertainment Management Company -
 Sherman Oaks, 818/994-8095

SEASON OF FEAR   MGM/UA, 1989, directed

KEVIN CAMPBELL
THE RETURN OF JAFAR (AHVF)   Buena Vista, 1994,
 w/Mirith J.S. Colao, Bill Motz, Steve Roberts, Bob Roth,
 Jan Strand & Brian Swenlin

JANE CAMPION
Agent: CAA - Beverly Hills, 310/288-4545

SWEETIE   Avenue Pictures, 1989, w/Gerard Lee, directed
THE PIANO ★★   Miramax, 1993, directed

CHRISTOPHER CANAAN*
Agent: Paradigm - Los Angeles, 310/277-4400

THE TEN MILLION DOLLAR GETAWAY   Alvin Cooperman
 Productions/Wilshire Court Productions, 1991

Screenplays:
CALEXICO
FULL COURT PRESS
OUT

ALEX CANAWATI
INEVITABLE GRACE   Silverstar Pictures, 1994, directed

DORAN WILLIAM CANNON*
Contact: WGA - Los Angeles, 310/550-1000

THE SQUARE ROOT OF ZERO   Mark-L Entertainment,
 1965, directed
SKIDOO   Paramount, 1968
BREWSTER McCLOUD   MGM, 1970

DYAN CANNON
Contact: Directors Guild of America - Los Angeles, 310/289-2000

NUMBER ONE (Short) ★   1976, directed
THE END OF INNOCENCE   Skouras Pictures, 1990, directed

MICHAEL ALAN CANTER*
Agent: Pleshette & Green - Los Angeles, 213/465-0428

Screenplays:
BAD MANNERS
THE LAST RESORT

JAY CANTOR
Agent: Michael Siegel & Associates - Los Angeles, 310/274-5222

Screenplays:
JANE EYRE
WALTZ INTO DARKNESS

DONALD CANTRELL
O.C. AND STIGGS   MGM/UA, 1987, w/Ted Mann

PETER CAPALDI
Agent: Ken McReddie, 91 Regent St., London W1R 7TB,
 071/439-1456, fax 734-6530

SOFT TOP HARD SHOULDER   Mayfair Entertainment
 International, 1993

LEON CAPETANOS*
Agent: William Morris Agency - Beverly Hills, 310/274-7451

SUMMER RUN   Lighthouse, 1974, directed
THE GUMBALL RALLY   Warner Bros., 1976
GREASED LIGHTNING   Warner Bros., 1977, w/Lawrence Dukone,
 Melvin Van Peebles & Kenneth Vose
TEMPEST   Columbia, 1982, w/Paul Mazursky
MOSCOW ON THE HUDSON   Columbia, 1984, w/Paul Mazursky
DOWN AND OUT IN BEVERLY HILLS   Buena Vista, 1986,
 w/Paul Mazursky
MOON OVER PARADOR   Universal, 1988, w/Paul Mazursky
FLETCH LIVES   Universal, 1989

Screenplays:
NIRVANA w/Paul Mazursky
MEET THE MORON
LAST MAN AT ARLINGTON
WHITE ON WHITE
LOST CITY
NIAGARA FALLS
MISSING PERSON
SCHOOL DAYS

DUANE CAPIZZI
THE RETURN OF JAFAR (AHVF)   Buena Vista, 1994,
 Story w/Douglas Langdale, Mark McCorkle, Robert Schooley &
 Tad Stories

LOREN-PAUL CAPLIN*
Agent: William Morris Agency - Beverly Hills, 310/274-7451

A SUBJECT OF CHILDHOOD (P)
MEN IN THE KITCHEN (P)
CITY MUSIC (P)
GANGS (P)   also screenplay
BATTLE IN THE EROGENOUS ZONE (Short)   Showtime, 1992,
 w/John Drimmer

Screenplays:
LOVE, FAME AND MONEY
BORDER RADIO
MICKEY'S MONKEY
KIT AND NEVADA

CARMINE CAPOBIANCO
CEMETARY HIGH   Titan Productions, 1989, w/Gorman Bechard

CARL CAPOTORTO
Contact: Chesterfield Film Co. - 818/777-3425

Screenplays:
FRAN'S THING

JAMES CAPPE*
Agent: Jim Preminger Agency - Los Angeles, 310/475-9491

THE ADVENTURES OF FORD FAIRLANE   20th Century Fox,
   1990, w/David Arnott & Daniel Waters

Screenplays:
A NIGHTMARE ON ELM STREET PART 6
GHOST OF A CHANCE (Shared)
THE INVADERS

FRANK CAPPELLO*
Manager: Jon Brown, The Brown Group - Burbank, 818/955-7040
Business Manager: Steve Warren, Hansen, Jacobsen & Teller -
   Los Angeles, 310/278-8622

SUBURBAN COMMANDO   New Line Cinema, 1991

Screenplays:
DUMMIES

BERNT CAPRA
Contact: Swiss Film Center, Munstergasse 18, 8001 Zurich,
   Switzerland, 01/472860

MINDWALK   Triton Pictures, 1991, Story, directed

JIM CARABATSOS*
Agent: Shapiro/Lichtman - Los Angeles, 310/859-8877

HEROES   Universal, 1977
BEYOND THE REEF   Universal, 1981, w/Louis LaRusso II
UNDERGROUND ACES   Filmways, 1981, w/Leonore Wright &
   Andrew Peter Marin
NO MERCY   Tri-Star, 1986
HEARTBREAK RIDGE   Warner Bros., 1986
HAMBURGER HILL   Tri-Star, 1987

Screenplays:
NATIONS
CRUISE w/Steven Seagal
UNWANTED ATTENTIONS

STEVEN W. CARABATSOS*
Contact: WGA - Los Angeles, 310/550-1000

EL CONDOR   National General, 1970, w/Larry Cohen
TENTACLES   20th Century-Fox, 1977, w/others
THE LAST FLIGHT OF NOAH'S ARK   Buena Vista, 1980,
   w/George Arthur Bloom & Sandy Glass
HOT PURSUIT   Paramount, 1987, w/Steven Lisberger

WALTER CARBONE
SOMETHING SPECIAL WILLY MILLY/I WAS A TEENAGE BOY
   Cinema Group, 1986, w/Carla Reuben

FRANK CARDEA*
Agent: Major Clients Agency - Los Angeles, 310/284-6400

DYING TO REMEMBER (CTF)   USA Network, 1993,
   w/Brian L. Ross & George Schenck

J. S. CARDONE*
(Joseph S. Cardone)
Agent: Jon Klane Agency - Beverly Hills, 310/278-0178

THE SLAYER   21st Century Distribution, 1982,
   w/William R. Ewing, directed
THUNDER ALLEY   Cannon, 1985, directed
CRASH AND BURN   Full Moon Entertainment, 1990
SHADOW ZONE   Paramount, 1990, directed
A ROW OF CROWS CLIMATE FOR KILLING   Propaganda Films,
   1991, directed
SHADOWHUNTER (CTF)   Republic Pictures, 1993, directed

Screenplays:
BLACK DAY, BLUE NIGHT (directing)
CONGO SQUARE
UNDER THE WIRE
COLD HEAT
THE MUMMY AND THE ARMADILLO
FALLOUT

MARK PATRICK CARDUCCI*
Agent: Susan Smith & Associates - Beverly Hills, 213/852-4777

PUMPKINHEAD   MGM/UA, 1988, w/Gary Gerani
BURIED ALIVE (CTF)   MCA Entertainment, 1990
FLYING SAUCERS OVER HOLLYWOOD: THE PLAN 9
   COMPANION (FD)   Atomic Pictures, 1993

Screenplays:
THE COMIC AND THE CON
LIGHT AT THE END
HOB
LITTLE ITALY
HALLOWEENIES

TOPPER CAREW*
Agent: ICM - Beverly Hills, 310/550-4000

D.C. CAB   Universal, 1983, Story w/Joel Schumacher
TALKIN' DIRTY AFTER DARK   New Line Cinema, 1991, directed

PETER CAREY
Agent: London Management - London, 011/441/493-1610

BLISS   New World, 1986, w/Ray Lawrence
UNTIL THE END OF THE WORLD   Warner Bros., 1991,
   w/Wim Wenders

CARLO CARLEI
Agent: ICM - Beverly Hills, 310/550-4000

THE FLIGHT OF THE INNNOCENT   MGM/UA, 1993,
   w/Gualtiero Rosella, directed
FLUKE   MGM/UA, 1995, w/James Carrington, directed

JOHN CARLEN*
Agent: The Gersh Agency - Beverly Hills, 310/274-6611
Manager: Stan Kamens - 310/288-4500

BLIND SIDE (CTF)   Chestnut Hill Productions, 1993,
   w/Stewart Lindh & Solomon Weingarten

Screenplays:
FIELDS OF VISION
TABLE DANCING
PARADISE ROAD

CLANCY CARLILE
HONKYTONK MAN   Warner Bros., 1982

ANNE CARLISLE
LIQUID SKY   Cinevista, 1983, w/Slava Tsukerman &
   Nina V. Kerova

LEWIS JOHN CARLINO*
Agent: CAA - Beverly Hills, 310/288-4545

TELEMACHUS (P)
SECONDS   Paramount, 1966
THE BROTHERHOOD   Paramount, 1968
THE FOX   Warner Bros., 1968, w/Howard Koch
THE MECHANIC   United Artists, 1972
A REFLECTION OF FEAR   Columbia, 1973, w/Edward Hume
CRAZY JOE   Columbia, 1974
THE SAILOR WHO FELL FROM GRACE WITH THE SEA
   Avco Embassy, 1976, directed
I NEVER PROMISED YOU A ROSE GARDEN ★   New World,
   1977, w/Gavin Lambert
THE GREAT SANTINI   THE ACE   Orion/Warner Bros.,
   1980, directed
RESURRECTION   Universal, 1980
HAUNTED SUMMER   Cannon, 1988

Screenplays:
CENTERFOLD
STRANGER IN A STRANGE LAND
SALINAS
THE ANDREASSON AFFAIR   PHENOMENON
KIN

JIM CARLSON*
Agent: Monteiro Rose Agency - Encino, 818/501-1177

POUND PUPPIES AND THE LEGEND OF BIG PAW (AF)
   Tri-Star, 1988, w/Terrence McDonnell

MATTHEW J. CARLSON*
Agent: CAA - Beverly Hills, 310/288-4545

WAGONS EAST!   TriStar, 1994

Screenplays:
BUZZ ORBIT

ROY CARLSON*
Agent: United Talent Agency - Beverly Hills, 310/273-6700

STAND ALONE   New World, 1985
THE WRONG MAN (CTF)   Polygram/Viacom Pictures, 1993, Story
CHINA MOON   Orion, 1994

Screenplays:
TILL DEATH DO US PART
YANKEE WHITE
DEEP UMBRA
LIME GREEN IN THE HIGH GROUND
COLLISION   (shared)
THE TENDER
MARTHA HONEY

CLARK CARLTON
VALET GIRLS   Empire Pictures, 1987

DON CARMODY
Agent: Gray/Goodman Inc. - Beverly Hills, 310/276-7070

WHISPERS   Live Home Video, 1990, Adaptation
THE HIT MAN   Cannon, 1991, w/Robert Geoffrion

MICHAEL CARMODY
SYNGENOR   South Gate Entertainment, 1990, Story

MATTHEW CARNAHAN*
Agent: CAA - Beverly Hills, 310/288-4545

KNEES OF A CELLIST (P)
BIG LOVE BURNING (P)

Screenplays:
BLACK CIRCLE BOYS

CHARLES ROBERT CARNER*
Agent: CAA - Beverly Hills, 310/288-4545
Business: South Side Films Inc., 1855 Westridge Rd., Los Angeles,
   CA 90049, 310/471-2758

GYMKATA   MGM/UA, 1985
LET'S GET HARRY   Tri-Star, 1986
BLIND FURY   Tri-Star, 1990

Screenplays:
THE FIXER
THE BATTLING SPUMONTI BROTHERS
THE ADVENTURES OF JONATHAN CABOT
AMERICAN PIE
CRIME OF THE CENTURY
DEAD HEAT OF SUMMER
THE DEFIER OF FATE
THE FOX
HOT CARGO
LION OF IRELAND
THE LONELY ONE
MAZE
MONEY TO BURN
THE PROTECTOR
QUEEN BEE
SILENT SERVICE
SIMON SAYS
WARLORD
YOUNG EVE

GLENN GORDON CARON*
Agent: CAA - Beverly Hills, 310/288-4545
Business: Picturemaker Productions, Paramount - 310/581-6608

CONDORMAN   Buena Vista, 1981, w/Mickey Rose &
   Marc Stirdivant

Screenplays:
EVITA
KNOWING DAMON

A.J. CAROTHERS*
Agent: The Coppage Company - North Hollywood, 818/980-1106

THE MIRACLE OF THE WHITE STALLIONS   Buena Vista, 1963
EMIL AND THE DETECTIVE   Buena Vista, 1964
THE HAPPIEST MILLIONAIRE   Buena Vista, 1967
NEVER A DULL MOMENT   Buena Vista, 1968
HERO AT LARGE   MGM/United Artists, 1980
THE SECRET OF MY SUCCESS   Universal, 1987, w/Jim Cash &
   Jack Epps Jr.

Screenplays:
IT'S NEVER TOO LATE (remake)
MERMAID w/Robert Towne
JAZZ BABIES
THE THIRTEEN CLOCKS
HANSEL & GRETEL
FANCY HARDWARE
PIANO SOLO
WHISKEY MAN
THE GIRL WITH THE GOLDEN HAIR
STAIRWAY TO HEAVEN
ADAM'S RIB
JEFFERSON McGRAW
FREE SPIRIT
TEMPTING FATE
EXECUTIVE PRIVILEGE

DAVID CARPENTER*
Agent: United Talent Agency - Beverly Hills, 310/273-6700

Screenplays:
MOM IS A TREASURE HUNTER w/Colin Greene & Tim Kirk
HACKER w/Tim Kirk

FRED CARPENTER
SMALL KILL   Rayfield Co., 1992, w/James McTernan

JOHN CARPENTER*
Agent: ICM - Beverly Hills, 310/550-4000

DARK STAR   Jack H. Harris Enterprises, 1974,
   w/Dan O'Bannon, directed
ASSAULT ON PRECINCT 13   Turtle Releasing Corporation,
   1976, directed
THE EYES OF LAURA MARS   Columbia, 1978,
   w/David Z. Goodman
HALLOWEEN   Compass International, 1978, w/Debra Hill, directed
HALLOWEEN II   Universal, 1981, w/Debra Hill
THE FOG   Avco Embassy, 1981, w/Debra Hill, directed
ESCAPE FROM NEW YORK   Avco Embassy, 1981,
   w/Nick Castle, directed
BLACK MOON RISING   New World, 1986, w/William Gray &
   Desmond Nakano
PRINCE OF DARKNESS   Universal, 1987,
   as "Martin Quatermass," directed
THEY LIVE   Universal, 1989, as "Frank Armitage," directed
EL DIABLO (CTF)   Wizan/Black Productions, 1990, w/Bill Philips &
   Tommy Lee Wallace

Screenplays:
MELTDOWN w/Robert Roy Pool (Miramax)

RICHARD CARPENTER
THE BORROWERS (CTF)   Working Title Television/BBC-TV/
   Turner Network, 1993

STEPHEN W. CARPENTER*
Agent: United Talent Agency - Beverly Hills, 310/273-6700
Contact: Lichter, Grossman & Nichols - Los Angeles, 310/205-6999

THE DORM THAT DRIPPED BLOOD   *PRANKS*   Artists Releasing
   Corporation/Film Ventures International, 1982, w/Jeffrey Obrow &
   Stacey Giachino, co-directed
THE POWER   Artists Releasing Corporation/Film Ventures
   International, 1984, w/Jeffrey Obrow, co-directed
THE KINDRED   FM Entertainment, 1987, w/others, co-directed
THE SERVANTS OF TWILIGHT   Trimark Pictures, 1991,
   w/Jeffrey Obrow

Screenplays:
HOUSE ARREST w/Jerry Leichtling & Arlene Sarner
BUSYBODIES
STEALING HEARTS
SEVENTH HEAVEN

ALLAN CARR*
Business: Allan Carr Enterprises, P.O. Box 691670, Los Angeles,
   CA 90069, 310/278-2490

CAN'T STOP THE MUSIC   AFD, 1980, w/Bronte Woodard

COLBY CARR
Agent: Broder-Kurland-Webb-Uffner - Beverly Hills, 310/281-3400

BLANK CHECK   Buena Vista, 1994, w/Blake Snyder

Screenplays:
THIRD GRADE w/Blake Snyder
HERBIE COME HOME w/Blake Snyder

RICHARD CARR
MAN FROM DEL RIO   United Artists, 1956
TOO LATE BLUES   Paramount, 1961, w/John Cassavetes
HELL IS FOR HEROES   Paramount, 1962, w/Robert Pirosh
HEAVEN WITH A GUN   MGM, 1969
AMERICANA   Crown International, 1983

MICHAEL CARRERAS
Contact: British Academy of Film & Television Arts, 195 Piccadilly,
   London W1, England, 71/734-0022

THE UNHOLY FOUR   *THE STRANGER CAME HOME*
   Exclusvie, 1954
CURSE OF THE MUMMY'S TOMB   Columbia, 1964,
   as "Henry Younger"
PREHISTORIC WOMEN   *SLAVE GIRLS*   Hammer,
   1966, directed
ONE MILLION YEARS B.C.   Hammer, 1966
CREATURES THE WORLD FORGOT   Columbia, 1970

JIM CARREY*
Agent: United Talent Agency - Beverly Hills, 310/273-6700

ACE VENTURA, PET DETECTIVE   Warner Bros., 1994,
   w/Jack Bernstein & Tom Shadyac

JEAN-CLAUDE CARRIERE
THE SUITOR   CAPAC, 1962, w/Pierre Etaix
THE DIARY OF A CHAMBERMAID   Speva, 1964,
   w/Luis Bunuel
VIVA MARIA!   United Artists, 1965, w/Louis Malle
HOTEL PARADISO   MGM, 1966, w/Peter Glenville
THE MILKY WAY   United Artists, 1967, w/Luis Bunuel
BELLE DE JOUR   Allied Artists, 1967, w/Luis Bunuel
BORSALINO   Paramount, 1970, w/Jean Cau, Jacues Deray &
   Claude Sautet
TAKING OFF   Universal, 1971, w/Milos Forman, John Guare &
   John Klein
THE DISCREET CHARM OF THE BOURGEOISIE ★
   20th Century-Fox, 1972, w/Luis Bunuel
THAT OBSCURE OBJECT OF DESIRE ★   First Artists, 1977,
   w/Luis Bunuel
A BUTTERFLY ON THE SHOULDER   *UN PAPILLON SUR
   L'EPAULE*   Gaumont, 1978, w/Tonino Guerra
THE TIN DRUM   New World, 1980, w/Franz Seitz &
   Volker Schlondorff
SAUVE QUIE PEUT LA VIE   *EVERY MAN FOR HIMSELF IN LIFE*
   New Yorker/Zoetrope, 1980, w/Anne-Marie Mieville &
   Jean-Luc Godard
THE ASSOCIATE   Quartet, 1982, w/Rene Gainville
CIRCLE OF DECEIT   United Artists Classics, 1982,
   w/Volker Schlondorff, Margarethe von Trotta & Kai Hermann
THE RETURN OF MARTIN GUERRE   European International,
   1983, w/Daniel Vigne
DANTON   Triumph, 1983
SWANN IN LOVE   Orion Classics, 1984, w/Peter Brook &
   Marie-Helen Estienne
THE UNBEARABLE LIGHTNESS OF BEING ★   Orion, 1988,
   w/Philip Kaufman
THE MAHABHARATA   MK2 USA, 1989
VALMONT   Orion, 1989
MAY FOOLS   Orion Classics, 1990, w/Louis Malle
CYRANO DE BERGERAC   Orion Classics, 1990,
   w/Jean-Paul Rappeneau
AT PLAY IN THE FIELDS OF THE LORD   Universal, 1991,
   w/Hector Babenco
THE RETURN OF CASANOVA   (No Distributor), 1992,
   w/Edouard Niermans
THE NIGHT AND THE MOMENT   Miramax, 1994,
   w/Anna-Maria Tato

Screenplays:
BLACK ANGEL w/Philip Kaufman

MATHIEU CARRIERE
BEETHOVEN'S NEPHEW   New World, 1988, w/Paul Morrissey

JAMES CARRINGTON
FLUKE   MGM/UA, 1995, w/Carlo Carlei

ROBERT B. CARRINGTON

Agent: Jerome S. Siegel Associates - Los Angeles, 213/850-1275

KALEIDOSCOPE   Warner Bros., 1966
WAIT UNTIL DARK   Warner Bros., 1967,
   w/Jane Howard-Carrington
FEAR IS THE KEY   Paramount, 1973
VENOM   Paramount, 1982

Screenplays:
A FESTIVAL OF FEAR
ARE YOU ALONE TONIGHT?
THE PLAYPEN
COLD WAR SWAP
DEATH TRACK
THE DONOR
DEATHWORK

J. LARRY CARROLL*

Agent: Shapiro/Lichtman - Los Angeles, 310/859-8877

THE DAY TIME ENDED   Compass International, 1979,
   w/Wayne Schmidt & David Schmoeller

JAMES CARROLL

Manager: Creative Alliance Management - Los Angeles,
   213/962-6090

Screenplays:
MADONNA RED   w/Arthur Sherman

JONATHAN CARROLL

Agent: Renaissance-H.N. Swanson - Los Angeles, 310/246-6000

Screenplays:
KISSING THE BEEHIVE
AFTER SILENCE

TOD CARROLL*

Agent: ICM - Beverly Hills, 310/550-4000

NATIONAL LAMPOON'S MOVIE MADNESS   United Artists, 1982,
   w/Shary Flenniken, Pat Mephitis, Gerald Sussman & Ellis Weiner
O.C. AND STIGGS   MGM/UA, 1987, Story
CLEAN AND SOBER   Warner Bros., 1988

Screenplays:
EVERYTHING IS BEAUTIFUL
REDEMPTION
WOMEN ON THE VERGE OF A NERVOUS BREAKDOWN   (remake)
BUTLERS
LA TULIPE
MY GOD THEY'VE GOT BOSCO
LES COMPERES   (remake)

WILLARD F. CARROLL*

Business: Hyperion Entertainment, 837 Tracton Avenue - Suite 402,
   Los Angeles, CA 90013, 213/625-2921

THE RUNESTONE   Hyperion Pictures, 1992, directed

Screenplays:
FULL MOON

RODNEY CARR-SMITH

BARTLEBY   Pantheon, 1970, w/Anthony Friedmann, directed
LOLLY MADONNA XXX   MGM, 1973, w/Sue Grafton

L. M. KIT CARSON*

Manager: Elkins Entertainment - 310/285-0700

DAVID HOLZMAN'S DIARY   Grove Press, 1967, w/Jim McBride
THE LEXINGTON EXPERIENCE (FD)   Korda, 1971
THE AMERICAN DREAMER (FD)   EYR, 1971, w/Dennis Hopper &
   Laurence Schiller

THE LAST WORD   Samuel Goldwyn Company, 1979,
   w/Greg Smith & Michael Varhol
BREATHLESS   Orion, 1983, w/Jim McBride
PARIS, TEXAS   TLC Films/20th Century-Fox, 1984, Adaptation
CHINESE BOXES   Chris Sievernich Productions/Palace
   Productions, 1984
THE TEXAS CHAINSAW MASSACRE PART 2   Cannon, 1986

Screenplays:
THE CHALLENGER   w/Jim McBride
HONEYSUCKLE COTTAGE   w/Jim McBride
ELEKTRA ASSASSIN   w/Jim McBride
THE MOVIEGOER   w/Jim McBride
CAGE
THE NEGOTIATOR (CTF)
NORIEGA VERDAD (CTF)
SWEETHEARTS
VAMPIRE BLUES

RUTH CARTER

COMING UP ROSES   Skouras Pictures, 1987

DEE CARUSO*

Contact: WGA - Los Angeles, 310/550-1000

WHICH WAY TO THE FRONT?   Warner Bros., 1970,
   w/Gerald Gardner
THE WORLD'S GREATEST ATHLETE   Buena Vista, 1973,
   w/Gerald Gardner
DOIN' TIME   The Ladd Company/Warner Bros., 1984,
   w/Franelle Silver & Ron Zwang

CARROLL CARTWRIGHT

Agent: Innovative Artists - Los Angeles, 310/553-5200

Screenplays:
HELLO, STRANGER   w/Topper Lilien
CLOSING ARGUMENT   w/Topper Lilien
YOU PLAY THE BLACK AND THE RED COMES UP   w/Topper Lilien

GARY D. CARTWRIGHT*

Contact: WGA - Los Angeles, 310/550-1000

J.W. COOP   Columbia, 1971, w/Cliff Robertson & Bud Shrake

STEVE CARVER

Agent: Shapiro/Lichtman - Los Angeles, 310/859-8877

BULLETPROOF   CineTel Films, 1987, w/T.L. Lankford, directed

CORT CASADY*

Contact: Ernest Del, Del, Rubel, Shaw, Mason & Derin -
   310/772-2000

Screenplays:
UNDERGROUND

DAVID CASCI*

Agent: Warden, White & Kane - Beverly Hills, 213/852-1028

EXTENDEND PLAY (Short)   1990, directed
THE PAGEMASTER   20th Century Fox, 1994, w/David Kirschner &
   Ernie Contreras

Screenplays:
CATCHING RAYS   w/Jeffrey Hilton
KIDSTUFF   w/Jeffrey Hilton
PANAMANIA   w/Jeffrey Hilton
TOM, DICK AND HARRY
TEMPORARY INCONVENIENCE
REMOTE
TOADY

F
I
L
M

W
R
I
T
E
R
S

RON CASDEN*
Agent: The Agency - Los Angeles, 310/551-3000

Screenplays:
TRIADS w/Michael Blodgett
THE ANSWERMAN
SUPERSTITION
MY UNCLE FELIX
RUNNING THE AMAZON

MARTY CASELLA*
Agent: Renaissance-H.N. Swanson - Los Angeles, 310/246-6000
Manager: Krost/Chapin Management - 310/281-3595

PAPER MOON (P)

Screenplays:
ONE NIGHT STAND (New Horizons/New World)

RICHARD CASEY
HELLBENT   Hellbent Productions, 1989, directed

JIM CASH*
Agent: CAA - Beverly Hills, 310/288-4545

TOP GUN   Paramount, 1986, w/Jack Epps Jr.
LEGAL EAGLES   Universal, 1986, w/Jack Epps Jr.
THE SECRET OF MY SUCCESS   Universal, 1987,
   w/A.J. Carothers & Jack Epps Jr.
TURNER & HOOCH   Buena Vista, 1989, w/Jack Epps Jr.,
   Daniel Petrie Jr., Michael Blodgett & Dennis Shryack
DICK TRACY   Buena Vista, 1990, w/Jack Epps Jr.

Screenplays:
HAWAII FIVE-0 w/Jack Epps Jr.
SUMMERTIME BLUES w/Jack Epps Jr.
REVENGE OF BLACKTHORN w/Jack Epps Jr.
WHEREABOUTS w/Jack Epps Jr.
DANGEROUSLY w/Jack Epps Jr. & Bennett Tramer
MR. MAYOR w/Jack Epps Jr.
MILWAUKEE CONFIDENTIAL w/Jack Epps Jr.
DIRTY FIVE w/Jack Epps Jr.
DIVIDING LINE w/Jack Epps Jr.

NICK CASSAVETES
Agent: ICM - Beverly Hills, 310/550-4000

Screenplays:
UNHOOK THE STARS (directing)
THE CARDS ARE WILD w/John Cassavetes

SHAUN CASSIDY*
Agent: ICM - Beverly Hills, 310/550-4000

STRAYS (CTF)   Niki Marvin Productions-MTE, 1991

P.J. CASTELLANETA
Agent: Renaissance-H.N. Swanson - Los Angeles, 310/246-6000

TOGETHER ALONE   Frameline, 1992, directed

SERGIO M. CASTILLA
THE GIRL IN THE WATERMELON   Mommy & Daddy Productions,
   1994, directed

ALAN CASTLE
STRANDED   New Line Cinema, 1987

ALIEN CASTLE
DESIRE & HELL AT SUNSET MOTEL   Two Moon Releasing,
   1992, directed
STREETWISE   Trimark, 1993, w/Robert Vincent O'Neil

NICK CASTLE▲
Agent: CAA - Beverly Hills, 310/288-4545

SKATETOWN, U.S.A.   Columbia, 1979
PRAY TV   Filmways, 1980
ESCAPE FROM NEW YORK   Avco Embassy, 1981,
   w/John Carpenter
TAG   New World, 1982, directed
KISS ME KILL ME   New World, 1982
THE BOY WHO COULD FLY   20th Century Fox, 1986, directed
TAP   Tri-Star, 1989, directed
HOOK   Tri-Star, 1991, Story w/Jim Hart

Screenplays:
HAROLD SQUARE w/Marc Mueller & Craig Safan
MY GENERATION

ROBERT CASWELL*
Agent: Sanford-Gross & Associates - Los Angeles, 310/208-2100

A CRY IN THE DARK   Warner Bros., 1988, w/Fred Schepisi
THE DOCTOR   Buena Vista, 1991
OVER THE HILL   Greater Union Distributors, 1992
A FAR OFF PLACE   Buena Vista, 1993, w/Jonathan Hensleigh &
   Sally Robinson

Screenplays:
FLOATING HEARTS
CHILDREN OF DUST
THUNDER

E.A. CAVALIER
Contact: Flipped Out Productions - 213/935-7810

Screenplays:
HELMET HEAD: GIRL HERO
DOG BREATH

THOMAS B. CAVANAGH*
Agent: The Wright Concept - Burbank, 818/954-8943

Screenplays:
THE MONSTER UNDER MY BED
THE PRESENCE
HOMETOWN HERO
SIGHT UNSEEN
IF ONLY

TONY CAVANAUGH
FATHER   Northern Arts Entertainment, 1992, w/Graham Hartley

JEFF CELENTANO
Agent: ICM - Beverly Hills, 310/550-4000
Contact: Jersey Born Pictures, 7920 Sunset Blvd. - 4th Floor,
   Los Angeles, CA 90046, 213/850—0919

DICKWAD (Short) 1993, directed

Screenplays:
UNDER THE HULA MOON w/Gregory Webb (directing)

MARIA ELENE CELLINO*
Contact: Ed Perlstein - Los Angeles, 213/859-7786

NO RETREAT, NO SURRENDER II   Shapiro Glickenhaus, 1989,
   w/Roy Horan & Keith W. Strandberg

CHRIS CERASO
HOME FIRES BURNING   Overseas Film Group, 1992,
   w/L.A. Puopolo, from his play

JANUS CERCONE*
Agent: United Talent Agency - Beverly Hills, 310/273-6700

LEAP OF FAITH   Paramount, 1992

Screenplays:
HOW TO STEAL A MILLION (remake)
SENATOR'S WIFE
VIRGINIA REEL
KNOCK-OUT
THE RUNAROUND
WAYS AND MEANS

GINNY CERRELLA*
Agent: Gold/Marshak - Burbank, 818/972-4300

SISTER, SISTER   New World, 1988, w/Joel Cohen & Bill Condon
TAINTED BLOOD (CTF)   Wilshire Court Productions, 1993,
    w/Kathleen Rowell

Screenplays:
CHOCOLATE w/Maryedith Burrell
PETALS IN THE WIND
NOBODY'S PERFECT
RONNIE FINKELHOF, SUPERSTAR
JERSEY SKYLINE
THE PRINCE OF POP
DEAD GIVEAWAY
VOODOO
UNNATURAL ACTS
THIEF OF TIME
GYPSY SWITCH
MARMALADE

BRUCE CERVI*
Manager: Jonathan Baruch, PRO Management - Los Angeles,
    310/478-5159

Screenplays:
CYBERTRYX w/John Lansing
THE ROSE CROSS w/John Lansing
DONE DEAL w/John Lansing

CLAUDE CHABROL
Contact: French Film Office, 745 Fifth Avenue, New York, NY 10151,
    212/832-8860

LE BEAU SERGE   United Motion Picture Organization,
    1958, directed
THE COUSINS   Films Around the World, 1959, directed
LES BICHES   VGC, 1968, directed
LA FEMME INFIDEL   Allied Artists, 1968, directed
LE BOUCHER   Cinerama Releasing Corporation, 1969, directed
THE CRY OF THE OWL   R5/S8, 1987, w/Odile Barski, directed
STORY OF WOMEN   MK2/New Yorker Films, 1989,
    w/Colo Tavernier O'Hagan, directed
QUIET DAYS IN CLICHY   Pathe, 1990, w/Ugo Leonzio, directed
MADAME BOVARY   Samuel Goldwyn Company, 1991, directed
BETTY   MK2, 1992, directed
L'ENFER   MK2, 1994, Adaptation, directed

PAUL CHADWICK*
Contact: Dark Horse Entertainment - Los Angeles, 310/396-5937

Screenplays:
CONCRETE w/Larry Wilson

NATALIE CHAIDEZ
Agent: Maggie Field Agency - Studio City, 818/980-2001

Screenplays:
RAVINE

PAM CHAIS*
Agent: Paradigm - Los Angeles, 310/277-4400

Screenplays:
GETTING HAL w/Diana Levitt

KITTY CHALMERS
JOURNEY TO THE CENTER OF THE EARTH   Cannon, 1987,
    w/Regina Davis, Rusty Lemorande & Debra Ricci
CYBORG   Cannon, 1989

JEAN CHALOPIN
RAINBROW BRITE AND THE STAR STEALER (AF)   Warner Bros.,
    1985, Story w/Howard R. Cohen

ERIC CHAMPNELLA
Agent: Premiere Artists - Los Angeles, 310/271-1414

Screenplays:
3,000 w/Keith Mitchell
LOVE ME TOMORROW w/Keith Mitchell

TONY CHAN
Agent: APA - Los Angeles, 310/273-0744

COMBINATION PLATTER   Arrow Releasing, 1993,
    w/Edwin Baker, directed

ROBERT CHANDLEE
THE KILLER INSIDE ME   Warner Bros., 1976, w/Edward Mann

ELIZABETH CHANDLER*
Agent: CAA - Beverly Hills, 310/288-4545

AFTERBURN (CTF)   Steve Tisch Co., 1992

Screenplays:
RENEGADES
WALK A CROOKED MILE

EVAN CHANDLER
ROBIN HOOD: MEN IN TIGHTS   20th Century Fox, 1993,
    w/J. David Shapiro & Mel Brooks

KIM CHANDLER
Agent: Maggie Field Agency - Studio City, 818/980-2001

Screenplays:
THE GARDEN OF ED w/Mark Sercomb

WARREN CHANEY
HAUNTED   Sandpiper Productions, 1990
BROKEN SPUR   Sandpiper Productions, 1990, directed

Screenplays:
BEHIND THE MASK

ANDREW CHAPMAN*
Agent: Sanford-Gross & Associates - Los Angeles, 310/208-2100

Screenplays:
THE SEA WOLF
WORLD ON FIRE

LEIGH CHAPMAN*
Agent: APA - Los Angeles, 310/273-0744

A SWINGIN' SUMMER   United Screen Hearts, 1965
TRUCK TURNER   American International, 1974
DIRTY MARY, CRAZY LARRY   20th Century-Fox, 1974,
    w/Antonio Santean
HOW COME NOBODY'S ON OUR SIDE?   American Films
    Limited, 1975

BOARDWALK   Atlantic Releasing Corporation, 1979,
   w/Stephen Verona
STEEL   *LOOK DOWN AND DIE*   World Northal, 1980
THE OCTAGON   American Cinema, 1980
IMPULSE   Warner Bros., 1990, w/John DeMarco
STORM AND SORROW (CTF)   Accent Entertainment/Hearst
   Entertainment, 1990

Screenplays:
CAPTAIN BUTTERFLY
DETROIT

MATTHEW CHAPMAN*
Agent: United Talent Agency - Beverly Hills, 310/273-6700

HUSSY   Watchgrove Ltd., 1980, directed
STRANGER'S KISS   Orion Classics, 1984,
   w/Blaine Novak, directed
SLOW BURN (CTF)   Joel Schumacher Productions/Universal
   Pay TV, 1986, directed
HEART OF MIDNIGHT   Virgin Vision, 1989, directed
CONSENTING ADULTS   Buena Vista, 1992
COLOR OF NIGHT   Buena Vista, 1994, w/Billy Ray

Screenplays:
CONVICTION
DR. JEKYLL AND MR. HYDE
NO FURTHER QUESTIONS
THE TELEKINETIC MAN
BAD DESIRE
SCINTILLA

PRISCILLA CHAPMAN
Contact: Weissmann, Wolff, Bergman, Coleman & Silverman -
   Beverly Hills, 310/858-7888

THE FAN   Paramount, 1981, w/John Hartwell

RICHARD E. CHAPMAN*
Agent: ICM - Beverly Hills, 310/550-4000

Screenplays:
LIVE FROM BAGDAD w/Robert Wiener
MY FELLOW AMERICANS w/Jack Kaplan
HOMEWORK
TWENTY-ONE THE HARD WAY
THE MAN WHO GAVE UP HIS NAME
AND NOW MY LOVE
50 FREE AND CLEAR
QUEEN FOR A DAY
THE JET PROPELLED COUCH
BRASS ANGELS
THE POLICEMAN

ROBIN CHAPMAN
TRIPLE ECHO   Hemdale, 1972
FORCE 10 FROM NAVARONE   American International, 1978

Screenplays:
LAST BLOSSOM OF THE PLUM TREE (RKO)

THOMAS C. CHAPMAN
Contact: 818/348-6535

HANGAR #18   Sunn Classic, 1980, Story w/James L. Conway
THE BOOGENS   Jensen Farley Pictures, 1982,
   Story w/David O'Malley

DAVID A. CHAPPE*
Contact: WGA - Los Angeles, 310/550-1000

Screenplays:
GALE FORCE w/Larry Konner & Mark Rosenthal
MAXWELL'S TRAIN
THE TREASURE OF GUNSIGHT BUTTE

ERIC CHAPPELL
RISING DAMP   ITC, 1980

JOE CHAPPELLE
THIEVES QUARTET   Headliner Entertainmetn Group,
   1994, directed

MEHDI CHAREF
Contact: French Film Office, 745 Fifth Avenue, New York, NY 10151,
   212/832-8860

TEA IN THE HAREM   Cinecom, 1986, directed

GLEN CHARLES*
Agent: Broder-Kurland-Webb-Uffner - Beverly Hills, 310/281-3400
Business: Triangle Entertainment, Paramount TV - 213/956-4000

Screenplays:
LADY TAKES AN ACE w/Les Charles

LARRY CHARLES*
Agent: United Talent Agency - Beverly Hills, 310/273-6700

Screenplays:
SOUL PATROL
OVER A BARREL
GREAT EXITS
ONE FOR THE MONEY
THE THIRD TESTAMENT

LES CHARLES*
Agent: Broder-Kurland-Webb-Uffner - Beverly Hills, 310/281-3400
Business: Triangle Entertainment, Paramount TV - 213/956-4000

Screenplays:
LADY TAKES AN ACE w/Glen Charles

REBECCA CHARLES
NEMESIS   Imperial Entertainment, 1993

ELISA J. CHAROUHAS
SOCIAL SUICIDE   Star Entertainment Group, 1992,
   w/Lawrence D. Foldes

DAVID H. CHASE*
Agent: United Talent Agency - Beverly Hills, 310/273-6700
Business Manager: Jess Morgan & Co. - Los Angeles, 213/937-1552

Screenplays:
TUNA HELL
LIARS
FEMALE SUSPECTS
CHANGING SIDES
NERVOUS SYSTEM
THE ARCHIE MOVIE

DAVID M. CHASKIN*
Agent: The Agency - Los Angeles, 310/551-3000

A NIGHTMARE ON ELM STREET, PART 2: FREDDY'S REVENGE
   New Line Cinema, 1985
THE CURSE   Trans World Entertainment, 1987
I, MADMAN   Trans World Entertainment, 1989

Screenplays:
THE VICTOR w/Richard Kletter
THE WELL
BOLTS!
HARDCOVER

DELLE CHATMAN*
Contact: WGA - Los Angeles, 310/550-1000

ENDINGS (P)
ALL AT ONCE (P)
ALL FOR NOTHING (P)
THE WOUND (P)

Screenplays:
THE EDUCATION OF NICOLE
TIME TO TELL
LISTEN TO ME
RED NIGHT
REST AREA

HOWARD CHAYKIN*
Agent: Warden, White & Kane - Beverly Hills, 213/852-1028

Screenplays:
POWER & GLORY
TIMING IS EVERYTHING w/John Moore
MIDNIGHT MEN
HOT RODS

PETER CHELSOM
Agent: William Morris Agency - Beverly Hills, 310/274-7451

HEAR MY SONG   Miramax, 1991, w/Adrian Dunbar, directed
FUNNY BONES   Buena Vista, 1995, directed

Screenplays:
SAM AND THE SERGEANT w/Adrian Dunbar
(Buena Vista, directing)
HUNCH

AYOKA CHENZIRA*
Contact: WGA - New York, 212/245-6180
Business: Crossgrain Pictures, 300 W. 55th St., New York, NY
10019, 212/757-6945

ZAJOTA AND THE BOOGIE SPIRIT (Short), 1993, directed
ALMA'S RAINBOW   Channel Four/U.S. Corporation for Public
Broadcasting, 1994, directed

CYNTHIA A. CHERBAK*
Agent: Dytman & Schwartz - Beverly Hills, 310/274-8844

THE KISSING PLACE (CTF)   Wilshire Court Productions, 1990,
w/Richard Altabef & Michael Wing

JOHN R. CHERRY III
ERNEST GOES TO CAMP   Buena Vista, 1987,
w/Coke Sams, directed
ERNEST SCARED STUPID   Buena Vista, 1991,
w/Coke Sams, directed
ERNEST RIDES AGAIN   Emshell Producers Group, 1993,
w/William K. Akers, directed

STANLEY Z. CHERRY*
Agent: Shapiro/Lichtman - Los Angeles, 310/859-8877
Business Manager: Cooper, Epstein, Hurewitz - Beverly Hills,
310/278-1111

BUNNY O'HARE   American International, 1971,
w/Coslough Johnson

STAN CHERVIN*
Manager: RKS Entertainment Group - Sherman Oaks, 818/788-3616

Screenplays:
SLAVES OF THE HOUSEHOLD

MARC D. CHESLER*
Contact: WGA - Los Angeles, 310/550-1000

Screenplays:
AMERICAN LADY w/Gail Fisher
DISTANT RELATIVE w/Gail Fisher
ME, MYSELF AND I w/Gail Fisher
MALE-FEMALE w/Gail Fisher
STIRRUPS w/Gail Fisher

HOWARD M. CHESLEY*
Agent: United Talent Agency - Beverly Hills, 310/273-6700

Screenplays:
POV
DORF
MEDICAL SCHOOL
LONGING TO FALL
RESISTING ARREST
LIKE HARRY
FLYBOY
CIVILIANS
SAN PEDRO
STOVER AT YALE
PEACE SHIP
BALLOON PAYMENT

LIONEL CHETWYND*
Agent: ICM - Beverly Hills, 310/550-4000

WE THE PEOPLE...200 (P)   shared
BLEEDING GREAT ORCHIDS (P)
MAYBE THAT'S YOUR PROBLEM (P)
THE APPRENTICESHIP OF DUDDY KRAVITZ ★   Paramount,
1974, Adaptation
TWO SOLITUDES   New World-Mutual, 1978, directed
QUINTET   20th Century-Fox, 1979, Story w/Robert Altman &
Patricia Resnick
THE HANOI HILTON   Cannon, 1987, directed
DOOMSDAY GUN (CTF)   Griffin Productions/HBO Showcase, 1994,
w/Walter Bernstein
JACOB (CTF)   Turner Pictures, 1994

ANDREW CHIARAMONTE
Contact: Weissmann, Wolff, Bergman, Coleman & Silverman -
Beverly Hills, 310/858-7888

TWOGETHER   Twogether Ltd. Partnership, 1992, directed

Screenplays:
DEATH AMONG STRANGERS w/Emmett Alston (directing)
AND THEN CAME HOMER (Story)

MARC CHIAT
Agent: United Talent Agency - Beverly Hills, 310/273-6700

Screenplays:
THE RIDE (directing)

BILLY CHICAGO
NETHERWORLD   Paramount Home Video/Full Moon
Entertainment, 1992

HELEN CHILDRESS*
Agent: CAA - Beverly Hills, 310/288-4545

REALITY BITES   Universal, 1994

Screenplays:
BLUE BY YOU

MARK CHILDRESS
Agent: Pleshette & Green - Los Angeles, 213/465-0428

Screenplays:
CRAZY IN ALABAMA

F I L M

W R I T E R S

CHARLES CHIODO
Business: Chiodo Brothers Productions, 818/842-5656

KILLER KLOWNS FROM OUTER SPACE   TransWorld
    Entertainment, 1988, w/Stephen Chiodo

STEPHEN CHIODO*
Business: Chiodo Brothers Productions, 818/842-5656

KILLER KLOWNS FROM OUTER SPACE   TransWorld
    Entertainment, 1988, w/Charles Chiodo, directed

DAVID CHISOLM*
Agent: CAA - Beverly Hills, 310/288-4545

THE WIZARD   Universal, 1989
DEAD MAN'S REVENGE (CTF)   MCA Television Entertainment,
    1994, w/Jim Byrnes

Screenplays:
THE DREAM CHILD
STREETWISE
SILENT SERVICES
DEVIL PUPS

MICHELE CHODOS*
Agent: United Talent Agency - Beverly Hills, 310/273-6700

POLICE ACADEMY VII: MISSION TO MOSCOW   Warner Bros.,
    1994, w/Randolph Davis

Screenplays:
TRIAL BY FIRE w/Randolph Davis
STAY TUNED FOR MURDER w/Randolph Davis

THOMAS CHONG*
Agent: Irvin Arthur Associates - Beverly Hills, 310/278-5934
Business Manager: Mannis & Barbakow - Los Angeles, 310/476-7311

UP IN SMOKE   Paramount, 1978, w/Richard "Cheech" Marin
CHEECH & CHONG'S NEXT MOVIE   Universal, 1980,
    w/Richard "Cheech" Marin
CHEECH & CHONG'S NICE DREAMS   Columbia, 1981,
    w/Richard "Cheech" Marin, directed
THINGS ARE TOUGH ALL OVER   Columbia, 1982,
    w/Richard "Cheech" Marin
CHEECH & CHONG: STILL SMOKIN'   Paramount, 1983,
    w/Richard "Cheech" Marin, directed
CHEECH & CHONG'S THE CORSICAN BROTHERS   Orion, 1984,
    w/Richard "Cheech" Marin, directed
FAR OUT MAN   New Line Cinema, 1990, directed

MICHAEL CHOQUETTE
STITCHES   International Film Marketing, 1985, w/Michael
    Paseornek

RANJIT CHOWDREY
SAM & ME   Sunrise Films Ltd. Toronto/Film Four International, 1991

H.R. (ROGER) CHRISTIAN
Contact: Directors Guild of America - Los Angeles, 310/289-2000

KING OF THE MOUNTAIN   Universal, 1981
NOSTRADAMUS   Orion Classics, 1994, Story w/Piers Ashworth &
    Knut Boeser, directed

NATHANIEL CHRISTIAN
CALIFORNIA CASANOVA   Academy Entertainment, 1991, directed

DAVID M. CHURCH*
Contact: WGA - Los Angeles, 310/550-1000

Screenplays:
PSYCHIC HOUSEWIFE
CLOUD FIVE

HALO
CONJUROR

GENE CHURCH
SNAPDRAGON (CTF)   Prism Pictures, 1994

DAVID CHUTE
Contact: 213/739-1682

CLICK: THE CALENDAR GIRL KILLER   Crown International, 1989,
    w/David Reskin, Ross Hagen & Hoke Howell

GERARD CICCORITTI
Business: Lightshow Communications, Inc., 19 Tennis Crescent -
    Suite 8, Toronto, Ontario M4K 1J4, Canada, 416/465-6465

SKULL: A NIGHT OF TERROR   Geonib Properties, 1989,
    w/Robert Bergman
A WHISPER TO A SCREAM   Distant Horizon and Lighthouse
    Communications, 1989, w/Robert Bergman

CYNTHIA CIDRE*
Agent: CAA - Beverly Hills, 310/288-4545

IN COUNTRY   Warner Bros., 1989, w/Frank Pierson
FIRES WITHIN   MGM-Pathe, 1991
THE MAMBO KINGS   Warner Bros., 1992

Screenplays:
THE IMMORTALS
DOUBLE EXPOSURE
RAISING HELL
BLUE MOON
FOOLS DIE
NERVE ENDINGS
VOODOO QUEEN
ANNA KARENINA

MATT CIMBER
BUTTERFLY   Analysis, 1981, w/John Goff, directed
YELLOW HAIR AND THE FORTRESS OF GOLD   Crown
    Inernational, 1984, w/John Kershaw, directed

MICHAEL CIMINO*
Agent: William Morris Agency - Beverly Hills, 310/274-7451

SILENT RUNNING   Universal, 1971, w/Steven Bochco &
    Deric Washburn
MAGNUM FORCE   Warner Bros., 1973, w/John Milius
THUNDERBOLT AND LIGHTFOOT   United Artists, 1974, directed
THE DEER HUNTER ★   Universal, 1978, Story w/Louis Garfinkle &
    Quinn K. Redeker, directed
HEAVEN'S GATE   United Artists, 1980, directed
YEAR OF THE DRAGON   MGM/UA, 1985, w/Oliver Stone, directed

Screenplays:
HEAVEN IS A SOME TIME THING
PARADISE JUNCTION
SERPENT'S TOOTH

TONY CINCIRIPINI
THE LAWLESS LAND   Concorde Pictures, 1989, w/Larry Leahy

PAUL CIOTTI
TED & VENUS   Double Helix Films, 1991, w/Bud Cort

CINDY CIRILE*
Contact: WGA - Los Angeles, 310/550-1000

RAPID FIRE   20th Century Fox, 1992, Story w/Alan McElroy

Screenplays:
PEACEMAKERS w/John Fasano (New Line Cinema)

JIM CIRILE*
Agent: William Morris Agency - Beverly Hills, 310/274-7451

Screenplays:
A CLEAN SWEEP
EARTHSHAKER
PET VIKING

PATRICK CIRILLO*
Agent: Broder-Kurland-Webb-Uffner - Beverly Hills, 310/281-3400

HOMER AND EDDIE   Skouras Pictures, 1990
DANGEROUS HEART (CTF)   MCA Telvision Entertainment, 1994

Screenplays:
EXQUISITE TENDERNESS w/Bernard Sloane (Capella)
CITY OF DARKNESS w/Joe Gayton
THE ENGLANDER w/Joe Gayton
DANCE WITH A PREACHER w/James Cady
PSYCHOTIC REACTION
SOJOURN

RAYMOND CISTHERI
BODY SNATCHERS   Warner Bros., 1993, Story w/Larry Cohen

TOM CITRANO*
Agent: Artists Agency - New York, 212/245-6960

NIGHT EYES   Amritraj-Baldwin Entertainment, 1990,
   w/Andrew Stevens

THOMAS CLABURN
THE HANGED MAN   Lot 49, 1993, directed

MICHAEL CLANCY*
Agent: William Morris Agency - Beverly Hills, 310/274-7451

Screenplays:
HIGHER EDUCATION

WES CLARIDGE*
Contact: WGA - Los Angeles, 310/550-1000

DEADLY GAME (CTF)   Osiris Productions/Wilshire Court
   Productions, 1991

Screenplays:
THE AMERICA'S CUP
THE ENCHANTMENT
THE FLYING DUTCHMAN
CIRCUS ROAD
FAR CENTAURI
NIGHTS OF EDEN
WILD WEST SHOW
STORM WARNING
YEAR OF THE TIGER

BOB CLARK*
Agent: Robert M. Kilgore, Fade In Productions, 1040 Country Club
   Lane, Escondido, CA 92926, 619/741-5501
Manager: Harold D. Cohen, Associated Management Co. -
   Los Angeles, 310/550-0570

PORKY'S   20th Century-Fox, 1982, directed
PORKY'S II: THE NEXT DAY   20th Century-Fox, 1983,
   w/Alan Ormsby & Roger Swaybill, directed
A CHRISTMAS STORY   MGM/UA, 1983, w/Jean Shepherd &
   Leigh Brown, directed
FROM THE HIP   DEG, 1987, w/David E. Kelly, directed
LOOSE CANNONS   Tri-Star, 1990, w/Richard Christian Matheson &
   Richard Matheson, directed
IT RUNS IN THE FAMILY   MGM/UA, 1995, w/Leigh Brown &
   Jean Shepherd, directed

Screenplays:
THE SHE MAN

BRIAN CLARK
Agent: Judy Daish Agency - London, 011/441/486-5405

WHOSE LIFE IS IT ANYWAY?   MGM/UA, 1981, w/Reginald Rose

Screenplays:
COMPUTER PROJECT
MEDICAL SCHOOL

BRUCE CLARK*
Contact: WGA - Los Angeles, 310/550-1000

GALAXY OF TERROR   New World, 1981, w/Marc Siegler, directed

DENNIS LYNTON CLARK*
Agent: The Brandt Company - Sherman Oaks, 818/783-7747

COMES A HORSEMAN   United Artists, 1978
THE KEEP   Paramount, 1983, Adaptation
THE COURTMARTIAL OF JACKIE ROBINSON (CTF)
   Turner Network Television, 1990, w/L. Travis Clark,
   Steve Duncan & Clayton Frohman

Screenplays:
FIDDLER'S GREEN (CTF)
FREEWALKERS (directing)
PORT ROYAL
PAUL BUNYAN
CHILDREN'S CRUSADE
AMAZING GRACE
BAND OF BROTHERS
VALLEY BOYS
THIRTEEN
THE LAST CHUCKER
SAVAGE HONOR
TRAILBLAZERS
THAI PIRATES (CTF)
WOUNDED KNEE THE DAY THE SUN DIED (CTF)

DUANE B. CLARK*
Agent: Shapiro/Lichtman - Los Angeles, 310/859-8877
Contact: Richard D. Thompson, Silverberg, Katz, Thompson & Braun -
   Los Angeles, 310/445-5800

SHAKING THE TREE   Miramax, 1992, w/Steven Wilde, directed

Screenplays:
PRINCE OF NEW YORK w/Steven Wilde
HOOPS w/Steven Wilde
WICCA
TRUE LOVE, HOPE & A REALLY BIG PEARL
ROADTRIP: AN AMERICAN ODYSSEY
THUNDER ROAD

GREYDON CLARK
ANGELS BRIGADE   Arista, 1980, w/Alvin L. Fast, directed
SKINHEADS   Amazing Movies, 1989, w/David Reskin

Screenplays:
TERROR OF MANHATTAN w/Michael J. Murray (directing)

KAREN CLARK*
Contact: WGA - Los Angeles, 310/550-1000

LISA   MGM/UA, 1990, w/Gary A. Sherman

RICHARD CLARK
Agent: Preferred Artists - Encino, 818/990-0305

Screenplays:
TREASURE OF THE SIERRA MADRE MALL

RON CLARK*
Agent: David Shapira & Associates - Sherman Oaks, 818/906-0322

WALLY'S CAFE (P)
MURDER AT THE HOWARD JOHNSON'S (P)   w/Sam Bobrick
NO HARD FEELINGS (P)
THE INCOMPARABLE LOULOU (P)
SILENT MOVIE   20th Century-Fox, 1976, w/Mel Brooks &
    Rudy DeLuca
NORMAN, IS THAT YOU?   MGM/United Artists, 1976,
    w/Sam Bobrick & George Schlatter, from his play w/Sam Bobrick
HIGH ANXIETY   20th Century-Fox, 1977, w/Mel Brooks,
    Rudy DeLuca & Barry Levinson
REVENGE OF THE PINK PANTHER   United Artists, 1978,
    w/Blake Edwards & Frank Waldman
THE FUNNY FARM   New World, 1983, directed
LIFE STINKS   MGM-Pathe, 1991, Story w/Mel Brooks,
    Rudy DeLuca & Steve Haberman

Screenplays:
BENITO w/Dom DeLuise
THE INCREDIBLE SHRINKING MAN
BUMPERS
BLOOMIES
SELLING SEASON
NOSE JOB
HARDWARE

WOODROW W. CLARK
THE HEALING FORCE   Woody Clark Productions,1983,
    w/Joanne Parrent & Jay Miracle

ARTHUR C. CLARKE
Agent: Scott Meredith Agency - New York, 212/245-5500

2001: A SPACE ODYSSEY ★   MGM, 1968, w/Stanley Kubrick

FRANK CLARKE
Agent: ICM - Beverly Hills, 310/550-4000

LETTER TO BREZHNEV   Circle Releasing Corporation, 1986
WONDERLAND   Vestron, 1989
BLONDE FIRST   Glinwood Films, 1991, directed

JOHN CLARKE
LONELY HEARTS   Samuel Goldwyn Company, 1982, w/Paul Cox

MALCOLM CLARKE
Agent: William Morris Agency - Beverly Hills, 310/274-7451

Screenplays:
COWGIRL KATE and other stories

MARY RUTH CLARKE
Contact: Academy of Canadian Cinema & Television, 753 Yonge St. -
    2nd Floor, Toronto M4Y 1Z9, Canada, 416/967-0315

MEET THE PARENTS   C.E.M. Productions, 1992, w/Greg Glienna

ROY CLARKE*
Agent: The Artists Agency - Los Angeles, 310/277-7779

HAWKS   Skouras Pictures, 1989
A FOREIGN FIELD   Fingertip Film, 1993

ANTHONY CLARVOE
Agent: Writers & Artists Agency - Los Angeles, 310/824-6300

PICK UP AXE (P)
LET'S PLAY TWO (P)
SHOW AND TELL (P)
THE LIVING (P)

Screenplays:
ALICE IN WONDERLAND
THE CASKET AND THE SWORD

TIM CLAWSON
Contact: 213/464-5808

THEY CALL ME BRUCE? *A FISTFUL OF CHOPSTICKS*
    Artists Releasing Corporation/Film Ventures International, 1982,
    w/Elliott Hong, David Randolf & Johnny Yune

ANDREW DICE CLAY*
(Andrew Clay Silverstein)
Agent: ICM - Beverly Hills, 310/550-4000

DICE RULES (FD)   7 Arts/Carolco, 1991,
    Concert Material and Story, "A Day in the Life"

MEL CLAY
WHITE TRASH   Fred Baker Film & Video Co., 1992, from his play

WALT CLAYTON*
Agent: Kaplan-Stahler - Beverly Hills, 213/653-4483

Screenplays:
FINDERS KILLERS
LETHAL TRINITY
SKY HIGH
TARGET GENOME

THOMAS M. CLEAVER
Contact: Lichter, Grossman & Nichols - Los Angeles, 310/205-6999

THE TERROR WITHIN   Concorde, 1989
HEROES STAND ALONE   Concorde, 1989
IMMORTAL SINS   Concorde, 1991, w/Beverly Gray

Screenplays:
WELCOME HOME
BROTHERS IN ARMS
CRADLE

JOHN CLEESE
Business: Prominent Features, Ltd., 68A Delancey St., London
    NW1 7RY, England, 01/284-1004

THE RISE AND RISE OF MICHAEL RIMMER   Warner Bros., 1970,
    w/Graham Chapman, Peter Cook & Kevin Billington
RENTADICK   Rank/Paradine/Virgin, 1972, w/Graham Chapman
AND NOW FOR SOMETHING COMPLETELY DIFFERENT
    Columbia, 1972, w/Graham Chapman, Terry Gilliam, Eric Idle,
    Terry Jones & Michael Palin
MONTY PYTHON AND THE HOLY GRAIL   Cinema 5, 1974,
    w/Graham Chapman, Terry Gilliam, Eric Idle, Terry Jones &
    Michael Palin
MONTY PYTHON'S LIFE OF BRIAN   Orion/Warner Bros., 1979,
    w/Graham Chapman, Terry Gilliam, Eric Idle, Terry Jones &
    Michael Palin
MONTY PYTHON LIVE AT THE HOLLYWOOD BOWL   Columbia,
    1982, w/Graham Chapman, Terry Gilliam, Eric Idle, Terry Jones &
    Michael Palin
MONTY PYTHON'S THE MEANING OF LIFE   Universal, 1983,
    w/Graham Chapman, Terry Gilliam, Eric Idle, Terry Jones &
    Michael Palin
A FISH CALLED WANDA ★   MGM/UA, 1988

TOM CLEGG
Agent: Peters, Fraser & Dunlop - London, 071/376-7676

McVICAR   Crown International, 1981, w/John McVicar, directed

BRIAN H. CLEMENS*
Agent: Paul Kohner, Inc. - Beverly Hills, 310/550-1060

THE DEPRAVED   Danzigers, 1957
AN HONOURABLE MURDER   Danziger, 1959, w/Eldon Howard
THE TELL-TALE HEART   1963
STATION SIX - SAHARA   Allied Artists, 1963, w/Bryan Forbes
THE CORRUPT ONES   *THE PEKING MEDALLION*
    Warner Bros., 1967

AND SOON THE DARKNESS   Levitt-Pickman, 1971,
   w/Terry Nation
SEE NO EVIL   Columbia, 1971
DR. JEKYLL AND SISTER HYDE   Hammer, 1971
CAPTAIN KRONOS, VAMPIRE HUNTER   Hammer/Paramount,
   1973, directed
THE GOLDEN VOYAGE OF SINBAD   Columbia, 1973,
   w/Ray Harryhausen
THE WATCHER IN THE WOODS   Buena Vista, 1980,
   w/Harry Spalding & Rosemary Anne Sisson
HIGHLANDER 2: THE QUICKENING   InterStar Releasing, 1991,
   Story w/William Panzer

PAUL CLEMENS
Agent: Susan Smith & Associates - Beverly Hills, 213/852-4777

Screenplays:
THE MANAGER w/Ron Magid

SAM CLEMENS
SLIPSTREAM   Entertainment Film, 1989, Story

DICK CLEMENT*
Agent: Broder-Kurland-Webb-Uffner - Beverly Hills, 310/281-3400

THE JOKERS   Universal, 1967, w/Ian LaFrenais
HANNIBAL BROOKS   United Artists, 1968, w/Ian LaFrenais
OTLEY   Columbia, 1969, w/Ian LaFrenais, directed
CATCH ME A SPY   Rank, 1971, w/Ian LaFrenais, directed
VILLAIN   EMI, 1971, w/Ian LaFrenais
THE LIKELY LADS   EMI, 1976, w/Ian LaFrenais
PORRIDGE   ITC, 1979, w/Ian LaFrenais, directed
THE PRISONER OF ZENDA   Universal, 1979, w/Ian LaFrenais
WATER   Atlantic Releasing Corporation, 1984, w/Ian LaFrenais &
   Bill Persky, directed
VICE VERSA   Columbia, 1988, w/Ian LaFrenais
THE COMMITMENTS   20th Century-Fox, 1991, w/Ian LaFrenais &
   Roddy Doyle

Screenplays:
SEEING RED w/Ian LaFrenais

RENE CLEMENT
Contact: French Film Office, 745 Fifth Avenue, New York, NY 10151,
   212/832-8860

LA BATAILLE DU RAIL   CGCF, 1945, directed
LES MAUDITS (THE DAMNED)   Speva Film, 1947,
   w/Henri Jeanson & Jacques Remy, directed
LOVERS, HAPPY LOVERS! *KNAVE OF HEARTS*
   20th Century-Fox, 1954, w/Hugh Mills, directed
JOY HOUSE *THE LOVE CAGE* MGM, 1964, w/Pascal Jardin &
   Charles Williams, directed

DULANY ROSS CLEMENTS
DANGER ZONE II: REAPER'S REVENGE   Skouras Pictures, 1989

R.C. CLEMENTS
Agent: Paradigm - Los Angeles, 310/277-4400

Screenplays:
UPON OTHER FIELDS
DELUSIONS OF GRANDEUR

RON CLEMENTS
Business: Walt Disney Productions, 818/560-1000

THE GREAT MOUSE DETECTIVE (AF)   Buena Vista, 1989,
   w/others, co-directed
THE LITTLE MERMAID (AF)   Buena Vista, 1989,
   w/John Musker, co-directed
ALADDIN (AF)   Buena Vista, 1992, w/John Musker, Ted Elliott &
   Terry Rossio, co-directed

Screenplays:
HERCULES (AF) w/John Musker

JAKE CLESI
BURIED ALIVE   21st Century Film Corporation, 1990, w/Stuart Lee

CHRISTOPHER CLEVELAND*
Agent: ICM - Beverly Hills, 310/550-4000

Screenplays:
THE PASSION OF RICHARD NIXON
THE WESTIES
GONE SOUTH
THE FOUNTAINHEAD (remake)

RICK CLEVELAND
Agent: The Gersh Agency - New York, 212/997-1818

TOM AND JERRY (P)
DOGMAN'S LAST STAND (P)
KIDS IN THE DARK (P)
BAD MOON (P)
THE RHINO'S POLICEMAN (P)
HOME GROWN (P)

Screenplays:
YOU SEND ME

GRAEME CLIFFORD
Agent: United Talent Agency - Beverly Hills, 310/273-6700

Screenplays:
FLASHER'S MAGIC

PATRICK CLIFTON
Agent: The Gersh Agency - Beverly Hills, 310/274-6611
Contact: 213/650-6412

SON-IN-LAW   Buena Vista, 1993, Story w/Susan McMartin &
   Peter Lenkov

Screenplays:
CROSSBONES
STORMY WEATHER
BIG MAN ON CAMPUS

EDWARD CLINTON*
Contact: WGA - New York, 212/245-6180

HONKY TONK FREEWAY   Universal/AFD, 1981

DARRAH CLOUD*
Contact: WGA - Los Angeles, 310/550-1000

THE STICK WIFE (P)   also screenplay
OH, PIONEERS!

Screenplays:
DREAM HOUSE

ROBERT CLOUSE
Agent: ICM - Beverly Hills, 310/550-4000

THE ULTIMATE WARRIOR   Warner Bros., 1975, directed
THE AMSTERDAM KILL   Columbia, 1978,
   w/Gregor Teifer, directed
THE PACK   Warner Bros., 1977, directed
THE BIG BRAWL   Warner Bros., 1980, directed
FORCE: FIVE   American Cinema, 1981, (based on screenplay by
   Emil Farkas & George Goldsmith), directed

CHRISTOPHER J. CLUESS*
Agent: Broder-Kurland-Webb-Uffner - Beverly Hills, 310/281-3400

Screenplays:
STARWRECK w/Stuart Kreisman
THE LAST HIGH SCHOOL MOVIE w/Stuart Kreisman

RAPHAEL CLUZEL
LIGHT YEARS   Miramax, 1988, w/Blaine Novak

CRAIG CLYDE
THE LEGEND OF WOLF MOUNTAIN   Hemdale, 1993,
   w/James Hennessy, directed

LEWIS COATES
(Luigi Cozzi)
Address: via Cassia 834, pal.F, Rome, Italy, 06/366-8116

STARCRASH   New World, 1979, w/Patrick Wachsberger, directed
HERCULES   MGM/UA/Cannon, 1983, directed
THE BLACK CAT   21st Century Film Corp, 1990, directed

HENRY COBBOLD*
Contact: WGA - Los Angeles, 310/550-1000

LAKE CONSEQUENCE (CTF)   Showtime Networks, 1993,
   w/Melanie Finn & Zalman King

RANDY SUE COBURN
MRS. PARKER AND THE VICIOUS CIRCLE   Fine Line Features,
   1994, w/Alan Rudolph

CHRISTINA COCEK
Agent: Warden, White & Kane - Beverly Hills, 213/852-1028

Screenplays:
COLUMBUS DAY (OBSERVED)
UNCERTAIN, TEXAS
THE SMITHS (Shared)

STACY COCHRAN
Agent: The Gersh Agency - Beverly Hills, 310/274-6611

COCKTAILS AT SIX (Short)   directed
ANOTHER DAMAGING DAY (Short)   directed
MY NEW GUN   I.R.S. Releasing, 1992, directed
BOYS   Buena Vista, 1995, directed

JAY COCKS*
Agent: CAA - Beverly Hills, 310/288-4545

THE AGE OF INNOCENCE ★   Columbia, 1993, w/Martin Scorcese

Screenplays:
AMERICAN REVOLUTION
GANGS OF NEW YORK
A CHAIN OF VOICES
SILENCE

ANDREI CODRESCU
Contact: National Public Radio - Santa Monica, 310/450-5183

ROAD SCHOLAR (FD)   Samuel Goldwyn Company, 1993, Shared

WAYNE COE
GRIM PRAIRIE TALES   East/West Film Partners Prods., 1990, directed

ETHAN COEN
Agent: United Talent Agency - Beverly Hills, 310/273-6700

CRIMEWAVE   Columbia, 1985, w/Joel Coen & Sam Raimi
BLOOD SIMPLE   Circle Films, 1986, w/Joel Coen
RAISING ARIZONA   20th Century Fox, 1987, w/Joel Coen
MILLER'S CROSSING   20th Century Fox, 1990, w/Joel Coen
BARTON FINK   20th Century Fox, 1991, w/Joel Coen
THE HUDSUCKER PROXY   Warner Bros., 1994, w/Joel Coen &
   Sam Raimi

Screenplays:
FARGO w/Joel Coen (Polygram)

JOEL COEN
Agent: United Talent Agency - Beverly Hills, 310/273-6700

CRIMEWAVE   Columbia, 1985, w/Ethan Coen & Sam Raimi
BLOOD SIMPLE   Circle Films, 1986, w/Ethan Coen, directed
RAISING ARIZONA   20th Century Fox, 1987,
   w/Ethan Coen, directed
MILLER'S CROSSING   20th Century Fox, 1990,
   w/Ethan Coen, directed
BARTON FINK   20th Century Fox, 1991, w/Ethan Coen, directed
THE HUDSUCKER PROXY   Warner Bros., 1994, w/Ethan Coen &
   Sam Raimi, directed

Screenplays:
FARGO w/Ethan Coen (Polygram, directing)

CHARLIE COFFEY*
Contact: Gary Nye, Inman, Weisz & Steinberg - 213/274-7111

EARTH GIRLS ARE EASY   Vestron, 1988, w/Julie Brown &
   Terrence E. McNally

MARTIN P. COHAN*
Agent: Paradigm - Los Angeles, 310/277-4400

HUMANOIDS FROM THE DEEP   New World, 1980,
   Story w/Frank Arnold

AMY COHEN
Agent: The Irv Schechter Company - Beverly Hills, 310/278-8070

Screenplays:
PLEASED TO MEET ME

BARNEY COHEN*
Business Manager: Richard Hofstetter, Frankfurt, Garbus, Klein &
   Selz - New York, 212/826-5537

FRIDAY THE 13TH, PART IV: THE FINAL CHAPTER
   Paramount, 1984
KILLER PARTY   MGM/UA, 1986
NEXT DOOR (CTF)   Nederlander Television/TriStar
   Television, 1994

BENNETT COHEN*
Contact: WGA - Los Angeles, 310/550-1000

RAINBOW DRIVE (CTF)   Viacom-Dove-ITC, 1990, w/Bill Philips

CHARLES ZEV COHEN*
Contact: WGA - Los Angeles, 310/550-1000

LADY BEWARE   Scotti Bros., 1987, w/Susan Miller
EDDIE AND THE CRUISERS II: EDDIE LIVES   Scotti Bros., 1989,
   w/Rick Doehring
BEYOND FORGIVENESS   Nu Image, 1995

Screenplays:
PENKNIFE

CHARLIE COHEN*
Agent: Broder-Kurland-Webb-Uffner - Beverly Hills, 310/281-3400

ERNEST GOES TO JAIL   Buena Vista, 1990

Screenplays:
TERROR AT THE DEWDROP INN

DAN COHEN
THE WHOLE TRUTH   Cinevista, 1993, co-directed

DAVID AARON COHEN*
Agent: Paradigm - Los Angeles, 310/277-4400

POINT OF VIEW   Contrast Ltd., 1990
V.I. WARSHAWSKI   Buena Vista, 1991, w/Edward Taylor &
   Nick Thiel

Screenplays:
FRIDAY NIGHT LIGHTS   w/Alan J. Pakula
RAP SQUAD
GO DOWN MOSES
BLOOD BROTHERS

DAVID G. COHEN
Contact: Nahin and Nahin Law Corp. - Los Angeles, 310/651-0171

THE TREASURE   Questar Pictures, 1990, w/Robert Cording

Screenplays:
CRUSADES
THE CREATION
SINGLE
MIRROR IMAGE
STREET DREAMS
THE JAZZBERRY CLUB
DESOLATION

DAVID M. COHEN*
Contact: Dept. of Theater, University of Texas - Austin, 512/471-5793

FRIDAY THE 13TH - A NEW BEGINNING   Paramount, 1985,
   w/Martin Kitrosser & Danny Steinmann
HOLLYWOOD ZAP   Troma, 1986, directed

ERIC COHEN
Agent: The Artists Group - Los Angeles, 310/552-1100

Screenplays:
LIBERTY SMITH   w/Marc Madnick

HOWARD R. COHEN
Agent: Epstein-Wyckoff-LaManna - Beverly Hills, 310/278-7222

SATURDAY THE 14TH   New World, 1981, directed
SPACE RAIDERS   New World, 1983, directed
STRYKER   New World, 1983
DEATHSTALKER   New World, 1984
RAINBOW BRITE AND THE STAR STEALER (AF)
   Warner Bros., 1985
DEATHSTALKER III: THE WARRIORS FROM HELL
   Concorde, 1988
LORDS OF THE DEEP   Concorde, 1989, w/Daryl Haney
SATURDAY THE 14TH STRIKES BACK   Concorde, 1990, directed
SPACE CASE   Lunar Bynne Limited Productions, 1990, directed

JOEL COHEN*
Contact: 213/876-8663

SISTER, SISTER   New World, 1988, w/Ginny Cerrella & Bill Condon
PASS THE AMMO   New Century/Vista, 1988, w/Neil Cohen

Screenplays:
MONEY TALKS   w/Alec Sokolow
FAMILY MAN   w/Alec Sokolow
TOY STORY (AF)   w/Alec Sokolow
THE GREAT KIDNAPPING   w/Alec Sokolow

JON COHEN*
Contact: WGA - New York, 212/245-6180

Screenplays:
CROSSOVER

KATHY COHEN*
Agent: CAA - Beverly Hills, 310/288-4545

Screenplays:
SACRED HEARTS
THE GOSSIP COLUMNIST
SKIRTS AND ZIPPERS
THE RED FERRARI

LARRY COHEN*
Business Manager: David Tiger, 818/999-4420

THE RETURN OF THE SEVEN   United Artists, 1966
DADDY'S GONE A HUNTING   Warner Bros., 1969,
   w/Lorenzo Semple Jr.
EL CONDOR   National General, 1970, w/Steven W. Carabatsos
HELL UP IN HARLEM   American International, 1973, directed
IT'S ALIVE   Warner Bros., 1974, directed
DEMON GOD TOLD ME TO   New World, 1977, directed
IT LIVES AGAIN   Warner Bros., 1978, directed
THE PRIVATE FILES OF J. EDGAR HOOVER
   American International, 1978, directed
THE AMERICAN SUCCESS CO. *SUCCESS* Columbia, 1979,
   w/William Richert
FULL MOON HIGH   Filmways, 1981, directed
I, THE JURY   20th Century-Fox, 1982
Q   United Film Distribution, 1982, directed
SCANDALOUS   Orion, 1984, Story w/John Byrum & Rob Cohen
SPECIAL EFFECTS   New Line Cinema, 1985, directed
PERFECT STRANGERS   New Line Cinema, 1985, directed
THE STUFF   New World, 1985, directed
RETURN TO SALEM'S LOT   Warner Bros., 1987,
   w/James Dixon, directed
IT'S ALIVE III: ISLAND OF THE ALIVE   Warner Bros., 1987, directed
BEST SELLER   Orion, 1987
MANIAC COP   Shapiro/Glickenhaus, 1988
DEADLY ILLUSION   CineTel Films, 1988, directed
WICKED STEPMOTHER   MGM/UA, 1989, directed
INTO THIN AIR   Triumph, 1990
MANIAC COP 2   The Movie House, 1990
THE AMBULANCE   Triumph, 1990, directed
GUILTY AS SIN   Buena Vista, 1993
BODY SNATCHERS   Warner Bros., 1993,
   Story w/Raymond Cistheri

Screenplays:
BRUTE FORCE (Axis Films)
THE SLAYER
PLAY THE HEAVY   w/James Dixon
THE MAN WHO LOVED HITCHCOCK
CAST OF CHARACTERS
KINGDOM COME
THE INSIDER
FEVER OF THE HUNT   w/Peter Lenkov
BEST FRIEND
SO HELP ME GOD
CANDIDATE FOR OBLIVION

LAWRENCE D. COHEN*
Agent: William Morris Agency - Beverly Hills, 310/274-7451

CARRIE   United Artists, 1976, play followed
GHOST STORY   Universal, 1981

Screenplays:
NIGHTMARE ON ALCATRAZ
A WOMAN OF INDEPENDENT MEANS
MOTHER AND TWO DAUGHTERS
SHARP PRACTICE

LAWRENCE J. COHEN*
Contact: WGA - Los Angeles, 310/550-1000

START THE REVOLUTION WITHOUT ME   Warner Bros., 1970,
   w/Fred Freeman
S*P*Y*S   20th Century-Fox, 1974, w/Fred Freeman &
   Malcolm Marmorstein

THE BIG BUS   Paramount, 1976, w/Fred Freeman
DELIRIOUS   MGM-Pathe, 1991, w/Fred Freeman

Screenplays:
THE PSYCHIATRIST & THE THIEF w/Fred Freeman
KARISTAN w/Fred Freeman

MURRAY COHEN
Agent: Richland/Wunsch/Hohman Agency - Los Angeles,
   310/278-1955

MIDAS (Short)   directed

Screenplays:
PARADISE COVE
THE GIRL NEXT DOOR   ANGEL PANGS

NEIL COHEN*
Agent: William Morris Agency - Beverly Hills, 310/274-7451

PASS THE AMMO   New Century/Vista, 1988, w/Joel Cohen
RICH BOYS   International Film Marketing, 1990, co-directed

Screenplays:
BEVERLY HILLS HOBOS
THE FLYING PELICAN
DESPERATE

ROB COHEN*
Agent: United Talent Agency - Beverly Hills, 310/273-6700

SCANDALOUS   Orion, 1984, w/John Byrum, directed
DRAGON: THE BRUCE LEE STORY   Universal, 1993,
   w/Ed Khmara & John Raffo, directed

Screenplays:
CAPITOL OFFENSE (directing)
THE RECOVERY w/John Byrum
THE RED MENACE

ROBERT H. COHEN*
Agent: United Talent Agency - Beverly Hills, 310/273-6700

Screenplays:
SHOWDOWN AT SHADY GLADE
THE TOWERING DISASTER w/David Cross

RONALD M. COHEN*
Agent: Barry Perelman Agency - Los Angeles, 310/274-5999

BLUE   Paramount, 1968, w/Meade Roberts
THE GOOD GUYS AND THE BAD GUYS   Warner Bros., 1969,
   w/Dennis Shryack
TWILIGHT'S LAST GLEAMING   Allied Artists, 1977,
   w/Edward Heubsch

MICHAEL COHN
WHEN THE BOUGH BREAKS   Prism, 1993, directed

HARLEY COKLISS
WARLORDS OF THE 21ST CENTURY   New World, 1982,
   w/Irviing Austin & John Beech

MIRITH J.S. COLAO
THE RETURN OF JAFAR (AHVF)   Buena Vista, 1994,
   w/Kevin Campbell, Bill Motz, Steve Roberts, Bob Roth,
   Jan Strand & Brian Swedlin

BRANDON COLE*
Agent: William Morris Agency - New York, 212/586-5100

SONS   Pacific Pictures, 1989, w/Alexandre Rockwell
MAC   Samuel Goldwyn Company, 1992, w/John Turturro

DOUG COLE*
Agent: Jon Klane Agency - Beverly Hills, 310/278-0178

Screenplays:
FALL OF THE SPARROW w/Colleen Craig
UNDER THE ROSE w/Colleen Craig
THE FIFTH WISH w/Colleen Craig

KELLY COLE
Contact: KellCole Productions - 213/876-6191

Screenplays:
THE APOTHECARY w/Christopher Coppola
ANOTHER VENICE

TOM COLE*
Agent: Innovative Artists - Los Angeles, 310/553-5200

MEDAL OF HONOR RAG (P)
THE EIGHTIES (P)   aka ABOUT TIME
FIGHTING BOB (P)
SMOOTH TALK   Spectrafilm, 1985
STREETS OF GOLD   20th Century Fox, 1986, w/Heywood Gould &
   Richard Price

Screenplays:
NEW LIFE

CLIFFORD COLEMAN
THE ICE RUNNER   Borde Film Releasing, 1993,
   w/Joshua Stallings & Joyce Warren

DAVID COLEMAN*
Agent: Jon Klane Agency - Beverly Hills, 310/278-0178

ENDLESS DESCENT   DEG, 1989
LOOSE ENDS (Short)   1994, directed

Screenplays:
CITY OF DARKNESS
HAT TRICK
SNAKE PIT
THE OVERLORD
SIGHTINGS

WANDA COLEMAN*
Agent: The Parness Agency - Santa Monica, 310/319-1664

Screenplays:
THE DUKE OF EARL
SHAWISHI

ADAM COLEMAN - HOWARD
Agent: William Morris Agency - Beverly Hills, 310/274-7451

DEAD GIRL   Cinetel, 1994, directed

RUSSELL W. COLGIN
YOUNG WARRIORS   Cannon, 1986, w/Lawrence D. Foldes

LEWIS A. COLICK*
Agent: CAA - Beverly Hills, 310/288-4545

THE DIRT BIKE KID   Concorde/Cinema Group, 1985,
   w/David Brandes
UNLAWFUL ENTRY   20th Century Fox, 1992
JUDGMENT NIGHT   Universal, 1993

Screenplays:
MEDGAR EVERS STORY
WHERE THE MONEY WAS
RADIANT CITY
THE PLUMBER

JERRY COLKER*
Contact: Mitchell, Silberberg & Knapp - Los Angeles, 310/312-3156

MAIL (P)
3 GUYS NAKED FROM THE WAIST DOWN (P)

Screenplays:
STANKY UNITED!
RAPUNZEL
CINDERELLA ROCK
IRON HEAT

MICHAEL COLLEARY*
Agent: The Irv Schechter Company - Beverly Hills, 310/278-8070

Screenplays:
STRETCH ARMSTRONG w/Mike Werb
FACE-OFF w/Mike Werb
ARCHANGELS

ROBERT COLLECTOR*
Agent: William Morris Agency - Beverly Hills, 310/274-7451

MEMOIRS OF AN INVISIBLE MAN   Warner Bros., 1992,
   w/Dana Olsen & William Goldman

Screenplays:
THE VULGARIANS w/Dana Olsen
MEN ON BASE w/Dana Olsen
GOLD LUST w/Dana Olsen
YOUR WISH IS MY COMMAND w/Dana Olsen

JOHN COLLEE
Agent: Peters, Fraser & Dunlop - London, 071/376-7676

PAPER MASK   Film Four International, 1991

PETER COLLEY
Business: Buckingham International Productions, 3960 Laurel Canyon
   Blvd. - Suite 259, Studio City, CA 91614-3791, 818/704-7720

BEYOND SUSPICION (P)
THE DONNELLYS (P)
YOU'LL GET USED TO IT! (P)
WHEN THE REAPER CALLS (P)
MARK OF CAIN   Vestron Video/Brighstar Films, 1990, from his play
ILLUSIONS   Paul International, 1992, from his play
   "I'll Be Back Before Midnight"

Screenplays:
THE LAST DUEL

RONALD COLLIER
CLOSE SHAVE   Tobann International, 1981, w/Robert Hendrickson

A.M. COLLINS*
Agent: Annette Van Duren Agency - Los Angeles, 213/650-3643

ANGRY HOUSEWIVES (P)   also screenplay

Screenplays:
DO IT FOR THE MONEY

CORBIN COLLINS
Manager: Addis-Wechsler - Los Angeles, 213/954-9000

Screenplays:
SHACKLES

JACKIE COLLINS*
Agent: William Morris Agency - Beverly Hills, 310/274-7451

THE STUD   Trans American, 1978
THE WORLD IS FULL OF MARRIED MEN   New Realm, 1979
YESTERDAY'S HERO   EMI, 1979

JOHN B. COLLINS*
Agent: The Coppage Company - North Hollywood, 818/980-1106

Screenplays:
LUNCH w/Robin Maxwell

ROBERT COLLINS*
Contact: WGA - Los Angeles, 310/550-1000

SAVAGE HARVEST   20th Century-Fox, 1981,
   w/Robert Blees, directed

ARTHUR COLLIS*
Contact: Stuart Berton, Berton & Feigen - 310/271-5123

BLUE DESERT   Neo Motion Pictures, 1991, w/Bradley Battersby

JENNIFER COLLOPY*
Agent: Writers & Artists Agency - Los Angeles, 310/824-6300

Screenplays:
ONE SUMMER, A MIRACLE
PRIVATE WARS
DOUBLE TIME
THE MEASURING WALL
A FEW GOOD WOMEN
LEPRECHAUN
BAD DREAMS
WIFE IN LAW
TAILSPIN

BILL COLOMBO
Agent: Neal Stevens & Associates - Beverly Hills, 310/275-7541

Screenplays:
WANDERING HOME (CTF)

HARRY COLOMBY*
Agent: CAA - Beverly Hills, 310/288-4545

JOHNNY DANGEROUSLY   20th Century Fox, 1987, w/Jeff Harris,
   Bernie Kukoff & Norman Steinberg
TOUCH AND GO   Tri-Star, 1987, w/Alan Ormsby & Bob Sand

CARL-JAN COLPAERT
Business: Cineville Inc., 225 Santa Monica Blvd. - 7th Floor,
   Santa Monica, CA 90401, 310/394-4699

DELUSION   I.R.S. Releasing, 1991, w/Kurt Voss, directed
THE CREW   Cineville, 1994, w/Lance Smith, directed

Screenplays:
THE SACRED AGE w/Benjamin Goldhagen

CHRIS COLUMBUS*
Agent: CAA - Beverly Hills, 310/288-4545
Contact: 1492, c/o 20th Century Fox - Los Angeles, 310/203-2368

RECKLESS   MGM/UA, 1984
GREMLINS   Warner Bros., 1984
THE GOONIES   Warner Bros., 1985
YOUNG SHERLOCK HOLMES   Paramount, 1985
HEARTBREAK HOTEL   Buena Vista, 1988, directed
ONLY THE LONELY   20th Century Fox, 1991, directed
LITTLE NEMO (AF)   Hemdale, 1992, w/Richard Outten
NINE MONTHS   20th Century Fox, 1995, directed

Screenplays:
MORE
THEATER OF BLOOD (remake)
WARPED ARROWS
I THINK I'M GOING TO LIKE IT HERE
STIFFS

PHIL COMBEST*
Contact: WGA - Los Angeles, 310/550-1000

Screenplays:
THREE WISHES w/Ruben Leder

MARK COMBS
Agent: The Parness Agency - Santa Monica, 310/319-1664

Screenplays:
THE GIRLS CLUB (Story)
BLOWN AWAY
BLACK MARIAH
STRIP SEARCH
LOVE SHACK

BETTY COMDEN*
Agent: ICM - New York, 212/556-5600

GOOD NEWS   MGM, 1947, w/Adolph Green
THE BARKLEYS OF BROADWAY   MGM, 1949, w/Adolph Green
ON THE TOWN   MGM, 1949, w/Adolph Green, from their play
SINGIN' IN THE RAIN   MGM, 1952, w/Adolph Green
THE BAND WAGON ★   MGM, 1953, w/Adolph Green
IT'S ALWAYS FAIR WEATHER ★   MGM, 1955, w/Adolph Green
AUNTIE MAME   Warner Bros., 1958, w/Adolph Green
BELLS ARE RINGING   MGM, 1960, w/Adolph Green,
    from their play
WHAT A WAY TO GO   20th Century-Fox, 1963, w/Adolph Green

ROBERT J. COMFORT*
Agent: Innovative Artists - Los Angeles, 310/553-5200

DOGFIGHT   Warner Bros., 1991

Screenplays:
CAR PICTURE
VINCE AND AL GO TO WAR
THE OX AND THE EYE
TEARIN' THE DRIVE-IN DOWN
HEAT LIGHTNING
FRIENDLY VOICES
ORANGE BLOSSOM DRIVE
WILD KINGDOM
THE KID w/Rick Kellard
SPIDER w/Rick Kellard
NICE GIRLS w/Rick Kellard
TOM WEST w/Rick Kellard

ELIZABETH COMICI*
Agent: Wallerstein*Kappelman Agency - Los Angeles, 213/782-0225

Screenplays:
LITTLE NAPOLEON w/Lou Comici
THE VISITOR w/Lou Comici
THE CHINESE MURDERS w/Lou Comici
RIVALS w/Lou Comici
NIGHTFALL w/Lou Comici
BLUE STAR w/Lou Comici
IVAN w/Lou Comici
BUMBURY w/Lou Comici
A BIT OF MAGIC w/Lou Comici
HERZL THE KING w/Lou Comici
THE PORTALS w/Lou Comici

LOU COMICI*
Agent: Wallerstein*Kappelman Agency - Los Angeles, 213/782-0225

Screenplays:
LITTLE NAPOLEON w/Liz Comici
THE VISITOR w/Liz Comici
THE CHINESE MURDERS w/Liz Comici
RIVALS w/Liz Comici
NIGHTFALL w/Liz Comici
BLUE STAR w/Liz Comici
IVAN w/Liz Comici

BUMBURY w/Liz Comici
A BIT OF MAGIC w/Liz Comici
HERZL THE KING w/Liz Comici
THE PORTALS w/Liz Comici

RICHARD COMPTON*
Contact: WGA - Los Angeles, 310/550-1000

RETURN TO MACON COUNTY   American International,
    1975, directed

RICHARD CONDON*
Agent: Harold Matson Company - New York, 212/679-4490

PRIZZI'S HONOR ★   20th Century Fox, 1985, w/Janet Roach

WILLIAM CONDON*
Agent: CAA - Beverly Hills, 310/288-4545

STRANGE BEHAVIOR *DEAD KIDS* World Northal, 1981,
    w/Michael Laughlin
STRANGE INVADERS   Orion, 1983, w/Michael Laughlin
SISTER, SISTER   New World, 1988, w/Ginny Cerrella &
    Joel Cohen, directed
MURDER 101 (CTF)   Alan Barnette/MCA Television, 1991,
    w/Roy Johansen
F/X 2: THE DEADLY ART OF ILLUSION   Orion, 1991

Screenplays:
RED EYE
THIRTEENTH DUKE w/Roger D. Manning
THE KID IN THE GREY FEDORA
BLOOD SECRETS
LAST KISS

J.C (CHRIS) CONKLING*
Contact: WGA - Los Angeles, 310/550-1000

THE LORD OF THE RINGS (AF)   United Artists, 1978,
    w/Peter S. Beagle

NICOLE CONN
Agent: Renaissance-H.N. Swanson - Los Angeles, 310/246-6000

CLAIRE OF THE MOON   Demi-Monde Productions, 1993, directed

SHANE CONNAUGHTON
Agent: William Morris Agency - Beverly Hills, 310/274-7451

THE DOLLAR BOTTOM (Short) ★★   Paramount, 1980
MY LEFT FOOT ★   Miramax, 1989, w/Jim Sheridan
THE PLAYBOYS   Samuel Goldwyn Company, 1992,
    w/Kerry Crabbe
O MARY, THIS LONDON   Samuel Goldwyn Company, 1994

Screenplays:
RUN OF THE COUNTRY (Columbia)
WAITING FOR MICHAEL

MYLES CONNELL
Agent: Writers & Artists Agency - Los Angeles, 310/824-6300

THE DEVIANT (Short) 1990, directed
IN UNCLE ROBERT'S FOOTSTEPS (Short) 1993, directed

Screenplays:
THE OPPORTUNISTS

MICHAEL CONNELLY
Agent: Renaissance-H.N. Swanson - Los Angeles, 310/246-6000

Screenplays:
THE BLACK ECHO

JON CONNOLLY*
Agent: CAA - Beverly Hills, 310/288-4545

THE DREAM TEAM   Universal, 1989, w/David Loucka

Screenplays:
MINIMUM SECURITY w/David Loucka
BIG SHOTS w/David Loucka
LITTLE LEAGUE CONFIDENTIAL w/David Loucka
INTO THE HEART w/David Loucka
PALS FOREVER w/David Loucka
THE OTHER WOMAN w/David Loucka
LENNIE'S HEART w/David Loucka
SINGLE AGAIN w/David Loucka
THE TRUTH w/David Loucka
THEY'VE LANDED w/David Loucka
A GOOD MAN w/David Loucka
AUGIE

RAY CONNOLLY
THAT'LL BE THE DAY   EMI, 1973
STARDUST   EMI, 1974
FOREVER YOUNG   Cinecom, 1986

Screenplays:
WORKING CLASS HERO
TRICK OR TREAT

PHILLIP D. CONNORS
EVILS OF THE NIGHT   Shapiro Entertainment, 1985,
   w/Mardi Rustam

CHRISTINE CONRAD*
Contact: Patty Felker - 310/207-8337

JUNIOR   Universal, 1994, w/Kevin Wade

STEVE CONRAD*
Agent: CAA - Beverly Hills, 310/288-4545

WRESTLING ERNEST HEMINGWAY   Warner Bros., 1993

Screenplays:
ROADSONG

PAT CONROY*
Contact: WGA - Los Angeles, 310/550-1000

THE PRINCE OF TIDES ★   Columbia, 1991, w/Becky Johnston

Screenplays:
EX w/Doug Marlette
ATLANTA BURNING

JOHN CONSIDINE*
Agent: Jim Preminger Agency - Los Angeles, 310/475-9491

A WEDDING   20th Century-Fox, 1978, w/Robert Altman,
   Allan Nicholls & Patricia Resnick

Screenplays:
A WAR

ROBERT CONTE*
Agent: ICM - Beverly Hills, 310/550-4000

ODD JOBS   Tri-Star, 1986, w/Peter Martin Wortmann
WHO'S HARRY CRUMB?   Tri-Star, 1988, w/Peter Martin Wortmann

Screenplays:
SWEET AUNTIE ROSE w/Peter Martin Wortmann
WOMEN ON THE VERGE w/Peter Martin Wortmann
HARRY SCARY w/Peter Martin Wortmann
DAYTIME w/Peter Martin Wortmann

FUGITIVE GUYS w/Peter Martin Wortmann
THE GREAT PRETENDER w/Peter Martin Wortmann
OFF THE GRID w/L.R. Lindbergh

ERNIE CONTRERAS*
Agent: CAA - Beverly Hills, 310/288-4545

THE PAGEMASTER   20th Century Fox, 1994, w/David Casci &
   David Kirschner

GARY CONWAY*
Contact: WGA - Los Angeles, 310/550-1000

AMERICAN NINJA 2   Cannon, 1987, w/James Booth
OVER THE TOP   Cannon, 1987, Story w/DavidEngelbach
AMERICAN NINJA 3: BLOOD HUNT   Cannon, 1989, Story

GERALD F. CONWAY*
Agent: Maggie Field Agency - Studio City, 818/980-2001

FIRE AND ICE (AF)   20th Century-Fox, 1983, w/Roy Thomas
CONAN THE DESTROYER   Universal, 1984, Story w/Roy Thomas

Screenplays:
THE LAST WARRIORS w/Roy Thomas
THE X-MEN w/Roy Thomas
DOC DYNAMO w/Roy Thomas
CAGE w/Roy Thomas
SNOW FURY w/Roy Thomas

JAMES L. CONWAY*
Agent: CAA - Beverly Hills, 310/288-4545

HANGAR #18   Sunn Classic, 1980,
   Story w/Tom Chapman, directed
THE PRESIDENT MUST DIE   Jensen Farley Pictures, 1981,
   w/Cliff Osmond, directed

TIM CONWAY*
Business Manager: Michael N. Cobin - Los Angeles, 213/461-3344

THEY WENT THAT-A-WAY & THAT-A-WAY   International Picture
   Show, 1978
THE PRIZE FIGHTER   New World, 1979, w/John Myhers
THE PRIVATE EYES   New World, 1980, w/John Myhers
THE LONGSHOT   Orion, 1986

DAVID COOK
WALTER AND JUNE *LOVING WALTER*   Film Forum, 1986
SECOND BEST   Warner Bros., 1994

DOUGLAS S. COOK*
Agent: Writers & Artists Agency - Los Angeles, 310/824-6300
Business: Aurora Productions, 8642 Melrose Ave. #100, Los Angeles,
   CA 90069, 310/854-6900

PAYOFF (CTF)   Viacom, 1991, w/David Weisberg
HOLY MATRIMONY   Buena Vista, 1994, w/David Weisberg

Screenplays:
THE ROCK w/David Weisberg

PETER COOK
Agent: David Wilkinson Associates, 115 Hazlebury Rd., London
   SW6 2Lx, 071/371-5188, fax 371-5161

BEDAZZLED   20th Century Fox, 1967
THE RISE AND RISE OF MICHAEL RIMMER   Warner Bros., 1970,
   w/Graham Chapman, John Cleese & Kevin Billington
THE HOUND OF THE BASKERVILLES   Atlantic Releasing
   Corporation, 1979, w/Dudley Moore & Paul Morrissey
YELLOWBEARD   Orion, 1983, w/Graham Chapman &
   Bernard McKenna

T. S. COOK*
(Thomas S. Cook)
Agent: William Morris Agency - Beverly Hills, 310/274-7451

THE CHINA SYNDROME ★   Columbia, 1979, w/Michael Gray &
   James Bridges
NIGHTBREAKER (CTF)   Turner Network Television, 1989

MARTIE COOKE
Agent: Writers & Artists Agency - Los Angeles, 310/824-6300

Screenplays:
ZACHARY'S TRUTH

JON COOKSEY*
Contact: WGA - Los Angeles, 310/550-1000

Screenplays:
TIL MARRIAGE DO US PART w/Ali Matheson
HIT PARADE w/Ali Matheson
REWIND w/Ali Matheson
BEAUTY SLEEP w/Ali Matheson

TONY COOKSON
Agent: The Artists Group - Los Angeles, 310/552-1100

AND YOU THOUGHT YOUR PARENTS WERE WEIRD   Trimark,
   1991, directed

BARRY MICHAEL COOPER*
Agent: Writers & Artists Agency - Los Angeles, 310/824-6300

WRITING ON THE WALL (P)   also screenplay
NEW JACK CITY   Warner Bros., 1991, w/Thomas Lee Wright
SUGAR HILL   20th Century Fox, 1993
ABOVE THE RIM   New Line Cinema, 1994, w/Jeff Pollack

Screenplays:
AMERICA'S OTHER CIVIL WAR: THE HISTORY OF
   GANGBANGING IN LOS ANGELES 1972-92 (CTF)
MAD FAME

DENNIS J. COOPER*
Agent: ICM - Beverly Hills, 310/550-4000
Business Manager: Michael Wolf - Los Angeles, 310/277-6991

Screenplays:
THE UNDEAD (from his play)

MATT COOPER*
Agent: William Morris Agency - Beverly Hills, 310/274-7451

A PIECE OF MY HEART (P)

Screenplays:
A VIEW FROM THE TOP

NATALIE COOPER*
Agent: Paradigm - Los Angeles, 310/277-4400

DESERT HEARTS   Samuel Goldwyn Company, 1986

Screenplays:
WHITE MAN'S BURDEN
OHIO SHUFFLE
YOUNG LILLY

PAUL COOPER*
Agent: Preferred Artists - Encino, 818/990-0305

Screenplays:
WHEN WE WERE COLORED (BET Films)

SUSAN COOPER*
Agent: ICM - Beverly Hills, 310/550-4000

Screenplays:
DINNER AT THE HOMESICK RESTAURANT w/Hume Cronyn

KEN COPEL
Agent: Paradigm - Los Angeles, 310/277-4400

TWO GUYS TALKING ABOUT GIRLS   Trimark, 1995

JEFF COPELAND
TALES OF THE UNKNOWN   AIP Home Video, 1990,
   "Warped," w/Roger Nygard

MARTIN COPELAND
THE HEAVENLY KID   Orion, 1985, w/Cary Medoway

Screenplays:
TOO DEEP FOR TEARS
BEST RIDE FROM NEW YORK

CHRISTOPHER COPPOLA
Contact: KellCole Productions - Los Angeles, 213/876-6191

DEADFALL   Trimark, 1993, w/Nick Vallelonga, directed

Screenplays:
THE APOTHECARY w/Kelly Cole

FRANCIS FORD COPPOLA
Agent: CAA - Beverly Hills, 310/288-4545
Business: American Zoetrope, Columbia Pictures,
   10202 W. Washington Blvd., Culver City, CA 90232, 310/280-8000
   & Sentinal Building, 916 Kearny Street, San Francisco, CA 94133,
   415/788-7500

TONIGHT FOR SURE   Premier Pictures, 1961, directed
DEMENTIA 13   American International, 1963, directed
THIS PROPERTY IS CONDEMNED   Paramount, 1966,
   w/Fred Coe & Edith Sommer
IS PARIS BURNING?   Paramount, 1966, w/Gore Vidal
YOU'RE A BIG BOY NOW   7 Arts, 1966, directed
THE RAIN PEOPLE   Warner Bros., 1969, directed
PATTON ★★   20th Century-Fox, 1970, w/Edmund H. North
THE GODFATHER ★   Paramount, 1972, w/Mario Puzo, directed
THE CONVERSATION ★   Paramount, 1974, directed
THE GODFATHER, PART II ★★   Paramount, 1974,
   w/Mario Puzo, directed
THE GREAT GATSBY   Paramount, 1974
APOCALYPSE NOW ★   United Artists, 1979,
   w/John Milius, directed
ONE FROM THE HEART   Columbia, 1982,
   w/Armyan Bernstein, directed
RUMBLE FISH   Universal, 1983, w/S.E. Hinton, directed
THE COTTON CLUB   Orion, 1984, w/William Kennedy, directed
NEW YORK STORIES   Buena Vista, 1989, "Life Without Zoe,"
   w/Sofia Coppola, directed
THE GODFATHER, PART III   Paramount, 1990,
   w/Mario Puzo, directed

ROMAN COPPOLA
Agent: William Morris Agency - Beverly Hills, 310/274-7451
Contact: ZZYZX Productions, 1632 5th St. - Suite 330, Santa Monica,
   CA 90401, 310/393-0200

THE SPIRIT OF '76   Columbia, 1990, Story w/Lucas Reiner

SOFIA COPPOLA
Contact: Screen Actors Guild - Los Angeles, 213/954-1600

NEW YORK STORIES   Buena Vista, 1989, "Life Without Zoe,"
   w/Francis Ford Coppola

SERGIO CORBUCCI
Address: via Donatello 15, Rome, Italy, 06/360-7610

SUPER FUZZ   Avco Embassy, 1981, w/Sabataino Ciuffini, directed

ROBERT CORDING
THE TREASURE   Questar Pictures, 1990,
   w/David G. Cohen, directed

NICHOLAS COREA*
Agent: David Shapira & Associates - Sherman Oaks, 818/906-0322

Screenplays:
R & R
LANEPLAY

JOHN CORK*
Agent: United Talent Agency - Beverly Hills, 310/273-6700

THE LONG WALK HOME   Miramax, 1990

Screenplays:
THE FUNERAL
THE NIGHT RIDER

AVERY CORMAN*
Agent: ICM - Beverly Hills, 310/550-4000

Screenplays:
MR. KAUFMAN w/Diane Sokolow
THE BIG HYPE

ROGER CORMAN
Business: Concorde Pictures, 11600 San Vicente Blvd., Los Angeles,
   CA 90049, 310/820-6733

FRANKENSTEIN UNBOUND   20th Century Fox, 1990,
   w/F.X. Feeney, directed

JOHN CORNELL
"CROCODILE" DUNDEE ★   Paramount, 1986,
   w/Paul Hogan & Ken Shadie, directed

STUART CORNFELD*
Agent: Broder-Kurland-Webb-Uffner - Beverly Hills, 310/281-3400

Screenplays:
SON OF DARKNESS w/David Goyer

PATRICIA CORNWELL
Agent: ICM - Beverly Hills, 310/550-4000

Screenplays:
CRUEL AND UNUSUAL

STEPHEN M. CORNWELL*
Agent: The Agency - Los Angeles, 310/551-3000
Business Manager: Hansen, Jacobsen & Teller - Los Angeles,
   310/278-8622

WHEN THAT I WAS (Short)   directed
GAS FOOD LODGING (Short)   directed
STATE OF FEAR (Short)   directed
THE KILLING STREETS   21st Century Film, 1990, directed

Screenplays:
M
BLOCK PARTY w/Nick Gregory
CRASH OUT w/Nick Paine
HAZARDOUS WASTE

EUGENE CORR*
Agent: Innovative Artists - Los Angeles, 310/553-5200

WILDROSE   Troma, 1984, w/John Hanson
DESERT BLOOM   Columbia, 1986, directed

MICHAEL CORRENTE
FEDERAL HILL   Trimark, 1994, directed

JOHN W. CORRINGTON
BOXCAR BERTHA   American International, 1972,
   w/Joyce Corrington
BATTLE FOR THE PLANET OF THE APES   20th Century-Fox,
   1973, w/Joyce Corrington

JOYCE H. CORRINGTON*
Agent: Jay Feldman Company - 310/829-9880

BOXCAR BERTHA   American International, 1972, w/John Corrington
BATTLE FOR THE PLANET OF THE APES   20th Century-Fox,
   1973, w/John Corrington

Screenplays:
THE LOST ONES

BUD CORT
Contact: Screen Actors Guild - Los Angeles, 213/954-1600

TED & VENUS   Double Helix Films, 1991, w/Paul Ciotti, directed

MICHAEL CORY
LOOSE SCREWS   Concorde, 1985

CHRISTOPHER COSBY*
Agent: Pleshette & Green - Los Angeles, 213/465-0428

BLOODSPORT   Cannon, 1988, w/Mel Friedman & Sheldon Lettich

Screenplays:
THE ATOMIC VETERAN w/Mel Friedman
SNOWBOUND w/Mel Friedman
SUPERBOXERS w/Mel Friedman
MAXIMUM MAXIMUM PRISONSHIP w/Mel Friedman
TRACKDOWN w/Mel Friedman
DEADLY METAL w/Mel Friedman
GOLDEN KNIGHTS w/Mel Friedman
ALIEN COP w/Mel Friedman

DON COSCARELLI*
Business: Starway International, 8033 Sunset Blvd. - Suite 405,
   Los Angeles, CA 90046, 213/650-6995

PHANTASM   Avco Embassy, 1979, directed
THE BEASTMASTER   MGM/UA, 1982, w/PaulPepperman, directed
PHANTASM II   Universal, 1988, directed
SURVIVAL QUEST   MGM/UA, 1990, directed
PHANTASM III   Starway International, 1993, directed

Screenplays:
THE BOY NEXT DOOR

GEORGE PAN COSMATOS
Agent: ICM - Beverly Hills, 310/550-4000

MASSACRE IN ROME   National General, 1973,
   w/Robert Katz, directed
THE CASSANDRA CROSSING   Avco Embassy, 1977,
   w/Robert Katz & Tom Mankiewicz, directed

JAMES COSTIGAN*
Contact: WGA - Los Angeles, 310/550-1000

KING DAVID   Paramount, 1985, w/Andrew Birkin
MR. NORTH   Samuel Goldwyn Company, 1988, w/John Huston &
   Janet Roach

LANNY COTLER
THE EARTHLING   Filmways, 1981

MANNY COTO*
Agent: United Talent Agency - Beverly Hills, 310/273-6700

JACK IN THE BOX (Short)   1986,   directed
DR. GIGGLES   Universal, 1992, w/Graeme Whifler, directed

Screenplays:
HOSTILE INTENT
THE WARRIOR OF WAVERLY STREET
THE TICKING MAN w/Brian Helgeland
VIRUS

JOHN COTTER
CHEETAH   Buena Vista, 1989, w/Griff DuRhone & Erik Tarloff

SUZETTE COUTURE*
Agent: The Gersh Agency - Beverly Hills, 310/274-6611

LA FLORIDA   Alliance Releasing, 1993, w/Pierre Sarrazin

BILL D. COUTURIÉ*
Agent: CAA - Beverly Hills, 310/288-4545

TWICE UPON A TIME (AF)   The Ladd Company/Warner Bros.,
    1983, w/Suella Kennedy, John Korty & Charles Swenson
DEAR AMERICA: LETTERS FROM VIETNAM (FD)   Taurus
    Entertainment, 1987, w/Richard Dewhurst, directed
EARTH AND THE AMERICAN DREAM (FD)   HBO Pictures, 1993,
    w/Ken Richards, directed
FAVORITE FILMS (FD)   Couturie Company/AFI, 1993, directed

Screenplays:
SPACE BROTHER w/Richard Dewhurst

GIL COWAN
OPPOSING FORCES   Orion, 1987

BRIAN COWDEN*
Manager: Jon Brown, The Brown Group - Burbank, 818/955-7040

Screenplays:
THE LONG WALK
THE EDGAR CASEY STORY
THE COLD JUNGLE

RONALD COWEN*
Agent: William Morris Agency - Beverly Hills, 310/274-7451

Screenplays:
FIREFLY w/Daniel Lipman
FAMILY DANCING w/Daniel Lipman

ALEX COX
Agent: Stephanie Mann Agency - Los Angeles, 213/653-7130

REPO MAN   Universal, 1984, directed
SID & NANCY   Samuel Goldwyn Company, 1986,
    w/Abbe Wool, directed
STRAIGHT TO HELL   Island Films, 1987, w/Dick Rude, directed

BRADLEY COX
Agent: Innovative Artists - Los Angeles, 310/553-5200
Manager: Addis-Wechsler - Los Angeles, 213/954-9000

Screenplays:
SPIKE TO THE ACHILLES

BRIAN COX
Business: Distant Horizon, 8282 Sunset Blvd. - Suite A, Los Angeles,
    CA 90046, 213/848-4140

DEADLY OBSESSION   Distant Horizon, 1989, w/Jeno Hodi &
    Paul Wolansky

DOUG COX*
Contact: WGA - Los Angeles, 310/550-1000

WHICH END'S UP? (P)   w/John Moody

Screenplays:
NO SMOKING w/John Moody

JAMES D. COX*
Agent: United Talent Agency - Beverly Hills, 310/273-6700

RITZVILLE (Short)   directed
EAT THE SUN (Short)   directed
NEPTUNE (Short)   directed
OLIVER & CO. (AF)   Buena Vista, 1988, w/Timothy J. Disney &
    James Mangold
THE RESCUERS DOWN UNDER (AF)   Buena Vista, 1990,
    w/Karvey Kirkpatrick, Joe Ranft & Byron Simpson
FERNGULLY: THE LAST RAINFOREST (AF)
    20th Century Fox, 1992

Screenplays:
THE FROG PRINCE (AF)
DON QUIXOTE

PAUL COX
Agent: Becsey/Wisdom/Kalajian Agency - Los Angeles, 310/550-0535

LONELY HEARTS   Samuel Goldwyn Company, 1982,
    w/John Clarke, directed
MAN OF FLOWERS   Spectrafilm, 1983, w/Bob Ellis, directed
MY FIRST WIFE   Spectrafilm, 1984, w/Bob Ellis, directed
CACTUS   Spectrafilm, 1986, w/Bob Ellis & Norman Kaye, directed
GOLDEN BRAID   Australian Film Commission/Film Victoria/
    Ilumination Films, 1990, w/Barry Dickins, directed
A WOMAN'S TALE   Orion Classics, 1991, directed
EXILE   Miramax, 1994, directed
EROTIC TALES   Mercure Distribution, 1994, "Touch Me,"
    w/Barry Dickins & Margot Wilburd, directed

CHRIS COYLE
Agent: The Gage Group - Los Angeles, 310/859-8777

Screenplays:
THE GODDESS OF ENCINO w/Julie Prendaville

KERRY CRABBE
Agent: William Morris Agency - Beverly Hills, 310/274-7451 &
    Judy Daish Agency - London, 486-5405

MEMOIRS OF A SURVIVOR   EMI, 1981, w/David Gladwell
THE PLAYBOYS   Samuel Goldwyn Company, 1992,
    w/Shane Connaughton

PETER CRABBE*
Agent: William Morris Agency - Beverly Hills, 310/274-7451

CAR 54, WHERE ARE YOU?   Orion, 1994, w/Peter McCarthy,
    Ebbe Roe Smith & Erik Tarloff

Screenplays:
SHORE LEAVE
HOME FOR THE HOLIDAYS
HUMPHREY

COLLEEN CRAIG*
Agent: Jon Klane Agency - Beverly Hills, 310/278-0178

Screenplays:
FALL OF THE SPARROW w/Doug Cole
UNDER THE ROSE w/Doug Cole
THE FIFTH WISH w/Doug Cole

H.A.L. CRAIG
WATERLOO Columbia, 1970, w/Sergie Bondarchuk
LION OF THE DESERT United Film Distribution, 1981

LAURIE CRAIG*
Manager: Linne Radmin, The Radmin Company - Beverly Hills,
310/274-9515

MODERN GIRLS Atlantic Releasing Corporation, 1986

Screenplays:
BAD DEATH w/Randee Russell
BAKED ALASKA

CLAUDE CRAMER
Agent: Jon Klane Agency - Beverly Hills, 310/278-0178

Screenplays:
STAR CROSSED
PARADISE CITY

WES CRAVEN*
Agent: ICM - Beverly Hills, 310/550-4000
Business: Wes Craven Films, 11112 Ventura Blvd. - 3rd Floor,
Studio City, CA 91604, 818/505-8110

THE HILLS HAVE EYES Vanguard, 1977, directed
DEADLY BLESSING United Artists/Polygram, 1981,
w/Glenn M. Benest & Matthew Barr
SWAMP THING Embassy, 1982
A NIGHTMARE ON ELM STREET New Line Cinema,
1984, directed
THE HILLS HAVE EYES II Castle Hill Productions, 1985, directed
A NIGHTMARE ON ELM STREET PART 3: DREAM WARRIORS
New Line Cinema, 1987, w/Bruce Wagner, Frank Darabont &
Chuck Russell
SHOCKER Universal, 1989, directed
THE PEOPLE UNDER THE STAIRS Universal, 1991, directed
WES CRAVEN'S NEW NIGHTMARE New Line Cinema,
1994, directed

Screenplays:
SHADOW OF GRAY

DARLENE CRAVIOTTO*
Agent: Pleshette & Green - Los Angeles, 213/465-0428

SQUANTO: A WARRIOR'S TALE Buena Vista, 1994

Screenplays:
IRONMAN
NO LANGUAGE BUT A CRY
SNAKEWALK
THE GIRL
SHADOWS
THE HARD RIDE
AMERICAN MADE

BOBBY CRAWFORD
A RAGE IN HARLEM Miramax, 1991, w/John Toles-Bey

JOANNA CRAWFORD*
Agent: John Taylor Williams, Palmer Dodge Agency - 617/573-0100

THE LITTLE ARK Cinema Center, 1971
BIRCH INTERVAL Gamma III, 1976

MARK McQUADE CRAWFORD
Agent: Renaissance-H.N. Swanson - Los Angeles, 310/246-6000

PSYCHIC (CTF) Trimark Pictures, 1992, Story w/William Crawford

NANCY VOYLES CRAWFORD*
Contact: WGA - Los Angeles, 310/550-1000

SIDEWINDER 1 Avco Embassy, 1977, w/Thomas McMahon
CARAVANS Universal, 1979, w/Thomas A. McMahon &
Lorraine Williams

WAYNE CRAWFORD*
Business: Gibraltar Entertainment, 14101 Valleyheart Dr. - Suite 205,
Sherman Oaks, CA 91423, 818/501-2076

VALLEY GIRL Atlantic Releasing Corporation, 1983,
w/Andrew Lane
JAKE SPEED New World, 1986, w/Andrew Lane

WILLIAM CRAWFORD*
Agent: Renaissance-H.N. Swanson - Los Angeles, 310/246-6000

PSYCHIC (CTF) Trimark Pictures, 1992,
Story w/Mark McQuade Crawford

MARIA CREAN
Agent: Warden, White & Kane - Beverly Hills, 213/852-1028

Screenplays:
QUIET HANDS

JAMES CRESSON*
(James Hicks)
Agent: William Morris Agency - Beverly Hills, 310/274-7451

THE MORNING AFTER 20th Century Fox, 1986
CHATAHOOCHEE Hemdale, 1990
DEFENSELESS 7 Arts/New Line Cinema, 1991

Screenplays:
WIT'S END

ANNE-MARIE CRICHTON
Agent: CAA - Beverly Hills, 310/288-4545

Screenplays:
TWISTER w/Michael Crichton

CHARLES CRICHTON
Agent: MLR Representation Ltd. - London, 71/351-5442

FLOODS OF FEAR Rank, 1958, directed
THE BOY WHO STOLE A MILLION Paramount, 1960,
w/John Eldridge, directed
A FISH CALLED WANDA ★ MGM/UA, 1988,
Story w/John Cleese, directed

MICHAEL CRICHTON*
Agent: CAA - Beverly Hills, 310/288-4545

EXTREME CLOSEUP National General, 1973
WESTWORLD MGM, 1973, directed
COMA MGM/UA, 1978, directed
THE GREAT TRAIN ROBBERY United Artists, 1979, directed
LOOKER The Ladd Company/Warner Bros., 1981, directed
RUNAWAY Tri-Star, 1984, directed
JURASSIC PARK Universal, 1993, w/David Koepp
RISING SUN 20th Century Fox, 1993, w/Michael Backes &
Philip Kaufman
CONGO Paramount, 1995, w/John Patrick Shanley

Screenplays:
TWISTER w/Anne-Marie Crichton
GENES

F I L M   W R I T E R S

STEVE CRIDER*
Agent: The Wright Concept - Burbank, 818/954-8943

Screenplays:
FAMILY MAN
JOHNNY B DEAD
DEAD MAN'S KEY

FRANK CRISTINA
(See Tom Laughlin)

TERESA CRISTINA
(See Tom Laughlin)

MICHAEL CRISTOFER*
Agent: CAA - Beverly Hills, 310/288-4545

SHADOW BOX (P)   also teleplay
LADY AND THE CLARINET (P)
BLACK ANGEL (P)
FALLING IN LOVE   Paramount, 1984
THE WITCHES OF EASTWICK   Warner Bros., 1987
THE BONFIRE OF THE VANITIES   Warner Bros., 1990
MR. JONES   TriStar, 1993, w/Eric Roth

Screenplays:
MISTRESS OF THE SEAS
BREAKING UP
CC PYLE & THE BUNION DERBY
MODIGLIANI
THE LADY & THE CLARINET
THE GREAT AMERICAN BELLY DANCE
GENTLE VENGENCE
THE MAIN
VANITIES
SILENCE
TRINITY

KEITH CRITCHLOW
VOLUNTEERS   Tri-Star, 1985, Story

JORDAN CRITTENDEN*
Contact: WGA - Los Angeles, 310/550-1000

UNEXPECTED GUESTS (P)
SOME PEOPLE, SOME OTHER PEOPLE, & WHAT THEY
    FINALLY DO (P)
GET TO KNOW YOUR RABBIT   Warner Bros., 1972

Screenplays:
THANKS, DAD w/Hal Dresner
DISAPPEARING ACT

DONALD CROMBIE
Business: Forest Home Films, 141 Penhurst St., Willoughby,
    NSW 2068, Australia, tel.:02/411-4972

ROUGH DIAMONDS   Beyond Films, 1994,
    w/Christopher Lee, directed

DAVID CRONENBERG*
Agent: CAA - Beverly Hills, 310/288-4545
Business: 217 Avenue Road, Toronto, Ontario M5R 2J3, Canada,
    416/961-3432

STEREO   Emergent Films, 1969, directed
CRIMES OF THE FUTURE   Emergent Films, 1970, directed
THEY CAME FROM WITHIN *SHIVERS* Trans-America,
    1976, directed
RABID   New World, 1977, directed
FAST COMPANY   Topar, 1979, w/Phil Savath &
    Courtney Smith, directed
THE BROOD   New World, 1979, directed
SCANNERS   Avco Embassy, 1981, directed
VIDEODROME   Universal, 1983, directed

THE FLY   20th Century Fox, 1986,
    w/Charles Edward Pogue, directed
DEAD RINGERS   20th Century Fox, 1988,
    w/Norman Snider, directed
NAKED LUNCH   20th Century Fox, 1991, directed

Screenplays:
RED CARS

KAREN CRONER*
Agent: William Morris Agency - Beverly Hills, 310/274-7451

GAS, FOOD, LODGING (Short)   directed

Screenplays:
THE BOY, THE DEVIL AND DIVORCE
DUE EAST
DEXTERITY
WILLIAM THE MAGNIFICENT

ISAAC CRONIN
CHAN IS MISSING   New Yorker, 1982, w/Wayne Wang &
    Terrel Seltzer

HUME CRONYN*
Agent: ICM - New York, 212/556-5600

Screenplays:
DINNER AT THE HOMESICK RESTAURANT w/Susan Cooper

JIM CROSBIE
BOY MEETS GIRL   Kino Eye, 1994, w/Jim Brady

ALISON CROSS*
Agent: CAA - Beverly Hills, 310/288-4545

Screenplays:
SPECIAL CIRCUMSTANCES
PALM BEACH
SAIGON
TWO ARE GUILTY

ANDREW CROSS
SHOCK 'EM DEAD   Academy Entertainment, 1991, w/Mark Freed

BEVERLY CROSS
THE LONG SHIPS   Columbia, 1963, w/Berkely Mather
JASON AND THE ARGONAUTS   Columbia, 1963, w/Jan Read
GENGIS KHAN   Columbia, 1964, w/Clarke Reynolds
HALF A SIXPENCE   Paramount, 1967
SINBAD AND THE EYE OF THE TIGER   Columbia, 1977
CLASH OF THE TITANS   United Artists, 1981

DAVID CROSS*
Manager: Tim Sarkas Management - 310/785-0444

Screenplays:
THE TOWERING DISASTER w/Rob Cohen

AVERY CROUNSE
Business: Elysian Pictures, 22049 Bobs Road, Long Beach,
    MS 39560, 213/871-8689

EYES OF FIRE   Aquarius Films, 1986, directed
THE INVISIBLE KID   Taurus Entertainment, 1988, directed

BILL CROUNSE
Agent: Barry Perelman Agency - Los Angeles, 310/274-5999

9 1/2 NINJAS   Republic Pictures, 1991, w/Don Pequignot
AMERICAN CYBORG: STEEL WARRIOR   Cannon, 1994,
    w/Don Peguignot & Brent Friedman

Screenplays:
FALSE SECURITY w/Don Pequignot
TO THE DEATH w/Don Pequignot

CAMERON CROWE*
Agent: CAA - Beverly Hills, 310/288-4545

FAST TIMES AT RIDGEMONT HIGH   Universal, 1982
THE WILD LIFE   Universal, 1984
SAY ANYTHING   20th Century Fox, 1989, directed
SINGLES   Warner Bros., 1992, directed

CHRISTOPHER CROWE
Agent: United Talent Agency - Beverly Hills, 310/273-6700

THE LAST CHASE   Crown International, 1981,
    as "C.R. O'Cristopher," w/Martyn Burke & Taylor Sutherland
NIGHTMARES   Universal, 1983, w/Jeffrey Bloom
THE MEAN SEASON   Orion, 1985, as "Leon Piedmont"
OFF LIMITS   20th Century Fox, 1988, w/Jack Thibeau, directed
WHISPERS IN THE DARK   Paramount, 1992, directed
THE LAST OF THE MOHICANS   20th Century Fox, 1992,
    w/Michael Mann
NO FEAR   Universal, 1995

Screenplays:
THE GENERAL'S DAUGHTER
AC/DC
GOODNIGHT MOON

MART CROWLEY*
Manager: Creative Alliance Management - Los Angeles,
    213/962-6090

A BREEZE FROM THE GULF (P)
REMOTE ASYLUM (P)
THE BOYS IN THE BAND   National General, 1970, from his play

JOHN CROWTHER
KILL AND KILL AGAIN   Film Ventures International, 1981
THE EVIL THAT MEN DO   Tri-Star, 1984, w/David Lee Henry
MISSING IN ACTION   Cannon, 1984, Story w/Lance Hool
THE WILD PAIR   Trans World Entertainment, 1987,
    Story w/Joseph Gunn
DAMNED RIVER   MGM/UA, 1990, w/Bayard Johnson

JIM CRUICKSHANK*
Agent: CAA - Beverly Hills, 310/288-4545
Business: Orr & Cruickshank Productions, Walt Disney Pictures,
    818/560-6423

BREAKING ALL THE RULES   New World, 1985, w/James Orr
TOUGH GUYS   Buena Vista, 1986, w/James Orr
THREE MEN AND A BABY   Buena Vista, 1987, w/James Orr
MR. DESTINY   Buena Vista, 1990, w/James Orr
SISTER ACT II: BACK IN THE HABIT   Buena Vista, 1993,
    w/James Orr & Judi Ann Mason

Screenplays:
MAN 2 MAN w/James Orr (Buena Vista)
FUN PARK w/James Orr
BANDIT w/James Orr

TOM CRUISE
Agent: CAA - Beverly Hills, 310/288-4545

DAYS OF THUNDER   Paramount, 1990, Story w/Robert Towne

JIM CRUMLEY*
Agent: William Morris Agency - Beverly Hills, 310/274-7451

Screenplays:
THE DANCING BEAR w/Tim Hunter
THE LAST GOOD KISS
TUNNELS OF CU CHI

BILLY CRYSTAL*
Agent: ICM - Beverly Hills, 310/550-4000
Business: Face Productions, Castle Rock - Los Angeles,
    310/285-2300

MEMORIES OF ME   MGM, 1988, w/Eric Roth
MR. SATURDAY NIGHT   Columbia, 1992, w/Lowell Ganz &
    Babaloo Mandel, directed
CITY SLICKERS II: THE LEGEND OF CURLY'S GOLD   Columbia,
    1994, w/Lowell Ganz & Babaloo Mandel
FORGET PARIS   Columbia, 1995, w/Lowell Ganz &
    Babaloo Mandel, directed

ROBERT CSETRI*
Contact: WGA - Los Angeles, 310/550-1000

Screenplays:
ATTILA THE HUN w/John Mendoza

CARLOS CUARON
Agent: William Morris Agency - Beverly Hills, 310/274-7451

Screenplays:
ROOTIE KAZOOTIE

FRANK CUCCI
LILY IN LOVE   New Line Cinema, 1985

FRED CUL CULLEN
THE MAN FROM SNOWY RIVER   20th Century-Fox,
    1983 (See John Dixon)

CULTURE CLASH
(See Richard Montoya, Ric Salinas & Herbert Siguenza)

CARMEN CULVER*
Agent: ICM - Beverly Hills, 310/550-4000

THE LAST PROSTITUTE (CTF)   BBK Productions/MCA Television
    Entertainment, 1991

JOSEPHINE CUMMINGS*
Contact: Amicus Entertainment - 818/760-3989

Screenplays:
ALTAR BOUND w/Richard Yalem

JAMES CUMMINS
Agent: Susan Smith & Associates - Beverly Hills, 213/852-4777

THE BONEYARD   Prism Entertainment, 1991, directed
STALKER   Proto Entertainment, 1992, directed

Screenplays:
LIGHTS OUT
SHADOW OF MAN
THE FIRST BEST STEP

RUSTY CUNDIEFF*
Agent: ICM - Beverly Hills, 310/550-4000

HOUSE PARTY 2: THE PAJAMA JAM!   New Line Cinema, 1991,
    w/Daryl G. Nickens
FEAR OF A BLACK HAT   Samuel Goldwyn Company,
    1994, directed

Screenplays:
TALES FROM THE HOOD w/Darin Scott (Savoy, directing)

RAY CUNNEFF
THE RAIN KILLER   Concorde, 1990

JERE P. CUNNINGHAM*
Agent: ICM - Beverly Hills, 310/550-4000
Business: Sky Blue Productions, Inc. - 818/907-9966

THE LAST OF THE FINEST   Orion, 1990, w/George Armitage &
   Thomas Lee Wright
JUDGMENT NIGHT   Universal, 1993, Story w/Lewis Colick

Screenplays:
CENTURION (directing)
CROCKETT AND BOWIE w/Crash Leyland
FLAMINGO
SHIVA
BUILDERS

LAURA CUNNINGHAM*
Agent: William Morris Agency - Beverly Hills, 310/274-7451

Screenplays:
PHONY FARM w/June Roberts

RICK CUNNINGHAM*
Agent: The Rothman Agency - Beverly Hills, 213/655-2020

Screenplays:
THE FISH

SEAN S. CUNNINGHAM
Agent: ICM - Beverly Hills, 310/550-4000
Business: Cunningham Productions, 4420 Hayvenhurst Ave.,
   Encino, CA 91436, 818/995-1585

Screenplays:
THE GYPSY'S CURSE (directing)

TIM CURNEN*
Agent: Peter Turner Agency - Santa Monica, 310/315-4772

FORBIDDEN WORLD   New World, 1982
GHOST WARRIOR *SWORDKILL*   Empire Pictures, 1986

Screenplays:
SCALAWAGS
BEASTIES
TUNNEL IN THE SKY

WILLIAM CURRAN*
Agent: Renaissance-H.N. Swanson - Los Angeles, 310/246-6000

LOVE, CHEAT & STEAL   (CTF)   Motion Picture Corporation
   of America, 1993, directed

LAUREN CURRIER
(See Barbara Turner)

VALERIE CURTIN*
Agent: CAA - Beverly Hills, 310/288-4545

...AND JUSTICE FOR ALL ★   Columbia, 1979, w/Barry Levinson
INSIDE MOVES   AFD, 1980, w/Barry Levinson
BEST FRIENDS   Warner Bros., 1982, w/Barry Levinson
UNFAITHFULLY YOURS   20th Century-Fox, 1984,
   w/Barry Levinson & Robert Klane
TOYS   20th Century Fox, 1992, w/Barry Levinson

Screenplays:
TWO LUCKY PEOPLE

DAN CURTIS*
Agent: ICM - Beverly Hills, 310/550-4000
Business: Dan Curtis Productions - 310/575-8999

BURNT OFFERINGS   United Artists, 1976, w/William F. Nolan

MICHAEL CURTIS*
Contact: WGA - Los Angeles, 310/550-1000

..AND GOD SPOKE   LIVE Entertainment, 1994, w/Gregory S. Malins

RICHARD CURTIS
Agent: Peters, Fraser & Dunlop - London, 071/376-7676

THE TALL GUY   Miramax, 1990
4 WEDDINGS AND A FUNERAL   Gramercy, 1994

STEPHEN J. CURWICK
Agent: United Talent Agency - Beverly Hills, 310/273-6700

POLICE ACADEMY 5: ASSIGNMENT MIAMI BEACH
   Warner Bros., 1988
POLICE ACADEMY 6: CITY UNDER SEIGE   Warner Bros., 1989

Screenplays:
MY NAME IS DADDY w/Sharee Gorman
WHITE MAGIC

DICK CUSACK*
Agent: William Morris Agency - Beverly Hills, 310/274-7451

Screenplays:
WIPE OUT

JOHN CUSACK
Agent: William Morris Agency - Beverly Hills, 310/274-7451

Screenplays:
GROSSE POINTE BLANK w/D.V. deVincentis & Steve Pink

CARLTON CUSE*
Agent: CAA - Beverly Hills, 310/288-4545

Screenplays:
NATIVES
SPACE CASE

HOWARD CUSHNIR*
Contact: 707/824-1236

SEXUAL HEALING (Short)   1993, directed

Screenplays:
DISTORTION
FLY AWAY HOME
IDIOT SAINT
NOTHING DOWN
COMING ATTRACTIONS

NEIL CUTHBERT*
Agent: William Morris Agency - New York, 212/586-5100

HOCUS POCUS   Buena Vista, 1993, w/Mick Garris

Screenplays:
SAUCER
PLUTO NASH
GLADIATOR OUTCASTS
SEDUCE AND DESTROY
CONNECTICUT YANKEE IN KING ARTHUR'S COURT

RON CUTLER*
Agent: Major Clients Agency - Los Angeles, 310/284-6400

LOCUSTS (Short)
WILLIE DYNAMITE   Universal, 1974
BLOOD RED   Hemdale, 1988
ARTICLE 99   Orion, 1991

Screenplays:
LUCY BOOMER
CLOSE RELATIONS

CATHERINE CYRAN
Agent: Innovative Artists - Los Angeles, 310/553-5200
Contact: 310/446-4795

A CRY IN THE WILD   Concorde/New Horizons, 1990,
   w/Gary Paulsen
DEEP SPACE   Califilm, 1991
SLUMBER PARTY MASSACRE 3   Concorde, 1991
UNCAGED   *ANGEL IN RED*   Califilm, 1991
WHITE WOLVES   Concorde, 1993, directed
NO MAN'S LAND   1994, directed

Screenplays:
AN OUTCAST OF THE ISLANDS (remake)

D

JOHN DAHL*
Agent: United Talent Agency - Beverly Hills, 310/273-6700

PRIVATE INVESTIGATIONS   MGM/UA, 1987, w/David Warfield
KILL ME AGAIN   MGM/UA, 1990, w/David Warfield, directed
RED ROCK WEST   Propaganda Films, 1993, w/Rick Dahl, directed

Screenplays:
MELTDOWN w/Rick Dahl & Scott Chestnut
BRIARPATCH

RICK DAHL*
Contact: WGA - Los Angeles, 310/550-1000

RED ROCK WEST   Propaganda Films, 1993, w/John Dahl

Screenplays:
MELTDOWN w/John Dahl & Scott Chestnut

BOB DAHLIN
Contact: Directors Guild of America - Los Angeles, 310/289-2000

MONSTER IN THE CLOSET   Troma, 1987, directed

ROBERT DALEY
Agent: Sterling Lord Literistic - New York, 212/696-2800

Screenplays:
THE INFORMANT w/Ken Friedman

WALTER DALLENBACH*
Contact: 805/565-3763

LAS VEGAS LADY   Crown International, 1986

DEBORAH DALTON*
Agent: ICM - Beverly Hills, 310/550-4000

WHORE   Trimark Pictures, 1991, w/Ken Russell

WALTER (WALLY) DALTON*
Contact: WGA - Los Angeles, 310/550-1000

Screenplays:
DOYLE TO DOYLE

GERRY DALY
BLACK MAGIC WOMAN   Trimark Pictures, 1991

FRANCIS DAMBERGER
Contact: Academy of Canadian Cinema & Television, 753 Yonge St. -
   2nd Floor, Toronto M4Y 1Z9, Canada, 416/967-0315

SOLITAIRE   Highway One Motion Pictures, 1992, directed

APRIL DAMMANN*
Contact: WGA - Los Angeles, 310/550-1000

ROSE & KATZ (Short)

Screenplays:
UNDER WRAPS
THE COLORS OF CHRISTMAS

LAMAR DAMON*
Agent: Paradigm - Los Angeles, 310/277-4400

Screenplays:
BOOTS
DESPERATE MEASURES
BOY AND ARROW w/Michael Ahn

BARBARA DANA*
Agent: Rosenstone/Wender - New York, 212/832-8330
Contact: 914/238-9696

CHU CHU AND THE PHILLY FLASH   20th Century-Fox, 1981

BILL DANA*
Contact: WGA - Los Angeles, 310/550-1000

THE NUDE BOMB   Universal, 1980, w/Arne Sultan &
   Leonard B. Stern

LAWRENCE DANE
Address: P.O. Box 310, Station F, Toronto MHY 2L7, Canada,
   416/923-6000

HEAVENLY BODIES   MGM/UA, 1985, w/Ron Base, directed

LOGAN N. DANFORTH
CROSS-COUNTRY   New World, 1983, w/William Gray

RODNEY DANGERFIELD*
Contact: WGA - Los Angeles, 310/550-1000

EASY MONEY   Orion, 1983, w/Dennis Blair, Michael Endler &
   P.J. O'Rourke
BACK TO SCHOOL   Orion, 1986, Story w/Greg Fields &
   Dennis Snee
ROVER DANGERFIELD (AF)   Warner Bros., 1991,
   Story developed w/Harold Ramis

JOHN R. DANIELS
GETTING OVER   Continental Films, 1981, Story w/Bernie Rollins

R.E. DANIELS
LONELY HEARTS   Live Entertainment, 1991, w/Andrew Lane

STAN DANIELS*
Agent: APA - Los Angeles, 310/273-0744

THE LONELY GUY   Universal, 1984, w/Ed. Weinberger
GLORY! GLORY! (CMS)   Atlantis Films Ltd./Orion TV, 1989
FOR RICHER, FOR POORER (CTF)   HBO Pictures/Citadel/Iron
   Mountain, 1992

Screenplays:
CARNIVAL

MAX DANN
THE EFFICIENCY EXPERT   Miramax, 1992, w/Andrew Knight

MARIA DANTE
SPACE MUTINY   Action International Pictures, 1989

MITCH DANTON
Agent: Leslie Kallen Agency - Sherman Oaks, 818/906-2785

Screenplays:
LURE OF THE MANTIS

RICHARD CHRISTIAN DANUS*
Contact: WGA - Los Angeles, 310/550-1000

XANADU   Universal, 1980, w/Marc Rubel
NO PLACE TO HIDE   Cannon, 1991, directed

KENNY D'AQUILA
Agent: Premiere Artists - Los Angeles, 310/271-1414

Screenplays:
NOT BEFORE ME
IF I HAD YOU
THE DEBT
NICK

FRANK DARABONT*
Agent: United Talent Agency - Beverly Hills, 310/273-6700

A NIGHTMARE ON ELM STREET PART 3: DREAM WARRIORS
   New Line Cinema, 1987, w/Chuck Russell, Wes Craven &
   Bruce Wagner
THE BLOB   Tri-Star, 1988, w/Chuck Russell
THE FLY II   20th Century Fox, 1989, w/Mick Garris, Jim Wheat &
   Ken Wheat
THE SHAWSHANK REDEMPTION   Columbia, 1994, directed
FRANKENSTEIN   TriStar, 1994, w/Steph Lady

Screenplays:
THE MIST
STRANGERS IN LEADVILLE w/Chuck Russell
COMMANDO II
A STITCH IN TIME
INFINITY CUBE (Shared)

JACK DARCUS
Contact: Academy of Canadian Cinema & Television, 753 Yonge St. -
   2nd Floor, Toronto M4Y 1Z9, Canada, 416/967-0315

THE PORTRAIT   Raincoast Releasing Ltd., 1992, directed

JULIE DASH
Agent: ICM - Beverly Hills, 310/550-4000

DAUGHTERS OF THE DUST   Geechee Girls Productions/
   American Playhouse, 1991, directed

Screenplays:
CROSSFIRE

SEAN DASH
Contact: Century Film Partners

ICE   PM Entertainment Group, 1993

Screenplays:
BREAKAWAY w/Eric Gardner (directing)

DAVID DASHEV
SMOKEY AND THE BANDIT PART 3   Universal, 1983,
   w/Stuart Birnbaum
THE ZOO GANG   Warner Bros., 1985, Story w/Stuart Birnbaum,
   Pen Densham & John Watson
SUMMER SCHOOL   Paramount, 1987, Story w/Stuart Birnbaum &
   Jeff Franklin

Screenplays:
THE SILVER CROSS w/Stuart Birnbaum
CHAMPAGNE FOR CAESAR CHANCE OF A LIFETIME
   w/Stuart Birnbaum
SOME OF MY BEST FRIENDS w/Stuart Birnbaum

JULES DASSIN
Address: Athinaeon Efivon 8, Athens 11521, Greece, tel. 721-1616

RIFFI   1955, w/Auguste le Breton & Rene Wheeler, directed
HE WHO MUST DIE   1957, w/Ben Barzman, directed
WHERE THE HOT WIND BLOWS LA LOI   MGM, 1958,
   w/Diego Fabbri, directed
NEVER ON SUNDAY ★   Lopert, 1960, directed
PHAEDRA   United Artists, 1961, directed
10:30 P.M. SUMMER   United Artists, 1966,
   w/Marguerite Duras, directed
UPTIGHT   Paramount, 1968, w/Ruby Dee &
   Julian Mayfield, directed
PROMISE AT DAWN   Avco Embassy, 1970, directed
A DREAM OF PASSION   Avco Embassy, 1978, directed

VICTOR DAVICH
Agent: Original Artists - Santa Monica, 310/394-1067

Screenplays:
TRY HARDER

LARRY DAVID*
Agent: United Talent Agency - Beverly Hills, 310/273-6700

Screenplays:
PROGNOSIS NEGATIVE
TWO BITS

MARJORIE S. DAVID*
Agent: Broder-Kurland-Webb-Uffner - Beverly Hills, 310/281-3400

MARIA'S LOVERS   Cannon, 1984, w/Gerard Brach,
   Andrei Konchalovsky & Paul Zindel
SHY PEOPLE   Cannon, 1987, w/Gerard Brach &
   Andrei Konchalovsky
INTO THE BADLANDS (CTF)   Ogiens/Kane Productions, 1991,
   w/Dick Beebe & Gordon Dawson

PETER DAVID
Business: To Be Continued Inc. - New York, 516/447-1599

OBLIVION   Fullmoon Entertainment, 1994

Screenplays:
HOWLING MAD
KNIGHT LIFE
SQUEEZE PLAY
BRAINS OVER BRAWN

PAUL DAVIDS*
Contact: Richard Rosen - Los Angeles, 213/466-9088

SHE DANCES ALONE   Continental, 1982
ROSWELL (CTF)   Viacom Pictures/Citadel Entertainment, 1994,
   Story w/Jeremy Kagan & Arthur Kopit

ADAM DAVIDSON*
Manager: The Roberts Company - Los Angeles, 310/552-7800

THE LUNCH DATE (Short) ★★   1990, directed

Screenplays:
HELL CAMP (shared)

ARLENE DAVIDSON*
Contact: Flatbush Films - 818/753-8280

EDDIE AND THE CRUISERS   Embassy, 1983, w/Martin Davidson

BOAZ DAVIDSON
Contact: Directors Guild of America - Los Angeles, 310/289-2000

IT'S A FUNNY, FUNNY WORLD   Noah Films, 1978, w/Zvi Shissel
LEMON POPSICLE   Noah Films, 1981, w/Eli Tabor, directed
THE LAST AMERICAN VIRGIN   Cannon, 1982, directed
HOT RESORT   Cannon, 1985, w/John Robins & Norman Hudis
SALSA   Cannon, 1988, w/Tomas Benitez &
   Shepard Goldman, directed
YOUNG COMMANDOS   Cannon, 1991, w/Greg Latter
DELTA FORCE 3: THE KILLING GAME   Cannon, 1992,
   w/Andy Deutsch & Greg Latter
AMERICAN CYBORG: STEEL WARRIOR   Cannon, 1994,
   Story w/Christopher Pearce, directed
BLOOD RUN   Nu-Image, 1994,
   Story w/Dennis Dimster Denk, directed

MARTIN DAVIDSON*
Agent: Innovative Artists - Los Angeles, 310/553-5200

IF EVER I SEE YOU AGAIN   Columbia, 1978, w/Joseph Brooks
ALMOST SUMMER   Universal, 1978, w/Judith Berg &
   Sandra Berg, directed
EDDIE AND THE CRUISERS   Embassy, 1983,
   w/Arlene Davidson, directed

ANDREW DAVIES
Agent: William Morris Agency - Beverly Hills, 310/274-7451

CONSUMING PASSIONS   Samuel Goldwyn Company, 1988,
   w/Paul D. Zimmerman
A PRIVATE LIFE   Totem Productions, 1989
CIRCLE OF FRIENDS   Savoy, 1995

Screenplays:
FOREIGN LANGUAGES
GOOD GIRLS

JACK DAVIES
CONVICT 99   Gainsborough, 1938, w/Marriott Edgar,
   Val Guest & Ralph Smart
LAUGHTER IN PARADISE   ABPC, 1951, w/Michael Pertwee
CURTAIN UP   Rank, 1952, w/Michael Pertwee
MR. POTTS GOES TO MOSCOW   *TOP SECRET*   ABP, 1952,
   w/Michael Pertwee
HAPPY EVER AFTER   *TONIGHT'S THE NIGHT*   ABP, 1954,
   w/Michael Pertwee & L.A.F. Strong
JUMPING FOR JOY   Rank, 1955, w/Henry E. Blyth
AN ALLIGATOR NAMED DAISY   Rank, 1955
DOCTOR AT SEA   Rank, 1955, w/Nicholas Phipps
UP IN THE WORLD   Rank, 1956, w/Peter Blackmore & Henry Blyth
TRUE AS A TURTLE   Rank, 1956, w/John Coates &
   Nicholas Phipps
THE SQUARE PEG   Rank, 1958
DON'T PANIC, CHAPS!   Hammer, 1959
FOLLOW A STAR   Rank, 1959, w/Henry Blyth & Norman Wisdom
THE BULLDOG BREED   Rank, 1960, w/Henry Blyth &
   Norman Wisdom
A COMING OUT PARTY   *VERY IMPORTANT PERSON*
   Rank, 1961
NEARLY A NASTY ACCIDENT   British Lion, 1961,
   w/Hugh Woodruff
ON THE BEAT   Rank, 1962
THE FAST LADY   Rank, 1962, w/Henry Blyth
CROOKS ANONYMOUS   Anglo Amalgamated, 1962, w/Henry Blyth
FATHER CAME TOO   Rank, 1963, w/Henry Blyth
A STITCH IN TIME   Rank, 1963
THE EARLY BIRD   Rank, 1965, w/Henry Blyth, Eddie Leslie &
   Norman Wisdom
THOSE MAGNIFICENT MEN IN THEIR FLYING MACHINES ★
   20th Century-Fox, 1965, w/Ken Annakin

DOCTOR IN CLOVER   Rank, 1966
GAMBIT   Universal, 1966, w/Alvin Sargent
THE CAVERN   20th Century-Fox, 1966, w/Michael Pertwee
THOSE DARING YOUNG MEN IN THEIR JAUNTY JALOPIES
   Paramount, 1969, w/Ken Annakin
DOCTOR IN TROUBLE   Rank, 1970
PAPER TIGER   Joseph E. Levine Presents, 1976
ffolkes   Universal, 1980

RAY DAVIES
Contact: British Academy of Film & Television Arts, 195 Picadilly,
   London W1, England, 01/734-0022

RETURN TO WATERLOO   New Line Cinema, 1985, directed

TERENCE DAVIES
Contact: Three Rivers Ltd., 46 Old Compton Street, London
   W1V 5PB, 071/287-2567, fax 287-3072

DISTANT VOICES, STILL LIVES   Alive Films, 1989, directed
THE LONG DAY CLOSES   Sony Pictures Classics, 1993, directed
THE NEON BIBLE   Miramax, 1995, directed

WILLIAM J. DAVIES*
Agent: United Talent Agency - Beverly Hills, 310/273-6700

TWINS   Universal, 1988, w/William Osborne, Timothy Harris &
   Herschel Weingrod
STOP! OR MY MOM WILL SHOOT   Universal, 1992,
   w/William Osborne & Blake Snyder
GHOST IN THE MACHINE   20th Century Fox, 1993,
   w/William Osborne
THE REAL McCOY   Universal, 1993, w/William Osborne

Screenplays:
EUREKA w/William Osborne & Chrarlie Peters
FOREIGN EXCHANGE w/William Osborne
EARTHQUAKE w/William Osborne
PRITCHARD COUNTY w/William Osborne

ALMER JOHN DAVIS
UNDER THE GUN   Marquis Pictures, 1989, w/James Devney &
   James Sbardellati

ANDREA DAVIS*
Contact: WGA - Los Angeles, 310/550-1000

Screenplays:
RUNNING IN PLACE

ANDREW DAVIS*
Agent: CAA - Beverly Hills, 310/288-4545
Contact: Bloom, Dekom, Hergott & Cook - Los Angeles, 310/278-8622

STONY ISLAND   World Northal, 1980, w/Tamar Hoffs, directed
BEAT STREET   Orion, 1984, w/David Gilbert & Paul Golding
ABOVE THE LAW   Warner Bros., 1988, w/Steven Pressfield &
   Ronald Shusett, directed

Screenplays:
STEAL BIG, STEAL LITTLE w/Lee Blessing & Jeanne Blake
   (Savoy, directing)
GROUNDBURST

BART DAVIS*
Contact: WGA - Los Angeles, 310/550-1000

IMPULSE   20th Century-Fox, 1984, w/Don Carlos Dunaway
LOVE OR MONEY   Hemdale, 1990, w/Elyse England &
   Michael Zausner
FULL FATHOM FIVE   Concorde, 1990

Screenplays:
ERNEST SAVES CAMELOT w/Michael Zausner

BILL C. DAVIS*
Agent: Renaissance-H.N. Swanson - Los Angeles, 310/246-6000

DANCING IN THE END ZONE (P)
SPINE (P)
MASS APPEAL   Universal, 1984, from his play

CARLOS DAVIS*
Agent: Maggie Field Agency - Studio City, 818/980-2001

PREPPIES (P)   w/Anthony Fingleton
BIMBO (Short)   w/Josh Brand
DROP DEAD, FRED   New Line Cinema, 1991, w/Anthony Fingleton

Screenplays:
BLAST FROM THE PAST w/Anthony Fingleton
LEAP YEAR w/Anthony Fingleton
TUG-OF-WAR w/Anthony Fingleton

CHARLES DAVIS
THUNDER RUN   Cannon, 1986, w/Carol Heyer

DEBORAH DEAN-DAVIS
(See Deborah DEAN-Davis)

DESMOND DAVIS
Contact: Lancer Film Productions - London, 071/485-1505

AN INSPECTOR CALLS   British Lion, 1954
THE UNCLE   Play-Pix, 1964, w/Margaret Abrams, directed
TIME LOST AND TIME REMEMBERED   *I WAS HAPPY HERE*
   Continental, 1966, w/Edna O'Brien

GLENN DAVIS*
Agent: Major Clients Agency - Los Angeles, 310/284-6400

Screenplays:
GOING FOR BROKE w/William Laurin
BLOOD WEEKEND w/William Laurin
MY GENERATION w/William Laurin
RACQUETS w/William Laurin
THE STAR PUPIL w/William Laurin
THE WET DETECTIVE w/William Laurin
OUR COTTAGE FROM HELL w/William Laurin

GREG DAVIS*
Agent: United Talent Agency - Beverly Hills, 310/273-6700

Screenplays:
US AND THEM w/Larry Garcia
HARRY SCARRY WANTS TO MARRY w/Larry Garcia
WIND IN THE WILLOWS w/Larry Garcia

GWEN DAVIS*
Contact: Dale Burgess - 415/771-5101; or Burton Mitchell -
   310/203-8080

Screenplays:
HOTEL BEL-AIR
DELUSION
WHAT A WAY TO GO!
BETTER LATE THAN NEVER

IAN DAVIS
THE HUNGER   MGM/UA, 1983, w/Michael Thomas

JEFFERSON DAVIS
THE TICKET OUTTA HERE   Black & White Pictures,
   1990, co-directed

JOEL DAVIS*
Agent: Schiowitz/Clay/Rose - Los Angeles, 213/650-7300

Screenplays:
REIGN OF TERROR
CROSSING THE LINE
ONE BY ONE
DIVERSIONS
IT TOOK FIRST PRIZE IN HOUSTON w/Winston A. Howlett
SILENT PARTNER
NEVER AGAIN

LUTHER DAVIS*
Agent: The Lantz Office - New York, 212/586-0200

B.F.'S DAUGHTER   MGM, 1948
BLACK HAND   MGM, 1949
A LION IS IN THE STREETS   Warner Bros., 1953
KISMET   MGM, 1955, w/Charles Lederer, from their play
THE GIFT OF LOVE   20th Century-Fox, 1958
HOLIDAY FOR LOVERS   20th Century-Fox, 1959
LADY IN A CAGE   American Entertainment Corp., 1964
ACROSS 110TH STREET   United Artists, 1972

MICHAEL PAUL DAVIS
Agent: The Gersh Agency - Beverly Hills, 310/274-6611

PINSTRIPE & STRAITJACKET (Short)   directed
IT'S A WONDERFUL ROSS (Short)   directed
PREHYSTERIA 2   Moonbeam Entertainment, 1993, Shared
PREHYSTERIA 3   Moonbeam Entertainment, 1993, Shared
DOUBLE DRAGON   Gramercy, 1994, w/Peter Gould
BEANSTALK   Moonbeam Entertainment, 1994, directed

Screenplays:
KINSEY REPORTS
THE AMAZING X-KIDS
NINJA MOM
THE SENSOR w/Peter Gould
THE DEADHEAD AND THE COED w/John Sulak
PENNY FOR YOUR THOUGHTS

MITCH DAVIS
WINDRUNNER   Leucadia Film Group, 1994

NORTHROP DAVIS*
Agent: Susan Smith & Associates - Beverly Hills, 213/852-4777
Manager: 3 Arts Entertainment - Los Angeles, 213/851-5700

THE BUS (Short)   directed
THE WELDER (Short)   directed

Screenplays:
MADLANDS
CYBER SHIP
THE FARM
INDEPENDENCE DAY

OSSIE DAVIS*
Agent: The Artists Agency - Los Angeles, 310/277-7779

GONE ARE THE DAYS   *PURLIE VICTORIOUS*   Trans-Lux,
   1963, from his play
COTTON COMES TO HARLEM   United Artists, 1970,
   w/Arnold Perl, directed
COUNTOWN FOR KUSINI   Columbia, 1976

PETER S. DAVIS
Business: Davis-Panzer Productions, 1754 N. Serrano - Suite 401,
   Hollywood, CA 90027, 213/463-2343

STEEL   *LOOK DOWN AND DIE*   World Northal, 1980,
   Story w/Rob Ewing & William N. Panzer

RANDOLPH DAVIS*
Agent: United Talent Agency - Beverly Hills, 310/273-6700

POLICE ACADEMY VII: MISSION TO MOSCOW   Warner Bros.,
   1994, w/Michele Chodos

Screenplays:
TRIAL BY FIRE w/Michele Chodos
STAY TUNED FOR MURDER w/Michele Chodos

ROBERT P. DAVIS
THE PILOT   Summit Featuers, 1981

SIDNEY DAVIS*
Contact: Ted Witzer - 310/474-6135

THE DOVE   Coe/Davis Ltd., 1968

STEPHEN DAVIS
Agent: Writers & Artists Agency - Los Angeles, 310/824-6300

RUBY   Triumph Releasing, 1992, from his play "Love Field"

TOM DAVIS*
Contact: WGA - Los Angeles, 310/550-1000

ONE MORE SATURDAY NIGHT   Columbia, 1986, w/Al Franken
CONEHEADS   Paramount, 1993, w/Dan Aykroyd, Bonnie Turner &
   Terry Turner

Screenplays:
SIRENS OF TITAN

WALTER HALSEY DAVIS*
Agent: Dytman & Schwartz - Beverly Hills, 310/274-8844

PANHANDLE (P)
TILDEN (P)
THE TAPIOCA MISANTHROPA (P)
SEVEN HOURS TO JUDGMENT   Trans World Entertainment, 1988,
   w/Steven E. deSouza

Screenplays:
CONFRONTATION

ZACH DAVIS
LIQUID DREAMS   Northern Arts, 1992, w/Mark Manos

ANNABEL DAVIS-GOFF*
Contact: WGA - Los Angeles, 310/550-1000

Screenplays:
NIGHT TENNIS
WOMEN IN JEOPARDY
AS THE WORM TURNS

ANTHONY M. DAWSON
Address: via Appia Antica 184, Rome, Italy, tel.: 06/782-2367

YOR, THE HUNTER FROM THE FUTURE   Columbia, 1983,
   w/Robert Bailey, directed

GORDON DAWSON*
Agent: The Coppage Company - North Hollywood, 818/980-1106

BRING ME THE HEAD OF ALFREDO GARCIA   United Artists,
   1974, w/Sam Peckinpah
INTO THE BADLANDS (CTF)   Ogiens/Kane Productions, 1991,
   w/Dick Beebe & Marjorie David

GERRY DAY*
Agent: Monteiro Rose Agency - Encino, 818/501-1177

THE BLACK HOLE   Buena Vista, 1979, w/Jeb Rosebrook

JONATHAN DAY*
Contact: WGA - New York, 212/245-6180

Screenplays:
BIG PINK
FOURTH OF JULY

RICHARD DAY*
Agent: United Talent Agency - Beverly Hills, 310/273-6700

Screenplays:
GOLD DIGGERS
LOVE KILLS

WARREN DEACON
Agent: Berzon Agency - Glendale, 818/548-1560

Screenplays:
DEE-JAY

DEBORAH DEAN-DAVIS*
Contact: WGA - Los Angeles, 310/550-1000

Screenplays:
TRADZEES
BETTER LATE THAN FOREVER
SCORPIO RISING
COULD THIS BE MAGIC
THE BOY NEXT DOOR
CONTENDERS

WILLIAM DEAR*
Agent: United Talent Agency - Beverly Hills, 310/273-6700

THE NORTHVILLE CEMETARY MASSACRE   Cannon, 1976,
   w/Thomas C. Dyke, co-directed
TIMERIDER   Jensen Farley Pictures, 1983,
   w/Michael Nesmith, directed
HARRY AND THE HENDERSONS   Universal, 1987,
   w/William E. Martin & Ezra D. Rappaport, directed
THE ROCKETEER   Buena Vista, 1991, Story w/Danny Bilson &
   Paul De Meo

Screenplays:
HOME FOR THE HOLIDAYS

JAMES DEARDEN*
Agent: ICM - Beverly Hills, 310/550-4000

FATAL ATTRACTION ★   Paramount, 1987,
   from his teleplay "Diversion"
PASCALI'S ISLAND   Avenue Pictures, 1988, directed
A KISS BEFORE DYING   Universal, 1991, directed

Screenplays:
A PHILOSOPHICAL INVESTIGATION
SYCAMORE DRIVE
RANSOM
PHANTOM
MADNESS OF A SEDUCED WOMAN
THE RINGER
SCARAMOUCHE

MICHAEL de AVILA
LOST PROPHET   Rockville Pictures, 1992, w/Shannon Goldman,
   Drew Morone & Larry O'Neil, directed

JOHN DeBELLO
ATTACK OF THE KILLER TOMATOES   1980, directed
HAPPY HOUR   TMS Pictures, 1987, w/Constantine Dillon &
   J. Stephen Peace, directed
RETURN OF THE KILLER TOMATOES   New World, 1988, directed

ALLEN N. DeBEVOISE
BREAKIN' MGM/UA/Cannon, 1984, w/Charles Parker & Gerald Scarfe

PHILLIPE de BROCA
Contact: French Film Office, 745 Fifth Ave., New York, NY 10151, 212/832-8860

CARTOUCHE Embassy, 1962, directed
THAT MAN FROM RIO ★ Lopert, 1964, w/others, directed
DEAR DETECTIVE *DEAR INSPECTOR* Cinema 5, 1978, w/Michael Audiard, directed

TOM DeCERCHIO*
Agent: ICM - Beverly Hills, 310/550-4000

Screenplays:
BATBOYS w/Bryan Buckley
SQUEEZE BOX
THE SANDBOX CLUB

JAMEE DECIO
Agent: William Morris Agency - Beverly Hills, 310/274-7451

Screenplays:
ROCKERS w/Jill Mazursky

DENISE DeCLUE*
Agent: CAA - Beverly Hills, 310/288-4545

GRIMM (P)
ABOUT LAST NIGHT Tri-Star, 1986, w/Tim Kazurinsky
FOR KEEPS Tri-Star, 1988, w/Tim Kazurinsky

Screenplays:
TUG OF WAR w/Tim Kazurinsky
ABOUT LAST NIGHT 2 w/Tim Kazurinsky
BIG SUCCESS w/Tim Kazurinsky
WEEKEND WARRIORS

EDWARD DECTER*
Agent: Broder-Kurland-Webb-Uffner - Beverly Hills, 310/281-3400

OPTIONS Vestron, 1989, w/John J. Strauss

Screenplays:
FOREVER MURRAY w/John J. Strauss
YARD WARS w/John J. Strauss
THERE'S SOMETHING ABOUT MARY w/John J. Strauss
LAST CHANCE TO DANCE BEFORE THE FREEWAY
AIRWAVES w/Paul Reiser

FRANK DEESE*
Agent: William Morris Agency - Beverly Hills, 310/274-7451

THE PRINCIPAL Tri-Star, 1987
JOSH AND S.A.M. Columbia, 1993

Screenplays:
UNDER THE ROCK PILE
LICENSED TO DRIVE
COMPANY MAN
BONES

CHRIS DeFARIA*
Contact: WGA - Los Angeles, 310/550-1000

Screenplays:
COMING ATTRACTIONS
SLAYER
AMITYVILLE 6

JAMES DeFELICE
WHY SHOOT THE TEACHER? Quartet, 1977
OUT OF THE DARK CineTel Films, 1989, w/Zane W. Levitt
ANGEL SQUARE Miramax, 1991, w/Anne Wheeler

FRANK deFELITTA*
Contact: Bernard Donnenfeld - Los Angeles, 310/277-1000

ZPG Paramount, 1972, w/Max Ehrlich
AUDREY ROSE United Artists, 1977
THE ENTITY 20th Century-Fox, 1983
SCISSORS Vidmark, 1991, directed

RAYMOND deFELITTA
Contact: 212/226-2686

BRONX CHEERS (Short) ★ 1990, directed

Screenplays:
CAFE SOCIETY (Tribeca/Cineville/Daylight, directing)
BEGIN THE BEGUINE
THE FABULOUS NOBODIES
CAN'T GET ARRESTED
THE WAR OF CHRISTMAS

FRANK DEFORD*
Agent: Sterling Lord Agency - New York, 212/751-2533

TRADING HEARTS New Century/Vista, 1988

Screenplays:
PEERS

MICHAEL DeGUZMAN*
Agent: Broder-Kurland-Webb-Uffner - Beverly Hills, 310/281-3400

JAWS THE REVENGE Universal, 1987

STEVE DeJARNATT
Agent: United Talent Agency - Beverly Hills, 310/273-6700

TARZANA (Short) 1979, directed
STRANGE BREW MGM/UA, 1983, w/Rick Moranis & Dave Thomas
MIRACLE MILE Hemdale, 1988, directed

Screenplays:
FUTUREBALL
INSOMNIA
HAIR OF THE DOG
DOODLEBUG SUPREME

COLMAN deKAY
BLOODHOUNDS OF BROADWAY Columbia, 1989, w/Howard Brookner

FRED DEKKER*
Agent: ICM - Beverly Hills, 310/550-4000

HOUSE New World, 1986, Story
NIGHT OF THE CREEPS Tri-Star, 1986, directed
THE MONSTER SQUAD Tri-Star, 1987, w/Shane Black, directed
IF LOOKS COULD KILL Warner Bros., 1991, Story
RICOCHET Warner Bros., 1991, Story w/Menno Meyjes
ROBOCOP 3 Orion, 1993, w/Frank Miller, directed

Screenplays:
MR. COOL w/David Arnott
THE FOREVER FACTOR
GODZILLA

JOHN deKLEIN
THE CARE BEARS ADVENTURE IN WONDERLAND (AF) Cineplex Odeon, 1987, w/Susan Snooks
BABAR: THE MOVIE (AF) New Line Cinema, 1989, w/Alan Bunce, Raymond Jeffelice & Peter Sauder

SHELAGH DELANEY
Agent: Pleshette & Green - Los Angeles, 213/465-0428

A TASTE OF HONEY   Continental, 1962, w/Tony Richardson
CHARLIE BUBBLES   Universal, 1968
DANCE WITH A STRANGER   Samuel Goldwyn Company, 1985
THE RAILWAY STATION MAN (CTF)   Turner Pictures, 1992

ROBERT De LAURENTIS*
Contact: Phil Klein, Browning, Jacobson & Klein - 310/247-0460

GREEN ICE   ITC, 1981, w/others
A LITTLE SEX   Universal, 1982

Screenplays:
BLACK TIE
KINGDOM OF DREAMS
TEENAGE GHOST STORY

BERNIE DeLEO
ILLEGAL MOTION (P)
TALES FROM THE CONCRETE BEACH (P)
BEACHED (P)
LAKE SHORE DRIVES (P)
DOUBLE CROSSED (P)
PAPAL BULL (P)
WE WERE BUT A HANDFUL (P)

Screenplays:
RESERVATIONS WITH LISA
WISHBONE

MARCUS DeLEON
Business: Together Brother Productions, 9505 W. Washington Blvd.,
   Culver City, CA 90230, 310/841-2301

KISS ME A KILLER   Califilm, 1991,
   w/Christopher Wooden,   directed

Screenplays:
BAKERSFIELD (directing)
BODY OF THE WOMAN

SEAN DELGADO
ALEXA   Platinum Pictures, 1989, w/Peggy Bruen, directed

BILL D'ELIA
Agent: Writers & Artists Agency - Los Angeles, 310/824-6300

THE FEUD   Castle Hill Productions, 1990, Shared, directed

Screenplays:
PRINCE SAM

FRANCIS DELIA
Agent: Stevens & Associates - Beverly Hills, 310/275-7541

FREEWAY   New World, 1988, w/Darrell Fetty
TROUBLE BOUND   ITC Entertainment, 1993, w/Darrell Fetty

WANDA DELL
Business: Dell Films, 1905 Powers Ferry Rd. - Suite 260, Atlanta,
   GA 30067, 404/955-6924

MARVIN AND TIGE   *LIKE FATHER AND SON*   20th Century-Fox
   International Classics, 1983, w/Eric Weston

DUANE DELL'AMICO*
Agent: The Gersh Agency - Beverly Hills, 310/274-6611

SLEEP WITH ME   MGM/UA, 1994, w/Roger Hedden, Neal Jimenez,
   Joe Keenan, Rory Kelly & Michael Steinberg

Screenplays:
BULLET'S DREAM
RAINBOW

THE STRANGER IN BETWEEN
I THOUGHT I HEARD MY BROTHER SAY
A BRIEF AND STOLEN LIFE
RIFF-RAFF
WHITE SONS

WILLIAM DELLIGAN*
Contact: WGA - Los Angeles, 310/550-1000

PRAYING MANTIS (CTF)   Fast Track Films/Wilshire Court
   Productions, 1993, w/Duane Poole
A PASSION TO KILL   A-Pix Entertainment, 1994
RULES OF OBSESSION (CTF)   Rysher, 1994

JEFFREY S. DELMAN
Personal Manager: Kenner Organization - Santa Monica,
   310/450-9497

VOODOO DAWN   Academy Entertainment, 1990, w/Evan Dunsky,
   Thomas Rendon & John Russo

PETER Del MONTE
Address: via Poerio 59/D, Rome, Italy, 06/585451

JULIA AND JULIA   Cinecom, 1987, w/Silvia Napolitano &
   Sandra Petraglia,   directed

GUILLERMO DEL TORO
Agent: The Gersh Agency - Beverly Hills, 310/274-6611

CHRONOS   October Films, 1994, directed

Screenplays:
SPANKY

MICHAEL DeLUCA*
Agent: William Morris Agency - Beverly Hills, 310/274-7451
Contact: New Line Cinema, 310/854-5811

FREDDY'S DEAD: THE FINAL NIGHTMARE
   New Line Cinema, 1991
IN THE MOUTH OF MADNESS   New Line Cinema, 1995

RUDY DeLUCA*
Agent: The Gersh Agency - Beverly Hills, 310/274-6611

THE WARM-UP (P) w/Greg Lewis & Sammy Shore
SILENT MOVIE   20th Century-Fox, 1976, w/Mel Brooks,
   Ron Clark & Barry Levinson
HIGH ANXIETY   20th Century-Fox, 1977, w/Mel Brooks,
   Ron Clark & Barry Levinson
CAVEMAN   United Artists, 1981, w/Carl Gottlieb
TRANSYLVANIA 6-5000   New World, 1985, directed
MILLION DOLLAR MYSTERY   DEG, 1987, w/Tim Metcalfe &
   Miguel Tejada-Flores
LIFE STINKS   MGM-Pathe, 1991, w/Mel Brooks & Steve Haberman

Screenplays:
DRACULA: DEAD AND LIKING IT w/Steve Haberman
LAND OF THE NICE

MICHAEL DeLUISE
Contact: Stoneface Entertainment - 818/901-7501

Screenplays:
PREY & INNOCENCE (directing)

ROBERT DeMAIO*
Agent: Sanford-Gross & Associates - Los Angeles, 310/208-2100

Screenplays:
ANNA OF THE SUBWAY
BEWITCHED, BOTHERED AND BEWILDERED

JOHN DeMARCO*
Agent: The Agency - Los Angeles, 310/551-3000

IMPULSE   Warner Bros., 1990, w/Leigh Chapman

J.M. DeMATTEIS
Agent: United Talent Agency - Beverly Hills, 310/273-6700

Screenplays:
THE STARDUST KID

RICHARD DEMBO
Contact: Swiss Film Center, Munstergasse 18, 8001 Zurich,
   Switzerland, 01/472860

DANGEROUS MOVES   Arthur Cohn Productions, 1984, directed

PAUL De MEO*
Agent: CAA - Beverly Hills, 310/288-4545
Business: Pet Fly Productions, Paramount TV, 213/956-8625

FUTURE COP   *TRANCERS*   Empire Pictures, 1985,
   w/Danny Bilson
ZONE TROOPERS   Empire Pictures, 1986, w/Danny Bilson
ELIMINATORS   Empire Pictures, 1986, w/Danny Bilson
THE WRONG GUYS   New World, 1988, w/Danny Bilson
ARENA   Empire Pictures, 1988, w/Danny Bilson
PULSEPOUNDERS   Empire Pictures, 1988, w/Danny Bilson
THE ROCKETEER   Buena Vista, 1991, w/Danny Bilson

Screenplays:
EDWIN MULLHOUSE   w/Danny Bilson
G-MEN   w/Danny Bilson

EAMES DEMETRIOS
THE GIVING   Northern Arts Entertainment, 1993, directed

PAUL De MIELCHE
Agent: The Artists Agency - Los Angeles, 310/277-7779

AMERICAN NINJA   Cannon, 1985

LOIS DEMKO
Agent: Berzon Agency - Glendale, 818/548-1560

Screenplays:
THE INSIDE KILL

JONATHAN DEMME*
Agent: CAA - Beverly Hills, 310/288-4545

ANGELS HARD AS THEY COME   New World, 1971, w/Joe Viola
THE HOT BOX   1972, w/Joe Viola
BLACK MAMA, WHITE MAMA   American International,
   1973, w/others
CAGED HEAT   New World, 1974, directed
FIGHTING MAD   20th Century-Fox, 1976, directed

JAMES DeMONACO
Agent: William Morris Agency - New York, 212/586-5100

Screenplays:
JACK   w/Gary Nadeau

KEN DENBOW
DECEPTIONS (CTF)   Republic Pictures, 1990, Story

SUSANNAH deNIMES*
Contact: WGA - Los Angeles, 310/550-1000

SURVIVAL GAME   Trans World Entertainment, 1987,
   w/Herb Freed & P.W. Swann

CLAIRE DENIS
Contact: French Film Office, 745 Fifth Avenue, New York, NY 10151,
   212/832-8860

CHOCOLAT   Orion Classics, 1989, w/Jean-Pol Fargeau, directed
NO FEAR, NO DIE   (No distributor), 1992,
   w/Jean-Pol Fargeau, directed

REINHARD DENKE
Manager: Atlas Entertainment - Los Angeles, 213/658-9100

Screenplays:
DOUBLE DOWN   w/Kirk Ellis

BRIAN DENNEHY
Agent: Susan Smith & Associates - Beverly Hills, 213/852-4777

Screenplays:
RYAN'S RULES   (directing)

CHARLES DENNIS*
Agent: Wallerstein*Kappelman Agency - Los Angeles, 213/782-0225

DOUBLE NEGATIVE   Best Film and Video, 1980, w/Janis Allen &
   Thomas Hedley, Jr.
FINDERS KEEPERS   Warner Bros., 1984, w/Ronny Graham &
   Terence Marsh
COVERGIRL   New World, 1984
RENO AND THE DOC (CTF)   Pan-Canada, 1994, directed

Screenplays:
THE BEARD
APRIL IN PARIS
LADY LUCK
SCREWBALL ACADEMY
CYRANO DE B
*T*W*I*C*U*S*
DEADLY COMPANION
THE THIRSTY DEAD

GILL DENNIS*
Agent: Broder-Kurland-Webb-Uffner - Beverly Hills, 310/281-3400

RETURN TO OZ   Buena Vista, 1985, w/Walter Murch
ON MY OWN   Alliance Communications Corp., 1992,
   w/John Frizzell & Antonio Tibaldi

Screenplays:
HERTZOG   w/Marc Norman

PEN DENSHAM*
Agent: ICM - Beverly Hills, 310/550-4000
Business: Trilogy Entertainment Group, MGM/UA - 310/449-3095

THE ZOO GANG   New World, 1985, w/John Watson, co-directed
ROBIN HOOD: PRINCE OF THIEVES   Warner Bros., 1991,
   w/John Watson
A GNOME NAMED NORM   7 Arts, 1992

Screenplays:
MOLL FLANDERS   (directing)
TREASURE ISLAND
FLYING TIGERS   w/John Watson
BLIND LUCK   w/John Watson
ACCELERATOR

BRIAN De PALMA*
Agent: CAA - Beverly Hills, 310/288-4545

GREETINGS   Sigman III, 1968, w/Charles S. Hirsch, directed
THE WEDDING PARTY   Powell Productions Plus/Ondine,
   1969, directed
HI, MOM!   Sigma III, 1970, directed
SISTERS   American International, 1973, w/Louise Rose, directed
PHANTOM OF THE PARADISE   20th Century-Fox, 1974, directed
HOME MOVIES   United Artists Classics, 1980, w/others, directed

DRESSED TO KILL   Filmways, 1980, directed
BLOW OUT   Filmways, 1981, directed
BODY DOUBLE   Columbia, 1984, w/Robert J. Avrech, directed
RAISING CAIN   Universal, 1992, directed

Screenplays:
DR. JEKYLL AND MR. HYDE
THE DEMOLISHED MAN w/Oliver Stone
TREASURE

FRANK De PALMA*
Manager: Jon Brown, The Brown Group - Burbank, 818/955-7040
Contact: Stephen F. Breimer, Bloom, Dekom, Hergott & Cook -
    Los Angeles, 310/278-8622

ATONEMENT (Short), 1978, directed
THE HIBAKUSHA GALLERY (Short), 1981, directed
PRIVATE WAR   Smart Egg, 1989, w/Terry Borst &
    Bjorn Carlstrom, directed
WING COMMANDER III: THE HEART OF THE TIGER
    Electronic Arts, 1994, w/Terry Borst

Screenplays:
THE WAR TRAIN w/Terry Borst
BOTH ENDS BURNING w/Terry Borst
THE RULES OF GRAVITY w/Terry Borst
BORDERLINE TANGO w/Terry Borst
A PLACE ON EARTH w/Terry Borst

SUZANNE de PASSE*
Business: De Passe Entertainment, 5750 Wilshire Blvd. - Suite 640,
    Los Angeles, CA 90036, 310/965-2580

LADY SINGS THE BLUES ★   Paramount, 1972, w/Chris Clark &
    Terence McCloy

JOHN DEREK
Contact: Directors Guild of America - Los Angeles, 310/289-2000

FANTASIES   *AND ONCE UPON A LOVE*   Joseph Brenner
    Associates, 1981, directed
BOLERO   Cannon, 1984, directed
GHOSTS CAN'T DO IT   Triumph, 1990, directed

SUSAN MURPHY DERMODY
BREATHING UNDER WATER   Periscope Productions,
    1991, directed

EVERETT DeROCHE
Agent: The Daniel Ostroff Agency - Los Angeles, 310/278-2020

THE LONG WEEKEND   1978
PATRICK   Cinema Shares International, 1979
THE DAY AFTER HALLOWEEN   *SNAPSHOT*   Group 1, 1979,
    w/Chris DeRoche
HARLEQUIN   Greater Union Film Distributors, 1980
ROAD GAMES   Avco Embassy, 1981
TREASURE OF THE YANKEE ZEPHYR   *RACE TO THE
    YANKEE ZEPHYR*   Artists Releasing Corporation/Film
    Ventures International, 1984
RAZORBACK   Warner Bros., 1985
THE QUEST   Miramax, 1986
LINK   Thorn-EMI, 1986
WINDRIDER   MGM/UA, 1987, w/Bonnie Harris

CLYDE DERRICK*
Agent: J. Michael Bloom & Associates - Los Angeles, 310/275-6800

Screenplays:
AFTERLIFE
THIS SPY'S IN LOVE WITH YOU

DOMINIQUE DeRUDDERE
Business: Antoine Dansuertstraat 95, B-1000 Brussels, Belgium

LOVE IS A DOG FROM HELL   Cineplex Odeon, 1987,
    w/Marc Didden, directed
WAIT UNTIL SPRING, BANDINI   Orion Classics, 1990, directed

TOM DeSIMONE*
Agent: APA - Los Angeles, 213/273-0744
Address: 6105 Westpark Dr., North Hollywood, CA 91606,
    818/761-7161

REFORM SCHOOL GIRLS   New World, 1986, directed
ANGEL III: THE FINAL CHAPTER   New World, 1988, directed

Screenplays:
WANTED DEAD OR ALIVE II

DICK DESMOND
ENTER THE NINJA   Cannon, 1981, w/Menahem Golan &
    Judd Bernard

STEVEN E. de SOUZA*
Agent: United Talent Agency - Beverly Hills, 310/273-6700

ARNOLD'S WRECKING COMPANY   Cine-Globe, 1973
48 HRS.   Paramount, 1982, w/Larry Gross, Walter Hill &
    Roger Spottiswoode
THE RETURN OF CAPTAIN INVINCIBLE   New World, 1983,
    w/Andrew Gaty
COMMANDO   20th Century Fox, 1985
THE RUNNING MAN   Tri-Star, 1987
SEVEN HOURS TO JUDGEMENT   Trans World Entertainment,
    1988, as "Elliot Stephens," w/Walter Halsey Davis
DIE HARD   20th Century Fox, 1988, w/Jeb Stuart
BAD DREAMS   20th Century Fox, 1988, w/Andrew Fleming
DIE HARD 2: DIE HARDER   20th Century Fox, 1990,
    w/Doug Richardson
HUDSON HAWK   Tri-Star, 1991, w/Dan Waters
RICOCHET   Warner Bros., 1991
BEVERLY HILLS COP III   Paramount, 1994
THE FLINTSTONES   Universal, 1994, w/Tom S. Parker &
    Jim Jennewein
STREET FIGHTER   Universal, 1995, directed

Screenplays:
888
THIN ICE
CRITICS CHOICE
DEAD RECKONING

ANDREW DETTMAN*
Agent: Broder-Kurland-Webb-Uffner - Beverly Hills, 310/281-3400

Screenplays:
WARLORD w/Daniel Truly
JUSTICE RISING w/Daniel Truly

ANDREW DEUTSCH
PLATOON LEADER   Cannon, 1988, w/Rick Marx & David Walker
RIVER OF DEATH   Cannon, 1989, w/Edward Simpson
DELTA FORCE 3: THE KILLING GAME   Cannon, 1992,
    w/Boaz Davidson & Greg Latter

Screenplays:
ROOT RETURNS
THORNY HAWKINS
THE GLOW

D.V. deVINCENTIS
Agent: William Morris Agency - Beverly Hills, 310/274-7451

Screenplays:
GROSSE POINTE BLANK w/John Cusack & Steve Pink

MATT DEVLEN
Contact: Wildcat Productions, 1137 N. McCadden Place,
Los Angeles, CA 90038

Screenplays:
CIVIL UNREST

ANNE DEVLIN
Agent: The Casarotto Company - London, 071/287-4450

EMILY BRONTE'S WUTHERING HEIGHTS   Paramount, 1993

BARRY DEVLIN
A MAN OF NO IMPORTANCE   Sony Pictures Classics, 1994

DEAN DEVLIN*
Agent: CAA - Beverly Hills, 310/288-4545

UNIVERSAL SOLDIER   TriStar, 1992, w/Christopher Leitch &
Richard Rothstein
STARGATE   MGM/UA, 1994, w/Roland Emmerich

Screenplays:
FINAL JUDGMENT
PHOTO OPPORTUNITY
MY FRIENDS (Shared)

DON DEVLIN*
Business Manager: Brad Ross, Ross & Bunyan - Los Angeles,
310/473-3717

LOVING   Columbia, 1970

JAMES DEVNEY
UNDER THE GUN   Marquis Pictures, 1989, w/Almer John Davis &
James Sbardellati

CHRISTOPHER DeVORE*
Agent: ICM - Beverly Hills, 310/550-4000

THE ELEPHANT MAN ★   Paramount, 1980, w/Eric Bergren &
David Lynch
FRANCES   Universal/AFD, 1982, w/Eric Bergren & Nicholas Kazan
HAMLET   Warner Bros., 1990, w/Franco Zefferelli

Screenplays:
BARON OF THE TREES
A WRINKLE IN TIME w/Eric Bergren
A GOOD DAY TO DIE

GARY M. DeVORE*
Agent: Innovative Artists - Los Angeles, 310/553-5200
Manager: Jon Brown, The Brown Group - Burbank, 818/955-7040

BACK ROADS   Warner Bros., 1981
THE DOGS OF WAR   United Artists, 1981, w/George Malko
SOLO   Dayton-Stewart Organization, 1984
RAW DEAL   DEG, 1986, w/Norman Wexler
RUNNING SCARED   MGM/UA, 1986, w/Jimmy Huston
TRAXX   DEG, 1988

Screenplays:
SPARE PARTS
PENTATHLON
TOO LATE TO DIE
HURRICANE CHASER
SIX SECOND HIGH
BLOODSHOT
HAPPY TRAILS
THE LIGHTS
HARD KNOX
THE SEARCH FOR JOSEPH TULLY

CAREY DeVUONO*
Contact: WGA - Los Angeles, 310/550-1000

Screenplays:
BAKERTON TC-1
ESCAPE FROM SUMMER CAMP

RICHARD DEWHURST*
Agent: Peter Turner Agency - Santa Monica, 310/315-4772

DEAR AMERICA: LETTERS HOME FROM VIETNAM (FD)
Taurus Entertainment, 1987, w/Bill Couturié

Screenplays:
SPACE BROTHER w/Bill Couturié
KIXI
MOMMY DON'T

NICOLE De WILDE
THE RAGGEDY RAWNEY   Four Seasons Entertainment, 1990,
w/Bob Hoskins

JACK DeWITT
BOMBA THE JUNGLE BOY   Monogram, 1949
CANADIAN PACIFIC   20th Century Fox, 1949, w/Kenneth Gamet
BATTLE OF CHIEF PONTIAC   Broder, 1953
SITTING BULL   United Artists, 1954, w/Sidney Sheldon
THE BAMBOO PRISON   Columbia, 1955
CELL 2455 DEATH ROW   Columbia, 1955
WOLF LARSEN   Allied Artists, 1958, w/Turnley Walker
JACK OF DIAMONDS   MGM, 1967, w/Sandy Howard
A MAN CALLED HORSE   Cinema Center, 1970
MAN IN THE WILDERNESS   Warner Bros., 1971
THE NEPTUNE FACTOR   20th Century-Fox, 1972
THE RETURN OF A MAN CALLED HORSE   United Artists, 1976
SKY RIDERS   20th Century-Fox, 1976, w/Stanley Mann &
Garry Michael White
TRIUMPHS OF A MAN CALLED HORSE   Jensen Farley Pictures,
1983, w/Carlos Aured & Ken Blackwell

THOMAS DeWOLFE
MISPLACED   Original Cinema, 1991, w/Louis Vansen

PETE DEXTER*
Agent: ICM - Beverly Hills, 310/550-4000

PARIS TROUT (CTF)   Showtime, 1991
RUSH   Paramount, 1991

Screenplays:
MULHOLLAND FALLS (MGM/UA)
MICHAEL w/Jim Quinlan
THE DEVIL AND DANIEL WEBSTER
BROTHERLY LOVE
THE HATS
DEADWOOD
THE LAST STOP

DAVID DIAMOND*
Agent: Original Artists - Santa Monica, 310/394-1067

Screenplays:
WHIZ KID w/David Weissman

JANIS DIAMOND*
Agent: Preferred Artists - Encino, 818/990-0305

TAGGET (CTF)   Mirisch-Tagget-MCA, 1991, w/Peter S. Fischer &
Richard T. Heffron

Screenplays:
SOUND BARRIER

PAUL DIAMOND*
Agent: Paradigm - Los Angeles, 310/277-4400

THE CHICKEN CHRONICLES   Avco Embassy, 1977

TOM DICILLO
Agent: William Morris Agency - Beverly Hills, 310/274-7451

JOHNNY SUEDE   Miramax, 1992, directed

ERNEST DICKERSON
Agent: United Talent Agency - Beverly Hills, 310/273-6700

JUICE   Paramount, 1992, w/Gerard Brown, directed

MICKI DICKOFF
Agent: Major Clients Agency - Los Angeles, 310/284-6400

IT'S NEVER TOO LATE: A PORTRAIT OF BUFFY (FD)
   1982, directed
MOTHER, MOTHER (Short)   1988, directed

JOAN DIDION*
Agent: ICM - Beverly Hills, 310/550-4000

PANIC IN NEEDLE PARK   20th Century-Fox, 1971,
   w/John G. Dunne
PLAY IT AS IT LAYS   Universal, 1972, w/John G. Dunne
A STAR IS BORN   Warner Bros., 1976, w/John G. Dunne &
   Frank R. Pierson
TRUE CONFESSIONS   United Artists, 1981, w/John G. Dunne

Screenplays:
UP CLOSE AND PERSONAL w/John G. Dunne
ZONE OF SILENCE w/John G. Dunne
COURT OF HONOR w/John G. Dunne
PLAYLAND w/John G. Dunne
KINGDOM w/John G. Dunne
DEER PARK w/John G. Dunne

WILLIAM DIEHL
Agent: William Morris Agency - Beverly Hills, 310/274-7451

Screenplays:
PRIMAL FEAR

ANTON DIETHER*
Agent: The Artists Group, Ltd. - Los Angeles, 310/552-1100

NIGHT GAMES   Avco Embassy, 1980, w/Clarke Reynolds

Screenplays:
MOSCOW EXCHANGE
THINGS THAT GO BUMP IN THE NIGHT
ROCK CITY

MICHAEL DiGAETANO*
Agent: CAA - Beverly Hills, 310/288-4545

HOUSEGUEST   Buena Vista, 1995, w/Lawrence Gay

Screenplays:
PLAYING SHORT w/Lawrence Gay
BACK TO SCHOOL II w/Lawrence Gay
MY FAVORITE LIFE w/Lawrence Gay
THE BIG ONES w/Lawrence Gay
DOUBLE VISION w/Lawrence Gay
LOOSE SHOES

ERIN DIGNAM
DENIAL *LOON* Filmstar, 1991, directed

Screenplays:
LOVED

MICHAEL DIJIACOMO
Agent: United Talent Agency - Beverly Hills, 310/273-6700

LOST TREASURE OF CAPTAIN CORNELIUS DEAD-EYE
   TUCKET (Short)   1993, directed

Screenplays:
SOULS WITHOUT REASON
THE WOLF AND THE DOVE
JULIAN MOLINAS PROJECT
SUNSET

RICHARD DiLELLO*
Agent: Paradigm - Los Angeles, 310/277-4400

BAD BOYS   Universal/AFD, 1983
COLORS   Orion, 1988, Story w/Michael Schiffer

Screenplays:
THE ORIGINAL GANGSTER
DARK MOON RISING
ESCAPE

FLINT DILLE*
(Robert Nichols Flint Dille)
Agent: ICM - Beverly Hills, 310/550-4000

AN AMERICAN TAIL: FIEVEL GOES WEST (AF)   Universal, 1991

Screenplays:
ABRACADABRA
BARR SINISTER
INSIDE OUT (AF)
HOME ON THE RANGE (AF)

CONSTANTIN DILLON
HAPPY HOUR   TMS Pictures, 1987, w/John De Bello &
   J. Stephen Peace

ROBERT DILLON*
Agent: ICM - Beverly Hills, 310/550-4000

CITY OF FEAR   Columbia, 1958, w/Steven Ritch
X - THE MAN WITH THE X-RAY EYES   American International,
   1963, w/Ray Russell
13 FRIGHTENED GIRLS   Columbia, 1963
THE OLD DARK HOUSE   Columbia, 1963
MUSCLE BEACH PARTY   American International, 1964
PRIME CUT   National General, 1972
99 AND 44/100 % DEAD   20th Century-Fox, 1974
FRENCH CONNECTION II   20th Century-Fox, 1975,
   w/Laurie Dillon & Alexander Jacobs
THE RIVER   Universal, 1984, w/Julian Barry
REVOLUTION   Warner Bros., 1985
THE SURVIVALIST   Lockstar Productions, 1986
FLIGHT OF THE INTRUDER   Paramount, 1991, w/David Shaber
DECEPTION   Miramax, 1993, w/Michael Thomas

Screenplays:
RODEO RIDERS
MICK w/Eoghan Harris
NORTH STAR

EDWARD DiLORENZO
THE IDOLMAKER   United Artists, 1980

ECKHARD DILSSNER
Business: FBW Productions, 279 S. Beverly Dr. - Suite 275,
   Beverly Hills, CA 90212

Screenplays:
DREAMS COME TRUE

MADELINE DiMAGGIO*
Agent: Media Artsts Group - Beverly Hills, 213/658-7434

STROKE OF MIDNIGHT   *IF THE SHOE FITS*   Media Home
   Entertainment 1991, w/Pamela Wallace

RICHARD DIMITRI*
Contact: WGA - Los Angeles, 310/550-1000

Screenplays:
HOTEL HAWAII
BIG TOP
PAROLE PETE

PAUL DINI*
Contact: WGA - Los Angeles, 310/550-1000

BATMAN: MASK OF THE PHANTASM (AF)   Warner Bros., 1993,
   w/Alan Burnett, Martin Pasko & Michael Reeves
DOUBLE DRAGON   Gramercy, 1994, Story w/Neal Shusterman

MARCIA DINNEEN*
Contact: WGA - Los Angeles, 310/550-1000

AN UNREMARKABLE LIFE   SVS, 1989

GREG DINNER
SHIPWRECKED   Buena Vista, 1991, w/Bob Foss, Nils Gaup &
   Nick Thiel

GERALD DI PEGO*
Agent: Broder-Kurland-Webb-Uffner - Beverly Hills, 310/281-3400

W   Cinerama Releasing Corporation, 1974, w/James Kelly
SHARKY'S MACHINE   Orion/Warner Bros., 1981
KEEPER OF THE CITY (CTF)   Viacom Pictures, 1991

Screenplays:
PARALLELS
REACH WELL WHERE YOU ARE GOING
WITH A VENGEANCE w/James Kelly
THE INSURANCE COMPANY
CISCO
ANNA LEE
THE OF
RAPTURE
SO LONG MAGGIE LOVE
ROMANCE

MARK DiSALLE
Business Manager: Jack Dwosh - Los Angeles, 310/203-8282

KICKBOXER   Pathe Entertainment, 1989,
   Story w/Jean-Claude Van Damme, directed

Screenplays:
BLOODSPORT II: THE NEXT KUMITE
   Story w/Jeffrey Schechter (directing)

TIMOTHY J. DISNEY
OLIVER & CO. (AF)   Buena Vista, 1988, w/Jim Cox &
   James Mangold

MARK DiSTEFANO
FRIENDS AND ENEMIES   Sideral Production, 1992,
   w/Tom McCluskey

Screenplays:
EDDIE FIVE FINGERS w/Tom McCluskey

LARRY DITILLIO*
(Lawrence Gabriel Ditillio)
Agent: Monteiro Rose Agency - Encino, 818/501-1177

THE MAD, MAD MOVIE MAKERS   *THE LAST PORNO FLICK*   1974
THE SECRET OF THE SWORD (AF)   Atlantic Releasing
   Corporation, 1985, w/Bob Forward

JAMES DIXON
Agent: Paradigm - Los Angeles, 310/277-4400

RETURN TO SALEMS LOT   Warner Bros., 1987, w/Larry Cohen
FAST GETAWAY   New Line Cinema, 1991

Screenplays:
PLAY THE HEAVY w/Larry Cohen

JOHN DIXON
THE MAN FROM SNOWY RIVER   20th Century-Fox, 1983
   (from a screenplay by Fred Cul Cullen)
RETURN TO SNOWY RIVER   Buena Vista, 1988,
   w/Geoff Burrowes

LESLIE DIXON*
Manager: Linne Radmin, The Radmin Company - Beverly Hills,
   310/274-9515

OUTRAGEOUS FORTUNE   Buena Vista, 1987
OVERBOARD   MGM/UA, 1987
LOVERBOY   Tri-Star, 1989, w/Robin Schiff & Tom Ropelewski
LOOK WHO'S TALKING NOW   TriStar, 1993, w/Tom Ropelewski
MRS. DOUBTFIRE   20th Century Fox, 1993,
   w/Randi Mayem Singer

Screenplays:
THAT OLD FEELING
JUNIOR ACHIEVEMENT
A.K.A.

EDWARD DMYTRYK
Contact: Directors Guild of America - Los Angeles, 310/289-2000

BLUEBEARD   Cinerama Releasing Corporation, 1972,
   w/Ennio di Concini & Maria Pia Fusco, directed

MICHAEL DOANE
Agent: Pleshette & Green - Los Angeles, 213/465-0428

Screenplays:
CITY OF LIGHT

RAY DOBBINS
WHEN PIGS FLY   Odyssey, 1993

FRANK Q. DOBBS*
Agent: Shapiro/Lichtman - Los Angeles, 310/859-8877

UPHILL ALL THE WAY   New World, 1986, directed

LEM DOBBS*
Agent: William Morris Agency - Beverly Hills, 310/274-7451

HIDER IN THE HOUSE   Vestron, 1989
THE HARD WAY   Universal, 1991, w/Daniel Pyne
KAFKA   Miramax, 1991

Screenplays:
THE DAY THE EARTH CAUGHT FIRE
EDWARD FORD (directing)
THE MARVEL OF THE HAUNTED CASTLE
LONG GONE AND FAR AWAY
DEVIL'S ISLAND
LIVE ROUNDS
WHITE ROSE
DOWNTOWN

JAMES J. DOCHERTY*
Contact: WGA - Los Angeles, 310/550-1000

HOLLYWOOD VICE SQUAD   Concorde/Cinema Group, 1986
NIGHTSTICK   Production Distribution Co., 1987
STREET JUSTICE   Lorimar, 1989

RUDY DOCHTERMANN*
(Rudolph Carl Dochtermann)
Agent: Media Artists Group - Hollywood, 213/463-5610

THE FIENDISH PLOT OF DR. FU MANCHU   United Artists, 1980,
   w/Jim Moloney

E.L. DOCTOROW*
Agent: ICM - New York, 212/556-5600

DRINKS BEFORE DINNER (P)
DANIEL   Paramount, 1983

ROBERT DODSON
NAKED OBSESSION   Concorde, 1991

RICK DOEHRING*
Agent: Preferred Artists - Encino, 818/990-0305

EDDIE AND THE CRUISERS II: EDDIE LIVES   Scotti Bros., 1989,
   w/Charles Zev Cohen

CHRISTOPHER DOHERTY
Agent: ICM - London, 071/636-6565

ROSALIE GOES SHOPPING   Four Seasons Entertainment, 1990,
   w/Eleonore Adlon & Percy Adlon
THE MILKY LIFE (LA VIDA LACTEA)   Cartel Films/Journal
   Film KG/Aries Production, 1993, w/Juan Esterlich

JAMES DOHERTY
NIGHT STICK   Production Distribution Co., 1987

BOB DOLMAN*
Agent: CAA - Beverly Hills, 310/288-4545

WILLOW   MGM/UA, 1988
FAR AND AWAY   Universal, 1992

Screenplays:
IT'S A FAIR WORLD w/Harry Shearer
MICHAEL BYE FALLDOWN
BRIDGE TO THE MOON
THE TOUR

MARTIN DOLMAN
AFTER THE FALL OF NEW YORK   Almi Pictures, 1985,
   w/Julian Berry & Gabriel Rossini,   directed

JEANNINE DOMINY*
Agent: CAA - Beverly Hills, 310/288-4545

Screenplays:
PAPESSE
ALINE
LILY

HENRY DOMONIC
(See John Brancato & Michael Ferris)

JAMES DONADIO*
Contact: WGA - Los Angeles, 310/550-1000

BY THE SWORD   The Movie Group, 1992, w/John McDonald

ANN DONAHUE*
Agent: ICM - Beverly Hills, 310/550-4000

Screenplays:
THOSE BEAUMONT GIRLS
PALER SHADE OF GREY
THE PROSPECT
THE INVITATION

ROGER DONALDSON
Agent: CAA - Beverly Hills, 310/288-4545

SMASH PALACE   Atlantic Releasing Corporation, 1981,
   w/Peter Hansard & Bruno Lawrence,   directed

SERGIO DONATI
Contact: Italy - tel.: 06/646-1569

THE BIG GUNDOWN   PEA, 1966, w/Sergio Sollima
ONCE UPON A TIME IN THE WEST   Paramount, 1969,
   w/Sergio Leone
ORCA   Paramount, 1977, w/Luciano Vincenzoni
HOLOCAUST 2000 *THE CHOSEN*   Rank, 1977,
   w/Alberto De Martino & Michael Robson
RAW DEAL   DEG, 1986, Story w/Luciano Vincenzoni
MAN ON FIRE   Tri-Star, 1987, w/Elie Chouraqui
TASHUNGA   AFCL, 1993

WALTER DONIGER*
Agent: Wile Enterprises - Santa Monica, 310/828-9768

ROPE OF SAND   Paramount, 1949
ALONG THE GREAT DIVIDE   Warner Bros., 1950, w/Lewis Meltzer
ALASKA SEAS   Paramount, 1953, w/Geoffrey Homes
DUFFY OF SAN QUENTIN   Warner Bros., 1953,   directed
HOLD BACK THE NIGHT   Universal-International, 1956,
   w/John C. Higgins
THE GUNS OF FORT PETTICOAT   Columbia, 1957
STONE COLD   Columbia, 1991

RICHARD DONN*
Agent: Watkins-Loomis Agency - New York, 212/532-0080

DIPLOMATIC IMMUNITY   Fries Distribution, 1991,
   w/Randall Frakes

BEN DONNELLY
LAST RITES   Cannon, 1980, w/Dominic Paris

THOMAS M. DONNELLY*
Contact: WGA - Los Angeles, 310/550-1000

DEFIANCE   American International, 1980
QUICKSILVER   Columbia, 1986,   directed
TALENT FOR THE GAME   Paramount, 1991, w/Larry Ferguson &
   David Himmelstein
BLINDSIDED (CTF)   MCA Television Entertainment, 1993

Screenplays:
REDEMPTION (directing)
ROUGH JUSTICE
JACK OF HEARTS
TIN MAN
SNAFU
GROWN UPS
THE LIFE OF RAFAELLE GALLO
THE BUFF

MARY AGNES DONOGHUE*
Agent: ICM - Beverly Hills, 310/550-4000

ME AND MAMIE O'ROURKE (P)
THE BUDDY SYSTEM   20th Century Fox, 1984
BEACHES   Buena Vista, 1988

DECEIVED   Buena Vista, 1991, Story
PARADISE   Buena Vista, 1991, directed

Screenplays:
THE BEAN TREES
HOT FLASHES
RULES OF ENGAGEMENT

MARTIN DONOVAN*
Contact: WGA - Los Angeles, 310/550-1000

LOVING COUPLES   20th Century-Fox, 1980

MARTIN DONOVAN*
Agent: United Talent Agency - Beverly Hills, 310/273-6700

APARTMENT ZERO   Skouras Pictures, 1989,
  w/David Koepp, directed
DEATH BECOMES HER   Universal, 1992, w/David Koepp

Screenplays:
WEDDINGS AND FUNERALS (Shared)

PAUL DONOVAN
Address: P.O. Box 2261, Station M, Halifax, Nova Scotia B3J 3L8,
  Canada, 902/420-1577

SELF-DEFENSE *SIEGE* New Line Cinema, 1983, directed
DEF-CON 4   New World, 1985, directed
NORMAN'S AWESOME EXPERIENCE   Norstar
  Entertainment, 1990
GEORGE'S ISLAND   New Line Cinema, 1991,
  w/Maura O'Connell, directed
BURIED ON SUNDAY   Alliance Releasing, 1992,
  w/Bill Fleming, directed
TOM   Saban Pictures, 1993, directed
PAINT CANS   Libra Films, 1994, directed

ANITA DOOHAN*
Agent: The Agency - Los Angeles, 310/551-3000

EMBRYO   Cine Artists, 1976, w/Jack W. Thomas
WHISPERS   Live Home Video, 1990

PAUL DOOLEY
Agent: ICM - Beverly Hills, 310/550-4000

HEALTH   20th Century-Fox, 1980, w/Robert Altman &
  Frank Barhydt

JOHN DOOLITTLE*
Contact: WGA - Los Angeles, 310/550-1000

Screenplays:
HOLLYWOOD SCANDAL w/Curtis Armstrong

MARGERY DOPPELT*
Contact: WGA - Los Angeles, 310/550-1000

TERROR IN THE AISLES (FD)   Universal, 1984

MATTHEW DORFF*
Agent: Innovative Artists - Los Angeles, 310/553-5200
Manager: Jonathan Baruch/PRO Management - Los Angeles,
  310/478-5159

CAMPUS MAN   Paramount, 1987, w/Geoffrey Baere & Alex Horvat

Screenplays:
CRUSADERS (CTF)
RANDOM ENCOUNTER
ASSIGNMENT: BERLIN
THE EXAMINER
REDLINES
SEX AND THE MARRIED WOMAN

CLOSER
PRIME OF LIFE
CLASSY KILL
I LOVE A VAMPIRE
THE CORONER
PIT BULLS FROM HELL

ARIEL DORFMAN*
Contact: WGA - Los Angeles, 310/550-1000

WIDOWS (P) w/Tony Kushner
DEATH AND THE MAIDEN   Fine Line Features, 1994,
  w/Rafael Yglesias, from his play

PHOEBE DORIN*
Agent: Warden, White & Kane - Beverly Hills, 213/852-1028

PERFECT FAMILY (CTF)   O.T.M.L./Wilshire Court, 1992,
  w/Christian Stoianovich

Screenplays:
BULLETPROOF w/Christian Stoianovich
BABY BLUE EYES w/Christian Stoianovich
DEEP SLEEP w/Christian Stoianovich
CONDUIT w/Christian Stoianovich
THE RUNAWAY WIFE w/Christian Stoianovich
WITHOUT MERCY w/Christian Stoianovich
THE 13TH FLOOR w/Christian Stoianovich

ROBERT DORN
OUT OF STYLE   BET Films, 1994

DORIS DÖRRIE
Agent: ICM - New York, 212/556-5600

STRAIGHT THROUGH THE HEART   1983, directed
IN THE BELLY OF THE WHALE   1984, directed
MEN...   New Yorker Films, 1986, directed
ME AND HIM   Columbia, 1989,
  Adaptation w/Michael Juncker, directed
HAPPY BIRTHDAY, TURKE!   Senator Film, 1992, directed

SHIMON DOTAN*
Agent: Shapiro/Lichtman - Los Angeles, 310/859-8877

REPEAT DIVE   Original Cinema, 19982, directed
THE SMILE OF THE LAMB   Original Cinema, 1986, directed
THE FINEST HOUR (CTF)   21st Century Film, 1993,
  w/Stuart Schoffman, directed

FERNANDO DOTY*
Contact: WGA - Los Angeles, 310/550-1000

Screenplays:
ABSOLUTE BLISS
FOOLPROOF
THE KITCHEN CABINET
SEX AND ARCHITECTURE

JOSEPH DOUGHERTY*
Agent: William Morris Agency - New York, 212/586-5100

DIGBY (P)   also screenplay
MY FAVORITE YEAR (P)
STEEL & LACE   Fries Distribution, 1990, w/Dave Edison
CAST A DEADLY SPELL (CTF)   Pacific Western, 1991
ATTACK OF THE 50-FOOT WOMAN (CTF)   HBO Pictures, 1993
WITCH HUNT (CTF)   HBO Pictures, 1994

Screenplays:
STOP THE VIOLENCE (CTF)
LADY LAZARUS
SAINT VALENTINE (CTF)
LUNATIC FRINGE
VERY OLD MONEY

MACGREGOR DOUGLAS*
Contact: WGA - Los Angeles, 310/550-1000

TWO MOON JUNCTION   Lorimar, 1988, Story w/Zalman King
LAKE CONSEQUENCE (CTF)   Showtime Networks, 1993, Story

PETER VINCENT DOUGLAS*
Agent: CAA - Beverly Hills, 310/288-4545

A TIGER'S TALE   Atlantic Releasing Corporation, 1987, directed

Screenplays:
ROSES ARE RED w/Meredith Baer & Gary Goldman
A WORK OF ART

NANCY DOWD
Agent: ICM - Beverly Hills, 310/550-4000

LOVE (Short) directed
SLAP SHOT   Universal, 1977
COMING HOME ★★   United Artists, 1978, Story
LADIES AND GENTLEMEN, THE FABULOUS STAINS   Paramount, 1982, as "Rob Morton"
SWING SHIFT   Warner Bros., 1983, w/Bo Goldman & Ron Nyswaner, as "Rob Morton"
HAPPY NEW YEAR   Columbia, 1987, as "Warner Lane"
LET IT RIDE   Warner Bros., 1989, as "Ernest Morton"

Screenplays:
PROFESSOR ROMEO
SEX IN THE 90'S
CENTERFOLD w/Ron Shelton
GOOD VIBES
R & R
JUST CRAZY ABOUT

ANSON DOWNES*
Contact: WGA - Los Angeles, 310/550-1000

BORIS & NATASHA (CTF)   MCEG Productions, 1992, w/Linda Favila & Charles Fradin

Screenplays:
PERFECT FIT w/Linda Favila

ROBERT DOWNEY
Agent: Henderson/Hogan Agency - Beverly Hills, 310/393-6227

CHAFED ELBOWS   Grove Press, 1965, directed
NO MORE EXCUSES   Rogosin, 1968, directed
PUTNEY SWOPE   Cinema 5, 1969, directed
POUND   United Artists, 1970, directed
GREASER'S PALACE   Greaser's Palace, 1972, directed
THE GONG SHOW MOVIE   Universal, 1980, w/Chuck Barris
AMERICA   ASA Communications, 1986, directed
TOO MUCH SUN   New Line Cinema, 1990, w/Laura Ernst & Al Schwartz, directed

RODDY DOYLE
Agent: Alexandra Cann Representation, 68e Redcliffe Gardens, London SW10 9HE, 071/835-2220, fax 835-1896

THE COMMITMENTS   20th Century Fox, 1991, w/Dick Clement & Ian La Frenais
THE SNAPPER   Miramax, 1993

Screenplays:
THE VAN

SHARON ELIZABETH DOYLE*
Agent: Maggie Field Agency - Studio City, 818/980-2001

STOLEN BABIES (CTF)   ABC Video Enterprises/Sander-Moss Productions, 1993

BRIAN DOYLE - MURRAY*
Contact: WGA - New York, 212/245-6180

CADDYSHACK   Orion/Warner Bros., 1980, w/Douglas Kenney & Harold Ramis
CLUB PARADISE   Warner Bros., 1985, w/Harold Ramis

AARON WILLIAM DOZIER
Agent: Metropolitan Talent Agency - Los Angeles, 213/857-4500

Screenplays:
RETURN TO SENDER w/J.D. Shapiro
PLAY BALL w/J.D. Shapiro
FRACTURED SKULL OF ICE w/J.D. Shapiro

ROBERT DOZIER*
Contact: WGA - Los Angeles, 310/550-1000

THE CARDINAL   Gamma, 1963
THE BIG BOUNCE   Warner Bros., 1969

BERT L. DRAGIN
Agent: Solomon Weingarten & Associates - Los Angeles, 310/479-4706

SUMMER CAMP NIGHTMARE THE BUTTERFLY REVOLUTION   Concorde, 1987, w/Penelope Spheeris, directed
TWICE DEAD   Concorde, 1989, w/Robert McDonnell, directed

STAN DRAGOTI*
Agent: CAA - Beverly Hills, 310/288-4545

DIRTY LITTLE BILLY   Columbia, 1972, w/Charles Moss, directed

DIANE DRAKE*
Agent: APA - Los Angeles, 310/273-0744

ONLY YOU   TriStar, 1994

Screenplays:
PRINCE AND PAWPER
DOG MEETS CAT

T.S. DRAKE*
Agent: Hamilburg Agency - Los Angeles, 310/657-1501

TERROR TRAIN   20th Century-Fox, 1980

AARON DRANE
Agent: Neal Stevens & Associates - Beverly Hills, 310/275-7541

Screenplays:
OUT OF THE PAST

ANTHONY DRAZAN*
Agent: United Talent Agency - Beverly Hills, 310/273-6700

ZEBRAHEAD   Triumph Releasing, 1992, directed

Screenplays:
SHELTER (directing)
LIVING WITHOUT YOU
BICYCLE DAYS
BIG BROTHER
THE SOFT TOUCH

DR. DRE
WHO'S THE MAN?   New Line Cinema, 1993, Story w/Ed Lover & Seth Greenland

CAROL DRECHSLER*
Agent: CAA - Beverly Hills, 310/288-4545

Screenplays:
GARDEN OF PALMS
SHE'S THE BOSS
KICK
POUND DOG
LOOSE WOMEN

PAUL DRESKIN
Agent: Leslie Kallen Agency - Sherman Oaks, 818/906-2785

Screenplays:
WEAVE OF WOMEN
THETA STATE
WHITE DEMON

HAL DRESNER*
(Harold A. Dresner)
Agent: Richland/Wunsch/Hohman Agency - Los Angeles, 310/278-1955

THE EXTRAORDINARY SEAMAN   MGM, 1969, w/Philip Rock
THE APRIL FOOLS   National General, 1969
Sssssssssss   Universal, 1973
THE EIGER SANCTION   Universal, 1974, w/Warren B. Murphy & Rod Whitaker
ZORRO, THE GAY BLADE   20th Century-Fox, 1981

Screenplays:
BROKE
THANKS, DAD w/Jordan Crittenden
BO-PEEP
EASY STREET
THE CHEAT

LORIN H. DREYFUSS
DETECTIVE SCHOOL DROP OUTS   *DUMB DICKS*   Cannon, 1986, w/David Landsberg
DUTCH TREAT   Cannon, 1987, w/David Landsberg

JOHN A. DRIMMER*
Agent: Major Clients Agency - Los Angeles, 310/284-6400
Contact: 213/935-6344

IMPULSE   20th Century-Fox, 1984, Story
ICEMAN   Universal, 1984, w/Chip Proser
BATTLE IN THE EROGENOUS ZONE (Short)   1992, w/Loren-Paul Caplin, directed

SARA DRIVER
SLEEPWALK   Ottoskop Filmproduktion/Driver Films, 1986, directed
WHEN PIGS FLY   Odyssey, 1993, Story w/Ray Dobbins, directed

GARY DRUCKER*
Contact: Sidewalk Studio - Los Angeles, 310/444-6538

Screenplays:
SOLDIERS OF FORTUNE
NEIGHBORHOOD WATCH
WEEGEE

MICHAEL B. DRUXMAN
KEATON'S COP   Cannon, 1990
CHEYENNE WARRIOR   Concorde/New Horizons, 1994

Screenplays:
DILLINGER AND CAPONE

LEE DRYSDALE
Agent: ICM - Beverly Hills, 310/550-4000

LEATHER JACKETS   Triumph Releasing, 1991, directed

Screenplays:
DEFENCELESS UNDER THE NIGHT
WASTELAND
NEEDLES (CTF)
LEGAL TENDER
JACK CARTER'S LAW
ROGUE TROOPER

BILL DuBAY
Agent: Berzon Agency - Glendale, 818/548-1560

Screenplays:
THE FUNNIES w/Frank Ridgeway

DAVID DuBOS
Agent: Writers & Artists Agency - Los Angeles, 310/824-6300

THE ROOMATE (Short)
FUTURE SHOCK (Short)   Hemdale, 1993

Screenplays:
STORM WARNING
DOUBTING THOMAS
LOUP-GAROU
MAXIMUM MAX w/Oley Sassone
POISENED WELL w/Oley Sassone

ADAM DUBOV*
Agent: William Morris Agency - Beverly Hills, 310/274-7451

THE GRAND POSEUR (Short)   directed
DEAD BEAT   Distant Horizon, 1994, w/Janice Shapiro, directed

Screenplays:
PURPLE WEST w/Janice Shapiro
WILD RIDE w/Janice Shapiro
UNFORGETTABLE w/Janice Shapiro
TUBESTEAK w/Janice Shapiro

JAMES DUFF*
Agent: Gold/Marshak - Burbank, 818/972-4300

A QUARREL OF SPARROWS (P)

Screenplays:
HOMEFRONT THE WAR AT HOME   *(from his play)*

PETER JOHN DUFFELL
Address: 13 Stratford Grove, Putney, London SW15 1NV, England, tel.: 071/785-9512

ENGLAND MADE ME   Cine Globe, 1973, w/Desmond Cory, directed

SHAY DUFFIN
Agent: Susan Smith & Associates - Beverly Hills, 213/852-4777

Screenplays:
CONFESIONS OF AN IRISH REBEL
REQUIEM FOR THE BLACK DONNELLYS

MICHAEL DUGAN*
Agent: Kopaloff Company - Los Angeles, 310/203-8430

Screenplays:
SPECIAL FAVORS w/Howard Smith
PENNILESS
OBJECT OF DESIRE
RED TAIL SQUADRON
RAGING HORMONES

THOMAS C. DUGAN
FATAL SKIES   AIP, 1990, Story w/James Eaton &
   William Zipp, directed

GEORGE DUGDALE
SLAUGHTER HIGH   Vestron, 1987, directed

JOHN DUIGAN
Agent: ICM - Beverly Hills, 310/550-4000

MOUTH TO MOUTH   Vega Film Productions, 1978, directed
WINTER OF OUR DREAMS   Satori, 1981, directed
FAR EAST   Filmco Australia, 1983, directed
THE YEAR MY VOICE BROKE   Avenue Pictures, 1987, directed
FLIRTING   Samuel Goldwyn Company, 1992, directed
WIDE SARGASSO SEA   New Line Cinema, 1993,
   w/Carole Angier & Jan Sharp, directed
SIRENS   Miramax, 1994, directed

Screenplays:
THE ICE DANCER

CAROL MUSKE DUKES
Agent: Shapiro/Lichtman - Los Angeles, 310/859-8877

Screenplays:
DEAR DIGBY
SHORTWAVE

TOM DULACK*
Agent: William Morris Agency - New York, 212/586-5100

INCOMMUNICADO (P)

Screenplays:
BREAKING LEGS (from his play)

DON CARLOS DUNAWAY*
Agent: The Rothman Agency - Beverly Hills, 213/655-2020

CUJO   Warner Bros., 1983, w/Lauren Currier
IMPULSE   20th Century-Fox, 1984, w/Bart Davis

ADRIAN DUNBAR
HEAR MY SONG   Miramax, 1991, w/Peter Chelsom

Screenplays:
SAM AND THE SERGEANT w/Peter Chelsom (Buena Vista)

CHARLES DUNCAN*
Agent: CAA - Beverly Hills, 310/288-4545

Screenplays:
AMERICAN BEAUTY

MICHAEL DUNCAN*
Contact: WGA - Los Angeles, 310/550-1000

EXPOSURE (P)

Screenplays:
TIME OUT OF JOINT w/Sam Hamm
SNAKES AND LADDERS
NO HANGUPS
ON THE ROAD AGAIN

PATRICK SHEANE DUNCAN*
Agent: Preferred Artists - Encino, 818/990-0305

BEACHGIRLS   Crown International, 1982, w/Phil Groves
84 CHARLIE MOPIC   New Century/Vista, 1989, directed
A HOME OF OUR OWN   Gramercy, 1993
THE PORNOGRAPHER   Charlie MoPic Co., 1994, directed
MR. HOLLAND'S OPUS   Buena Vista, 1995

Screenplays:
NICK OF TIME
EXILES ON MAIN STREET
PRISONER OF THE ROAD
TRUE SPORT
HOME BEFORE MORNING
ELFIN
THE FINEST KIND
WAYWARD ANGELS
ROOKIE COP
PAYBACK
HEART OF GOLD
BLOOD MONEY
DEL MAR HEIST
KILLSQUAD
HAVANA DREAMING

STEVE DUNCAN*
Contact: WGA - Los Angeles, 310/550-1000

THE COURTMARTIAL OF JACKIE ROBINSON (CTF)
   Turner Network Television, 1990, w/L. Travis Clark,
   Dennis L. Clark & Clayton Frohman

Screenplays:
UNDER ONE ROOF

NINIAN DUNETT
RESTLESS NATIVES   Orion Classics, 1985

AMY DUNKELBERGER
Agent: Renaissance-H.N. Swanson - Los Angeles, 310/246-6000

THE WAITING (Short)   1984

Screenplays:
STRANGE DESIRE
CRACKERJACK COWBOY

VIC DUNLOP*
Agent: The Gersh Agency - Beverly Hills, 310/274-6611

BREAKFAST OF ALIENS   Hemdale, 1993, w/David Lee Miller

Screenplays:
JOHN DOE w/David Lee Miller
SISTER MARY BUTCH w/David Lee Miller

GEOFFREY FRANCIS DUNN
VOYAGE OF THE HEART   Teacup Films, 1989

HARRY S. DUNN*
Agent: Dytman & Schwartz - Los Angeles, 310/274-8844

COYOTE SUMMER (P)

Screenplays:
ON THE AIR
THE HONEYMOON

ROBERT J. DUNN*
Agent: Sanford-Gross & Associates - Los Angeles, 310/208-2100

Screenplays:
OZONE
IS YOUR BROTHER BLUE?
SWEET LIES
THE LONG SATURDAY NIGHT

JAMES PATRICK DUNNE*
Agent: United Talent Agency - Beverly Hills, 310/273-6700

Screenplays:
I OWE YOU MY LIFE
MOE'S WORLD
FIRE AND ICE
CHOICES   THE SIXTH MAN

JOHN GREGORY DUNNE*
Agent: ICM - Beverly Hills, 310/550-4000

PANIC IN NEEDLE PARK   20th Century-Fox, 1971, w/Joan Didion
PLAY IT AS IT LAYS   Universal, 1971, w/Joan Didion
A STAR IS BORN   Warner Bros., 1976, w/Joan Didion &
    Frank R. Pierson
TRUE CONFESSIONS   United Artists, 1981, w/Joan Didion

Screenplays:
UP CLOSE AND PERSONAL   w/Joan Didion
ZONE OF SILENCE   w/Joan Didion
COURT OF HONOR   w/Joan Didion
PLAYLAND   w/Joan Didion
KINGDOM   w/Joan Didion
DEER PARK   w/Joan Didion

EVAN DUNSKY*
Agent: Sanford-Gross & Associates - Los Angeles, 310/208-2100

VOODOO DAWN   Academy Entertainment, 1990,
    w/Jeffrey Delman, Thomas Rendon & John Russo

CHRISTOPHER DURANG*
Agent: CAA - Beverly Hills, 310/288-4545

SISTER MARY IGNATIUS EXPLAINS IT ALL FOR YOU (P)
THE MARRIAGE OF BETTE AND BOO (P)
LAUGHING WILD (P)
A HISTORY OF THE AMERICAN FILM (P)
BEYOND THERAPY   New World, 1987, w/Robert Altman,
    from his play

Screenplays:
THE ADVENTURES OF LOLA

MARGUÉRITE DURAS
Contact: French Film Office, 745 Fifth Avenue, New York, NY 10151,
    212/832-8860

HIROSHIMA, MON AMOUR ★   Zenith, 1960
UNE AUSSI LONGUE ABSENCE (THE LONG ABSENCE)
    Procinex, 1961, w/Gerald Jarlot
10:30 P.M. SUMMER   United Artists, 1966, w/Jules Dassin

TODD DURHAM*
Agent: Richland/Wunsch/Hohman Agency - Los Angeles,
    310/278-1955
Business: Straightjacket Productions, P.O. Box 1804, Beverly Hills,
    CA 90213, 213/650-2142

VISIONS OF SUGAR-PLUMS   Regency Entertainment,
    1984, directed
BLACK CREEK   Regency Entertainment, 1985, w/W.H. Keeter
HYPERSPACE   Regency Entertainment, 1986, directed

Screenplays:
NATIONAL LAMPOON'S COUSIN EDDIE
PRACTICAL DEMONKEEPING
DREAMBUSTERS
DEADLINE
WALKING TARGET
SIGNED, SEALED, DELIVERED
ANIMAL PASSION
THE LIFE AND ADVENTURES OF SANTA CLAUS
BEAUTY BECOMES THE BEAST
MR. SMITH GOES TO HELL
GOV
WILD BILL BEETHOVEN
POISON APPLES
WIMPS FROM SPACE
PEE-WEE HERMAN VS. THE FLYING SAUCERS

GRIFF DuRHONE*
Contact: WGA - Los Angeles, 310/550-1000

CHEETAH   Buena Vista, 1989, w/John Cotter & Erik Tarloff

PHILIP DUSENBERRY*
Contact: Pinder Lane Productions - New York, 212/489-0880

HAIL TO THE CHIEF   20th Century Fox, 1973, w/others
THE NATURAL   Tri-Star, 1984, w/Roger Towne

ROBERT DUVALL
Agent: William Morris Agency - Beverly Hills, 310/274-7451

ANGELO, MY LOVE   Cinecom, 1983, directed

Screenplays:
THE APOSTLE (directing)

LAURENCE DWORET*
Agent: ICM - Beverly Hills, 310/550-4000

OUTBREAK   Warner Bros., 1995, Story w/Robert Roy Pool

Screenplays:
ULTIMATUM   w/Robert Roy Pool
UNDERGROUND   w/Robert Roy Pool
THE PRACTICE   w/Robert Roy Pool
CROSSING   w/Denise DiNovi
CODE BLUE

JOHN DWYER*
Agent: William Morris Agency - Beverly Hills, 310/274-7451

CAPTAIN RON   Buena Vista, 1992, w/Tom Eberhardt

H. KAYE DYAL
LONE WOLF McQUADE   Orion, 1983, Story w/B.J. Nelson
PROJECT ELIMINATOR   South Gate Entertainment, 1991, directed

DALE DYE*
Agent: Paradigm - Los Angeles, 310/277-4400

FIRE BIRDS   Buena Vista, 1990, Story w/John K. Swenson &
    Step Tyner

ANNE DYER
BATTLE BEYOND THE STARS   New World, 1980,
    Story w/John Sayles

ROBERT DYKE*
Agent: APA - Los Angeles, 310/273-0744

Screenplays:
LINES OF FORCE   w/Tex Ragsdale
RETRO   w/Tex Ragsdale

E

KENNETH EASTAUGH
MR. LOVE   Warner Bros., 1986

JEFF EASTIN
Agent: Sanford-Gross & Associates - Los Angeles, 310/208-2100

Screenplays:
INCONVENIENCED

CAROLE EASTMAN*
(Adrien Joyce)
Agent: William Morris Agency - Beverly Hills, 310/274-7451
Business Manager: Guild Management, 310/277-9711

THE SHOOTING   American International, 1966
THE MODEL SHOP   Columbia, 1969
FIVE EASY PIECES ★   Columbia, 1970
PUZZLE OF A DOWNFALL CHILD   Universal, 1970
THE FORTUNE   Columbia, 1975
MAN TROUBLE   20th Century Fox, 1992
RUNNING MATES (CTF)   HBO Pictures, 1992, as "A.L. Appling"

Screenplays:
I KNOW WHERE I'M GOING!

CHARLES EASTMAN
Contact: Armstrong & Hirsch - Los Angeles, 310/553-0305

LITTLE FAUSS AND BIG HALSY   Paramount, 1970
THE ALL-AMERICAN BOY   Warner Bros., 1973, directed
SECOND-HAND HEARTS   Lorimar/Paramount, 1981

JAMES EATON
FATAL SKIES   AIP, 1990, w/William Zipp

MICHAEL EATON
Contact: 310/660-9049

THE TRAGEDY OF FLIGHT 103: THE INSIDE STORY (CTF)
   HBO Showcase/Granada Films, 1990
FELLOW TRAVELLER (CTF)   British Film Institute/BBC/
   HBO Showcase, 1990

FRAN LEWIS EBELING
THE LADIES CLUB   New Line Cinema, 1986, w/Paul Mason

THOM EBERHARDT*
Agent: The Daniel Ostroff Agency - Los Angeles, 310/278-2020

NIGHT OF THE COMET   Atlantic Releasing Corporation,
   1984, directed
THE NIGHT BEFORE   Kings Road Productions, 1987,
   w/Gregory Scherick, directed
ALL I WANT FOR CHRISTMAS   Paramount, 1991,
   w/Richard Kramer
HONEY I BLEW UP THE KID   Buena Vista, 1992,
   w/Peter Elbling & Garry Goodrow
CAPTAIN RON   Buena Vista, 1992, w/John Dwyer, directed

ROGER EBERT
Contact: Donald M. Ephraim - Chicago, 312/321-9700

BEYOND THE VALLEY OF THE DOLLS   20th Century-Fox, 1970

DANIEL MARTIN ECKHARD
Agent: Writers & Artists Agency - Los Angeles, 310/824-6300

Screenplays:
OUT THERE
NOT MINDING THE HURT
BREAKFAST IN ATLANTIS

MICHAEL ALAN EDDY*
Agent: Jim Preminger Agency - Los Angeles, 310/475-9491

BEDROOM EYES   Aquarius Releasing, 1984

Screenplays:
SINS OF THE FATHER
EASTERN/WESTERN
THE CHINA GUN
CAPTAIN HOOK
CRUNCH
STEAL THE NIGHT
THE COUNSELOR
PEN PALS
GUN SHY
STAR WITNESS
THE GIFT
BLACK ON WHITE
BABY BLUE EYES
LITTLE GIRL LOST

DEAN EDELSON
Agent: The Gage Group - Los Angeles, 310/859-8777

Screenplays:
MY BROTHER

RICK EDELSTEIN*
Contact: WGA - Los Angeles, 310/550-1000

SEXUAL SERENDIPITY (P)

Screenplays:
A MATTER OF CHOICE

MARK EDWARD EDENS*
Agent: Monteiro Rose Agency - Encino, 818/501-1177

LIFE ON THE EDGE   Festival Entertainment, 1992

Screenplays:
ORLANDO FURIOUS

DAVID EDGAR
Agent: Michael Imison, Playwrights - London, 011/441/354-3274

NICHOLAS NICKLEBY (P)
MARY BARNES (P)
LADY JANE   Paramount, 1986

PATRICK EDGEWORTH
RAW DEAL   Greater Union Film Distributors, 1977
DRIVING FORCE   J&M Entertainment, 1990

DAVE EDISON
STEEL & LACE   Fries Distribution, 1990, w/Joseph Dougherty

DON EDMONDS
BARE KNUCKLES   Intercontinental, 1978, directed

ERIC EDSON*
Contact: WGA - Los Angeles, 310/550-1000

THE ROSE AND THE JACKAL (CTF)   Steve White Productions/
   Spectator Films/PWD Productions, 1990
DIVING IN   Skouras Pictures, 1990

Screenplays:
THE HERO
SOLOMON'S MIND
SCALAWAGS
CHASER
SNOOKUMS

BLAKE EDWARDS*
Agent: William Morris Agency - Beverly Hills, 310/274-7451
Business: Blake Edwards Co., 11777 San Vicente Blvd., Los Angeles,
   CA 90049, 310/571-2828

PANHANDLE   Allied Artists, 1948, w/John C. Champion
SOUND OFF   Columbia, 1952, w/Richard Quine
ALL ASHORE   Columbia, 1952, w/Richard Quine
DRIVE A CROOKED ROAD   Columbia, 1954
THE ATOMIC KID   Republic, 1954, Story
MY SISTER EILEEN   Columbia, 1955, w/Richard Quine
BRING YOUR SMILE ALONG   Columbia, 1955, directed
HE LAUGHED LAST   Columbia, 1956, directed
OPERATION MAD BELL   Columbia, 1957, w/Arthur Carter &
   Jed Harris
MISTER CORY   Universal-International, 1957, directed
THIS HAPPY FEELING   Universal-International, 1958, directed
SOLDIER IN THE RAIN   Allied Artists, 1963, w/Maurice Richlin
THE PINK PANTHER   United Artists, 1964,
   w/Maurice Richlin, directed
A SHOT IN THE DARK   United Artists, 1964,
   w/William Peter Blatty, directed
WHAT DID YOU DO IN THE WAR, DADDY?   United Artists, 1966,
   w/William Peter Blatty, directed
GUNN   Warner Bros., 1967, w/William Peter Blatty, directed
THE PARTY   United Artists, 1968, w/Frank Waldman &
   Tom Waldman, directed
DARLING LILI   Paramount, 1970, w/William Peter Blatty, directed
WILD ROVERS   MGM, 1971, directed
THE TAMARIND SEED   Avco Embassy, 1974, directed
RETURN OF THE PINK PANTHER   United Artists, 1975,
   w/Frank Waldman, directed
THE PINK PANTHER STRIKES AGAIN   United Artists, 1976,
   w/Frank Waldman, directed
REVENGE OF THE PINK PANTHER   United Artists, 1978,
   w/Ron Clark & Frank Waldman, directed
10   Orion/Warner Bros., 1979, directed
S.O.B.   Paramount, 1981, directed
VICTOR/VICTORIA ★   MGM/United Artists, 1982, directed
TRAIL OF THE PINK PANTHER   MGM/United Artists, 1982,
   w/Geoffrey Edwards, Tom Waldman & Frank Waldman, directed
CURSE OF THE PINK PANTHER   MGM/UA, 1983,
   w/Geoffrey Edwards, directed
THE MAN WHO LOVED WOMEN   Columbia, 1983,
   w/Geoffrey Edwards & Milton Wexler, directed
CITY HEAT   Warner Bros., 1l984, w/Joseph C. Stinson,
   as "Sam O. Brown"
A FINE MESS   Columbia, 1986, directed
THAT'S LIFE!   Columbia, 1986, w/Milton Wexler, directed
SUNSET   Tri-Star, 1987, directed
SKIN DEEP   20th Century Fox, 1989, directed
SWITCH   Warner Bros., 1991, directed
SON OF THE PINK PANTHER   MGM , 1993,
   w/Madeline Sunshine & Steve Sunshine, directed

E. PAUL EDWARDS*
Contact: WGA - Los Angeles, 310/550-1000

Screenplays:
MY CUBA

GEOFFREY B. EDWARDS
Business Manager: Glass/Rosen/Orkin - 818/907-1600

TRAIL OF THE PINK PANTHER   MGM/United Artists, 1982,
   w/Blake Edwards, Tom Waldman & Frank Waldman
CURSE OF THE PINK PANTHER   MGM/UA, 1983,
   w/Blake Edwards
THE MAN WHO LOVED WOMEN   Columbia, 1983,
   w/Blake Edwards & Milton Wexler
RAD   Tri-Star, 1986, w/Sam Bernard

HENRY EDWARDS*
Contact: WGA - Los Angeles, 310/550-1000

SGT. PEPPER'S LONELY HEARTS CLUB BAND   Universal, 1978

PAUL F. EDWARDS*
Agent: ICM - Beverly Hills, 310/550-4000

TRACKDOWN   United Artists, 1976
HIGH-BALLIN'   American International, 1978
FIRE BIRDS   Buena Vista, 1990, w/David Taylor & Nick Thiel

Screenplays:
LOOSE CANNON   w/Larry Ferguson
TULKU   STAR OF TIBET
THE WILD BIG RED
LEONARD PELTIER STORY   IN THE SPIRIT OF CRAZY HORSE
STEALING THUNDER

TOM EDWARDS*
Manager: Creative Alliance Management - Los Angeles,
   213/962-6090

WIZARDS OF THE LOST KINGDOM   Concorde/Cinema
   Group, 1985

CHRISTINE EDZARD
Address: Sands Films Ltd., Grices Warf, 169 Rotherhithe St., London
   SE16 1QU, England, 071/231-2209, fax 271-2119

STORIES FROM A FLYING TRUNK   EMI, 1979, directed
LITTLE DORRIT, PART 1: NOBODY'S FAULT ★   Cannon,
   1989, directed
LITTLE DORRIT, PART 2: LITTLE DORRIT'S STORY ★
   Cannon, 1989, directed
THE FOOL   Sands Films, 1991, w/Olivier Stockman, directed

PAMELA EELLS*
Contact: WGA - Los Angeles, 310/550-1000

Screenplays:
BAMBOO   w/Sally Lapiduss

SAM EGAN*
Contact: WGA - Los Angeles, 310/550-1000

ELVIRA: MISTRESS OF THE DARK   New World, 1988,
   w/John Paragon & Cassandra Peterson
IMAGINE: JOHN LENNON (FD)   Warner Bros., 1988,
   w/Andrew Solt

Screenplays:
THE BORROWER

CHARLES H. EGLEE*
Agent: ICM - Beverly Hills, 310/550-4000

DEADLY EYES   *NIGHT EYES*   Warner Bros., 1983

JAN EGLESON
Agent: ICM - Beverly Hills, 310/550-4000

BILLY IN THE LOWLANDS   Theater Co. of Boston, 1979, directed
THE DARK END OF THE STREET   First Run Features,
    1981, directed
THE LITTLE SISTER   American Playhouse, 1985, directed

Screenplays:
MANCHESTER ANGEL

ATOM EGOYAN
Business: Ego Film Arts, 490 Adelaide Street West - Suite 102,
    Toronto, Ontario M5V 1T3, 416/365-2137

NEXT OF KIN   Ego Film Arts, 1985, directed
FAMILY VIEWING   Ego Film Arts, 1987, directed
SPEAKING PARTS   Cinephile, 1990, directed
THE ADJUSTER   Orion Classics, 1991, directed
CALENDAR   Zeitgeist Films, 1993, directed
EXOTICA   Miramax, 1994, directed

JOHN EHLE
THE JOURNEY OF AUGUST KING   Miramax, 1995

GRETEL EHRLICH*
Agent: ICM - Beverly Hills, 310/550-4000

Screenplays:
HEART MOUNTAIN

ROSANNE EHRLICH
CHANTILLY LACE (CTF)   Showtime, 1993, w/Linda Yellen

JON EIG
Agent: Berzon Agency - Glendale, 818/548-1560

Screenplays:
LOVE IS A MYSTERY

ROBERT H. EISELE*
Agent: Ken Sherman & Associates - Beverly Hills, 310/273-8840

A DARK NIGHT OF THE SOUL (P)
ANIMALS ARE PASSING FROM OUR LIVES (P)
A GARDEN IN LOS ANGELES (P)
THE GREENROOM (P)
GOATS (P)
THE MURDER OF EINSTEIN (P)
BREACH OF CONTRACT   Atlantic Releasing Corporation,
    1984, Shared
LAST LIGHT (CTF)   Showtime Entertainment/Stillwater
    Productions, 1993
THE BIRDS II: LAND'S END (CTF)   Rosemont/MCA Television
    Entertainment, 1994, w/Jim Wheat & Ken Wheat
LILY IN THE WINTER (CTF)   USA Pictures, 1994

Screenplays:
THE INNOCENT (CTF) (Shared)
THE INVITATION (Shared)
THE FOREST CHILD
TWO OF THE MISSING

D. E. EISENBERG
DREAM A LITTLE DREAM   Vestron, 1989, w/Daniel Jay Franklin &
    Marc Rocco

MAX EISENBERG*
Contact: WGA - Los Angeles, 310/550-1000

Screenplays:
THE CROSSING
ME, MYSELF AND I
PERSONAL INJURY

ALAN EISENSTOCK*
Agent: Writers & Artists Agency - Los Angeles, 310/824-6300

Screenplays:
SOLD w/Larry Mintz
DIE RISE w/Larry Mintz

JO EISINGER
NIGHT AND THE CITY   20th Century-Fox, 1950
THE SLEEPING CITY   Universal-International, 1950
THE SYSTEM   Warner Bros., 1953
BEDEVILLED   MGM, 1955
CRIME OF PASSION   United Artists, 1956
THE BIG BOODLE   United Artists, 1957
OSCAR WILDE   Vantage, 1959
HOUSE OF THE SEVEN HAWKS   MGM, 1959
THE BOY WHO STOLE A MILLION   British Lion, 1960,
    w/Charles Crichton
THEY CAME TO ROB LOS VEGAS   Warner Bros., 1969,
    w/Antonio Isasi
THE JIGSAW MAN   United Film Distribution, 1984

PHILIP EISNER*
Agent: Lisa Callamaro Literary Agency- Beverly Hills, 310/274-6783

Screenplays:
I, ASSASSIN
WIREHEAD
EVENT HORIZON
WEAPON
SCANNERS
MUTANT CHRONICLES
CENTURIONS

ED ELBERT
HOTEL OKLAHOMA   European American Entertainment, 1991,
    w/Bobby Houston & Terry Kahn

PETER ELBLING*
Contact: WGA - Los Angeles, 310/550-1000

HONEY, I BLEW UP THE KID   Buena Vista, 1992,
    w/Thom Eberhardt & Garry Goodrow

LONNE ELDER III
Agent: Preferred Artists - Encino, 818/990-0305

SOUNDER ★   20th Century-Fox, 1972
PART 2 SOUNDER   Gamma III, 1976
BUSTIN' LOOSE   Universal, 1981, Adaptation

KEVIN ELDERS*
Business Manager: Marvin Meyer, Rosenfelt, Meyer and Susman,
    9601 Wilshire Boulevard, Beverly Hills, CA 90210, 310/858-7700

IRON EAGLE   Tri-Star, 1986, w/Sidney J. Furie
IRON EAGLE II   Tri-Star, 1988, w/Sidney J. Furie
ACES: IRON EAGLE III   New Line Cinema, 1992

Screenplays:
ROOM 502 (EFG Entertainment, directing)
STREET (MCEG Sterling Entertainment)
RAVEN HAWK
FIRST STRIKE
ONE NATION INVISIBLE
MEGASCANNER
LOVE AND DARKNESS

LAURICE ELEHWANY*
Agent: ICM - Beverly Hills, 310/550-4000

MY GIRL   Columbia, 1991
LITTLE PANDA   Warner Bros., 1995, w/Jeff Rothberg

Screenplays:
THE FRONT LINES

DANNY ELFMAN*
Contact: Bloom, Dekom, Hergott & Cook - Los Angeles, 310/278-8622

Screenplays:
JULIEN
THE WORLD OF JIMMY CALLICUT

RICHARD ELFMAN
FORBIDDEN ZONE   Sutton Marketing, 1980, w/Matthew Bright,
   Nick L. Martinson & Nick James

HARRY ELFONT*
Agent: ICM - Beverly Hills, 310/550-4000
Manager: Ogden House - Los Angeles, 213/851-0458

Screenplays:
THE FAMILY WAY w/Deborah Kaplan

MICHAEL ELIAS *
Agent: CAA - Beverly Hills, 310/288-4545

THE FRISCO KID   Warner Bros., 1979, w/Frank Shaw
THE JERK   Universal, 1979, w/Carl Gottlieb & Steve Martin
SERIAL   Paramount, 1980, w/Richard Eustis
YOUNG DOCTORS IN LOVE   20th Century-Fox, 1982,
   w/Richard Eustis
LUSH LIFE (CTF)   Showtime/Chanticleer Films, 1994, directed

Screenplays:
ON THE BRINK w/Richard Eustis
BANDIES (P) w/Richard Eustis
DIRE STRAITS w/Richard Eustis
BLACKJACK & SALTY w/Richard Eustis

JAN ELIASBERG*
Agent: William Morris Agency - Beverly Hills, 310/274-7451
Manager: Elsboy Entertainment - Los Angeles, 310/851-5700

Screenplays:
GROWING UP FAST
TRAVELLING LIGHT
CELINA'S WORLD

JOYCE ELIASON*
Agent: ICM - Beverly Hills, 310/550-4000

TELL ME A RIDDLE   Filmways, 1980, w/Alev Lyttle

Screenplays:
HEAVEN SCENT w/Ken Friedman
SECOND TIME LUCKY
HEARTS

STEVE ELKINS*
Manager: Creative Alliance Management - Los Angeles,
   213/962-6090

MEDUSA CHALLENGER (Short)

Screenplays:
THE NONESUCH MAN

ROBERT ELLIOT*
Contact: WGA - Los Angeles, 310/550-1000

RICH GIRL   Studio Three Film Corporation, 1991

SAM ELLIOTT
Agent: United Talent Agency - Beverly Hills, 310/273-6700

CONAGHER (CTF)   Imagine Film Entertainment, 1991,
   w/Jeffrey M. Meyer & Katherine Ross

STEPHAN ELLIOTT
Agent: William Morris Agency - Beverly Hills, 310/274-7451

FRAUDS   LIVE Entertainment/J&M Entertainment, 1993, directed
THE ADVENTURES OF PRISCILLA, QUEEN OF THE DESERT
   Gramercy, 1994, directed

TED ELLIOTT*
Agent: William Morris Agency - Beverly Hills, 310/274-7451

LITTLE MONSTERS   Vestron, 1989, w/Terry Rossio
ALADDIN (AF)   Buena Vista, 1992, w/Terry Rossio,
   Ron Clements & John Musker
THE PUPPET MASTERS   Buena Vista, 1994, w/Terry Rossio &
   David Goyer

Screenplays:
GODZILLA w/Terry Rossio
SANDMAN w/Terry Rossio
ZORRO w/Terry Rossio
PRINCESS OF MARS w/Terry Rossio
DUNN'S CONUNDRUM w/Terry Rossio

BOB ELLIS
Agent: Cameron Creswell Agency - Sydney, Australia,
   tel.: 02/356-4677

MAN OF FLOWERS   Spectrafilm, 1983, w/Paul Cox
MY FIRST WIFE   Spectrafilm, 1984, w/Paul Cox
CACTUS   Spectrafilm, 1986, w/Paul Cox & Norman Kaye
WARM NIGHTS ON A SLOW MOVING TRAIN   Miramax, 1987,
   w/Deny Lawrence, directed
THE NOSTRADAMUS KID   Ronin Films, 1993, directed

BRET EASTON ELLIS*
Agent: ICM - New York, 212/556-5600

Screenplays:
RULES OF ATTRACTION

GARY ELLIS
TALES OF THE UNKNOWN   AIP Home Video, 1990,
   "Living on Video"

KIRK ELLIS
Manager: Atlas Entertainment - Los Angeles, 213/658-9100

Screenplays:
THE GRASS HARP
DOUBLE DOWN w/Reinhard Denke

MICHAEL ELLIS
Agent: Sanford-Gross & Associates - Los Angeles, 310/208-2100

Screenplays:
LET THEM EAT CAKE w/Pamela Falk

PETE ELLIS
SECOND COUSIN, ONCE REMOVED   Intrepid Ventures Group,
   1994, w/Dave Bussan, John McColpin & John Shorney

TREY ELLIS*
Agent: ICM - Beverly Hills, 310/550-4000

THE INKWELL   Buena Vista, 1994, as "Tom Ricostranza,"
   w/Paris Qualles

Screenplays:
HOME REPAIRS

HARLAN ELLISON*
Agent: Shapiro/Lichtman - Los Angeles, 310/859-8877

THE OSCAR   Paramount, 1966, w/Clarence Greene &
    Russel Rouse

Screenplays:
WOULD YOU DO IT FOR A PENNY?
STRANGLEHOLD
HARLAN ELLISON'S MOVIE
BLIND VOICES
SEVEN WORLDS, SEVEN WARRIORS
THE WHIMPER OF WHIPPED DOGS
I, ROBOT
NICK THE GREEK
BEST BY FAR
SWING LOW, SWEET HARRIET
THE DREAM MERCHANTS
RUMBLE
KHADIM
BUG JACK BARRON

EDWARD EMANUEL
Agent: Lynne & Reilly - Hollywood, 213/850-1984

3 NINJAS   Buena Vista, 1992

MAX EMBER*
Agent: Robert Littman Company - Beverly Hills, 310/278-1572

Screenplays:
KNIGHT AND DAY
THE PRINCE OF PARK AVENUE
THE FROG PRINCE
FRATS
HOLLYWOOD HIGH
BIMBO

JIM EMERSON*
Contact: WGA - Los Angeles, 310/550-1000

IT'S PAT, THE MOVIE   Buena Vista, 1994, w/Steve Hibbert &
    Julia Sweeney

JOHN EMERY
FREEDOM   Satori, 1985

IAN EMES
Agent: ICM - Beverly Hills, 310/550-4000

KNIGHTS AND EMERALDS   Warner Bros., 1986, directed

ROLAND EMMERICH
Agent: CAA - Beverly Hills, 310/288-4545

STARGATE   MGM/UA, 1994, w/Dean Devlin, directed

MERVYN EMRYS
MINISTRY OF VENGEANCE   Concorde, 1989,
    w/Brian D. Jeffries & Ann Narus

JOHN ENBOM
Contact: Man Way Inc., 7047 Franklin Ave. - #121, Hollywood,
    CA 90028

Screenplays:
THE LOW LIFE w/George Hickenlooper

ROBERT ENDERS*
Agent: Peter Crouch & Associates - London, 71/734-2167

VOICES   Hemdale, 1973, w/George Kirgo
THE MAIDS   American Film Theatre, 1975, w/Christopher Miles
CONDUCT UNBECOMING   Allied Artists, 1975
NASTY HABITS   Brut Productions, 1977

CY ENDFIELD
Contact: British Academy of Film & Television Arts, 195 Picadilly,
    London W1, England, 01/734-0022

THE MASTER PLAN   Astor, 1954, as "Hugh Raker," directed
CHILD IN THE HOUSE   Eros, 1956
HELL DRIVERS   Rank, 1957, w/John Kruse, directed
SEA FURY   Rank, 1958, w/John Kruse, directed
JET STORM   British Lion, 1959, w/Sigmund Miller, directed
ZULU   Embassy, 1964, w/John Prebble, directed
SANDS OF THE KALAHARI   Paramount, 1965, directed
UNIVERSAL SOLDIER   Appaloosa, 1971, directed
ZULU DAWN   New World, 1982, w/Anthony Storey

MICHAEL S. ENDLER
Contact: 818/783-8110

EASY MONEY   Orion, 1983, w/Dennis Blair, Rodney Dangerfield &
    P. J. O'Rourke

MORRIS ENGEL
Contact: Marc Jacobson, Phillips Nizer - New York

THE LITTLE FUGITIVE   1953, Shared, co-directed

STEPHEN ENGEL*
Agent: CAA - Beverly Hills, 310/288-4545

Screenplays:
THE REAL WORLD w/Robert Burnett

DAVID ENGELBACH*
Agent: Above the Line - West Hollywood, 310/859-6115

DEATH WISH II   Filmways, 1982
AMERICA 3000   Cannon, 1986, directed
OVER THE TOP   Cannon, 1987, Story w/Gary Conway

Screenplays:
THE SORCERER'S APPRENTICE w/John Wolff
VAROOM w/John Wolff

TOM ENGELMAN
THE TEMP   Paramount, 1993, Story w/Kevin Falls

ROBERT ENGELS*
Agent: CAA - Beverly Hills, 310/288-4545

TWIN PEAKS: FIRE WALK WITH ME   New Line Cinema, 1992,
    w/David Lynch

Screenplays:
ACTION PHOTOGRAPHY

ELYSE ENGLAND
LOVE OR MONEY   Hemdale, 1990, w/Bart Davis &
    Michael Zausner

DIANE ENGLISH*
Agent: William Morris Agency - Beverly Hills, 310/274-7451
Business: Shukovsky-English Entertainment, Warner Bros. TV,
    818/760-6100

Screenplays:
THE WOMEN (remake)
A MARRIED LIFE
DRIVE ME CRAZY
PERFECT TIMING
THREE DAYS, FOUR NIGHTS

DON ENRIGHT*
Contact: Ziffren, Brittenham & Branca - Beverly Hills, 310/552-3388

SEARCH AND DESTROY   Film Ventures International, 1981
SPASMS   Producers Distribution Company, 1983

NICK ENRIGHT
Agent: ICM - Beverly Hills, 310/550-4000

LORENZO'S OIL ★   Universal, 1992, w/George Miller

ANNIE ENSCOE
Agent: The Gersh Agency - Beverly Hills, 310/274-6611

Screenplays:
LITTLE FIXIT w/Larry Enscoe

LARRY ENSCOE
Agent: The Gersh Agency - Beverly Hills, 310/274-6611

Screenplays:
LITTLE FIXIT w/Annie Enscoe

AMY EPHRON*
Agent: J. Michael Bloom & Associates - Los Angeles, 310/275-6800

Screenplays:
THE WILD SWANS (AF)
CORDUROY THE BEAR
SHADOWS IN THE WINDOW
GOING GREEN

DELIA EPHRON*
Agent: CAA - Beverly Hills, 213/550-4000

BRENDA STARR   Triumph Releasing, 1992, as "Jenny Wolkind,"
    w/James David Buchanan & Noreen Stone
THIS IS MY LIFE   20th Century Fox, 1992, w/Nora Ephron
MIXED NUTS   TriStar, 1994, w/Nora Epron

Screenplays:
FUNNY SAUCE

NORA EPHRON*
Agent: ICM - New York, 212/556-5600

SILKWOOD ★   20th Century-Fox, 1983, w/Alice Arlen
HEARTBURN   Paramount, 1985
WHEN HARRY MET SALLY... ★   Columbia, 1989
COOKIE   Warner Bros., 1989, w/Alice Arlen
MY BLUE HEAVEN   Warner Bros., 1990
THIS IS MY LIFE   20th Century Fox, 1992,
    w/Delia Ephron, directed
SLEEPLESS IN SEATTLE ★   TriStar, 1993, w/Jeffrey Arch &
    David S. Ward, directed
MIXED NUTS   TriStar, 1994, w/Delia Ephron, directed

Screenplays:
HIGGINS AND BEECH w/Alice Arlen
MODERN BRIDE w/Alice Arlen & Joan Taylor
ENCORE

TOM EPPERSON*
Agent: William Morris Agency - Beverly Hills, 310/274-7451

ONE FALSE MOVE   I.R.S. Releasing, 1992, w/Billy Bob Thornton

Screenplays:
CAMOUFLAGE w/Billy Bob Thornton
THE BOND w/Billy Bob Thornton
THE OTIS REDDING STORY w/Billy Bob Thornton

JACK EPPS, JR.*
Agent: CAA - Beverly Hills, 310/288-4545

TOP GUN   Paramount, 1986, w/Jim Cash
LEGAL EAGLES   Universal, 1986, w/Jim Cash
THE SECRET OF MY SUCCESS   Universal, 1987,
    w/A.J. Carothers & Jim Cash
TURNER & HOOCH   Buena Vista, 1989, w/Jim Cash,
    Daniel Petrie Jr., Michael Blodgett & Dennis Shryack
DICK TRACY   Buena Vista, 1990, w/Jim Cash

Screenplays:
HAWAII FIVE-0 w/Jim Cash
SUMMERTIME BLUES w/Jim Cash (directing)
REVENGE OF BLACKTHORN w/Jim Cash
WHEREABOUTS w/Jim Cash
DANGEROUSLY w/Jim Cash & Bennett Tramer
MR. MAYOR w/Jim Cash
MILWAUKEE CONFIDENTIAL w/Jim Cash
DIRTY FIVE w/Jim Cash
DIVIDING LINE w/Jim Cash

MICKEY EPPS
JOYSTICKS   Jensen Farley Pictures, 1983, w/Al Gomez

ALEXANDER EPSTEIN
Contact: Attorney Alfred Sapse - Century City, 310/277-4481

WARRIORS   Nu Image, 1993, w/Benjamin Gold

DAVID EPSTEIN*
Agent: Broder-Kurland-Webb-Uffner - Beverly Hills, 310/281-3400

Screenplays:
DEAD AIR

JULIUS J. EPSTEIN*
Agent: The Gersh Agency - Beverly Hills, 310/274-6611

CONFESSION   Warner Bros., 1937, w/Margaret Le Vino
DAUGHTERS COURAGEOUS   Warner Bros., 1939,
    w/Philip G. Epstein
FOUR WIVES   Warner Bros., 1939, w/Philip G. Epstein &
    Maurice Hanline
NO TIME FOR COMEDY   Warner Bros., 1940, w/Philip G. Epstein
THE BRIDE CAME C.O.D.   Warner Bros., 1940,
    w/Philip G. Epstein
SATURDAY'S CHILDREN   Warner Bros., 1940, w/Philip G. Epstein
THE STRAWBERRY BLONDE   Warner Bros., 1941,
    w/Philip G. Epstein
THE MAN WHO CAME TO DINNER   Warner Bros., 1941,
    w/Philip G. Epstein
ARSENIC AND OLD LACE   Warner Bros., 1942,
    w/Philip G. Epstein
MRS. SKEFFINGTON   Warner Bros., 1944, w/Philip G. Epstein
CASABLANCA ★★   Warner Bros., 1943, w/Philip G. Epstein &
    Howard Koch
ONE MORE TOMORROW   Warner Bros., 1946,
    w/Philip G. Epstein, Charles Hoffman & Catherine Turney
ROMANCE ON THE HIGH SEAS   Warner Bros., 1948,
    w/Philip G. Epstein & I.A.L. Diamond
MY FOOLISH HEART   Goldwyn, 1949, w/Philip G. Epstein
TAKE CARE OF MY LITTLE GIRL   20th Century-Fox, 1951,
    w/Philip G. Epstein
FOREVER FEMALE   Paramount, 1953, w/Philip G. Epstein
THE LAST TIME I SAW PARIS   MGM, 1954, w/Philip G. Epstein &
    Richard Brooks
YOUNG AT HEART   Warner Bros., 1954, w/Leonore Coffee
THE TENDER TRAP   MGM, 1955
KISS THEM FOR ME   20th Century-Fox, 1957
TAKE A GIANT STEP   United Artists, 1958, w/Louis S. Peterson
FANNY   Warner Bros., 1960
TALL STORY   Warner Bros., 1960
THE LIGHT IN THE PIAZZA   MGM, 1962
SEND ME NO FLOWERS   Universal International, 1964
RETURN FROM THE ASHES   United Artists, 1965
ANY WEDNESDAY   Warner Bros., 1966
PETE'N'TILLIE ★   Universal, 1972
ONCE IS NOT ENOUGH   Paramount, 1975
CROSS OF IRON   EMI-Rapid Film, 1977, w/Herbert Asmodi
HOUSE CALLS   Universal, 1978, w/Alan Mandel, Max Shulman &
    Charles Shyer
REUBEN, REUBEN ★   20th Century-Fox, 1983

Screenplays:
HAPPY ALL THE TIME

GORDON ERIKSEN*
Contact: Susan Bodine, Esq. - 212/888-1777
Address: 116 Prospect Place - Apt. 3, Brooklyn, NY 11217

THE BIG DIS   Pyramid Films, 1989, w/Robert Pilotte, co-directed
SCENES FROM THE NEW WORLD   1994,
   w/Heather Johnston, directed

PATRICK ERSGARD
Agent: The Chasin Agency - Los Angeles, 310/278-7505

Screenplays:
TRACE OF RED
PERIL

JOHN ESKOW*
Agent: CAA - Beverly Hills, 310/288-4545

PINK CADILLAC   Warner Bros., 1989
AIR AMERICA   Tri-Star, 1990, w/Richard Rush

Screenplays:
RUSSIAN MAFIA PROJECT
GONE TO TEXAS
NEW CANTERBURY TALES
BLAST FROM THE PAST
SMOKESTACK LIGHTING
THE BRITISH DIPLOMAT
THE GREAT PRETENDER
CIVIL DEFENSE
ROBINSON & CARUSO
MINDREADER

JOHN ESPOSITO*
Agent: Susan Smith & Associates - Beverly Hills, 213/852-4777

GRAVEYARD SHIFT   Paramount, 1990

Screenplays:
TELL TALE TAVERN

LAURA ESQUIVEL
Contact: Arau Films - Mexico, tel.: 52/5-5493060

LIKE WATER FOR CHOCOLATE   Miramax, 1993

Screenplays:
REGINA w/Alfonso Arau

ALLEN ESROCK*
Agent: Preferred Artists - Encino, 818/990-0305

Screenplays:
FLASH

LUIS ESTEBAN
ONLY THE STRONG   20th Century Fox, 1993, w/Sheldon Lettich

JUAN ESTERLICH
THE MILKY LIFE (LA VIDA LACTEA)   Cartel Films/Journal Film KG/
   Aries Production, 1993, w/Chris Doherty, directed

EMILIO ESTEVEZ*
Agent: CAA - Beverly Hills, 310/288-4545
Business: Avatar Entertainment, Walt Disney Studios - 818/560-4300

THAT WAS THEN, THIS IS NOW   Paramount, 1985
WISDOM   20th Century Fox, 1987, directed
MEN AT WORK   Triumph Releasing, 1990, directed

KEITH ESTRADA
Agent: Metropolitan Talent Agency - Los Angeles, 213/857-4500

Screenplays:
SAINT NICK w/Peter Fedorenko
JOHN WESLEY HARDIN w/Peter Fedorenko
THE ENEMY WIND w/Peter Fedorenko

ALLEN ESTRIN*
Agent: William Morris Agency - Beverly Hills, 310/274-7451

Screenplays:
OUR HOUSE w/Mark Estrin
MODEL COP
HOW TO MURDER YOUR PARENTS

ERIC ESTRIN*
Agent: Paradigm - Los Angeles, 310/277-4400

Screenplays:
MIRROR IMAGE w/Michael Berlin (World Vision)
TAX MAN w/Michael Berlin
RED BIRD DOWN w/Michael Berlin

JONATHAN ESTRIN*
Agent: CAA - Beverly Hills, 310/288-4545

Screenplays:
AMNESTY INTERNATIONAL (CTF) w/Shelley List
DELANCEY STREET w/Shelley List

MARK G. ESTRIN*
Agent: William Morris Agency - Beverly Hills, 310/274-7451

Screenplays:
OUR HOUSE w/Allen Estrin

JOE ESZTERHAS*
Agent: ICM - Beverly Hills, 310/550-4000

F.I.S.T.   United Artists, 1978, w/Sylvester Stallone
FLASHDANCE   Paramount, 1983, w/Thomas Hedley
JAGGED EDGE   Columbia, 1985
BIG SHOTS   20th Century Fox, 1987
HEARTS OF FIRE   Lorimar, 1988, w/Scott Richardson
BETRAYED   MGM/UA, 1988
CHECKING OUT   Warner Bros., 1989
MUSIC BOX   Tri-Star, 1989
BASIC INSTINCT   TriStar, 1992
NOWHERE TO RUN   Columbia, 1993, w/Les Bohem &
   Randy Feldman
SLIVER   Paramount, 1993
JADE   Paramount, 1995
SHOWGIRLS   MGM/UA, 1995

Screenplays:
FOREPLAY (Savoy)
GANGLAND
ONE NIGHT STAND
SACRED COWS
ORIGINAL SIN
MAGIC MAN
BEAT THE EAGLE
CITY HALL w/J. Morgan
PALS
DIESHOT
NARC
PLATINUM
ROWDY

JOHN T. EUBANK
THE FINAL ALLIANCE   RC/Columbia Pictures Home Video, 1991,
   w/Havel Goldstein

RICHARD D. EUSTIS*
Agent: CAA - Beverly Hills, 310/288-4545

SERIAL   Paramount, 1980, w/MichaelElias
YOUNG DOCTORS IN LOVE   20th Century-Fox, 1982,
    w/Michael Elias

Screenplays:
ON THE BRINK w/Michael Elias
BANDIES (P) w/Michael Elias
DIRE STRAITS w/Michael Elias
BLACKJACK & SALTY w/Michael Elias

BRUCE A. EVANS *
Agent: CAA - Beverly Hills, 310/288-4545

A MAN, A WOMAN AND A BANK   Avco Embassy, 1979,
    w/Ray Gideon
STARMAN   Columbia, 1984, w/Ray Gideon
STAND BY ME ★   Columbia, 1986, w/Ray Gideon
MADE IN HEAVEN   Lorimar, 1988, w/Ray Gideon
KUFFS   Universal, 1992, w/Ray Gideon, directed

Screenplays:
THE DAY BEFORE MIDNIGHT w/Ray Gideon
BLACK RICE w/Ray Gideon
THE BETHUNE w/Ray Gideon
CHRISTMAS IN JULY w/Ray Gideon

DAVID MICKEY EVANS*
Agent: United Talent Agency - Beverly Hills, 310/273-6700
Contact: Evans/de la Torre Productions - Twentieth Century Fox,
    310/203-2683

RADIO FLYER   Columbia, 1992
THE SANDLOT   20th Century Fox, 1993, w/Robert Gunter, directed

Screenplays:
THE DEVIL'S PLAYGROUND
HIGHWAY TO HELL

JENNIFER EVANS
Agent: Susan Smith & Associates - Beverly Hills, 213/852-4777

Screenplays:
IT'S ONLY LOVE

JOSH EVANS
INSIDE THE GOLDMINE   Cineville, 1994,
    w/Uri Zighelboim, directed

LEO EVANS*
Contact: WGA - Los Angeles, 310/550-1000

HELL HIGH   JGM Enterprises, 1989, w/Douglas Grossman

NICHOLAS EVANS
Agent: CAA - Beverly Hills, 310/288-4545

MURDER BY THE BOOK (CTF)   TVS International, 1990
JUST LIKE A WOMAN   Samuel Goldwyn Company, 1994

Screenplays:
LIFE AND LIMB
COME AGAIN?

SHELLEY EVANS*
Agent: The Tantleff Office - New York, 212/941-3939

LADYKILLER (CTF)   MCA Television Entertainment, 1992

ANDY EVANSON
CAUGHT IN THE ACT (CTF)   Davis Entertainment/Meltzer/Viviano
    Productions/MCA Television Entertainment, 1993,
    Story w/Ken Hixon

CHARLES EVERED*
Agent: William Morris Agency - Beverly Hills, 310/274-7451

DRIFT (P)   also screenplay (directing)

Screenplays:
HOMESPUN
ASTEROID MAN
WALKER'S DREAM
NATION'S FINEST
A PRINCE IN NEW JERSEY

GIMEL EVERETT
Agent: CAA - Beverly Hills, 310/288-4545
Personal Manager: Steve Freedman - Studio City, 818/508-5155
Attorney: Dennis Cline, Behr and Robinson, 2049 Century Park East,
    Suite 2690, Los Angeles, CA 90067, 310/556-9210

THE LAWNMOWER MAN   New Line Cinema, 1992,
    w/Brett Leonard

Screenplays:
THE LAWNMOWERMAN II: MINDFIRE w/Brett Leonard
THE IMMORTALS w/Brett Leonard
HIDDEN AGENDAS w/Brett Leonard

ROB EWING
STEEL   *LOOK DOWN AND DIE*   World Northal, 1980,
    Story w/Peter S. Davis & William N. Panzer

WILLIAM R. EWING*
Contact: 818/345-2790

THE SLAYER   21st Century Distribution, 1982, w/J.S. Cardone

CLIVE EXTON
Agent: Rochelle Stevens & Co. - London, 071/359-3900
Business Manager: Teresa C. Deane, CPA, 2516 Via Tejon -
    Suite 216, Palos Verdes Estates, CA 90274, 310/373-9741

MURDER IS EASY (P)   Adaptation
A PLACE TO GO   British Lion, 1963, w/Michael Relph
NIGHT MUST FALL   MGM, 1964
ISADORA   *THE LOVES OF ISADORA*   Universal, 1968,
    w/Melvyn Bragg
ENTERTAINING MR. SLOANE   Pathe, 1969
TEN RILLINGTON PLACE   Columbia, 1970
RUNNING SCARED   Paramount, 1972, w/David Hemmings
DOOMWATCH   Tigon, 1972
THE HOUSE IN NIGHTMARE PARK   EMI, 1973, w/Terry Nation
THE AWAKENING   EMI, 1980, w/Chris Bryant & Allan Scott
RED SONJA   MGM/UA, 1985, w/George Macdonald Fraser

D.M. (DAVID) EYRE JR.*
Agent: The Artists Agency - Los Angeles, 310/277-7779

CATTLE ANNIE AND LITTLE BRITCHES   Universal, 1981,
    w/Robert S. Ward
WOLFEN   Orion/Warner Bros., 1981, w/Michael Wadleigh
LAGUNA HEAT (CTF)   HBO Pictures/Jay Weston Productions,
    1987, w/Pete Hamill & David Burton Morris
PAST TIME   Miramax, 1991

Screenplays:
CHECKMAN
THE ENEMY
HAIL, ALMA MATER

JOHN EZRINE*
Contact: WGA - Los Angeles, 310/550-1000

A DANGEROUS GAME   Hemdale, 1989

Screenplays:
SATAN'S LITTLE SISTER

F

CHRISTIAN FABER
BAIL JUMPER   Angelika Films, 1990, w/Josephine Wallace

CHRISTOPHER V. FABER*
Agent: United Talent Agency - Beverly Hills, 310/273-6700

HANG 'EM REALLY HIGH (Short)   1989, w/Danniel Baron

Screenplays:
ASSAULT ON EMPIRE STATE MOUNTAIN (CTF) w/Danniel Baron
MUCKRAKER w/Danniel Baron
THE BIG PLUNGE w/Danniel Baron
FAT CHANCE w/Danniel Baron
JACKPOT w/Danniel Baron

RACHEL FABIEN
LA VIE CONTINUE   Triumph/Columbia, 1982, w/Moshe Mizrahi
EVERY TIME WE SAY GOODBYE   Tri-Star, 1988, w/Leah Appet &
   Moshe Mizrahi

RAMSEY FADIMAN*
Agent: United Talent Agency - Beverly Hills, 310/273-6700

Screenplays:
THE WILL
FASHION AVENUE
GOOD DAYS   MIDDAY MOON
RESCUE ME
THE NORMAL HEART

PAMELA FALK
Agent: Sanford-Gross & Associates - Los Angeles,
   310/208-2100

Screenplays:
LET THEM EAT CAKE w/Michael Ellis

DAVID FALLON*
Agent: United Talent Agency - Beverly Hills, 310/273-6700

SPLIT DECISIONS   New Century/Vista, 1988
WHITE FANG   Buena Vista, 1991, w/Jeanne Rosenberg &
   Nick Thiel
WHITE FANG 2: MYTH OF THE WHITE WOLF   Buena Vista, 1994

Screenplays:
SUPERBOXERS
SEVEN SUMMITS
HARDBALL
STREETWISE

MICHAEL FALLON*
Contact: WGA - Los Angeles, 310/550-1000

THE MASK   New Line Cinema, 1994, Story w/Mark Verheiden

Screenplays:
CARVER'S BOX

JEFF FALLS
THE CHANNELER   Magnum Entertainment, 1991,
   w/Peter Mead & Jeb Seibel

KEVIN M. FALLS*
Agent: United Talent Agency - Beverly Hills, 310/273-6700

THE TEMP   Paramount, 1993

Screenplays:
BREAKING BALLS AND BROKEN HEARTS
LEFT COAST
DOVE
BACHELOR MOM
BABY IN THE SILO
PUFFS
TENLEY'S MEN
SEPARATE WAYS
GARBEY

JAMAA FANAKA
Contact: Sanford Gilbert, 2115 Main Street, Santa Monica, CA 90405,
   310/399-3245

WELCOME HOME, BROTHER CHARLES   Crown International,
   1975, directed
EMMA MAE   Pro-International, 1976, directed
PENITENTIARY   Jerry Gross Organization, 1979, directed
PENITENTIARY II   MGM/UA, 1982, directed
PENITENTIARY III   Cannon, 1987, directed
STREET WARS   Medallion Entertainment Corp., 1993, directed

BARRY FANARO*
Agent: United Talent Agency - Beverly Hills, 310/273-6700

Screenplays:
KINGPIN w/Mort Nathan

HAMPTON FANCHER*
Agent: United Talent Agency - Beverly Hills, 310/273-6700

BLADE RUNNER   The Ladd Company/Warner Bros., 1982,
   w/David Peoples
THE MIGHTY QUINN   MGM/UA, 1989

Screenplays:
STEALING ALASKA
THE PAINTER
CHINESE BANDITS
MRS. CALIBAN
PRISM
TOUCH
SALVATION

CELIA FANNON
Agent: Writers & Artists Agency - Los Angeles, 310/824-6300

GREEN ICEBERGS (P)
TO DISTRACTION (P)

JACQUES FANSTEN
Contact: Holland Film Production, P.O. Box 5048, 1007 AA,
   Amsterdam, The Netherlands, tel. 20/799-261

CROSS MY HEART   MK2 Productions, 1991, directed

MICHAEL FARGAS
PRIME RISK   Almi Pictures, 1985, directed

EMIL FARKAS
FORCE: FIVE   American Cinema, 1981, w/George Goldsmith

FRANK FARMER
SLUMBER PARTY '57   Cannon, 1977

GRAEME FARMER
DARLINGS OF THE GODS (CMS)   Simpson Le Mesurier Films
   Production/Australian Broadcasting Corporation/Thames TV, 1990,
   w/Roger Simpson

F
I
L
M

W
R
I
T
E
R
S

RALPH FARQUHAR*
Agent: CAA - Beverly Hills, 310/288-4545

KRUSH GROOVE   Warner Bros., 1985

DANIEL FARRANDS
RAVE: DANCING TO A DIFFERENT BEAT
   Smart Egg Pictures, 1993

Screenplays:
JOSEPH CONRAD'S LORD JIM   (Intrazone Ltd.)
HALLOWEEN VI   (Miramax)

TREVOR A. FARRANT*
Business: Punchline Pty. Ltd. - Australia, tel. 08/512-930

THE PIRATE MOVIE   20th Century-Fox, 1982
STRUCK BY LIGHTNING   Beyond International Group, 1990

JUDY FARRELL*
Agent: The Wright Concept - Burbank, 818/954-8943

Screenplays:
THE INVASION OF GARRETT PORTER w/Joe Bratcher
CONNECTIONS w/Joe Bratcher
SHADES OF GREY w/Joe Bratcher
WHY ME?

BOB FARRELLY*
Agent: CAA - Beverly Hills, 310/288-4545
Manager: 3 Arts Entertainment - Los Angeles, 213/851-5700

DUMB AND DUMBER   New Line Cinema, 1994, w/Peter Farrelly &
   Bennett Yellin

Screenplays:
TENDERFOOTS w/Peter Farrelly

PETER FARRELLY*
Agent: CAA - Beverly Hills, 310/288-4545
Manager: 3 Arts Entertainment - Los Angeles, 213/851-5700

DUMB AND DUMBER   New Line Cinema, 1994, w/Bob Farrelly &
   Bennett Yellin, directed

Screenplays:
TENDERFOOTS w/Bob Farrelly
ADULT EDUCATION w/Bennett Yellin
DUST TO DUST w/Bennett Yellin
YOUNG LOVERS w/Bennett Yellin
FREE SPIRITS w/Bennett Yellin
OUR PLANET TONIGHT w/Bennett Yellin
BLACK TIE w/Bennett Yellin
POISON IVY w/Bennett Yellin

JOHN FARRIS*
Contact: WGA - Los Angeles, 310/550-1000

DEAR DEAD DELILAH   Southern Star, 1975, directed
THE FURY   20th Century-Fox, 1978

JOHN FASANO*
Agent: ICM - Beverly Hills, 310/550-4000

ANOTHER 48 HRS.   Paramount, 1990, w/Larry Gross & Jeb Stuart

Screenplays:
PEACEMAKER w/Cindy Cirile (New Line Cinema)
HUNCHBACK (CTF)
POE
MUSKATEERS
GIRL'S CLUB
BLUE BLOOD
BATTLETECH
THE POINT

ALVIN L. FAST
DEATHTRAP   Mars, 1976, w/Mardi Rustam
ANGEL'S BRIGADE   Arista, 1980, w/Greydon Clark

LINDA R. FAVILA*
Contact: WGA - Los Angeles, 310/550-1000

BORIS & NATASHA (CTF)   MCEG, 1992, w/Charles E. Fradin &
   Anson Downes

Screenplays:
PERFECT FIT w/Anson Downes

WILLIAM FAY
RISING STORM   Gibraltar Releasing, 1989, w/Gary Rosen

JEFF FAZIO*
Agent: Warden, White & Kane - Beverly Hills, 213/852-1028

Screenplays:
THE HUNTERS
AL DENTE
AIRBORNE
PARIS AMERICAN
IN THE BAG

JACQUELINE FEATHER*
Agent: Innovative Artists - Los Angeles, 310/553-5200

Screenplays:
THE BOXER w/David Seidler
CLOSE TO HOME w/David Seidler
GLITTERBUG w/David Seidler

PETER FEDORENKO
Agent: Metropolitan Talent Agency - Los Angeles, 213/857-4500

Screenplays:
SAINT NICK w/Keith Estrada
JOHN WESLEY HARDIN w/Keith Estrada
THE ENEMY WIND w/Keith Estrada

F.X. FEENEY
FRANKENSTEIN UNBOUND   20th Century Fox, 1990,
   w/Roger Corman

JARRE FEES*
Agent: United Talent Agency - Beverly Hills, 310/273-6700

LATE NIGHT WITH LOIS AND LESTER (P)
PERMANENT RECORD   Paramount, 1988, w/Larry Ketron &
   Alice Liddle

Screenplays:
THE MANON RHEAUME STORY
SABRINA FACE THE MUSIC
WAITING FOR MR. CONNERY
PICTURE THIS
MAN OF THE HOUR

LINDA FEFERMAN*
Contact: WGA - Los Angeles, 310/550-1000

SEVEN MINUTES IN HEAVEN   Warner Bros., 1986,
   w/Jane Bernstein, directed

JULES FEIFFER*
Agent: The Lantz Office - New York, 212/586-0200

GROWN-UPS (P)
A THINK PIECE (P)
ELLIOT LOVES (P)
LITTLE MURDERS   20th Century-Fox, 1970
CARNAL KNOWLEDGE   Avco Embassy, 1971

POPEYE   Paramount, 1980
I WANT TO GO HOME   MK2, 1989

Screenplays:
EVERYBODY'S FINE (remake)
BABY PICTURES
ANSWERS
LITTLE BRUCIE
TERRY & THE PIRATES

J. D. FEIGELSON*
Business Manager: Dick de Blois - 310/273-7769

Screenplays:
ASTRONAUTS WIVES
ALMOST HUMAN

JUDITH FEIN*
Agent: CAA - Beverly Hills, 310/288-4545

SCRUTINY (P)
CHANNELS (P)
DANCING TO DOVER (P)
LILITH (P)
SAARDA VARDAK (P)
VISITING DAD (P)
BACK IN THE WORLD (P)
RICHARD RAWLEY'S DRINK (P)

Screenplays:
THE NIGHT OF THE WEEPING WOMEN
FINISHED
MAJOR MOM
HORIZONTAL WOMAN IN A VERTICAL WORLD
STREET SMART
DIRTY DANCING II
HARRIET THE SPY
SISTERS (CTF)
THE INTIMATE WRITINGS OF THEODORE HAMMER

STEVE FEINBERG
Agent: J. Michael Bloom & Associates - Los Angeles, 310/275-6800

Screenplays:
THE HAPPY WORKER w/Gerald Pierson

STEVEN FEINBERG
Contact: Lloyd Braun, Silverberg, Katz, Thompson & Braun - Los Angeles, 310/445-5801
Office: 213/857-0405

FORTRESS   Miramax, 1993, w/Troy Neighbors, Terry Curtis Fox & David Venable

Screenplays:
SEAHUNTER w/Troy Neighbors
FORTRESS 2 w/Troy Neighbors
RUNAROUND SUE w/Troy Neighbors
U.F.O. SCOUTS w/Troy Neighbors
CRIMESTOPPERS w/Troy Neighbors
PAINKILLER w/Troy Neighbors
THE EXTRAORDINARY VOYAGE OF VERNE AND WELLS w/Troy Neighbors

BRUCE FEIRSTEIN*
Contact: Bloom, Dekom, Hergott & Cook - Los Angeles, 310/278-8622

HOME (Short)   1990

Screenplays:
OUR GANG
THE HISTORY OF CELEBRITY IN AMERICA
LOVE AND MONEY
AIRPORT SUMMER

FORMERLY BERMAN'S w/Alan King
KISSING w/Gene Wilder
REAL MEN DON'T EAT QUICHE
FIRST AVENUE ROMANCE
HIGH FINANCE

STEPHEN J. FEKE*
Agent: Camden-ITG - Los Angeles, 310/289-2700

WHEN A STRANGER CALLS   Columbia, 1979,
   w/Fred Walton
HADLEY'S REBELLION   American Film Distributors, 1984,
   w/Fred Walton
PAPA WAS A PREACHER   La Rose Distributors, 1986
MAC & ME   Orion, 1988, w/Stewart Raffill
TRAPPED (CTF)   USA/MCA Television, 1989, w/Fred Walton
KEYS TO FREEDOM   RPB Pictures/Queens Cross Productions, 1990, directed

Screenplays:
RECKONING
AMONG HONORABLE MEN
ST. JOHN'S BREAD
OUT OF THE DARK LOCKERS

MARK L. FELDBERG*
Contact: WGA - Los Angeles, 310/550-1000

LET'S GET HARRY   Tri-Star, 1987, Story w/Samuel Fuller
DISORDERLIES   Warner Bros., 1987, w/Mitchell Klebanoff

Screenplays:
BLACK MAGNOLIA w/Mitchell Klebanoff
BEVERLY HILLS NINJA w/Mitchell Klebanoff

DENNIS J. FELDMAN*
Agent: ICM - Beverly Hills, 310/550-4000

JUST ONE OF THE GUYS   Columbia, 1985, w/Jeff Franklin
THE GOLDEN CHILD   Paramount, 1986
REAL MEN   MGM/UA, 1987, directed
SPECIES   MGM/UA, 1995

Screenplays:
THE PIRANDELLO FACTOR
BUDDHA OF BRANDENBERG
MONSTER NIGHT
DAYWORLD

JOHNATHAN H. FELDMAN*
Agent: ICM - Beverly Hills, 310/550-4000

ALLIGATOR EYES   Castle Hill, 1990, directed

Screenplays:
LONG ISLAND

JOHNATHAN M. FELDMAN
Agent: CAA - Beverly Hills, 310/288-4545

SWING KIDS   Buena Vista, 1993

Screenplays:
BAND OF ANGELS
PROOF POSITIVE (CTF)

JUDY FELDMAN*
Agent: Writers & Artists Agency - Los Angeles, 310/824-6300

Screenplays:
NEEDLES w/Sarah Gallagher

RANDY FELDMAN*
Agent: United Talent Agency - Beverly Hills, 310/273-6700

HELL NIGHT   Aquarius, 1981
TANGO & CASH   Warner Bros., 1989
NOWHERE TO RUN   Columbia, 1993, w/Les Bohem &
   Joe Eszterhas

Screenplays:
THE DISCIPLE
MAN TO MAN
RENEGADES
CASE CLOSED

J.P. FELIX
EDGE OF SANITY   Millimeter Films, 1989, w/Ron Raley

ANDREW J. FENADY*
Business: Fenady Associates, Inc., 249 N. Larchmont Blvd. - Suite 6,
   Los Angeles, CA 90004, 213/466-6375

STAKEOUT ON DOPE STREET   Warner Bros., 1958,
   w/Irvin Kershner & Irwin Schwartz
RIDE BEYOND VENGEANCE   Columbia, 1966
CHISUM   Warner Bros., 1970
THE MAN WITH BOGART'S FACE   *SAM MARLOW, PRIVATE EYE*
   20th Century-Fox, 1980
THE SEA WOLF (CTF)   Bob Banner & Associates, 1993

DUKE FENADY
Agent: William Morris Agency - Beverly Hills, 310/274-7451

Screenplays:
HONOR BOUND

PABLO FENJVES*
Agent: Paradigm - Los Angeles, 310/277-4400

A CASE FOR MURDER (CTF)   Bodega Bay Productions/MCA
   Television Entertainment, 1993, w/Duncan Gibbons
BITTER VENGEANCE (CTF)   Fast Track Films/Wilshire Court, 1994

Screenplays:
RANDOM ACCESS
THE TAX MAN
THE LAST BACHELOR

JULIE FERBER
Agent: Susan Smith & Associates - Beverly Hills, 213/852-4777

I DO? (Short)

Screenplays:
DRIVE
DREAM A LITTLE DREAM

BLAIR FERGUSON*
Agent: Candace Lake - Beverly Hills, 310/289-0600

Screenplays:
THE MOVES MAKE THE MAN
STONE WINGS
TUNNEL BOYS
MUD SWEAT AND GEARS
PEACHES POINT

JAMES FERGUSON*
Agent: William Morris Agency - Beverly Hills, 310/274-7451

LITTLE GIANTS   Warner Bros., 1994, w/Robert Shallcross,
   Michael Goldberg & Tommy Swerdlow

LARRY FERGUSON*
Agent: ICM - Beverly Hills, 310/550-4000

ST. HELENS   Davis-Panzer Productions, 1981, w/Peter Bellwood
HIGHLANDER   20th Century Fox, 1986, w/Peter Bellwood &
   Gregory Widen
BEVERLY HILLS COP II   Paramount, 1987, w/Warren Skaaren
THE PRESIDIO   Paramount, 1988
THE HUNT FOR RED OCTOBER   Paramount, 1990,
   w/Donald Stewart
TALENT FOR THE GAME   Paramount, 1991,
   w/Tom Donnelly & David Himmelstein
ALIEN 3   20th Century Fox, 1992, w/David Giler & Walter Hill
NAILS (CTF)   Viacom, 1992
BEYOND THE LAW (CTF)   Poplar Entertainment/Capitol Films,
   1994, directed

Screenplays:
THE MONEY TRAIN (Columbia)
GUNFIGHTER'S MOON
THE LAST LAUGH w/Peter Bellwood
MALACHI w/Peter Bellwood
BLOOD LEGACY
THE LAWBREAKERS
SID

GEORGE FERNANDEZ
CEASE FIRE   Cineworld, 1985, from his play "Vietnam Trilogy"

ABEL FERRARA
Contact: Directors Guild of America - Los Angeles, 310/289-2000

BAD LIEUTENANT   Aries, 1992, w/Zoe Lund, directed

BETH FERRIS
HEARTLAND   Levitt-Pickman, 1979

MICHAEL FERRIS*
Agent: United Talent Agency - Beverly Hills, 310/273-6700

WATCHERS II   Concorde, 1990, w/John Brancato as
   "Henry Domonic"
FLIGHT OF BLACK ANGEL (CTF)   Hess-Kallberg Productions,
   1991, w/John Brancato as "Henry Domonic"
THE UNBORN   Califilm, 1991, w/John Brancato as
   "Henry Domonic"
FEMME FATALE   Republic Pictures, 1991, w/John Brancato
INTO THE SUN   Trimark, 1992, w/John Brancato
INTERCEPTOR   Trimark, 1993, w/John Brancato

Screenplays:
PHASING w/John Brancato
THE GAME w/John Brancato
LOWLIFE w/John Brancato
THE FLYING DUTCHMAN w/John Brancato
THE NET w/John Brancato
GUYS w/John Brancato & Peter Gaffney

DAN E. FESMAN*
Contact: WGA - Los Angeles, 310/550-1000

Screenplays:
SHOCKED w/Chris Brancato (Savoy)

DARRELL FETTY*
Agent: APA - Los Angeles, 310/273-0744

FREEWAY   New World, 1988, w/Francis Delia
TROUBLE BOUND   ITC Entertainment, 1993, w/Francis Delia

Screenplays:
NICKY DUCKS
DEFIANCE, OHIO

MANUEL FIDELLO
FRIDAY THE 13TH, PART VII: THE NEW BLOOD   Paramount,
1988, w/Daryl Haney

DAVID M. FIELD*
Agent: William Morris Agency - Beverly Hills, 310/274-7451

AMAZING GRACE AND CHUCK   Tri-Star, 1987

Screenplays:
LIME'S CRISIS w/Ron Bass
HEART'S DESIRE

PAT FIELDER*
Agent: Preferred Artists - Encino, 818/990-0305

GERONIMO   United Artists, 1962

RICHARD FIELDER*
Agent: Major Clients Agency - Los Angeles, 310/284-6400

A DISTANT TRUMPET   Apex, 1952
ADAM'S WOMAN   Warner Bros., 1970

GREG FIELDS*
Contact: 213/460-5955

BACK TO SCHOOL   Orion, 1986, Story w/Rodney Dangerfield &
Dennis Snee

MARIA FIELDS
DEADLY DANCER   Action International Pictures, 1990,
w/David Halpern

SCOTT G. FIELDS*
Agent: United Talent Agency - Beverly Hills, 310/273-6700

DANGEROUSLY CLOSE   Cannon, 1986, w/Marty Ross &
John Stockwell
UNDER COVER   Cannon, 1987, w/John Stockwell

Screenplays:
JUPITER BROWN w/John Stockwell
DOUBLE CROSS w/John Stockwell
SEE JANE RUN w/John Stockwell
DEAD SLEEP w/John Stockwell
SICILIAN OVERTURE w/John Stockwell
STORK CLUB w/John Stockwell
POINT PANIC w/John Stockwell

HARVEY FIERSTEIN*
Agent: William Morris Agency - New York, 212/586-5100

LA CAGE AUX FOLLES (P)
SPOOKHOUSE (P)
TORCH SONG TRILOGY   New Line Cinema, 1988, from his play
TIDY ENDINGS (CTF)   HBO/Sandollar Productions, 1988

Screenplays:
PLUCKED
SINGING SISTERS

MIKE FIGGIS
Agent: CAA - Beverly Hills, 310/288-4545

STORMY MONDAY   Atlantic Releasing Corporation,
1986, directed
LIEBESTRAUM   MGM-Pathe, 1991, directed
LEAVING LAS VEGAS   Lumiere, 1995, directing

PETER FILARDI*
Agent: ICM - Beverly Hills, 310/550-4000

FLATLINERS   Columbia, 1990

Screenplays:
TOM CAT
THE CRAFT

CHARLES FINCH*
Business Manager: Laventhol & Horvath - 310/553-1040
Business: Ruddy & Morgan Organization, 9300 Wilshire Blvd. -
Suite 508, Beverly Hills, CA 90212, 310/271-7698

PRICELESS BEAUTY   Republic Pictures, 1986, shared, directed
WHERE SLEEPING DOGS LIE   August Entertainment, 1992,
w/Yolande Turner Finch, directed
BAD GIRLS   20th Century Fox, 1994, Story w/Gray Frederickson &
Albert S. Ruddy

Screenplays:
RED, SIZE SIX w/YolandeTurner Finch

JEREMY BERTRAND FINCH*
Agent: Media Artsts Group - Beverly Hills, 213/658-7434

Screenplays:
THE GIVER
WHIPLASH
OUTCALLS

MARTINA S. FINCH*
Agent: The Gage Group - Los Angeles, 310/859-8777
Manager: RKS Entertainment Group - Sherman Oaks, 818/788-3616

Screenplays:
FALSE PAPERS

MIKE FINCH
Agent: Wile Enterprises - Santa Monica, 310/828-9768

Screenplays:
CONFRONTATION

YOLANDE TURNER FINCH
WHERE SLEEPING DOGS LIE   August Entertainment, 1992,
w/Charles Finch
BAD GIRLS   20th Century Fox, 1994, w/Ken Friedman

Screenplays:
RED, SIZE SIX w/Charles Finch

ADRIANNE FINCHAM
Agent: Ken Sherman & Associates -213/273-8840

Screenplays:
KIT BRANDON w/Elliott Anderson
MINUS ONE w/Elliott Anderson

ALAN FINE*
Agent: Ken Sherman & Associates - Los Angeles, 213/273-8840

Screenplays:
HASTINGS HIGH

TRAVIS FINE
Agent: Susan Smith & Associates - Beverly Hills, 213/852-4777

Screenplays:
ONE-EYED JACK & THE LORDS OF THE SEA

CARMEN FINESTRA*
Agent: Bruce Brown Agency - Los Angeles, 310/208-1835

Screenplays:
HARV, THE BARBARIAN

ANTHONY J. FINGLETON*
Agent: Maggie Field Agency - Studio City, 818/980-2001

OVER MY DEAD BODY (P)   shared
PREPPIES (P) w/Carlos Davis
DROP DEAD, FRED   New Line Cinema, 1991, w/Carlos Davis

Screenplays:
BLAST FROM THE PAST w/Carlos Davis
TUG-OF-WAR w/Carlos Davis
LEAP YEAR w/Carlos Davis
TYPHOON SHIPMENT w/Phillip Dearborn

WILLIAM M. FINKELSTEIN*
Contact: WGA - Los Angeles, 310/550-1000

TOM CONNOVER (P)
LONG ODDS FROM JERSEY (P)   also screenplay

Screenplays:
CLOSE OUT

KENNETH FINKLEMAN*
Agent: CAA - Beverly Hills, 310/288-4545

GREASE 2   Paramount, 1982
AIRPLANE II: THE SEQUEL   Paramount, 1983, directed
ILLEGALLY YOURS   DEG, 1986, w/Michael Kaplan &
   John Levenstein, as "Max Dickens & M.A. Stewart"
HEAD OFFICE   Tri-Star, 1986, directed
WHO'S THAT GIRL?   Warner Bros., 1987, w/Andrew Smith

Screenplays:
ALAMO GORDO w/Donald Cammell
NEWS w/Gary Ross
TWO LITTLE RICH GIRLS
COMEBACK
ASSASSINATION ON EMBASSY ROAD
SUNNY WITH RAIN
DANGEROUSLY

WILLIAM FRANKLIN FINLEY*
Agent: Becsey/Wisdom/Kalajian Agency - Los Angeles, 310/550-0535

THE FIRST TIME   New Line Cinema, 1982, w/Charlie Loventhal &
   Susan Weiser-Finley

STEVE FINLY
Agent: Metropolitan Talent Agency - Los Angeles, 213/857-4500

Screenplays:
RAINY SEASON
GUILT
IMPLIED CONSENT

MELANIE FINN*
Contact: WGA - Los Angeles, 310/550-1000

LAKE CONSEQUENCE (CTF)   Showtime Networks, 1993,
   w/Henry Cobbold & Zalman King

JOHN FINNEGAN
ALL'S FAIR   Moviestore Entertainment, 1989, w/William Pace,
   Tom Rondinella & Randee Russell

RICHARD FINNEY*
Agent: Innovative Artists - Los Angeles, 310/553-5200

Screenplays:
EVOLUTION w/James Bonny
VEXERS w/James Bonny
MEN IN BLACK w/James Bonny
PUPPET MASTERS w/James Bonny

RICHARD FIRE*
Contact: WGA - Los Angeles, 310/550-1000

HENRY...PORTRAIT OF A SERIAL KILLER   Greycat Films, 1989
THE BORROWER   Cannon, 1991, w/Mason Nage

Screenplays:
STEP RIGHT UP w/John McNaughton
MEETING EVIL

LES FIRESTEIN*
Agent: United Talent Agency - Beverly Hills, 310/273-6700

Screenplays:
FULLY AUTOMATIC
F-TROOP

SAM FIRSTENBERG
Contact: Gendece Film Co., 999 Doheny Drive - Suite 411,
   Los Angeles, CA 90069, 310/271-8596

ONE MORE CHANCE   Cannon, 1981, directed

MICHAEL FIRTH
Business: P.O. Box 37-177, Parnell, Auckland, New Zealand,
   tel.: 09/399-699

SYLVIA   MGM/UA Classics, 1985, w/F. Fairfax &
   Michele Quill, directed

JANICE FISCHER*
Agent: David Shapira & Associates - Sherman Oaks, 818/906-0322

THE LOST BOYS   Warner Bros., 1987, w/Jeffrey Boam &
   James Jeremias

Screenplays:
THE WITCH'S REVENGE w/Robert Kosberg
INTER-GALACTIC HIGH w/James Jeremias
MERLYN w/James Jeremias
HELL OF A DEAL w/J. Tappis
MISSING LINKS w/M. Ganzel
DR. VOODOO

MAX FISCHER
Address: 4691 Bonquista Avenue, Montreal, Quebec H3W 2C6
   Canada, 514/482-5827

THE LUCKY STAR   Pickman Films, 1981, w/Jack Rosenthal

PETER S. FISCHER*
Agent: CAA - Beverly Hills, 310/288-4545

TAGGET (CTF)   Mirisch-Tagget-MCA, 1991, w/Janis Diamond &
   Richard T. Heffron

STEPHEN C. FISCHER*
Contact: WGA - Los Angeles, 310/550-1000

Screenplays:
SOMETHING LINGERS
WHEN A MAN LOVES A WOMAN (THE INSIDE STORY)
PHYSICAL CHEMISTRY

LAURENCE FISHBURNE
Agent: Paradigm - Los Angeles, 310/277-4400
Contact: Loa Productions

RIFF RAFF (P)

Screenplays:
SIMPLE

DEIRDRE FISHEL
RISK   Seventh Art Releasing, 1994, directed

ANTWONE "FISH" FISHER
Business Manager: Armstrong, Hirsch, Jackoway, Tyerman &
   Wertheimer - Los Angeles, 310/553-0305

Screenplays:
THE ANTWONE FISHER STORY

CARRIE FISHER*
Agent: CAA - Beverly Hills, 310/288-4545

POSTCARDS FROM THE EDGE   Columbia, 1990

Screenplays:
THE OTHER WOMAN w/Meryl Streep
CHRISTMAS IN LAS VEGAS
SURRENDER THE PINK
THE STORK CLUB

DAVID FISHER
Address: 14144 Dickens, Apt. 115, Sherman Oaks, CA 91423,
   818/907-1368

LIAR'S MOON   Crown International, 1982, directed
TOY SOLDIERS   New World, 1984, w/Walter Fox, directed

FRANCESCA FISHER
WILD BLUE MOON   Quetzal Films, 1992,
   w/Taggart Siegel, co-directed

JIM FISHER*
Agent: ICM - Beverly Hills, 310/550-4000

THE BEVERLY HILLBILLIES   20th Century Fox, 1993,
   w/Jim Staahl, Larry Konner & Mark Rosenthal

Screenplays:
BLOW HARD w/Jim Staahl
CHUMP TOWER w/Jim Staahl
UNDER SURVEILLANCE w/Jim Staahl
DUH BOAT S.O.S. w/Jim Staahl

MICHAEL FISHER*
Agent: Stone Manners Agency - Los Angeles, 213/654-7575

EARTHBOUND   Taft International, 1981

ROBERT FISHER*
Contact: WGA - Los Angeles, 310/550-1000

THE IMPOSSIBLE YEARS (P) w/Arthur Marx
A GLOBAL AFFAIR   Seven Arts, 1963, w/Arthur Marx &
   Charles Lederer
I'LL TAKE SWEDEN   United Artists, 1965, w/Arthur Marx &
   Nat Perrin
EIGHT ON THE LAM   United Artists, 1966, w/Arthur Marx,
   Albert E. Lewin & Burt Styler
CANCEL MY RESERVATION   Naho Enterprises, 1972,
   w/Arthur Marx

TERRY LOUISE FISHER*
Agent: CAA - Beverly Hills, 310/288-4545

SECOND THOUGHTS   Universal, 1983, Story w/Steve Brown

Screenplays:
JAG

BILL FISHMAN
Agent: The Gersh Agency - Beverly Hills, 310/274-6611
Business: Fallout Films, 1310 Main Street, Venice, CA 90291

TAPEHEADS   Avenue Pictures, 1988, w/Peter McCarthy, directed

Screenplays:
DREAMING OF BABYLON

JEFFREY ALAN FISKIN*
Agent: CAA - Beverly Hills, 310/288-4545

ANGEL UNCHAINED   American International, 1969
CUTTER'S WAY   United Artists Classics, 1981
THE PURSUIT OF D.B. COOPER   Universal, 1981
CRACKERS   Universal, 1984
REVENGE   Columbia, 1990, w/Jim Harrison

Screenplays:
BLACK PANTHER
CRAVAN
FIRST CLASS
A CHRONICLE OF BRIMSTONE
CHANGE OF PLANS
FLASHDANCE II
THE BOURNE IDENTITY

BENEDICT FITZGERALD*
Agent: Renaissance-H.N. Swanson - Los Angeles, 310/246-6000

WISE BLOOD   New Line Cinema, 1979, w/Michael Fitzgerald
ZELDA (CTF)   Turner Pictures/ZDF Enterprises, 1993,
   w/Anthony Ivor
HEART OF DARKNESS (CTF)   Turner Pictures/Chris Rose
   Productions, 1994

Screenplays:
MUD, BLOOD AND GLORY
EGYPT, ILLINOIS
CHANEL
L.A. MONOGATARI

MICHAEL FITZGERALD
WISE BLOOD   New Line Cinema, 1979, w/Benedict Fitzgerald

GREGORY FITZPATRICK
Agent: ICM - Beverly Hills, 310/550-4000

Screenplays:
MAELSTROM

FANNIE FLAGG*
Agent: CAA - Beverly Hills, 310/288-4545

FRIED GREEN TOMATOES ★   Universal, 1991, w/Carol Sobieski

Screenplays:
DAISY FAY AND THE MIRACLE MAN

JOE FLAHERTY*
Contact: WGA - Los Angeles, 310/550-1000

Screenplays:
BIG BROADCAST

PAUL FLAHERTY*
Agent: William Morris Agency - Beverly Hills, 310/274-7451

Screenplays:
ANGIE O'MARA

FIONNULA FLANAGAN
JAMES JOYCE'S WOMEN   Universal, 1985

SARA FLANIGAN*
(Sara Flanigan Carter)
Contact: WGA - Los Angeles, 310/550-1000

SUDIE AND SIMPSON (CTF)   Freed/Laufer, 1990, w/Ken Koser
WILDFIRE (CTF)   Freed-Laufer Productions/Carroll Newman
    Productions/Polone Co./Hearst Entertainment Productions, 1992

GRAHAM FLASHNER
Agent: Susan Smith & Associates - Beverly Hills, 213/852-4777

THE SECRETARY   Republic Pictures, 1994

Screenplays:
BASICALLY UNATTRACTIVE

GARY FLEDER*
Agent: William Morris Agency - Beverly Hills, 310/274-7451

AIRTIME (Short)   1991, Story w/Scott Rosenberg, directed

GREGORY FLEEMAN
F/X   Orion, 1986, w/Robert Megginson

Screenplays:
TWO COPS w/Robert Megginson

BUD FLEISHER
HARDCASE AND FIST   United Entertainment, 1989,
    w/Tony Zarindast

ANDREW FLEMING*
Agent: United Talent Agency - Beverly Hills, 310/273-6700

BAD DREAMS   20th Century Fox, 1988,
    w/Steven de Souza, directed
EVERY BREATH   Motion Picture Corporation of America, 1993,
    w/Steve Bing & Judd Nelson
THREESOME   TriStar, 1994, directed

RODMAN FLENDER
Agent: ICM - Beverly Hills, 310/550-4000

IN THE HEAT OF PASSION   Concorde, 1992, directed

Screenplays:
DRACULA RISING (Concorde)

SHARY FLENNIKEN*
Contact: WGA - Los Angeles, 310/550-1000

NATIONAL LAMPOON'S MOVIE MADNESS   United Artists, 1982,
    w/Tod Carroll, Pat Mephitis, Gerald Sussman & Ellis Weiner

CHARLIE FLETCHER*
Agent: United Talent Agency - Beverly Hills, 310/273-6700

Screenplays:
FAIR GAME (Warner Bros.)
THUNDER
ICEBREAKER w/Jake Bowman
KISS THE SKY
KISS AND TELL

SETH FLICKER*
Agent: Sanford-Gross & Associates - Los Angeles,
    310/208-2100

Screenplays:
SHOCK CORRIDOR
TURKS OF BRIGHTON
BROTHERS IN CRIME

THEODORE J. FLICKER*
Business Manager: Marvin Freedman, Freedman, Kinzelberg &
    Broder - Los Angeles, 310/277-0700

SPINOUT   MGM, 1966, w/George Kirgo
THE PRESIDENT'S ANALYST   Paramount, 1967, directed
UP IN THE CELLAR   American International, 1970, directed

DENNY MARTIN FLINN*
Agent: Paradigm - Los Angeles, 310/277-4400

STAR TREK VI: THE UNDISCOVERED COUNTRY   Paramount,
    1991, w/Nicholas Meyer

Screenplays:
FORBIDDEN PLANET (remake)
CARLA

MIGUEL TEJADA-FLORES
(See Miguel TEJADA-FLORES)

JOHN FLYNN*
Agent: The Gersh Agency - Beverly Hills, 310/274-6611

THE OUTFIT   MGM, 1974, directed

TOM FLYNN*
Agent: United Talent Agency - Beverly Hills, 310/273-6700

WATCH IT   Skouras Pictures, 1993, directed

Screenplays:
STAND THE HEAT
PREVIOUS COMMITMENT
MAN'S BEST FRIEND
THE OVERUNDER
THE AMBULANCE CHASER
...ANSWERS TO SANDY
INDECENT AROUSAL

ELLEN L. FOGLE*
Agent: CAA - Beverly Hills, 310/288-4545

Screenplays:
FILTHY RICH

LAWRENCE D. FOLDES
Contact: Ronald G. Gabler - Beverly Hills, 310/205-8908
Business: Star Cinema Production Group, Inc., 6523 Hollywood
    Blvd. - Suite 927, Los Angeles, CA 90028, 213/463-2000

YOUNG WARRIORS   Cannon, 1983, w/Russell W. Colgin, directed
SOCIAL SUICIDE   Star Entertainment Group, 1992,
    w/Elisa J. Charouhas, directed

PETER FOLDY
HOT MOVES   Cardinal Pictures Corp., 1985, w/Larry Anderson
HOMEBOYS   DB Media, 1991
DEADLY EXPOSURE   21st Century, 1992, directed

Screenplays:
SMOKESCREEN (directing)
LUNA PARK
POSTCARD FROM PARADISE

PETER FOLEG
THE UNSEEN   World Northal, 1981, Story w/Michael L. Grace,
   Kim Henkel & Nancy Rifkin

JAMES FOLEY*
Agent: CAA - Beverly Hills, 310/288-4545

AFTER DARK, MY SWEET   Avenue Pictures, 1990,
   w/Robert Redlin, directed

Screenplays:
FAR FROM HOME

ALLAN R. FOLSOM*
Agent: The Marion Rosenberg Office - Los Angeles, 213/653-7383

Screenplays:
DEADLY FORCE
VICTORIO

PETER FONDA
Agent: United Talent Agency - Beverly Hills, 310/273-6700

EASY RIDER ★   Columbia, 1969, w/Dennis Hopper &
   Terry Southern
FATAL MISSION   Funahara, 1990, w/others

NAOMI FONER*
Agent: CAA - Beverly Hills, 310/288-4545

VIOLETS ARE BLUE   Columbia, 1986
RUNNING ON EMPTY ★   Warner Bros., 1988
A DANGEROUS WOMAN   Gramercy Pictures, 1993
LOSING ISAIAH   Paramount, 1995

Screenplays:
THE HOMESMAN
FIRST LIGHT
TRIANGLE
BABY, BABY
LOOKING FOR WORK
VERY GOOD GIRLS
RANDOM HEARTS
ALIBIS

FERNANDO FONSECA*
Contact: WGA - New York, 212/245-6180

THE UNHOLY   Vestron, 1988, w/Philip Yordan

RUBEN FONSECA
EXPOSURE   Miramax, 1991

PAUL FONTAINE-SALAIS
DARK AT NOON   Sideral Productions/Canal Plus, 1992

LLOYD FONVIELLE
Manager: Addis-Wechsler - Los Angeles, 213/954-9000

LORDS OF DISCIPLINE   Paramount, 1983, w/Thomas Pope
THE BRIDE   Columbia, 1985
CHERRY 2000   Orion, 1986, Story
GOTHAM (CTF)   Showtime/Phoenix Entertainment Group/Keith
   Addis & Associates, 1988, directed

Screenplays:
THE KING LIVES
WOMEN, MONEY & RESTAURANTS
FOOLISH THINGS
EVE'S RIB
ATLANTIS

HORTON FOOTE*
Agent: Lucy Kroll Agency - New York, 212/877-0627

COURTSHIP (P) also teleplay
TALKING PICTURES (P)
THE ROADS TO HOME (P)
STORM FEAR   United Artists, 1955
TO KILL A MOCKINGBIRD ★★   Universal, 1962
BABY, THE RAIN MUST FALL   Columbia, 1965,
   from his play "The Travelling Lady"
THE CHASE   Columbia, 1966
HURRY, SUNDOWN   Paramount, 1967, w/Thomas C. Ryan
FOOLS PARADE   Columbia, 1971
TOMORROW   Filmgroup, 1972
TENDER MERCIES ★★   Universal/AFD, 1983
1918   Cinecom International, 1985, from his play
THE TRIP TO BOUNTIFUL ★   Island Pictures, 1985, from his play
ON VALENTINES DAY   Angelika Films, 1986, from his play
   "Valentines Day"
CONVICTS   MCEG, 1991, from his play
THE HABITATION OF DRAGONS (CTF)   TNT Screenworks, 1992,
   from his play
OF MICE AND MEN   MGM, 1992

Screenplays:
MIZ LIL AND THE CHRONICLES OF GRACE
BESSIE
THE WIDOW CLAIRE (from his play)
SPRING MOON
ROOTS IN A PARCHED GROUND
HEART MOUNTAIN
MY FIRST LADY

BRYAN FORBES*
Agent: The Marion Rosenberg Office - Los Angeles, 213/653-7383 or
   Chatto & Linnit - London, 71/930-6677

COCKLESHELL HEROES   Columbia, 1955, w/Richard Maibaum
HOUSE OF SECRETS   Rank, 1956, w/Robert Buckner
THE BLACK TENT   Rank, 1956, w/Robin Maugham
THE BABY AND THE BATTLESHIP   British Lion, 1956,
   w/Jay Lewis & Gilbert Hackforth-Jones
I WAS MONTY'S DOUBLE   NTA Pictures, 1958
THE CAPTAIN'S TABLE   Rank, 1958, w/Nicholas Phipps &
   John Whiting
DANGER WITHIN   British Lion, 1959, w/Frank Harvey
THE ANGRY SILENCE   British Lion, 1960
MAN IN THE MOON   Allied Film Makers, 1960, w/Michael Relph
THE LEAGUE OF GENTLEMEN   Rank, 1960
ONLY TWO CAN PLAY   British Lion, 1962
THE L-SHAPED ROOM   British Lion, 1962, directed
STATION SIX-SAHARA   Allied Artists, 1963, w/Brian Clemens
SEANCE ON A WET AFTERNOON   Rank, 1964, directed
OF HUMAN BONDAGE   MGM, 1964
KING RAT   Columbia, 1965, directed
THE WHISPERERS   United Artists, 1966, directed
DEADFALL   20th Century-Fox, 1968, directed
THE RAGING MOON   *LONG AGO TOMORROW*   EMI,
   1970, directed
THE SLIPPER AND THE ROSE: THE STORY OF CINDERELLA
   Universal, 1976, w/Richard M. Sherman &
   Robert B. Sherman, directed
INTERNATIONAL VELVET   MGM/United Artists, 1978, directed
HOPSCOTCH   Avco Embassy, 1980
BETTER LATE THAN NEVER   Warner Bros., 1983, directed
THE NAKED FACE   Cannon, 1985, directed
CHAPLIN   TriStar, 1992, w/William Boyd & William Goldman

JEAN FORD*
Contact: WGA - Los Angeles, 310/550-1000

Screenplays:
THE PRIOR LIFE OF MICKEY SLATER w/S. Michael Cole
IMMACULATE DECEPTION w/S. Michael Cole

JESSE HILL FORD*
Business Manager: Tom Holbrook - Los Angeles, 213/962-1695

THE LIBERATION OF L.B. JONES   Columbia, 1970,
   w/Stirling Silliphant

KATIE FORD*
Agent: United Talent Agency - Beverly Hills, 310/273-6700

Screenplays:
THE SURFER
OUT IN AMERICA
A DAY AT THE CAPRI
SKIRTS

PHILIP R. FORD
VEGAS IN SPACE   Troma, 1993, w/Doris Fish & Miss X, directed

RICHARD FORD*
Agent: ICM - New York, 212/556-5600

BRIGHT ANGEL   Hemdale, 1991

TIMOTHY FORDER
THE MYSTERY OF EDWIN DROOD   Mayfair Entertainment,
   1993, directed

Screenplays:
ADOLPHE

RICHARD FOREMAN
STRONG MEDICINE   Film Forum, 1981

STEPHEN H. FOREMAN*
Agent: Maggie Field Agency - Studio City, 818/980-2001

THE JAZZ SINGER   AFD, 1980, Adaptation

Screenplays:
COLT
DESPERADO
WOMAN IN THE WILDERNESS
SUPERSTITION
KEY WEST
THE JOURNEY OF AUGUST KING
COUGAR
BEN & JOANNA
PINK MOUNTAIN TINNY

MILOS FORMAN*
Agent: The Lantz Office - New York, 212/586-0200

LOVES OF A BLONDE   Prominent, 1966, w/Ivan Passer &
   Jaroslav Papusek, directed
THE FIREMAN'S BALL   Cinema 5, 1968, w/Ivan Passer &
   Jaroslav Papousek, directed
TAKING OFF   Universal, 1971, w/Jean-Claude Carriere,
   John Guare & John Klein, directed

DOUG FORSMITH
LIBERTY & BASH   Fries Home Video, 1990

BILL FORSYTH*
Agent: CAA - Beverly Hills, 310/288-4545

THAT SINKING FEELING   Samuel Goldwyn Company,
   1979, directed
GREGORY'S GIRL   Samuel Goldwyn Company, 1982, directed
LOCAL HERO   Warner Bros., 1983, directed
COMFORT AND JOY   Universal, 1984, directed
HOUSEKEEPING   Columbia, 1987, directed
BEING HUMAN   Warner Bros., 1994, directed

FREDERICK FORSYTH
Agent: Curtis Brown, Ltd. - New York, 212/473-5400

THE FOURTH PROTOCOL   Lorimar, 1987

ROB FORSYTH
CLEARCUT   Northern Arts, 1991

WILLIAM W. FORSYTHE
THE KILLING MIND (CTF)   Hearst Entertainment Productions, 1991,
   w/Pat A. Victor

BOB FORWARD*
Agent: Monteiro Rose Agency - Encino, 818/501-1177

THE SECRET OF THE SWORD (AF)   Atlantic Releasing
   Corporation, 1985, w/Larry Ditillio

Screenplays:
THE DEMON RUMM
MAX DAMAGE
METRO
WIZARDRY

BOB FOSS
SHIPWRECKED   Buena Vista, 1991, w/Greg Dinner, Nils Gaup &
   Nick Thiel

ROBERT O. FOSTER*
Agent: The Gersh Agency - Beverly Hills, 310/274-6611

CLINTON AND NADINE (CTF)   HBO Pictures/ITC, 1988
DEAD-BANG   Warner Bros., 1989

TONY FOSTER*
Contact: Screen Star Group - 902/443-2456

THE SOUND AND THE SILENCE (CTF)   Screen Star Entertainment/
   Atlantis Films, 1993, w/William Schmidt

ROBERT FOWLER*
Agent: Harold R. Greene Inc. - Marina Del Rey, 310/823-5393

BELOW THE BELT   Atlantic Releasing Corporation, 1980,
   w/Sherrie Sonnett

ALAN C. FOX
THE PARTY ANIMAL   International Film Marketing, 1985, Story

ERICA FOX
DEAD WOMEN IN LINGERIE   Seagate Films, 1990,
   w/John Romo, directed

FRED S. FOX*
Agent: The Cooper Agency - Los Angeles, 310/277-8422

OH GOD! BOOK II   Warner Bros., 1980, w/Josh Greenfeld,
   Hal Goldman, Seaman Jacobs & Melissa Miller

ROBBIE FOX*
Agent: CAA - Beverly Hills, 310/288-4545

THE GREAT O'GRADY (Short)   directed
SHOOTING ELIZABETH   Live Entertainment, 1993
SO I MARRIED AN AXE-MURDERER   TriStar, 1993
IN THE ARMY NOW   Buena Vista, 1994, Story w/Steve Zacharias &
   Jeff Buhai

Screenplays:
ONCE IN LOVE WITH JAMIE (directing)
FOUR MONTHS 12 MINUTES
SLIGHTLY PANICKED
JOEY ON THE 31ST FLOOR
FINDING M

TERRY CURTIS FOX*
Agent: United Talent Agency - Beverly Hills, 310/273-6700

COPS (P)   also screenplay
JUSTICE (P)
SUMMER GARDEN (P)
THE PORNOGRAPHER'S DAUGHTER (P)
THE PERFECT WITNESS (CTF)   HBO Premiere Films, 1989,
   w/Ron Hutchinson
FORTRESS   Miramax, 1993, w/Steven Feinberg,
   Troy Neighbors & David Venable

Screenplays:
JUNGLELAND
BYLINE
SUNSTROKE
FLASH OF EDEN
THE PROSECUTION
13
THE LIFE OF RAFELLO GALLO

WALTER FOX
TOY SOLDIERS   New World, 1984, w/David Fisher

VICTORIA FOYT
Contact: International Rainbow Pictures, The Penthouse,
   9165 Sunset Blvd., Los Angeles, CA 90069, 310/271-0202

BABYFEVER   Rainbow Film Co., 1994, w/Henry Jaglom

CHARLES E. FRADIN*
Contact: WGA - Los Angeles, 310/550-1000

BORIS & NATASHA (CTF)   MCEG, 1992, w/Linda R. Favila &
   Andson Downes

Screenplays:
DELIVERY BOY

CLAUDIO FRAGASSO
THE SEVEN MAGNIFICENT GLADIATORS   Cannon, 1985

RANDALL FRAKES
ROLLER BLADE   New World, 1986, w/Donald G. Jackson
HELL COMES TO FROGTOWN   New World, 1988
DIPLOMATIC IMMUNITY   Fries Distribution, 1991, w/Richard Donn

Screenplays:
DEATHLOK
SIXTY SIX
THE LAST THIRTY DAYS OF LIBERTY
SYNNERS
BLACK WATER

JOSEPH R. FRALEY*
Business Manager: Tim O'Connor, 818/769-1425

SILENT RAGE   Columbia, 1982

MIKE FRANCE*
Agent: APA - Los Angeles, 310/273-0744

CLIFFHANGER   TriStar, 1993, w/Sylvester Stallone

Screenplays:
GOLDENEYE
TEAGUE

JAMES FRANCISCUS
Contact: Screen Actors Guild - Los Angeles, 213/954-1600

29TH STREET   20th Century Fox, 1991, Story w/Frank Pesce

RICARDO FRANCO
BLOOD AND SAND   Overseas Film Group, 1989,
   w/Rafael Azcona & Thomas Fucci
BERLIN BLUES   Cannon, 1989, directed

CAROL FRANK*
Contact: WGA - Los Angeles, 310/550-1000

SORORITY HOUSE MASSACRE   Concorde, 1987, directed

HARRIET FRANK, JR. *
Agent: William Morris Agency - Beverly Hills, 310/274-7451

SILVER RIVER   Warner Bros., 1948, w/Stephen Longstreet
WHIPLASH   Warner Bros., 1948, w/Maurice Geraghty
TEN WANTED MEN   Columbia, 1955, Story w/Irving Ravetch
THE LONG HOT SUMMER   MGM, 1958, w/Irving Ravetch
THE SOUND AND THE FURY   20th Century-Fox, 1959,
   w/Irving Ravetch
HOME FROM THE HILL   MGM, 1959, w/Irving Ravetch
THE DARK AT THE TOP OF THE STAIRS   Warner Bros., 1960,
   w/Irving Ravetch
HUD ★   Paramount, 1963, w/Irving Ravetch
HOMBRE   20th Century-Fox, 1967, w/Irving Ravetch
THE REIVERS   National General, 1969, w/Irving Ravetch
THE COWBOYS   Warner Bros., 1972, w/Irving Ravetch
THE SPIKES GANG   United Artists, 1974, w/Irving Ravetch
CONRACK   20th Century-Fox, 1974, w/Irving Ravetch
NORMA RAE ★   20th Century-Fox, 1979, w/Irving Ravetch
MURPHY'S ROMANCE   Columbia, 1985, w/Irving Ravetch
STANLEY & IRIS   MGM/UA, 1990, w/Irving Ravetch

Screenplays:
BEGINNERS w/Barbara Benedek & Irving Ravetch
MIXED FEELINGS w/Irving Ravetch
SINGLE w/Irving Ravetch

LAURIE FRANK*
Agent: APA - Los Angeles, 310/273-0744

MAKING MR. RIGHT   Orion, 1987, w/Floyd Byars
LOVE CRIMES   Millimeter Films, 1992, w/Allan Moyle

Screenplays:
ASSUME THE POSITION
HARD TO GET
IN DEEP w/Jocko Potter
BEAUTY AND BRAINS

SCOTT FRANK*
(A. Scott Frank)
Agent: CAA - Beverly Hills, 310/288-4545

PLAIN CLOTHES   Paramount, 1988
DEAD AGAIN   Paramount, 1991
LITTLE MAN TATE   Orion, 1991
MALICE   Columbia, 1993, w/Aaron Sorkin
GET SHORTY   MGM/UA, 1995

Screenplays:
GLORY DAYS
SECOND NATURE

DAVID FRANKEL*
Agent: ICM - Beverly Hills, 310/550-4000

FUNNY ABOUT LOVE   Paramount, 1990, w/Norman Steinberg
NERVOUS TICKS   I.R.S. Releasing, 1992
MIAMI RHAPSODY   Buena Vista, 1995, directed

DEBRA FRANKEL*
Contact: WGA - Los Angeles, 310/550-1000

Screenplays:
NANCY NEWTON, R.N.
NO T.V.
DEVIL'S FOOD

AL FRANKEN*
Agent: Martin Hurwitz Associates - Beverly Hills, 310/274-0240
Personal Manager: Barry Secunda - New York, 212/247-4790

ONE MORE SATURDAY NIGHT   Columbia, 1986, w/Tom Davis
WHEN A MAN LOVES A WOMAN   Buena Vista, 1994, w/Ron Bass
STUART SAVES HIS FAMILY   Paramount, 1995

CARL FRANKLIN
Agent: Broder-Kurland-Webb-Uffner - Beverly Hills, 310/281-3400

PUNK (Short)   directed
EYE OF THE EAGLE II: INSIDE THE ENEMY   Concorde, 1989,
   w/Dan Gagliasso,   directed
DEVIL IN A BLUE DRESS   TriStar, 1995,   directed

Screenplays:
SHOOTING FROM THE HEART   w/Robert Johnson

DANIEL JAY FRANKLIN
DREAM A LITTLE DREAM   Vestron, 1989, w/D.E. Eisenberg &
   Marc Rocco

GEORGE FRANKLIN
THE INCUBUS   Film Ventures International, 1982

HOWARD FRANKLIN*
Agent: CAA - Beverly Hills, 310/288-4545

THE NAME OF THE ROSE   20th Century Fox, 1986,
   w/Andrew Birkin, Gerard Brach & Alain Godard
SOMEONE TO WATCH OVER ME   Columbia, 1987
QUICK CHANGE   Warner Bros., 1990, co-directed
THE PUBLIC EYE   Universal, 1992, directed

Screenplays:
THE HUNDRETH MONKEY
QUEEN OF KINGDOM
HOOVERVILLE
THE SHADOW
THE MAN WHO SAVED THE WORLD

JEFF FRANKLIN*
Agent: ICM - Beverly Hills, 310/550-4000
Business: Franklin/Waterman Entertainment, 2644 30th St. -
   1st Floor, Santa Monica, CA 90405, 310/452-9100

JUST ONE OF THE GUYS   Columbia, 1985, w/Dennis Feldman
SUMMER SCHOOL   Paramount, 1987

DAVID H. FRANZONI*
Agent: CAA - Beverly Hills, 310/288-4545

JUMPIN' JACK FLASH   20th Century Fox, 1986, w/Patricia Irving,
   J.W. Melville & Christopher Thompson
CITIZEN COHN (CTF)   HBO-Viacom-Breakheart-Spring Creek, 1992

Screenplays:
BODIES ELECTRIC
THE MAYOR OF CASTRO STREET
THE SKULL
AL CAPONE
BRUNO MANSER
L.A. GOLD   w/Bob Swaim
THE 9TH FOX
TORN
THE CLUB
FIRE

BRAD FRASER
Manager: International Arts Entertainment - Los Angeles,
   310/551-0014

LOVE AND HUMAN REMAINS   Sony Pictures Classics, 1994,
   from his play "Unidentified Human Remains and the
   True Nature of Love"

GEORGE MACDONALD FRASER
Contact: British Film Institute, 011/44/071/437-4355

THE THREE MUSKETEERS   20th Century-Fox, 1974
THE FOUR MUSKETEERS   20th Century-Fox, 1975
ROYAL FLASH   20th Century-Fox, 1976
CROSSED SWORDS   *THE PRINCE AND THE PAUPER*
   20th Century-Fox, 1977
OCTOPUSSY   MGM/UA, 1983, w/Richard Maibaum &
   Michael G. Wilson
RED SONJA   MGM/United Artists, 1985, w/Clive Exton
THE RETURN OF THE MUSKETEERS   Universal, 1990

Screenplays:
STILLWELL   w/Calder Willingham
COLOSSUS
THE ICE PEOPLE
OUT OF TIME

VICTORIA FRASER
Agent: The Gersh Agency - Beverly Hills, 310/274-6611

Screenplays:
BLOODLINE   w/Marc Weinberg

MICHAEL FRAYN
Agent: Peters, Fraser & Dunlop - London, 071/376-7676

BENEFACTORS (P)
NOISES OFF (P)
CLOCKWISE   Universal, 1986

GRAY FREDERICKSON
BAD GIRLS   20th Century Fox, 1994,   Story w/Charles Finch &
   Albert S. Ruddy

BILL FREED*
Contact: WGA - Los Angeles, 310/550-1000

WATCHERS   Tri-Star, 1988, w/Damian Lee

DAVE FREED
Agent: Maggie Field Agency - Studio City, 818/980-2001

Screenplays:
GREENLIGHT
SUPERGRAMPS

DONALD FREED*
Agent: The Gersh Agency - Beverly Hills, 310/274-6611

VETERAN'S DAY (P)
INQUEST: THE U.S. VS. JULIUS AND ETHEL ROSENBERG (P)
THE WHITE CROW: EICHMANN IN JERUSALEM (P)
   also screenplay
ALFRED AND VICTORIA: A LIFE (P)
THE QUARTERED MAN (P)   also screenplay
OUR MAN IN NICARAGUA (P)
IS HE STILL DEAD? (P)
CIRCE AND BRAVO (P)
EXECUTIVE ACTION   EA Enterprises, 1973, Story w/Mark Lane
SECRET HONOR   Cinecom International, 1985, w/Arnold M. Stone,
   from his play "Secret Honor: The Last Testament of Richard M. Nixon"
OF LOVE AND SHADOWS   Betka Film Ltd., 1994, w/Betty Kaplan

Screenplays:
SLAY THE DREAMER   w/Mark Lane
RICHARDSON   w/Mark Lane

HERB FREED*
Contact: Slaff, Mosk & Rudman - Los Angeles, 310/275-5351

BEYOND EVIL   IFI-Scope III, 1980, w/Paul Ross, directed
GRADUATION DAY   IFI/Scope III, 1981, w/Anne Marisse
SURVIVAL GAME   Trans World Entertaiment, 1987,
   w/Susannah de Nimes & P.W. Swann

Screenplays:
THE DAY THE EARTH STRUCK BACK w/Marion Segal

MARK FREED
SHOCK 'EM DEAD   Academy Entertainment, 1991,
   w/Andrew Cross, directed

JERROLD FREEDMAN*
Business Manager: Julie Miller, Oberman, Tivoli & Miller -
   Los Angeles, 310/471-9300

BORDERLINE   AFD, 1980, w/Steve Kline, directed

TERENCE FREELY
DUEL OF HEARTS (CTF)   TNT/Grade Company, 1992

DAVID FREEMAN*
Agent: ICM - Beverly Hills, 310/550-4000

FIRST LOVE   Paramount, 1977, w/Jane Stanton Hitchcock
THE BORDER   Universal, 1982, w/Walon Green & Deric Washburn
STREET SMART   Cannon, 1987

Screenplays:
AMERICAN ROULETTE
MADE IN AMERICA
TOUGH CUSTOMERS
HUMORESQUE
TREASURE ISLAND
PLAY CRAZY
INNER FIRE
CHASER

FRED FREEMAN*
Agent: CAA - Beverly Hills, 310/288-4545

START THE REVOLUTION WITHOUT ME   Warner Bros., 1970,
   w/Lawrence J. Cohen
S*P*Y*S   20th Century-Fox, 1974, w/Lawrence J. Cohen &
   Malcolm Marmorstein
THE BIG BUS   Paramount, 1976, w/Lawrence J. Cohen
DELIRIOUS   MGM-Pathe, 1991, w/Lawrence J. Cohen

Screenplays:
THE PSYCHIATRIST AND THE THIEF w/Lawrence J. Cohen
KARISTAN w/Lawrence J. Cohen

LYN FREEMAN*
Contact: WGA - Los Angeles, 310/550-1000

WITHOUT WARNING   Filmways, 1980, w/Daniel Grodnick,
   Ben Nett & Steve Mathis

M.S. FREEMAN
Agent: Original Artists - Santa Monica, 310/394-1067

Screenplays:
MANHATTAN ISLAND

FRED FREIBERGER*
Contact: WGA - Los Angeles, 310/550-1000

THE BEAST FROM TWENTY THOUSAND FATHOMS
   Warner Bros., 1953, w/Lou Morheim

JEFF FREILICH*
Agent: Major Clients Agency - Los Angeles, 310/284-6400

Screenplays:
GLORY DAYS
TWO SCOOPS
OUTTA SIGHT
DYNAMITE
PARADISE FLATS
DEVIL'S BARGAIN

CAROLINE FREISEN
Agent: Berzon Agency - Glendale, 818/548-1560

Screenplays:
THE EMPEROR WHO

LANA FREISTAT - MELMAN
Agent: Richland/Wunsch/Hohman Agency - Los Angeles,
   310/278-1955

Screenplays:
HUNGRY HEARTS
A PERFECT BRIDE
LOVE WITH A PERFECT STRANGER

ROB FRESCO*
Contact: 310/470-7571

INTIMATE STRANGER   South Gate Entertainment, 1991

Screenplays:
DEEP SECRETS

JUDY FREUDBERG*
Contact: WGA - New York, 212/245-6180

SESAME STREET PRESENTS FOLLOW THAT BIRD   Warner Bros.,
   1985, w/Tony Geiss
AN AMERICAN TAIL (AF)   Universal, 1986, w/Tony Geiss
THE LAND BEFORE TIME (AF)   Universal, 1987,
   Story w/Tony Geiss

Screenplays:
OPERATION AMANDA   NAVY BRATS   w/Tony Geiss

HEIDI FREY
Agent: Renaissance-H.N. Swanson - Los Angeles, 310/246-6000

Screenplays:
SEX

RANDALL FRIED
Agent: The Artists Group - Los Angeles, 310/552-1100

HEAVEN IS A PLAYGROUND   New Line Cinema,
   1991, directed

Screenplays:
RIP CITY

RICHARD L. FRIEDENBERG*
Agent: The Daniel Ostroff Agency - Los Angeles, 213/278-2020

DYING YOUNG   20th Century Fox, 1991
A RIVER RUNS THROUGH IT ★   Columbia, 1992
PRIVATE DEBTS (Short)   Showtime, 1993

Screenplays:
THE EDUCATION OF LITTLE TREE

WILLIAM FRIEDKIN*
Agent: ICM - Beverly Hills, 310/550-4000

CRUISING   United Artists, 1980, directed
TO LIVE AND DIE IN L.A.   MGM/UA, 1985,
   w/Gerald Petievich, directed
THE GUARDIAN   Universal, 1990, w/Dan Greenburg &
   Stephen Volk, directed
RAMPAGE   Miramax, 1992, directed, filmed in 1987

Screenplays:
TRACKER (directing)

CYNTHIA FRIEDLOB*
Agent: Jim Preminger Agency - Los Angeles, 310/475-9491

CLASS ACT   Warner Bros., 1992, w/John Semper

ADAM FRIEDMAN
RAPPIN'   Cannon, 1985, w/Robert Litz

Screenplays:
ONE FELL SWOOP
STRAY DANCER

BRENT V. FRIEDMAN
SYNGENOR   South Gate Entertainment, 1990
THE RESURRECTED   Scotti Bros., 1992
NECROMICON   Davis Film/August Entertainment, 1993
AMERICAN CYBORG: STEEL WARRIOR   Cannon, 1994,
   w/Bill Crounse & Don Pequignot

Screenplays:
TICKS

BRUCE JAY FRIEDMAN*
Agent: William Morris Agency - New York, 212/586-5100

STIR CRAZY   Columbia, 1980
DOCTOR DETROIT   Universal, 1983, w/Robert Boris &
   Carl Gottlieb
SPLASH ★   Buena Vista, 1984, w/Lowell Ganz &
   Babaloo Mandel

Screenplays:
BODY POLITIC
PX
OUR LADY OF THE LOCKERS
DEEP TROUBLE
YOUR BASIC LOUSY MARRIAGE
ABOUT HARRY TOWNS
LIFE ENDS AT FORTY
DETROIT ABE
SCUBA DUBA
LET'S HEAR IT FOR A BEAUTIFUL GUY
TOKYO WOES

IRIS FRIEDMAN*
Contact: WGA - Los Angeles, 310/550-1000

NOBODY'S CHILDREN (CTF)   Winkler/Daniels-Quinta-USA
   Network, 1993, w/Petru Popescu

JOSH FRIEDMAN
Agent: Sanford-Gross & Associates - Los Angeles,
   310/208-2100

Screenplays:
DEAD DROP
TATUM'S HAIRCUT

KENNETH FRIEDMAN*
Agent: Sanford-Gross & Associates - Los Angeles,
   310/208-2100

DEATH BY INVITATION   1971, directed
WHITE LINE FEVER   Columbia, 1975, w/Jonathan Kaplan
MR. BILLION   20th Century-Fox, 1976, w/Jonathan Kaplan
HEART LIKE A WHEEL   20th Century-Fox, 1983
MADE IN USA   DEG, 1986, directed
JOHNNY HANDSOME   Tri-Star, 1989
CADILLAC MAN   Orion, 1990

Screenplays:
SVENGALI
THE INFORMANT w/Robert Daley
ZODIAC DIRTY WATER
GARBAGE
HEAVEN SCENT w/Joyce Eliason
NIGHTSIDE
KEY WEST DRUG SMUGGLING
THE BOOSTER

MEL FRIEDMAN*
Agent: Pleshette & Green - Los Angeles, 213/465-0428

BLOODSPORT   Cannon, 1988, w/Chris Cosby & Sheldon Lettich

Screenplays:
THE ATOMIC VETERAN w/Chris Cosby
SNOWBOUND w/Chris Cosby
SUPERBOXERS w/Chris Cosby
MAXIMUM MAXIMUM PRISONSHIP w/Chris Cosby
TRACKDOWN w/Chris Cosby
DEADLY METAL w/Chris Cosby
GOLDEN KNIGHTS w/Chris Cosby
ALIEN COP w/Chris Cosby

RICHARD S. FRIEDMAN*
Agent: Broder-Kurland-Webb-Uffner - Beverly Hills, 310/281-3400

SCARED STIFF   International Film Marketing, 1987,
   w/Daniel F. Bacanar & Mark Frost
STREET KNIGHT   Paramount, 1993

ROBERT L. FRIEDMAN*
Agent: ICM - New York, 212/556-5600

Screenplays:
MANIC w/Selma Thompson

RON FRIEDMAN*
Agent: Shapiro/Lichtman - Los Angeles, 310/859-8877

THE TRANSFORMERS: THE MOVIE (AF)   DEG, 1986

STEPHEN FRIEDMAN
LOVIN' MOLLY   Columbia, 1974

THOMAS FRIEDMAN*
Contact: 617/492-2777

TIME WALKER   New World, 1982, w/Karen Levitt
DANGER ZONE II: REAPER'S REVENGE   Skouras Pictures, 1989,
   Story w/Jason Williams

AVA OSTERN FRIES
(See Ava OSTERN-Fries)

JOHN FRIZZELL
ON MY OWN   Alliance Communications Corp., 1992,
   w/Gill Dennis & Antonio Tibaldi

BILL FROEHLICH*
Agent: Paradigm - Los Angeles, 310/277-4400

RETURN TO HORROR HIGH   New World, 1987, w/Mark Lisson,
   Dana Escalante & Greg H. Sim

CLAYTON S. FROHMAN*
Agent: The Irv Schechter Company - Beverly Hills, 310/278-8070

UNDER FIRE   Orion, 1983, w/Ron Shelton
THE DELINQUENTS   Warner Bros., 1990, w/Mac Gudgeon
THE COURTMARTIAL OF JACKIE ROBINSON (CTF)
   Turner Network Television, 1990, w/L. Travis Clark,
   Dennis Clark & Steve Duncan

Screenplays:
MAKING THUNDERBIRDS
PRECIOUS METAL
SUNBELT
CHEERLEADER OF THE NEW LEFT
GIANT KILLER

MEL FROHMAN*
Contact: WGA - Los Angeles, 310/550-1000

...ALL THE MARBLES   MGM/United Artists, 1981
LIES OF THE TWINS (CTF)   MCA Television Entertainment, 1991,
   w/Wally Klenhard

DIANE FROLOV*
Agent: Richland/Wunsch/Hohman Agency - Los Angeles,
   310/278-1955

Screenplays:
COME GET MAGGIE
LOWFLYERS
MEN
BACK IN STEP w/Andy Schneider

SETH FRONT*
Agent: APA - Los Angeles, 310/273-0744

NICKEL & DIME   August Entertainment, 1992, w/Eddy Polon

MARK C. FROST*
Agent: CAA - Beverly Hills, 310/288-4545

THE BELIEVERS   Orion, 1987
SCARED STIFF   International Film Marketing, 1987,
   w/Daniel F. Bacaner & Richard Friedman
STORYVILLE   20th Century Fox, 1992, w/Lee Reynolds, directed

Screenplays:
THE LIST OF SEVEN
ONE SALIVA BUBBLE w/David Lynch
BLIND LUCK w/R. Lance Hill
GOOD MORNING, CHICAGO
72-HOUR CLUB
THE SECOND EXPEDITION
LUNCH AT FIRST SIGHT
BLIND VOICES
GHOST DIARY
TRUE ROMANCE
GRIDLOCK
TRACES
VENUS DESCENDING

SCOTT FROST*
Agent: APA - Los Angeles, 310/273-0744

PAST TENSE (CTF)   Showtime Entertainment, 1994,
   w/Miguel Tejada-Flores

Screenplays:
SILO
SPUTNICK
SURRENDER DOROTHY
A LITTLE TOUCHED

WILLIAM FRUET
Business: Jaguar Productions Ltd., 51 Olive Avenue, Toronto, Ontario
   M6G 1T7, Canada, 416/535-3569

GOIN' DOWN THE ROAD   Chevron, 1970
RIP-OFF   Alliance, 1972, directed
WEDDING IN WHITE   Avco Embassy, 1973, directed
SLIPSTREAM   Pacific Rim Films, 1974
THE HOUSE BY THE LAKE   *DEATH WEEKEND*   American
   International, 1977, directed

BORIS FRUMIN
Agent: Neal Stevens & Associates - Beverly Hills, 310/275-7541
Contact: New York University Film School - New York

BLACK AND WHITE   MN Productions, 1992, directed

ROY FRUMKES
Agent: Rajeer Hgarwal - New York
Business: Bat Track Productions, 166 W. 83rd St., New York,
   NY 10024, 212/873-6626

STREET TRASH   Lightning Pictures, 1987

Screenplays:
DUST w/Rocco Simonelli

MICHAEL FRY*
Contact: WGA - Los Angeles, 310/550-1000

Screenplays:
MIND, BODY & SOUL

RICK FRY
BRIDE OF RE-ANIMATOR   Troma, 1991, Story w/Brian Yuzna
SOCIETY   Zecca Productions, 1992, w/Woody Keith

E. MAX FRYE*
Agent: ICM - Beverly Hills, 310/550-4000

SOMETHING WILD   Orion, 1986
AMOS & ANDREW   Columbia, 1993, directed

Screenplays:
TWISSLEMAN
DEAR JOHNNY POGUE
THE BIG PLUNGE

STEPHEN FRYE
Agent: William Morris Agency - Beverly Hills, 310/274-7451

Screenplays:
A CONFEDERACY OF DUNCES

JACKIE FRYSCMAN
Business: Starwatcher Graphics - 213/467-0121

Screenplays:
STARWATCHER (AF) w/Moebius (Paramount)

ROBERT FUEST
Agent: Leading Players, 31 Kings Rd., London SW3, England

JUST LIKE A WOMAN   Monarch, 1966, directed
DR. PHIBES RISES AGAIN   American International, 1972,
   w/Robert Blees, directed
THE LAST DAYS OF MAN ON EARTH   *THE FINAL PROGRAM*
   New World, 1974, directed

ATHOL FUGARD
Agent: William Morris Agency - New York, 212/586-5100

TSOTSI (P)
MASTER HAROLD AND THE BOYS (P)
THE ROAD TO MECCA (P)

A LESSON FROM ALOES (P)
THE ISLAND (P)
SIZWE BANZI IS DEAD (P)
MY CHILDREN! MY AFRICA! (P)
BOESMAN AND LENA (P)
PLAYLAND (P)
MARIGOLDS IN AUGUST   RM Productions, 1984
THE GUEST   RM Productions, 1984

KATHERINE FUGATE
Agent: Susan Smith & Associates - Beverly Hills, 213/852-4777

Screenplays:
LAYOVER
OTIS

BRIAN FULD
Contact: Prelude Pictures, Paramount, 213/956-8646

Screenplays:
SWORDFIGHT

LEE FULKERSON
FREE RIDE   Galaxy International, 1986, w/Robert Bell &
   Ronald Zwang

CHARLES H. FULLER*
Agent: William Morris Agency - New York, 212/586-5100

BURNER'S FROLIC (P)
ZOOMAN AND THE SIGN (P)
A SOLDIER'S STORY ★   Columbia, 1984,
   from his play "A Soldier's Play"

Screenplays:
THE BROWNSVILLE ROAD
SIMPLE JUSTICE
KINGSBLOOD

DAVID FULLER*
Agent: The Daniel Ostroff Agency - Los Angeles, 213/278-2020

THE HEIST (CTF)   HBO Pictures, 1989, w/Rick Natkin
THE TAKING OF BEVERLY HILLS   Columbia, 1991,
   w/Rick Natkin & David Burke
NECESSARY ROUGHNESS   Paramount, 1991, w/Rick Natkin

FLEMING B. FULLER
PREY OF THE CHAMELEON (CTF)   Showtime, 1992,
   w/April Campbell Jones

KIM FULLER*
Contact: Crucial Films - London, 071/287-6153

LENNY LIVE AND UNLEASHED   Miramax, 1989, w/Lenny Henry

LESLIE A. FULLER*
Agent: William Morris Agency - Beverly Hills, 310/274-7451

Screenplays:
SHAMELESS
REC ROOM
BLOOD RELATIONS

SAMUEL FULLER*
Contact: WGA - Los Angeles, 310/550-1000

CONFIRM OR DENY   20th Century-Fox, 1941, w/Jo Swerling &
   Henry Wales
I SHOT JESSE JAMES   Screen Guild, 1949, directed
SHOCKPROOF   Columbia, 1949, w/Helen Deutsch
THE BARON OF ARIZONA   Lippert, 1950, directed
FIXED BAYONETS!   20th Century-Fox, 1951, directed
PARK ROW   United Artists, 1952, directed
PICKUP ON SOUTH STREET   20th Century-Fox, 1953, directed
HELL AND HIGH WATER   20th Century-Fox, 1954, directed

RUN OF THE ARROW   Global, 1956, directed
FORTY GUNS   20th Century-Fox, 1957, directed
CHINA GATE   20th Century-Fox, 1957, directed
THE CRIMSON KIMONO   Columbia, 1959, directed
UNDERWORLD USA   Columbia, 1960, directed
MERRILL'S MARAUDERS   Warner Bros., 1962,
   w/Milton Sperling, directed
SHOCK CORRIDOR   Allied Artists, 1963, directed
CAPETOWN AFFAIR   20th Century-Fox, 1967, w/Harold Medford
SHARK!   Heritage, 1970, w/John Kingsbridge, directed
DEAD PIGEONS ON BEETHOVEN STREET   Emerson,
   1972, directed
THE KLANSMAN   Paramount, 1974, w/Millard Kaufman
THE BIG RED ONE   United Artists, 1980, directed
WHITE DOG   Paramount, 1982, w/Curtis Hanson, directed
LET'S GET HARRY   Tri-Star, 1987, Story w/Mark L. Feldberg
STREET OF NO RETURN   BAC Films, 1991,
   w/Jacques Bral, directed
GIRLS IN PRISON (CTF)   Showtime/Drive-In Classic Cinema,
   1994, w/Christa Lang

CHOSEI FUNAHARA
FATAL MISSION   Funahara, 1990, w/Peter Fonda, Anthony Gentile,
   John Gentile & George Rowe

SIDNEY J. FURIE
Agent: ICM - Beverly Hills, 310/550-4000
Business: Furie Productions Inc., 9169 Sunset Blvd., Los Angeles,
   CA 90069

DURING ONE NIGHT   *NIGHT OF PASSION*   Astor, 1961, directed
THE LAWYER   Paramount, 1970, w/Harold Buchman, directed
THE BOYS IN COMPANY C   Columbia, 1978,
   w/Rick Natkin, directed
PURPLE HEARTS   The Ladd Company/Warner Bros., 1984,
   w/Rick Natkin, directed
IRON EAGLE   Tri-Star, 1986, w/Kevin Elders, directed
IRON EAGLE II   Tri-Star, 1988, w/Kevin Elders, directed
THE TAKING OF BEVERLY HILLS   Nelson Entertainment, 1991,
   Story w/David Fuller & Rick Natkin, directed

STEPHEN FURST
Agent: Rogers & Associates - North Hollywood, 818/509-1010

NINJA KID   PM Entertainment, 1993, directed
MAGIC KID 2   PM Entertainment, 1994, directed

GEORGE FURTH*
Contact: Ralph R. Turner, CPA - 310/273-4260

Screenplays:
AMERICA'S SWEETHEART
PRECIOUS SONS

JOHN FUSCO*
Agent: William Morris Agency - Beverly Hills, 310/274-7451

CROSSROADS   Columbia, 1986
YOUNG GUNS   20th Century Fox, 1988
YOUNG GUNS II   20th Century Fox, 1990
THUNDERHEART   TriStar, 1992
THE BABE   Universal, 1992
LOCH NESS   Gramercy, 1995

Screenplays:
TRUE NORTH
BOY'S LIFE
BLUES WATER
SMACK IN THE MIDDLE w/L. Craig
FABLECHASE
TOWNIES

PAUL FUSCO*
Manager: Brillstein-Grey - Beverly Hills, 310/275-6135

Screenplays:
SUNSET MANOR

G

PAL GABOR
BRADY'S ESCAPE   Satori Releasing, 1984, Story

MITCHELL GABOURI
BUYING TIME   MGM/UA, 1989, w/Richard Gabouri, directed

RICHARD GABOURI
BUYING TIME   MGM/UA, 1989, w/Mitchell Gabouri

REG GADNEY
Agent: Peters, Fraser & Dunlop - London, 071/376-5999

IRAN: DAYS OF CRISIS (CMS)   Gerald Rafshoon/Consolidated,
   1991, w/Tim Wells

GEORGE GAGE
Contact: Directors Guild of America - Los Angeles, 310/289-2000

SKATEBOARD   Universal, 1978, w/Dick Wolf, directed
FLESHBURN   Crown International, 1984, w/Beth Gage, directed

DAN GAGLIASSO
EYE OF THE EAGLE II: INSIDE THE ENEMY   Concorde Pictures,
   1989, w/Carl Franklin

CHARLES L. GAINES*
Contact: WGA - Los Angeles, 310/550-1000

STAY HUNGRY   United Artists, 1976, w/Bob Rafelson

RUDY GAINES
Agent: J. Michael Bloom & Associates - Los Angeles, 310/275-6800

Screenplays:
IVANHOE w/John Rice
LEWIS & CLARK, THE EXPEDITION w/John Rice
JOURNAL OF ADVENTURE w/John Rice
LEVITICUS WAR w/John Rice
BUFFALO COMMONS w/John Rice
TO DIE FOR w/John Rice
SHELTER FROM THE STORM w/John Rice
GREENHOUSE EFFECT

FRANK GALATI*
Agent: William Morris Agency - Beverly Hills, 310/274-7451

THE GRAPES OF WRATH (P)
EARTHLY POSSESSIONS (P)
THE ACCIDENTAL TOURIST ★   Warner Bros., 1988,
   w/Lawrence Kasdan
THE AMERICAN CLOCK (CTF)   TNT/Amblin/Michael
   Brandman, 1993

Screenplays:
PINNOCHIO
THE QUIET AMERICAN
A CONFEDERACY OF DUNCES
TRACER
THE LIVING END

BOB GALE
Agent: CAA - Beverly Hills, 310/288-4545

I WANNA HOLD YOUR HAND   Universal, 1978, w/Robert Zemeckis
1941   Universal/Columbia, 1979, w/Robert Zemeckis
USED CARS   Columbia, 1980, w/Robert Zemeckis
BACK TO THE FUTURE ★   Universal, 1985, w/Robert Zemeckis
BACK TO THE FUTURE II   Universal, 1989
BACK TO THE FUTURE III   Universal, 1990
TRESPASS   Universal, 1992, w/Robert Zemeckis

Screenplays:
GANGLAND w/Robert Zemeckis
JIMBO'S STAND
HENRY STAR, OUTLAW
DIPLOMATIC IMMUNITY
CARPOOL

CHARLES R. GALE*
Agent: CAA - Beverly Hills, 310/288-4545

MAKING THE GRADE   MGM/UA/Cannon, 1984,
   Story w/Gene Quintano
GUILTY AS CHARGED   I.R.S. Releasing, 1991
ERNEST SCARED STUPID   Buena Vista, 1991, w/Coke Sams
TATTLETALE   The Movie Group, 1992
CAPTAIN NUKE AND THE BOMBER BOYS   Concorde, 1995

Screenplays:
PLASTIC MAN
HI, I'M FROM HELL
COMMON STOCK
THIS MAGIC MOMENT   SCARECROW

JOHN GALE
THE FIRING LINE   AIP, 1991, w/Sonny Sanders, directed,
   filmed in 1988

TIMOTHY GALFAS*
Contact: WGA - Los Angeles, 310/550-1000

MATILDA   American International, 1978, w/Albert S. Ruddy
SUNNYSIDE   American International, 1979, w/Jeff King, directed

JOHN ANDREW GALLAGHER
Agent: The Parks Agency - New York, 212/254-9067

BEACH HOUSE   New Line Cinema, 1982,
   w/Marino Amaruso, directed
POSED FOR MURDER   Double Helix Films, 1988
STREET HUNTER   21st Century Film Corporation, 1990,
   w/Steve James, directed
MEN LIE   Lexington Pictures, 1994, directed

Screenplays:
BLUE HIGHWAYS
SCREWDRIVER
THE TIME OF THEIR LIVES
VINNEY D. w/Frank Vincent
MYSTERIOUS WAYS w/Sylvia Caminer
BLOODY FELLOWS w/Ethan Reiff
FIREWOLF w/Steve James
NIGHT EAGLE w/Steve James
HELL SOLDIER w/Steve James
TRACKDOWN w/Robert Ginty
SOMEWHERE IN THE MEDITERRANEAN w/Denis Leary

MARY GALLAGHER*
Agent: The Artists Agency - Los Angeles, 310/277-7779

FATHER DREAMS (P)
LITTLE BIRD (P)
CHOCOLATE CAKE (P)
BUDDIES (P)
DOG EAT DOG (P)
LOVE MINUS (P)

HOW TO SAY GOODBYE (P)
LITTLE MISS FRESNO (P)   w/Ara Watson
¿DE D´ØNDE? (P)

Screenplays:
NOBODY HOME

SARAH GALLAGHER*
Agent: Writers & Artists Agency - Los Angeles, 310/824-6300

Screenplays:
NEEDLES w/Judy Feldman

STEPHEN GALLAGHER
CHIMERA (CTF)   Zenith Productions/Anglia Films, 1992

GEORGE GALLO*
Agent: ICM - Beverly Hills, 310/550-4000

WISE GUYS   MGM/UA, 1986
MIDNIGHT RUN   Universal, 1988
29TH STREET   20th Century Fox, 1991, directed
TRAPPED IN PARADISE   20th Century Fox, 1994, directed

Screenplays:
BAD BOYS (Columbia)
AMERICAN MELTDOWN w/E. Olsiewicz
PROS & CONS
THE GRASS IS GREENER
MAESTRO & ME AMERICAN BRASS
003 STOOGES
DEBS
STOLEN FLOWER
SLAUGHTER IN CHINATOWN
TV MAN

GUY J. GALLO*
Agent: Susan Smith & Associates - Beverly Hills, 213/852-4777

UNDER THE VOLCANO   Universal, 1984

Screenplays:
MEDICINE BEAR
PRINCE OF PEACE
GOING AFTER CACCIATO
A FLAG FOR SUNRISE
ALMOST INNOCENT
THE LIGHT PRINCESS (AF)

BRIAN GAMBLE
RED SURF   Arrowhead Entertainment, 1990,
   Story w/Jason Hoffs & Vincent Robert

TOM W. GAMMILL*
Agent: William Morris Agency - Beverly Hills, 310/274-7451

Screenplays:
THEY ARE US w/Max Pross

GLENDA GANIS*
Contact: WGA - Los Angeles, 310/550-1000

Screenplays:
DIVINE RAPTURE
BLUE DREAMS
CHESSA
MAMA MIA
ONCE MORE ONCE
SKINNY LEGS
THE OTHER ANNE FLETCHER

ROBERTS GANNAWAY*
Agent: Maggie Field Agency - Studio City, 818/980-2001

Screenplays:
CATS DON'T DANCE (AF) w/Elana Lesser & Cliff Ruby
   (Turner Pictures)
FLESH AND INK
HOUSE-O-MATIC

JOSEPH M. GANNON*
Agent: Jim Preminger Agency - Los Angeles, 310/475-9491

SOLAR CRISIS   Scochiku-Fuji, 1990, w/Ted Sarafian
STARFIRE   Inter-Ocean Film, 1992, w/Crispen Bolt

LUCY GANNON
Agent: Lemon Unna & Durbridge - London, 071/727-1346

A SMALL DANCE   Thames Television International, 1991

LOWELL GANZ*
Agent: CAA - Beverly Hills, 310/288-4545

WRONG TURN AT LUNGFISH (P)   w/Garry Marshall
NIGHTSHIFT   The Ladd Company/Warner Bros., 1982,
   w/Babaloo Mandel
SPLASH ★   Buena Vista, 1984, w/Bruce Jay Friedman &
   Babaloo Mandel
SPIES LIKE US   Warner Bros., 1985, w/Dan Aykroyd &
   Babaloo Mandel
GUNG HO   Paramount, 1986, w/Babaloo Mandel
VIBES   Columbia, 1988, w/Babaloo Mandel
PARENTHOOD   Univeral, 1989, w/Babaloo Mandel
CITY SLICKERS   Columbia, 1991, w/Babaloo Mandel
A LEAGUE OF THEIR OWN   Columbia, 1992, w/Babaloo Mandel
MR. SATURDAY NIGHT   Columbia, 1992, w/Babaloo Mandel &
   Billy Crystal
GREEDY   Universal, 1994, w/Babaloo Mandel
CITY SLICKERS II: THE LEGEND OF CURLY'S GOLD   Columbia,
   1994, w/Babaloo Mandel & Billy Crystal
FORGET PARIS   Columbia, 1995, w/Babaloo Mandel & Billy Crystal

Screenplays:
MULTIPLICITY w/Babaloo Mandel
CRAZY w/Babaloo Mandel
INTO THE WOODS w/Babaloo Mandel
OVER MY DEAD BODY w/Babaloo Mandel
THE PERFECT COUPLE w/Babaloo Mandel
DANCE SKINS w/Babaloo Mandel
C. DMIAS w/Garry Marshall
HAPPY HOUR
KIAMESHA
THE GREATEST SHOW ON EARTH

LARRY GARCIA*
Agent: United Talent Agency - Beverly Hills, 310/273-6700

Screenplays:
US AND THEM w/Greg Davis
HARRY SCARRY WANTS TO MARRY w/Greg Davis
WIND IN THE WILLOWS w/Greg Davis

GERALD GARDNER*
Agent: Shapiro/Lichtman - Los Angeles, 310/859-8877

WHICH WAY TO THE FRONT?   Warner Bros., 1970, w/Dee Caruso
THE WORLD'S GREATEST ATHLETE   Buena Vista, 1973,
   w/Dee Caruso

HERB GARDNER*
Agent: The Lantz Office - New York, 212/586-0200

I'M NOT RAPPAPORT (P)
CONVERSATIONS WITH MY FATHER (P)
A THOUSAND CLOWNS ★   United Artists, 1965, from his play

WHO IS HARRY KELLERMAN AND WHY IS HE SAYING
ALL THESE TERRIBLE THINGS ABOUT ME?
National General, 1971
THIEVES Paramount, 1977, from his play
THE GOODBYE PEOPLE Embassy, 1984, from his play, directed

LEONARD C. GARDNER*
Agent: Ron Lescher, Lescher & Lescher - 212/529-1790

FAT CITY Columbia, 1972
VALENTINO RETURNS Skouras Pictures, 1989

LEO GAREN*
Agent: The Cooper Agency - Santa Monica, 310/277-8422

BAND OF THE HAND Tri-Star, 1986, w/Jack Baran

Screenplays:
DON'T HOLD BACK w/Jack Baran
HEX
DOUBLE EAGLE
SNAKEBITE AND TNT

BRIAN GARFIELD*
Agent: The Coppage Company - North Hollywood, 818/980-1106

HOPSCOTCH Avco Embassy, 1980, w/Bryan Forbes
THE STEPFATHER New Century/Vista, 1987,
Story w/Caroline Lefcourt & Donald E. Westlake

LOUIS A. GARFINKLE*
Contact: WGA - Los Angeles, 310/550-1000

THE DOBERMAN GANG Dimension, 1973, w/Frank Ray Perilli
LITTLE CIGARS 1973, w/Frank Ray Perilli
THE DEER HUNTER ★ Universal, 1978, Story w/Michael Cimino &
Quinn K. Redeker

Screenplays:
PRODIGY w/Frank Ray Perilli
SHANGHAI TANGO w/Quinn Redeker
VOSA w/Quinn Redeker
THE EEZMO w/Quinn Redeker
BENYA THE KING

GERRY GARIBALDI*
Contact: WGA - Los Angeles, 310/550-1000

Screenplays:
RAINBOWS
CORNER BOYS

ROBERT GARLAND*
Agent: ICM - Beverly Hills, 310/550-4000

THE ELECTRIC HORSEMAN Columbia, 1979
NO WAY OUT Orion, 1987
THE BIG BLUE Columbia/WEG, 1988, w/Luc Besson

Screenplays:
CITY OF LIGHT
GIANT
DOUBLE
CAPE DISAPPOINTMENT
LANCELOT
THE GULF OF MOSQUITOS
DELAYED REACTION

RAY GARMON
THE LAST RIDERS PM Home Video, 1991, w/Joseph Mehri &
Addison Randall

HELEN GARNER
MONKEY GRIP Cinecom, 1982, w/Ken Cameron
THE LAST DAYS OF CHEZ NOUS Fine Line Features, 1992

TONY GARNETT*
Business Manager: Michael Mesnick, 310/473-9101
Contact: Island World Pictures - London

PROSTITUTE Mainline Films, 1979, directed
DEEP IN THE HEART *HANDGUN* Warner Bros., 1981, directed

JOSEPH GAROFALO*
Contact: WGA - Los Angeles, 310/550-1000

EVIL SPEAK The Frank Moreno Co., 1982, w/Eric Weston

MICK GARRIS*
Agent: CAA - Beverly Hills, 310/288-4545

CRITTERS 2 New Line Cinema, 1988, w/D.T. Twohy, directed
COMING SOON (CTD) Universal Pay TV, 1983, w/John Landis
BATTERIES NOT INCLUDED Universal, 1987, Story
THE FLY II 20th Century Fox, 1989, w/Frank Darabont,
Jim Wheat & Ken Wheat
HOCUS POCUS Buena Vista, 1993, w/Neil Cuthbert

Screenplays:
ALMOST IRRESISTIBLE
DOUBLE VISION
BLACK SHEEP
BLOODSTONE
UNCLE WILLIE
HALLOWEEN HOUSE
RED SLEEP w/Richard Matheson

PAUL GARSON
CYCLONE CineTel Films, 1987, w/T.L. Lankford

LLOYD GARVER*
Agent: Broder-Kurland-Webb-Uffner - Beverly Hills, 310/281-3400

Screenplays:
CHANGE OF HEART

BONNIE GARVIN*
Agent: Candace Lake - Beverly Hills, 310/289-0600
Manager: Lasher McManus Robinson - Los Angeles, 310/446-1466

Screenplays:
SERENADING SIMONE
THE ERNIE GOODMAN STORY
TIME OUT

GEORGE GARY
LOVE IS LIKE THAT Boomerang, 1992

JEROME GARY
Agent: William Morris Agency - Beverly Hills, 310/274-7451

DRAGSTRIP GIRL (CTF) Showtime/Drive-In Classic Cinema, 1994

Screenplays:
TIGER, TIGER

KEN GASS
THE SQUAMISH FIVE CBC Film, 1989, w/Terence McKenna

HAROLD GAST*
Agent: Shapiro/Lichtman - Los Angeles, 310/859-8877

IRONCLADS (CTF) Rosemont Productions, 1991

JOHN GATLIFF
DEATH BEFORE DISHONOR New World, 1987,
w/Lawrence Kubik

ANDREW GATY
Business: AG Productions - Universal Pictures, 818/777-2178

THE RETURN OF CAPTAIN INVINCIBLE   New World, 1983,
   w/Steven E. de Souza

SHANNON GAUGHAN*
Agent: United Talent Agency - Beverly Hills, 310/273-6700

Screenplays:
RAZZLE DAZZLE (CTF)

NILS GAUP
PATHFINDER   International Film Exchange Ltd., 1990, directed
SHIPWRECKED   Buena Vista, 1991, w/Greg Dinner, Bob Foss &
   Nick Thiel, directed

ELEANOR E. GAVER*
Manager: Creative Alliance Management - Los Angeles,
   213/962-6090

DEAD IN THE WATER (CTF)   Kevin Bright Productions/MTE,
   1991, w/Walter Klenhard & Robert Seidenberg

COSTA - GAVRAS
Agent: CAA - Beverly Hills, 310/288-4545

THE SLEEPING CAR MURDERS   7 Arts, 1966,
   Adaptation, directed
Z ★   Cinema 5, 1969, w/Jorge Semprun, directed
MISSING ★★   Universal, 1982, w/Donald Stewart, directed
FAMILY BUSINESS   European Classics, 1987
THE LITTLE APOCALYPSE   K.G. Productions, 1993,
   w/Jean-Claude Grumberg, directed

LAWRENCE GAY*
Agent: CAA - Beverly Hills, 310/288-4545

HOUSEGUEST   Buena Vista, 1995, w/Michael DiGaetano

Screenplays:
PLAYING SHORT w/Michael DiGaetano
BACK TO SCHOOL II w/Michael DiGaetano
DOUBLE VISION w/Michael DiGaetano
THE BIG ONES w/Michael DiGaetano

STEVEN GAYDOS*
Agent: The Parness Agency - Santa Monica, 310/319-1664

Screenplays:
TEQUILA! (Ventana Films)
ARMED RESPONSE w/Rene Balcer

MICHAEL GAYLIN*
Agent: United Talent Agency - Beverly Hills, 310/273-6700

NO ESCAPE   Savoy, 1994, w/Joel Gross

Screenplays:
DOUBLE
SCORPION AND THE SEA
THE KILLING SEASON
SIEGE
THE COVER
BABCOCK ON BAKER STREET (CTF)

ANTHONY GAYTON
Contact: WGA - Los Angeles, 310/550-1000

Screenplays:
CITY KIDS w/Joe Gayton
CHASING KILROY w/Joe Gayton
EDDIE DIBBS MUST DIE! w/Joe Gayton

JOE GAYTON*
Agent: ICM - Beverly Hills, 310/550-4000

UNCOMMON VALOR   Paramount, 1983
WARM SUMMER RAIN   Trans World Entertainment, 1989, directed
SHOUT   Universal, 1991

Screenplays:
THE ENGLANDER w/Pat Cirillo
CITY OF DARKNESS w/Pat Cirillo
CITY KIDS w/Tony Gayton
CHASING KILROY w/Tony Gayton
EDDIE DIBBS MUST DIE! w/Tony Gayton
OF PAWNS AND KNIGHTS
KNIGHTLY DREAMS
KID IRISH SMOKER
PALOOKA

DAN GAZZANIGA
SPECIAL DELIVERY   American International, 1976

DAVID GEEVES
AMERICAN NINJA 4: THE ANNIHILATION   Cannon, 1991

PLEASANT GEHMAN
THE RUNNIN' KIND   MGM/UA, 1990, w/Max Tash

JOHN GEILFUSS*
Agent: Sanford-Gross & Associates - Los Angeles,
   310/208-2100

Screenplays:
HUNTING PYGMIES

TONY GEISS*
Contact: 212/627-5510

SESAME STREET PRESENTS FOLLOW THAT BIRD   Warner Bros.,
   1985, w/Judy Freudberg
AN AMERICAN TAIL (AF)   Universal, 1986, w/Judy Freudberg
THE LAND BEFORE TIME (AF)   Universal, 1987,
   Story w/Judy Freudberg

Screenplays:
OPERATION AMANDA NAVY BRATS w/Judy Freudberg

ARNIE GELBART
THE GUNRUNNER   New World, 1989

LARRY GELBART*
Agent: CAA - Beverly Hills, 310/288-4545
Business Manager: Barry Pollack - Los Angeles, 310/550-4525

SLY FOX (P)   also screenplay
POWER FAILURE (P)
CITY OF ANGELS (P)
A FUNNY THING HAPPENED ON THE WAY TO THE FORUM (P)
   w/Burt Shevelove
THE NOTORIOUS LANDLADY   Columbia, 1962, w/Richard Quine
NOT WITH MY WIFE YOU DON'T   Warner Bros., 1966,
   w/Peter Barnes & Norman Panama
THE WRONG BOX   Columbia, 1966, w/Burt Shevelove
THE CHASTITY BELT   *ON THE WAY TO THE CRUSADES I MET
   A GIRL WHO...*   Warner Bros., 1967, w/Luigi Magri
A FINE PAIR   1968, w/others
OH, GOD! ★   Warner Bros., 1977
MOVIE, MOVIE   Warner Bros., 1978, w/Sheldon Keller
ROUGH CUT   Paramount, 1980, as "Francis Burns"
NEIGHBORS   Columbia, 1981
TOOTSIE ★   Columbia, 1982, w/Murray Schisgal
BLAME IT ON RIO   20th Century Fox, 1984, w/Charlie Peters
MASTERGATE (CTF)   Showtime Entertainment/Rollins-Joffe,
   1992, from his play
BARBARIANS AT THE GATE (CTF)   HBO Pictures, 1993

Screenplays:
THE NUTTY PROFESSOR (remake)
NOTHING SACRED
JAZZ BABIES
KILL-IN
NOBODY LIKES AN HONEST COP
UNITED STATES
HOTEL ROYALE
MOVIE, MOVIE II
TWO + TWO

MARK GELDMAN*
Agent: Stone Manners Agency - Los Angeles, 213/654-7575

CYBORG 2: GLASS SHADOW   Trimark, 1993,
   w/Michael Scroeder & Ron Yanover
THE JUNGLE BOOK   Buena Vista, 1994, w/Ron Yanover &
   Stephen Sommers

Screenplays:
TOM THUMB w/Ron Yanover (MDP Worldwide)

STEPHEN GELLER*
Agent: Joel Behr, Behr & Robinson - 310/556-9222

SLAUGHTERHOUSE FIVE   Universal, 1971
ASHANTI   Columbia, 1970
SEE NO EVIL   Columbia, 1971
THE VALACHI PAPERS   *JOE VALACHI: I SEGRETI DI*
   COSA NOSTRA Columbia, 1972

Screenplays:
GOOD AS GOLD

JONATHAN GEMS*
Agent: William Morris Agency - Beverly Hills, 310/274-7451

WHITE MISCHIEF   Columbia, 1988, w/Michael Radford

Screenplays:
HOUSE OF USHER
BLACK ICE (Story)

MICHAEL GENET
Agent: William Morris Agency - New York, 212/586-5100

Screenplays:
PORK PIE
STAGGER LEE

PETER GENT*
Agent: Sterling Lord Literistic - New York, 212/696-2800
Contact: 616/382-3784

NORTH DALLAS FORTY   Paramount, 1979, w/Ted Kotcheff &
   Frank Yablans

ANTHONY GENTILE*
Contact: WGA - Los Angeles, 310/550-1000

FATAL MISSION   Funahara, 1990, w/Peter Fonda,
   Chosei Funahara, John Gentile & George Rowe

JOHN GENTILE*
Contact: WGA - Los Angeles, 310/550-1000

FATAL MISSION   Funahara, 1990, w/Peter Fonda,
   Anthony Gentile, Chosei Funahara & George Rowe

LANCE GENTILE
Agent: Media Artsts Group - Beverly Hills, 213/658-7434

STATE OF EMERGENCY (CTF)   Chestnut Hill, 1994,
   w/Susan Black

ROBERT GEOFFRION
Agent: Gray/Goodman Inc. - Beverly Hills, 310/276-7070

HONEYMOON   International Film Marketing, 1987,
   w/Patrick Jamian & Phillipe Setbon
THE HIT MAN   Cannon, 1991, w/Don Carmody

Screenplays:
SCREAM OF STONE
EDEN RIVER

JIM GEOGHAN*
Agent: The Irv Schechter Company - Beverly Hills, 310/278-8070

ONLY KIDDING (P)
LIGHT SENSITIVE (P)
STOOGEMANIA   Atlantic Releasing Corporation, 1986,
   w/Chuck Workman

JON A. GEORGE*
Agent: Preferred Artists - Encino, 818/990-0305

ESCAPE 2000   New World, 1983, w/Neill Hicks
THE FINAL TERROR   Comworld, 1983, w/Neill Hicks &
   Ronald Shusett
DON'T TALK TO STRANGERS (CTF)   MCA Television
   Entertainment, 1994, w/Neill Hicks & Nevin Schreiner

NELSON GEORGE*
Contact: WGA - New York, 212/245-6180

STRICTLY BUSINESS   Warner Bros., 1991, w/Pam Gibson
CB4   Universal, 1993, w/Robert LoCash & Chris Rock

PETER GEORGE
YOUNG GOODMAN BROWN   50th Street Films, 1993, directed

TERRY GEORGE*
Agent: ICM - Beverly Hills, 310/550-4000

IN THE NAME OF THE FATHER ★   Universal, 1993,
   w/Jim Sheridan

Screenplays:
THE GIRL IN THE AIR (remake)

ALEX GEORGES
CULTIVATING CHARLIE   GMS Productions, 1994, directed

GARY GERANI
PUMPKINHEAD   MGM/UA, 1988, w/Mark Patrick Carducci

BILL GERBER*
Manager: Arlene Rothberg Management - 310/276-2214

Screenplays:
DADDY'S LITTLE GIRL
HER SIDE OF THE FAMILY

CRAIG GERBER
Agent: Annette Van Duren Agency - Los Angeles, 213/650-3643

Screenplays:
GRANDALUSIAN

CHRIS GEROLMO*
Agent: CAA - Beverly Hills, 310/288-4545

MILES FROM HOME   Cinecom International, 1988
MISSISSIPPI BURNING   Orion, 1989
WITNESS (Short)   Showtime Entertainment, 1993, directed

Screenplays:
CITIZEN X (CTF)
NO EXCUSE

F
I
L
M

W
R
I
T
E
R
S

GLENN GERS
Agent: Lisa Callamaro Literary Agency- Beverly Hills, 310/274-6783

Screenplays:
ANONYMOUS MEN IN SUITS

LEONARD GERSHE*
Contact: WGA - Los Angeles, 310/550-1000

FUNNY FACE ★   Paramount, 1956
SILK STOCKINGS   MGM, 1957, w/Leonard Spiegelgass
BUTTERFLIES ARE FREE   Columbia, 1972, from his play
FORTY CARATS   Columbia, 1973, from his play

TED GERSHUNY*
Agent: Kaplan-Stahler - Beverly Hills, 213/653-4483

FAR FROM HOME   Vestron, 1989, Story

Screenplays:
"M" w/David Loucka

DOUCHAN GERSI
Contact: Cineville, 310/394-4699

Screenplays:
JOURNEY INTO THE HEART OF DARKNESS
   w/Kurt Voss (directing)

ALEXANDRA GERSTEN
Agent: Writers & Artists Agency - New York, 212/947-8765

MY THING OF LOVE (P)

NICHOLAS GESSNER
QUICKER THAN THE EYE   Eural Films/FR3/Condor Films, 1988,
   w/Joseph Morhaim, directed

ROBERT GETCHELL
Agent: CAA - Beverly Hills, 310/288-4545

ALICE DOESN'T LIVE HERE ANY MORE ★   Warner Bros., 1974
BOUND FOR GLORY ★   United Artists, 1976
MOMMIE DEAREST   Paramount, 1981, w/Frank Perry,
   Tracy Hotchner & Frank Yablans
SWEET DREAMS   Tri-Star, 1985
STELLA   Buena Vista, 1990
POINT OF NO RETURN   Warner Bros., 1993, w/Alexandra Seros
THIS BOY'S LIFE   Warner Bros., 1993
THE CLIENT   Warner Bros., 1994, w/Akiva Goldsman

Screenplays:
FROM ALICE TO OCEAN
SHIBUMI
ROADSHOW w/James Bridges
THE LIGHT FANTASTIC
CIVIL WARS

ERIC GETHERS*
Contact: WGA - Los Angeles, 310/550-1000

Screenplays:
THE MAVEN
HILDY
LIFE UPSIDE DOWN

CRAIG GHOLSON
ADJUSTABLE POSITIONS (P)   also screenplay

STACEY GIACHINO
THE DORM THAT DRIPPED BLOOD   *PRANKS*
   Artists Releasing Corporation/Film Ventures International,
   1982, w/Jeffrey Obrow & Stephen Carpenter

JOE GIANNONE
MADMAN   Jensen Farley Pictures, 1982, directed

JOE GIBBONS
THE GENIUS   Fugitive Productions, 1993,
   w/Emily Breer, co-directed

PETER GIBBS
ARTHUR'S HALLOWED GROUND   Cinecom, 1986

STUART GIBBS
Manager: Ogden House - Los Angeles, 213/851-0458

Screenplays:
TEN WOMEN, NO SANDWICH

BRIAN GIBSON
Agent: ICM - Beverly Hills, 310/550-4000

BREAKING GLASS   Paramount, 1980, directed

PAM GIBSON*
Contact: WGA - New York, 212/245-6180

STRICTLY BUSINESS   Warner Bros., 1991, w/Nelson George

WILLIAM GIBSON*
Agent: Shapiro/Lichtman - Los Angeles, 310/859-8877

JOHNNY MNEUMONIC   TriStar, 1995

NELSON GIDDING*
Agent: Wile Enterprises - Santa Monica, 310/828-9768

THE HELEN MORGAN STORY   Warner Bros., 1957,
   w/Oscar Saul, Dean Reisner & Stephen Longstreet
I WANT TO LIVE! ★   United Artists, 1958, w/Don Mankiewicz
ONIONHEAD   Warner Bros., 1958
ODDS AGAINST TOMORROW   United Artists, 1959,
   w/John O. Killens
THE INSPECTOR   20th Century-Fox, 1961
NINE HOURS TO RAMA   20th Century-Fox, 1962
THE HAUNTING   MGM, 1963
THE LOST COMMAND   Columbia/Red Lion, 1966
SKULLDUGGERY   Universal, 1970
THE ANDROMEDA STRAIN   Universal, 1971
THE HINDENBURG   Universal, 1975
BEYOND THE POSEIDON ADVENTURE   Warner Bros., 1979

Screenplays:
FORBIDDEN PLANET (remake)

RAYNOLD GIDEON*
Agent: CAA - Beverly Hills, 310/288-4545

A MAN, A WOMAN AND A BANK   Avco Embassy, 1979,
   w/Bruce Evans
STARMAN   Columbia, 1984, w/Bruce Evans
STAND BY ME ★   Columbia, 1986, w/Bruce Evans
MADE IN HEAVEN   Lorimar, 1987, w/Bruce Evans
KUFFS   Universal, 1992, w/Bruce Evans

Screenplays:
BLACK RICE w/Bruce Evans
THE BETHUNE w/Bruce Evans
CHRISTMAS IN JULY w/Bruce Evans
THE DAY BEFORE MIDNIGHT w/Bruce Evans

JAMES GIERMAN*
Agent: Lucy Kroll Agency - New York, 212/877-0627

Screenplays:
CLIPPED w/Kim Buckley

MARIA GIESE
Agent: Camden-ITG - Los Angeles, 310/289-2700

A DRY HEAT (Short) 1991, directed
JEWISH WATER (Short) 1993, directed

Screenplays:
A PINT OF BITTER
CHE GUEVARA
ELECTRIC WARRIOR

CAMILLE GIFFORD
DIRTY TRICKS   Avco Embassy, w/Thomas Gifford,
   Eleanor Elias Norton & William W. Norton Sr.

THOMAS GIFFORD*
Contact: The Robbins Office - New York, 212/223-0720

DIRTY TRICKS   Avco Embassy, w/Camille Gifford,
   Eleanor Elias Norton & William W. Norton Sr.

JONATHAN D. GIFT
VALHALLA   Arclight Film, 1992, directed

KEITH GIGLIO
Agent: Innovative Artists - Los Angeles, 310/553-5200
Manager: Jonathan Baruch, PRO Management - Los Angeles,
   310/478-5159

Screenplays:
THE BROADWAY BRAWLER w/Juliet Aires
WELCOME TO THE FAMILY w/Juliet Aires
VERONA w/Juliet Aires
THE SENTINEL w/Juliet Aires
STRINGER

BEE GILBERT
SALT ON OUR SKIN   Warner Bros. Transatlantic, 1993,
   w/Andrew Birkin

BRAD GILBERT
Contact: Monument Pictures, 8391 Beverly Blvd. - Suite 141,
   Los Angeles, CA 90048, 213/243-5277

TOUCH OF A STRANGER   Raven-Star Pictures, 1990,
   w/Joslyn Barnes, directed

BRIAN GILBERT
Agent: CAA - Beverly Hills, 310/288-4545

FRENCH LESSON   *THE FROG PRINCE*   Warner Bros.,
   1984, Adaptation, directed
SHARMA AND BEYOND   Cinecom, 1986, directed

BRUCE GILBERT
Contact: American Filmworks, 222 N. Canon Dr. - Suite 201,
   Beverly Hills, CA 90210, 310/288-0566

BY DAWN'S EARLY LIGHT (CTF)   HBO/Panavision
   International, 1990

HUGO GILBERT
Contact: Ziffren, Brittenham & Branca - Beverly Hills, 310/552-3388

HOT TO TROT   Warner Bros., 1988, w/Stephen Neigher &
   Charlie Peters

LEWIS GILBERT
Contact: Gang, Tyre & Brown - Los Angeles, 213/463-4863

HUNDRED HOUR HUNT   *EMERGENCY CALL*   Greshler, 1952,
   w/Vernon Harris, directed
THE GOOD DIE YOUNG   United Artists, 1954,
   w/Vernon Harris, directed

THE SEA SHALL NOT HAVE THEM   Eros, 1954,
   w/Vernon Harris, directed
REACH FOR THE SKY   Rank, 1956, directed
CARVE HER NAME WITH PRIDE   Lopert, 1958,
   w/Vernon Harris, directed
FERRY TO HONG KONG   20th Century-Fox, 1958,
   w/Vernon Harris, directed
THE ADVENTURERS   Paramount, 1970,
   w/Michael Hastings, directed
HAUNTED   Lumiere, 1995, directed

VIRGINIA GILBERT
THE FINAL MISSION   Trimark, 1993, w/Sam Montgomery, Lee
   Redmond & Ernest Sheldon Jr.

DAVID K. GILER*
Agent: ICM - Beverly Hills, 310/550-4000

MYRA BRECKINRIDGE   20th Century-Fox, 1970, w/Mike Sarne
THE PARALLAX VIEW   Paramount, 1974, w/Lorenzo Semple Jr.
THE BLACK BIRD   Columbia, 1975, directed
FUN WITH DICK AND JANE   Columbia, 1977, w/Jerry Belson &
   Mordecai Richler
SOUTHERN COMFORT   20th Century-Fox, 1981, w/Walter Hill &
   Michael Kane
THE MONEY PIT   Universal, 1986
ALIENS   20th Century Fox, 1986, Story w/James Cameron &
   Walter Hill
ALIEN 3   20th Century Fox, 1992, w/Larry Ferguson & Walter Hill

Screenplays:
THE KILLER w/Walter Hill (remake)
RICH PEOPLE HAVING FUN w/Lynne Giler
LA CAGE AUX FOLLES, USA w/Reinhold Weege
SPIRITS

LYNNE D. GILER*
Contact: WGA - Los Angeles, 310/550-1000

Screenplays:
RICH PEOPLE HAVING FUN w/David Giler
TALKING DIRTY
SILHOUETTES
SEX TIPS FOR GIRLS
KRIPPENDORF'S TRIBE

STUART GILLARD*
Agent: ICM - Beverly Hills, 310/550-4000
Manager: Jon Brown, The Brown Group - Burbank, 818/955-7040

PARADISE   Avco Embassy, 1982, directed
IF YOU COULD SEE WHAT I HEAR   Jensen FarleyPictures, 1982
SPRING FEVER   Comworld, 1983, w/Fred Stefan
A MAN CALLED SARGE   Cannon, 1990, directed
TEENAGE MUTANT NINJA TURTLES III: THE TURTLES ARE
   BACK...IN TIME   New Line Cinema, 1993, directed

Screenplays:
THE GOLDEN IDOL (directing)

TERRY GILLIAM
Agent: CAA - Beverly Hills, 310/288-4545

AND NOW FOR SOMETHING COMPLETELY DIFFERENT
   Columbia, 1972, w/Graham Chapman, John Cleese, Eric Idle,
   Terry Jones & Michael Palin
MONTY PYTHON AND THE HOLY GRAIL   Cinema 5, 1974,
   w/Graham Chapman, John Cleese, Eric Idle, Terry Jones &
   Michael Palin, directed
JABBERWOCKY   Cinema 5, 1977,
   w/Charles Alverson, directed
MONTY PYTHON'S LIFE OF BRIAN   Orion/Warner Bros., 1979,
   w/Graham Chapman, John Cleese, Eric Idle, Terry Jones &
   Michael Palin
TIME BANDITS   Avco Embassy, 1981, w/Michael Palin, directed

**F
I
L
M

W
R
I
T
E
R
S**

MONTY PYTHON LIVE AT THE HOLLYWOOD BOWL   Columbia,
   1982, w/Graham Chapman, John Cleese, Eric Idle, Terry Jones &
   Michael Palin
MONTY PYTHON'S THE MEANING OF LIFE   Universal, 1983,
   w/Graham Chapman, John Cleese, Eric Idle, Terry Jones &
   Michael Palin, directed
BRAZIL ★   Universal, 1985, w/Charles McKeown &
   Tom Stoppard, directed
THE ADVENTURES OF BARON MUNCHAUSEN   Columbia, 1988,
   w/Charles McKeown, directed

Screenplays:
THE DEFECTIVE DETECTIVE w/Richard La Gravenese

VINCE GILLIGAN*
(George Vincent Gilligan Jr.)
Agent: Broder-Kurland-Webb-Uffner - Beverly Hills, 310/281-3400

WILDER NAPALM   TriStar, 1993

Screenplays:
HOME FRIES (Warner Bros.)
TWO FACE

ERIC GILLILAND*
Agent: ICM - Beverly Hills, 310/550-4000

EYE OF THE STORM   World Wide Pictures, 1992,
   w/John Shepherd

BETTINA GILOIS*
Agent: ICM - Beverly Hills, 310/550-4000

Screenplays:
THE MISTS OF AVALON
PARADISE, KANSAS

DAN GILROY*
Agent: CAA - Beverly Hills, 310/288-4545

FREEJACK   Warner Bros., 1992, w/Steven Pressfield &
   Ronald Shusett
CHASERS   Warner Bros., 1994, w/Joe Batteer & John Rice

FRANK D. GILROY*
Contact: WGA - New York, 212/245-6180

ANY GIVEN DAY (P)
THE FASTEST GUN ALIVE   MGM, 1956, w/Russel Rouse
THE GALLANT HOURS   United Artists, 1959, w/Beirne Lay Jr.
THE SUBJECT WAS ROSES   MGM, 1968, from his play
THE ONLY GAME IN TOWN   20th Century-Fox, 1969, from his play
DESPERATE CHARACTERS   ITC, 1971, directed
FROM NOON TIL THREE   United Artists, 1976, directed
ONCE IN PARIS...   Atlantic Releasing Corporation, 1978, directed
JINXED   MGM/UA, 1982, as "Bert Blessing," w/David Newman
THE GIG   Castle Hill Productions, 1985, directed
THE LUCKIEST MAN IN THE WORLD   Co-Star Entertainment,
   1989, directed

Screenplays:
WHAT I DID THAT SUMMER

TONY GILROY*
Agent: ICM - Beverly Hills, 310/550-4000

THE CUTTING EDGE   MGM, 1992
DOLORES CLAIBORNE   Columbia, 1995

Screenplays:
DESPERATION ANGELS
PRAY FOR RAIN
R.S.V.P.

BRYAN GINDOFF*
Contact: WGA - Los Angeles, 310/550-1000

HARD TIMES   Columbia, 1975, w/Bruce Henstell & Walter Hill
LOSIN' IT   Embassy, 1983, Story w/B.W.L. Norton

STEVE GINSBERG
Agent: The Rothman Agency - Beverly Hills, 213/655-2020

FAMILY PRAYERS   Arrow Entertainment, 1993

ROBERT GINTY*
Agent: ICM - Beverly Hills, 310/550-4000

WOMAN OF DESIRE   Nu Image, 1993, directed

Screenplays:
NEW YORK COP (Sunstripe Pictures)
DEVIL AND THE DEEP BLUE SEA w/Tony Palmer
TRACKDOWN w/John A. Gallagher

UGO GIORGETTI
FESTA   NDR Films, 1990, directed

BUDDY GIOVINAZZO
SHE'S BACK   Vestron, 1989

GEORGE GIPE
THE LIVING END (P)
DEAD MEN DON'T WEAR PLAID   Universal, 1982,
   w/Steve Martin & Carl Reiner
THE MAN WITH TWO BRAINS   Warner Bros., 1983,
   w/Steve Martin & Carl Reiner

Screenplays:
HOT SHEET
THE PICTURE OF GORIAN DAY
DOMINANT GENES
BULL
PRINCE CHARMING
MANHATTAN STAGECOACH
ROAD TO RUIN
THE ADVENTURES OF WILLIE & MADELINE
OPUS ONE
ACES

BERNARD GIRARD
THE BIG PUNCH   Warner Bros., 1948
BREAKTHROUGH   Warner Bros., 1950, w/Joseph L. Breen Jr. &
   Ted Sherdeman
DEAD HEAT ON A MERRY-GO-ROUND   Paramount,
   1966, directed
THE MAD ROOM   Columbia, 1969, w/A.Z. Martin, directed

FRANCOIS GIRARD
Agent: Becsey/Wisdom/Kalajian Agency - Los Angeles, 310/550-0535

THIRTY-TWO SHORT FILMS ABOUT GLENN GOULD
   Samuel Goldwyn Company, 1994, w/Don McKellar, directed

MICHAEL PAUL GIRARD
GETTING LUCKY   Vista Street Productions, 1990, directed

JEAN GIRAUD
(MOEBIUS)
LITTLE NEMO: ADVENTURES IN SLUMBERLAND (AF)   Hemdale,
   1992, Story w/Yukata Fujioka

Screenplays:
STARWATCHER (AF) w/Jackye Fryscman (Paramount)

GILBERT GIRION
AMERICAN BLUE NOTE   Panorama Entertainment, 1991

JACKELYN GIROUX
FOREVER   Triax Entertainment Group, 1992, w/Thomas Palmer Jr.

Screenplays:
BOLT (Multipix Productions)

RICK GITELSON*
Agent: William Morris Agency - Beverly Hills, 310/274-7451

Screenplays:
FAMILY MAN
DUKE AND FLUFFY w/Eric Freiser
ABOVE AND BEYOND w/Eric Freiser

ANTHONY H. GITTELSON*
Agent: William Morris Agency - Beverly Hills, 310/274-7451

Screenplays:
WITCHCRAFT w/Celia Gittelson
DAYS OF AWE KABALAH w/Celia Gittelson

CELIA GITTELSON*
Agent: William Morris Agency - Beverly Hills, 310/274-7451

Screenplays:
WITCHCRAFT w/Tony Gittelson
DAYS OF AWE KABALAH w/Tony Gittelson

ROBERT GITTLER
THE BUDDY HOLLY STORY   Columbia, 1978

JOYCE GITTLIN*
Agent: William Morris Agency - Beverly Hills, 310/274-7451

Screenplays:
NEXT OF KIN w/Jeffrey Richman
DIRTY WORDS w/Jeffrey Richman

RICHARD N. GLADSTEIN
SILENT NIGHT, DEADLY NIGHT III: YOU BETTER WATCH OUT!
   Quiet Fims, 1989, Story w/Monte Hellman & Carlos Lazlo

STEPHEN GLANTZ*
Agent: The Agency - Los Angeles, 310/551-3000

SHOWDOWN IN LITTLE TOKYO   Warner Bros., 1991,
   w/Caliope Brattlestreet

Screenplays:
THE GOLDEN 13 w/Caliope Brattlestreet
DANCING CROSS THE RIVER w/Caliope Brattlestreet
JUNKYARD DOGS w/Caliope Brattlestreet
MEN OF BRONZE w/Caliope Brattlestreet
GROWING UP RICH w/Caliope Brattlestreet
SKIPTRACER w/Caliope Brattlestreet

ROBERT GLASS*
Contact: WGA - Los Angeles, 310/550-1000

RUNNING AGAINST TIME (CTF)   Finnegun-Pinchuk Productions,
   1990, w/Stanley Shapiro
DEATH DREAMS (CTF)   Ultra Entertainment/Dick Clark Film
   Group Inc., 1991

Screenplays:
NIGHT VISIONS
ACTS OF GOD (CTF)

SANDY GLASS*
Contact: WGA - Los Angeles, 310/550-1000

THE LAST FLIGHT OF NOAH'S ARK   Buena Vista, 1980,
   w/Steve Carabatsos & George Arthur Bloom

BARRY GLASSER
Agent: The Brandt Company - Sherman Oaks, 818/783-7747

GOLD DIGGERS   Universal, 1995

LEONARD GLASSER*
Agent: Preferred Artists - Encino, 818/990-0305

OUT COLD   Hemdale, 1989, w/George Malko

RICHARD GLATZER*
Agent: United Talent Agency - Beverly Hills, 310/273-6700

GRIEF   Strand Releasing, 1994, directed

MITCH GLAZER*
(Mitchell Aram Glazer)
Agent: CAA - Beverly Hills, 310/288-4545

MR. MIKE'S MONDO VIDEO   New Line Cinema, 1979,
   w/Michael O'Donoghue, Emily Prager & Dirk Wittenborn
SCROOGED   Paramount, 1988, w/Michael O'Donoghue
OFF AND RUNNING   Rank Film Distribution, 1992
THREE OF HEARTS   New Line Cinema, 1993, w/Adam Greenman

Screenplays:
MOON OVER MIAMI
ARRIVE ALIVE w/Michael O'Donoghue
LOLA w/Michael O'Donoghue
THE HOUSE GUEST w/Michael O'Donoghue
A FISH STORY
KINGPIN
BUNCO

MICHAEL GLEASON*
Agent: ICM - Beverly Hills, 310/550-4000

FAST CHARLIE...THE MOONBEAM RIDER   Universal, 1979

MICHIE GLEASON
SUMMER HEAT   Atlantic Releasing Corporation, 1987, directed

JAMES GLICKENHAUS
Business: Shapiro Glickenhaus Entertainment, 12001 Ventura Place -
   Suite 404, Studio City, CA 91604, 818/766-8500

THE ASTROLOGER   Interstar, 1977, directed
THE EXTERMINATOR   Avco Embassy, 1980, directed
THE SOLDIER   Embassy, 1982, directed
THE PROTECTOR   Warner Bros., 1985, directed
SHAKEDOWN   Universal, 1988, directed
ROOM AT THE END OF THE UNIVERSE   Shapiro-Glickenhaus,
   1989, directed
McBAIN   Shaprio-Glickenhaus, 1991, directed
SLAUGHTER OF THE INNOCENTS   Shapiro-Glickenhaus,
   1993, directed

GREG GLIENNA
Agent: ICM - Beverly Hills, 310/550-4000

MEET THE PARENTS   C.E.M. Productions, 1992
   w/Mary Ruth Clarke, directed

ALAN JAY GLUECKMAN*
Contact: Bloom, Dekom, Hergott & Cook - Los Angeles, 310/278-8622

NIGHT WARNING   Comworld, 1983, w/Stephen Breimer &
   Boom Collins
RUSSKIES   New Century Entertainment, 1988, w/Sheldon Lettich &
   Michael Nankin
GROSS ANATOMY   Buena Vista, 1990, Story w/Stanley Isaacs,
   Howard Rosenman & Mark Spragg
THE FEAR INSIDE (CTF)   Viacom Pictures, 1992, Story

Screenplays:
THE WORST MOVIE EVER MADE
THE DICK AND THE DOC
DAREDEVILS OF THE GOLDEN LEGION
THE NEXT PRESIDENT OF THE U.S.A.
BRIDE AND GROOM
SAVAGE RED
PEEL MY BANANA

JEAN-LUC GODARD
Contact: French Film Office, 745 Fifth Avenue, New York, NY 10151, 212/832-8860

BAND OF OUTSIDERS   Royal Films International, 1964, directed
THE MARRIED WOMAN   Royal Films International, 1964, directed
ALPHAVILLE   Pathe Contemporary, 1965, directed
THE OLDEST PROFESSION   Goldstone, 1967, Shared, directed
SAUVE QUI PEUT LA VIE   *EVERY MAN FOR HIMSELF IN LIFE*
   New Yorker/Zoetrope, 1980, w/Jean-Claude Carriere &
   Anne-Marie Mieville, directed
PASSION   United Artists Classics, 1983, directed
DETECTIVE   Spectrafilm, 1985, w/Anne-Marie Mieville,
   Alain Sarde & Philippe Setbon
NOUVELLE VOGUE (NEW WAVE)   Vega Film SA, 1990, directed
GERMANY NINE ZERO   Brainstorm-Antenne 2, 1991, directed
HELAS POUR MOI (OH, WOE IS ME)   Vega Film, 1993, directed

GARY W. GODDARD*
Agent: CAA - Beverly Hills, 310/288-4545

TARZAN, THE APE MAN   MGM/United Artists, 1981, w/Tom Rowe

Screenplays:
MAJOR, MAJOR
SPACE COMMANDS

MARK GODDARD
BIG GIRLS DON'T CRY...THEY GET EVEN   New Line Cinema,
   1992, Story w/Melissa Goddard & Frank Mugavero

MELISSA GODDARD
Contact: Joshua Grode, Silverberg, Katz, Thompson & Braun
Business: MG Entertainment, New World Entertainment -
   Los Angeles, 310/444-8189

BIG GIRLS DON'T CRY...THEY GET EVEN   New Line Cinema,
   1992, Story w/Mark Goddard & Frank Mugavero

LIBERTY GODSHALL*
Agent: United Talent Agency - Beverly Hills, 310/273-6700

Screenplays:
FRANKIE IN THE RAIN

IVAN GOFF*
Contact: WGA - Los Angeles, 310/550-1000

BACKFIRE   Warner Bros., 1949, w/Larry Marcus & Ben Roberts
GOODBYE MY FANCY   Warner Bros., 1951, w/Ben Roberts
CAPTAIN HORATIO HORNBLOWER   Warner Bros., 1951,
   w/Aeneas Mackenzie & Ben Roberts
COME FILL THE CUP   Warner Bros., 1951, w/Ben Roberts
GREEN FIRE   MGM, 1954, w/Ben Roberts
KING OF THE KYBER RIFLES   20th Century-Fox, 1954,
   w/Ben Roberts
SERENADE   Warner Bros., 1956, w/Ben Roberts & John Twist
MAN OF A THOUSAND FACES   Universal-International, 1957,
   w/Ben Roberts & R. Wright Campbell
BAND OF ANGELS   Warner Bros., 1957, w/Ben Roberts &
   John Twist
SHAKE HANDS WITH THE DEVIL   United Artists, 1959,
   w/Ben Roberts
PORTRAIT IN BLACK   Universal-International, 1960,
   w/Ben Roberts
MIDNIGHT LACE   Universal, 1960, w/Ben Roberts
THE LEGEND OF THE LONE RANGER   Universal/AFD, 1981,
   w/Michael Kane, Ben Roberts & William Roberts

JOHN GOFF*
Contact: WGA - Los Angeles, 310/550-1000

BUTTERFLY   Analysis, 1981, w/Matt Cimber
THE NIGHT STALKER   Almi Pictures, 1987, w/Don Edmonds
DEADLY INTENT   Fries Entertainment, 1988
HIT LIST   New Line Cinema, 1989, w/Peter Brosnan

MENAHEM GOLAN*
Contact: WGA - Los Angeles, 310/550-1000
Business: International Dynamic Pictures

DIAMONDS   Avco Embassy, 1975, w/David Paulsen, directed
THE MAGICIAN OF LUBLIN   Cannon, 1979,
   w/Irving S. White, directed
THE APPLE   Cannon, 1980, directed
ENTER THE NINJA   Cannon, 1981, w/Dick Desmond &
   Judd Bernard, directed
SAHARA   MGM/UA, 1984, Story
HOT CHILI   Cannon, 1985, w/William Sachs
THE DELTA FORCE   Cannon, 1986, w/James Bruner, directed
HANNA'S WAR   Cannon, 1988, w/Stanley Mann, directed
THE FORBIDDEN DANCE   Columbia, 1990,
   Story as "Joseph Goldman"
MACK THE KNIFE   21st Century Film Corp, 1990, directed
HIT THE DUTCHMAN!   21st Century Film Corp, 1992,
   as "Joseph Goldman," directed
DEADLY HEROS   Trimark, 1993

LEE GOLD
A CAPTIVE IN THE LAND   Vision International, 1991

LUCKY GOLD
Agent: The Tantleff Office - New York, 212/941-3939

THE SECRET PASSION OF ROBERT CLAYTON (CTF)
   Wilshire Court Productions, 1992, Story w/Brian Ross

Screenplays:
THROUGH THE NIGHTSHADE
BEFORE I WAKE

SANDRA GOLDBACHER
Agent: Rochelle Stevens & Co. - London, 071/359-3900

SEVENTEEN (Short)   directed

Screenplays:
BLISS (directing)

DAN GOLDBERG*
Agent: CAA - Beverly Hills, 310/288-4545
Business: Ivan Reitman Productions, Universal Studios -
   818/777-8080

MEATBALLS   Paramount, 1979, w/Janis Allen, Len Blum &
   Harold Ramis
STRIPES   Columbia, 1981, w/Len Blum & Harold Ramis
HEAVY METAL (AF)   Columbia, 1981, w/Len Blum
SPACEHUNTER: ADVENTURES IN THE
FORBIDDEN ZONE   Columbia, 1983, w/Len Blum, Edith Rey &
   David Preston
FEDS   Warner Bros., 1988, w/Len Blum, directed

Screenplays:
RABBIT BOY   w/Len Blum
WIDOWS   w/Len Blum

DICK GOLDBERG*
Agent: Ken Sherman & Associates - Beverly Hills, 310/273-8840

THE LONG, COLD SUMMER (P)
COMRADES (P)
SLICK SLOAN AND THE CASE OF THE MISSING EGGS (P)
WONDROUS VISIONS (P)
FAMILY BUSINESS (P)
THE IMAGEMAKER   Castle Hill Productions, 1986, w/Hal Weiner

GARY DAVID GOLDBERG*
Agent: United Talent Agency - Beverly Hills, 310/273-6700

DAD   Universal, 1989, directed
BYE, BYE LOVE   20th Century Fox, 1995, w/Brad Hall

Screenplays:
COMING OF AGE IN NEW YORK CITY   MARVIN AND SARA
SON OF GREASE   GREASIER
SILKY
REEL TO REEL

HARRIS GOLDBERG*
Contact: WGA - Los Angeles, 310/550-1000

Screenplays:
SOCIAL STUDIES   w/Nancy Miller
ESCAPE FROM WANNA WANNA   w/Tom Nursall
GETTING EVEN   w/Tom Nursall

HOWARD GOLDBERG
SPONTANEOUS COMBUSTION   Taurus Entertainment, 1990,
   w/Tobe Hooper

Screenplays:
APPLE PIE
EDEN

LEE GOLDBERG*
Agent: Shapiro/Lichtman - Los Angeles, 310/859-8877

Screenplays:
.357 VIGILANTE   w/Bill Rabkin
BLADE   w/Bill Rabkin

MARSHALL GOLDBERG*
Agent: William Morris Agency - Beverly Hills, 310/274-7451

Screenplays:
HOLY WARS

MICHAEL GOLDBERG*
Agent: CAA - Beverly Hills, 310/288-4545

COOL RUNNINGS   Buena Vista, 1993, w/Tommy Swerdlow &
   Lynn Siefert
LITTLE GIANTS   Warner Bros., 1994, w/Tommy Swerdlow,
   James Ferguson & Robert Shallcross

PHILIP GOLDBERG*
Agent: Wile Enterprises - Santa Monica, 310/828-9768

Screenplays:
THIS IS NEXT YEAR

DAN GOLDEN
NAKED OBSESSION   Concorde, 1991,
   Story w/Roger Dodson, directed

DAVID GOLDEN
Agent: Renaissance-H.N. Swanson - Los Angeles, 310/246-6000

Screenplays:
TWO BY TWO   w/Jay Rosen
O POSITIVE   w/Jay Rosen

JOHN GOLDEN*
Contact: WGA - New York, 212/245-6180

SAMANTHA   Planet Productions Corp., 1992,
   w/Stephen La Rocque

MICHAEL GOLDENBERG*
Agent: ICM - Beverly Hills, 310/550-4000

AMELIA AND THE KING OF PLANTS   New Line Cinema, 1995, directed

Screenplays:
THE INTERPRETATION OF DREAMS

MARTHA GOLDHIRSH*
Agent: United Talent Agency - Beverly Hills, 310/273-6700

SIBLING RIVALRY   Columbia, 1990

Screenplays:
BABY PICTURES
MY TWO HUSBANDS
FAMILY MAN
AUGUST IN MANHATTAN

DANIEL GOLDIN*
Agent: ICM - Beverly Hills, 310/550-4000

DARKMAN   Universal, 1990, w/Josh Goldin, Chuck Pfarrer,
   Ivan Raimi & Sam Raimi
OUT ON A LIMB   Universal, 1992, w/Josh Goldin

Screenplays:
JEFFREY OF ARABIA   w/Josh Goldin
LIFE AFTER LIFE   w/Josh Goldin
MATES   w/Josh Goldin

JOSHUA P. GOLDIN*
Agent: ICM - Beverly Hills, 310/550-4000

DARKMAN   Universal, 1990, w/Daniel Goldin, Chuck Pfarrer,
   Ivan Raimi & Sam Raimi
OUT ON A LIMB   Universal, 1992, w/Daniel Goldin

Screenplays:
JEFFREY OF ARABIA   w/Dan Goldin
LIFE AFTER LIFE   w/Dan Goldin
MATES   w/Dan Goldin

MARILYN GOLDIN
Contact: French Film Office, 745 Fifth Avenue, New York, NY 10151,
   212/832-8860

BAROCCO   1976
CAMILLE CLAUDEL   Orion Classics, 1989, w/Bruno Nuytten

PAUL GOLDING*
Contact: WGA - Los Angeles, 310/550-1000

BEAT STREET   Orion, 1984, w/Andy Davis & David Gilbert
PULSE   Columbia, 1988, directed

Screenplays:
BREAKFAST OF CHAMPIONS

B.J. GOLDMAN
TRIPWIRE   CineTel Films, 1989, w/James Lemmo

BO GOLDMAN*
Agent: CAA - Beverly Hills, 310/288-4545

ONE FLEW OVER THE CUCKOO'S NEST ★★   United Artists, 1976,
   w/Lawrence Hauben
THE ROSE   20th Century-Fox, 1979, w/Bill Kerby
MELVIN AND HOWARD ★★   Universal, 1980
SHOOT THE MOON   MGM/UA, 1982
SWING SHIFT   Warner Bros., 1983, w/Nancy Dowd &
   Ron Nyswaner as "Rob Morton"
LITTLE NIKITA   Columbia, 1988, w/John Hill
SCENT OF A WOMAN ★   Universal, 1992
CITY HALL   Columbia, 1995, w/Ken Lipper

Screenplays:
FIRST KNIGHT (Columbia)
HOT SHOT w/Neal Marshall
TIME STEPS
SWITCHING
PEARL
THE OLD NEIGHBORHOOD
THE FOUR HUNDRED
YOU FOR ME
THE ANITA FACTOR
MONKEYS
MURDER ON THE BRIDGE

GARY L. GOLDMAN*

Agent: ICM - Beverly Hills, 310/550-4000
Contact: Fox Animation Studios, 2747 E. Camelback Rd., Phoenix, AZ 85016, fax 602/224-0160

THE SECRET OF NIMH (AF)   MGM/UA, 1982,
   Story Adaptation w/Don Bluth, Will Finn & John Pomeroy
BIG TROUBLE IN LITTLE CHINA   20th Century Fox, 1986,
   w/David Weinstein
ALL DOGS GO TO HEAVEN (AF)   MGM/UA, 1989, Story w/others
TOTAL RECALL   Tri-Star, 1990, w/Dan O'Bannon & Ronald Shusett
NAVY SEALS   Orion, 1990, w/Chuck Pfarrer

Screenplays:
TOTAL RECALL II w/Ron Shusett
NEW ORLEANS MUSICAL
HALLELUJAH
WARRIORS
ROSES ARE RED
GENES

HAL GOLDMAN*

Contact: WGA - Los Angeles, 310/550-1000

OH GOD! BOOK II   Warner Bros., 1980, w/Fred Fox,
   Josh Greenfeld, Seaman Jacobs & Melissa Miller

JAMES A. GOLDMAN*

Agent: William Morris Agency - Beverly Hills, 310/274-7451

A FAMILY AFFAIR (P)   w/William Goldman & John Kander
FOLLIES (P)
BLOOD, SWEAT AND STANLEY POOLE (P)   w/William Goldman
THE LION IN WINTER ★★   Avco Embassy, 1968, from his play
THEY MIGHT BE GIANTS   Universal, 1971, from his play
NICHOLAS AND ALEXANDRA   Columbia, 1971
ROBIN AND MARIAN   Columbia, 1976
WHITE NIGHTS   Columbia, 1985, w/Eric Hughes

Screenplays:
CHINA HAND
GONE WITH THE WIND - PART II
MAN FROM GREEK AND ROMAN w/C. Forman
BANNER BUSINESS

JOSEPH GOLDMAN
(See Menahem Golan)

LINDA GOLDMAN

Agent: Susan Smith & Associates - Beverly Hills, 213/852-4777

Screenplays:
EXTRA BAGGAGE
CITY WOMEN
ILLICIT BEHAVIOR
FREUDIAN SLEEP

MATT GOLDMAN*

Contact: WGA - Los Angeles, 310/550-1000

Screenplays:
BUNK BED BROTHERS w/Pat Hazell (from their play)

MIA GOLDMAN*

Agent: United Talent Agency - Beverly Hills, 310/273-6700

Screenplays:
DIZZINESS
TO HAVE AND TO HOLD

SHANNON GOLDMAN

LOST PROPHET   Rockville Pictures, 1992, w/Michael de Avila,
   Drew Morone & Larry O'Neil

WENDY GOLDMAN*

Agent: CAA - Beverly Hills, 310/288-4545

CASUAL SEX?   Universal, 1988, w/Judy Toll, from their play

Screenplays:
THE SECRET LIFE OF GIRLS w/Judy Toll

WILLIAM GOLDMAN*

Agent: CAA - Beverly Hills, 310/288-4545

A FAMILY AFFAIR (P)   w/James A. Goldman & John Kander
BLOOD, SWEAT AND STANLEY POOLE (P)   w/James A. Goldman
MASQUERADE   United Artists, 1965, w/Michael Relph
HARPER   Warner Bros., 1966
BUTCH CASSIDY AND THE SUNDANCE KID ★★
   20th Century-Fox, 1969
THE HOT ROCK   20th Century-Fox, 1972
THE GREAT WALDO PEPPER   Universal, 1975
THE STEPFORD WIVES   Columbia, 1975
ALL THE PRESIDENT'S MEN ★★   Warner Bros., 1976
MARATHON MAN   Paramount, 1976
A BRIDGE TOO FAR   United Artists, 1977
MAGIC   20th Century-Fox, 1978
THE PRINCESS BRIDE   20th Century Fox, 1987
HEAT   Paramount, 1987
MISERY   Columbia, 1990
THE YEAR OF THE COMET   Columbia, 1992
MEMOIRS OF AN INVISIBLE MAN   Warner Bros., 1992,
   w/Robert Collector & Dana Olsen
CHAPLIN   TriStar, 1992, w/William Boyd & Bryan Forbes
MAVERICK   Warner Bros., 1994

Screenplays:
THE CHAMBER
SINGING OUT LOUD w/Stephen Sondheim
LOW FIVES
THE GHOST AND THE DARKNESS
NATIONAL PASTTIME
RESCUE
THE SEA KINGS
THE SKI BUM

RAY GOLDRUP

Agent: Jack Scagnetti Agency - North Hollywood, 818/762-3871

WINDWALKER   Pacific International, 1980

AKIVA GOLDSMAN*

Agent: ICM - Beverly Hills, 310/550-4000

THE CLIENT   Warner Bros., 1994, w/Robert Getchell
SILENT FALL   Warner Bros., 1994
BATMAN FOREVER   Warner Bros., 1995, w/Janet Scott Batchler &
   Lee Batchler

Screenplays:
LOST IN SPACE
FLESH AND INK
DR. STRANGE (Shared)

PETER GOLDSMID

THE ROAD TO MECCA   Distant Horizon/Videovision Enterprises,
   1992, co-directed

BRUCE L. GOLDSMITH*
Contact: WGA - Los Angeles, 310/550-1000

Screenplays:
KID STUFF

GEORGE H. GOLDSMITH*
Contact: WGA - Los Angeles, 310/550-1000

FORCE: FIVE   American Cinema, 1981, w/Emil Farkas
CHILDREN OF THE CORN   New World, 1984
BLUE MONKEY   Spectrafilm, 1987
NOWHERE TO HIDE   New Century/Vista, 1987, w/Alex Rebar

ALLAN A. GOLDSTEIN
Agent: William Morris Agency - Beverly Hills, 310/274-7451

DEATHWISH V: THE FACE OF DEATH   Trimark, 1994, directed

ALLEN S. GOLDSTEIN*
Contact: 818/766-8628

ROOFTOPS   New Century/Vista, 1989, Story w/Tony Mark

AMY GOLDSTEIN*
Manager: 3 Arts Entertainment - Los Angeles, 213/851-5700

THE SILENCER   Crown International, 1992, w/Scott Kraft, directed

GARY GOLDSTEIN*
Contact: WGA - Los Angeles, 310/550-1000

Screenplays:
STRESS TEST
THIS MAGIC MOMENT
JUST MY IMAGINATION
LIKE A VIRGIN
THE CRAVING

HAVEL GOLDSTEIN
THE FINAL ALLIANCE   RCA/Columbia Pictures Home Video,
   1991, w/John T. Eubank

JOSHUA GOLDSTEIN*
Contact: WGA - Los Angeles, 310/550-1000

18 AGAIN!   New World, 1988, w/Jonathan Prince
PARTNERS 'N LOVE (CTF)   Atlantis Films Ltd., 1992,
   w/Jonathan Prince

Screenplays:
THE FINE TOUCH   w/Jonathan Prince
THE SKY$ THE LIMIT   w/Jonathan Prince

MARTIN M. GOLDSTEIN*
Agent: Wile Enterprises - Santa Monica, 310/828-9768

EMMA AND ELVIS   Northern Arts Entertainment, 1992,
   w/Steven Bognar & Julia Reichert

SCOTT GOLDSTEIN
Agent: The Chasin Agency - Los Angeles, 310/278-7505

Screenplays:
ON THE BORDER
EROICA

DEENA GOLDSTONE*
Agent: Pleshette & Green - Los Angeles, 213/465-0428

SAFE PASSAGE   New Line Cinema, 1994

BOBCAT GOLDTHWAIT*
Business Manager: Jane Tani, Grant & Tani - 310/273-9494

SHAKES THE CLOWN   I.R.S. Releasing, 1992, directed

LARRY GOLIN
Contact: Propaganda Films, 940 N. Mansfield Ave., Los Angeles,
   CA 90038, 213/462-6400

LIGHTS OUT   Gramercy, 1993
FINAL COMBINATION   Rank, 1994

Screenplays:
THE UPTOWN LOCAL DANNY SANCHEZ w/Lynn Geller
THE BIG DANCE

BRYAN GOLUBOFF*
Agent: William Morris Agency - New York, 212/586-5100

THE OTHER FIVE PERCENT (P)
MY SIDE OF THE STORY (P)
IN-BETWEENS (P)
BIG AL (Short)   1993, based on his play
THE BASKETBALL DIARIES   New Line Cinema, 1995

Screenplays:
SAFEST PLACE ON EARTH

STEVE GOMER
Agent: Susan Smith & Associates - Beverly Hills, 213/852-4777
Manager: 3 Arts Entertainment - Los Angeles, 213/851-5700

SWEET LORRAINE   Angelika Films, 1987, Story w/Shelly Altman,
   George Malko & Michael Zettler, directed

AL GOMEZ
JOYSTICKS   Jensen Farley Pictures, 1983, w/Mickey Epps

MARGA GOMEZ
Agent: William Morris Agency - Beverly Hills, 310/274-7451

MARGA GOMEZ IS PRETTY, WITTY AND GAY (P)

Screenplays:
MEMORY TRICKS (from her play)

NICK GOMEZ
Agent: ICM - Beverly Hills, 310/550-4000

NO PICNIC (Short)   directed
WILD KINGDOM (Short)   directed
LAWS OF GRAVITY   RKO Pictures, 1992, directed
NEW JERSEY DRIVE   Gramercy, 1995, directed

DIANE GONCIARZ
STREETWALKIN'   Concorde/Cinema Group, 1985,
   w/Robert Alden & Joan Freeman

JEAN GONICK*
Agent: CAA - Beverly Hills, 310/288-4545

Screenplays:
THE FROG PRINCE

LAURENCE GONZALES*
Agent: Pleshette & Green - Los Angeles, 213/465-0428

Screenplays:
LITTLE BROTHER
UNDERGROUND JUNGLE
GOLD

REUBEN GONZALEZ*
Agent: The Gersh Agency - Beverly Hills, 310/274-6611

Screenplays:
NOCTURNE
HOLIDAY CITY
NYDIA'S CHULETAS

GREG GOODELL*
Agent: Shapiro/Lichtman - Los Angeles, 310/859-8877

Screenplays:
FACE OF EVIL

WILLIAM GOODHART*
Contact: Ronald S. Konecky, Esq., 485 Madison Avenue, New York, NY 10022, 212/980-0120

GENERATION   Avco Embassy, 1969, from his play
THE HERETIC: EXORCIST II   Warner Bros., 1977
CLOUD DANCER   Blossom, 1980

Screenplays:
THE MOVIEGOER
CONJUNCTION
TOO FAR TO WALK
LOOKING OUT
THE TOUR
WARRIOR OF THE RAINBOW
NO TRANSFER
SOME KIND OF PROGRESS
THE DEATHBIRTH OF HOUDINI
THE SANDMAN
THE SIXTH COMMANDMENT

DAVID ZELAG GOODMAN
Manager: Creative Alliance Management - Los Angeles, 213/962-6090
Business Manager: Stanley Karp, 12100 Wilshire Blvd., Los Angeles, CA 90025

THE STRANGLERS OF BOMBAY   Columbia, 1959
LOVERS AND OTHER STRANGERS ★   Cinerama Releasing Corporation, 1970, w/Joseph Bologna & ReneeTaylor
MONTE WALSH   National General, 1970, w/Lukas Heller
STRAW DOGS   Cinerama Releasing Corporation, 1972, w/Sam Peckinpah
MAN ON A SWING   Paramount, 1975
FAREWELL, MY LOVELY   Avco Embassy, 1975
LOGAN'S RUN   MGM/UA, 1976
MARCH OR DIE   Columbia, 1977
THE EYES OF LAURA MARS   Columbia, 1978, w/John Carpenter
FIGHTING BACK   Paramount, 1982, w/Thomas Hedley
MAN, WOMAN AND CHILD   Paramount, 1983, w/Erich Segal

Screenplays:
IN A LONELY PLACE w/Michael Grais & Mark Victor
BEYOND THE LAW
THE DEEP (Sequel)
THE RELIGION
HOLLOW POINT

MICHAEL PATRICK GOODMAN*
Agent: Gray/Goodman Inc. - Beverly Hills, 310/276-7070
Business Manager: David Rotman - 310/829-5455

WANTED DEAD OR ALIVE   New World, 1987, w/Gary A. Sherman & Brian Taggart

Screenplays:
NO MERCY ASKED w/George Christie Jr.
FALLING OF ANGELS
FIREPOWER

FRANCES GOODRICH
EASTER PARADE   MGM, 1948, w/Albert Hackett & Sidney Sheldon
FATHER OF THE BRIDE ★   MGM, 1950, w/Albert Hackett
FATHER'S LITTLE DIVIDEND   MGM, 1951, w/Albert Hackett
GIVE A GIRL A BREAK   MGM, 1953, w/Albert Hackett
THE LONG LONG TRAILER   MGM, 1954, w/Albert Hackett
GABY   MGM, 1956, w/Albert Hackett & Charles Lederer
A CERTAIN SMILE   20th Century-Fox, 1958, w/Albert Hackett
THE DIARY OF ANNE FRANK   20th Century-Fox, 1959, w/Albert Hackett, from their play
FIVE FINGER EXERCISE   Columbia, 1962, w/Albert Hackett
FATHER OF THE BRIDE   Buena Vista, 1991, w/Albert Hackett, Nancy Meyers & Charles Shyer

GARRY GOODROW*
Manager: Silver, Kass & Massetti - New York, 212/391-4545

HONEY, I BLEW UP THE KID   Buena Vista, 1992, w/Thom Eberhardt & Peter Elbling

BERNARD GORDON*
Contact: WGA - Los Angeles, 310/550-1000

THE LAWLESS BREED   Universal-International, 1952
FLESH AND FURY   Universal-International, 1952
55 DAYS AT PEKING   Bronston, 1962, w/Philip Yordan
CUSTER OF THE WEST   Cinerama Releasing, 1967, w/Julian Halevy
KRAKATOA, EAST OF JAVA   ABC, 1968, w/Clifford Newton Gould

BERT I. GORDON*
Contact: WGA - Los Angeles, 310/550-1000

CYCLOPS   American International, 1957, directed
THE AMAZING COLOSSAL MAN   American International, 1957, w/Mark Hanna, directed
THE MAD BOMBER   Cinemation, 1973, directed
NECROMANCY   Cinerama Releasing Corporation, 1973, directed
THE FOOD OF THE GODS   American International, 1976, directed
FOOD OF THE GODS II   Concorde-Centaur, 1989, as "Richard Bennett," w/E. Kim Brewster

BRYAN GORDON*
Agent: ICM - Beverly Hills, 310/550-4000

RAY'S MALE HETEROSEXUAL DANCE HALL (Short) ★★   1987, directed

Screenplays:
PIE IN THE SKY
KISS THE BABY
URIAH
WORTH WINNING
MARY WANTS TO HAVE AN AFFAIR

DAN GORDON*
Agent: The Agency - Los Angeles, 310/551-3000

TRAIN RIDE TO HOLLYWOOD   Taylor-Laughlin, 1975
TANK   Universal, 1984
GOTCHA!   Universal, 1985
GULAG (CTF)   Lorimar Productions/HBO PremiereFilms, 1985
PASSENGER 57   Warner Bros., 1992, w/David Loughery
SURF NINJAS   New Line Cinema, 1993
TAKING THE HEAT (CTF)   Viacom Pictures, 1993
WYATT EARP   Warner Bros., 1994, w/Lawrence Kasdan
MURDER IN THE FIRST   Warner Bros., 1995

Screenplays:
THE MECHANIC (remake)
GONE BUT NOT FORGOTTEN
HEAT WAVE
THE GOOD BOOK
JACKALS
A MATTER OF HONOR

**F
I
L
M

W
R
I
T
E
R
S**

DAVID GORDON*
Manager: The Anthony Elliot Company - Los Angeles, 310/284-6804

Screenplays:
ROCKETMAN
TWISTER w/Lawrence Alexander

EDWIN GORDON*
Contact: 818/343-8288

THE CHOSEN   20th Century-Fox International Classics, 1982

FRITZ GORDON
SLEEPAWAY CAMP 3: TEENAGE WASTELAND   Double Helix
   Films, 1989

JILL GORDON
Agent: ICM - Beverly Hills, 310/550-4000
Manager: 3 Arts Entertainment - Los Angeles, 213/851-5700

Screenplays:
ANGUS (New Line Cinema, 1995)
SMELLS LIKE TEEN

KEITH GORDON*
Agent: The Gersh Agency - Beverly Hills, 310/274-6611

THE CHOCOLATE WAR   MCEG, 1988, directed
STATIC   Sandstar Releasing, 1989, w/Mark Romanek
A MIDNIGHT CLEAR   InterStar Releasing, 1992, directed

Screenplays:
WAKING THE DEAD

MARK GORDON*
Agent: Jim Preminger Agency - Los Angeles, 310/475-9491

Screenplays:
HER MAJESTY
HOTEL SCHOOL

ROBERT N. GORDON*
Agent: The Gersh Agency - Beverly Hills, 310/274-6611

Screenplays:
ADDICTED TO LOVE
TELL ME ALL ABOUT IT
CARTOONED

RUEBEN GORDON
Contact: Lloyd Braun, Silverberg, Katz, Thompson & Braun -
   Los Angeles, 310/445-5801

LEGION OF IRON   Epic Productions, 1989, w/Steven Schoenberg
KING OF THE STREETS *ALIEN WARRIOR* Shapiro Entertainment,
   1986, w/Steven Schoenberg, Edward Hunt & Barry Pearson

Screenplays:
MIDNIGHT HEAT w/Steven Schoenberg
HEART OF GOLD w/Steven Schoenberg

STUART GORDON*
Agent: United Talent Agency - Beverly Hills, 310/273-6700

H.P. LOVECRAFT'S RE-ANIMATOR   Empire Pictures, 1985,
   w/William J. Norris & Dennis Paoli, directed
FROM BEYOND   Empire Pictures, 1986,
   Adaptation w/Dennis Paoli & Brian Yuzma, directed
HONEY, I SHRUNK THE KIDS   Buena Vista, 1989,
   Story w/Ed Naha & Brian Yuzna
ROBOTJOX   Triumph Releasing, 1990, Story, directed
BODY SNATCHERS   Warner Bros., 1993, w/Dennis Paoli &
   Nicholas St. John
CASTLE FREAK   Fullmoon, 1994, Story

Screenplays:
SPACE TRUCKERS (Story w/Ted Mann)

NICK GORE*
Contact: WGA - Los Angeles, 310/550-1000

Screenplays:
THE NOMINATION w/Jerry Jacobius
BLOOMER GIRLS w/Jerry Jacobius
WISHFUL THINKING w/Jerry Jacobius

JOE GORES*
Agent: Renaissance-H.N. Swanson - Los Angeles, 310-246-6000

Screenplays:
INTERFACE
COME MORNING
COVER STORY
FALLEN ANGEL
GANGBUSTERS
PAPER CRIMES
PARADISE ROAD
RUN CUNNING

CLAUDE GORETTA
Contact: Swiss Film Center, Munstergasse 18, 8001 Zurich,
   Switzerland, 01/472860

THE LACEMAKER   New Yorker, 1977, w/Pascal Laine, directed
THE DEATH OF MARIO RICCI   New Line Showcase, 1983,
   w/Georges Haldas, directed

KATHY GORI
Agent: Paradigm - Los Angeles, 310/277-4400

SAVE THE LAST DANCE FOR ME   Swann American Pictures,
   1981, w/Alan Berger

Screenplays:
LIFE RIGHTS w/Alan Berger
THE BUFF w/Alan Berger
THE GOLD COAST w/Alan Berger
MERCY GIRLS w/Alan Berger
I'M NOT CHARLIE w/Alan Berger
THE MAN SHE KNEW w/Alan Berger
HER SAINTED HUSBAND w/Alan Berger
GOODBYE FOREVER w/Alan Berger
RICH LITTLE POOR GIRLS w/Alan Berger & Joan Rivers
FOR BETTER OR FOR WORSE w/Alan Berger
ROCKET MAN LIFE ON EARTH w/Alan Berger
NATIONAL PARK w/Alan Berger
LADIES DAY w/Alan Berger
UNDER WRAPS w/Alan Berger
SHAGGY w/Alan Berger

JIM GORMAN*
Agent: ICM - Beverly Hills, 310/550-4000

Screenplays:
CUTTHROAT ISLAND Story w/Michael Beckner (MGM/UA)
TEXAS LEAD AND GOLD w/Michael Beckner
HOSTILE TAKEOVER w/Michael Beckner

SHAREE GORMAN
Agent: United Talent Agency - Beverly Hills, 310/273-6700

Screenplays:
MY NAME IS DADDY w/Steve Curwick

CHARLES GORMLEY
Contact: British Academy of Film & Television Arts, 195 Piccadilly,
   London W1, England, 01/734-0022

GOSPEL ACCORDING TO VIC   Skouras Pictures, 1987, directed

PHIL GORN
Agent: Berzon Agency - Glendale, 818/548-1560

Screenplays:
THE RAINFOREST

F
I
L
M

W
R
I
T
E
R
S

EDDIE GORODETSKY*
Contact: WGA - Los Angeles, 310/550-1000

Screenplays:
MY MOTHER CAN FLY

ROBERT E. GOSNELL*
Contact: 303/838-2724

FIREWALKER   Cannon, 1986

PHILIP KAN GOTANDA*
Agent: Helen Merrill Agency - New York, 212/591-5326

FISH HEAD SOUP (P)
DAY STANDING ON ITS HEAD (P)
THE WASH   Skouras Pictures, 1988, from his play

CARL GOTTLIEB*
Business Manager: Edward D. Astrin, 16633 Ventura Blvd. -
   Suite 1450, Encino, CA 91436, 818/501-3022

JAWS   Universal, 1975, w/Peter Benchley
WHICH WAY IS UP?   Universal, 1978, w/Cecil Brown
JAWS II   Universal, 1978, w/Howard Sackler
THE JERK   Universal, 1979, w/Michael Elias & Steve Martin
CAVEMAN   United Artists, 1981, w/Rudy DeLuca, directed
DOCTOR DETROIT   Universal, 1983, w/Robert Boris &
   Bruce Jay Friedman
JAWS 3-D   Universal, 1983, w/Richard Matheson

Screenplays:
SHE-HULK
PAUL BUNYAN
HIGHWAY PATROL

MICHAEL GOTTLIEB*
Agent: APA - Los Angeles, 310/273-0744
Business: Harmony Pictures, 2921 W. Alameda Avenue, Burbank,
   CA 91505, 818/846-6700

MANNEQUIN   20th Century Fox, 1987, w/Ed Rugoff, directed
MR. NANNY   New Line Cinema, 1993, w/Ed Rugoff, directed

Screenplays:
THE VULGARIANS w/Ed Rugoff
SEEING STARS w/Ed Rugoff
SOMETHING REAL w/Ed Rugoff
WHOPPER w/Ed Rugoff

PAUL GOTTLIEB
IN PRAISE OF OLDER WOMEN   Avco Embassy, 1978

ROBERT GOTTLIEB
Agent: Jon Klane Agency - Beverly Hills, 310/278-0178

Screenplays:
SHINE ON
DIGGING IN THE DIRT

ALFRED GOUGH
Agent: Warden, White & Kane - Beverly Hills, 213/852-1028
Manager: Ogden House - Los Angeles, 213/851-0458

Screenplays:
MANGO w/Miles Millar
ICE w/Miles Millar

HEYWOOD GOULD*
Agent: ICM - Beverly Hills, 310/550-4000

ROLLING THUNDER   American International, 1978,
   w/Paul Schrader
THE BOYS FROM BRAZIL   20th Century-Fox, 1978
FORT APACHE, THE BRONX   20th Century-Fox, 1981

STREETS OF GOLD   20th Century Fox, 1986, w/Tom Cole &
   Richard Price
COCKTAIL   Buena Vista, 1988
ONE GOOD COP   Buena Vista, 1991, directed
TRIAL BY JURY   Warner Bros., 1994, w/Jordan Katz, directed

Screenplays:
DIPLOMATIC IMMUNITY
DOUBLE BANG
THE FIFTH PROFESSION

PETER GOULD
Manager: 3 Arts Entertainment - Los Angeles, 213/851-5700

DIRTY LITTLE SECRETS (Short)   directed
DOUBLE DRAGON   Gramercy, 1994, w/Michael Davis

Screenplays:
THE SENSOR w/Michael Davis
DIXIE COP
96 TEARS

DAVID S. GOYER*
Agent: United Talent Agency - Beverly Hills, 310/273-6700

DEATH WARRANT   MGM/UA, 1990
KICKBOXER 2   Trimark Pictures, 1991
THE SUBSTITUTE (CTF)   Pacific Motion Pictures/Wilshire Court,
   1993, as "Cynthia Verlaine"
THE PUPPET MASTERS   Buena Vista, 1994, w/Ted Elliott &
   Terry Rossio

Screenplays:
SON OF DARKNESS w/Stuart Cornfeld
BLADE
CASCA
LIBERATOR
ARCADE
ALIAS
JACK OF HEARTS
ICE AGE

MICHAEL L. GRACE*
Agent: Maggie Field Agency - Studio City, 818/980-2001

JFK: OF CABBAGES AND KINGS (P)
SNOOPY, THE MUSICAL (P)
FINAL CUT (P)
RAZZLE DAZZLE (P)
THE UNSEEN   World Northal, 1981

Screenplays:
LADYKILLER
DANGEROUS
JUDGMENT CALL
BOTTOM LINE
THE SWINDLE
TRUE BLUE
KING'S X
MILLIONAIRES

ED GRACYZYK
COME BACK TO THE 5 & DIME, JIMMY DEAN, JIMMY DEAN
   Cinecom, 1982, from his play

Screenplays:
LOVE, JANIS

JAMES GRADY*
Agent: William Morris Agency - New York, 212/586-5100

Screenplays:
LONG SHOT

WENDY GRAF*
Agent: Pleshette & Green - Los Angeles, 213/465-0428

Screenplays:
LIFESAVERS w/Lisa Stotsky
ALL MINE w/Lisa Stotsky
FINAL ARGUMENTS w/Lisa Stotsky

TODD GRAFF*
Agent: CAA - Beverly Hills, 310/288-4545

USED PEOPLE   20th Century Fox, 1992,
   based on material from his "The Grandma Plays"
THE VANISHING   20th Century Fox, 1993
FLY BY NIGHT   Arrow Entertainment, 1993
ANGIE   Buena Vista, 1994

Screenplays:
THE CROWDED ROOM
WOKE UP LAUGHING
BACKSTAB

SUE GRAFTON*
Agent: Sanford-Gross & Associates - Los Angeles,
   310/208-2100

LOLLY MADONNA XXX   MGM, 1973, w/Rodney Carr-Smith

BRUCE GRAHAM*
Agent: United Talent Agency - Beverly Hills, 310/273-6700

A VERY NICE NEIGHBORHOOD (P)
CHAMPAGNE CHARLIE STAKES (P)
BELMONT AVENUE SOCIAL CLUB (P)
DEVIOUS MEANS (P)
MOON OVER THE BREWERY (P)
MINOR DEMONS (P) also screenplay
DESPERATE AFFECTION (P) also screenplay

Screenplays:
MIXED NUTS
ASSUMED IDENTITY
IN THE CORPS
LIAR LIAR
DANGER SIGN
BRILLIANT FAILURES
THE RETURN OF PHILO MCGIFFIN
THE GOOD CITIZEN
REILLY'S LAST REQUEST
A LITTLE ADVENTURE

JANICE LEE GRAHAM*
Contact: WGA - Los Angeles, 310/550-1000

UNTIL SEPTEMBER   MGM/UA, 1984

Screenplays:
ALEXANDER & NEIL

JESSE GRAHAM
OUT OF TIME   Motion Pictures International, 1989

MELANIE GRAHAM*
Agent: The Chasin Agency - Los Angeles, 310/278-7505

A SINFUL LIFE   New Line Cinema, 1989, from her play
   "Just Like the Pom-Pom Girls"

MICHAEL AXEL GRAHAM*
Contact: WGA - Los Angeles, 310/550-1000

Screenplays:
THE POLICEMAN

RONNY GRAHAM*
Agent: Paradigm - Los Angeles, 310/277-4400

TO BE OR NOT TO BE   20th Century-Fox, 1983,
   w/Thomas Meehan
FINDERS KEEPERS   Warner Bros., 1984, w/Terence Marsh &
   Charles Dennis
SPACEBALLS   MGM/UA, 1987, w/Mel Brooks & Thomas Meehan

RUTH GRAHAM
BECOMING COLETTE   Castle Hill Productions, 1992

Screenplays:
THE FIFTH CHILD
TRACKS

MICHAEL GRAIS*
Agent: CAA - Beverly Hills, 310/288-4545

THE THIN LINE   New Yorker, 1980, w/Mark Victor
DEATH HUNT   20th Century-Fox, 1981, w/Mark Victor
POLTERGEIST   MGM/UA, 1980, w/Steven Spielberg & Mark Victor
POLTERGEIST II: THE OTHER SIDE   MGM/UA, 1986,
   w/Mark Victor
MARKED FOR DEATH   20th Century Fox, 1990, w/Mark Victor
COOL WORLD   Paramount, 1992, w/Mark Victor

Screenplays:
CAFE BERLIN w/Mark Victor
WARP w/Mark Victor
TRUEST SPORT w/Mark Victor
IN A LONELY PLACE w/Mark Victor & David Z. Goodman
BRAIN w/Mark Victor
TURN LEFT OR DIE w/Mark Victor
OCTOBER CIRCLE w/Mark Victor

MAURICE GRAN*
Contact: WGA - Los Angeles, 310/550-1000

BULLSEYE!   21st Century Film, 1991, w/Leslie Bricusse &
   Laurence Marks

DEREK GRANGER
Agent: Peters, Fraser & Dunlop - London, 071/376-7676

A HANDFUL OF DUST   New Line Cinema, 1988,
   w/Charles Sturridge & Tim Sullivan
WHERE ANGELS FEAR TO TREAD   Fine Line Features, 1992,
   w/Charles Sturridge & Tim Sullivan

PERCY GRANGER*
Contact: WGA - Los Angeles, 310/550-1000

Screenplays:
BLIND LOVE
FISHER'S ISLAND
FROZEN MUSIC
DISAPPEARING ACTS
MUSTANGS
A DIME TO DANCE BY
JUST BEYOND

BARRA GRANT*
Contact: WGA - Los Angeles, 310/550-1000

A MOTHER, A DAUGHTER, AND A GUN (P)
SLOW DANCING IN THE BIG CITY   United Artists, 1978
MISUNDERSTOOD   MGM/UA, 1984

Screenplays:
HEY MR. FANTASY
INTENSIVE CARE

SUSANNAH GRANT
Agent: APA - Los Angeles, 310/273-0744

Screenplays:
ISLAND GIRL

ROBERT GRASMERE
Agent: APA - Los Angeles, 310/273-0744

A MILLION TO JUAN   Samuel Goldwyn Company, 1994,
   w/Francesca Matos

GARY GRAVER
Agent: Smith/Gosnell/Nicholson - Pacific Palisades, 310/459-0307

TEXAS LIGHTNING   Film Ventures International, 1981, directed
TRICK OR TREAT   Lone Star, 1983, directed

BEVERLY GRAY
IMMORTAL SINS   Concorde, 1991, w/Tom Cleaver

JAMES GRAY
Agent: United Talent Agency - Beverly Hills, 310/273-6700

LITTLE ODESSA   Fine Line Features, 1995, directed

Screenplays:
MECCA

JOHN GRAY*
Agent: ICM - Beverly Hills, 310/550-4000

BILLY BISHOP GOES TO WAR (P)
BILLY GALVIN   Vestron, 1986, directed
THE LOST CAPONE (CTF)   Patchett-Kaufman Entertainment, 1990

Screenplays:
KATIE w/John Bunzel & Paul Young (directing)
THE LITTLE DRUMMER BOY
NO LIGHTS, NO SIRENS w/Robert Lea

MIKE GRAY*
Agent: William Morris Agency - Beverly Hills, 310/274-7451

THE CHINA SYNDROME ★   Columbia, 1979,
   w/T.S. Cook & James Bridges
WAVELENGTH   New World, 1983, directed
CODE OF SILENCE   Orion, 1985, w/Michael Blodgett &
   Dennis Shyrack

PAMELA GRAY*
Agent: Monteiro Rose Agency - Encino, 818/501-1177

Screenplays:
THE BLOUSE MAN

SIMON GRAY
Agent: Judy Daish Agency - London, 011/44/071/486-5405

OTHERWISE ENGAGED (P)
QUARTERMAINE'S TERMS (P)
THE HOLY TERROR (P)
COMMON PURSUIT (P)   also teleplay
BUTLEY   American Film Theatre, 1974, from his play
A MONTH IN THE COUNTRY   Orion Classics, 1987
UNNATURAL PURSUITS (CTF)   BBC-TV, 1994

Screenplays:
REGENERATIONS

SPALDING GRAY
Agent: ICM - Beverly Hills, 310/550-4000

Plays/Monologues Include: *Sex and Death to the Age of 14,*
   Booze Cars and College Girls, A Personal History of the American
   Theater, Terrors of Pleasure, Three Places in Rhode Island (trilogy),
   Gray's Anatomy

SWIMMING TO CAMBODIA   Cinecom, 1987, from his play
MONSTER IN A BOX   Fine Line Features, 1992, from his play

WILLIAM GRAY*
Agent: Dytman & Schwartz - Los Angeles, 310/274-8844

PROM NIGHT   Avco Embassy, 1980
THE CHANGELING   AFD, 1980, w/Diana Maddox
AN EYE FOR AN EYE   Avco Embassy, 1981, w/James Bruner
HUMONGOUS   Embassy, 1982
CROSS-COUNTRY   New World, 1983, w/Logan N. Danforth
THE PHILADELPHIA EXPERIMENT   New World, 1984,
   w/Michael Janover
BLACK MOON RISING   New World, 1986, w/John Carpenter &
   Desmond Nakano

Screenplays:
DARK SHADOWS

BRIAN GRAZER
Agent: CAA - Beverly Hills, 310/288-4545
Business: Imagine Entertainment, 1925 Century Park East -
   23rd Floor, Los Angeles, CA 90067, 310/277-1665

SPLASH ★   Buena Vista, 1984, Story
ARMED AND DANGEROUS   Columbia, 1986,
   Story w/James Keach & Harold Ramis
HOUSESITTER   Universal, 1992, Story w/Mark Stein

MIKE GRECO
ALOHA SUMMER   Spectrafilm, 1988, w/Bob Benedetto

ADOLPH GREEN*
Agent: ICM - New York, 212/556-5600

GOOD NEWS   MGM, 1947, w/Adolph Green
THE BARKLEYS OF BROADWAY   MGM, 1949, w/Betty Comden
ON THE TOWN   MGM, 1949, w/Betty Comden, from their play
SINGIN' IN THE RAIN   MGM, 1952, w/Betty Comden
THE BAND WAGON ★   MGM, 1953, w/Betty Comden
IT'S ALWAYS FAIR WEATHER ★   MGM, 1955, w/Betty Comden
AUNTIE MAME   Warner Bros., 1958, w/Betty Comden
BELLS ARE RINGING   MGM, 1960, w/Betty Comden,
   from their play
WHAT A WAY TO GO   20th Century-Fox, 1963, w/Betty Comden

CLIFF GREEN
PICNIC AT HANGING ROCK   Atlantic Releasing Corporation, 1975
SUMMERFIELD   Greater Union Film Distributors, 1977

CLIFFORD GREEN*
Agent: William Morris Agency - Beverly Hills, 310/274-7451

BABY - SECRET OF THE LOST LEGEND   Buena Vista, 1985,
   w/Ellen Green
SPACECAMP   20th Century Fox, 1986, w/Ellen Green &
   Casey T. Mitchell, as "W.W. Wicket"
THE SEVENTH SIGN   Tri-Star, 1988, w/Ellen Green as
   "George Kaplan & W.W. Wicket"

Screenplays:
THREE WISHES Story w/Ellen Green (Rysher)
THE PRESIDENT STEPS OUT w/Ellen Green
MAGIC HOUR   ORPHEUS PROJECT w/Ellen Green
WHITE ANGEL w/Ellen Green

ELLEN GREEN*

Agent: William Morris Agency - Beverly Hills, 310/274-7451

BABY - SECRET OF THE LOST LEGEND   Buena Vista, 1985,
   w/Cliff Green
SPACECAMP   20th Century Fox, 1986, w/Cliff Green &
   Casey T. Mitchell, as "W.W. Wicket"
THE SEVENTH SIGN   Tri-Star, 1988, w/Cliff Green as
   "George Kaplan & W.W. Wicket"

Screenplays:
THREE WISHES   Story w/Cliff Green (Rysher)
THE PRESIDENT STEPS OUT w/Cliff Green
MAGIC HOUR   ORPHEUS PROJECT w/Cliff Green
WHITE ANGEL w/Cliff Green

GERALD GREEN*

Contact: WGA - New York, 212/245-6180

THE LAST ANGRY MAN   Columbia, 1959

Screenplays:
O JERUSALEM
THE PLOT TO MURDER THE POPE
EL PUEBLO

LEWIS GREEN*

Agent: The Artists Group - Los Angeles, 310/552-1100 or
   Jon Klane Agency - Beverly Hills, 310/278-0178

Screenplays:
THE WIRE (CTF)
VIRGIN MARY
NEVER TALK TO STRANGERS w/Jordan Rush
DUDES w/Jordan Rush

WALON GREEN*

Agent: ICM - Beverly Hills, 310/550-4000

THE WILD BUNCH ★   Warner Bros., 1969, w/Sam Peckinpah
SORCERER   WAGES OF FEAR   Universal/Paramount, 1977
THE BRINK'S JOB   Universal, 1978
THE SECRET LIFE OF PLANTS (FD)   Paramount, 1978,
   w/Michael Braun & Peter Thompson, directed
THE BORDER   Universal, 1982, w/David Freeman &
   Deric Washburn
SOLARBABIES   MGM/UA, 1986, w/Douglas Anthony Metrov
CRUSOE   Island Pictures, 1988, w/Christopher Logue
ROBOCOP 2   Orion, 1990, w/Frank Miller

Screenplays:
CRUSADES
SADE
RED DRAGON
CENTERFOLD
L.A. WOMAN
PARLOR GAMES
THE DUPLICATED MAN
WASTED
DINOSAUR (AF)
DUE PROCESS

PETER GREENAWAY

Contact: British Academy of Film & Television Arts, 195 Piccadilly,
   London W1, England, 071/734-0022

THE DRAUGHTSMAN'S CONTRACT   United Artists Classics,
   1983, directed
A ZED AND TWO NOUGHTS   Skouras Pictures, 1985, directed
THE BELLY OF AN ARCHITECT   Skouras Pictures, 1987, directed
DROWNING BY NUMBERS   Galaxy International, 1988, directed
THE COOK, THE THIEF, HIS WIFE AND HER LOVER   Miramax,
   1990, directed
PROSPERO'S BOOKS   Miramax, 1991, directed
THE BABY OF MACON   (No Distributor), 1993, directed

EVERETT GREENBAUM*

Agent: Preferred Artists - Encino, 818/990-0305

GOOD NEIGHBOR SAM   Columbia, 1964, w/James Fritzell &
   David Swift
THE GHOST AND MR. CHICKEN   Universal, 1965,
   w/James Fritzell
THE RELUCTANT ASTRONAUT   1967
ANGEL IN MY POCKET   Universal, 1969, w/James Fritzell

ALAN GREENBERG*

Contact: WGA - Los Angeles, 310/550-1000

Screenplays:
DANCE ME OUTSIDE
THE LAND THEY LEFT BEHIND
LOVE IN VAIN

BOB GREENBERG

LOBSTER MAN FROM MARS   Electric Pictures, 1989

MATT GREENBERG

Agent: APA - Los Angeles, 310/273-0744

THE GREY KNIGHT   Motion Picture Corporation, 1993

Screenplays:
CULTIVATING CHARLIE (CMS Productions)
THE BIG BRASS RING w/George Hickenlooper

RICHARD GREENBERG*

Agent: William Morris Agency - Beverly Hills, 310/274-7451

EASTERN STANDARD (P)
THE EXTRA MAN (P)
NIGHT AND HER STARS (P)

STANLEY R. GREENBERG*

Agent: Major Clients Agency - Los Angeles, 310/284-6400

THE BIRDS (P)
SOYLENT GREEN   MGM, 1972
SKYJACKED   MGM, 1972

STEVE GREENBERG

DEFENSE PLAY   Trans World Entertainment, 1988,
   w/Aubrey Solomon

DAN GREENBURG*

Agent: William Morris Agency - Beverly Hills, 310/274-7451

I COULD NEVER HAVE SEX WITH ANY MAN WHO HAS SO
   LITTLE RESPECT FOR MY HUSBAND   Cinema 5, 1973
FOREPLAY   Cinema National, 1975, w/David Odell &
   Jack Richardson
PRIVATE LESSONS   Jensen Farley Pictures, 1981
PRIVATE SCHOOL   Universal, 1983, w/Suzanne O'Malley
THE GUARDIAN   Universal, 1990, w/William Friedkin &
   Stephen Volk
MORE PRIVATE LESSONS   Carnegie Film Group, 1993

Screenplays:
SHELLY
EXES

CLARENCE GREENE*

Contact: WGA - Los Angeles, 310/550-1000

D.O.A.   Buena Vista, 1988, Story w/Charles Edward Pogue &
   Russell Rouse

DAVID GREENE*
Agent: CAA - Beverly Hills, 310/288-4545

GODSPELL   Columbia, 1973, w/John Michael Tebelak, directed

KIMBERLY GREENE
Agent: United Talent Agency - Beverly Hills, 310/273-6700

SWEET POTATO RIDE (Short)   1993,
     w/Camille Tucker, co-directed

Screenplays:
M'LADY w/Camille Tucker

STEVEN S. GREENE*
Contact: WGA - Los Angeles, 310/550-1000

HARDBODIES   Columbia, 1984, w/Eric Alter & Mark Griffiths
THE EXPERTS   Paramount, 1988, w/Eric Alter & Nick Thiel

Screenplays:
MARRYING UP w/Eric Alter
NOSEJOB w/Stan Sheff
SLEEPING BEAUTY

AMY GREENFIELD
ANTIGONE/RITES OF PASSION   Eclipse Productions,
     1991, directed

JOSH GREENFELD*
Contact: WGA - Los Angeles, 310/550-1000

HARRY AND TONTO ★   20th Century-Fox, 1974, w/Paul Mazursky
OH GOD! BOOK II   Warner Bros., 1980, w/Fred Fox, Hal Goldman,
     Seaman Jacobs & Melissa Miller

SETH GREENLAND*
Contact: WGA - Los Angeles, 310/550-1000

GIRLS IN MOVIES (P)
WHO'S THE MAN?   New Line Cinema, 1993

Screenplays:
BAD WITH NUMBERS (Savoy)

ADAM GREENMAN*
Agent: William Morris Agency - Beverly Hills, 310/274-7451

THREE OF HEARTS   New Line Cinema, 1993, w/Mitch Glazer

Screenplays:
LITTLE ODESSA
JEOPARDY
ANNE FLETCHER
ALBY'S HOUSE OF BONDAGE
SEX ADDICTS (CTF)

MAGGIE GREENWALD*
Agent: ICM - Beverly Hills, 310/550-4000
Contact: Brenda Goodman - 212/206-6698

HOME REMEDY   Xerox Productions, 1988, directed
THE KILL OFF   Films Around the World, 1990, directed
THE BALLAD OF LITTLE JO   Fine Line Features, 1993, directed

Screenplays:
SAVAGE NIGHT

DAVID GREENWALT*
Agent: ICM - Beverly Hills, 310/550-4000

UTILITIES *GETTING EVEN* New World, 1983, w/James Kouf
WACKO   Jensen Farley Pictures, 1983, w/James Kouf,
     Dana Olsen & Michael Spound
CLASS   Orion, 1983, w/James Kouf

AMERICAN DREAMER   Warner Bros., 1984, w/James Kouf
SECRET ADMIRER   Orion, 1985, w/James Kouf, directed
SHAKER RUN   Challenge Film Corp., 1985, w/James Kouf

Screenplays:
GREED w/James Kouf
AIRPLANE III w/James Kouf
BIGAMY w/James Kouf
THE LAKE w/James Kouf
HONEYMOON w/James Kouf
LOVE BEHIND BARS

DAN GREER
BAKER'S HAWK   Doyt-Dayton, 1976

STEVEN GREGG
Agent: United Talent Agency - Beverly Hills, 310/273-6700

THE LARGEST ELIZABETH IN THE WORLD (P)   also screenplay
A PRIVATE MOMENT (P)
SEX LIVES OF SUPERHEROES (P)
THIS IS A TEST (P)

Screenplays:
NUCLEAR FAMILY
WEETZIE BAT

ANDRE GREGORY
Contact: Screen Actors Guild - Los Angeles, 213/954-1600

MY DINNER WITH ANDRE   New Yorker, 1981, w/Wallace Shawn

JOHN GREGORY
Agent: Berzon Agency - Glendale, 818/548-1560

Screenplays:
THE BONUS

RICHARD GREGSON*
Contact: WGA - Los Angeles, 310/550-1000

THE ANGRY SILENCE   British Lion, 1960, Story w/Michael Craig
EMINENT DOMAIN   Triumph, 1991, w/Andrzej Krakowski

LESLIE GREIF*
Contact: Bloom, Dekom, Hergott & Cook - Los Angeles, 310/278-8622

Screenplays:
THE MADDENING w/Henry Slesar (Trimark)
THE LEGEND OF WOLF LODGE
PARAMEDICS

GORDON GREISMAN*
Agent: CAA - Beverly Hills, 310/288-4545

Screenplays:
LOST
PRELUDE
A LIVING WAGE
SILENCES
CASTAWAYS
FELLOW TRAVELERS
AGAINST THE WIND

SHANI S. GREWAL
DOUBLE X: THE NAME OF THE GAME   Feature Film Co.,
     1992, directed

BABS GREYHOSKY*
Agent: Major Clients Agency - Los Angeles, 310/284-6400

Screenplays:
CUPID

JOHN GREYSON
ZERO PATIENCE   Cinevista, 1994, directed

Screenplays:
URINAL
THE MAKING OF MONSTER

NANCY GREYSTONE
Agent: Pleshette & Green - Los Angeles, 213/465-0428

Screenplays:
STARS NIGHT OUT
NELLY BLY
WESTWARD WHEELING
ALONG FOR THE RIDE
OUR LADY OF THE PARKWAY DINER
ACROSS THE LAKE

STEVE GRIEGER
Agent: Berzon Agency - Glendale, 818/548-1560

Screenplays:
FATHER HUSTLE w/Tim Irving
FUTUREMAN w/Tim Irving
OUR GANG w/Tim Irving
THE RETURN OF THE TERRIBLE TOTS w/Tim Irving

ANDREW GRIEVE
Agent: Lemon Unna & Durbridge - London, 071/727-1346

ON THE BLACK HILL   Roxie Releasing Co., 1991, directed

EDDIE GRIFFIN
Contact: Screen Actors Guild - Los Angeles, 213/954-1600

Screenplays:
BLUELIGHT w/Preston Whitmore

TOM GRIFFIN*
Agent: William Morris Agency - Beverly Hills, 310/274-7451

THE BOYS NEXT DOOR (P)
EINSTEIN AND THE POLAR BEAR (P)
DINNER AT EIGHT (CTF)   Think Entertainment, 1989

Screenplays:
FIDELITY
MR. AMBASSADOR

TONY GRIFFIN
DROP ZONE   Paramount, 1994, Story w/Guy Manos &
   Peter Barsochini

CHARLES B. GRIFFITH
A BUCKET OF BLOOD   American International, 1957
ATTACK OF THE CRAB MONSTERS   Allied Artists, 1957
NOT OF THIS EARTH   Allied Artists, 1957, w/Mark Hanna
THE WILD ANGELS   American International, 1966
EAT MY DUST   New World, 1976, directed
DR. HECKYL AND MR. HYPE   Cannon, 1980, directed

LISSA LEFF GRIFFITH
Agent: Jim Preminger Agency - Los Angeles, 310/475-9491

SUMMER LESSONS (Short)   directed

Screenplays:
INDIAN SUMMER
THE STAR SPANGLED GIRL w/Suzy Witten
WHAT TO DO WITH DANNY

THOMAS IAN GRIFFITH*
Agent: CAA - Beverly Hills, 310/288-4545

NIGHT OF THE WARRIOR   Trimark, 1991
EXCESSIVE FORCE   New Line Cinema, 1993, w/Erwin Stoff

MARK L. GRIFFITHS*
Agent: The Turtle Agency - Studio City, 818/506-6898
Contact: Shelley Surpin, Surpin, Mayersohn & Edelstone -
   Los Angeles, 310/552-1808

RUNNING HOT   New Line Cinema, 1984, directed
HARDBODIES   Columbia, 1984, w/Steven Greene &
   Eric Alter, directed
HARDBODIES 2   CineTel Films, 1986, w/Eric Alter, directed

TREVOR GRIFFITHS*
Contact: Peters, Fraser & Dunlop - London, 071/376-7676

COMEDIANS (P)
THE PARTY (P)
SAM (P)
OCCUPATIONS (P)
THE WAGES OF THIN (P)
REDS ★   Paramount, 1981, w/Warren Beatty
SINGING THE BLUES IN RED   Angelika Films, 1988

CHRISTOPHER GRIMM
RHYTHM THIEF   Film Crash, 1994, w/Matthew Harrison

MARIA GRIMM
THE FEMININE TOUCH   Flamingo Films, 1994

TONY GRISONI*
Agent: Sanford-Gross & Associates - Los Angeles,
   310/208-2100

THE INSIDE MAN (Short)   1980
POSSESSIONS (Short)   1982
DARK WATER   ITC, 1980, w/Andrew Bergman
QUEEN OF HEARTS   Cinecom, 1989
EBBTIDE (Short)   1993

KENNETH W. GRISWOLD
CHAMPIONS FOREVER (FD)   Ion Pictures, 1989

RAJKO GRLIC
THAT SUMMER OF WHITE ROSES   Amy International/Jadran Film,
   1989, w/Simon MacCorkindale & Borislav Pekic, directed

TINUS GROBLER
BRUTAL GLORY   Quintex Entertainment, 1991

GEOFF GRODE*
Contact: WGA - Los Angeles, 310/550-1000

Screenplays:
TWO GUYS FROM ITALY
SINGLE FILE
SANTA CRUZ
THE FOURTH DICK
THIEF TAKER

CHARLES GRODIN*
Agent: United Talent Agency - Beverly Hills, 310/273-6700

PRICE OF FAME (P)
ONE OF THE ALL TIME GREATS (P)
MOVERS & SHAKERS   MGM/UA, 1985

Screenplays:
THE SECRET LIFE OF MEN

MICHAEL GRODNER
Agent: Susan Smith & Associates - Beverly Hills, 213/852-4777

Screenplays:
COURTING DISASTER
THE TAKING OF P.S. 196
GUN SHY
I SHOT THE SHERIFF
BARE KNUCKLES
DARK HORSE

DANIEL GRODNIK*
Agent: Paradigm - Los Angeles, 310/277-4400
Business: Itasca Pictures, 345 N. Maple Drive - Suite 278,
   Beverly Hills, CA 90210, 310/273-6505

WITHOUT WARNING   Filmways, 1980, w/Lyn Freeman,
   Ben Nett & Steve Mathis

FERDE GROFE JR.*
Contact: Sal Lawrence, 310/275-5114

JUDGMENT DAY   Rockport/Ferde Grofe Films, 1989, directed

ALAN GROSS*
Contact: WGA - Los Angeles, 310/550-1000

THE MAN IN 605 (P)
LUNCHING (P)

Screenplays:
THE LOVE SONG OF RUDY KAZOO
AMERICAN GOTHIC

JOEL GROSS*
Agent: William Morris Agency - New York, 212/586-5100

MESMER (P)
PORTRAIT (P)
HAVEN (P)
BLIND MAN'S BLUFF (CTF)   Wilshire Court Productions/
   Pacific Motion Pictures, 1992
NO ESCAPE   Savoy Pictures, 1994, w/Michael Gaylin

Screenplays:
SYNDICATE WIFE
LA VS. NY
THE BEGGARS ALIBI
AGAINST ALL HOPE
TEARS OF THE SUN w/Ron Bass
SPRINGTIME GIRL
WIDOW

LARRY GROSS*
Agent: CAA - Beverly Hills, 310/288-4545

HEADIN' FOR BROADWAY   20th Century-Fox, 1980,
   w/Joseph Brooks & Hilary Henkin
48 HRS.   Paramount, 1982, w/Walter Hill, Steven de Souza &
   Roger Spottiswoode
STREETS OF FIRE   Universal, 1984, w/Walter Hill
ANOTHER 48 HRS.   Paramount, 1990, w/John Fasano & Jeb Stuart
GERONIMO: AN AMERICAN LEGEND   Columbia, 1993,
   w/John Milius

Screenplays:
THE ROYAL WAY w/Andrei Konchalovsky (Miramax)
SMILLA'S SENSE OF SNOW
CANDIDE
SUCCESS w/Mary Robison
NOT A THROUGH STREET
SNOW BLIND
MAD LOVE
THE BARTENDER
SMALL COLLEGE IN THE WOODS
LIFE LINE

BROADWAY
ADULTERY
NEON
QUEEN OF MIDNIGHT
L.A. AT NIGHT
THROB
THE EXECUTIONER

MARJORIE L. GROSS*
Agent: William Morris Agency - Beverly Hills, 310/274-7451
Manager: 3 Arts Entertainment - Los Angeles, 213/851-5700

Screenplays:
THE BEST MAN w/Ron Zimmerman
HAPPILY EVER AFTER
SPOOKY

DOUGLAS GROSSMAN*
Contact: Andrew Rigrod - 310/858-0682

UP THE CREEK   Orion, 1984, Story w/Jim Kouf & Jeffrey Sherman
HELL HIGH   JGM Enterprises, 1989, w/Leo Evans, directed

LYNN GROSSMAN*
Agent: United Talent Agency - Beverly Hills, 310/273-6700

TOKYO POP   Spectrafilm, 1988, w/Fran Rubel Kuzui

Screenplays:
THE PUTNAM PROJECT
HE'S ALL MINE
HOME FOR THE HOLIDAYS
CANARSIE
CLEAR CUT
WANTED (Shared)
GROWING UP
MARRIED LIFE
DAVID AT 40
LINER NOTES

JOHN P. GROVES*
Contact: WGA - Los Angeles, 310/550-1000

THE GOLDEN SEAL   Samuel Goldwyn Company, 1983
AMERICAN GLADIATOR   Buena Vista, 1985
BIGGLES   New Century/Vista, 1988, w/Kent Walwin

Screenplays:
DEATH PROBE
SQUAW MAN
KLUDGE

PHIL GROVES
BEACHGIRLS   Crown International, 1982, w/Patrick Duncan

JEAN GRUAULT
Contact: French Film Office, 745 Fifth Avenue, New York, NY 10151,
   212/832-8860

JULES ET JIM   Janus, 1961, w/Francois Truffaut
THE WILD CHILD   United Artists, 1970, w/Francois Truffaut
THE STORY OF ADELE H.   New World, 1975,
   w/Suzanne Schiffman & Francois Truffaut
MON ONCLE D'AMERIQUE ★   New World, 1980
L'AMOUR A MORT   Roissy Film, 1984
LIFE IS A BED OF ROSES   Spectrafilm, 1984
LES ANNEES 80S   World Artists, 1985, w/Chantal Akerman
THE MYSTERY OF ALEXINA   European Classics, 1985,
   w/Rene Feret

LISA GRUNWALD*
Agent: Pleshette & Green - Los Angeles, 213/465-0428

Screenplays:
SUMMER
OTHER HUSBAND'S WIVES

LARRY M. GRUSIN*
Agent: Gold/Marshak - Burbank, 818/972-4300
Manager: Krost/Chapin Management - Los Angeles, 310/281-3585

GARBO TALKS   MGM/UA, 1984

Screenplays:
IRREPLACEABLE KID
CHROMIUM BLUE
EARTHLY DELIGHTS
LIVING ARROWS
ADAM & EVE THE SECOND
BACKWARDS ON A HORSE
ONE IN A MILLION
IVAN

JOHN GUARE*
Agent: ICM - New York, 212/556-5600

LYDIE BREEZE (P)
THE HOUSE OF BLUE LEAVES (P)
LANDSCAPE OF THE BODY (P)
BOSOMS AND NEGLECT (P)
RICH AND FAMOUS (P)
GARDENIA (P)
MOON OVER MIAMI (P)   also screenplay
FOUR BABOONS ADORING THE SUN (P)
TAKING OFF   Universal, 1971, w/Jean-Claude Carriere,
    Milos Forman & John Klein
ATLANTIC CITY ★   Paramount, 1981
SIX DEGREES OF SEPARATION   MGM, 1993, from his play

Screenplays:
DIETRICH
THE STARK TRUTH
GERSHWIN
SALUTE THE ARTIST
THE BIG KISS
BAMBOOZLE
STEPPENWOLF
EYE CONTACT

PAUL GUAY*
Agent: Innovative Artists - Los Angeles, 310/553-5200
Manager: The Roberts Company - Los Angeles, 310/552-7800

THE LITTLE RASCALS   Universal, 1994, w/Stephen Mazur &
    Penelope Spheeris

Screenplays:
MR. MAGOO w/Stephen Mazur
ABRA-CADAVER w/Stephen Mazur
MAGICIAN'S ANONYMOUS w/Stephen Mazur
THE CHRISTMAS SPIRIT w/Stephen Mazur
THE C-NOTE w/Stephen Mazur
TAKE TWO w/Stephen Mazur
THE LAST LAUGH w/Marcus Cootsona & Craig Lachman
CENTRAL PARK

RICHARD GUAY*
Agent: United Talent Agency - Beverly Hills, 310/273-6700
Business: Forward Films, 2445 Herring Avenue, Bronx, NY 10469

TRUE LOVE   MGM/UA, 1989, w/Nancy Savoca
HOUSEHOLD SAINTS   Fine Line Features, 1993, w/Nancy Savoca

Screenplays:
GRACE UNDER PRESSURE w/Nancy Savoca

CHRISTIAN GUDEGAST
Agent: The Irv Schechter Company - Beverly Hills, 310/278-8070

Screenplays:
BLACK OCEAN
ECLIPSE

MAC GUDGEON
GROUND ZERO   Avenue Pictures, 1988, w/Jan Sardi
THE DELINQUENTS   Warner Bros., 1990, w/Clayton Frohman
WIND   TriStar, 1992, w/Rudy Wurlitzer

ANN GUEDES
BEARSKIN: AN URBAN FAIRYTALE   Film Four International/
    British Screen/Cinema Action IPC/RPT, 1989,
    w/Eduardo Guedes, co-directed

EDUARDO GUEDES
BEARSKIN: AN URBAN FAIRYTALE   Film Four International/
    British Screen/Cinema Action IPC/RPT, 1989,
    w/Ann Guedes, co-directed

ROBERT GUENETTE*
Agent: ICM - Beverly Hills, 310/550-4000

THE DEFECTOR   PECF, 1966, w/Raoul Levy
THE MYSTERIOUS MONSTERS (FD)   Sunn Classic,
    1976, directed
THE MAN WHO SAW TOMORROW (FD)   Warner Bros., 1981,
    w/Alan Hopgood, directed

ANDREW GUERDAT*
Agent: CAA - Beverly Hills, 310/288-4545

FOURTH STORY (CTF)   Viacom Pictures Inc./
    Konigsberg-Sanitsky Co., 1991

TONINO GUERRA
LA NOTTE   Lopert, 1961, w/Michelangelo Antonioni & Ennio Flaiano
L'AVVENTURA   Janus, 1961, w/Michelangelo Antonioni &
    Elio Bertolini
L'ECLISSE (THE ECLIPSE)   Paris Film, 1952, w/others
LA NOIA (THE EMPTY CANCAS)   CC Chapion, 1964, w/others
RED DESERT   Rizzoli, 1965, w/Michelangelo Antonioni
CASANOVA '70 ★   Embassy, 1965, w/others
THE TENTH VICTIM   Avco Embassy, 1965, w/others
BLOW-UP ★   Premier, 1966, w/Michelangelo Antonioni &
    Edward Bond
IN SEARCH OF GREGORY   Universal, 1969, w/Lucile Laks
ZABRISKIE POINT   MGM, 1970, w/Michelangelo Antonioni,
    Fred Gardner, Clare Peploe & Sam Shepard
AMARCORD ★   New World, 1974, w/Federico Fellini
CADAVERIA ECCELLENTI (ILLUSTRIOUS CORPSES)
    United Artists, 1975, w/Francesco Rosi & Lino Jannuzzi
A BUTTERFLY ON THE SHOULDER   UN PAPILLON SUR
    L'EPAULE   Gaumont, 1978, w/Jean-Claude Carriere
EBOLI   CHRIST STOPPED AT EBOLI   Franklin Media, 1980,
    w/Raffaele La Capria & Francesco Rosi
THE NIGHT OF THE SHOOTING STARS   LA NOTTE DI SANS
    LORENZO   United Artists Classics, 1982, w/Paolo Taviani,
    Vittorio Taviani & Guiliana G. DeNegri
AND THE SHIP SAILS ON   Triumph/Columbia, 1983,
    w/Federico Fellini
NOSTALGHIA   Grange Communications, 1984, w/Andre Tarkovsky
HENRY IV   Orion Classics, 1985, w/Marco Bellocchio
GINGER AND FRED   MGM/UA, 1986, w/Federico Fellini &
    Tullio Pinelli
NIGHT SUN   1990, Shared
JOURNEY OF LOVE   Centaur Releasing, 1990
EVERYBODY'S FINE   Miramax, 1991, w/Giuseppe Tornatore
ESPECIALLY ON SUNDAY   Miramax, 1993, directed

CHRISTOPHER GUEST*
Agent: CAA - Beverly Hills, 310/288-4545

THIS IS SPINAL TAP   Embassy, 1984, w/Michael McKean,
    Harry Shearer & Rob Reiner
THE BIG PICTURE   Columbia, 1989, w/Michael McKean &
    Michael Varhol, directed

JUDITH A. GUEST*
Agent: Patricia Karlan Agency - Burbank, 818/846-8666

RACHEL RIVER   Taurus Entertainment, 1989

VAL GUEST
Agent: ICM - London, 071/629-8080

CONVICT 99   Gainsborough, 1938, w/Jack Davies,
   Marriott Edgar & Ralph Smart
ASK A POLICEMAN   Gainsborough, 1938, w/Marriott Edgar &
   J.O.C. Orton
BAND WAGON   Gainsborough, 1939, w/Marriott Edgar
CHARLEY'S BIG-HEARTED AUNT   Gainsborough, 1940,
   w/Marriott Edgar
BACK ROOM BOY   General Film Distributors, 1942,
   w/Marriott Edgar
MISS LONDON LTD.   General Film Distributors, 1943,
   w/Marriott Edgar, directed
GIVE US THE MOON   General Film Distributors, 1944, directed
BEES IN PARADISE   General Film Distributors, 1944,
   w/Marriott Edgar, directed
I'LL BE YOUR SWEETHEART   General Film Distributors, 1945,
   w/Val Valentine, directed
MURDER AT THE WINDMILL   Grand National, 1949, directed
PAPER ORCHARD   Columbia, 1949
HAPPY GO LOVELY   ABP, 1950
MISS PILGRIM'S PROGRESS   Grand National, 1950, directed
MISTER DRAKE'S DUCK   United Artists, 1951, directed
ANOTHER MAN'S POISON   United Artists, 1952
PENNY PRINCESS   Rank, 1952, directed
THE RUNAWAY BUS   Eros, 1954, directed
DANCE LITTLE LADY   Renown, 1954,
   w/Doreen Montgomery, directed
BREAK IN THE CIRCLE   20th Century-Fox, 1955, directed
THE CREEPING UNKNOWN   *THE QUARTERMASS EXPERIMENT*
   Hammer, 1955, w/Richard Landau, directed
ENEMY FROM SPACE   *QUATERMASS II*   Hammer, 1957,
   w/Nigel Kneale, directed
UP THE CREEK   Byron, 1958, directed
THE CAMP ON BLOOD ISLAND   Columbia, 1958,
   w/Jon Manchip White, directed
HELL IS A CITY   Columbia, 1960, directed
STOP ME BEFORE I KILL   *THE FULL TREATMENT*   Columbia,
   1961, w/R.S. Thorn, directed
THE DAY THE EARTH CAUGHT FIRE   Universal, 1962,
   w/Wolf Mankowitz, directed
JIGSAW   British Lion, 1962, directed
EIGHTY THOUSAND SUSPECTS   Rank, 1963, directed
CONTEST GIRL   *THE BEAUTY JUNGLE*   Continental, 1964,
   w/Robert Muller, directed
WHERE THE SPIES ARE   MGM, 1965, w/Wolf Mankowitz, directed
ASSIGNMENT K   Columbia, 1968, w/Maurice Foster &
   Bill Strutton, directed
WHEN DINOSAURS RULED THE EARTH   Hammer, 1969, directed
THE BOYS IN BLUE   MAM Ltd./Apollo Leisure Group,
   1983, directed

ANGELO GUGLIELMO
Agent: Writers & Artists Agency - Los Angeles, 310/824-6300

Screenplays:
FALLEN FROM GRACE   w/Paul Raczakowski

FREELING DAMON GUINN
Agent: The Artists Group - Los Angeles, 310/552-1100

Screenplays:
HARVEST DAY DANCE

PAUL JOSEPH GULINO
MURDEROUS VISION (CTF)   Gary Sherman/Wilshire Court
   Productions, 1991

STEPHEN GULSVIG
Agent: Berzon Agency - Glendale, 818/548-1560

Screenplays:
THE MONEY TREE

JOSEPH A. GUNN*
Contact: WGA - Los Angeles, 310/550-1000

THE WILD PAIR   Trans World Entertainment, 1987

ROBERT GUNTER*
Agent: Innovative Artists - Los Angeles, 310/553-5200

THE SANDLOT   20th Century Fox, 1993, w/David Mickey Evans

Screenplays:
RUN WITH THE WIND (AF)
MAYHEM
THE DREAD BOYS
FALSE PROFIT
MOMMA'S BOY
THE LEMON

DANIEL J. GUNTZELMAN*
Agent: ICM - Beverly Hills, 310/550-4000

REVENGE OF THE NERDS II   20th Century Fox, 1987,
   w/Steve Marshall

Screenplays:
HOT WATER   w/Steve Marshall
PAPARAZZI   w/Steve Marshall

PAUL GURION*
Contact: WGA - Los Angeles, 310/550-1000

Screenplays:
ICELANDIC SAGAS   (New Line Cinema)
HACKSAW

A.R. "PETE" GURNEY*
Agent: William Morris Agency - New York, 212/586-5100

THE DAVID SHOW (P)
SCENES FROM AMERICAN LIFE (P)
RICHARD CORY (P)
THE WAYSIDE MOTOR INN (P)
WHAT I DID LAST SUMMER (P)
THE GOLDEN AGE (P)
THE PERFECT PARTY (P)
SWEET SUE (P)
THE DINING ROOM (P)
THE COCKTAIL HOUR (P)
THE MIDDLE AGES (P)
ANOTHER ANTIGONE (P)
LOVE LETTERS (P)   also screenplay
SNOW BALL (P)
THE OLD BOY (P)
LATER LIFE (P)
THE FOURTH WALL (P)
A CHEEVER EVENING (P)

Screenplays:
HURDLES
THE HOUSE OF MIRTH

DAN GURSKIS*
Agent: The Gersh Agency - Beverly Hills, 310/274-6611

CIVIL WARS (P)
PATER NOSTER (P)
THE STRANGER   Columbia, 1987
BODY LANGUAGE (CTF)   Wilshire Court Productions, 1992,
   w/Brian Ross

Screenplays:
THE LOCKED ROOM

ERIC GUSTAVSON
Agent: The Chasin Agency - Los Angeles, 310/278-7505

Screenplays:
LIARS

BETH R. GUTCHEON*
Agent: CAA - Beverly Hills, 310/288-4545

WITHOUT A TRACE   20th Century-Fox, 1983
THE GOOD FIGHT (CTF)   Freyda Rothstein Productions/Hearst
   Entertainment, 1993

Screenplays:
THE MARRIAGE STORY
MATINEE

LARRY GUTERMAN*
Contact: WGA - Los Angeles, 310/550-1000

Screenplays:
SHORT CIRCUIT III w/Irving Belateche
JACK SPRINGER w/Irving Belateche

VINCENT A. GUTIERREZ*
Agent: Annette Van Duren Agency - Los Angeles, 213/650-3643

INSIDE EDGE   Life Entertainment, 1992

Screenplays:
HEARTBREAKER
BLESS ME ULTIMA
WELCOME HOME
WOMAN OF THE RING
A FLAG TO FLY
THE JOURNEY OF MARIA LOPEZ

RICHARD A. GUTTMAN
HIGHPOINT   New World, 1984, w/Ian Sutherland
THE LAST ELEPHANT (CTF)   RHI Entertainment/Quintex
   Entertainment, 1990, w/Bill Bozzone

Screenplays:
COVER OF DARKNESS
MOST WANTED

ROBERT GUZA JR.*
Agent: The Irv Schechter Company - Beverly Hills, 310/278-8070

PROM NIGHT   Avco Embassy, 1980, Story
CURTAINS   Jensen Farley Pictures, 1983

STEPHEN R. GYLLENHAAL*
Agent: CAA - Beverly Hills, 310/288-4545

THE NEW KIDS   Columbia, 1985

H

BELINDA HAAS
Agent: United Talent Agency - Beverly Hills, 310/273-6700

THE MUSIC OF CHANCE   I.R.S. Releasing, 1993, w/Philip Haas
ANGELS & INSECTS   Samuel Goldwyn Company, 1995,
   w/Philip Haas

CHARLIE S. HAAS*
Agent: CAA - Beverly Hills, 310/288-4545

OVER THE EDGE   Orion/Warner Bros., 1979, w/Tim Hunter
TEX   Buena Vista, 1982, w/Tim Hunter
RECKLESS DISREGARD (CTF)   Telecom Entertainment/Polar Film
   Corporation/Fremantle of Canada Ltd., 1985
MARTIANS GO HOME   Taurus Entertainment, 1990
GREMLINS 2 THE NEW BATCH   Warner Bros., 1990
MATINEE   Universal, 1993
RUNAWAY DAUGHTERS (CTF)   Showtime/Drive-In
   Classic Cinema, 1994

Screenplays:
THE LAVENDER HILL MOB (remake)
TERMITE TERRACE
TRAP DOOR w/Tim Hunter
HOMELANDS
DEATH MAKES THE CHART
BACK ON TOP

PHILIP HAAS
Agent: United Talent Agency - Beverly Hills, 310/273-6700

THE MUSIC OF CHANCE   I.R.S. Releasing, 1993,
   w/Belinda Haas, directed
ANGELS & INSECTS   Samuel Goldwyn Company, 1995,
   w/Belinda Haas, directed

STEVE HABERMAN*
Agent: Amsel, Eisenstadt & Frazier - Los Angeles, 310/939-1188

BLIND CURVES (Short)   directed
LIFE STINKS   MGM-Pathe, 1991, w/Mel Brooks & Rudy DeLuca

Screenplays:
DRACULA: DEAD AND LIKING IT w/Rudy DeLuca
SCOOP
NOT HUMAN

MICHAEL HACKER
Agent: Metropolitan Talent Agency - Los Angeles, 213/857-4500

LONG TIME COMING (P)

Screenplays:
IRONMEN w/Jeff Miller
FEVER w/Jeff Miller

ALBERT HACKETT*
Agent: Flora Roberts Inc. - New York, 212/355-4165

EASTER PARADE   MGM, 1948, w/Frances Goodrich &
   Sidney Sheldon
FATHER OF THE BRIDE ★   MGM, 1950, w/Frances Goodrich
FATHER'S LITTLE DIVIDEND   MGM, 1951, w/Frances Goodrich
GIVE A GIRL A BREAK   MGM, 1953, w/Frances Goodrich
THE LONG LONG TRAILER   MGM, 1954, w/Frances Goodrich
GABY   MGM, 1956, w/Frances Goodrich & Charles Lederer

A CERTAIN SMILE   20th Century-Fox, 1958, w/Frances Goodrich
THE DIARY OF ANNE FRANK   20th Century-Fox, 1959,
    w/Frances Goodrich, from their play
FIVE FINGER EXERCISE   Columbia, 1962, w/Frances Goodrich
FATHER OF THE BRIDE   Buena Vista, 1991, w/Frances Goodrich,
    Nancy Meyers & Charles Shyer

TOD HACKETT
(See Alan Ormsby)

DENNIS E. HACKIN*
Agent: The Artists Agency - Los Angeles, 310/277-7779

WANDA NEVADA   United Artists, 1979
BRONCO BILLY   Warner Bros., 1980
NO HOLDS BARRED   New Line Cinema, 1989

Screenplays:
THUNDERBOAT w/Stuart Birnbaum

MOSHE HADAR
CARTEL   Shapiro Glickenhaus, 1990

NICHOLAS HADJI
Contact: KellCole Productions - 213/876-6191

Screenplays:
TUSKAGEE AIRMEN 332

HORATIUS HAEBERLE
THE LAST WORD   Samuel Goldwyn Company, 1979, Story

ROLF HAEDRICH
AMONG THE CINDERS   New World, 1985,
    w/John O'Shea, directed

ZION HAEN
TRIUMPH OF THE SPIRIT   Nova International Films, 1989,
    Story w/Shimon Arama

GEORGE D. HAGEN*
Agent: United Talent Agency - Beverly Hills, 310/273-6700

Screenplays:
STIFFS
SMALL FEARS
PAJAMA PRINCESS

ROSS L. HAGEN*
Agent: Barry Perelman Agency - Los Angeles, 213/274-5999

CLICK: THE CALENDAR GIRL KILLER   Crown International, 1991,
    w/Hoke Howell, David Chute & David Reskin, co-directed

STEVEN J. HAGER*
Contact: WGA - New York, 212/245-6180

BEAT STREET   Orion, 1984, Story

JAMES HAGGIN*
Agent: Innovative Artists - Los Angeles, 310/553-5200

Screenplays:
NUCLEAR FAMILY w/Blake Snyder
TROUBLESHOOTER

PAUL HAGGIS*
Manager: I.R.S./Harris Management - Culver City, 310/841-4169

RED HOT   SC Entertainment International, 1993,
    w/Michael Maurer, directed

DAVID W. HAHN*
Business: Otter Productions - Los Angeles, 213/969-0195

IN A REHEARSAL ROOM (Short)   1975, directed
RUTH PAGE: AN AMERICAN ORIGINAL (FD)   Films Inc.,
    1978, directed

Screenplays:
A VENGEFUL HEART
HARVEST MOON
SUMMER DREAMS
CURSE OF THE STARVING CLASS
EVENING IN PARIS w/John Byrum

OLIVER D. HAILEY
FOR THE USE OF THE HALL (P)
JUST YOU AND ME KID   Columbia, 1979, w/Leonard B. Stern

RICHARD HAINES
SPACE AVENGER   Manley Productions, 1990,
    w/Lynwood Sawyer, directed

MERVYN HAISMAN
JANE AND THE LOST CITY   New World, 1987

JOE HALDEMAN*
Contact: WGA - New York, 212/245-6180

ROBOTJOX   Triumph Releasing, 1990

MARY HALE
Agent: APA - Los Angeles, 310/273-0744

Screenplays:
MULTIPLICITY w/Chris Miller

JONATHAN HALES
LOOPHOLE   MGM/United Artists, 1980
THE MIRROR CRACK'D   EMI, 1980, w/Barry Sandler
YOUNG INDIANA JONES AND THE HOLLYWOOD FOLLIES (CTF)
    Lucasfilm Ltd./Family Channel, 1994, w/Matthew Jacobs

JOHN HALFPENNY
ROCK & RULE (AF)   MGM/UA, 1985, w/Peter Sauder

BENJAMIN HALL
Agent: Lisa Callamaro Literary Agency- Beverly Hills, 310/274-6783

Screenplays:
BASE NATURE w/Winter Mead
PAPER PRISONS w/Winter Mead

BRAD HALL*
Agent: CAA - Beverly Hills, 310/288-4545

BORIS & NATASHA (CTF)   MCEG Productions, 1992,
    Story w/Charles Fradin
BYE, BYE LOVE   20th Century Fox, 1995, w/Gary David Goldberg

KENNETH J. HALL
THE TOMB   Trans World Entertainment, 1986
DR. ALIEN   Phantom Productions, 1989
PUPPET MASTER   Full Moon, 1989, Story w/Charles Band

PARNELL HALL*
Contact: WGA - New York, 212/245-6180

C.H.U.D.   New World, 1984

RANDY HALL
Agent: Berzon Agency - Glendale, 818/548-1560

Screenplays:
THEREAFTER
SHAKESPEARE MOUSE
DAD THE DUDE

LASSE HALLSTROM
Agent: ICM - Beverly Hills, 310/550-4000

MY LIFE AS A DOG ★ Skouras Pictures, 1987,
   w/Reidar Jonsson, Brasse Brannstrom &
   Per Berglund, directed

Screenplays:
PETER PAN

DENISE HALMA*
Agent: Camden-ITG - Los Angeles, 310/289-2700

Screenplays:
PRETTY WOMAN II
DAD'S WEEK OFF w/Elliot Stern

DAVID HALPERN
DEADLY DANCER Action International Pictures, 1990,
   w/Maria Fields

ALANNA HAMILL*
Contact: WGA - Los Angeles, 310/550-1000

THE SPIDER AND THE FLY (CTF) Haft/Nasatir-Wilshire Court,
   1994, w/Robert Pucci

DENIS M. HAMILL
Contact: 914/876-2794

TURK 182 20th Century Fox, 1985, w/John Hamill &
   James Gregory Kingston
CRITICAL CONDITION Paramount, 1987,
   w/John Hamill

Screenplays:
CALL ME A COP w/John Hamill
STOMPING GROUND w/John Hamill
A KILLING FOR CHRIST w/John Hamill
REFORM SCHOOL PROJECT w/John Hamill
DIPLOMATIC IMMUNITY w/John Hamill
ENCORE w/John Hamill
WHERE THERE'S A WILL w/John Hamill
DIVERSIONS w/John Hamill

JOHN P. HAMILL
Contact: 914/876-2794

TURK 182 20th Century Fox, 1985, w/Denis Hamill &
   James Gregory Kingston
CRITICAL CONDITION Paramount, 1987, w/Denis Hamill

Screenplays:
CALL ME A COP w/Denis Hamill
STOMPING GROUND w/Denis Hamill
A KILLING FOR CHRIST w/Denis Hamill
REFORM SCHOOL PROJECT w/Denis Hamill
DIPLOMATIC IMMUNITY w/Denis Hamill
ENCORE w/Denis Hamill
WHERE THERE'S A WILL w/Denis Hamill
DIVERSIONS w/Denis Hamill

PETE HAMILL*
Agent: ICM - Beverly Hills, 310/550-4000

DOC United Artists, 1971
BADGE 373 Paramount, 1973
LAGUNA HEAT (CTF) HBO Pictures/Jay Weston Productions,
   1987, w/D.M. Eyre & David Burton Morris
THE NEON EMPIRE (CTF) Fries Entertainment/Richard Maynard
   Productions, 1989

Screenplays:
THE YELLOW HANDKERCHIEF (Universal)
PANCHO VILLA
CAR RACING STORY
HORSE RACING
DIRTY LAUNDRY
JACK THE RIPPER
JUDGMENT DAY

ANN LEWIS HAMILTON*
Agent: United Talent Agency - Beverly Hills, 310/273-6700

Screenplays:
FLING
THE GIRLS OF SUMMER
ELLEN FOSTER
NEON CITY
FRESH AIR

DEAN HAMILTON
SAVAGE LAND Hemdale, 1994, directed

GUY HAMILTON
Agent: ICM - Beverly Hills, 310/550-4000

THE COLDITZ STORY Republic, 1955, w/Ivan Foxwell, directed
A TOUCH OF LARCENY Paramount, 1959, w/Ivan Foxwell &
   Roger MacDougall, directed

JOHN HAMILTON
Agent: Berzon Agency - Glendale, 818/548-1560

Screenplays:
HAGAR THE HORRIBLE w/Jim Olloff
GHOST MARSHALL w/Jim Olloff

SAM HAMM*
Agent: Warden, White & Kane - Beverly Hills, 213/852-1028

NEVER CRY WOLF Buena Vista, 1983, w/Curtis Hanson &
   Richard Kletter
BATMAN Warner Bros., 1989, w/Warren Skaaren
BATMAN RETURNS Warner Bros., 1992, Story w/Dan Waters

Screenplays:
DEMOLISHED MAN
TIME OUT OF JOINT w/Michael Duncan
WATCHMEN
THE AVENGERS
RENEGADE
PULITZER PRIZE
DUMBLUCK
HANG TIME
WHITE WEDDING

JANE-HOWARD HAMMERSTEIN*
Agent: The Marion Rosenberg Office - Los Angeles, 213/653-7383

Screenplays:
TECUMSEH (CTF)

DIANA HAMMOND*
Agent: Writers & Artists Agency - Los Angeles, 310/824-6300

Screenplays:
EDEN ROC
BLOOD RED ROSE
TEARS OF AUTUMN
DON'T GET THE GIRL?
LIBBY
SHADOW OF GOD
FATHER'S DAY
ARE YOU OUT OF MY MIND?
HOLY BLOOD, HOLY GRAIL
MOUSE PACKS
WILDCARD
VIRGIN

JEFFREY LEE HAMMOND*
Agent: Richland/Wunsch/Hohman Agency - Los Angeles, 310/278-1955

Screenplays:
COLD EYE w/Mark Kruger
THE APOSTASY w/Mark Kruger
DARK HORSE w/Mark Kruger
CANDIDE (AF) w/Mark Kruger
POST-MORTEM (CTF) w/Mark Kruger

CHRISTOPHER HAMPTON*
Agent: William Morris Agency - Beverly Hills, 310/274-7451

THE PHILANTHROPIST (P)
WHITE CAMELEON (P)
TREATS (P)
TOTAL ECLIPSE (P)   also screenplay
SUNSET BLVD. (P)   w/Don Black
A DOLL'S HOUSE   Elkins, 1973
TALES FROM THE VIENNA WOODS   Cinema 5, 1981,
   w/Maximilian Schell
BEYOND THE LIMIT   Paramount, 1983
THE WOLF AT THE DOOR   International Film Marketing, 1986
THE GOOD FATHER   Skouras Pictures, 1987
DANGEROUS LIAISONS ★★   Warner Bros., 1988, from his play
CARRINGTON   Polygram, 1994
MARY REILLY   TriStar, 1995

Screenplays:
A BRIGHT SHINING LIE
NOSTROMO w/Robert Bolt
IMAGINING ARGENTINA
THE LAST SECRET
THE MOON & SIXPENCE
RUSSIAN STORY
THE PORTAGE TO SAN CRISTOBAL
THE FLORENTINES

JOHN HANCOCK*
Agent: Camden-ITG - Los Angeles, 310/289-2700

WEEDS   DEG, 1987, w/Dorothy Tristan, directed

JOHN LEE HANCOCK*
Agent: Broder-Kurland-Webb-Uffner - Beverly Hills, 310/281-3400

A PERFECT WORLD   Warner Bros., 1993

Screenplays:
RIVETHEAD
THE SANTA CLAUS BANK ROBBERY
CREEPY KARPIS

CHIP HAND*
Contact: 805/584-0268

LOVELINES   Tri-Star, 1984, w/William Hillman

PETER HANDKE
THE GOALIE'S ANXIETY AT THE PENALTY KICK
   Bauer International, 1972
THE WRONG MOVE   New Yorker, 1975
THE LEFT-HANDED WOMAN   1978, directed
WINGS OF DESIRE   DER HIMMEL UBER BERLIN   Orion Classics,
   1987, w/Wim Wenders

KEN HANDLER
DELIVERY BOYS   New World, 1985, directed

MARK HANDLEY
NELL   Fox, 1994, w/William Nicholson, from his play "Idioglossia"

Screenplays:
THE EDUCATION OF A NEW PIONEER

DARYL HANEY
DADDY'S BOYS   Concorde, 1988
FRIDAY THE 13TH, PART VII: THE NEW BLOOD   Paramount,
   1988, w/Manuel Fidello
LORDS OF THE DEEP   Concorde, 1989, w/Howard Cohen
CRIME ZONE   Concorde, 1989
MASQUE OF THE RED DEATH   Concorde, 1989, w/Larry Brand
CRACKDOWN   Concorde, 1991, w/Ross Bell
WATCHERS II   Concorde, 1993
ANIMAL INSTINCTS 2   Academy Entertainment, 1993

PETER J. HANKOFF*
Manager: RKS Entertainment Group - Sherman Oaks, 818/788-3616

Screenplays:
SANTERIA w/David Madsen
RED CAR w/David Madsen
INSIDE JOB w/David Madsen
RHYTHM & BLUES w/David Madsen
BORROWED TIME w/David Madsen
NIGHTFALL w/Brian Grant
HELL SPA
BREAKTHROUGH
THE CHAINLETTER
THE CRIMINAL MIND OF J. C. LOOMIS
MR. HAPPY
PARKLAND

BRIAN HANNANT
THE ROAD WARRIOR   MAD MAX II   Warner Bros., 1982,
   w/Terry Hayes

ROB HANNING*
Agent: William Morris Agency - Beverly Hills, 310/274-7451

CLUB XII (P)   w/Randy Weiner, also screenplay
THE GANG'S NEW THREADS (P)   w/Randy Weiner

Screenplays:
YO' JULIETTE w/Randy Weiner

ERIK HANSEN*
Agent: Broder-Kurland-Webb-Uffner - Beverly Hills, 310/281-3400

HEART AND SOULS   Universal, 1993, w/Gregory Hansen,
   Brent Maddock & S.S. Wilson

Screenplays:
THE PROMOTER w/Gregory Hansen
MUM'S THE WORD w/Gregory Hansen

GREGORY HANSEN*
Agent: Broder-Kurland-Webb-Uffner - Beverly Hills, 310/281-3400

HEART AND SOULS   Universal, 1993, w/Erik Hansen,
   Brent Maddock & S.S. Wilson

Screenplays:
THE PROMOTER w/Erik Hansen
MUM'S THE WORD w/Erik Hansen

CURTIS HANSON*
Agent: United Talent Agency - Beverly Hills, 310/273-6700

THE DUNWICH HORROR   American International, 1970,
   w/Henry Rosenbaum & Ronald Silkowsky
THE AROUSERS   *SWEET KILL*   New World, 1976
THE SILENT PARTNER   EMC Films/Aurora, 1979
WHITE DOG   Paramount, 1982, w/Samuel Fuller
NEVER CRY WOLF   Buena Vista, 1983, w/Sam Hamm &
   Richard Kletter
THE BEDROOM WINDOW   DEG, 1987, directed

Screenplays:
THE BROTHERHOOD OF THE GRAPE

JOHN HANSON
Agent: Becsey/Wisdom/Kalajian Agency - Los Angeles, 310/550-0535
Business: New Front Films, 125 W. Richmond Avenue,
   Point Richmond, CA 94801, 415/231-0225

NORTHERN LIGHTS   Cinemanifest/New Front Films, 1978,
   w/Rob Nilsson, co-directed
WILDROSE   Troma, 1984, w/Eugene Corr, directed

MASATO HARADA
THE PAINTED DESERT   New Dawn Pictures, 1993,
   w/Rebecca Ross, directed

STEWART HARDING
SPACEHUNTER: ADVENTURES IN THE FORBIDDEN ZONE
   Columbia, 1983, Story w/Jean LaFleur

EVA HARDY
SHE'LL BE WEARING PINK PAJAMAS   Film Forum, 1986

JONATHAN HARDY
BREAKER MORANT ★   New World/Quartet, 1980,
   w/Bruce Beresford & David Stevens

ROBIN HARDY
Address: c/o Robert Lasky, 1150 Fifth Avenue, New York, NY 10128

THE FANTASIST   ITC, 1986, directed
FORBIDDEN SUN   Academy Entertainment, 1989

DAVID HARE
Agent: ICM - Beverly Hills, 310/550-4000

SAIGON - YEAR OF THE CAT (P)   also teleplay
SLAG (P)
THE GREAT EXHIBITION (P)
RACING DEMON (P)
THE KNIFE (P)
BRASSNECK (P)   w/Howard Brenton
KNUCKLE (P)
FANSHEN (P)
LICKING HITLER (P)
DREAMS OF LEAVING (P)
PRAVDA (P)   w/Howard Brenton
MURMURING JUDGES (P)
MAP OF THE WORLD (P)
PLENTY   20th Century Fox, 1985, from his play, directed
WETHERBY   MGM/UA Classics, 1985, directed
STRAPLESS   Miramax, 1990, directed
PARIS BY NIGHT   Cineplex Odeon, 1990, directed
HEADING HOME (CTF)   BBC TV, 1992
DAMAGE   New Line Cinema, 1992
THE SECRET RAPTURE   Castle Hill, 1994, from his play

DEAN HARGROVE*
Agent: Broder-Kurland-Webb-Uffner - Beverly Hills, 310/281-3400

THE MANCHU EAGLE MURDER MYSTERY   United Artists, 1975,
   w/Gabriel Dell, directed

ROBERT HARGROVE
Agent: Preferred Artists - Encino, 818/990-0305

Screenplays:
RECON ONE w/Frank Hale
WELCOME TO THE WAR w/Frank Hale

ERIC HARLACHER*
Agent: Monteiro Rose Agency - Encino, 818/501-1177

HOMEWRECKER (CTF)   Joss Communications/Wilshire Court
   Productions, 1992, w/Fred Walton

Screenplays:
THE FORK AT DEVIL'S GLEN
PRO BONO

RENNY HARLIN
Agent: ICM - Beverly Hills, 310/550-4000

BORN AMERICAN   Cinema Group, 1986, w/Markus Selin, directed

ROBERT M. HARLING*
Agent: CAA - Beverly Hills, 310/288-4545

STEEL MAGNOLIAS   Tri-Star, 1989, from his play
SOAPDISH   Paramount, 1991, w/Andrew Bergman

Screenplays:
THE FIRST WIVES CLUB
RADIO FREE ALASKA
THE EVENING STAR

BARRY HARMON
Agent: Writers & Artists Agency - New York, 212/947-8765

OLYMPUS ON MY MIND (P)
ROMANCE ROMANCE (P)

Screenplays:
BROADWAY BABES
ONCE UPON A MATTRESS
THE BUTTERFLY REVOLUTION
THE JUDAS GOSPEL
SECOND WIND

JUANITA HARMON
Agent: Writers & Artists Agency - Los Angeles, 310/824-6300

Screenplays:
MOTHER'S DAY

SAMUEL H. HARPER*
Agent: Richland/Wunsch/Hohman Agency - Los Angeles,
   310/278-1955

ROOKIE OF THE YEAR   20th Century Fox, 1993

Screenplays:
ACROSS THE BRIDGE
UNCLE SCRATCHY
THE THIRD WHEEL

MICHAEL HARRESCHOU*
Contact: Lew Grimes - New York, 212/974-9505

SAFARI 3000   MGM/United Artists, 1982

STEPHEN HARRIGAN*
Agent: Broder-Kurland-Webb-Uffner - Beverly Hills, 310/281-3400

THE LAST OF HIS TRIBE (CTF)   River City, 1992

Screenplays:
RIN TIN TIN

ALFRED HARRIS*
Agent: Preferred Artists - Encino, 818/990-0305

Screenplays:
TEMPLE OF THE MOON
MY BEAUTIFUL BRIDES

BONNIE HARRIS
WINDRIDER   MGM/UA, 1987, w/Everett DeRoche

DAMIAN HARRIS*
Agent: CAA - Beverly Hills, 310/288-4545
Manager: Addis-Wechsler - Los Angeles, 213/954-9000

THE RACHEL PAPERS   MGM/UA, 1989, directed

DANIEL HARRIS*
Contact: WGA - Los Angeles, 310/550-1000

Screenplays:
MAMA WANTS A BRAND NEW GRAVE! w/Tino Magnatta

FRANK HARRIS
KILLPOINT   Crown International, 1984, directed

HAL HARRIS*
Business Manager: Hansen, Jacobsen & Teller - Los Angeles,
   310/278-8622

Screenplays:
GREYSTOKE II
CORONADO'S GOLD
SPORTSMAN OF THE YEAR

JAMES B. HARRIS*
Contact: Ringer - 310/277-5521
Business: James B. Harris Productions, 248-1/2 Lasky Drive,
   Beverly Hills, CA 90212, 310/273-4270

SOME CALL IT LOVING   CineGlobe, 1973, directed
FAST-WALKING   Pickman Films, 1982, directed
COP   Atlantic Releasing Corporation, 1988, directed
BOILING POINT   Warner Bros., 1993, directed

KIRK HARRIS
Contact: 818/386-5897

Screenplays:
COUNTED OUT (directing)
REASON TO BELIEVE

LESLIE HARRIS
Business: Truth 24 F.P.S., Brooklyn, New York

JUST ANOTHER GIRL ON THE I.R.T.   Miramax, 1993, directed

MARK HARRIS*
Contact: Henry Harris -212/669-0106

BANG THE DRUM SLOWLY   Paramount, 1973

PAUL HARRIS
NICE GIRLS DON'T EXPLODE   New World, 1987

RICHARD HARRIS
Contact: Writers Guild of Great Britain - London, 071/723-8074

I START COUNTING   United Artists, 1969
THE LADY IN THE CAR WITH GLASSES AND A GUN   Lira Film,
   1969, w/El Perry
STEPPING OUT   Paramount, 1991, from his play

SUSAN HARRIS*
Agent: CAA - Beverly Hills, 310/288-4545

Screenplays:
FATHER'S DAY

TIMOTHY H. HARRIS*
Agent: CAA - Beverly Hills, 310/288-4545
Business: Myrtos Productions, 20th Century Fox, 310/277-2211

CHEAPER TO KEEP HER   American Cinema, 1980,
   w/Herschel Weingrod
TRADING PLACES   Paramount, 1983, w/Herschel Weingrod
BREWSTER'S MILLIONS   Universal, 1985, w/Herschel Weingrod
MY STEPMOTHER IS AN ALIEN   WEG, 1988,
   w/Jonathan Reynolds, Herschel Weingrod & Jericho Stone
TWINS   Universal, 1988, w/Herschel Weingrod, William Davies &
   William Osborne
KINDERGARTEN COP   Universal, 1990, w/Herschel Weingrod &
   Murray Salem
PURE LUCK   Universal, 1991, w/Herschel Weingrod

Screenplays:
DUMMIES w/Herschel Weingrod
SIBERIAN EXPRESS w/Herschel Weingrod
THE FRENCH KISS w/Herschel Weingrod
THE PIED PIPER   MOTHER'S DAY w/Herschel Weingrod
THE FUGITIVE PIGEON w/Herschel Weingrod
BIGFINGER w/Herschel Weingrod
MICKEY w/Herschel Weingrod
BEAUTY SCHOOL w/Herschel Weingrod
THE LITTLE BROTHER w/Herschel Weingrod
DISASTER w/Herschel Weingrod

TRENT HARRIS
ORKLY KID (Short)   directed
RUBIN AND ED   I.R.S. Releasing, 1992, directed

Screenplays:
PLAN 10 FROM OUTER SPACE (directing)
ZYZZYX

WENDELL B. HARRIS, JR.
CHAMELEON STREET   Films Around the World, 1990, directed

Screenplays:
NEGROPOLIS (directing)
JOE LOUIS

JIM HARRISON*
Agent: Phoenix Literary Agency - Montana, 406/222-2848

A FAR EDGE (P)
COLD FEET   Avenue Pictures, 1989, w/Tom McGuane
REVENGE   Columbia, 1990, w/Jeffrey Fiskin
WOLF   Columbia, 1994, w/Wesley Strick

Screenplays:
BETWEEN WARS

JOHN KENT HARRISON*
Agent: William Morris Agency - Beverly Hills, 310/274-7451

MURDER BY PHONE   New World, 1982, w/Michael Butler &
   Dennis Shryack
BEAUTIFUL DREAMERS   Hemdale, 1992, directed
THE SOUND AND THE SILENCE (CTF)   Screen Star
   Entertainment/Atlantis Films, 1993, w/Tony Foster &
   William Schmidt, directed

Screenplays:
ROAST BEEF ON SUNDAY
FUR TRADING IN AMERICA

JOHN S. HARRISON*
Agent: CAA - Beverly Hills, 310/288-4545

MEMORIES OF MURDER (CTF) Houston Lady Co./Viacom, 1990,
    w/Nevin Schreiner
FLOATING GUN Trans World Entertainment, 1993

Screenplays:
CORAZON (CTF)
GLORY ROAD w/Randy Johnson
CLONE
IN DEEP

LINDSAY HARRISON*
Agent: Bruce Brown Agency - Los Angeles, 310/208-1835

FRATERNITY VACATION New World, 1985

Screenplays:
AT 17 w/Kathleen Rowell
COMING OF AGE
HOLIDAY ADVENTURE
CUSTODY
WOMEN OF BEVERLY HILLS

MATTHEW HARRISON
RHYTHM THIEF Film Crash, 1994, w/Christopher Grimm, directed

PAUL CARTER HARRISON
YOUNGBLOOD American International, 1978

WILLIAM HARRISON*
Agent: William Morris Agency - New York, 212/586-5100

ROLLERBALL United Artists, 1975
MOUNTAINS OF THE MOON Tri-Star, 1990, w/Bob Rafelson

Screenplays:
UP RIVER

LEE HARRY
SILENT NIGHT, DEADLY NIGHT PART II Ascot Entertainment
    Group, 1987, w/Joseph H. Earle, directed

T. MICHAEL HARRY
IN THE SHADOW OF KILIMANJARO Scotti Bros., 1986,
    w/Jeffrey M. Sneller

CHRISTOPHER HART*
Agent: The Artists Agency - Los Angeles, 310/277-7779

EAT AND RUN New World, 1987, w/Stan Hart, directed

Screenplays:
A KNIGHT IN NEW YORK

JACOBSEN HART
T-FORCE PM Entertainment, 1994

Screenplays:
DIRECT HIT (PM Entertainment)
GUARDIAN ANGEL (PM Entertainment)

JIM V. HART*
Agent: CAA - Beverly Hills, 310/288-4545

GIMME AN F 20th Century Fox, 1985
HOOK Tri-Star, 1991, w/Malia Scotch Marmo
BRAM STOKER'S DRACULA Columbia, 1992

Screenplays:
ENCHANTED COTTAGE
CRISIS IN THE HOT ZONE
HONOR AMONG THIEVES

CONTACT
FRAT RATS
STILL CRAZY w/Bill Kerby
TROUBLE IN BIG D
HOSE JOB
BLOOD MAN
PROTEKTOR
WINTER
HONEYMOON
OLD FRIEND OF THE FAMILY
DRAGONS
WARRIOR BLUE

JOE HART
REPO JAKE PM Home Video, 1991

KENNETH HARTFORD
HELL SQUAD Cannon, 1987

GRAHAM HARTLEY
FATHER Northern Arts Entertainment, 1992, w/Tony Cavanaugh

HAL HARTLEY
Business: True Fiction Pictures, 12 W. 27th St., 10th Floor, New York,
    NY 10001, 212/684-4284

THE UNBELIEVABLE TRUTH Miramax, 1990, directed
TRUST Fine Line Features, 1991, directed
THEORY OF ACHIEVEMENT (Short) 1991, directed
AMBITION (Short) 1991, directed
SURVIVING DESIRE (Short) 1992, directed
SIMPLE MEN Fine Line Features, 1992, directed
AMATEUR Sony Pictures Classics, 1994, directed

Screenplays:
FLIRT (directing)

JESSE HARTMAN
RIVER OF GRASS Plan B Pictures, 1994, w/Kelly Reichardt

PHIL HARTMAN*
Agent: William Morris Agency - Beverly Hills, 310/274-7451

PEE WEE'S BIG ADVENTURE Warner Bros., 1985,
    w/Paul Reubens & Michael Varhol

Screenplays:
*THE CASE OF THE PURPLE TERROR: A CHICK
    HAZARD MYSTERY*
MR. FIX-IT
THE LIAR

RAYMOND C. HARTUNG*
Agent: United Talent Agency - Beverly Hills, 310/273-6700

SNOW KILL (CTF) Wilshire Court Productions, 1990,
    w/Harv Zimmel
FATAL EXPOSURE (CTF) GC Group/Wilshire Court
    Productions, 1991

Screenplays:
OVEREXPOSED
SMART MONEY
TEMPTING FATE
SCREENPLAY
TRASH PATROL

DAVID HARTWELL*
Agent: Sanford-Gross & Associates - Los Angeles,
    310/208-2100

LOVE IS A GUN Trimark, 1994, directed

Screenplays:
SINNERS

JOHN HARTWELL
THE FAN   Paramount, 1981, w/Priscilla Chapman

RON HARVEY
FIST OF FEAR TOUCH OF DEATH   Aquarius, 1980

RONALD HARWOOD
Agent: William Morris Agency - Beverly Hills, 310/274-7451

ANOTHER TIME (P)
REFLECTED GLORY (P)
PRIVATE POTTER   MGM, 1962, from his play
A HIGH WIND IN JAMAICA   20th Century-Fox, 1965,
   w/Dennis Cannan & Stanley Mann
DIAMONDS FOR BREAKFAST   Paramount, 1968,
   w/Pierre Rouve & N.F. Simpson
EYEWITNESS   ITC, 1970
ONE DAY IN THE LIFE OF IVAN DENISOVICH   Group W, 1971
OPERATION DAYBREAK   Warner Bros., 1975
THE DRESSER ★   Columbia, 1983, from his play
THE DOCTOR AND THE DEVILS   20th Century Fox, 1985
A FINE ROMANCE   Castle Hill Productions, 1992
THE BROWNING VERSION   Paramount, 1994

Screenplays:
CRY, THE BELOVED COUNTRY

PATRICK B. HASBURGH*
Agent: CAA - Beverly Hills, 310/288-4545

ASPEN EXTREME   Buena Vista, 1993, directed

Screenplays:
FINAL TOUR
ABEL RAISED A CAIN

WILLIAM HASLEY*
Agent: The Artists Group - Los Angeles, 310/552-1100

Screenplays:
DEFIANE
ROUGHSTOCK
EIGHT SECONDS
A DEADLY SILENCE
HARRY AND ROLLO
BODY COUNT

MICHAEL HASTINGS
Contact: British Academy of Film & Television Arts, 195 Piccadilly,
   London W1, England, 071/734-0022

THE CHANGELING (CTF)   BBC TV, 1994
TOM & VIV   Miramax, 1994, w/Adrian Hodges, based on his play

RICHARD HATEM
Contact: The Goldstein Company - Los Angeles, 310/659-9511

DARK TERRITORY: UNDER SIEGE II   Warner Bros., 1995,
   w/Matt Reeves

CHARLIE HAUCK*
Contact: WGA - Los Angeles, 310/550-1000

Screenplays:
ENGAGED TO BE MARRIED
OFFICE ROMANCE

REX HAUCK*
Contact: WGA - Los Angeles, 310/550-1000

Screenplays:
TWAS THE NIGHT   w/Bryce Zabel

ALAN HAUGE
Contact: GMT Productions, 5751 Buckingham Parkway,
   Culver City, CA 90230

Screenplays:
JAMES DEAN: AN AMERICAN LEGEND   (directing)

WILLIAM HAUPTMAN*
Agent: Broder-Kurland-Webb-Uffner - Beverly Hills, 310/281-3400

HEAT (P)
GILLETTE (P)
BIG RIVER (P)

Screenplays:
THE STORM SEASON

JEFFREY C. HAUSE*
Agent: Warden, White & Kane - Beverly Hills, 213/852-1028

ONCE BITTEN   Samuel Goldwyn Company, 1985, w/Dave Hines &
   Jonathan Roberts

Screenplays:
FATHER FIGURE   w/Dave Hines
A DREAM COME TRUE   w/Dave Hines
EXCHANGE STUDENT   w/Dave Hines
MIRACLE SEASON   w/Dave Hines
THE RIGHT HAND MEN   w/Dave Hines
NUCLEAR REACTIONS   w/Dave Hines

KEN HAUSER
BEASTMASTER 2: THROUGH THE PORTAL OF TIME
   New Line Cinema, 1991, w/Doug Miles, Sylvio Tabet,
   R.J. Robertson & Jim Wynorski

CHRIS HAUTY*
Agent: Original Artists - Santa Monica, 310/394-1067

Screenplays:
DON COYOTE
AVENUE OF THE GIANTS
INCREDIBLE JOURNEY 2
ROULEZ-GEUNESSE   (remake)

MICHAEL A. HAWES*
Contact: WGA - Los Angeles, 310/550-1000

ONE DARK NIGHT   Comworld, 1983, w/Tom McLoughlin

DIANA HAWKINS
CHAPLIN   TriStar, 1992, Story

RICHARD HAWLEY*
Agent: Paradigm - Los Angeles, 310/277-4400

MOTHER'S BOYS   Dimension, 1994, w/Barry Schneider

Screenplays:
THE HUNTED (CTF)

CHRISTOPHER HAWTHORNE*
Agent: The Irv Schechter Company - Beverly Hills, 310/278-8070

PARENTS   Vestron, 1989

Screenplays:
PROWLER

DAVID HAY
Agent: Warden, White & Kane - Beverly Hills, 213/852-1028

Screenplays:
SUSPICIOUS MINDS
UNPROTECTED
EXILES

JIM HAYDEN
Agent: William Morris Agency - Beverly Hills, 310/274-7451

Screenplays:
THE RECOVERY

CLYDE ALLEN HAYES*
Agent: Paradigm - Los Angeles, 310/277-4400

RUBDOWN (CTF)   Wilshire Court Productions, 1993

JOHN MICHAEL HAYES*
Agent: Morgan & Martindale - 310/274-5143
Manager: Jon Brown, The Brown Group - Burbank, 818/955-7040

RED-BALL EXPRESS   Universal-International, 1952
THUNDER BAY   Universal-International, 1953, w/Gil Doud
TORCH SONG   MGM, 1953, w/Jan Lustig
REAR WINDOW ★   Paramount, 1954
TO CATCH A THIEF   Paramount, 1955
THE TROUBLE WITH HARRY   Paramount, 1955
THE BAR SINISTER   MGM, 1955
THE ROSE TATTOO   Paramount, 1955
PEYTON PLACE   20th Century-Fox, 1957
BUT NOT FOR ME   Paramount, 1959
BUTTERFIELD EIGHT   MGM, 1960, w/Charles Schnee
THE CARPETBAGGERS   Paramount, 1964
THE CHALK GARDEN   Universal-International, 1964
WHERE LOVE HAS GONE   Paramount, 1964
HARLOW   Paramount, 1965
JUDITH   Paramount, 1965
IRON WILL   Buena Vista, 1994, w/Jeffrey Arch & Djordje Milicevic

JOSEPH HAYES*
Agent: Renaissance-H.N. Swanson - Los Angeles, 310/246-6000

THE DESPERATE HOURS   Paramount, 1955, from his play
THE YOUNG DOCTORS   United Artists, 1961
DESPERATE HOURS   MGM/UA, 1990, w/Lawrence Konner &
   Mark Rosenthal

STEVEN HAYES*
Agent: David Shapira & Associates - Sherman Oaks, 818/906-0322

Screenplays:
THE WHITE SHERPA

TERRY HAYES*
Agent: ICM - Beverly Hills, 310/550-4000

THE ROAD WARRIOR *MAD MAX II*   Warner Bros., 1982,
   w/George Miller & Brian Hannant
MAD MAX BEYOND THUNDERDOME   Warner Bros., 1985,
   w/George Miller
DEAD CALM   Warner Bros., 1989
BANGKOK HILTON (CTF)   Kennedy Miller Productions, 1990

Screenplays:
THE SAINT
THE DEVIL'S ADVOCATE
PLANET OF THE APES
FROM HELL

BRIAN HAYLES
NOTHING BUT THE NIGHT   Rank, 1972
WARLORDS OF ATLANTIS   Columbia, 1978
ARABIAN ADVENTURE   Badger Films, 1979

LAURA HAYNES*
Contact: WGA - Los Angeles, 310/550-1000

Screenplays:
MINIMUM SECURITY
THE CATCH
FAMILY MATTERS

TODD HAYNES
SUPERSTAR: THE KAREN CARPENTER STORY (Short)   directed
POISON   Zeitgeist Films, 1991, directed
SAFE   Sony Pictures Classics, 1994, directed

JACK HAZAN
Contact: British Academy of Film & Television Arts, 195 Piccadilly,
   London W1, England, 071/734-0022

RUDE BOY   Atlantic Releasing Corporation, 1980,
   w/David Mingay & Ray Gange,   directed

PAT HAZELL*
Agent: Richland/Wunsch/Hohman Agency - Los Angeles,
   310/278-1955

GROUNDED FOR LIFE (P)   w/Ben Habeeb

Screenplays:
BUNK BED BROTHERS w/Matt Goldman *(from their play)*

BARRY HEALEY
ONE MAGIC CHRISTMAS   Buena Vista, 1985,
   Story w/Phillip Borsos & Thomas Meehan

MICHAEL P. HEALY
Contact: CBS Entertainment, 7800 Beverly Blvd., Los Angeles,
   CA 90036, 213/852-2345

VAMPING   Atlantic Releasing Corporation, 1984

JANET HEANEY*
Agent: William Morris Agency - Beverly Hills, 310/274-7451

POWWOW HIGHWAY   Warner Bros., 1989, w/Jean Stawarz

JONATHAN HEAP
Manager: Creative Alliance Management - Los Angeles,
   213/962-6090

12:01 (Short) ★   1990, w/Stephen Tolkin, directed

Screenplays:
HONOR BOUND w/Philip Morton
WHAT NICK SAW w/Philip Morton
THE SUN w/Philip Morton & Tom Read

DALE HEARD
Manager: Addis-Wechsler - Los Angeles, 213/954-9000

Screenplays:
WARRIOR

LAURENCE HEATH*
Contact: WGA - Los Angeles, 310/550-1000

TRIUMPH OF THE SPIRIT   Nova International Films, 1989,
   w/Andrzej Krakowski

MERRILL HEATTER*
Contact: WGA - Los Angeles, 310/550-1000

SNAPSHOT   Group 1, 1979

DAVID HEAVENER
Business: Hero Films - Los Angeles, 213/662-6095

TWISTED JUSTICE   Seymour Borde & Associates, 1990, directed
KILL CRAZY   Media Home Entertainment, 1991, directed
PRIME TARGET   Hero Films, 1991, directed
EYE OF THE STRANGER   Monarch Films, 1993, directed

AMY HECKERLING*
Agent: CAA - Beverly Hills, 310/288-4545

LOOK WHO'S TALKING   Tri-Star, 1989, directed
LOOK WHO'S TALKING TOO   Tri-Star, 1990,
   w/Neal Israel, directed
CLUELESS   Paramount, 1995, directed

Screenplays:
RAT RACE

ROB HEDDEN*
Agent: The Daniel Ostroff Agency - Los Angeles, 310/278-2020

FRIDAY THE 13TH PART VIII: JASON TAKES MANHATTAN
   Paramount, 1989, directed

Screenplays:
CLOCK STOPPERS

ROGER HEDDEN*
Agent: William Morris Agency - New York, 212/586-5100

BODIES, REST & MOTION   Fine Line Features, 1993, from his play
SLEEP WITH ME   MGM/UA, 1994, w/Duane Dell'Amico,
   Neal Jimenez, Joe Keenan, Rory Kelly & Michael Steinberg

PETER HEDGES
Agent: William Morris Agency - Beverly Hills, 310/274-7451

WHAT'S EATING GILBERT GRAPE?   Paramount, 1993

THOMAS HEDLEY, JR.*
Contact: Barry Haldeman - 310/201-7423

MR. PATMAN   Film Consortium, 1980
DOUBLE NEGATIVE   Best Film and Video, 1980, w/Janis Allen &
   Charles Dennis
CIRCLE OF TWO   World Northal, 1981
FIGHTING BACK   Paramount, 1982, w/David Z. Goodman
FLASHDANCE   Paramount, 1983, w/Joe Eszterhas
HARD TO HOLD   Universal, 1984

Screenplays:
TOUGH TANGO
STREET DANDY
VALENTINO PLACE
BLOOD MAN
PROTEKTOR
WINTER

GREG HEFFERNAN*
Agent: The Artists Group - Los Angeles, 310/552-1100

Screenplays:
LESSON PLAN (Captor Films/Saban Entertainment)
RIVER'S END

TERRANCE HEFFERNAN
HEARTACHES   MPM, 1982

RICHARD T. HEFFRON
Agent: CAA - Beverly Hills, 310/288-4545

TAGGET (CTF)   Mirisch-Tagget-MCA, 1991, w/Janis Diamond &
   Peter S. Fischer, directed

RICHARD HEFT
LASER MISSION   Bavaria Filmworks, 1989

Screenplays:
THE STINGER
THE SWIMMING POOL
ZONE TWO

CAROL HEIKKINEN*
Agent: William Morris Agency - Beverly Hills, 310/274-7451

THE THING CALLED LOVE   Paramount, 1993
EMPIRE   Warner Bros., 1995

Screenplays:
MEDIA DARLINGS
ALIVE AND WELL

DAVID HEISLER
PRIVATE COLLECTIONS   Red Wing Productions, 1990,
   w/Bruce Williams

BRUCE HELFORD*
Agent: United Talent Agency - Beverly Hills, 310/273-6700

Screenplays:
GUN SHY

MATS HELGE
RUSSIAN TERMINATOR   Arena Home Video, 1991, directed

BRIAN HELGELAND*
Agent: United Talent Agency - Beverly Hills, 310/273-6700

A NIGHTMARE ON ELM STREET 4: THE DREAM MASTER
   New Line Cinema, 1988, w/Scott Pierce
976-EVIL   New Line Cinema, 1989, w/Rhet Topham
HIGHWAY TO HELL   Hemdale, 1992

Screenplays:
THE POSTMAN
ELEMENTARY
FOREVER KING
MOO
THE VOYAGE OF THE BLACK SERPENT
THE LONG ROAD WEST
THE FIFTH PROFESSION
THE TICKING MAN w/Manny Coto
DUKE STEAMER: WORLD'S GREATEST BODYGUARD
MUTATION

CRAIG HELLER*
Contact: WGA - Los Angeles, 310/550-1000

Screenplays:
READY OR NOT w/Guy Shulman
SEPARATE WAYS w/Guy Shulman

GREGORY HELLER
ALPHABET CITY   Atlantic Releasing Corporation, 1984,
   w/Amos Poe

JOSEPH HELLER*
Agent: ICM - New York, 212/556-5600

SEX AND THE SINGLE GIRL   Warner Bros., 1964,
   w/David R. Schwartz
DIRTY DINGUS MAGEE   MGM, 1970, w/Frank Waldman &
   Tom Waldman

Screenplays:
GOOD AS GOLD

ZOE HELLER
Contact: The Independent on Sunday, 40 City Road, London
   EC1Y 2DB, 071/253-1222

TWENTY-ONE   Anglo International Films Ltd., 1991, w/Don Boyd

MONTE HELLMAN
SILENT NIGHT, DEADLY NIGHT III: YOU BETTER WATCH OUT!
   Quiet Fims, 1989, Story w/Richard N. Gladstein &
   Carlos Lazlo, directed

SIMON HEMINGWAY*
Manager: Lasher McManus Robinson - Los Angeles, 310/446-1466

Screenplays:
THE TIDE POOL

JOHN HEMPHILL
SODBUSTERS (CTF)   Showtime/Atlantis Films, 1994,
   w/Eugene Levy

JANICE HENDLER
BAD COMPANY   Moonstone Entertainment, 1993, w/Larry Brody

ROBERT HENDRICKSON
CLOSE SHAVE   Tobann International, 1981, w/Ronald Collier

T. MICHAEL HENDRICKSON
Agent: Paradigm - Los Angeles, 310/277-4400

Screenplays:
NICK IN TIME w/Debby Shively

ALEX HENDRIE*
Agent: Jon Klane Agency - Beverly Hills, 310/278-0178

Screenplays:
TEXAS JACK
McFEE'S LAST CASE
THE RIDE

SHIRL HENDRYX*
Agent: Media Artsts Group - Beverly Hills, 213/658-7434

RUNNING BRAVE   Buena Vista, 1983, w/Henry Bean

FRANK HENENLOTTER
Business: Lievins/Henenlotter, 443 West 43rd Street #1,
   New York, NY 10036, 212/265-2166

BASKET CASE   Analysis, 1982, directed
BASKET CASE 2   Shapiro Glickenhaus, 1990, directed
FRANKENHOOKER   Shapiro Glickenhaus, 1990,
   w/Robert Martin, directed
BASKET CASE 3: THE PROGENY   Shaprio Glickenhaus, 1992,
   w/Robert Martin, directed

KIM HENKEL*
Contact: 512/749-5701

THE TEXAS CHAINSAW MASSACRE   Bryanston, 1974,
   w/Tobe Hooper
THE UNSEEN   World Northal, 1981, Story w/Peter Foleg,
   Michael L. Grace & Nancy Rifkin
LAST NIGHT AT THE ALAMO   Cinecom, 1983
DOC'S FULL SERVICE   Brazos Films, 1994, w/Eagle Pennel &
   Henry Wideman Jr.

HILARY HENKIN*
Agent: CAA - Beverly Hills, 310/288-4545

HEADIN' FOR BROADWAY   20th Century-Fox, 1980,
   w/Joseph Brooks & Larry Gross
FATAL BEAUTY   MGM/UA, 1987, w/Dean Reisner
ROAD HOUSE   MGM/UA, 1989, w/David Lee Henry
ROMEO IS BLEEDING   Gramercy, 1994

Screenplays:
V FOR VENDETTA
THE STARS MY DESTINATION
EXECUTIONER
STOLEN FLOWER
ANNA & JAKE
FOREIGN BODIES
DIVINE COMEDY

BETH HENLEY*
Agent: William Morris Agency - Beverly Hills, 310/274-7451

THE WAKE OF JAMIE FOSTER (P)
THE DEBUTANTE BALL (P)
THE LUCKY SPOT (P)
ABUNDANCE (P)
CONTROL FREAKS (P)
TRUE STORIES   Warner Bros., 1986, w/David Byrne &
   Stephen Tobolowsky
CRIMES OF THE HEART ★   DEG, 1986, from her play
NOBODY'S FOOL   Island Pictures, 1986
MISS FIRECRACKER   Corsair, 1989, from her play
   "The Miss Firecracker Contest"

Screenplays:
STRAWBERRY
LONG & HAPPY LIFE

JAMES HENNESSY
THE LEGEND OF WOLF MOUNTAIN   Hemdale, 1993,
   w/Craig Clyde

PAUL W. HENNING*
Contact: Gang, Tyre, Ramen & Brown - Los Angeles, 213/463-4863

LOVER COME BACK ★   Universal International, 1961,
   w/Stanley Shapiro
BEDTIME STORY   Universal International, 1964,
   w/Stanley Shapiro
DIRTY ROTTEN SCOUNDRELS   Orion, 1989, w/Stanley Shapiro &
   Dale Launer

CHRIS HENRIKSON
Agent: ICM - Beverly Hills, 310/550-4000

Screenplays:
BIG HAIR
BREAKDOWN

BUCK HENRY*
Agent: William Morris Agency - Beverly Hills, 310/274-7451

THE TROUBLEMAKER   Janus, 1964
THE GRADUATE ★   Avco Embassy, 1967,
   w/Calder Willingham
CANDY   Selmor, 1968
CATCH-22   Paramount, 1970
THE OWL AND THE PUSSYCAT   Columbia, 1970
WHAT'S UP DOC?   Warner Bros., 1972, w/Robert Benton &
   David Newman
THE DAY OF THE DOLPHIN   Avco Embassy, 1973
FIRST FAMILY   Warner Bros., 1980, directed
PROTOCOL   Warner Bros., 1984
TO DIE FOR   Columbia, 1995

Screenplays:
JAILBIRD
GUSHER
BABE WEST
AMERICAN ROULETTE
APE
COMRADES

DAVID LEE HENRY
(See R. Lance Hill)

LENNY HENRY
Contact: Crucial Films - London, 071/287-6153

LENNY LIVE AND UNLEASHED   Miramax, 1989, w/Kim Fuller

JONATHAN HENSLEIGH*
Agent: CAA - Beverly Hills, 310/288-4545

A FAR OFF PLACE   Buena Vista, 1993, w/Robert Caswell &
   Sally Robinson
DIE HARD 3   20th Century Fox, 1995

Screenplays:
JUMANJI (TriStar)
THE SHORES OF TRIPOLI (CTF, directing)
CAPTAIN BLOOD
GOLF AND THE KINGDOM

PAUL G. HENSLER*
Agent: Candace Lake - Beverly Hills, 310/289-0600

DON'T CRY, IT'S ONLY THUNDER   Sanrio, 1982
GOTCHA!   Universal, 1985, Story w/Dan Gordon

J. MIYOKO HENSLEY*
Contact: WGA - Los Angeles, 310/550-1000

Screenplays:
THE DANCING BANDIT w/Steven Hensley
NEON DREAMS w/Steven Hensley

STEVEN HENSLEY*
Contact: WGA - Los Angeles, 310/550-1000

Screenplays:
THE DANCING BANDIT w/J. Miyoko Hensley
NEON DREAMS w/J. Miyoko Hensley

PAUL HENUGGE
THE ROSE GARDEN   Cannon, 1989

BOBBY HERBECK*
Contact: 20th Century Fox - Los Angeles, 310/277-2211

TEENAGE MUTANT NINJA TURTLES   New Line Cinema, 1990,
   w/Todd W. Langen

BOB HERBERT
REBEL   Vestron, 1986, w/Michael Jenkins,
   from his play "No Names...No Pack Drill"

STEPHEN HEREK
Agent: ICM - Beverly Hills, 310/550-4000

CRITTERS   New Line Cinema, 1985, w/Domonic Muir, directed

TIM HERLIHY
Agent: CAA - Beverly Hills, 310/288-4545

BILLY MADISON   Universal, 1995, w/Adam Sandler

MARK HERMAN
Agent: William Morris Agency - Beverly Hills, 310/274-7451

BLAME IT ON THE BELLBOY   Buena Vista, 1992, directed

Screenplays:
NEPTUNE'S FEAST w/Jack Rosenthal
THE SHANNON STONE

MAXINE HERMAN*
Agent: Innovative Artists - Los Angeles, 310/553-5200

Screenplays:
BLUE HEAVEN

PEE-WEE HERMAN
(See Paul Reubens)

LEONARD HERMES
STRYKER   New World, 1983, Story

JAIME HUMBERTO HERMOSILLO
Agent: Rene Fuentes-Chao, Cinevista, Inc., 353 West 39th St.,
   New York, NY 10018, 212/947-4373

MATINEE   Azteca Films, 1978, directed
DONA HERLINDA AND HER TWO SONS   Cinevista, 1985, directed
THE HOMEWORK   Clasa Films, 1992, directed

JOAN VICENZA HERNDON
Agent: Berzon Agency - Glendale, 818/548-1560

Screenplays:
MR. PARK AVENUE

VENABLE HERNDON*
Contact: WGA - Los Angeles, 310/550-1000

ALICE'S RESTAURANT   United Artists, 1969, w/Arthur Penn

MICHAEL HERR*
Agent: ICM - New York, 212/556-5600

FULL METAL JACKET ★   Warner Bros., 1987, w/Gustav Hasford &
   Stanley Kubrick

ROWDY HERRINGTON*
Agent: William Morris Agency - Beverly Hills, 310/274-7451

JACK'S BACK   Cinema Group, 1988, directed
STRIKING DISTANCE   Columbia, 1993, w/Martin Kaplan, directed

Screenplays:
THE PATRIOT
OCEAN BOULEVARD w/Greg Taylor

NANCY HERSAGE*
Agent: Favored Artists Agency - Los Angeles, 213/653-3191

Screenplays:
THE ADVENTURES OF JADE STARR w/Shirley Tallman

ALEX HERSCHLAG
Agent: Abrams Artists & Associates - Los Angeles, 310/859-0625

Screenplays:
NO MORE MR. NICE GUY w/Rob Schneider
THE MEANEST MAN IN THE WORLD

JOEL HERSHMAN
Contact: Hershman/Swords Productions, Warner Bros. - Burbank,
   818/954-3288

HOLD ME, THRILL ME, KISS ME   October Films, 1993, directed

PATRICIA HERSKOVIC*
Contact: Jack Freedman Productions, 818/789-9306

BODY PARTS   Paramount, 1991, Story w/Joyce Taylor

MARSHALL HERSKOVITZ*
Agent: CAA - Beverly Hills, 310/288-4545

Screenplays:
BABY GENIUS w/Ed Zwick
DRAWING FIRE
SECRET SEVENTEEN (CTF)

JIM HERZFELD*
Agent: ICM - Beverly Hills, 310/550-4000

TAPEHEADS   Avenue Pictures, 1988, Story w/Bill Fishman,
   Peter McCarthy & Ryan Rowe

Screenplays:
GENIE BOB   w/Ryan Rowe

JOHN M. HERZFELD*
Agent: William Morris Agency - Beverly Hills, 310/274-7451

VOICES   MGM/UA, 1979
HARD FEELINGS   Astral Bellevue, 1981
TWO OF A KIND   20th Century Fox, 1983, directed
THE LAST WINTER   Tri-Star, 1984
HANG TOUGH   Moviestore Entertainment, 1990, w/W.D. Richter,
   filmed in 1980

Screenplays:
THE MIDNIGHT CLUB   (directing)
SECOND CHANCE
TAILS, I DIE
ON EASY STREET
RESCUE
SEASIDE HEIGHTS
JAMAICA

WERNER HERZOG
Contact: German Film & TV Academy, Pommernallee 1, 1 Berlin 19,
   West Germany, 0311/302-6096

SIGNS OF LIFE   Werner Herzog Filmproduction, 1968, directed
AGUIRRE, THE WRATH OF GOD   New Yorker, 1973, directed
HEART OF GLASS   New Yorker, 1976, directed
NOSFERATU THE VAMPYRE   20th Century-Fox, 1979, directed
FITZCARRALDO   New World, 1982, directed
WHERE THE GREEN ANTS DREAM   Orion Classics,
   1984, directed

KIT HESKETH-HARVEY
Agent: Valerie Hoskins Associates, 20 Charlotte St., London
   WIP 1HJ, 071/637-4490

MAURICE   Cinecom, 1987, w/James Ivory

EUGENE HESS
Business: Hess/Lippert Films, 1045 Ocean Ave., Santa Monica,
   CA 90403, 310/394-1121

DON'T DO IT   Hess/Lippert Films, 1994, directed

GORDON HESSLER
Contact: Directors Guild of America - Los Angeles, 310/289-2000

THE GIRL IN A SWING   Millimeter Films, 1989, directed

CHARLTON HESTON
Agent: ICM - Beverly Hills, 310/550-4000

ANTONY AND CLEOPATRA   Rank, 1973, directed

FRASER CLARKE HESTON*
Agent: Writers & Artists Agency - Los Angeles, 310/824-6300
Business: Agamemnon Films, Inc., 650 N. Bronson - Suite B225,
   Los Angeles, CA 90004, 213/960-4066

THE MOUNTAIN MEN   Columbia, 1980
MOTHER LODE   Agamemnon Films, 1982, w/Peter Snell
TREASURE ISLAND (CTF)   Agamemnon Films/British Lion,
   1990, directed
CRUCIFER OF BLOOD (CTF)   Agamemnon Films/British Lion,
   1991, directed

Screenplays:
THE STRANDING
SEE YOU LATER, ALLIGATOR
KIDNAPPED
WOLF IN THE HEART

ROD HEWITT
Agent: Barry Perelman Agency - Los Angeles, 310/274-5999

Screenplays:
THE DANGEROUS   (West Side Studios, directing)

CASSIDY HEYDT
Agent: United Talent Agency - Beverly Hills, 310/273-6700

Screenplays:
OUTLAWS   w/Boaz Yakin

CAROL HEYER
THUNDER RUN   Cannon, 1986, w/Charles Davis

LOUIS M. HEYWARD
SERGEANT DEADHEAD   American International, 1965
WAR-GODS OF THE DEEP *CITY UNDER THE SEA*   American
   International, 1965, w/Charles Bennett
DR. GOLDFOOT AND THE GIRL BOMBS   American International,
   1966, w/Robert Kaufman
THE GHOST IN THE INVISIBLE BIKINI   American International,
   1966, w/Elwood Ullman
THE GLASS SPHINX   American International, 1968,
   w/Adriano Bolsoni

STEVE HIBBERT*
Agent: Above the Line - West Hollywood, 310/859-6115

IT'S PAT, THE MOVIE   Buena Vista, 1994, w/Jim Emerson &
   Julia Sweeney

GEORGE HICKENLOOPER
Agent: Broder-Kurland-Webb-Uffner - Beverly Hills, 310/281-3400

SOME FOLKS CALL IT A SLING BLADE (Short), 1994, directed
PICTURE THIS: THE LIFE AND TIMES OF PETER BOGDANOVICH
   IN ARCHER CITY, TEXAS (FD)   Nelson Entertainment,
   1991, directed
HEARTS OF DARKNESS: A FILMMAKER'S APOCALYPSE (FD)
   Triton, 1992, w/Fax Bahr, co-directed

Screenplays:
THE LOW LIFE   w/John Enbom   (directing)
THE BIG BRASS RING   w/Matt Greenberg   (directing)

BRUCE HICKEY
NECROPOLIS   Empire Pictures, 1987, directed

MICHAEL HICKEY
SILENT NIGHT, DEADLY NIGHT   Tri-Star, 1984

PAMELA HICKEY*
Agent: Shapiro/Lichtman - Los Angeles, 310/859-8877

Screenplays:
ACE OF THE NEWSREELS   w/Dennys McCoy
HARRY THE LION   w/Dennys McCoy
FULL RECOVERY   w/Dennys McCoy

GAIL MORGAN HICKMAN*
Contact: WGA - Los Angeles, 310/550-1000

THE BIG SCORE   Almi Pictures, 1983
THE ENFORCER   1986
MURPHY'S LAW   Cannon, 1987
NUMBER ONE WITH A BULLET   Cannon, 1987,
   w/Andrew Kurtzman, James Belushi & Rob Riley
DEATHWISH 4: THE CRACKDOWN   Cannon, 1987

**F
I
L
M
W
R
I
T
E
R
S**

GAIL PATRICK HICKMAN*
Agent: Monteiro Rose Agency - Encino, 818/501-1177

Screenplays:
AGAINST ALL ENEMIES

ANTHONY HICKOX
Business: Hickox Films - Los Angeles, 213/876-8423

WAXWORK   Vestron, 1988, directed
SUNDOWN: THE VAMPIRE IN RETREAT   Vestron, 1989,
   w/John Burgess, directed
WAXWORK II: LOST IN TIME   Electric Pictures, 1991, directed

Screenplays:
THE MUMMY

GREG HICKS
THE LAST BOY SCOUT   Warner Bros., 1991, Story w/Shane Black

JAMES HICKS
(See James Cresson)

NEILL D. HICKS*
Contact: WGA - Los Angeles, 310/550-1000

ESCAPE 2000   New World, 1983, w/Jon George
THE FINAL TERROR   Comworld, 1983, w/Jon George &
   Ronald Shusett
DEAD RECKONING (CTF)   MCA Entertainment, 1990,
   w/Andie McCuaig
DON'T TALK TO STRANGERS (CTF)   MCA Television
   Entertainment, 1994, w/Jon George & Nevin Schreiner

JULIE HICKSON*
Agent: United Talent Agency - Beverly Hills, 310/273-6700

Screenplays:
MAN-MOTH
TRUE LOVE
TUNNELS OF LOVE
MEMOIRS OF A MIDGET
CLEO FROM NINE TO FIVE
CONFESSIONS OF AN EX-SECRET SERVICE AGENT   (Shared)

LARRY HILBRAND
THE IRON TRIANGLE   Scotti Bros., 1989, w/John Bushelman &
   Eric Weston

DEBRA HILL*
Agent: The Gersh Agency - Beverly Hills, 310/274-6611

HALLOWEEN   Compass International, 1978, w/John Carpenter
HALLOWEEN II   Universal, 1981, w/John Carpenter
THE FOG   Avco Embassy, 1981, w/John Carpenter
CONFESSIONS OF A SORORITY GIRL (CTF)   Showtime/Drive-In
   Classic Cinema, 1994, w/Gigi Vorgan
JAILBREAKERS (CTF)   Showtime/Drive-In Classic Cinema, 1994,
   w/Gigi Vorgan

Screenplays:
HOMETOWN   w/Gigi Vorgan
DOGFIGHTER

JACKSON HILL*
Contact: WGA - Los Angeles, 213/550-1000

SPIDER BABY   *THE LIVER EATERS/CANNIBAL ORGY*
   1968, directed
PIT STOP   Distributors International, 1969, directed
THE BIG DOLL HOUSE   New World, 1971, directed
COFFY   American International, 1973, directed
FOXY BROWN   American International, 1974, directed
CITY ON FIRE   Astral-Bellevue, 1979, w/Celine LaFreniere &
   David P. Lewis
DEATH SHIP   Avco Embassy, 1980, Story w/David P. Lewis

JOHN HILL*
Agent: Broder-Kurland-Webb-Uffner - Beverly Hills, 310/281-3400

HEARTBEEPS   Universal, 1981
LITTLE NIKITA   Columbia, 1988, w/Bo Goldman
QUIGLEY DOWN UNDER   Warner Bros., 1990

Screenplays:
SHRINK WRAPPED
CONTROL FREAK
RICH KID
MRS. MERLIN
GOOD LUCK
THIN ICE
CHOPPER & THE FLASH
FAR AS THE EYE CAN SEE
HIGHWAYMAN OF CONCORD
THOSE OF US WITHOUT KEYS
VICTOR'S BIG SCORE
HARD-BOILED
WORLD'S GREATEST HUMAN FLY

R. LANCE HILL*
(David Lee Henry)
Agent: The Gersh Agency - Beverly Hills, 310/274-6611

HARRY TRACY   Quartet Films Inc., 1983
THE EVIL THAT MEN DO   Tri-Star, 1984, w/John Crowther
8 MILLION WAYS TO DIE   Tri-Star, 1986, w/Oliver Stone
ROAD HOUSE   MGM/UA, 1989, w/Hilary Henkin
OUT FOR JUSTICE   Warner Bros., 1991

Screenplays:
FAST JACK BLACK
TRIPWIRE   w/Paul Leo Freedman
BLIND LUCK   w/Mark Frost

WALTER HILL*
Agent: William Morris Agency - Beverly Hills, 310/274-7451
Business: Walter Hill Productions, Paramount Pictures - 213/956-8083

THE GETAWAY   National General, 1972
HICKEY AND BOGGS   United Artists, 1972
THE MACKINTOSH MAN   Warner Bros., 1973
THE THIEF WHO CAME TO DINNER   Warner Bros., 1973
HARD TIMES   Columbia, 1975, w/Bryan Gindorff &
   Bruce Henstell, directed
THE DROWNING POOL   Warner Bros., 1975, w/Lorenzo Semple &
   Tracy Keenan Wynn
THE DRIVER   20th Century-Fox, 1978, directed
THE WARRIORS   Paramount, 1979, w/David Shaber, directed
SOUTHERN COMFORT   20th Century-Fox, 1981, w/David Giler &
   Michael Kane, directed
48 HRS.   Paramount, 1982, w/Steven de Souza, Larry Gross &
   Roger Spottiswoode, directed
STREETS OF FIRE   Universal, 1984, w/Larry Gross, directed
BLUE CITY   Paramount, 1986, w/Lukas Heller
ALIENS   20th Century Fox, 1986, Story w/James Cameron &
   David Giler
RED HEAT   Tri-Star, 1988, w/Harry Kleiner &
   Troy Kennedy Martin, directed
ALIEN 3   20th Century Fox, 1992, w/Larry Ferguson & David Giler
THE GETAWAY   Universal, 1994, w/Amy Holden Jones
WILD BILL   MGM/UA, 1994, directed

Screenplays:
YOJIMBO   (remake, directing)
THE KILLER   w/David Giler   (remake)
HOOD
THE LAST GOOD KISS

SHIRLEY HILLARD
Agent: Susan Smith & Associates - Beverly Hills, 213/852-4777

SEASON OF CHANGE   Jaguar Pictures, 1994

Screenplays:
MONTANA

ROBERT HILLIARD*
Agent: Omni Artists - Beverly Hills, 310/858-0085

VASECTOMY, A DELICATE MATTER   Seymour Borde &
   Associates, 1986, w/Robert Burge

WILLIAM BYRON HILLMAN*
Agent: The Brustein Company - Los Angeles, 310/470-8342

DOUBLE EXPOSURE   Crown International, 1982, directed
LOVE LINES   Tri-Star, 1984, w/Chip Hand

HOWARD HIMELSTEIN*
Agent: Susan Smith & Associates - Beverly Hills, 213/852-4777

Screenplays:
A SECOND CHANCE
RING OF TRUTH
SMOKING GUN
HOLY MATRIMONY
RUNAROUND SUE
MY SEXIEST YEAR

DAVID J. HIMMELSTEIN*
Agent: CAA - Beverly Hills, 310/288-4545

POWER   20th Century Fox, 1986
TALENT FOR THE GAME   20th Century Fox , 1991,
   w/Tom Donnelly & Larry Ferguson
VILLAGE OF THE DAMNED   Universal, 1995

Screenplays:
U.S. MARSHALL
SPECIAL ELECTION
SILENT SERVICE
THE GENERAL'S DAUGHTER

GRANT HINDEN-MILLER
STARLIGHT HOTEL   Republic Pictures, 1987

JOSEPH HINDY
Agent: The Artists Group - Los Angeles, 310/552-1100

Screenplays:
SANTA & CLAUS (Ganesha Partners)
THE LIFE OF EMERY CARLTON

ALAN HINES*
Agent: ICM - Beverly Hills, 310/550-4000

SQUARE DANCE   Island Pictures, 1987

BARRY HINES
KES   United Artists, 1969, w/Tony Garnett & Ken Loach
THE GAMEKEEPER   ATV, 1980

DAVID S. HINES*
Agent: Warden, White & Kane - Beverly Hills, 213/852-1028

ONCE BITTEN   Samuel Goldwyn Company, 1985, w/Jeff Hause &
   Jonathan Roberts

Screenplays:
FATHER FIGURE w/Jeff Hause
A DREAM COME TRUE w/Jeff Hause
EXCHANGE STUDENT w/Jeff Hause
MIRACLE SEASON w/Jeff Hause
THE RIGHT HAND MEN w/Jeff Hause
NUCLEAR REACTIONS w/Jeff Hause

S. E. HINTON*
Agent: Curtis Brown, Ltd. - New York, 212/473-5400

RUMBLE FISH   Universal, 1983, w/Francis Coppola

CHARLES S. HIRSCH*
Personal Manager: Carol Akiyama - Sherman Oaks, 818/906-3639

GREETINGS   Sigma III, 1968, w/Brian DePalma
HI, MOM!   Sigma III, 1970, Story w/Brian DePalma

JAMES G. HIRSCH*
Agent: Broder-Kurland-Webb-Uffner - Beverly Hills, 310/281-3400
Business: Papazian-Hirsch, 500 S. Sepuliveda Blvd. - Suite 600,
   Los Angeles, CA 90049, 310/471-2332

DRIVE LIKE LIGHTNING (CTF)   Papazian-Hirsch/Canal Plus, 1992
DEEP TROUBLE (CTF)   Papazian-Hirsch Entertainment, 1993

NEAL HIRSCHFELD*
Agent: Richland/Wunsch/Hohman Agency - Los Angeles,
   310/278-1955

Screenplays:
OPERATION C-CHASE (CTF)
DIAMONDS IN THE ROUGH
IN FROM THE COLD

ROGER O. HIRSON*
Contact: WGA - New York, 212/245-6180

PIPPIN (P)
DEMON SEED   MGM/UA, 1977, w/Robert J. Jaffe

MICHAEL D. HIRST*
Agent: ICM - Beverly Hills, 310/550-4000

THE DECEIVERS   Cinecom, 1988
FOOLS OF FORTUNE   New Line Cinema, 1990
THE BALLAD OF THE SAD CAFE   Angelika Films, 1991
MEETING VENUS   Warner Bros., 1991, w/Istvan Szabo
UNCOVERED   CIBY 2000, 1994, w/Jack Baran &
   Jim McBride, directed

MICHAEL HITCHCOCK*
Manager: Jonathan Baruch/PRO Management - Los Angeles,
   310/478-5159

WHERE THE DAY TAKES YOU   New Line Cinema, 1992,
   w/Marc Rocco & Kurt Voss

Screenplays:
HOUSE ARREST (Savoy)
SERIOUS TROUBLE
THIRD WHEEL

KEN HIXON*
Agent: The Irv Schechter Company - Beverly Hills, 310/278-8070

GRANDVIEW, U.S.A.   Warner Bros., 1984
MORGAN STEWART'S COMING HOME   New Century/Vista, 1987,
   w/David Titcher
CAUGHT IN THE ACT (CTF)   Davis Entertainment/Meltzer/Viviano
   Productions/MCA Television Entertainment, 1993

Screenplays:
SPICE OF LIFE
MY FATHER'S SON
INVENTING THE ABBOTS

WILLIAM HJORTSBERG*
Contact: WGA - Los Angeles, 310/550-1000

THUNDER AND LIGHTNING   20th Century-Fox, 1977
LEGEND   Universal, 1986

Screenplays:
FALLING ANGEL
SIX WHITE HORSES
NOMAD

DAVID HOAG*
Agent: Innovative Artists - Los Angeles, 310/553-5200

Screenplays:
THE INAMORATA
120-VOLT MIRACLES

FREDERICA HOBIN*
Contact: WGA - Los Angeles, 310/550-1000

Screenplays:
BIMBOS
THE BATTLE OF MAPLE GLEN

VICKI HOCHBERG*
(Victoria G. Hochberg)
Contact: WGA - Los Angeles, 310/550-1000

CRUMBS (Short)   directed
'57 CAD (Short)   directed

Screenplays:
FRIES w/Danny Opatoshu
SAM AND YETTA

JOHN HODGE
Agent: Peters, Fraser & Dunlop - London, 071/376-7676

SHALLOW GRAVE   Film Four International, 1994

ADRIAN HODGES
Agent: Lemon Unna & Durbridge - London, 071/727-1346

THE BRIDGE   British Screen/Film Four International, 1991
TOM & VIV   Miramax, 1994, w/Michael Hastings

MIKE HODGES
Agent: Lemon Unna & Durbridge - London, 071/727-1346

GET CARTER   MGM, 1971, directed
PULP   United Artists, 1972, directed
THE TERMINAL MAN   Warner Bros., 1974, directed
DAMIEN - OMEN II   20th Century-Fox, 1978, w/Stanley Mann
BLACK RAINBOW   Goldcrest Film & Television, 1990, directed
THE LIFEFORCE EXPERIMENT (CTF)   Lillian-Gallo Entertainment,
   1994, w/Gerard MacDonald

DAVID HODGIN*
Agent: Writers & Artists Agency - Los Angeles, 310/824-6300
Manager: Creative Alliance Management - Los Angeles,
   213/962-6090

Screenplays:
EXECUTIVE PRIVILEGE w/Wayne Beach
EX w/Wayne Beach

HELEN HODGMAN
THE RIGHT HAND MAN   FilmDallas, 1987

JENO HODI
DEADLY OBSESSION   Distant Horizon, 1989, w/Brian Cox &
   Paul Wolansky, directed

ALICE S. HOFFMAN*
Agent: The Gersh Agency - Beverly Hills, 310/274-6611

INDEPENDENCE DAY   Warner Bros., 1983

Screenplays:
TURTLE MOON w/Tom Martin
SEVENTH HEAVEN w/Tom Martin
GOOD HOUSEKEEPING w/Tom Martin
RAIN OR SHINE
HEAT WAVE

GARY HOFFMAN*
Contact: Marjorie Rubin - 818/972-4920

TAKING THE HEAT (CTF)   Viacom Pictures, 1993, Story

LAURAN HOFFMAN
BAR GIRLS   Lavender Hill Mob, 1994, from her play

MICHAEL HOFFMAN*
Agent: ICM - Beverly Hills, 310/550-4000

PRIVILEGED   New Yorker, 1982, w/Rupert Walters &
   David Woolcambe, directed
RESTLESS NATIVES   Orion Classics, 1985, directed
PROMISED LAND   Vestron, 1987, directed

JASON HOFFS
Contact: Amblin Entertainment, 818/777-4600

RED SURF   Arrowhead Entertainment, 1990,
   Story w/Brian Gamble & Vincent Robert

TAMAR SIMON HOFFS*
Agent: The Gersh Agency - Beverly Hills, 310/274-6611
Contact: Bloom, Dekom, Hergott & Cook - Los Angeles, 310/278-8622

LEPKE   Warner Bros., 1974, w/Wesley Lau
STONEY ISLAND   World Northal, 1980, w/Andrew Davis
THE ALLNIGHTER   Universal, 1987, w/Margot L. Kessler, directed

BRETT HOGAN
"CROCODILE" DUNDEE II   Paramount, 1988, w/Paul Hogan

CHUCK HOGAN
Agent: ICM - Beverly Hills, 310/550-4000

Screenplays:
THE STANDOFF

PAUL HOGAN
Agent: CAA - Beverly Hills, 310/288-4545

"CROCODILE" DUNDEE ★   Paramount, 1986, w/John Cornell &
   Ken Shadie
"CROCODILE" DUNDEE II   Paramount, 1988, w/Brett Hogan
ALMOST AN ANGEL   Paramount, 1990
LIGHTNING JACK   Savoy Pictures, 1994

P.J. HOGAN
Agent: William Morris Agency - Beverly Hills, 310/274-7451

MURIEL'S WEDDING   Miramax, 1994, directed

BOB HOGE
Agent: Premiere Artists - Los Angeles, 310/271-1414

Screenplays:
GOOFMAN w/Marc Sedaka
A CLEAN SLATE
THE GODSON
THE LOTUS MAN
BUCKING THE ODDS

BRIAN HOHLFELD*
Agent: Sanford-Gross & Associates - Los Angeles, 310/208-2100

HE SAID SHE SAID   Paramount, 1991

Screenplays:
HENRY IN LOVE

LAWRENCE R. HOLBEN*
Agent: Solomon Weingarten & Associates - Los Angeles,
310/479-4706

THE HIDING PLACE   World Wide, 1974
NO LONGER ALONE   World Wide, 1978

Screenplays:
LUKE'S SUMMER

AGNIESZKA HOLLAND
Agent: William Morris Agency - Beverly Hills, 310/274-7451

ROUGH TREATMENT   Film Polski, 1980, w/Andrzej Wajda
A WOMAN ALONE   *WOMAN ON HER OWN*   1981,
   w/Maciej Karpinsk, directed
DANTON   Triumph/Columbia, 1983, Shared
A LOVE IN GERMANY   Triumph/Columbia, 1983,
   w/Boleslaw Michalek & Andrzej Wajda
ANGRY HARVEST   European Classics, 1986,
   w/Paul Hengge, directed
ANNA   Vestron, 1987
TO KILL A PRIEST   Columbia, 1990, w/Jean-Yves Pitoun, directed
KORCZAK   New Yorker Films, 1991
EUROPA, EUROPA ★   Orion Classics, 1991, directed
OLIVIER, OLIVIER   Sony Classics, 1992, w/Regis Debray &
   Yves LaPointe, directed
THREE COLORS: BLUE   Miramax, 1993, w/others

Screenplays:
MITIGATING CIRCUMSTANCES w/Jean-Yves Pitoun   (directing)

CHARLES HOLLAND*
Contact: WGA - Los Angeles, 310/550-1000

Screenplays:
BLACK PANTHER

GERRY HOLLAND*
Contact: 212/861-3051

JAWS OF SATAN   United Artists, 1984

JOE HOLLAND
Contact: Amber Waves Productions, 1555 Cassil Place,
   Hollywood, CA 90028

Screenplays:
AMBER WAVES   (directing)

SAVAGE STEVE HOLLAND*
Agent: CAA - Beverly Hills, 310/288-4545

BETTER OFF DEAD   Warner Bros., 1985, directed
ONE CRAZY SUMMER   Warner Bros., 1986, directed

Screenplays:
THE SITTER   (Cineville, directing)
STATION TO STATION

TOM HOLLAND*
Agent: Becsey/Wisdom/Kalajian Agency - Los Angeles, 310/550-0535

THE BEAST WITHIN   MGM/United Artists, 1982
PSYCHO II   Universal, 1983
CLASS OF '84   United Film Distribution, 1984,
   w/Mark Lester & John Saxton
CLOAK AND DAGGER   Universal, 1984
SCREAM FOR HELP   Lorimar, 1984
FRIGHT NIGHT   Columbia, 1985, directed
CHILD'S PLAY   MGM/UA, 1988, w/Don Mancini &
   John Lafia, directed

Screenplays:
BLIND SPOT
DAY OF THE TRIFFIDS
CRYSTAL TOWER

ALLAN HOLLEB*
Agent: Peter Turner Agency - Santa Monica, 310/315-4772

CANDY STRIPE NURSES   New World, 1974, directed

Screenplays:
CITY HALL
FOOLS PARADISE
DEADWOOD
THE STRETCH
FREESTYLE

DON HOLLEY*
Agent: Premiere Artists - Los Angeles, 310/271-1414
Manager: Jon Brown, The Brown Group - Burbank, 818/955-7040

NATIONAL LAMPOON'S LOADED WEAPON 1   New Line Cinema,
   1993, w/Gene Quintano

Screenplays:
MIRACLE MAN
LOVE AT FIRST OVERSIGHT
MONTANA SERENADE

ELAINE HOLLIMAN
CHICKS IN WHITE SATIN (FD) ★ 1994, w/Susan Lambert,
   directed, also screenplay

RUPERT HOLMES*
Agent: APA - Los Angeles, 310/273-0744

THE MYSTERY OF EDWIN DROOD (P)
ACCOMPLICE (P)
SOLITARY CONFINEMENT (P)

Screenplays:
TRAPS
SCHOOL FOR SCANDAL   (remake)
SPEAKEASY

MERRIN HOLT*
Agent: Camden-ITG - Los Angeles, 310/289-2700

BUY AND CELL   Empire Pictures, 1988, w/Ken Krauss

Screenplays:
LAST STAND   w/Ken Krauss

ROGER S. HOLZBERG*
Agent: APA - Los Angeles, 310/273-0744
Manager: Chris Black Management - 213/848-3699

MIDNIGHT CROSSING   Vestron, 1988, w/Doug Weiser, directed

Screenplays:
WHALESONG

WINNIE HOLZMAN*
Agent: CAA - Beverly Hills, 310/288-4545

Screenplays:
TILL THERE WAS YOU

MARK HOMER
Agent: Susan Smith & Associates - Beverly Hills, 213/852-4777

Screenplays:
NIGHTWATCH
GUILTY CONSCIENCE
INTO THE FIRE

ELLIOTT HONG
THEY CALL ME BRUCE? *A FISTFUL OF CHOPSTICKS*
   Artists Releasing Corporation/Film Ventures International, 1982,
   w/Tim Clawson, David Randolf & Johnny Yune, directed

BRENDAN HOOD
Agent: ICM - Beverly Hills, 310/550-4000

Screenplays:
MOUSETRAP

HARRY HOOK
Agent: CAA - Beverly Hills, 310/288-4545

THE KITCHEN TOTO   Cannon, 1987, directed

Screenplays:
PEACEMAKER

TOBE HOOPER
Agent: Major Clients Agency - Los Angeles, 310/284-6400

THE TEXAS CHAINSAW MASSACRE   Bryanston, 1974,
   w/Kim Henkel, directed
SPONTANEOUS COMBUSTION   Taurus Entertainment, 1990,
   w/Howard Goldberg, directed

ARTHUR HOPCRAFT
Agent: A.P. Watt Ltd., 20 John St., London WC1N 2DR,
   071/405-6774, fax 831-2154

AGATHA   Warner Bros., 1979, w/Kathleen Tynan

MARGOT HOPE
FEMME FONTAINE: KILLER BABE FOR THE C.I.A.   Troma,
   1994, directed

JOHN HOPKINS
Agent: Above the Line - West Hollywood, 310/859-6115

Screenplays:
PRIME MATES

JOHN HOPKINS*
Contact: WGA - New York, 212/245-6180

TWO LEFT FEET   British Lion, 1963, w/Roy Baker
THUNDERBALL   United Artists, 1964, w/Richard Maibaum
VIRGIN SOLDIERS   Columbia, 1969
THE OFFENCE   United Artists, 1973, from his play
   "This Story of Yours"
MURDER BY DECREE   Avco Embassy, 1979
THE POWER   Artists Releasing Corporation/Film Ventures
   International, 1984, Story w/Stephen Carpenter,
   Jeffrey Obrow & John Penny
THE HOLCROFT COVENANT   Universal, 1985,
   w/Edward Anhalt & Richard Maibaum
TORMENT   New World, 1986, w/Samson Aslanian, directed

Screenplays:
JOURNEY TO OHM
ALLARD LOWENSTEIN STORY (CTF)
A VIEW FROM THE SQUARE

KAREN LEIGH HOPKINS*
Agent: United Talent Agency - Beverly Hills, 310/273-6700

WELCOME HOME, ROXY CARMICHAEL   Paramount, 1990

Screenplays:
FIRST COMES LOVE w/Jessie Nelson
THE BLUE CHAIR
A WOMAN'S A HELLUVA THING
KISS A BLONDE
BURNING VIOLETS
ONCE UPON A SKY
GUNS AND ROSES

DENNIS HOPPER
Agent: CAA - Beverly Hills, 310/288-4545

EASY RIDER ★   Columbia, 1969, w/Peter Fonda &
   Terry Southern, directed
THE AMERICAN DREAMER (FD)   EYR, 1971, w/L.M. Kit Carson &
   Laurence Schiller
THE LAST MOVIE   Universal, 1971,
   Story w/Stewart Stern, directed

ROY HORAN
NO RETREAT, NO SURRENDER II   Shapiro Glickenhaus, 1989,
   w/Maria Elen Cellino & Keith W. Strandberg

LANNY HORN
FAST FOOD   Fries Entertainment, 1989, w/Clark Brandon

Screenplays:
SECOND UNIT w/Clark Brandon
SKEETER w/Clark Brandon

ROBERT HORN*
Agent: William Morris Agency - Beverly Hills, 310/274-7451

Screenplays:
GOOD ADVICE w/Daniel Margosis

CHRISTOPHER HORNER
ACCIDENTAL MEETING (CTF)   Fast Track Film/Wilshire Court
   Productions, 1994, w/Pete Best

ISRAEL HOROVITZ*
Agent: William Morris Agency - Beverly Hills, 310/274-7451

THE INDIAN WANTS THE BRONX (P)
LINE (P)
IT'S CALLED THE SUGAR PLUM (P)
MORNING (P)
DR. HERO (P)
THE PRIMARY ENGLISH CLASS (P)
SHOOTING GALLERY RATS (P)
THE REASON WE EAT (P)
MACKEREL (P)
THE WIDOW'S BLIND DATE (P)
SUNDAY RUNNERS IN THE RAIN (P)
SCROOGE & MARLEY (P)
RATS (P)
THE WAKEFIELD TRILOGY (P)
PARK YOUR CAR IN HARVARD YARD (P)
THE STRAWBERRY STATEMENT   MGM, 1970
BELIEVE IN ME   MGM, 1971
AUTHOR! AUTHOR!   20th Century-Fox, 1982
A MAN IN LOVE   Cinecom, 1987, w/Diane Kurys

Screenplays:
JAMES DEAN
THE DEUCE GLOUCESTER WATERFRONT
ASTOR HAIR
LETTERS TO IRIS
FELL
HOW TO GET MARRIED
DADDY'S BOY
THE BOOTH
PAYOFSKY'S DISCOVERY
THE BIG QUESTION

JED HOROVITZ
ROCK'N'ROLL HIGH SCHOOL FOREVER   Concorde, 1991, Story

ANTHONY HOROWITZ
DIAMOND'S EDGE   Castle Hill Productions, 1990

ED HOROWITZ*
Agent: ICM - Beverly Hills, 310/550-4000

ON DEADLY GROUND   Warner Bros., 1994, w/Robin Russin

Screenplays:
DOWNWIND

JORDAN HOROWITZ
ALAN & NAOMI   Triton Pictures, 1992

MARK HOROWITZ*
Contact: WGA - Los Angeles, 310/550-1000

ALMOST YOU   20th Century-Fox, 1984

Screenplays:
GALATEA
AMERICAN SPIRIT

CRAIG HORRALL
SEX APPEAL   Platinum Pictures, 1986, w/Chuck Vincent
BAD BLOOD   Platinum Pictures, 1989
WILDEST DREAMS   Platinum Pictures, 1990

JAMIE HORTON
TOP OF THE WORLD   Denver Center Productions, 1993,
   w/Brockman Seawell

ALEX HORVAT*
Contact: 310/449-4049

CAMPUS MAN   Paramount, 1987, w/Geoffrey Baere & Matt Dorff

Screenplays:
KISSING MIRANDA (KM Productions, directing)

DAVID HOSELTON*
Agent: The Rothman Agency - Beverly Hills, 213/655-2020

CLARENCE (CTF)   Atlantis Films/Northstar Entertainment/South
   Pacific Pictures, 1990, w/Lorne Cameron

Screenplays:
FIRST KNIGHT w/Lorne Cameron (Columbia)

BOB HOSKINS
Agent: CAA - Beverly Hills, 310/288-4545

THE RAGGEDY RAWNEY   Four Seasons Entertainment, 1990,
   w/Nicole De Wilde, directed

DAN HOSKINS
PRETTY SMART   New World, 1987
CHROME HEARTS   Image Organization, 1990
CHOPPER CHICKS IN ZOMBIE TOWN   Troma, 1991, directed

A.E. HOTCHNER*
Business: Newman's Own, Westport, CT

ALICE IN BLUNDERLAND (P)
HEMINGWAY'S ADVENTURES OF A YOUNG MAN
   20th Century-Fox, 1962

TRACEY HOTCHNER*
Contact: WGA - Los Angeles, 310/550-1000

MOMMIE DEAREST   Paramount, 1981, w/Frank Perry,
   Frank Yablans & Robert Getchell

ARIES HOUGH
Agent: Susan Smith & Associates - Beverly Hills, 213/852-4777

Screenplays:
SAN YSIDRO

RON HOUSE*
Contact: WGA - Los Angeles, 310/550-1000

BULLSHOT!   Island Alive, 1983, w/Alan Shearman & Diz White
THE SHRIMP ON THE BARBIE   Unity Pictures Corp., 1990,
   w/Alan Shearman & Grant Morris

DIANNE HOUSTON*
Agent: CAA - Beverly Hills, 310/288-4545

OVERRIDE (Short)   Showtime, 1994

Screenplays:
EM
THE FISHERMAN

PAM HOUSTON
Agent: Pleshette & Green - Los Angeles, 213/465-0428

Screenplays:
WEDDING CAKE ON THE SIDE OF THE ROAD

ROBERT (BOBBY) HOUSTON*
Agent: Jim Preminger Agency - Los Angeles, 310/475-9491

BAD MANNERS *GROWING PAINS* New World, 1984,
   w/Joseph Kwong, directed
TRUST ME   Cinecom, 1989, w/Gary Rigdon, directed
HOTEL OKLAHOMA   European American Entertainment, 1991,
   w/Lisa Sutton, directed

ADAM COLEMAN HOWARD
(See Adam COLEMAN-Howard)

ELIZABETH JANE HOWARD
GETTING IT RIGHT   MCEG, 1989

GREG HOWARD
(See Bull Dog E.)

KARIN HOWARD
Business: Distant Diesel Productions, Inc., 3541 Landa Street,
   Los Angeles, CA 90039, 213/662-9411

THE NEVERENDING STORY II: THE NEXT CHAPTER
   Warner Bros., 1990
THE TIGRESS   Vidmark, 1993, directed

Screenplays:
THE NEVERENDING STORY III (Story)
WOMAN IN THE DARK

KEN HOWARD
CHALLENGE THE WIND   Sell Entertainment, 1990,
   w/William Blackburn & Marla Young

RALPH HOWARD
Agent: Camden-ITG - Los Angeles, 310/289-2700

Screenplays:
RADIO ZERO

RANCE HOWARD*
Business: Major H Studios, 310/468-5000

GRAND THEFT AUTO   New World, 1978, w/Ron Howard

Screenplays:
WOMAN WARRIOR (CTF)

RON HOWARD*

Agent: CAA - Beverly Hills, 310/288-4545
Business: Imagine Entertainment, 1925 Century Park East - 23rd Floor, Los Angeles, CA 90067, 310/277-1665

GRAND THEFT AUTO   New World, 1978,
   w/Rance Howard, directed
LEO AND LOREE   United Artists, 1980, Story w/James Ritz
PARENTHOOD   Universal, 1989, Story w/Lowell Ganz & Babaloo Mandel, directed
FAR AND AWAY   Universal, 1992, Story w/Bob Dolman, directed

SANDY HOWARD*

Contact: WGA - Los Angeles, 310/550-1000

JACK OF DIAMONDS   MGM, 1967, w/Jack DeWitt
VICE SQUAD   Avco Embassy, 1982, w/Kenneth Peters & Robert Vincent O'Neill

TINA HOWE*

Agent: The Gage Group - Los Angeles, 310/859-8777 or Flora Roberts - New York, 212/355-4165

COASTAL DISTURBANCES (P)
THE ART OF DINING (P)
ONE SHOE OFF (P)
PAINTING CHURCHES (P)   also screenplay

HOKE HOWELL*

Contact: WGA - Los Angeles, 310/550-1000

CLICK: THE CALENDAR GIRL KILLER   Crown International, 1991, w/Ross Hagen, David Chute & David Reskin

JANA HOWINGTON

Contact: Josh Grode, Christiansen, White, Miller, Fink & Jacobs - Los Angeles, 310/553-3000

Screenplays:
THE NARROW ROAD w/Steve LuKanic
MIRROR RORRIM w/Steve LuKanic
FULL COUNT w/Steve LuKanic

FRANK HOWSON

HEAVEN TONIGHT   Boulevard Films, 1990, w/Alister Webb
MY FORGOTTEN MAN   Boulevard Films, 1993, w/Alister Webb, directed

PERRY HOWZE*

Agent: William Morris Agency - Beverly Hills, 310/274-7451

MAID TO ORDER   New Century/Vista, 1987, w/Randy Howze & Amy Jones
MYSTIC PIZZA   Samuel Goldwyn Company, 1988, w/Randy Howze, Amy Jones & Alfred Uhry
CHANCES ARE   Tri-Star, 1988, w/Randy Howze

Screenplays:
MARY POPPINS II w/Randy Howze
HOTEL METROPOL w/Randy Howze
AUDOBON EERIE w/Randy Howze
JOY AS IT FLIES w/Randy Howze & Philip Dunne

RANDY HOWZE*

Agent: William Morris Agency - Beverly Hills, 310/274-7451

MAID TO ORDER   New Century/Vista, 1987, w/Perry Howze & Amy Jones
MYSTIC PIZZA   Samuel Goldwyn Company, 1988, w/Perry Howze, Amy Jones & Alfred Uhry
CHANCES ARE   Tri-Star, 1988, w/Perry Howze

Screenplays:
MARY POPPINS II w/Perry Howze
HOTEL METROPOL w/Perry Howze
AUDOBON EERIE w/Perry Howze
JOY AS IT FLIES w/Perry Howze & Philip Dunne

GEORGE HUANG

Agent: United Talent Agency - Beverly Hills, 310/273-6700

THE BUDDY FACTOR   Trimark, 1995, directed

NORMAN HUDIS*

Agent: Eric Glass - London, 071/629-7162

THE HIGH TERRACE   CIPA, 1956, w/Alfred Shaughnessy
PASSPORT TO TREASON   Eros, 1956, w/Kenneth Hales
THE HOUR OF DECISION   Eros, 1957
CARRY ON SERGEANT   Anglo Amalgamated, 1958
THE DUKE WORE JEANS   Insignia, 1958
PLEASE TURN OVER   Anglo Amalgamated, 1959
BEWARE OF THE CHILDREN   *NO KIDDING*
   American International, 1960, w/Robin Estridge
TWICE AROUND THE DAFFODILS   Anglo-Amalgamated, 1962
CARRY ON CRUISING   Governor, 1962
NURSE OF WHEELS   Anglo Amalgamated, 1963
HOT RESORT   Cannon, 1985, w/Boaz Davidson & John Robins

Screenplays:
SPUR OF THE MOMENT

REGINALD HUDLIN*

Agent: ICM - Beverly Hills, 310/550-4000

THE KOLD WAVES (Short)   directed
REGGIE'S WORLD OF SOUL (Short)   directed
HOUSE PARTY   New Line Cinema, 1990, directed
BEBE'S KIDS (AF)   Paramount, 1992

BILL HUDSON

Agent: Annette Van Duren Agency - Los Angeles, 213/650-3643

Screenplays:
THE BROWNIE AFFAIR
TANGLEWOOD
TINDERBOX

MATTHEW HUFFMAN

Agent: ICM - Beverly Hills, 310/550-4000

SECRET SANTA (Short)   1994, directed, also screenplay

ROY HUGGINS*

Agent: William Morris Agency - Beverly Hills, 310/274-7451

TOO LATE FOR TEARS   United Artists, 1949
HANGMAN'S KNOT   Columbia, 1952, directed
GUN FURY   Columbia, 1953, w/Irving Wallace
PUSHOVER   Columbia, 1954
A FEVER IN THE BLOOD   Warner Bros., 1960, w/Harry Kleiner

Screenplays:
GREED

ALBERT HUGHES

Contact: Caravan Pictures, Walt Disney Studios

MENACE II SOCIETY   New Line Cinema, 1993, Story w/Allen Hughes & Tyger Williams, co-directed

ALLEN HUGHES

Contact: Caravan Pictures, Walt Disney Studios

MENACE II SOCIETY   New Line Cinema, 1993, Story w/Albert Hughes & Tyger Williams, co-directed

CAROL V. HUGHES*

Contact: WGA - Los Angeles, 310/550-1000

MISSING LINK   Universal, 1989, w/David Hughes, co-directed

CHUCK HUGHES*

Agent: Renaissance-H.N. Swanson - Los Angeles, 310/246-6000

ED AND HIS DEAD MOTHER   ITC Distribution, 1993

Screenplays:
THE LION SLEEPS TONIGHT

DAVID A. HUGHES*

Contact: WGA - Los Angeles, 310/550-1000

MISSING LINK   Universal, 1989, w/Carol Hughes, co-directed

ERIC HUGHES*

Agent: Renaissance-H.N. Swanson - Los Angeles, 310/246-6000
Manager: Creative Alliance Management - Los Angeles,
   213/962-6090

RAISE THE TITANIC   AFD, 1980, w/Adam Kennedy
AGAINST ALL ODDS   Columbia, 1984
WHITE NIGHTS   Columbia, 1985, w/James Goldman

Screenplays:
NOCTURNE
WAR DANCE
A LOUSY KILLING

GERALD VAUGHN HUGHES*

Contact: WGA - Los Angeles, 310/550-1000

SEBASTIAN   Paramount, 1968
THE DUELLISTS   Paramount, 1978

JOHN HUGHES*

Agent: CAA - Beverly Hills, 310/288-4545
Business: Hughes Entertainment, 254 Market Street, Lake Forest,
   IL 60045, 708/615-0030

NATIONAL LAMPOON'S CLASS REUNION
   20th Century-Fox, 1982
NATIONAL LAMPOON'S VACATION   Warner Bros., 1983
MR. MOM   20th Century-Fox, 1983
NATE AND HAYES   Paramount, 1983, w/David Odell
SIXTEEN CANDLES   Universal, 1984, directed
THE BREAKFAST CLUB   Universal, 1985, directed
WEIRD SCIENCE   Universal, 1985, directed
NATIONAL LAMPOON'S EUROPEAN VACATION   Warner Bros.,
   1985, w/Robert Klane
PRETTY IN PINK   Paramount, 1986
FERRIS BUELLER'S DAY OFF   Paramount, 1986, directed
SOME KIND OF WONDERFUL   Paramount, 1987
PLANES, TRAINS AND AUTOMOBILES   Paramount,
   1987, directed
SHE'S HAVING A BABY   Paramount, 1988, directed
THE GREAT OUTDOORS   Universal, 1988
UNCLE BUCK   Universal, 1989, directed
NATIONAL LAMPOON'S CHRISTMAS VACATION
   Warner Bros., 1989
HOME ALONE   20th Century Fox, 1990
CAREER OPPORTUNITIES   Universal, 1990
DUTCH   20th Century Fox, 1991
CURLY SUE   Warner Bros., 1991, directed
BEETHOVEN   Universal, 1992, as "Edmund Dantes,"
   w/Amy Holden Jones
HOME ALONE 2: LOST IN NEW YORK   20th Century Fox, 1992
DENNIS THE MENACE   Warner Bros., 1993
BABY'S DAY OUT   20th Century Fox, 1994
MIRACLE ON 34TH STREET   Buena Vista, 1994, w/George Seaton

Screenplays:
THE BEE
DAMN YANKEES
BLACK CAT BONE: THE RETURN OF HUCKLEBERRY FINN
OIL & VINEGAR
MOTORHEADS VS. SPORTOS
PRISON PLANET   KHAN
SPY VS. SPY
MUSCLE CARS

DALLAS DEBUTANTE
SCHOOL SPIRIT
THREE SECRETARIES
THE DANCE
THE NANNY
BALL AND CHAIN
THE BUGSTER
LARRY'S LATE FOR LIFE

KEN HUGHES*

Agent: Robert Eisenbach Agency - Los Angeles, 213/962-5809

THE BRAIN MACHINE   RKO Radio, 1955, directed
THE DEADLIEST SIN   *CONFESSION*   Allied Artists, 1955, directed
PORTRAIT IN SMOKE   *WICKED AS THEY COME*   Columbia,
   1956, directed
TOWN ON TRIAL   Columbia, 1956, w/Robert Westerby
HIGH FLIGHT   Columbia, 1957, w/Joseph Landon
JAZZBOAT   Columbia, 1959, w/John Antrobus, directed
THE MAN WITH THE GREEN CARNATION   *POSTMARK FOR
   DANGER*   Anglo-Amalgamated, 1955, w/Guy Green
THE SMALL WORLD OF SAMMY LEE   Bryanston, 1962, directed
ARRIVEDERCI, BABY!   *DROP DEAD, DARLING*   Paramount,
   1966, directed
CHITTY CHITTY BANG BANG   United Artists, 1968,
   w/Roald Dahl, directed
CROMWELL   Columbia, 1970, directed
ALFIE DARLING   *OH! ALFIE*   EMI, 1975, directed

RON HUGO

Agent: William Morris Agency - Beverly Hills, 310/274-7451

Screenplays:
THIN WALLS
THE ADVERTISER
REVENGE OF THE POTATO
DREAMLAND
TINGLER

JAY HUGUELY*

Agent: The Irv Schechter Company - Beverly Hills, 310/278-8070

JASON GOES TO HELL: THE FINAL FRIDAY   New Line Cinema,
   1993, w/Dean Lorey

EDWARD C. HUME*

Agent: Broder-Kurland-Webb-Uffner - Beverly Hills, 310/281-3400

SUMMERTREE   Columbia, 1971, w/Stephen Yafa
A REFLECTION OF FEAR   Columbia, 1973, w/Lewis John Carlino
TWO-MINUTE WARNING   Universal, 1976
THE TERRY FOX STORY (CTF)   HBO Premiere Films/Robert
   Cooper Films II, 1983

Screenplays:
STEEL TIGER
THE POWER OF THE DOG
LOOKING FOR HARRY

JOEL DON HUMPHREYS*

Agent: The Gersh Agency - Beverly Hills, 310/274-6611

MY HEROES HAVE ALWAYS BEEN COWBOYS   Samuel Goldwyn
   Company, 1991

CYRIL HUMPHRIES

Contact: 071/937-1719

FAMILY TREE (P)

Screenplays:
HAM ON RYE   w/Kevin Lygo

DAVID HUMPHRIES

QUADROPHENIA   World Northal, 1979, w/Franc Roddam &
   Martin Stellman
THE HAUNTING OF JULIA   Discovery, 1981

JACKSON HUNSICKER
Business: Ravenhill Films, 818/506-0249

THE FROG PRINCE   Cannon, 1986, directed
TEN LITTLE INDIANS   Cannon, 1989, w/Gerry O'Hara
ODDBALL HALL   The Movie Group, 1990, directed

EDWARD HUNT
STARSHIP INVASIONS   Warner Bros., 1977, directed
KING OF THE STREETS   *ALIEN WARRIOR*
   Shapiro Entertainment, 1986, w/Ruben Gordon,
   Barry Pearson & Steven Shoenberg, directed
BLOODY BIRTHDAY   Judica Productions, 1986,
   w/Barry Pearson, directed

EVAN HUNTER*
(Ed McBain)
Agent: Paul Kohner, Inc. - Beverly Hills, 310/550-1060

STRANGERS WHEN WE MEET   Columbia, 1960
THE BIRDS   Universal, 1963
FUZZ   United Artists, 1972
WALK PROUD   Universal, 1979

FREDERIC HUNTER*
Agent: Warden, White & Kane - Beverly Hills, 213/852-1028

Screenplays:
A GIFT NO ONE WANTS
PEGGY AND CLAIRE
SOMEONE SPECIAL
TOUCHING EVIL
SOMETHING TERRIBLE MAY HAPPEN

JAMES GRANBY HUNTER
CABO BLANCO   Avco Embassy, 1981, Story w/Milton Gelman

JOHN C. HUNTER*
Contact: WGA - Los Angeles, 310/550-1000

THE GREY FOX   United Artists Classics, 1983

LEW HUNTER*
Contact: WGA - Los Angeles, 310/550-1000

Screenplays:
THE SOUND OF LOVE
JONI
GLORIA JO
NIKITA, NATASHA, NEW YORK
THE SOWERS

RUSSELL HUNTER
THE CHANGELING   AFD, 1980, Story

THOMAS HUNTER
THE FINAL COUNTDOWN   United Artists, 1980, w/David Ambrose,
   Gerry Davis & Peter Powell

TIM HUNTER*
Agent: William Morris Agency - Beverly Hills, 310/274-7451

OVER THE EDGE   Orion/Warner Bros., 1979, w/Charlie Haas
TEX   Buena Vista, 1982, w/Charlie Haas, directed

Screenplays:
TRAP DOOR w/Charlie Haas
THE DANCING BEAR w/James Crumely
NIGHTWOOD BAR

GEORGIE HUNTINGTON
Agent: Paul Kohner, Inc. - Beverly Hills, 310/550-1060

TABLE TALK...OR HOW WOMEN TALK WHEN MEN AREN'T
   AROUND (P)
TERESA'S TATTOO   Cinetel, 1994

Screenplays:
SNAPSHOT w/Marc Cushman
DEADLY DESIRE w/Marc Cushman
JACK'S VOTE

CAROLINE HUPPERT
Contact: French Film Office, 745 Fifth Avenue, New York, NY 10151,
   212/832-8860

SINCERELY CHARLOTTE   New Line Cinema, 1986,
   w/Luc Beraud & Joelle Gordon, directed

GALE ANNE HURD
Business: Pacific Western Productions, Paramount Pictures,
   213/956-8601

THE TERMINATOR   Orion, 1984, w/James Cameron

MAURICE E. HURLEY*
Agent: Shapiro/Lichtman - Los Angeles, 310/859-8877

Screenplays:
TANGLED WEB
THE PATRIOT'S GAME
THE WAY OUT
THE MOE BURG STORY

DAVID M. HURWITZ*
Agent: United Talent Agency - Beverly Hills, 310/273-6700

Screenplays:
MULTIPLE CHOICES w/Larry Arnstein
THE ACCIDENTAL DON w/Stu Silver

HARRY HURWITZ*
Business: RSM Productions, Inc., 450 North Rossmore Avenue -
   Suite 202, Los Angeles, CA 90004, 213/466-5225

THE PROJECTIONIST   Maron Films Ltd., 1971, directed
THE COMEBACK TRAIL   Dynamite Entertainment/Rearguard
   Productions, 1971, directed
RICHARD   Billings, 1972, w/Lovees Yerby, directed
UNDER THE RAINBOW   Orion/Warner Bros., 1981,
   w/Pat McCormick, Martin Smith, Pat Bradley & Fred Bauer
THAT'S ADEQUATE   South Gate Entertainment, 1989, directed
FLESHTONE   Prism Pictures, 1994, directed

Screenplays:
THE SACRIFICER

JIMMY HUSTON*
Business Manager: 310/557-1158

FINAL EXAM   MPM, 1981, directed
RUNNING SCARED   MGM/UA, 1986, w/Gary DeVore

Screenplays:
ROBONANNY w/Lynn Mills
MOT
THE BIG PLAYER
BAD BLOOD

TONY HUSTON
Agent: Paul Kohner, Inc. - Beverly Hills, 310/550-1060

THE DEAD ★   Vestron, 1987

RON HUTCHINSON*
Agent: ICM - Beverly Hills, 310/550-4000

RAT IN THE SKULL (P)
THE PERFECT WITNESS (CTF)   HBO Premiere Films, 1989,
   w/Terry Curtis Fox
RED KING, WHITE KNIGHT (CTF)   Entertainment Productions/
   Zenith, 1989

THE JOSEPHINE BAKER STORY (CTF)   HBO Pictures/RHI
    Entertainment/Anglia Television Ltd., 1991
PRISONER OF HONOR (CTF)   HBO Pictures/Etude, 1991
BLUE ICE   Guild Film Distributors, 1992
AGAINST THE WALL (CTF)   HBO/The Producers Entertainment
    Group, 1994
THE BURNING SEASON (CTF)   HBO Pictures, 1994,
    w/William Mastrosimone & Michael Tolkin
FATHERLAND (CTF)   HBO Pictures, 1994, w/Stanley Weiser

Screenplays:
SLAVE OF DREAMS (DeLaurentis Productions)
BODIES

WILLARD M. HUYCK*
Agent: CAA - Beverly Hills, 310/288-4545

THE DEVIL'S EIGHT   American International, 1968,
    w/John Milius & James Gordon White
AMERICAN GRAFFITI ★   Universal, 1973, w/Gloria Katz &
    George Lucas
MESSIAH OF EVIL   International Cinefilm, 1975,
    w/Gloria Katz, directed
LUCKY LADY   20th Century-Fox, 1975, w/Gloria Katz
FRENCH POSTCARDS   Paramount, 1979, w/Gloria Katz, directed
INDIANA JONES AND THE TEMPLE OF DOOM   Paramount,
    1984, w/Gloria Katz
BEST DEFENSE   Paramount, 1984, w/Gloria Katz, directed
HOWARD THE DUCK   Universal, 1986, w/Gloria Katz, directed
RADIOLAND MURDERS   Universal, 1994, w/Gloria Katz,
    Ron Osborn & Jeff Reno

Screenplays:
MISSION: IMPOSSIBLE w/Gloria Katz
NIGHT RIDE DOWN w/Gloria Katz
THE AIR-CONDITIONED DREAM w/Gloria Katz
NIAGRA FALLS w/Gloria Katz
A YELLOW RAFT IN BLUE WATER w/Gloria Katz

DAVID HENRY HWANG*
Agent: CAA - Beverly Hills, 310/288-4545

RICH RELATIONS (P)
FAMILY DEVOTIONS (P)
THE DANCE AND THE RAILROAD (P)
FACE VALUE (P)
M. BUTTERFLY   Warner Bros., 1993, from his play
GOLDEN GATE   Samuel Goldwyn Company, 1994

Screenplays:
THE ALIENIST
THE FOUNDATION
POSSESSION
THE IDIOT
SEVEN YEARS IN TIBET
BATTLE OF ONO w/Gary Tieche

PETER HYAMS*
Agent: ICM - Beverly Hills, 310/550-4000

T.R. BASKIN   Paramount, 1971
BUSTING   United Artists, 1973, directed
TELEFON   MGM/UA, 1977, w/Stirling Silliphant
CAPRICORN ONE   20th Century-Fox, 1978, directed
HANOVER STREET   Columbia, 1979, directed
THE HUNTER   Paramount, 1980, w/Ted Leighton
OUTLAND   The Ladd Company/Warner Bros., 1981, directed
THE STAR CHAMBER   20th Century-Fox, 1983,
    w/Roderick Taylor, directed
2010   MGM/UA, 1984, directed
NARROW MARGIN   Tri-Star, 1990, directed

NOEL HYND
Agent: Renaissance-H.N. Swanson - Los Angeles, 310/246-6000

AGENCY   Jensen Farley Pictures, 1981

I

JEREMY IACONE*
Agent: CAA - Beverly Hills, 310/288-4545

BOUND BY HONOR   Buena Vista, 1993, w/Jimmy Santiago Baca &
    Floyd Mutrux

Screenplays:
MAN OF DESTINY
WILLIE THE HAT'S KID
TOMMY SWIFT
PRIMO
DANGEROUS RELATIONS
WINTER CHILDREN
DANCING QUEEN

LEON ICHASO*
Agent: CAA - Beverly Hills, 310/288-4545

EL SUPER   Columbia, 1979, w/Manuel Arce, directed
CROSSOVER DREAMS   Miramax, 1985, w/Manuel Arce &
    Ruben Blades, directed

JOE IDE*
Agent: APA - Los Angeles, 310/273-0744

Screenplays:
WEDLOCK
PAYBACK
SAMSON
HEARTLESS
LAWFULLY WEDDED WIFE

ERIC IDLE*
Agent: William Morris Agency - Beverly Hills, 310/274-7451

AND NOW FOR SOMETHING COMPLETELY DIFFERENT
    Columbia, 1972, w/Graham Chapman, John Cleese, Terry Gilliam,
    Terry Jones & Michael Palin
MONTY PYTHON AND THE HOLY GRAIL   Cinema 5, 1974,
    w/Graham Chapman, John Cleese, Terry Gilliam, Terry Jones &
    Michael Palin
ALL YOU NEED IS CASH   THE RUTLES   Rutles Corps
    Productions, 1978, co-directed
MONTY PYTHON'S LIFE OF BRIAN   Orion/Warner Bros., 1979,
    w/Graham Chapman, John Cleese, Terry Gilliam, Terry Jones &
    Michael Palin
MONTY PYTHON LIVE AT THE HOLLYWOOD BOWL   Columbia,
    1982, w/Graham Chapman, John Cleese, Terry Gilliam,
    Terry Jones & Michael Palin
MONTY PYTHON'S THE MEANING OF LIFE   Universal, 1983,
    w/Graham Chapman, John Cleese, Terry Gilliam, Terry Jones &
    Michael Palin
SPLITTING HEIRS   Universal, 1993

Screenplays:
HOW I WON THE LOTTERY
ROAD TO MARS
RUTLAND ISLES THE RUTLAND TRIANGLE

MICHAEL IGNATIEFF
1919   Spectrafilm, 1986, w/Hugh Brody

ALEXANDER IGNON*
Agent: Jon Klane Agency - Beverly Hills, 310/278-0178

Screenplays:
RANSOM

F I L M W R I T E R S

HASSAN ILDARI
Business: Golden Quill, 8439 Sunset Blvd. - Suite 103, Los Angeles, CA 90069, 213/656-7075
Manager: I.R.S./Harris Management - Culver City, 310/841-4169

FACE OF THE ENEMY   Tri-Culture Pictures, 1989, Story, directed

Screenplays:
CAN'T CATCH A BREAK w/Joe Bevilacqua & Louis Bonoma (directing)
FLOWERMAN w/Les Standiford

W. PETER ILIFF*
Agent: ICM - Beverly Hills, 310/550-4000

POINT BREAK   20th Century Fox, 1991
PRAYER OF THE ROLLERBOYS   Castle Hill Productions, 1991
PATRIOT GAMES   Paramount, 1993, w/Donald Stewart

Screenplays:
TAKING LIBERTY w/Peter Linett
CAGE
ROCKET'S RED GLARE
HACKSAW
THE STORM CHASER
PEACH FUZZ

LOU ILLAR*
Business Manager: Corbett Ourso - 504/542-5762

SIDEKICKS   Triumph Releasing, 1993, w/Donald G. Thompson

NEIL ILLINGSWORTH
HEART OF THE STAG   New World, 1984

DON INGALLS*
Agent: Shapiro/Lichtman - Los Angeles, 310/859-8877

AIPORT 1975   Universal, 1974

Screenplays:
CHRYSANTHEMUM COVENANT

ALBERT INNAURATO*
Agent: William Morris Agency - New York, 212/586-5100

GEMINI (P)
EARTHWORMS (P)
MAGDA AND CALLAS (P)
THE RETURN OF MAGDA DA SILVA (P)   also screenplay

Screenplays:
RETURN TO MYSTIC PIZZA w/Jenny Tripp

MARKUS INNOCENTI
Agent: William Morris Agency - Beverly Hills, 310/274-7451

MURDER STORY   Contracts International/Elsevier-Vendex Film, 1989, w/Eddie Arno, co-directed

TINO INSANA*
Contact: WGA - Los Angeles, 310/550-1000

MASTERS OF MENACE   CineTel Films/New Line Cinema, 1990

Screenplays:
HIGH HOPES
THE BIG BANG (CTF)
THE MONARCHS OF MANHATTAN
MOTLEY'S CREW

JANE IREDALE*
Contact: Robert Freedman, Leavy, Rosenweig & Hyman - New York, 212/983-0400

Screenplays:
CHECKPOINT CHARLIE

MATTHEW IRMAS
Business: Emby Eye, 3000 W. Olympic Blvd. - Suite 1431, Santa Monica, CA 90404, 310/315-4826

WHEN THE PARTY'S OVER   WTPO, 1992, Story w/Amy Wycoff

DANIEL IROM
Address: 7077 Alvern St. - Apt. A325, Los Angeles, CA 90045, 310/641-5667

BUM RAP   Millenium Productions, 1993, directed, filmed in 1988

MICHAEL IRONSIDE
Contact: Screen Actors Guild - Los Angeles, 213/954-1600

CHAINDANCE   Festival Films, 1991, w/Alan Aylward

DAVID IRVING
RUMPELSTILTSKIN   Cannon, 1987, directed
THE EMPEROR'S NEW CLOTHES   Cannon, 1988, directed

Screenplays:
THE PIED PIPER (21st Century)

JOHN IRVING
Agent: Sterling Lord Literistic - New York, 212/696-2800

Screenplays:
CIDER HOUSE RULES

PATRICIA IRVING*
Contact: WGA - Los Angeles, 310/550-1000

JUMPIN' JACK FLASH   20th Century Fox, 1986, w/David H. Franzoni, J.W. Melville & Christopher Thompson

TIM IRVING
Agent: Berzon Agency - Glendale, 818/548-1560

Screenplays:
FATHER HUSTLE w/Steve Grieger
FUTUREMAN w/Steve Grieger
OUR GANG w/Steve Grieger
THE RETURN OF THE TERRIBLE TOTS w/Steve Grieger

DAVID A. ISAACS*
Agent: Broder-Kurland-Webb-Uffner - Beverly Hills, 310/281-3400

VOLUNTEERS   Tri-Star, 1985, w/Ken Levine
MANNEQUIN TWO: ON THE MOVE   20th Century Fox, 1991, w/Ken Levine, Betsy Israel & Ed Rugoff

Screenplays:
GETTING AWAY w/Ken Levine
HOME FRONT w/Ken Levine
STAR SPANGLED ADVENTURE w/Ken Levine
THE LIVING LEGEND w/Ken Levine

JILL ISAACS*
Agent: CAA - Beverly Hills, 310/288-4545

Screenplays:
THE ENTERPRISE
ANGEL'S FLIGHT

STANLEY ISAACS*
Contact: Keith Fleer, Fleer, Sinclair, Tenenbaum & Co. -
   Los Angeles, 310/285-6222

GROSS ANATOMY   Buena Vista, 1990, Story w/Mark Spragg,
   Howard Rosenman & Alan Jay Glueckman

Screenplays:
DUE PROCESS (Story w/Judy Nogg)

SUSAN ISAACS*
Agent: William Morris Agency - New York, 212/586-5100

COMPROMISING POSITIONS   Paramount, 1985
HELLO AGAIN   Buena Vista, 1987

TARA ISON*
Agent: CAA - Beverly Hills, 310/288-4545

DON'T TELL MOM THE BABYSITTER'S DEAD   Warner Bros.,
   1991, w/Neil Landau

Screenplays:
TRUE TO LIFE w/Neil Landau
BELOVED SON w/Neil Landau
INSIDE OUT w/Neil Landau
TRANSYLVANIA-PENNSYLVANIA w/Neil Landau

BETSY ISRAEL
Agent: Melanie Jackson Agency - New York, 212/582-8585

MANNEQUIN TWO: ON THE MOVE   20th Century Fox, 1991,
   w/David Isaacs, Ken Levine & Ed Rugoff

BOB ISRAEL
BACHELOR PARTY   20th Century Fox, 1984, Story

CHARLES E. ISRAEL
ANGELA   Embassy, 1984

NEAL ISRAEL*
Agent: William Morris Agency - Beverly Hills, 310/274-7451

TUNNEL VISION   Worldwide, 1976,
   w/Michael Mislove, directed
BACHELOR PARTY   20th Century-Fox, 1984,
   w/Pat Proft, directed
POLICE ACADEMY   The Ladd Company/Warner Bros., 1984,
   w/Pat Proft & Hugh Wilson
MOVING VIOLATIONS   20th Century Fox, 1985,
   w/Pat Proft, directed
REAL GENIUS   Tri-Star, 1985, w/Pat Proft & Peter Torokvei
LOOL WHO'S TALKING TOO   Tri-Star, 1990, w/Amy Heckerling

Screenplays:
DAD'S WEEK OFF
FACE THE MUSIC THE MOTHER-IN-LAW w/Gail Parent
DAVY CROCKETT AFTER THE ALAMO w/Pat Proft
REPULSIVE ATTRACTION w/Ed Naha
UP FOR GRABS w/Pat Proft
THE CHILDREN'S CRUSADE w/F. Abatemarco & J. Roth
OPERATION U.F.O.

JUZO ITAMI
Agent: ICM - Beverly Hills, 310/550-4000

THE FUNERAL   New Yorker, 1987, directed
TAMPOPO   New Yorker, 1987, directed
A TAXING WOMAN   New Yorker, 1988, directed
A TAXING WOMAN RETURNS   New Yorker, 1989, directed
THE GENTLE ART OF JAPANESE EXTORTION   Capitol Films,
   1993, directed

DAVID IVES
Agent: Writers & Artists Agency - Los Angeles, 310/824-6300

ALL IN THE TIMING (P)
SURE THING (P)
WORDS WORDS WORDS (P)
VARIATIONS ON THE DEATH OF TROTSKY (P)

Screenplays:
THE HUNTED
THE MAN IN THE WHITE SUIT
MR. BLANCO'S MILLIONS
THE ENCHANTMENT

ANTHONY IVOR
ZELDA (CTF)   Turner Pictures/ZDF Enterprises, 1993,
   w/Benedict Fitzgerald

JAMES IVORY
Agent: CAA - Beverly Hills, 310/288-4545
Business: Merchant Ivory Productions, 250 W. 57th St. - Suite 1913 A,
   New York, NY 10019, 212/582-8049

SHAKESPEARE WALLAH   Continental, 1966,
   w/Ruth Prawer-Jhabvala, directed
THE GURU   20th Century-Fox, 1969,
   w/Ruth Prawer-Jhabvala, directed
BOMBAY TALKIE   Dia Films, 1970,
   w/Ruth Prawer-Jhabvala, directed
MAURICE   Cinecom, 1987, w/Kit Hesketh-Harvey, directed

Screenplays:
A SOLDIER'S DAUGHTER NEVER CRIES

STEVEN IYAMA
LAST CALL   Prism Entertainment, 1990

J

ARNALDO JABAR
I LOVE YOU   Atlantic Releasing Corporation, 1982, directed

MAX JACK*
Contact: WGA - Los Angeles, 310/550-1000

THE AMBASSADOR   MGM/UA/Cannon, 1985

DAVID S. JACKSON*
Home: 344 E. Rustic Road, Santa Monica, CA 90402, 310/573-6264

ALISTAIR MACLEAN'S DEATH TRAIN (CTF)   USA Network,
   1993, directed

DONALD G. JACKSON
Address: 7007 Comanche Ave., Canoga Park, CA 91306,
   818/716-9539

ROLLER BLADE   New World, 1986, w/Randall Frakes, directed
HELL COMES TO FROGTOWN   New World, 1988,
   Story w/Randall Frakes, directed

LEWIS JACKSON*
Contact: WGA - New York, 212/245-6180

YOU BETTER WATCH OUT   *CHRISTMAS EVIL*
   Edward R. Pressman Productions, 1980, directed

MARK JACKSON
EYES OF A STRANGER   Warner Bros., 1981, w/Eric L. Bloom

PAUL JACKSON*
Agent: Major Clients Agency - Los Angeles, 310/284-6400

Screenplays:
DEAD MATCH w/Tony Blake

PETER JACKSON
Agent: ICM - Beverly Hills, 310/550-4000

BAD TASTE   1987, directed
MEET THE FEEBLES   1989, directed
DEAD/ALIVE   Wingnut Films Ltd./New Zealand Film Commission,
    1993, w/Stephen Sinclair & Frances Walsh, directed
HEAVENLY CREATURES   Miramax, 1994,
    w/Frances Walsh, directed

Screenplays:
THE FRIGHTENERS w/Frances Walsh (Universal, directing)

TRACEY JACKSON*
Contact: WGA - Los Angeles, 310/550-1000

Screenplays:
THE ROSENBERGS AND JULIETTE
LAUGH LINES

JERRY JACOBIUS*
Contact: WGA - Los Angeles, 310/550-1000

Screenplays:
THE NOMINATION w/Nick Gore
BLOOMER GIRLS w/Nick Gore
WISHFUL THINKING w/Nick Gore

ALAN JACOBS
Agent: ICM - Beverly Hills, 310/550-4000

NINA TAKES A LOVER   Triumph, 1994, directed

Screenplays:
SFO (directing)

BARRY A. JACOBS*
Contact: WGA - Los Angeles, 310/550-1000

THE FURTHER ADVENTURES OF TENNESSEE BUCK
    Trans World Entertainment, 1988, w/Stuart Jacobs

JACK JACOBS*
Business Manager: Arthur Dreifuss/G. Michaud, 818/981-6680

IN SEARCH OF HISTORIC JESUS   Sunn Classic, 1979,
    w/Melvin Wald

LAWRENCE-HILTON JACOBS
ANGELS OF THE CITY   Raedon Home Video, 1989,
    w/Raymond Martino & Joseph Merhi, directed

MATTHEW JACOBS*
Agent: ICM - Beverly Hills, 310/550-4000

LASSIE   Paramount, 1994, w/Elizabeth Anderson & Gary Ross
YOUNG INDIANA JONES AND THE HOLLYWOOD FOLLIES (CTF)
    Lucasfilm Ltd./Family Channel, 1994, w/Jonathan Hales

Screenplays:
THE ADVENTURES OF HUCKLEBERRY FINN

MICHAEL PATRICK JACOBS*
Agent: Neal Stevens & Associates - Beverly Hills, 310/275-7541

CERTAIN FURY   New World, 1985
3:15   Dakota Entertainment, 1986, w/Sam Bernard
HALLOWEEN 5: THE REVENGE OF MICHAEL MYERS
    Galaxy International, 1989, w/Shem Bitterman &
    Dominique Othenin-Girard

NEIL JACOBS
Agent: The Artists Group - Los Angeles, 310/552-1100

Screenplays:
30 DAY WONDER

ROBERT NELSON JACOBS*
Agent: Innovative Artists - Los Angeles, 310/553-5200

Screenplays:
WORLDS APART
FADE TO HEAT
RUNNING MATES

SEAMAN JACOBS*
Agent: The Cooper Agency - Santa Monica, 310/277-8422

IT HAPPENED AT THE WORLD'S FAIR   MGM, 1962, w/Si Rose
OH GOD! BOOK II   Warner Bros., 1980, w/Fred Fox,
    Josh Greenfeld, Hal Goldman & Melissa Miller

STUART JACOBS
THE FURTHER ADVENTURES OF TENNESSEE BUCK
    Trans World Entertainment, 1988, w/Barrry Jacobs

WILL JACOBS*
Contact: WGA - Los Angeles, 310/550-1000

Screenplays:
THE TROUBLE WITH GIRLS
ALL SHOOK UP

JOSEPH JACOBY*
Business Manager: Royal E. Blakeman - New York, 212/421-4100

HURRY UP OR I'LL BE 30   Avco Embassy, 1973,
    w/David Wiltse, directed
THE GREAT BANK HOAX   *SHENANIGANS*   Warner Bros.,
    1978, directed

JUST JAECKIN
Contact: Directors Guild of America - Los Angeles, 310/289-2000

LADY CHATTERLEY'S LOVER   Cannon, 1982,
    w/Christopher Wicking, directed
THE PERILS OF GWENDOLINE IN THE LAND OF THE YIK YAK
    GWENDOLINE   Samuel Goldwyn Company, 1984, directed

RICK JAFFA*
Agent: William Morris Agency - Beverly Hills, 310/274-7451

Screenplays:
HELL BENT - AND BACK w/Doug Richardson
CROSS RIVER
HELL & HIGH WATER (CTF)

ROBERT J. JAFFE*
Contact: WGA - Los Angeles, 310/550-1000

DEMON SEED   MGM/UA, 1977, w/Roger O. Hirson
MOTEL HELL   United Artists, 1980, w/Steven-Charles Jaffe
NIGHTFLYERS   New Century/Vista, 1987

Screenplays:
THE WORSHIPPERS

STEVEN-CHARLES JAFFE*
Contact: Stan Coleman, Weissmann, Wolff, Bergman, Coleman &
   Silverman - Beverly Hills, 310/858-7888
Business: Meyer/Jaffe Productions, Paramount Pictures -
   Los Angeles, 213/956-5841

MOTEL HELL   United Artists, 1980, w/Robert Jaffe

HENRY JAGLOM
Business: International Rainbow Pictures, The Penthouse, 9165
   Sunset Blvd., Los Angeles, CA 90069, 310/271-0202

A SAFE PLACE   Columbia, 1971, directed
TRACKS   Castle Hill Productions, 1976, directed
SITTING DUCKS   Specialty Films, 1979, directed
CAN SHE BAKE A CHERRY PIE?   Castle Hill Productions/
   Quartet Films, 1983, directed
ALWAYS   Samuel Goldwyn Company, 1985, directed
SOMEONE TO LOVE   Rainbow/Castle Hill Productions,
   1987, directed
NEW YEAR'S DAY   International Rainbow Pictures, 1989, directed
EATING   International Rainbow Pictures, 1990, directed
VENICE/VENICE   International Rainbow Pictures, 1992, directed
BABYFEVER   Rainbow Film Company, 1994,
   w/Victoria Foyt,   directed
A HOUSE IN THE HAMPTONS   Rainbow Film Company,
   1995, directed

DON JAKOBY*
Agent: William Morris Agency - Beverly Hills, 310/274-7451

BLUE THUNDER   Columbia, 1983, w/Dan O'Bannon
THE PHILADELPHIA EXPERIMENT   New World, 1984,
   Story w/Wallace Bennett
LIFEFORCE   Tri-Star, 1985, w/Dan O'Bannon
INVADERS FROM MARS   Cannon, 1986, w/Dan O'Bannon
ARACHNOPHOBIA   Buena Vista, 1990, w/Wesley Strick

Screenplays:
THE TOURING OPTION
II
D.C. THRILLER
TELEKINETIC MAN w/Dan O'Bannon
THE PRIMITIVE w/Dan O'Bannon
HEAVY ARMOR
BURN THIS w/Linda Yellen
GENESIS

PATRICK JAMAIN
Contact: French Film Office, 745 Fifth Avenue, New York, NY 10151,
   212/832-8860

HONEYMOON   International Film Marketing, 1987,
   w/Robert Geoffrion & Philippe Setbon,   directed

FREDERICK JAMES*
Contact: WGA - Los Angeles, 310/550-1000

HUMANOIDS FROM THE DEEP   New World, 1980

LISA JAMES*
Contact: WGA - Los Angeles, 310/550-1000

Screenplays:
FAMILY VALUES w/Richard Romanus

NICHOLAS JAMES
Agent: Stephanie Mann Agency - Los Angeles, 213/653-7130

Screenplays:
DOUBLE EDGE
TOTAL RECALL 2 (Story)

NICK JAMES
FORBIDDEN ZONE   Sutton Marketing, 1980, w/Matthew Bright,
   Richard Elfman & Nick L. Martinson

STEVE JAMES
STREET HUNTER   21st Century, 1990, w/John A. Gallagher

Screenplays:
FIREWOLF w/John A. Gallagher
NIGHT EAGLE w/John A. Gallagher
HELL SOLDIER w/John A. Gallagher

SYRIE A. JAMES*
Agent: Richland/Wunsch/Hohman Agency - Los Angeles,
   310/278-1955

Screenplays:
CAT AND MOUSE
STAGECOACH (AF)

ALAN JANES
BUDDY: THE BUDDY HOLLY STORY (P)
WINTER FLIGHT   Cinecom, 1984

LANE JANGER
Agent: William Morris Agency - Beverly Hills, 310/274-7451

Screenplays:
BEYOND THE LIMIT

TOM JANKIEWICZ
Agent: William Morris Agency - Beverly Hills, 310/274-7451

Screenplays:
GROSSE POINTE BLANK (Story)

STEVE JANKOWSKI
Contact: Linda Lichter, Lichter, Grossman & Nichols - Los Angeles,
   310/205-6999
Home: 310/558-0188

TEENAGE BONNIE AND KLEPTO CLYDE   Trimark, 1994,
   w/John Shepphird

Screenplays:
GARAGE BAND w/John Shepphird
RENEGADE BLADE w/John Shepphird
RUNNER
NOT TOO CLOSE

MICHAEL JANOVER*
Agent: Maggie Field Agency - Studio City, 818/980-2001

HARDLY WORKING   20th Century-Fox, 1981, w/Jerry Lewis
THE PHILADELPHIA EXPERIMENT   New World, 1984,
   w/William Gray

Screenplays:
EVEN IN PARADISE
TRESPASSERS
HEROS FOR HIRE
SMASH BAND
SNATCHED
CHEAP THRILLS
B-MOVIE

TAMA JANOWITZ
Agent: ICM - Beverly Hills, 310/550-4000

SLAVES OF NEW YORK   Tri-Star, 1989

SUSAN ESTELLE JANSEN*
Agent: United Talent Agency - Beverly Hills, 310/273-6700

LAST WORDS (Short)

Screenplays:
THE CHICKEN, THE FOX AND THE BAG OF GRAIN

LEN JANSON*
Agent: The Irv Schechter Company - Beverly Hills, 310/278-8070

STOP, LOOK & LISTEN (Short) ★ (Shared)

Screenplays:
VICIOUS CYCLES (Shared)

KAREN JANSZEN*
Agent: Richland/Wunsch/Hohman Agency - Los Angeles,
310/278-1955

FREE WILLY 2 Warner Bros., 1995, w/Corey Blechman &
John Mattson

Screenplays:
DIGGING TO CHINA
SOLD

JIM JARMUSCH
Contact: Frankfurt, Garbus, Klein & Selz - New York, 212/980-0120
Business: Black Snake Productions, Inc., 24 Prince Street - Suite 7,
New York, NY 10012, 212/226-1341

PERMANENT VACATION Gray City, 1982, directed
STRANGER THAN PARADISE Samuel Goldwyn Company,
1984, directed
DOWN BY LAW Island Pictures, 1986, directed
MYSTERY TRAIN Orion, 1989, directed
NIGHT ON EARTH Fine Line Features, 1992, directed
DEAD MAN Twelve Gauge Productions, 1995, directed

KEVIN JARRE
Agent: William Morris Agency - Beverly Hills, 310/274-7451

RAMBO: FIRST BLOOD PART II Tri-Star, 1985, Story
GLORY Tri-Star, 1989
TOMBSTONE Buena Vista, 1993

Screenplays:
FATHER AND SON VALHALLA'S WAKE
DEAD OR ALIVE (CTF)
MAGNIFICENT SEVEN
GOLDEN GATE IRON
THE DEVIL'S OWN

JOHN JARRELL*
Agent: Above the Line - West Hollywood, 310/859-6115

Screenplays:
GARBAGE MAN
STOPOVER

PAUL JARRICO*
Business: Jarrico Productions, 2017 California Ave., Santa Monica,
CA 90403, 310/453-5073

TOM, DICK AND HARRY ★ RKO, 1940
THOUSANDS CHEER MGM, 1943, w/Richard Collins
SONG OF RUSSIA MGM, 1944, w/Richard Collins
THE SEARCH MGM, 1948, w/Richard Schweitzer &
David Wechsler
THE WHITE TOWER RKO, 1950
THE DAY THE HOT LINE GOT HOT Commonwealth United,
1968, w/others
MESSENGER OF DEATH Cannon, 1988

CHARLES JARROTT
Agent: The Chasin Agency - Beverly Hills, 310/278-7505

MORNING GLORY Academy Entertainment, 1993,
w/Deborah Raffin

HARVEY JASON*
Contact: 310/657-5515

Screenplays:
THE SPYMASTERS
REWIND

VADIM JEAN
Agent: Peters, Fraser & Dunlop - London, 071/376-7676

BEYOND BEDLAM Feature Film Company, 1994,
w/Rob Walker, directed

RICHARD JEFFERIES*
Agent: William Morris Agency - Beverly Hills, 310/274-7451

BLOOD TIDE 21st Century Film Corporation, 1982,
w/Donald Langdon & Nico Mastorakis, directed
THE VAGRANT MGM, 1992

Screenplays:
BEWARE THE WILKIES (directing)
THE FLY III
SAMSONITE WARHEAD
SCARECROW
THE BAD PLACE
PETER'S EARTH
THE REAL ROMEO
JUST MET
PALS FOREVER

BRIAN D. JEFFRIES
MINISTRY OF VENGEANCE Concorde, 1989, w/Mervyn Emrys &
Ann Narus
HANGFIRE Motion Picture Corporation, 1991

LIONEL JEFFRIES
Agent: ICM - London, 071/629-8080

THE RAILWAY CHILDREN EMI, 1970, directed
THE AMAZING MR. BLUNDEN Goldstone, 1973, directed
WOMBLING FREE Rank, 1977, directed

GUY JENKIN
Agent: London Management - London, 071/493-1610

REBECCA'S DAUGHTERS Astralma Erste Filmproduktion, 1992,
based on original screenplay by Dylan Thomas

LEN JENKIN*
Agent: Flora Roberts, Inc. - New York, 212/355-4165

AMERICAN NOTES (P)
POOR FOLKS' PLEASURE (P)
BLAME IT ON THE NIGHT Tri-Star, 1984

DAN JENKINS*
Agent: ICM - New York, 212/556-5600

BAJA OKLAHOMA HBO Pictures/Rastar Productions, 1988,
w/Bobby Roth
DEAD SOLID PERFECT (CTF) HBO Pictures/David Merrick
Productions, 1988, w/Bobby Roth

Screenplays:
FLAT OUT SPEED w/Edwin Shrake
SLIM AND NONE w/Edwin Shrake
LOOSE WOMEN w/Edwin Shrake
DAMN YANKEES w/Edwin Shrake
DINOSAUR WINE w/Edwin Shrake

LIMO w/Edwin Shrake
DEATH DEFYING T.S. BABCOCK w/R. Biheller
LIFE ITS OWN SELF
GREAT AMERICA

JOHN JENKINS
PATTI ROCKS   FilmDallas, 1988, w/David Burton Morris,
   Chris Mulkey & Karen Landry

MICHAEL JENKINS
Agent: The Artists Agency - Los Angeles, 310/277-7779

CAREFUL HE MIGHT HEAR YOU   TLC Films/
   20th Century-Fox, 1984
REBEL   Vestron, 1986, w/Bob Herbert, directed
THE HEARTBREAK KID   Roadshow Pictures, 1993,
   w/Richard Barnett, directed

VICTORIA JENKINS*
Agent: Shapiro/Lichtman - Los Angeles, 310/859-8877

STACKING   Spectrafilm, 1987

BART JENNETT*
Agent: The Wright Concept - Burbank, 818/954-8943

Screenplays:
TERMINAL INTELLIGENCE
CATCHING CASSANOVA
OUT OF THE GUTTER

JIM JENNEWEIN*
Agent: United Talent Agency - Beverly Hills, 310/273-6700

STAY TUNED   Warner Bros., 1992, w/Tom S. Parker
MAJOR LEAGUE II   Warner Bros., 1994, Story w/Tom S. Parker &
   R.J. Stewart
THE FLINTSTONES   Universal, 1994, w/Tom S. Parker &
   Steven deSouza
GETTING EVEN WITH DAD   MGM/UA, 1994, w/Tom S. Parker
RICHIE RICH   Warner Bros., 1994, w/Tom S. Parker

Screenplays:
THE FAMILY MAN w/Tom S. Parker

MICHAEL JENNING
Agent: William Morris Agency - Beverly Hills, 310/274-7451

NEXT OF KIN   Warner Bros., 1989

Screenplays:
CAPONE IN LAREDO w/John Norville
LEWD CONDUCT
STREET SMARTS
CINDERELLA UNIVERSE
LETHAL GAS
DEADBEATS
ACT OF LOVE
DARKNESS AT PEMBERLY
DARK CITY
LAST GOOD KISS

SANDRA JENNINGS*
Agent: The Artists Agency - Los Angeles, 310/277-7779

BEWARE THE JUBJUB BIRD (P)
TOOTH OF THE LION (P)   also teleplay
   "The Summer My Father Grew Up"
LOUIS QUINZE (P)
THE WITCH PIE (P)
PINK PUFFERS (P)

Screenplays:
SWEET BABE AND DIVA
CHRISTINA'S WORLD
WAGNER ELECTRIC

JAMES JEREMIAS*
Contact: WGA - Los Angeles, 310/550-1000

THE LOST BOYS   Warner Bros., 1987, w/Jeffrey Boam &
   Janice Fischer

Screenplays:
INTER-GALACTIC HIGH w/Janice Fischer
MERLYN w/Janice Fischer

JERICO*
(Jerico Stone)
Contact: 213/653-2952

MY STEPMOTHER IS AN ALIEN   WEG, 1989, w/Timothy Harris,
   Herschel Weingrod & Jonathan Reynolds
MATINEE   Universal, 1993, Story w/Charlie Haas

Screenplays:
HE'S A REBEL: THE PHIL SPECTOR STORY

SUE JETT*
Contact: WGA - Los Angeles, 310/550-1000

Screenplays:
FIRST, LAST & ALWAYS
LOOKING FOR LOVE

BOB JEWSON
STIR   Hoyts, 1980

RUTH PRAWER JHABVALA*
Agent: CAA - Beverly Hills, 310/288-4545

THE HOUSEHOLDER   Royal Films International, 1963
SHAKESPEARE WALLAH   Continental, 1966, w/James Ivory
THE GURU   20th Century-Fox, 1969, w/James Ivory
BOMBAY TALKIE   Dia Films, 1970, w/James Ivory
SWEET SOUNDS   Merchant-Ivory Productions, 1976
ROSELAND   Cinema Shares International, 1977
THE EUROPEANS   Levitt-Pickman, 1979
HULLABALOO OVER GEORGIE & BONNIE'S PICTURES
   Corinth, 1979
JANE AUSTEN IN MANHATTAN   Contemporary, 1980
QUARTET   New World, 1981
HEAT & DUST   Universal Classics, 1983
THE BOSTONIANS   Almi Pictures, 1984
A ROOM WITH A VIEW ★★   Cinecom International, 1986
MADAME SOUSATZKA   Universal, 1988, w/John Schlesinger
MR. AND MRS. BRIDGE   Miramax, 1990
HOWARD'S END ★★   Orion Classics, 1992
REMAINS OF THE DAY ★   Columbia, 1993
JEFFERSON IN PARIS   Buena Vista, 1995

Screenplays:
PORTRAIT OF A LADY
SURVIVING PICASSO (Warner Bros.)

PENN JILLETTE*
Agent: William Morris Agency - New York, 212/586-5100

PENN & TELLER GET KILLED   Warner Bros., 1989, w/Teller

NEAL JIMENEZ*
Agent: Richland/Wunsch/Hohman Agency - Los Angeles,
   310/278-1955

WHERE THE RIVER RUNS BLACK   MGM/UA, 1986,
   w/Peter Silverman
RIVER'S EDGE   Hemdale, 1987
FOR THE BOYS   20th Century Fox, 1991, w/Marshall Brickman &
   Lindy Laub
THE WATER DANCE   Samuel Goldwyn Company,
   1992, co-directed
THE DARK WIND   Le Studio Canal/7 Arts, 1993, w/Eric Bergren

SLEEP WITH ME   MGM/UA, 1994, w/Duane Dell'Amico,
    Roger Hedden, Joe Keenan, Rory Kelly & Michael Steinberg
HIDEAWAY   TriStar, 1995, w/Andrew Kevin Walker

Screenplays:
MR. STONE (directing)
THE SWEET HEREAFTER
LOST UNDERCOVER
BLUE ANGEL
SON OF ELVIS
IT ONLY RAINS AT NIGHT
STAINED GLASS

ROBERT E. JIRAS*
Contact: WGA - New York, 212/245-6180

I AM THE CHEESE   Libra Cinema 5, 1983, w/David Lange

PETER JOBIN*
Contact: WGA - New York, 212/245-6180

HAPPY BIRTHDAY TO ME   Columbia, 1981, w/John Saxton &
    Timothy Bond

Screenplays:
STAR LEGION w/Jeff Begun (Blue Ridge Entertainment)

ARTHUR JOFFE
Contact: French Film Office, 745 Fifth Avenue, New York, NY 10151,
    212/832-8860

HAREM   Sara Films, 1985, w/Richard Prieur &
    Tom Rayfiel, directed

ROLAND JOFFÉ*
Business: Lightmotive, 662 N. Robertson Blvd., Los Angeles,
    CA 90069, 310/659-6200

FAT MAN AND LITTLE BOY   Paramount, 1989,
    w/Bruce Robinson, directed

ROY JOHANSEN*
Agent: Patricia Karlan Agency - Burbank, 818/846-8666

BACK TO HANNIBAL: THE RETURN OF TOM SAWYER
    AND HUCKLEBERRY FINN (CTF)   Gay-Jay Productions/
    The Disney Channel, 1990
MURDER 101 (CTF)   Alan Barnette/MCA Television, 1991,
    w/William Condon

Screenplays:
KING OF THE HILL
THE ANSWER MAN

TIM JOHN*
Agent: ICM - Beverly Hills, 310/550-4000

Screenplays:
REMOTE w/Oliver Butcher
A REAL MOTHER KEEPING MUM w/Oliver Butcher
NEEDLES & PINS

BAYARD JOHNSON
DAMNED RIVER   MGM/UA, 1990, w/John Crowther

CHARLES JOHNSON*
Contact: WGA - Los Angeles, 310/550-1000

THE MONKEY HUSTLE   American International, 1976

CINDY LOU JOHNSON*
Agent: William Morris Agency - New York, 212/586-5100

CLAUDE   JJ Films, 1992, directed
TRUSTING BEATRICE   Castle Hill Productions, 1993, directed

COSLOUGH JOHNSON*
Agent: CAA - Beverly Hills, 310/288-4545
Contact: 310/276-2176

BUNNY O'HARE   American International, 1971, w/Stanley Z. Cherry

Screenplays:
MY PET HUSBAND w/Jeremy Lloyd

DAVE ALAN JOHNSON*
Agent: William Morris Agency - Beverly Hills, 310/274-7451

Screenplays:
PERPETUAL JULY w/Michael Pavone
THE GOOD HUMOR MAN w/Michael Pavone

D. CLARK JOHNSON
Agent: The Gersh Agency - New York, 212/997-1818

THE DROP SQUAD   Gramercy, 1994, from his short film,
    w/Butch Robinson, directed

Screenplays:
WITHERSPOON
WOO
LINE OF FIRE

DENIS JOHNSON*
Agent: Pleshette & Green - Los Angeles, 213/465-0428

Screenplays:
ICE CREAM DIMENSION
ANGELS
UP ABOVE THE WORLD
STARS AT NOON (CTF)
CIVIL WAR IN HELL
AND THEN CAME HOMER

DIANE JOHNSON
Agent: Flora Roberts, Inc. - New York, 212/355-4165

THE SHINING   Warner Bros., 1980, w/Stanley Kubrick

Screenplays:
CURE

GEORGE CLAYTON JOHNSON*
Contact: WGA - Los Angeles, 310/550-1000

OCEAN'S 11   Warner Bros., 1960
TWILIGHT ZONE - THE MOVIE   Warner Bros, 1983, Segment 2,
    w/Richard Matheson & Josh Rogan

JODI A. JOHNSON
Agent: APA - Los Angeles, 310/273-0744

Screenplays:
MAMA & ME

KENNETH JOHNSON*
Agent: William Morris Agency - Beverly Hills, 310/274-7451

Screenplays:
DO YOU BELIEVE IN MAGIC
SATURN RISING
THE MADWOMAN OF NEW YORK
THE FIRSTBORN
THE CORSICAN BROTHERS

KRISTINE JOHNSON
IMAGINARY CRIMES   Warner Bros., 1994, w/Davia Nelson

LARRY H. JOHNSON*
Contact: WGA - Los Angeles, 310/550-1000

LORD LOVE A DUCK   United Artists, 1966, w/George Axelrod

MALCOLM JOHNSON
Agent: Susan Smith & Associates - Beverly Hills, 213/852-4777

Screenplays:
REPUTATION: THE LEGEND OF BASS REEVES
AMERICAN WINGS
KOKOYAH: THE BEAST OF THE NORTH
TO THE STARS WE ASPIRE

MARK STEVEN JOHNSON*
Agent: William Morris Agency - Beverly Hills, 310/274-7451

GRUMPY OLD MEN   Warner Bros., 1993

Screenplays:
FROSTY (Warner Bros.)
GRUMPY OLD MEN II
BALLS
CYPRESS HILLS
DRAGON TEARS
BIG BULLY
THE PRO
FRAIDY CATS

MONICA JOHNSON*
Agent: Innovative Artists - Los Angeles, 310/553-5200

AMERICATHON   United Artists, 1979, w/Michael Mislove
REAL LIFE   Paramount, 1979, w/Albert Brooks & Harry Shearer
MODERN ROMANCE   Columbia, 1981, w/Albert Brooks
JEKYLL AND HYDE...TOGETHER AGAIN   Paramount, 1982,
   w/Jerry Belson, Michael Leeson & Harvey Miller
LOST IN AMERICA   Warner Bros./The Geffen Company, 1985,
   w/Albert Brooks
THE SCOUT   20th Century Fox, 1994, w/Albert Brooks &
   Andrew Bergman

Screenplays:
THE CLINIC
BATTLE FOR PALM SPRINGS
THANK GOD THERE'S A ROOF

PATRICIA A. JOHNSON
A FORCE OF ONE   American Cinema, 1979,
   Story w/Ernest Tidyman

PATRICK READ JOHNSON*
Agent: William Morris Agency - Beverly Hills, 310/274-7451
Manager: Melinda Jason - Beverly Hills, 310/289-6134

SPACED INVADERS   Buena Vista, 1990,
   w/Scott Lawrence Alexander,   directed

Screenplays:
SPEED RACER w/John Lau
US AND THEM w/John Lau
BIOSPHERE w/Eric Bergren
STAR SAILOR w/Ron Bass
DRAGONHEART
SUMMERTIME
SANTIAGO

RANDY JOHNSON*
(J. Randal Johnson)
Agent: ICM - Beverly Hills, 310/550-4000

DUDES   New Century/Vista, 1987
THE DOORS   Tri-Star, 1991, w/Oliver Stone

Screenplays:
ZORRO
TESLA
SLAUGHTER ALLEY
SENIOR YEARS
URBAN LEGENDS w/Gregory Widen, Ethan Wiley,
   William Judkins & Donald Knowlton
GLORY ROAD w/John S. Harrison

ROBERT JOHNSON
Agent: Broder-Kurland-Webb-Uffner - Beverly Hills, 310/281-3400

Screenplays:
FIRE AND FEAR: THE INSIDE STORY OF MIKE TYSON (CTF)
THE TUNNEL

ROSS JOHNSON*
Agent: The Gersh Agency - Beverly Hills, 310/274-6611

Screenplays:
HOUSE OF LOVE

STEPHEN JOHNSON*
Contact: WGA - Los Angeles, 310/550-1000

STOP AT NOTHING (CTF)   Empty Chair Productions, 1991

TERRY JOHNSON
Agent: Curtis Brown - London, 071/872-0331

INSIGNIFICANCE   Island Alive, 1985, from his play

TODD JOHNSON
Agent: Warden, White & Kane - Beverly Hills, 213/852-1028

Screenplays:
EUGENE AND HIS SEAMLESS PANTS w/Patrick Ranahan
HEAD DOWN TILT w/Patrick Ranahan
THE LIMBIC REGION w/Patrick Ranahan

TONI ANN JOHNSON
Agent: ICM - Beverly Hills, 310/550-4000

Screenplays:
GRAMERCY PARK IS CLOSED TO THE PUBLIC (from her play)

DWAYNE JOHNSON-COCHRAN*
Agent: United Talent Agency - Beverly Hills, 310/273-6700

Screenplays:
THE CAR THIEF
ED'S FISH STORY
SLAM THE NIGHT
THE LAST SET
THE SECOND AMENDMENT
THE LIBERATORS
MY TRIBE IS LOST
TURF

AARON KIM JOHNSTON
THE LAST WINTER   Rode Pictures Inc., 1989, directed
FOR THE MOMENT   John Aaron Features II, 1994, directed

Screenplays:
GIRLS TOWN
HARDBOILED

BECKY JOHNSTON*
Agent: ICM - Beverly Hills, 310/550-4000

UNDER THE CHERRY MOON   Warner Bros., 1986
THE PRINCE OF TIDES ★   Columbia, 1991, w/Pat Conroy

Screenplays:
THE MAYOR OF CASTRO STREET
LENYA
STRANGE NEW WORLD

HEATHER S. JOHNSTON*
Contact: Susan Bodine - New York, 212/888-1777

SCENES FROM THE NEW WORLD   1994, w/Gordon Eriksen

TONY JOHNSTON
THE SIEGE OF FIREBASE GLORIA   Fries Entertainment, 1989,
    w/William Nagle

TUCKER JOHNSTON
BLOOD SALVAGE   Paragon Arts International, 1990,
    w/Ken Sanders, directed

Screenplays:
THE DOBERMAN GANG (remake, directing)

CHRIS JOHNSTONE
BUFFALO JUMP   Machipongo Inlet Films, 1992, directed

AMY HOLDEN JONES*
Agent: United Talent Agency - Beverly Hills, 310/273-6700

LOVE LETTERS   New World, 1983, directed
MAID TO ORDER   New Century/Vista, 1987, w/Perry Howze &
    Randy Howze, directed
MYSTIC PIZZA   Samuel Goldwyn Company, 1988, w/Perry Howze,
    Randy Howze & Alfred Uhry
BEETHOVEN   Universal, 1992, w/Edmund Dantes
INDECENCY (CTF)   Point of View Productions/MCA Television
    Entertainment, 1992, w/Holly Goldberg Sloan & Alan Ormsby
INDECENT PROPOSAL   Paramount, 1993
THE GETAWAY   Universal, 1994, w/Walter Hill

Screenplays:
WHEN SHE WAS GOOD
RELIC
MAGGIE AND JINX

APRIL CAMPBELL JONES*
Agent: Ken Sherman & Associates - Beverly Hills, 310/273-8840

PREY OF THE CHAMELEON (CTF)   Showtime, 1992,
    w/Fleming B. Fuller

Screenplays:
ARICHMAN'S WIFE
SOMERSET HOLMES
JERKWATER
OLD COPS
HARD RAIN

BRIAN THOMAS JONES
OCEAN DRIVE WEEKEND   Troma, 1985, directed
ESCAPE FROM SAFEHAVEN   SVS Films, 1989,
    w/James McCalmont, directed

CAM JONES
Agent: Susan Smith & Associates - Beverly Hills, 213/852-4777

Screenplays:
GAME OVER w/Rick Spitznass
INHERIT THE EARTH w/Rick Spitznass

DEBORAH JONES*
Agent: Innovative Artists - Los Angeles, 310/553-5200

Screenplays:
VALADON
LIBERTY STREET

EDWARD R. JONES*
("Hacksaw" Jones)
Agent: Renaissance-H.N. Swanson - Los Angeles, 310/246-6000

Screenplays:
SOUL SURVIVORS
SEXUAL HEALING

EVAN JONES
Contact: Writers Guild of Great Britain - London, 071/723-8074

THESE ARE THE DAMNED   Columbia, 1962
EVA   Times, 1962, w/Hugo Butler
KING AND COUNTRY   Allied Artists, 1965
MODESTY BLAISE   20th Century-Fox, 1966
FUNERAL IN BERLIN   Paramount, 1967
OUTBACK   *WAKE IN FRIGHT*   United Artists, 1971
VICTORY   Lorimar/Paramount, 1981, w/Yabo Yablonsky
THE KILLING OF ANGEL STREET   Forest Home Films, 1981,
    w/Michael Craig & Cecil Holmes
CHAMPIONS   Embassy, 1984
KANGAROO   Cineplex Odeon, 1987
A SHOW OF FORCE   Paramount, 1990, w/John Strong
SHADOW OF THE WOLF   Triumph Releasing, 1993,
    w/Rudy Wurlitzer

IAN JONES
NED KELLY   United Artists, 1970, w/Tony Richardson
THE LIGHTHORSEMEN   Cinecom, 1988

LAURA JONES
HIGH TIDE   Tri-Star, 1987
AN ANGEL AT MY TABLE   Fine Line Features, 1991
PORTRAIT OF A LADY   Gramercy, 1995

Screenplays:
TIRRA LIRRA BY THE RIVER
THE WELL
OSCAR AND LUCINDA

LAURIE JONES
IN THE SPIRIT   Castle Hill Productions, 1990, w/Jeannie Berlin

MARK JONES
Agent: Jim Preminger Agency - Los Angeles, 310/475-9491

LEPRECHAUN   Trimark Pictures, 1993, directed

MARTIN JONES*
Contact: WGA - New York, 212/245-6180

PRISON STORIES: WOMEN ON THE INSIDE (CTF)
    Francine LeFrak Productions/HBO Showcase, 1991,
    "Esperanza"; "New Chicks", w/Dick Beebe & Jule Selbo

Screenplays:
WEST MEMPHIS MOJO (from his play)

PATRICIA JONES
Agent: United Talent Agency - Beverly Hills, 310/273-6700

MONA MUST DIE   Jones & Reiker, 1994, w/Donald Reiker

ROBERT C. JONES*
Agent: The Marion Rosenberg Office - Los Angeles, 213/653-7383

COMING HOME ★★   United Artists, 1978, w/Waldo Salt

Screenplays:
GOD BLESS YOU, MR. ROSEWATER
VITAL PARTS

SCOTT DAVIS JONES*
Agent: The Coppage Company - North Hollywood, 818/980-1106

Screenplays:
MAVIS KEATES
GIRL HOOPS

TERRY JONES
Agent: CAA - Beverly Hills, 310/288-4545

CONSUMING PASSIONS (P) w/Michael Palin
AND NOW FOR SOMETHING COMPLETELY DIFFERENT
   Columbia, 1972, w/Graham Chapman, John Cleese,
   Terry Gilliam, Eric Idle & Michael Palin
MONTY PYTHON AND THE HOLY GRAIL Cinema 5, 1974,
   w/Graham Chapman, John Cleese, Terry Gilliam, Eric Idle &
   Michael Palin, directed
MONTY PYTHON'S LIFE OF BRIAN Orion/Warner Bros., 1979,
   w/Graham Chapman, John Cleese, Terry Gilliam, Eric Idle &
   Michael Palin, directed
MONTY PYTHON LIVE AT THE HOLLYWOOD BOWL Columbia,
   1982, w/Graham Chapman, John Cleese, Terry Gilliam,
   Eric Idle & Michael Palin
MONTY PYTHON'S THE MEANING OF LIFE Universal, 1983,
   w/Graham Chapman, John Cleese, Terry Gilliam, Eric Idle &
   Michael Palin, directed
LABYRINTH Tri-Star, 1986
ERIK THE VIKING Orion, 1989, directed

Screenplays:
MIRACLE MAN

TOMMY LEE JONES
Agent: ICM - Beverly Hills, 310/550-4000

THE GOOD OLD BOYS (CTF) Turner Pictures, 1994,
   w/J.T. Allen, directed

DONNA MATSON JONSSON*
Agent: Paradigm - Los Angeles, 310/277-4400

Screenplays:
MY FATHER, HIS SON w/Reidar Jonsson
NORTH STAR w/Reidar Jonsson
THE HUNT w/Reidar Jonsson

REIDAR JONSSON*
Agent: Paradigm - Los Angeles, 310/277-4400

MY LIFE AS A DOG ★ Skouras Pictures, 1987, w/Per Berglund,
   Brasse Branstrom & Lasse Hallstrom

Screenplays:
MY FATHER, HIS SON w/Donna Matson Jonsson
NORTH STAR w/Donna Matson Jonsson
THE HUNT w/Donna Matson Jonsson

NEIL JORDAN
Agent: ICM - Beverly Hills, 310/550-4000 & Casaratto Company -
   London, 071/287-4450

DANNY BOY ANGEL Triumph/Columbia, 1983, directed
THE COMPANY OF WOLVES Cannon, 1984,
   w/Angela Carter, directed
MONA LISA Island Pictures, 1986, w/David Leland, directed
HIGH SPIRITS Tri-Star, 1988, directed
THE MIRACLE Miramax, 1991, directed
THE CRYING GAME ★★ Miramax, 1992, directed

Screenplays:
BROKEN DREAMS w/John Boorman

ROBERT L. JOSEPH*
Agent: CAA - Beverly Hills, 310/288-4545

ECHOES OF A SUMMER CineArtists, 1976

WALTER JOSTEN
Business: Blue Rider Pictures, Republic Pictures, 2800 28th St. -
   Suite 105, Santa Monica, CA 90405, 310/314-8246

NIGHT ANGEL Fries Entertainment, 1990, w/Joe Augustyn

ADRIEN JOYCE
(See Carole Eastman)

PATRICIA JOYCE*
Agent: Preferred Artists - Encino, 818/990-0305

Screenplays:
LOVELY BUT DEADLY

C. COURTNEY JOYNER
Contact: Cathryn James, Jaymes and Co., 310/762-7831

THE OFFSPRING TMS Pictures, 1987, w/Jeff Burr & Darin Scott
PRISON Empire Pictures, 1988
CATACOMBS Empire Pictures, 1988
VIETNAM, TEXAS Epic Productions, 1990, w/Tom Badal
CLASS OF 1999 Taurus Entertainment, 1990
PUPPETMASTER III: TOULON'S REVENGE Full Moon, 1991
DOCTOR MORDRID Full Moon, 1992, w/Charles Band
TRANCERS III: DETH LIVES! Full Moon, 1992, directed
THE LURKING FEAR Full Moon, 1993, directed

Screenplays:
G.I. JOE w/Sheldon Lettich
WHEN A MAN LOVES A WOMAN
THE GYPSY ANGELS EAST OF THE SUN w/Virgil W. Vogel
SCORPION w/Kevin Meyer
DARK STREET w/Warren Peters
DOUBLE ACTION MAN
A DELICATE LINK
THE WHITE ZONE
THE PENALTY BOX
FAMILY REUNION

MIKE JUDGE
Agent: CAA - Beverly Hills, 310/288-4545
Manager: 3 Arts Entertainment - Los Angeles, 213/851-5700

Screenplays:
ESCAPE FROM CAMP WANNABARF w/Larry Wilson

WILLIAM JUDKINS
Agent: Pleshette & Green - Los Angeles, 213/465-0428

Screenplays:
GODS
98 MINUTES
THE CURE
ACT OF LOVE
THE UNFORTUNATE MULE INCIDENT
THE SCORE (Shared)

JERRY R. JUHL*
Business Manager: Paul White, White, Zuckerman & Warsavsky -
   Los Angeles, 213/462-2885

THE MUPPET MOVIE AFD, 1979, w/Jack Burns
THE GREAT MUPPET CAPER Universal/AFD, 1981,
   w/Tom Patchett, Jack Rose & Jay Tarses
THE MUPPET CHRISTMAS CAROL Buena Vista, 1992

ARTHUR JULIAN*
Business Manager: Murphy & Kress - Santa Monica, 310/396-7000

THE HAPPY ROAD MGM, 1956, w/Harry Kurnitz &
   Joseph Morhaim
THE BOATNIKS Buena Vista, 1970

AARON JULIEN*
Agent: Broder-Kurland-Webb-Uffner - Beverly Hills, 310/281-3400

DIRTY WORK (CTF) Wilshire Court Productions, 1992

ISAAC JULIEN
Agent: The Casarotto Company - London, 071/287-4450

YOUNG SOUL REBELS   Miramax, 1991, w/Paul Hallam &
   Derrick Saldaan McClintock,   directed

JOHN JUNKERMAN
MR. BASEBALL   Universal, 1992, Story w/Theo Pelletier

JAMES JUSTICE*
Agent: Leslie Kallen Agency - Sherman Oaks, 818/906-2785

Screenplays:
HOT SAUCE

K

GEORGE KACZENDER
Agent: The Chasin Agency - Los Angeles, 310/278-7505

Screenplays:
ROMANCE WITH MURDER
INQUISITOR

KEITH KACZOREK*
Agent: The Rothman Agency - Beverly Hills, 213/655-2020

LADY AVENGER   Marco Colombo, 1989, w/Will Schmitz

JEREMY KAGAN*
Agent: Becsey/Wisdom/Kalajian Agency - Los Angeles, 310/550-0535

ROSWELL (CTF)   Viacom Pictures/Citadel Entertainment, 1994,
   Story w/Paul Davids & Arthur Kopit,   directed

MARCY KAHAN
Agent: Sheil Land Associates - London

ANTONIA AND JANE   Miramax, 1991

JAMES KAHN*
Contact: WGA - Los Angeles, 310/550-1000

Screenplays:
PEARLHART
DEAD POINT

JEFF KAHN*
Agent: William Morris Agency - Beverly Hills, 310/274-7451

Screenplays:
TRAITORS, SPIES AND INNKEEPERS w/Ben Stiller

JEFF KAHN
REVOLUTION!   Northern Arts Entertainment, 1991,   directed

JONATHAN KAHN*
Agent: CAA - Beverly Hills, 310/288-4545

THE CHILI CON CARNE CLUB (Short)   1993,
   w/James Melkonian,   directed

TERRY C. KAHN
FOX   Eagle Entertainment, 1991,   directed
HOTEL OKLAHOMA   European American Entertainment, 1991,
   Story w/Ed Elbert & Bobby Houston

CONSTANCE KAISERMAN
Business: Merchant Ivory Productions, 250 West 57th St., Suite 1913,
   New York, NY 10023, 212/582-8049

MY LITTLE GIRL   Hemdale, 1987, w/Nan Mason,   directed

LEE KALCHEIM*
Agent: Broder-Kurland-Webb-Uffner - Beverly Hills, 310/281-3400

Screenplays:
ATOMIC FOLLIES

MICHAEL KALESNIKO*
Agent: United Talent Agency - Beverly Hills, 310/273-6700

Screenplays:
PRIVATE PARTS (Savoy)
TO HAVE AND TO HOLD
MY KIND OF TOWN
COCK N' BULL
KINGDOM COME
JOE CITIZEN
SUNDOWNER
BOTCHED
ANTWORLD

TOM KALIN
SWOON   Fine Line Features, 1992,   directed

LAETA KALOGRIDIS
Agent: ICM - Beverly Hills, 310/550-4000

Screenplays:
IN NOMINE DEI

JAY KAMEN*
Agent: Warden, White & Kane - Beverly Hills, 213/852-1028

Screenplays:
THE JEWELER w/Robert Kizer
S.W.M.
HOT HOUSE

ROBERT MARK KAMEN*
Agent: CAA - Beverly Hills, 310/288-4545

TAPS   20th Century-Fox, 1981, w/Darryl Ponicsan
SPLIT IMAGE   Orion, 1982, w/Robert Kaufman & Scott Spencer
THE KARATE KID   Columbia, 1984
THE KARATE KID PART II   Columbia, 1986
THE KARATE KID PART III   Columbia, 1989
THE POWER OF ONE   Warner Bros., 1992
GLADIATOR   Columbia, 1992, w/Lyle Kesler
LETHAL WEAPON 3   Warner Bros., 1992, w/Jeffrey Boam
A WALK IN THE CLOUDS   20th Century Fox, 1995

Screenplays:
A CONNECTICUT YANKEE IN KING ARTHUR'S COURT
*   (Warner Bros.)*
CROSSINGS
RYOMA
AFGHAN PROJECT

STUART KAMINSKY*
Contact: WGA - New York, 212/245-6180

ENEMY TERRITORY   Empire Pictures, 1987, w/Bobby Liddell

Screenplays:
HIDDEN FEARS

STEVEN W. KAMPMANN*
Agent: The Gersh Agency - Beverly Hills, 310/274-6611

BACK TO SCHOOL   Orion, 1986, w/Will Aldis, Harold Ramis & Peter Torokvei
THE COUCH TRIP   Orion, 1988, w/Will Aldis & Sean Stein
STEALING HOME   Warner Bros., 1988, w/Will Aldis, directed
CLIFFORD   Orion, 1992, w/Will Aldis, as "Bobby Bon Hayes & Jay Dee Rock," directed

Screenplays:
THE DINK

JOHN KAMPS*
Agent: United Talent Agency - Beverly Hills, 310/273-6700

Screenplays:
MIGHTY MORPHIN' POWER RANGERS
SILENT PARTNER
JAVA NARCISSUS
HUNTER'S POINT
ADVENTURE I w/David Koepp
LITTLE BOHEMIA
GALATEA
THE FANATIC

STEPHEN KANDEL*
Agent: Paradigm - Los Angeles, 310/277-4400

BATTLE OF THE CORAL SEA   Columbia, 1959, w/Dan Ullman
CHAMBER OF HORRORS   Warner Bros., 1966
CANNON FOR CORDOBA   United Artists, 1970

BRUCE KANE*
Manager: Creative Alliance Management - Los Angeles, 213/962-6090

Screenplays:
UNFORGETTABLE

MICHAEL KANE
SMOKEY AND THE BANDIT II   Universal, 1977
FOOLIN' AROUND   Columbia, 1978, w/David Swift
HOT STUFF   Columbia, 1979, w/Donald E. Westlake
THE LEGEND OF THE LONE RANGER   Universal/AFD, 1981, w/Ben Roberts, William Roberts & Ivan Goff
HARD COUNTRY   Universal, 1981
SOUTHERN COMFORT   20th Century-Fox, 1981, w/Walter Hill & David Giler
ALL THE RIGHT MOVES   20th Century-Fox, 1983
THE BEAR   Embassy, 1984
THE CISCO KID (CTF)   Esparza-Katz/Goodman-Rosen, 1994, w/Luis Valdez

Screenplays:
ICECREAM MAN w/Kim Bass (Cappella International)
LONG DAN
GHOST TOWN
SATURDAY'S CHILD
THE DEEP II
DEEP TROUBLE
SARATOGA
STRIKE THREE CALLED
SEVEN THE HARD WAY
JAYWALKING
ESCROW
BANDMAN

ROBERT G. KANE*
Contact: WGA - Los Angeles, 310/550-1000

KISSES FOR MY PRESIDENT   Warner Bros., 1964, w/Claude Binyon
THE VILLAIN   Columbia, 1979

ROLFE KANEFSKY
Contact: Valkhn Film & Video - New York, 212/586-1603

THERE'S NOTHING OUT THERE   Arrow Entertainment, 1993, directed

Screenplays:
UNDYING THIRST
PHOTOGRAPHS

JEFF KANEW
Agent: Above the Line - West Hollywood, 310/859-6115

NATURAL ENEMIES   Cinema 5, 1979, directed
EDDIE MACON'S RUN   Universal, 1983, directed

CHARLES T. KANGANIS
L.A. HEAT   PM Entertainment, 1989
A TIME TO DIE   PM Entertainment, 1991, directed
FIST OF HONOR   PM Entertainment, 1993
NO ESCAPE, NO RETURN   PM Entertainment, 1993, directed

MICHAEL KANIECKI
THE LOST WORDS   Film Crash, 1994, w/Dan Keoppel & Scott Saunders

FAY KANIN*
Contact: WGA - Los Angeles, 310/550-1000

GOODBYE MY FANCY (P)
RASHOMON (P)   w/Michael Kanin
BLONDIE FOR VICTORY   Columbia, 1942
MY PAL GUS   20th Century-Fox, 1952, w/Michael Kanin
RHAPSODY   MGM, 1954, w/Michael Kanin
THE OPPOSITE SEX   MGM, 1956, w/Michael Kanin
TEACHER'S PET ★   Paramount, 1958, w/Michael Kanin
THE RIGHT APPROACH   20th Century-Fox, 1961, w/Michael Kanin
SWORDMAN OF SIENA   MGM, 1962, w/Michael Kanin

Screenplays:
THE SURROGATE
THE SOURCE

HAL KANTER*
Contact: 818/788-4026

HERE COME THE GIRLS   Paramount, 1953, w/Edmund Hartmann
ABOUT MRS. LESLIE   Paramount, 1954, w/Ketti Frings
CASANOVA'S BIG NIGHT   Paramount, 1954, w/Edmund Hartmann
LOVING YOU   Paramount, 1957, w/Herbert Baker, directed
ONCE UPON A HORSE   Universal, 1958, directed
BACHELOR IN PARADISE   MGM, 1961, w/Valentine Davies
BLUE HAWAII   Paramount, 1961
MOVE OVER DARLING   20th Century-Fox, 1963, w/Jack Sher
DEAR BRIGITTE   20th Century-Fox, 1965

ANDREW KAPLAN*
Agent: The Coppage Company - North Hollywood, 818/980-1106

THE DISPUTATION (P)
THE REVOLUTIONARY (P)

Screenplays:
BEYOND COURAGE
TRACK OF THE JAGUAR
WAR OF THE RAVEN

BETTY KAPLAN*
Agent: ICM - Beverly Hills, 310/550-4000

OF LOVE AND SHADOWS   Betka Film Ltd., 1994, w/Donald Freed, directed

CAROL KAPLAN
Agent: Writers & Artists Agency - Los Angeles, 310/824-6300

Screenplays:
FIELDS OF FIRE w/Kate Robbins

DEBORAH KAPLAN
Agent: ICM - Beverly Hills, 310/550-4000
Manager: Ogden House - Los Angeles, 213/851-0458

Screenplays:
THE FAMILY WAY w/Harry Elfont

ED KAPLAN*
Agent: Innovative Artists - Los Angeles, 310/553-5200

ALL IN A SUMMER'S DAY (Short)   directed

Screenplays:
SUMMERHOUSE
SUGAR & SPIKE
GEORGIA ON MY MIND
ACCIDENT PRONE
SO HELP ME GOD
A WOMAN'S PLACE
RAINBOW'S END
CRUSH
A MAN WITHOUT WORDS

GEORGE KAPLAN
(See Clifford Green & Ellen Green)

JACK KAPLAN*
Contact: WGA - Los Angeles, 310/550-1000

Screenplays:
MY FELLOW AMERICANS w/Richard Chapman
WHISTLING DIXIE
LAND OF OPPORTUNITY w/Jonathan Lynn

JAMES KAPLAN*
Agent: ICM - New York, 212/556-5600

Screenplays:
NATIVE GENIUS w/Peter Kaplan
BLACK WALLS

JONATHAN KAPLAN*
Agent: CAA - Beverly Hills, 310/288-4545

WHITE LINE FEVER   Columbia, 1975, w/KenFriedman, directed
MR. BILLION   20th Century-Fox, 1976, w/KenFriedman, directed

MARTIN KAPLAN
STRIKING DISTANCE   Columbia, 1993, w/Rowdy Herrington

MARTY KAPLAN*
(Martin H. Kaplan)
Agent: ICM - Beverly Hills, 310/550-4000

NOISES OFF   Buena Vista, 1992
THE DISTINGUISHED GENTLEMAN   Buena Vista, 1992

Screenplays:
MAX Q

MICHAEL A. KAPLAN*
Agent: ICM - Beverly Hills, 310/550-4000

ILLEGALLY YOURS   DEG, 1986, w/Ken Finkelman &
   John Levenstein, as "Max Dickens & M.A. Stewart"

Screenplays:
CARLESS w/John Levenstein
TALES OF THE NEW DEPRESSION

MITCHELL KAPNER*
Agent: Richland/Wunsch/Hohman Agency - Los Angeles,
   310/278-1955

Screenplays:
POUND OF FLESH
TRUST ME
HAROLD AND THE PURPLE CRAYON
THE LITTLE WIFE
LES COMPERES

LARRY KARASZEWSKI*
Agent: ICM - Beverly Hills, 310/550-4000

PROBLEM CHILD   Universal, 1990, w/Scott Alexander
PROBLEM CHILD 2   Universal, 1991, w/Scott Alexander
ED WOOD   Buena Vista, 1994, w/Scott Alexander

Screenplays:
LARRY FLYNT w/Scott Alexander
THAT DARN CAT w/Scott Alexander
LITTLE DEMONS w/Scott Alexander
SLUSHY (Story) w/Scott Alexander
JUPITER NEEDS PARKING w/Scott Alexander
BLACKBALLED w/Scott Alexander
HOMEWRECKERS w/Scott Alexander
SEVEN DEADLY TIMS w/Scott Alexander
L.A. TALES

PETER KARLIN
Agent: Writers & Artists Agency - Los Angeles, 310/824-6300

Screenplays:
STRIKE ZONE

JANICE KARMAN
THE CHIPMUNK ADVENTURE (AF)   Samuel Goldwyn Company,
   1986, w/Ross Bagdasarian, directed

THOMAS KARNOWSKI
THE SWORD AND THE SORCERER   Group 1, 1982,
   w/Albert Pyun & John Stuckmeyer

TOM KARTOZIAN*
Agent: The Irv Schechter Company - Beverly Hills, 310/278-8070

FROZEN ASSETS   RKO Pictures, 1992, w/Don Klein

LAWRENCE KASDAN*
Agent: United Talent Agency - Beverly Hills, 310/273-6700
Business: Kasdan Pictures, 20th Century Fox, 310/203-1890

THE EMPIRE STRIKES BACK   20th Century-Fox, 1980,
   w/Leigh Brackett
CONTINENTAL DIVIDE   Universal, 1981
RAIDERS OF THE LOST ARK   Paramount, 1981
BODY HEAT   Warner Bros., 1981, directed
RETURN OF THE JEDI   20th Century-Fox, 1983, w/George Lucas
THE BIG CHILL ★   Columbia, 1983, w/Barbara Benedek, directed
SILVERADO   Columbia, 1985, w/Mark Kasdan, directed
THE ACCIDENTAL TOURIST ★   Warner Bros., 1988,
   w/Frank Galati, directed
GRAND CANYON ★   20th Century Fox, 1991, w/Meg Kasdan, directed
THE BODYGUARD   Warner Bros., 1992
WYATT EARP   Warner Bros., 1994, w/Dan Gordon, directed

Screenplays:
INNS OF NEW ENGLAND w/Meg Kasdan

MARK KASDAN*
Agent: CAA - Beverly Hills, 310/288-4545

SILVERADO   Columbia, 1985, w/Lawrence Kasdan
CRIMINAL LAW   Hemdale, 1989

Screenplays:
THE MAGNIFICENT SEVEN w/Terry Swann

MEG KASDAN*
Business Manager: Breslauer, Jacobson & Rutman - 310/282-0477

GRAND CANYON ★   20th Century Fox, 1991, w/Lawrence Kasdan

Screenplays:
INNS OF NEW ENGLAND w/Lawrence Kasdan

MARYANNE KASICA*
Agent: Shapiro/Lichtman - Los Angeles, 310/859-8877

Screenplays:
BUZZARDS LUCK w/Michael Scheff

JEROME A. KASS*
Agent: Richland/Wunsch/Hohman Agency - Los Angeles,
310/278-1955

THE BLACK STALLION RETURNS   MGM/UA, 1983,
w/Richard Kletter

SAM HENRY KASS
Agent: ICM - Beverly Hills, 310/550-4000

DICE AND CARDS (P)
LUSTING AFTER PIPINO'S WIFE (P)
SIDDOWN!!! (P)
SIDE STREET SCENES (P)
FAMILY SNAPSHOTS (P)
THE SEARCH FOR ONE-EYE JIMMY   Grenda Films,
1993, directed

PHIL KASSEL
Agent: The Agency - Los Angeles, 310/551-3000

Screenplays:
SMALL IN THE SADDLE

MICHAEL KASSIN*
Agent: CAA - Beverly Hills, 310/288-4545

Screenplays:
ZERO HOUR w/Michael Wolk

MATTIEU KASSOVITZ
Contact: French Film Office, 745 Fifth Avenue, New York, NY 10151,
212/832-8860

CAFE AU LAIT   New Yorker Films, 1994, directed

LEONARD KASTLE
THE HONEYMOON KILLERS   Cinerama Releasing Corporation,
1969, directed

Screenplays:
CHANGE OF HEART
THE WEDDING AT CANA
SHAKESPEARE'S DOG

DAPHNA KASTNER
Contact: Screen Actors Guild - Los Angeles, 213/954-1600

JULIA HAS TWO LOVERS   South Gate Entertainment, 1991,
w/Bashar Shbib

Screenplays:
FRENCH EXIT w/Michael Alan Lerner (Cineville, directing)

JOHN KATCHMER*
Contact: WGA - Los Angeles, 310/550-1000

UNLAWFUL ENTRY   20th Century Fox, 1992,
Story w/Lewis Colick & George D. Putnam

JASON KATIMS*
Agent: CAA - Beverly Hills, 310/288-4545

WHO MADE ROBERT DENIRO KING OF AMERICA? (P)
DRIVING LESSONS (P)

Screenplays:
THE PALLBEARER w/Matt Reeves (Miramax)

MITCHEL L. KATLIN*
Agent: CAA - Beverly Hills, 310/288-4545

OPPORTUNITY KNOCKS   Universal, 1990, w/Nat Bernstein

Screenplays:
ON THE AIR w/Nat Bernstein
WHEN THE WIFE'S AWAY w/Nat Bernstein
LORD OF THE MANOR w/Nat Bernstein

A. L. KATZ*
Manager: Allen Kassirer - 818/340-9800

CHILDREN OF THE CORN II: THE FINAL SACRIFICE   Dimension
Entertainment, 1993, w/Gilbert Adler

Screenplays:
FAT TUESDAY w/Gil Adler & J.P. Kelly (Universal)

ALLAN D. KATZ*
Agent: Paradigm - Los Angeles, 310/277-4400
Business Manager: Brentwood Management Group - 310/826-0909

BIG MAN ON CAMPUS   Vestron, 1989

DOUGLAS KATZ
LIFE IN THE FOOD CHAIN   Katzfilms, 1992, directed

EVAN KATZ*
Agent: ICM - Beverly Hills, 310/550-4000

LOVE MATTERS (CTF)   Chanticleer Productions, 1993,
w/Eb Lottimer

Screenplays:
COUNTERFEIT FATHER w/Tom Ropelewski

GLORIA KATZ*
Agent: CAA - Beverly Hills, 310/288-4545

AMERICAN GRAFFITI ★   Universal, 1973, w/Willard Huyck &
George Lucas
MESSIAH OF EVIL   International Cinefilm, 1975, w/Willard Huyck
LUCKY LADY   20th Century-Fox, 1975, w/Willard Huyck
FRENCH POSTCARDS   Paramount, 1979, w/Willard Huyck
INDIANA JONES AND THE TEMPLE OF DOOM   Paramount, 1984,
w/Willard Huyck
BEST DEFENSE   Paramount, 1984, w/Willard Huyck
HOWARD THE DUCK   Universal, 1986, w/Willard Huyck
RADIOLAND MURDERS   Universal, 1994, w/Willard Huyck,
Ron Osborn & Jeff Reno

Screenplays:
MISSION: IMPOSSIBLE w/Willard Huyck
NIGHT RIDE DOWN w/Willard Huyck
THE AIR-CONDITIONED DREAM w/Willard Huyck
NIAGRA FALLS w/Willard Huyck
A YELLOW RAFT IN BLUE WATER w/Willard Huyck

JONATHAN KATZ*
Contact: WGA - New York, 212/245-6180

HOUSE OF GAMES   Orion, 1987, Story w/David Mamet

Ka

F
I
L
M

W
R
I
T
E
R
S

JORDAN KATZ*
Agent: ICM - Beverly Hills, 310/550-4000

TRIAL BY JURY   Warner Bros., 1994, w/Heywood Gould

Screenplays:
INCOGNITO (Warner Bros.)

ROBERT KATZ*
Agent: Sterling Lord Literistic - New York, 212/696-2800

MASSACRE IN ROME   National General, 1973,
   w/George Pan Cosmatos
THE CASSANDRA CROSSING   Avco Embassy, 1977,
   w/George Pan Cosmatos & Tom Mankiewicz
THE SALAMANDER   ITC, 1983
HOTEL COLONIAL   Columbia, 1987, w/Ira Barmak,
   Enzo Monteleone & Cinzia Torrini

Screenplays:
FATHER DAMIEN OF MOLOKAI

STEPHEN KATZ*
Contact: 214/491-1511

SATAN'S PRINCESS   Paramount Home Video/Sun Heat
   Pictures, 1991

Screenplays:
THE VIRGIN SUICIDES
AMERICAN GOTHIC
DESIGNATED HITTER
KNEE DEEP IN ALLIGATORS
MORNINGSIDE HEIGHTS
SHADOW OF THE VAMPIRE

JONATHAN KAUFER*
Agent: Hilary Wayne - Beverly Hills, 310/289-6186
Contact: Bloom, Dekom, Hergott & Cook - Los Angeles,
   310/278-8622

SOUP FOR ONE   Warner Bros., 1982, directed

Screenplays:
WAR BABIES
ALL CONQUERS LOVE
HORROR HOLIDAY
COMPUTER
THE EDUCATION OF LINUS DOOLEY
SLEEPWALKER

CHARLES KAUFMAN
Business: Troma, Inc., 733 Ninth Avenue, New York, NY 10019,
   212/757-4555

MOTHER'S DAY   United Film Distribution, 1980,
   w/Warren D. Leight, directed
WAITRESS!   Troma, 1982, w/Michael Stone
WHEN NATURE CALLS   Troma, 1985, directed

Screenplays:
ELVES w/Larry B. Williams
WENDELL WILCOX AND THE MONSTER MAKERS
   w/Larry B. Williams

KEN KAUFMAN*
Agent: The Daniel Ostroff Agency - Los Angeles, 310/278-2020

IN THE ARMY NOW   Buena Vista, 1994, w/Stu Krieger,
   Daniel Petrie Jr., Fax Bahr & Adam Small

Screenplays:
WHAT'S UP BUGS?

KEVIN KAUFMAN
ROMEO & JULIA   Kaufman Films, 1992, directed

LLOYD KAUFMAN
Business: Troma, Inc., 733 Ninth Avenue, New York, NY 10019,
   212/757-4555

STUCK ON YOU!   Troma, 1983, w/others, co-directed
THE TOXIC AVENGER, PART III: THE LAST TEMPTATION OF
   TOXIE   Troma, 1989, w/Gay Parrington Terry, co-directed
CLASS OF NUKE 'EM HIGH PART 2: SUBHUMANOID MELTDOWN
   Troma, 1991, w/Eric Louzil, Carl Morano, Marcus Rolling,
   Jeffrey W. Sass & Matt Unger

MILLARD KAUFMAN
Agent: Jim Preminger Agency - Los Angeles, 310/475-9491

TAKE THE HIGH GROUND ★   MGM, 1953
BAD DAY AT BLACK ROCK ★   MGM, 1954
RAINTREE COUNTRY   MGM, 1958
NEVER SO FEW   MGM, 1959
CONVICTS FOUR   *REPRIEVE*   Allied Artists, 1962, directed
THE WAR LORD   Universal, 1965, w/John Collier
THE KLANSMAN   Paramount, 1974, w/Samuel Fuller

PHILIP KAUFMAN*
Agent: CAA - Beverly Hills, 310/288-4545

GOLDSTEIN   Altura, 1965, co-directed
FEARLESS FRANK   American International, 1969, directed
THE GREAT NORTHFIELD, MINNESOTA RAID   Universal,
   1972, directed
THE OUTLAW JOSEY WALES   Warner Bros., 1976,
   w/Sonia Chernus
THE WANDERERS   Orion/Warner Bros., 1979,
   w/Rose Kaufman, directed
RAIDERS OF THE LOST ARK   Paramount, 1981,
   Story w/George Lucas
THE RIGHT STUFF   The Ladd Company/Warner Bros.,
   1983, directed
THE UNBEARABLE LIGHTNESS OF BEING ★   Orion, 1988,
   w/Jean-Claude Carriere, directed
HENRY & JUNE   Universal, 1990, w/Rose Kaufman, directed
RISING SUN   20th Century Fox, 1993, w/Michael Backes &
   Michael Crichton, directed

Screenplays:
BLACK ANGEL w/Jean-Claude Carriere

ROSE L. KAUFMAN*
Contact: 415/421-3374

THE WANDERERS   Orion/Warner Bros., 1979, w/Philip Kaufman
HENRY & JUNE   Universal, 1990, w/Philip Kaufman

LAURA KAVANAU
Agent: Renaissance-H.N. Swanson - Los Angeles, 310/246-6000

Screenplays:
DEEP COVER (CTF) DOWN FOR BLOOD w/Michael Levine

DUSTY KAY*
Contact: WGA - Los Angeles, 310/550-1000

Screenplays:
WANTED

KAREN KAY
CALL ME   Vestron, 1988

TERRY KAY
Agent: CAA - Beverly Hills, 310/288-4545

Screenplays:
SHADOW SONG

TONY KAYDEN
Agent: The Brandt Company - Sherman Oaks, 818/783-7747

OUT OF BOUNDS   Columbia, 1986
SLIPSTREAM   Entertainment Film, 1989

Screenplays:
DON'T THINK TWICE
THE AVENGER
POLICE PYTHON .357
MIDNIGHT BLUE
NOVEMBER MAN
HOUSE DETECTIVE
DIRE STRAITS

JOHN KAYE*
Agent: The Coppage Company - North Hollywood, 818/980-1106

CHERRY TERRY, THE ROCKIN' ROBIN (P)
RAFFERTY AND THE GOLD DUST TWINS   Warner Bros., 1975
AMERICAN HOT WAX   Paramount, 1978
WHERE THE BUFFALO ROAM   Universal, 1980

Screenplays:
MERCY SPRINGS
MAGNETIC NORTH
TELEPHONE JACK

NORMAN KAYE
CACTUS   Spectrafilm, 1986, w/Paul Cox & Bob Ellis

PHOEBE KAYLOR
CARNY   United Artists, 1980, Story w/Robert Kaylor & Robbie Robertson

ROBERT KAYLOR
Contact: Directors Guild of America - Los Angeles, 310/289-2000

CARNY   United Artists, 1980, Story w/Phoebe Kaylor & Robbie Robertson, directed

ELIA KAZAN*
Business: 174 East 95th St., New York, NY 10128

AMERICA, AMERICA ★   Warner Bros., 1963, directed
THE VISITORS   United Artists, 1972, directed
THE ARRANGEMENT   Warner Bros., 1969, directed

NICHOLAS KAZAN*
Agent: Sanford-Gross & Associates - Los Angeles, 310/208-2100

BLOOD MOON (P)
SOUTHERN COMFORT (P)
SAFE HOUSE (P)
FRANCES   Universal/AFD, 1982, w/Eric Bergren & Christopher DeVore
AT CLOSE RANGE   Orion, 1986
PATTY HEARST   Atlantic Releasing Corporation, 1988
REVERSAL OF FORTUNE ★   Warner Bros., 1990
MOBSTERS   Universal, 1991, w/Mike Mahern
DREAM LOVER   Gramercy, 1994, directed

Screenplays:
MATILDA w/Robin Swicord (Universal)
CORTES
ANIMALS
THE RIDE-ALONG
OUTLAWS
SINGLE WOMEN
THE SURVIVALIST
PUNK DADDY
THE BEARD

TIM KAZURINSKY*
Agent: CAA - Beverly Hills, 310/288-4545

ABOUT LAST NIGHT   Tri-Star, 1986, w/Denise De Clue
FOR KEEPS   Tri-Star, 1988, w/Denise De Clue

Screenplays:
TUG OF WAR w/Denise DeClue
ABOUT LAST NIGHT 2 w/Denise DeClue
BIG SUCCESS w/Denise De Clue

JAMES KEACH*
Agent: Metropolitan Talent Agency - Los Angeles, 213/857-4500

THE LONG RIDERS   United Artists, 1980, w/Bill Bryden, Stacy Keach & Steven Philip Smith
ARMED AND DANGEROUS   Columbia, 1986, w/Brian Grazer & Harold Ramis

STACY KEACH
Contact: Screen Actors Guild - Los Angeles, 213/954-1600

THE LONG RIDERS   United Artists, 1980, w/Bill Bryden, James Keach & Steven Philip Smith

LAURENCE KEANE
BIG MEAT EATER   New Line Cinema, 1984, w/Phil Savath & Chris Windsor

JIM KEARNS*
Contact: WGA - Los Angeles, 310/550-1000

Screenplays:
JOHN Q

ROBERT KEATS*
Contact: WGA - Los Angeles, 310/550-1000

THE CLOSER   Ion Pictures, 1991, w/Louis La Russo II

Screenplays:
FLEX
NANETTE OF THE NORTH

BARRY KEEFFE
Agent: London Management - London, 071/493-1610

THE LONG GOOD FRIDAY   Embassy, 1982

Screenplays:
THE TIGHTROPE MAN
THE BLUNDERER (CTF)

JOE KEENAN*
Agent: ICM - Beverly Hills, 310/550-4000

THE TIMES (P)
SLEEP WITH ME   MGM/UA, 1994, w/Duane Dell'Amico, Roger Hedden, Neal Jimenez, Rory Kelly & Michael Steinberg

Screenplays:
LORD BUTLER (shared)

P. JAMES KEITEL
BELOW 30/ABOVE 10,000   Damaged Californians, 1994, directed

HARVEY KEITH
Contact: Directors Guild of America - Los Angeles, 310/289-2000

JEZEBEL'S KISS   Shapiro Glickenhaus, 1990, directed

F
I
L
M

W
R
I
T
E
R
S

WOODY KEITH
INITIATION: SILENT NIGHT, DEADLY NIGHT 4   Silent Films, 1990
BRIDE OF RE-ANIMATOR   Troma, 1991, w/Rick Fry
SOCIETY   Zecca Corp., 1992, w/Rick Fry

JOHN KELLEHER
Business: Liberty Films, The Forum, 74-80 Camden St.,
   London NW1 0JL, England, 071/387-5733

EAT THE PEACH   Skouras, 1987, w/Peter Ormrod

TIM KELLEHER*
Agent: William Morris Agency - Beverly Hills, 310/274-7451

Screenplays:
FIRST KID
LEISURE SUIT LARRY

FREDERICK KING KELLER
TUCK EVERLASTING   Coe Films, 1981, directed
VAMPING   Atlantic Releasing Corporation, 1984, Story, directed

SHELDON KELLER*
Contact: WGA - Los Angeles, 310/550-1000

BUONA SERA MRS. CAMPBELL   United Artists, 1968,
   w/Melvin Frank & Denis Norden
CLEOPATRA JONES   Warner Bros., 1973, w/Max Julien

DAVID E. KELLEY*
Agent: CAA - Beverly Hills, 310/288-4545

FROM THE HIP   DEG, 1987, w/Bob Clark

Screenplays:
STRANGERS
EDDIE'S BACK

HUGH KELLEY
CAGE   New Century/Vista, 1989

J.P. KELLEY*
Agent: William Morris Agency - Beverly Hills, 310/274-7451

Screenplays:
FAT TUESDAY w/Gil Adler & A.L. Katz (Universal)
THE WITCHING HOUR
THE LOCUSTS

WILLIAM KELLEY*
Agent: Reece Halsey Agency - Los Angeles, 213/652-2409

WITNESS ★★   Paramount, 1985, w/Earl Wallace

Screenplays:
CALLED HOME w/Earl Wallace

D.A. KELLOGG
BITTERSWEET LOVE   Avco Embassy, 1976, w/Adrian Morrall

MARJORIE KELLOGG*
Agent: Gold/Marshak - Burbank, 818/972-4300

TELL ME THAT YOU LOVE ME, JUNIE MOON   Paramount, 1969
THE BELL JAR   Avco Embassy, 1979

CASEY KELLY*
Agent: Broder-Kurland-Webb-Uffner - Beverly Hills, 310/281-3400

DADDY LONG LEGS (P)
ERRAND OF MERCY (P)
THE OTHER WOMAN (P)

Screenplays:
SOMEPLACE ELSE
GREENER PASTURES
LETTERS TO SCHWARTZY
BURNING TIME

CHRIS KELLY
ANY MAN'S DEATH   INI Entertainment, 1990, w/Iain Roy

KEVIN KELLY
Agent: CAA - Beverly Hills, 310/288-4545

Screenplays:
DOWN THE DRAIN

MARGARET KELLY
PUBERTY BLUES   Universal Classics, 1983

MAUREEN KELLY
Agent: Susan Smith & Associates - Beverly Hills, 213/852-4777

Screenplays:
BIPPIDY, BOPPIDY, BOO AND THE AMERICAN DREAM

PATRICK SMITH KELLY*
Agent: United Talent Agency - Beverly Hills, 310/273-6700

Screenplays:
REGULATOR
TOUGH CROWD
SOLO WEAPON
NATURE OF THE BEAST

RORY KELLY
Agent: United Talent Agency - Beverly Hills, 310/273-6700

SLEEP WITH ME   MGM, 1994, w/Duane Dell'Amico,
   Roger Hedden, Neal Jimenez, Joe Keenan &
   Michael Steinberg, directed

WILLIAM KELMAN*
Contact: BFD Entertainment, P.O. Box 1705, Santa Monica,
   CA 90294, 310/305-7262

MORTUARY ACADEMY   Taurus Entertainment, 1987
THE ALMIGHTY FRED   BFD Entertainment, 1993, directed

Screenplays:
TOUGH COOKIES

THOMAS KELSEY
PURPLE HAZE   Triumph/Columbia, 1983,
   Story w/David Burton Morris & Victoria Wozniak

KEVIN KELTON*
Agent: ICM - Beverly Hills, 310/550-4000

Screenplays:
DEVIL'S ADVOCATE
NATIONAL LAMPOON'S COLLEGE BOUND

PAUL KEMBER
Agent: The Casarotto Company - London, 071/287-4450

NOT QUITE PARADISE   New World, 1985, from his play

TOM (ZBIGNIEW) KEMPINSKI*
Contact: WGA - Los Angeles, 310/550-1000

SEPARATION (P)   also teleplay
TIMBUCTOO (P)
PAPER MARRIAGES (P)
DUET FOR ONE   Cannon, 1987, w/Andrei Konchalovsky &
   Jeremy Lipp, from his play

THOMAS KENEALLY
THE CHANT OF JIMMIE BLACKSMITH   New Yorker, 1978, Story
SILVER CITY   Samuel Goldwyn Company, 1985,
   w/Sophia Turkiewicz

PETER KENNA
THE GOOD WIFE   Atlantic Releasing Corporation, 1986

ADAM KENNEDY*
Contact: Egon Dumler - New York, 212/759-4850

THE DOVE   Paramount, 1974, w/Peter Beagle
THE DOMINO PRINCIPLE   Avco Embassy, 1977
RAISE THE TITANIC   AFD, 1980, w/Eric Hughes

BURT KENNEDY*
Agent: Borinstein Oreck Bogart Agency - Los Angeles, 213/658-7500
Business: Brigade Productions, 13138 Magnolia Blvd.,
   Sherman Oaks, CA 91403, 818/986-8759

SEVEN MEN FROM NOW   Batjac, 1956
FORT DOBBS   Warner Bros., 1957, w/George W. George
THE TALL T   Columbia, 1957
RIDE LONESOME   Columbia, 1959
YELLOWSTONE KELLY   Warner Bros., 1959
COMANCHE STATION   Columbia, 1960
THE CANADIANS   20th Century-Fox, 1961, directed
SIX BLACK HORSES   Universal-International, 1962
MAIL ORDER BRIDE   MGM, 1963, directed
THE ROUNDERS   MGM, 1965, directed
WELCOME TO HARD TIMES   MGM, 1967, directed
YOUNG BILLY YOUNG   United Artists, 1969, directed
HANNIE CAULDER   Paramount, 1971,
   w/David Haft as "Z.X. Jones," directed
THE TRAIN ROBBERS   Warner Bros., 1973, directed
THE TROUBLE WITH SPIES   DEG, 1987, directed
WHITE HUNTER, BLACK HEART   Warner Bros., 1990,
   w/James Bridges & Peter Viertel

Screenplays:
THE SAVAGE LAND (directing)

DUNCAN KENNEDY
Agent: United Talent Agency - Beverly Hills, 310/273-6700

Screenplays:
ZERO GRAVITY w/John Zinman

JAMES KENNEDY
Agent: Joseph/Knight Agency - Los Angeles, 213/465-5474

THE WINNERS CIRCLE (P)
STATEN ISLAND FERRY (P)
THE GANDY DANCER (P)
SWIFTY (P)
MAD VINCENT (P)
PERFUME (P)
THE HOLDING COMPANY (P)
DOGFIGHT (P)
HIT AND RUN (P)
THE SESSION (P)
CEREMONY FOR THE MIDGET (Short)

Screenplays:
SUCCESS
KEY WEST
JIMMY JONES
BABY BABY BABY
BULLETPROOF
BODIE
HEARTLAND U.S.A.

KERRY KENNEDY
Agent: Writers & Artists Agency - Los Angeles, 310/824-6300

Screenplays:
HOPE

LEON ISAAC KENNEDY
BODY AND SOUL   Cannon, 1981, from a screenplay by
   Abraham Polonsky
KNIGHTS OF THE CITY   New World, 1986

MICHAEL KENNEDY
Agent: Great North Artists Management, 350 Dupont Street, Toronto,
   Ontario M5R 1V9, Canada, 416/925-2051

THE SWORDSMAN   SC Entertainment International, 1992, directed

SUELLA KENNEDY
TWICE UPON A TIME (AF)   The Ladd Company/Warner Bros.,
   1983, w/Bill Couterie, John Korty & Charles Swenson

WILLIAM KENNEDY*
Agent: Pleshette & Green - Los Angeles, 213/465-0428

THE COTTON CLUB   Orion, 1984, w/Francis Coppola
IRONWEED   Tri-Star, 1987

Screenplays:
BILLY PHELAN'S GREATEST GAME
LEGS
THE SPORTSWRITER

TONY KENRICK*
Agent: Innovative Artists - Los Angeles, 310/553-5200

NOBODY'S PERFEKT   Columbia, 1981

Screenplays:
MOMMA KNOWS BEST
DEAD END

DAN KEOPPEL
THE LOST WORDS   Film Crash, 1994, w/Michael Kaniecki &
   Scott Saunders

BILL KERBY*
Agent: CAA - Beverly Hills, 310/288-4545

THE LAST AMERICAN HERO   20th Century-Fox, 1973,
   w/William Roberts
THE GRAVY TRAIN   Columbia, 1974, w/David Whitney
FIREPOWER   ITC, 1977, Story w/Michael Winner
HOOPER   Warner Bros., 1978, w/Thomas Rickman
THE ROSE   20th Century-Fox, 1979, w/Bo Goldman
LAKOTA WOMAN: SIEGE AT WOUNDED KNEE (CTF)
   TNT/Fonda Films, 1994

Screenplays:
THE ANYTHING GUYS
STILL CRAZY w/Jim Hart
THE TOWER
MOONTRAP
TRAP DOOR
OUT OF BODY
THE WAR HORSE

RONNI KERN*
Agent: ICM - Beverly Hills, 310/550-4000

A CHANGE OF SEASONS   20th Century-Fox, 1980,
   w/Erich Segal & Fred Segal
AMERICAN POP (AF)   Columbia, 1981

Screenplays:
SOLOMON AND SHEBA (DeLaurentis)
REUNION
THE BUST OUT KING
FAST COMPANY
FISHTAIL
SOLD
RAISING TWAIN

F
I
L
M

W
R
I
T
E
R
S

SHIP MOVEMENTS
PRINCESS OF PAROLE
THE TROUBLE WITH LARRY
LOVE STORY '78

SARAH M. KERNOCHAN*
Agent: United Talent Agency - Beverly Hills, 310/273-6700

9 1/2 WEEKS   MGM/UA, 1986, w/Zalman King & Patricia L. Knop
DANCERS   Cannon, 1987
IMPROMPTU   Hemdale, 1991
SOMMERSBY   Warner Bros., 1993, w/Nicholas Meyer

Screenplays:
NANCY DREW
THE PLEDGE
DELTA OF VENUS w/Colo Tavernier O'Hagan
THE PSYCHIC
THE GIRL IN THE BLACK
HELMET
THE HAIRY BIRD

JEFFREY KERNS
DOUBLE TROUBLE   Motion Picture Corporation of America, 1992,
   w/Chuck Osbourne & Kurt Wimmer

NINA V. KEROVA
LIQUID SKY   Cinevista, 1983, w/Slava Tsukerman & Anne Carlisle

FRANK KERR*
Contact: 617/925-9555

TRUE BLOOD   Fries Entertainment, 1989, directed

Screenplays:
THE CHILDREN OF THE EARTH
THE SECOND COMING
UNDERGROUND
WAR BABY

LODGE KERRIGAN
CLEAN SHAVEN   DSM III Films, 1993, directed

JOHN KERSHAW
Contact: WGA - New York, 212/245-6180

THE LONELY LADY   Universal, 1983, w/Shawn Randall
YELLOWHAIR AND THE FORTRESS OF GOLD
   Crown International, 1984, w/Matt Cimber

CLAUDE KERVEN*
Agent: United Talent Agency - Beverly Hills, 310/273-6700

CANDY STORE (Short)
MORTAL THOUGHTS   Columbia, 1991, w/William Reilly

Screenplays:
THE SHADOW WAR w/Dan Cahill

BRADLEY KESDEN
MEATBALLS III   TMS Pictures, 1986, w/Michael Paseornek

ELLEN KESEND*
Agent: Candace Lake - Beverly Hills, 310/289-0600

Screenplays:
BETWEEN THE WARS
IN'N'OUT
SPACE CASE
CONVICTIONS

ALEK KESHISHIAN*
Agent: CAA - Beverly Hills, 310/288-4545

Screenplays:
CHARMED (directing)

LYLE D. KESSLER*
Agent: United Talent Agency - Beverly Hills, 310/273-6700 or
   The Tantleff Office - New York, 212/941-3939

ROBBERS (P)
THE WATERING PLACE (P)
POSSESSION (P)
THE VIEWING (P)
TOUCHED   Lorimar Productions/Wildwood Partners, 1983
ORPHANS   Lorimar, 1987, from his play
GLADIATOR   Columbia, 1992, w/Robert Mark Kamen
THE SAINT OF FORT WASHINGTON   Warner Bros., 1993

Screenplays:
LIFE'S COMPANION
AL AND CAMILLE
RIFFIFI
WAYWARD ANGEL

MARGOT L. KESSLER*
Manager: Carol Lees, The Lees Company - 818/760-7784

THE STRAINS OF AFFECTION (P)
THE ALLNIGHTER   Universal, 1987, w/Tamar S. Hoffs

MERLE KESSLER
(Ian Shoales)
Contact: National Public Radio - Santa Monica, 310/450-5183

ZADAR! COW FROM HELL   Stone Peach Productions, 1989

LARRY KETRON*
Agent: APA - Los Angeles, 310/273-0744

LAUREEN'S WHEREABOUTS (P)
PERMANENT RECORD   Paramount, 1988, w/Jarre Fees &
   Alice Liddle
FRESH HORSES   Weintraub Entertainment, 1988, from his play
VITAL SIGNS   20th Century Fox, 1990, w/Jeb Stuart

Screenplays:
AFRICAN FACTOR
SUN BEARING DOWN
RACHEL FATE
ASIAN SHADE
DEATH OF A DIRTY BLONDE
CAPTAIN AMANDA

CARLA KETTNER*
Agent: Innovative Artists - Los Angeles, 310/553-5200

Screenplays:
JOURNEY'S END

MICHAEL KEUSCH
LENA'S HOLIDAY   Prism Entertainment, 1991,
   w/Deborah Tilton, directed

TED KEY*
Contact: WGA - Los Angeles, 310/550-1000

THE CAT FROM OUTER SPACE   Buena Vista, 1978

CHRISTOPHER KEYSER*
Agent: CAA - Beverly Hills, 310/288-4545

BENEFIT OF THE DOUBT   Miramax, 1993, w/Jeffrey Polman

Screenplays:
SISTER
THE POINT
SOUTHERN CROSS
DEAD OF SUMMER
JAG
OUT OF CHARACTER
MANHATTAN ISLAND

RIFFAT A. KHAN
FEELIN' SCREWY   Raedon Entertainment, 1991, directed

EDWARD KHMARA*
Agent: William Morris Agency - Beverly Hills, 310/274-7451

LADYHAWKE   Warner Bros., 1985, w/Tom Mankiewicz &
   Michael Thomas
ENEMY MINE   20th Century Fox, 1985
NECROPOLIS   Empire Pictures, 1986
DRAGON: THE STORY OF BRUCE LEE   Universal, 1993,
   w/Rob Cohen & John Raffo

Screenplays:
ROLLER DISCO
THE INVITATION w/R. Eisele
THE BIG FIGHT

CALLIE KHOURI*
Agent: ICM - Beverly Hills, 310/550-4000

THELMA AND LOUISE ★★   MGM-Pathe, 1991

Screenplays:
GRACE UNDER PRESSURE (Warner Bros.)

JOHN KILLORAN
Agent: Susan Smith & Associates - Beverly Hills, 213/852-4777

Screenplays:
TWILIGHT
IOWA STARS
JUST SAY BOO

KENNY KIM
3 NINJAS   Buena Vista, 1992, Story

BRUCE KIMMEL
Address: 3680 Fredonia Dr., Los Angeles, CA 90068, 213/874-1571

THE FIRST NUDIE MUSICAL   Paramount, 1976, co-directed
SPACESHIP *THE CREATURE WASN'T NICE*   Almi Cinema 5,
   1982, directed

JUD KINBERG*
Agent: Shapiro/Lichtman - Los Angeles, 310/859-8877

EAST OF SUDAN   Columbia, 1965

TIM KINCAID
ESCAPE FROM BAD GIRLS DORMITORY   Films Around the World,
   1985, directed
BREEDERS   Empire Pictures, 1986, directed
MUTANT HUNT   Empire Pictures, 1986, directed
ROBOT HOLOCAUST   Empire Pictures, 1987, directed
THE OCCULTIST   Empire Pictures, 1987, directed

JEFFREY KINDLEY*
Agent: Bret Adams Ltd. - New York, 212/765-5630

THE HITCHHIKERS (P)

Screenplays:
WESTLANDER
IS THERE LIFE AFTER HIGH SCHOOL?
FIRST OFFENDER (CTF)

ANDREA KING
Agent: CAA - Beverly Hills, 310/288-4545

Screenplays:
BODY LANGUAGE
ANIMAL ATTRACTION

DAVID KING
Contact: Academy of Canadian Cinema & Television, 753 Yonge St. -
   2nd Floor, Toronto M4Y 1Z9, Canada, 416/967-0315

HARMONY CATS   BC Film/NFB/CBC, 1993

LARRY L. KING*
Contact: Attorney Barbara S. Blaine, 700 13th St. NW,
   Washington, DC 20005

THE BEST LITTLE WHOREHOUSE GOES PUBLIC (P)
   w/Peter Masterson
THE BEST LITTLE WHOREHOUSE IN TEXAS   Universal, 1982,
   w/Peter Masterson, from their play

LAURA KING*
Agent: United Talent Agency - Beverly Hills, 310/273-6700

Screenplays:
THE NATURE OF ANNIE BEEN
EL NINO
BLESSING IN DISGUISE
CHEEK TO CHEEK

LESLIE KING*
Contact: WGA - Los Angeles, 310/550-1000

SON OF DARKNESS: TO DIE FOR II   Trimark, 1991

MARLENE KING*
Agent: ICM - Beverly Hills, 310/550-4000
Contact: Joshua Grode, Silverberg, Katz, Thompson & Braun

NATIONAL LAMPOON'S SENIOR TRIP   New Line Cinema, 1995,
   w/Roger Kumble
THE GAS LIGHT ADDITION   New Line Cinema, 1995

Screenplays:
MOBY DICK w/Roger Kumble & Charles Banks

RICK KING
Agent: Jim Preminger Agency - Los Angeles, 310/475-9491

HARD CHOICES   Lorimar, 1986, directed
HOTSHOT   International Film Marketing, 1987, w/Joe Sauter, directed
POINT BREAK   20th Century Fox, 1991, Story w/Peter Iliff

Screenplays:
WATCHING THE DETECTIVE

ROBERT P. KING*
Agent: Paradigm - Los Angeles, 310/277-4400

THE NEST   Concorde, 1987
UNDER THE BOARDWALK   New World, 1989
BLOODFIST   Concorde, 1989
PHANTOM OF THE MALL: ERIC'S REVENGE   Fries Entertainment,
   1989, w/Tony Michelman & Scott J. Schneid

CLEAN SLATE   MGM/UA, 1994
SPEECHLESS   MGM/UA, 1994

Screenplays:
RED CORNER
EL DORADO

STEPHEN KING*
Agent: CAA - Beverly Hills, 310/288-4545

CREEPSHOW   Warner Bros., 1982
STEPHEN KING'S CAT'S EYE   MGM/UA, 1985
SILVER BULLET   Paramount, 1985
MAXIMUM OVERDRIVE   DEG, 1986, directed
CREEPSHOW 2   New World, 1987, Story
PET SEMATARY   Paramount, 1989
STEPHEN KING'S SLEEPWALKERS   Columbia, 1992

TY KING
Agent: United Talent Agency - Beverly Hills, 310/273-6700

Screenplays:
TILL MONDAY

ZALMAN KING*
Agent: William Morris Agency - Beverly Hills, 310/274-7451

ROADIE   United Artists, 1980, Story w/Big Boy Medlin,
   Alan Rudolph & Michael Ventura
9 1/2 WEEKS   MGM/UA, 1986, w/Sarah Kernochan &
   Patricia L. Knop
WILDFIRE   Cinema Group, 1988, w/Matthew Bright
TWO MOON JUNCTION   Lorimar, 1988, directed
WILD ORCHID   Triumph, 1990, w/Patricia L. Knop, directed
WILD ORCHID 2: BLUE MOVIE BLUE   Vision International,
   1992, directed
LAKE CONSEQUENCE (CTF)   Showtime Networks, 1993,
   w/Henry Cobbold & Melanie Finn

Screenplays:
HOT w/Patricia L. Knop
BAKERSFIELD BLUES
ANGELS FLIGHT
GUITAR DOLLS
STREET HEAT
FIRST AMERICAN REBEL
COMPOSURE
GOD'S HEAD
PULL THE TRIGGER
GOOD-BYE

BEN KINGSLEY
Agent: ICM - Beverly Hills, 310/550-4000

Screenplays:
THE CIRCLE OF THE WHITE ROSE w/Jed Tullett (directing)

BARBARA KINGSOLVER
Agent: The Gersh Agency - Beverly Hills, 310/274-6611

Screenplays:
PIGS IN HEAVEN (CTF)

JAMES GREGORY KINGSTON*
Contact: WGA - Los Angeles, 310/550-1000

TURK 182   20th Century Fox, 1985, w/Denis Hamill & John Hamill

ERNEST KINOY*
Agent: William Morris Agency - New York, 212/586-5100

BROTHER JOHN   Columbia, 1970
BUCK AND THE PREACHER   Columbia, 1971
LEADBELLY   Paramount, 1976

MURROW (CTF)   HBO Premiere Films/Titus Productions/TVS Ltd.
   Productions, 1986
WHITE WATER SUMMER   Columbia, 1987, w/Mayna Starr
CHERNOBYL: THE FINAL WARNING (CTF)   Roger Gimbel
   Productions/Carolco Television, 1991

Screenplays:
MAGNIFICAT

WILLIAM KINSOLVING*
Agent: The Marion Rosenberg Office - Los Angeles, 213/653-7383

Screenplays:
MR. CHRISTIAN
BORN WITH THE CENTURY
JADE

GEORGE KIRGO*
Agent: CAA - Beverly Hills, 310/288-4545

RED LINE 7000   Paramount, 1965
SPINOUT   MGM, 1966, w/Theodore J. Flicker
DON'T MAKE WAVES   MGM, 1967, w/Ira Wallach
VOICES   Hemdale, 1973, w/Robert Enders

TIM KIRK*
Agent: United Talent Agency - Beverly Hills, 310/273-6700

Screenplays:
INTO THIN AIR w/David Carpenter
MOM IS A TREASURE HUNTER w/David Carpenter & Colin Greene
HACKER w/David Carpenter

D. SHONE KIRKPATRICK*
Contact: WGA - Los Angeles, 310/550-1000

BROTHERS IN ARMS   Ablo, 1989

Screenplays:
HATTERAS
WHITER SHADE OF PALE
SMITH AND WESSON
THE YUKON KID

BRUCE KIRSCHBAUM*
Agent: Broder-Kurland-Webb-Uffner - Beverly Hills, 310/281-3400

BACK TO THE BEACH   Paramount, 1987,
   Story w/James Komack & B.W.L. Norton

Screenplays:
MISTY BLUE RIVER
PIGSKINS (shared)

DAVID KIRSCHNER*
Agent: CAA - Beverly Hills, 310/288-4545

AN AMERICAN TAIL (AF)   Universal, 1986,
   Story w/Judy Freudberg & Tony Geiss
HOCUS POCUS   Buena Vista, 1993, Story w/Mick Garris
THE PAGEMASTER   20th Century Fox, 1994, w/David Casci &
   Ernie Contreras

MARY ANN KIRSCHNER
Agent: Leslie Kallen Agency - Sherman Oaks, 818/906-2785

Screenplays:
BLACK DIRT

TIM KISSEL
IN THE SOUP   Cacous Films Inc., 1992, w/Alexandre Rockwell

ROY KISSIN
ON THE EDGE   Skouras Pictures, 1986, Story w/Rob Nilsson

MARTIN KITROSSER
FRIDAY THE 13TH PART 3   Paramount, 1982, w/Carol Watson
MEATBALLS PART II   Tri-Star, 1984, Story w/Carol Watson
FRIDAY THE 13TH - A NEW BEGINNING   Paramount, 1985,
   w/David Cohen & Danny Steinmann

ROBERT KLANE*
Agent: William Morris Agency - Beverly Hills, 310/274-7451

WHERE'S POPPA?   United Artists, 1970
EVERY LITTLE CROOK AND NANNY   MGM, 1972,
   w/Jonathan Axelrod & Cy Howard
FIRE SALE   20th Century-Fox, 1977
THANK GOD IT'S FRIDAY   Columbia, 1978, directed
UNFAITHFULLY YOURS   20th Century Fox, 1984,
   w/Valerie Curtin & Barry Levinson
THE MAN WITH ONE RED SHOE   20th Century Fox, 1985
NATIONAL LAMPOON'S EUROPEAN VACATION   Warner Bros.,
   1985, w/John Hughes
WALK LIKE A MAN   MGM/UA, 1987
WEEKEND AT BERNIE'S   20th Century Fox, 1989
FOLKS!   20th Century Fox, 1992
WEEKEND AT BERNIE'S II   TriStar, 1993, directed

Screenplays:
ODD COUPLE
JURY DUTY
POST OFFICE
TRANSYLVANIA MUSICAL
LA CAGE AUX FOLLES, U.S.A.
THE HORSE IS DEAD
RUBY RED
GREASIER
PLAY MONEY

DAVID KLASS
Agent: Pleshette & Green - Los Angeles, 213/465-0428

Screenplays:
SHELTER w/Jeffrey Abrams
CALIFORNIA BLUE
ICEBREAKER
DOGSTAR
DESPERATE MEASURES

RIC KLASS
ELLIOT FAUMAN, PH.D.   Taurus Entertainment, 1990, directed

ANDREW KLAVAN*
Agent: Innovative Artists - Los Angeles, 310/553-5200

A SHOCK TO THE SYSTEM   Corsair Pictures, 1990

Screenplays:
THE OUTSIDER
ROUGH JUSTICE
DON'T SAY A WORD

LAURENCE KLAVAN*
Agent: The Tantleff Office - New York, 212/941-3939

Screenplays:
TOIL AND TROUBLE
ONE BEDROOM
THE USUAL SUSPECTS

STEVEN MICHAEL KLAYMAN*
Contact: WGA - Los Angeles, 310/550-1000

THE HUSTLER OF MONEY (Short)   Shared, co-directed

Screenplays:
MR. SCHNEIDERMAN PLEASE GO HOME
SPLIT DECISION
BABY MAKES THREE

MITCHELL S. KLEBANOFF*
Manager: Patricia Estrin - 818/780-4704

DISORDERLIES   Warner Bros., 1987, w/Mark Feldberg

Screenplays:
BLACK MAGNOLIA w/Mark Feldberg
BEVERLY HILLS NINJA w/Mark Feldberg

DENA KLEIMAN*
Agent: ICM - New York, 212/556-5600

STRAPPED (CTF)   HBO Showcase, 1993

DENNIS KLEIN*
Agent: United Talent Agency - Beverly Hills, 310/273-6700

Screenplays:
SEX & VIOLENCE
THE GOOD DOCTOR (directing)
LAST DANCE OF THE GOLDEN WEST (CTF)

DON KLEIN
FROZEN ASSETS   RKO Pictures, 1992, w/Tom Kartozian

JAIME B. KLEIN
PANDEMONIUM   MGM/UA, 1982, w/Richard Whitley

Screenplays:
ROAD TO RUIN w/Richard Whitley
REGATTA w/Richard Whitley
MR. NICE GUY
760 NO. MAPLE
MILLION DOLLAR TOWN
THINGS INVISIBLE TO SEE

JON KLEIN*
Agent: Lois Berman Agency - New York, 212/684-1835

T BONE N WEASEL (CTF)   Turner Pictures, 1992, from his play

LEWIS KLEINBERG*
Agent: Susan Smith & Associates - Beverly Hills, 213/852-4777

Screenplays:
RUNNING FOR COVER
GOING FOR BROKE
YOUNG AT HEART

RICHERD KLEINBERG
Contact: Bloom, Dekom, Hergott & Cook - Los Angeles, 310/278-8622

Screenplays:
SLEIGHT OF HAND
DEAD GIVEAWAY
PILOT ERROR

AVI KLEINBERGER
AMERICAN NINJA   Cannon, 1985, Story w/Gideon Amir
P.O.W. THE ESCAPE   Cannon, 1986, Story w/Gideon Amir

HARRY KLEINER
FALLEN ANGEL   20th Century-Fox, 1945
THE STREET WITH NO NAME   20th Century-Fox, 1948
RED SKIES OF MONTANA   20th Century-Fox, 1952
KANGAROO   20th Century-Fox, 1952
SALOME   Columbia, 1953, w/Jesse Lasky Jr.
CARMEN JONES   20th Century-Fox, 1954
THE VIOLENT MEN   *ROUGH COMPANY*   Columbia, 1955
THE GARMENT JUNGLE   Columbia, 1957
ICE PALACE   Warner Bros., 1960
A FEVER IN THE BLOOD   Warner Bros., 1960, w/Roy Huggins
FANTASTIC VOYAGE   20th Century-Fox, 1966
BULLITT   Warner Bros., 1968, w/Alan R. Trustman

LE MANS   National General, 1970
EXTREME PREJUDICE   Tri-Star, 1987, w/Deric Washburn
RED HEAT   Tri-Star, 1988,   w/Walter Hill & Troy Kennedy Martin

MAGGIE KLEINMAN*
Agent: J. Michael Bloom & Associates - Los Angeles, 310/275-6800

WELCOME HOME   Columbia, 1989

Screenplays:
ANNAPOLIS
HOME FOR THE HOLIDAYS
WHITE HUNTERS
CAUGHT DEAD w/Diane Wagner
FINAL BALLOT
SLUMLORD
PRINCE CHARMING

CARL D. KLEINSCHMIDT*
Contact: WGA - Los Angeles, 310/550-1000

MIDDLE AGE CRAZY   20th Century-Fox, 1980

RANDAL KLEISER*
Agent: ICM - Beverly Hills, 310/550-4000
Business Manager: Gregory Hinton, 3050 Runyon Canyon Rd.,
   Los Angeles, CA 90046, 213/851-5224

STREET PEOPLE   American International, 1976, w/others
SUMMER LOVERS   Filmways, 1982, directed
NORTH SHORE   Universal, 1987, Story w/William Phelps

Screenplays:
IT'S MY PARTY (directing)

WALTER KLENHARD*
Agent: Paradigm - Los Angeles, 310/277-4400

SWEET POISON (CTF)   Smart Money Productions Inc./MCA
   Television Entertainment, 1991
DEAD IN THE WATER (CTF)   Kevin Bright Productions/MCA
   Television Entertainment, 1991, w/Eleanor E. Gaver &
   Robert Seidenberg
LIES OF THE TWINS (CTF)   MCA Television Entertainment, 1991,
   w/Mel Frohman
THE LAST HIT (CTF)   Garson Studios/MCA Television
   Entertainment, 1993, w/Alan Sharp
THE HAUNTING OF SEA CLIFF INN (CTF)   May Day Productions,
   1994, directed

Screenplays:
GOODNIGHT MOON
DANCER'S TOUCH

LENORE KLETTER*
Agent: William Morris Agency - Beverly Hills, 310/274-7451

Screenplays:
BEST FRIENDS
SONNY ALL THE TIME
HUSBAND AND WIFE
MAN ABOUT TOWN

RICHARD C. KLETTER*
Agent: ICM - Beverly Hills, 310/550-4000

TEACH 109 (Short)   directed
NEVER CRY WOLF   Buena Vista, 1983, w/Sam Hamm &
   Curtis Lee Hanson
THE BLACK STALLION RETURNS   MGM/UA, 1983,
   w/Jerome Kass

Screenplays:
THE VICTOR w/David Chaskin
AMERICAN EXPRESS w/Craig Bolotin

QUINT'S LAST CASE w/E. Ellison, R.Nilsson & S. Wax
FLYING
DIAMONDS

MAX KLEVEN*
Contact: WGA - Los Angeles, 310/550-1000

RUCKUS   *THE LONER*   New World, 1981, directed

STEVEN E. KLINE*
Contact: WGA - Los Angeles, 310/550-1000

BORDERLINE   AFD, 1980, w/Jerrold Freedman

WOODY KLING
HERE COME THE LITTLES   Atlantic Releasing Corporation, 1985

JUDSON KLINGER*
Agent: Becsey/Wisdom/Kalajian Agency - Los Angeles, 310/550-0535

ENDANGERED SPECIES   MGM/UA, 1982, Story w/Richard Woods

STEVE KLOVES*
Agent: United Talent Agency - Beverly Hills, 310/273-6700

RACING WITH THE MOON   Paramount, 1984
THE FABULOUS BAKER BOYS ★   20th Century Fox,
   1989, directed
FLESH AND BONE   Paramount, 1993, directed

Screenplays:
SWINGS
SANTEE

STEVE KLUGER
ONCE UPON A CRIME   MGM-Pathe, 1992, w/Nancy Meyers &
   Charles Shyer

Screenplays:
KID STUFF w/David Kohn

DANIEL KNAUF
Agent: Broder-Kurland-Webb-Uffner - Beverly Hills, 310/281-3400

BLIND JUSTICE (CTF)   Heyman/Moritz Pictures/HBO Pictures, 1994

Screenplays:
CANAAN'S WAY (CTF)
DOWNSTREAMERS

NIGEL KNEALE
Contact: British Academy of Film & Television Arts, 195 Piccadilly,
   London W1, England, 071/734-0022

THE ABOMINABLE SNOWMAN   20th Century-Fox, 1957
ENEMY FROM SPACE   *QUATERMASS II*   Hammer, 1957,
   w/Val Guest
LOOK BACK IN ANGER   Warner Bros., 1958
THE ENTERTAINER   British Lion, 1960, w/John Osborne
HMS DEFIANT   *DAMN THE DEFIANT*   Columbia, 1962,
   w/Edmund H. North
FIRST MEN IN THE MOON   Columbia, 1964, w/Jan Read
THE DEVIL'S OWN   *THE WITCHES*   Hammer, 1966
FIVE MILLION YEARS TO EARTH   *QUATERMASS AND THE PIT*
   Hammer, 1967

ANDREW KNIGHT
THE EFFICIENCY EXPERT   Miramax, 1992, w/Max Dann

CHRISTOPHER KNIGHT
Business: The Knight Company, 1337 Ocean Ave. - South Penthouse,
   Santa Monica, CA 90401, 310/395-7100

WINNERS TAKE ALL   Apollo Pictures, 1987, Story w/Tom Tatum

PATRICIA LOUISIANNA KNOP*
Agent: Camden-ITG - Los Angeles, 310/289-2700

THE PASSOVER PLOT   Atlas, 1977, w/Millard Cohan
LADY OSCAR   Toho, 1978
SILENCE OF THE NORTH   Universal, 1982
9 1/2 WEEKS   MGM/UA, 1986, w/Sarah Kernochan & Zalman King
SIESTA   Lorimar, 1987
WILD ORCHID   Triumph, 1990, w/Zalman King

Screenplays:
FOUR DAYS IN FEBRUARY
HOT w/Zalman King
FOR THE FIRST TIME
THIRD TIME LUCKY

CHRISTOPHER E. KNOPF*
Agent: Bruce Brown Agency - Los Angeles, 310/208-1835

THE TALL STRANGER   Allied Artists, 1957
TWENTY MILLION MILES TO EARTH   Columbia, 1957,
   w/Bob Williams
EMPEROR OF THE NORTH POLE   *SHACK!*
   20th Century-Fox, 1973
POSSE   Paramount, 1975, w/William Roberts
THE CHOIRBOYS   Universal, 1977
SCOTT JOPLIN   Universal, 1977

Screenplays:
SCARLET & THE BLACK

FLIP KOBLER*
Agent: Paradigm - Los Angeles, 310/277-4400

WILD DUST (P)

Screenplays:
KINGDOM BY THE SEA w/Cindy Marcus
WHITE NOISE w/Cindy Marcus

C. J. KOCH
THE YEAR OF LIVING DANGEROUSLY   MGM/UA, 1983,
   w/David Williamson & Peter Weir

HERMAN KOCH
WINGS OF FAME   First Floor Features, 1990, w/Otakar Votocek

HOWARD KOCH*
Contact: WGA - Los Angeles, 310/550-1000

THE SEA HAWK   Warner Bros., 1940, w/Seton I. Miller
CASABLANCA ★   Warner Bros., 1943, w/Julius J. Epstein &
   Philip G. Epstein
RHAPSODY IN BLUE   Warner Bros., 1945, w/Elliot Paul
THREE STRANGERS   Warner Bros., 1946, w/John Huston
NO SAD SONGS FOR ME   Columbia, 1950
THE THIRTEENTH LETTER   20th Century-Fox, 1951
THE GREENGAGE SUMMER   *LOSS OF INNOCENCE*
   Columbia, 1961
THE WAR LOVER   Columbia, 1962
633 SQUADRON   United Artists, 1964, w/James Clavell
THE FOX   Claridge, 1968, w/Lewis John Carlino

Screenplays:
THE GARDENER

PHILLIP KOCH
PINK NIGHTS   Koch-Marschall Productions, 1991, directed,
   filmed in 1987

LAIRD KOENIG*
Agent: Paul Kohner, Inc. - Beverly Hills, 310/550-1060

SCENE OF THE CRIME (P)
RED SUN   National General, 1972, w/Denne Bart Petitclerc,
   William Roberts & Lawrence Roman

THE LITTLE GIRL WHO LIVES DOWN THE LANE
   American International, 1977
SIDNEY SHELDON'S BLOODLINE   Paramount, 1979
INCHON!   MGM/UA, 1982, w/Robin Moore
TWIST OF FATE   Condor Productions/Nelson Entertainment, 1991

Screenplays:
TENNESSEE NIGHTS w/Nicholas Gessner
RISING SUN

RAYMOND KOENIG*
Contact: WGA - Los Angeles, 310/550-1000

BLACULA   American International, 1972, w/Joan Torres

DAVID KOEPP*
Agent: United Talent Agency - Beverly Hills, 310/273-6700

APARTMENT ZERO   Skouras Pictures, 1989, w/Martin Donovan
BAD INFLUENCE   Trans World Entertainment, 1990
TOY SOLDIERS   Tri-Star, 1991, w/Daniel Petrie Jr.
DEATH BECOMES HER   Universal, 1992, w/Martin Donovan
JURASSIC PARK   Universal, 1993, w/Michael Crichton
CARLITO'S WAY   Universal, 1993
THE PAPER   Universal, 1994, w/Steve Koepp
THE SHADOW   Universal, 1994

Screenplays:
MISSION: IMPOSSIBLE (Paramount)
TRIGGER EFFECT (directing)
ADVENTURE I w/John Kamps

STEVE KOEPP
Agent: United Talent Agency - Beverly Hills, 310/273-6700

THE PAPER   Universal, 1994, w/David Koepp

NICK KOFF*
Contact: Carlos Goodman, Esq. - Los Angeles, 310/205-6999
Contact: Emotion Pictures, 8310 Willoughby Avenue, West
   Hollywood, CA 90069, 213/852-0381

Screenplays:
BLOOD TIES w/Lee Ford Parker
MOUTHPIECE
AFTERMATH

ARNIE KOGEN*
Agent: The Irv Schechter Company - Beverly Hills, 310/278-8070

BIRDS DO IT   Columbia, 1966

DAVID KOHAN*
Agent: United Talent Agency - Beverly Hills, 310/273-6700

Screenplays:
CRICKET IN TIMES SQUARE w/Max Mutchnick

HOWARD KOHN*
Contact: WGA - Los Angeles, 310/550-1000

ROLLOVER   Orion/Warner Bros., 1981, Story w/David Shaber &
   David Weir

JOHN KOHN*
Contact: WGA - Los Angeles, 310/550-1000

THE SIEGE OF THE SAXONS   Columbia, 1963, w/Jud Kinberg
THE COLLECTOR ★   Columbia, 1965, w/Stanley Mann
GOLDEN GIRL   Avco Embassy, 1979
SHANGHAI SURPRISE   MGM/UA, 1986, w/Robert Bentley

F
I
L
M

W
R
I
T
E
R
S

LENNY KOLINSKY
Agent: Stephanie Mann Agency - Los Angeles, 213/653-7130

Screenplays:
ABOUT FACE w/Beatrice Levavi
SWEET LADY JANE w/Beatrice Levavi
BLOOD TIES w/Beatrice Levavi

AMOS KOLLEK
Contact: Israel Film Centre, Ministry of Industry & Trade, 30 Agron
Street, P.O. Box 299, Jerusalem, Israel, 02/210297

GOODBYE NEW YORK Castle Hill Productions, 1985, directed
FOREVER, LULU Tri-Star, 1987, directed
HIGH STAKES Vestron, 1990, directed
DOUBLE EDGE Castle Hill Productions, 1992, directed
FIVE GIRLS Castle Hill Productions, 1993, directed

XAVIER KOLLER
Agent: ICM - Beverly Hills, 310/550-4000

JOURNEY OF HOPE Miramax, 1990, directed

JAMES KOMACK*
Agent: Paradigm - Los Angeles, 310/277-4400

BACK TO THE BEACH Paramount, 1987,
Story w/Bruce Kirschbaum & B.W.L. Norton

ANDREI KONCHALOVSKY*
Agent: CAA - Beverly Hills, 310/288-4545

ANDREI RUBLEV Mosfilm, 1966, w/Andrei Tarkovsky
A NEST OF GENTRY Corinth, 1969, w/Valentin Yezhov, directed
MARIA'S LOVERS Cannon, 1984, w/Gerard Brach,
Marjorie David & Paul Zindel, directed
DUET FOR ONE Cannon, 1987, w/Tom Kempinski &
Jeremy Lipp, directed
SHY PEOPLE Cannon, 1987, w/Gerard Brach &
Marjorie David, directed
THE INNER CIRCLE Columbia, 1991, w/Anatoli Usov, directed

Screenplays:
THE ROYAL WAY w/Larry Gross (Miramax, directing)
TATIANA w/Floyd Byars

KAREN KONDAZIAN
Contact: Screen Actors Guild - Los Angeles, 213/954-1600
Agent: Abrams, Ruboloff & Lawrence - Los Angeles, 213/935-1700

Screenplays:
THE WHIP

JACKIE KONG
THE BEING BFV Films, 1983, directed
NIGHT PATROL New World, 1984, w/Murray Langston &
Bill Osco, directed

LAWRENCE KONNER*
Agent: CAA - Beverly Hills, 310/288-4545
Manager: 3 Arts Entertainment - Los Angeles, 213/851-5700

THE LEGEND OF BILLIE JEAN Tri-Star, 1985, w/Mark Rosenthal
THE JEWEL OF THE NILE 20th Century Fox, 1985,
w/Mark Rosenthal
SUPERMAN IV: THE QUEST FOR PEACE Warner Bros., 1987,
w/Mark Rosenthal
THE IN CROWD Orion, 1988, w/Mark Rosenthal
DESPERATE HOURS Warner Bros., 1990, w/Mark Rosenthal &
Joseph Hayes
STAR TREK VI: THE UNDISCOVERED COUNTRY Paramount,
1991, Story w/Mark Rosenthal & Leonard Nimoy
FOR LOVE OR MONEY Universal, 1993, w/Mark Rosenthal
THE BEVERLY HILLBILLIES 20th Century Fox, 1993,
w/Mark Rosenthal, Jim Fisher & Jim Staahl

Screenplays:
SECOND STRING w/Mark Rosenthal
GALE FORCE w/Mark Rosenthal & David A. Chappe
FORTRESS w/Mark Rosenthal
THE HIT (remake) w/Mark Rosenthal

JEFFREY S. KONVITZ*
Contact: 213/655-9335

THE SENTINEL Universal, 1976, w/Michael Winner
GORP Filmways, 1980

ARTHUR KOPIT*
Agent: The Tantleff Office - New York, 212/941-3939

PHANTOM (P)
ROAD TO NIRVANA (P)
ROSWELL (CTF) Viacom Pictures/Citadel Entertainment, 1994

Screenplays:
BETWEEN THE WARS

HOWARD R. KORDER*
Agent: The Tantleff Office - New York, 212/941-3939

FUN (P)
NOBODY (P)
EPISODE 26 (P)
NIGHT MANEUVERS (P)
IMAGINING "AMERICA" (P)
BOYS' LIFE (P) also screenplay
SEARCH AND DESTROY (P)
LIP SERVICE (CTF) Cinehaus, 1988, from his play

Screenplays:
LOVE AND BULLETS

MARI KORNHAUSER*
Agent: Writers & Artists Agency - Los Angeles, 310/824-6300

ZANDALEE New Line Cinema, 1991
F.T.W. Nu-Image, 1994

Screenplays:
THEY DON'T DANCE MUCH
HEART AND SOUL
THE TORRID ZONE
SCORPIONS
BURMA

JOHN V. KORTY*
Agent: Richland/Wunsch/Hohman Agency - Los Angeles,
310/278-1955

CRAZY QUILT Farallon, 1965, directed
FUNNYMAN New Yorker, 1967, w/Peter Bonerz, directed
OLIVER'S STORY Paramount, 1978, w/Erich Segal, directed
TWICE UPON A TIME (AF) The Ladd Company/Warner Bros.,
1983, w/Charles Swenson, Suella Kennedy &
Bill Couturie, co-directed

Screenplays:
KINGDOM

ANNIE KORZEN
NOBODY'S PERFECT Moviestore Entertainment, 1990,
w/Joel Block

ROBERT A. KOSBERG*
Business: Robert Kosberg Productions, TriStar Pictures -
Los Angeles, 310/280-4774

IN THE MOOD Lorimar, 1987, Story w/Phil Alden Robinson &
David Simon

Screenplays:
THE WITCH'S REVENGE w/Janice Fischer

KEN KOSER*
Contact: WGA - New York, 212/245-6180

SUDIE AND SIMPSON (CTF) Freed/Laufer, 1990,
   w/Sara Flanigan Carter

RON KOSLOW*
Agent: ICM - Beverly Hills, 310/550-4000

LIFEGUARD Paramount, 1976
FIRSTBORN Paramount, 1984
INTO THE NIGHT Universal, 1985

Screenplays:
LAST DANCE (Buena Vista)
WOLF & ROSE
THE GLORY BOYS
TAPPING THE SOURCE

IREN KOSTER*
Agent: ICM - Beverly Hills, 310/550-4000

Screenplays:
INVISIBLE KIDS w/Tracey Silvers (AKS Entertainment, directing)

JOHN H. KOSTMAYER*
Agent: United Talent Agency - Beverly Hills, 310/273-6700

WHERE'S THE BODY (P)
ON THE MONEY (P)
THE HISTORY OF FEAR (P)
I LOVE YOU TO DEATH Tri-Star, 1990

Screenplays:
BRITTLE INNINGS
THANKSGIVING STORY

TED KOTCHEFF
Contact: Directors Guild of America - Los Angeles, 310/289-2000

NORTH DALLAS FORTY Paramount, 1979, w/Peter Gent &
   Frank Yablans, directed

WILLIAM KOTZWINKLE*
Agent: The Gersh Agency - Beverly Hills, 310/274-6611

A NIGHTMARE ON ELM STREET PART IV: THE DREAM MASTER
   New Line Cinema, 1988, Story w/Brian Helgeland
BOOK OF LOVE New Line Cinema, 1991

Screenplays:
NIGHTINGALE AND THE SATIN WOMAN
FATA MORGANA

JIM KOUF*
Agent: ICM - Beverly Hills, 310/550-4000
Business: Kouf-Bigelow Productions, Walt Disney Pictures,
   818/560-5103

THE BOOGENS Jensen Farley Pictures, 1982,
   as "Bob Hunt" w/David O'Malley
PINK MOTEL New Image, 1982
UTILITIES GETTING EVEN New World, 1983,
   w/David Greenwalt
WACKO Jensen Farley Pictures, 1983, w/David Greenwalt,
   Dana Olsen & Michael Spound
CLASS Orion, 1983, w/David Greenwalt
UP THE CREEK Orion, 1983
AMERICAN DREAMER Warner Bros., 1984,
   w/David Greenwalt
SECRET ADMIRER Orion, 1985, w/David Greenwalt
SHAKER RUN Challenge Film Corporation, 1985,
   w/David Greenwalt
MIRACLES Orion, 1986, directed
STAKEOUT Buena Vista, 1987

THE HIDDEN New Line Cinema, 1987, as "Bob Hunt"
DISORGANIZED CRIME Buena Vista, 1989, directed
STAKEOUT 2 Buena Vista, 1993

Screenplays:
OPERATION DUMBO DROP (Buena Vista)
GREED w/David Greenwalt
AIRPLANE III w/David Greenwalt
BIGAMY w/David Greenwalt
THE LAKE w/David Greenwalt
HONEYMOON w/David Greenwalt

EDWARD KOVACH
THINK BIG Concorde, 1990, w/David Tausik & Jon Turtletaub

PAUL KOVAL
PSYCHIC (CTF) Trimark, 1992, w/Miguel Tejada-Flores

Screenplays:
HEAVEN SENT w/Ed Fitzgerald
THE TRADE OFF w/Ed Fitzgerald

JANET KOVALCIK*
Agent: The Irv Schechter Company - Beverly Hills, 310/278-8070

MARRIED TO IT Orion, 1993
MY GIRL 2 Columbia, 1994

Screenplays:
DEAR DIGBY
AMERICAN BEAUTY
THE SHOWER
AFTER ALL THESE YEARS
DURNER'S SPRING
THE JAMAICAN AND THE RAISIN
SENIOR YEAR
STANDING IN THE SHADOWS OF LOVE
A WOMAN'S PLACE

RON KOVIC
Agent: ICM - Beverly Hills, 310/550-4000

BORN ON THE FOURTH OF JULY ★ Universal, 1989,
   w/Oliver Stone

MICHAEL KOZOLL*
Agent: Becsey/Wisdom/Kalajian Agency - Los Angeles, 310/550-0535
Contact: 310/202-3377

FIRST BLOOD Orion, 1982, w/William Sackheim &
   Sylvester Stallone
THE HARD WAY Universal, 1991, Story w/Lem Dobbs

Screenplays:
NATURAL ACTS

ROBERT KRAFT
Agent: CAA - Beverly Hills, 310/288-4545

HUDSON HAWK Tri-Star, 1991, Story w/Bruce Willis

ROBERT S. KRAFT*
Agent: Hilary Wayne - Beverly Hills, 310/289-6186

Screenplays:
AS YOUNG AS YOU FEEL w/Ted Pushinsky
MAKING MONEY w/Ted Pushinsky

SCOTT KRAFT*
Manager: 3 Arts Entertainment - Los Angeles, 213/851-5700

THE SILENCER Crown International, 1992, w/Amy Goldstein

**F
I
L
M

W
R
I
T
E
R
S**

ANDRZEJ KRAKOWSKI
THE CALIFORNIA REICH (FD) ★   Yasny Talking Pictures, 1975
TRIUMPH OF THE SPIRIT   Nova International Films, 1989,
    w/Laurence Heath
EMINENT DOMAIN   Triumph Releasing, 1991, w/Richard Gregson

Screenplays:
THE WEDDING WAS BEAUTIFUL, PEOPLE WERE CRYING
LANTON MILLS

MARK KRAM
Agent: United Talent Agency - Beverly Hills, 310/273-6700

Screenplays:
BLOW AWAY w/David Loucka & Dean Selmier
JOEY FAMOUS w/David Loucka
THE DREAM CASE w/David Loucka
WEEKEND WARRIORS w/David Loucka
MARATHON

LARRY KRAMER*
Contact: Arthur B. Kramer - 212/715-9264

THE NORMAL HEART (P)
THE DESTINY OF ME (P)
WOMEN IN LOVE ★   United Artists, 1969
LOST HORIZON   Columbia, 1972

RICHARD L. KRAMER*
Agent: William Morris Agency - Beverly Hills, 310/274-7451

ALL I WANT FOR CHRISTMAS   Paramount, 1991,
    w/Thom Eberhardt

Screenplays:
SAVING GRACE
THE BOYS NEXT DOOR
LIBBY
PETTING ZOO
SECOND HEAVEN
ALUMNI
BEST IS YET TO BE

SUSAN KRAMER*
Agent: CAA - Beverly Hills, 310/288-4545

Screenplays:
THE GOLDBERGS AND THE ROMANOS (Savoy)
ISN'T IT ROMANTIC
EVERY WOMAN LOVES A RUSSIAN POET

JONATHAN KRANE
Business: The Krane Group, TriStar Pictures, 213/650-0942

Screenplays:
SPECTACULAR DISCOVERY
DISCOVERIES DAD
UNDERGROUND LOVE w/Cherie Lee Jensen
TEDDY BOY w/Richard Perry

SARA L. KRANE*
Agent: Wile Enterprises - Santa Monica, 310/828-9768

Screenplays:
THE RED FERRARI
SHE SAID SHE LIKED THE WAY SHE HELD THE MICROPHONE
DIRTY DANCING II

ROBERT KRANTZ*
Contact: Leah Antonio, Mayer, Glassman & Gaines, 310/207-0007

Screenplays:
THE WHISTLE BLOWER (TriStar)
POINT OF DECEPTION
DO YOU WANNA DANCE?

JEFF KRASK*
Agent: Paradigm - Los Angeles, 310/277-4400

Screenplays:
SECRET AGENT MAN

RIC KRAUSE
Agent: The Gage Group - Los Angeles, 310/859-8777

CALENDAR GIRL (P)
DR. JIMMY'S HEARTBREAK HOUR (P)

Screenplays:
PUSH
LIKE A TRAIN

KEN KRAUSS*
Agent: Camden-ITG - Los Angeles, 310/289-2700

BUY AND CELL   Empire Pictures, 1988, w/Merrin Holt

Screenplays:
LAST STAND w/Merrin Holt

STEVEN M. KRAUZER*
Agent: Virginia Barber Literary Agency, 101 Fifth Ave.,
    New York, NY 10003

COCAINE WARS   Concorde/Cinema Group, 1985
SWEET REVENGE   Concorde, 1987, w/Tim McCoy

STUART G. KREISMAN*
Agent: Broder-Kurland-Webb-Uffner - Beverly Hills, 310/281-3400

Screenplays:
STARWRECK w/Chris Cluess
THE LAST HIGH SCHOOL MOVIE w/Chris Cluess

HOWARD B. KREITSEK*
Contact: WGA - Los Angeles, 310/550-1000

THE ILLUSTRATED MAN   Warner Bros., 1969
BREAKOUT   Columbia, 1975, w/Frank Kowalski

EDDIE KRELL
DELIRIUM   Odyssey Pictures, 1980, Story w/Jim Loew

STU KRIEGER*
Agent: The Daniel Ostroff Agency - Los Angeles, 310/278-2020

WHERE THE BOYS ARE   Tri-Star, 1984, w/Jeff Burkhart
THE LAND BEFORE TIME (AF)   Universal, 1984
A TROLL IN CENTRAL PARK (AF)   Warner Bros., 1993
MONKEY TROUBLE   New Line Cinema, 1994, w/Franco Amurri
IN THE ARMY NOW   Buena Vista, 1994, w/Ken Kaufman,
    Daniel Petrie Jr., Fax Bahr & Adam Small

HELENA KRIEL*
Agent: The Daniel Ostroff Agency - Los Angeles, 310/278-2020

Screenplays:
KAMA SUTRA w/Mira Nair

PETER A. KRIKES*
Agent: William Morris Agency - Beverly Hills, 310/274-7451

STAR TREK IV: THE VOYAGE HOME   Paramount, 1986,
    w/Harve Bennett, Steve Meerson & Nicholas Meyer
BACK TO THE BEACH   Paramount, 1987, w/Steve Meerson &
    Christopher Thompson
DOUBLE IMPACT   Columbia, 1991, Story w/Steve Meerson,
    Sheldon Lettich & Jean-Claude Van Damme

Screenplays:
GIGANTOR w/Steve Meerson
RING OF BLOOD w/Steve Meerson
BEST ENEMIES w/Steve Meerson
THAT'S LIFE, 1986 w/Steve Meerson
A NEW KIND OF LOVE w/Steve Meerson
RIVER OAKS w/Steve Meerson
THE LONG WAY HOME w/Steve Meerson
ON GUARD w/Steve Meerson
19 PURCHASE STREET w/Steve Meerson
PLANET OF THE TEENAGERS w/Steve Meerson
MONEY FROM THE SKY w/Steve Meerson

R. TIMOTHY KRING*
Agent: ICM - Beverly Hills, 310/550-4000

TEEN WOLF TOO   Atlantic Releasing Corporation, 1987

Screenplays:
NIGHT CALLINGS w/Norman Morrill
SUBLET
SLIPPED DISC

DAVID KRINSKY*
Agent: ICM - Beverly Hills, 310/550-4000

Screenplays:
HEADHUNTERS w/John Altschuler
BRAINMAN w/John Altschuler & David Palmer
DOUBLE HITCH w//John Altschuler & David Palmer

MARC KRISTAL
Agent: Paradigm - Los Angeles, 310/277-4400

TORN APART   Castle Hill Productions, 1990

KIM KRIZAN
BEFORE SUNRISE   Columbia, 1995, w/Richard Linklater

MICHAEL H. KROHN*
Agent: Above the Line - West Hollywood, 310/859-6115

Screenplays:
GREEN LANTERN
GUNSLINGER

STEPHEN D. KRONISH*
Agent: Douroux & Co. - Beverly Hills, 310/552-0900

Screenplays:
DEADLY HONEYMOON

JEREMY JOE KRONSBERG*
Business Manager: Leonard Grainger - Los Angeles, 310/858-1573

EVERY WHICH WAY BUT LOOSE   Warner Bros., 1978
GOING APE!   Paramount, 1981, directed

Screenplays:
POINT AFTER
LOVE LUCK

SANDY KROOPF*
Agent: William Morris Agency - Beverly Hills, 310/274-7451

BIRDY   Tri-Star, 1984, w/Jack Behr

Screenplays:
B STREET w/Jack Behr
PUBLIC SECRETS w/Jack Behr
MATINEE w/Jack Behr
RUNAWAY w/Jack Behr
ALIAS EDDIE SHERBERT w/Jack Behr
WITNESS TO WAR w/Jack Behr
BOOK OF EPPE w/Jack Behr

THE MONKEY WRENCH GANG w/Jack Behr
PERFECT COUNTERFEIT w/Jack Behr
SPEECHLESS w/Jack Behr
SERIOUS LIVING w/Jack Behr
IT HAPPENED TOMORROW w/Jack Behr

MARK KRUGER*
Agent: Paradigm - Los Angeles, 310/277-4400

Screenplays:
COLD EYE w/Jeffrey Hammond
THE APOSTASY w/Jeffrey Hammond
DARK HORSE w/Jeffrey Hammond
CANDIDE (AF) w/Jeffrey Hammond
POST-MORTEM (CTF) w/Jeffrey Hammond

SPENCER KRULL
Contact: 213/874-2294

Screenplays:
CITIZEN SANE w/Gerry E. Kahn
EDDIE KRETTS' FINAL EXAM
LIFE OF THE PARTY

RICHARD KRZEMIEN*
Contact: WGA - Los Angeles, 310/550-1000

Screenplays:
IT'S A WONDERFUL DOG

LAWRENCE KUBIK*
Contact: WGA - Los Angeles, 310/550-1000

DEATH BEFORE DISHONOR   New World, 1987, w/John Gatliff

STANLEY KUBRICK*
Agent: CAA - Beverly Hills, 310/288-4545

FEAR AND DESIRE   Joseph Burstyn, Inc., 1954, directed
KILLER'S KISS   United Artists, 1955, directed
THE KILLING   United Artists, 1956, directed
PATHS OF GLORY   United Artists, 1957, w/Calder
Willingham & Jim Thompson, directed
DR. STRANGELOVE, OR: HOW I LEARNED TO STOP WORRYING
   AND LOVE THE BOMB ★   Columbia, 1964, w/Peter George &
   Terry Southern, directed
2001: A SPACE ODYSSEY ★   MGM, 1968,
   w/Arthur C. Clarke, directed
A CLOCKWORK ORANGE ★   Warner Bros., 1971, directed
BARRY LYNDON ★   Warner Bros., 1975, directed
THE SHINING   Warner Bros., 1980, w/Diane Johnson, directed
FULL METAL JACKET ★   Warner Bros., 1987, w/Gustav Hasford &
   Michael Herr, directed

NORBERT KUCKELMANN
MAN UNDER SUSPICION   Spectrafilm, 1985, directed

MARK KUDLOW*
Contact: WGA - Los Angeles, 310/550-1000

Screenplays:
LAUGHTER IN THE DARK (Treehouse Pictures)

ROBERT KUHN*
Agent: The Wright Concept - Burbank, 818/954-8943

HIGH STRUNG   Film Brigade, 1993, w/Steve Oedekerk
THE CURE   Universal, 1995

Screenplays:
ROYAL COACH TAXI
ALL TIME
HONESTY

**F
I
L
M
W
R
I
T
E
R
S**

BERNIE KUKOFF*
Agent: Paradigm - Los Angeles, 310/277-4400

JOHNNY DANGEROUSLY   20th Century Fox, 1984,
    w/Harry Colomby, Jeff Harris & Norman Steinberg

ROGER KUMBLE*
Agent: ICM - Beverly Hills, 310/550-4000
Contact: Joshua Grode, Silverberg, Katz, Thompson & Braun

PAY OR PLAY (P)
NATIONAL LAMPOON'S SENIOR TRIP   New Line Cinema, 1995,
    w/Marlene King

Screenplays:
MOBY DICK w/Marlene King & Charles Banks
PROVOCATEUR

STEVEN M. KUNES*
Agent: Susan Smith & Associates - Beverly Hills, 213/852-4777

Screenplays:
FIRST COMES LOVE
DINNER AT THE HOMESICK RESTAURANT
RUM RUNNERS
LOOK HOMEWARD ANGEL
A CONFEDERACY OF DUNCES
LOVE, ROGER

DARRYL KUNTZ
DAKOTA   Miramax, 1988, w/Lynn Kuntz

LYNN KUNTZ
DAKOTA   Miramax, 1988, w/Darryl Kuntz

HANIF KUREISHI
Agent: The Artists Agency - Los Angeles, 310/277-7779

MY BEAUTIFUL LAUNDRETTE ★   Orion Classics, 1986
SAMMY AND ROSIE GET LAID   Cinecom, 1987
LONDON KILLS ME   Fine Line Features, 1992, directed

JOHN A. KURI
Agent: Paradigm - Los Angeles, 310/277-4400
Business: Sheffield Entertainment Corporation, 16133 Ventura Blvd. -
    Suite 700, Encino, CA 91436, 818/501-8471

CAPTIVE HEARTS   MGM/UA, 1987, w/Pat Morita

CARL L. KURLANDER*
Agent: William Morris Agency - Beverly Hills, 310/274-7451

ST. ELMO'S FIRE   Columbia, 1985, w/Joel Schumacher

Screenplays:
RUNAWAY MOM
BABY TALK
HANDSOME DEVILS

PAUL KURTA
Contact: Creative Group Productions, 6126 Rhodes Avenue,
    North Hollywood, CA 91606, 818/508-8212

KEY EXCHANGE   20th Century Fox, 1985, w/John Romano

CASEY KURTTI*
Agent: Shapiro/Lichtman - Los Angeles, 310/859-8877

THREE WAYS HOME (P)   also screenplay
CATHOLIC SCHOOL GIRLS (P)

Screenplays:
COACH (CTF)

ANDREW KURTZMAN*
Agent: ICM - Beverly Hills, 310/550-4000

NUMBER ONE WITH A BULLET   Cannon, 1987,
    w/Gail Morgan Hickman, Rob Riley & James Belushi
SEE NO EVIL, HEAR NO EVIL   Tri-Star, 1989, w/Earl Barret,
    Arne Sultan, Eliot Wald & Gene Wilder
CAMP NOWHERE   Buena Vista, 1994, w/Eliot Wald

Screenplays:
THE WILLIAMS FAMILY w/Eliot Wald
THE SCOUT w/Eliot Wald

ROBERT KURTZMAN
Agent: Susan Smith & Associates - Beverly Hills, 213/852-4777

Screenplays:
FROM DUSK TILL DAWN (Story)

DIANE KURYS
Agent: William Morris Agency - Beverly Hills, 310/274-7451

PEPPERMINT SODA *DIABOLO MENTHE*   New Yorker,
    1977, directed
COCKTAIL MOLOTOV   Putnam Square, 1980, directed
ENTRE NOUS *COUP DE FOUDRE*   United Artists Classics,
    1983, directed
A MAN IN LOVE   Cinecom, 1987, w/Israel Horovitz, directed
C'EST LA VIE   Samuel Goldwyn Company, 1990,
    w/Alain le Henry, directed
SIX DAYS SIX NIGHTS   Fine Line Features, 1994, directed
APRES L'AMOUR (LOVE AFTER LOVE)   Rainbow Releasing,
    1994, directed

RONALD G. KURZ*
Contact: WGA - New York, 212/245-6180

FRIDAY THE 13TH PART 2   Paramount, 1981

TONY KUSHNER
Agent: CAA - Beverly Hills, 310/288-4545

SLAVS! (P)
A BRIGHT ROOM CALLED DAY (P)
WIDOWS (P)   w/Ariel Dorfman
ANGELS IN AMERICA, PART 1: MILLENNIUM APPROACHES (P)
    also screenplay
ANGELS IN AMERICA, PART 2: PERESTROIKA (P)
    also screenplay

EMIR KUSTURICA
Agent: CAA - Beverly Hills, 310/288-4545

TIME OF THE GYPSIES   Columbia, 1989, directed

SAM KUTE*
Agent: Wile Enterprises - Santa Monica, 310/828-9768

Screenplays:
CHAMPIONS OF HEART

DONNA KUYPER*
Agent: Paradigm - Los Angeles, 310/277-4400

Screenplays:
SANDMAN

FRAN RUBEL KUZUI
Agent: United Talent Agency - Beverly Hills, 310/273-6700
Business: Kuzui Enterprises, 7920 Sunset Blvd., 4th Floor,
    Los Angeles, CA 90046, 213/851-9047

TOKYO POP   Spectrafilm, 1988, w/Lynn Grossman, directed

KEN KWAPIS*
Agent: CAA - Beverly Hills, 310/288-4545

Screenplays:
SEXUAL LIFE (Gramercy, directing)

L

CLAIRE LABINE*
Agent: William Morris Agency - New York, 212/586-5100

Screenplays:
SUMMER OF THE FALCON

RICHARD LABRIE
BLOOD AND CONCRETE: A LOVE STORY   I.R.S. Media, 1991,
   w/Jeff Reiner

DIANE LADD
Contact: Screen Actors Guild - Los Angeles, 213/954-1600

MRS. MUNCK (AF)   Showtime, 1995, directed

STEPH LADY*
Contact: WGA - Los Angeles, 310/550-1000

FRANKENSTEIN   TriStar, 1994, w/Frank Darabont

DANY LaFERRIERE
HOW TO MAKE LOVE TO A NEGRO WITHOUT GETTING TIRED
   Angelika Films, 1990, w/Richard Sadler

GEORGE LAFIA
DEADLY WEAPON   Empire Pictures, 1989, Story w/Michael Miner

JOHN J. LAFIA*
Agent: CAA - Beverly Hills, 310/288-4545

THE BLUE IGUANA   Paramount, 1988, directed
CHILDS PLAY   MGM/UA, 1989, w/Tom Holland & Don Mancini
MAN'S BEST FRIEND   New Line Cinema, 1993, directed

Screenplays:
THE BLACK GLASS
DAGGER, INC.
SOB'S

JEAN LaFLEUR
SPACEHUNTER: ADVENTURES IN THE FORBIDDEN ZONE
   Columbia, 1983, Story w/Stewart Harding

IAN LaFRENAIS*
Agent: Broder-Kurland-Webb-Uffner - Beverly Hills, 310/281-3400

THE JOKERS   Universal, 1967, w/Dick Clement
HANNIBAL BROOKS   United Artists, 1968, w/Dick Clement
OTLEY   Columbia, 1969, w/Dick Clement
CATCH ME A SPY   Rank, 1971, w/Dick Clement
VILLAIN   EMI, 1971, w/Dick Clement
THE LIKELY LADS   EMI, 1976, w/Dick Clement
PORRIDGE   ITC, 1979, w/Dick Clement
THE PRISONER OF ZENDA   Universal, 1979, w/Dick Clement
WATER   Atlantic Releasing Corporation, 1984,
   w/Dick Clement & Bill Persky
VICE VERSA   Columbia, 1988, w/Dick Clement

THE COMMITMENTS   20th Century-Fox, 1991, w/Dick Clement &
   Roddy Doyle

Screenplays:
SEEING RED w/Dick Clement

CELINE La FRIENERE
CITY ON FIRE   Astral-Bellevue, 1979, w/Jack Hill & David P. Lewis
FOREIGN BODY   Orion, 1986

RICHARD LaGRAVENESE*
Agent: CAA - Beverly Hills, 310/288-4545

RUDE AWAKENING   Orion, 1989, w/Neil Levy
THE FISHER KING ★   Tri-Star, 1991
THE REF   Buena Vista, 1994, w/Marie Weiss
THE LITTLE PRINCESS   Warner Bros., 1995
THE BRIDGES OF MADISON COUNTY   Warner Bros., 1995
UNSTRUNG HEROS   Buena Vista, 1995

Screenplays:
THE DEFECTIVE DETECTIVE w/Terry Gilliam
OH, THE PLACES YOU'LL GO
THE MIRROR HAS TWO FACES
SKIRTS
WIDOWS
CATS
THE TALISMAN

MARTIN LAIKS*
Agent: William Morris Agency - Beverly Hills, 310/274-7451

Screenplays:
THE GRANDMOTHER WARS

MURDO LAIRD
Agent: Warden, White & Kane - Beverly Hills, 213/852-1028

Screenplays:
RUBY RED
YOSHIKO
DANIELLA
PANAMA
PROLOGUES

RITA LAKIN*
Business Manager: Harold Cohen - 310/275-6133

VOICE OF THE HEART (CTF)   Worldvision, 1990

EDWARD J. LAKSO*
Agent: Maggie Field Agency - Studio City, 818/980-2001

Screenplays:
COTATI
THE STORK
GODMOTHERS
TONY & IRENE

FRANK LaLOGGIA*
Agent: Becsey/Wisdom/Kalajian Agency - Los Angeles, 310/550-0535
Business: LaLoggia Productions - Los Angeles, 213/462-3055

FEAR NO EVIL   Avco Embassy, 1981, directed
LADY IN WHITE   New Century/Vista, 1988, directed

ROSS La MANNA*
Agent: William Morris Agency - Beverly Hills, 213/274-7451

CHROME SOLDIERS (CTF)   Wilshire Court, 1992,
   Story w/John McCormick & Jonas McCord

Screenplays:
ARCTIC BLUE
DNA w/John McCormick
TORPEDOS w/John McCormick
PRIDE AND JOY w/John McCormick

GREGORY LAMBERSON
UNDYING LOVE   Slaughtered Lamb Productions, 1991, directed

GAVIN LAMBERT*
Manager: Creative Alliance Management - Los Angeles,
   213/962-6090

BITTER VICTORY   Columbia, 1957, w/Nicholas Ray & Rene Hardy
SONS AND LOVERS ★   20th Century-Fox, 1960, w/T.E.B. Clarke
THE ROMAN SPRING OF MRS. STONE   Warner Bros., 1961
INSIDE DAISY CLOVER   Warner Bros., 1965
I NEVER PROMISED YOU A ROSE GARDEN ★   New World, 1977,
   w/Lewis John Carlino
DEAD ON THE MONEY (CTF)   Perfect Circle Corp./Voyage
   Productions Inc., 1991

SUSAN LAMBERT
CHICKS IN WHITE SATIN (FD)   1994, w/Elaine Holliman,
   also screenplay

TED LAMBERT*
Contact: WGA - New York, 212/245-6180

Screenplays:
THE CHERRY ORCHARD

BILL LaMOND*
Agent: Bennett Agency - Los Angeles, 310/471-2251

THIS TIME FOREVER   (No Distributor), 1985, w/Jo LaMond

Screenplays:
THE EX-MR. WINFIELD w/Jo LaMond
WILD BLUE YONDER w/Jo LaMond

JO LaMOND*
Agent: Bennett Agency - Los Angeles, 310/471-2251

THIS TIME FOREVER   (No Distributor), 1985, w/Bill LaMond

Screenplays:
THE EX-MR. WINFIELD w/Bill LaMond
WILD BLUE YONDER w/Bill LaMond

MILLARD LAMPELL*
Agent: William Morris Agency - Beverly Hills, 310/274-7451

BLIND DATE   Rank, 1959, w/Ben Barzman
ESCAPE FROM EAST BERLIN *TUNNEL 28*   MGM, 1962,
   w/Peter Berneis & Gabrielle Upton
THE IDOL   Embassy, 1966
EAGLE IN A CAGE   Group W, 1970

KEN LAMPLUGH
Agent: Jon Klane Agency - Beverly Hills, 310/278-0178

CIA: CODE NAME ALEXA   PM Entertainment, 1993,
   w/John Weidner

Screenplays:
INDESTRUCTIBLE w/John Weidner

MIKE LANAHAN
(See Jeff BUHAI, David OBST & Steve ZACHARIAS)

BILL LANCASTER*
Contact: Jack M. Ostrow - Los Angeles, 310/272-2141

THE BAD NEWS BEARS   Paramount, 1976
THE BAD NEWS BEARS GO TO JAPAN   Paramount, 1978
THE THING   Universal, 1982

Screenplays:
MONKEY KING
THE BAD NEWS BEARS GO TO CUBA

CALIFORNIA ROUGH AND TUMBLE
VIDA

PETER LANCE*
Agent: Dytman & Schwartz - Beverly Hills, 310/274-8844

Screenplays:
ANGELS OF DEATH
THE COVER UP

ELAINE OVERBEY LANDAU*
Contact: WGA - Los Angeles, 310/550-1000

Screenplays:
KILL BILL w/Neil Landau
SAM AND NORA w/Mona Lyden
DATE WITH A GENIE

NEIL LANDAU*
Agent: CAA - Beverly Hills, 310/288-4545

MAPS FOR DROWNERS (P)
DON'T TELL MOM THE BABYSITTER'S DEAD   Warner Bros.,
   1991, w/Tara Ison

Screenplays:
KILL BILL w/Elaine Overbey Landau
FLUSHING IN PARIS
TRUE TO LIFE w/Tara Ison
BELOVED SON w/Tara Ison
INSIDE OUT w/Tara Ison
TRANSYLVANIA-PENNSYLVANIA w/Tara Ison

JOHN LANDIS*
Agent: CAA - Beverly Hills, 310/288-4545

SCHLOCK   Jack H. Harris Enterprises, 1973, directed
THE BLUES BROTHERS   Universal, 1980,
   w/Dan Aykroyd, directed
AN AMERICAN WEREWOLF IN LONDON   Universal,
   1981, directed
COMING SOON (CTD)   Universal Pay TV, 1983,
   w/Mick Garris, directed
TWILIGHT ZONE - THE MOVIE   Warner Bros., 1983,
   Prologue & Segment 1, directed
CLUE   Paramount, 1985, Story w/Jonathan Lynn

JOSEPH S. LANDON*
Agent: Pleshette & Green - Los Angeles, 213/465-0428

Screenplays:
RETURN TO MYSTIC PIZZA

KAREN LANDRY
Agent: Susan Smith & Associates - Beverly Hills, 213/852-4777

PATTI ROCKS   FilmDallas, 1988, w/John Jenkins,
   David Burton Morris & Chris Mulkey

DAVID LANDSBERG*
Contact: WGA - Los Angeles, 310/550-1000

DETECTIVE SCHOOL DROPOUTS *DUMB DICKS*   Cannon, 1986,
   w/Lorin Dreyfuss
DUTCH TREAT   Cannon, 1987, w/Lorin Dreyfuss

ANDREW J. LANE*
Agent: The Marion Rosenberg Office - Los Angeles, 213/653-7383
Business: Gibraltar Entertainment, 14101 Valleyheart Dr., #205,
   Sherman Oaks, CA 91423, 818/501-2076

VALLEY GIRL   Atlantic Releasing Corporation, 1983,
   w/Wayne Crawford
JAKE SPEED   New World, 1986, w/Wayne Crawford
LONELY HEARTS   Live Entertainment, 1991,
   w/R.E. Daniels, directed

BRIAN LANE*
Agent: Kaplan-Stahler - Beverly Hills, 213/653-4483

Screenplays:
SHIBUMI
MOB RULES
EVIL WAYS
MONSTER
THE CATERER

BRIAN ALAN LANE*
Business Manager: Dern & Donaldson - Los Angeles, 310/557-0417

THE GIRL FROM MARS (CTF) Atlantis Films Ltd., 1991

CHARLES LANE
Agent: Paradigm - Los Angeles, 310/277-4400

A PLACE IN TIME (Short) directed
SIDEWALK STORIES Island Pictures, 1989, directed

Screenplays:
INERTIA
SKINS

JAMES LANE
Contact: Easystreet Filmworks, 3038 E. Corte St., W. Covina,
CA 91791

HOUSEWIFE FROM HELL Crown International, 1993, co-directed

Screenplays:
MY HAUNTED HOUSE

ROCKY LANE
Agent: Susan Smith & Associates - Beverly Hills, 213/852-4777

Screenplays:
PETER AND THE WOLF

WARNER LANE
(See Nancy Dowd)

LANIER LANEY
Contact: Hansen, Jacobson & Teller - Los Angeles, 310/271-8777

LOVE AT STAKE *BURNIN' LOVE* Tri-Star, 1988,
w/Terry Sweeney
SHAG: THE MOVIE Hemdale, 1989, w/Terry Sweeney &
Robin Swicord

CHRISTA LANG
GIRLS IN PRISON (CTF) Showtime/Drive-In Classic Cinema,
1994, w/Samuel Fuller

MICHEL LANG
THE GIFT Samuel Goldwyn Company, 1983, directed

PERRY LANG*
Agent: Douroux & Co. - Beverly Hills, 310/552-0900

LITTLE VEGAS I.R.S. Releasing, 1990, directed

DOUGLAS LANGDALE
THE RETURN OF JAFAR (AHVF) Buena Vista, 1994,
Story w/Duane Capizzi, Mark McCorkle, Robert Schooley &
Tad Stories

DONALD LANGDON
BLOOD TIDE 21st Century, 1982, w/Richard Jeffries &
Nico Mastorakis

DAVID LANGE
I AM THE CHEESE Almi, 1983, w/Robert Jiras

MONIQUE LANGE
THE TROUT Triumph, 1982, w/Joseph Losey

TODD W. LANGEN*
Agent: The Wright Concept - Burbank, 818/954-8943

TEENAGE MUTANT NINJA TURTLES New Line Cinema, 1990,
w/Bobby Herbeck
TEENAGE MUTANT NINJA TURTLES II: THE SECRET OF
THE OOZE New Line Cinema, 1991

Screenplays:
I...DO
IN NO PARTICULAR ORDER
ONE ANGRY MAN
THE PENNY RAFFLE
JOINT MISSION
MAKING OF SEX & VIOLENCE

JOHN LANGLEY
Contact: Browning, Jacobson & Klein - Beverly Hills, 310/247-8777

P.O.W. THE ESCAPE Cannon, 1986, w/James Bruner,
Malcolm Barbour & Jeremy Lipp

Screenplays:
VESPERS w/Malcolm Barbour

ROY LANGSDON
THE FORBIDDEN DANCE Columbia, 1990, w/John Platt
OUT OF SIGHT, OUT OF MIND Spectrum Entertainment Group,
1990, w/John Platt

MURRAY LANGSTON
NIGHT PATROL New World, 1984, w/Jackie Kong & Bill Osco

KATE J. LANIER*
Agent: Broder-Kurland-Webb-Uffner - Beverly Hills, 310/281-3400

WHAT'S LOVE GOT TO DO WITH IT? Buena Vista, 1993

Screenplays:
CINDERELLAS

T. L. LANKFORD
ARMED RESPONSE CineTel Films, 1986
CYCLONE CineTel Films, 1987, w/Paul Garson
BULLETPROOF CineTel Films, 1987, w/Steve Carver
DEEP SPACE Trans World Entertainment, 1988, w/Fred Olen Ray
SOUTH OF RENO Castle Hill Productions, 1988, w/Mark Rezyka
MOB BOSS Vidmark Entertainment, 1990

BRUCE LANSBURY*
Agent: Rogers & Associates - North Hollywood, 818/509-1010

I'M DANGEROUS TONIGHT (CTF) MCA Television, 1990,
w/Philip John Taylor

JOHN LANSING*
Manager: Jonathan Baruch, PRO Management - Los Angeles,
310/478-5159

Screenplays:
CYBERTRYX w/Bruce Cervi
THE ROSE CROSS w/Bruce Cervi
DONE DEAL w/Bruce Cervi

SALLY LAPIDUSS*
Contact: WGA - Los Angeles, 310/550-1000

Screenplays:
BAMBOO w/Pamela Eels

LYNDA LaPLANTE
Agent: ICM - Beverly Hills, 310/550-4000

PRIME SUSPECT (CMS)   Granada TV, 1991
PRIME SUSPECT 2 (CMS)   Granada TV, 1992
PRIME SUSPECT 3 (CMS)   Granada TV, 1994
FRAMED (CMS)   Anglia Films, 1993

Screenplays:
PRIME SUSPECT
RED MERCURY

RING LARDNER, JR.*
Agent: Jim Preminger Agency - Los Angeles, 310/475-9491

TOMORROW THE WORLD   United Artists, 1944, w/Leopold Atlas
WOMAN OF THE YEAR ★★   MGM, 1942, w/Michael Kanin
THE CROSS OF LORRAINE   MGM, 1944, w/Robert Andrews,
   Alexander Esway & Michael Kanin
CLOACK AND DAGGER   U.S. Pictures, 1946, w/Albert Matz
THE FORBIDDEN STREET   *BRITTANIA MEWS*
   20th Century-Fox, 1948
THE CINCINNATI KID   MGM, 1965, w/Terry Southern
M*A*S*H ★★   20th Century-Fox, 1970
THE GREATEST   Columbia, 1977

JEREMY LARNER*
Agent: Diskant & Associates - Los Angeles, 310/824-3773

DRIVE, HE SAID   Columbia, 1971, w/Jack Nicholson
THE CANDIDATE ★★   Warner Bros., 1972

Screenplays:
WATER DANCER
JOSHUA MACHINE

STEPHEN La ROCQUE*
Agent: APA - Los Angeles, 310/273-0744

SAMANTHA   Planet Productions, 1992, w/John Golden, directed

JIM LARSEN
Business: Jim Larsen Productions, P.O. Box 415, Aldie, VA 22001

Screenplays:
AT UNCLE LEO'S HOUSE NEAR THE EDGE OF TOWN (directing)

SHANA LARSEN
Agent: Paradigm - Los Angeles, 310/277-4400

Screenplays:
200 CIGARETTES

NANCY LARSON*
Contact: WGA - Los Angeles, 310/550-1000

COACH   Crown International, 1978, w/Stephen Bruce Rose
THE WIZARD OF LONELINESS   Skouras Pictures, 1988

Screenplays:
ZORRO
ISABEL EBERHARDT
MOTHERLOAD
LEGEND OF THE GRAIL

LOUIS La RUSSO II*
Agent: William Morris Agency - Beverly Hills, 310/274-7451

LAMPPOST REUNION (P)
BEYOND THE REEF   Universal, 1981, w/Jim Carabatsos
THE CLOSER   Ion Pictures, 1991, w/Robert Keats,
   from his play "Wheelbarrow Closers"

Screenplays:
MANHATTAN CHARMER
TIME FOR WEDDING CAKE
LOUIE'S WIDOW

JASON LASKAY
Agent: Abrams Artists & Associates - Los Angeles, 310/859-0625

Screenplays:
MAN FACING SOUTHEAST (IRS, remake, directing)

ALEX LASKER*
Agent: ICM - Beverly Hills, 310/550-4000

FIREFOX   Warner Bros., 1982, w/Wendell Wellman
DOUBLECROSSED (CTF)   Green/Epstein Productions/Lorimar TV,
   1991, Story w/Roger Young
BEYOND RANGOON   Columbia, 1995, w/Bill Rubenstein

LAWRENCE LASKER*
Contact: WGA - Los Angeles, 310/550-1000

WARGAMES ★   MGM/UA, 1983, w/Walter F. Parkes
PROJECT X   20th Century Fox, 1987, Story w/Stanley Weiser
SNEAKERS   Universal, 1992, w/Walter F. Parkes &
   Phil Alden Robinson

Screenplays:
PETER PAN w/Walter F. Parkes
NEVER SAY DIE

AARON LATHAM*
Agent: CAA - Beverly Hills, 310/288-4545

URBAN COWBOY   Paramount, 1980, w/Jim Bridges
PERFECT   Columbia, 1985, w/Jim Bridges
THE PROGRAM   Buena Vista/Samuel Goldwyn, 1993,
   w/David Ward

Screenplays:
ATTITUDE COWBOYS
THE ZERO CLUB

LYNN MARIE LATHAM*
Contact: WGA - Los Angeles, 310/550-1000

Screenplays:
COMING OUT w/Bernard Lechowick

GREG LATTER
JOBMAN   Blue Rock Films, 1990, w/Darrell Roodt
YOUNG COMMANDOS   Cannon, 1991, w/Boaz Davidson
DELTA FORCE 3: THE KILLING GAME   Cannon Home Video,
   1992, w/Boaz Davidson & Andy Deutsch

JOHN LAU*
Agent: The Coppage Company - North Hollywood, 818/980-1106

Screenplays:
SPEED RACER w/Patrick Read Johnson
US AND THEM w/Patrick Read Johnson
TOM, DICK AND HARRY

LINDY LAUB*
Contact: WGA - Los Angeles, 310/550-1000

SHIKSE (Short)   directed
FOR THE BOYS   20th Century Fox, 1991, w/Marshall Brickman &
   Neal Jimenez

Screenplays:
LUDLOW, 1914
TWO VIRGINS
REFUGE

MICHAEL LAUGHLIN
STRANGE BEHAVIOR   *DEAD KIDS*   World Northal, 1981,
   w/William Condon, directed
STRANGE INVADERS   Orion, 1983, w/William Condon, directed
MESMERIZED   RKO/Challenge Corporation Services,
   1984, directed

TOM LAUGHLIN
Contact: Directors Guild of America - Los Angeles, 310/289-2000

BORN LOSERS   American International, 1967, directed
BILLY JACK   Warner Bros., 1973,
   as "Frank & Teresa Cristina," directed
BILLY JACK GOES TO WASHINGTON   Taylor-Laughlin, 1978,
   as "Frank & Teresa Cristina," directed

DALE LAUNER*
Business: 20th Century Fox, 310/203-2081

RUTHLESS PEOPLE   Buena Vista, 1986
BLIND DATE   Tri-Star, 1987
DIRTY ROTTEN SCOUNDRELS   Orion, 1988, w/Paul Henning &
   Stanley Shapiro
MY COUSIN VINNIE   20th Century Fox, 1992
LOVE POTION #9   20th Century Fox, 1992, directed

Screenplays:
MY COUSIN VINNIE 2

GERALD LAURENCE
FINAL APPROACH   Trimark Pictures, 1991, w/Eric Steven Stahl

MICHAEL LAURENCE*
Contact: WGA - New York, 212/245-6180

WHICH WAY HOME (CTF)   TNT/McElroy & McElroy, 1991

ARTHUR LAURENTS
SCREAM (P)
THE TIME OF THE CUCKOO (P)
NICK & NORA (P)
CAUGHT   Enterprise, 1948
ROPE   Warner Bros., 1948
ANNA LUCASTA   Columbia, 1949, w/Philip Yordan
ANASTASIA   Fox, 1956
BONJOUR TRISTESSE   Columbia, 1957
GYPSY   Warner Bros., 1962, from his play
THE WAY WE WERE   Columbia, 1973
THE TURNING POINT ★   20th Century-Fox, 1977

WILLIAM LAURIN*
Agent: Major Clients Agency - Los Angeles, 310/284-6400

Screenplays:
GOING FOR BROKE w/Glenn Davis
BLOOD WEEKEND w/Glenn Davis
MY GENERATION w/Glenn Davis
RACQUETS w/Glenn Davis
THE STAR PUPIL w/Glenn Davis
THE WET DETECTIVE w/Glenn Davis
OUR COTTAGE FROM HELL w/Glenn Davis

JEAN-CLAUDE LAUZON
Contact: Academy of Canadian Cinema and Television, 633 Yonge
   St. - 2nd Floor, Toronto, Ontario M4Y 1Z9, Canada, 416/967-0315

NIGHT ZOO   FilmDallas, 1987, directed
LEOLO   Alliance Releasing, 1992, directed

TOM LAVAGNINO
Agent: Warden, White & Kane - Beverly Hills, 213/852-1028

Screenplays:
WYLD WIDOWS
WALKING AFTER MIDNIGHT

JULIANNA LAVIN
Contact: Republic Pictures- 310/306-4040

LIVE NUDE GIRLS   Republic Pictures, 1994, directed

Screenplays:
RED DRESS

KIRK LaVINE*
Agent: Warden, White & Kane - Beverly Hills, 213/852-1028

Screenplays:
UPTOWN GIRL w/Ken Liotti

JAMES LAWLER
Agent: Annette Van Duren Agency - Los Angeles, 213/650-3643

Screenplays:
THE MUSIC OF STALE PRETZELS

BRUNO LAWRENCE
SMASH PALACE   Atlantic Releasing Corporation, 1981,
   w/Roger Donaldson & Peter Hansard
THE QUIET EARTH   Skouras Pictures, 1985, w/Bill Baer &
   Sam Pillsbury

DAVID LAWRENCE*
Agent: The Agency - Los Angeles, 310/551-3000

ESCAPE 2000   New World, 1983, Story w/George Schenck &
   Robert Williams

JEROME LAWRENCE*
Contact: Charles A. Scott, Gang, Tyre, Ramen & Brown -
   Los Angeles, 213/463-4863

TOAST OF THE TOWN (P)   w/Robert E. Lee
AUNTIE MAME (P)   w/Robert E. Lee
THE GANG'S ALL HERE (P)   w/Robert E. Lee
THE NIGHT THOREAU SPENT IN JAIL (P)   w/Robert E. Lee
INHERIT THE WIND (P)   w/Robert E. Lee
FIRST MONDAY IN OCTOBER   Paramount, 1981, w/Robert E. Lee,
   from their play

Screenplays:
THE CLOCK STRUCK ONE w/Robert E. Lee

MARC LAWRENCE*
Agent: United Talent Agency - Beverly Hills, 310/273-6700

LIFE WITH MIKEY   Buena Vista, 1993

Screenplays:
PARADISE MISPLACED

PETER LAWRENCE
THE BURNING   Filmways/Orion, 1982, w/Bob Weinstein
TERMINAL CHOICE   Almi Pictures, 1985, w/Neal Bell

RAY LAWRENCE
Agent: Becsey/Wisdom/Kalajian Agency - Los Angeles, 310/550-0535

BLISS   New World, 1986, w/Peter Carey, directed

JAMES LAWSON
Agent: United Talent Agency - Beverly Hills, 310/273-6700

Screenplays:
THE MADMAN'S KISS

J. F. LAWTON*
(Jonathan Frederick Lawton)
Agent: United Talent Agency - Beverly Hills, 310/273-6700
Manager: The Goldstein Company - Los Angeles, 310/659-9511

THE ARTIST (Short)
RENESANCE (Short)
CANNIBAL WOMEN IN THE AVOCADO JUNGLE OF DEATH
   Megalomania Productions, 1989, as "J.D. Athens," directed
PRETTY WOMAN   Buena Vista, 1990
PIZZA MAN   Megalomania Productions, 1991,
   as "J.D. Athens," directed
MISTRESS   International Rainbow Pictures, 1992, w/Barry Primus
UNDER SIEGE   Warner Bros., 1992
BLANKMAN   MGM/UA, 1994, w/Damon Wayans
THE HUNTED   Universal, 1994, directed

Screenplays:
BLUE TEARS
FIRE
RED SNEAKERS
INDIGO CAT
SLEEPLESS NIGHTS

RICHARD LAWTON
Agent: Warden, White & Kane - Beverly Hills, 213/852-1028

Screenplays:
SHOOT THE MESSENGER
REVENGE ROMANCE
IN THE SHADOW OF THE BIG CHEESE
WHITE MAN'S BURDEN
A NIGHT LIKE THIS

MICHAEL LAZAROU*
Agent: ICM - Beverly Hills, 310/550-4000

JERSEY DEVIL AND THE SHEILA FROM OZ (P)
HEAT WAVE (CTF)   Avnet/Kerner Co., 1990

Screenplays:
RAZZMATAZZ
TAKE THE A TRAIN

JERRY LAZARUS*
Agent: William Morris Agency - Beverly Hills, 310/274-7451
Contact: 213/464-8381

TREASURE OF THE FOUR CROWNS   Cannon, 1983,
   w/Lloyd Battista & Jim Bryce
HONEYMOON ACADEMY   Triumph, 1990, w/Gene Quintano
SURVIVE THE NIGHT (CTF)   Heartstar Productions/
   Once Upon a Time, 1993, Story w/Steve Whitney
ABOVE SUSPICION (CTF)   Rysher, 1994, w/W.H. Macy &
   Steven Schachter, directed

Screenplays:
FULL PARTNERSHIP

PHILIP LAZEBNIK*
Agent: United Talent Agency - Beverly Hills, 310/273-6700

Screenplays:
POCAHONTAS (AF)
SILLY HILLBILLIES ON MARS

CARLOS LAZLO
SILENT NIGHT, DEADLY NIGHT III: YOU BETTER WATCH OUT!
   Quiet Films, 1989

PAUL LEADON
AROUND THE WORLD IN 80 WAYS   Alive Films, 1987,
   w/Stephen MacLean

LARRY LEAHY
THE LAWLESS LAND   Concorde Pictures, 1989, w/Tony Cinciripini

NORMAN LEAR *
Business: Act III Communications, 310/553-3636
Business Manager: Perry & Neidorf - Beverly Hills, 310/550-1254

COME BLOW YOUR HORN   Paramount, 1962
DIVORCE AMERICAN STYLE ★   Columbia, 1967
THE NIGHT THEY RAIDED MINSKY'S   United Artists, 1968,
   w/Sidney Michaels & Arnold Schulman
COLD TURKEY   United Artists, 1971, directed

DENIS LEARY
Agent: William Morris Agency - Beverly Hills, 310/274-7451
Business: Apostle Pictures, New York (Walt Disney Studios)

Screenplays:
THE KING'S WAKE (CTF)
TWO IF BY SEA w/Michael Armstrong
NOOSE w/Michael Armstrong

MARY LEASE
DOLLY DEAREST   Trimark Pictures, 1992, directed

STEPHEN LEATHER
Agent: Sterling Lord Literistic - New York, 212/696-2800

Screenplays:
TWENTY MINUTES

RON LEAVITT*
Agent: United Talent Agency - Beverly Hills, 310/273-6700

Screenplays:
BELLHOP
BLITZ

FRED LeBOW*
Agent: William Morris Agency - Beverly Hills, 310/274-7451

WHILE YOU WERE SLEEPING   Buena Vista, 1995,
   w/Daniel Sullivan

Screenplays:
NEW YEAR'S EVE w/Daniel Sullivan
SNOWFLAKES w/Daniel Sullivan
SANTA'S DAUGHTER w/Daniel Sullivan
FAMILY BOOK w/Daniel Sullivan
MOONLES MIDNIGHT w/Daniel Sullivan
BAR SONG w/Daniel Sullivan
TERROR RANCH w/Daniel Sullivan

BERNARD LECHOWICK*
Contact: WGA - Los Angeles, 310/550-1000

Screenplays:
COMING OUT w/Lynn Marie Latham

PATRICE LECONTE
Agent: APA - Los Angeles, 310/273-0744

MONSIEUR HIRE   Orion Classics, 1989, directed
THE HAIRDRESSER'S HUSBAND   Triton Pictures, 1992, directed
TANGO   AMLF, 1993, w/Patrick DeWolf, directed
YVONNE'S PERFUME   President Films, 1994, directed

PAUL LEDER*
Contact: WGA - Los Angeles, 310/550-1000

GOIN' TO CHICAGO   Poor Robert Productions, 1990, directed
MURDER BY NUMBERS   Burnhill Productions, 1990, directed
FRAME UP II: THE COVER UP   Promark Entertainment,
   1992, directed
MOLLY & GINA   Curb Entertainment, 1994, w/Reuben Leder

REUBEN LEDER*
Agent: The Irv Schechter Company - Beverly Hills, 310/278-8070

MOLLY & GINA   Curb Entertainment, 1994, w/Paul Leder

Screenplays:
THREE WISHES w/Phil Combest

RICHARD LEDER*
Agent: Paradigm - Los Angeles, 310/277-4400

Screenplays:
ELEANOR
THE COLOR WAR

RICHARD LEDERER
THE HOLLYWOOD KNIGHTS   Columbia, 1980,
   Story w/Floyd Mutrux & William Tennant

ANG LEE
Contact: Department of Motion Picture Affairs, 2 Tientsin St.,
   Taipei, Taiwan, ROC, tel.: 2/351-6591

THE WEDDING BANQUET   Samuel Goldwyn Company, 1993,
   w/James Schamus & Hui Ling Wang, directed
EAT DRINK MAN WOMAN   Samuel Goldwyn Company, 1994,
   w/James Schamus & Hui Ling Wang, directed

CINQUE LEE
Contact: Forty Acres & A Mule Filmworks, 124 DeKalb Ave.,
   Brooklyn, NY 11217, 718/624-3703

CROOKLYN   Universal, 1994, w/Joie Susannah Lee & Spike Lee

Screenplays:
NO IT U LOVER

DAMIAN LEE
Business: Rose & Ruby Productions, Inc., 33 Howard St., Toronto,
   Ontario M4X 1J6, Canada, 416/961-0555

BUSTED UP   Shapiro Entertainment, 1987
WATCHERS   Tri-Star, 1988, w/Bill Freed
CRIME AND PUNISHMENT   21st Century Film Corporation, 1993

Screenplays:
NATIONAL LAMPOON'S SCUBA SCHOOL (21st Century, directing)

GALEN LEE
ROADHOUSE 66   Atlantic Releasing Corporation, 1984,
   w/George Simpson

GERARD LEE
SWEETIE   Avenue Pictures, 1989, w/Jane Campion

JOIE SUSANNAH LEE
Contact: Forty Acres & A Mule Filmworks, 124 DeKalb Ave.,
   Brooklyn, NY 11217, 718/624-3703

CROOKLYN   Universal, 1994, w/Cinque Lee & Spike Lee

LESLIE LEE*
Agent: Fifi Oscard Associates - New York, 212/764-1100

THE KILLING FLOOR   Public Forum Productions/American
   Playhouse, 1992

MARK W. LEE*
Agent: Jon Klane Agency - Beverly Hills, 310/278-0178

REBEL ARMIES DEEP INTO CHAD (P)
PIRATES (P)
CALIFORNIA DOGFIGHT (P)
PARADISE (P)
CHAIN OF COMMAND (P)
THE NEXT KARATE KID   Columbia, 1994
FORTUNES OF WAR (CTF)   HBO Pictures, 1994

Screenplays:
SKULL & BONES
CAPITAL PAGES
MULTIPLE CHOICE
WHITE DRAGON
CRAZY FOR KATE
SPARE PARTS
KAMPALA
FINAL VOWS
BOY EATING TIGER

PATRICK LEE
PERFUME OF THE CYCLONE   Movie Group, 1990

SPIKE LEE
(Shelton Jackson Lee)
Agent: ICM - Beverly Hills, 310/550-4000
Contact: Frankfurt, Garbus, Klein & Selz - New York, 212/980-0120
Business: Forty Acres & A Mule Filmworks, 124 DeKalb Ave.,
   Brooklyn, NY 11217, 718/624-3703

JOE'S BED-STUY BARBERSHOP: WE CUT HEADS   First Run
   Features, 1983, directed
SHE'S GOTTA HAVE IT   Island Pictures, 1986, directed
SCHOOL DAZE   Columbia, 1988, directed
DO THE RIGHT THING ★   Universal, 1989, directed
MO' BETTER BLUES   Universal, 1990, directed
JUNGLE FEVER   Universal, 1991, directed
MALCOLM X   Warner Bros., 1992, w/Arnold Perl, directed
CROOKLYN   Universal, 1994, w/Cinque Lee & Joie Lee, directed

STUART LEE
BURIED ALIVE   21st Century Film, 1990, w/Jake Clesi

MICHAEL J. LEESON*
Agent: CAA - Beverly Hills, 310/288-4545

JEKYLL AND HYDE...TOGETHER AGAIN   Paramount, 1982,
   w/Jerry Belson, Monica Johnson & Harvey Miller
THE SURVIVORS   Columbia, 1983
NO SMALL AFFAIR   Columbia, 1984, w/Craig Bolotin,
   as "Terence Mulcahy"
THE WAR OF THE ROSES   20th Century Fox, 1989
I.Q.   Paramount, 1994, w/Andy Breckman

Screenplays:
LES COMPERES
A YEAR AND A DAY
THE MAN WHO COULD WORK MIRACLES

CAROLINE LEFCOURT
THE STEPFATHER   New Century/Vista, 1987,
   Story w/Brian Garfield & Donald E. Westlake

PETER LEFCOURT*
Agent: Paradigm - Los Angeles, 310/277-4400

SWEET TALK (P)
LA RONDE DE LUNCH (P)
THE AUDIT (P)

Screenplays:
THE DREYFUS AFFAIR: A LOVE STORY
INHERIT THE MOB

ADAM B. LEFF*
Agent: ICM - Beverly Hills, 310/550-4000

LAST ACTION HERO   Columbia, 1993, Story w/Zak Penn
P.C.U.   20th Century Fox, 1994, w/Zak Penn

Screenplays:
CENTRAL PARK w/Zak Penn

GEORGE LEFFERTS*
Agent: George Lefferts Associates - New Jersey, 201/592-0374

MEAN DOG BLUES   American International, 1978

DOUGLAS A. LEFLER*
Agent: Rogers & Associates - North Hollywood, 818/509-1010

STEEL DAWN   Vestron, 1987

MARK JORDAN LEGAN*
Agent: Broder-Kurland-Webb-Uffner - Beverly Hills, 310/281-3400

NICKEL & DIME (P)   also screenplay

Screenplays:
KNEESLAPPER
SAY UNCLE

LAURIAN LEGGETT*
Agent: The Irv Schechter Company - Beverly Hills, 310/278-8070

DOC HOLLYWOOD   Warner Bros., 1990, Adaptation

Screenplays:
DETOUR TOUGH N GO
LIP SERVICE
ROMAN NOLIDAY

JOHN LEGUIZAMO
Agent: William Morris Agency - Beverly Hills, 310/274-7451

SPIC-O-RAMA (P)

Screenplays:
WHITE CHOCOLATE

ERNEST LEHMAN*
Agent: The Gersh Agency - Beverly Hills, 310/274-6611

EXECUTIVE SUITE   MGM, 1954
SABRINA ★   Paramount, 1954, w/Samuel Taylor & Billy Wilder
THE KING AND I   20th Century-Fox, 1956
SOMEBODY UP THERE LIKES ME   MGM, 1956
SWEET SMELL OF SUCCESS   United Artists, 1957,
   w/Clifford Odets
NORTH BY NORTHWEST ★   MGM, 1959
FROM THE TERRACE   20th Century-Fox, 1960
WEST SIDE STORY ★   United Artists, 1961
THE PRIZE   MGM, 1963
THE SOUND OF MUSIC   20th Century-Fox, 1965
WHO'S AFRAID OF VIRGINIA WOOLF? ★   Warner Bros., 1966
HELLO DOLLY   20th Century-Fox, 1969
PORTNOY'S COMPLAINT   Warner Bros., 1972, directed
BLACK SUNDAY   Paramount, 1976, w/Ivan Moffat & Kenneth Ross
FAMILY PLOT   Universal, 1976

MICHAEL LEHMANN
Agent: CAA - Beverly Hills, 310/288-4545

MEET THE APPLEGATES   *THE APPLEGATES*   Triton Pictures,
   1991, w/Redbeard Simmons, directed

Screenplays:
LE SURF HOT w/Redbeard Simmons
DREAMDATE

JERRY LEICHTLING*
Agent: CAA - Beverly Hills, 310/288-4545

PEGGY SUE GOT MARRIED   Tri-Star, 1986, w/Arlene Sarner
BLUE SKY   Orion, 1994, w/Arlene Sarner &
   Rama Laurie Stagner

Screenplays:
HOUSE ARREST w/Arlene Sarner & Steven Carpenter
THE TALISMAN w/Arlene Sarner
HONKY TONK SUE w/Arlene Sarner

MIKE LEIGH
Agent: William Morris Agency - Beverly Hills, 310/274-7451 or
   Peters, Fraser & Dunlop - London, 071/376-7676

BLEAK MOMENTS   Autumn/Memorial/BFI, 1971, directed
HIGH HOPES   Skouras Pictures, 1989, directed
LIFE IS SWEET   October Films, 1991, directed
NAKED   Fine Line Features, 1993, directed

WARREN D. LEIGHT*
Agent: William Morris Agency - Beverly Hills, 310/274-7451

PAY-PER-KILL (P)
MAYOR (P)
HIGH HEELED WOMAN CABARET ACT (P)
MOTHER'S DAY   United Film Distribution, 1980,
   w/Charles Kaufman
STUCK ON YOU!   Troma, 1983, w/others
BEFORE THE NICKELODEON   First Run Features, 1983,
   w/Charles Musser
ME AND HIM   Columbia, 1989
THE NIGHT WE NEVER MET   Miramax, 1993, directed

Screenplays:
POOR LITTLE LAMBS

MICHAEL W. LEIGHTON*
Contact: 310/390-1000

RUSH WEEK   RCA/Columbia Home Video, 1991,
   w/Russell Y. Manzatt

TED LEIGHTON
THE HUNTER   Paramount, 1980, w/Peter Hyams

MOLLY-ANN LEIKIN*
Contact: WGA - Los Angeles, 310/550-1000

Screenplays:
ABBY & SOCKS
FRENCH DRESSING
DOOLITTLE & STICK
LEFTY'S PIANO

MATT LEIPZIG
Contact: Jerry Weintraub Productions, Warner Bros. - Burbank,
   818/954-2500

HOUR OF THE ASSASSIN   Concorde, 1987

CHRISTOPHER LEITCH*
Agent: Paradigm - Los Angeles, 310/277-4400

UNIVERSAL SOLDIER   TriStar, 1992, w/Dean Devlin &
   Richard Rothstein

Screenplays:
ALONG FOR THE RIDE w/Ted Tobin

DAVID LELAND*
Agent: The Casarotto Company - London, 071/287-4450

MONA LISA   Island Pictures, 1986, w/Neil Jordan
PERSONAL SERVICES   Vestron, 1987
WISH YOU WERE HERE   Atlantic Releasing Corporation,
   1987, directed

Screenplays:
RUNNING WILD
THE WHITE RIVER KID

CLAUDE LELOUCH
Contact: French Film Office, 745 Fifth Avenue, New York, NY 10151,
   212/832-8860

A MAN AND A WOMAN ★   Allied Artists, 1966,
   w/Pierre Uytterhoeven, directed
LIVE FOR LIFE   United Artists, 1967,
   w/Pierre Uytterhoeven, directed
HAPPY NEW YEAR   *LA BONNE ANNEE*   Avco Embassy,
   1973, directed
AND NOW MY LOVE   *TOUTE UNE VIE* ★   Avco Embassy, 1975,
   w/Pierre Uytterhoeven, directed
SECOND CHANCE   *SI C'ETAIT A REFAIR*   United Artists Classics,
   1976, directed
ANOTHER MAN, ANOTHER CHANCE   United Artists,
   1977, directed
ROBERT ET ROBERT   Quartet, 1978, directed
BOLERO   *LES UNS ET LES AUTRES/WITHIN MEMORY*
   Double 13/Sharp Features, 1982, directed
A MAN AND A WOMAN: 20 YEARS LATER   Warner Bros.,
   1986, directed
THE BEAUTIFUL STORY   AFMD, 1992, directed
ALL THAT...FOR THIS?   Bac Films, 1993, directed

JONATHAN LEMKIN*
Agent: CAA - Beverly Hills, 310/288-4545

Screenplays:
RED SUN RISING
NO DEPOSIT, NO RETURN   *THE SIEGE*

JAMES LEMMO
HEART   New World, 1987, w/Randy Jurgenson, directed
TRIPWIRE   CineTel Films, 1989, w/B.J. Goldman, directed
WE'RE TALKIN' SERIOUS MONEY   Cinetel, 1992,
   w/Leo Rossi, directed
BODILY HARM   Rysher Entertainment, 1994, w/Ronda Barendse &
   Joseph Whaley, directed

Screenplays:
THE RETREAT   (Shared, directing)

KASI LEMMONS*
Agent: Innovative Artists - Los Angeles, 310/553-5200

Screenplays:
TABLOID

RUSTY LEMORANDE*
Business Manager: Hansen, Jacobsen & Teller - Los Angeles,
   310/278-8622

ELECTRIC DREAMS   MGM/UA, 1984
JOURNEY TO THE CENTER OF THE EARTH   Cannon, 1987,
   w/Kitty Chalmers, Regina Davis & Debra Ricci, directed
THE TURN OF THE SCREW   Electric Pictures, 1991, directed

Screenplays:
THE FRIENDLY
GHOST TOWN U.S.A.

PETER LENKOV*
Agent: United Talent Agency - Beverly Hills, 310/273-6700

SON-IN-LAW   Buena Vista, 1993, Story w/Patrick Clifton &
   Susan McMartin
DEMOLITION MAN   Warner Bros., 1993, w/Rob Reneau &
   Dan Waters

Screenplays:
TRAIL OF THE GODS
THE SHOOTING STAR
MEASURE OF DARKNESS
VIRUS

GARY LENNON
Agent: Writers & Artists Agency - Los Angeles, 310/824-6300

DATES AND NUTS (P)
DRUNKS (P)   also screenplay

Screenplays:
CONCHETTE

ROBERT W. LENSKI*
Agent: William Morris Agency - Beverly Hills, 310/274-7451

Screenplays:
BEVERLY HILLS BOX 33
WANDERLUST
MILITARY MAN

DEAN LENT
BORDER RADIO   International Film Marketing, w/Allison Anders &
   Kurt Voss, co-directed

NORMAN LENZER
Business: 7471 Melrose Ave. - Suite 8, Los Angeles, 213/653-1011

THE ADVENTURES OF THE AMERICAN RABBIT (AF)
   Atlantic Releasing Corporation, 1986

MALCOLM LEO*
Business: Malcolm Leo Productions, 6536 Sunset Blvd., Hollywood,
   CA 90028, 213/464-4448

THIS IS ELVIS (FD)   Warner Bros., 1981, w/Andrew Solt

BRETT LEONARD
Agent: CAA - Beverly Hills, 310/288-4545
Personal Manager: Steve Freedman - Studio City, 818/508-5115
Attorney: Dennis Cline, Behr and Robinson, 2049 Century Park East,
   Suite 2690, Los Angeles, CA 90067, 310/556-9210

THE LAWNMOWER MAN   New Line Cinema, 1992,
   w/Gimel Everett, directed

Screenplays:
THE IMMORTALS w/Gimel Everett
HIDDEN AGENDAS w/Gimel Everett
THE LAWNMOWER MAN II: MINDFIRE w/Gimel Everett

ELMORE LEONARD*
Agent: Michael Siegel & Associates - Los Angeles, 310/274-5222

THE MOONSHINE WAR   MGM, 1970
JOE KIDD   Universal, 1972
MR. MAJESTYK   United Artists, 1974
STICK   Universal, 1985, w/Joseph Stinson
52 PICK-UP   Cannon, 1986, w/John Steppling
THE ROSARY MURDERS   New Line Cinema, 1987, w/Fred Walton
CAT CHASER   Vestron, 1990, w/Jim Borrelli & Alan Sharp

Screenplays:
JUVENILE

HUGH LEONARD*
Agent: William Morris Agency - New York, 212/586-5100

BROTH OF A BOY (P)
THE MASK OF MORIARITY (P)
INTERLUDE   Columbia, 1968, w/Lee Langley
GREAT CATHERINE   Warner Bros., 1968
PERCY   MGM, 1971
OUR MISS FRED   EMI, 1972
DA   FilmDallas Pictures, 1988, from his play
WIDOW'S PEAK   Fine Line Features, 1994

Screenplays:
MATTIE (Fine Line Features)
O'NEIL
THE PATRICK PIERCE MOTEL
STEPHEN "D"

JOHN LEONE
TOUGH ENOUGH   20th Century-Fox, 1983

GLENN LEOPOLD*
Contact: Wayne Alexander, Alexander, Halloran, Nau & Shanker -
   Los Angeles, 310/552-0035

THE PROWLER   Sandhurst Corporation, 1982, w/Neal F. Barbera
TOO SCARED TO SCREAM   Moviestore Entertainment, 1985,
   w/Neal F. Barbera

TOM LEOPOLD*
Contact: WGA - Los Angeles, 310/550-1000

HENRY AND THE SECOND GUNMAN (P)
J. EDGAR! (P) w/Harry Shearer
CLUB PARADISE   Warner Bros., 1986, Story w/Chris Miller,
   Ed Roboto & David Standish

Screenplays:
SAVE ME AN ANGEL

DANNY LERNER
NEVER SAY DIE   Nu-Image, 1994, w/Jeff Albert & Yossi Wein

ERIC LERNER*
Contact: Tom Hunter, Bloom, Dekom, Hergott & Cook - Los Angeles,
   310/278-8622

BIRD ON A WIRE   Universal, 1990, w/David Seltzer &
   Louis Venosta

MICHAEL LERNER*
Contact: WGA - Los Angeles, 310/550-1000

Screenplays:
PANIC

ROBIN LERNER
Agent: The Rothman Agency - Beverly Hills, 213/655-2020

Screenplays:
EAST OF THE SUN, WEST OF THE MOON
FLEA CIRCUS (AF)
JUST SO (AF)
THE WILD SWANS

GEN LeROY*
Contact: 212/769-0536

Screenplays:
BORN WITH A TRUNK
THE THIN MAN'S LAST CASE
IT'S A CRIME
GREASEPAINT

DENNIS LESS
LABYRINTH   Tri-Star, 1986, Story w/Jim Henson

MICHAEL LESSAC*
Agent: United Talent Agency - Beverly Hills, 310/273-6700

HOUSE OF CARDS   Miramax, 1993, directed

ELANA LESSER*
Agent: David Shapira & Associates - Sherman Oaks,
   818/906-0322

Screenplays:
CAT'S DON'T DANCE (AF) (Turner Pictures)
   w/Roberts Gannaway & Cliff Ruby
SNOWBALLS (AF)
THE MIGHTY CASEY

MARK L. LESTER
Contact: Directors Guild of America - Los Angeles, 310/289-2000

STEEL ARENA   L.-T. Films, 1973, directed
CLASS OF '84   United Film Distribution, 1982, w/John Saxton &
   Tom Holland, directed
CLASS OF 1999   Taurus Entertainment, 1990,
   Story, directed

MICHAEL LESTER
CODENAME: WILDGEESE   New World, 1986

SHELDON B. LETTICH*
Agent: William Morris Agency - Beverly Hills, 310/274-7451

TRACERS (P)   shared
FIREFIGHT (Short)   1986, directed
RUSSKIES   New Century Entertainment, 1987,
   w/Alan Glueckman & Michael Nankin
RAMBO III   Tri-Star, 1988, w/Sylvester Stallone
BLOODSPORT   Cannon, 1988, w/Chris Cosby & Mel Friedman
LIONHEART   Universal, 1991,
   w/Jean-Claude Van Damme, directed
DOUBLE IMPACT   Columbia, 1991,
   w/Jean-Claude Van Damme, directed
ONLY THE STRONG   20th Century Fox, 1993,
   w/Luis Esteban, directed

Screenplays:
G.I. JOE (directing)

GIGI LEVANGIE*
Agent: CAA - Beverly Hills, 310/288-4545

Screenplays:
THE STEPMOTHER

BRIAN LEVANT*
Agent: United Talent Agency - Beverly Hills, 310/273-6700

Screenplays:
THAT'S ALL FOLKS
HONEY, THE DOG ATE THE KIDS
BLOW HARD

BEATRICE LEVAVI
Agent: Stephanie Mann Agency - Los Angeles, 213/653-7130

Screenplays:
ABOUT FACE w/Lenny Kolinsky
SWEET LADY JANE w/Lenny Kolinsky
BLOOD TIES w/Lenny Kolinsky

JEREMY LEVEN*
Agent: ICM - Beverly Hills, 310/550-4000

CREATOR Universal, 1985
PLAYING FOR KEEPS Universal, 1986, w/Bob Weinstein & Harvey Weinstein
DON JUAN DeMARCO AND THE CENTERFOLD New Line Cinema, 1994, directed

Screenplays:
THE DOUBLE
BRAIN MAN
SATAN, CRAZY AS HELL
ACE TRUCKING CO.

JOHN LEVENSTEIN*
Agent: Susan Smith & Associates - Beverly Hills, 213/852-4777

ILLEGALLY YOURS DEG, 1986, w/Ken Finkelman & Michael Kaplan, as "Max Dickens & M.A. Stewart"

Screenplays:
CARLESS w/Michael Kaplan
BREADWINNER

A. A. LEVER
PRIMO BABY Victory Film, 1990

FRANK LEVERING
PARASITE Embassy, 1982, w/Alan J. Adler & Michael Shoob

JAY LEVEY
U.H.F. Orion, 1989, w/Al Yankovic, directed

CATHERINE MAY LEVIN
THE BOY WHO CRIED BITCH Pilgrims 3 Corp., 1991

JEFF LEVIN*
Contact: WGA - Los Angeles, 310/550-1000

Screenplays:
LATE BLOOMERS w/Leann Lantos & Jeff Lantos
TIGHT QUARTERS w/Leann Lantos & Jeff Lantos
EVERYTHING COUNTS w/Leann Lantos & Jeff Lantos

JOHN LEVIN*
Agent: Shapiro/Lichtman - Los Angeles, 310/859-8877

Screenplays:
THE CONTRACTOR

LEAR LEVIN*
Manager: Creative Alliance Management - Los Angeles, 213/962-6090

Screenplays:
THE FOURTH ESTATE
BALL'N CHAIN

MARC LEVIN
BLOWBACK Northern Arts Entertainment, 1991, directed

MARK LEVIN*
Agent: ICM - Beverly Hills, 310/550-4000

Screenplays:
THE SWORD

SHIRA LEVIN*
Contact: WGA - Los Angeles, 310/550-1000

Screenplays:
IF MORNING EVER COMES w/Gary Weiner

VICTOR LEVIN*
Agent: Broder-Kurland-Webb-Uffner - Beverly Hills, 310/281-3400

Screenplays:
LITTLE FEET
THE DICK

EMILY B. LEVINE*
Contact: WGA - Los Angeles, 310/550-1000

Screenplays:
THE FLING

KEN LEVINE*
Agent: Broder-Kurland-Webb-Uffner - Beverly Hills, 310/281-3400

VOLUNTEERS Tri-Star, 1985, w/David Isaacs
MANNEQUIN TWO: ON THE MOVE 20th Century Fox, 1991, w/David Isaacs, Betsy Israel & Ed Rugoff

Screenplays:
GETTING AWAY w/David Isaacs
HOME FRONT w/David Isaacs
STAR SPANGLED ADVENTURE w/David Isaacs
LIVING LEGEND w/David Isaacs

LAURA S. LEVINE*
Contact: WGA - Los Angeles, 310/550-1000

Screenplays:
DUMPED

MICHAEL LEVINE
Agent: Renaissance-H.N. Swanson - Los Angeles, 310/246-6000

Screenplays:
DEEP COVER (CTF) DOWN FOR BLOOD w/Laura Kavanau

PAUL LEVINE*
Agent: Camden-ITG - Los Angeles, 310/289-2700

BEST OF THE BEST Taurus Entertainment, 1989

RICHARD B. LEVINE*
Contact: WGA - Los Angeles, 310/550-1000

Screenplays:
BLACK TIDE

BARRY LEVINSON
THE INTERNECINE PROJECT Allied Artists, 1974, w/Jonathan Lynn
STREET GIRLS New World, 1975, w/Michael Miller

BARRY LEVINSON*
Agent: CAA - Beverly Hills, 310/288-4545
Business: Baltimore Pictures, Warner Bros. - 818/954-2666

SILENT MOVIE 20th Century-Fox, 1976, w/Mel Brooks, Ron Clark & Rudy DeLuca
HIGH ANXIETY 20th Century-Fox, 1977, w/Mel Brooks, Ron Clark & Rudy DeLuca
...AND JUSTICE FOR ALL ★ Columbia, 1979, w/Valerie Curtin
INSIDE MOVES AFD, 1980, w/Valerie Curtin
BEST FRIENDS Warner Bros., 1982, w/Valerie Curtin
DINER ★ MGM/United Artists, 1982, directed
UNFAITHFULLY YOURS 20th Century-Fox, 1984, w/Valerie Curtin & Robert Klane
TIN MEN Buena Vista, 1987, directed
AVALON ★ Tri-Star, 1990, directed
TOYS 20th Century Fox, 1992, w/Valerie Curtin, directed
JIMMY HOLLYWOOD Paramount, 1994, directed

DAVID LEVINSON*
Agent: Warden, White & Kane - Beverly Hills, 213/852-1028

Screenplays:
JAZZ BABIES
SEEING STARS
SHOULDER TO SHOULDER
SOME KIDS ARE REALLY WEIRD
JANE Q. PUBLIC

LARRY LEVINSON
MISSING IN ACTION 2: THE BEGINNING   Cannon, 1985,
    w/Arthur Silver & Steve Bing

DIANA LEVITT
Agent: Paradigm - Los Angeles, 310/277-4400

Screenplays:
GETTING HAL w/Pam Chais

KAREN LEVITT
TIME WALKER   New World, 1982, w/Tom Friedman

STEVE LEVITT
Agent: Broder-Kurland-Webb-Uffner - Beverly Hills, 310/281-3400

Screenplays:
DEAF HEAVEN

ZANE W. LEVITT
Business: Zeta Entertainment Ltd., 909/983-0897

OUT OF THE DARK   CineTel Films, 1989, w/J. Greg DeFelice

ALAN LEVY
Agent: William Morris Agency - Beverly Hills, 310/274-7451
Manager: 3 Arts Entertainment - Los Angeles, 213/851-5700

Screenplays:
THE REST OF US

EUGENE LEVY*
Agent: William Morris Agency - Beverly Hills, 310/274-7451

SODBUSTERS (CTF)   Showtime/Atlantis Films, 1994,
    w/John Hemphill

JEFERY LEVY*
Agent: United Talent Agency - Beverly Hills, 310/273-6700

GHOULIES   Empire Pictures, 1986, w/Luca Bercovici
ROCKULA   Cannon, 1989, w/Luca Bercovici & Christopher Verwiel
DRIVE   Megagiant Entertainment, 1992, directed
S.F.W.   Gramercy, 1995, w/Danny Rubin, directed

Screenplays:
THE TUNGSTEN KISS
UNARMED AND DANGEROUS

NEIL A. LEVY*
Contact: WGA - Los Angeles, 310/550-1000

RUDE AWAKENING   Orion, 1989, w/Richard LaGravenese

Screenplays:
DAYS OF GRACE
CHASING THE DRAGON

ROBERT LEVY*
Business Manager: Harabedian & Hall - 213/380-7130

A KID IN KING ARTHUR'S COURT   Buena Vista, 1995,
    w/Michael Part

SHUKI LEVY
ROUND TRIP TO HEAVEN   Saban Pictures International, 1992,
    w/Winston Richard

BEN LEWIN
Agent: Innovative Artists - Los Angeles, 310/553-5200

GEORGIA   Jethro Films, 1988, directed
THE FAVOUR, THE WATCH, AND THE VERY BIG FISH
    Trimark Pictures, 1992, directed
LUCKY BREAK   Samuel Goldwyn Company, 1994, directed

ANDY LEWIS
UNDERGROUND   United Artists, 1970, w/Ron Bishop
KLUTE ★   Warner Bros., 1971, w/Dave Lewis

Screenplays:
THE TRIUMPH OF LINCOLN CLUN w/Dave Lewis
PANAMA
THEO
ZANDE
PANIC
BRANT
THE ARMS MERCHANT
BINARY PROJECT
MARCO
ALLIE
NINA

EDWARD LEWIS*
Business Manager: Barbara Rosenbaum, Krees & Rosenbaum -
    Los Angeles, 213/872-2132

BROTHERS   Warner Bros., 1977, w/Mildred Lewis

EVERETT LEWIS
THE NATURAL HISTORY OF PARKING LOTS   Little Deer
    Productions, 1989, directed

Screenplays:
SUZI AND THE MECHANIC (directing)

FIONA LEWIS*
Contact: WGA - Los Angeles, 310/550-1000

Screenplays:
EASY VIRTUE
WHITE GOLD
AMERICAN RHAPSODY
ABOVE SUSPIC'ON
LAST WEEKEND
GOING FOR BROKE
REALM 7
IN GOOD HANDS
LIBELED LADY
DIPLOMATIC IMMUNITY
HARDBALL
AMATEURS
CLASS CONFLICT

JEFFERSON LEWIS
A PAPER WEDDING   Capitol Entertainment Release, 1991,
    w/Andree Pelletier
ORDINARY MAGIC   The Film Works, 1993
MON AMIE MAX   Les Productions du Verseau/Les Productions
    La Zennec, 1994

JERRY LEWIS*
Agent: William Morris Agency - Beverly Hills, 310/274-7451

THE BELLBOY   Paramount, 1960, directed
THE LADIES' MAN   Paramount, 1961, w/Bill Richmond, directed
THE ERRAND BOY   Paramount, 1962, directed
THE NUTTY PROFESSOR   Paramount, 1963,
    w/Bill Richmond, directed

THE PATSY   Paramount, 1964, directed
THE FAMILY JEWELS   Paramount, 1965,
   w/Bill Richmond, directed
THE BIG MOUTH   Columbia, 1967, w/Bill Richmond, directed
HARDLY WORKING   20th Century-Fox, 1981,
   w/Michael Janover, directed
SMORGASBORD   Warner Bros., 1985, w/Bill Richmond, directed

MICHAEL LEWIS
THE SEVENTH COIN   Hemdale, 1993, w/Dror Soref

MILDRED LEWIS
BROTHERS   Warner Bros., 1977, w/Edward Lewis

RICHARD J. LEWIS
Contact: Academy of Canadian Cinema & Television, 753 Yonge St. -
   2nd Floor, Toronto M4Y 1Z9, Canada, 416/967-0315

WHALE MUSIC   Alliance Releasing, 1994,
   w/Paul Quarrington, directed

WARREN LEWIS*
Agent: Paradigm - Los Angeles, 310/277-4400

BLACK RAIN   Paramount, 1989, w/Craig Bolotin

WILLIAM W. LEWIS*
Agent: Rosenstone/Wender - New York, 212/832-8330

BRADY'S ESCAPE   Satori Releasing, 1984

DENIS LEWISTON
HOT TARGET   Crown International, 1985, directed

ELLIOTT LEWITT
AT CLOSE RANGE   Orion, 1986, Story w/Nicholas Kazan

CRASH LEYLAND*
(Mark St. David Leyland)
Agent: ICM - Beverly Hills, 310/550-4000

SNIPER   TriStar, 1993, w/Michael Frost Beckner

Screenplays:
JUDGE DREDD (Buena Vista)
CROCKETT AND BOWIE w/Jere Cunningham
GARDEN OF EDEN (Shared)
WITH FLYING COLORS
MOTHER HUBBARD
CITADEL
CANYON
ONE CUT FROM PARADISE

HOWARD LIBOV
Agent: Paradigm - Los Angeles, 310/277-4400

MIDNIGHT EDITION   Shapiro Glickenhaus, 1993,
   w/Michael Stewart & Yuri Zeltser, directed

ALICE LIDDLE
PERMANENT RECORD   Paramount, 1988, w/Jarre Fees &
   Larry Ketron

BOBBY LIDELL
ENEMY TERROR   Empire Pictures, 1987, Story w/Stuart Kaminsky

MICHAEL LIEBER*
Contact: WGA - Los Angeles, 310/550-1000

BENEFIT OF THE DOUBT   Miramax, 1993, Story

JEFF LIEBERMAN*
Agent: Renaissance-H.N. Swanson - Los Angeles, 310/246-6000

SQUIRM   American International, 1976, directed
BLUE SUNSHINE   Cinema Shares International, 1979, directed

Screenplays:
THE NEVERENDING STORY III
US

MARC LIEBERMAN
LOVE KILLS (CTF)   OMTL Productions Inc./Wilshire Court Prods.,
   1991, w/Corey Mandell

RAY LIEN
BAD APPLES   You Betcha, 1994, directed

TOPPER LILIEN*
Agent: Innovative Artists - Los Angeles, 310/553-5200

MR. FIXIT (Short)   1988

Screenplays:
YOU PLAY THE BLACK AND THE RED COMES UP
   w/Carroll Cartwright
HELLO, STRANGER w/Carroll Cartwright
CLOSING ARGUMENT w/Carroll Cartwright

JOHN LINDE
AFTER SCHOOL   Moviestore Entertainment, 1989, w/Rod McBrien,
   Hugh Parks & Joe Tankersley

STEWART LINDH
BLIND SIDE (CTF)   Chestnut Hill Productions, 1993,
   w/John Carlen & Solomon Weingarten

Screenplays:
RETRIBUTION
THE SEA HORSE
DIXIE
THE DIVIDED HEART
BLUE BLOOD
LINCOLN FLATS
THE SIREN
DARK MATTER
STILLWATER COVE
PELICAN BAY

MARK LINDQUIST*
Contact: WGA - Los Angeles, 310/550-1000

Screenplays:
AFTER THE PEEPSHOW

JIM LINDSAY*
Manager: Carlyle Management - Los Angeles, 213/469-3086

TRIAL & ERROR (CTF)   Alliance Communications/USA Network,
   w/Rick Way & N.D. Schreiner

Screenplays:
CONVICT COWBOY w/Rick Way
MY MOTHER WEARS ARMY BOOTS w/Rick Way

MICHAEL LINDSAY-HOGG
Agent: William Morris Agency - Beverly Hills, 310/274-7451

THE OBJECT OF BEAUTY   Avenue Pictures, 1991, directed

JONNIE LINDSELL
I DON'T BUY KISSES ANYMORE   Skouras Pictures, 1992
LIGHTNING IN A BOTTLE   Curb Entertainment, 1994

PETER LINETT*
Agent: Susan Smith & Associates - Beverly Hills, 213/852-4777

Screenplays:
TAKING LIBERTY w/Peter Iliff

WILLIAM LINK*
Agent: CAA - Beverly Hills, 310/288-4545
Business: Foxcroft Productions, Columbia Television

ROLLERCOASTER   Universal, 1977, w/Richard Levinson

Screenplays:
THE HIT w/Doug Barr

RICHARD LINKLATER*
Agent: William Morris Agency - Beverly Hills, 310/274-7451

SLACKER   Orion Classics, 1991, directed
DAZED AND CONFUSED   Gramercy, 1993, directed
BEFORE SUNRISE   Columbia, 1995, w/Kim Krizan, directed

KEN LIOTTI*
Agent: Warden, White & Kane - Beverly Hills, 213/852-1028

Screenplays:
UPTOWN GIRL w/Kirk LaVine

EUGENE LIPINSKI
Contact: Academy of Canadian Cinema & Television, 633 Yonge St. -
   2nd Floor, Toronto, Ontario M4Y 1Z9, Canada, 416/967-0315

PERFECTLY NORMAL   Four Seasons Entertainment, 1991,
   w/Paul Quarrington

DANIEL LIPMAN*
Agent: William Morris Agency - Beverly Hills, 310/274-7451

Screenplays:
FIREFLY w/Ron Cowen
FAMILY DANCING w/Ron Cowen

JEREMY D. LIPP*
Agent: Major Clients Agency - Los Angeles, 310/284-6400

P.O.W. THE ESCAPE   Cannon, 1986, w/Malcolm Barbour,
   James Bruner & John Langley
DUET FOR ONE   Cannon, 1987, w/Andrei Konchalovsky &
   Tom Kempinski

Screenplays:
THE SIMULATOR

KEN LIPPER*
Contact: WGA - New York, 212/245-6180

CITY HALL   Columbia, 1995, w/Bo Goldman

DHANI LIPSIUS*
Contact: WGA - Los Angeles, 310/550-1000

HALLOWEEN 4   Galaxy International, 1988, Story w/Alan McElroy,
   Benjamin Ruffner & Larry Rattner

AARON LIPSTADT
CITY LIMITS   Atlantic Releasing Corporation, 1985,
   w/Don Opper & James Reigle, directed

STEVEN LISBERGER*
Agent: The Chasin Agency - Beverly Hills, 310/278-7505

ANIMALYMPICS (AF)   Lisberger Studios, 1980, directed
TRON   Buena Vista, 1982, directed
HOT PURSUIT   Paramount, 1987, w/Steve Carabatsos, directed

Screenplays:
DANIEL BOONE: SON OF THE SHAWNEE INDIANS

DAN LISHNER
MONTANA RUN   Greycat Films, 1992, w/Ron Reid &
   Randy Thompson

STEPHANIE LISS
Agent: United Talent Agency - Beverly Hills, 310/273-6700
Manager: Creative Alliance Management - Los Angeles,
   213/962-6090

Screenplays:
SILHOUETTE
THE GERTA KLEIN STORY

MARK L. LISSON*
Agent: Paradigm - Los Angeles, 310/277-4400

RETURN TO HORROR HIGH   New World, 1987,
   w/Dana Escalanta & Bill Froehlich

SHELLEY P. LIST*
Agent: CAA - Beverly Hills, 310/288-4545

Screenplays:
DELANCEY STREET w/Jonathan Estrin
AMNESTY INTERNATIONAL (CTF) w/Jonathan Estrin

ROBERT LITTELL
Agent: Annette Van Duren Agency - Los Angeles, 213/650-3643

THE AMATEUR   20th Century-Fox, 1982, w/Diana Maddox

Screenplays:
OUCH!
BUZZING OFF

ROBERT JAY LITZ*
Contact: Seth D. Gelblum, Frankfurt, Garbus, Klein & Selz -
   New York, 212/826-5534
Address: 325 E. 12th St. - Suite 4F, New York, NY 10003,
   212/260-2601

RAPPIN'   Cannon, 1985, w/Adam Friedman
HOUSE OF CARDS   Miramax, 1993, Story w/Michael Lessac

Screenplays:
IMPOSSIBLE FROM HERE

JERRY LIU
PING PONG   Samuel Goldwyn Company, 1987

HAROLD LIVINGSTON*
Contact: WGA - New York, 212/245-6180

THE HELL WITH HEROS   Universal, 1968, w/Halstead Welles
STAR TREK - THE MOTION PICTURE   Paramount, 1979

JENNIE LIVINGSTON
Agent: William Morris Agency - Beverly Hills, 310/274-7451

PARIS IS BURNING (FD)   Prestige, 1991, directed

Screenplays:
NOT FOR PROFIT (directing)

KIMBALL LIVINGSTON*
Contact: WGA - Los Angeles, 310/550-1000

WIND   TriStar, 1992, Story w/Jeff Benjamin & Roger Vaughn

DANIEL W. LJOKA*
Contact: 213/655-7416

THE ARRIVAL   Del Mar Entertainment, 1990

Screenplays:
FIND AMANDA A HUSBAND

JEREMY LLOYD
VAMPIRA   Columbia, 1974
THE BAWDY ADVENTURES OF TOM JONES   Universal, 1975
ARE YOU BEING SERVED?   EMI, 1977, w/David Croft

Screenplays:
MY PET HUSBAND   w/Coslough Johnson

MICHAEL LLOYD
LOVELINES   Tri-Star, 1984, Story w/Chip Hand & William Hillman

KENNETH LOACH
Agent: Judy Daish Agency - London, 071/486-5405

POOR COW   Anglo Amalgamated, 1967, w/Nell Dunn, directed
KES   United Artists, 1970, w/Tony Garnet & Barry Hines, directed

ROBERT LoCASH*
Agent: United Talent Agency - Beverly Hills, 310/273-6700

CB4   Universal, 1993, w/Nelson George & Chris Rock
NAKED GUN 33 1/3: THE FINAL INSULT   Paramount, 1994,
   w/Pat Proft & David Zucker

Screenplays:
CROCKETT
BECAUSE WE'RE YOUNG
BONUS BABY
TOMMY HOLIDAY STORY

RICHARD S. LOCHTE*
Contact: WGA - Los Angeles, 310/550-1000

ESCAPE TO ATHENA   ITC, 1979, w/Edward Anhalt

JOSEPH LOEB III*
Agent: CAA - Beverly Hills, 310/288-4545

TEEN WOLF   Atlantic Releasing Corporation, 1985,
   w/Matthew Weisman
COMMANDO   20th Century Fox, 1985, Story w/Steven deSouza &
   Matthew Weisman
TEEN WOLF TOO   Atlantic Releasing Corporaiton, 1987,
   Story w/Matthew Weisman
BURGLAR   Warner Bros., 1987, w/Matthew Weisman &
   Hugh Wilson

Screenplays:
INSPECTOR DAD   w/Matthew Weisman
ACCIDENTS WILL HAPPEN   w/Matthew Weisman
SILENT PARTNERS   w/Matthew Weisman
NIGHTTIME GUY   w/Matthew Weisman
VALLEY GIRL II

JIM LOEW
DELIRIUM   Odyssey Pictures, 1980, Story w/Eddie Krell

RANDY LOFFICIER
Contact: Starwatcher Graphics - 213/467-0121

Screenplays:
MOEBIUS' AIRTIGHT GARAGE (AF)

NORMAN LOFTIS
SMALL TIME   Panorama Entertainment, 1990, directed

ROBERT LOGAN*
Agent: Elliot Wax & Associates - Los Angeles, 310/273-8217

REPOSSESSED   7 Arts/New Line Cinema, 1990, directed
MEATBALLS 4   Moviestore Entertainment, 1992, directed

Screenplays:
F-TROOP (directing)
STRINGERS (directing)

JEFFREY J. LoGROSSO
Agent: Renaissance-H.N. Swanson - Los Angeles, 310/246-6000

Screenplays:
WHITE HOUSE PARTY   w/Joseph B. Bellissimo

CHRISTOPHER LOGUE
Address: c/o Private Eye, 6 Carlisle St., London W1V 5RG,
   071/437-4017, fax 437-0705

SAVAGE MESSIAH   MGM, 1972
CRUSOE   Island Pictures, 1988, w/Walon Green

ULLI LOMMEL
Business: Horizons Productions, 1134 N. Ogden Drive,
   West Hollywood, CA 90046, 213/654-6911

A TASTE OF SIN   Ambassador, 1983, w/John P. Marsh &
   Ron Norman, directed
BRAINWAVES   MPM, 1983, directed
THE DEVONSVILLE TERROR   MPM, 1983, w/George T. Lindsey &
   Suzanna Love, directed
WARBIRDS   Vidmark Entertainment, 1989,
   w/Clifford B. Wellman, directed

BRITT LOMOND
SWORDS OF HEAVEN   Trans World Entertainment, 1985,
   w/James Bruner, William P. O'Hagan & Joseph Randazzo

RICHARD LONCRAINE
Agent: Broder-Kurland-Webb-Uffner - Beverly Hills, 310/281-3400
Address: 223 Westbourne Grove, London W11 2SE, England,
   071/221-5380

BELLMAN AND TRUE   Island Pictures, 1987,
   w/Desmond Lowden & Michael Wearing

R.M. LONDON
DRIVING ME CRAZY   Motion Picture Corporation of America, 1991,
   w/David Tausik & Jon Turteltaub

ROBBY LONDON*
Contact: 818/995-3800

PINOCCHIO AND THE EMPEROR OF THE NIGHT (AF)
   New World, 1987, w/Barry O'Brien & Dennis O'Flaherty
HAPPILY EVER AFTER   First National Film Corporation, 1993,
   w/Martha Moran

JOAN LONG
THE PICTURE SHOW MAN   Roadshow Distributors, 1977
CADDIE   Atlantic Releasing Corporation, 1981

HARRY S. LONGSTREET*
Agent: The Coppage Company - North Hollywood, 818/980-1106

SEX, LOVE AND COLD HARD CASH (CTF)   Citadel Pictures/MCA
   Television Entertainment, 1993, directed

Screenplays:
A VOW TO KILL (CTF)   w/Renee Longstreet (directing)

RENEE LONGSTREET*
Agent: The Coppage Company - North Hollywood, 818/980-1106

Screenplays:
A VOW TO KILL (CTF) w/Harry Longstreet

LISA LOOMER*
Agent: Paradigm - Los Angeles, 310/277-4400

¡BOC´ØN! (P)
LOOKING FOR ANGELS (P)
CUTS (P)
CHAIN OF LIFE (P)
BIRDS (P)
ACCELERANDO (P)
THE WAITING ROOM (P)

Screenplays:
JUST DESSERTS

MARTIN LOPEZ
MUTANT ON THE BOUNTY   Skouras Pictures, 1989

TEMISTOCOLES LOPEZ
Contact: Cineville, 310/315-5340

EXQUISITE CORPSES   ASA Communicatios, 1988, directed
CHAIN OF DESIRE   October Films, 1993, directed

Screenplays:
ONE THOUSAND DAYS OF PASSION (directing)

STEPHEN LORD*
Agent: Shapiro/Lichtman - Los Angeles, 310/859-8877

BEYOND AND BACK   Sunn Classic, 1978
THE BERMUDA TRIANGLE   Sunn Classic, 1979

LIDDY LOREE
Agent: Warden, White & Kane - Beverly Hills, 213/852-1028

Screenplays:
ANIMAL ATTRACTION w/Jackie Rabinowtiz
THE BRIDE OF FRANK w/Jackie Rabinowitz
BUSYBODIES w/Jackie Rabinowitz

DEAN LOREY*
Agent: ICM - Beverly Hills, 310/550-4000

MY BOYFRIEND'S BACK   Buena Vista, 1993
JASON GOES TO HELL: THE FINAL FRIDAY   New Line Cinema,
   1993, w/Jay Huguely
MAJOR PAYNE   Universal, 1995, w/Gary Rosen & Damon Wayans

Screenplays:
THEY
THE MOVE

ALEC LORIMORE*
Agent: Peter Turner Agency - Santa Monica, 310/315-4772

Screenplays:
FIVE CAR STUD w/Terry Winkless
SEQUENCE w/Terry Winkless
FAST LANE w/Terry Winkless
OUT OF THE BOX w/Terry Winkless
TOO GOOD TO BE TRUE w/Terry Winkless
THE GREAT CAPE GIRARDEAU LEAP w/Terry Winkless
WASHINGTON PAGES w/Terry Winkless
THE JETSONS w/Terry Winkless
VODONE w/Terry Winkless
THE RUNNER w/Terry Winkless
PARTNERS IN TIME w/Terry Winkless

JAMES LORINZ
ME AND THE MOB   Arrow Releasing, 1994, w/Frank Rainone &
   Rocco Simonelle

PATRICIA LOSEY
STEAMING   New World, 1984

EMIL LOTEANU
Contact: Union of Soviet Filmmakers, Vassilievskaya 13, Moscow,
   U.S.S.R., tel.: 250-4114

THE SHOOTING PARTY   Mosfilm, 1978, directed

EB LOTTIMER
Agent: Premiere Artists - Los Angeles, 310/271-1414

LOVE MATTERS (CTF)   Chanticleer Productions, 1993,
   w/Evan Katz, directed

Screenplays:
DIVORCE: A CONTEMPORARY WESTERN

DAVID LOUCKA*
Agent: United Talent Agency - Beverly Hills, 310/273-6700

THE DREAM TEAM   Universal, 1989, w/Jon Connolly

Screenplays:
MINIMUM SECURITY w/Jon Connolly
BIG SHOTS w/Jon Connolly
LITTLE LEAGUE CONFIDENTIAL w/Jon Connolly
INTO THE HEART w/Jon Connolly
PALS FOREVER w/Jon Connolly
THE OTHER WOMAN w/Jon Connolly
LENNIE'S HEART w/Jon Connolly
SINGLE AGAIN w/Jon Connolly
THE TRUTH w/Jon Connolly
THEY'VE LANDED w/Jon Connolly
A GOOD MAN w/Jon Connolly
SPY VS. SPY w/Steve Dunn
HIGH FIDELITY w/Steve Dunn
BLOW AWAY w/Mark Kram & Dean Selmier
JOEY FAMOUS w/Mark Kram
THE DREAM CASE w/Mark Kram
WEEKEND WARRIORS w/Mark Kram
"M" w/Ted Gershuny
THE ASSOCIATE (Shared)
AMEROSA PLACE (Shared)
BEVERLY HILLS NINJA (Shared)
VALENTINE
12 BAR BLUES

DAVID LOUGHERY*
Agent: United Talent Agency - Beverly Hills, 310/273-6700

DREAMSCAPE   20th Century-Fox, 1984, w/Joe Ruben &
   Chuck Russell
STAR TREK V: THE FINAL FRONTIER   Paramount, 1989
FLASHBACK   Paramount, 1990
PASSENGER 57   Warner Bros., 1992, w/Dan Gordon
THE THREE MUSKETEERS   Buena Vista, 1993

Screenplays:
CABIN FEVER
THE MAN WITH NINE LIVES
NIGHT ON THE TOWN
MAD MISS MANTON
SON OF A GUN

ERIC LOUZIL
CLASS OF NUKE E'M HIGH PART 2: SUBHUMANOID MELTDOWN
   Troma, 1991, w/Lloyd Kaufman, Carl Morano, Marcus Rolling,
   Jeffrey W. Sass & Matt Unger, directed

Screenplays:
LUKAS' CHILD (directing)

MICHAEL JAMES LOVE*
Agent: The Gersh Agency - Beverly Hills, 310/274-6611

GABY - A TRUE STORY   Tri-Star, 1987, w/Martin Salinas

Screenplays:
HEIR NOT APPARENT w/Martin Salinas
FLY AWAY HOME w/Martin Salinas

CHARLES LOVENTHAL*
Contact: WGA - Los Angeles, 310/550-1000

HOME MOVIES   United Artists Classics, 1980, w/others
THE FIRST TIME   New Line Cinema, 1982,
    w/Susan Wieser-Finley & W. Franklin Finley, directed
HIGHER EDUCATION   Sicom Productions, 1987

Screenplays:
STAR SCHOOL (directing)
THE REAL WORLD

ED LOVER
WHO'S THE MAN?   New Line Cinema, 1993, Story w/Dr. Dre &
    Seth Greenland

BERT LOVITT
PRINCE JACK   Castle Hill Productions, 1984, directed

ROBERT LOVY
CIRCUITRY MAN   Skouras Pictures, 1990, w/Steven Lovy

Screenplays:
CIRCUITRY MAN II: PRINCE OF PLUGS w/Steven Lovy (IRS)

STEVEN LOVY
CIRCUITRY MAN   Skouras Pictures, 1990, w/Robert Lovy, directed

Screenplays:
*CIRCUITRY MAN II: PRINCE OF PLUGS w/Robert Lovy
    (IRS, directing)*

DESMOND LOWDEN
Agent: Lemon, Unna & Durbridge - London, 071/727-1346

BELLMAN AND TRUE   Island Pictures, 1987,
    w/Richard Loncraine & Michael Wearing

RICHARD LOWENSTEIN
Agent: Cameron Creswell Agency - Sydney, Australia,
    tel.: 02/356-4677

STRIKEBOUND   TRM Productions, 1985, directed
DOGS IN SPACE   Skouras Pictures, 1987, directed

Screenplays:
SAY A LITTLE PRAYER (directing)

WOLF LOWENTHAL
COMIN' AT YA!   Filmways, 1981, w/Lloyd Battista & Eugen
    Quintano

CRAIG LUCAS*
Agent: William Morris Agency - New York, 212/586-5100

THREE POSTCARDS (P)
BLUE WINDOW (P) also screenplay
MARRY ME A LITTLE (P)
THE DYING GAUL (P)
LONGTIME COMPANION   Samuel Goldwyn Company, 1990
PRELUDE TO A KISS   20th Century Fox, 1992, from his play
RECKLESS   Samuel Golwyn, 1995, from his play

Screenplays:
SAINT MAYBE
THE SECRET LIVES OF DENTISTS

GEORGE LUCAS
Business: Lucasfilm Ltd., P.O. Box 668, San Anselmo, CA 94960

THX 1138   Warner Bros., 1971, w/Walter Murch, directed
AMERICAN GRAFFITI ★   Universal, 1973, w/Willard Huyck &
    Gloria Katz, directed
STAR WARS ★   20th Century-Fox, 1977, directed
RAIDERS OF THE LOST ARK   Paramount, 1981,
    Story w/Philip Kaufman
RETURN OF THE JEDI   20th Century-Fox, 1983,
    w/Lawrence Kasdan
INDIANA JONES AND THE TEMPLE OF DOOM   Paramount,
    1984, Story
WILLOW   MGM/UA, 1988, Story
INDIANA JONES AND THE LAST CRUSADE   Paramount, 1989,
    Story w/Menno Meyjes
RADIOLAND MURDERS   Universal, 1994, Story

WILLIAM LUCE*
Agent: William Morris Agency - Beverly Hills, 310/274-7451

Screenplays:
THE PROPHET
CURRER BELL, ESQ.

COLEMAN LUCK*
Agent: Major Clients Agency - Los Angeles, 310/284-6400

Screenplays:
ESCAPE FROM L.A.

MICHAEL LUCKER
Agent: Richland/Wunsch/Hohman Agency - Los Angeles,
    310/278-1955

Screenplays:
THE BOO BROTHERS w/Chris Parker
LITTLE OUTLAWS w/Chris Parker
REPEAT OFFENDER w/Chris Parker

JERRY LUDWIG*
Agent: Richland/Wunsch/Hohman Agency - Los Angeles,
    310/278-1955

DEADLY DESIRE (CTF)   Skylark Films/Wilshire Court
    Productions, 1991

TOBY LUDWIG
DEADLY DESIRE (CTF)   Skylark Films/Wilshire Court Productions,
    1991, Story w/Jerry Ludwig

KURT LUEDTKE*
Agent: CAA - Beverly Hills, 310/288-4545

ABSENCE OF MALICE ★   Columbia, 1981
OUT OF AFRICA ★★   Universal, 1985

Screenplays:
THE DISTANT SHORE
HEARTS
WALLS
SILENCE WILL SPEAK

BUZ LUHRMANN
Agent: ICM - Beverly Hills, 310/550-4000

STRICTLY BALLROOM   Miramax, 1992,
    w/Craig Pearce, directed

Screenplays:
ROMEO AND JULIET w/Craig Pearce (directing)

F
I
L
M

W
R
I
T
E
R
S

Lu

FILM
WRITERS

STEVE LuKANIC
Contact: Josh Grode, Christiansen, White, Miller, Fink & Jacobs -
    Los Angeles, 310/553-3000

Screenplays:
THE NARROW ROAD w/Jana Howington
MIRROR RORRIM w/Jana Howington
FULL COUNT w/Jana Howington

ERIC LUKE*
Agent: Sanford-Gross & Associates - Los Angeles,
    310/208-2100

EXPLORERS   Paramount, 1985
STILL NOT QUITE HUMAN (CTF)   Resnick-Margellos Productions,
    1992, directed

Screenplays:
WEATHERMAN
ATTACK FROM OUTER SPACE
NIGHTMARE
HARRY
THE JETSONS
THE WITCH   THE GUESTS

SIDNEY LUMET*
Agent: ICM - Beverly Hills, 310/550-4000

PRINCE OF THE CITY ★   Orion/Warner Bros., 1981,
    w/Jay Presson Allen, directed
Q & A   Tri-Star, 1990, directed

Screenplays:
NIGHT FALLS ON MANHATTAN

STEPHANIE LUNA
Agent: Berzon Agency - Glendale, 818/548-1560

Screenplays:
PROBABLE LOGIC

ZOE LUND
Contact: Screen Actors Guild - Los Angeles, 213/954-1600

BAD LIEUTENANT   Aries, 1992, w/Abel Ferrara

STEVEN LUOTTO
IRON WARRIOR   Tri-Star, 1987, w/Al Bradley

TONY LURASCHI
THE OUTSIDER   Paramount, 1980, directed

STEVE LUSTGARTEN
AMERICAN TABOO   Lustgarten Entertainment Organization,
    1991, directed

JOHN LUTZ
Agent: Pleshette & Green - Los Angeles, 213/465-0428

Screenplays:
THE EX (American World/Cinetel)

DAVID LUX
Agent: Renaissance-H.N. Swanson - Los Angeles, 310/246-6000

Screenplays:
SKINWALKER w/Chris Mollo

KEVIN LYGO
Contact: 071/937-1719

Screenplays:
HAM ON RYE w/Cyril Humphries

LESLIE LYLES
ME AND VERONICA   True One/True Pictures, 1992

BRAD LYNCH
MR. FROST   Triumph, 1990, w/Philippe Setbon

DAVID LYNCH*
Agent: CAA - Beverly Hills, 310/288-4545

ERASERHEAD   Libra, 1978, directed
THE ELEPHANT MAN ★   Paramount, 1980, w/Eric Bergren &
    Christopher DeVore, directed
DUNE   Universal, 1984, directed
BLUE VELVET   DEG, 1986, directed
WILD AT HEART   Samuel Goldwyn Company, 1990, directed
TWIN PEAKS: FIRE WALK WITH ME   New Line Cinema, 1992,
    w/Robert Engels, directed

Screenplays:
MULHOLLAND DRIVE   (CIBY 2000, directing)
THE DREAM OF THE BOVINE
ONE SALIVA BUBBLE w/Mark Frost
RONNIE ROCKET

GREGORY LYNCH
Agent: Berzon Agency - Glendale, 818/548-1560

Screenplays:
THE OLD COUNTRY
PSYCHIC NEWS

JENNIFER CHAMBERS LYNCH
Agent: CAA - Beverly Hills, 310/288-4545
Manager: Atlas Entertainment - Los Angeles, 213/658-9100

BOXING HELENA   Orion, 1993, directed

MARTIN LYNCH
A PRAYER FOR THE DYING   Samuel Goldwyn Company, 1987,
    w/Edmund Ward

CAROL LYNN
CLICK: THE CALENDAR GIRL KILLER   Crown International, 1991,
    Story w/John Stewart

JONATHAN LYNN*
Agent: ICM - Beverly Hills, 310/550-4000

GINGERBREAD MAN (P)
ARMS & THE MAN (P)
TONIGHT AT 8:30 (P)
SONGBOOK (P)
PASS THE BUTLER (P)
HOTEL PARADISE (P)
MICK'S PEOPLE (Short)
THE INTERNECINE PROJECT   Allied Artists, 1974,
    w/Barry Levinson
CLUE   Paramount, 1985, directed
NUNS ON THE RUN   20th Century Fox, 1990, directed

Screenplays:
LAND OF OPPORTUNITY w/Jack Kaplan
ROCKITS
BIG DEAL

ROBIN LYONS
THE PRINCESS AND THE GOBLIN (AF)   Hemdale, 1994

ALEV LYTLE
TELL ME A RIDDLE   Filmways, 1980, w/Joyce Eliason

SHEL LYTTON
BODY SLAM   DEG, 1987, w/Steve Burkow

M

DICK MAAS
Agent: William Morris Agency - Beverly Hills, 310/274-7451
Business: First Floor Features, P.O. Box 53221, 1007 RE
 Amsterdam, Netherlands, tel.: 20/664-7471

THE LIFT   Island Alive/Media Home Entertainment,
 1983, directed
FLODDER   Concorde Films, 1986, directed
AMSTERDAMNED   Vestron, 1987, directed

JOHN MAASS
Agent: United Talent Agency - Beverly Hills, 310/273-6700

CURDLED (Short)   1994, w/Reb Braddock, co-directed,
 also screenplay

BILL MACCHI*
Contact: 201/324-0130

Screenplays:
CLICK

SIMON MacCORKINDALE
Contact: Screen Actors Guild - Los Angeles, 213/954-1600

THAT SUMMER OF WHITE ROSES   Amy International/Jadran Film,
 1989, w/Rajko Grlic & Borislav Pekic

GERALD MacDONALD
MARILYN & BOBBY: HER FINAL AFFAIR (CTF)   Barry Weitz/
 The Auerbach Co., 1993

GERARD MacDONALD
THE LIFEFORCE EXPERIMENT (CTF)   Lillian Gallo Entertainment,
 1994, w/Mike Hodges

EDUARDO MACHADO*
Agent: ICM - Beverly Hills, 310/550-4000

MODERN LADIES OF GUANABACOA (P)
BROKEN EGGS (P)
SECOND GENERATION (P)
FABIOLA (P)
WHEN IT'S OVER (P)   w/Geraldine Sherman
WHY TO REFUSE (P)
ONCE REMOVED (P)
DON JUAN IN NEW YORK (P)
BURNING BEACH (P)
STEVIE WANTS TO PLAY THE BLUES (P)
FLOATING ISLANDS (P)

Screenplays:
CHINA RIOS (CTF)
FIELDER'S CHOICE

PETER M. MacKENZIE
Contact: Robert Zipser, 2121 Ave. of the Stars - Suite 1700,
 Los Angeles, CA 90067, 310/203-8600

MISSION MANILA   Overseas Filmgroup, 1988, directed
MERCHANTS OF WAR   Triax Entertainment, 1988,
 w/Asher Brauner & Eric Weston, directed

Screenplays:
SOUTH OF MEMPHIS

THE HAWK'S EYE
MACHINE MAN
GRAND CRU

GILLIES MacKINNON
Agent: ICM - Beverly Hills, 310/550-4000

Screenplays:
EASTERHOUSE w/Bill MacKinnon (directing)

BERNARD MacLAVERTY
Agent: Lemon Unna & Durbridge - London, 071/727-1346

CAL   Warner Bros., 1984
LAMB   Film Forum, 1986
HOSTAGES (CTF)   HBO Showcase/Granada Film, 1993

ALISON MacLEAN
Agent: William Morris Agency - Beverly Hills, 310/274-7451

KITCHEN SINK (Short)   1989, directed
CRUSH   Strand Releasing, 1992, w/Anne Kennedy, directed

ALISTAIR MacLEAN
WHERE EAGLES DARE   MGM, 1969
WHEN EIGHT BELLS TOLL   Winkast, 1971
PUPPET ON A CHAIN   Cinerama Releasing Company, 1972,
 w/Don Sharp & Paul Wheeler
BREAKHEART PASS   United Artists, 1976

STEPHEN J. MacLEAN
STARSTRUCK   Cinecom International, 1982
AROUND THE WORLD IN 80 WAYS   Alive Films, 1987,
 w/Paul Leadon, directed

Screenplays:
THE TROPICS

ANDREW MacLEAR
DEALERS   Skouras Pictures, 1989

COLIN MacLEOD
DRIVE   Megagiant Entertainment, 1992,
 in collaboration w/Jefery Levy

MATT MacMANUS*
Contact: WGA - Los Angeles, 310/550-1000

FLIGHT OF THE NAVIGATOR   Buena Vista, 1986,
 w/Michael Burton

DON MacPHERSON
Agent: Casaratto Company - London, 071/287-4450

ABSOLUTE BEGINNERS   Orion, 1986, w/Richard Burridge &
 Christopher Wicking
CROSSING THE LINE   Miramax, 1992

Screenplays:
CRIMINAL CONVERSATIONS
THE AVENGERS
JONATHAN WILD
A TALE OF TWO CITIES
FRANKENSTEIN
DARK ANGEL

MALCOLM MacRURY
Agent: Lisa Callamaro Literary Agency- Beverly Hills, 310/274-6783

THE MAN WITHOUT A FACE   Warner Bros., 1993
HARVEST FOR THE HEART (CTF)   Atlantis Films, 1994

W.H. MACY*
Contact: WGA - New York, 212/245-6180

ABOVE SUSPICION (CTF)   Rysher, 1994, w/Jerry Lazarus &
   Steven Schachter

DAVID MADDEN
Business: Interscope Communications, 10900 Wilshire Blvd. -
   Suite 1400, Los Angeles, CA 90024, 310/208-8525

A PART OF THE FAMILY (CTF)   Interscope, 1994, directed

GUY MADDIN
Contact: Academy of Canadian Cinema & Television, 753 Yonge St. -
   2nd Floor, Toronto M4Y 1Z9, Canada, 416/967-0315

TALES FROM THE GIMLI HOSPITAL   1988, directed
ARCHANGEL   Zeitgeist Films Ltd., 1991,
   w/George Toles, directed

BRENT MADDOCK*
Manager: The Roberts Company - Los Angeles, 310/552-7800

SHORT CIRCUIT   Tri-Star, 1986, w/S.S. Wilson
BATTERIES NOT INCLUDED   Universal, 1986, w/Brad Bird,
   Matthew Robbins & S.S. Wilson
SHORT CIRCUIT II   Tri-Star, 1988, w/S.S. Wilson
TREMORS   Universal, 1990, w/S.S. Wilson
GHOST DAD   Universal, 1990, w/S.S. Wilson & Chris Reese
HEART AND SOULS   Universal, 1993, w/S.S. Wilson,
   Erik Hansen & Greg Hansen

Screenplays:
LINES OF FORCE w/S.S. Wilson

DIANA MADDOX*
Agent: Larry Grossman & Associates - Beverly Hills, 310/550-8127

THE CHANGELING   AFD, 1980, w/William Gray
THE AMATEUR   20th Century-Fox, 1982, w/Robert Littell

MARC MADNICK
Agent: The Artists Group - Los Angeles, 310/552-1100

Screenplays:
LIBERTY SMITH w/Eric Cohen

DAVID MADSEN*
Agent: Renaissance-H.N. Swanson - Los Angeles, 310/246-6000

Screenplays:
COPY CAT
THE RED CAR (Shared)
SANTERIA (Shared)
THE SOLID GOLD ALAMO (Shared)
BORROWED TIME (Shared)

STEVEN MAEDA
Agent: APA - Los Angeles, 310/273-0744

Screenplays:
SANDBLAST

GUY MAGAR
Contact: Directors Guild of America - Los Angeles, 310/289-2000
Business: Magar Films, 3518 Cahuenga Blvd. West - Suite 307,
   Los Angeles, CA 90068, 213/436-0344

RETRIBUTION   Taurus Entertainment, 1988, w/Lee Wasserman
STEPFATHER III (CTF)   ITC Entertainment, 1992,
   w/Marc B. Ray, directed
LOOKIN' ITALIAN   Showcase Entertainment, 1994, directed

ALLAN MAGEE
Contact: Academy of Canadian Cinema & Television, 753 Yonge St. -
   2nd Floor, Toronto M4Y 1Z9, Canada, 416/967-0315

HIGHWAY 61   Skouras Pictures, 1992, Story w/Bruce McDonald &
   Don McKellar

DOUG MAGEE*
Agent: Sanford-Gross & Associates - Los Angeles,
   310/208-2100

SOMEBODY HAS TO SHOOT THE PICTURE (CTF)   Alan Barnette
   Productions, 1990

RON MAGID
Agent: Susan Smith & Associates - Beverly Hills, 213/852-4777

Screenplays:
THE MANAGER w/Paul Clemens

MARK MAGILL
WAITING FOR THE MOON   Skouras Pictures, 1987

Screenplays:
FAITH & CREDIT

ALBERT MAGNOLI*
Business Manager: Ernest & Young - Los Angeles, 310/551-5500

PURPLE RAIN   Warner Bros., 1984, w/William Blinn, directed

JEFFREY P. MAGUIRE*
Agent: United Talent Agency - Beverly Hills, 310/273-6700

VAMPIRE LUST   Demos Films, 1975, w/Djordje Milicevic
RECKLESS   Can-America Productions, 1979, w/Djordje Milicevic
VICTORY   Lorimar/Paramount, 1981, Story w/Djordje Milicevic
TOBY MCTEAGUE   Spectrafilm, 1986, w/Jamie Brown &
   Djordje Milicevic
IN THE LINE OF FIRE ★   Columbia, 1993

Screenplays:
GRIDIRON GANG (Columbia)
ENDURANCE
LAST KISS w/Djordje Millicevic

ROBERT MAGUIRE
Agent: Warden, White & Kane - Beverly Hills, 213/852-1028

Screenplays:
A KISS IN THE STARLIGHT

DEZSO MAGYAR*
Home: 864 Harvard St., Santa Monica, CA 90403, 310/450-4247

OFF BEAT   Buena Vista, 1986, Story
STREETS OF GOLD   20th Century Fox, 1986, Story
NO SECRETS   I.R.S. Releasing, 1991, w/Ken Selden, directed

ANTHONY MAHARJ
CROSS FIRE   Silvertree Pictures, 1989, w/Noah Blough, directed
FUTURE HUNTERS   Lightning Pictures, 1989, Story

Screenplays:
RAGE (directing)

MIKE MAHERN*
(Anthony M. Mahern)
Agent: United Talent Agency - Beverly Hills, 310/273-6700

MOBSTERS   Universal, 1991, w/Nick Kazan

Screenplays:
THE HEIRESS
PREY

INSIDE THE BELTWAY
TRUST
FREEDOM SUMMER
JUSTICE

KEVIN A. MAHONEY*
Contact: WGA - Los Angeles, 310/550-1000

SORORITY QUEEN IN A MOBILE HOME (P)
PAPER PLATES (P)
FOUR STARS (P)
SHORT WAVE (P)
TOM AT NIGHT (P)
ALL ABOUT STEVE (P)
ONE FOR THE MONEY (P)
FADED HOME (P)
THANK YOU, GOODNIGHT (P)
THE INITIATE (P)
PUBLISHED BY GROVE PRESS (P)

Screenplays:
ONE LUCKY GIRL
CLAYTON
A LA CARTE

WILLIAM MAI*
Contact: Shelly Surpin - Los Angeles, 213/552-188

THE LIGHTSHIP   Castle Hill Productions, 1986, w/David C. Taylor

NORMAN MAILER*
Agent: ICM - Beverly Hills, 310/550-4000

WILD 90   Supreme Mix, 1968, directed
BEYOND THE LAW   Grove Press, 1968, directed
MAIDSTONE   Supreme Mix, 1971, directed
TOUGH GUYS DON'T DANCE   Cannon, 1985, directed

Screenplays:
HAVANA

STUART MAIN
Contact: New Zealand Film Commission, 36 Allen St., Wellington,
   New Zealand, tel.: 4/859-754

DESPERATE REMEDIES   Miramax, 1993,
   w/Peter Wells, co-directed

DUSAN MAKAVEJEV
Contact: Institut za Film, CikaLjubina 15/11, 1100 Belgrade,
   Yugoslavia 38, tel. 11/62-51-31

MAN IS NOT A BIRD   Grove Press, 1965, directed
LOVE AFFAIR: OR THE CASE OF THE MISSING SWITCHBOARD
   OPERATOR   Brandon, 1966, directed
INNOCENCE UNPROTECTED   Grove Press, 1968, directed
WR - MYSTERIES OF THE ORGANISM   Cinema 5, 1971, directed
SWEET MOVIE   Biograph, 1975, directed
MONTENEGRO   *MONTENEGRO, OR PIGS AND PEARLS*
   Atlantic Releasing Corporation, 1981, directed
MANIFESTO   Cannon, 1989, directed
GORILLA BATHES AT NOON   Alert Film, 1993, directed

BOB MAKELA*
Contact: WGA - Los Angeles, 310/550-1000

Screenplays:
ADVENTURES IN BACHELORHOOD

ANNE MAKEPEACE*
Agent: Preferred Artists - Encino, 818/990-0305

WILDEST DREAMS (Short)   1990, directed
THOUSAND PIECES OF GOLD   American Playhouse, 1991
ISHI: THE LAST YAHI (FD)   Rattlesnake Productions, 1992
NIGHT DRIVING (Short)   Chanticleer Films, 1993, directed

TERRENCE MALICK*
Business Manager: Henry Bamberger - Los Angeles, 310/446-2780

SANSHO THE BAILIFF (P)
DEADHEAD MILES   Paramount, 1971
POCKET MONEY   National General, 1972
BADLANDS   Warner Bros., 1974, directed
GRAVY TRAIN   *THE DION BROTHERS*   Columbia, 1974
DAYS OF HEAVEN   Paramount, 1978, directed

Screenplays:
THE ENGLISH-SPEAKER   *(directing)*
THE MOVIEGOER
COUNTRYMAN
THE JERRY LEE LEWIS PROJECT
THE THIN RED LINE   *(directing)*
Q   THE BEGINNING OF THE WORLD
HUNGRY HEART
DESERT ROSE

GREGORY MALINS
Agent: ICM - Beverly Hills, 310/550-4000

...AND GOD SPOKE   LIVE Entertainment, 1994, w/Michael Curtis

GEORGE MALKO*
Agent: Paradigm - Los Angeles, 310/277-4400

THE DOGS OF WAR   United Artists, 1981, w/Gary M. DeVore
SWEET LORRAINE   Angelika Films, 1987, Story w/Shelly Altman,
   Steve Gomer & Michael Zettler
OUT COLD   Hemdale, 1989, w/Howard Glasser

Screenplays:
SLOW BURN
KISS OFF
SOB SISTERS   w/Anthony Fingleton
ROGUE FROM MOTOR CITY

LOUIS MALLE*
Agent: ICM - New York, 212/556-5600
Business Manager: Gelfand, Rennert & Feldman - 212/682-0234

FRANTIC   *ASCENSEUR POUR L'ECHAFAUD/ELEVATOR TO
   THE GALLOWS/LIFT TO THE SCAFFOLD*   Times, 1957,
   w/Roger Nimier, directed
THE LOVERS   Zenith International, 1958, directed
ZAZIE   *ZAZIE DANS DE METRO*   Astor, 1960,
   w/Jean-Paul Rappeneu, directed
THE FIRE WITHIN (LE FEU FOLLET)   Governor, 1963, directed
VIVA MARIA!   United Artists, 1965,
   w/Jean-Claude Carriere, directed
MURMUR OF THE HEART   *LE SOUFFLE AU COEUR* ★
   Palomar, 1972, directed
LACOMBE LUCIEN   20th Century-Fox, 1974, directed
BLACK MOON   20th Century-Fox, 1975, directed
AU REVOIR, LES ENFANTS ★   Orion Classics, 1987, directed
MAY FOOLS   Orion Classics, 1990,
   w/Jean-Claude Carriere, directed

BRUCE MALMUTH*
Agent: Becsey/Wisdom/Kalajian Agency - Los Angeles, 310/550-0535

Screenplays:
MAMA'S BOY
JUDGMENT DAY

RENE MALO
Business: The Image Organization, 9000 Sunset Blvd. - Suite 915,
   Los Angeles, CA 90069, 310/278-8751

SCANNERS III: THE TAKEOVER   Republic Pictures, 1992,
   w/B.J. Nelson, David Preston & Julie Richard

MARK MALONE*
Agent: ICM - Beverly Hills, 310/550-4000

SENSE OF LOSS (P)
THE ART OF CONVERSATION (P)
DEAD OF WINTER   MGM/UA, 1987, w/Marc Shmuger
SIGNS OF LIFE   Avenue Pictures, 1989
BULLET PROOF HEARTS   *KILLER*   InterCoast Pictures, 1994,
   Story, directed

Screenplays:
WASPS
HOOD
THE WRIGHT BROS. FLYERS

WILLIAM MALONE
CREATURE   Cardinal Releasing, 1985, w/Allan Reed, directed

DAVID MAMET*
Agent: Rosenstone/Wender - New York, 212/832-8330

AMERICAN BUFFALO (P)
EDMOND (P)   also screenplay
REUNION (P)
DARK PONY (P)
SEXUAL PERVERSITY IN CHICAGO (P)
THE DUCK VARIATIONS (P)
THE SHAWL (P)
PRAIRIE DU CHIEN (P)
MR. HAPPINESS (P)
THE WOODS (P)
SPEED-THE-PLOW (P)
BOBBY GOULD IN HELL (P)
THE CRYPTOGRAM (P)
THE POSTMAN ALWAYS RINGS TWICE   Paramount, 1981
THE VERDICT ★   20th Century-Fox, 1982
THE UNTOUCHABLES   Paramount, 1987
HOUSE OF GAMES   Orion, 1987, directed
THINGS CHANGE   Columbia, 1988, w/Shel Silverstein, directed
WE'RE NO ANGELS   Paramount, 1989
HOMICIDE   Triumph, 1991, directed
THE WATER ENGINE (CTF)   TNT/Brandman Productions/
   Amblin Television, 1992, from his play
GLENGARRY GLEN ROSS   New Line Cinema,
   1992, from his play
HOFFA   20th Century Fox, 1992
A LIFE IN THE THEATER (CTF)   Brandman Productions/
   Amblin Television, 1993, from his play
TEXAN (Short)   Showtime/Chanticleer, 1994
OLEANNA   Samuel Goldwyn Company, 1994,
   from his play, directed
VANYA ON 42ND STREET   Sony Pictures Classics, 1994
LAKEBOAT   Freedman/Greene Productions, 1995, from his play

Screenplays:
HIGH AND LOW (remake)
CHARLIE CHAN
ACE IN THE HOLE
KINGDOM
STATE & MAIN
DEERSLAYER

LYNN MAMET*
Agent: Innovative Artists - Los Angeles, 310/553-5200

ON HOPE (Short)   Showtime/Chanticleer, 1994
LESLIE'S FOLLY (Short)   Showtime/Chanticleer, 1994

Screenplays:
BEHIND EVERY GOOD MAN

MILCO MANCHEVSKI
BEFORE THE RAIN   Gramercy, 1995, directed

DON MANCINI*
Agent: United Talent Agency - Beverly Hills, 310/273-6700

CHILD'S PLAY   MGM/UA, 1989, w/Tom Holland & John Lafia
CHILD'S PLAY 2   Universal, 1990
CHILD'S PLAY 3   Universal, 1991

Screenplays:
DOG WHO CRIED WOLF
GREEN HORNET

GREGG MANCUSO
Agent: Stephanie Mann Agency - Los Angeles, 213/653-7130

Screenplays:
SAVED BY THE SPELL
PAINTED INTO A CORNER

ALAN R. MANDEL*
Contact: WGA - Los Angeles, 310/550-1000

SMOKEY AND THE BANDIT   Universal, 1977,
   w/James Lee Barrett & Charles Shyer
HOUSE CALLS   Universal, 1978, w/Julius J. Epstein,
   Max Shulman & Charles Shyer
GOIN' SOUTH   Paramount, 1979, w/Al Ramrus,
   John Herman Shaner & Charles Shyer

Screenplays:
BREAKFAST ON BEDFORD DRIVE w/Charles Shyer
THE LONG RAINBOW w/Charles Shyer
BIG DEAL ON MACARTHUR BOULEVARD w/Charles Shyer
TICKETS w/Charles Shyer
LADIES DAY
MOTHER NATURE'S DAUGHTER
DOMESTIC RELATIONS
JAKE'S THING
JUST ONE OF THOSE THINGS
JOE COLLEGE

BABALOO MANDEL*
Agent: CAA - Beverly Hills, 310/288-4545

NIGHT SHIFT   The Ladd Company/Warner Bros., 1982,
   w/Bruce Jay Friedman & Lowell Ganz
SPLASH ★   Buena Vista, 1984, w/Bruce Jay Friedman &
   Lowell Ganz
SPIES LIKE US   Warner Bros., 1985, w/Dan Aykroyd &
   Lowell Ganz
GUNG HO   Paramount, 1986, w/Lowell Ganz
VIBES   Columbia, 1988, w/Lowell Ganz
PARENTHOOD   Universal, 1989, w/Lowell Ganz
CITY SLICKERS   Columbia, 1991, w/Lowell Ganz
A LEAGUE OF THEIR OWN   Columbia, 1992, w/Lowell Ganz
MR. SATURDAY NIGHT   Columbia, 1992, w/Lowell Ganz &
   Billy Crystal
GREEDY   Universal, 1994, w/Lowell Ganz
CITY SLICKERS II: THE LEGEND OF CURLY'S GOLD   Columbia,
   1994, w/Lowell Ganz & Billy Crystal
FORGET PARIS   Columbia, 1995, w/Lowell Ganz & Billy Crystal

Screenplays:
MULTIPLICITY w/Lowell Ganz
CRAZY w/Lowell Ganz
INTO THE WOODS w/Lowell Ganz
OVER MY DEAD BODY w/Lowell Ganz
DANCE SKINS w/Lowell Ganz
PERFECT COUPLE w/Lowell Ganz

GEOFFREY MANDEL
Agent: Gold/Marshak - Burbank, 818/972-4300

KILL THE DIRECTOR (Short)   directed

Screenplays:
THE WEAPON SHOP

Ma

FILM
WRITERS
GUIDE

F
I
L
M

W
R
I
T
E
R
S

LORING MANDEL*
Agent: Jim Preminger Agency - Los Angeles, 310/475-9491

ALL THE WAY HOME (P)
TOO CONFUSED, THE ANGEL (P)
ADVISE AND CONSENT (P)
PROJECT IMMORTALITY (P)
COUNTDOWN   Warner Bros., 1968
PROMISES IN THE DARK   Orion/Warner Bros., 1979
THE LITTLE DRUMMER GIRL   Warner Bros., 1984

Screenplays:
JULY'S PEOPLE
SHORELINES
COUNTDOWN
ENTEBBE
REBELLION
CLOSING TIME

COREY MANDELL
Agent: ICM - Beverly Hills, 310/550-4000

LOVE KILLS (CTF)   OMTL Productions Inc./Wilshire Court Prods.,
    1991, w/Marc Lieberman

Screenplays:
THRILL SEEKERS

JEFF MANDELL
FIREHEAD   A.I.P. Studios, 1991, w/Peter Yuval

JAMES MANGOLD
Agent: Susan Smith & Associates - Beverly Hills, 213/852-4777

BARN (Short)   directed
HUNTERS IN THE SNOW (Short)   directed
VICTOR (Short)   directed
OLIVER & CO. (AF)   Buena Vista, 1988, w/James Cox &
    Timothy J. Disney

Screenplays:
UPSTATE STORY   (directing)
COPLAND

DON M. MANKIEWICZ*
Agent: Shapiro/Lichtman - Los Angeles, 310/859-8877

HOUSE OF NUMBERS   MGM, 1957, w/Russell Rouse
I WANT TO LIVE ★   United Artists, 1958, w/Nelson Gidding
THE HOODLUM PRIEST   United Artists, 1961, w/Joseph Landon
THE CHAPMAN REPORT   Warner Bros., 1962, w/Wyatt Cooper

JOHN MANKIEWICZ*
Agent: United Talent Agency - Beverly Hills, 310/273-6700

Screenplays:
WILKES
FULL TERM
AMERICAN IRON   w/Dan Pyne
GREENWICH KILLING TIME

TOM MANKIEWICZ*
Agent: ICM - Beverly Hills, 310/550-4000

THE SWEET RIDE   20th Century-Fox, 1968
DIAMONDS ARE FOREVER   United Artists, 1971,
    w/Richard Maibaum
LIVE AND LET DIE   United Artists, 1973
THE MAN WITH THE GOLDEN GUN   United Artists, 1974,
    w/Richard Maibaum
MOTHER, JUGS & SPEED   20th Century-Fox, 1976
THE EAGLE HAS LANDED   Columbia, 1977
THE CASSANDRA CROSSING   Avco Embassy, 1977,
    w/George Pan Cosmatos & Robert Katz

LADYHAWKE   Warner Bros., 1985, w/Edward Khmara &
    Michael Thomas
DRAGNET   Universal, 1987, w/Dan Aykroyd &
    Alan Zweibel,   directed

Screenplays:
HALFWAY HOME
WASHINGTON GIRLS   w/Colin Higgins
THE PRACTICE
FATHER'S DAY

TOM MANKLE
Agent: ICM - Beverly Hills, 310/550-4000

Screenplays:
SLUSHY

WOLF MANKOWITZ
A KID FOR TWO FARTHINGS   London Films, 1955
THE BESPOKE OVERCOAT   Remus, 1956
EXPRESSO BONGO   British Lion, 1959, from his play
THE MILLIONAIRESS   20th Century-Fox, 1960
HOUSE OF FRIGHT   THE TWO FACES OF DR. JEKYLL
    Hammer, 1960
THE DAY THE EARTH CAUGHT FIRE   British Lion, 1961,
    w/Val Guest
THE WALTZ OF THE TOREADORS   Rank, 1962
WHERE THE SPIES ARE   MGM, 1965, w/Val Guest
THE TWENTY-FIFTH HOUR   Concordia, 1967, w/Francois Boyer &
    Henri Verneuil
CASINO ROYALE   Columbia, 1967, w/John Law & Michael Sayers
BLOOMFIELD   THE HERO   World Film Services, 1969
TREASURE ISLAND   Massfilms, 1971, w/Orson Welles
BLACK BEAUTY   Tigon, 1971
THE HIRELING   Columbia, 1973
ALMONDS AND RAISINS (FD)   Brook Productions, 1983

ABBY MANN*
Agent: APA - Los Angeles, 310/273-0744

JUDGMENT AT NUREMBERG ★★   United Artists, 1961,
    from his play
THE CONDEMNED OF ALTONA   20th Century-Fox, 1962,
    w/Cesare Zavattini
A CHILD IS WAITING   United Artists, 1963
SHIP OF FOOLS ★   Columbia, 1965
THE DETECTIVE   20th Century-Fox, 1968
REPORT TO THE COMMISSIONER   United Artists, 1974,
    w/Ernest Tidyman
WAR AND LOVE   Cannon, 1985
MURDERERS AMONG US: THE SIMON WIESENTHAL
    STORY (CTF)   HBO Pictures/Robert Cooper Productions/
    TVS Films, 1989, w/Ron Hutchinson & Robin Vote
TEAMSTER BOSS: THE JACKIE PRESSER STORY (CTF)
    HBO Pictures, 1992

Screenplays:
THE NAKED MOVIE STAR GAME (CTF)
LIFE ON THE HIGH WIRE (CTF)

DIANE RUDNICK - MANN*
(See Diane RUDNICK-Mann)

EDWARD MANN*
Agent: Shapiro/Lichtman - Los Angeles, 310/859-8877

ISLAND OF TERROR   Planet, 1966, w/Alan Ramsen
THE KILLER INSIDE ME   Warner Bros., 1976, w/Robert Chandlee

EMILY MANN*
Agent: William Morris Agency - New York, 212/586-5100

STILL LIFE (P)

Screenplays:
WINNIE

MICHAEL MANN*
Agent: CAA - Beverly Hills, 310/288-4545

THIEF   United Artists, 1981, directed
THE KEEP   Paramount, 1983, directed
MANHUNTER   DEG, 1986, directed
THE LAST OF THE MOHICANS   20th Century Fox, 1992,
   w/Christopher Crowe, directed
HEAT   Warner Bros., 1995, directing

Screenplays:
PUBLIC ENEMY NO. 1

RACHEL KRONSTADT MANN*
Contact: WGA - Los Angeles, 310/550-1000

BACKTRACK (CTF)   Dick Clark Cinema Production/Vestron
   Pictures Inc., 1991, w/Ann Louise Bardach

STANLEY MANN*
Agent: The Gersh Agency - Beverly Hills, 310/274-6611

ANOTHER TIME, ANOTHER PLACE   Paramount, 1958
THE MOUSE THAT ROARED   Columbia, 1959,
   w/Roger Macdougall
HIS AND HERS   Eros, 1960, w/Jan Lowell & Mark Lowell
THE MARK   20th Century-Fox, 1961, w/Sidney Buchman
WOMAN OF STRAW   United Artists, 1964, w/Robert Muller &
   Michael Relph
RAPTURE   20th Century-Fox International Classics, 1965
UP FROM THE BEACH   20th Century-Fox, 1965, w/Claude Brule
A HIGH WIND IN JAMAICA   20th Century-Fox, 1965,
   w/Denis Cannan & Ronald Harwood
THE COLLECTOR ★   Columbia, 1965, w/John Kohn
THE NAKED RUNNER   Warner Bros., 1967
THE STRANGE AFFAIR   Paramount, 1968
FRAULEIN DOKTOR   Paramount, 1968, w/others
RUSSIAN ROULETTE   Avco Embassy, 1975, w/Tom Ardies &
   Arnold Margolin
SKY RIDERS   20th Century-Fox, 1976, w/Jack DeWitt &
   Garry Michael White
BREAKING POINT   20th Century-Fox, 1976, w/Roger Swaybill
THE SILENT FLUTE   Volare, 1978, w/Stirling Silliphant
DAMIEN - OMEN II   20th Century-Fox, 1978, w/Michael Hodges
METEOR   American International, 1979, w/Edmund H. North
CIRCLE OF IRON   Avco Embassy, 1979, w/Stirling Silliphant
EYE OF THE NEEDLE   United Artists, 1981
FIRESTARTER   Universal, 1984
CONAN THE DESTROYER   Universal, 1984
TAI-PAN   DEG, 1986, w/John Briley
HANNA'S WAR   Cannon, 1988, w/Menahem Golan

Screenplays:
POWELL
THIRD TIME LUCKY
EVENING FLIGHT

TED MANN*
Agent: Warden, White & Kane - Beverly Hills, 213/852-1028

O.C. AND STIGGS   MGM/UA, 1987, w/Donald Cantrell

Screenplays:
SPACE TRUCKERS
THE BUTLER SCHOOL
CAMPUS COPS
THE VULGARIANS
BLOWN OFF THE MAP
MALIBU BUZZARDS
DRIVE AWAY
FINAL TOUR
NEVERLAND   w/John McNaughton
LOVE HURTS
BIKINI

ROGER D. MANNING
Contact: John Dellaverson, Loeb & Loeb - Los Angeles,
   310/282-2057

GRUNT! THE WRESTLING MOVIE   New World, 1985

Screenplays:
THE THIRTEENTH DUKE   w/Bill Condon
ALBERT'S PIANO
GO GET 'EM

GUY MANOS
DROP ZONE   Paramount, 1994, Story w/Tony Griffin &
   Peter Barsochini

MARK MANOS
LIQUID DREAMS   Northern Arts Entertainment, 1992,
   w/Zach Davis, directed

JOHN MANTLEY*
Contact: WGA - Los Angeles, 310/550-1000

Screenplays:
A PIECE OF THE SKY

DENNIS MANUEL*
Contact: WGA - Los Angeles, 310/550-1000

Screenplays:
LADY IN WAITING

RUSSELL V. MANZATT*
Agent: Paul Kohner, Inc. - Beverly Hills, 310/550-1060

RUSH WEEK   RCA/Columbia Home Video, 1991,
   w/Michael W. Leighton

LINDSAY MARACOTTA*
Contact: WGA - Los Angeles, 310/550-1000

Screenplays:
UNRAVELLED
PARALLEL WORLDS

ROBERT MARASCO*
Contact: WGA - New York, 212/245-6180

CHILD'S PLAY (P)

Screenplays:
MIMIC

TERRY MARCEL
Agent: Friend Entertainment - Los Angeles, 213/962-9584

HAWK THE SLAYER   ITC, 1976, w/Harry Robertson
THERE GOES THE BRIDE   Lonsdale, 1980,
   w/Ray Cooney, directed

TIMOTHY MARCH
A PIECE OF THE ACTION   Warner Bros., 1977, Story
FAST FORWARD   Columbia, 1985, Story

DAVID MARCONI*
Agent: William Morris Agency - Beverly Hills, 310/274-7451

THE HARVEST   Arrow Entertainment, 1993, directed

ADAM MARCUS
JASON GOES TO HELL: THE FINAL FRIDAY   New Line Cinema,
   1993, Story w/Jay Huguely, directed

C I N D Y   M A R C U S *
Agent: Paradigm - Los Angeles, 310/277-4400

Screenplays:
KINGDOM BY THE SEA w/Flip Kobler
WHITE NOISE w/Flip Kobler

J A M E S   M A R C U S
TANK MALLING   Pointlane Films, 1989,
    w/Mick Southworth, directed

L A W R E N C E   B .   M A R C U S *
Contact: WGA - Los Angeles, 310/550-1000

BACKFIRE   Warner Bros., 1949, w/Ivan Goff & Ben Roberts
DARK CITY   Paramount, 1950, w/John Meredyth Lucas
THE UNGUARDED MOMENT   Universal-International, 1956,
    w/Herb Meadow
THE VOICE IN THE MIRROR   Universal-International, 1958
A COVENANT WITH DEATH   Warner Bros., 1966, w/Saul Levitt
PETULIA   Warner Bros., 1968
JUSTINE   20th Century-Fox, 1969
GOING HOME   MGM, 1971
ALEX & THE GYPSY   20th Century-Fox, 1976
THE STUNT MAN ★   20th Century-Fox, 1980

Screenplays:
THE HOMESMAN
RAGS

M I T C H E L L   M A R C U S *
Contact: WGA - Los Angeles, 310/550-1000

Screenplays:
THE FORCE w/Steve Kallaugher (Image Organization)
WILD KINGDOM

A R L E N E   M A R E C H A L
Agent: Broder-Kurland-Webb-Uffner - Beverly Hills, 310/281-3400

Screenplays:
NOON HOUR
REAL MEN

E V E   R O S E   M A R E M O N T
Contact: Radiant Productions, TriStar Pictures, 310/280-7101

Screenplays:
HOMESICK

P A U L   B .   M A R G O L I S *
Agent: The Irv Schechter Company - Beverly Hills, 310/278-8070

Screenplays:
MIRAGE
CHROMIUM YELLOW
MISSING WIVES

D A N I E L   M A R G O S I S *
Agent: William Morris Agency - Beverly Hills, 310/274-7451

Screenplays:
GOOD ADVICE w/Robert Horn

D O N A L D   M A R G U L I E S *
Agent: United Talent Agency - Beverly Hills, 310/273-6700

FOUND A PEANUT (P)
WHAT'S WRONG WITH THIS PICTURE? (P)
THE LOMAN FAMILY PICNIC (P)
THE MODEL APARTMENT (P)
SIGHT UNSEEN (P)   also screenplay

Screenplays:
DON'T WORRY, HE WON'T GET FAR ON FOOT
CAPA

BOY MOST LIKELY
PRESIDENTIAL SUITE
BETWEEN THE MOON AND WOODSTOCK

A N D R E W   P E T E R   M A R I N *
Agent: CAA - Beverly Hills, 310/288-4545

HOG WILD   Avco Embassy, 1980
UNDERGROUND ACES   Filmways, 1981, w/Jim Carabatsos &
    Lenore Wright
TRIAL & ERROR (CTF)   Alliance Communications/USA Network,
    1993, Story

R I C H A R D   "C H E E C H"   M A R I N *
Agent: CAA - Beverly Hills, 310/288-4545
Business Manager: Betty M. Beall - Los Angeles, 310/558-8110

UP IN SMOKE   Paramount, 1978, w/Tommy Chong
CHEECH & CHONG'S NEXT MOVIE   Universal, 1980,
    w/Tommy Chong
CHEECH & CHONG'S NICE DREAMS   Columbia, 1981,
    w/Tommy Chong
THINGS ARE TOUGH ALL OVER   Columbia, 1982,
    w/Tommy Chong
CHEECH & CHONG: STILL SMOKIN'   Paramount, 1983,
    w/Tommy Chong
CHEECH & CHONG'S THE CORSICAN BROTHERS   Orion, 1984,
    w/Tommy Chong
BORN IN EAST L.A.   Universal, 1987, directed

Screenplays:
THE GARDENER w/Roger Simon
ANGEL OF OXNARD

A N N E   M A R I S S E
GRADUATION DAY   IFI-Scope III, 1981, w/Herb Freed

M A R Y   E L L E N   M A R K
AMERICAN HEART   Triton Pictures, 1993, Story w/Martin Bell &
    Peter Silverman

T O N Y   M A R K *
Business Manager: Greg Reneau - 310/453-7070

ROOFTOPS   New Century/Vista, 1989, Story w/Allan Goldstein

P E T E R   M A R K L E *
Agent: CAA - Beverly Hills, 310/288-4545

THE PERSONALS   New World, 1982, directed
YOUNGBLOOD   MGM/UA, 1986, directed

Screenplays:
SKULL & BONES

M E R R I L L   M A R K O E *
Business Manager: Nigro, Karlen & Segal - Los Angeles,
    310/277-4657

Screenplays:
JUST ANOTHER LOVE STORY
LIVING THE ALTERNATIVE LIFE

M I T C H   M A R K O W I T Z *
Agent: Larry Grossman & Associates - Beverly Hills, 310/550-8127

GOOD MORNING VIETNAM   Buena Vista, 1987
CRAZY PEOPLE   Paramount, 1990

Screenplays:
MONKEY BUSINESS (remake)
FALSE LABOR
GETTING GIRLS
BREAKING UP IS HARD TO DO
THE LAST HASIDIC COMIC
ROBBERS

ARTHUR R. MARKS*
Contact: Arthur Productions, Inc. - 818/887-1007

BONNIE'S KIDS   General Film Corporation, 1974, directed
THE ROOM MATES   General Film Corporation, 1973, directed

DENNIS MARKS*
Agent: Elliot Wax & Associates - Los Angeles, 310/273-8217

THE JETSONS (AF)   Universal, 1990
TOM AND JERRY: THE MOVIE (AF)   Turner Pictures, 1993

ROSS MARKS*
Agent: William Morris Agency - Beverly Hills, 310/274-7451

SHOWDOWN ON RIO ROAD (Short)   AFI, 1993,
    w/Mark Medoff, directed

Screenplays:
THE KRAMER

NEAL MARLENS*
Business: The Black/Marlens Company, 17351 Sunset Blvd. -
    Suite 504, Pacific Palisades, CA 90272, 310/573-1717

Screenplays:
THE JUMPING OFF POINT w/Carol Black

DOUG MARLETTE*
Contact: WGA - Los Angeles, 310/550-1000

Screenplays:
EX w/Pat Conroy

ANDREW MARLOWE
Agent: ICM - Beverly Hills, 310/550-4000

Screenplays:
APOGEE
LEHIGH PIRATES

BRAD MARLOWE
Manager: Charles Melnicker - Los Angeles, 310/550-7470

THE WEBBERS   Blue Ridge Entertainment, 1993, directed

DEREK MARLOWE*
Agent: Paradigm - Los Angeles, 310/277-4400

A DANDY IN ASPIC   Columbia, 1968

MALIA SCOTCH MARMO*
Agent: ICM - Beverly Hills, 310/550-4000

ONCE AROUND   Universal, 1991
HOOK   Tri-Star, 1991, w/Jim V. Hart

Screenplays:
SIMPLE PRAYERS
SIGHTINGS

MALCOLM MARMORSTEIN*
Agent: Preferred Artists - Encino, 818/990-0305

S*P*Y*S   20th Century-Fox, 1974, w/Lawrence J. Cohen &
    Fred Freeman
WHIFFS   20th Century-Fox, 1975
PETE'S DRAGON   Buena Vista, 1977
RETURN FROM WITCH MOUNTAIN   Buena Vista, 1978
DEAD MEN DON'T DIE   Castle Hill, 1991, directed
THE RELUCTANT VAMPIRE   Waymar Productions, 1992,
    from his play, directed

Screenplays:
TERRY AND THE PIRATES
WEAK LINKS
THE CLOUD
THE PROFESSOR
THE SILENT NINE
CLICK OF THE HAMMER
ROMAN JOY
HEROES AND VILLAINS
A CRY OF WHITENESS
MOTHER IS A COUNTRY
PRISMOIDS

EUGENE MARNER*
Contact: WGA - New York, 212/245-6180

BEAUTY AND THE BEAST   Cannon, 1987, directed

HUDSON MARQUEZ
A TASTE FOR KILLING (CTF)   Bodega Bay Productions, 1992,
    Story w/Allen Rucker

LEON MARR
Address: 19 Beech Avenue, Toronto, Ontario M4E 3H3, Canada,
    416/691-1215

DANCING IN THE DARK   New World, 1986, directed

TERENCE MARSH*
Agent: Sandra Marsh Management - Sherman Oaks, 818/905-6961

FINDERS KEEPERS   Warner Bros., 1984, w/Charles Dennis &
    Ronny Graham
HAUNTED HONEYMOON   Orion, 1986, w/Gene Wilder

ANDREW MARSHALL
Contact: 011/441-8056

THE MISADVENTURES OF MR. WILT   Samuel Goldwyn Company,
    1990, Adaptation w/David Renwick

Screenplays:
MUSHROOM BUTTON w/David Renwick
JINGLE BELLS w/David Renwick

GARRY MARSHALL*
Agent: ICM - New York, 212/556-5600
Business Manager: Diane Frazen, Henderson Productions, 10067
    Riverside Drive, North Hollywood, CA 91602, 818/985-6417

WRONG TURN AT LUNGFISH (P) w/Lowell Ganz
HOW SWEET IT IS   National General, 1968, w/Jerry Belson
THE GRASSHOPPER   National General, 1979, w/Jerry Belson
THE FLAMINGO KID   20th Century Fox, 1984,
    w/Neal Marshall, directed

Screenplays:
LOVE, ROGER w/Jerry Belson
C. DMIAS w/Lowell Ganz

GEORGE LEE MARSHALL*
Agent: The Chasin Agency - Los Angeles, 310/278-7505

CRACK IN THE KREMLIN WALL (CTF)   Viacom, 1993,
    w/David Taylor

Screenplays:
TWILIGHT TIME
STORM FRONT
INQUIRY AGENT
SWEET TABOO
SNAFU
CRYSTAL SHIPS
THE WILD BIG RED
TANGO IN DIEGO

NEAL MARSHALL*
Contact: WGA - Los Angeles, 310/550-1000

THE FLAMINGO KID   20th Century Fox, 1984, w/Garry Marshall

Screenplays:
G.I. JONES
THE CAB DRIVER
PAJAMA PRINCESS
WIFE MISTRESS

STEVE K. MARSHALL*
Agent: Paradigm - Los Angeles, 310/277-4400

REVENGE OF THE NERDS II   20th Century Fox, 1987,
    w/Dan Guntzelman

Screenplays:
HOT WATER w/Dan Guntzelman
PAPARAZZI w/Dan Guntzelman

BILL MARSILII
Agent: Warden, White & Kane - Beverly Hills, 213/852-1028

Screenplays:
THE INVISIBLE CHOIR
THE FORGOTTEN HELPER
THE RAIDER ALABAMA w/Russell Shorto

WILLIAM C. MARTELL
Contact: Murder Mysteries Served with a Twist, 8306 Wilshire Blvd. -
    Suite 989, Beverly Hills, CA 90211, 818/988-1283

NINJA BUSTERS   GPD Inc., 1984
TREACHEROUS   Ulysse Entertainment, 1993, w/Kevin Brodie
RIPTIDES   Hemdale, 1994
DOUBLE ACTION   Hemdale, 1994
DOWN FOR THE COUNT   World Screen Associates, 1994

Screenplays:
COURTING DEATH
LIGHTNING STRIKES w/Paul Kyriazi
TAKE BACK THE NIGHT
HARD EVIDENCE
MOONLIGHT EXPRESS
THE LAST STAND
THE VICTIM'S WIFE
LETHAL DECEPTION
UNDERCURRENTS
SHOOTER ON THE SIDE
THE BAKER TOUCH

DARNELL MARTIN
Agent: William Morris Agency - Beverly Hills, 310/274-7451
Address: 91 First Avenue, New York, NY 10003, 212/529-6875

SUSPECT (Short)   directed
I LIKE IT LIKE THAT   Columbia, 1994, directed

Screenplays:
LISTENING TO THE DEAD

JEFF MARTIN*
Contact: WGA - Los Angeles, 310/550-1000

Screenplays:
COUSIN EDDY   (Shared)

JOHN MARTIN*
Contact: WGA - Los Angeles, 310/550-1000

Screenplays:
FORGOTTEN IMPULSES w/Jay Roach

MARDIK MARTIN*
Agent: The Partos Company - Los Angeles, 213/876-5500

MEAN STREETS   Warner Bros., 1973, w/Martin Scorsese
NEW YORK, NEW YORK   United Artists, 1977, w/Earl Mac Rauch
RAGING BULL   United Artists, 1978, w/Paul Schrader

Screenplays:
ROCK 'N' ROLL STORY
WEEGIE

PAMELA SUE MARTIN
Contact: Screen Actors Guild - Los Angeles, 213/954-1600

TORCHLIGHT   International Film Marketing, 1984,
    w/Eliza Moorman

RICHARD WAYNE MARTIN
NO JUSTICE   Richfield's Releasing, 1989, co-directed

ROBERT MARTIN
FRANKENHOOKER   Shapiro Glickenhaus, 1990,
    w/Frank Henenlotter
BASKET CASE 3: THE PROGENY   Shapiro Glickenhaus, 1992,
    w/Frank Henenlotter

STEVE MARTIN*
Agent: ICM - Beverly Hills, 310/550-4000

PICASSO AT THE LAPIN AGILE (P)
THE JERK   Universal, 1979, w/Michael Elias & Carl Gottlieb
DEAD MEN DON'T WEAR PLAID   Universal, 1982,
    w/George Gipe & Carl Reiner
THE MAN WITH TWO BRAINS   Warner Bros., 1983,
    w/George Gipe & Carl Reiner
THREE AMIGOS   Orion, 1986, w/Lorne Michaels & Randy Newman
ROXANNE   Columbia, 1987
L.A. STORY   Tri-Star, 1991
A SIMPLE TWIST OF FATE   Buena Vista, 1994

Screenplays:
THE TOUCH

THOMAS E. MARTIN
Agent: The Gersh Agency - Beverly Hills, 310/274-6611

Screenplays:
TURTLE MOON w/Alice Hoffman
SEVENTH HEAVEN w/Alice Hoffman
GOOD HOUSEKEEPING w/Alice Hoffman

TROY KENNEDY MARTIN
Agent: Sanford-Gross & Associates - Los Angeles, 310/208-2100

THE ITALIAN JOB   Paramount, 1969
KELLY'S HEROES   MGM, 1970
THE JERUSALEM FILE   MGM, 1971
SWEENEY 2   EMI, 1978
RED HEAT   Tri-Star, 1988, w/Walter Hill & Harry Kleiner

Screenplays:
TROPPO

WILLIAM E. MARTIN*
Contact: WGA - Los Angeles, 310/550-1000

HARRY AND THE HENDERSONS   Universal, 1987,
    w/William Dear & Ezra D. Rappaport

WRYE MARTIN
ASWANG   Young American Films, 1994,
    w/Barry Polterman, co-directed

GREG MARTINELLI*
Contact: WGA - New York, 212/245-6180

MORTAL SINS (CTF)   Blake Edwards Television/Barry Weitz Films/
   USA Pictures, 1992, w/Dennis Paoli

DAN MARTINEZ
Agent: Leslie Kallen Agency - Sherman Oaks, 818/906-2785

Screenplays:
PRANKSTERS

RICHARD MARTINI*
Contact: WGA - Los Angeles, 310/550-1000

THREE FOR THE ROAD   New Century/Vista, 1987,
   w/Miguel Tejada-Flores & Tim Metcalfe
YOU CAN'T HURRY LOVE   MCEG, 1988, directed
LIMIT UP   MCEG, 1990, w/Lu Anders, directed

RAYMOND MARTINO
Agent: CAA - Beverly Hills, 310/288-4545

ANGELS OF THE CITY   Raedon Home Video, 1989,
   w/Lawrence-Hilton Jacobs & Joseph Merhi
AMERICAN BORN   PM Home Video, 1990,
   w/Addison Randall, directed

Screenplays:
CODY AND WHEEZE w/William Stroum

NICK L. MARTINSON
FORBIDDEN ZONE   Sutton Marketing, 1980, w/Matthew Bright,
   Richard Elfman & Nick James

MIKE MARVIN*
Agent: The Agency - Los Angeles, 310/551-3000

SIX PACK   20th Century-Fox, 1982, w/Alex Matter
HOT DOG - THE MOVIE   MGM/UA, 1984
THE WRAITH   New Century/Vista, 1986, directed
WISHMAN   Monarch Releasing, 1993, directed

Screenplays:
BED & BREAKFAST w/Andy Tennant
HALF BAKED! w/Andy Tennant

ARTHUR MARX*
Agent: Peter Sabiston - 310/826-9732

THE IMPOSSIBLE YEARS (P)   w/Robert Fisher
A GLOBAL AFFAIR   Seven Arts, 1963, w/Robert Fisher &
   Charles Lederer
I'LL TAKE SWEDEN   United Artists, 1965, w/Robert Fisher &
   Nat Perrin
EIGHT ON THE LAM   United Artists, 1966, w/Robert Fisher,
   Albert E. Lewin & Burt Styler
CANCEL MY RESERVATION   Naho Enterprises, 1972,
   w/Robert Fisher

RICK (R.J.) MARX
Contact: 914/232-6781

C.O.D.   Lone Star, 1982
PREPPIES   Platinum, 1984, w/Chuck Vincent
POMPEII *WARRIOR QUEEN*   Seymour Borde & Associates, 1987
DRAGONARD   Cannon, 1987
GOR   Cannon, 1988
DEAD MAN WALKING   Metropolis Productions/Hit Films, 1988,
   w/John Weidner
PLATOON LEADER   Cannon, 1988, w/Andrew Deutsch &
   David Walker
OUTLAW OF GOR   Cannon, 1989, w/Harry Alan Towers
MASTER OF DRAGONARD HILL   Cannon, 1990,
   w/Harry Alan Towers
DOUBLE OBSESSION   Columbia, 1994

JACK MASON
A MATTER OF DEGREES   Backbeat Productions, 1989,
   w/W.T. Morgan & Randall Poster

JOHN MASON
Agent: Susan Smith & Associates - Beverly Hills, 213/852-4777

Screenplays:
ALL ABOUT ED
OUR MAN IN MONGOA

JUDI ANN MASON*
Agent: ICM - Beverly Hills, 310/550-4000

INDIGO BLUES (P)
SISTER ACT II: BACK IN THE HABIT   Buena Vista, 1993,
   w/Jim Cruickshank & James Orr

Screenplays:
HOLLOW SPRINGS

NAN MASON
MY LITTLE GIRL   Hemdale, 1987, w/Connie Kaiserman

PAUL MASON*
Contact: Bloom, Dekom, Hergott & Cook - Los Angeles, 310/278-8622

THE LADIES CLUB   New Line Cinema, 1986, w/FranLewis Ebeling
THE FURTHER ADVENTURES OF TENNESSEE BUCK
   Trans World Entertainment, 1988, Story

ED MAST
BOMBS AWAY   Shapiro Entertainment, 1985, w/Bruce Wilson

WILLIAM E. MASTERS*
Agent: ICM - Beverly Hills, 310/550-4000

Screenplays:
GOOD NEWS/BAD NEWS
THE MONEY TRAIN

MARY STUART MASTERSON
Agent: William Morris Agency - Beverly Hills, 310/274-7451

Screenplays:
AROUND THE BLOCK (Savoy, directing)

PETER MASTERSON*
Business: Tejas Productions, 1165 Fifth Avenue - Apt. 15A,
   New York, NY 10029, 212/427-4055

THE BEST LITTLE WHOREHOUSE GOES PUBLIC (P)
   w/Larry L. King
THE BEST LITTLE WHOREHOUSE IN TEXAS   Universal, 1982,
   w/Larry L. King, from their play

NICO MASTORAKIS
Business: Omega Entertainment, 8760 Shoreham Drive - Suite 501,
   Los Angeles, CA 90069, 310/855-0516

BLOOD TIDE   21st Century, 1982, w/Richard Jeffries &
   Donald Langdon
BLIND DATE   New Line Cinema, 1984, w/Fred C. Perry, directed
GLITCH!   Omega Pictures, 1988, directed
BLOODSTONE   Omega Pictures, 1989, w/Curt Allen

WILLIAM MASTROSIMONE*
Agent: William Morris Agency - New York, 212/586-5100

SUNSHINE (P)
CAT'S PAW (P)
TAMER OF HORSES (P)   also screenplay
EXTREMITIES   Atlantic Releasing Corporation, 1986, from his play
THE BEAST   Columbia, 1988, from his play "Nanawatai"

WITH HONORS   Warner Bros., 1994
THE BURNING SEASON (CTF)   HBO Pictures, 1994,
   w/Ron Hutchinson & Michael Tolkin

Screenplays:
LITTLE THINGS

EDDY MATALON
SWEET KILLING   Skouras Pictures, 1994, directed

JAMES MATHERS
Agent: Susan Smith & Associates - Beverly Hills, 213/852-4777

Screenplays:
LES SPLENDIDES w/Reed Bernstein

ALI MATHESON*
Contact: WGA - Los Angeles, 310/550-1000

Screenplays:
TIL MARRIAGE DO US PART w/Jon Cooksey
HIT PARADE w/Jon Cooksey
REWIND w/Jon Cooksey
BEAUTY SLEEP w/Jon Cooksey

CHRISTIAN L. MATHESON*
Agent: Above the Line - West Hollywood, 310/859-6115

BILL & TED'S EXCELLENT ADVENTURE   Orion, 1989,
   w/Ed Solomon
BILL & TED'S BOGUS JOURNEY   Orion, 1991, w/Ed Solomon
MOM AND DAD SAVE THE WORLD   Warner Bros., 1992,
   w/Ed Solomon

Screenplays:
KILLER BEACH BABES (directing)
A PAIR OF JACKS

RICHARD MATHESON*
Agent: ICM - Beverly Hills, 310/550-4000

NOW YOU SEE IT (P)
RANSOM   MGM, 1955, w/Cyril Hume
INCREDIBLE SHRINKING MAN   Universal, 1957
THE BEAT GENERATION   Albert Zugsmith, 1959, w/Lewis Meltzer
HOUSE OF USHER   American International, 1960
MASTER OF THE WORLD   American International, 1961
TALES OF TERROR   American International, 1961
THE PIT AND THE PENDULUM   American International, 1961
BURN, WITCH, BURN *NIGHT OF THE EAGLE*   American
   International, 1962, w/Charles Beaumont & George Baxt
THE COMEDY OF TERRORS   American International, 1963
THE RAVEN   American International, 1963
DIE, DIE, MY DARLING *FANATIC*   Columbia, 1965
THE YOUNG WARRIORS   Universal, 1967
THE DEVIL'S BRIDE   Hammer, 1968
DE SADE   American International, 1969
THE LEGEND OF HELL HOUSE   20th Century-Fox, 1974
SOMEWHERE IN TIME   Universal, 1980
TWILIGHT ZONE- THE MOVIE   Warner Bros., 1983,
   Segments 3 & 4
JAWS 3-D   Universal, 1983, w/Carl Gottlieb
DUEL   Universal, 1983
LOOSE CANNONS   Tri-Star, 1990, w/Richard C. Matheson &
   Bob Clark

Screenplays:
SHIFTER w/Richard C. Matheson
FACE-OFF
WHAT DREAMS MAY COME
BIG TIME RETURN
IMPLOSION
FORBIDDEN LAND
DEDMAN
SKEDADDLE
THE LAST REVOLUTION

NOVUM
CREATURE
RED SLEEP w/Mick Garris

RICHARD CHRISTIAN MATHESON*
Agent: ICM - Beverly Hills, 310/550-4000

THREE O'CLOCK HIGH   Universal, 1987, w/Tom Szollosi
IT TAKES TWO   MGM/UA, 1989, w/Tom Szollosi
LOOSE CANNONS   Tri-Star, 1990, w/Richard Matheson &
   Bob Clark

Screenplays:
SHIFTER w/Richard Matheson
RED SLEEP w/Mick Garris
MAN'S BEST FRIEND

SCOTT MATHEWS
Contact: 310/453-3977

CANNIBALS (P)
QUEEN OF THE STARLIGHT LOUNGE (P)

Screenplays:
JOHN WESLEY HARDIN
RODEO FRY

TEMPLE MATHEWS*
Agent: APA - Los Angeles, 310/273-0744

Screenplays:
LUCY'S MOON
THE TROPHY WIFE
CHERRY PINK
ESCAPE FROM HELL
TUNNEL RAT
OFF THE MARK
BATTLEAXE

SEAN MATHIAS
THE LOST LANGUAGE OF CRANES   BBC Television, 1991

STEVE MATHIS
WITHOUT WARNING   Filmways, 1980, w/Lyn Freeman,
   Dan Grodnick & Ben Nett

MELISSA MATHISON*
Agent: CAA - Beverly Hills, 310/288-4545

THE BLACK STALLION   United Artists, 1979,
   w/Jeanne Rosenberg & William Wittliff
THE ESCAPE ARTIST   Orion/Warner Bros., 1982, w/Stephen Zito
E.T.: THE EXTRATERRESTRIAL ★   Universal, 1982
THE INDIAN IN THE CUPBOARD   Paramount, 1995

Screenplays:
E.T. II
WINTER'S TALE
TINTIN

MICHAEL MATLOCK
TALES OF THE UNKNOWN   AIP Home Video, 1990,
   "Jack Falls Down"

FRANCISCA MATOS
Agent: APA - Los Angeles, 310/273-0744

A MILLION TO JUAN   Samuel Goldwyn Company, 1994,
   w/Robert Grasmere

ALEX MATTER
SIX PACK   20th Century-Fox, 1982, w/Mike Marvin

CHARLES MATTERA*
Agent: Paradigm - Los Angeles, 310/277-4400

BLOODFIST III: FORCED TO FIGHT   Concorde, 1992,
    w/Allison Burnett

Screenplays:
SHOOTING LARGE w/Allison Burnett

TOM MATTHEWS
Agent: United Talent Agency - Beverly Hills, 310/273-6700

Screenplays:
MAD CITY
THE NINE O'CLOCK MURDERS
THE SHARPER OF THE TWO
UNLOADING LAUGHING BOY

BURNY MATTISON
Business: Walt Disney Co., 818/560-1000

THE FOX AND THE HOUND (AF)   Buena Vista, 1981,
    Story w/others
THE GREAT MOUSE DETECTIVE (AF)   Buena Vista, 1986,
    w/others, co-directed

JOHN MATTSON*
Agent: United Talent Agency - Beverly Hills, 310/273-6700

MILK MONEY   Paramount, 1994
FREE WILLY 2   Warner Bros., 1995, w/Corey Blechman &
    Karen Janszen

Screenplays:
HONEYMOON
GRACE
ME

NAT MAULDIN*
Agent: Dytman & Schwartz - Beverly Hills, 310/274-8844

DOWNTOWN   20th Century Fox, 1990

Screenplays:
ROGER RABBIT II

J. STEPHEN MAUNDER
TALONS OF THE EAGLE   Shapiro Glickenhaus, 1993
OPERATION GOLDEN PHOENIX   Alliance Releasing, 1994,
    w/Kevin Ward

Screenplays:
EXPECT NO MERCY

JOSHUA D. MAURER
Business: City Entertainment, 1360 S. Roxbury Dr., Los Angeles,
    CA 90035, 310/284-7925

Screenplays:
THE DELI BOYS w/Gregg Ostrin

MICHAEL MAURER*
Agent: The Irv Schechter Company - Beverly Hills, 310/278-8070

RED HOT   SC Entertainment International, 1993, w/Paul Haggis

Screenplays:
SPARE PARTS w/Rick Merwyn

JOHN MAXIM
Agent: Renaissance-H.N. Swanson - Los Angeles, 310/246-6000

Screenplays:
THE BANNERMAN SOLUTION

IAN MAXTONE-GRAHAM*
Agent: ICM - Beverly Hills, 310/550-4000

Screenplays:
LOSERS

GARTH MAXWELL
Agent: William Morris Agency - Beverly Hills, 310/274-7451

JACK BE NIMBLE   Essential Productions/New Zealand
    Film Commission, 1993

RICHARD MAXWELL*
Agent: United Talent Agency - Beverly Hills, 310/273-6700

THE CHALLENGE   Embassy, 1982, w/John Sayles
THE SERPENT AND THE RAINBOW   Universal, 1988,
    w/Adam Rodman
SHADOW OF CHINA   New Line Cinema, 1991,
    w/Mitsuo Yanagimachi

Screenplays:
STOLEN MOMENTS
IN GOD'S NAME
SHEET LIGHTNINGS
DOUBLE SUNRISE
HANDCARVED COFFINS
SNAKEHEAD
INTRUDERS
FALSE FLAG

RONALD F. MAXWELL
Agent: William Morris Agency - Beverly Hills, 310/274-7451
Contact: Weissmann, Wolff, Bergman, Coleman & Silverman -
    Beverly Hills, 310/858-7888

GETTYSBURG   New Line Cinema, 1993, directed

Screenplays:
MALDOROR Story w/Andy Wolk
RAVEN WARRIOR Story w/Leo Aylen

ELAINE MAY*
(Elaine Berlin)
Agent: CAA - Beverly Hills, 310/288-4545
Business Manager: Scott Bercu - New York, 212/391-4900

MR. GOGOL AND MR. PREEN (P)
SUCH GOOD FRIENDS   Paramount, 1971
A NEW LEAF   Paramount, 1971, directed
MIKEY AND NICKY   Paramount, 1977, directed
HEAVEN CAN WAIT ★   Paramount, 1978, w/Warren Beatty
ISHTAR   Columbia, 1987, directed

Screenplays:
BIRDS OF A FEATHER (MGM/UA)
MEN (remake)
THE ONE-HUNDRED DOLLAR MISUNDERSTANDING

BERNARD MAYBECK
THE COVER GIRL MURDERS (CTF)   River Enterprises/Wilshire
    Court, 1993, w/Douglas Barr

PAUL MAYERSBERG
THE MAN WHO FELL TO EARTH   Cinema 5, 1976
THE DISAPPEARANCE   Levitt-Pickman, 1977
MERRY CHRISTMAS, MR. LAWRENCE   Universal, 1983,
    w/Nagisa Oshima
EUREKA   United Artists Classics, 1984
CAPTIVE *HEROINE*   CineTel Films, 1986, directed
NIGHTFALL   Concorde, 1988, directed

TONY MAYLAM
Contact: Directors Guild of America - Los Angeles, 310/289-2000

WHITE ROCK (FD) EMI, 1977, directed
THE RIDDLE OF THE SANDS Satori, 1979,
  w/John Bailey, directed

MELANIE MAYRON*
Agent: The Gersh Agency - Beverly Hills, 310/274-6611

STICKY FINGERS Spectrafilm, 1988, w/Catlin Adams

MICHAEL MAYSON
Agent: CAA - Beverly Hills, 310/288-4545
Contact: Frankfurt, Garbus, Klein & Selz - New York, 212/980-0120

BILLY TURNER'S SECRET (Short) directed

Screenplays:
THROWIN' BASS

ADAM MAZER
Agent: Susan Smith & Associates - Beverly Hills, 213/852-4777

FOREVER YOUNG (Short) 1989, Shared, directed

Screenplays:
THE LAST RIDE OF WATERLOO CLYDE
HARLEQUIN
WATCHIN' DEBIRDIE w/Jason Blumenthal

DAN MAZUR*
Contact: WGA - Los Angeles, 310/550-1000

Screenplays:
RAND ROBINSON, ROBOT REPAIRMAN w/David Tausik
SCARECROW w/Reed Steiner

STEPHEN MAZUR*
Agent: Innovative Artists - Los Angeles, 310/553-5200
Manager: The Roberts Company - Los Angeles, 310/552-7800

THE LITTLE RASCALS Universal, 1994, w/Paul Guay &
  Penelope Spheeris

Screenplays:
MR. MAGOO w/Paul Guay
ABRA-CADAVER w/Paul Guay
MAGICIAN'S ANONYMOUS w/Paul Guay
THE CHRISTMAS SPIRIT w/Paul Guay
THE C-NOTE w/Paul Guay
TAKE TWO w/Paul Guay

JILL MAZURSKY*
Agent: ICM - Beverly Hills, 310/550-4000

TAKING CARE OF BUSINESS Buena Vista, 1990,
  w/Jeffrey Abrams

Screenplays:
ROCKERS w/Jamee Decio
UNDER THE GUN w/Jeffrey Abrams
GONE FISHIN' w/Jeffrey Abrams
SPOILED ROTTEN

PAUL MAZURSKY*
Agent: ICM - Beverly Hills, 310/550-4000

I LOVE YOU, ALICE B. TOKLAS Warner Bros., 1968,
  w/Larry Tucker
BOB & CAROL & TED & ALICE ★ Columbia, 1969,
  w/Larry Tucker, directed
ALEX IN WONDERLAND MGM, 1970, w/Larry Tucker, directed
BLUME IN LOVE Warner Bros., 1973, directed

HARRY AND TONTO ★ 20th Century-Fox, 1974,
  w/Josh Greenfeld, directed
NEXT STOP, GREENWICH VILLAGE 20th Century-Fox,
  1976, directed
AN UNMARRIED WOMAN ★ 20th Century-Fox, 1978, directed
WILLIE AND PHIL 20th Century-Fox, 1980, directed
TEMPEST Columbia, 1982, w/Leon Capetanos, directed
MOSCOW ON THE HUDSON Columbia, 1984,
  w/Leon Capetanos, directed
DOWN AND OUT IN BEVERLY HILLS Buena Vista, 1986,
  w/Leon Capetanos, directed
MOON OVER PARADOR Univeral, 1988,
  w/Leon Capetanos, directed
ENEMIES, A LOVE STORY ★ 20th Century Fox, 1989,
  w/Roger L. Simon, directed
SCENES FROM A MALL Buena Vista, 1991,
  w/Roger L. Simon, directed
THE PICKLE Columbia, 1993, directed

Screenplays:
POOR (Warner Bros., directing)
NIRVANA w/Leon Capetanos

THOMAS MAZZIOTTI
UNDERTOW Capstone Films, 1991, directed

REPARTA MAZZOLA*
Contact: WGA - Los Angeles, 310/550-1000

Screenplays:
DEADLY ICE (GEL Distribution)

ED McBAIN
(See Evan Hunter)

JIM McBRIDE*
Agent: The Daniel Ostroff Agency - Los Angeles, 310/278-2020

DAVID HOLZMAN'S DIARY Grove Press, 1967,
  w/L.M. Kit Carson, directed
MY GIRLFRIEND'S WEDDING 1968, directed
GLEN AND RANDA UMC, 1971, w/Lorenzo Mars & Rudy Wurlitzer
HOT TIMES *A HARD DAY FOR ARCHIE* 1973, directed
BREATHLESS Orion, 1983, w/L.M. Kit Carson, directed
GREAT BALLS OF FIRE! Orion, 1989, w/Jack Baran, directed
UNCOVERED CIBY2000, 1994, w/Jack Baran &
  Michael Hirst, directed

ROD McBRIEN
AFTER SCHOOL Moviestore Entertainment, 1989, w/John Linde,
  Hugh Parks & Joe Tankersley

ROD McCALL*
Agent: Becsey/Wisdom/Kalajian Agency - Los Angeles, 310/550-0535

SALLY & BUDDY & LORETTA (Short) directed
EARLY WINTER 1976, unreleased, directed
CHEATIN' HEARTS *PAPER HEARTS* King/Moonstone,
  1993, directed

Screenplays:
WITH OPEN ARMS w/Luis Puenzo
HOT MOON w/Suzanne Blum
BIRTHDAY
CABOOSE
HENRY LEAVES HOME
JO AND THE LIZARDS
ROADWAY
KOHCHEE
NINO
RADIO KILLERS FROM OUTER SPACE

JAMES McCALMONT
ESCAPE FROM SAFEHAVEN SVS Films, 1989,
  w/Brian Thomas Jones

TIMOTHY B. McCANLIES*
Agent: ICM - Beverly Hills, 310/550-4000

NORTH SHORE   Universal, 1987, w/William Phelps

Screenplays:
SECOND TO NONE   FLY BY aka THAI PIRATES
HARLEM
DEVIL'S BARGAIN
LOUISIANA RUN
MONTE CARLO COPS

BRYAN McCANN
BULLIES   Universal, 1986, w/John Sheppard

ANDREW McCARTHY
Agent: Leslie Kallen Agency - Sherman Oaks, 818/906-2785

Screenplays:
MY CRAZY FAMILY

FRANCIS X. McCARTHY*
Agent: Camden-ITG - Los Angeles, 310/289-2700

Screenplays:
BOGUS
EARLY RETIREMENT
REMOTE CONTROL
RED SQUARE
OUT OF CONTROL
RED ALERT

PETER McCARTHY
Agent: William Morris Agency - Beverly Hills, 310/274-7451

TAPEHEADS   Avenue Pictures, 1988, w/Bill Fishman
CAR 54, WHERE ARE YOU?   Orion, 1994, w/Peter Crabbe,
   Ebbe Roe Smith & Erik Tarloff
FLOUNDERING   Strand Releasing, 1994, directed

TODD McCARTHY
Contact: Daily Variety, 5700 Wilshire Blvd. - Suite 120, Los Angeles,
   CA 90036, 213/857-6600

PRESTON STURGES: THE RISE AND FALL OF AN AMERICAN
   DREAMER (FD)   Barking Dog Productions, 1989
HOLLYWOOD MAVERICKS (FD)   American Film Institute/NHK
   Enterprises, Inc., 1989, w/Michael Henry Wilson
VISIONS OF LIGHT: THE ART OF CINEMATOGRAPHY (FD)
   American Film Institute/NHK Enterprises, 1992, co-directed

PAUL McCARTNEY
Agent: ICM - Beverly Hills, 310/550-4000

GIVE MY REGARDS TO BROAD STREET   20th Century-Fox, 1984

SEAN McCARVER*
Contact: 213/960-4769

Screenplays:
KIDSTUFF
FALLING INTO FIENDISH
NIKKI & ME
BRIGADOON
STIR IT UP
SHOOT THE DEGROODTS

JIM McCLAIN
Agent: United Talent Agency - Beverly Hills, 310/273-6700

Screenplays:
TRACK DOWN w/Ron Mita
THE FRENCH TEACHER w/Ron Mita
URBAN LEGEND w/Ron Mita

TOM McCLUSKEY
FRIENDS AND ENEMIES   Sideral Production, 1992,
   w/Mark DiStefano

Screenplays:
EDDIE FIVE FINGERS w/Mark DiStefano

JOHN McCOLPIN
SECOND COUSIN, ONCE REMOVED   Intrepid Ventures Group,
   1994, w/Dave Bussan, Pete Ellis & John Shorney

JONAS McCORD*
Agent: CAA - Beverly Hills, 310/288-4545

CHROME SOLDIERS (CTF)   Wilshire Court Productions, 1992,
   Story w/Ross La Manna & John McCormick
MALICE   Columbia, 1993, Story

Screenplays:
STAGECOACH MARY
THE BODY

MARK McCORKLE
THE RETURN OF JAFAR (AHVF)   Buena Vista, 1994,
   Story w/Duane Capizzi, Douglas Langdale, Robert Schooley &
   Tad Stories

DAN McCORMACK
MINOTAUR   RFPL, 1994, directed

JOHN P. McCORMICK*
Contact: WGA - Los Angeles, 310/550-1000

LIVING ON TOKYO TIME   Skouras Pictures, 1987,
   w/Steven Okazaki
CHROME SOLDIERS (CTF)   Wilshire Court Productions, 1992,
   Story w/Ross La Manna & Jonas McCord

Screenplays:
DNA w/Ross La Manna
TORPEDOS w/Ross La Manna
PRIDE AND JOY w/Ross La Manna

PATRICK B. McCORMICK*
Contact: WGA - Los Angeles, 310/550-1000

UNDER THE RAINBOW   Orion/Warner Bros., 1981,
   w/Harry Hurwitz, Martin Smith, Pat Bradley & Fred Bauer

RANDALL McCORMICK*
Agent: ICM - Beverly Hills, 310/550-4000

Screenplays:
THE NORTHMEN

TOM McCOWN
Contact: 310/838-4728

HEART OF DIXIE   Orion, 1989

Screenplays:
BRIDGE TO TERABITHIA
THE ROSE OF SHARON
LIGHT YEARS

ARCH McCOY
HERE COME THE TIGERS   American International, 1978

DENNYS McCOY*
Agent: Shapiro/Lichtman - Los Angeles, 310/859-8877

Screenplays:
ACE OF THE NEWSREELS w/Pamela Hickey
HARRY THE LION w/Pamela Hickey
FULL RECOVERY wPamela Hickey

TIM McCOY
SWEET REVENGE   Concorde, 1987, w/Steven M. Krauzer

JUDY McCREARY*
Agent: ICM - Beverly Hills, 310/550-4000

Screenplays:
RUNNER
WAITING TO EXHALE

LAURA ANNE McCREARY
Agent: CAA - Beverly Hills, 310/288-4545

Screenplays:
THE FOURTH JOHN

ANDIE McCUAIG
DEAD RECKONING (CTF)   Houston Lady Co./MCA Entertainment,
   1990, w/Neill D. Hicks

PAUL McCUDDEN
Agent: United Talent Agency - Beverly Hills, 310/273-6700

Screenplays:
THE BRAVE
JOAN OF ARC
HARD RAIN
ALL THAT GLITTERS
JOSHUA CHAMBERLAIN

JIM McCULLOUGH, JR.
MOUNTAINTOP MOTEL MASSACRE   New World, 1986

BRUCE McDONALD
Contact: Academy of Canadian Cinema & Television, 753 Yonge St. -
   2nd Floor, Toronto M4Y 1Z9, Canada, 416/967-0315

HIGHWAY 61   Skouras Pictures, 1992, Story w/Allan Magee &
   Don McKellar, directed
DANCE ME OUTSIDE   Cineplex Odeon, 1994,
   w/Don McKellar, directed

JOHN R. McDONALD*
Contact: WGA - New York, 212/245-6180

BY THE SWORD   The Movie Group, 1992, w/James Donadio

LEROY McDONALD
Contact: Quiet Monday Productions, 1990 S. Bundry Dr.,
   Los Angeles, CA 90025

Screenplays:
TUSKEGEE SUBJECT #626

MICHAEL JAMES McDONALD
Contact: Groundlings - Los Angeles, 213/934-4747

Screenplays:
HOW MUCH ARE THOSE CHILDREN IN THE WINDOW?
   (Concorde, directing)
REVENGE OF THE RED BARON (New Horizons)

ROBERT C. McDONNELL*
Manager: Creative Alliance Management - Los Angeles,
   213/962-6090

TWICE DEAD   Concorde, 1989, w/Bert L. Dragin

Screenplays:
OBIT w/John Lowry Lamb

TERRANCE McDONNELL*
Agent: Monteiro Rose Agency - Encino, 818/501-1177

POUND PUPPIES AND THE LEGEND OF BIG PAW (AF)   TriStar,
   1988, w/Jim Carlson

Screenplays:
COWBOY LOGIC

MICHAEL M. McDOWELL*
Agent: William Morris Agency - Beverly Hills, 310/274-7451

BEETLEJUICE   The Geffen Company/Warner Bros., 1988,
   w/Warren Skaaren
TALES FROM THE DARKSIDE: THE MOVIE   Paramount, 1990,
   "Lot 249" & "Lover's Vow"
THE NIGHTMARE BEFORE CHRISTMAS (AF)   Buena Vista,
   1993, Adaptation

Screenplays:
THINNER
TALES FROM THE DARKSIDE: THE MOVIE II w/Gahan Wilson
PET PEOPLE
WOMEN BEHIND BARS
NIGHTCLUB CONFIDENTIAL
ESP MCGREE
MUMMIES

MATTHEW McDUFFIE*
Agent: Broder-Kurland-Webb-Uffner - Beverly Hills, 310/281-3400

Screenplays:
FRUITCAKE WEATHER
YOU ONLY DIE ONCE (Story) w/Jim Byrnes (CTF)
BILLY HELL
ANGELS ON HORSEBACK
KISS THE GROUND
WISHBONES

ALAN B. McELROY*
Agent: CAA - Beverly Hills, 310/288-4545
Manager: Jon Brown, The Brown Group - Burbank, 818/955-7040

HALLOWEEN 4   Galaxy International, 1989
WHEELS OF TERROR (CTF)   Once Upon a Time, 1990
RAPID FIRE   20th Century Fox, 1992
UNDER THE CAR (Short)   Fried Films/Chanticleer, 1993, directed

Screenplays:
SILENT SHIELD
CUTTHROAT
WIND CHILL FACTOR
CRUSADER

JOHN McELWEE
Agent: Warden, White & Kane - Beverly Hills, 213/852-1028

Screenplays:
SERPENT'S TOOTH
KUEL KIDS
BLACK SHEEP

STEPHEN McEVEETY
AIRBORNE   Warner Bros., 1993, Story w/Bill Apablasa

IAN McEWAN
Agent: CAA - Beverly Hills, 310/288-4545

THE PLOUGHMAN'S LUNCH   Samuel Goldwyn Company, 1984
THE GOOD SON   20th Century Fox, 1993
THE INNOCENT   Miramax, 1994

Screenplays:
SOURSWEET

MARK THOMAS McGEE
INNER SANCTUM   RCA/Columbia Pictures Home Video, 1991

REX McGEE*
Agent: Innovative Artists - Los Angeles, 310/553-5200
Manager: Jon Brown, The Brown Group - Burbank,
   818/955-7040
Business: 9507 Santa Monica Blvd. - Suite 206, Beverly Hills,
   CA 90210, 310/859-8156

PURE COUNTRY   Warner Bros., 1991

Screenplays:
COMMUNITY STANDARDS
PAL SMURCH
UNTYING THE KNOT
THE LIFE OF THE PARTY
THE HONEYMOON
WALTZ IN MARATHON
MEET MR. BRINK
EASY LIVING
DECEPTION
THE HARDY BOYS

SCOTT McGEHEE
Agent: William Morris Agency - Beverly Hills, 310/274-7451
Contact: Kino-Korsakoff, 606 N. Larchmont - Suite 308,
   Los Angeles, CA 90004, 213/466-7683

SUTURE   Kino-Korsakoff, 1993, w/David Siegel, co-directed

KATHLEEN McGHEE-ANDERSON*
Agent: ICM - Beverly Hills, 310/550-4000

MOTHERS (P)

Screenplays:
COACH

JOSANN McGIBBON*
Agent: The Daniel Ostroff Agency - Los Angeles, 310/278-2020

WORTH WINNING   20th Century Fox, 1989, w/Sara Parriott
THREE MEN AND A LITTLE LADY   Buena Vista, 1990,
   Story w/Sara Parriott
THE FAVOR   Orion, 1994, w/Sara Parriott

Screenplays:
MRS. CALIFORNIA w/Sara Parriott
RUNAWAY BRIDE w/Sara Parriott

DAVID McGILLIVRAY
TERROR   Crown International, 1979

JIMMY McGOVERN
Contact: British Academy of Film & Television Arts, 195 Piccadilly,
   London W1, England, 01/734-0022

PRIEST   Miramax, 1995

DOUGLAS McGRATH*
Agent: ICM - Beverly Hills, 310/550-4000

THE BIG DAY (P)
BORN YESTERDAY   Buena Vista, 1993
BULLETS OVER BROADWAY   Miramax, 1994, w/Woody Allen

Screenplays:
JUST MARRIED
TOM SAWYER

GEORGE McGRATH*
Agent: Broder-Kurland-Webb-Uffner - Beverly Hills, 310/281-3400

BIG-TOP PEE WEE   Paramount, 1988, w/Paul Reubens

Screenplays:
MARATHON MOVIE
SILLY HILLBILLIES FROM MARS (AF)

JOHN McGRATH
Agent: The Casarotto Company - London, 071/287-4450

BILLION DOLLAR BRAIN   United Artists, 1967
THE VIRGIN SOLDIERS   Columbia, 1968, Adaptation
THE BOFORS GUN   Rank, 1968
THE RECKONING   Columbia, 1969
THE DRESSMAKER   Euro-American, 1988
THE LONG ROADS   BBC TV, 1993

PATRICK McGRATH*
Agent: Writers & Artists Agency - Los Angeles, 310/824-6300

Screenplays:
THE GROTESQUE (I.R.S.)
MIAMI GOTHIC

THOMAS McGRATH
INDEPENDENCE   20th Century-Fox, 1976, w/Joyce Ritter &
   Lloyd Ritter

JOHN McGREEVY*
Agent: Preferred Artists - Encino, 818/990-0305

HOT ROD GIRL   American International, 1956
DEATH IN SMALL DOSES   Mirisch Productions, 1957
CAST A LONG SHADOW   United Artists, 1959,
   w/Martin H. Goldsmith
HELLO DOWN THERE   Paramount, 1969, w/Frank Telford
NIGHT CROSSING   Buena Vista, 1982

THOMAS McGUANE*
Agent: ICM - Beverly Hills, 310/550-4000

92 IN THE SHADE   United Artists, 1975, directed
RANCHO DELUXE   United Artists, 1975
THE MISSOURI BREAKS   United Artists, 1976
TOM HORN   Warner Bros., 1980, w/Edwin Shrake
COLD FEET   Avenue Pictures, 1989, w/Jim Harrison

Screenplays:
SOLDIERS OF MISFORTUNE
NOBODY'S ANGEL
BOULEVARD WEST
TROPICAL WHOLESALE
TOKYO BAY
FLYING COLORS
THE EL WESTERN

DON McGUIRE*
Contact: WGA - Los Angeles, 310/550-1000

MEET DANNY WILSON   Universal-International, 1951
WALKING MY BABY BACK HOME   Universal-International, 1953,
   w/Oscar Brodney
THREE RING CIRCUS   Paramount, 1954, w/Joseph Pevney
ARTISTS AND MODELS   Paramount, 1955, w/Frank Tashlin
JOHNNY CONCHO   United Artists, 1956,
   w/David P. Harmon, directed
HEAR ME GOOD   Paramount, 1957, directed
THE DELICATE DELINQUENT   Paramount, 1957, directed
SUPPOSE THEY GAVE A WAR AND NOBODY CAME?   Cinerama
   Releasing Corporation, 1970, w/Hal Captain
TOOTSIE ★   Columbia, 1982, Story w/Larry Gelbart

JAY McINERNEY*
Agent: ICM - New York, 212/556-5600

BRIGHT LIGHTS, BIG CITY   MGM/UA, 1988

Screenplays:
DAMON AND PATRICE

DOUGLAS LLOYD McINTOSH*
Agent: Camden-ITG - Los Angeles, 310/289-2700

NOTORIOUS (CTF)   Hamster-ABC, 1992

Screenplays:
BAD WOMAN BLUES
THE LAUGHING MAN

CHRIS McINTYRE
DEAD WRONG   Prism Pictures, 1993, directed

DOUG McINTYRE*
Agent: The Wright Concept - Burbank, 818/954-8943

Screenplays:
BIG FAT ELVIS w/Doug Steckler
RIDE THE WIND

ELIZABETH McKAY
AN UNSUITABLE JOB FOR A WOMAN   Castle Hill
   Productions, 1985

STEVEN McKAY*
Agent: Broder-Kurland-Webb-Uffner - Beverly Hills, 310/281-3400

HARD TO KILL   Warner Bros., 1990
DIGGSTOWN   MGM, 1992

Screenplays:
JOHN & MARY
THIN ICE
BODY HUNTER

MICHAEL McKEAN*
Agent: William Morris Agency - Beverly Hills, 310/274-7451

THIS IS SPINAL TAP   Embassy, 1984, w/Christopher Guest,
   Harry Shearer & Rob Reiner
THE BIG PICTURE   Columbia, 1989, w/Christopher Guest &
   Michael Varhol

ROBERT McKEE*
Contact: WGA - Los Angeles, 310/550-1000

ABRAHAM (CTF)   Turner Network Television/LUX/RAI, 1994

DON McKELLAR
Contact: Academy of Canadian Cinema & Television, 753 Yonge St. -
   2nd Floor, Toronto M4Y 1Z9, Canada, 416/967-0315

HIGHWAY 61   Skouras Pictures, 1992
DANCE ME OUTSIDE   Cineplex Odeon, 1994, w/Bruce McDonald
THIRTY-TWO SHORT FILMS ABOUT GLENN GOULD
   Samuel Goldwyn Company, 1993, w/Francois Girard

T.C. McKELVEY
DUNE WARRIORS   Califilm, 1991

BERNARD McKENNA
Agent: Jill Foster, 3 Lonsdale Road, London SW 13 9ED,
   081/741-9410, fax 741-2916

THE ODD JOB   Columbia, 1978, w/Graham Chapman
YELLOWBEARD   Orion, 1983, w/Graham Chapman & Peter Cook

TERENCE McKENNA
THE SQUAMISH FIVE   CBC Film, 1989, w/Ken Gass

BLEU McKENZIE
KING OF THE CITY *CLUB LIFE*   Troma, 1986,
   Story w/Norman Thaddeus Vane

CHARLES McKEOWN
Agent: CAA - Beverly Hills, 310/288-4545

BRAZIL ★   Universal, 1985, w/Terry Gilliam & Tom Stoppard
THE ADVENTURES OF BARON MUNCHAUSEN   Columbia, 1988,
   w/Terry Gilliam

VINCE McKEWIN*
Agent: United Talent Agency - Beverly Hills, 310/273-6700

Screenplays:
THE CLIMB
FLORIDA STRAITS
VETERAN'S DAY
EMPEROR NORTON
YEAGER
A COP AND A CRIMINAL
COLLISION

W.R. (BILL) McKINNEY, JR.*
Agent: Stephanie Mann Agency - Los Angeles, 213/653-7130

TEACHERS   MGM/UA, 1984

Screenplays:
ABEL BAKER CAIN
THE EXCHANGE STUDENT
PRIDE AND JOY
BAREHUNTIN'
CHINA
WINSTON COME HOME, YOUR DOG DIED TUESDAY
THE PHENOM
THE BUTLER

JOHN McLAUGHLIN
THE LAST GOOD TIME   Samuel Goldwyn Company, 1994,
   w/Bob Balaban

STEVE McLEAN
POSTCARDS FROM AMERICA   Islet, 1994, directed

DON McLENNAN
Agent: Susan Smith & Associates - Beverly Hills, 213/852-4777

HARD KNOCKS   Andromeda Productions, 1980,
   w/Hilton Bonner, directed
SLATE, WYN & ME   Hemdale, 1987, directed

Screenplays:
NAOMI'S ROOM
APPARENT WIND
BEFORE YOUR VERY EYES w/Hilton Bonner
KING ISLAND w/Zbigniew Friedrich
MOST WANTED MAN w/Larry Held
JAILBAIT w/Tom Burstall
WHITE HEAT
UNFINISHED BUSINESS
COMEDY OF ERRORS

TOM McLOUGHLIN*
Business Manager: Armstrong, Hirsch, Jackoway, Tyerman &
   Wertheimer - Los Angeles, 310/553-0305

ONE DARK NIGHT   Comworld, 1983, w/Michael Hawes, directed
FRIDAY THE 13TH, PART VI: JASON LIVES   Paramount,
   1986, directed
DATE WITH AN ANGEL   DEG, 1987, directed

THOMAS McMAHON*
Contact: WGA - Los Angeles, 310/550-1000

SIDEWINDER 1   Avco Embassy, 1977, w/Nancy Voyles Crawford

SUSAN McMARTIN
Agent: Premiere Artists - Los Angeles, 310/271-1414

WINGS (P)
PARKED (P)
SON-IN-LAW   Buena Vista, 1993, Story w/Patrick Clifton &
    Peter Lenkov

Screenplays:
I, MOLLY

KEN McMULLEN
Contact: British Academy of Film & Television Arts, 195 Piccadilly,
    London W1, England, 71/734-0022

PIECES (Short)   1971,   directed
ROOM TO MOVE (Short)   1972,   directed
LOVELIES AND DOWDIES (Short)   1974,   directed
BEING AND DOING (Short)   1984,   directed
1867 (Short)   1990,   directed
GHOST DANCE   Film Four International, 1983, directed
ZINA   Palan Entertainment, 1985, w/Terry James, directed
PARTITION   Film Four International, 1987, w/Tariq Ali, directed
1871   Film Four International, 1990, w/Terry James &
    James Leahy,   directed

LARRY McMURTRY*
Agent: William Morris Agency - Beverly Hills, 310/274-7451

THE LAST PICTURE SHOW ★   Columbia, 1971,
    w/Peter Bogdanovich
MONTANA (CTF)   Turner Network TV, 1989
MEMPHIS (CTF)   Propaganda Films/River Siren, 1992,
    w/Cybill Shepherd & Susan Rhinehart
FALLING FROM GRACE   Columbia, 1992

Screenplays:
PRETTY BOY FLOYD w/Diana Ossana
FATHER KNOWS BEST w/Diana Ossana
THE STANDOFF w/Diana Ossana
DANCE WITH ME OUTSIDE w/L. Silko
DESERT ROSE
SOMEBODY'S DARLING
ALL MY FRIENDS ARE GOING TO BE STRANGERS
JUBILEE
HONKY TONK SUE
CROSSING NIAGARA

KEITH McNALLY
END OF THE NIGHT   In Absentia Productions, 1991,   directed

TERRENCE McNALLY*
Agent: William Morris Agency - New York, 212/586-5100

THIS SIDE OF THE DOOR (P)
AND THINGS THAT GO BUMP IN THE NIGHT (P)
NEXT (P)
WHERE HAS TOMMY FLOWERS GONE? (P)
BAD HABITS (P)
THE TUBS (P)
IT'S ONLY A PLAY (P)
THE LISBON TRAVIATA (P)
LIPS TOGETHER, TEETH APART (P)
KISS OF THE SPIDER WOMAN (P)
LOVE! VALOUR! COMPASSION! (P)
THE RITZ   Warner Bros., 1976, from his play
FRANKIE AND JOHNNY   Paramount, 1991,
    from his play "Frankie and Johnny in the Clair De Lune"

Screenplays:
PUCCINI

TERRENCE E. McNALLY
EARTH GIRLS ARE EASY   Vestron, 1988, w/Julie Brown &
    Charlie Coffey

JOHN McNAUGHTON
Agent: ICM - Beverly Hills, 310/550-4000

HENRY...PORTRAIT OF A SERIAL KILLER   Greycat, 1989,
    w/Richard Fire,   directed

Screenplays:
STEP RIGHT UP w/Richard Fire
NEVERLAND w/Ted Mann
THE LAST WORDS OF DUTCH SCHULTZ w/Scott Vehill

JERRY McNEELY*
Agent: Paul Kohner, Inc. - Beverly Hills, 310/550-1060

BLIND VENGEANCE (CTF)   Spanish Trail Productions, 1990,
    Story w/Howard Rodman

LESLIE McNEIL*
Contact: WGA - Los Angeles, 310/550-1000

BENNY & JOON   MGM, 1993, Story w/Barry Berman

STEPHEN F. McPHERSON*
Agent: Richland/Wunsch/Hohman Agency - Los Angeles,
    310/278-1955

COCOON: THE RETURN   20th Century Fox, 1987

Screenplays:
DOCTOR GOODNIGHT w/Elizabeth Bradley
GOING HOME w/Elizabeth Bradley
OUTWARD BOUND w/Elizabeth Bradley
MAD DASH w/Elizabeth Bradley
TO THE MANOR BORN w/Elizabeth Bradley
THE GRAY GHOST MIDNIGHT FLYER w/Elizabeth Bradley

JAMES C. McQUAIDE*
Agent: William Morris Agency - Beverly Hills, 310/274-7451

Screenplays:
THE DOOMSDAY CONSPIRACY w/Mark Verheiden
SHERLOCK HOLMES

CHRISTOPHER McQUARRIE
Agent: ICM - Beverly Hills, 310/550-4000

PUBLIC ACCESS   Cinemabeam, 1993, w/Michael Feit Dugan &
    Bryan Singer

Screenplays:
THE USUAL SUSPECTS

LAURIE McQUILLAN
MOTORCYCLE GANG (CTF)   Showtime/Drive-In Classic Cinema,
    1994, w/Kent Anderson

JAMES McTERNAN
SMALL KILL   Rayfield Co., 1992, w/Fred Carpenter

JOHN McTIERNAN*
Agent: CAA - Beverly Hills, 310/288-4545

NOMADS   Atlantic Releasing Corporation, 1985, directed

Screenplays:
BITTER ROOT
QUEST OF ST. JAMES ELK
TREASURE HUNT

KATHY McWORTER*
Agent: ICM - Beverly Hills, 310/550-4000
Manager: RKS Entertainment Group - Sherman Oaks, 818/788-3616

THE WAR   Universal, 1994

Screenplays:
THE CHEESE STANDS ALONE
BATS
THE BOY WHO EATS ROCKS

NICK MEAD
BULLSEYE!   21st Century Film, 1991, Story w/Leslie Bricusse &
   Michael Winner
BANK ROBBER   I.R.S. Releasing, 1993, directed

Screenplays:
PARTING SHOTS w/Michael Winner

PETER MEAD
THE CHANNELER   Magnum Entertainment, 1991, w/Jeff Falls &
   Jeb Seibel

WINTER MEAD
Agent: Lisa Callamaro Literary Agency- Beverly Hills, 310/274-6783

Screenplays:
BASE NATURE w/Benjamin Hall
PAPER PRISONS w/Benjamin Hall

BRUCE MEADE
REFORM SCHOOL GIRLS (CTF)   Showtime/Drive-In Classic
   Cinema, 1994

HERB MEADOW*
Contact: WGA - Los Angeles, 310/550-1000

Screenplays:
ANNE OF THE SPANISH MAIN (Cinemagic Pictures)

IRENE MECCHI*
Agent: William Morris Agency - Beverly Hills, 310/274-7451

THE LION KING (AF)   Buena Vista, 1994, w/Jonathan Roberts &
   Linda Woolverton

BENNY MEDINA*
Contact: WGA - Los Angeles, 310/550-1000

ABOVE THE RIM   New Line Cinema, 1994, Story w/Jeff Pollack

JAMES E. MEDLIN*
(Big Boy Medlin)
Contact: WGA - Los Angeles, 310/550-1000

ROADIE   United Artists, 1981, w/Michael Ventura

Screenplays:
MEANWHILE BACK AT THE KREMLIN w/Michael Ventura
HOWLING AT THE MOON w/Michael Ventura
MONTREAUX
THE JOKER AND THE DEALER
SHOT NIGHT
BEACH PARTY '85
LOW POWER

MURRAY MEDNICK*
Contact: WGA - Los Angeles, 310/550-1000

THE HAWK (P)
THE DEER KILL (P)
THE HUNTER (P)
CARTOON (P)
SAND (P)
AR YOU COOKIN? (P)

THE COYOTE CYCLE (P)
TAXES (P)
HEADS (P)
SEE YOU IN NAIROBI (P)
SHATTER'N'WADE (P)
SCAR (P)   also screenplay

MARK MEDOFF*
Agent: William Morris Agency - Beverly Hills, 310/274-7451

THE TURNAROUND (P)
THE MAGESTIC KID (P)
THE HANDS OF ITS ENEMY (P)
THE HEART OUTRIGHT (P)
THE BAD BOYS (P)   also screenplay
FREE (P)   also screenplay
CAPTAIN SUNTAN RIDES AGAIN (P)   also screenplay
THE KRAMER (P)
GOOD GUYS WEAR BLACK   American Cinema, 1978,
   w/Bruce Cohn
WHEN YOU COMIN' BACK RED RYDER?   Columbia, 1979,
   from his play
CHILDREN OF A LESSER GOD ★   Paramount, 1986,
   w/Hesper Anderson, from his play
OFF BEAT   Buena Vista, 1986
APOLOGY (CTF)   Roger Gimbel Productions/Peregrine
   Entertainment/ASAP Productions/HBO, 1986
CLARA'S HEART   Warner Bros., 1988
CITY OF JOY   TriStar, 1992
SHOWDOWN ON RIO ROAD (Short)   AFI, 1993, w/Ross Marks,
   from his play
HOMAGE   Skyline Entertainment, 1994,
   from his play "The Homage That Follows"

Screenplays:
PRIZED POSSESSIONS
FOURTH FURY
BULLY
LAST WISH
MISS ONE THOUSAND SPRING BLOSSOMS
DECEPTION

CARY MEDOWAY
Agent: Shapiro/Lichtman - Los Angeles, 310/859-8877

THE HEAVENLY KID   Orion, 1985, w/Martin Copeland, directed

THOMAS MEEHAN*
Agent: David Shapira & Associates - Sherman Oaks, 818/906-0322
Contact: Alan U. Schwartz - 310/278-1111

ANNIE (P)
AIN'T BROADWAY GRAND (P) w/Lee Adams
TO BE OR NOT TO BE   20th Century-Fox, 1983, w/Ronny Graham
ONE MAGIC CHRISTMAS   Buena Vista, 1985
SPACEBALLS   MGM/UA, 1987, w/Mel Brooks & Ronny Graham

STEVE MEERSON*
Agent: William Morris Agency - Beverly Hills, 310/274-7451

STAR TREK IV: THE VOYAGE HOME   Paramount, 1986,
   w/Harve Bennett, Peter Krikes & Nicholas Meyer
BACK TO THE BEACH   Paramount, 1987, w/Peter Krikes &
   Christopher Thompson
DOUBLE IMPACT   Columbia, 1991, Story w/Peter Krikes,
   Sheldon Lettich & Jean-Claude Van Damme

Screenplays:
GIGANTOR w/Peter Krikes
RING OF BLOOD w/Peter Krikes
BEST ENEMIES w/Peter Krikes
THAT'S LIFE, 1986 w/Peter Krikes
A NEW KIND OF LOVE w/Peter Krikes
RIVER OAKS w/Peter Krikes
THE LONG WAY HOME w/Peter Krikes
ON GUARD w/Peter Krikes
19 PURCHASE STREET w/Peter Krikes
PLANET OF THE TEENAGERS w/Peter Krikes
MONEY FROM THE SKY w/Peter Krikes

LESLIE MEGAHY
Agent: Peters, Fraser & Dunlop - London, 071/376-7676

THE ADVOCATE   Miramax, 1994, directed

ROBERT T. MEGGINSON*
Agent: Shapiro/Lichtman - Los Angeles, 310/859-8877

F/X   Orion, 1986, w/Gregory Fleeman

Screenplays:
TWO COPS w/Gregory Fleeman
DOUBTING THOMAS
FLAWLESS

JOSEPH MEHRI
ANGELS OF THE CITY   Raedon Home Video, 1989,
   w/Lawrence Hilton-Jacobs & Raymond Martino
THE LAST RIDERS   PM Home Video, 1991, w/Ray Garmon &
   Addison Randall, directed

GORDON MELBOURNE
BULLET PROOF HEARTS   *KILLER*   InterCoast Pictures, 1994

STEVE MELCHING
Agent: ICM - Beverly Hills, 310/550-4000
Manager: Ogden House - Los Angeles, 213/851-0458

Screenplays:
PARENT'S NIGHT

JIM MELKONIAN
Agent: ICM - Beverly Hills, 310/550-4000

THE CHILI CON CARNE CLUB   (Short), 1993, w/Jonathan Kahn
THE STONED AGE   Trimark, 1994, w/Rich Wilkes, directed
THE JERKY BOYS   Buena Vista, 1995, w/Rich Wilkes,
   Kamal Ahmed & John G. Brennan

JAMES MELLON
Contact: Sneak Preview Productions - Los Angeles, 213/962-0295

AN UNFINISHED SONG (P)

Screenplays:
BIRD OF PREY

LANA FREISTAT - MELMAN
(See Lana FREISTAT-Melman)

IVAN MENCHELL*
Agent: The Tantleff Office - New York, 212/941-3939

THE CEMETARY CLUB   Buena Vista, 1993, from his play

Screenplays:
EIGHT DAYS A WEEK

GEORGE MENDELUK
Business: World Classic Pictures, 6263 Tapia Drive, Malibu,
   CA 90265, 310/457-9911

STONE COLD DEAD   Dimension, 1979, directed

RAMON MENENDEZ*
Agent: United Talent Agency - Beverly Hills, 310/273-6700

STAND AND DELIVER   Warner Bros., 1988, w/Tom Musca
MONEY FOR NOTHING   Buena Vista, 1993, w/Tom Musca &
   Carol Sobieski, directed

ROBIN MENKEN
YOUNG LUST   RSO Films, 1982, w/Bruce Wagner
TEEN WITCH   Trans World Entertainment, 1989,
   w/Vernon Zimmerman

NINA MENKES
QUEEN OF DIAMONDS   Menkes Film Productions, 1991, directed

JOE MENOSKY*
Contact: WGA - Los Angeles, 310/550-1000

HIDING OUT   DEG, 1987, w/Jeff Rothberg

PAT MEPHITIS
NATIONAL LAMPOON'S MOVIE MADNESS   United Artists, 1982,
   w/Tod Carroll, Shary Flenniken, Gerald Sussman & Ellis Weiner

ANNE MEREDITH*
Agent: Broder-Kurland-Webb-Uffner - Beverly Hills, 310/281-3400

Screenplays:
TANDEM BLUES

MONTE MERRICK*
Agent: Above the Line - West Hollywood, 310/859-6115

HELL OF A TOWN (P)
PRIDE AND JOY (P)
STAYING TOGETHER   Hemdale, 1989
MEMPHIS BELLE   Warner Bros., 1990
MR. BASEBALL   Universal, 1992, w/Gary Ross & Kevin Wade
8 SECONDS   New Line Cinema, 1994

Screenplays:
OLIVER TWIST
STARRY EYED
TENDERFOOT
THE CONTENDER
PRIVATE PROPERTY

BOB MERRILL
W.C. FIELDS AND ME   Universal, 1976

KEITH MERRILL
Contact: Directors Guild of America - Los Angeles, 310/289-2000

TAKE DOWN   Buena Vista, 1979, w/Eric Herdershot, directed
HARRY'S WAR   Taft International, 1981, directed

RICK MERWYN
Agent: The Irv Schechter Company - Beverly Hills, 310/278-8070

Screenplays:
SPARE PARTS w/Michael Maurer

PHILIP FRANK MESSINA*
Agent: Paul Kohner, Inc. - Beverly Hills, 310/550-1060

BRAINSTORM   MGM/UA, 1983, w/Robert Stitzel

ALEXANDER METCALF
Agent: Sanford-Gross & Associates - Los Angeles,
   310/208-2100

Screenplays:
INFINTY WALTZ
HEARTLESS

KEN METCALFE
FIRECRACKER   New World, 1981, w/Cirio Santiago

STEPHEN B. METCALFE*
Agent: United Talent Agency - Beverly Hills, 310/273-6700

PILGRIMS (P)
SORROWS AND SONS (P)
THE INCREDIBLY FAMOUS WILLY RIVERS (P)
WHITE LINEN (P)
WHITE MAN DANCING (P)
DIVERTIMENTI (P)
EMILY (P)   also screenplay
VIKINGS (P)   also screenplay
FLORIDA STRAITS (CTF)   HBO Premiere Films/Robert Cooper
   Productions, 1986
JACKNIFE   Cineplex Odeon, 1989, from his play "Strange Snow"
COUSINS   Paramount, 1989
ROOMMATES   Buena Vista, 1994, w/Max Apple

Screenplays:
MACHINE GUN KELLY
HALF A LIFETIME (CTF)
EVERLOVIN' BROWN
THE TIME BETWEEN
BOYS FROM GALILEE
LAST SEPTEMBER
THE BIG NOISE
TIME FLIES
COMMENCEMENT

TIMOTHY J. METCALFE*
Agent: William Morris Agency - Beverly Hills, 310/274-7451

REVENGE OF THE NERDS   20th Century Fox, 1984,
   Story w/Jeff Buhai, Miguel Tejada-Flores & Steve Zacharias
THREE FOR THE ROAD   New Century/Vista, 1987,
   w/Richard Martini & Miguel Tejada-Flores
MILLION DOLLAR MYSTERY   DEG, 1987,
   w/Miguel Tejada-Flores & Rudy DeLuca
FRIGHT NIGHT PART 2   New Century/Vista, 1989,
   w/Miguel Tejada-Flores & Tommy Lee Wallace
IRON MAZE   Iron Maze Productions, 1991
KALIFORNIA   Gramercy, 1993

Screenplays:
KILLER (directing)

DOUGLAS ANTHONY METROV*
Contact: 404/924-9938

SOLARBABIES   MGM/UA, 1986, w/Walon Green

RADLEY METZGER
THE LICKERISH QUARTET   Audobon, 1970, directed
THE CAT AND THE CANARY   Quartet, 1982, directed

JEFFREY M. MEYER*
Contact: WGA - Los Angeles, 310/550-1000

CONAGHER (CTF)   Imagine Film Entertainment, 1991,
   w/Sam Elliott & Katherine Ross

JOHN MEYER
NOT FOR PUBLICATION   Samuel Goldwyn Company, 1984,
   w/Paul Bartel

KEVIN MEYER*
Agent: Broder-Kurland-Webb-Uffner - Beverly Hills, 310/281-3400

ACROSS FIVE APRILS   *CIVIL WAR DIARY* (CTF)   New World
   Entertainment, 1990, directed
INVASION OF PRIVACY (CTF)   Amritraj Entertainment/Promark
   Entertainment/Prism Pictures, 1992, directed
UNDER INVESTIGATION   Saban Entertainment, 1993, directed
PERFECT ALIBI   Rysher Entertainment, 1994, directed

MARLANE X. MEYER*
Agent: The Gersh Agency - Beverly Hills, 310/274-6611

ETTA JENKS (P)
MOE'S LUCKY SEVEN (P)
PRISON STORIES: WOMEN ON THE INSIDE (CTF)   Francine
   LeFrak Productions/HBO Showcase, 1991, "Parole Board"
BETTER OFF DEAD (CTF)   Viacom Productions, 1993

NICHOLAS MEYER*
Agent: CAA - Beverly Hills, 310/288-4545
Business: Meyer/Jaffe Productions, Paramount Pictures,
   213/956-5841

LOCO MOTIVES (P)
INVASION OF THE BEE GIRLS   1973
THE SEVEN-PERCENT SOLUTION ★   Universal, 1976
TIME AFTER TIME   Orion/Warner Bros., 1977, directed
STAR TREK IV: THE VOYAGE HOME   Paramount, 1986,
   w/Harve Bennett, Peter Krikes & Steve Meerson
COMPANY BUSINESS   MGM-Pathe, 1991, directed
STAR TREK VI : THE UNDISCOVERED COUNTRY   Paramount,
   1992, w/Denny Martin Flinn, directed
SOMMERSBY   Warner Bros., 1993, w/Sarah Kernochan

Screenplays:
THE WHITE COMPANY
DON QUIXOTE
BLACK ORCHID
CHARMED LIVES
CONJURING
THE FRAME-UP
UNDERSTUDY

PATRICIA K. MEYER
Agent: CAA - Beverly Hills, 310/288-4545

Screenplays:
IN CASE OF EMERGENCY
THE BLUE BRIGADE
KNOCKOUT

RUSS MEYER
Business: RM Films International Inc., P.O. Box 3748, Hollywood,
   CA 90028, 213/466-7791

THE IMMORAL MR. TEAS   Pedram, 1959, directed
EVE AND THE HANDYMAN   Eve, 1961, directed
EROTICA   Eve, 1961, directed
THE IMMORTAL WEST AND HOW IT WAS LOST   Eve,
   1961, directed
LORNA   Eve, 1965, directed
MOTOR PSYCHO   Eve, 1965, Shared, directed
FASTER, PUSSYCAT! KILL! KILL!   Eve, 1965, Shared, directed
GOOD MORNING...AND GOODBYE   Eve, 1967, directed
FINDERS KEEPERS, LOVERS WEEPERS   Eve, 1968, directed
CHERRY, HARRY AND RAQUEL   Eve, 1969, Shared, directed
BEYOND THE VALLEY OF THE DOLLS   20th Century-Fox, 1970,
   Story, shared, directed
SWEET SUZY! *BLACKSNAKE*   Signal 166, 1975,
   Shared, directed
SUPERVIXENS   RM Films, 1975, Shared, directed
RUSS MEYER'S UP!   RM Films, 1976, directed
BENEATH THE VALLEY OF THE ULTRAVIXENS   RM Films,
   1979, directed

TURI MEYER
Agent: Warden, White & Kane - Beverly Hills, 213/852-1028

LEPRECHAN 2   Trimark, 1994, w/Al Septien

Screenplays:
CHAIRMAN OF THE BOARD   w/Al Septien (Trimark)
SLEEPSTALKER   w/Al Septien
THE CONQUERORS   w/Al Septien
FLASH POINT   w/Al Septien
THE TERRORIST   w/Al Septien

STORM WARNING w/Al Septien
THE THIRD RAIL w/Al Septien
CROSS OF WOOD w/Al Septien
CRIMINAL PAST w/Al Septien
THE CARRIER w/Al Septien

NANCY J. MEYERS*
Agent: ICM - Beverly Hills, 310/550-4000

PRIVATE BENJAMIN ★   Warner Bros., 1980, w/Harvey Miller &
    Charles Shyer
IRRECONCILABLE DIFFERENCES   Warner Bros., 1984,
    w/Charles Shyer
PROTOCOL   Warner Bros., 1984, Story w/Harvey Miller &
    Charles Shyer
BABY BOOM   MGM/UA, 1987, w/Charles Shyer
FATHER OF THE BRIDE   Buena Vista, 1991, w/Charles Shyer,
    Frances Goodrich & Albert Hackett
ONCE UPON A CRIME   MGM-Pathe, 1992, w/Charles Shyer &
    Steve Kluger
I LOVE TROUBLE   Buena Vista, 1994, w/Charles Shyer
FATHER OF THE BRIDE 2   Buena Vista, 1995, w/Charles Shyer

Screenplays:
TOAST OF THE TOWN w/Charles Shyer
LOVE CRAZY w/Charles Shyer

PATRICK MEYERS
K2   Paramount, 1992, w/Scott Roberts, from his play

PETER MEYERSON*
Contact: WGA - Los Angeles, 310/550-1000

THE LATE SIXTIES (P)
THE LAST FAMILY (P)

Screenplays:
BRONX STORY
THE LAST HOUSE
CITY OF ANGELS
BULLETPROOF
BRINGING IT ALL BACK HOME w/Alan Myerson
THE FASTEST MAN IN THE WORLD
FRIENDS

MENNO MEYJES*
Agent: CAA - Beverly Hills, 310/288-4545

THE COLOR PURPLE ★   Warner Bros., 1985
LIONHEART   Orion, 1987, w/Richard Outten
INDIANA JONES AND THE LAST CRUSADE   Paramount, 1989,
    Story w/George Lucas
RICOCHET   Warner Bros., 1991, Story w/Fred Dekker
FOREIGN STUDENT   Gramercy, 1994

Screenplays:
MANOLETE (Miramax, directing)
THE LION, THE WITCH AND THE WARDROBE
TREASURE ISLAND
CAPA
RACING IN THE STREETS
DEATH OF ROCK & ROLL
LORENZO DEMICI

MICHAEL MICHAELIAN*
Contact: WGA - Los Angeles, 310/550-1000

MIRACLE IN THE WILDERNESS (CTF)   Ruddy & Morgan
    Productions/Turner Pictures, 1991, w/Jim Byrnes

LEONARD MICHAELS
Contact: 415/642-3467

THE MEN'S CLUB   Atlantic Releasing Corporation, 1986

LORNE MICHAELS*
Business: Broadway Video, 1619 Broadway, 9th Floor, New York,
    NY 10019, 212/265-7621

THREE AMIGOS   Orion, 1986, w/Steve Martin & Randy Newman

MURRAY MICHAELS
TUFF TURF   New World, 1985, Story w/Gregg Collins O'Neill

TONY MICHELMAN
Agent: Innovative Artists - Los Angeles, 310/553-5200

PHANTOM OF THE MALL: ERIC'S REVENGE   Fries Entertainment,
    1989, w/Robert King & Scott J. Schneid

Screenplays:
MOUNT MANHATTAN w/Scott J. Schneid
DOWNFALL w/Scott J. Schneid
THE RED HOUR LEGACY w/Scott J. Schneid
INVASION OF THE BODY BUILDERS w/Scott J. Schneid

DAVID MICHENER
THE FOX AND THE HOUND (AF)   Buena Vista, 1981,
    Story w/others
THE GREAT MOUSE DETECTIVE (AF)   Buena Vista, 1986,
    w/others, co-directed

THOMAS MIDDLETON
THE CHANGELING (CTF)   BBC-TV, 1994, w/William Rowley

BETTE MIDLER
Business: All-Girl Pictures, Walt Disney Pictures, 818/560-5000

DIVINE MADNESS   Warner Bros., 1980, w/Jerry Blatt &
    Bruce Vilanch

ANNE-MARIE MIEVILLE
Contact: French Film Office, 745 Fifth Avenue, New York, NY 10151,
    212/832-8860

SAUVE QUI PEUT LA VIE   *EVERY MAN FOR HIMSELF N LIFE*
    New Yorker/Zoetrope, 1980, w/Jean-Luc Godard &
    Jean-Claude Carriere
FIRST NAME: CARMEN   Spectrafilm, 1984
DETECTIVE   Spectrafilm, 1985, w/Jean-Luc Godard, Alain Sarde &
    Philippe Setbon

JOHN MIGLIS*
Agent: CAA - Beverly Hills, 310/288-4545

KEEP THE CHANGE (CTF)   Steve Tisch Co./High
    Horse Films, 1992

Screenplays:
GERONIMO HOPE

DAVID MILES
Agent: Writers & Artists Agency - Los Angeles, 310/824-6300

Screenplays:
MANSON IN THE DESERT

DOUG MILES
BEASTMASTER 2: THROUGH THE PORTAL OF TIME
    New Line Cinema, 1991, w/Ken Hauser, Sylvio Tabet,
    R.J. Robertson & Jim Wynorski

DAVID MILHAUD
SHADOW OF THE WOLF   Triumph, 1993, Adaptation

DJORDJE MILICEVIC*
Business Manager: Singer, Lewak, Greenbaum - Los Angeles,
310/477-3924

WET RAINBOW   Demos Films, 1974, w/Paul Baerwold, directed
VAMPIRE LUST   Demos Films, 1975, w/Jeff Maguire, directed
RECKLESS   Can-America Productions, 1979,
   w/Jeff Maguire, directed
VICTORY   Lorimar/Paramount, 1981, Story w/Jeff Maguire
RUNAWAY TRAIN   Cannon, 1985, w/Edward Bunker & Paul Zindel
TOBY McTEAGUE   Spectrafilm, 1986, w/Jamie Brown &
   Jeff Maguire
GLADIATOR   Columbia, 1992, Story w/Robert Mark Kamen
IRON WILL   Buena Vista, 1994, w/Jeffrey Arch &
   John Michael Hayes

Screenplays:
ABOVE SUSPICION
DEATH OF A STOCKBROKER
ENTERPRISE w/David Wheeler
FLAG FOR SUNRISE
GIRL ON A GOLDEN LEASH
HAMMER HAND
HIGHWAY ONE
LAST KISS w/Jeff Maguire
REMORA
ROCK AND GOAL
SECOND CHANCE
SHADOW 81
SHOOTER
SIEGE OF SILENCE
WOUNDED KNEE

FRANK MILITARY, JR.*
Agent: William Morris Agency - New York, 212/586-5100

Screenplays:
THE LOTTERY ROSE
BIRDS OF PREY
THE SILENCE
ANATOMY OF A JURY
THE PIECE
BEYOND REASON

JOHN MILIUS*
Agent: ICM - Beverly Hills, 310/550-4000

THE DEVIL'S EIGHT   American International, 1968,
   w/James Gordon White & Willard Hyuck
EVEL KNIEVEL   MGM, 1971, w/Alan Caillou
THE LIFE AND TIMES OF JUDGE ROY BEAN
   National General, 1972
JEREMIAH JOHNSON   Warner Bros., 1972, w/Edward Anhalt
MAGNUM FORCE   Warner Bros., 1973, w/Michael Cimino
DILLINGER   American International, 1973, directed
THE WIND AND THE LION   MGM/United Artists, 1975, directed
BIG WEDNESDAY   Warner Bros., 1978,
   w/Dennis Aaberg, directed
1941   Universal/Columbia, 1979, Story
APOCALYPSE NOW ★   United Artists, 1979, w/Francis Coppola
CONAN THE BARBARIAN   Universal, 1982,
   w/Oliver Stone, directed
RED DAWN   MGM/UA, 1984, w/Kevin Reynolds, directed
EXTREME PREJUDICE   Tri-Star, 1987, Story w/Fred Rexer
FAREWELL TO THE KING   Orion, 1989, directed
GERONIIMO: AN AMERICAN LEGEND   Columbia, 1993,
   w/Larry Gross
CLEAR AND PRESENT DANGER   Paramount, 1994,
   w/Donald Stewart & Steven Zaillian

Screenplays:
THE TEXAS RANGERS
THE SIEGE OF LENINGRAD
THE VIKING

JEFF MILLAR*
Contact: 713/467-2730

DEAD AND BURIED   Avco Embassy, 1981, Story w/Alex Stern

Screenplays:
F'BALL

MILES MILLAR
Agent: Warden, White & Kane - Beverly Hills, 213/852-1028
Manager: Ogden House - Los Angeles, 213/851-0458

Screenplays:
MANGO w/Alfred Gough
ICE w/Alfred Gough

ANNIE MILLER
Contact: French Film Office, 745 Fifth Avenue, New York, NY 10151,
   212/832-8860

THE LITTLE THIEF   Miramax, 1989

ARTHUR MILLER*
Agent: ICM - New York, 212/556-5600

ALL MY SONS (P)
DEATH OF A SALESMAN (P)
THE CRUCIBLE (P)   also screenplay
A MEMORY OF TWO MONDAYS (P)
A VIEW FROM THE BRIDGE (P)
AFTER THE FALL (P)
INCIDENT AT VICHY (P)
THE PRICE (P)
THE CREATION OF THE WORLD AND OTHER BUSINESS (P)
THE ARCHBISHOP'S CEILING (P)
THE AMERICAN CLOCK (P)
DANGER: MEMORY! (P)
THE RIDE DOWN MOUNT MORGAN (P)
CLARA (P)
THE LAST YANKEE (P)
BROKEN GLASS (P)
THE MISFITS   United Artists, 1961
EVERYBODY WINS   Orion, 1990

BRODERICK MILLER*
Agent: William Morris Agency - Beverly Hills, 310/274-7451

DEADLOCK (CTF)   Frederick S. Pierce-Spectator, 1991

BRUCE MILLER*
Contact: WGA - Los Angeles, 310/550-1000

Screenplays:
CRAZY FOR YOU

CHRIS MILLER*
Agent: APA - Los Angeles, 310/273-0744

NATIONAL LAMPOON'S ANIMAL HOUSE   Universal, 1978,
   Douglas Kenney & Harold Ramis
CLUB PARADISE   Warner Bros., 1986, Story w/Tom Leopold,
   Ed Roboto & David Standish

Screenplays:
MULTIPLICITY w/Mary Hale
VOODOO w/Michael Sutton
KEYSTONE COPS w/Michael Sutton
THE CO-EDS w/Michael Sutton
THE TECHNICOLOR TIME MACHINE w/Michael Sutton
ANIMAL HOUSE NOW w/Michael Sutton
NO SUCH LUCK w/Michael Sutton
WITCHCRAFT w/Michael Sutton
BEL-AIR BUTLER w/Michael Sutton
JUST LIKE A WOMAN w/Michael Sutton

DAVID LEE MILLER*
Agent: The Gersh Agency - Beverly Hills, 310/274-6611

BREAKFAST OF ALIENS   Hemdale, 1993,
    w/Vic Dunlop, directed

Screenplays:
JOHN DOE w/Vic Dunlop
SISTER MARY BUTCH w/Vic Dunlop

FRANK MILLER*
Agent: Shapiro/Lichtman - Los Angeles, 310/859-8877

ROBOCOP 2   Orion, 1990, w/Walon Green
ROBOCOP 3   Orion, 1993, w/Fred Dekker

Screenplays:
SIN CITY

GEOF MILLER*
Contact: 206/524-3163

DEEPSTAR SIX   Tri-Star, 1989, w/Lewis Abernathy

GEORGE MILLER
Agent: ICM - Beverly Hills, 310/550-4000
Business: Kennedy Miller Productions, 30 Orwell Street,
    Kings Cross, Sydney, Australia

MAD MAX   American International, 1979,
    w/James McCausland, directed
THE ROAD WARRIOR *MAD MAX II* Warner Bros., 1982,
    w/Brian Hannant & Terry Hayes, directed
MAD MAX BEYOND THUNDERDOME   Warner Bros., 1985,
    w/Terry Hayes, directed
LORENZO'S OIL ★   Universal, 1992, w/Nick Enright, directed

HARVEY MILLER*
Agent: ICM - Beverly Hills, 310/550-4000

PRIVATE BENJAMIN ★   Warner Bros., 1980, w/Nancy Meyers &
    Charles Shyer
JEKYLL AND HYDE...TOGETHER AGAIN   Paramount, 1982,
    w/Jerry Belson, Monica Johnson & Michael Leeson
CANNONBALL RUN II   Warner Bros., 1984, w/Hal Needham &
    Albert Ruddy
PROTOCOL   Warner Bros., 1984, Story w/Nancy Meyers &
    Charles Shyer
BAD MEDICINE   20th Century Fox, 1985, directed
GETTING AWAY WITH MURDER   Savoy, 1995, directed

JASON MILLER*
Agent: The Artists Agency - Los Angeles, 310/277-7779

LOU GEHRIG DID NOT DIE OF CANCER (P)
THAT CHAMPIONSHIP SEASON   Cannon, 1982,
    from his play, directed

Screenplays:
SHAKE DOWN THE THUNDER

JEFF MILLER
Agent: Metropolitan Talent Agency - Los Angeles, 213/857-4500

Screenplays:
IRONMEN w/Michael Hacker
FEVER w/Michael Hacker

MARK MILLER
SAVANNAH SMILES   Embassy, 1982

MARK C. MILLER*
Agent: Lenhoff/Robinson - Los Angeles, 310/558-4700

Screenplays:
I REALLY REALLY DIDN'T DO IT!
WIFE FOR SALE
JURY DUTY

MELISSA MILLER
OH GOD! BOOK II   Warner Bros., 1980, w/Fred S. Fox,
    Josh Greenfeld, Hal Goldman & Seaman Jacobs

MICHAEL A. MILLER*
Agent: Warden, White & Kane - Beverly Hills, 213/852-1028

DREAM MAN   Republic Pictures, 1994

Screenplays:
MOUNT WEATHER
JOAN
ORION POKER
HELLBENT
LAWYERS, GUNS AND MONEY

MOLLIE D. MILLER*
Agent: CAA - Beverly Hills, 310/288-4545

Screenplays:
GIRL CRAZY
SOLO
MODERN DOLLS

NANCY MILLER*
Agent: Maggie Field Agency - Studio City, 818/980-2001

Screenplays:
SOCIAL STUDIES w/Harris Goldberg

RANDALL MILLER*
Agent: CAA - Beverly Hills, 310/288-4545

MARILYN HOTCHKISS BALLROOM DANCING &
    CHARM SCHOOL (Short)   directed

Screenplays:
PRESUMED IMPOTENT w/Jody Savin (directing)
PIRATE TOM w/Jody Savin

REBECCA MILLER
Agent: William Morris Agency - Beverly Hills, 310/274-7451

ANGELA   1995, directed

SUSAN MILLER*
Agent: Major Clients Agency - Los Angeles, 310/284-6400

LADY BEWARE   Scotti Bros., 1987, w/Charles Zev Smith

Screenplays:
BLESSING IN DISGUISE

VICTOR MILLER*
Agent: Rick Hashagen & Associates - New York, 212/315-3130

FRIDAY THE 13TH   Paramount, 1980
A STRANGER IS WATCHING   MGM/UA, 1982, w/Earl Mac Rauch

PETER MILLIGAN
Contact: Prelude Pictures, Paramount, 213/956-8646

Screenplays:
PILGRIM

GREG MILLIN
THE CLINIC   Satori, 1985

WILLIAM P. MILLING
Agent: Solomon Weingarten & Associates - Los Angeles,
   310/479-4706

WOLFPACK   JER, 1986, directed
LAUDERDALE   Omega Pictures, 1988, directed
FORBIDDEN AMERICA   1982
SILENT MADNESS   Almi Pictures, 1984, Shared
SAVAGE DAWN   MAG Enterprises/Gregory Earls
   Productions, 1985
WOLFPACK   JER, 1986
CAGED FURY   21st Century Film Corp., 1989, directed
JOKER'S WILD   Omega Pictures, 1991, directed

LYNN MILLS*
Contact: WGA - Los Angeles, 310/550-1000

Screenplays:
ROBONANNY w/Jimmy Huston

PAULA MILNE
Agent: CAA - Beverly Hills, 310/288-4545

MAD LOVE   Buena Vista, 1995

RON MILNER
CHECKMATES (P)
THE KILLING FLOOR   Public Forum Productions/American
   Playhouse, 1992, Adaptation

Screenplays:
THE JAMES BROWN STORY

MAX MILO
KISS AND BE KILLED   Monarch Home Video,
   1991, directed

DAVID SCOTT MILTON*
Agent: Shapiro/Lichtman - Los Angeles, 310/859-8877

DUET (P)
DUET FOR SOLO VOICE AND BREAD (P)
SKIN (P)
BORN TO WIN   United Artists, 1971

MICHAEL MINER*
Agent: United Talent Agency - Beverly Hills, 310/273-6700

ROBOCOP   Orion, 1987, w/Edward Neumeier
DEADLY WEAPON   Empire Pictures, 1989, directed

Screenplays:
LAWNMOWER MAN 2
THE SECRET AGENT
NEW JACK CITY II w/Edward Neumeier
STRATT w/Edward Neumeier
THE EXECUTIONER w/Edward Neumeier
COMPANY MAN w/Edward Neumeier
HITMAN w/Edward Neumeier (co-directing)
WHITE TRASH w/Edward Neumeier
UPSIDE-DOWN
IRONMAN
BEAT THE DEVIL
ANIMAL
SAVAGES

ANTHONY MINGHELLA*
Agent: William Morris Agency - Beverly Hills, 310/274-7451

MADE IN BANGKOK (P)   also screenplay
TRULY, MADLY, DEEPLY   Samuel Goldwyn Company,
   1991, directed

Screenplays:
THE ENGLISH PATIENT (directing)

JOSEPH MINION*
Contact: WGA - Los Angeles, 310/550-1000

AFTER HOURS   The Geffen Company/Warner Bros., 1985
VAMPIRE'S KISS   Hemdale, 1989
MOTORAMA   Two Moon Releasing, 1993

Screenplays:
MRS. DUKE'S MILLIONS

CECILIA MINIUCCHI
Contact: River One Films, 1619 Broadway - 5th Floor, New York,
   NY 10019

Screenplays:
CLUCK (directing)

JOE MINJARES
Agent: The Gage Group - Los Angeles, 310/859-8777

Screenplays:
THE KING OF THE KOSHER GROCERS

ROY MINTON
SCUM   Berwick Street Films, 1979
SCRUBBERS   Orion Classics, 1984, w/Jeremy Watt &
   Mai Zetterling

LARRY MINTZ*
Agent: Writers & Artists Agency - Los Angeles, 310/824-6300

Screenplays:
SOLD w/Alan Eisenstock
DIE RISE w/Alan Eisenstock

MELANIE I. MINTZ*
Business Manager: Scott Shukat, Shukat Company - New York,
   212/582-7614

LEADER OF THE PACK (P)
JUST ONCE (P)

Screenplays:
POWER: THE PHIL SPECTOR STORY
IN SUBMISSION

MURRAY MINTZ*
Agent: Mitchell J. Hamilburg Agency - Los Angeles, 310/657-1501

Screenplays:
RED SCARE w/Joshua Smith
COLD CASH w/Joshua Smith
HIGH MOON
HEIR APPARENT
CARDIAC ARREST

JAY MIRACLE
THE HEALING FORCE   Woody Clark Productions, 1983,
   w/Woodrow W. Clark & Joanne Parrent

DAVID MIRKIN*
Agent: The Rothman Agency - Beverly Hills, 213/655-2020

THE LAST RESORT   Concorde/Cinema Group, 1986

Screenplays:
GUERILLA VIDEO
TRIMMING THE FAMILY TREE
THE LAST RESORT

BRAD A. MIRMAN*
Agent: Hilary Wayne - Beverly Hills, 310/289-6186

BODY OF EVIDENCE   MGM, 1993
KNIGHT MOVES   InterStar Releasing, 1993
HIGHLANDER 3: THE SORCERER   Miramax, 1995,
   Story w/William Panzer

Screenplays:
ABSOLON
PARTNERS IN CRIME
THE SET-UP
G.I. JILL

DAVID A. MISCH*
Agent: William Morris Agency - Beverly Hills, 310/274-7451

Screenplays:
DISTURBING THE PEACE
CONVENTIONS
GIRLGRABBERS FROM VENUS

RENÉE MISSEL*
Business: Renee Missel Productions, 7920 Sunset Blvd. - Suite 200,
   Los Angeles, CA 90046, 213/845-0300

MY MAN ADAM   Tri-Star, 1985, w/Roger L. Simon

RON MITA
Agent: United Talent Agency - Beverly Hills, 310/273-6700

Screenplays:
TRACK DOWN w/Jim McClain
THE FRENCH TEACHER w/Jim McClain
URBAN LEGEND w/Jim McClain

JULIAN MITCHELL
Agent: Peters, Fraser & Dunlop - London, 071/376-7676

ARABESQUE   Universal, 1966, w/Stanley Price & Pierre Marton
ANOTHER COUNTRY   20th Century-Fox, 1984, from his play
VINCENT AND THEO   Hemdale, 1990
AUGUST   Majestic Films, 1994

KEITH MITCHELL
Agent: Premiere Artists - Los Angeles, 310/271-1414

Screenplays:
3,000 w/Eric Champnella
LOVE ME TOMORROW w/Eric Champnella

SOLLACE MITCHELL*
Agent: CAA - Beverly Hills, 310/288-4545

Screenplays:
DOUBLE TAKE
PRESENT LAUGHTER
COLLEGE BOWL
THE WEDDING
SHELTER ISLAND
HATCHECK
HELLUVA DEAL
PG

STEVE MITCHELL
CHOPPING MALL   *KILLBOTS*   Concorde, 1986, w/Jim Wynorski

STEVEN LONG MITCHELL*
Agent: The Wright Concept - Burbank, 818/954-8943

SKI PATROL   Triumph, 1990, w/Craig Van Sickle

Screenplays:
PUMPKINHEADS II w/Craig Van Sickle

MOSHE MIZRAHI
Agent: The Gersh Agency - Beverly Hills, 310/274-6611
Business: Rosa Productions, 5 rue D'Artois, 75008 Paris,
   France, 04/359-4704

MADAME ROSA   Lira Films, 1977, directed
I SENT A LETTER TO MY LOVE   *CHERE INCONNUE*   Atlantic
   Releasing Corporation, 1980, w/Gerard Brach, directed
LA VIE CONTINUE   Triumph/Columbia, 1982,
   w/Rachel Fabien, directed
EVERY TIME WE SAY GOODBYE   Tri-Star, 1986,
   w/Rachel Fabien & Leah Appet, directed

JORDAN H. MOFFET*
Agent: United Talent Agency - Beverly Hills, 310/273-6700

Screenplays:
ROCK BOTTOM
FAMILY ROYALTY

PETER MOHAN
RACE TO FREEDOM: THE UNDERGROUND RAILROAD (CTF)
   The Family Channel/BET, 1994, w/Nancy Trites Botkin &
   Diana Braithwaite

CHRIS MOLLO
Agent: Renaissance-H.N. Swanson - Los Angeles, 310/246-6000

Screenplays:
SKINWALKER w/David Lux

JAMES C. MOLONEY
THE FIENDISH PLOT OF DR. FU MANCHU   United Artists, 1980,
   w/Rudy Dochtermann

ROBERT MOLONEY*
Agent: ICM - Beverly Hills, 310/550-4000

Screenplays:
NEED TO KNOW
JAKE'S TOMATOES
THE ID & I
HALLEY'S CONNECTION
BACK NINE
FOR ONE NIGHT ONLY

PAUL MONASH*
Agent: Paradigm - Los Angeles, 310/277-4400

BAIL OUT AT 43,000   United Artists, 1957
THE SAFECRACKER   MGM, 1958
THE SCARFACE MOB   Desilu, 1958
THE GUN RUNNERS   United Artists, 1958, w/Daniel Mainwaring
THE FRIENDS OF EDDIE COYLE   Paramount, 1973
STALIN (CTF)   HBO Pictures, 1992

PAUL S. MONES*
Agent: The Marion Rosenberg Office - Los Angeles, 213/653-7383
Manager: Addis-Wechsler - Los Angeles, 213/954-900
Contact: Signature A Film Company

THE BEAT   Vestron, 1987, directed
FATHERS AND SONS   Addis/Wechsler, 1992, directed
SAINTS AND SINNERS   MDP Worldwide, 1994, directed

Screenplays:
MEAN TIME
MADRAS

CHRISTOPHER MONGER*
Agent: The Artists Agency - Los Angeles, 310/277-7779

WAITING FOR THE LIGHT   Triumph, 1990, directed
AN ENGLISHMAN WHO WENT UP A HILL BUT CAME DOWN
   A MOUNTAIN   Miramax, 1995, directed

Screenplays:
PEN PALS
MY WIFE'S SISTERS

VINCENT MONGOL
CHAINED HEAT   Jensen Farley Pictures, 1983, w/Paul Nicolas
WARD B   *HELLHOLE*   Arkoff International Pictures, 1985

MEREDITH MONK
BOOK OF DAYS   The Stutz Company, 1991, w/Tone Blevins

CAROL MonPERE*
Agent: William Morris Agency - Beverly Hills, 310/274-7451

THE MOUSE AND HIS CHILD (AF)   Sanrio, 1977

Screenplays:
MIDNIGHT SOLDIER
THE LIMIT
UNFINISHED BUSINESS
COMBAT ZONE

MARCEL MONTECINO*
Agent: CAA - Beverly Hills, 310/288-4545

Screenplays:
BRACKISH BAYOU
PANCHO'S WAR
ABOVE CANAL
IMPROPER CONDUCT
THE CROSS-KILLER
BIG TIME
TUSKE GI ARMEN   RED TAILS

ART MONTERASTELLI*
Agent: Broder-Kurland-Webb-Uffner - Beverly Hills, 310/281-3400

WORKING STIFFS (Short)   1992, directed

Screenplays:
RECOIL
BLUE LIGHTNING

CLAIRE MONTGOMERY*
Contact: WGA - Los Angeles, 310/550-1000

THE PERFECT BRIDE (CTF)   Image Organization, 1991,
   w/Monty Montgomery

KATE MONTGOMERY
Agent: Susan Smith & Associates - Beverly Hills, 213/852-4777

Screenplays:
CHRISTMAS IN THE CLOUDS

MARK MONTGOMERY*
Agent: Candace Lake - Beverly Hills, 310/289-0600

VOYAGE (CTF)   Davis Entertainment/Quinta Communications, 1993

Screenplays:
THE GENERAL'S DAUGHTER
MONTANA BLUE w/John Montgomery
WRONG TURN w/John Montgomery
UNDERTOW w/John Montgomery

MICHAEL T. MONTGOMERY
Agent: The Adler Agency - Studio City, 818/769-5003

EYE OF THE TIGER   Scotti Bros., 1986
ROLLING VENGEANCE   Apollo Pictures, 1987

MONTY MONTGOMERY*
Contact: WGA - Los Angeles, 310/550-1000

THE LOVELESS   Atlantic Releasing Corporation, 1981,
   w/Kathryn Bigelow, co-directed
THE PERFECT BRIDE (CTF)   Image Organization, 1991,
   w/Claire Montgomery

SAM MONTGOMERY
THE FINAL MISSION   Trimark, 1993, w/Virginia Gilbert,
   Lee Redmond & Ernest Sheldon Jr.

RICHARD MONTOYA*
(with Ric Salinas & Herbert Siguenza: Culture Clash)
Agent: William Morris Agency - Beverly Hills, 310/274-7451

A BOWL OF BEINGS (P)   w/Ric Salinas & Herbert Siguenza
THE MISSION (P)   w/Ric Salinas & Herbert Siguenza

Screenplays:
GOMEZ, GOMEZ AND GOMEZ w/Ric Salinas &
   Herbert Siguenza (UA)

JOHN MOODY*
Contact: WGA - Los Angeles, 310/550-1000

WHICH END'S UP? (P)   w/Doug Cox

Screenplays:
NO SMOKING w/Doug Cox

PAUL MOONEY
Business Manager: Helen Shaw - Los Angeles, 310/474-8032

JO JO DANCER, YOUR LIFE IS CALLING   Columbia, 1986,
   w/Richard Pryor & Rocco Urbisci

BRIAN MOORE*
Agent: ICM - Beverly Hills, 310/550-4000

THE LUCK OF GINGER COFFEY   Continental, 1964
TORN CURTAIN   Universal, 1966
THE BLOOD OF OTHERS (CMS)   HBO Premiere Films/ICC/Filmax
   Productions, 1984
CONTROL (CTF)   HBO Showcase/Alliance Entertainment Corp/
   Cristaldifilm/Les Films Ariane, 1987
BLACK ROBE   Samuel Goldwyn Company, 1991

Screenplays:
NO OTHER LIFE

DUDLEY MOORE*
Agent: ICM - Beverly Hills, 310/550-4000

THIRTY IS A DANGEROUS AGE, CYNTHIA   Columbia, 1967,
   w/Joe McGrath & John Wells
BEDAZZLED   20th Century-Fox, 1967, Story w/Peter Cook
THE HOUND OF THE BASKERVILLES   Atlantic Releasing
   Corporation, 1979, w/Peter Cook & Paul Morrissey

ELLEN MOORE
Contact: Chesterfield Film Co. - 818/777-3425

Screenplays:
LADY IN THE LAKE

JOHN F. MOORE*
Contact: WGA - Los Angeles, 310/550-1000

Screenplays:
TIMING IS EVERYTHING w/Howard Chaykin

MICHAEL MOORE
Agent: ICM - New York, 212/556-5600

ROGER & ME (FD) Warner Bros., 1989, directed
CANADIAN BACON MGM/UA, 1995, directed

PETER S. MOORE*
Contact: WGA - Los Angeles, 310/550-1000

Screenplays:
NIGHTHUNT
GOING FOR THE JUGGLER

ROBIN MOORE
INCHON! MGM/UA, 1982, w/Laird Koenig

RON MOORE*
Agent: Richland/Wunsch/Hohman Agency - Los Angeles,
  310/278-1955

STAR TREK: GENERATIONS Paramount, 1994, w/Brannon Braga

SIMON MOORE
Agent: Sanford-Gross & Associates - Los Angeles, 310/208-2100 or
  Rochelle Steves & Co. - London, 071/359-3900

UP ON THE ROOF (P)
MISERY (P)
UNDER SUSPICION Columbia, 1992, directed
THE QUICK AND THE DEAD TriStar, 1995

Screenplays:
HIT AND RUN (directing)
THE PHARAOH OF IDAHO
THE DARK HORIZON
THE TENTH KINGDOM
THE BIG BREAK
REBEL MAGIC

TERRY MOORE
Contact: Screen Actors Guild - Los Angeles, 213/954-1600

BEVERLY HILLS BRATS Taurus Entertainment, 1989,
  Story w/Jerry Rivers

WESLEY MOORE*
Contact: WGA - New York, 212/245-6180

SWIM VISIT (P)
APPRENTICE TO MURDER New World, 1988, w/Allan Scott
ARE YOU LONESOME TONIGHT (CTF) OTML Productions/
  Wilshire Court Productions, 1992

Screenplays:
DOUBLE TAKE
TELEGRAPH HILL

WILLIAM MOORE
FIVE DAYS FROM HOME Universal, 1978

FRANK MOORHOUSE
THE COCA COLA KID Cinecom/Film Gallery, 1985
BETWEEN WARS Satori, 1985
THE EVERLASTING SECRET FAMILY International Film
  Exchange, 1989

JOCELYN MOORHOUSE*
Agent: William Morris Agency - Beverly Hills, 310/274-7451

PROOF Fine Line Features, 1992, directed

ELIZA MOORMAN
TORCHLIGHT International Film Marketing, 1984,
  w/Pamela Sue Martin

PHILLIPPE MORA
BROTHER, CAN YOU SPARE A DIME? (FD) Dimension,
  1975, directed
MAD DOG MAD DOG MORGAN Cinema Shares International,
  1976, directed
HOWLING III THE MARSUPIALS: THE HOWLING III
  Square Pictures, 1987, directed
ART DECO DETECTIVE Trident Releasing, 1994, directed

Screenplays:
PTERODACTYL WOMAN OF BRENTWOOD (directing)

MARTHA MORAN
HAPPILY EVER AFTER First National Film Corp., 1993,
  w/Robby London

Screenplays:
NO DESSERT DAD, UNTIL YOU MOW THE LAWN w/Jennifer Moran

RICK MORANIS*
Agent: ICM - Beverly Hills, 310/550-4000

STRANGE BREW MGM/UA, 1983, w/Dave Thomas &
  Steve DeJarnatt, directed

Screenplays:
KILLER CHARLIE FIVE (Shared)

CARL MORANO
CLASS OF NUKE E'M HIGH PART 2: SUBHUMANOID MELTDOWN
  Troma, 1991, w/Lloyd Kaufman, Eric Louzil, Marcus Rolling,
  Jeffrey W. Sass & Matt Unger, directed

RAFAEL MOREAU
Agent: William Morris Agency - Beverly Hills, 310/274-7451

HACKERS MGM/UA, 1995

ANDRE MORGAN
Business: Ruddy-Morgan Productions, 120 El Camino Dr. -
  Suite 112, Beverly Hills, CA 90212, 310/271-7698

MEGAFORCE 20th Century-Fox, 1982, w/James Whittaker,
  Albert S. Ruddy & Hal Needham

DARIN J. MORGAN*
Contact: WGA - Los Angeles, 310/550-1000

Screenplays:
BEL AIR PATROL
HELLBOUND

GLEN MORGAN*
Agent: CAA - Beverly Hills, 310/288-4545

THE BOYS NEXT DOOR New World, 1985, w/James Wong

Screenplays:
HANGMAN w/James Wong

PETER MORGAN
THE SILENT TOUCH Castle Hill Releasing, 1993, w/Mark Wadlow

W.T. MORGAN
Address: 733 Levering Avenue, Los Angeles, CA 90024,
310/208-4198

A MATTER OF DEGREES   Backbeat Productions, 1989,
w/Jack Mason & Randall Poster, directed

JOSEPH MORHAIM*
Agent: Shapiro/Lichtman - Los Angeles, 310/859-8877

THE HAPPY ROAD   MGM, 1956, w/Arthur Julian & Harry Kurnitz
DOC SAVAGE, MAN OF BRONZE   Warner Bros., 1975,
w/George Pal
QUICKER THAN THE EYE   Eural Films/FR3/Condor Films, 1988,
w/Nicholas Gessner

LOU MORHEIM*
Agent: Shapiro/Lichtman - Los Angeles, 310/859-8877

FOR MEN ONLY   Lippert, 1952, w/Herbert Margolies
THE BEAST FROM TWENTY THOUSAND FATHOMS
Warner Bros., 1953, w/Fred Freiburger
THE LAST BLITZKRIEG   Columbia, 1959
THE HUNTING PARTY   United Artists, 1971,
w/Gilbert Alexander & William Norton

DON MORIARTY
ZORRO, THE GAY BLADE   20th Century-Fox, 1981,
Story w/Greg Alt, Hal Dresner & Bob Randall

ROBERT MORIN
Contact: Academy of Canadian Cinema & Television, 753 Yonge St. -
2nd Floor, Toronto M4Y 1Z9, Canada, 416/967-0315

WINDIGO   Allegro Films, 1994, directed

PAT MORITA
Contact: 310/552-2020

CAPTIVE HEARTS   MGM/UA, 1987, w/John A. Kuri

DREW MORONE
LOST PROPHET   Rockville Pictures, 1992, w/Michael de Avila,
Shannon Goldman & Larry O'Neil

TONY MORPHETT
THE LAST WAVE   United Artists, 1977, w/Petru Popescu
SWEET TALKER   New Visions, 1991
CRIME BROKER   Pinnacle Pictures, 1993

Screenplays:
THE SEVENTH FLOOR (Pinnacle Pictures)

MICHAEL MORPUGO
WHEN THE WHALES CAME   20th Century Fox, 1989

ADRIAN MORRALL
BITTERSWEET LOVE   Avco Embassy, 1976, w/D.A. Kellogg

DAVID BURTON MORRIS*
Agent: Paradigm - Los Angeles, 310/277-4400
Business Manager: Craig Jacobson, Hansen, Jacobsen & Teller -
Los Angeles, 310/278-8622

PURPLE HAZE   Triumph/Columbia, 1983,
Story w/Thomas Kelsey & Victoria Wozniak, directed
LAGUNA HEAT (CTF)   HBO Pictures/Jay Weston Productions,
1987, w/D.M. Eyre & Pete Hamill
PATTI ROCKS   FilmDallas, 1988, w/John Jenkins, Karen Landry &
Chris Mulkey, directed

Screenplays:
ASSUMING ROOM TEMPERATURE (directing)

GRANT MORRIS
Agent: The Irv Schechter Company - Beverly Hills, 310/278-8070

THE RETURN OF SWAMP THING   Lightyear Entertainment, 1989,
w/Derek Spencer
THE SHRIMP ON THE BARBIE   Unity Pictures Corp., 1990,
w/Ron House & Alan Shearman

Screenplays:
THE AMERICAN WAY w/Louis Venosta

HOWARD J. MORRIS*
Agent: Broder-Kurland-Webb-Uffner - Beverly Hills, 310/281-3400

MR. WRITE   Shapiro Glickenhaus, 1994, from his play

JUDY MORRIS
LUIGI'S LADIES   TraLaLa Films Ltd., 1989, w/Ranald Allan,
Jennifer Claire & Wendy Hughes, directed

JOHN MORRISEY
9 1/2 NINJAS   Republic Pictures, 1991, Story w/Bill Crounse &
Don Pequignot

PAUL MORRISSEY
ANDY WARHOL'S DRACULA   *BLOOD FOR DRACULA*   Bryanston,
1974, directed
ANDY WARHOL'S FRANKENSTEIN   *FLESH FOR FRANKENSTEIN*
Bryanston, 1974, directed
THE HOUND OF THE BASKERVILLES   Atlantic Releasing
Corporation, 1979, w/Peter Cook & Dudley Moore, directed
MIXED BLOOD   Sara Films, 1984, directed
BEETHOVEN'S NEPHEW   New World, 1988,
w/Mathieu Carriere, directed
SPIKE OF BENSONHURST   FilmDallas, 1988,
w/Alan Bowne, directed

Screenplays:
STRAY DOG w/Jule Selbo

BARRY MORROW*
Agent: CAA - Beverly Hills, 310/288-4545

RAIN MAN ★★   MGM/UA, 1987, w/Ron Bass

Screenplays:
RACE THE SUN (TriStar)
AT LARGE
ELEPHANTS
BELLY UP
BLOOD ON THE TRACKS
DELICATE ARRANGEMENTS
TREVOR

JOHN MORTIMER
Agent: Peters, Fraser & Dunlop - London, 071/376-7676

A LITTLE HOTEL ON THE SIDE (P)   Adaptation
GUNS OF DARKNESS   ABP, 1962
THE DOCK BRIEF   MGM, 1962, w/Pierre Rouve, from his play
THE RUNNING MAN   Columbia, 1963
BUNNY LAKE IS MISSING   Columbia, 1965, w/Penelope Mortimer
A FLEA IN HER EAR   20th Century-Fox, 1968
JOHN AND MARY   20th Century-Fox, 1969
NO SEX PLEASE, WE'RE BRITISH   Columbia, 1973,
w/Brian Cooke & Anthony Marriott

Screenplays:
THE MAN WHO WAS THURSDAY
THE STAND IN
AMOK
CAUSE CELEBRE
DR. FISCHER OF GENEVA
PARADISE POSTPONED

PENELOPE MORTIMER
Agent: Curtis Brown - London, 071/872-0331

BUNNY LAKE IS MISSING   Columbia, 1965, w/John Mortimer
A SUMMER STORY   Atlantic Releasing Corporation, 1988
PORTRAIT OF A MARRIAGE   BBC/WGBH/Boston Television, 1992

ERNEST MORTON
(See Nancy Dowd)

LISA MORTON
MEET THE HOLLOWHEADS   Moviestore Entertainment, 1989,
   w/Tom Burman

PHILIP MORTON*
Manager: Creative Alliance Management - Los Angeles,
   213/962-6090

WHO'S WRITING THIS (P)   w/Bruce Paddock
IN THE WINGS (P)   w/Bruce Paddock

Screenplays:
HARRY'S LOT (directing)
THE SUN w/Jonathan Heap & Tom Reed
HONOR BOUND w/Jonathan Heap
CAUGHT w/Jonathan Heap
WHAT NICK SAW w/Jonathan Heap
PARENTAL DISCRETION ADVISED w/Tommy Blaze
ROCK THUNDER w/Tommy Blaze
ROUGH JUSTICE
TELEPATH

ROB MORTON
(See Nancy Dowd, Bo Goldman & Ron Nyswaner)

HARRY MOSES*
Contact: WGA - New York, 212/245-6180

ASSAULT AT WEST POINT (CTF)   Ultra Entertainment/Mosaic
   Group/Showtime, 1994, directed

Screenplays:
CONDUCT UNBECOMING: THE COURTMARTIAL OF JOHNSON
   WHITAKER (CTF)

RICHARD MOSES
ON THE RIGHT TRACK   20th Century-Fox, 1981,
   w/Avery Buddy & Tina Pina

ALAN MOSKOWITZ*
Agent: APA - Los Angeles, 310/273-0744

MORTAL PASSIONS   Gibraltar Releasing, 1990
ACTING ON IMPULSE (CTF)   Spectator Films, 1993,
   w/Mark Pittman

Screenplays:
TRICKS

JULIE MOSKOWITZ*
Agent: The Gersh Agency - Beverly Hills, 310/274-6611

HUSH LITTLE BABY (CTF)   Power Pictures/Hearst International/
   USA Pictures, 1994, w/Gary Stephens

WILLIAM MOSLEY-PAYNE*
Agent: Broder-Kurland-Webb-Uffner - Beverly Hills, 310/281-3400

LIVIN' LARGE   Samuel Goldwyn Company, 1991

Screenplays:
OFF THE BOARD
MONARCH PICTURES
A STONE COLD WAR
MINIMUM SECURITY

BETTINA MOSS
Agent: Sanford-Gross & Associates - Los Angeles, 310/208-2100

Screenplays:
THE INVENTOR OF EVERYTHING

GARY MOSS
Agent: Paul Kohner, Inc. - Beverly Hills, 310/550-1060

Screenplays:
WILDERNESS

D. BRENT MOTE*
Agent: Favored Artists Agency - Los Angeles, 213/653-3191

DEEP RED (CTF)   Dave Bell Associates/MCA Television, 1994

GREG MOTTOLA
Agent: William Morris Agency - Beverly Hills, 310/274-7451

Screenplays:
LUSH LIFE

BILL MOTZ
THE RETURN OF JAFAR (AHVF)   Buena Vista, 1994,
   w/Kevin Campbell, Mirith J.S. Colao, Steve Roberts, Bob Roth,
   Jan Strand & Brian Swenlin

CAROLINE MOURIS
BEGINNER'S LUCK   New World, 1986, w/Frank Mouris

FRANK MOURIS
FRANK FILM (Short) ★   directed
BEGINNER'S LUCK   New World, 1986,
   w/Caroline Mouris, co-directed

MALCOLM MOWBRAY
Agent: Peters, Fraser & Dunlop - London, 071/376-7676

A PRIVATE FUNCTION   Island Alive, 1985,
   Story w/Allan Bennett, directed

MICHAEL MOYE*
Agent: United Talent Agency - Beverly Hills, 310/273-6700

Screenplays:
BELLHOP
BLITZ

ALLAN MOYLE*
Agent: William Morris Agency - Beverly Hills, 310/274-7451

THE RUBBER GUN   Schuman-Katzka, 1978, directed
EAST END HUSTLE   Troma, 1979, as "Alan Bozo Moyle,"
   w/Frank Vitale
TIMES SQUARE   AFD, 1980, Story w/Leanne Unger, directed
PUMP UP THE VOLUME   New Line Cinema, 1990, directed
LOVE CRIMES   Millimeter Films, 1992, w/Laurie Frank

Screenplays:
REDEMPTION (directing)
HEAD HUNTER

ELAINE MUELLER*
Agent: Warden, White & Kane - Beverly Hills, 213/852-1028

Screenplays:
SAVING GRACES
PERSUASION
SPACES IN THE DARK
GARDENA MIRACLE
LEAD STORY
BLOWIN' IN THE WIND

ERIC MUELLER
WORLD AND TIME ENOUGH   1 in 10 Films, 1994,   directed

FRANK MUGAVERO
Agent: Jon Klane Agency - Beverly Hills, 310/278-0178

BIG GIRLS DON'T CRY...THEY GET EVEN
   New Line Cinema, 1992

Screenplays:
EASYLAND
SOMETHING FOREVER
CURSE OF THE REDHEAD

BRIAN DOMONIC MUIR*
Manager: Creative Alliance Management - Los Angeles,
   213/962-6090

CRITTERS   New Line Cinema, 1986, w/Stephen Herek

Screenplays:
THE TRAFFIC VIGILANTES
SKINS
NIGHTMARES IN THE SKY
OLD SOLDIERS
A MURDER OF CROWS
BAT OUT OF HELL

TERENCE MULCAHY
(See Michael Leeson)

JIM MULHOLLAND*
Agent: Broder-Kurland-Webb-Uffner - Beverly Hills, 310/281-3400

THE RATINGS GAME (CTF)   Imagination-New Street Productions,
   1984, w/Michael Barrie
AMAZON WOMEN ON THE MOON   Universal, 1987,
   w/Michael Barrie
OSCAR   Buena Vista, 1991, w/Michael Barrie

CHRIS MULKEY
Agent: Paradigm - Los Angeles, 310/277-4400

PATTI ROCKS   FilmDallas, 1988, w/John Jenkins, Karen Landry &
   David Burton Morris

MARTIN MULL*
Contact: WGA - Los Angeles, 310/550-1000

RENTED LIPS   Cineworld Enterprises, 1988

KEVIN MULLIGAN*
Contact: WGA - Los Angeles, 310/550-1000

Screenplays:
KID BROTHER

MARK MULLIN*
Contact: WGA - Los Angeles, 310/550-1000

COOL BLUE   Cinema Corp of America, 1990,
   w/Richard Shepard, co-directed

Screenplays:
RED DOG
STREETGANG CONVENTIONS AND INFINITY
SILHOUETTE
THE DEEP END
MADAM, I'M ADAM
MURDER A MINUTE (Shared)
PROJECT METAL
RAGE TO LIVE

CHRISTOPHER MUNCH
Agent: William Morris Agency - Beverly Hills, 310/274-7451

IN LAURA'S GARDEN   1987, directed
THE HOURS AND TIMES   Antartic Pictures, 1992, directed

Screenplays:
COLOR OF A BRISK AND LEAPING DAY

JAG MUNDHRA
Agent: Gold/Marshak - Burbank, 818/972-4300

IMPROPER CONDUCT   Everest Pictures, 1994,
   Story w/Carl Austin, directed

ROBERT MUNDY*
Agent: Susan Smith & Associates - Beverly Hills, 213/852-4777

THE VISITOR   International Picture Show, 1980, w/Luciano Comici
CHATTANOOGA CHOO CHOO   April Fools, 1984,
   w/Steven Philip Smith

Screenplays:
STANDARDS AND PRACTICES
MAXWELL: THE OUTSIDER (CTF)
21
SERVANT'S ENTRANCE
BLACK PANTHER
CASANOVA SLEPT HERE

IAN MUNE
Agent: Susan Smith & Associates - Beverly Hills, 213/852-4777
Address: Stony Creek Rd. RD1, Kaukapakapa, New Zealand

SLEEPING DOGS   Aardvark Films, 1977, w/Arthur Baysting
GOODBYE PORK PIE   Samuel Goldwyn Company, 1980,
   w/Geoff Murphy
CAME A HOT FRIDAY   Orion Classics, 1985,
   w/Dean Parker, directed
THE END OF THE GOLDEN WEATHER   South Pacific Pictures,
   1991, directed

Screenplays:
THE WHALERIDER (Shared)
ON THE LAM

RONA MUNRO
Contact: British Academy of Film & Television Arts, 195 Piccadilly,
   London W1, England, 01/734-0022

LADYBIRD LADYBIRD   Samuel Goldwyn Company, 1994

WALTER MURCH*
Agent: The Mirisch Agency - Los Angeles, 310/282-9940
Contact: Bloom, Dekom, Hergott & Cook - Los Angeles, 310/278-8622

THX 1138   Warner Bros., 1971, w/George Lucas
RETURN TO OZ   Buena Vista, 1985, w/Gill Dennis, directed

FREDI M. MURER
Contact: Swiss Film Center, Munstergasse 18, 8001 Zurich,
   Switzerland, 01/472-860

ALPINE FIRE   Vestron, 1987, directed

CHRISTOPHER MURPHEY
Agent: Writers & Artists Agency - Los Angeles, 310/824-6300

Screenplays:
BEYOND THE SEA

MICHAEL MURPHEY
HARD COUNTRY   Universal, 1981, Story w/Michael Kane

MICHAEL S. MURPHEY
Business: Bodega Bay Productions, 9301 Wilshire Blvd. - Suite 310, Beverly Hills, CA 90210, 310/273-3157

HAMBONE AND HILLIE   New World, 1984, w/Sandra K. Bailey & Joel Soisson
THE SUPERNATURALS   Republic Entertainment/Sandy Howard Productions, 1985, w/Joel Soisson
TRICK OR TREAT   DEG, 1986, w/Joel Soisson & Rhet Topham

BLAIR MURPHY
JUGULAR WINE   Cinequanon Pictures, 1993, directed

CHARLIE MURPHY
Agent: Innovative Artists - Los Angeles, 310/553-5200

Screenplays:
A VAMPIRE IN BROOKLYN w/Eddie Murphy & Vernon Lynch Jr.

COLLEEN MURPHY
Contact: Academy of Canadian Cinema & Television, 753 Yonge St. - 2nd Floor, Toronto M4Y 1Z9, Canada, 416/967-0315

TERMINI STATION   Northern Arts Entertainment, 1991

EDDIE MURPHY*
Agent: CAA - Beverly Hills, 310/288-4545

EDDIE MURPHY RAW   Paramount, 1987, w/Keenen Ivory Wayans
BEVERLY HILLS COP II   Paramount, 1987, Story w/Robert D. Wachs
COMING TO AMERICA   Paramount, 1988, Story
HARLEM NIGHTS   Paramount, 1989, directed
BOOMERANG   Paramount, 1992, Story

Screenplays:
A VAMPIRE IN BROOKLYN w/Charlie Murphy & Vernon Lynch Jr.

GARY MURPHY*
Agent: William Morris Agency - Beverly Hills, 310/274-7451

WITHOUT A CLUE   Orion, 1989, w/Larry Strawther

Screenplays:
8:24 TO HEAVEN w/Larry Strawther

GEOFF MURPHY
Agent: CAA - Beverly Hills, 310/288-4545

GOODBYE PORK PIE   Samuel Goldwyn Company, 1980, w/Ian Mune, directed
UTU   Pickman Films, 1983, w/Keith Aberdein, directed

RICHARD MURPHY*
Contact: WGA - Los Angeles, 310/550-1000

Screenplays:
RADIO MAN w/Stan Seidel
STORMY WEATHER

RYAN MURPHY
Agent: Lisa Callamaro Literary Agency- Beverly Hills, 310/274-6783

Screenplays:
SORORITY CONFIDENTIAL
THE BOY WHO CRIED WEREWOLF

TAB MURPHY*
Agent: Peter Turner Agency - Santa Monica, 310/315-4772

MY BEST FRIEND IS A VAMPIRE   Kings Road Entertainment, 1988
GORILLAS IN THE MIST ★   Universal, 1988, Story w/Anna Hamilton Phelan
THE LAST OF THE DOG MEN   Savoy, 1995, directed

Screenplays:
M.I.A.
ECLIPSE OF THE BEAST
BLACK MASK
KING FOR A DAY
DUTCH HARBOR
HEAVEN & EARTH
QUEEN OF ST. JAMES ELK
TREASURE HUNT

WARREN MURPHY*
Contact: WGA - Los Angeles, 310/550-1000

THE EIGER SANCTION   Universal, 1975, w/Hal Dresner & Rod Whitaker
LETHAL WEAPON 2   Warner Bros., 1989, Story w/Shane Black

Screenplays:
THE FOREVER KING

BILL MURRAY*
Agent: CAA - Beverly Hills, 310/288-4545

THE RAZOR'S EDGE   Columbia, 1984, w/John Byrum

DAVID MURRAY*
Contact: WGA - Los Angeles, 310/550-1000

Screenplays:
DONOVAN'S MIRACLE

JOHN FENTON MURRAY*
Contact: WGA - Los Angeles, 310/550-1000

THE ATOMIC KID   Republic, 1954, w/Benedict Freeman
IT'S ONLY MONEY   Paramount, 1962
DID YOU HEAR THE ONE ABOUT THE TRAVELLING SALESLADY   Universal, 1967
ARNOLD   Avco Embassy, 1973, w/Jameson Brewer

MICHAEL J. MURRAY*
Agent: Paradigm - Los Angeles, 310/277-4400

LOVE KILLS (CTF)   OMTL Productions/Wilshire Court Productions, 1991, based on a screenplay by Marc Lieberman & Corey Mandell

Screenplays:
ATLAS
TERROR OF MANHATTAN w/Greydon Clark
THE LIGHTNING FIELD (CTF)
THE PARROT
THE FALL OF THE HOUSE OF USHER
MASK OF THE RED DEATH
THE RAVEN
THE MUMMY

TOM MUSCA*
Agent: United Talent Agency - Beverly Hills, 310/273-6700

STAND AND DELIVER   Warner Bros., 1988, w/Ramon Menendez
LITTLE NIKITA   Columbia, 1988, Story w/Terry Schwartz
MONEY FOR NOTHING   Buena Vista, 1993, w/Ramon Memendez & Carol Sobieski

STEVE MUSCARELLA*
Contact: WGA - Los Angeles, 310/550-1000

ECHOES (Short)   directed

Screenplays:
COLD STORAGE
CLUB DEAD

JOHN MUSKER
Business: Walt Disney Studios, 818/560-1000

THE GREAT MOUSE DETECTIVE (AF)   Buena Vista, 1989,
    w/others, co-directed
THE LITTLE MERMAID (AF)   Buena Vista, 1989,
    w/Ron Clements, co-directed
ALADDIN (AF)   Buena Vista, 1992, w/Ron Clements, Ted Elliott &
    Terry Rossio, co-directd

Screenplays:
HERCULES (AF) w/Ron Clements

MAX MUTCHNICK*
Agent: United Talent Agency - Beverly Hills, 310/273-6700

Screenplays:
CRICKET IN TIMES SQUARE w/David Kohan

FLOYD MUTRUX*
Agent: ICM - Beverly Hills, 310/550-4000

THE CHRISTIAN LICORICE STORE   National General, 1971
DUSTY AND SWEETS McGEE   Warner Bros., 1971, directed
FREEBIE AND THE BEAN   Warner Bros., 1974, Story
ALOHA, BOBBY AND ROSE   Columbia, 1975, directed
THE HOLLYWOOD KNIGHTS   Columbia, 1980, directed
AMERICAN ME   Universal, 1992, w/Desmond Nakano
BOUND BY HONOR   Buena Vista, 1993,
    w/Jimmy Santiago Baca & Jeremy Iacone
THERE GOES MY BABY   Orion, 1994, directed

Screenplays:
DE-FENSE w/Ice Cube
COMMON GROUND
KISS TOMORROW GOODBYE
THE BALTIMORON
WESTERN SWING
THE LEGEND OF MARY SHELLEY
TELL CASPAR GOOD NIGHT
BANK JOB w/H. Matofsky
GO TO WORK
HILLSIDE STRANGLER
SKYLINE DRIVE
MAX THE FOX
HAPPY HOUR SANTA ANA WINDS
HEAT WAVE
ALONG CAME JONES

NANCYLEE MYATT*
Agent: Becsey/Wisdom/Kalajian Agency - Los Angeles,
    310/550-0535

little secrets   Cinecom, 1991, from her play "Slumber Party"

CINDY MYERS*
Agent: Innovative Artists - Los Angeles, 310/553-5200

FORGOTTEN PRISONERS: THE AMNESTY FILES (CTF)
    Turner Pictures, 1990, w/Rex Weiner
BED & BREAKFAST   Hemdale, 1992

Screenplays:
PEACOCK RAG
TELLING TALES
SNAKES

MIKE MYERS*
Agent: United Talent Agency - Beverly Hills, 310/273-6700

WAYNE'S WORLD   Paramount, 1992, w/Bonnie Turner &
    Terry Turner
WAYNE'S WORLD 2   Paramount, 1993, w/Bonnie Turner &
    Terry Turner

Screenplays:
COFFEETALK

SCOTT B. MYERS*
Agent: CAA - Beverly Hills, 310/288-4545

K-9   Universal, 1989, w/Steven Siegel

Screenplays:
ALASKA w/Andy Burg
HAMLET (Shared)
FROGS (Shared)
MYSTERIOUS ISLAND (Shared)
THE ADVENTURES OF RADMAN (Shared)
BAZOOKA JOE (Shared)
THE MOVE (Shared)
LOST BOYS II (Shared)
PEOPLE'S CHOICE (Shared)
LEGACY

N

GARY NADEAU
Agent: William Morris Agency - New York, 212/586-5100

RED (Short)   1994, directed

Screenplays:
JACK w/James DeMonaco (directing)

MASON NAGE
THE BORROWER   Cannon, 1991, w/Richard Fire

WILLIAM NAGLE
DEATH OF A SOLDIER   Scotti Bros., 1986
THE SIEGE OF FIREBASE GLORIA   Fries Entertainment, 1989,
    w/Tony Johnston

ED NAHA*
Agent: ICM - Beverly Hills, 310/550-4000

TROLL   Empire Pictures, 1986
DOLLS   Empire Pictures, 1987
HONEY, I SHRUNK THE KIDS   Buena Vista, 1989,
    w/Tom Schulman
CHUD II: BUD THE CHUD   Vestron, 1989,
    as "M. Kane Jeeves"
SPELLCASTER   Empire Pictures, 1992,
    Story, filmed in 1986

Screenplays:
REPULSIVE ATTRACTION w/Neal Israel
THE LAUGHING SUTRA
THE UNKNOWN SOLDIER
ERNEST SPACED OUT
BREAKDOWN
HEX

MIRA NAIR
Agent: ICM - Beverly Hills, 310/550-4000

Screenplays:
KAMA SUTRA w/Helena Kriel

DESMOND NAKANO*
Agent: William Morris Agency - Beverly Hills, 310/274-7451

BOULEVARD NIGHTS   Warner Bros., 1979
BODY ROCK   New World, 1984

BLACK MOON RISING   New World, 1986, w/John Carpenter &
    William Gray
LAST EXIT TO BROOKLYN   Constantin Films, 1990
AMERICAN ME   Universal, 1992, w/Floyd Mutrux

Screenplays:
WHITE MAN'S BURDEN
GOLD OF GALDIAZ

SPENSER NAKASAKO*
Contact: WGA - Los Angeles, 310/550-1000

LIFE IS CHEAP...BUT TOILET PAPER IS EXPENSIVE
    Silverlight Entertainment, 1990, co-directed

STEVEN NALEVANSKY
BLOOD BEACH   Jerry Gross Organization, 1981,
    Story w/Jeffrey Bloom

FRANK NAMEI*
Contact: WGA - Los Angeles, 310/550-1000

COLLISION COURSE   DEG, 1987, w/Robert Resnikoff

MICHAEL NANKIN*
Agent: ICM - Beverly Hills, 310/550-4000

MIDNIGHT MADNESS   Buena Vista, 1980,
    w/David Wechter, co-directed
THE GATE   New Century/Vista, 1987
RUSSKIES   New Century, 1987, w/Alan Glueckman &
    Sheldon Lettich
THE GATE II   Triumph Releasing, 1992

Screenplays:
FORTY

SUSAN NANUS*
Agent: William Morris Agency - Beverly Hills, 310/274-7451

THE SURVIVOR (P)

Screenplays:
MAJORITY RULES HIP TO BE SQUARE w/Rachel Feldman
SMOTHERED w/Rachel Feldman
AMERICAN HARVEST
THE MOST ELIGIBLE MAN IN NEW YORK
BEAT THE EAGLE

JO NAPOLEON*
Contact: WGA - Los Angeles, 310/550-1000

Screenplays:
AFTER THE BEAR HUNT
JAGUAR
THE SMASHBOX

ANN V. NARUS*
Contact: WGA - Los Angeles, 310/550-1000

MINISTRY OF VENGEANCE   Concorde, 1989,
    w/Brian D. Jeffries & Mervyn Emrys

JAMES NASALLA
O'HARA'S WIFE   Davis-Panzer Productions, 1982,
    w/William S. Bartman

N. RICHARD NASH*
Agent: Writers & Artists Agency - Los Angeles, 310/824-6300

THE RAINMAKER   Paramount, 1956, from his play
PORGY AND BESS   Goldwyn, 1959
ONE SUMMER LOVE   *DRAGONFLY*
    American International, 1976

JAMES A. NATHAN
THE KILLING TIME   New World, 1987, w/Don Bohlinger &
    Bruce Franklin Singer

Screenplays:
SMOKESCREEN w/Dan Bohlinger

MORT NATHAN*
Agent: United Talent Agency - Beverly Hills, 310/273-6700

Screenplays:
KINGPIN w/Barry Fanaro

STEVE NATHAN*
Agent: ICM - Beverly Hills, 310/550-4000

Screenplays:
THE ENGAGEMENT w/Paul Price
LOOSE WOMEN w/Paul Price
IN THE PROCESS w/Paul Price
THE AILEEN QUINN STORY w/Paul Price
UTILITIES w/Paul Price

JEFF NATHANSON*
Agent: United Talent Agency - Beverly Hills, 310/273-6700

STRANGER THINGS   Columbia, 1995

Screenplays:
THE SEDUCER
POPS
SECRET SERVICE
THE FACE

MICHAEL J. NATHANSON*
Business Manager: Matt Sauer, Rosenfield, Meyer & Susman -
    Beverly Hills, 310/858-7700

SHE'S OUT OF CONTROL   Columbia, 1989, w/Seth Winston
THE BULKIN TRAIL (CTF)   Upstart Productions, 1993,
    w/Mitchell Newman, directed

TERRY NATION*
Contact: 310/459-8057

AND SOON THE DARKNESS   Associated British, 1970,
    w/Brian Clemens
THE HOUSE IN NIGHTMARE PARK   EMI, 1973, w/Clive Exton

RICK NATKIN*
Agent: The Daniel Ostroff Agency - Los Angeles, 310/278-2020

THE BOYS IN COMPANY C   Columbia, 1978, w/Sidney Furie
NIGHT OF THE JUGGLER   Columbia, 1980, w/Bill Norton Sr.
PURPLE HEARTS   The Ladd Company/Warner Bros., 1984,
    w/Sidney Furie
THE HEIST (CTF)   HBO Pictures, 1989, w/David Fuller
THE TAKING OF BEVERLY HILLS   Columbia, 1991,
    w/David Fuller & David Burke
NECESSARY ROUGHNESS   Paramount, 1991, w/David Fuller

BILL NAUD
NECROMANCER   Bonnaire Films & Spectrum Entertainment, 1989

GREGORY NAVA*
Agent: ICM - Beverly Hills, 310/550-4000

THE CONFESSIONS OF AMANS   Bauer International, 1977,
    w/Anna Thomas, directed
THE END OF AUGUST   Quartet, 1982, w/Anna Thomas,
    Eula Seaton & Leon Heller
EL NORTE ★   Cinecom/Island Alive, 1984,
    w/Anna Thomas, directed
A TIME OF DESTINY   Columbia, 1988, w/Anna Thomas, directed
MY FAMILY   New Line Cinema, 1995, w/Anna Thomas, directed

R O D   N A V E
DOLLY DEAREST   Trimark Pictures, 1992, Story w/Mary Lease &
   Peter Sutcliffe

Screenplays:
BIKINI BIKER BEACH BABES   (directing)

J E F F R E Y   W .   N E A L *
Agent: ICM - Beverly Hills, 310/550-4000

Screenplays:
LONE JUSTICE
BACKSTREETS

J A C K   N E A R Y
Contact: New Century Theatre, Smith College, New York

TO FORGIVE, DIVINE (P)
FIRST NIGHT (P)
JERRY FINNEGAN'S SISTER (P)
FIVE NICKLES (P)
THE GOD THING (P)

H A R O L D   N E B E N Z A L *
Contact: WGA - Los Angeles, 310/550-1000

THE WILBY CONSPIRACY   United Artists, 1975, w/Rod Amateau
KINJITE: FORBIDDEN SUBJECTS   Cannon, 1989

Screenplays:
PURSUIT MANUMIT w/Rod Amateu

H A L   N E E D H A M *
Agent: Camden-ITG - Los Angeles, 310/289-2700
Business: Bandit Productions, 3518 Cahuenga Blvd West -
   Suite 110, Los Angeles, CA 90068, 213/876-8052

MEGAFORCE   20th Century-Fox, 1982, w/James Whittaker,
   Albert S. Ruddy & Andre Morgan, directed
STROKER ACE   Universal, 1983, w/Hugh Wilson, directed
CANONBALL RUN II   Warner Bros., 1984, w/Harvey Miller &
   Albert S. Ruddy, directed

J A K E   R A Y M O N D   N E E D H A M
NATURAL CAUSES   Pacific Rim Productions, 1994, directed

T O M   N E F F
Contact: Wild Wolf Productions, 10401 Venice Blvd. - Suite 200,
   Los Angeles, CA 90034, 310/280-6800

RUNNING MATES   Shapiro Entertainment, 1985, directed
FREDERIC REMINGTON: THE TRUTH OF OTHER DAYS (FD)
   1991, directed

Screenplays:
A PIECE OF THE FED
ONE OF A KIND w/Pablo Fenjves
THE MAGIC BIRD
GATES OF PEARL w/Steve Neff

A N D R E W   N E I D E R M A N
Agent: Paradigm - Los Angeles, 310/277-4400

DUPLICATES (CTF)   Sankan Productions, 1992, w/Sandor Stern

T R O Y   N E I G H B O R S
Contact: Lloyd Braun, Silverberg, Katz, Thompson & Braun -
   Los Angeles, 310/445-5801
Office: 213/857-0405

FORTRESS   Miramax, 1993, w/Steven Feinberg,
   Terry Curtis Fox & David Venable

Screenplays:
SEAHUNTER w/Steven Feinberg
FORTRESS 2 w/Steven Feinberg

RUNAROUND SUE w/Steven Feinberg
U.F.O. SCOUTS w/Steven Feinberg
CRIMESTOPPERS w/Steven Feinberg
PAINKILLER w/Steven Feinberg
THE EXTRAORDINARY VOYAGE OF VERNE AND WELLS
   w/Steven Feinberg

S T E P H E N   C .   N E I G H E R *
Agent: The Rothman Agency - Beverly Hills, 213/655-2020

HOT TO TROT   Warner Bros., 1988, w/Hugo Gilbert &
   Charlie Peters

Screenplays:
TOUCHING GOLIATH
KING OF THE USA
STAYING ON TOP

S T E V E N   N E I L L
THE DAY TIME ENDED   Compass International, 1979, Story

B . J .   N E L S O N *
Contact: James Mulholland - Los Angeles, 310/278-1111

LONE WOLF McQUADE   Orion, 1983
APT PUPIL   New Century/Vista, 1989
SCANNERS II: THE NEW ORDER   Triton Pictures, 1991
SCANNERS III: THE TAKEOVER   Republic Pictures, 1992,
   w/Rene Malo, David Preston & Julie Richard

Screenplays:
BUDDY COPS w/David O'Malley

B R I A N   N E L S O N
Agent: The Gage Group - Los Angeles, 310/859-8777

Screenplays:
TIGER WOMAN

C A R L   N E L S O N
TALKING ABOUT SEX   Curb Entertainment, 1994, w/Aaron Speiser

D A V I A   N E L S O N
IMAGINARY CRIMES   Warner Bros., 1994, w/Kristine Johnson

D O N A L D   R .   N E L S O N *
Contact: WGA - Los Angeles, 310/550-1000

ONE MORE TRAIN TO ROB   Universal, 1971, w/Don Tait
NO DEPOSIT, NO RETURN   Buena Vista, 1976, w/Arthur Alsberg
GUS   Buena Vista, 1976, w/Arthur Alsberg
HERBIE GOES TO MONTE CARLO   Buena Vista, 1977,
   w/Arthur Alsberg
HOT LEAD AND COLD FEET   Buena Vista, 1978,
   w/Arthur Alsberg & Joe McEveety

J E S S I E   N E L S O N
Agent: United Talent Agency - Beverly Hills, 310/273-6700

TO THE MOON ALICE (Short)   directed
CORRINA, CORRINA   New Line Cinema, 1994, directed

Screenplays:
FIRST COMES LOVE w/Karen Leigh Hopkins (directing)
OFF THE FLOOR
THE RUNNING

J O H N   A L A N   N E L S O N
BEST OF THE BEST 2   20th Century Fox, 1993, w/Max Strom

Screenplays:
YAKUZA w/Max Strom (Neo Motion Pictures)
MIDNIGHT SUN BURNING BRIDGES w/Max Strom

JUDD NELSON
Contact: Screen Actors Guild - Los Angeles, 213/954-1600

EVERY BREATH   Motion Picture Corporation of America, 1993,
 w/Steve Bing & Andrew Fleming

PETER NELSON*
Agent: Paradigm - Los Angeles, 310/277-4400

THE LONELY PASSION OF JUDITH HEARNE
 Island Pictures, 1987
GETTING UP AND GOING HOME (CTF)   Carroll Newman
 Productions/Polone Co./Hearst Entertainment, 1992
UNTAMED LOVE (CTF)   CLC Productions/Carroll Newman
 Productions/Polone Co., 1994

RICHARD NELSON
Agent: William Morris Agency - Beverly Hills, 310/274-7451

ETHAN FROME   Miramax, 1993

ROGERS NELSON
(See Prince)

JOSEPH C. NEOLA*
Contact: 818/763-9866

Screenplays:
FIVE O'CLOCK FOXTROT w/Mary Neola

MARY NEOLA*
Contact: 818/763-9866

Screenplays:
FIVE O'CLOCK FOXTROT w/Joe Neola

AVI NESHER
Agent: The Gersh Agency - Beverly Hills, 310/274-6611

TIMEBOMB   MGM-Pathe, 1992, directed

Screenplays:
DOPPELGANGER (ITC, directing)
THE TAXMAN (directing)
THE STRAW MAN
THE HEAT OF RAMADAN

MICHAEL NESMITH*
Business: Pacific Arts, 50 N. La Cienega Blvd. - Suite 210,
 Beverly Hills, CA 90211, 310/657-2233

TIMERIDER   Jensen Farley Pictures, 1983, w/William Dear

LEONARD NEUBAUER*
Contact: WGA - Los Angeles, 310/550-1000

NEW YEAR'S EVIL   Cannon, 1981

CHRIS NEUFELD
THE BIG PLUNGE   Embassy International, 1985

EDWARD NEUMEIER*
Agent: United Talent Agency - Beverly Hills, 310/273-6700

ROBOCOP   Orion, 1987, w/Michael Miner

Screenplays:
NEW JACK CITY II w/Michael Miner
STRATT w//Michael Miner
THE EXECUTIONER w/Michael Miner
COMPANY MAN w/Michael Miner
HITMAN w/Michael Miner (co-directing)
WHITE TRASH w/Michael Miner
STARSHIP TROOPERS
ROCKETS REDGLARE

CRAIG J. NEVIUS*
Contact: WGA - Los Angeles, 310/550-1000

CLASS DISMISSED (P)
THE MEN'S ROOM (P)
WHERE THE HEART IS (P)
HAPPY TOGETHER   Borde Releasing Corp., 1990
FANTASTIC FOUR   Concorde Pictures, 1993

MARSHALL NEW
Agent: Leslie Kallen Agency - Sherman Oaks, 818/906-2785

Screenplays:
CLOSE ENOUGH FOR ROCK'N'ROLL w/Ethlie Ann Vare

ROBERT NEWCOMBE*
Agent: The Agency - Los Angeles, 310/551-3000

Screenplays:
YOU SHOULD SEE THE CONKLIN'S LIVING ROOM
OUIKES AS IN "YIKES!"

ANTHONY NEWLEY*
Contact: WGA - Los Angeles, 310/550-1000

ROAR OF THE GREASEPAINT, SMELL OF THE CROWD (P)
 w/Leslie Bricusse
STOP THE WORLD - I WANT TO GET OFF   Warner Bros., 1966,
 w/Leslie Bricusse
CAN HIERONYMUS MERKIN EVER FORGET MERCY HUMPPE &
 FIND TRUE HAPPINESS?   Universal, 1969,
 w/Herman Raucher, directed

BRENDA NEWMAN
CANVAS   Optima Productions/ABC Distribution, 1992,
 w/Alain Zaloum

DAVID NEWMAN*
Agent: APA - Los Angeles. 310/273-0744

BONNIE AND CLYDE ★   Warner Bros., 1967,
 w/Robert Benton
THERE WAS A CROOKED MAN...   United Artists, 1970,
 w/Robert Benton
WHAT'S UP DOC?   Warner Bros., 1972, w/Robert Benton &
 Buck Henry
BAD COMPANY   Paramount, 1972, w/Robert Benton
SUPERMAN   Warner Bros., 1978, w/Robert Benton,
 Leslie Newman & Mario Puzo
SUPERMAN II   Warner Bros., 1980, w/Leslie Newman &
 Mario Puzo
JINXED   MGM/UA, 1982, w/Frank Gilroy
STILL OF THE NIGHT   MGM/UA, 1982,
 Story w/Robert Benton
SUPERMAN III   Warner Bros., 1983, w/Leslie Newman
SHEENA   Columbia, 1984, w/Lorenzo Semple
SANTA CLAUS: THE MOVIE   Tri-Star, 1985

Screenplays:
THE NAKED TRUTH w/Leslie Newman
THREE-QUARTER MOON
JUNE BABY
THE VISITOR
SMOOTH CRIMINAL
CAPTAIN ZAP AND THE BRUTE (CTF)

ELAINE NEWMAN*
Agent: The Artists Group - Los Angeles, 310/552-1100

Screenplays:
THE MARRIAGE THING w/Ed Burnham

LESLIE NEWMAN*
Agent: ICM - New York, 212/556-5600

SUPERMAN   Warner Bros., 1978, w/Robert Benton,
   David Newman & Mario Puzo
SUPERMAN II   Warner Bros., 1980, w/David Newman &
   Mario Puzo
SUPERMAN III   Warner Bros., 1983, w/David Newman

Screenplays:
THE NAKED TRUTH w/David Newman
GATHERING FORCE
HAPPILY EVER AFTER

MITCHELL NEWMAN
THE BULKIN TRAIL (CTF)   Upstart Productions, 1993,
   w/Michael J. Nathanson

PAUL NEWMAN*
Agent: CAA - Beverly Hills, 310/288-4545

HARRY & SON   Orion, 1984, w/Ronald L. Buck, directed

RANDY NEWMAN*
Agent: Gorfaine/Schwartz - Los Angeles, 213/969-1011
Business Manager: Gelfand, Rennert & Feldman - Los Angeles,
   310/553-1707

THREE AMIGOS   Orion, 1986, w/Steve Martin & Lorne Michaels

ROBERT NEWTON
Agent: The Gersh Agency - Beverly Hills, 310/274-6611

Screenplays:
MERCURY RISING

MBONGENI NGEMA
SARAFINA!   Miramax/Buena Vista, 1992, w/William Nicholson,
   from his play

MAURIZIO NICHETTI
Agent: William Morris Agency - Beverly Hills, 310/274-7451

THE ICICLE THIEF   Aries Releasing, 1990,
   w/Mauro Monti, directed
VOLERE/VOLARE   Fine Line Features, 1993, directed
STEFANO QUANTESTORIE   Penta Distribuzione, 1993,
   w/Laura Fischetto, directed

ANDREW NICCOL*
Agent: Pleshette & Green - Los Angeles, 213/465-0428

Screenplays:
THE TRUMAN SHOW
THE UNDRESSING OF SOPHIE DEANE

PAUL NICHOLAS
Contact: Directors Guild of America - Los Angeles, 310/289-2000

CHAINED HEAT   Jensen Farley Pictures, 1983,
   w/Vincent Mongol, directed
THE NAKED CAGE   Cannon, 1986, directed

ALLAN F. NICHOLLS*
Business: P.O. Box 165, New York, NY 10014, 212/664-2458

A WEDDING   20th Century-Fox, 1978, w/Robert Altman,
   John Considine & Patricia Resnick
A PERFECT COUPLE   20th Century-Fox, 1979, w/Robert Altman
DEAD RINGER   Feature Films, 1991, directed, filmed in 1981

JOHN NICHOLS*
Agent: Curtis Brown, Ltd. - New York, 212/473-5400

THE MILAGRO BEANFIELD WAR   Universal, 1988,
   w/David S. Ward

PETER NICHOLS
Agent: William Morris Agency - Beverly Hills, 310/274-7451 &
   The Casarotto Company - London, 071/287-4450

HAVING A WILD WEEKEND *CATCH US IF YOU CAN*
   Warner Bros., 1965
GEORGY GIRL   Columbia, 1966, w/Margaret Forster
A DAY IN THE DEATH OF JOE EGG   Columbia, 1971,
   from his play
THE NATIONAL HEALTH   Columbia, 1973, from his play
PRIVATES ON PARADE   Orion Classics, 1984, from his play

JACK NICHOLSON*
Contact: Sandy Bresler, Bresler, Kelly & Kipperman - Encino,
   818/905-1155

THUNDER ISLAND   1963, Shared
RIDE IN THE WHIRLWIND   American International, 1966
FLIGHT TO FURY   Harold Goldman Associates, 1966
THE TRIP   American Internation, 1967
HEAD   Columbia, 1968, w/Bob Rafelson
DRIVE, HE SAID   Columbia, 1970, w/Jeremy Larner, directed

WILLIAM NICHOLSON*
Agent: CAA - Beverly Hills, 310/288-4545

A PRIVATE MATTER (CTF)   Longbow-Mirage-HBO Pictures, 1992
THE MARCH (CTF)   BBC-TV/One World Consortium, 1992
SARAFINA!   Miramax/Buena Vista, 1992, w/Mbongeni Ngema
SHADOWLANDS ★   Savoy Pictures, 1993, from his play
NELL   20th Century Fox, 1994, w/William Handley

Screenplays:
CRIME OF THE CENTURY

NICHOLAS NICIPHOR*
Agent: Barry Perelman Agency - Los Angeles, 310/274-5999

OUR WINNING SEASON   American International, 1978
FATAL CHARM (CTF)   Jonathan D. Krane, 1992
CANDLES IN THE DARK (CTF)   Taska Films/Kushner-Locke, 1993

DARYL G. NICKENS*
Agent: Maggie Field Agency - Studio City, 818/980-2001

HOUSE PARTY 2: THE PAJAMA JAM!   New Line Cinema, 1991,
   w/Rusty Cundieff

Screenplays:
AT YOUR SERVICE

TED NICOLAOU
SOUTHERN HOSPITALITY (Short)   directed
TERRORVISION   Empire Pictures, 1986, directed
ASSAULT OF THE KILLER BIMBOS   Empire Pictures, 1988

BRUCE NICOLAYSEN
THE PASSAGE   United Artists, 1979

RICHARD NIELSEN
OH, WHAT A NIGHT   Norstar Entertainment, 1992

ALISON NIGH*
Contact: WGA - Los Angeles, 310/550-1000

Screenplays:
OUT THERE w/Thomas Strelich (I.R.S.)

ROB NILSSON
Business: Snowball Pictures, 415/567-4404

NORTHERN LIGHTS   Cinemanifest/New Front Films, 1978,
   w/John Hanson, co-directed
ON THE EDGE   Skouras Pictures, 1986, directed
SIGNAL SEVEN   One Pass Pictures, 1986, directed
HEAT AND SUNLIGHT   New Front Alliance/Snowball Productions,
   1987, directed

Screenplays:
CHALK w/Don Bajema (Tenderloin Action Group, directing)

LEONARD NIMOY*
Agent: The Gersh Agency - Beverly Hills, 310/274-6611
Business Manager: Richard B. Francis, Francis & Freedman -
   Beverly Hills, 310/277-7351

STAR TREK IV: THE VOYAGE HOME   Paramount, 1986,
   Story w/Harve Bennett, directed
STAR TREK VI: THE UNDISCOVERED COUNTRY   Paramount,
   1991, Story w/Larry Konner & Mark Rosenthal

BRIAN NISSEN
Contact: Nest Entertainment - 818/846-9850

THE SWAN PRINCESS (AF)   New Line Cinema, 1994,
   w/Richard Rich

Screenplays:
FEATHERTOP (AF) w/Richard Rich

MICKEY NIVELLI
HEAVEN BECOMES HELL   Taurus Entertainment, 1989, directed

TIM NOAH
DAREDREAMER   Lensman Co., 1989, Story w/Barry Caillier &
   Pat Royce

JUDY NOGG*
Agent: Jim Preminger Agency - Los Angeles, 310/475-9491

Screenplays:
DUE PROCESS Story w/Stanley Isaacs
EXCESS BAGGAGE SMUGGLER
THE WHISPER

KEN NOLAN
Agent: Renaissance-H.N. Swanson - Los Angeles, 310/246-6000

Screenplays:
IN CONTEMPT

ELISABETH NONAS
Manager: The Anthony Elliot Company - Los Angeles, 310/284-6804

Screenplays:
AFTERLIFE

DIANE NOOMIN*
Contact: WGA - Los Angeles, 310/550-1000

Screenplays:
ZIPPYVISION w/Bill Griffith

DAVID NOONAN*
Agent: ICM - Beverly Hills, 310/550-4000

Screenplays:
MEMOIRS OF A CADDY
THE CRASH ROOM w/Gene Stone

THOMAS P. NOONAN*
Agent: The Gersh Agency - New York, 212/997-1818

RED WIND (CTF)   MCA Television, 1991
WHAT HAPPENED WAS   Samuel Goldwyn Company,
   1994, directed
THE WIFE   (no distributor), 1995, directed, from his play "Wifey"

MICHAEL NORELL*
Agent: Bruce Brown Agency - Los Angeles, 310/208-1835

LONG GONE (CTF)   HBO Pictures/The Landsburg Company, 1987
THE DIAMOND FLEECE (CTF)   Moving Image Productions, 1992

Screenplays:
CALL ME A COP
BARNUM
PALS

GLENN NORMAN
Agent: Writers & Artists Agency - Los Angeles, 310/824-6300

Screenplays:
POWER DOWN

HOWARD NORMAN
Agent: CAA - Beverly Hills, 310/288-4545

Screenplays:
THE BIRD ARTISTS w/Arne Glimcher
3-D w/Martin Goldstein

MARC NORMAN*
Agent: ICM - Beverly Hills, 310/550-4000

OKLAHOMA CRUDE   Columbia, 1973
ZANDY'S BRIDE   Warner Bros., 1974
THE KILLER ELITE   United Artists, 1975, w/ Stirling Silliphant
THE AVIATOR   MGM/UA, 1985
BAT-21   Tri-Star, 1988, as "George Gordon,"
   w/William C. Anderson

Screenplays:
SHAKESPEARE IN LOVE
MAHAD
2 GOOD 2 BE FORGOTTEN
SHADOW CATCHER
THE LOCK NESS MONSTER
FAHAD & LENA
HERZOG w/Gill Dennis
STATION CHIEF

MARSHA NORMAN*
Agent: United Talent Agency - Beverly Hills, 310/273-6700 or
   The Tantleff Office - New York, 212/941-3939

GETTING OUT (P)
THE SECRET GARDEN (P)
SARAH AND ABRAHAM (P)
THE RED SHOES (P)
THE LAUNDROMAT (CTF)   Byck-Lancaster Productions/Sandcastle
   5 Productions, 1985
'NIGHT, MOTHER   Universal, 1986, from her play
THIRD AND OAK: THE POOL HALL (CTF)   Nederlander
   Television and Film, 1989

Screenplays:
THE TRUMPET OF THE SWAN (AF)
MADELINE
CROSS MY HEART (remake)
MEDICINE WOMAN
CHILDREN WITH EMERALD EYES
MY SHADOW

MICHAEL NORMAND
LEON THE PIG FARMER   Cinevista/Unapix, 1993, w/Gary Sinyor

BILL NORRETT
Agent: Kaplan-Stahler - Beverly Hills, 213/653-4483

Screenplays:
FAMILY GUNPLAY

STEPHEN NORRINGTON
DEATH MACHINE   Trimark, 1994, directed

AARON NORRIS*
Contact: Henry Holmes - 310/205-8320

INVASION U.S.A.   Cannon, 1985, Story w/James Bruner

CHUCK NORRIS*
Agent: ICM - Beverly Hills, 310/550-4000
Contact: Myron D. Emery - 310/557-1333

INVASION U.S.A.   Cannon, 1985, w/James Bruner
BRADDOCK: MISSING IN ACTION III   Cannon, 1988,
   w/James Bruner

PAMELA R. NORRIS*
Agent: The Gersh Agency - Beverly Hills, 310/274-6611

TROOP BEVERLY HILLS   WEG, 1989,
   w/Margaret Grieco Oberman

Screenplays:
LUCKY NUMBER
PAROLE OFFICER

WILLIAM H. NORRIS
H.P. LOVECRAFT'S RE-ANIMATOR   Empire Pictures, 1985,
   w/Stuart Gordon & Dennis Paoli

B.W.L. NORTON, JR.*
Agent: CAA - Beverly Hills, 310/288-4545

CISCO PIKE   Columbia, 1971, directed
OUTLAW BLUES   Warner Bros., 1977
CONVOY   United Artists, 1978
MORE AMERICAN GRAFFITI   Universal, 1979, directed
LOSIN' IT   Embassy, 1983
BACK TO THE BEACH   Paramount, 1987,
   Story w/Bruce Kirschbaum & James Komack

Screenplays:
LOCKDOWN
BULL
KITELINE
BULLROAR

ELEANOR ELIAS NORTON*
Contact: WGA - Los Angeles, 310/550-1000

THE DAY OF THE ANIMALS   Film Ventures International, 1976,
   w/William Norton
DIRTY TRICKS   Avco Embassy, 1981, w/William Norton,
   Thomas Gifford & Camille Gifford

WILLIAM W. NORTON, SR.*
Agent: David Shapira & Associates - Sherman Oaks, 818/906-0322

THE SCALPHUNTERS   United Artists, 1968
SAM WHISKEY   United Artists, 1969
THE MACKENZIE BREAK   United Artists, 1970
THE HUNTING PARTY   United Artists, 1971,
   w/Gilbert Alexander & Lou Morheim
WHITE LIGHTNING   United Artists, 1973
TRADER HORN   MGM, 1973, w/Edward Harper
BIG BAD MAMA   New World, 1974, w/Frances Doel
BRANNIGAN   United Artists, 1975, w/Michael Butler,
   William P. McGivern & Christopher Trumbo

THE DAY OF THE ANIMALS   Film Ventures International, 1976,
   w/Eleanor Norton
MOVING VIOLATION   20th Century-Fox, 1976,
   w/David R. Osterhout
GATOR   United Artists, 1976
A SMALL TOWN IN TEXAS   American International, 1976
NIGHT OF THE JUGGLER   Columbia, 1980, w/Rick Natkin
DIRTY TRICKS   Avco Embassy, 1981, w/Eleanor Elias Norton,
   Thomas Gifford & Camille Gifford

JOHN NORVILLE*
Agent: William Morris Agency - Beverly Hills, 310/274-7451

Screenplays:
TIN CUP
CAPONE IN LAREDO w/Michael Jenning
THE AMERICAN SPORTSMAN
AN EXILE'S BAGGAGE
LOUIE LOUIE
MORGAN'S CAY

FRANK NORWOOD*
Contact: WGA - Los Angeles, 310/550-1000

PAST MIDNIGHT (CTF)   Cinetel Films, 1992

Screenplays:
BLIND SIDE
CLIMAX
PEACEMAKER
WALKING ON GLASS

CLAIR NOTO*
Agent: Jon Klane Agency - Beverly Hills, 310/278-0178

Screenplays:
JULIA PASTRANA
THE TOURIST
THE HEAVENLY
PAPARAZZI
SLAVE, A TRUE STORY
PRODIGY

BLAINE NOVAK*
Agent: Innovative Artists - Los Angeles, 310/553-5200

STRANGER'S KISS   Orion Classics, 1984, w/Matthew Chapman
GOOD TO GO   Island Pictures, 1986, directed
LIGHT YEARS   Miramax, 1988, w/Raphael Cluzel

Screenplays:
BLUE CHAMPAGNE (directing)
BEAUTIFUL ENEMIES
THE DRIFT
SUNSET UNLIMITED
BEAT THE BURDEN

CYRUS NOWRASTEH*
Agent: CAA - Beverly Hills, 310/288-4545

Screenplays:
NIGHT EYES
EMMA AND THE HOBO KING
THE DEVIL SOLDIERS

PHILLIP NOYCE
Agent: ICM - Beverly Hills, 310/550-4000 or Cameron Creswell
   Agency - Sydney, Australia, tel.: 02/356-4677

NEWSFRONT   New Yorker, 1979, directed
HEATWAVE   New Line Cinema, 1982,
   w/Marc Rosenberg, directed

VICTOR NUÑEZ
Agent: Paul Kohner, Inc. - Beverly Hills, 310/550-1060

GAL YOUNG UN   Nunez Films, 1979, directed
A FLASH OF GREEN   Spectrafilm, 1985, directed
RUBY IN PARADISE   October Films, 1993, directed

Screenplays:
SCAR (directing)

KEM NUNN*
Agent: United Talent Agency - Beverly Hills, 310/273-6700

Screenplays:
STREEETRACERS
TAPPING THE SOURCE
UNASSIGNED TERRITORY
CHILDREN OF LIGHT

TREVOR NUNN
Agent: ICM - Beverly Hills, 310/550-4000
Address: Homevale Ltd., Gloucester Mansions, Cambridge Circus,
   London WC2H 8HD England, tel. 071/240-5435

HEDDA   Brut Productions, 1975, directed

BRUNO NUYTTEN
Contact: French Film Office, 745 Fifth Avenue, New York, NY 10151,
   212/832-8860

CAMILLE CLAUDEL   Orion Classics, 1989,
   w/Marilyn Goldin, directed
ALBERT SUFFERS   AMLF, 1992, directed

RICHARD NYGARD
TALES OF THE UNKNOWN   AIP Home Video, 1990,
   "Warped" w/Jeff Copeland

DANIEL NYIRI
Contact: 7505 Hampton Ave. - Suite 17, West Hollywood, CA 90046,
   213/874-7519

A FEW MINUTES WITH LUDWIG (Short)   1990, directed

Screenplays:
ONE-WAY TICKET (Shared)
BATTLEFIELDS (Shared)
SECRET FEAR (Shared)

RON NYSWANER*
Agent: Sanford-Gross & Associates - Los Angeles, 310/208-2100

F/10 SPLIT (P)
SURVIVING DAUGHTER (P)
THE F WORD (P)
SMITHEREENS   New Line Cinema, 1982, w/Peter Askin
SWING SHIFT   Warner Bros., 1983, w/Nancy Dowd &
   Bo Goldman, as "Rob Morton"
PURPLE HEARTS   Warner Bros., 1984
MRS. SOFFEL   MGM/UA, 1984
THE PRINCE OF PENNSYLVANIA   New Line Cinema,
   1988, directed
GROSS ANATOMY   Buena Vista, 1989, w/Mark Spragg
LOVE HURTS   Vestron, 1991
PHILADELPHIA ★   TriStar, 1993

Screenplays:
THE WINNER
SHELLEY'S LEG
HEARTACHES INTO THE FIRE

VERN OAKLEY
MR. 247   Tribe Production, 1994,
   Story w/Paul Zimmerman, directed

DAVID OAS
(See Jeff BUHAI, David OBST & Steve ZACHARIAS)

DAN O'BANNON*
Business Manager: 310/277-0298

DARK STAR   Jack H. Harris Enterprises, 1974, w/John Carpenter
ALIEN   20th Century-Fox, 1979
HEAVY METAL (AF)   Columbia, 1981, Shared Story
DEAD AND BURIED   Avco Embassy, 1981, w/ Ronald Shusett
BLUE THUNDER   Columbia, 1983, w/Don Jakoby
LIFEFORCE   Tri-Star, 1985, w/Don Jakoby
THE RETURN OF THE LIVING DEAD   Orion, 1985, directed
INVADERS FROM MARS   Cannon, 1986, w/Don Jakoby
TOTAL RECALL   Tri-Star, 1990, w/Gary Goldman & Ronald Shusett
SCREAMERS   Triumph Films, 1995

Screenplays:
THE ROSTOV RIPPER
QUARTERMASS EXPERIMENT
TELEKINETIC MAN w/Don Jakoby
THE PRIMITIVE w/Don Jakoby
HEMOGOBLIN

ROCKNE S. O'BANNON*
Agent: CAA - Beverly Hills, 310/288-4545

ALIEN NATION   20th Century Fox, 1988
FEAR (CTF)   Vestron, 1989

Screenplays:
HEP

MARGARET GRIECO OBERMAN*
Agent: Richland/Wunsch/Hohman Agency - Los Angeles,
   310/278-1955

TROOP BEVERLY HILLS   WEG, 1989, w/Pamela Norris

Screenplays:
BAD TO THE BONE w/Jim Piddock
MR. DARLING w/Rosie Shuster
THE BROTHER-IN-LAW
THE STAND-UP GUY w/Jim Piddock
STRANGERS IN THE NIGHT w/Jim Piddock
UNDERCOVER w/Jim Piddock
DWAYNE w/Jim Piddock

BARRY O'BRIEN*
Contact: 310/201-0892

PINOCCHIO AND THE EMPEROR OF THE NIGHT (AF)
   New World, 1987, w/Robby London & Dennis O'Flaherty

CONAN O'BRIEN*
Agent: United Talent Agency - Beverly Hills, 310/273-6700

Screenplays:
HANZ AND FRANZ GO TO HOLLYWOOD

JOHN O'BRIEN
VERMONT IS FOR LOVERS   Zeitgeist Films, 1994, directed

LORENZO O'BRIEN
Business: 9505 W. Washington Blvd., Culver City, CA 90230,
   310/841-2301

HIGHWAY PATROLMAN   First Look Pictures, 1994

RICHARD O'BRIEN
THE ROCKY HORROR PICTURE SHOW   20th Century-Fox,
   1976, w/Jim Sharman, from his play
SHOCK TREATMENT   20th Century-Fox, 1981,
   w/Jim Sharman

Screenplays:
*THE ROCKY HORROR PICTURE SHOW II: REVENGE OF
   THE OLD QUEEN*

JEFFREY OBROW
Agent: APA - Los Angeles, 310/273-0744

THE POWER   Artists Releasing Corporation/Film Ventures
   Internatioal, 1982, w/Stephen Carpenter, co-directed
THE DORM THAT DRIPPED BLOOD   *PRANKS*   Artists Releasing
   Corporation/Film Ventures International, 1983,
   w/Stephen Carpenter & Stacey Giachino, co-directed
THE KINDRED   FM Entertainment, 1987, w/others, co-directed
THE SERVANTS OF TWILIGHT   Trimark, 1991,
   w/Stephen Carpenter, directed

DAVID OBST*
Agent: Writers & Artists Agency - Los Angeles, 310/824-6300
Business Manager: Zeiderman, Friedman & LaRosa - New York,
   212/688-65333

THE WHOOPEE BOYS   Paramount, 1986, w/Jeff Buhai &
   Steve Zacharias
JOCKS   Crown International, 1987, w/Jeff Buhai &
   Steve Zacharias, as "Mike Lanahan & David Oas"
JOHNNY BE GOOD   Orion, 1988, w/Jeff Buhai &
   Steve Zacharias
PERFECT HARMONY (CTF)   Sea Breeze Productions, 1991

Screenplays:
MAN OF THE YEAR

C.R. O'CHRISTOPHER
(See Christopher Crowe)

MAURA O'CONNELL
Contact: Academy of Canadian Cinema & Television, 753 Yonge St. -
   2nd Floor, Toronto M4Y 1Z9, Canada, 416/967-0315

GEORGE'S ISLAND   New Line Cinema, 1991, w/Paul Donovan

GAVIN O'CONNOR
Contact: Eli Kabillio, The Shooting Gallery, 359 Broadway -
   2nd Floor, New York, NY 10013, 212/334-8370

THE BET (Short)   1993

Screenplays:
COMFORTABLY NUMB (directing)

PATRICK J. O'CONNOR*
Agent: Michael Siegel & Associates - Los Angeles, 310/274-5222

Screenplays:
ZOO
RICOCHET RIVER

DAVID ODELL*
Contact: Bloom, Dekom, Hergott & Cook - Los Angeles,
   310/278-8622

CRY UNCLE   Cambist, 1971
DEALING: OR THE BERKELEY-TO-BOSTON-FORTY-BRICK-LOST-
   BAG BLUES   Warner Bros., 1972
FOREPLAY   Cinema National, 1975, w/Dan Greenberg &
   Jack Richardson
THE PRESIDENT'S WOMEN   Krona, 1981
THE DARK CRYSTAL   Universal, 1982
NATE AND HAYES   Paramount, 1983, w/John Hughes
SUPERGIRL   Warner Bros., 1984
MASTERS OF THE UNIVERSE   Cannon, 1987

Screenplays:
VOODOO w/Petru Popescu
THE STORK
DIRTY EDDIE
SWAMPOUT
NOVEL LIFE
MARIE LAVEAU
THE CATHODE MONSTER

MIKE O'DELL
PERFECT PROFILE   Magnum Entertainment, 1991

MICHAEL O'DONOGHUE†
MR. MIKE'S MONDO VIDEO   New Line Cinema, 1979,
   w/Mitch Glazer, Emily Prager & Dirk Wittenborn, directed
SCROOGED   Paramount, 1988, w/Mitch Glazer

Screenplays:
ARRIVE ALIVE w/Mitch Glazer
LOLA w/Mitch Glazer
THE HOUSE GUEST w/Mitch Glazer
DROP DEAD
SLAMMER
THE BADGER

STEVE OEDEKERK*
Agent: William Morris Agency - Beverly Hills, 310/274-7451

HIGH STRUNG   Film Brigade, 1993, w/Robert Kuhn

Screenplays:
ACE VENTURA 2
FURIOUS GEORGE
PATCH ADAMS
SINGLE WHITE FAMILY
NOTHING TO LOSE

DENNIS O'FLAHERTY*
Agent: Camden-ITG - Los Angeles, 310/289-2700

HAMMETT   Orion/Warner Bros., 1982, w/ Ross Thomas
PINOCCHIO AND THE EMPEROR OF THE NIGHT (AF)
   New World, 1987, w/Robby London & Barry O'Brien

Screenplays:
SOUND OFF
FEVER
LACKAWANNA
MOST LIKELY TO SUCCEED
HIGH STEEL
RINO
SUNSHINE FLYER
BROTHERHOOD OF THE GRAPE

COLO TAVERNIER O'HAGAN
Contact: French Film Office, 745 Fifth Avenue, New York, NY 10151, 212/832-8860

A WEEK'S VACATION   *UNE SEMAINE DE VACANCES*
   Biograph, 1982, w/Marie-Francois Hans & Bertrand Tavernier
A SUNDAY IN THE COUNTRY   MGM/UA Classics, 1984,
   w/Bertrand Tavernier
BEATRICE   *LA PASSION BEATRICE*   Samuel Goldwyn
   Company, 1987
SUMMER INTERLUDE   *COMEDIE D'ETE*   Ariel/Zeitan, 1989,
   w/Daniel Vigne
STORY OF WOMEN   MK2/New Yorker Film, 1989,
   w/Claude Chabrol
DADDY NOSTALGIA   Avenue Pictures, 1991

Screenplays:
DELTA OF VENUS   w/Sarah Kernochan

WILLIAM P. O'HAGAN
SWORDS OF HEAVEN   Trans World Entertainment, 1989,
   w/James Bruner, Britt Lomond & Joseph Randazzo

GERRY O'HARA
Address: Flat K, 51 Elm Park Gardens, London SW10 9PA,
   England, 071/352-6153

THE PLEASURE GIRLS   Times, 1965, directed
ALL THE RIGHT NOISES   20th Century-Fox, 1971, directed
THE BITCH   Brent Walker Productions, 1979, directed
TEN LITTLE INDIANS   Cannon, 1989, w/Jackson Hunsicker
THE PHANTOM OF THE OPERA   21st Century Film Corp.,
   1989, Story

STEVEN OKAZAKI
LIVING ON TOKYO TIME   Skouras Pictures, 1987,
   w/John McCormick, directed
THE LISA THEORY   Farallon Pictures/Colossal Pictures,
   1994, directed

JOHN O'KEEFE*
Manager: Christine Owens - 415/255-1048

SHIMMER   American Playhouse Theatrical Films, 1993,
   from his play

SAMUEL MARTIN OLDHAM
DEADLY AMAZONS   Amazon Productions, 1992

ENRICO OLDOINI
BYE BYE BABY   Seymour Borde & Associates, 1989,
   w/Liliana Betti & Paolo Costella, directed

HENRY OLEK*
Contact: WGA - Los Angeles, 310/550-1000

A DIFFERENT STORY   Avco, 1978
TULIPS   Avco Embassy, 1981
ALL OF ME   Universal, 1984, Adaptation

Screenplays:
WAVES
HEAVEN SCENT
A FEW MURDERS IN THE NEIGHBORHOOD
PARTY BALL
ENTICE & CONSENT
FRIEND OF THE COURT

JOEL OLIANSKY*
Agent: United Talent Agency - Beverly Hills, 310/273-6700

COUNTERPOINT   Universal, 1967, w/James Lee
THE TODD KILLINGS   National General, 1971, w/Dennis Murphy
THE COMPETITION   Columbia, 1980, directed

BIRD   Warner Bros., 1988
THE SILENCE AT BETHANY   Keener Productions/American
   Playhouse Theatrical Films, 1988, directed

Screenplays:
SALERNO & FINNEGAN
FREE JOANIE LITTLE
THE ANTAGONISTS
THE CHILL
THE BIG BROKERS
THE BELLS

DAVID OLIVER
CAVEGIRL   Crown International, 1985, directed

DEANNA OLIVER*
Agent: ICM - Beverly Hills, 310/550-4000

CASPER   Universal, 1995, w/Sherri Stoner

RON OLIVER
HELLO MARY LOU: PROM NIGHT II   Samuel Goldwyn
   Company, 1987
THE LAST KISS: PROM NIGHT III   Norstar Entertainment,
   1990, co-directed
LIAR'S EDGE (CTF)   New Line Cinema/Norstar Entertainment,
   1992, directed

Screenplays:
GROUNDED

RUBY L. OLIVER
LOVE YOUR MAMA   Hemdale, 1993, directed

JIM OLLOFF
Agent: Berzon Agency - Glendale, 818/548-1560

Screenplays:
HAGAR THE HORRIBLE   w/John Hamilton
GHOST MARSHALL   w/John Hamilton

MARTY OLLSTEIN*
Contact: Sidewinder Productions - 310/828-6598

DANGEROUS LOVE   Concorde, 1988, directed

ARNE OLSEN*
Agent: Paradigm - Los Angeles, 310/277-4400

RED SCORPION   Shapiro Glickenhaus, 1989
COP AND A HALF   Universal, 1993
BLACK ICE (CTF)   Saban Entertainment, 1993,
   w/John Alan Schwartz

Screenplays:
THE MIGHTY MORPHIN POWER RANGERS
HOOLIGANS
C.O.D.
FRANK
CRIME FIGHTER
SHOOTING STARS
BRAINDAZZLED
RAPID FIRE

DANA R. OLSEN*
Agent: ICM - Beverly Hills, 310/550-4000

IT CAME FROM HOLLYWOOD   Paramount, 1982
WACKO   Jensen Farley Pictures, 1983, w/James Kouf,
   David Greenwalt & Michael Spound
GOING BERSERK   Universal, 1983, w/David Steinberg
THE 'BURBS   Universal, 1989
MEMOIRS OF AN INVISIBLE MAN   Warner Bros., 1992,
   w/Robert Collector & William Goldman

Screenplays:
THE VULGARIANS w/Robert Collector
MEN ON BASE w/Robert Collector
GOLD LUST w/Robert Collector
YOUR WISH IS MY COMMAND w/Robert Collector
PEANUT BUTTER SANDWICHES
TRAFFIC SCHOOL
HALLS OF SHAME

DOUG OLSEN
THE AMITYVILLE CURSE Allegro Films, 1990,
   Adaptatioan w/Michael Krueger & Norvell Rose

WILLIAM OLSEN
GETTING IT ON Comworld, 1983, directed

MARTIN OLSON*
Agent: Annette Van Duren Agency - Los Angeles, 213/650-3643

Screenplays:
YANKEE MAN
THE MAN WHO WAS THURSDAY
JEFF
DIMENSION OF MIRACLES
IT'S A WONDERFUL WORLD
LITTLE DRACULA

MICHAEL O'MAHONY
Agent: Hilary Wayne - Beverly Hills, 310/289-6186

Screenplays:
UNCOMMON CRIMINAL

DAVID O'MALLEY*
Agent: The Daniel Ostroff Agency - Los Angeles, 310/278-2020

THE BOOGENS Jensen Farley Pictures, 1982, w/Bob Hunt
KID COLTER TMS Pictures, 1985, directed
EASY WHEELS Fries Entertainment, 1989, w/Celia Abrams &
   Ivan Raimi, directed
EDGE OF HONOR Wind River, 1991, w/Mark Rosenbaum &
   Michael Spence
FATAL INSTINCT MGM, 1993

JASON O'MALLEY
BACKSTREET DREAMS Vidmark Entertainment, 1990

Screenplays:
BOARDWALK

SUZANNE O'MALLEY*
Agent: APA - Los Angeles, 310/273-0744

PRIVATE SCHOOL Universal, 1983, w/Dan Greenburg

Screenplays:
LADY BODYGUARDS
THE WORST PERSON IN N.Y.
THE DUMBBELL

DENIS R. O'NEIL*
Agent: J. Michael Bloom & Associates - Los Angeles, 310/275-6800

THE RIVER WILD Universal, 1994

Screenplays:
TRAPPED
ALL AROUND THE TOWN
MURDER AMONG FRIENDS
SOUTH FROM BLUIE WEST
THE BLUE MAN
SPY HOTEL
CALL ME BOB
UNFINISHED BUSINESS
JOE HOUSE

LARRY O'NEIL
LOST PROPHET Rockville Pictures, 1992, w/Michael de Avila,
   Shannon Goldman & Drew Morone

ROBERT VINCENT O'NEIL
Agent: Preferred Artists - Encino, 818/990-0305

PACO Cinema National, 1975, directed
THE BALTIMORE BULLET Avco Embassy, 1980,
   w/John F. Brascia
VICE SQUAD Avco Embassy, 1982, w/Sandy Howard &
   Kenneth Peters
DEADLY FORCE Embassy, 1983, w/Ken Blackwell &
   Barry Schneider
ANGEL New World, 1984, w/Joseph M. Cala, directed
AVENGING ANGEL New World, 1985, w/Joseph M.Cala, directed
STREETWISE Trimark, 1993, w/Alien Castle

Screenplays:
FOR WHOM THE BELL TOLLS
KILLSHOT
SECRETS OF LOST CAVERNS
SUDDENLY DANGEROUS

DAVID O'NEILL
Agent: William Morris Agency - Beverly Hills, 310/274-7451

Screenplays:
MARTIN EDEN (directing)

GENE O'NEILL*
Agent: Don Walerstein, Rohner & Walerstein - 310/477-5001

DOWN TWISTED Cannon, 1987, w/Noreen Tobin

GREG COLLINS O'NEILL*
Contact: 213/651-1075

TUFF TURF New World, 1985, Story w/Murray Michaels
THE SLEEPING CAR Triax Entertainment, 1990

DANNY OPATOSHU
THE STUDENT TEACHERS New World, 1973
GET CRAZY Embassy, 1983, w/Henry Rosenbaum & David Taylor

Screenplays:
FRIES w/Vicki Hochburg

BARRY OPPER
Business: Sho Films, 2300 Duane St. - Suite 9, Los Angeles,
   CA 90039, 213/665-9088

CRITTERS 3 New Line Cinema, 1992, Story

DON KEITH OPPER*
Manager: Creative Alliance Management - Los Angeles,
   213/962-6090

ANDROID New World, 1982, w/James Reigle
CITY LIMITS Atlantic Releasing Corporation, 1985,
   w/Aaron Lipstadt & James Reigle
SLAM DANCE Island Pictures, 1987

Screenplays:
STARTING FIVE

RENEE ORIN*
Agent: Omni Artists - Beverly Hills, 310/858-0085
Contact: 310/827-0529

Screenplays:
TIL DEATH DO US PART
UNFINISHED BUSINESS

279

HARIS ORKIN*
Contact: WGA - Los Angeles, 310/550-1000

Screenplays:
IN YOUR SHOES
JOE AND ROSALIA
THE PASADENA KID
TAKING CHANCES
ANOTHER FINE MESS
THE LAVENDAR HILL MOB
MOST WANTED
SIN CITY
BIGMALLION
ADOPT-A-CON
HARD TO MISS

PETER ORMROD
Contact: Irish Film Institute, 6 Eustace St., Dublin 2, Ireland,
tel. 795744

EAT THE PEACH   Skouras Pictures, 1986,
w/John Kelleher, directed

ALAN ORMSBY*
Agent: Innovative Artists - Los Angeles, 310/553-5200

CHILDREN SHOULDN'T PLAY WITH DEAD THINGS
Gemini Film, 1972
DEATHDREAM   1972
DERANGED   1974, directed
MY BODYGUARD   20th Century-Fox, 1980
THE LITTLE DRAGONS   Aurora, 1980, w/Harvey Applebaum,
Louis G. Atlee & Rudolph Borchert
CAT PEOPLE   Universal, 1982
PORKY'S II: THE NEXT DAY   20th Century-Fox, 1983,
w/Bob Clark & Roger Swaybill
TOUCH AND GO   Tri-Star, 1986, w/Harry Colomby & Bob Sand
POPCORN   Studio Three Film Corp., 1991, as "Tod Hackett"
INDECENCY (CTF)   Point of View Productions/MCA Television
Entertainment, 1992, w/Amy Jones & Holly Goldberg Sloan

Screenplays:
THE MUMMY
THE POOL
MEMORY BOY
FAMILY PORTRAIT
NORTHEAST KINGDOM
CONDUCT UNBECOMING
HUMBOLDT COUNTY
TWISTED!

P.J. O'ROURKE
Agent: Phoenix Literary Agency - Montana, 406/222-2848

EASY MONEY   Orion, 1983, w/Dennis Blair, Rodney Dangerfield &
Michael Endler

Screenplays:
MARGARITAVILLE

JAMES ORR*
Agent: CAA - Beverly Hills, 310/288-4545
Business: Orr & Cruickshank Productions, Walt Disney Pictures,
818/560-6423

BREAKING ALL THE RULES   New World, 1985,
w/Jim Cruickshank, directed
TOUGH GUYS   Buena Vista, 1986, w/Jim Cruickshank
THREE MEN AND A BABY   Buena Vista, 1987, w/Jim Cruickshank
MR. DESTINY   Buena Vista, 1990, w/Jim Cruickshank, directed
SISTER ACT II: BACK IN THE HABIT   Buena Vista, 1993,
w/Jim Cruickshank & Judi Ann Mason

Screenplays:
MAN 2 MAN w/Jim Cruickshank (Buena Vista)
FUN PARK w/Jim Cruickshank
BANDIT w/Jim Cruickshank

RON OSBORN*
Agent: Warden, White & Kane - Beverly Hills, 213/852-1028

RADIOLAND MURDERS   Universal, 1994, w/Jeff Reno,
Willard Huyck & Gloria Katz

Screenplays:
DEATH TAKES A HOLIDAY w/Jeff Reno

JOHN OSBORNE
Contact: British Academy of Film & Television Arts, 195 Piccadilly,
London W1, England, 071/734-0022

LOOK BACK IN ANGER (P)
LUTHER (P)
DEJA VU (P)
THE ENTERTAINER   British Lion, 1960, w/Nigel Kneale,
from his play
TOM JONES ★★   United Artists, 1963
INADMISSABLE EVIDENCE   Paramount, 1968, from his play

WILLIAM H. OSBORNE*
Agent: United Talent Agency - Beverly Hills, 310/273-6700

TWINS   Universal, 1988, w/William Davies, Timothy Harris &
Herschel Weingrod
STOP! OR MY MOM WILL SHOOT   Universal, 1992,
w/William Davies & Blake Snyder
GHOST IN THE MACHINE   20th Century Fox, 1993,
w/William Davies
THE REAL McCOY   Universal, 1993, w/William Davies

Screenplays:
EUREKA w/William Davies & Charlie Peters
FOREIGN EXCHANGE w/William Davies
EARTHQUAKE w/William Davies
PRITCHARD COUNTY w/William Davies

CHUCK OSBOURNE
DOUBLE TROUBLE   Motion Picture Corporation of America, 1992,
w/Jeffrey Kerns & Kurt Wimmer

WILLIAM OSCO
NIGHT PATROL   New World, 1981, w/Jackie Kong &
Murray Langston

JOHN O'SHEA
AMONG THE CINDERS   New World, 1985, w/Rolf Haedrich

SUZANNE OSHRY*
Contact: WGA - Los Angeles, 310/550-1000

Screenplays:
DOING BUSINESS

CLIFF OSMOND*
Contact: 310/454-3717

THE PRESIDENT MUST DIE   Jensen Farley Pictures, 1981,
w/James L. Conway
THE PENITENT   Cineworld, 1988, directed

DIANA OSSANA
Agent: William Morris Agency - Beverly Hills, 310/274-7451

Screenplays:
PRETTY BOY FLOYD w/Larry McMurtry
THE STANDOFF w/Larry McMurtry
FATHER KNOWS BEST w/Larry McMurtry

SUZANNE OSTEN
THE GUARDIAN ANGEL   Sandrew Film, 1990, w/Etienne Glaser &
Madeleine Gustafsson, directed

PETER OSTERLUND*
Agent: United Talent Agency - Beverly Hills, 310/273-6700

Screenplays:
COUNTERMEASURE w/Amy Brooke Baker
SPIN w/Amy Brooke Baker
THE CANTOR'S DILEMMA w/Amy Brooke Baker
SYCAMORE DRIVE w/Amy Brooke Baker
MEMORY BOY w/Amy Brooke Baker

AVA OSTERN-FRIES
Business: Avanti Enterprises, c/o Fries Entertainment,
 6922 Hollywood Blvd., Los Angeles, CA 90028-6133,
 213/468-8306

TROOP BEVERLY HILLS   WEG, 1989, Story

GREGG OSTRIN
Business: City Entertainment, 1360 S. Roxbury Dr., Los Angeles,
 CA 90035, 310/284-7925

Screenplays:
THE DELI BOYS w/Joshua D. Maurer

DOMINIQUE OTHENIN-GIRARD
Manager: Sarah Jackson, Carthay Circle - 310/657-5454

HALLOWEEN 5: THE REVENGE OF MICHAEL MYERS
 Galaxy International, 1989, w/Shem Bitterman &
 Michael Jacobs, directed

BRIAN O'TOOLE
Agent: Leslie Kallen Agency - Sherman Oaks, 818/906-2785

Screenplays:
TIS THE SEASON
APOCALYPSE COW
WEREWOLF MOON

JEAN-PAUL OULLETTE
THE UNNAMEABLE   Vidmark Entertainment, 1988

GERARD OURY
Contact: French Film Office, 745 Fifth Avenue, New York,
 NY 10151, 212/832-8860

DON'T LOOK NOW...WE'RE BEING SHOT AT
 LA GRANDE VADROVILLE Cinepix, 1966, directed
THE BRAIN   Paramount, 1969, w/Marcel Julian &
 Daniel Thompson, directed

RICHARD OUTTEN*
Agent: ICM - Beverly Hills, 310/550-4000

LIONHEART   Orion, 1987, w/Menno Meyjes
LITTLE NEMO (AF)   Hemdale, 1992, w/Chris Columbus
PET SEMATARY TWO   Paramount, 1992

Screenplays:
THE ENCHANTING
GLOBAL P.D.
SPACE CASE
ON MY HONOR
TRANSYLVANIA-PENNSYLVANIA
GOONIES 2

WILLIAM OVERGARD
THE LAST DINOSAUR (AF)   Rankin & Bass Productions, 1977
THE BUSHIDO BLADE   Trident, 1981

ERIC OVERMYER*
Agent: William Morris Agency - Beverly Hills, 310/274-7451

THE HELIOTROPE BOUQUET BY SCOTT JOPLIN AND
 LOUIS CHAUVIN (P)

Screenplays:
DARK RAPTURE

JAN OXENBERG
THANK YOU AND GOODNIGHT! (FD)   Aries Film, 1992, directed

Screenplays:
ONE FOR MY BABY (directing)

FRANK OZ*
Agent: CAA - Beverly Hills, 310/288-4545

THE MUPPETS TAKE MANHATTAN   Tri-Star, 1984,
 w/Tom Patchett & Jay Tarses, directed

P

DAVID PABIAN*
Agent: Warden, White & Kane - Beverly Hills, 213/852-1028

PUPPET MASTER II   Full Moon, 1991

Screenplays:
PRINCE VALIANT (Neue Constantin)
ROGUE'S MOON
REINMAR
MIRAGE CANYON
PRIME EVIL
MANWOLF
BROTHERS

WILLIAM R. PACE
Contact: 212/340-8001

ECHO CANYON (Short)   1986, directed
BLADES   Troma, 1988, w/Tom Rondinella
ALL'S FAIR   Moviestore Entertainment, 1989, w/John Finnegan,
 Tom Rondinella & Randee Russell
A GIRL'S GUIDE (CTF)   USA Network/Six Shooter Productions,
 1993, w/Tom Rondinella

Screenplays:
TREETOPS w/Tom Rondinella
FAMILY RITES w/Tom Rondinella
VOODOO LOUNGE

TOM PAGE*
Contact: WGA - Los Angeles, 310/550-1000

Screenplays:
HOUSE OF CHROME
MASK OF MICHAEL
HITTING CHARLOTTE

MARNIE PAIGE
HYPER SAPIEN   Tri-Star, 1986, w/Richard Adcock &
 Christopher Blue

**F
I
L
M

W
R
I
T
E
R
S**

NICK PAINE
THE PHILADELPHIA EXPERIMENT 2   Trimark, 1993,
   w/Kevin Rock

Screenplays:
CRASHOUT w/Stephen Cornwell

ALAN J. PAKULA*
Agent: ICM - Beverly Hills, 310/550-4000
Business: The Pakula Company, 330 West 58th Street - Suite 5H,
   New York, NY 10019, 212/664-0640

SOPHIE'S CHOICE ★   Universal/AFD, 1982, directed
SEE YOU IN THE MORNING   Lorimar, 1988, directed
PRESUMED INNOCENT   Warner Bros., 1990,
   w/Frank Pierson, directed
THE PELICAN BRIEF   Warner Bros., 1993, directed

Screenplays:
MOO

DOUG PALAU*
Agent: Innovative Artists - Los Angeles, 310/553-5200

Screenplays:
PRINCE CHARMING
FIXIN"TO DIE
DOGSPELL

EUZHAN PALCY
Agent: William Morris Agency - Beverly Hills, 310/274-7451

SUGAR CANE ALLEY   Orion, 1983, directed
A DRY WHITE SEASON   MGM/UA, 1989,
   w/Colin Welland, directed

SARAH C. PALEY*
Agent: William Morris Agency - New York, 212/586-5100

Screenplays:
IT CAME FROM POLAND
FAIRY GODMOTHER
WHAT HAPPENED TO HARRY
ALMOST HUMAN
MISTER MAGOO

MICHAEL PALIN
Business: Prominent Features Ltd., 68A Delancey St., London
NW1 7RY, England, 01/284-1004

CONSUMING PASSIONS (P) w/Terry Jones
AND NOW FOR SOMETHING COMPLETELY DIFFERENT
   Columbia, 1972, w/ Graham Chapman, John Cleese,
   Terry Gilliam, Eric Idle & Terry Jones
MONTY PYTHON AND THE HOLY GRAIL   Cinema 5, 1974,
   w/Graham Chapman, John Cleese, Terry Gilliam, Eric Idle &
   Terry Jones
MONTY PYTHON'S LIFE OF BRIAN   Orion/Warner Bros., 1979,
   w/Graham Chapman, John Cleese, Terry Gilliam, Eric Idle &
   Terry Jones
TIME BANDITS   Avco Embassy, 1981, w/Terry Gilliam
MONTY PYTHON LIVE AT THE HOLLYWOOD BOWL   Columbia,
   1982, w/Graham Chapman, John Cleese, Terry Gilliam,
   Eric Idle & Terry Jones
THE MISSIONARY   Columbia, 1982
THE SECRET POLICEMAN'S OTHER BALL   Miramax, 1982,
   w/Marty Feldman & Martin Lewis
MONTY PYTHON'S THE MEANING OF LIFE   Universal, 1983,
   w/Graham Chapman, John Cleese, Terry Gilliam, Eric Idle &
   Terry Jones
AMERICAN FRIENDS   Prominent Features, 1991,
   w/Tristram Powell

ROSPO PALLENBERG*
Agent: The Gersh Agency - Beverly Hills, 310/274-6611

EXCALIBUR   Orion/Warner Bros., 1981
THE EMERALD FOREST   20th Century Fox, 1985

Screenplays:
ROBOTS RULE

PETER PALLISER*
Contact: WGA - New York, 212/245-6180

LANDSLIDE   Northern Screen, 1992

ANDERS PALM
MURDER ON LINE ONE   Academy Entertainment, 1990, directed

ANTHONY PALMER*
Contact: WGA - Los Angeles, 310/550-1000

NIGHT GAME   Trans World Entertainment, 1989,
   w/Spencer Eastman

MELINDA PALMER
Agent: Janklow & Associates - Westlake Village, 310/785-9550

THE GARBAGE PAIL KIDS MOVIE   Atlantic Releasing Corporation,
   1987, w/Rod Amateau

THOMAS PALMER JR.
FOREVER   Triax Entertainment Group, 1992,
   w/Jackelyn Giroux, directed

TONY PALMER
Business: Ladbroke Films Ltd. - London, 071/727-3541

TESTIMONY   Isolde Films, 1988, w/David Rudkin, directed

MATT PALMIERI
Agent: ICM - Beverly Hills, 310/550-4000

CRUISE CONTROL (Short) ★   1993, directed

CHAZZ PALMINTERI*
Agent: CAA - Beverly Hills, 310/288-4545

A BRONX TALE   Savoy, 1993, from his play
FAITHFUL   Savoy, 1995, from his play

DENNIS J. PALUMBO*
Contact: WGA - Los Angeles, 310/550-1000

ALL THE PLEASURES PROVE (P)
MY FAVORITE YEAR   MGM/UA, 1982, w/Norman Steinberg

Screenplays:
KIDD
THE MAN WHO GAVE UP HIS NAME
THE GHOST OF HELL'S KITCHEN
DOUBLES
THE WORKS
POE
THE GRAND GAME
WORKING TRASH
RITES OF SUMMER
THURSDAY'S CHILD

NORMAN PANAMA*
Agent: Kaplan-Stahler - Beverly Hills, 213/653-4483

AND THE ANGELS SING   Paramount, 1943, w/Melvin Frank &
   Claude Binyon
THANK YOUR LUCKY STARS   Warner Bros., 1943,
   w/Melvin Frank & James V. Kern

DUFFY'S TAVERN   Paramount, 1945, w/Melvin Frank
MONSIEUR BEAUCAIRE   Paramount, 1945, w/Melvin Frank
THE ROAD TO UTOPIA ★   Paramount, 1945, w/Melvin Frank
OUR HEARTS WERE GROWING UP   Paramount, 1946,
    w/Melvin Frank
THE RETURN OF OCTOBER   Columbia, 1948, w/Melvin Frank
MR. BLANDINGS BUILDS HIS DREAM HOUSE   RKO, 1948,
    w/Melvin Frank
THE REFORMER AND THE REDHEAD   MGM, 1950,
    w/Melvin Frank, co-directed
STRICTLY DISHONORABLE   MGM, 1951,
    w/Melvin Frank, co-directed
CALLAWAY WENT THATAWAY   MGM, 1951, w/Melvin Frank
ABOVE AND BEYOND   MGM, 1952, w/Melvin Frank, co-directed
KNOCK ON WOOD ★   Paramount, 1954,
    w/Melvin Frank, co-directed
WHITE CHRISTMAS   Paramount, 1954, w/Melvin Frank &
    Norman Krasna
THE COURT JESTER   Paramount, 1955,
    w/Melvin Frank, co-directed
THAT CERTAIN FEELING   Paramount, 1956, w/Melvin Frank,
    William Altman & I.A.L. Diamond, co-directed
THE TRAP   THE BAITED TRAP   Paramount, 1958,
    w/Richard Alan Simmons, directed
L'IL ABNER   Paramount, 1959, w/Melvin Frank
THE FACTS OF LIFE ★   United Artists, 1960, w/Melvin Frank
ROAD TO HONG KONG   United Artists, 1962,
    w/Melvin Frank, co-directed
NOT WITH MY WIFE, YOU DON'T!   Warner Bros., 1966,
    w/Peter Barnes & Larry Gelbart, directed
I WILL, I WILL...FOR NOW   20th Century-Fox, 1976,
    w/Albert E. Lewin

WILLIAM N. PANZER
Business: Davis-Panzer Productions, 1754 N. Serrano - Suite 401,
    Hollywood, CA 90027, 213/463-2343

STEEL   LOOK DOWN AND DIE   World Northal, 1980,
    Story w/Peter S. Davis & Rob Ewing
HIGHLANDER 2: THE QUICKENING   InterStar Releasing, 1991,
    Story w/Brian Clemens
HIGHLANDER 3: THE SORCERER   Miramax, 1995,
    Story w/Brad A. Mirman

DENNIS PAOLI*
Agent: William Morris Agency - Beverly Hills, 310/274-7451

H.P. LOVECRAFT'S RE-ANIMATOR   Empire Pictures, 1985,
    w/Stuart Gordon & William H. Norris
FROM BEYOND   Empire Pictures, 1986
THE PIT AND THE PENDULUM   Full Moon Entertainment, 1991
SPELLCASTER   Empire Pictures, 1992, w/Charles Bogel,
    filmed in 1986
MORTAL SINS (CTF)   Blake Edwards Television/Barry Weitz Films,
    1992, w/Greg Martinelli
BODY SNATCHERS   Warner Bros., 1993, w/Stuart Gordon &
    Nicholas St. John
CASTLE FREAK   Fullmoon, 1994

Screenplays:
MIDNIGHT

MICHAEL J. PARADISE
(Giulio Paradisi)
THE VISITOR   International Picture Show, 1980,
    Story w/Ovidio Assontis

MITCH PARADISE*
Agent: ICM - Beverly Hills, 310/550-4000

Screenplays:
JUST IN TIME
DEAD EVEN
DEATH SPA
BORN TO RUN

JOHN PARAGON*
Agent: Broder-Kurland-Webb-Uffner - Beverly Hills, 310/281-3400

ELVIRA: MISTRESS OF THE DARK   New World, 1988,
    w/Sam Egan & Cassandra Peterson

Screenplays:
TWIN SITTERS (Guts & Glory Productions)
BORN TO SUFFER
BUZZWORD

GAIL PARENT*
Agent: William Morris Agency - Beverly Hills, 310/274-7451

SHEILA LEVINE IS DEAD AND LIVING IN NEW YORK   Paramount,
    1975, w/Kenny Solms
THE MAIN EVENT   Warner Bros., 1979, w/ Andrew Smith
CROSS MY HEART   Universal, 1987, w/Armyan Bernstein

Screenplays:
FACE THE MUSIC THE MOTHER-IN-LAW w/Neal Israel
SLAVES OF LOVE
DOCTORS IN HOLLYWOOD

DOMINIC PARIS
LAST RITES   Cannon, 1980, w/Ben Donnelly

HENRY C. PARKE*
Agent: Warden, White & Kane - Beverly Hills, 213/852-1028

Screenplays:
UNFINISHED BUSINESS
WHITE LIES
ROAR OF THE PRESS
ON THE LAM
STRAWBERRY FIELDS
HONEYMOON
DEADLY ERNEST

ALAN PARKER*
Agent: CAA - Beverly Hills, 310/288-4545

MELODY   Hemdale, 1971
BUGSY MALONE   Paramount, 1976, directed
ANGEL HEART   Tri-Star, 1987, directed
COME SEE THE PARADISE   20th Century Fox, 1990, directed
THE ROAD TO WELLVILLE   Columbia, 1994, directed

CARY PARKER
THE GIRL IN THE PICTURE   Samuel Goldwyn Company,
    1986, directed

CHARLES PARKER
(See David Zito)

CHRIS PARKER
Agent: Richland/Wunsch/Hohman Agency - Los Angeles,
    310/278-1955

Screenplays:
THE BOO BROTHERS w/Michael Lucker
LITTLE OUTLAWS w/Michael Lucker
REPEAT OFFENDER w/Michael Lucker

DAVID PARKER
Agent: CAA - Beverly Hills, 310/288-4545

MALCOLM   Vestron, 1986
RIKKY AND PETE   MGM/UA, 1988
THE BIG STEAL   Overseas Film Group, 1991

Screenplays:
OPPY w/Peter Yeldham

G. ROSS PARKER*
Agent: ICM - New York, 212/556-5600

Screenplays:
HIGH HEELED SNEAKERS
DOLL FACE
KNOCK WOOD

JOAN H. PARKER*
Agent: Flora Roberts - New York, 212/355-4165

SPENSER: CEREMONY (CTF)   Norstar Entertainment, 1993,
   w/Robert B. Parker
SPENSER: PALE KINGS AND PRINCES (CTF)   Norstar
   Entertainment, 1994, w/Robert B. Parker

LEE FORD PARKER
Manager: The Anthony Elliot Company - Los Angeles, 310/284-6804

Screenplays:
BLOOD TIES w/Nick Koff

MONICA PARKER*
Contact: WGA - Los Angeles, 310/550-1000

ALL DOGS GO TO HEAVEN (AF)   MGM/UA, 1989, Story w/others

Screenplays:
TURN ME LOOSE

ROBERT B. PARKER
Agent: Flora Roberts - New York, 212/355-4165

SPENSER: CEREMONY (CTF)   Norstar Entertainment, 1993,
   w/Joan H. Parker
SPENSER: PALE KINGS AND PRINCES (CTF)   Norstar
   Entertainment, 1994, w/Joan H. Parker

RONALD PARKER*
Agent: The Marion Rosenberg Office - Los Angeles, 213/653-7383

Screenplays:
THE NEW WORLD
BABE RUTH (CTF)
FIVE GOOD GUYS

SCOTT PARKER*
Agent: Annette Van Duren Agency - Los Angeles, 213/650-3643
Manager: Michael Meitzer - Los Angeles, 310/289-0701

DIE LAUGHING   Orion/Warner Bros., 1980, w/Robby Benson &
   Jerry Segal
HE KNOWS YOU'RE ALONE   MGM/UA, 1980

Screenplays:
KID MIDAS
SATURDAY AFTERNOON w/Eric Bloom
THE WRONG DOOR
BEMS
CAREER MOVE
GO TO HELL
MUSHROOM
IF YOU BELIEVE
FLATBUSH GAS
GROWN-UPS
GRIMOIRE

TOM S. PARKER*
Agent: United Talent Agency - Beverly Hills, 310/273-6700

STAY TUNED   Warner Bros., 1992, w/Jim Jennewein
MAJOR LEAGUE II   Warner Bros., 1994, w/Jim Jennewein &
   R.J. Stewart
THE FLINTSTONES   Universal, 1994, w/Jim Jennewein &
   Steven deSouza

GETTING EVEN WITH DAD   MGM/UA, 1994, w/Jim Jennewein
RICHIE RICH   Warner Bros., 1994, w/Jim Jennewein

Screenplays:
THE FAMILY MAN w/Jim Jennewein

WALTER F. PARKES*
Agent: CAA - Beverly Hills, 310/288-4545
Business: Amblin Entertainment, Universal Pictures, 818/777-4600

WARGAMES ★   MGM/UA, 1983, w/Lawrence Lasker
SNEAKERS   Universal, 1992, w/Lawrence Lasker &
   Phil Alden Robinson

Screenplays:
PETER PAN w/Lawrence Lasker

ERIC PARKINSON
SOULTAKER   Taurus Entertainment, 1990, Story w/Vivian Schilling

ADRIENNE PARKS*
Contact: Dixon Dearn, Dearn & Donaldson - Los Angeles,
   310/557-0417

Screenplays:
KING OF THE BOWL-O-RAMA

HUGH PARKS
AFTER SCHOOL   Moviestore Entertainment, 1989, w/John Linde,
   Rod McBrien & Joe Tankersley

RICK PARKS*
Agent: Broder-Kurland-Webb-Uffner - Beverly Hills, 310/281-3400

Screenplays:
CUPID w/Andy Tennant

PETER PARNELL*
Agent: William Morris Agency - Beverly Hills, 310/274-7451

Screenplays:
REALLY ROSIE

JOANNE PARRENT*
Agent: Maggie Field Agency - Studio City, 818/980-2001

THE HEALING FORCE   Woody Clark Productions, 1983,
   w/Woodrow 'V. Clark & Jay Miracle

Screenplays:
WITCH-HUNT

JAMES D. PARRIOTT*
Agent: CAA - Beverly Hills, 310/288-4545

HEART CONDITION   New Line Cinema, 1990, directed

Screenplays:
COLORMAN

SARA PARRIOTT*
Agent: The Daniel Ostroff Agency - Los Angeles, 310/278-2020

WORTH WINNING   20th Century Fox, 1989, w/Josann McGibbon
THREE MEN AND A LITTLE LADY   Buena Vista, 1990,
   Story w/Josann McGibbon
THE FAVOR   Orion, 1994, w/Josann McGibbon

Screenplays:
MRS. CALIFORNIA w/Josann McGibbon
RUNAWAY BRIDE w/Josann McGibbon

MICHAEL PART*
Agent: Hilary Wayne - Beverly Hills, 310/289-6186

A KID IN KING ARTHUR'S COURT   Buena Vista, 1995,
    w/Robert Levy

Screenplays:
BLACK WATER
DOORNAIL
WEATHERMAKER
THE REPLACEMENTS
SALEM

ARTO PARTAGAMIAN
BECAUSE WHY   Aska Film Productions, 1994, directed

MICHAEL PASEORNEK*
Contact: Cinepix, New York

STITCHES   International Film Marketing, 1985, w/Michael Coquette
MEATBALLS III   TMS Pictures, 1986, w/Bradley Kesden
SNAKEEATER'S REVENGE   Image Organization, 1990,
    w/Don Carmody & John Dunning

Screenplays:
CYBERSTORM (directing)

MARTIN PASKO
BATMAN: MASK OF THE PHANTASM (AF)   Warner Bros., 1993,
    w/Alan Burnett, Paul Dini & Michael Reeves

ELIZABETH PASSARELLI*
Agent: The Gersh Agency - Beverly Hills, 310/274-6611

Screenplays:
PRODIGAL SON
OTHERWISE ENGAGED
ZOMBIE HIGH

IVAN PASSER*
Agent: The Agency - Los Angeles, 310/551-3000

LOVES OF A BLONDE   Prominent, 1966, w/Milos Forman &
    Jaroslav Papousek
THE FIREMAN'S BALL   Cinema 5, 1968, w/Milos Forman &
    Jaroslav Papousek
LAW AND DISORDER   Columbia, 1974, w/Ken Harris Fishman &
    William Richert, directed

Screenplays:
PORTHOLE TO PARADISE (directing)

ACE PASSMORE
Agent: William Morris Agency - Beverly Hills, 310/274-7451

Screenplays:
BLUE BLAZES w/Eric Small

TOM PATCHETT*
Agent: CAA - Beverly Hills, 310/288-4545
Business Manager: Tanner, Mainstain, Hoffer - Los Angeles,
    310/446-2700

WOLVERINES (P)
MAD MAGAZINE PRESENTS UP THE ACADEMY   Warner Bros.,
    1980, w/Jay Tarses
THE GREAT MUPPET CAPER   Universal/AFD, 1981,
    w/ Jay Tarses, Jerry Juhl & Jack Rose
THE MUPPETS TAKE MANHATTAN   Tri-Star, 1984,
    w/Frank Oz & Jay Tarses

Screenplays:
THE BRAVE YOUNG MEN OF WEINBERG w/JayTarses
THE KID WHO COULD GO TO HIS LEFT w/Jay Tarses
CROOKS w/Jay Tarses

MICHAEL PATE
Business: Pisces Productions, 21 Bundarra Road, Bellevue Hill,
    NSW, 2023, Australia, tel.: 02/30-4208

TIM   Satori, 1979, directed
THE MANGO TREE   Satori, 1982

JOHN PATERSON
ANNIE'S COMING OUT   Film Australia, 1984, w/Chris Borthwick
A TEST OF LOVE   Universal, 1985, w/Chris Borthwick

VICKIE PATIK*
Agent: Dytman & Schwartz - Beverly Hills, 310/274-8844

Screenplays:
FAMILY MELODRAMA
INTERSLOPE

RANDY PATRICK
Agent: APA - Los Angeles, 310/273-0744

Screenplays:
WHITE TRASH IN A TRAILER PARK
RETURN TO SENDER
LITTLE FEET

VINCENT PATRICK*
Agent: United Talent Agency - Beverly Hills, 310/273-6700

THE POPE OF GREENWICH VILLAGE   MGM/UA, 1984
FAMILY BUSINESS   Tri-Star, 1989

Screenplays:
MAFIA COP
FREEING THE WHALES
IN FROM THE COLD
OF THE LORD
JOE II
MY NEW PARTNER
HARLEM UNIVERSITY
AT PLAY

WILLI PATTERSON
Agent: Susan Smith & Associates - Beverly Hills, 213/852-4777

Screenplays:
FASCINATED

CINCO PAUL
Agent: Innovative Artists - Los Angeles, 310/553-5200
Manager: 3 Arts Entertainment - Los Angeles, 213/851-5700

Screenplays:
BAND OF GOLD
STEP BY STEP

DON MICHAEL PAUL*
Agent: The Gersh Agency - Beverly Hills, 310/274-6611

HARLEY DAVIDSON AND THE MARLBORO MAN
    MGM-Pathe, 1991

DOROTHY KOSTER PAUL
Business: Crystal Sky, 1800 Century Park East - 6th Floor,
    Los Angeles, CA 90067, 310/843-0223

ETERNITY   Paul Entertainment, 1990, w/Steven Paul & Jon Voight

HENRY PAUL
Business: Crystal Sky, 1800 Century Park East - 6th Floor,
    Los Angeles, CA 90067, 310/843-0223

FALLING IN LOVE AGAIN   International Picture Show, 1980,
    Story w/Steven Paul

F I L M W R I T E R S

STEVEN PAUL

Business: Crystal Sky, 1800 Century Park East - 6th Floor, Los Angeles, CA 90067, 310/843-0223

FALLING IN LOVE AGAIN   International Picture Show, 1980, w/Ted Allan & Susannah York,   directed
SLAPSTICK OF ANOTHER KIND   *SLAPSTICK*   Entertainment Releasing Corp./International FilmMarketing, 1983,   directed
NEVER TOO YOUNG TO DIE   Paul Releasing, 1986, w/Gil Bettman & Anton Fitz
ETERNITY   Paul Entertainment, 1990, w/Dorothy Koster Paul & Jon Voight,   directed

DAVID PAULSEN*

Contact: The Hemisphere Group - 818/789-3013

DIAMONDS   Avco Embassy, 1975, w/Menahem Golan
SAVAGE WEEKEND   *THE UPSTATE MURDERS*   Cannon, 1976,   directed
THE URANIUM CONSPIRACY   Noah Films, 1978
SCHIZOID   Cannon, 1980,   directed

GARY PAULSEN*

Agent: Innovative Artists - Los Angeles, 310/553-5200

A CRY IN THE WILD   Concorde/New Horizons, 1990, w/Catherine Cryan

Screenplays:
THE FOXMAN
WOODSONG
NIGHTJOHN (CTF)

MICHAEL PAVONE*

Agent: William Morris Agency - Beverly Hills, 310/274-7451

Screenplays:
PERPETUAL JULY w/Dave Alan Johnson
THE GOOD HUMOR MAN w/Dave Alan Johnson

ALEXANDER PAYNE*

Agent: CAA - Beverly Hills, 310/288-4545

THE PASSION OF MARTIN   (Short), 1991,   directed

Screenplays:
THE COWARD
THE LIVING END w/Jim Taylor
MARTIANS

ANDREW PAYNE

SPACED OUT   Miramax, 1981

DAVID PAYNE

Agent: Berzon Agency - Glendale, 818/548-1560

Screenplays:
SCORCHER
WORM

WILLIAM MOSLEY-PAYNE
(See William MOSLEY-Payne)

J. STEPHEN PEACE

HAPPY HOUR   The Movie Store, 1987, w/John De Bello & Constantine Dillon

GREG PEAD
(See Yahoo Serious)

CRAIG PEARCE

STRICTLY BALLROOM   Miramax, 1994, w/Buz Luhrmann

Screenplays:
ROMEO AND JULIET w/Buz Luhrmann

CHRISTOPHER PEARCE

AMERICAN CYBORG: STEEL WARRIOR   Cannon, 1994, Story w/Boaz Davidson

STEVEN PEARL*

Agent: Paradigm - Los Angeles, 310/277-4400

THE DOG ATE IT   (Short)   1991,   directed

Screenplays:
LIFE IS HOMEWORK

BARRY PEARSON

KING OF THE STREETS   *ALIEN WARRIOR*   Shapiro Entertainment, 1986, w/Ed Hunt, Ruben Gordon & Steven Shoenberg
BLOODY BIRTHDAY   Judica Productions, 1986, w/Ed Hunt

DURK PEARSON*

Contact: WGA - Los Angeles, 310/550-1000

THE DEAD POOL   Warner Bros., 1988, Story w/Steve Sharon & Sandy Shaw

KIMI PECK*

Agent: The Gersh Agency - Beverly Hills, 310/274-6611

LITTLE DARLINGS   Paramount, 1980, w/Dalene Young

Screenplays:
HOW TO MARRY A MILLIONAIRE

MITCHELL PECK

Agent: ICM - Beverly Hills, 310/550-4000

Screenplays:
FOLK HEROES

TONY PECKHAM*

Agent: Paradigm - Los Angeles, 310/277-4400

Screenplays:
BURNOUT

DAVID E. PECKINPAH*

Agent: Broder-Kurland-Webb-Uffner - Beverly Hills, 310/281-3400

Screenplays:
THE PAPER BOY (Allegro Films)
PALS FOREVER
OUTLAW SKIES

QUENTIN PEEPLES

AN AMBUSH OF GHOSTS   Stress Fiesta Films, 1993

ROBERT L. PEETE*

Agent: Wile Enterprises - Santa Monica, 310/828-9768

IT'S CALLED SURVIVAL   (P)
THE CENTERFOLD GIRLS   Dimension, 1974
DRIVE-IN   Columbia, 1976

HANAN PELED

DEADLINE   Skouras Pictures, 1987

ANDREE PELLETIER

Contact: Academy of Canadian Cinema & Television, 753 Yonge St. - 2nd Floor, Toronto M4Y 1Z9, Canada, 416/967-0315

A PAPER WEDDING   Capitol Entertainment Release, 1991, w/Jefferson Lewis

THEO PELLETIER
MR. BASEBALL   Universal, 1992, Story w/John Junkerman

HOWARD C. PEN
SWORD OF THE VALIANT   Cannon, 1984, w/Stephen Weeks &
   Philip M. Breen

ARTHUR PENN
Agent: William Morris Agency - Beverly Hills, 310/274-7451
Business Manager: Evan R. Bell, Kraft, Haiken & Bell - New York,
   212/687-4500

ALICE'S RESTAURANT   United Artists, 1969,
   w/Venable Herndon, directed

LEO PENN
Contact: Directors Guild of America - Los Angeles, 310/289-2000

JUDGMENT IN BERLIN   New Line Cinema, 1988,
   w/Joshua Sinclair, directed

SEAN PENN
Agent: William Morris Agency - Beverly Hills, 310/274-7451

INDIAN RUNNER   MGM-Pathe, 1991, directed
THE CROSSING GUARD   Miramax, 1994, directed

ZAK PENN*
Agent: ICM - Beverly Hills, 310/550-4000

LAST ACTION HERO   Columbia, 1993, Story w/Adam Leff
P.C.U.   20th Century Fox, 1994, w/Adam Leff

Screenplays:
CENTRAL PARK w/Adam Leff

EAGLE PENNELL
THE WHOLE SHOOTIN' MATCH   First Run Features,
   1978, directed
DOC'S FULL SERVICE   Brazos Films, 1994, w/Kim Henkel &
   Henry Wideman Jr., directed

JONATHAN PENNER*
Agent: Susan Smith & Associates - Beverly Hills, 213/852-4777

DOWN ON THE WATERFRONT (Short) ★   1993, w/Stacy Title

Screenplays:
WALL PEOPLE w/Stacy Title
DREAD w/Stacy Title
PAYBACK w/Stacy Title
BE STILL, MY HEART w/Stacy Title
KILKRAVEN w/Stacy Title
ALL FOR ONE w/Stacy Title

JOHN V. PENNEY*
Agent: Innovative Artists - Los Angeles, 310/553-5200

THE POWER   Artists Releasing Corporation/Film Ventures
   International, 1982, Story w/Stephen Carpenter,
   John Hopkins & Jeffrey Obrow
THE KINDRED   FM Entertainment, 1987, w/others
RETURN OF THE LIVING DEAD III   Trimark, 1993

Screenplays:
BROTHERS IN ARMS SIEGE

DORNE M. PENTES
THE GREAT UNPLEASANTNESS   Crescent Pictures,
   1993, directed

JAMES PENZI
NIGHT OF THE DEMONS 2   Republic Pictures, 1994,
   w/Joe Augustyn, Story

DAVID WEBB PEOPLES*
Agent: Shapiro/Lichtman - Los Angeles, 310/859-8877

BLADE RUNNER   The Ladd Company/Warner Bros., 1982,
   w/Hampton Fancher
LEVIATHAN   MGM/UA, 1989, w/Jeb Stuart
THE BLOOD OF HEROES   New Line Cinema, 1990, directed
DEADFALL   ITC, 1990
UNFORGIVEN ★   Warner Bros., 1992
HERO   Columbia, 1992

Screenplays:
12 MONKEYS w/Janet Peoples (Universal)
PAIR-A-DICE
SGT. ROCK
LADY HAWKS
VINDICATORS
TIME BOMB
JOURNEY OF THE 14 PRESIDENTS
TAXI TO GLORY
GRABBERS
CHINESE BANDIT
GUATEMALA
JOINT ACCOUNT

JANET PEOPLES*
Agent: Shapiro/Lichtman - Los Angeles, 310/859-8877

Screenplays:
12 MONKEYS w/David Webb Peoples (Universal)

CLARE PEPLOE
Agent: ICM - London, 071/636-6565

ZABRISKIE POINT   MGM, 1970, w/Michelangelo Antonioni,
   Fred Gardner, Tonino Guerra & Sam Shepard
LUNA   20th Century-Fox, 1979, w/Bernardo Bertolucci &
   Giuseppe Bertolucci
HIGH SEASON   Hemdale, 1988, w/Mark Peploe, directed
ROUGH MAGIC   Savoy, 1995, w/William Brockfeld, directed

MARK PEPLOE*
Agent: ICM - Beverly Hills, 310/550-4000

THE PIED PIPER   Paramount, 1972, w/Andrew Birkin &
   Jacques Demy
THE PASSENGER   *PROFESSIONE: REPORTER*   MGM/United
   Artists, 1975, w/Michelangelo Antonioni & Peter Wollen
THE LAST EMPEROR ★   Columbia, 1987, w/Bernardo Bertolucci
HIGH SEASON   Hemdale, 1988, w/Clare Peploe
THE SHELTERING SKY   Warner Bros., 1990,
   w/Bernardo Bertolucci
AFRAID OF THE DARK   Fine Line Features, 1992,
   w/Frederick Seidel, directed
LITTLE BUDDHA   Miramax, 1993, w/Rudy Wurlitzer

Screenplays:
VICTORY w/Frederick Seidel (Miramax, directing)
THE CREW w/Michelangelo Antonioni
OUT OF THE BLUE
CATFISH TANGLE

PAUL PEPPERMAN*
Contact: WGA - Los Angeles, 310/550-1000

THE BEASTMASTER   MGM/UA, 1982, w/Don Coscarelli

DON PEQUIGNOT
Agent: Barry Perelman Agency - Los Angeles, 310/274-5999

9 1/2 NINJAS   Republic Pictures, 1991, w/Bill Crounse
AMERICAN CYBORG: STEEL WARRIOR   Cannon, 1994,
   w/Bill Crounse & Brent Friedman

Screenplays:
FALSE SECURITY w/Bill Crounse
TO THE DEATH w/Bill Crounse

MIGUEL PEREIRA
VERONICO CRUZ Cinevista, 1990, directed

FRANK RAY PERILLI*
Contact: 213/850-5160

LITTLE CIGARS 1973, w/Louis Garfinkle
THE DOBERMAN GANG Dimension, 1973, w/Louis Garfinkle
DRACULA'S DOG Crown International, 1978
ALLIGATOR Group 1, 1980, Story w/John Sayles
THE LAND OF NO RETURN International Picture Show, 1981,
   w/Kent Bateman
JOEY TAKES A CAB Bandwagon Productions, 1991

Screenplays:
PRODIGY w/Louis Garfinkle
THE GODMOTHER w/Louis Garfinkle
TIJUANA DONKEY w/Louis Garfinkle

HEIDE PERLMAN*
Agent: CAA - Beverly Hills, 310/288-4545

Screenplays:
MR. POPPER'S PENGUINS
THE SHOWER

STEVEN PEROS*
Agent: Sterling Lord Literistic - New York, 212/696-2800

Screenplays:
EVERYBODY CHARLESTON!
SOCRATES PARK
GLOW IN THE DARK
BLOOD MAGIC
THE FAMILY MAN w/James McManus

MARJORIE PERRELLI
Agent: William Morris Agency - Beverly Hills, 310/274-7451

Screenplays:
ROMEO AND RAMONA

FRANK PERRY
Contact: Directors Guild of America - Los Angeles, 310/289-2000

MOMMIE DEAREST Paramount, 1981, w/Robert Getchell,
   Tracy Hotchner & Frank Yablans, directed

FRED C. PERRY
BLIND DATE New Line Cinema, 1984, w/Nico Mastorakis

MICHAEL PERRY
Agent: United Talent Agency - Beverly Hills, 310/273-6700

Screenplays:
NONNIE

WILLIAM PERSKY*
Agent: CAA - Beverly Hills, 310/288-4545

WATER Atlantic Releasing Corporation, 1984, w/Dick Clement &
   Ian La Frenais

FRANK PESCE
Contact: Screen Actors Guild - Los Angeles, 213/954-1600

29TH STREET 20th Century Fox, 1991, Story w/James Franciscus

P.J. PESCE
Agent: United Talent Agency - Beverly Hills, 310/273-6700

THE AFTERLIFE OF GRANDPA (Short) directed
BODY WAVES Concorde, 1992, directed
THE DESPERATE TRAIL M.P.C.A./Turner Entertainment, 1994,
   w/Tom Abrams, directed

Screenplays:
WHORE II (Shared)
LEO'S MISERABLE AFFLICTIONS AND UNFORTUNATE MISHAPS
CASEY SPEAKS w/Adam Belanoff

CHARLIE PETERS*
Agent: ICM - Beverly Hills, 310/550-4000

PATERNITY Paramount, 1981
KISS ME GOODBYE 20th Century-Fox, 1982
BLAME IT ON RIO 20th Century-Fox, 1984, w/Larry Gelbart
HOT TO TROT Warner Bros., 1988, w/Hugo Gilbert &
   Stephen Neigher
HER ALIBI Warner Bros., 1989
THREE MEN AND A LITTLE LADY Buena Vista, 1990
PASSED AWAY Buena Vista, 1992, directed
MY FATHER, THE HERO Buena Vista, 1994, w/Francis Veber

Screenplays:
EUREKA w/Willl Davies & William Osborne
MUSIC FROM ANOTHER ROOM
THE MAN IN THE WHITE SUIT (remake)
EXPECTING MIRACLES
THE JUGGLER
HONEYCHILD
HOPELESS ROMANTIC

KENNETH PETERS
VICE SQUAD Avco Embassy, 1982, w/Sandy Howard &
   Robert Vincent O'Neil

STEPHEN PETERS
Contact: Weissmann, Wolff, Bergman, Coleman & Silverman -
   Beverly Hills, 310/858-7888

THE PARK IS MINE (CTF) HBO Premiere Films/Astral Film
   Productions/ICC, 1985
THE FOURTH WAR Cannon, 1990, w/Kenneth Ross
DEATH WISH V 21st Century Distribution, 1993

Screenplays:
BABYLON
FIFTEEN MINUTES ALONE
HIGH SPEED
THE STAND OUT
THE BINGE
AMERICAN COUP

WOLFGANG PETERSEN
Agent: CAA - Beverly Hills, 310/288-4545

DAS BOOT (THE BOAT) ★ Triumph/Columbia, 1981, directed
THE NEVERENDING STORY Warner Bros., 1984,
   w/Herman Weigel, directed
SHATTERED MGM-Pathe, 1991, directed

Screenplays:
FIELDS OF HONOR w/Andrew Birkin

CASSANDRA PETERSON*
Contact: Mark Pierson, Creative Minds Management - 213/469-8354

ELVIRA: MISTRESS OF THE DARK New World, 1988,
   w/Sam Egan & John Paragon

CHRISTOPHER PETERSON
Agent: William Morris Agency - Beverly Hills, 310/274-7451

Screenplays:
FREQUENT FLYER

DANIEL M. PETERSON
GIRLFRIEND FROM HELL IVE, 1990, directed

DAVID PETERSON
FINE FOOD, FINE PASTRIES, OPEN 6 TO 9 (Short) ★ 1989

Screenplays:
I RUN AND FEEL RAIN (Circle Releasing, directing)

DON PETERSON
AN ALMOST PERFECT AFFAIR Paramount, 1979,
    w/Walter Bernstein
TARGET Warner Bros., 1985, w/Howard Berk

MAURICE PETERSON*
Agent: ICM - New York, 212/556-5600

HOMEWORK Jensen Farley Pictures, 1982, w/Don Saffran

GERALD D. PETIEVICH*
Agent: ICM - Beverly Hills, 310/550-4000

TO LIVE AND DIE IN L.A. MGM/UA, 1985, w/William Friedkin

Screenplays:
ONE-SHOT DEAL

DENNE BART PETITCLERC*
Agent: Innovative Artists - Los Angeles, 310/553-5200

RED SUN National General, 1972, w/Laird Koenig,
    William Roberts & Lawrence Roman
AN OPEN SEASON Impala/Arpa, 1974
ISLANDS IN THE STREAM Paramount, 1977

Screenplays:
THE KILLING GROUND
WINTER SONG
LANCERS
DESTINIES
DOUBLE EAGLE
MEN OF THE DRAGON
PIECES OF SEVEN
PROMETHEUS
A FAREWELL TO ARMS
SILENT NIGHT
LORD OF THE AMAZON

DANIEL PETRIE
Agent: CAA - Beverly Hills, 310/288-4545
Business: 13201 Haney Place, Los Angeles, CA 90049,
    310/451-9157

THE BAY BOY Orion, 1984, directed

Screenplays:
THE SECOND COMING

DANIEL PETRIE, JR.*
Agent: Richland/Wunsch/Hohman Agency - Los Angeles,
    310/278-1955

BEVERLY HILLS COP ★ Paramount, 1984
THE BIG EASY Columbia, 1987
SHOOT TO KILL Buena Vista, 1988, w/Michael Burton &
    Harv Zimmel
TURNER & HOOCH Buena Vista, 1989, w/Michael Blodgett,
    Dennis Shryack, Jim Cash & Jack Epps
TOY SOLDIERS Tri-Star, 1991, w/David Koepp, directed
IN THE ARMY NOW Buena Vista, 1994, w/Ken Kaufman,
    Stu Krieger, Fax Bahr & Adam Small, directed

Screenplays:
FINAL TOUR (directing)
FIRESTAR
OUT OF TIME

P.J. PETTIETTE
BAD DREAMS 20th Century Fox, 1988, Story w/Michael Dick,
    Andrew Fleming & Yuri Zeltser

PAMELA PETTLER*
Agent: William Morris Agency - Beverly Hills, 310/274-7451

Screenplays:
SNOW WHITE AND THE GUYS

KATHY PEYSER*
Agent: The Gersh Agency - Beverly Hills, 310/274-6611
Contact: Tom Fineman, Hyman, Abell, Fineman & Greenspan -
    Los Angeles, 310/820-7717

Screenplays:
FIELD TRIP w/Tony Peyser

TONY PEYSER*
Agent: The Gersh Agency - Beverly Hills, 310/274-6611
Contact: Tom Fineman, Hyman, Abell, Fineman & Greenspan -
    Los Angeles, 310/820-7717

Screenplays:
FIELD TRIP w/Kathy Peyser

HARLEY PEYTON*
Agent: CAA - Beverly Hills, 310/288-4545

LESS THAN ZERO 20th Century Fox, 1987
HEAVEN'S PRISONERS Savoy, 1995

Screenplays:
KEYS TO TULSA (ITC)
WILD BOYS
HOT WIRE
LIFE DURING WARTIME

CHUCK PFAFFER*
Agent: Broder-Kurland-Webb-Uffner - Beverly Hills, 310/281-3400

NAVY SEALS Orion, 1990, w/Gary Goldman
DARK MAN Universal, 1990, w/Daniel Goldin, Joshua Goldin,
    Ivan Raimi & Sam Raimi
HARD TARGET Universal, 1993

Screenplays:
VIRUS
THE GREEN HORNET
HOLLOWPOINT
MEDAL OF VALOR

ANNA HAMILTON PHELAN*
Agent: CAA - Beverly Hills, 310/288-4545

MASK Universal, 1985
GORILLAS IN THE MIST ★ Universal, 1988
INTO THE HOMELAND (CTF) HBO Pictures/Capistrano
    Pictures, 1987

Screenplays:
PARTING THE WATERS
JOHNNY SPAIN aka CHAINS
MACHINE GUN KELLY
ONE MORE TIME
THE HOME FRONT

WILLIAM W. PHELPS*
Agent: ICM - Beverly Hills, 310/550-4000

NORTH SHORE Universal, 1987, w/Tim McCanlies, directed

Screenplays:
BROTHER TO BROTHER
ETHICAL CHOICE

BILL PHILLIPS*
Agent: The Gersh Agency - Beverly Hills, 310/274-6611

CHRISTINE   Columbia, 1983
FIRE WITH FIRE   *CAPTIVE HEARTS*   Paramount, 1986,
   w/Paul Boorstin, Sharon Boorstin & Warren Skaaren
PHYSICAL EVIDENCE   Columbia, 1989
RISING SON (CTF)   Sarabande Productions, 1990
EL DIABLO (CTF)   Wizan/Black Productions, 1990,
   w/John Carpenter & Tommy Lee Wallace
RAINBOW DRIVE (CTF)   Viacom-Dove-ITC, 1990,
   w/Bennett Cohen
THERE GOES THE NEIGHBORHOOD   Paramount, 1992, directed
THE BEANS OF EGYPT, MAINE   I.R.S. Releasing, 1994

LOU DIAMOND PHILLIPS
Agent: Innovative Artists - Los Angeles, 310/553-5200

AMBITION   Miramax, 1991
DANGEROUS TOUCH   Trimark, 1993, w/Kurt Voss,   directed

LUCY PHILLIPS
STEAL AMERICA   Tara Releasing, 1992,
   w/Glen Scantlebury,   directed

MAURICE PHILLIPS
Agent: Paradigm - Los Angeles, 310/277-4400 or
   Rochelle Stevens & Co. - London, 071/359-3900

ENID IS SLEEPING   Vestron, 1991, w/A.J. Tipping &
   James Whaley,   directed

MAURICE PIALAT
Contact: French Film Office, 745 Fifth Avenue, New York, NY 10151,
   213/832-8860

UNDER THE SUN OF SATAN   Alive Films, 1987,
   w/Sylvie Danton,   directed
VAN GOGH   Sony Pictures Classics, 1991,   directed

REX PICKETT*
Agent: Writers & Artists Agency - New York, 212/947-8765

CALIFORNIA WITHOUT END   Nightfilm Productions,
   1983,   directed
FROM HOLLYWOOD TO DEADWOOD   Island Pictures,
   1989,   directed

Screenplays:
BAJA HIDEAWAY
KNIFE IN THE HEART
DECOY
THE ROAD BACK
LILY
RED WIND
WHO SHOT SAMUEL RAY?
OPERATION CULIACAN
CRITICAL MASS   w/Howard Cohen

JIM PIDDOCK*
Agent: Richland/Wunsch/Hohman Agency - Los Angeles,
   310/278-1955

TRACES OF RED   Samuel Goldwyn Company, 1992

Screenplays:
BAD TO THE BONE   w/Margaret Oberman
GOOD TIMES/BAD TIMES
THE BOY'S OWN STORY
STRANGERS IN THE NIGHT   w/Margaret Oberman
UNDERCOVER   w/Margaret Oberman
DWAYNE   w/Margaret Oberman

LEON PIEDMONT
(See Christopher Crowe)

JOHN PIELMEIER*
Agent: Curtis Brown, Ltd. - Los Angeles, 213/461-0148

SLEIGHT OF HAND (P)
HAUNTED LIVES (P)
THE BOYS OF WINTER (P)
EVENING (P)
JASS (P)
VOICES IN THE DARK (P)
AGNES OF GOD   Columbia, 1985, from his play

Screenplays:
SERENADE
ASCENT

CHARLES B. PIERCE
THE LEGEND OF BOGGY CREEK   Howco International,
   1973, directed
WINTERHAWK   Howco International, 1975, directed
THE WINDS OF AUTUMN   Howco International, 1976, directed
GREYEAGLE   American International, 1977, directed
THE NORSEMEN   American International, 1978, directed
THE EVICTORS   American International, 1979, w/Paul Fisk &
   Gary Rusoff, directed
SACRED GROUND   Pacific International, 1983, directed
SUDDEN IMPACT   Warner Bros., 1983, Story w/Earl E. Smith
BOGGY CREEK II   Howco International, 1985, directed

SCOTT PIERCE
(See Jim Wheat & Ken Wheat)

SHIRLEY PIERCE*
Agent: The Gersh Agency - Beverly Hills, 310/274-6611

Screenplays:
AIDA

DORI PIERSON*
Business Manager: Ann Massie - 310/450-7644

SPOT MARKS THE X (CTF)   Catalina Production Group, 1986
BIG BUSINESS   Buena Vista, 1988, w/Marc Rubel

Screenplays:
QUEEN FOR A DAY
ONE FINE DAY
EXCESS BAGGAGE
RETURN ENGAGEMENT
FRIENDLY RELATIONS
HIGH AND LONESOME
CONTINENTAL CIRCUS

FRANK R. PIERSON*
Agent: United Talent Agency - Beverly Hills, 310/273-6700

CAT BALLOU ★   Columbia, 1965, w/Walter Newman
COOL HAND LUKE ★   Warner Bros., 1967, w/Donn Pearce
THE HAPPENING   Columbia, 1967, w/Ronald Austin &
   James D. Buchanan
THE LOOKING GLASS WAR   Columbia, 1969, directed
THE ANDERSON TAPES   Columbia, 1971
DOG DAY AFTERNOON ★★   Warner Bros., 1975
A STAR IS BORN   Warner Bros., 1976, w/Joan Didion &
   John Gregory Dunne, directed
KING OF THE GYPSIES   Paramount, 1978, directed
IN COUNTRY   Warner Bros., 1989, w/Cynthia Cidre
PRESUMED INNOCENT   Warner Bros., 1990, w/Alan J. Pakula

Screenplays:
HARD RAIN   (directing)
COPY CAT
DAKOTA WOMAN (CTF)
CITY HALL (CTF)
AIN'T THAT AMERICA
HANDCARVED COFFINS
THE EVANGELIST
MEN OF BRONZE
DESIRE

GERALD PIERSON
Agent: J. Michael Bloom & Associates - Los Angeles, 310/275-6800

Screenplays:
THE HAPPY WORKER w/Steve Feinberg

JEREMY PIKSER*
Agent: William Morris Agency - New York, 212/586-5100

THE LEMON SISTERS Miramax, 1990

Screenplays:
ALMOST NORMAL

NICHOLAS PILEGGI*
Agent: CAA - Beverly Hills, 310/288-4545

GOOD FELLAS ★ Warner Bros., 1990, w/Martin Scorsese
CASINO Universal, 1995, w/Martin Scorsese

Screenplays:
THE COP WHO CAME IN FROM THE HEAT
TIN FOR SALE

SAM PILLSBURY
Agent: Paradigm - Los Angeles, 310/277-4400

THE SCARECROW Oasis, 1981, w/Michael Heath, directed
THE QUIET EARTH Skouras Pictures, 1985, w/Bill Baer &
    Bruno Lawrence

ROBERT PILOTTE
THE BIG DIS Pyramid Films, 1989, w/Gordon Eriksen

GREGORY K. PINCUS*
Agent: ICM - Beverly Hills, 310/550-4000

LITTLE BIG LEAGUE Columbia, 1994, w/Adam Scheinman

TINA PINE*
Contact: 516/654-5045

ON THE RIGHT TRACK 20th Century-Fox, 1981,
    w/Buddy Avery & Richard Moses

MIGUEL PINERO
SHORT EYES The Film League, 1978, from his play

WENDY PINI
Contact: WaRP Graphics, 5 Reno Road, Poughkeepsie, NY 12603,
    914/462-0588

Screenplays:
ELFQUEST

STEVE PINK
Agent: William Morris Agency - Beverly Hills, 310/274-7451

Screenplays:
GROSSE POINTE BLANK w/D.V. deVincentis & John Cusack

JOHN PINKNEY
THIRST Greater Union Film Distributors, 1979

SETH PINKSER*
Agent: Amsel, Eisenstadt & Frazier - Los Angeles, 310/939-1188
Contact: 213/934-5115

STRANGE FRUIT (Short) directed
OVERTURE (Short) directed
PUPAE (Short) directed
SEE NO EVIL (Short) directed
LOVING (Short) directed
THE HIDDEN 2 New Line Cinema, 1993, directed

Screenplays:
JAKE'S RUN
THE SUBSTITUTE

HAROLD PINTER
Agent: Judy Daish Agency - London, 011/441/486-5405
Business: c/o ACTAC Ltd., 16 Cadogan Lane, London SW1,
    England, 01/235-2797

THE HOTHOUSE (P)   also teleplay
OLD TIMES (P)   also teleplay
NO MAN'S LAND (P)
THE DUMB WAITER (P)   also teleplay
A SLIGHT ACHE (P)
THE ROOM (P)   also teleplay
THE COLLECTION (P)
THE LOVER (P)
LANDSCAPE (P)
MOUNTAIN LANGUAGE (P)
ONE FOR THE ROAD (P)
PARTY TIME (P)
THE SERVANT Landau, 1964
THE CARETAKER THE GUEST Caretaker Films, 1964,
    from his play
THE PUMPKIN EATER Columbia, 1964
THE QUILLER MEMORANDUM Rank, 1966
ACCIDENT Cinema 5, 1967
THE BIRTHDAY PARTY Palomar, 1968, from his play
THE GO-BETWEEN EMI, 1970
THE HOMECOMING American Express, 1973, from his play
THE LAST TYCOON Paramount, 1976
THE FRENCH LIEUTENANT'S WOMAN ★ United Artists, 1981
BETRAYAL ★ 20th Century-Fox International Classics, 1983,
    from his play
TURTLE DIARY Samuel Goldwyn Company, 1985
THE HANDMAID'S TALE Cinecom, 1990
THE COMFORT OF STRANGERS Skouras Pictures, 1991
REUNION Les Films Ariane/FR3 Films, 1991
THE TRIAL Angelika Films, 1993

Screenplays:
REMEMBRANCE OF THINGS PAST

DAVID PIRIE
Agent: London Management - London, 071/493-1610

Screenplays:
DREAM DEMONS
LOVE ACT
TOTAL ECLIPSE OF THE HEART

MARK PIRRO
DEATHROW GAMESHOW Crown International, 1987
MY MOM'S A WEREWOLF Crown International, 1988

DEAN PITCHFORD*
Agent: Richland/Wunsch/Hohman Agency - Los Angeles,
    310/278-1955

FOOTLOOSE Paramount, 1984
SING Tri-Star, 1989
THE WASHING MACHINE MAN (Short) Showtime/Chanticleer,
    1992, directed

Screenplays:
LAST BLOSSOM
PARALLELS
ELSEWHERE

JEAN-YVES PITOUN*
Agent: United Talent Agency - Beverly Hills, 310/273-6700

TO KILL A PRIEST Columbia, 1990, w/Agnieszka Holland

Screenplays:
MITIGATING CIRCUMSTANCES w/Agnieszka Holland
MYSTERIOUS ISLAND

**F
I
L
M

W
R
I
T
E
R
S**

LOVE AND CHAOS
OFF SHORE
THE ROSE OF TIBET
MISTAKEN IDENTITY
DUE PROCESS
LOVE KILLS
THE PARTNER
FRENCH KISS

GLEN PITRE
BELIZAIRE THE CAJUN   Skouras Pictures, 1986, directed

Screenplays:
REDFISH

AMY PITTA
Agent: Premiere Artists - Los Angeles, 310/271-1414

Screenplays:
LOVE, GRACIE

MARK PITTMAN
Agent: Neal Stevens & Associates - Beverly Hills, 310/275-7541

ACTING ON IMPULSE (CTF)   Spectator Films, 1993,
   w/Alan Moskowitz

Screenplays:
EYES OF A STRANGER

ANGELO PIZZO*
Agent: ICM - Beverly Hills, 310/550-4000

HOOSIERS   Orion, 1986
RUDY   TriStar, 1993

Screenplays:
INDY
THE STREAK
KNIGHTS OF TERROR
SATURDAYS HEROS

BRET T. PLATE*
Agent: Innovative Artists - Los Angeles, 310/553-5200

Screenplays:
MASTER OF THE LAMP
DOWN EAST

ALAN PLATER
Agent: The Casarotto Company - London, 071/287-4450

THE VIRGIN AND THE GYPSY   Chevron, 1970
IT SHOULDN'T HAPPEN TO A VET   EMI, 1976
PRIEST OF LOVE   Filmways, 1981

JOHN PLATT
THE FORBIDDEN DANCE   Columbia, 1990, w/Roy Langsdon
OUT OF SIGHT, OUT OF MIND   Spectrum Entertainment Group,
   1990, w/Roy Langsdon

POLLY PLATT*
Business: Gracie Films, Sony Film Corp., 310/203-3772

TARGETS   Paramount, 1968, Story w/Peter Bogdanovich
GOOD LUCK, MISS WYCOFF   Bel Air-Gradison, 1972
PRETTY BABY   Paramount, 1978

Screenplays:
THE ASSISTANT

JEFF PLATTS
Agent: Berzon Agency - Glendale, 818/548-1560

Screenplays:
JACKPOT

JOHN PLEFFER
THE SINGER AND THE DANCER   Columbia, 1977,
   w/Gillian Armstrong

JOHN PLESHETTE*
Agent: Pleshette & Green - Los Angeles, 213/465-0428

Screenplays:
FIRST LIGHT
ASSIGNED RISK w/Rogers Turrentine
JENNY BE GOOD
VADIM'S LOUISE

BILL PLYMPTON
THE TUNE (AF)   October Films, 1992, w/Maureen McElheron &
   P.C. Vey, directed

Screenplays:
J. LYLE

RICK PODELL*
Agent: The Irv Schechter Company - Beverly Hills, 310/278-8070
Business Manager: Mucci, Webber & Lagnese - Los Angeles,
   213/938-7900

NOTHING IN COMMON   Tri-Star, 1986, w/Michael Preminger

Screenplays:
HIGHER EDUCATION w/Michael Preminger
TUXEDO TERRACE w/Michael Preminger
LAWRENCE MANOR w/Michael Preminger
AN AMERICAN COUPLE w/Michael Preminger
LIES AND MORE LIES
THE LAST VIRGIN IN AMERICA

AMOS POE*
Agent: William Morris Agency - New York, 212/586-5100

THE FOREIGNER   Amos Poe Visions, 1978, directed
SUBWAY RIDERS   Hep Pictures, 1981, directed
ALPHABET CITY   Atlantic Releasing Corporation, 1984,
   w/Gregory Heller, directed
ROCKET GIBRALTAR   Columbia, 1988
TRIPLE BOGEY *ON A PAR FIVE HOLE*   Island World,
   1992, directed
DEAD WEEKEND   I.R.S. Media, 1995, Story, directed

Screenplays:
THE TIDES
PORT OF CALL
BEACH HOUSE

S. LEE POGOSTIN*
Agent: Shapiro/Lichtman - Los Angeles, 310/859-8877

PRESSURE POINT   United Artists, 1962, w/Hubert Cornfield
SYNANON *GET OFF MY BACK*   Columbia, 1965, w/Ian Bernard
HARD CONTRACT   20th Century-Fox, 1969, directed
GOLDEN NEEDLES   American International, 1974,
   w/Sylvia Schneble
HIGH ROAD TO CHINA   Warner Bros., 1983,
   w/Sandra Weintraub Roland

CHARLES EDWARD POGUE*
Agent: ICM - Beverly Hills, 310/550-4000

WHO DONE IT, DARLING? (P)
SINBAD (P)
THE EBONY APE (P)
DOUBLE-ENTENDRE (P)
VAPOR OF GLORY (P)
SIGN OF THE FOUR   Mapleton Films/Paramount
   Home Video, 1983
THE HOUND OF THE BASKERVILLES   Mapleton Films/
   Paramount Home Video, 1983
PSYCHO III   Universal, 1986

THE FLY   20th Century Fox, 1986, w/David Cronenberg
D.O.A.   Buena Vista, 1988
DRAGONHEART   Universal, 1995

Screenplays:
KULL THE CONQUEROR
AN ARABIAN NIGHT
THE UNINVITED
MAGIC COTTAGE
BLOOD OF THE GODS
THE GREYSTONE
THE KINGMAKERS
SATAN'S SORROW
BLOOD & SEX
FRANKENSTEIN

JOHN POGUE
Agent: Favored Artists Agency - Los Angeles, 213/653-3191

Screenplays:
MAN WITH A FOOTBALL

WILLIAM POHLAD
OLD EXPLORERS   Taurus Entertainment, 1991, directed

GREGORY POIRIER
Agent: ICM - Beverly Hills, 310/550-4000

DANGER ZONE III: STEEL HORSE WAR   Danger Zone Company,
   1990, w/Jason Williams

Screenplays:
THE IRON HORSEMAN
BOOM TOWN

SIDNEY POITIER*
Agent: CAA - Beverly Hills, 310/288-4545

FOR LOVE OF IVY   Cinerama Releasing Corporation, 1968, Story

DAVID POLAND*
Contact: WGA - Los Angeles, 310/550-1000

Screenplays:
UNDER SURVEILLANCE w/Ethan Rieff & Chris Voris

ROMAN POLANSKI
Agent: ICM - Beverly Hills, 310/550-4000

KNIFE IN THE WATER   Kanawha, 1963, w/Jakub Goldberg &
   Jerzy Skolimowski, directed
DO YOU LIKE WOMEN?   Francoriz, 1964, w/Gerard Brach
REPULSION   Royal Films International, 1965,
   w/Gerard Brach, directed
CUL-DE-SAC   Sigma III, 1966, w/Gerard Brach, directed
THE FEARLESS VAMPIRE KILLERS, OR PARDON ME BUT
   YOUR TEETH ARE IN MY NECK   *DANCE OF THE VAMPIRES*
   MGM, 1967, w/Gerard Brach, directed
ROSEMARY'S BABY ★   Paramount, 1968, directed
A DAY AT THE BEACH   Paramount, 1970, unreleased
WHAT?   Avco Embassy, 1973, w/Gerard Brach, directed
THE TENANT   Paramount, 1976, w/Gerard Brach, directed
TESS   Columbia, 1980, w/Gerard Brach &
   John Brownjohn, directed
PIRATES   Cannon, 1986, w/Gerard Brach, directed
FRANTIC   Warner Bros., 1988, w/Gerard Brach, directed
BITTER MOON   Fine Line Features, 1993, w/Gerard Brach &
   John Brownjohn, directed

STEPHEN POLIAKOFF
Contact: British Academy of Film & Television Arts, 195 Piccadilly,
   London W1, England, 071/734-0022

RUNNERS   Goldcrest, 1983
SHE'S BEEN AWAY   BBC Films, 1989
CLOSE MY EYES   Castle Hill, 1991, directed
CENTURY   I.R.S. Releasing, 1994, directed

BARRY POLLACK*
Contact: 818/889-1499

COOL BREEZE   MGM, 1972, directed

JEFF POLLACK*
Contact: WGA - Los Angeles, 310/550-1000

ABOVE THE RIM   New Line Cinema, 1994,
   w/Barry Michael Cooper, directed

JEFFREY POLMAN
BENEFIT OF THE DOUBT   Miramax, 1993, w/Chris Keyser

EDDY POLON*
Contact: WGA - Los Angeles, 310/550-1000

NICKEL & DIME   August Entertainment, 1992, w/Seth Front

VICKI POLON*
Agent: Paradigm - Los Angeles, 310/277-4400

PLEASANTVILLE (TF)   PBS, 1978, shared, directed
GIRLFRIENDS   Warner Bros., 1978
DEADLY MEDICINE (TF)   NBC, 1991
MR. WONDERFUL   Warner Bros., 1993, w/Amy Schor

Screenplays:
MY PERFECT WIFE
MEDALLION
MOUNTAIN CHARLY
DOWN TO EARTH
MOM

ABRAHAM POLONSKY*
Agent: The Gersh Agency - Beverly Hills, 310/274-6611

BODY AND SOUL   Enterprise, 1947
FORCE OF EVIL   MGM, 1948, w/Ira Wolfert, directed
I CAN GET IT FOR YOU WHOLESALE   *THIS IS MY AFFAIR*
   20th Century-Fox, 1951
MADIGAN   Universal, 1968, w/Howard Rodman
TELL THEM WILLIE BOY IS HERE   Universal, 1969, directed
AVALANCHE EXPRESS   20th Century-Fox, 1979
MONSIGNOR   20th Century-Fox, 1982, w/Wendell Mayes

BARRY POLTERMANN
ASWANG   Young American Films, 1994, w/Wrye Martin, co-directed

JASON POMERANCE
Agent: The Gersh Agency - Beverly Hills, 310/274-6611

Screenplays:
RUN WITH THE DOGS

EDWARD POMERANTZ*
Agent: The Artists Agency - Los Angeles, 310/277-7779

QUACKS AND HORNERS (P)
MO'S MOVIE (P)   also screenplay
BRISBURIAL (P)
KID (P)
NOTHING PERSONAL (P)
A CHANGE OF PACE (P)
THE GARDEN (P)
ONLY A GAME (P)

Screenplays:
DOGSPELL
FOR ADULTS ONLY
INTO IT
OUTBACK CITY DREAMING w/Christopher Lee
GORILLA!
MAN RUNNING
MISSIE
LAS VEGAS STRIP
ANGELA
DEAD CENTER
THE KISS

JOHN POMEROY
THE SECRET OF NIMH (AF)   MGM/UA, 1982,
    Story Adaptation w/Don Bluth, Will Finn & Gary Goldman
ALL DOGS GO TO HEAVEN (AF)   MGM/UA, 1989, Story w/others

DARRYL PONICSAN*
Agent: CAA - Beverly Hills, 310/288-4545

CINDERELLA LIBERTY   20th Century-Fox, 1974
TAPS   20th Century-Fox, 1981, w/Robert Mark Kamen
VISION QUEST   Warner Bros., 1985
NUTS   Warner Bros., 1987, w/Alvin Sargent & Tom Topor
THE BOOST   Hemdale, 1988
SCHOOL TIES   Paramount, 1992, w/Dick Wolf
THE ENEMY WITHIN (CTF)   Vincent Pictures/HBO Pictures, 1994,
    w/Ron Bass

Screenplays:
WHISPERS IN BEDLAM
MATARESE CIRCLE w/R. Dupont & K. Hughes
LETHAL GAS
REAL PROPERTY
THE TRUEST SPORT
THE RINGER

LEA POOL
Contact: Academy of Canadian Cinema & Television, 753 Yonge St. -
    2nd Floor, Toronto M4Y 1Z9, Canada, 416/967-0315

DESIRE IN MOTION   Alliance-Vivafilm, 1994, directed

ROBERT ROY POOL*
Agent: ICM - Beverly Hills, 310/550-4000

THE BIG TOWN   Columbia, 1987
OUTBREAK   Warner Bros., 1995, Story w/Laurence Dworet

Screenplays:
MELTDOWN w/John Carpenter (Miramax)
ULTIMATUM w/Laurence Dworet
THE PRACTICE w/Laurence Dworet
UNDERGROUND w/Laurence Dworet
GOLD COAST

DUANE POOLE*
Agent: Major Clients Agency - Los Angeles, 310/284-6400

CHOMPS   American International, 1979, w/Dick Robbins
SUNSTROKE (CTF)   Wilshire Court Productions, 1992
PRAYING MANTIS (CTF)   Fast Track Films/Wilshire Court
    Productions, 1993, w/William Delligan

ELAINE POPE*
Agent: United Talent Agency - Beverly Hills, 310/273-6700

RESTLESS UNDERWEAR (P)
LOOKALIKES (Short)   1990

Screenplays:
THE FAST TRACK
PRISON WIVES
THE LAST AMERICAN FAMILY
BETTE CAIN
HAPPILY EVER AFTER
CAGED

JEFF POPE
FOOL'S GOLD: THE STORY OF THE BRINK'S-MAT ROBBERY
    LWT Production/ITV, 1994, w/Terry Windsor

THOMAS POPE*
Agent: Writers & Artists Agency - Los Angeles, 310/824-6300

FRATERNITY ROW   1976, shared
THE MANITOU   Herman Weist Productions, 1978, w/Jon Cedar &
    William Girdler

A GREAT RIDE   Mason International, 1979, w/Walter Dallenbach
THE BLACK HOLE   Buena Vista, 1979
THE LORDS OF DISCIPLINE   Paramount, 1983, w/Lloyd Fonvielle
HAMMETT   Orion/Warner Bros., 1983, Story Adaptation
COLD DOG SOUP   HandMade Films, 1989

Screenplays:
BAD BOYS (Columbia)
MAMA'S BOY
THE VOID
THE CURIOUS CASE OF BENJAMIN BUTTON
THE EAGLE OF BROADWAY
YOUNG TEDDY ROOSEVELT
EINSTEIN
TOM MIX AND PANCHO VILLA
CROSSING NIAGARA
PEERS
JEDEDIAH SMITH
PROHIBITION STORY
WOMAN NEXT DOOR
PROVIDENCE
WORD OF HONOR

PETRU S. POPESCU*
Contact: WGA - Los Angeles, 310/550-1000

THE LAST WAVE   United Artists, 1977, w/Tony Morphett &
    Peter Weir
DEATH OF AN ANGEL   20th Century Fox, 1985, directed
NOBODY'S CHILDREN (CTF)   Winkler/Daniels-Quinta-USA
    Network, 1994, w/Iris Friedman

Screenplays:
VOODOO w/David Odell
BEFORE & AFTER EDITH

BENEDICTE POPPER
TARGET OF SUSPICION (CTF)   USA Pictures, 1994,
    Story w/Christian Biegalski

DANNY PORFIRO
DOMINICK & EUGENE   Orion, 1988, Story

LON PORTER
Agent: Hilary Wayne - Beverly Hills, 310/289-6186

URTH/BONE/MORT (P)
TWO DOLLAR ROMANCE (P)

Screenplays:
A REASONABLE MADNESS
DEADLINE AT DAWN
ALTER EGO
SUMMER JOB
THE TREASURE OF BOCA MACAVA

ROBERT PORTER*
Agent: Pleshette & Green - Los Angeles, 213/465-0428

Screenplays:
DUEL IN THE SUN
RANGERS
WINGED VICTORY

WILL PORTER
(See Will Aldis)

SCOTT POSNER
Contact: Kenoff & Machtinger - Los Angeles, 310/552-0808

Screenplays:
SPRING BREAK ADVENTURE w/Jimmy Zeilinger

GAIL POSTAL
PENPAL MURDERS   Cinevue/Steve Postal Prods., 1991,
    w/Steve Postal

STEVE POSTAL
PENPAL MURDERS   Cinevue/Steve Postal Prods., 1991, w/Gail Postal, directed

RANDALL POSTER
A MATTER OF DEGREES   Backbeat Productions, 1989, w/Jack Mason & W.T. Morgan

SALLY POTTER
Agent: London Management - London, 071/493-1610

ORLANDO   Adventure Films, 1993, directed

MICHAEL POTTS
SCHWEITZER   Sugar Entertainment, 1990
ILLICIT BEHAVIOR (CTF)   Prism Entertainment/Promark Entertainment, 1992

LYNN C. POUNIAN
Contact: Carol Lees, Moving Pictures, 818/760-7784

Screenplays:
HIGHER EDUCATION

JON POVILL*
Contact: WGA - Los Angeles, 310/550-1000

TOTAL RECALL   Tri-Star, 1990, Story w/Dan O'Bannon & Ronald Shusett

Screenplays:
SPECIES UNKNOWN
BROKEN PROMISES, MENDED DREAMS w/Richard Meryman
THE NINE w/Gene Roddenberry
IN PURSUIT OF ANGEL LOVE w/Deke Simon
SECOND CHANCES
OUT OF CONTROL w/Jaron Summers
ELEMENTARY, MY DEAR w/Jaron Summers
A SPANGLE IN DARKNESS
STARCROSSED
HARRY'S BOY
TRANAI
HARVEST (Story)
THE NEW HOPE CONSPIRACY

ANN POWELL*
Agent: Martin Hurwitz Associates - Beverly Hills, 310/274-0240

NIGHT OWL (CTF)   Morgan Hill Films/Hearst Entertainment, 1993, w/Rose Schacht

Screenplays:
LUCKY STRIKE w/Rose Schacht

MICHAEL NORIEGA POWELL
Agent: The Coppage Company - North Hollywood, 818/980-1106

Screenplays:
ON DANGEROUS GROUND w/Joe Stinson
SPIRIT LAKE w/Joe Stinson
BEYOND THE APOGEE
KILLER COPS

ROBERT POWELL*
Agent: APA - Los Angeles, 310/273-0744

Screenplays:
DIVINE INTERVENTION
RIDING WITH THE BUTTERFLY

TRISTRAM POWELL
Agent: The Casarotto Company - London, 71/287-4450

AMERICAN FRIENDS   Prominent Features, 1991, w/Michael Palin, directed

DONNA POWERS*
Agent: United Talent Agency - Beverly Hills, 310/273-6700

Screenplays:
A WHISPER IN THE ATTIC w/Wayne Powers (Paramount)
BANSHEE w/Wayne Powers
NIKKIE w/Wayne Powers
MEXICAN STAND-OFF w/Wayne Powers

WAYNE POWERS*
Agent: United Talent Agency - Beverly Hills, 310/273-6700

Screenplays:
A WHISPER IN THE ATTIC w/Donna Powers (Paramount)
BANSHEE w/Donna Powers
NIKKIE w/Donna Powers
MEXICAN STAND-OFF w/Donna Powers

MATT PRAGER
Agent: Maggie Field Agency - Studio City, 818/980-2001

Screenplays:
THE FRY GIRL w/Pam Brady

TIMOTHY PRAGER
STROKE OF MIDNIGHT   *IF THE SHOE FITS*   Media Home Entertainment, 1991, based on screenplay by Madeline DiMaggio & Pamela Wallace

CHARLES PRATT, JR.*
Agent: The Irv Schechter Company - Beverly Hills, 310/278-8070

THE INITIATION   New World, 1984

DENNIS A. PRATT*
Agent: Wallerstein*Kappelman Agency - Los Angeles, 213/782-0225

AMERICAN JUSTICE   The Movie Store, 1986

Screenplays:
BLUE TANGO
NICO
HIT MAN
SHOWDOWN OVER RIO
SPOOKY BLANKETS CIA BABIES
EMPEROR OF THE PIRATES
TICKER
DOLAN'S WALK

RUTH PRAWER JHABVALA
(See Ruth Prawer JHABVALA)

JANEY PREGER
THAT SUMMER   Columbia, 1979

BURT PRELUTSKY*
Agent: Cindy Turtle & Associates - Studio City, 818/506-6898
Business Manager: Jon Mercedes - Los Angeles, 310/657-5030

Screenplays:
FOR SINGLES ONLY
NOT GUILTY
A ROYAL MESS

MICHAEL A. PREMINGER*
Agent: The Irv Schechter Company - Beverly Hills, 310/278-8070

NOTHING IN COMMON   Tri-Star, 1986, w/Rick Podell

Screenplays:
HIGHER EDUCATION w/Rick Podell
TUXEDO TERRACE w/Rick Podell
LAWRENCE MANOR w/Rick Podell
AN AMERICAN COUPLE w/Rick Podell

JULIE PRENDAVILLE
Agent: The Gage Group - Los Angeles, 310/859-8777

Screenplays:
THE GODDESS OF ENCINO w/Chris Coyle

STEVEN PRESSFIELD*
Agent: Innovative Artists - Los Angeles, 310/553-5200
Manager: 3 Arts Entertainment - Los Angeles, 213/851-5700

KING KONG LIVES   DEG, 1986, w/Ronald Shusett
ABOVE THE LAW   Warner Bros., 1988, w/Andrew Davis &
    Ronald Shusett
FREEJACK   Warner Bros., 1992, w/Ronald Shusett & Dan Gilroy

Screenplays:
BAGGER VANCE
SEPARATE LIVES
JOSHUA TREE
BORN TO RUN

KENNETH PRESSMAN*
Agent: Writers & Artists Agency - New York, 212/391-1112

DIARY OF A HIT MAN   Vision International, 1992,
    from his play "Insider's Price"

JAY PRESSON ALLEN
(See Jay Presson ALLEN)

DAVID PRESTON
SPACEHUNTER: ADVENTURES IN THE FORBIDDEN ZONE
    Columbia, 1983, w/Len Blum, Dan Goldberg & Edith Rey
SCANNERS III: THE TAKEOVER   Republic Pictures, 1992,
    w/Rene Malo, B.J. Nelson & Julie Richmond

Screenplays:
TWIN SISTERS w/Andre Koob & Jean-Marc Paland

GAYLENE PRESTON
Contact: New Zealand Film Commission, P.O. Box 11546,
    Wellington, New Zealand, 4/859-754

DARK OF THE NIGHT   *MR. WRONG*   Quartet, 1985,
    w/Geoff Murphy & Graham Tetley, directed

TREVOR PRESTON
SLAYGROUND   Universal, 1984
BILLY THE KID AND THE GREEN BAIZE VAMPIRE   ITC, 1985
PARKER   Birgin Films, 1985
THICKER THAN WATER (CTF)   BBC, 1994

JEFFREY PRICE*
Agent: CAA - Beverly Hills, 310/288-4545

TRENCHCOAT   Buena Vista, 1983, w/Peter Seaman
WHO FRAMED ROGER RABBIT   Buena Vista, 1988,
    w/Peter Seaman
DOC HOLLYWOOD   Warner Bros., 1991, w/Peter Seaman &
    Daniel Pyne

Screenplays:
HOUDINI w/Peter Seaman
MR. WHISTLE w/Peter Seaman
SPEND, SPEND, SPEND w/Peter Seaman
LAST HOLIDAY w/Peter Seaman
GOOD KING HARRY w/Peter Seaman
MISS MOTHERWELL w/Peter Seaman

PAUL PRICE*
Contact: WGA - Los Angeles, 310/550-1000

Screenplays:
THE ENGAGEMENT w/Steve Nathan
LOOSE WOMEN w/Steve Nathan

IN THE PROCESS w/Steve Nathan
THE AILEEN QUINN STORY w/Steve Nathan
UTILITIES w/Steve Nathan

R. BARKER PRICE*
Agent: Renaissance-H.N. Swanson - Los Angeles, 310/246-6000

CATACOMBS   Empire Pictures, 1988

Screenplays:
CAFE RACER
THE GROTTO

RICHARD PRICE*
Agent: Sanford-Gross & Associates - Los Angeles, 310/208-2100

STREETS OF GOLD   20th Century Fox, 1986, w/Tom Cole &
    Heywood Gould
THE COLOR OF MONEY ★   Buena Vista, 1986
NEW YORK STORIES   Buena Vista, 1989, "Life Lessons"
SEA OF LOVE   Universal, 1989
NIGHT AND THE CITY   20th Century Fox, 1992
MAD DOG AND GLORY   Universal, 1993
KISS OF DEATH   20th Century Fox, 1995
CLOCKERS   Universal, 1995

Screenplays:
EAST COAST HIGH
DREAMSTREET
EMPIRE   STEEL ANGEL
COLOR WAR
WINGO

STANLEY PRICE
Agent: Lemon Unna & Durbridge - London, 071/727-1346

CLOSE RELATIONS (CTF)   Lionheart Television, 1990
GENGHIS COHN (CTF)   BBC-TV, 1994

TIM ROSE PRICE
Agent: The Casarotto Company - London, 071/287-4450

DARK OBSESSION   *DIAMOND SKULLS*   Circle Releasing, 1991
SHUTTLECOCK   ICM Films, 1991
RAPA NUI   Warner Bros., 1994, w/Kevin Reynolds

Screenplays:
THE SERPENT'S KISS   (RPB Productions)
INCIDENT AT BARROW CREEK

BARRY PRIMUS
Agent: Innovative Artists - Los Angeles, 310/553-5200

FINAL STAGE (Short)   directed
MISTRESS   International Rainbow Pictures, 1992,
    w/J.F. Lawton, directed

PRINCE
(Rogers Nelson)
Agent: CAA - Beverly Hills, 310/288-4545

GRAFFITI BRIDGE   Warner Bros., 1990, directed

JONATHAN PRINCE*
Agent: United Talent Agency - Beverly Hills, 310/273-6700

18 AGAIN!   New World, 1988, w/Josh Goldstein
PARTNERS 'N LOVE (CTF)   Atlantis Films Ltd., 1992,
    w/Josh Goldstein

Screenplays:
THE FINE TOUCH w/Josh Goldstein
THE SKY$ THE LIMIT w/Josh Goldstein

PETER PRINCE
Agent: ICM - Beverly Hills, 310/550-4000

THE HIT   Island Alive, 1984
WATERLAND   Fine Line Features, 1992

Screenplays:
CHEATERS
RASPUTIN
OPPENHEIMER

DAVID A. PRIOR
HELL ON THE BATTLEGROUND   Action International Pictures,
   1989, directed
DEADLY DANCER   Action International Pictures, 1990, Story
THE FINAL SANCTION   Action International Pictures,
   1990, directed
RAW NERVE   Action International Pictures, 1991,
   w/Lawrence L. Simeone, directed
CENTER OF THE WEB   Pyramid Distribution, 1992, directed
DOUBLE THREAT   Pyramid Distribution, 1992, directed
GOOD COP, BAD COP   West Side Studios, 1993, directed

DAVID PRITCHARD
VIOLENT ZONE   Arista Films, 1989, w/John Bushelman

PATRICIA KROFT PRITCHARD*
Contact: WGA - Los Angeles, 310/550-1000

Screenplays:
SINGLE WHITE FAMILY
JUST MARRIED

ANDREW PRITZKER
Agent: Jon Klane Agency - Beverly Hills, 310/278-0178

Screenplays:
SANDMAN
NOTES NOT PLAYED
A BOY AND HIS SAUCE
MR. SPEAKER

LEON PROCHNIK*
Agent: Broder-Kurland-Webb-Uffner - Beverly Hills, 310/281-3400

CHILD'S PLAY   Paramount, 1972
FOUR EYES AND SIX-GUNS (CTF)   Turner Pictures, 1993

Screenplays:
THE STIRRING
AGAIN
FOOLS GOLD
TIME PIECE

ELAINE PROCTOR
Agent: Peters, Fraser & Dunlop - London, 071/376-7676

ON THE WIRE   NFTS, 1990, directed
FRIENDS   Chrysalide Films/Rio Films, 1993, directed

PAT PROFT*
Agent: ICM - Beverly Hills, 310/550-4000
Contact: 310/449-4008

BACHELOR PARTY   20th Century Fox, 1984, w/ Neal Israel
POLICE ACADEMY   The Ladd Company/Warner Bros., 1984,
   w/ Neal Israel & Hugh Wilson
MOVING VIOLATIONS   20th Century Fox, 1985, w/Neal Israel
REAL GENIUS   Tri-Star, 1985, w/Neal Israel & Peter Torokvei
THE NAKED GUN   Paramount, 1988, w/Jim Abrahams,
   David Zucker & Jerry Zucker
LUCKY STIFF   New Line Cinema, 1989
NAKED GUN 2 1/2: THE SMELL OF FEAR   Paramount, 1991,
   w/David Zucker
HOT SHOTS!   20th Century Fox, 1991, w/Jim Abrahams

BRAIN DONORS   Paramount, 1992
HOT SHOTS! PART DEUX   20th Century Fox, 1993,
   w/Jim Abrahams
THE NAKED GUN 33 1/3: THE FINAL INSULT   Paramount, 1994,
   w/David Zucker & Robert Locash

Screenplays:
WRONGFULLY ACCUSED (directing)
LADY SALISBURY, PRIVATE CITIZEN
DAVY CROCKETT AFTER THE ALAMO w/Neal Israel
UP FOR GRABS w/Neil Israel
THE GOSSIP COLUMNIST
HUSTLE BUNS
ROLLIN" STONED...A ROADIE'S RIOTOUS REVELATIONS
SUMMIT KILL

CHIP PROSER*
(Charles M. Proser)
Agent: William Morris Agency - Beverly Hills, 310/274-7451

ICEMAN   Universal, 1984, w/John Drimmer
INNERSPACE   Warner Bros., 1987, w/Jeffrey Boam

Screenplays:
ZODIAC
INTERFACE

FEDERICO PROSPERI
CURSE II: THE BITE   Trans World Entertainment, 1989,
   w/Susan Zelouf

MAX PROSS*
Agent: William Morris Agency - Beverly Hills, 310/274-7451

Screenplays:
THEY ARE US w/Tom Gammill

SARAH PROVOST*
Agent: Writers & Artists Agency - Los Angeles, 310/824-6300

A NO PLAY (P)
SIX OF ONE (P)
THE HOME TEAM (P)

Screenplays:
THE SCARLET PIMPERNEL
BLOOD RELATIVE
SUNSHINE GARDENS
OPENINGS

ALEX PROYAS
Agent: CAA - Beverly Hills, 310/288-4545

SPIRITS OF THE AIR, GREMLINS OF THE CLOUDS
   1989, directed

Screenplays:
DARK CITY (Buena Vista, directing)

GREG PRUSS*
Agent: ICM - Beverly Hills, 310/550-4000

Screenplays:
BODY HUNTER
NICK FURY

DEBORAH PRYOR
Agent: Writers & Artists Agency - New York, 212/947-8765

Screenplays:
REBELS
BRIAR PATCH

RICHARD PRYOR*
Agent: ICM - Beverly Hills, 310/550-4000

BUSTIN' LOOSE   Universal, 1981, Story
RICHARD PRYOR LIVE ON THE SUNSET STRIP (FD)
   Columbia, 1982
RICHARD PRYOR HERE AND NOW (FD)   Columbia,
   1983, directed
JO JO DANCER, YOUR LIFE IS CALLING   Columbia, 1986,
   w/Paul Mooney & Rocco Urbisci, directed

GEOF PRYSIRR*
Contact: Sandra Siegal Management - 818/995-0619

UN-BECOMING AGE   Castle Hill, 1993, w/Meredith Baer

ROBERT PUCCI*
Agent: Monteiro Rose Agency - Encino, 818/501-1177

THE SPIDER AND THE FLY (CTF)   Haft/Nasatir-Wilshire Court,
   1994, w/Alanna Hamill

Screenplays:
SUNSTROKE
HEART & SOLE
MISS CONCEPTION & THE OLYMPIAN
FULL HONEYMOON
JUSTICE CALHOUN

LUIS PUENZO
Agent: William Morris Agency - Beverly Hills, 310/274-7451

THE OFFICIAL STORY ★   Historias Cinematograficas, 1985,
   w/Aida Bortnik, directed
OLD GRINGO   Columbia, 1989, w/Aida Bortnik, directed
THE PLAGUE   Gaumont Pictures, 1992, directed

FRANK PUGLIESE*
Agent: United Talent Agency - Beverly Hills, 310/273-6700

AVEN'U BOYS (P)
KING OF CONNECTICUT (P)
DEM BUMS (P)
WARM SUMMER WIND (P)
THE ALARM (P)
SNUFF (P)

Screenplays:
MOB GIRL
YO OLIVER
DION
THE QUARTER MILE
FRANKY'S STREETS
DA BOYS
GEORGE MILLER ADDRESS UNKNOWN (Shared)

ELINOR PULLEN
Agent: The Irv Schechter Company - Beverly Hills, 310/278-8070

Screenplays:
WAR BRIDES

L.A. PUOPOLO
Business: Puopolo Productions Inc., Tribeca Film Center, 375
   Greenwich St. - Suite 700, New York, NY 10013, 212/941-3885

HOME FIRES BURNING   Overseas Film Group, 1992,
   w/Chris Ceraso, directed

JIM PURDY
Agent: Wallerstein*Kappelman Agency - Los Angeles, 213/782-0225

WHERE'S PETE (Short)   1986, directed
LEFT OUT (Short)   directed
DESTINY TO ORDER   Cineplex-Odeon, directed
CONCRETE ANGELS   Cineplex-Odeon, directed

JON PURDY
REFLECTION ON A CRIME   Concorde, 1994, directed

Screenplays:
THE GUYVER

CHARLES G. PURPURA*
Agent: Richland/Wunsch/Hohman Agency - Los Angeles,
   310/278-1955

HEAVEN HELP US   Tri-Star, 1984
SATISFACTION   20th Century Fox, 1988

Screenplays:
REPLAY
THE HITMAN (CTF)
THE MORALIST OF ALPHABET STREET
ROOMMATES

DAVID PURSALL
COUNT FIVE AND DIE   20th Century-Fox, 1957, w/Jack Seddon
VILLAGE OF DAUGHTERS   MGM, 1961, w/Jack Seddon
THE SECRET PARTNER   MGM, 1961, w/Jack Seddon
MURDER SHE SAID   MGM, 1961, w/Jack Seddon
KILL OR CURE   MGM, 1962, w/Jack Seddon
THE LONGEST DAY   20th Century-Fox, 1962, w/Jack Seddon,
   Romain Gary, James Jones & Cornelius Ryan
MURDER AHOY   MGM, 1964, w/Jack Seddon
MURDER MOST FOUL   MGM, 1964, w/Jack Seddon
THE ALPHABET MURDERS   MGM, 1965, w/Jack Seddon
THE BLUE MAX   20th Century-Fox, 1966, w/Jack Seddon
THE SOUTHERN STAR   Columbia, 1968, w/Jack Seddon
WHAT CHANGED CHARLEY FARTHING   Patina-Hildago, 1975,
   w/Jack Seddon
TOMORROW NEVER COMES   Rank, 1978, w/Jack Seddon &
   Sydney Banks

NEAL PURVIS
Agent: Lemon Unna & Durbridge - London, 071/727-1346

LET HIM HAVE IT   Fine Line Features, 1991, w/Robert Wade

Screenplays:
GUILT-EDGED w/Robert Wade

TONY PURYEAR*
Manager: 3 Arts Entertainment - Los Angeles, 213/851-5700
Contact: Peter Nichols, Lichter, Grossman & Nichols - Los Angeles,
   310/205-6999

Screenplays:
ERASER

TED PUSHINSKY*
Agent: Hilary Wayne - Beverly Hills, 310/289-6186

Screenplays:
AS YOUNG AS YOU FEEL w/Robert Kraft
MAKING MONEY w/Robert Kraft

GEORGE D. PUTNAM*
Contact: WGA - Los Angeles, 310/550-1000

TO KILL FOR   Moviestore Entertainment, 1991
UNLAWFUL ENTRY   20th Century Fox, 1992,
   Story w/Lewis Colick & John Katchmer

MARIO PUZO*
Contact: Bert Fields, Greenberg, Glusker, Fields, Clamen &
   Machtinger - Los Angeles, 310/553-3610

THE GODFATHER ★★   Paramount, 1972, w/Francis Ford Coppola
THE GODFATHER, PART II ★★   Paramount, 1974,
   w/Francis Ford Coppola
EARTHQUAKE   Universal, 1974, w/George Fox

SUPERMAN   Warner Bros., 1978, w/Robert Benton,
   David Newman & Leslie Newman
SUPERMAN II   Warner Bros., 1980, w/David Newman &
   Leslie Newman
THE COTTON CLUB   Orion, 1984, Story w/Francis Ford Coppola &
   William Kennedy
THE GODFATHER, PART III   Paramount, 1990,
   w/Francis Ford Coppola
CHRISTOPHER COLUMBUS: THE DISCOVERY   Warner Bros.,
   1992, w/Cary Bates & John Briley

Screenplays:
CARNIVAL

DANIEL PYNE*
Agent: United Talent Agency - Beverly Hills, 310/273-6700

PACIFIC HEIGHTS   20th Century Fox, 1990
THE HARD WAY   Universal, 1991, w/Lem Dobbs
DOC HOLLYWOOD   Warner Bros., 1991, w/Jeffrey Price &
   Peter Seaman
WHITE SANDS   Warner Bros., 1992

Screenplays:
DAVY CROCKETT
RED ROOSTER
MYTHAGO WOOD
SEVEN
WINNING UGLY
AMERICAN IRON w/John Mankiewicz

ALBERT PYUN*
Agent: United Talent Agency - Beverly Hills, 310/273-6700
Contact: John La Violette, Bloom, Dekom, Hergott & Cook -
   Los Angeles, 310/278-8622

THE SWORD AND THE SORCERER   Group 1, 1982,
   w/Tom Karnowski & John Stuckmeyer, directed
RADIOACTIVE DREAMS   DEG, 1986, directed
VICIOUS LIPS   Empire Pictures, 1987, directed
DOWN TWISTED   Cannon, 1987, Story, directed
ALIEN FROM L.A.   Cannon, 1988, w/Regina Davis &
   Debra Ricci, directed
BRAIN SMASHER...A LOVE STORY   Moonstone Entertainment,
   1993, directed

Screenplays:
SAM & ED

PARIS QUALLES*
Agent: Major Clients Agency - Los Angeles, 310/284-6400

THE INKWELL   Buena Vista, 1994, w/Tom Ricostranza
SILENT WITNESS: WHAT A CHILD SAW (CTF)   Power Pictures/
   The Movie Network/Hearst Entertainment, 1994

Screenplays:
BROTHERS

PAUL QUARRINGTON
PERFECTLY NORMAL   Four Seasons Entertainment, 1991,
   w/Eugene Lipinski
GIANT STEPS   Cinephile, 1992, w/Greg Dummett
WHALE MUSIC   Alliance Releasing, 1994, w/Richard Lewis
CAMILLA   Miramax, 1994

MARTIN QUATERMASS
(See John Carpenter)

FLORENCE QUENTIN
Contact: French Film Office, 745 Fifth Avenue, New York, NY 10151,
   212/832-8860

TATIE DANIELLE   Prestige Films, 1991

MOE QUIGLEY
COLD STEEL   CineTel Films, 1987, w/Michael D. Sonye

MICHELE QUILL
SYLVIA   MGM/UA Classics, 1985, w/F. Fairfax & Michael Firth

KEVIN QUINN
Agent: Writers & Artists Agency - Los Angeles, 310/824-6300

Screenplays:
PRESENT DANGER
OPHELIA
THE FUNERAL PARTY
SHADOW OF DEATH
FRIEND OF THE BRIDE
WAY OUT WEST
THE DEPUTY
PRESSURE
I LOVE NEW YORK
LEGMAN
THE DAY THE EARTH CAUGHT FIRE

NICOLE QUINN*
Agent: APA - Los Angeles, 310/273-0744

Screenplays:
SECTION EIGHT

TOM QUINN
Agent: Leslie Kallen Agency - Sherman Oaks, 818/906-2785

Screenplays:
DEADLY VISIONS

EUGENE QUINTANO*
Agent: ICM - Beverly Hills, 310/550-4000
Manager: 3 Arts Entertainment - Los Angeles, 213/851-5700

COMIN' AT YA!   Filmways, 1981, w/Wolf Lowenthal & Lloyd Battista
MAKING THE GRADE   MGM/UA/Cannon, 1984
KING SOLOMON'S MINES   Cannon, 1985, w/James R. Silke
ALLAN QUATERMAIN AND THE LOST CITY OF GOLD   Cannon,
   1987, w/Lee Reynolds
POLICE ACADEMY 3: BACK IN TRAINING   Warner Bros., 1986
POLICE ACADEMY 4: CITIZENS ON PATROL   Warner Bros., 1987
HONEYMOON ACADEMY   Triumph, 1989,
   w/Jerry Lazarus, directed
NATIONAL LAMPOON'S LOADED WEAPON 1   New Line Cinema,
   1993, w/Don Holley, directed
SUDDEN DEATH   Universal, 1995

Screenplays:
SCRATCH w/Tony Anthony (CTF)
SPY VS. SPY
A DOLLAR FOR THE DEAD
SPEAR
OUR FATHER
THE QUEST
D'ARTAGNAN
BEAUTY
BAR STARS
THE LONG HILL
HOUSESITTING IN BEVERLY HILLS
COMMANDO SCHOOL

F
I
L
M

W
R
I
T
E
R
S

R

DAVID RABE*
Agent: United Talent Agency - Beverly Hills, 310/273-6700 or
   The Tantleff Office - New York, 212/941-3939

HURLY BURLY (P)
STICKS AND BONES (P)
THE BASIC TRAINING OF PAVLO HUMMEL (P)
THE ORPHAN (P)
IN THE BOOM BOOM ROOM (P)
GOOSE AND TOM TOM (P)
THOSE THE RIVER KEEPS (P)
I'M DANCING AS FAST AS I CAN   Paramount, 1982
STREAMERS   United Artists Classics, 1983, from his play
CASUALTIES OF WAR   Columbia, 1989
THE FIRM   Paramount, 1993, w/David Rayfiel & Robert Towne

Screenplays:
DESPERADOES

JACKIE RABINOWITZ
Agent: Warden, White & Kane - Beverly Hills, 213/852-1028

Screenplays:
SALES OF A DEATHMAN w/Liddy Loree
ANIMAL ATTRACTION w/Liddy Loree
THE BRIDE OF FRANK w/Liddy Loree
BUSYBODIES w/Liddy Loree

WILLIAM RABKIN*
Contact: WGA - Los Angeles, 310/550-1000

Screenplays:
.357 VIGILANTE w/Lee Goldberg
BLADE w/Lee Goldberg
SHATTERDOLL

GLENN RABNEY*
Contact: WGA - Los Angeles, 310/550-1000

Screenplays:
THE QUEEN OF SPADES w/Bart Baker

PAUL RACZAKOWSKI
Agent: Writers & Artists Agency - Los Angeles, 310/824-6300

Screenplays:
FALLEN FROM GRACE w/Angelo Guglielmo

LISA - MARIA RADANO*
Contact: WGA - Los Angeles, 310/550-1000

BROOKLYN LAUNDRY (P)

Screenplays:
I MARRIED A DEAD MAN

PETER RADER*
Agent: CAA - Beverly Hills, 310/288-4545

WATERWORLD   Universal, 1995, w/David Twohy

Screenplays:
MUSE w/Michelle Weissman
REDHANDED
ABSOLUTE ZERO (Story w/P.K. Simonds)

MICHAEL RADFORD
Agent: Sanford-Gross & Associates - Los Angeles, 310/208-2100
Address: 3B Pickering Mews, London W2 5AD, England

ANOTHER TIME, ANOTHER PLACE   Samuel Goldwyn Company,
   1983, directed
1984   Atlantic Releasing Corporation, 1984, directed
WHITE MISCHIEF   Columbia, 1987, w/Jonathan Gems, directed

BOB RAFELSON*
Agent: ICM - Beverly Hills, 310/550-4000
Business: Marmont Productions, 8439 Sunset Blvd. - Suite 108,
   Los Angeles, CA 90069, 310/650-3195

HEAD   Columbia, 1968, w/Jack Nicholson, directed
FIVE EASY PIECES ★   Columbia, 1970,
   Story w/Carole Eastman, directed
STAY HUNGRY   United Artists, 1976, w/Charles Gaines, directed
MOUNTAINS OF THE MOON   Tri-Star, 1990,
   w/William Harrison, directed
EROTIC TALES   Mercure Distribution, 1994, "Wet," directed

PICCIO RAFFANINI
OBSESSION: A TASTE FOR FEAR   Titanus Produzione, 1989,
   w/Lidia Ravera, directed

STEWART RAFFILL
Agent: Preferred Artists - Encino, 818/990-0305

NAPOLEON AND SAMANTHA   Buena Vista, 1972
THE ADVENTURES OF THE WILDERNESS FAMILY
   Pacific International, 1975, directed
ACROSS THE GREAT DIVIDE   Pacific International, 1976, directed
THE SEA GYPSIES   Warner Bros., 1978, directed
HIGH RISK   American Cinema, 1981, directed
THE ICE PIRATES   MGM/UA, 1983, w/Stanford Sherman, directed
MAC AND ME   Orion, 1988, w/Stephen Feke, directed
PASSENGER 57   Warner Bros., 1992, Story w/Dan Gordon
LOST IN AFRICA   Pyramide, 1994, directed

DEBORAH RAFFIN
Contact: Dove Audio - Los Angeles, 310/273-7722

MORNING GLORY   Academy Entertainment, 1993,
   w/Charles Jarrott

JOHN RAFFO*
Agent: ICM - Beverly Hills, 310/550-4000

BIG AND MEAN (Short)   directed
DRAGON: THE BRUCE LEE STORY   Universal, 1993,
   w/Rob Cohen & Ed Khmara

Screenplays:
PINCUSHION
DAYBREAKER
WARRIOR

TEX RAGSDALE*
Agent: APA - Los Angeles, 310/273-0744

MOONTRAP   Shapiro-Glickenhaus, 1989

Screenplays:
LINES OF FORCE w/Robert Dyke
RETRO w/Robert Dyke
HUNTER IN THE HOUSE

PHILIP W. RAILSBACK
Agent: Metropolitan Talent Agency - Los Angeles, 213/857-4500

THE STARS FELL ON HENRIETTA   Warner Bros., 1995

Screenplays:
GARDEN OF THORNS

IVAN RAIMI*
Contact: WGA - New York, 212/245-6180

EASY WHEELS   Fries Entertainment, 1989, w/Celia Adams &
   David O'Malley
DARK MAN   Universal, 1990, w/Daniel Goldin, Josh Goldin,
   Chuck Pfarrer & Sam Raimi
ARMY OF DARKNESS   Universal, 1993, w/Sam Raimi

SAM RAIMI*
Agent: ICM - Beverly Hills, 310/550-4000
Business: Renaissance Motion Pictures, Inc., 6381 Hollywood Blvd. -
   Suite 680, Los Angeles, CA 90028, 213/463-9965

THE EVIL DEAD   New Line Cinema, 1983, directed
CRIMEWAVE   Columbia, 1985, w/Ethan Coen &
   Joel Coen, directed
EVIL DEAD 2   DEG, 1987, w/Scott Spiegel, directed
DARK MAN   Universal, 1990, w/Daniel Goldin, Josh Goldin,
   Chuck Pfarrer & Ivan Raimi, directed
ARMY OF DARKNESS   Universal, 1993, w/Ivan Raimi, directed
THE HUDSUCKER PROXY   Warner Bros., 1994, w/Ethan Coen &
   Joel Coen

Screenplays:
THE NUTTY NUT w/Scott Spiegel & Ron Zwang

YVONNE RAINER
PRIVILEGE   Zeitgeist Films, 1991, directed

FRANK RAINONE
WHO DO I GOTTA KILL?   Castle Hill Productions, 1993,
   Shared, directed
ME AND THE MOB   Arrow Releasing, 1994, w/James Lorinz &
   Rocco Simonelle, directed

RONALD L. RALEY*
Contact: WGA - Los Angeles, 310/550-1000

EDGE OF SANITY   Millimeter Films, 1989, w/J.P. Felix

GILBERT A. RALSTON*
Agent: Reece Halsey Agency - Los Angeles, 213/652-2409

BEN   Cinerama Releasing, 1972

RICK RAMAGE*
Agent: ICM - Beverly Hills, 310/550-4000

Screenplays:
THE SCARLET LETTER
KILLOBYTE
MR. SANDMAN
BAT BOMB
THE FICTIONIST
SHAKESPEARE'S SISTER
BICENTENNIAL MAN

ALEXANDER D. RAMATI
THE ASSISI UNDERGROUND   Cannon, 1985, directed

HAROLD A. RAMIS*
Agent: CAA - Beverly Hills, 310/288-4545
Business: Ocean Pictures, 2821 Main St., Santa Monica, CA 90405,
   310/399-9271

NATIONAL LAMPOON'S ANIMAL HOUSE   Universal, 1978,
   w/Douglas Kenney & Chris Miller
MEATBALLS   Paramount, 1979, w/Janis Allen, Len Blum &
   Dan Goldberg
CADDYSHACK   Orion/Warner Bros., 1980, w/Douglas Kenney &
   Brian Doyle Murray, directed
STRIPES   Columbia, 1981, w/Len Blum & Dan Goldberg
NATIONAL LAMPOON'S VACATION   Warner Bros., 1983,
   w/Chevy Chase & John Hughes, directed
GHOSTBUSTERS   Columbia, 1984, w/Dan Aykroyd

CLUB PARADISE   Warner Bros., 1986,
   w/Brian Doyle Murray, directed
BACK TO SCHOOL   Orion, 1986, w/Steven Kampmann,
   Will Aldis & Peter Torokvei
ARMED AND DANGEROUS   Columbia, 1987, w/Peter Torokvei
CADDYSHACK II   Warner Bros., 1988, w/PeterTorokvei
GHOSTBUSTERS II   Columbia, 1989, w/Dan Aykroyd
ROVER DANGERFIELD (AF)   Warner Bros., 1991,
   Story developed w/Rodney Dangerfield
GROUNDHOG DAY   Columbia, 1993, w/Danny Rubin, directed

Screenplays:
CHAMPAGNE NIGHTS w/Peter Torokvei

AL RAMRUS*
Agent: Preferred Artists - Encino, 818/990-0305

HALLS OF ANGER   United Artists, 1970, w/John Herman Shaner
THE ISLAND OF DR. MOREAU   American International, 1977,
   w/John Herman Shaner
GOIN' SOUTH   Paramount, 1978, w/Alan Mandel,
   John Herman Shaner & Charles Shyer

Screenplays:
ROOMS OF THE HEART

ROBERT RAMSEY*
Agent: Paradigm - Los Angeles, 310/277-4400

Screenplays:
DESTINY TURNS ON THE RADIO w/Matt Stone (Savoy)
INTOLERABLE CRUELTY w/Matt Stone

PATRICK RANAHAN*
Agent: Warden, White & Kane - Beverly Hills, 213/852-1028

Screenplays:
EUGENE AND HIS SEAMLESS PANTS w/Todd Johnson
HEAD DOWN TILT w/Todd Johnson
THE LIMBIC REGION w/Todd Johnson

ADDISON RANDALL
AMERICAN BORN   PM Home Video, 1990, w/Raymond Martino
THE KILLING ZONE   PM Home Video, 1991, directed
THE LAST RIDERS   PM Home Video, 1991, w/Ray Garmon &
   Joseph Mehri, directed

BOB RANDALL*
Agent: Gold/Marshak - Burbank, 818/972-4300

DAVID'S MOTHER (P) also teleplay
ZORRO, THE GAY BLADE   20th Century-Fox, 1981,
   Story w/Greg Alt, Hal Dresner & Don Moriarty

Screenplays:
LAST MAN ON THE LIST

NICK RANDALL
CHROME SOLDIERS (CTF)   Wilshire Court Productions, 1992

SHAWN RANDALL
THE LONELY LADY   Universal, 1983, w/John Kershaw

JOHN RANDAZZO
SWORDS OF HEAVEN   Trans World Entertainment, 1985,
   w/James Bruner, Britt Lomond & William P. O'Hagan

CRAIG RANDELMAN
Manager: I.R.S./Harris Management - Culver City, 310/841-4169
Contact: Karl Austen, Armstrong, Hirsch, Jackoway, Tyerman &
   Wertheimer - Los Angeles, 310/553-0305

Screenplays:
SOFT KILL w/Michael Berlly
LITTLE NAPOLEON w/Michael Berlly
COUP D'ETAT w/Michael Berlly

301

DAVID RANDOLF
THEY CALL ME BRUCE? *A FISTFUL OF CHOPSTICKS*
   Artists Releasing Corporation/Film Ventures International, 1982,
   w/Tim Clawson, Elliott Hong & Johnny Yune

TIMNA RANON*
Agent: Barry Perelman Agency - Los Angeles, 310/274-5999
Contact: Michael Donaldson, Dern & Donaldson - Los Angeles,
   310/557-0417

Screenplays:
THE EAGLE
HOLD FAST MY WORLDS   REBEKAH

MORT RANSEN
FALLING OVER BACKWARDS   Astral Films, 1990, directed

WHITNEY RANSICK
Agent: William Morris Agency - Beverly Hills, 310/274-7451

HANDGUN   Workin' Man Films, 1994, directed

PETER RANSLEY
Agent: Peters, Fraser & Dunlop - London, 071/376-7676

THE HAWK   Castle Hill, 1994

MARTIN RANSOHOFF
Business: Albacore Films, 9460 Wilshire Blvd. - Suite 415,
   Beverly Hills, CA 90212, 310/274-4585

A CHANGE OF SEASONS   20th Century-Fox, 1980,
   Story w/Erich Segal

STEVE RANSOHOFF
PHYSICAL EVIDENCE   Columbia, 1989, Story w/Bill Phillips

FREDERIC RAPHAEL
Agent: William Morris Agency - Beverly Hills, 310/274-7451

BACHELOR OF HEARTS   Rank, 1958, w/Leslie Bricusse
WHY BOTHER TO KNOCK   ABP, 1961, w/Dennis Cannan &
   Frederick Gotfurt
NOTHING BUT THE BEST   Anglo Amalgamated, 1964
DARLING ★★   Anglo Amalgamated, 1965
TWO FOR THE ROAD ★   20th Century-Fox, 1966
FAR FROM THE MADDING CROWD   EMI, 1967
A SEVERED HEAD   Columbia, 1970
DAISY MILLER   Paramount, 1974
RICHARD'S THINGS   New World, 1981
THE KING'S WHORE   J & M Entertainment, 1990, w/Axel Corti &
   Daniel Vigne

Screenplays:
DESIRE w/Henry Bean & Leora Barish
FREE SPIRIT
UNITED STATES
THE RIGHT MAN
WE THREE   CAESAR AND ROSALIE
A NEW WIFE
LIBBY HOLMAN
SONG BIRD
IN THOSE DAYS
LOVE AFFAIR
THE BIG ONE
ROSES, ROSES
THE CURSE OF GENIUS

JERRY RAPP*
Agent: Maggie Field Agency - Studio City, 818/980-2001

Screenplays:
THE TOURISTS w/Jeff Berman
ON THE AIR w/Jeff Berman
STRAY KIDS w/Jeff Berman

WISHING w/Jeff Berman
I SEE YOU, MR. BRIGGS
THE HUFF BROTHERS w/Christopher Joyce & John Perry
WE, THE OTHER PEOPLE w/Christopher Joyce, John Perry &
   Mark Hertzog

EZRA D. RAPPAPORT*
Agent: Shapiro/Lichtman - Los Angeles, 310/859-8877

DEJA VU   Cannon, 1985, w/Anthony Richmond & Arnold Schmidt
HARRY AND THE HENDERSONS   Universal, 1987,
   w/William Dear & William E. Martin

I.C. RAPPAPORT*
Agent: The Agency - Los Angeles, 310/551-3000

JERICHO FEVER (CTF)   Sankan Produtions/Wilshire Court, 1993

JARED RAPPAPORT*
Contact: Prelude Pictures, Paramount, 213/956-8646

Screenplays:
SENIOR TRIP

MARK RAPPAPORT
IMPOSTORS   First Run Features, 1981

JEAN-PAUL RAPPENEAU
Agent: William Morris Agency - Beverly Hills, 310/274-7451

ZAZIE   *ZAZIE DANS LE METRO*   Astor, 1960, w/Louis Malle
THAT MAN FROM RIO ★   Lopert, 1964, w/others
LE SAUVAGE   1978, w/Elisabeth Rappeneau &
   Jean-Loup Dabadie, directed
CYRANO DE BERGERAC   Orion Classics, 1990,
   w/Jean-Claude Carriere, directed

JUDITH RASCOE*
Agent: William Morris Agency - Beverly Hills, 310/274-7451

ROAD MOVIE   Grove Press, 1974
WHO'LL STOP THE RAIN   United Artists, 1978
A PORTRAIT OF THE ARTIST AS A YOUNG MAN
   Howard Mahler Films, 1979
ENDLESS LOVE   Universal, 1981
EAT A BOWL OF TEA   Columbia, 1989
HAVANA   Universal, 1990, w/David Rayfiel

Screenplays:
THE RUTH ETTING STORY
THE FORTUNE TELLER
HANDCARVED COFFINS
PICTURES FROM THE WATER TRADE

RICHARD RASHKE*
Agent: Ken Sherman & Associates -213/273-8840

Screenplays:
SCHEMES

TINA RATHBORNE
Agent: The Irv Schechter Company - Beverly Hills, 310/278-8070

ZELLY & ME   Columbia, 1988, directed

Screenplays:
HOUSE OF MIRTH (directing)

LARRY RATTNER*
Contact: Attorney Shelly Browning, 310/858-7700

HALLOWEEN 4   Galaxy International, 1988, Story w/Dhani Lipsius,
   Alan McElroy & Benjamin Ruffner
THE HORSEPLAYER   Relentless Entertainment, 1989, w/Kurt Voss
GENUINE RISK   I.R.S. Releasing, 1990, Story w/Kurt Voss

EARL MAC RAUCH*

Agent: Shapiro/Lichtman - Los Angeles, 310/859-8877

NEW YORK, NEW YORK   United Artists, 1977, w/Mardik Martin
A STRANGER IS WATCHING   MGM/UA, 1982, w/Victor Miller
THE ADVENTURES OF BUCKAROO BANZAI ACROSS THE
   8TH DIMENSION   20th Century-Fox, 1984
WIRED   Taurus Entertainment, 1989

Screenplays:
NATIVE TONGUE
SCI-FI HIGH
TAPPING THE SOURCE
GRASS ROOTS
NOBLE ENEMIES
BIG BAND OF BLUES
THE LAST RIDE
JET CAR
WILD SANCTUARY
BOYS IN BLUES

HERMAN RAUCHER*

Agent: Lew Grimes - New York, 212/974-9505
Contact: Arthur B. Greene - 212/661-8200

SWEET NOVEMBER   Warner Bros., 1968
CAN HIERONYMUS MERKIN EVER FORGET MERCY HUMPPE &
   FIND TRUE HAPPINESS?   Universal, 1969, w/Anthony Newley
WATERMELON MAN   Columbia, 1970
SUMMER OF '42 ★   Warner Bros., 1971
CLASS OF '44   Warner Bros., 1973
ODE TO BILLY JOE   Warner Bros., 1976
THE OTHER SIDE OF MIDNIGHT   20th Century-Fox, 1977,
   w/Daniel Taradash

Screenplays:
THERE SHOULD HAVE BEEN CASTLES
GLORY DAY
CHARLIE IS MY DARLING
CRY GORF
IT'S ME AGAIN
HIT ME EASY
MAYNARD'S HOUSE
THREE FEET TO GERMANY
TUTTO E. FINITO
TWO WAYS TO GO

IRVING RAVETCH*

Agent: William Morris Agency - Beverly Hills, 310/274-7451

THE OUTRIDERS   MGM, 1950
VENGEANCE VALLEY   MGM, 1951
TEN WANTED MEN   Columbia, 1955, Story w/Harriet Frank Jr.
THE LONG HOT SUMMER   MGM, 1958, w/Harriet Frank Jr.
THE SOUND AND THE FURY   20th Century-Fox, 1959,
   w/Harriet Frank Jr.
HOME FROM THE HILL   MGM, 1959, w/Irving Ravetch
THE DARK AT THE TOP OF THE STAIRS   Warner Bros., 1960,
   w/Harriet Frank, Jr.
HUD ★   Paramount, 1963, w/Harriet Frank, Jr.
HOMBRE   20th Century-Fox, 1967, w/Harriet Frank, Jr.
THE REIVERS   National General, 1969, w/Harriet Frank, Jr.
THE COWBOYS   Warner Bros., 1972, w/Harriet Frank, Jr.
THE SPIKES GANG   United Artists, 1974, w/Harriet Frank, Jr.
CONRACK   20th Century-Fox, 1974, w/Harriet Frank, Jr.
NORMA RAE ★   20th Century-Fox, 1979, w/Harriet Frank, Jr.
MURPHY'S ROMANCE   Columbia, 1985, w/Harriet Frank, Jr.
STANLEY & IRIS   MGM/UA, 1990, w/Harriet Frank, Jr.

Screenplays:
BEGINNERS w/Barbara Benedek & Harriet Frank, Jr.
MIXED FEELINGS w/Harriet Frank, Jr.
SINGLE w/Harriet Frank, Jr.

RAND RAVICH*

Agent: CAA - Beverly Hills, 310/288-4545

CRIME LORDS   Image Organization, 1991
CANDYMAN 2: FAREWELL TO THE FLESH   Gramercy, 1995

Screenplays:
THE MAKER
GRANDFATHER
PLATFORM 18
THE CONJURER w/Stephen Berger
HOLD
HOMER JONES
KAIMERA
AFTER THE RIPENING MOON
MR. W

WENDELL RAWLS*

Agent: CAA - Beverly Hills, 310/288-4545

Screenplays:
ABOVE THE FOLD

BILLY RAY*

Agent: Broder-Kurland-Webb-Uffner - Beverly Hills, 310/281-3400

COLOR OF NIGHT   Buena Vista, 1993, w/Matthew Capman

Screenplays:
SHOOTER w/Yves Martin & Meg Thayer
CUSTODY
HONG KONG THRILLER
KISS THE BRIDE
MODEL COP

FRED OLEN RAY

Business: American-Independent Productions, P.O. Box 1901,
   Hollywood, CA 90078, 818/995-6610

BIOHAZARD   21st Century, 1985, directed
BULLETPROOF   CineTel Films, 1987, Story w/T.L. Lankford
DEEP SPACE   Trans World Entertainment, 1988,
   w/T.L. Lankford, directed

KAREN RAY

Agent: Pleshette & Green - Los Angeles, 213/465-0428

Screenplays:
ONE FOR THE MONEY w/Stacy Sherman
POOR HOLLY w/Stacy Sherman

LESLIE A. RAY*

Agent: Dytman & Schwartz - Los Angeles, 310/274-8844

MY DEMON LOVER   New Line Cinema, 1987

Screenplays:
MORGAN w/Michael Taav
STREET HEARTS
MAKING WAVES

MARC RAY*

Contact: WGA - Los Angeles, 310/550-1000

STEPFATHER III (CTF)   ITC Entertainment Group, 1992,
   w/Guy Magar

Screenplays:
BOOK OF THE CHILD

DAVID RAYFIEL*

Agent: CAA - Beverly Hills, 310/288-4545
Contact: 212/772-2221

CASTLE KEEP   Columbia, 1969, w/Daniel Taradash
VALDEZ IS COMING   United Artists, 1970, w/Roland Kibbee
THREE DAYS OF THE CONDOR   Paramount, 1975, w/Lorenzo Semple
LIPSTICK   Paramount, 1976
DEATH WATCH   Quartet, 1980, w/Bertrand Tavernier
ROUND MIDNIGHT   Warner Bros., 1986, w/Bertrand Tavernier
HAVANA   Universal, 1990, w/Judith Rascoe
THE FIRM   Paramount, 1993, w/Robert Towne & David Rabe
INTERSECTION   Paramount, 1994, w/Marshall Brickman

Screenplays:
MARY AND RICHARD
THE TRIANGLE FACTORY
BOYS & GIRLS TOGETHER
WELCOME HOME, WELL DONE
SILENCE

THOMAS G. RAYFIEL*

Contact: WGA - New York, 212/245-6180

HAREM   UGC, 1985, w/Arthur Joffe & Richard Prieur

KATHERINE J. REBACK*

Business Manager: Armstrong, Hirsch, Jackoway, Tyerman & Wertheimer - Los Angeles, 310/553-0305

Screenplays:
THE RECEPTIONIST

ALEX REBAR

NOWHERE TO HIDE   New Century/Vista, 1987, w/George Goldsmith

THERESA REBECK*

Agent: William Morris Agency - Beverly Hills, 310/274-7451

SPIKE HEELS (P)
LOOSE KNIT (P)
THE FAMILY OF MANN (P)

Screenplays:
PAROLE OFFICE

ERIC RED*

Agent: ICM - Beverly Hills, 310/550-4000

THE HITCHER   Tri-Star, 1986
NEAR DARK   DEG, 1987, w/Kathryn Bigelow
COHEN & TATE   Nelson Entertainment, 1988, directed
BLUE STEEL   MGM/UA, 1990, w/Kathryn Bigelow
BODY PARTS   Paramount, 1991, w/Norman Snider, directed
THE LAST OUTLAW (CTF)   Davis Entertainment/ HBO Pictures, 1993

Screenplays:
THOR (directing)
UNDERTOW w/Kathryn Bigelow
CANAL STREET
LOST BOYS II

JAY A. REDACK*

Contact: Howard Borris - 213/655-3991

RABBIT TEST   Avco Embassy, 1978, w/Joan Rivers

KEITH REDDIN*

Agent: William Morris Agency - New York, 212/586-5100

RUM AND COKE (P)
LIFE DURING WARTIME (P)

THE INNOCENTS CRUSADE (P)   also screenplay
THE HEART OF JUSTICE (CTF)   TNT Screenworks, 1993, from his play

QUINN K. REDEKER*

Contact: WGA - Los Angeles, 310/550-1000

THE DEER HUNTER ★   United Artists, 1978, Story w/Michael Cimino & Louis Garfinkle

Screenplays:
SHANGHAI TANGO w/Louis Garfinkle
VOSA w/Louis Garfinkle
THE EEZMO w/Louis Garfinkle

JAMES REDFORD*

Agent: William Morris Agency - Beverly Hills, 310/274-7451

Screenplays:
ROCKY ROAD
TERRA INCOGNITA

ROBERT REDLIN*

Agent: Abrams Artists & Associates - Los Angeles, 310/859-0625

AFTER DARK, MY SWEET   Avenue Pictures, 1990, w/James Foley

Screenplays:
LIMITED PARTNERSHIPS w/Galen Johnson
PHONECALLS FROM THE DEAD

LEE REDMOND

THE FINAL MISSION   Trimark, 1993, w/Virginia Gilbert, Sam Montgomery & Ernest Sheldon Jr., directed

ALLAN REED

CREATURE   Cardinal Releasing, 1985, w/William Malone

JIM REED

Agent: Susan Smith & Associates - Beverly Hills, 213/852-4777

Screenplays:
TROUBLE ON 162
THE SINS OF ANGELS

JOEL M. REED

NIGHT OF THE ZOMBIES   NMD, 1981

JERRY REES

Agent: United Talent Agency - Beverly Hills, 310/273-6700

THE BRAVE LITTLE TOASTER (AF)   Hyperion-Kushner-Locke Productions, 1987 directed

Screenplays:
BETTY BOOP
THE KISS w/Steve Leiva (directing)

CHRISTOPHER REEVE*

Contact: WGA - New York, 212/767-7800

SUPERMAN IV: THE QUEST FOR PEACE   Warner Bros., 1987, Story w/Lawrence Konner & Mark Rosenthal

MATT REEVES*

Agent: CAA - Beverly Hills, 310/288-4545

DARK TERRITORY: UNDER SIEGE II   Warner Bros., 1995, w/Richard Hatem

Screenplays:
THE PALLBEARER w/Jason Katims (Miramax, directing)

MICHAEL REEVES
BATMAN: MASK OF THE PHANTASM (AF)   Warner Bros., 1993,
   w/Alan Burnett, Paul Dini & Martin Pasko

BRIAN REHAK*
Manager: The Roberts Company - Los Angeles, 310/552-7800

THE IMAGE (CTF)   Citadel Entertainment Productions, 1990

Screenplays:
1968
TRAFFIC SCHOOL

FRANK REHWALT
Agent: David Shapira & Associates - Sherman Oaks, 818/906-0322

Screenplays:
DOOMED w/Mara Treffecante

KELLY REICHARDT
RIVER OF GRASS   Plan B Pictures, 1994,
   w/Jesse Hartman, directed

JULIE REICHERT*
Contact: 505/242-7176

BREAKIN' 2: ELECTRIC BOOGALOO   Tri-Star, 1984,
   w/Jan Ventura
EMMA AND ELVIS   Northern Arts Entertainment, 1992,
   w/Steven Bognar & Martin M. Goldstein, directed

MARK REICHERT
UNION CITY   Kinesis Ltd., 1980, directed

ALASTAIR REID
Agent: Peters, Fraser & Dunlop - London, 071/376-7676

BABY LOVE   Avco Embassy, 1969, w/Guido Coen &
   Michael Klinger, directed
SOMETHING TO HIDE   Avton, 1971, directed

RON REID
MONTANA RUN   Greycat Films, 1992, w/Dan Lishner &
   Randy Thompson

ETHAN REIFF
Agent: United Talent Agency - Beverly Hills, 310/273-6700

DEMON KNIGHT   Universal, 1995, w/Cyrus Voris

Screenplays:
PIECE OF MIND w/Cyrus Voris
SLAYER w/Cyrus Voris
JOSH KIRBY: TIMEMASTER! w/Cyrus Voris
MAN-AT ARMS w/Cyrus Voris

JAMES REIGLE
ANDROID   New World, 1982, w/Don Opper
CITY LIMITS   Atlantic Releasing Corporation, 1985,
   w/Aaron Lipstadt & Don Opper

DONALD REIKER*
Contact: WGA - Los Angeles, 310/550-1000

MONA MUST DIE   Jones & Reiker, 1994,
   w/Patricia Jones, directed

TOM REILLY*
Agent: ICM - Beverly Hills, 310/550-4000

Screenplays:
FOOL'S GOLD w/Hogan Sheffer
THE BLACK ROSE w/Hogan Sheffer

WILLIAM REILLY*
Agent: Broder-Kurland-Webb-Uffner - Beverly Hills, 310/281-3400

THE BROAD COALITION   *WHAT DO I TELL THE BOYS AT
   THE STATION?* August, 1972
MEN OF RESPECT   Columbia, 1991, directed
MORTAL THOUGHTS   Columbia, 1991, w/Claude Kerven

CARL REINER*
Agent: CAA - Beverly Hills, 310/288-4545

THE THRILL OF IT ALL   Universal-International, 1963
THE ART OF LOVE   Universal, 1965
ENTER LAUGHING   Columbia, 1967, w/Joseph Stein,
   from his play, directed
THE COMIC   Columbia, 1969, w/Aaron Rubin, directed
DEAD MEN DON'T WEAR PLAID   Universal, 1979,
   w/George Gipe & Steve Martin, directed
THE MAN WITH TWO BRAINS   Warner Bros., 1983,
   w/George Gipe & Steve Martin, directed
BERT RIGBY, YOU'RE A FOOL   Warner Bros., 1989, directed

JEFF REINER
Agent: The Artists Group - Los Angeles, 310/552-1100

BLOOD AND CONCRETE: A LOVE STORY   I.R.S. Media, 1991,
   w/Richard LaBrie, directed

LUCAS REINER
Agent: ICM - Beverly Hills, 310/550-4000

THE SPIRIT OF '76   Columbia, 1990, directed

Screenplays:
THE GOLD CUP (Picture Entertainment Corp., directing)
APRIL FOOLS (directing)

ROB REINER*
Agent: CAA - Beverly Hills, 213/288-4545
Business: Castle Rock Entertainment, 335 N. Maple Drive - Suite 135,
   Beverly Hills, CA 90210, 310/285-2300

THIS IS SPINAL TAP   Embassy, 1984, w/Christopher Guest,
   Michael McKean & Harry Shearer, directed

AL REINHART
Agent: CAA - Beverly Hills, 310/288-4545

APOLLO 13   Universal, 1995, w/William Broyles Jr.

GUSTAVE V. REININGER*
Agent: Camden-ITG - Los Angeles, 310/289-2700

Screenplays:
WALK WITH ANGELS
GULF COAST
TEN TENTHS

BRUCE REISMAN
Contact: Gilder Entertainment, 4333 Stern - Suite 103,
   Sherman Oaks, CA 91423

Screenplays:
BLADE BOXER w/William Katt (directing)
THE HIGHER GROUND
WISH

MARK A. REISMAN *
Agent: The Irv Schechter Company - Beverly Hills, 310/278-8070

SUMMER RENTAL   Paramount, 1985, w/Jeremy Stevens

Screenplays:
BIG HOSPITAL w/Jeremy Stevens
NINETY MINUTES w/Jeremy Stevens

IVAN REITMAN
Agent: CAA - Beverly Hills, 213/288-4545
Business: Ivan Reitman Productions, Universal Pictures,
818/777-8080

LEGAL EAGLES   Universal, 1986, Story w/Jim Cash &
Jack Epps Jr., directed

LINDA REMY*
Contact: 415/381-0390

DESERT BLOOM   Columbia, 1986, Story w/Eugene Corr

SHELDON RENAN*
Contact: WGA - Los Angeles, 310/550-1000

LAMBADA   Warner Bros., 1990, w/Joel Silberg

Screenplays:
HOLLOW POINT
SNAKE
THE GAMELAN KEY
THE SAMAURI KIDS
SPLITTERZ

THOMAS RENDON
VOODOO DAWN   Academy Entertainment, 1990,
w/Jeffrey Delman, Evan Dunsky & John Russo

ROBERT SCOTT RENEAU*
Contact: WGA - Los Angeles, 310/550-1000

ACTION JACKSON   Lorimar, 1988
DEMOLITION MAN   Warner Bros., 1993, w/Peter Lenkov &
Dan Waters

JEFF W. RENO*
Agent: Warden, White & Kane - Beverly Hills, 213/852-1028

RADIOLAND MURDERS   Universal, 1994, w/Ron Osborn,
Willard Huyck & Gloria Katz

Screenplays:
DEATH TAKES A HOLIDAY w/Ron Osborn

DAVID RENWICK
Contact: 011/441-8056

THE MISADVENTURES OF MR. WILT   Samuel Goldwyn Company,
1990, Adaptation w/Andrew Marshall

Screenplays:
MUSHROOM BUTTON w/Andrew Marshall
JINGLE BELLS w/Andrew Marshall

FRANK RENZULLI*
Agent: Major Clients Agency - Los Angeles, 310/284-6400

Screenplays:
WHERE'S BROOKLYN

DAVID RESKIN
Contact: 213/462-2275

ACTION U.S.A.   Stewart & Berger Inc., 1989
SKINHEADS   Amazing Movies, 1989, w/Greydon Clark
CLICK: THE CALENDAR GIRL KILLER   Crown International, 1989,
w/David Chute, Ross Hagen & Hoke Howell
HIDDEN OBSESSION   Broadstar Entertainment, 1993
RUSSIAN HOLIDAY   Greydon Clark Productions, 1993

ADAM RESNICK*
Agent: United Talent Agency - Beverly Hills, 310/273-6700

CABIN BOY   Buena Vista, 1994, directed

Screenplays:
HOPETOWN
PROPOSING TO PENNY

PATRICIA RESNICK*
Agent: William Morris Agency - Beverly Hills, 310/274-7451

LADIES IN WAITING (P)
A WEDDING   20th Century-Fox, 1978, w/Robert Altman,
John Considine & Allan Nichols
QUINTET   20th Century-Fox, 1979, w/Robert Altman &
Frank Barhydt
NINE TO FIVE   20th Century-Fox, 1980, w/Colin Higgins
MAXIE   Orion, 1985
SECOND SIGHT   Warner Bros., 1989, w/Tom Schulman
STRAIGHT TALK   Buena Vista, 1992, w/Craig Bolotin
GRANDPA'S FUNERAL (Short)   Chanticleer, 1994, directed

Screenplays:
TEACHER'S PET
THE DEVIL AND MISS JONES w/Bruce Vilanch
SORORITY
THREE AFTER THIRTY
FIRST BOOK OF EPPIE
FAMILY SECRETS
CROSSTOWN
HELL CAN WAIT
WRONG PLANET (Story w/Lee Rose)
ROUGH TRADE (Story w/Lee Rose)

ROBERT D. RESNIKOFF*
Agent: Innovative Artists - Los Angeles, 310/553-5200

THE JOGGER (Short)   directed
COLLISION COURSE   DEG, 1987, w/Frank Namei
THE FIRST POWER   Orion, 1990, directed

Screenplays:
MINE
SHADOW DEAL
THE 400

CARLA REUBEN
SOMETHING SPECIAL   *WILLY MILLY/I WAS A TEENAGE BOY*
Cinema Group, 1986, w/Walter Carbone

PAUL REUBENS*
(Pee-Wee Herman)
Personal Manager: Michael McLean - 818/505-0945

PEE-WEE'S BIG ADVENTURE   Warner Bros., 1985,
w/Phil Hartman & Michael Varhol
BIG TOP PEE-WEE   Paramount, 1988, w/George McGrath

FRED REXER*
Contact: WGA - Los Angeles, 310/550-1000

EXTREME PREJUDICE   Tri-Star, 1987, Story w/John Milius

EDITH REY
SPACEHUNTER: ADVENTURES IN THE FORBIDDEN ZONE
Columbia, 1983, w/Len Blum, Dan Goldberg & David Preston
BREAKING ALL THE RULES   New World, 1985,
Story w/Rafal Zielinski

CHRISTOPHER REYNOLDS
OFFERINGS   Arista Films, 1989, directed

CLARKE REYNOLDS*
Contact: Morgan & Martindale - Los Angeles, 310/474-0810

SON OF A GUNFIGHTER   MGM, 1964
THE VIKING QUEEN   Warner Bros., 1967
OPERATION THUNDERBOLT   Cinema Shares
    International, 1978
NIGHT GAMES   Avco Embassy, 1980, w/Anton Diether

JONATHAN REYNOLDS*
Agent: The Gersh Agency - Beverly Hills, 310/274-6611

GENIUSES (P)
MICKI AND MAUDE   Columbia, 1984
LEONARD PART 6   Columbia, 1987
SWITCHING CHANNELS   Tri-Star, 1988
MY STEPMOTHER IS AN ALIEN   WEG, 1988, w/Timothy Harris,
    Herschel Weingrod & Jericho Stone
THE DISTINGUISHED GENTLEMAN   Buena Vista, 1992,
    Story w/Marty Kaplan

Screenplays:
THE PHILADELPHIA FLASH
THE SURVIVALISTS
KATE
WHEREABOUTS
HAR'LD

KEVIN H. REYNOLDS*
Agent: William Morris Agency - Beverly Hills, 310/274-7451
Business: Windmill Films Inc., 248 Westminster Ave., Venice,
    CA 90291, 310/399-1448

RED DAWN   MGM/UA, 1984, w/John Milius
FANDANGO   Warner Bros., 1985, directed
RAPA NUI   Warner Bros., 1994, w/Tim Rose Price, directed

Screenplays:
LITTLE THINGS
THE FIRE

LEE D. REYNOLDS*
Agent: Warden, White & Kane - Beverly Hills, 213/852-1028
Contact: Bloom, Dekom, Hergott & Cook - Los Angeles,
    310/278-8622

ALLAN QUATERMAIN AND THE LOST CITY OF GOLD   Cannon,
    1987, w/Gene Quintano
DELTA FORCE 2   MGM/UA, 1990
STORYVILLE   20th Century Fox, 1992, w/Mark Frost

Screenplays:
COTTON WHITE
WITHOUT A TRACE
THE NEW SOUTH
SHERLOCK HOLMES ON THE ORIENT EXPRESS
STRANGER IN A STRANGE LAND
HOT OFF THE WIRE
TWO OF THE MISSING
BALEFIRE
HANG ON TIGHT
WISHFUL THINKING
PIGEON BOY

REBECCA REYNOLDS*
Agent: Bret Adams Agency - New York, 212/765-5630

OVEREXPOSED   Concorde, 1990, w/Larry Brand

RICK REYNOLDS*
Agent: ICM - Beverly Hills, 310/550-4000
Personal Manager: Jack Rollins/Charles Joffe, 130 West 57th St.,
    New York, NY, 212/582-1940

ONLY THE TRUTH IS FUNNY (CTF)   Rollins-Joffe Productions,
    1993, from his play

Screenplays:
COULD THIS BE MAGIC
TUCSON
THE BOY IN THE BASEMENT

MARK REZYKA
SOUTH OF RENO   Castle Hill Productions, 1988,
    w/T.L. Lankford, directed

PHILLIP RHEE
BEST OF THE BEST   Taurus Entertainment, 1989,
    Story w/Paul Levine

SUSAN RHINEHART*
Agent: Writers & Artists Agency - Los Angeles, 310/824-6300

MEMPHIS (CTF)   Propaganda Films/River Siren, 1992,
    w/Larry McMurtry & Cybill Shepherd

Screenplays:
DESPERATE WOMEN

DON RHYMER*
Agent: The Gersh Agency - Beverly Hills, 310/274-6611

Screenplays:
CARPOOL

GRIFF RHYS-JONES
MORONS FROM OUTER SPACE   Universal, 1985, w/Mel Smith

RONALD RIBMAN*
Agent: Sam Gelfman, BDP & Associates - North Hollywood,
    818/506-7615

THE RUG MERCHANTS OF CHAOS (P)
COLD STORAGE (P)
THE ANGEL LEVINE   United Artists, 1970, w/Bill Gunn

RUDY RICCI
THE RETURN OF THE LIVING DEAD   Orion, 1985,
    Story w/John Russo & Russell Streiner

ANNE RICE*
Agent: ICM - Beverly Hills, 310/550-4000

INTERVIEW WITH A VAMPIRE   Warner Bros., 1994

Screenplays:
THE BRIDE OF FRANKENSTEIN

JOHN M. RICE*
Agent: J. Michael Bloom & Associates - Los Angeles, 310/275-6800

CURIOSITY KILLS (CTF)   MCA Television Entertainment, 1990,
    w/Joe Batteer
CHASERS   Warner Bros., 1994, w/Joe Batteer & Dan Gilroy
BLOWN AWAY   MGM/UA, 1994, w/Joe Batteer

Screenplays:
IVANHOE w/Rudy Gaines
LEWIS & CLARK, THE EXPEDITION w/Rudy Gaines
JOURNAL OF ADVENTURE w/Rudy Gaines
LEVITICUS WAR w/Rudy Gaines
BUFFALO COMMONS w/Rudy Gaines
TO DIE FOR w/Rudy Gaines
SHELTER FROM THE STORM w/Rudy Gaines
CROSSFIRE
THE FORGOTTEN MAN
HOOLIGANS
DEAD RUN

Ri

FILM
WRITERS
GUIDE

F
I
L
M

W
R
I
T
E
R
S

SEAN MICHAEL RICE
Agent: Lenhoff/Robinson - Los Angeles, 310/558-4700

Screenplays:
ENTWINE

SUSAN C. RICE*
Agent: United Talent Agency - Beverly Hills, 310/273-6700

GOOD SPORTS (P)
ENORMOUS CHANGES AT THE LAST MINUTE   TC Films
   International, 1985, w/John Sayles
ANIMAL BEHAVIOR   Millimeter Films, 1989

Screenplays:
ABOUT TIME
ENOUGH ROPE w/Diane Sokolow
STRAIGHT A'S
THE WOMAN WHO ATE 14TH STREET
TELL ME ON A SUNDAY
MAGGIE
STRANGERS
THE RUNNING MATE
LOVE 30

WAYNE RICE*
Agent: ICM - Beverly Hills, 310/550-4000
Business: Dayjob Films, Universal Pictures, 818/777-8322

CLASS ACT   Warner Bros., 1992, Story w/Richard Brenne &
   Michael Swerdlick
ONLY YOU   LIVE Entertainment/Highlight Communications, 1992

Screenplays:
JUST LIKE DAD (Leucadia Films)
GENTLE BEN
DESPERATE MEASURES w/Gregg Hoffman
DATE WITH MOM AND DAD
MOST ELIGIBLE BACHELOR

DAVID N. RICH*
Contact: Chrsitine Cuddy - 310/312-3246

RENEGADES   Universal, 1989

MATTY RICH
Agent: The Gersh Agency - Beverly Hills, 310/274-6611
Business: Blacks 'n Progress Productions, TriStar

STRAIGHT OUT OF BROOKLYN   Samuel Goldwyn Company,
   1991, directed

Screenplays:
FORTY THIEVES

RICHARD RICH
Contact: Nest Entertainment - 818/846-9850

THE BLACK CAULDRON (AF)   Buena Vista, 1985,
   w/others, directed
THE SWAN PRINCESS (AF)   New Line Cinema, 1994,
   w/Brian Nissen

Screenplays:
FEATHERTOP (AF) w/Brian Nissen

RON RICH
GHOST FEVER   Miramax, 1987, w/Oscar Brodney

JULIE RICHARD
SCANNERS III: THE TAKEOVER   Republic Pictures, 1992,
   w/Rene Malo, B.J. Nelson & David Preston

WINSTON RICHARD
ROUND TRIP TO HEAVEN   Saban Pictures International, 1992,
   w/Shuki Levy

BENJAMIN MICHAEL RICHARDS*
Contact: WGA - Los Angeles, 310/550-1000

Screenplays:
THE KIDS FROM NOWHERE

KEN RICHARDS*
Contact: WGA - Los Angeles, 310/550-1000

Screenplays:
YOU SHOULD SEE THEM PLAY

RON RICHARDS*
.\ddress: P.O. Box 12014, Marina Del Rey, CA 90295, 310/578-2074

Screenplays:
KISS OF VENUS
GRADUATE'S PRIZE
THE FORBIDDEN KILL
REBIRTH
THE PORNOGRAPHERS
CRUSADE FOR HEAVEN
ELLIE
THE HONEYMOON
A GIRL CALLED BOOTS

DOUG RICHARDSON*
Agent: CAA - Beverly Hills, 310/288-4545

DIE HARD 2: DIE HARDER   20th Century Fox, 1990,
   w/Steven E. deSouza

Screenplays:
THE MONEY TRAIN (Columbia)
HELL BENT - AND BACK w/Rick Jaffa
CRY MERCY
TELEGRAPH ROAD
PRAVDA
HONOR BRIGHT
LAWYERS, GUNS AND MONEY
FINAL APPEAL

MIKE RICHARDSON
Contact: Dark Horse Entertainment - 310/396-5937

TIMECOP   Universal, 1994, Story w/Mark Verheiden

PETER RICHARDSON
Contact: Comic Strip Ltd., 43a Berwick St., London W1V 3RE,
   071/439-9509, fax 734-2793

THE SUPERGRASS   Hemdale, 1986,
   w/Peter Richens, directed
EAT THE RICH   New Line Cinema, 1987,
   w/Peter Richens, directed
THE POPE MUST DIE   Miramax, 1991,
   w/Peter Richens, directed

SCOBIE RICHARDSON
WILD CARD (CTF)   Davis Entertainment/MCA Television
   Entertainment, 1992

SCOTT RICHARDSON*
Contact: WGA - Los Angeles, 310/550-1000

HEARTS OF FIRE   Lorimar, 1988, w/Joe Eszterhas

Screenplays:
LOST WEEKEND

SY RICHARDSON
POSSE   Gramercy, 1993, w/Dario Scardapane

JACE RICHDALE*
Agent: United Talent Agency - Beverly Hills, 310/273-6700

Screenplays:
INCURABLE ROMANTIC
SOUL PATROL
DARE TO BE GREAT

WILLIAM RICHERT*
Agent: The Marion Rosenberg Office - Los Angeles, 213/653-7383

LAW AND DISORDER   Columbia, 1974,
   w/Kenneth Harris Fishman & Ivan Passer
THE HAPPY HOOKER   Double H, 1975
WINTER KILLS   Avco Embassy, 1979, directed
THE AMERICAN SUCCESS CO.   *SUCCESS* Columbia, 1979,
   w/Larry Cohen, directed
A NIGHT IN THE LIFE OF JIMMY REARDON   20th Century Fox,
   1988, directed

Screenplays:
MAN IN THE IRON MASK (directing)
MEDICINE WOMAN
PRIZZI'S FAMILY
THE PRESIDENT ELOPES
SUGARPUSS

MORDECAI RICHLER
Agent: ICM - New York, 212/556-5600

NO LOVE FOR JOHNNIE   Rank, 1960, w/Nicholas Phipps
YOUNG AND WILLING   *THE WILD AND THE WILLING* Rank,
   1962, w/Nicholas Phipps
LIFE AT THE TOP   Columbia, 1965
THE APPRENTICESHIP OF DUDDY KRAVITZ ★   Paramount, 1974
FUN WITH DICK AND JANE   Columbia, 1977, w/Jerry Belson &
   David Giler
JACOB TWO-TWO MEETS THE HOODED FANG
   Cinema Shares International, 1978
JOSHUA THEN AND NOW   20th Century Fox, 1985

Screenplays:
THE BOYS
ST. URBAIN'S HORSEMAN

JEFFREY RICHMAN*
Agent: William Morris Agency - Beverly Hills, 310/274-7451

Screenplays:
NEXT OF KIN w/Joyce Gittlin
DIRTY WORDS w/Joyce Gittlin

MEG RICHMAN*
Agent: APA - Los Angeles, 310/273-0744

Screenplays:
WINGS OF AN ANGEL
SISTER'S KEEPER
SUMMER OF LOVE
QUICKSAND
THE LIVING LAGOON
SHOUTED FIRE

ANTHONY RICHMOND
Agent: Paul Gerard Agency - Newport Beach, 714/644-7950

DEJA VU   Cannon, 1985, w/Ezra D. Rappaport &
   Arnold Schmidt, directed

BILL RICHMOND*
Agent: Paradigm - Los Angeles, 310/277-4400

THE LADIES' MAN   Paramount, 1961, w/Jerry Lewis
THE NUTTY PROFESSOR   Paramount, 1963, w/Jerry Lewis
THE FAMILY JEWELS   Paramount, 1965, w/Jerry Lewis

THE BIG MOUTH   Columbia, 1967, w/Jerry Lewis
SMORGASBORD   Warner Bros., 1985, w/Jerry Lewis

Screenplays:
OFF AND RUNNING
THE NUTTY PROFESSOR II

JOSHUA C. RICHMOND
Agent: Emile Gladstone, The Agency - Los Angeles, 310/551-3000

Screenplays:
FROM BEHIND THE SUN
DARK STAR
MY FRIEND IN PARIS w/Ellen Sussman
RED LIGHT w/Ellen Sussman
U-239 w/Stuart Goldberg

LEN RICHMOND
Agent: Paul Kohner, Inc. - Beverly Hills, 310/550-1060

AGONY   1993, directed

Screenplays:
GUYS
RISKY KISSES

ERIC A. RICHTER
THE INHERITORS   Island Alive, 1985, w/Walter Bannert

W.D. RICHTER*
Agent: Shapiro/Lichtman - Los Angeles, 310/859-8877

SLITHER   MGM, 1972
PEEPER   *FAT CHANCE* 20th Century-Fox, 1975
NICKELODEON   Columbia, 1976, w/Peter Bogdanovich
INVASION OF THE BODY SNATCHERS   United Artists, 1978
DRACULA   Universal, 1979
BRUBAKER ★   20th Century-Fox, 1980, w/Arthur Ross
ALL NIGHT LONG   Universal, 1981
HARD FEELINGS   Astral Bellvue, 1981
BIG TROUBLE IN LITTLE CHINA   20th Century Fox,
   1986, Adaptation
HANG TOUGH   Moviestore Entertainment, 1990, w/John Herzfeld,
   filmed in 1980
NEEDFUL THINGS   Columbia, 1993

Screenplays:
HOME FOR THE HOLIDAYS (Poly Gram)
EVERYONE'S IN LOVE
DRAWN BY DESIRE
EXTREME MEASURES
JUST LIKE NEW YORK
WORDS AND MUSIC
LES REPOUX
SECOND MARRIAGE
THE CHRIS LUKAS PROJECT
ROBOTO
ALLEY OOP
THE BUSINESS STORY
THE NINJA
HOME OF THE BRAVE
PURSUIT
TERROR SHIP
WINGING IT
BEFORE WE SAY GOODBYE
NIGHT PEOPLE
SUDDEN TURNS
GYROSCOPE
JUMBO MURDERS
DEADLY HONEYMOON
TERROR ON DUNCAN ISLAND
THE MASTER
SILENT NIGHT
RIOTOUS ASSEMBLY
MANIAC SLAYS BLONDE
RUBY RED
ROCKY MOUNTAIN TIME
STARLIGHT PARADE
TERATOMA

F
I
L
M

W
R
I
T
E
R
S

WILLIAM HARLAN RICHTER*
Agent: CAA - Beverly Hills, 310/288-4545

Screenplays:
REVOLVER
BURNING DAYLIGHT

THOMAS RICKMAN*
Agent: CAA - Beverly Hills, 310/288-4545

KANSAS CITY BOMBER MGM, 1972, w/Calvin Clements
THE LAUGHING POLICEMAN 20th Century-Fox, 1973
THE WHITE DAWN Paramount, 1976, w/James Houston
W.W. AND THE DIXIE DANCEKINGS 20th Century-Fox, 1975
HOOPER Warner Bros., 1978, w/Bill Kerby
COAL MINER'S DAUGHTER ★ Universal, 1980
THE RIVER R'T Paramount, 1984, directed
EVERYBODY'S ALL-AMERICAN Warner Bros., 1988

Screenplays:
BLESS THE CHILD
THE SEA WOLF
STARS FELL ON ALABAMA w/Billy Field
TWO-PENNY SPARROW
THE LEAVINGS OF B.T. WOMECK
WORLDBEATER
COLOR MAN
THE ZIG-ZAG MAN

RICK RIDGEWAY
Manager: Creative Alliance Management - Los Angeles,
  213/962-6090

Screenplays:
MAN-EATER
FLYING FREE

PHILIP RIDLEY
Agent: A.P. Watt Ltd., 20 John St., London WC1N 2DR,
  071/405-6774, fax 831-2154

THE KRAYS Miramax, 1990
THE REFLECTING SKIN Prestige Films, 1991, directed

WILLIAM RIEAD
SCORPION Crown International, 1986, directed

JOHN RIECK
Agent: William Morris Agency - Beverly Hills, 310/274-7451

Screenplays:
STOVE CITY

GUY RIEDEL*
(Michael G. Riedel)
Agent: Sherry Robb, AFH Management - Los Angeles, 213/965-8780

Screenplays:
FLAWLESS

DEAN F. RIESNER*
Contact: WGA - Los Angeles, 310/550-1000

THE HELEN MORGAN STORY Warner Bros., 1957,
  w/Nelson Gidding, Stephen Longstreet & Oscar Saul
COOGAN'S BLUFF Universal, 1968, w/Herman Miller &
  Howard Rodman
PLAY MISTY FOR ME Universal, 1971, w/Jo Heims
DIRTY HARRY Warner Bros., 1971, w/Harry Julian Fink &
  Rita M. Fink
CHARLEY VARRICK Universal, 1973, w/Howard Rodman
THE TAKE 1974
THE ENFORCER Warner Bros., 1976, w/Stirling Silliphant
FATAL BEAUTY MGM/UA, 1987, w/Hilary Henkin

Screenplays:
HIGH COUNTRY
I LOVE YOU

ADAM RIFKIN*
Agent: William Morris Agency - Beverly Hills, 310/274-7451

NEVER ON TUESDAY Palisades Entertainment, 1990, directed
THE DARK BACKWARD Greycat Films, 1991, directed
THE CHASE 20th Century Fox, 1994, directed

Screenplays:
WEIRDSVILLE
HELLBREAK
PICKLE ON MY TONGUE
MAMA'S BOY

NANCY RIFKIN
THE UNSEEN World Northal, 1981, Story w/Peter Foleg,
  Michael L. Grace & Kim Henkel

JOHN RILEY*
Agent: Alan Mehi, The Adam Green Agency - 310/277-1541

Screenplays:
DEADLOCK

ROB RILEY*
Contact: 312/929-3355

NUMBER ONE WITH A BULLET Cannon, 1987,
  w/Gail Morgan Hickman, Andrew Kurtzman & James Belushi

JETTE RINCK*
Contact: WGA - Los Angeles, 310/550-1000

TUFF TURF New World, 1985

Screenplays:
TRIBES
GLASS HOUSE

DAVID W. RINTELS*
Agent: CAA - Beverly Hills, 310/288-4545

SCORPIO United Artists, 1972, w/Gerald Wilson
NOT WITHOUT MY DAUGHTER MGM-Pathe, 1991

Screenplays:
ANDERSONVILLE (CTF)

JONATHAN RINTELS*
Agent: Jim Preminger Agency - Los Angeles, 310/475-9491

Screenplays:
BREAKING THE CHAIN
LAND'S END
SUPERBABY

MICHAEL RISSI*
Agent: United Talent Agency - Beverly Hills, 310/273-6700

Screenplays:
FEAR BOOK
BORDERLINE

MICHAEL RITCHIE*
Contact: WGA - New York, 212/245-6180

COOL RUNNINGS Buena Vista, 1993, Story w/Lynn Siefert

ROB RITCHIE
THE INVESTIGATION: INSIDE A TERRORIST BOMBING (CTF)
  Granada Television, 1990

JOE RITTER
THE TOXIC AVENGER   Troma, 1985

JOYCE RITTER
INDEPENDENCE   20th Century-Fox, 1976, w/Thomas McGrath &
   Lloyd Ritter

LLOYD RITTER
INDEPENDENCE   20th Century-Fox, 1976, w/Thomas McGrath &
   Joyce Ritter

JAMES J. RITZ*
Contact: WGA - Los Angeles, 310/550-1000

LEO AND LOREE   United Artists, 1980

THOMAS RITZ
Contact: Linda Lichter, Lichter, Grossman & Nichols - Los Angeles,
   310/205-6999
Business: Maverick Productions, 818/766-9984 (also fax)

MARTIAL OUTLAW   Republic Pictures, 1993

Screenplays:
OPEN FIRE   (Image Organization)
GOOD MORNING HEARTACHE
SMOKING GUN
TEN DEGREES SOUTHWEST
DOG'S LIFE
ON THE LINE

JERRY RIVERS
BEVERLY HILLS BRATS   Taurus Entertainment, 1989,
   Story w/Terry Moore

JOAN RIVERS*
Business Manager: Nigro, Karlin & Segal - 310/277-4657

SALLY MARR...AND HER ESCORTS (P) w/Lonny Price &
   Erin Sanders
RABBIT TEST   Avco Embassy, 1978,
   w/Jay A. Reback, directed

DAVID ROACH
YOUNG EINSTEIN   Warner Bros., 1989, w/Yahoo Serious
RECKLESS KELLY   Warner Bros., 1993, w/Yahoo Serious,
   Warwick Ross & Lulu Serious

JANET ROACH*
Agent: United Talent Agency - Beverly Hills, 310/273-6700

PRIZZI'S HONOR ★   20th Century Fox, 1985,
   w/Richard Condon
MR. NORTH   Samuel Goldwyn Company, 1988,
   w/John Huston & James Costigan

Screenplays:
PROSPECT
FIRST WIVE'S CLUB
BUCK ISLAND
FREUD'S HAT
CAPER
IN HER OWN IMAGE

M. JAY ROACH*
Agent: ICM - Beverly Hills, 310/550-4000

BLOWN AWAY   MGM/UA, 1994, Story w/Joe Batteer &
   John Rice

Screenplays:
FORGOTTEN IMPULSES w/John Martin

ALLISON ROBBINS*
Agent: CAA - Beverly Hills, 310/288-4545

METROPOLITAN PRAIRIE (P)
THE READING LESSON (P)
YOU AIN'T KNOWN TRUE HATRED TIL YOUR CAR'S
   BEEN TOWED (P)

Screenplays:
SERIOUS MONEY
SLOW TIME
CONEY ISLAND
TIL DEATH DO US PART w/Mario Radosta
THE ARRANGEMENT w/Mario Radosta

KATE ROBBINS
Agent: Writers & Artists Agency - Los Angeles, 310/824-6300

Screenplays:
FIELDS OF FIRE w/Carol Kaplan

MATTHEW L. ROBBINS*
Agent: ICM - Beverly Hills, 310/550-4000

THE SUGARLAND EXPRESS   Universal, 1974, w/Hal Barwood &
   Steven Spielberg
THE BINGO LONG TRAVELING ALL-STARS & MOTOR KINGS
   Universal, 1976, w/Hal Barwood
MACARTHUR   Universal, 1977, w/Hal Barwood
CORVETTE SUMMER   MGM/United Artists, 1978,
   w/Hal Barwood, directed
DRAGONSLAYER   Paramount, 1981, w/Hal Barwood, directed
WARNING SIGN   20th Century Fox, 1985, w/Hal Barwood
BATTERIES NOT INCLUDED   Universal, 1987, w/Brad Bird,
   Brent Maddock & S.S. Wilson, directed

Screenplays:
THE GRID w/Hal Barwood
NEWSREEL w/Hal Barwood
WITNESSES w/Hal Barwood
HOME FREE w/Hal Barwood
NIGHT SHADE w/Hal Barwood

RICHARD P. ROBBINS*
Contact: WGA - Los Angeles, 310/550-1000

CHOMPS   American-International, 1979, w/Duane Poole

TIM ROBBINS
Agent: ICM - Beverly Hills, 310/550-4000

CARNAGE (P)
MAYHEM: THE INVASION (P)
BOB ROBERTS   Miramax/Paramount, 1992, directed

Screenplays:
DEAD MAN WALKING (directing)

VINCENT ROBERT*
Agent: Writers & Artists Agency - Los Angeles, 310/824-6300
Contact: 213/931-0730

RED SURF   Arrowhead Entertainment, 1990

Screenplays:
BONES
THE GHOULS
BROTHERS OF THE COAST
LONG SHADOWS
SECOND CHANCE

BARRY ROBERTS
LEGAL TENDER   Prism Entertainment, 1991

DARRYL ROBERTS

Contact: Avant Garde Productions, 312/488-4787

HOW U LIKE ME NOW   Shapiro Glickenhaus, 1993, directed

Screenplays:
IF WE RAN IT

JOE ROBERTS

MY TUTOR   Crown International, 1983

JONATHAN ROBERTS*

Agent: United Talent Agency - Beverly Hills, 310/273-6700

ONCE BITTEN   Samuel Goldwyn Company, 1985, w/Jeff Hause &
   David Hines
THE SURE THING   Embassy, 1985, w/Steven Bloom
THE LION KING (AF)   Buena Vista, 1994, w/Irene Mecchi &
   Linda Woolverton

Screenplays:
JAMES AND THE GIANT PEACH (AF)
FRANKENSTEIN GOES TO HARLEM
DREAM DATE   w/Steven Bloom

JUNE ROBERTS*

Agent: CAA - Beverly Hills, 310/288-4545

EXPERIENCE PREFERRED BUT NOT ESSENTIAL
   Samuel Goldwyn Company, 1983
MERMAIDS   Orion, 1990

Screenplays:
FUNNY PECULIAR (Samuel Goldwyn Company)
PHONY FARM w/Laura Cunningham
TWO BIT ROMANCE w/Randi Mayem Singer
WORLD WAR II
KICK

SCOTT ROBERTS

THE AMERICAN WAY   *RIDERS OF THE STORM*   Miramax, 1987
K2   Paramount, 1992, w/Patrick Meyers

Screenplays:
ONCE UPON A TIME IN THE UNIVERSE

STEVE ROBERTS*

Agent: Writers & Artists Agency - Los Angeles, 310/824-6300

Screenplays:
THE TRACKER (New Line Cinema)
BACKFIRE
CYBERPUNK
EXTRA TIME
TITUS GROAN

STEVE ROBERTS

THE RETURN OF JAFAR (AHVF)   Buena Vista, 1994,
   w/Kevin Campbell, Mirith J.S. Colao, Bill Motz, Bob Roth,
   Jan Strand & Brian Swenlin

WILLIAM ROBERTS*

Contact: WGA - Los Angeles, 310/550-1000

YOU FOR ME   MGM, 1952
EASY TO LOVE   MGM, 1953, w/Laslo Vadnay
FAST COMPANY   MGM, 1953
HER TWELVE MEN   MGM, 1954, w/Laura Z. Hobson
THE MATING GAME   MGM , 1959
THE MAGNIFICENT SEVEN   United Artists, 1960
COME FLY WITH ME   MGM, 1962
THE WONDERFUL WORLD OF THE BROTHERS GRIMM   MGM,
   1962, w/Charles Beaumont & David P. Herman
THE BRIDGE AT REMAGEN   United Artists, 1968,
   w/Richard Yates

DEVIL'S BRIGADE   United Artists, 1968
ONE MORE TRAIN TO ROB   Universal, 1971
RED SUN   National General, 1972, w/Laird Koenig,
   Denne Bart Petitclerc & Lawrence Roman
THE LAST AMERICAN HERO   20th Century-Fox, 1973,
   w/Bill Kerby
POSSE   Paramount, 1975, w/Christopher Knopf
THE LEGEND OF THE LONE RANGER   Universal/AFD, 1981,
   w/Ivan Goff, Michael Kane & Ben Roberts
10 TO MIDNIGHT   Cannon, 1983

Screenplays:
SAM BASS: THE MAKING OF AN OUTLAW w/Al Ruggerio
THE RETURN OF MAGDA LA SELVA

BILL ROBERTSON

THE EVENTS LEADING UP TO MY DEATH   Flat Rock Films,
   1992, directed

CLIFF ROBERTSON*

Contact: Robertson & Associates - 818/988-1130

J.W. COOP   Columbia, 1971, w/Gary Cartwright &
   Bud Shrake, directed

HARRY ROBERTSON

HAWK THE SLAYER   ITC, 1976, w/Terry Marcel

MICHAEL ROBERTSON

Contact: Peter Martin Nelson, Nelson, Guggenheim & Felker -
   Los Angeles, 310/207-8337

Screenplays:
BACK OF BEYOND w/Rick Sawyer (directing)

ROBBIE ROBERTSON*

Manager: Addis-Wechsler - Los Angeles, 213/954-9000

CARNY   United Artists, 1980, Story w/Phoebe Kaylor &
   Robert Kaylor

WILLIAM PRESTON ROBERTSON*

Contact: WGA - Los Angeles, 310/550-1000

Screenplays:
JOHNNY SKIDMARKS (Shared)
CULT COP
WITCHES
DECEIT (Shared)

JOHN M. ROBINS

DEATH SHIP   Avco Embassy, 1980
HOT RESORT   Cannon, 1985, w/Boaz Davidson &
   Norman Hudis, directed

OLIVER ROBINS

Agent: Writers & Artists Agency - Los Angeles, 310/824-6300

Screenplays:
LOOT

BRUCE C. ROBINSON*

Agent: CAA - Beverly Hills, 310/288-4545

THE KILLING FIELDS ★   Warner Bros., 1984
WITHNAIL AND I   Cineplex Odeon, 1987, directed
HOW TO GET AHEAD IN ADVERTISING   Warner Bros.,
   1989, directed
FAT MAN AND LITTLE BOY   Paramount, 1989, w/Roland Joffe
JENNIFER 8   Paramount, 1992, directed

Screenplays:
AN ACT OF LOVE

BUTCH ROBINSON
THE DROP SQUAD   Gramercy, 1994, w/D. Clark Johnson

LEE ROBINSON
THE HIGHEST HONOR   New World, 1984

PHIL ALDEN ROBINSON*
Agent: CAA - Beverly Hills, 310/288-4545 & Peter Turner Agency -
   Santa Monica, 310/315-4772
Business: Universal Pictures, 818/777-5055

RHINESTONE   20th Century Fox, 1984, w/Sylvester Stallone
ALL OF ME   Universal, 1984
IN THE MOOD *THE WOO WOO KID*   Lorimar, 1987, directed
FIELD OF DREAMS ★   Universal, 1989, directed
RELENTLESS   New Line Cinema, 1989, as "Jack T.D. Robinson"
SNEAKERS   Universal, 1992, w/Lawrence Lasker &
   Walter Parkes, directed

Screenplays:
ZLATA'S DIARY

RICHARD ROBINSON
KINGDOM OF THE SPIDERS   Dimension, 1977, w/Alan Cailou

SALLY ROBINSON*
Manager: International Arts Entertainment - Los Angeles,
   310/551-0014
Business: Dayjob Films, Universal Pictures, 818/777-8322

MEDICINE MAN   Buena Vista, 1992, w/Tom Schulman
A FAR OFF PLACE   Buena Vista, 1993, w/Robert Caswell &
   Jonathan Hensleigh

Screenplays:
WANTED

TODD ROBINSON*
Agent: Paradigm - Los Angeles, 310/277-4400

Screenplays:
THE FOUR DIAMONDS
WHITE SQUALL
A PASSAGE HOME

TOM ROBINSON
SALVATION!   Circle Releasing, 1987, w/Beth B & Scott B

ED ROBOTO
CLUB PARADISE   Warner Bros., 1986, Story w/Tom Leopold,
   Chris Miller & David Standish

MICHAEL ROBSON
HOLOCAUST 2000 *THE CHOSEN*   Rank, 1977,
   w/Alberto De Martino & Sergio Donati
THE 39 STEPS   International Picture Show, 1978
THE WATER BABIES   Pethurst International/Film Polski, 1978

MARC ROCCO
Agent: CAA - Beverly Hills, 310/288-4545
Business: Yankee Entertainment Group, 3815 W. Olive Ave. -
   Suite 201, Burbank, CA 91505, 818/954-0780

DREAM A LITTLE DREAM   Vestron, 1989, w/D.E. Eisenberg &
   Daniel Jay Franklin, directed
WHERE THE DAY TAKES YOU   New Line Cinema, 1992,
   w/Michael Hitchcock & Kurt Voss, directed

ERIC ROCHANT
Contact: French Film Office, 745 Fifth Avenue, New York,
   NY 10151, 212/832-8860

TOO MUCH   Cannon, 1987, directed
THE 5TH MONKEY   21st Century Film Corporation, 1990, directed
LOVE WITHOUT PITY   UGC, 1991, directed

CHRIS ROCK*
Agent: William Morris Agency - Beverly Hills, 310/274-7451

CB4   Universal, 1993, w/Nelson George & Robert LoCash

JAY DEE ROCK
(See Will Aldis & Steven Kampmann)

KEVIN ROCK
THE PHILADELPHIA EXPERIMENT 2   Trimark, 1993, w/Nick Paine
WARLOCK: THE ARMAGEDDON   Trimark, 1993, w/Sam Bernard

Screenplays:
PHANTOMS (Miramax)
THE SPIRIT REALM w/David Markov
THE DAHAK

ALEXANDRE ROCKWELL
Agent: United Talent Agency - Beverly Hills, 310/273-6700
Business Manager: Guild Management Company - Los Angeles,
   310/277-9711

SONS   Pacific Pictures, 1989, w/Brandon Cole, directed
IN THE SOUP   Triton Pictures, 1992, w/Tim Kissell, directed
SOMEBODY TO LOVE   Lumiere Pictures, 1994,
   w/Sergei Bodrov, directed
FOUR ROOMS   Miramax, 1995, "Two Sides of a Plate," directed

ROBERT RODAT*
Agent: The Irv Schechter Company - Beverly Hills, 310/278-8070

THE COMRADES OF SUMMER (CTF)   Grossbart/Barnett, 1992
TALL TALE   Buena Vista, 1994, w/Steve Bloom

Screenplays:
THE RIPPER
THE CHRISTMAS CONSPIRACY
INSPECTOR GENERAL
THE EX-MR. WINFIELD
STRANGE HEARTS
ROGUES w/Steve Bloom
HUCKSTERS
DANCING IN THE DARK
FATHER GOOSE

MARY RODGERS*
Agent: Paramuse Artists - New York, 212/758-5055

FREAKY FRIDAY   Buena Vista, 1977
THE DEVIL AND MAX DEVLIN   Buena Vista, 1981

ADAM D. RODMAN*
Agent: Preferred Artists - Encino, 818/990-0305

THE SERPENT AND THE RAINBOW   Universal, 1987,
   w/Richard Maxwell, as "A.R. Simoun"

Screenplays:
THE SILENT MAN
ACT OF FAITH
BUG JACK BARRON
DOUBTING THOMAS
THE BIG THICKET
D.E.A.

HOWARD A. RODMAN*
Agent: CAA - Beverly Hills, 310/288-4545

Screenplays:
THE THREE STIGMATA OF PALMER ELDRITCH
SOUTH OF HEAVEN
DADDY EMPIRE
DESTINY EXPRESS
SOMEBODY ELSE

ROBERT RODRIGUEZ*
Agent: ICM - Beverly Hills, 310/550-4000

BEDHEAD (Short)   directed
EL MARIACHI   Columbia, 1993, directed
ROADRACERS (CTF)   Showtime/Drive-In Classic Cinema, 1994,
   w/Tommy Nix,   directed
FOUR ROOMS   Miramax, 1995, "The Misbehavers," directed

Screenplays:
RETURN OF THE MARIACHI (directing)
TIL DEATH DO US PART

MICHAEL ROEMER
Contact: Yale School of Art, Box 1605A, Yale Station, New Haven,
   CT 06520, 203/432-2600

NOTHING BUT A MAN   Cinema 5, 1965, co-directed
THE PLOT AGAINST HARRY   New Yorker, 1990, directed,
   filmed in 1968

Screenplays:
FAMOUS LONG AGO

JOSH ROGAN
TWILIGHT ZONE - THE MOVIE   Warner Bros., 1983,
   Segment 2 w/George Clayton Johnson & Richard Matheson

BRIAN ROGERS
Agent: Elliot Wax & Associates - Los Angeles, 310/273-8217

Screenplays:
THE BUSINESS TRIP

STEVEN ROGERS
Agent: United Talent Agency - Beverly Hills, 310/273-6700

Screenplays:
KATE AND LEOPOLD

TOM ROGERS
Agent: Paradigm - Los Angeles, 310/277-4400

Screenplays:
NEVERMORE
COLD FEET

ROY ROGOSIN
Contact: 603/433-4472

WEEKEND WARRIORS   The Movie Store, 1986, w/Bruce Belland

MARCUS ROLLING
CLASS OF NUKE 'EM HIGH 2: SUBHUMANOID MELTDOWN
   Troma, 1991, w/Lloyd Kaufman, Eric Louzil, Carl Morano,
   Jeffrey W. Sass & Matt Unger

BERNIE ROLLINS
Agent: Schiowitz/Clay/Rose - Los Angeles, 213/650-7300

GETTING OVER   Continental Films, 1981

LAWRENCE ROMAN*
Agent: Paradigm - Los Angeles, 310/277-4400

ALONE TOGETHER (P)
P.S. I LOVE YOU (P)
COULDA, WOULDA, SHOULDA (P)
MOVING MOUNTAINS (P)
GRAPES AND RAISINS (P)
VICE SQUAD   United Artists, 1953
DRUMS ACROSS THE RIVER   Universal-International, 1954,
   w/John K. Butler
NAKED ALIBI   Universal-International, 1954

ONE DESIRE   Universal-International, 1955, w/Robert Blees
THE MAN FROM BITTER RIDGE   Universal-International, 1955
A KISS BEFORE DYING   United Artists, 1956
THE SHARK FIGHTERS   United Artists, 1956, w/John Robinson
SLAUGHTER ON TENTH AVENUE   Universal-International, 1957
UNDER THE YUM YUM TREE   Columbia, 1963, w/David Swift,
   from his play
THE SWINGER   Paramount, 1966
PAPER LION   United Artists, 1968
RED SUN   National General, 1972, w/Laird Koenig,
   Denne Bart Petitclerc & William Roberts
A WARM DECEMBER   National General, 1973
McQ   Warner Bros., 1974
FINAL VERDICT (CTF)   Turner Pictures, 1991
THE ERNEST GREEN STORY (CTF)   Walt Disney Co., 1993

Screenplays:
THE BOSTON MASSACRE (CTF)
COULDA, WOULDA, SHOULDA

MARK ROMANEK
Contact: 213/462-6400

STATIC   Sandstar Releasing, 1989, w/Keith Gordon, directed

Screenplays:
CRASH
GHOST BOY MOON

NEIL ROMANEK
Agent: Jon Klane Agency - Beverly Hills, 310/278-0178

Screenplays:
CARNIVAL EARTH
JACK OF HEARTS
BOUDICA
NEMO

GITA ROMANO*
Agent: Susan Smith & Associates - Beverly Hills, 213/852-4777

Screenplays:
STILL
MAN'S WORLD
PARUMP
DREAMSEX ·

JOHN ROMANO*
Agent: CAA - Beverly Hills, 310/288-4545

KEY EXCHANGE   20th Century Fox, 1985, under pseudonym,
   w/Paul Kurta

Screenplays:
TRAIL OF THE FOX
A WOMAN'S PLACE
ACTS
MARRIAGE OR BUST
PERFUME

RICHARD ROMANUS*
Contact: WGA - Los Angeles, 310/550-1000

Screenplays:
FAMILY VALUES w/Lisa James

GEORGE A. ROMERO*
Agent: The Gersh Agency - Beverly Hills, 310/274-6611

THE CRAZIES *CODE NAME: TRIXIE* Cambist, 1972, directed
HUNGRY WIVES   Jack H. Harris Enterprises, 1973, directed
MARTIN   Libra, 1978, directed
DAWN OF THE DEAD   United Film Distribution, 1979, directed
KNIGHTRIDERS   United Film Distribution, 1981
DAY OF THE DEAD   United Film Distribution, 1985, directed
CREEPSHOW 2   New World, 1987

MONKEY SHINES   Orion, 1988, directed
TALES FROM THE DARKSIDE   Paramount, 1990,
   "Cat From Hell"
NIGHT OF THE LIVING DEAD   21st Century Film
   Corporation, 1990
TWO EVIL EYES   Taurus Entertainment, 1991,
   "The Curious Facts in the Case of Mr. Valdemar," directed
THE DARK HALF   Orion, 1993, directed

Screenplays:
FLYING HORSES

JOHN ROMO
DEAD WOMEN IN LINGERIE   Seagate Films, 1990, w/Erica Fox

THOMAS R. RONDINELLA
Contact: 201/736-5221

BLADES   Troma, 1988, w/William Pace, directed
ALL'S FAIR   Moviestore Entertainment, 1989, w/John Finnegan,
   William Pace & Randee Russell
A GIRL'S GUIDE (CTF)   USA Network/Six Shooter Productions,
   1993, w/William Pace, directed

Screenplays:
TREETOPS   w/William Pace
FAMILY RITES   w/William Pace
HEART OF FORTUNE   (Shared)

DARRELL ROODT
Contact: Showdata, Johan Blignant, 11 Frost Ave., Auckland
   Park 2092, Johannesburg, South Africa, 27-11/482-1382

PLACE OF WEEPING   New World, 1986, directed
JOBMAN   Blue Rock Films, 1990, w/Gregg Latter, directed

KEVIN ROONEY*
Agent: United Talent Agency - Beverly Hills, 310/273-6700

Screenplays:
FOOLS PARADISE   w/J.J. Wall
CARTOON   w/Brant Von Hoffman

MICKEY ROONEY
Contact: Harstad/Lund Productions - 505/982-7100

THE LEGEND OF O.B. TAGGART   Northern Arts
   Entertainment, 1995

DONALD P. ROOS*
Agent: ICM - Beverly Hills, 310/550-4000

SINGLE WHITE FEMALE   Columbia, 1992
LOVE FIELD   Orion, 1992
BOYS ON THE SIDE   Warner Bros., 1995

Screenplays:
DIABOLIQUE

TOM ROPELEWSKI*
Manager: Linne Radmin, The Radmin Company - Beverly Hills,
   310/274-9515

THE KISS   Tri-Star, 1988, w/Stephen Volk
LOVERBOY   Tri-Star, 1989, w/Leslie Dixon & Robin Schiff
MADHOUSE   Orion, 1990, directed
LOOK WHO'S TALKING NOW   TriStar, 1993,
   w/Leslie Dixon, directed

Screenplays:
THE NEXT BEST THING   (directing)
COUNTERFEIT FATHER   w/Evan Katz

CYD ROPP
Agent: APA - Los Angeles, 310/273-0744

Screenplays:
VR WORLD

ANDY ROSE*
Contact: WGA - Los Angeles, 310/550-1000

Screenplays:
PLAY MONEY   FUNNY MONEY   w/Alex Gorby
SPAGHETTI MEN
McHALE'S NAVY

BERNARD ROSE*
Agent: CAA - Beverly Hills, 310/288-4545

PAPER HOUSE   Vestron, 1988, directed
CANDYMAN   TriStar, 1992, directed
IMMORTAL BELOVED   Columbia, 1994, directed

JACK ROSE*
Contact: WGA - Los Angeles, 310/550-1000

ROAD TO RIO   Paramount, 1947, w/Edmund Beloin
SORROWFUL JONES   Paramount, 1949, w/Mel Shavelson &
   Edmund Hartmann
ALWAYS LEAVE THEM LAUGHING   Warner Bros., 1949,
   w/Mel Shavelson
THE DAUGHTER OF ROSIE O'GRADY   Warner Bros., 1950,
   w/Peter Milne & Mel Shavelson
ON MOONLIGHT BAY   Warner Bros., 1951, w/Mel Shavelson
ROOM FOR ONE MORE   Warner Bros., 1952, w/Mel Shavelson
APRIL IN PARIS   Warner Bros., 1952, w/Mel Shavelson
I'LL SEE YOU IN MY DREAMS   Warner Bros., 1952,
   w/Mel Shavelson
TROUBLE ALONG THE WAY   Warner Bros., 1953,
   w/Mel Shavelson
LIVING IT UP   Paramount, 1954, w/Mel Shavelson
THE SEVEN LITTLE FOYS ★   Paramount, 1955, w/Mel Shavelson
BEAU JAMES   Paramount, 1957, w/Mel Shavelson
HOUSEBOAT   Paramount, 1958, w/Mel Shavelson
THE FIVE PENNIES   Paramount, 1959, w/Mel Shavelson
IT STARTED IN NAPLES   Paramount, 1960, w/Mel Shavelson &
   Susi Cecchi d'Amico
ON THE DOUBLE   Paramount, 1961, w/Mel Shavelson
WHO'S GOT THE ACTION?   Paramount, 1962
PAPA'S DELICATE CONDITION   Paramount, 1963
WHO'S BEEN SLEEPING IN MY BED?   Paramount, 1963
A TOUCH OF CLASS ★   Avco Embassy, 1973, w/Melvin Frank
LOST AND FOUND   Columbia, 1979, w/Melvin Frank
THE GREAT MUPPET CAPER   Universal/AFD, 1981, w/Jerry Juhl,
   Tom Patchett & Jay Tarses

JOEL ROSE*
Agent: William Morris Agency - New York, 212/586-5100

DEAD WEEKEND   I.R.S. Media, 1995

Screenplays:
IT'S NOT SUPERSTITION
KILL THE POOR   w/Alan Taylor

LEE ROSE*
Manager: Carlyle Management - Los Angeles, 213/469-3086

DECONSTRUCTING SARAH (CTF)   Carla Singer Productions/
   MCA Television, 1994

Screenplays:
WRONG PLANET
BACK BY 10
LEAVE OF ABSENCE
ON A WING AND A PRAYER

MICKEY ROSE*
Agent: Larry Grossman & Associates - Beverly Hills, 310/550-8127

TAKE THE MONEY AND RUN   Cinerama Releasing Corporation, 1969, w/Woody Allen
BANANAS   United Artists, 1971, w/Woody Allen
STUDENT BODIES   Paramount, 1981, directed
CONDORMAN   Buena Vista, 1981, w/Glenn Gordon Caron & Marc Stirdivant

NORVELL ROSE
THE AMITYVILLE CURSE   Allegro Films, 1990, w/Michael Krueger

REGINALD ROSE*
Contact: WGA - New York, 212/245-6180

CRIME IN THE STREETS   Allied Artists, 1956, from his teleplay
TWELVE ANGRY MEN ★   United Artists, 1957, from his play
THE MAN IN THE NET   United Artists, 1958
MAN OF THE WEST   United Artists, 1958
BAXTER   EMI, 1972
THE WILD GEESE   Rank, 1978
SOMEBODY KILLED HER HUSBAND   Columbia, 1978
WHOSE LIFE IS IT ANYWAY?   MGM/United Artists, 1981, w/Brian Clark
THE SEA WOLVES   Paramount/Lorimar, 1981
WHO DARES WINS   Rank, 1982
THE FINAL OPTION   MGM/UA, 1983
WILD GEESE II   Universal, 1986

SI ROSE*
Agent: Preferred Artists - Encino, 818/990-0305

IT HAPPENED AT THE WORLD'S FAIR   MGM, 1962, w/Seaman Jacobs
MCHALE'S NAVY   Universal, 1964

JEB ROSEBROOK*
Agent: Paul Kohner, Inc. - Beverly Hills, 310/550-1060

JUNIOR BONNER   ABC Films, 1972
THE BLACK HOLE   Buena Vista, 1979, w/Gerry Day

Screenplays:
FAST FRIENDS w/Joe Byrne

DAN ROSEN
Agent: Paradigm - Los Angeles, 310/277-4400

Screenplays:
THE LAST SUPPER

GARY ROSEN*
Agent: The Irv Schechter Company - Beverly Hills, 310/278-8070
Manager: Carlyle Management - Los Angeles, 213/469-3086

RISING STORM   Gibraltar Releasing, 1989, w/William Fay
FRAMED (CTF)   HBO Pictures, 1990
MAJOR PAYNE   Universal, 1995, w/Dean Lorey & Damon Wayans

Screenplays:
SNAP

HERBERT H. ROSEN
COASTER   Atlantic Film Group, 1981

JAY ROSEN
Agent: Renaissance-H.N. Swanson - Los Angeles, 310/246-6000

Screenplays:
TWO BY TWO w/David Golden
O POSITIVE w/David Golden

MARTIN ROSEN
Address: 305 San Anselmo Avenue, San Anselmo, CA 94960, 415/456-1414

WATERSHIP DOWN (AF)   Avco Embassy, 1978, directed
THE PLAGUE DOGS (AF)   Nepenthe Productions, 1982, directed

HENRY ROSENBAUM*
Agent: Paradigm - Los Angeles, 310/277-4400

A BULLET FOR PRETTY BOY   American International, 1970
THE DUNWICH HORROR   American International, 1970, w/Curtis Hanson & Ronald Silkowsky
BLACK MAMA, WHITE MAMA   American International, 1973
HANKY PANKY   Columbia, 1982, w/David Taylor
GET CRAZY   Embassy, 1983, w/Danny Opatoshu & David Taylor
LOCK UP   Tri-Star, 1989, w/Richard Smith & Jeb Stuart

Screenplays:
OFF SUNSET
KNOCKOUT
MR. MAUI

JEFFREY ROSENBAUM
FIREWALKER   Cannon, 1986, Story w/Norman Aladjem & Robert Gosnell

MARK ROSENBAUM
EDGE OF HONOR   Wind River, 1991, w/David O'Malley & Michael Spence

ANITA ROSENBERG*
Contact: Linda Lichter, Lichter, Grossman & Nichols - Los Angeles, 310/205-6999

MODERN GIRLS   Atlantic Releasing Corporation, 1986, Story w/Laurie Craig
ASSAULT OF THE KILLER BIMBOS   Empire Pictures, 1988, Story w/Patti Astor & Ted Nicolau, directed

CRAIG ROSENBERG
Agent: Sanford-Gross & Associates - Los Angeles, 310/208-2100

Screenplays:
ELIOT LOVES GABRIELLA

JEANNE ROSENBERG*
Agent: Innovative Artists - Los Angeles, 310/553-5200

THE BLACK STALLION   United Artists, 1979, w/Melissa Mathison & William D. Witliff
THE JOURNEY OF NATTY GANN   Buena Vista, 1985
WHITE FANG   Buena Vista, 1991, w/David Fallon & Nick Thiel
HEIDI (CTF)   Harmony Gold, 1993

Screenplays:
WOLFDOG
JACKSON HOLE

MARC ROSENBERG
HEATWAVE   New Line Cinema, 1983, w/Phillip Noyce
ENCOUNTER AT RAVEN'S GATE   Hemdale, 1987, w/Rold de Heer
DINGO   Greycat Films, 1994

MELISSA ROSENBERG*
Agent: The Irv Schechter Company - Beverly Hills, 310/278-8070

Screenplays:
A MAMBO MAN
UNTITLED DANCE MOVIE

PHIL ROSENBERG*
Agent: Favored Artists Agency - Los Angeles, 213/653-3191

Screenplays:
LYING IN WAIT (Republic Pictures)

SCOTT ROSENBERG*
Agent: ICM - Beverly Hills, 310/550-4000

AIRTIME (Short)   1991, w/Gary Fleder
THINGS TO DO IN DENVER WHEN YOU'RE DEAD
   Miramax, 1995

Screenplays:
DISTURBING BEHAVIOR (New Line Cinema)
BEAUTIFUL GIRLS
FIVE O'CLOCK SHADOW
REPEAT OFFENDER
BAD MOON RISING
BLACK ICE

DALE ROSENBLOOM*
Contact: WGA - Los Angeles, 310/550-1000

INSTANT KARMA   MGM/UA, 1990, w/Bruce A. Taylor

SETH ZVI ROSENFELD*
Agent: William Morris Agency - New York, 212/586-5100

SERVY-N-BERNICE 4EVER (P)   also screenplay
WRITING ON THE WALL (P)   also screenplay

Screenplays:
COACH
ROUND THE WAY GIRL

DAVID ROSENFELT*
Agent: Shapiro/Lichtman - Los Angeles, 310/859-8877

Screenplays:
LORD CHARLIE
DEADLOCKED

HOWARD ROSENMAN
Business: Brillstein-Grey - Beverly Hills, 310/275-6135

GROSS ANATOMY   Buena Vista, 1990,
   Story w/Alan Jay Glueckman, Stanley Isaacs & Mark Spragg

JACK ROSENTHAL*
Agent: William Morris Agency - Beverly Hills, 310/274-7451

THE KNOWLEDGE (P)   also screenplay
ANOTHER SUNDAY & SWEET PEA (P)
SMASH (P)
THE LOVERS!   British Lion, 1973
THE LUCKY STAR   Pickman Films, 1981, w/Max Fischer
YENTL   MGM/UA, 1983, w/Barbra Streisand
KIPPERBANG   *P'TANG, YANG, KIPPERBANG*
   MGM/UA Classics, 1984
THE CHAIN   Rank, 1985
THE WEDDING GIFT   Miramax, 1994

Screenplays:
NEPTUNE'S FEAST w/Mark Herman
FAMILY MATTERS
THE BEST
GABRIELA
NON-WHITE COMEDY
AND A NIGHTINGALE SANG....
CONVENTIONS

MARK D. ROSENTHAL*
Agent: CAA - Beverly Hills, 310/288-4545

THE JEWEL OF THE NILE   20th Century Fox, 1985,
   w/Larry Konner
THE LEGEND OF BILLIE JEAN   Tri-Star, 1985, w/Larry Konner
SUPERMAN IV: THE QUEST FOR PEACE   Warner Bros., 1987,
   w/Larry Konner
THE IN CROWD   Orion, 1988, w/Larry Konner, directed
DESPERATE HOURS   Warner Bros., 1990, w/Larry Konner &
   Joseph Hayes
STAR TREK VI: THE UNDISCOVERED COUNTRY   Paramount,
   1991, Story w/Larry Konner & Leonard Nimoy
FOR LOVE OR MONEY   Universal, 1993, w/Larry Konner
THE BEVERLY HILLBILLIES   20th Century Fox, 1993,
   w/Larry Konner, Jim Fisher & Jim Staahl

Screenplays:
SECOND STRING w/Larry Konner
GALE FORCE w/Larry Konner & David A. Chappe
FORTRESS w/Larry Konner
THE HIT w/Larry Konner

ROBERT J. ROSENTHAL
Contact: Gunther Schiff - 310/557-9081
Business: Apple-Rose Productions, 3961 Landmark St., Culver City,
   CA 90232, 310/204-1000

MALIBU BEACH   Crown International, 1978, w/Celia Susan Cotelo
ZAPPED!   Embassy, 1982, w/Bruce Rubin, directed

CHARLES ROSIN*
Agent: Broder-Kurland-Webb-Uffner - Beverly Hills, 310/281-3400

SILENT WITNESS: WHAT A CHILD SAW (CTF)   Power Pictures/
   The Movie Network/Hearst Entertainment, 1994, Story

MARK ROSMAN*
Contact: WGA - Los Angeles, 310/550-1000

THE HOUSE ON SORORITY ROW   Film Ventures, 1983, directed

Screenplays:
EVOLVER (directing)

MARK ROSNER*
Contact: WGA - Los Angeles, 310/550-1000

SAVE THE LAST DANCE FOR ME (Short)   directed
ON OCEAN FRONT WALK (FD)   1977, directed

Screenplays:
RIVALS
STRANGLEHOLD COACH
COMBAT ZONE

ALAN DUNCAN ROSS*
Contact: Irell & Manella - Los Angeles, 310/203-7945

Screenplays:
CALIFORNIA DREAMIN
DOUBLE BLIND

ARTHUR ROSS*
Contact: WGA - Los Angeles, 310/550-1000

THE STAND AT APACHE RIVER   Universal-International, 1953
THE CREATURE FROM THE BLACK LAGOON
   Universal-International, 1954, w/Harry Essex
THE THREE WORLDS OF GULLIVER   Columbia, 1959,
   w/Jack Sher
BRUBAKER ★   20th Century-Fox, 1980, Story w/W.D. Richter

BRIAN L. ROSS*
Agent: Camden-ITG - Los Angeles, 310/289-2700

THE SECRET PASSION OF ROBERT CLAYTON (CTF)
   Wilshire Court Productions, 1992
BODY LANGUAGE (CTF)   Wilshire Court Productions, 1992,
   w/Dan Gurskis
DYING TO REMEMBER (CTF)   USA Network, 1993,
   w/Frank Cardea &George Schenck
TARGET OF SUSPICION (CTF)   USA Pictures, 1994
AGAINST HER WILL: THE CARRIE BUCK STORY (CTF)
   Viacom, 1994

DONALD H. ROSS*
Contact: WGA - Los Angeles, 310/550-1000

HAMBURGER...THE MOTION PICTURE   FM Entertainment, 1986

GARY A. ROSS*
Agent: CAA - Beverly Hills, 310/288-4545

BIG ★   20th Century Fox, 1988, w/Anne Spielberg
MR. BASEBALL   Universal, 1992, w/Monte Merrick & Kevin Wade
DAVE ★   Warner Bros., 1993
LASSIE   Paramount, 1994, w/Elizabeth Anderson &
   Matthew Jacobs

Screenplays:
A COUPLE OF POINTS (directing)
NEWS w/Ken Finkelman

JUDITH ROSS*
Contact: WGA - Los Angeles, 310/550-1000

AN ALMOST PERFECT PERSON (P)
VIA GALACTICA (P)
HAPPILY EVER AFTER (P)
RICH KIDS   United Artists, 1979

Screenplays:
PALEY (CTF)
PEERS
COVER STORY
THE OTHER MAN
JANE'S HOUSE
PARADISE
A WOMAN IN THE HOUSE

KATHERINE ROSS
Contact: Screen Actors Guild - Los Angeles, 213/954-1600

CONAGHER (CTF)   Imagine Film Entertainment, 1991,
   w/Sam Elliott & Jeffrey M. Meyer

KENNETH ROSS*
Contact: WGA - Los Angeles, 310/550-1000

THE DAY OF THE JACKAL   Universal, 1973
THE ODESSA FILE   Columbia, 1974, w/George Markstein
BLACK SUNDAY   Paramount, 1977, w/Ernest Lehman &
   Ivan Moffatt
THE FOURTH WAR   Cannon, 1990, w/Stephen Peters

MARTIN K. (MARTY) ROSS*
Agent: The Gersh Agency - New York, 212/997-1818

DANGEROUSLY CLOSE   Cannon, 1986, w/Scott Fields &
   John Stockwell
THE IMPOSSIBLE SPY (CTF)   BBC TV/Quartet International/IMGC,
   1987, w/Douglas Livingstone

PAUL ROSS
BEYOND EVIL   IFI-Scope III, 1980, w/Herb Freed

REBECCA ROSS
THE PAINTED DESERT   New Dawn Pictures, 1993,
   w/Masato Harada

STEVEN JAMES ROSS
Agent: William Morris Agency - Beverly Hills, 310/274-7451

Screenplays:
THE MONK w/Martin Schwartz (Gramercy)

STUART ROSS
Agent: Innovative Artists - Los Angeles, 310/553-5200

THE HEEBIE JEEBIES (P)
NOT-SO-NEW FACES (P)
NASTY LITTLE SECRETS (P)
FUN WITH DICK AND JANE-THE MUSICAL (P)
THE LUNCH GIRLS (P)
CONRACK (P)
CREEPS (P)
FOREVER PLAID (P)   also screenplay

LEO ROSSI
Contact: Screen Actors Guild - Hollywood, 213/465-4600

WE'RE TALKIN' SERIOUS MONEY   Cinetel, 1992,
   w/James Lemmo

TERRY P. ROSSIO*
Agent: William Morris Agency - Beverly Hills, 310/274-7451

LITTLE MONSTERS   Vestron, 1989, w/Ted Elliott
ALADDIN (AF)   Buena Vista, 1992, w/Ted Elliott, Ron Clements &
   John Musker
THE PUPPET MASTERS   Buena Vista, 1994, w/Ted Elliott &
   David Goyer

Screenplays:
GODZILLA w/Ted Elliott
SANDMAN w/Ted Elliott
ZORRO w/Ted Elliott
PRINCESS OF MARS w/Ted Elliott
DUNN'S CONUNDRUM w/Ted Elliott

EUGENIE ROSS-LEMING*
Agent: ICM - Beverly Hills, 310/550-4000
Business: B & E Enterprises, Paramount TV, 213/956-5959

Screenplays:
ANNIE AND THE CASTLE OF TERROR w/Brad Buckner
CADETS w/Brad Buckner
LOOSE WOMEN w/Brad Buckner
UFO w/Brad Buckner
ROMANTIC FOOLS w/Brad Buckner
SVENGALI w/Brad Buckner
FOREIGNERS w/Brad Buckner
LAMB OF GOD w/Brad Buckner
THE KID w/Brad Buckner
FORGET ME NOT w/Brad Buckner

RICHARD ROSSNER*
Contact: WGA - Los Angeles, 310/550-1000

Screenplays:
SON OF A GUN w/M.J. Anderson

ARI ROTH
Agent: Writers & Artists Agency - New York, 212/947-8765

Screenplays:
BORIS GUILTY

BOB ROTH
THE RETURN OF JAFAR (AHVF)   Buena Vista, 1994,
    w/Kevin Campbell, Mirith J.S. Colao, Bill Motz, Steve Roberts,
    Jan Strand & Brian Swenlin

BOBBY ROTH*
Agent: William Morris Agency - Beverly Hills, 310/274-7451

INDEPENDENCE DAY   Unifilm, 1977, directed
THE BOSS' SON   Circle Associates, 1980, directed
HEARTBREAKERS   Orion, 1984, directed
BAJA OKLAHOMA   HBO Pictures/Rastar Productions,
    w/Dan Jenkins, directed
DEAD SOLID PERFECT (CTF)   HBO Pictures/David Merrick
    Productions, 1988, w/Dan Jenkins, directed
THE MAN INSIDE   New Line Cinema, 1990, directed

Screenplays:
WALLRAFF
NATIVES

ERIC ROTH*
Agent: CAA - Beverly Hills, 310/288-4545

THE NICKEL RIDE   20th Century-Fox, 1975
THE CONCORDE - AIRPORT '79   Universal, 1979
SUSPECT   Tri-Star, 1987
MEMORIES OF ME   MGM/UA, 1988, w/Billy Crystal
MR. JONES   TriStar, 1993, w/Michael Cristofer
FORREST GUMP   Paramount, 1994

Screenplays:
THE HORSE WHISPERER
SLOW WALTZ IN CEDAR BEND
THE POSTMAN
THE BOP
CHEEK TO CHEEK
NICK THE GREEK
MA BELL
LOVERS
MURDER AT THE MOVIES
US
WONDER BOY
INTENSIVE CARE
BODIE
LOUIE
WILLIE
GOODNIGHT MOON
NERVE ENDING
THE DANGER
GOSPEL

LYNN ROTH*
(Tamara Lynn Roth)
Agent: Broder-Kurland-Webb-Uffner - Beverly Hills, 310/281-3400

THE PORTRAIT (CTF)   Atticus Corp./Greenwald Productions, 1993

Screenplays:
THE COLOR OF EVENING

PHILIP J. ROTH
APEX   Republic Pictures, 1994, w/Ronald Schmidt, directed

JEFF ROTHBERG*
Agent: William Morris Agency - Beverly Hills, 310/274-7451

HIDING OUT   DEG, 1987, w/Joe Menosky
LITTLE PANDA   Warner Bros., 1995, w/Laurice Elehwany

Screenplays:
BOGUS (Story)
JACK AND THE BEANSTALK
DOWNTIME
PRIVATE ENEMY
MR. WRONG
ANNIE II
THE INSIDER

JASON ROTHENBERG
Agent: United Talent Agency - Beverly Hills, 310/273-6700

Screenplays:
DEA PROJECT
HOBSON'S CHOICE

ROBERT ROTHMAN
SAM AND SARAH   Full Circle Films, 1991, w/John Strysik

ELISA ROTHSTEIN*
Agent: Innovative Artists - Los Angeles, 310/553-5200

DELTA OF VENUS   New Line Cinema, 1995

RICHARD ROTHSTEIN*
Agent: Martin Hurwitz Associates - Beverly Hills, 310/274-0240

DEATH VALLEY   Universal, 1982
HARD TO HOLD   Universal, 1984, Story w/Tom Hedley
UNIVERSAL SOLDIER   TriStar, 1992, w/Dean Devlin &
    Christopher Leitch

Screenplays:
A MURDEROUS INTENT

CHRISTINE ROUM*
Agent: Jim Preminger Agency - Los Angeles, 310/475-9491

SOMEWHERE IN BEDROCK (Short)   1986, directed
BELINDA IN THE WATER (Short)   1987, directed

Screenplays:
WITHOUT REMORSE
DON'T SAY A WORD
THE BODYGUARD 2
DEAD RECKONING
THE EXPERIMENT
DEN OF THIEVES
SHAGGY
ALOHA
COMRADES

ROBERT ROVNER
Agent: United Talent Agency - Beverly Hills, 310/273-6700

Screenplays:
EXILE w/Jim Cowan

ERLINDA QUILAOIT ROWE
FATAL MISSION   Funahara, 1990, Story

FREDDIE ROWE
HOWLING IV...THE ORIGINAL NIGHTMARE   Allied Entertainment,
    1988, w/Clive Turner

GEORGE ROWE
FATAL MISSION   Funahara, 1990, w/Peter Fonda,
    Chosei Funahara, Anthony Gentile & John Gentile, directed

RYAN ROWE*
Agent: Above the Line - West Hollywood, 310/859-6115

TAPEHEADS   Avenue Pictures, 1988, Story w/Bill Fishman,
    Jim Herzfeld & Peter McCarthy

Screenplays:
TOTALLY LONDON
KILLER BEACH BABES (Story w/Chris Matheson)
THE MAN WITH 9 LIVES   JACK, YOU'RE DEAD
BESIDE MYSELF
LOSERS
GENIE BOB w/Jim Herzfeld
RUB OF THE GREEN

THOMAS L. ROWE*
Contact: WGA - Los Angeles, 310/550-1000

TARZAN, THE APE MAN   MGM/United Artists, 1981,
    w/Gary Goddard

Screenplays:
NO LAUGHING MATTER

KATHLEEN K. ROWELL*
Agent: The Gersh Agency - Beverly Hills, 310/274-6611

THE OUTSIDERS   Warner Bros., 1983
JOY OF SEX   Paramount, 1984, w/J.J. Salter
HEAR NO EVIL   20th Century Fox, 1993, w/R.M. Badat
TAINTED BLOOD (CTF)   Wilshire Court Productions, 1993

MARK ROWEN*
Contact: WGA - Los Angeles, 310/550-1000

Screenplays:
NO ONE TO KISS AT MIDNIGHT

WILLIAM ROWLEY
THE CHANGELING (CTF)   BBC-TV, 1994, w/Thomas Middleton

IAIN ROY
ANY MAN'S DEATH   INI Entertainment, 1990, w/Chris Kelly

PATRICIA ROYCE
DAREDREAMER   Lensman Co., 1989, w/Barry Caillier
TO CROSS THE RUBICON   Lensman Co., 1991, w/Lorraine Devon

ROBB ROYER*
Contact: WGA - Los Angeles, 310/550-1000

Screenplays:
LOCKED OUT w/Sean Finnegan

PATRICIA ROZEMA
Address: 212 Robert St., Toronto, Ontario M5S 2K7, Canada

I'VE HEARD THE MERMAIDS SINGING   Miramax, 1987, directed
WHITE ROOM   Alliance Releasing, 1990, directed
WHEN NIGHT IS FALLING   Alliance Releasing, 1995, directed

JOHN RUANE
DEATH IN BRUNSWICK   Overseas Film Group, 1990,
    w/Boyd Oxlade, directed

MARC R. RUBEL*
Contact: WGA - Los Angeles, 310/550-1000

XANADU   Universal, 1980, w/Richard Christian Danus
BIG BUSINESS   Buena Vista, 1988, w/Dori Pierson

ALBERT RUBEN*
Contact: WGA - New York, 212/245-6180

THE SEVEN-UPS   20th Century-Fox, 1973, w/Alexander Jacobs
VISIT TO A CHIEF'S SON   United Artists, 1974

ANDY RUBEN*
Agent: ICM - Beverly Hills, 310/550-4000

THE PATRIOT   Crown International, 1986, w/Katt Shea Ruben
STRIPPED TO KILL   Concorde, 1987, w/Katt Shea Ruben
DANCE OF THE DAMNED   Concorde, 1989, w/Katt Shea Ruben
STREETS   Concorde, 1990, w/Katt Shea Ruben
POISON IVY   New Line Cinema, 1992, w/Katt Shea Ruben

Screenplays:
PRINCE HOMBRA

JOSEPH RUBEN*
Agent: United Talent Agency - Beverly Hills, 310/273-6700

THE POM-POM GIRLS   Crown International, 1976, directed
JOYRIDE   American International, 1977, w/Peter Rainer, directed
DREAMSCAPE   20th Century Fox, 1984, w/David Loughery &
    Chuck Russell, directed

Screenplays:
JUICE
NIGHT ON THE TOWN

BILL RUBENSTEIN*
Contact: WGA - Los Angeles, 310/550-1000

BEYOND RANGOON   Columbia, 1995, w/Alex Lasker

BRUCE RUBIN*
Contact: WGA - Los Angeles, 310/550-1000

ZAPPED!   Embassy, 1982, w/Robert J. Rosenthal

BRUCE JOEL RUBIN*
Agent: Sanford-Gross & Associates - Los Angeles, 310/208-2100

BRAINSTORM   MGM/UA, 1983, Story
DEADLY FRIEND   Warner Bros., 1986
GHOST ★★   Paramount, 1990
JACOB'S LADDER   Tri-Star, 1990
MY LIFE   Columbia, 1993, directed

Screenplays:
DEEP IMPACT (Paramount)

DANNY RUBIN*
Agent: ICM - Beverly Hills, 310/550-4000

GROUNDHOG DAY   Columbia, 1993, w/Harold Ramis
HEAR NO EVIL   20th Century Fox, 1993, Story w/R.M. Badat
S.F.W.   Gramercy, 1995, w/Jefery Levy

Screenplays:
CORDUROY

DENIS RUBIN*
Manager: Creative Alliance Management - Los Angeles,
    213/962-6090

Screenplays:
SPEAK OF THE DEVIL w/Jon Rubin

JON RUBIN*
Manager: Creative Alliance Management - Los Angeles,
    213/962-6090

Screenplays:
SPEAK OF THE DEVIL w/Denis Rubin

MANN RUBIN*
Agent: William Morris Agency - Beverly Hills, 310/274-7451
Contact: 213/271-5398

THE BEST OF EVERYTHING   20th Century-Fox, 1959,
    w/Edith Sommer
BRAINSTORM   Warner Bros., 1965
AN AMERICAN DREAM   Warner Bros., 1966
WARNING SHOT   Paramount, 1966
THE FIRST DEADLY SIN   Filmways, 1980
THE HUMAN SHIELD   Cannon, 1992

Screenplays:
THE MAGNIFICENT IDIOT

RICHARD RUBIN
NEVER FORGET (CTF)   Turner Network Television, 1991

RONALD RUBIN*
Agent: Major Clients Agency - Los Angeles, 310/284-6400

Screenplays:
THE BOYS OF SUMMER
THE ANNULMENT
I'LL GET THERE...I HOPE IT'S WORTH THE TRIP
THE SWISS CONNECTION

SCOTT RUBIN
Agent: The Wright Concept - Burbank, 818/954-8943

Screenplays:
COVER ME, I'M GOING FOR THE PAPER

CLIFF RUBY*
Agent: David Shapira & Associates - Sherman Oaks, 818/906-0322

Screenplays:
CAT'S DON'T DANCE (AF) (Turner Pictures)
    w/Roberts Gannaway & Elana Lesser

ALLEN RUCKER*
Contact: Morra, Brezner & Steinberg - Los Angeles, 310/203-1090

HOMETOWN BOY MAKES GOOD (CTF)   HBO Television, 1990
A TASTE FOR KILLING (CTF)   Bodega Bay Productions, 1992,
    w/Hudson Marquez

ALBERT S. RUDDY
Business: Ruddy-Morgan Productions, 9300 Wilshire Blvd. -
    Suite 508, Beverly Hills, CA 90212, 310/271-7698

MATILDA   American International, 1978, w/Timothy Galfas
MEGAFORCE   20th Century-Fox, 1982, w/James Whittaker,
    Hal Needham & Andre Morgan
CANONBALL RUN II   Warner Bros., 1984, w/Harvey Miller &
    Hal Needham
BAD GIRLS   20th Century Fox, 1994, Story w/Charles Finch &
    Gray Frederickson

DAVID RUDKIN
Agent: The Casarotto Company - London, 071/287-4450

TESTIMONY   Isolde Films, 1988, w/Tony Palmer
DECEMBER BRIDE   Film Four Productions, 1991

RITA RUDNER*
Agent: ICM - Beverly Hills, 310/550-4000

PETER'S FRIENDS   Samuel Goldwyn Company, 1992,
    w/Martin Bergman

Screenplays:
GREEN ACRES w/Martin Bergman
WILD KINGDOM w/Martin Bergman

DIANE RUDNICK-MANN*
Contact: Patti C. Felker, Nelson, Guggenheim & Felker -
    Los Angeles, 310/207-8337

Screenplays:
HER CHILDREN

PAUL RUDNICK*
Agent: CAA - Beverly Hills, 310/288-4545

I HATE HAMLET (P)
THE NAKED TRUTH (P)
SISTER ACT   Buena Vista, 1992, as "Joseph Howard"
ADDAMS FAMILY VALUES   Paramount, 1993
JEFFREY   Workin Man Films, 1994, from his play

Screenplays:
POOR LITTLE LAMBS
MAGIC TIME
GOSSIP COLUMNIST

STEVE RUDNICK*
Agent: United Talent Agency - Beverly Hills, 310/273-6700

THE SANTA CLAUSE   Buena Vista, 1994, w/Leo Benvenuti

Screenplays:
LEGAL MISFITS w/Leo Benvenuti

MARK RUDNITSKY*
Agent: Wile Enterprises - Santa Monica, 310/828-9768

Screenplays:
CRITICAL MASS

ALAN S. RUDOLPH*
Agent: William Morris Agency - Beverly Hills, 310/274-7451
Business Manager: William Goldstein - 818/999-3601

PREMONITION   Transvue, 1972, directed
BUFFALO BILL AND THE INDIANS, or SITTING BULL'S
    HISTORY LESSON   United Artists, 1976, w/Robert Altman
WELCOME TO L.A.   United Artists/Lions Gate, 1977, directed
REMEMBER MY NAME   Columbia/Lagoon Associates,
    1979, directed
ROADIE   United Artists, 1980, Story w/Zalman King,
    Big Boy Medlin & Michael Ventura,   directed
ENDANGERED SPECIES   MGM/UA, 1982,
    w/John Binder,   directed
CHOOSE ME   Island Alive/New Cinema, 1984, directed
TROUBLE IN MIND   Alive Films, 1985, directed
THE MODERNS   Alive Films, 1988, w/Jon Bradshaw, directed
LOVE AT LARGE   Orion, 1990, directed
EQUINOX   SC Entertainment International, 1992, directed
MRS. PARKER AND THE VICIOUS CIRCLE   Fine Line Features,
    1994, w/Randy Sue Coburn,   directed

Screenplays:
BANDITS (directing)
THE FAR SIDE

BENJAMIN RUFFNER*
Contact: Ilan Bialer - Los Angeles, 310/550-4515

HALLOWEEN 4   Galaxy International, 1988, Story w/Dhani Lipsius,
    Alan McElroy & Larry Rattner

AL RUGGERIO*
(Alfonse M. Ruggerio Jr.)
Agent: ICM - Beverly Hills, 310/550-4000

Screenplays:
SAM BASS: THE MAKING OF AN OUTLAW w/William Roberts
OUTLAWS

ED RUGOFF*
Agent: Jim Preminger Agency - Los Angeles, 310/475-9491

MANNEQUIN   20th Century Fox, 1987, w/Michael Gottlieb
MANANEQUIN TWO: ON THE MOVE   20th Century Fox, 1991,
    w/David Isaacs, Betsy Israel & Ken Levine
MR. NANNY   New Line Cinema, 1993, w/Michael Gottlieb

Screenplays:
PUNCHY w/Michael Gottlieb
THE VULGARIANS w/Michael Gottlieb
SOMETHING REAL w/Michael Gottlieb
SEEING STARS w/Michael Gottlieb
WHOPPER w/Michael Gottlieb

CHRIS RUPPENTHAL*
Agent: CAA - Beverly Hills, 310/288-4545

VIOLENT DEATH, A MUSICAL (Short)   directed,
   based on his play, Shared

Screenplays:
WE'RE IN THE MONEY
FIREDOGS w/Ira Besserman
MAN OF GOD

CHRISTOPHER RUSH
VENUS PETER   British Film Institute, 1989, w/Ian Sellar

JORDAN RUSH*
Agent: Jon Klane Agency - Beverly Hills, 310/278-0178

CLUB FED   Prism Entertainment, 1991, w/Peter Stone

Screenplays:
NEVER TALK TO STRANGERS w/Lewis Green
DUDES w/Lewis Green
LATE BLOOMER
TOP DOG
HELLO GIRLS w/Barry Halpin

RICHARD RUSH*
Agent: William Morris Agency - Beverly Hills, 310/274-7451

OF LOVE AND DESIRE   New World, 1963,
   w/Laslo Gorag, directed
PSYCH-OUT   American International, 1968, directed
THE STUNT MAN ★   20th Century-Fox, 1980, Story, directed
AIR AMERICA   Tri-Star, 1990, w/John Eskow

Screenplays:
THE FAT LADY
THE LONG DARK TEATIME OF THE SOUL

LOU RUSOFF
RUNAWAY DAUGHTERS (CTF)   Showtime/Drive-In Classic
   Cinema, 1994, Story w/Charlie Haas

BRIAN RUSSELL*
Contact: WGA - Los Angeles, 310/550-1000

THE ANNIHILATORS   New World, 1985

CHUCK RUSSELL*
Agent: United Talent Agency - Beverly Hills, 310/273-6700

DREAMSCAPE   20th Century Fox, 1984, w/David Loughery &
   Joe Ruben
A NIGHTMARE ON ELM STREET PART 3: DREAM WARRIORS
   New Line Cinema, 1987, w/Wes Craven, Frank Darabont &
   Bruce Wagner, directed
THE BLOB   Tri-Star, 1988, w/Frank Darabont, directed

Screenplays:
SHADOW OF DEATH
SHIVA
NEUROMANCER
STRANGERS IN LEADVILLE w/Frank Darabont

DAVID O. RUSSELL
Agent: United Talent Agency - Beverly Hills, 310/273-6700

HAIRWAY TO THE STARS (Short)   1991, directed
SPANKING THE MONKEY   Fine Line Features, 1994, directed

Screenplays:
FLIRTING WITH DISASTER (Miramax, directing)
SOUTH OF HEAVEN

JAY W. RUSSELL*
Agent: The Gersh Agency - Beverly Hills, 310/274-6611

END OF THE LINE   Orion Classics, 1988,
   w/John Wohlbruck, directed

KEN RUSSELL
Agent: ICM - Beverly Hills, 310/550-4000

THE DEVILS   Warner Bros., 1971, directed
THE BOY FRIEND   MGM, 1971, directed
MAHLER   Mayfair, 1974, directed
TOMMY   Columbia, 1975, directed
LISZTOMANIA   Warner Bros., 1975, directed
VALENTINO   United Artists, 1977, w/John Byrum, directed
SALOME'S LAST DANCE   Vestron, 1988, directed
THE LAIR OF THE WHITE WORM   Vestron, 1988, directed
THE RAINBOW   Vestron, 1989, w/Vivian Russell, directed
WHORE   Trimark Pictures, 1991, w/Deborah Dalton, directed
EROTIC TALES   Mercure Distribution, 1994,
   "The Insatiable Mrs. Kirsch," directed

RANDEE Y. RUSSELL*
Agent: Broder-Kurland-Webb-Uffner - Beverly Hills, 310/281-3400

ALL'S FAIR   Moviestore Entertainment, 1989, w/John Finnegan,
   William Pace & Tom Rondinella

Screenplays:
FACE THE MUSIC (Chrysalide Films)
BAD DEATH w/Laurie Craig

VIVIAN RUSSELL
THE RAINBOW   Vestron, 1989, w/Ken Russell

WILLY RUSSELL
Agent: The Casarotto Company - London, 071/287-4450

JOHN PAUL GEORGE RINGO AND BURT (P)
BLOODBROTHERS (P)
EDUCATING RITA ★   Columbia, 1983, from his play
SHIRLEY VALENTINE   Paramount, 1989, from his play
DANCIN' THRU THE DARK   Palace Pictures/British Screen/BBC
   Films/Formost Films, 1990

ROBIN RUSSIN*
Contact: Weissmann, Wolff, Bergman, Coleman & Silverman -
   Beverly Hills, 310/858-7888

ON DEADLY GROUND   Warner Bros., 1994, w/Ed Horowitz

JOHN A. RUSSO*
Agent: Shapiro/Lichtman - Los Angeles, 310/859-8877

NIGHT OF THE LIVING DEAD   Continental, 1968
THE RETURN OF THE LIVING DEAD   Orion, 1985,
   Story w/Rudy Ricci & Russell Streiner
VOODOO DAWN   AIP, 1990, w/Jeffrey Delman, Evan Dunsky &
   Thomas Rendon

MARDI RUSTAM
DEATHTRAP   Mars, 1976, w/Alvin L. Fast
EVILS OF THE NIGHT   Shapiro Entertainment, 1985,
   w/Phillip D. Connors, directed

RICHARD RUTOWSKI*
Contact: WGA - Los Angeles, 310/550-1000

NATURAL BORN KILLERS   Warner Bros., 1994, w/David Veloz &
   Oliver Stone

NEIL RUTTENBERG*
Agent: APA - Los Angeles, 310/273-0744

THE MASK OF SARNAT (Short)   directed
DEATHSTALKERS II: NECROPOLIS   Concorde, 1986
MAD DOG COLL   21st Century Film Corporation, 1992

Screenplays:
PIPE CLEANERS
MISTER TWISTER
TIGER AND PET
SPIDER MAN
ANT MAN
DEATHCATHALON

MORRIE RUVINSKY*
Agent: Paradigm - Los Angeles, 310/277-4400

IMPROPER CHANNELS   Crown International, 1981,
   w/Adam Arkin & Ian Sutherland

Screenplays:
CHEAP PARTS
RAINY DAYS, RAINY NIGHTS
DISTANT SHORES
THE PLASTIC MILE
THE FINISHING TOUCH

JAMES RYAN
Agent: William Morris Agency - Beverly Hills, 310/274-7451

IRON TOMMY (P)
DENNIS (P)
PORTRAIT OF MY BIKINI (P)
ARAB BRIDE (P)
NOT SHOWING (P)
SOUTH PACIFIC SNOW (P)
DOOR TO CUBA (P)
IN CAHOOTS (P)
MINK ON A GOLD HOOK (P)

ROBERT RYDER*
Agent: Jon Klane Agency - Beverly Hills, 310/278-0178

Screenplays:
THANKSGIVING
TAKE ME TO THE RIVER SINK OR SWIM
DEAD BY MORNING

JOHN RYMAN
GALAXIES ARE COLLIDING   SC Entertainment International,
   1992, directed

S

MARC SACHNOFF
PENNY ANTE   Andrew Solt Productions, 1990

WILLIAM SACHS*
Contact: Hollywood Independent Pictures - 818/907-5667

THERE IS NO THIRTEEN   Film Ventures International,
   1977, directed
THE INCREDIBLE MELTING MAN   American International,
   1978, directed
VAN NUYS BLVD.   Crown International, 1979, directed
GALAXINA   Crown International, 1980, directed
EXTERMINATOR II   Cannon, 1984, w/Mark Buntzman
HOT CHILI   Cannon, 1985, w/Menahem Golan, directed
JUDGMENT   Promark, 1991, directed

WILLIAM B. SACKHEIM*
Business Manager: EV Associates - Los Angeles, 310/274-8565

BARRICADE   Warner Bros., 1949
PAULA *THE SILENT VOICE* Columbia, 1952, w/James Poe
FORBIDDEN   Universal-International, 1953, w/Gil Doud
BORDER RIVER   Universal-International, 1953
THE HUMAN JUNGLE   Allied Artists, 1954, w/Daniel Fuchs
THE COMPETITION   Columbia, 1980, Story w/Joel Oliansky
FIRST BLOOD   Orion, 1982, w/Michael Kozoll & Sylvester Stallone

HOWARD SACKLER
THE GREAT WHITE HOPE   20th Century-Fox, 1970, from his play
GRAY LADY DOWN   Universal, 1978, w/James Whitaker
SAINT JACK   New World, 1979, w/Peter Bogdanovich &
   Paul Theroux

ALAN SACKS*
Agent: Annette Van Duren Agency - Los Angeles, 213/650-3643
Business: Heritage Entertainment, 7920 Sunset Blvd. - Suite 200,
   Los Angeles, CA 90046, 213/850-5858

THRASHIN' Fries Entertainment, 1986, w/Paul Brown
THE COWBOY POETRY GATHERING (Short)   1994,
   also screenplay

Screenplays:
MASTER OF LIES
MY TEACHER IS AN ALIEN

EZRA M. SACKS*
Agent: CAA - Beverly Hills, 310/288-4545

FM   Universal, 1978
A SMALL CIRCLE OF FRIENDS   United Artists, 1980
WILDCATS   Warner Bros., 1986

Screenplays:
CONEY ISLAND COWBOYS

FRANK SACKS
EXTREME JUSTICE (CTF)   Trimark, 1993, w/Robert Boris

MICHAEL SADLER
Agent: Lemon Unna & Durbridge - London, 071/727-1346

A YEAR IN PROVENCE (CMS)   BBC TV, 1993

RICHARD SADLER
HOW TO MAKE LOVE TO A NEGRO WITHOUT GETTING TIRED
   Angelika Films, 1990, w/Dany LaFerriere

JAMES SADWITH*
Agent: ICM - Beverly Hills, 310/550-4000

Screenplays:
THE MATCH
IN THE EYE OF THE STORM
MALIBU WARS

DON SAFRAN*
Contact: 818/954-3851

HOMEWORK   Jensen Farley Pictures, 1982, w/Maurice Peterson

HENRI SAFRAN
Contact: Mitch Consultancy, 98 Bay Road, Waverton, NSW, 2060,
   Australia, tel.: 02/922-6566

NORMAN LOVES ROSE   Atlantic Releasing Corporation,
   1981, directed
THE WILD DUCK   RKR Releasing, 1983, w/Peter Smalley &
   John Lind, directed

KEN SAGOES
ON PROMISED LAND (CTF)   Anasazi Productions, 1994

MARK SAHA*
Agent: United Talent Agency - Beverly Hills, 310/273-6700

Screenplays:
THE TIME OF OUR LIVES
CHINA RIFLES
DOODLEBUG DAYS

BRUCE HIDEMI SAKOU
FRIDAY THE 13TH, PART IV: THE FINAL CHAPTER   Paramount,
   1984, Story

C. L. SALASKI
Agent: Jack Scagnetti Agency - North Hollywood, 818/762-3871

Screenplays:
WITHIN REACH
THROUGH MY EYES

MURRAY SALEM*
Agent: Camden-ITG - Los Angeles, 310/289-2700

KINDERGARTEN COP   Universal, 1990, w/Timothy Harris &
   Herschel Weingrod

Screenplays:
JURY DUTY
DETECTIVE SCHOOL
ONE OF THE GIRLS
SONSHIA PASS
I SPY
BARRACK BOYS
LUCIFER: A LOVE STORY
FOR BETTER OR WORSE (CTF)

MARTIN SALINAS*
Agent: The Gersh Agency - Beverly Hills, 310/274-6611

GABY - A TRUE STORY   Tri-Star, 1987, w/Michael Love

Screenplays:
FLY AWAY HOME w/Michael Love
HEIR NOT APPARENT w/Michael Love

RIC SALINAS*
(w/Richard Montoya & Herbert Siguenza: Culture Clash)
Agent: William Morris Agency - Beverly Hills, 310/274-7451

A BOWL OF BEINGS (P)   w/Richard Montoya & Herbert Siguenza
THE MISSION (P)   w/Richard Montoya & Herbert Siguenza

Screenplays:
GOMEZ, GOMEZ AND GOMEZ w/Richard Montoya &
   Herbert Siguenza (UA)

CLAUDIA SALTER*
Contact: WGA - Los Angeles, 310/550-1000

ACE ELI AND ROGER OF THE SKIES   20th Century-Fox, 1973

Screenplays:
WASHINGTON SLEPT HERE

JAMES SALTER*
Agent: Sterling Lord Literistic - New York, 212/696-2800

THREE   United Artists, 1969, directed
THE APPOINTMENT   MGM, 1969
DOWNHILL RACER   Paramount, 1969
THRESHOLD   20th Century-Fox International Classics, 1983

JOEL S. SALTZMAN*
Agent: The Agency - Los Angeles, 310/551-3000

Screenplays:
THE WIZARD FROM FLATBUSH w/Harv Zimmel
ROMANCE ARTIST

MARK P. SALTZMAN*
Agent: William Morris Agency - New York, 212/586-5100

THE ADVENTURES OF MILO AND OTIS   Columbia, 1989
3 NINJAS KICK BACK   TriStar, 1994

Screenplays:
PIGMALION
SINBAD (AF)
THE GUARDIANS OF GOOD
ROMEO, ROMEO

VICTOR SALVA
Contact: 310/273-6505

CLOWNHOUSE   Commercial Pictures, 1989, directed
NATURE OF THE BEAST   New Line Cinema, 1994, directed

Screenplays:
THE POWDER (directing)

HAROLD SALWEN*
Agent: The Gersh Agency - New York, 212/997-1818

DEADLY SURVEILLANCE (CTF)   Westwind Productions, 1991,
   w/Paul Ziller
PROBABLE CAUSE (CTF)   Wilmont Prods./Showtime Ent., 1994

Screenplays:
DENISE CALLS UP (directing)
GIRLS TALK
SO LONG, NEW JERSEY

AUDREY THALER SALZBERG*
Agent: J. Michael Bloom & Associates - Los Angeles, 310/275-6800

Screenplays:
THE GHOST OF THE GREEN MONKEY w/Steven Salzberg
MARTHA MITCHELL PROJECT w/Steven Salzberg
DEAD INSIDE (CTF) w/Steven Salzberg
WORKING THE WIRE w/Steven Salzberg

STEVEN SALZBERG*
Agent: J. Michael Bloom & Associates - Los Angeles, 310/275-6800

Screenplays:
THE GHOST OF THE GREEN MONKEY w/Audrey Thaler Salzberg
MARTHA MITCHELL PROJECT w/Audrey Thaler Salzberg
DEAD INSIDE (CTF) w/Audrey Thaler Salzberg
WORKING THE WIRE w/Audrey Thaler Salzberg

MARK SALZMAN
IRON AND SILK   Sun Productions, 1990, w/Shirley Sun

Screenplays:
GHOST STORY

JEANNE SALZMANN
MEETINGS WITH REMARKABLE MEN   Libra, 1979

COKE SAMS*
Contact: WGA - Los Angeles, 310/550-1000

ERNEST GOES TO CAMP   Buena Vista, 1987,
   w/John R. Cherry III
ERNEST SCARED STUPID   Buena Vista, 1991,
   Story w/John R. Cherry III

MILCA SANCHEZ-SCOTT
Contact: KCET/WMG/American Playhouse, 4401 Sunset Blvd.,
   Los Angeles, CA 90027

EL DORADO (P)
ROOSTERS   American Playhouse Theatrical Films, 1993,
   from her play

ROBERT L. SAND*
Agent: Broder-Kurland-Webb-Uffner - Beverly Hills, 310/281-3400

TOUCH AND GO   Tri-Star, 1987, w/Harry Colomby & Alan Ormsby

DUKE SANDEFUR*
(Donald D. Sandefur)
Contact: WGA - Los Angeles, 310/550-1000

GHOST TOWN   Trans World Entertainment, 1988
THE PHANTOM OF THE OPERA   21st Century Film
   Corporation, 1989
PHANTOM OF MANHATTAN   21st Century Film Corporation, 1990

B. LAMAR SANDERS*
Contact: New York University - New York, 212/998-1780

THE KIRLIAN WITNESS   Sarno, 1981, w/Jonathan Sarno

KEN SANDERS
BLOOD SALVAGE   Paragon Arts International, 1990,
   w/Tucker Johnston

SONNY SANDERS
THE FIRING LINE   AIP Home Video/Silver Screen International,
   1991, w/John Gale

ADAM SANDLER
Agent: CAA - Beverly Hills, 310/288-4545

BILLY MADISON   Universal, 1995, w/Tim Herlihy

BARRY SANDLER*
Agent: Candace Lake - Beverly Hills, 310/289-0600

THE LONERS   Fanfare, 1972, w/J. Lawrence
GABLE AND LOMBARD   Universal, 1976
THE DUCHESS AND THE DIRTWATER FOX   20th Century-Fox,
   1976, w/Melvin Frank

THE MIRROR CRACK'D   EMI, 1980, w/Jonathan Hales
MAKING LOVE   20th Century-Fox, 1982
CRIMES OF PASSION   New World, 1984
ALL-AMERICAN MURDER   Prism Entertainment, 1992

Screenplays:
STAR LADIES w/J. Rivers
JULIO AND STEIN
FAMILY VALUES

SUSAN SANDLER*
Agent: ICM - Beverly Hills, 310/550-4000

CROSSING DELANCEY   Warner Bros., 1988, from her play

Screenplays:
SAVED BY ROCK'N'ROLL   MAMAROCK
I SLEPT FOR SCIENCE
LONELYVILLE

ANNA SANDOR*
Contact: WGA - Los Angeles, 310/550-1000

AMELIA EARHART: THE FINAL FLIGHT (CTF)
   Avenue Pictures, 1994

DONALD S. SANFORD*
Agent: Ben Kamsler Ltd. - Van Nuys, 818/785-4167

SUBMARINE X-1   United Artists, 1967, w/Guy Elmes
MOSQUITO SQUADRON   United Artists, 1968, w/Joyce Perry
MIDWAY   Universal, 1976
RAVAGERS   Columbia, 1979

JIMMY SANGSTER*
Agent: Shapiro/Lichtman - Los Angeles, 310/859-8877

X THE UNKNOWN   Hammer, 1956
THE CURSE OF FRANKENSTEIN   Warner Bros., 1957
THE CRAWLING EYE   *THE TROLLENBERG TERROR*   Eros, 1958
THE SNORKEL   Columbia, 1958, w/Anthony Dawson &
   Peter Myers
THE REVENGE OF FRANKENSTEIN   Columbia, 1958,
   w/Hurford Janes
BLOOD OF THE VAMPIRE   Artists Alliance, 1958
HORROR OF DRACULA   *DRACULA*   Universal, 1958
INTENT TO KILL   20th Century-Fox, 1958
JACK THE RIPPER   Mid Century, 1958
THE MAN WHO COULD CHEAT DEATH   Paramount, 1959
THE MUMMY   Hammer, 1959
BRIDE OF DRACULA   Universal-International, 1960,
   w/Peter Bryan & Edward Percy
THE TERROR OF THE TONGS   Hammer, 1960
THE SIEGE OF SIDNEY STREET   Midcentury, 1960,
   w/Alexander Baron
THE HELLFIRE CLUB   New World, 1960, w/Leon Griffiths
THE CONCRETE JUNGLE   *THE CRIMINAL*   Fanfare, 1960,
   w/Alun Owen
SCREAM OF FEAR   *TASTE OF FEAR*   Columbia, 1961
DEVIL SHIP PIRATES   ABP, 1963
MANIAC   Columbia, 1963
PARANOIAC   Universal-International, 1963
NIGHTMARE   Universal-International, 1964
HYSTERIA   MGM, 1964
THE NANNY   ABP, 1965
DEADLIER THAN THE MALE   Rank, 1967,
   w/Liz Charles-Williams & David Osborn
THE ANNIVERSARY   Hammer, 1968
CRESCENDO   Warner Bros., 1969, w/Alfred Shaughnessy
THE HORROR OF FRANKENSTEIN   EMI, 1970, directed
FEAR IN THE NIGHT   Hammer, 1972, w/Michael Syson, directed
WHO SLEW AUNTIE ROO?   United Artists, 1978, w/Robert Blees
THE LEGACY   Columbia, 1978, w/Patrick Tilley & Paul Wheeler
THE DEVIL AND MAX DEVLIN   Buena Vista, 1981,
   Story w/Mary Rodgers
PHOBIA   Paramount, 1981, w/Peter Bellwood, Lew Lehman,
   Gary A. Sherman & Ronald Shusett

DAMON SANTOSTEFANO*
Contact: WGA - New York, 212/245-6180

Screenplays:
THE BRANDENBURG w/Nicholas Felacci

DAVID SAPERSTEIN*
Business: Ebbets Field Productions, 16 Carlton Lane, New Rochelle,
NY 10804, 914/636-1281

COCOON   20th Century-Fox, 1984, Story
A KILLING AFFAIR   Hemdale, 1988, directed
PERSONAL CHOICE   Moviestore Entertainment, 1989, directed

DERAN SARAFIAN*
Agent: William Morris Agency - Beverly Hills, 310/274-7451

ALIEN PREDATOR   Trans World Entertainment, 1987, directed
INTERZONE   Trans World Entertainment, 1987, directed

Screenplays:
MAN PLUS w/Tedi Serafian

TEDI SARAFIAN*
Agent: William Morris Agency - Beverly Hills, 310/274-7451

SOLAR CRISIS   Scochiku-Fuji, 1990, w/Joe Gannon
ROADFLOWER   Miramax, 1994
TANK GIRL   MGM/UA, 1995

Screenplays:
TERRITORIES
MAN PLUS w/Deran Serafian
WICKED WAYS
GEORGE

JAN SARDI
Agent: A.A. Williams Management - in association w/William Morris
Agency - Beverly Hills, 310/274-7451
Business: Victorian International Pictures Pty. Ltd., 30 Lalor Street,
Port Melbourne, 3207 Victoria, Australia, 03/646-4777

STREET HERO   1983
MOVING OUT   Satori, 1985
GROUND ZERO   Avenue Pictures, 1988, w/Mac Gudgeon
SECRETS   Beyond Films Ltd., 1992, directed

ALVIN SARGENT*
Agent: William Morris Agency - Beverly Hills, 310/274-7451

GAMBIT   Universal, 1966, w/Jack Davies
THE STALKING MOON   National General, 1968
THE STERILE CUCKOO   Paramount, 1969
I WALK THE LINE   Columbia, 1970
THE EFFECT OF GAMMA RAYS ON MAN-IN-THE-MOON
MARIGOLDS   20th Century-Fox, 1972
PAPER MOON ★   Paramount, 1973
LOVE AND PAIN AND THE WHOLE DAMNED THING
Columbia, 1973
BOBBY DEERFIELD   Columbia, 1977
JULIA ★★   20th Century-Fox, 1977
STRAIGHT TIME   Warner Bros., 1978, w/Jeffrey Boam &
Edward Bunker
ORDINARY PEOPLE ★★   Paramount, 1980
NUTS   Warner Bros., 1987, w/Darryl Ponicsan & Tom Topor
DOMINICK & EUGENE   Orion, 1988, w/Corey Blechman
WHITE PALACE   Universal, 1990, w/Ted Tally
WHAT ABOUT BOB?   Buena Vista, 1991, Story w/Laura Ziskin
OTHER PEOPLE'S MONEY   Warner Bros., 1991
HERO   Columbia, 1992, Story w/Laura Ziskin &
David Webb Peoples

Screenplays:
BOGUS (Warner Bros.)
EVERYTHING MUST CHANGE w/ R. Voller
SECOND WIND w/R. Gould
SILENT VOWS

TWO LIVES
JOSHUA
ANYWHERE BUT HERE
MADLY IN LOVE

ARLENE SARNER*
Agent: CAA - Beverly Hills, 310/288-4545

PEGGY SUE GOT MARRIED   Tri-Star, 1986, w/Jerry Leichtling
BLUE SKY   Orion, 1994, w/Jerry Leichtling & Rama Laurie Stagner

Screenplays:
HOUSE ARREST w/Jerry Leichtling & Steven Carpenter
THE TALISMAN w/Jerry Leichtling
THE MAN WHO COULD WORK MIRACLES w/Jerry Leichtling
HONKY TONK SUE w/Jerry Leichtling

JONATHAN SARNO
THE KIRLIAN WITNESS   Sarno, 1981, w/Lamar Sanders
RAMONA   CNI Cinema, 1991, directed
BEACH BEVERLY HILLS   CNI Cinema, 1993,
w/Gloria Pryor,   directed

ROBERT SARNO*
Agent: William Morris Agency - Beverly Hills, 310/274-7451

HOWLING II...YOUR SISTER IS A WEREWOLF   Thorn-EMI, 1986,
w/Gary Brandner

Screenplays:
DECOY (Prism Pictures)
HUNTED
HARDWIRED
AFTERNOON SESSIONS w/Billy Brown
GETTING DOWN w/Billy Brown

PETER SASDY
COUNTESS DRACULA   20th Century-Fox, 1972, w/Alexander Paul,
Jeremy Paul & Gabriel Ronay,   directed

JEFFREY W. SASS
Business: Troma Inc., 733 Ninth Ave., New York, NY 10019,
212/757-4555

CLASS OF NUKE 'EM HIGH 2: SUBHUMANOID MELTDOWN
Troma, 1991, w/Lloyd Kaufman, Eric Louzil, Carl Morano,
Marcus Rolling & Matt Unger

OLEY SASSONE
(Francis Sassone)
Agent: APA - Los Angeles, 310/273-0744

WILD HEARTS CAN'T BE BROKEN   Buena Vista, 1991,
w/Matt Williams

CAROLE LUCIA SATRINA*
Contact: WGA - New York, 212/245-6180

PUSS IN BOOTS   Cannon, 1989

PETER SAUDER
ROCK & RULE (AF)   MGM/UA, 1985, w/John Halfpenny
THE CARE BEARS MOVIE (AF)   Samuel Goldwyn Company, 1985
CARE BEARS MOVIE II: A NEW GENERATION (AF)
Columbia, 1986
BABAR: THE MOVIE (AF)   New Line Cinema, 1989, w/Alan Bunce,
John DeKlein, Raymond Jaffelice & J.D. Smith

CYNTHIA SAUNDERS*
Agent: Broder-Kurland-Webb-Uffner - Beverly Hills, 310/281-3400

Screenplays:
LAY YOUR BODY DOWN
RIDE THE WIND
DECEPTION

GEORGE SAUNDERS

Agent: APA - Los Angeles, 310/273-0744
Contact: Howard M. Frumes, Manatt, Phelps, Phillips & Kantor -
 Los Angeles, 310/312-4166
Business: 213/882-4104

TEEN ANGEL   Cannon, 1991, w/John Bryant
MISSION OF JUSTICE   Image/Westwind, 1992, w/John Bryant
MARTIAL OUTLAW   Republic, 1993, Story w/John Bryant
LITTLE NINJA MAN   Cannon, 1993, w/John Bryant
SCANNER COP   Image Organization, 1993, w/John Bryant

Screenplays:
BOMB SQUAD w/John Bryant
MAGIC BUS w/John Bryant
CUSTODY w/John Bryant
LONE JUSTICE w/John Bryant
MALICIOUS
CONCRETE COWBOY
BLOOD TEST
BIG GUNS, SMALL MEN

JAMES SAUNDERS

Agent: The Casarotto Company - London, 071/287-4450

THE SAILOR'S RETURN   Euston Films Ltd., 1980

SCOTT SAUNDERS

THE LOST WORDS   Film Crash, 1994, w/Michael Kaniecki &
 Dan Keoppel, directed

JOSEPH M. SAUTER*

Contact: WGA - New York, 212/245-6180

HOTSHOT   International Film Marketing, 1987, w/Rick King

CLAUDE SAUTET

Contact: French Film Office, 745 Fifth Avenue, New York, NY 10151,
 212/832-8860

THE THINGS OF LIFE   Columbia, 1970, w/Jean-Loup Dabadie &
 Paul Guimard, directed
CESAR AND ROSALIE   Cinema 5, 1972,
 w/Jean-Loup Dabadie, directed
A FEW DAYS WITH ME   Galaxy International, 1988,
 w/Jacques Fieschi & Jerome Tonnerre, directed

PAUL SAVAGE*

Contact: WGA - Los Angeles, 310/550-1000

INCHON   MGM/UA, 1982, Story w/Robin Moore

PHILIP S. SAVATH*

Contact: WGA - Los Angeles, 310/550-1000

FAST COMPANY   Topar, 1979, w/David Cronenberg &
 Courtney Smith
BIG MEAT EATER   New Line Cinema, 1984, w/Laurence Keane &
 Chris Windsor
THE OUTSIDE CHANCE OF MAXIMILIAN GLICK
 Southgate Entertainment, 1989

JODY SAVIN*

Agent: CAA - Beverly Hills, 310/288-4545

Screenplays:
PRESUMED IMPOTENT w/Randall Miller
PIRATE TOM w/Randall Miller

JOSEPH SAVINO*

Agent: Jim Preminger Agency - Los Angeles, 310/475-9491

DETROIT ROLL (Short)   also screenplay
QUEEN'S LOGIC   7 Arts/New Line Cinema, 1991,
 Story w/Tony Spiridakis

Screenplays:
SEND IN THE CLOWNS
SEMINARY HILL
THE ELEVENTH FLOOR

NANCY SAVOCA*

Agent: United Talent Agency - Beverly Hills, 310/273-6700
Business: Forward Films, 2445 Herring Avenue, Bronx, NY 10469

TRUE LOVE   MGM/UA, 1989, w/Richard Guay, directed
HOUSEHOLD SAINTS   Fine Line Features, 1993,
 w/Richard Guay, directed

Screenplays:
GRACE UNDER PRESSURE w/Richard Guay (directing)

BEVERLY M. SAWYER*

Agent: Maggie Field Agency - Studio City, 818/980-2001

Screenplays:
ADOPTION PROJECT
JUMP CHILDREN
SOMETHING'S COMING
PEPSI
QUARTER POUND BLUES

LYNWOOD SAWYER

SPACE AVENGER   Manley Productions, 1990, w/Richard Haines

JOHN T. SAYLES*

Agent: Paradigm - Los Angeles, 310/277-4400

PIRANHA   New World, 1978
THE LADY IN RED   New World, 1979
BATTLE BEYOND THE STARS   New World, 1979
ALLIGATOR   Group 1, 1980
RETURN OF THE SECAUCUS SEVEN   Libra/Specialty Films,
 1980, directed
THE HOWLING   Avco Embassy, 1981, w/Terry Winkless
THE CHALLENGE   Embassy, 1982, w/Richard Maxwell
LIANNA   United Artists Classics, 1983, directed
BABY IT'S YOU   Paramount, 1983, directed
THE BROTHER FROM ANOTHER PLANET   Cinecom,
 1984, directed
ENORMOUS CHANGES AT THE LAST MINUTE   TC Films
 International, 1985, w/Susan Rice
THE CLAN OF THE CAVE BEAR   Warner Bros., 1986
WILD THING   Atlantic Releasing Corporation, 1987
MATEWAN   Cinecom International, 1987, directed
EIGHT MEN OUT   Orion, 1988, directed
BREAKING IN   Samuel Goldwyn Company, 1989
CITY OF HOPE   Samuel Goldwyn Company, 1991, directed
PASSION FISH ★   Miramax, 1992, directed
THE SECRET OF ROAN INNISH   Jones Entertainment Group,
 1994, directed

Screenplays:
COMMANDER
A SAFE PLACE MEN OF WAR
KILLING MR. WATSON (CTF)
BEDLAM

JULIE SAYRES*

Contact: WGA - Los Angeles, 310/550-1000

Screenplays:
UNDER A YELLOW MOON
CLOVER

JAMES SBARDELLATI

UNDER THE GUN   Marquis Pictures, 1989, w/Almer John Davis &
 James Devney, directed

GERALD SCALFE

BREAKIN'   MGM/UA/Cannon, 1984, w/Allen DeBevoise &
 Charles Parker

GLEN SCANTLEBURY
STEAL AMERICA   Tara Releasing, 1992, w/Lucy Phillips

DARIO SCARDAPANE
Agent: The Gersh Agency - Beverly Hills, 310/274-6611

POSSE   Gramercy, 1993, w/Sy Richardson

Screenplays:
RAINY DAY MEN
A TIME FOR HEROES
CYCLES w/Josh Becker

ROMANO SCAVOLINI
NIGHTMARE   21st Century Distribution, 1981
DOG TAGS   Cinevest Entertainment Group, 1989, directed

ROSE A. SCHACHT*
Agent: Martin Hurwitz Associates - Beverly Hills, 310/274-0240

NIGHT OWL (CTF)   Morgan Hill Films/Hearst Entertainment, 1993,
   w/Ann Powell

Screenplays:
LUCKY STRIKE w/Ann Powell

STEVEN SCHACHTER*
Agent: ICM - Beverly Hills, 310/550-4000

MARY SILLIMAN'S WAR (CTF)   Heritage Films/Citadel Films, 1994,
   w/Louisa Burns Bisogno
ABOVE SUSPICION (CTF)   Rysher, 1994, w/Jerry Lazarus &
   W.H. Macy

BLAKE SCHAEFER
CRACK HOUSE   Cannon, 1989

ERIC SCHAEFFER
Agent: CAA - Beverly Hills, 310/288-4545

MY LIFE'S IN TURNAROUND   Arrow Releasing, 1994,
   w/Donal Lardner Ward, co-directed

Screenplays:
WHAT EVER HAPPENED TO LOVE AT FIRST SIGHT
   w/Donal Lardner Ward
IF LUCY FELL
DAD'S THE NEW SAVIOR
LIKE AL AND ME
MAY I SEE YOU AGAIN
METER MADNESS
SAL'S PIZZA MOVIE
WHAT ABOUT LOVE

FRANCIS (FRANKY) SCHAEFFER
Agent: Becsey/Wisdom/Kalajian Agency - Los Angeles, 310/550-0535

WIRED TO KILL   American Distribution Group, 1986, directed

KEN SCHAFER
Agent: Irvin Arthur Associates - Beverly Hills, 310/278-5934

Screenplays:
A DEATH WITH BRUSH
SHATTER GAME

JOHN J. SCHALTER*
Agent: Jon Klane Agency - Beverly Hills, 310/278-0178

Screenplays:
SIR FRANCIS
BEATING THE ODDS
DALLAS TEXANS
THE GAME

NIGHTCALLER
PROFESSOR HOLMES
COACH MOM
ESCAPE
OVERTIME
DREAM LOVERS
THE QUID PRO QUO
BLOOD GAMES
PEACEKEEPERS AT WAR
AUTUMN DANCE
DOWN MEXICO WAY

MIMI SCHAPIRO*
Agent: The Irv Schechter Company - Beverly Hills, 310/278-8070

DROP DEAD GORGEOUS (CTF)   Power Pictures Corp., 1991,
   w/Thomas Baum & Bill Wells

JEFFREY SCHECHTER*
Agent: William Morris Agency - Beverly Hills, 310/274-7451
Manager: Jonathan Baruch/PRO Management - Los Angeles,
   310/478-5159

Screenplays:
BLOODSPORT II: THE NEXT KUMITE (Odyssey)
JADE FOG RISING
DEAR MR. TURNER
ME TOO
LITTLE BIG FOOT

MICHAEL B. SCHEFF*
Agent: Shapiro/Lichtman - Los Angeles, 310/859-8877

AIRPORT '77   Universal, 1977, w/David Spector
WELCOME TO L.A. (Short)   1993, directed

Screenplays:
BUZZARDS LUCK w/Mary Anne Kasica

ADAM SCHEINMAN*
Contact: WGA - Los Angeles, 310/550-1000

LITTLE BIG LEAGUE   Columbia, 1994, w/Gregory K. Pincus

ANDREW SCHEINMAN
Business: Castle Rock, 310/285-2300

NORTH   Columbia, 1994, w/Alan Zweibel

MAXMILLIAN SCHELL
Agent: Camden-ITG - Los Angeles, 310/289-2700

END OF THE GAME   20th Century-Fox, 1976,
   w/Friedrich Durrenmatt, directed

GEORGE W. SCHENCK*
Agent: Major Clients Agency - Los Angeles, 310/284-6400

MORE DEAD THAN ALIVE   United Artists, 1968
BARQUERO   United Artists, 1970, w/William Marks
FUTUREWORLD   American International, 1976, w/Mayo Simon
ESCAPE 2000   New World, 1983, Story w/David Lawrence &
   Robert Williams
DYING TO REMEMBER (CTF)   USA Network, 1993,
   w/Frank Cardea & Brian L. Ross

CARL SCHENKEL
Agent: CAA - Beverly Hills, 310/288-4545

SILENCE LIKE GLASS   Moviestore Entertainment, 1989,
   w/Bea Hellman, directed

ROBERT SCHENKKAN*
Agent: Writers & Artists Agency - Los Angeles, 310/824-6300

THE KENTUCKY CYCLE (P)   also screenplay
FINAL PASSAGES (P)
TACHINOKI (P)
THE SURVIVALIST (P)
HEAVEN ON EARTH (P)
MAGIC (P)
THE WALL (Short)   directing

FRED SCHEPISI*
Agent: ICM - New York, 212/556-5600

THE DEVIL'S PLAYGROUND   Entertainment Marketing,
    1976, directed
THE CHANT OF JIMMIE BLACKSMITH   New Yorker,
    1978, directed
A CRY IN THE DARK   Warner Bros., 1988, w/Robert Caswell

SHAWN SCHEPPS*
Agent: ICM - Beverly Hills, 310/550-4000
Business: Hollywood Pictures - 818/560-1000

THE STEVEN WEED SHOW (P)
CONSPICIOUS CONSUMPTION (P)
ENCINO MAN   Buena Vista, 1992
SON-IN-LAW   Buena Vista, 1993, w/Fax Bahr & Adam Small
MANY ARE CALLED (Short)   1993

Screenplays:
CAT AND ALLISON ARE HAVING A BAD WEEK

J. NOYES SCHER
Business: Northwinds Entertainment, 3 Sheridan Square - Apt. 8A,
    New York, NY 10014

PRISONERS OF INERTIA   Northwinds Entertainment,
    1989, directed

GREGORY SCHERICK*
Contact: WGA - Los Angeles, 310/550-1000

THE NIGHT BEFORE   Kings Road Productions, 1987,
    w/Thom Eberhardt

GARRETT K. SCHIFF*
Agent: The Agency - Los Angeles, 310/551-3000

Screenplays:
THE FINEST IN THE FIELD
MY OWN BACKYARD

LAURA SCHIFF
JULES VERNE'S 800 LEAGUES DOWN THE AMAZON   Concorde,
    1993, w/Jackson Barr

NADINE SCHIFF
Business: Stonebridge Entertainment, Columbia Pictures -
    Los Angeles, 310/280-6800

MADE IN AMERICA   Warner Bros., 1993,
    Story w/Marcia Brandwynne & Holly Goldberg Sloan

ROBIN L. SCHIFF*
Agent: Broder-Kurland-Webb-Uffner - Beverly Hills, 310/281-3400

THE LADIES ROOM (P)
LOVERBOY   Tri-Star, 1989, w/Leslie Dixon & Tom Ropelewski

Screenplays:
ROMY AND MICHELE'S HIGH SCHOOL REUNION
LET'S CALL THE WHOLE THING OFF
VENUS IN BLUE JEANS
RSVP

MICHAEL SCHIFFER*
Agent: CAA - Beverly Hills, 310/288-4545

COLORS   Orion, 1988
LEAN ON ME   Warner Bros., 1989
CRIMSON TIDE   Buena Vista, 1995

Screenplays:
BLUE AND GOLD
THE RIVERKEEPER
RUN DON'T WALK
SEE JANE RUN
THE POST-DOC
THE GUN MOLL

SUZANNE SCHIFFMAN
Contact: French Film Office, 745 Fifth Avenue, New York, NY 10151,
    212/832-8860

DAY FOR NIGHT ★   Warner Bros., 1974, w/Jean-Louis Richard &
    Francois Truffaut
THE STORY OF ADELE H.   New World, 1975, w/Jean Gruault &
    Francois Truffaut
SMALL CHANGE *L'ARGENT DE POCHE*   New World, 1976,
    w/Francois Truffaut
THE MAN WHO LOVED WOMEN   Cinema 5, 1977,
    w/Michel Fermaud & Francois Truffaut
THE LAST METRO   United Artists, 1981, w/Francois Truffaut
THE WOMAN NEXT DOOR   United Artists Classics, 1981,
    w/Jean Aurel & Francois Truffaut
VIVEMENT DIMANCHE   Spectrafilm, 1983, w/Jean Aurel &
    Francois Truffaut
CONFIDENTIALLY YOURS   Spectrafilm, 1984, w/Jean Aurel &
    Francois Truffaut
LOVE ON THE GROUND   Spectrafilm, 1986, w/others
SORCERESS *LA MOINE ET LA SORCIERE*   European Classics,
    1987, directed

WILLIAM SCHIFRIN*
Agent: William Morris Agency - Beverly Hills, 310/274-7451

Screenplays:
THE NEXT BIG THING w/Joel Wilf
NOWHERE GIRL

TOM SCHILLER*
Contact: Marc Chamlin, Loeb & Loeb - New York, 212/692-4855

NOTHING LASTS FOREVER   MGM/UA Classics, 1984, directed

Screenplays:
SAFARI w/Sandy Krinski

FRANK SCHILLING
Contact: David Kingsdale - Los Angeles, 310/447-3666

Screenplays:
THE SHORT CUT
TELEVISION, ROMANCE & INFIDELITY
BITING RITA

VIVIAN SCHILLING
SOULTAKER   Taurus Entertainment, 1990

Screenplays:
BLACK CREEK

ROBERT SCHIRMER
Agent: Renaissance-H.N. Swanson - Los Angeles, 310/246-6000

Screenplays:
STORM CHASERS

F
I
L
M

W
R
I
T
E
R
S

MURRAY SCHISGAL*
Agent: Arthur B. Greene - New York, 212/661-8200
Business: Punch Productions Inc., 75 Rockefeller Plaza, New York,
  NY 10019, 212/484-6900

LUV (P)
ALL OVER TOWN (P)
JIMMY SHINE (P)
TWICE AROUND THE PARK (P)
A NEED FOR BRUSSEL SPROUTS (P)
THE TIGER MAKES OUT   Columbia, 1967,
  from his play "The Typists & The Tiger"
TOOTSIE ★   Columbia, 1982, w/Larry Gelbart

Screenplays:
THE STAND IN
DAYS AND NIGHTS OF A FRENCH HORN PLAYER
CHEAP LAUGHS

GEORGE SCHLATTER*
Business: George Schlatter Productions, 8321 Beverly Blvd.,
  Los Angeles, CA 90048, 213/655-1400

FIRE AND ICE   Concorde, 1987, w/Digby Wolfe

CRAIG SCHLATTMAN
AT GROUND ZERO   Proletariat Pictures/Roadfilm Productions,
  1994, directed

JOHN SCHLESINGER
Agent: United Talent Agency - Beverly Hills, 310/273-6700

TERMINUS (FD)   British Transport Films, 1961, directed
MADAME SOUSATZKA   Universal, 1988,
  w/Ruth Prawer Jhabvala, directed

Screenplays:
GOOD DAYS w/David Leavitt (directing)

VOLKER SCHLONDORFF
Agent: ICM - New York, 212/556-5600

THE TIN DRUM   United Artists, 1979, w/Jean-Claude Carriere &
  Franz Seitz
CIRCLE OF DECEIT   *DIE FALSCHUNG*   United Artists Classics,
  1982, w/Jean-Claude Carriere, Margarethe von Trotta &
  Kai Hermann, directed
VOYAGER   Castle Hill Productions, 1991,
  w/Rudy Wurlitzer, directed

RANDY B. SCHLOSSMAN*
Agent: APA - Los Angeles, 310/273-0744

Screenplays:
STUCK IN THE MIDDLE

ARNE L. SCHMIDT
Agent: ICM - Beverly Hills, 310/550-4000

Screenplays:
DEAD DROP w/Rick Seaman (Story)

ARNOLD SCHMIDT
DEJA VU   Cannon, 1985, w/Ezra D. Rappaport &
  Anthony Richmond

MARLENE SCHMIDT
THEY'RE PLAYING WITH FIRE   New World, 1984,
  w/Hikmet Avedis
THE FIFTH FLOOR   Film Ventures International, 1980,
  Story w/Hikmet Avedis
MORTUARY   Artists Releasing Corporation/Film Ventures
  International, 1983, w/Hikmet Avedis

RICK SCHMIDT
MORGAN'S CAKE   L.L. Productions, 1989, directed
AMERICAN ORPHEUS   L.L. Production, 1992, directed

RONALD SCHMIDT
APEX   Republic Pictures, 1994, w/Philip J. Roth

WAYNE SCHMIDT
THE DAY TIME ENDED   Compass International, 1979,
  w/J. Larry Carroll & David L. Schmoeller

WILLIAM SCHMIDT*
Agent: Dytman & Schwartz - Beverly Hills, 310/274-8844

THE SOUND AND THE SILENCE (CTF)   Screen Star Entertainment/
  Atlantis Films, 1993, w/Tony Foster

WILL SCHMITZ
LADY AVENGER   Marco Colombo, 1989, w/Keith Kaczorek

JONATHAN SCHMOCK*
Agent: Paradigm - Los Angeles, 310/277-4400

Screenplays:
THE SANDAL BROTHERS w/Jim Vallely

DAVID L. SCHMOELLER*
Agent: Shapiro/Lichtman - Los Angeles, 310/859-8877
Business: The Schmoeller Corporation, 2244 Stanley Hills Dr.,
  Los Angeles, CA 90046, 213/654-0748

TOURIST TRAP   Compass International, 1979,
  w/J. Larry Carroll, directed
THE DAY TIME ENDED   Compass International, 1979,
  w/J. Larry Carroll & Wayne Schmidt
THE SEDUCTION   Avco Embassy, 1982, directed
CRAWLSPACE   Empire Pictures, 1986, directed
GHOST TOWN   Empire Pictures, 1988, Story, directed
CATACOMBS   Empire Pictures, 1988, under pseudonym, directed
PUPPET MASTER   Full Moon Entertainment, 1989,
  under pseudonym, directed
NETHERWORLD   Full Moon Entertainment, 1991,
  under pseudonym, directed

Screenplays:
THE DATE (directing)

STEPHEN SCHNECK*
Agent: Stone Manners Agency - Los Angeles, 213/654-7575

WELCOME TO BLOOD CITY   EMI, 1977, w/Michael Winder
TEHACHAPI   Hemdale, 1993

SCOTT J. SCHNEID*
Agent: Innovative Artists - Los Angeles, 310/553-5200
Contact: Jared Levine, Gruber, Wender, Levine, 315 S. Beverly Dr. -
  Suite 400, Beverly Hills, CA 90212

PHANTOM OF THE MALL: ERIC'S REVENGE   Fries Entertainment,
  1989, w/Robert King & Tony Michelman

Screenplays:
MOUNT MANHATTAN w/Tony Michelman
DOWNFALL w/Tony Michelman
THE RED HOUR LEGACY w/Tony Michelman
INVASION OF THE BODY BUILDERS w/Tony Michelman

BARRY SCHNEIDER
Agent: Premiere Artists - Los Angeles, 310/271-1414

RUBY   Dimension, 1977, w/George Edwards
HARPER VALLEY P.T.A.   April Fools, 1978, w/George Edwards
ROLLER BOOGIE   United Artists, 1979
TAKE THIS JOB AND SHOVE IT   Avco Embassy, 1981

DEADLY FORCE   Embassy, 1983, w/Ken Blackwell &
   Robert Vincent O'Neil
MOTHER'S BOYS   Dimension, 1994, w/Richard Hawley

Screenplays:
SEX IN THE FORBIDDEN ZONE
BEHIND BLUE EYES

MITCHELL SCHNEIDER*
Agent: The Coppage Company - North Hollywood, 818/980-1106

Screenplays:
BUSTIN' OUT
THE ART OF DECEPTION
POOR BOYS
RIDING THE WIND
UNSTRUNG HERO

STEVEN SCHOENBERG*
Agent: United Talent Agency - Beverly Hills, 310/273-6700
Contact: Lloyd Braun, Silverberg, Katz, Thompson & Braun -
   Los Angeles, 310/445-5801

LEGION OF IRON   Epic Productions, 1989, w/Rueben Gordon
KING OF THE STREETS   ALIEN WARRIOR   Shapiro Entertainment,
   1986, w/Rueben Gordon, Edward Hunt & Barry Pearson

Screenplays:
MIDNIGHT HEAT w/Rueben Gordon
HEART OF GOLD w/Rueben Gordon

STUART SCHOFFMAN*
Agent: Maggie Field Agency - Studio City, 818/980-2001

THE FINEST HOUR (CTF)   21st Century Film Corporation, 1993,
   w/Shimon Dotan

Screenplays:
FLAMINGO FOLLIES (AF)
RAPUNZEL
STACY OF ARABIA
GIVE A GIRL A BREAK
RED TAPE
GENTLE VENGEANCE
JAMAICA
QUEENIE & JACK
FULL MOON
GENESIS

ROBERT SCHOOLEY
THE RETURN OF JAFAR (AHVF)   Buena Vista, 1994,
   Story w/Duane Capizzi, Douglas Langdale, Mark McCorkle &
   Tad Stories

AMY SCHOR*
Contact: WGA - Los Angeles, 310/550-1000

MR. WONDERFUL   Warner Bros., 1993, w/Vicki Polon

Screenplays:
THE SUMMER I SHRUNK MY GRANDMOTHER
THE 27-YEAR ITCH
SOMETHING BORROWED, SOMETHING BLUE

DAVID J. SCHOW*
Agent: United Talent Agency - Beverly Hills, 310/273-6700

LEATHERFACE: TEXAS CHAINSAW MASSACRE III
   New Line Cinema, 1990
CRITTERS 3   New Line Cinema, 1992
CRITTERS 4   New Line Cinema, 1992
THE CROW   Miramax, 1994, w/John Shirley

LEONARD SCHRADER*
Agent: Writers & Artists Agency - Los Angeles, 310/824-6300
Business Manager: Cooper, Epstein, Hurewitz - Beverly Hills,
   310/278-1111

THE YAKUZA   Warner Bros., 1975, Story
BLUE COLLAR   Universal, 1978, w/Paul Schrader
OLD BOYFRIENDS   Avco Embassy, 1978, w/Paul Schrader
THE MAN WHO STOLE THE SUN   Kitty, 1982,
   w/Kazuhiko Hasegawa
MISHIMA: A LIFE IN FOUR CHAPTERS   Warner Bros., 1985,
   w/Paul Schrader
KISS OF THE SPIDER WOMAN ★   New Yorker Films, 1985
NAKED TANGO   August Entertainment, 1990, directed

PAUL SCHRADER*
Agent: ICM - Beverly Hills, 310/550-4000

THE YAKUZA   Warner Bros., 1975, w/Robert Towne
TAXI DRIVER   Columbia, 1976
OBSESSION   Columbia, 1976
ROLLING THUNDER   Universal, 1978, w/Heywood Gould
BLUE COLLAR   Universal, 1978, w/Leonard Schrader, directed
OLD BOYFRIENDS   Avco Embassy, 1978, w/Leonard Schrader
HARDCORE   Columbia, 1979, directed
AMERICAN GIGOLO   Paramount, 1980, directed
RAGING BULL   United Artists, 1980, w/Mardik Martin
MISHIMA: A LIFE IN FOUR CHAPTERS   Warner Bros., 1985,
   w/Leonard Schader, directed
THE MOSQUITO COAST   Warner Bros., 1986
LIGHT OF DAY   Tri-Star, 1987, directed
THE LAST TEMPTATION OF CHRIST   Universal, 1988
LIGHT SLEEPER   Fine Line Features, 1992, directed

Screenplays:
GOTTI
INVESTIGATION
HEAVEN BELOW w/H. Miller
FOREVER MINE
8 SCENES FROM THE LIFE OF HANK WILLIAMS
COVERT PURPLE
HOLY BLOOD, HOLY GRAIL
GERSHWIN
QUEBECOIS
PIPELINER

NEVIN D. SCHREINER*
Agent: Peter Turner Agency - Santa Monica, 310/315-4772

MEMORIES OF MURDER (CTF)   Houston Lady Co./Viacom, 1990,
   w/John Harrison
THIS GUN FOR HIRE (CTF)   BBK Productions/MTE, 1991
MISSING PARENTS (Short)   Showtime, 1991
WHITE LIE (CTF)   MCA Television Entertainment, 1991
TRIAL & ERROR (CTF)   Alliance Communications/USA Network,
   1993, w/Jim Lindsay & Rick Way
LINDA (CTF)   Wilshire Court Productions, 1993
DON'T TALK TO STRANGERS (CTF)   MCA Television
   Entertainment, 1994, w/Jon George & Neill Hicks

Screenplays:
KEEPERS
THE CHINA LAKE MURDERS (CTF)
GARCIA
BOOKWORM
THE NEWCOMER
NEW MOON

BARBET SCHROEDER
Agent: CAA - Beverly Hills, 310/288-4545

THE VALLEY obscured by clouds   Lagoon Associates,
   1972, directed
MAITRESSE   Gaumont, 1976, w/Paul Voujargol, directed
LES TRICHEURS   Filmsan Galatee, 1983, w/Pascal Bonitzer &
   Steve Baes, directed

MICHAEL SCHROEDER
CYBORG 2: GLASS SHADOW   Trimark, 1993, w/Mark Geldman &
    Ron Yanover, directed

BUDD SCHULBERG*
Agent: The Artists Agency - Los Angeles, 310/277-7779

WINTER CARNIVAL   United Artists, 1939, w/Lester Cole
ON THE WATERFRONT ★★   Columbia, 1954
A FACE IN THE CROWD   Warner Bros., 1957
WIND ACROSS THE EVERGLADES   Warner Bros., 1958

Screenplays:
WHAT MAKES SAMMY RUN?

SANDRA SCHULBERG
WILDROSE   Troma, 1985, Story w/John Hansen

ARNOLD SCHULMAN*
Agent: ICM - Beverly Hills, 310/550-4000
Business Manager: Starr & Co., 350 Park Ave., New York,
    NY 10022, 212/759-6556

WILD IS THE WIND   Paramount, 1957
A HOLE IN THE HEAD   United Artists, 1959, from his play
CIMARRON   MGM, 1960
LOVE WITH THE PROPER STRANGER ★   Paramount, 1963
THE NIGHT THEY RAIDED MINSKY'S   United Artists, 1968,
    w/Norman Lear & Sidney Michaels
GOODBYE, COLUMBUS ★   Paramount, 1969
TO FIND A MAN   Columbia, 1971
FUNNY LADY   Columbia, 1975, w/Jay Presson Allen
WON TON TON, THE DOG WHO SAVED HOLLYWOOD
    Paramount, 1976, w/Cy Howard
PLAYERS   Paramount, 1979
A CHORUS LINE   Columbia, 1985
TUCKER: THE MAN AND HIS DREAM   Paramount, 1988,
    w/David Seidler
AND THE BAND PLAYED ON (CTF)   HBO Pictures, 1993

TOM SCHULMAN*
Agent: CAA - Beverly Hills, 310/288-4545

DEAD POETS SOCIETY ★★   Buena Vista, 1989
HONEY, I SHRUNK THE KIDS   Buena Vista, 1989, w/Ed Naha
SECOND SIGHT   Warner Bros., 1989, w/Patricia Resnick
WHAT ABOUT BOB?   Buena Vista, 1991
MEDICINE MAN   Buena Vista, 1992, w/Sally Robinson

Screenplays:
THE DANCING MAN

JEFF SCHULTZ
NORTH OF PITTSBURGH   Cinephile, 1992

CHARLES M. SCHULZ
Contact: United Features Syndicate

A BOY NAMED CHARLIE BROWN (AF)   National General, 1968
SNOOPY, COME HOME (AF)   National General, 1972
RACE FOR YOUR LIFE, CHARLIE BROWN (AF)   Paramount, 1978
BOY VOYAGE CHARLIE BROWN (AND DON'T COME BACK) (AF)
    Paramount, 1980

JOEL SCHUMACHER*
Agent: CAA - Beverly Hills, 310/288-4545

SPARKLE   Warner Bros., 1976
CAR WASH   Universal, 1976
THE WIZ   Universal, 1978
D.C. CAB   Universal, 1983, directed
ST. ELMO'S FIRE   Columbia, 1985, w/Carl Kurlander, directed

Screenplays:
HOBGOBLINS
EXPENSIVE SHOES

LEON SCHUSTER
KWAGGA STRIKES BACK   Genesis Releasing, 1991,
    w/Paul Slabolepszy, Australian

AL SCHWARTZ
LOOKIN' TO GET OUT   Paramount, 1982, w/Jon Voight
TOO MUCH SUN   New Line Cinema, 1990, w/Robert Downey &
    Laura Ernst

BEN SCHWARTZ
Agent: Original Artists - Santa Monica, 310/394-1067

Screenplays:
THE EAGLE KING
FURIOUS GEORGE

JOHN ALAN SCHWARTZ*
Contact: WGA - Los Angeles, 310/550-1000

BLACK ICE (CTF)   Saban Entertainment, 1993, w/Arne Olsen

LLOYD J. SCHWARTZ*
Agent: Lenhoff/Robinson - Los Angeles, 310/558-4700

GILLIGAN'S ISLAND: THE MUSICAL (P)   w/Sherwood Schwartz
THE BRADY BUNCH MOVIE   Paramount, 1995,
    w/Sherwood Schwartz

MARJORIE SCHWARTZ*
Contact: WGA - Los Angeles, 310/550-1000

THE BUTCHER'S WIFE   Paramount, 1991, w/Ezra Litwak

Screenplays:
RADIO FREE ALASKA w/Ezra Litwak
WINGS OF DESIRE w/Ezra Litwak
DANCING IN THE DARK w/Ezra Litwak
JUST DESERT w/Ezra Litwak

MARTIN SCHWARTZ
Agent: William Morris Agency - Beverly Hills, 310/274-7451

Screenplays:
THE MONK w/Steven James Ross (Gramercy)

SHERWOOD SCHWARTZ*
Contact: Rose Schwartz, Schwartz & Mark - Los Angeles,
    310/284-7882

GILLIGAN'S ISLAND: THE MUSICAL (P)   w/Lloyd Schwartz
THE BRADY BUNCH MOVIE   Paramount, 1995, w/Lloyd Schwartz

STEVEN S. SCHWARTZ*
Agent: Jon Klane Agency - Beverly Hills, 310/278-0178
Address: 53 Curtiss Rd., New Preston, CT 06177, 203/868-0627

Screenplays:
CRITICAL CARE
THE TREEMAKER
THE BLUE HOUR

TERRY SCHWARTZ
LITTLE NIKITA   Columbia, 1988, Story w/Tom Musca

DAVID SCHWIMMER
Contact: Screen Actors Guild - Los Angeles, 213/954-1600

THE PERSISTENCE OF MEMORY (P)
THE JUNGLE (P)   Adaptation

Screenplays:
BROKEN TIME w/Susan Black

ETTORE SCOLA
Address: via Bertoloni, 1/E, Rome, Italy, 06/875-174

ADUA E LE COMPAGNE   Zebra Film, 1960, w/Ruggero Maccari,
   Antonio Pietrangeli & Tullio Pinelli
DOWN AND DIRTY   *BRUTTI, SPORCHI E CATTIVI*
   New Line Cinema, 1976, directed
A SPECIAL DAY   Cinema 5, 1977, w/Ruggero Maccari, directed
PASSIONE D'AMORE   Putnam Square, 1982,
   w/Ruggero Maccari, directed
LA NUIT DE VARENNES   Triumph/Columbia, 1982,
   w/Sergio Amidei, directed
LE BAL   Almi Classics, 1983, w/Ruggero Maccari,
   Jean-Claude Penchenat & Furio Scarpelli, directed
MACARONI   Paramount, 1985, w/Furio Scarpelli &
   Ruggero Maccari
THE FAMILY   Vestron, 1987, directed

MARTIN SCORSESE*
Agent: CAA - Beverly Hills, 310/288-4545
Business: Tribeca Film Center, 375 Greenwich St., New York,
   NY 10013, 212/941-4000

MEAN STREETS   Warner Bros., 1973, w/Mardik Martin, directed
GOOD FELLAS ★   Warner Bros., 1990,
   w/Nicholas Pileggi, directed
THE AGE OF INNOCENCE ★   Columbia, 1993,
   w/Jay Cocks, directed
CASINO   Universal, 1995, w/Nicholas Pileggi, directed

ALEXANDER R. SCOTT
Agent: Paradigm - Los Angeles, 310/277-4400

THE HEARTH(P)

Screenplays:
KNIGHT TO KING ONE

ALLAN G. SCOTT*
Agent: ICM - Beverly Hills, 310/550-4000

THE MAN WHO HAD POWER OVER WOMEN   Avco Embassy,
   1971, w/Chris Bryant
DON'T LOOK NOW   Paramount, 1974, w/Chris Bryant
THE GIRL FROM PETROVKA   Universal, 1974, w/Chris Bryant
THE SPIRAL STAIRCASE   Warner Bros., 1975, w/Chris Bryant
JOSEPH ANDREWS   Paramount, 1977, w/Chris Bryant
THE AWAKENING   Orion/Warner Bros., 1980, w/Chris Bryant &
   Clive Exton
MARTIN'S DAY   MGM/UA, 1985, w/Chris Bryant
D.A.R.Y.L.   Paramount, 1985, w/David Ambrose & Jeffrey Ellis
CASTAWAY   Cannon, 1987
APPRENTICE TO MURDER   New World, 1988, w/Wesley Moore
THE WITCHES   Warner Bros., 1990
COLD HEAVEN   Hemdale, 1992

Screenplays:
MORGAN'S PASSING
LILAH
THE KILLING KIND
THE LAST SPY
TRUE BLUE
THE PRACTICAL HEART
IN TIME OF WAR
THE FOURTH ANGEL
THE MATING BIRDS
NINE TIGER MAN w/Chris Bryant
GOODBYE CALIFORNIA w/Chris Bryant
THE CHALLENGER
ACROSS THE RIVER AND INTO THE TREES
DON COYOTE
ABRACADAVER
ALEXANDRA

CYNTHIA SCOTT
Agent: Becsey/Wisdom/Kalajian Agency - Los Angeles, 310/550-0535
Address: 225 Clarke, Montreal, Quebec H3Ü 2E3, Canada

STRANGERS IN GOOD COMPANY   First Run Features/Castle Hill
   Releasing, 1991, w/Sally Bochner, Gloria Demers &
   David Wilson, directed

DARIN SCOTT
Agent: Irene Robinson Group - Los Angeles, 213/274-5101

THE OFFSPRING   TMS Pictures, 1987, w/Jeff Burr &
   C. Courtney Joyner

Screenplays:
TALES FROM THE HOOD w/Rusty Cundieff (Savoy)
PEE WEES
THE PERFECT GIRL

GAVIN SCOTT*
Agent: William Morris Agency - Beverly Hills, 310/274-7451

Screenplays:
SMALL SOLDIERS

JAMES SCOTT
Address: P.O. Box 69799, Los Angeles, CA 90069

STRIKE IT RICH   Miillimeter Films, 1990, directed

JEFFREY A. SCOTT*
Contact: WGA - Los Angeles, 310/550-1000

STARCHASER: THE LEGEND OF ORIN   Atlantic Releasing
   Corporation, 1985

JOHN SCOTT
Agent: Neal Stevens & Associates - Beverly Hills, 310/275-7541

Screenplays:
AGAINST THE WIND w/Kent Wilson

MIKE SCOTT*
Agent: The Irv Schechter Company - Beverly Hills, 310/278-8070

THE LITTLE RASCALS   Universal, 1994,
   Story w/Robert Wolterstorff & Penelope Spheeris

MILCA SANCHEZ-SCOTT
(See Milca SANCHEZ-Scott)

ROBERT OWENS SCOTT
KNOWING LISA   Imagining Things Enterprises, 1992

NELL SCOVELL*
Agent: United Talent Agency - Beverly Hills, 310/273-6700

Screenplays:
REUNIONS

SUSAN SCRANTON
GAS   Paramount, 1981, Story w/Dick Wolf

MIKE SCULLY*
Agent: The Irv Schechter Company - Beverly Hills, 310/278-8070

Screenplays:
SUMO WRESTLER PROJECT

STEVEN SEAGAL*
Agent: CAA - Beverly Hills, 310/288-4545
Business: Steamroller Productions, Warner Bros. Pictures,
818/954-4267

ABOVE THE LAW   Warner Bros., 1988,
Story w/Andrew Davis

Screenplays:
MAN OF HONOR
CRUISE w/Jim Carabatsos

PETER S. SEAMAN*
Agent: CAA - Beverly Hills, 310/288-4545

TRENCHCOAT   Buena Vista, 1983, w/Jeffrey Price
WHO FRAMED ROGER RABBIT   Buena Vista, 1988,
w/Jeffrey Price
DOC HOLLYWOOD   Warner Bros., 1991, w/Jeffrey Price &
Daniel Pyne

Screenplays:
HOUDINI w/Jeffrey Price
MR. WHISTLE w/Jeffrey Price
SPEND, SPEND, SPEND w/Jeffrey Price
LAST HOLIDAY w/Jeffrey Price
GOOD KING HARRY w/Jeffrey Price
MISS MOTHERWELL w/Jeffrey Price

BROCKMAN SEAWELL
TOP OF THE WORLD   Denver Center Productions, 1993,
w/Jamie Horton

DAVIN R. SEAY*
Agent: William Morris Agency - Beverly Hills, 310/274-7451

Screenplays:
THE WANDERER
HOME FREE

BEVERLY SEBASTIAN
THE AMERICAN ANGELS: BAPTISM OF BLOOD   Sebastian
International Pictures, 1990, w/Ferd Sebastian, co-directed
RUNNING COOL   Sebastian International Pictures/Paramount
Home Video, 1994, w/Ferd Sebastian, co-directed

FERD SEBASTIAN
THE AMERICAN ANGELS: BAPTISM OF BLOOD   Sebastian
International Pictures, 1990, w/Beverly Sebastian, co-directed
RUNNING COOL   Sebastian International Pictures/Paramount
Home Video, 1994, w/Beverly Sebastian, co-directed

MARC SEDAKA
Agent: Premiere Artists - Los Angeles, 310/271-1414

Screenplays:
OVERNIGHT DELIVERY
JUDGE BOB
THE MAYOR OF NEW YORK
GOOFMAN w/Bob Hoge

JOHN WILLIAM SEE*
Contact: 503/231-8294

FEAR OF ACTING (P)
THE LADY CRIES MURDER (P)
GETTING EVEN   New World, 1983

Screenplays:
REVENGE ROMANCE
BODYGUARD

IAN SEEBERG*
Agent: APA - Los Angeles, 310/273-0744

THE COMPANION (CTF)   USA/Michael Phillips Productions, 1994,
w/Valerie Bennett

Screenplays:
MYSTERY BENEATH w/Valerie Bennett
WAKE UP CALL w/Valerie Bennett
TIMERS w/Valerie Bennett
HIGHER GROUND TEMPTATION w/Valerie Bennett
MORT w/Valerie Bennett
CAT & MOUSE w/Valerie Bennett

ERICH SEGAL*
Business Manager: Albert Rettig, Esq., 11777 San Vicente Blvd. -
Suite 601, Los Angeles, CA 90049, 310/826-6330

YELLOW SUBMARINE (AF)   King Features, 1968, w/others
RPM   Columbia, 1970
THE GAMES   20th Century-Fox, 1970
LOVE STORY ★   Paramount, 1970
JENNIFER ON MY MIND   United Artists, 1971
OLIVER'S STORY   Paramount, 1978, w/John Korty
A CHANGE OF SEASONS   20th Century-Fox, 1980,
w/Fred Segal & Ronni Kern
MAN, WOMAN AND CHILD   Paramount, 1983,
w/David Z. Goodman

JERRY SEGAL*
Contact: WGA - Los Angeles, 310/550-1000

ONE ON ONE   Warner Bros., 1977, w/Robby Benson
DIE LAUGHING   Orion/Warner Bros., 1980, w/Robby Benson &
Scott Parker

LINDA A. SEGALL*
Contact: WGA - Los Angeles, 310/550-1000

Screenplays:
TROUBLE IN TARZANA
CUBBIE

JEB SEIBEL
THE CHANNELER   Magnum Entertainment, 1991, w/Jeff Falls &
Peter Mead

FREDERICK SEIDEL
Agent: Peters, Fraser & Dunlop - London, 071/376-7676

AFRAID OF THE DARK   Fine Line Features, 1992, w/Mark Peploe

Screenplays:
VICTORY w/Mark Peploe (Miramax)

STAN SEIDEL*
Agent: Sanford-Gross & Associates - Los Angeles, 310/208-2100

Screenplays:
RADIO MAN w/Richard Murphy
HIGH RESOLUTION
THE HONEYMOON
DIRECT TO THE TOP
ROOT OF ALL EVIL

SUSAN SEIDELMAN
Agent: William Morris Agency - Beverly Hills, 310/274-7451

SMITHEREENS   New Line Cinema, 1982,
Story w/Ron Nyswaner, directed
CONFESSIONS OF A SUBURBAN GIRL   BBC Scotland,
1992, directed
EROTIC TALES ★   Mercure Distribution, 1994, "The Dutch Master,"
w/Jonathan Brett, 1993, directed

Screenplays:
OZONE

ROBERT SEIDENBERG
DEAD IN THE WATER (CTF)   Kevin Bright Productions/MTE,
   1991, w/Eleanor E. Gaver & Walter Klenhard

DAVID SEIDLER*
Agent: Innovative Artists - Los Angeles, 310/553-5200

TUCKER: THE MAN AND HIS DREAM   Paramount, 1988,
   w/Arnold Schulman

Screenplays:
THE BOXER w/Jacqueline Feather
CLOSE TO HOME w/Jacqueline Feather
GLITTERBUG w/Jacqueline Feather

MERY SEIGLER
MOVIES MONEY MURDER   Hills Entertainment Group, 1992

ROY SEKOFF*
Agent: CAA - Beverly Hills, 310/288-4545

Screenplays:
BACK ON THE MAP w/Jeff Stolzer
UNHAPPY RETURNS w/Jeff Stolzer

JACK SEKOWSKI
Agent: Susan Smith & Associates - Beverly Hills, 213/852-4777

Screenplays:
DREAM MAN w/Maria Veltre
A DOG'S LIFE w/Maria Veltre
BIRTHDAY WISHES w/Maria Veltre
SHOOTING STAR

JULE SELBO*
Agent: CAA - Beverly Hills, 310/288-4545

PRISON STORIES: WOMEN ON THE INSIDE (CTF)
   Francine Letvak Productions/HBO Showcase, 1991,
   "New Chicks" w/Dick Beebe & Martin Jones
HARD PROMISES   Columbia, 1991

Screenplays:
GANGSTERS IN LOVE
STRAY DOG w/Paul Morrissey
MRS. CALIBAN
AGGIE
CHEERS
BIG SKY ROMANCE

KEN SELDEN
Agent: United Talent Agency - Beverly Hills, 310/273-6700

VACANT LOT (Short)   directed
NO SECRETS   I.R.S. Releasing, 1991, w/Dezso Magyar

Screenplays:
WHITE LIES

NICHOLAS SELDON*
Agent: The Gersh Agency - Beverly Hills, 310/274-6611

Screenplays:
THE BRINK w/Robert Skotak

DAVID SELF
Agent: Leslie Kallen Agency - Sherman Oaks, 818/906-2785

Screenplays:
VECTORS
FIELDS OF FIRE

HENRY SELICK
Agent: CAA - Beverly Hills, 310/288-4545

Screenplays:
NIGHTGAMES w/Michael Shea

MARKUS SELIN
BORN AMERICAN   Cinema Group, 1986, w/Renny Harlin

IAN SELLAR
Agent: The Artists Agency - Los Angeles, 310/277-7779

VENUS PETER   British Film Institute, 1989,
   w/Christopher Rush, directed
PRAGUE   Christopher Young Films-BBC-UGC,
   1992, directed

PETER SELLARS
Agent: CAA - Beverly Hills, 310/288-4545

THE CABINET OF DR. RAMIREZ   Capital Entertainment,
   1991, directed

ARTHUR D. SELLERS*
Agent: Shapiro/Lichtman - Los Angeles, 310/859-8877

TOFU ON THE RAMPAGE (P)
MODERN PROBLEMS   20th Century-Fox, 1981,
   w/Ken Shapiro & Tom Sherohman

Screenplays:
THE BAND
KISS-OFF
FUNGUS THE BOGEYMAN
JUNGLE BOY

KEVIN S. SELLERS*
Contact: WGA - Los Angeles, 310/550-1000

BLUE SKIES AGAIN   Warner Bros., 1983

DAVID SELTZER*
Agent: CAA - Beverly Hills, 310/288-4545

THE HELLSTROM CHRONICLE (FD)   Cinema 5, 1971
KING, QUEEN, KNAVE   Avco Embassy, 1972, w/David Shaw
ONE IS A LONELY NUMBER   MGM, 1972
THE OTHER SIDE OF THE MOUNTAIN   Universal, 1975
THE OMEN   20th Century-Fox, 1976
PROPHECY   Paramount, 1979
TABLE FOR FIVE   Warner Bros., 1983
SIX WEEKS   Polygram, 1985
LUCAS   20th Century Fox, 1986, directed
PUNCHLINE   Columbia, 1988, directed
BIRD ON A WIRE   Universal, 1990, w/Eric Lerner &
   Louis Venosta
SHINING THROUGH   20th Century Fox, 1992, directed

Screenplays:
A PERFECT DAY FOR RASPBERRY RIPPLE
THE CAMEL DRIVE OF 1890
MEGGIDO
OTHER MEN'S DAUGHTERS
HOME AQUATICUS
KILLERS
EQUAL TIME
COOL, CLEAR WATER
ASHES
WHISTLIN' DIXIE

TERREL SELTZER*
Agent: Paradigm - Los Angeles, 310/277-4400

CHAN IS MISSING   New Yorker, 1982, w/Isaac Cronin & Wayne Wang
DIM SUM: A LITTLE BIT OF HEART   Orion Classics, 1985
HOW I GOT INTO COLLEGE   20th Century Fox, 1989

Screenplays:
ALIEN TIMES
DEFENDANT
TAKING LUCY
THE BEAUTY OF IT

JOHN SEMPER*
Agent: Jim Preminger Agency - Los Angeles, 310/475-9491

CLASS ACT   Warner Bros., 1992, w/Cynthia Friedlob

LORENZO SEMPLE, JR.*
Agent: CAA - Beverly Hills, 310/288-4545

BATMAN   20th Century-Fox, 1966
FATHOM   20th Century-Fox, 1967
PRETTY POISON   20th Century-Fox, 1968
DADDY'S GONE A-HUNTING   Warner Bros., 1969, w/Larry Cohen
THE SPORTING CLUB   Avco Embassy, 1971
THE MARRIAGE OF A YOUNG STOCKBROKER   20th Century-Fox, 1971
PAPILLON   Allied Artists, 1973, w/Dalton Trumbo
THE SUPERCOPS   United Artists, 1974
THE PARALLAX VIEW   Paramount, 1974, w/David Giler
THE DROWNING POOL   Warner Bros., 1975, w/Walter Hill & Tracy Keenan Wynn
THREE DAYS OF THE CONDOR   Paramount, 1975, w/David Rayfiel
KING KONG   Paramount, 1976
HURRICANE   Paramount, 1979
FLASH GORDON   Universal, 1980
NEVER SAY NEVER AGAIN   Warner Bros., 1983
SHEENA   Columbia, 1984, w/David Newman

Screenplays:
THE DESTROYER
MANDRAKE
MILE HIGH
GOOD RIDDANCE
THE BENGAL LANCERS
WHERE THE SUN NEVER SETS
THE STARS MY DESTINATION
MUTATION
IMPATIENT

MARIA SEMPLE*
Agent: United Talent Agency - Beverly Hills, 310/273-6700

Screenplays:
AFTER VENUS
HARRIET THE SPY
UNTIL FOREVER
WILD SIDE
EASY TO LOVE

JORGE SEMPRUN
LA GUERRE EST FINIE (THE WAR IS OVER)   Bramlon, 1966
Z ★   Cinerama 5, 1969, w/Costa-Gavras
THE CONFESSION   Paramount, 1970
STAVISKY   Cinemation, 1974

AL SEPTIEN
Agent: Warden, White & Kane - Beverly Hills, 213/852-1028

TEAMMATES (P)
LEPRECHAUN 2   Trimark, 1994, w/Turi Meyer

Screenplays:
CHAIRMAN OF THE BOARD w/Turi Meyer (Trimark)
SLEEPSTALKER w/Turi Meyer
THE CONQUERORS w/Turi Meyer
FLASH POINT w/Turi Meyer
THE TERRORIST w/Turi Meyer
STORM WARNING w/Turi Meyer
THE THIRD RAIL w/Turi Meyer
CROSS OF WOOD w/Turi Meyer
CRIMINAL PAST w/Turi Meyer
THE CARRIER w/Turi Meyer

MICHAEL SERAFIN*
Agent: Warden, White & Kane, Inc. - Beverly Hills, 213/852-1028

Screenplays:
MIND YOUR OWN BUSINESS
TWO ON THE AISLE
EMBRACABLE YOU
AMERICAN BOY

YAHOO SERIOUS
(Greg Pead)
YOUNG EINSTEIN   Warner Bros., 1989, w/David Roach, directed
RECKLESS KELLY   Warner Bros., 1993, w/David Roach, Warwick Ross & Lulu Serious, directed

ALEXANDRA SEROS*
Agent: ICM - Beverly Hills, 310/550-4000

POINT OF NO RETURN   Warner Bros., 1993, w/Robert Getchell
THE SPECIALIST   Warner Bros., 1994

Screenplays:
LIBRA: THE STORY OF LEE HARVEY OSWALD

DEBORAH SERRA*
Agent: CAA - Beverly Hills, 310/288-4545

Screenplays:
PRIMAL
HONEY WEST

COLINE SERREAU*
Agent: William Morris Agency - Beverly Hills, 310/274-7451

3 MEN AND A CRADLE   Samuel Goldwyn Company, 1985, directed
MAMA, THERE'S A MAN IN YOUR BED   *ROUMALD ET JULIETTE*   Miramax, 1990, directed
LA CRISE (CRISIS-GO-ROUND)   AMLF, 1992, directed

Screenplays:
RANDALL AND JULIET (remake of MAMA..)
JOVA

PHILIPPE SETBON
Contact: French Film Office, 745 Fifth Ave., New York, NY 10151, 212/832-8860

DETECTIVE   Spectrafilm, 1985, w/Jean-Luc Godard, Anne-Marie Mieville & Alain Sarde
HONEYMOON   International Film Marketing, 1987, w/Robert Geoffrion & Patrick Jamain
MR. FROST   Triumph, 1990, w/Brad Lynch, directed

MARK SEVI
Agent: APA - Los Angeles, 310/273-0744

RELENTLESS II: DEAD ON   Cinetel, 1991
CLASS OF 1999 II: THE SUBSTITUTE   Cinetel/Trimark, 1993
GHOULIES IV   Cinetel, 1993
FAST GETAWAY II: FASTER GETAWAY   Cinetel/LIVE, 1994
RELENTLESS IV: ASHES TO ASHES   Cinetel/New Line, 1994
SCANNER COP II   Republic Pictures, 1994

Screenplays:
FORCE ON FORCE (Cinetel)
INFERNO (Image Organization)
RAINDOGS w/Rutger Hauer & Michael Lally
WALKING ON GLASS w/Joseph Shields
CARNIVAL w/Mario Puzo
HIT LIST II
DREAM A LITTLE DREAM II (Story)
NEMESIS
CLONE w/James Womer
STATE OF FEAR w/James Womer

JEFF SEYMOUR
RAVE REVIEW   Wildebeest Company, 1994, directed

DAVID SHABER*
Agent: CAA - Beverly Hills, 310/288-4545

LAST EMBRACE   United Artists, 1979
THE WARRIORS   Paramount, 1979, w/Walter Hill
THOSE LIPS, THOSE EYES   United Artists, 1980
ROLLOVER   Orion/Warner Bros., 1981
NIGHTHAWKS   Universal, 1981
FLIGHT OF THE INTRUDER   Paramount, 1991,
    w/Robert Dillon

Screenplays:
FORBIDDEN SEQUENCE
CHINESE BANDIT
GROWING MAN
THE LIMEY
LUCY
SCOTCH SOUR
RIGHTS OF PASSAGE
THE PRINCE OF 47TH STREET
FREEDOM SONG
THE CLOWN
HIGH RISE
WHEELS
VERNA, THE USC GIRL
POLYGAMIST HEAVEN SENT
STROKES
PROPATIA

SAMANTHA SHAD*
Agent: APA - Los Angeles, 310/273-0744

CLASS ACTION   20th Century Fox, 1991, w/Christopher Ames &
    Carolyn Shelby

Screenplays:
RULES OF EVIDENCE

SUSAN SHADBURNE
Business: Millenium Pictures, Inc., 2580 N.W. Upshur, Portland,
    OR 97210, 503/227-7041

THE ADVENTURES OF MARK TWAIN (AF)   Atlantic Releasing
    Corporation, 1986
SHADOW PLAY   New World, 1986, directed

KEN SHADIE
"CROCODILE" DUNDEE ★   Paramount, 1980, w/John Cornell &
    Paul Hogan

TOM SHADYAC*
Agent: United Talent Agency - Beverly Hills, 310/273-6700

ACE VENTURA, PET DETECTIVE   Warner Bros., 1994,
    w/Jack Bernstein & Jim Carrey, directed

ANTHONY SHAFFER
Agent: Renaissance-H.N. Swanson - Los Angeles, 310/246-6000

WHODUNNIT (P)
MR. FORBUSH AND THE PENGUINS   CRY OF THE PENGUINS
    EMI, 1971
FRENZY   Universal, 1972
SLEUTH   20th Century-Fox, 1972
THE WICKER MAN   Warner Bros., 1975
DEATH ON THE NILE   Paramount, 1978
EVIL UNDER THE SUN   Universal/AFD, 1982
ABSOLUTION   Trans World Entertainment, 1988
APPOINTMENT WITH DEATH   Cannon, 1988,
    w/Peter Buckman & Michael Winner
SOMMERSBY   Warner Bros., 1993, Story w/Nicholas Meyer

Screenplays:
DEATH COMES AT THE END
BO-PEEP

PETER SHAFFER
Agent: The Lantz Office - New York, 212/586-0200

SHRIVINGS (P)
BLACK COMEDY (P)
THE ROYAL HUNT OF THE SUN (P)
THE PRIVATE EAR AND THE PUBLIC EYE (P)
LETTICE & LOVAGE (P)
YONADAB (P)
FIVE FINGER EXERCISE (P)
FOLLOW ME   Universal, 1971, from his play "The Public Eye"
EQUUS ★   United Artists, 1977, from his play
AMADEUS ★★   Orion, 1984, from his play

SUSAN HALLI SHAFFER*
Agent: William Morris Agency - Beverly Hills, 310/274-7451

Screenplays:
OUT OF THE HOUSE
STRAWBERRY CANYON
DADDY LONG LEGS
MISS CONCEPTION
LEFTOVERS

STEVE SHAGAN*
Agent: ICM - Beverly Hills, 310/550-4000

TERRIFIC...TERRIFIC! (P)
SAVE THE TIGER ★   Paramount, 1973
HUSTLE   Paramount, 1975
VOYAGE OF THE DAMNED ★   ITC, 1976, w/David Butler
NIGHTWING   Columbia, 1979, w/Edwin Shrake
THE FORMULA   MGM/UA, 1980
THE SICILIAN   20th Century Fox, 1987

Screenplays:
PRIMAL FEAR
SACRED GROUND
BOSS OF BOSSES
A CAST OF THOUSANDS
HOLY MEN
TRICKS
THE ELECTRIC COTILLION
FIELDS OF EDEN
THEY SHALL NOT PASS

ROBERT SHALLCROSS*
Agent: William Morris Agency - Beverly Hills, 310/274-7451

LITTLE GIANTS   Warner Bros., 1994, w/James Ferguson,
    Michael Goldberg & Tommy Swerdlow

JOHN HERMAN SHANER*
Agent: Paradigm - Los Angeles, 310/277-4400

HALLS OF ANGER   United Artists, 1970, w/Al Ramrus
THE ISLAND OF DR. MOREAU   American International, 1977,
   w/Al Ramrus
GOIN' SOUTH   Paramount, 1979, w/Alan Mandel, Al Ramrus &
   Charles Shyer
THE LAST MARRIED COUPLE IN AMERICA   Universal, 1979

Screenplays:
SPARK
BEVERLY HILLS DOCTOR
CASHFLOW
AMERICAN NONSENSE

PETER SHANER
Agent: ICM - Beverly Hills, 310/550-4000

LOVER'S KNOT   Two Pauls Entertainment, 1994, directed

JOHN PATRICK SHANLEY*
Agent: William Morris Agency - Beverly Hills, 310/274-7451

DANNY AND THE DEEP BLUE SEA (P)
SAVAGE IN LIMBO (P)
the dreamer examines his pillow (P)
ITALIAN AMERICAN RECONCILIATION (P)
WOMEN OF MANHATTAN (P)
BEGGARS IN THE HOUSE OF PLENTY (P)
FOUR DOGS AND A BONE (P)
THE BIG FUNK (P)
FIVE CORNERS   Handmade Films, 1987
MOONSTRUCK ★★   MGM, 1987
THE JANUARY MAN   MGM/UA, 1989
JOE VERSUS THE VOLCANO   Warner Bros., 1990, directed
ALIVE   Buena Vista/Paramount, 1993
WE'RE BACK (AF)   Universal, 1993
CONGO   Paramount, 1995, w/Michael Crichton

Screenplays:
BELL, BOOK AND CANDLE (directing)
NIGHT TRAIN TO VALHALLA
WILD BIG RED

ALAN M. SHAPIRO*
Agent: William Morris Agency - Beverly Hills, 310/274-7451

TIGERTOWN (CTF)   Buena Vista, 1984, directed
THE CRUSH   Warner Bros., 1993, directed

Screenplays:
FLIPPER
STONYBROOK
BUT WHAT ABOUT ME
MY FAMILY
HAUNTED GUITAR
3 TO GET READY

J. DAVID SHAPIRO*
Agent: Metropolitan Talent Agency - Los Angeles, 213/857-4500

ROBIN HOOD: MEN IN TIGHTS   20th Century Fox, 1993,
   w/Evan Chandler & Mel Brooks

Screenplays:
RETURN TO SENDER w/Aaron William Dozier
PLAY BALL w/Aaron William Dozier
FRACTURED SKILL OF ICE w/Aaron William Dozier

JANICE SHAPIRO*
Contact: WGA - Los Angeles, 310/550-1000

THIS YEAR'S MODEL (Short)   directed
NIGHT DADDY (Short)   directed
DEAD BEAT   Dustant Horizon, 1994, w/Adam Dubov

Screenplays:
PURPLE WEST w/Adam Dubov
WILD RIDE w/Adam Dubov
TUBESTEAK w/Adam Dubov
UNFORGETTABLE w/Adam Dubov
THE CADILLAC KID

KEN S. SHAPIRO*
Address: 20115 Observation Drive, Topanga, CA 90290,
   310/455-1222

THE GROOVE TUBE   Levitt-Pickman, 1974, directed
MODERN PROBLEMS   20th Century-Fox, 1981,
   w/Tom Sherohman & Arthur Sellers, directed

LISA SHAPIRO
Agent: The Artists Group - Los Angeles, 310/552-1100

LABOR PAINS (P)   also screenplay

PAUL W. SHAPIRO*
Agent: ICM - Beverly Hills, 310/550-4000

BREAKING THE RULES   Miramax, 1992
CALENDAR GIRL   Columbia, 1993

RICHARD SHAPIRO*
Contact: Franklin B. Rohner/Donald Walerstein, 310/477-5001

THE GREAT SCOUT AND CATHOUSE THURSDAY
   American International, 1976

JOHN SHARKEY
OMEGA SYNDROME   New World, 1987
DOUBLE REVENGE   Smart Egg Releasing, 1988, w/Brian Tobin

JIM SHARMAN
Contact: M & L Casting Consultants, 49 Darlinghurst Road,
   Kings Cross, NSW, 2100, Australia, 02/358-3111

THE ROCKY HORROR PICTURE SHOW   20th Century-Fox, 1976,
   w/Richard O'Brien, directed
SHOCK TREATMENT   20th Century-Fox, 1981,
   w/Richard O'Brien, directed

STEVE SHARON*
Contact: WGA - Los Angeles, 310/550-1000

THE DEAD POOL   Warner Bros., 1988

Screenplays:
SARGEANT K.

ALAN SHARP*
Agent: CAA - Beverly Hills, 310/288-4545

THE LAST RUN   MGM, 1971
THE HIRED HAND   Universal, 1971
ULZANA'S RAID   Universal, 1972
BILLY TWO HATS   United Artists, 1973
NIGHT MOVES   Warner Bros., 1975
DAMNATION ALLEY   20th Century-Fox, 1977, w/Lukas Heller
THE OSTERMAN WEEKEND   20th Century-Fox, 1983,
   w/Ian Masters
LITTLE TREASURE   Tri-Star, 1985, directed
CAT CHASER   Vestron, 1990, w/Jim Borrelli & Elmore Leonard
DESCENDING ANGEL (CTF)   Fredya Rothstein, 1990,
   w/Robert Siegel & Grace Woodards
THE LAST HIT (CTF)   Garson Studios/MCA Television
   Entertainment, 1993, w/Walter Klenhard
ROB ROY   MGM/UA, 1994

Screenplays:
HARD KNOX

DON SHARP

Agent: ICM - London, 071/629-8080

BACKGROUND *EDGE OF DIVORCE* Group Three, 1953,
w/Warren Cheatham Strode
CONFLICT OF WINGS *FUSS OVER FEATHERS* Group Three,
1953, w/John Pudney
THE BLUE PETER British Lion, 1955, w/John Pudney
A TASTE OF EXCITEMENT Trio Films, 1964,
w/Brian Carton, directed
PUPPET ON A CHAIN Cinerama Releasing Corporation, 1972,
w/Alistair Maclean & Paul Wheeler, directed
BEAR ISLAND Taft International, 1980, w/David Butler &
Murray Smith, directed

KRISCHNA SHAS

HARD ROCK ZOMBIES Cannon, 1985, w/David Ball, directed

WILLIAM SHATNER

Agent: William Morris Agency - Beverly Hills, 310/274-7451

STAR TREK V: THE FINAL FRONTIER Paramount, 1989,
Story w/Harve Bennett & David Loughery, directed

MELVILLE SHAVELSON*

Contact: WGA - Los Angeles, 310/550-1000

WHERE THERE'S LIFE Paramount, 1947, w/Allen Boretz
SORROWFUL JONES Paramount, 1949, w/Jack Rose &
Edmund Hartmann
ALWAYS LEAVE THEM LAUGHING Warner Bros., 1949,
w/Jack Rose
THE DAUGHTER OF ROSIE O'GRADY Warner Bros., 1950,
w/Peter Milne & Jack Rose
DOUBLE DYNAMITE RKO, 1951, w/Harry Crane & Leo Rosten
ON MOONLIGHT BAY Warner Bros., 1951, w/Jack Rose
APRIL IN PARIS Warner Bros., 1952, w/Jack Rose
ROOM FOR ONE MORE Warner Bros., 1952, w/Jack Rose
I'LL SEE YOU IN MY DREAMS Warner Bros., 1952, w/Jack Rose
TROUBLE ALONG THE WAY Warner Bros., 1953, w/Jack Rose
LIVING IT UP Paramount, 1954, w/Jack Rose
THE SEVEN LITTLE FOYS ★ Paramount, 1955,
w/Jack Rose, directed
BEAU JAMES Paramount, 1957, w/Jack Rose, directed
HOUSEBOAT Paramount, 1958, w/Jack Rose, directed
THE FIVE PENNIES Paramount, 1959, w/Jack Rose, directed
IT STARTED IN NAPLES Paramount, 1960, w/Jack Rose &
Susi Cecchi d'Amico, directed
ON THE DOUBLE Paramount, 1961, w/Jack Rose, directed
THE PIGEON THAT TOOK ROME Paramount, 1962, directed
A NEW KIND OF LOVE Paramount, 1963, directed
CAST A GIANT SHADOW United Artists, 1966, directed
YOURS, MINE AND OURS United Artists, 1968,
w/Mort Lachman, directed
THE WAR BETWEEN MEN AND WOMEN National General,
1972, w/Danny Arnold, directed
MIXED COMPANY United Artists, 1974,
w/Mort Lachman, directed

CHRIS SHAW

Agent: Jon Klane Agency - Beverly Hills, 310/278-0178

SPLIT Starker Films, 1991, filmed in 1988, directed

Screenplays:
MORPHOGENESIS
EVERYTHING YOU WANT

DAVID SHAW*

Contact: WGA - Los Angeles, 310/550-1000

IF IT'S TUESDAY, THIS MUST BE BELGIUM United Artists, 1969
KING, QUEEN, KNAVE Avco Embassy, 1972, w/David Seltzer

LOU SHAW*

Agent: The Wright Concept - Burbank, 818/954-8943

Screenplays:
THE BUCKET
THE DRIFT

SANDY SHAW*

Contact: WGA - Los Angeles, 310/550-1000

THE DEAD POOL Warner Bros., 1988, Story w/Durk Pearson &
Steve Sharon

WALLACE SHAWN

Contact: Screen Actors Guild - Los Angeles, 213/954-1600

MARIE AND BRUCE (P) also screenplay
THE HOTEL PLAY (P)
AUNT DAN AND LEMON (P)
THE FEVER (P)
MY DINNER WITH ANDRE New Yorker, 1981, w/Andre Gregory

LINDA SHAYNE*

Agent: Abrams Artists & Associates - Los Angeles, 310/859-0625
Business Manager: L. Miller Management - 310/454-7196

SCREWBALLS New World, 1983, w/Jim Wynorski
CRYSTAL HEART New World, 1987
PURPLE PEOPLE EATERS Concorde, 1988, directed

BASHAR SHBIB

Address: 5437 Park Ave., Montreal, Quebec H2V 4G9, Canada

JULIA HAS TWO LOVERS South Gate Entertainment, 1991,
w/Dapha Kastner, directed
LOVE$GREED Oneira Pictures, 1991, w/Gabor Zsigovic, directed

Screenplays:
EVERY WOMAN LOVES A RUSSIAN POET
w/Susan Kramer (directing)

KATT SHEA*

(Katt Shea Ruben)
Agent: ICM - Beverly Hills, 310/550-4000

THE PATRIOT Crown International, 1986,
w/Andy Ruben, directed
STRIPPED TO KILL Concorde, 1987, w/Andy Ruben, directed
DANCE OF THE DAMNED Concorde, 1989,
w/Andy Ruben, directed
STRIPPED TO KILL 2 Concorde, 1990, directed
STREETS Concorde, 1990, w/Andy Ruben, directed
POISON IVY New Line Cinema, 1992, w/Andy Ruben, directed

HARRY SHEARER*

Agent: Metropolitan Talent Agency - Los Angeles, 213/857-4500

J. EDGAR! (P) w/Tom Leopold
REAL LIFE Paramount, 1979, w/Albert Brooks & Monica Johnson
THIS IS SPINAL TAP Embassy, 1984, w/Christopher Guest,
Michael McKean & Rob Reiner

Screenplays:
IT'S A FAIR WORLD w/Bob Dolman
BOHEMIAN GROVE

ALAN SHEARMAN*

Contact: WGA - Los Angeles, 310/550-1000

THE SHRIMP ON THE BARBIE Unity Pictures Corp., 1990,
w/Ron House & Grant Morris

MARTIN SHEEN
(Ramon Estevez)
Business: Symphony Pictures, 5711 W. Slauson Blvd. - Suite 226,
 Culver City, CA 90230, 310/649-3668

CADENCE   New Line Cinema, 1990, w/Dennis Shryack, directed

SIMON SHEEN
Business: Sheen Productions

3 NINJAS KICK BACK   TriStar, 1994, (Screenplay by Mark
 Saltzman based on screenplay by Simon Sheen)

Screenplays:
THE LEGEND OF GALGAMETH (Story)

HOGAN SHEFFER*
Agent: ICM - Beverly Hills, 310/550-4000

Screenplays:
FOOL'S GOLD w/Tom Reilly
THE BLACK ROSE w/Tom Reilly

DAVID SHEFFIELD*
Agent: CAA - Beverly Hills, 310/288-4545

POLICE ACADEMY 2: THEIR FIRST ASSIGNMENT   Warner Bros.,
 1983, w/Barry Blaustein
COMING TO AMERICA   Paramount, 1988, w/Barry Blaustein
BOOMERANG   Paramount, 1992, w/Barry Blaustein

Screenplays:
THE NUTTY PROFESSOR w/Barry Blaustein (remake)
KNOCKOUT! w/Barry Blaustein
THE GELFAN w/Barry Blaustein
OPTIMUM w/Barry Blaustein
BUTTERSCOTCH KID w/Barry Blaustein
LAST HOLIDAY w/Barry Blaustein
BROTHERS KEEPERS w/Barry Blaustein

CAROLYN J. SHELBY*
Agent: Richland/Wunsch/Hohman Agency - Los Angeles,
 310/278-1955
Business: North Beach Productions, 818/591-2222

CLASS ACTION   20th Century Fox, 1991, w/Christopher Ames &
 Samantha Shad

Screenplays:
THE MAGIC COTTAGE w/Christopher Ames
CHAPEL OF LOVE w/Christopher Ames
BLACK AND BLUE w/Christopher Ames
IT'S NOT THE MONEY w/Christopher Ames
LEADER OF THE PACK w/Christopher Ames

DAVID SHELDON*
Agent: Preferred Artists - Encino, 818/990-0305

GRIZZLY *KILLER GRIZZLY* Film Ventures International, 1976,
 w/Harvey Flaxman

ERNEST SHELDON JR.
THE FINAL MISSION   Trimark, 1993, w/Virginia Gilbert,
 Sam Montgomery & Lee Redmond

SIDNEY SHELDON*
Agent: ICM - Beverly Hills, 310/550-4000

THE BACHELOR AND THE BOBBY SOXER ★★   RKO, 1947
EASTER PARADE   MGM, 1948, w/Frances Goodrich &
 Albert Hackett
ANNIE GET YOUR GUN   MGM, 1950
NANCY GOES TO RIO   MGM, 1950
NO QUESTIONS ASKED   MGM, 1951
THREE GUYS NAMED MIKE   MGM, 1951

RICH, YOUNG AND PRETTY   MGM, 1951, w/Dorothy Cooper
REMAINS TO BE SEEN   MGM, 1953
DREAM WIFE   MGM, 1953, w/Herbert Baker &
 Alfred L. Levitt, directed
YOU'RE NEVER TOO YOUNG   Paramount, 1955
PARDNERS   Paramount, 1956
THE BIRDS AND THE BEES   Paramount, 1956
ANYTHING GOES   Paramount, 1956
THE BUSTER KEATON STORY   Paramount, 1957,
 w/Robert Smith, directed
ALL IN A NIGHT'S WORK   Paramount, 1961, w/Edmund Beloin &
 Maurice Richlin
JUMBO *BILLY ROSE'S JUMBO*   MGM, 1962

RON SHELTON*
Agent: Sanford-Gross & Associates - Los Angeles, 310/208-2100
Business: Raleigh Studios, 650 N. Bronson, Los Angeles, CA 90004,
 213/462-5095

UNDER FIRE   Orion, 1983, w/Clayton Frohman
THE BEST OF TIMES   Universal, 1986
BULL DURHAM ★   Orion, 1988, directed
BLAZE   Buena Vista, 1989, directed
WHITE MAN CAN'T JUMP   20th Century Fox, 1992, directed
BLUE CHIPS   Paramount, 1994
COBB   Warner Bros., 1994, directed

Screenplays:
THE GREAT WHITE HYPE
CENTERFOLD w/Nancy Dowd
ANTELOPE VALLEY
THE BUTTON
THE BOXER & THE BLONDE
TROPICANA

NINA SHENGOLD*
Contact: WGA - Los Angeles, 310/550-1000

HOMESTEADERS (P)   also screenplay

Screenplays:
FREE LUNCH
LABOR OF LOVE

RICHARD SHEPARD
Agent: The Marion Rosenberg Office - Los Angeles, 213/653-7383

COOL BLUE   Cinema Corp of America, 1990,
 w/Mark Mullin, co-directed
THE LINGUINI INCIDENT   Academy Entertainment, 1992,
 w/Tamar Brott, directed

SAM SHEPARD*
Agent: ICM - Beverly Hills, 310/550-4000

RED CROSS (P)
A LIE OF THE MIND (P)
TRUE WEST (P)
BURIED CHILD (P)
CURSE OF THE STARVING CLASS (P)
SHAVED SPLITS (P)
MAD DOG BLUES (P)
THE UNSEEN HAND (P)
4-H CLUB (P)
SUICIDE IN B FLAT (P)
OPERATION: SIDEWINDER (P)
TOOTH OF CRIME (P)
MELODRAMA PLAY (P)
FORENSIC & THE NAVIGATOR (P)
LA TURISTA (P)
COWBOYS (P)
ROCK GARDEN (P)
SEDUCED (P)
STATES OF SHOCK (P)
THE UNSEEN HAND (P)
SIMPATICO (P)

ZABRISKIE POINT   MGM, 1970, w/Michelangelo Antonioni,
    Fred Gardner, Tonino Guerra & Clare Peploe
PARIS, TEXAS   TLC Films/20th Century-Fox, 1984
FOOL FOR LOVE   Cannon, 1985, from his play
FAR NORTH   Alive Films, 1988, directed
SILENT TONGUE   Trimark, 1994, directed

CYBILL SHEPHERD
Agent: United Talent Agency - Beverly Hills, 310/273-6700

MEMPHIS (CTF)   Propaganda Films/River Siren, 1992,
    w/Larry McMurtry & Susan Rhinehart

JEAN P. SHEPHERD*
Contact: WGA - New York, 212/245-6180

A CHRISTMAS STORY   MGM/UA, 1983, w/Bob Clark &
    Leigh Brown
IT RUNS IN THE FAMILY   MGM/UA, 1995, w/Bob Clark &
    Leigh Brown

JOHN SHEPHERD
EYE OF THE STORM   World Wide Pictures, 1992, w/Eric Gilliland

JOHN SHEPPARD*
Agent: Barry Perelman Agency - Los Angeles, 213/274-5999

BULLIES   Universal, 1986, w/Bryan McCann
HIGHER EDUCATION   Norstar Entertainment, 1987,
    w/Hal Lieberman

JOHN SHEPPHIRD
Contact: Linda Lichter, Lichter, Grossman & Nichols - Los Angeles,
    310/205-6999
Home: 310/395-7773

TEENAGE BONNIE AND KLEPTO CLYDE   Trimark, 1994,
    w/Steve Jankowski

Screenplays:
GARAGE BAND w/Steve Jankowski
RENEGADE BLADE w/Steve Jankowski
SQUEAL
MISFIT HERO
STREET LUNCH

JIM SHERIDAN
Agent: CAA - Beverly Hills, 310/288-4545
Business: Ferndale Films, Universal Pictures, 818/777-5851

MY LEFT FOOT ★   Miramax, 1989,
    w/Shane Connaughton, directed
THE FIELD   Avenue Pictures, 1990, directed
INTO THE WEST   Miramax, 1993, directed
IN THE NAME OF THE FATHER ★   Universal, 1993,
    w/Terry George, directed

ARTHUR SHERMAN
Manager: Creative Alliance Management - Los Angeles,
    213/962-6090

Screenplays:
MADONNA RED w/James Carroll

GARY A. SHERMAN*
Contact: WGA - Los Angeles, 310/550-1000

PHOBIA   Paramount, 1981, w/Peter Bellwood, Lew Lehman,
    James Sangster & Ronald Shusett
WANTED DEAD OR ALIVE   New World, 1986,
    w/Michael Patrick Goodman & Brian Taggert, directed
POLTERGEIST III   MGM/UA, 1988, w/Brian Taggert, directed
LISA   MGM/UA, 1990, w/Karen Clark, directed
AFTER THE SHOCK (CTF)   Wilshire Court Productions,
    1990, directed

JEFFREY C. SHERMAN*
Agent: Abrams Artists & Associates - Los Angeles, 310/859-0625

UP THE CREEK   Orion, 1983, Story w/Jim Kouf &
    Douglas Grossman

Screenplays:
CUT OUT
HOT DELIVERIES
SUMMER JOB
TEEN TOUR
REVERSE ANGEL

JONATHAN MARC SHERMAN
Agent: ICM - Beverly Hills, 310/550-4000

WOMEN AND WALLACE (P)
SERENDIPITY AND SERENITY (P)
JESUS ON THE OIL TANK (P)
VEINS AND THUMBTACKS (P)
SOPHISTRY (P)

MARTIN SHERMAN*
Agent: The Casarotto Company - London, 071/287-4450

BENT (P)
MESSIAH (P)
MADHOUSE IN GOA (P)
WHEN SHE DANCED (P)
THE SUMMER HOUSE   Samuel Goldwyn Company, 1993

Screenplays:
THE CLOTHES IN THE WARDROBE (Goldwyn)
SEA UNDER LOVE

ROBBIE SHERMAN
Agent: Berzon Agency - Glendale, 818/548-1560

Screenplays:
THE PENGUIN PIRATE

ROBERT SHERMAN*
Contact: WGA - Los Angeles, 310/550-1000

PICTURE MOMMY DEAD   Embassy, 1966

STACY SHERMAN
Agent: Pleshette & Green - Los Angeles, 213/465-0428

Screenplays:
ONE FOR THE MONEY w/Karen Ray
POOR HOLLY w/Karen Ray

STANFORD L. SHERMAN*
Contact: WGA - Los Angeles, 310/550-1000

ANY WHICH WAY YOU CAN   Warner Bros., 1980
KRULL   Columbia, 1983
THE MAN WHO WASN'T THERE   Paramount, 1983
THE ICE PIRATES   MGM/UA, 1983, w/Stewart Raffill

Screenplays:
SEVENTH WORLD
SURPRISE OF THE DEEP
SWEETER THAN HONEY
KID KONG
TOM, NICK & MARY
UNDER PRESSURE
THE DISAPPEARANCE OF THE USS MAKO
SEPTEMBER RUN
THE NIGHT THAT REVEREND CLANCY'S HOME
ONE MORE SONG FOR JESUS
JAKE
THE SHEIKS OF ARABY
THE SABERS OF KANDAHAR
EMPIRES OF THE DEEP

TOM SHEROHMAN
MODERN PROBLEMS   20th Century-Fox, 1981, w/Arthur Sellers & Ken Shapiro

SUSAN SHILLIDAY*
Agent: United Talent Agency - Beverly Hills, 310/273-6700

LEGENDS OF THE FALL   TriStar, 1994, w/William Witliff

Screenplays:
A WRINKLE IN TIME

COLIN SHINDLER
Agent: Renaissance-H.N. Swanson - Los Angeles, 310/246-6000

BUSTER   Hemdale, 1988

JOHN SHIRLEY*
Agent: William Morris Agency - Beverly Hills, 310/274-7451

THE CROW   Miramax, 1994, w/David Schow

Screenplays:
HER HUNGER
THE MARSHAL OF CENTRAL PARK
NEW ROSE HOTEL

MARK SHIRREFS
THE GIRL FROM TOMORROW (CTF)   Film Australia/Nine Network, 1991, w/John Thomson

MARC I. SHMUGER*
Contact: WGA - New York, 212/245-6180

DEAD OF WINTER   MGM/UA, 1987, w/Mark Malone

Screenplays:
KING OF AMERICA

JACK SHOLDER*
Agent: ICM - Beverly Hills, 310/550-4000

THE TATTOOED HITMAN   New Line Cinema, 1977
ALONE IN THE DARK   New Line Cinema, 1982, directed
WHERE ARE THE CHILDREN   Columbia, 1986

MICHAEL SHOOB*
Contact: Trianon Productions - Los Angeles, 310/451-0314

PARASITE   Embassy, 1982, w/Alan J. Adler & Frank Levering

WANDA BIRDSONG SHOPE*
Contact: WGA - Los Angeles, 310/550-1000

Screenplays:
FAMILY MAN

FREDERIC SHORE*
Contact: WGA - Los Angeles, 310/550-1000

SURVIVAL RUN   *SPREE*   Film Ventures, 1978, w/G.M. Cahill & Larry Spiegel

SIG SHORE
SUDDEN DEATH   Marvin Films, 1985, directed

DEL SHORES*
Agent: Broder-Kurland-Webb-Uffner - Beverly Hills, 310/281-3400

CHEATIN' (P)
DAUGHERS OF THE LONE STAR STATE (P)
DADDY'S DYIN'...WHO'S GOT THE WILL   MGM/UA, 1990, from his play

JOHN SHORNEY
SECOND COUSIN, ONCE REMOVED   Intrepid Ventures Group, 1994, w/Dave Bussan, Pete Ellis & John McColpin, directed

MICHAEL J. SHORT*
Contact: 416/628-4884

SPEED ZONE   Orion, 1989

ROBERT SHORT*
Agent: Barry Perelman Agency - Los Angeles, 310/274-5999
Business: Robert Short Productions, 4228 Glencoe Avenue, Marina del Rey, CA 90292, 310/306-6842

RAGE OF HONOR   Trans World Entertainment, 1987, w/Wallace Bennet
PROGRAMMED TO KILL   Trans World Entertainment, 1987, co-directed

Screenplays:
A.I.

EDWIN (BUD) SHRAKE*
Agent: ICM - Beverly Hills, 310/550-4000

J.W. COOP   Columbia, 1972, w/Gary Cartwright & Cliff Robertson
KID BLUE   20th Century-Fox, 1973
NIGHTWING   Columbia, 1979, w/Steve Shagan
TOM HORN   Warner Bros., 1980, w/Thomas McGuane
SONGWRITER   Tri-Star, 1984

Screenplays:
FLAT OUT SPEED w/Dan Jenkins
SLIM & NONE w/Dan Jenkins
LOOSE WOMEN w/Dan Jenkins
DAMN YANKEES w/Dan Jenkins
DINOSAUR WINE w/Dan Jenkins
LIMO w/Dan Jenkins
RIP w/G. Cartwright
THE BIG MAMOO
FIRST AMONG THE BEST

DON SHROLL*
Agent: J. Michael Bloom & Associates - Los Angeles, 310/275-6800

Screenplays:
THE BLUE TRAIN
AN ECLIPSE OF MEN
THE GIFT

DENNIS SHRYACK*
Agent: The Agency - Los Angeles, 310/551-3000

THE GOOD GUYS AND THE BAD GUYS   Warner Bros., 1969, w/Ronald M. Cohen
THE CAR   Universal, 1977, w/Michael Butler & Lane Slate
THE GAUNTLET   Warner Bros., 1977, w/Michael Butler
MURDER BY PHONE   New World, 1982, w/Michael Butler & John Kent Harrison
FLASHPOINT   Tri-Star, 1984, w/Michael Butler
PALE RIDER   Warner Bros., 1985, w/Michael Butler
CODE OF SILENCE   Orion, 1985, w/Michael Butler & Mike Gray
RENT-A-COP   Kings Road, 1988, w/Michael Blodgett
HERO AND THE TERROR   Cannon, 1988, w/Michael Blodgett
TURNER & HOOCH   Buena Vista, 1989, w/Michael Blodgett, Jim Cash & Jack Epps
CADENCE   New Line Cinema, 1990, w/Martin Sheen
RUN   Buena Vista, 1991, w/Michael Blodgett
FIFTY FIFTY   Cannon, 1993, w/Michael Blodgett

Screenplays:
WEAVEWORLD (CMS) w/Peter Bellwood
THE DOCTOR AND THE DRAGON LADY w/Peter Bellwood
GORILLAS w/Peter Bellwood
THE KILLING SEED w/Peter Bellwood
THE DOC AND DONNA w/Bill Peterson

THE EXECUTIONER w/Michael Butler
METZGER'S DOG w/Michael Butler
SEIZURE w/Michael Butler
IRIS w/Michael Butler
TWO WEEKS WITH PAY w/Michael Butler

BARBARA SHULGASSER
Agent: William Morris Agency - Beverly Hills, 310/274-7451

READY TO WEAR (PRET-A-PORTER) Miramax, 1994,
   w/Robert Altman

GUY SHULMAN*
Contact: WGA - Los Angeles, 310/550-1000

ALL DOGS GO TO HEAVEN (AF) MGM/UA, 1989, Story w/others

Screenplays:
READY OR NOT w/Craig Heller
SEPARATE WAYS w/Craig Heller

RONALD SHUSETT*
Agent: ICM - Beverly Hills, 310/550-4000

W Cinerama Releasing Corporation, 1974, Story w/James Kelly
ALIEN 20th Century-Fox, 1979, Story
DEAD AND BURIED Avco Embassy, 1981, w/Dan O'Bannon
PHOBIA Paramount, 1981, w/Peter Bellwood, Lew Lehman,
   James Sangster & Gary Sherman
THE FINAL TERROR Comworld, 1983, w/Jon George & Neill Hicks
KING KONG LIVES DEG, 1986, w/Steven Pressfield
ABOVE THE LAW Warner Bros., 1988, w/Andrew Davis &
   Steven Pressfield
TOTAL RECALL Tri-Star, 1990, w/Gary Goldman & Dan O'Bannon
FREEJACK Warner Bros., 1992, w/Steven Pressfield & Dan Gilroy

Screenplays:
TOTAL RECALL II w/Gary Goldman
JANUARY HOUR
THE BIG SCORE

ROSIE SHUSTER*
Agent: Innovative Artists - Los Angeles, 310/553-5200

GILDA LIVE (FD) Warner Bros., 1980, w/others

Screenplays:
THE DISAPPEARANCE w/Richard Maxwell
MR. DARLING w/Margaret Oberman
BAD GIRLS w/Nell Cox
JUST IN TIME
MY GIRLFRIEND'S BOYFRIEND
WHAT I DID WITH THE PRESIDENT'S DAUGHTER

NEAL D. SHUSTERMAN*
Agent: Innovative Artists - Los Angeles, 310/553-5200

TIME SCAVENGERS New Line Cinema, 1990
DOUBLE DRAGON Gramercy, 1994, Story w/Paul Dini

Screenplays:
DISSIDENTS
PILGRIMAGE
EYES OF KID MIDAS
SHADOW CLUB
BRIDGES BURNED
HIDE AND SEEK

M. NIGHT SHYAMALAN
Agent: Gold/Marshak - Burbank, 818/972-4300

PRAYING WITH ANGER Cinevista/Unapix, 1993, directed

Screenplays:
LABOR OF LOVE

CHARLES R. SHYER*
Agent: ICM - Beverly Hills, 310/550-4000

SMOKEY AND THE BANDIT Universal, 1977,
   w/James Lee Barrett & Alan Mandel
GOIN' SOUTH Paramount, 1978, w/Alan Mandel,
   John Herman Shaner & Al Ramrus
HOUSE CALLS Universal, 1978, w/ Alan Mandel & Max Shulman
PRIVATE BENJAMIN ★ Warner Bros., 1980, w/Harvey Miller &
   Nancy Meyers
IRRECONCILABLE DIFFERENCES Warner Bros., 1984,
   w/Nancy Meyers, directed
PROTOCOL Warner Bros., 1984, Story w/Harvey Miller &
   Nancy Meyers
BABY BOOM MGM/UA, 1987, w/Nancy Meyers, directed
FATHER OF THE BRIDE Buena Vista, 1991, w/Nancy Meyers,
   Frances Goodrich & Albert Hackett, directed
ONCE UPON A CRIME MGM-Pathe, 1992, w/Nancy Meyers &
   Steve Kluger
I LOVE TROUBLE Buena Vista, 1994, w/Nancy Meyers, directed
FATHER OF THE BRIDE 2 Buena Vista, 1995,
   w/Nancy Meyers, directed

Screenplays:
LOVE CRAZY w/Nancy Meyers
TOAST OF THE TOWN w/Nancy Meyers
BREAKFAST ON BEDFORD DRIVE w/Alan Mandel
THE LONG RAINBOW w/Alan Mandel
BIG DEAL ON MACARTHUR BOULEVARD w/Alan Mandel
TICKETS w/Alan Mandel

MUSSEF SIBAY
Business: Apsicon Productions, 9600 Kirkside Rd., Los Angeles,
   CA 90035, 310/558-0531

A WOMAN, HER MEN AND HER FUTON Interpersonal Film,
   1992, directed

ANDY SIDARIS
Business: The Sidaris Company, 9229 Sunset Blvd. - Suite 208,
   Los Angeles, CA 90069, 310/278-5056

STACEY New World, 1973, directed
SEVEN American International, 1979, directed
MALIBU EXPRESS Malibu Bay Films, 1984, directed
HARD TICKET TO HAWAII Malibu Bay Films, 1987, directed
PICASSO TRIGGER Malibu Bay Films, 1988, directed
SAVAGE BEACH Malibu Bay Films, 1989, directed
GUNS Malibu Bay Films, 1990, directed
DO OR DIE Malibu Bay Films, 1991, directed
HARD HUNTED Malibu Bay Films, 1993, directed
FIT TO KILL Malibu Bay Films, 1993, directed

ASHLEY SIDAWAY
Contact: Winchester Pictures - Canada, 514/288-5888

Screenplays:
RAINBOW w/Robert Sidaway (Vine International)

ROBERT SIDAWAY
Contact: Winchester Pictures - Canada, 514/288-5888

Screenplays:
RAINBOW w/Ashley Sidaway (Vine International)

ABDULAH SIDRAN
WHEN FATHER WAS AWAY ON BUSINESS Cannon, 1985

LYNN SIEFERT*
Agent: CAA - Beverly Hills, 310/288-4545

COOL RUNNINGS Buena Vista, 1993, w/Michael Goldberg &
   Tommy Swerdlow

Screenplays:
PLUTO BY JOEY
SYLVIE

BARRY SIEGEL
WINDOWS   United Artists, 1980

DAVID SIEGEL
Agent: William Morris Agency - Beverly Hills, 310/274-7451
Contact: Kino-Korsakoff, 606 N. Larchmont - Suite 308, Los Angeles,
    CA 90004, 213/466-7683

SUTURE   Kino-Korsakoff, 1993, w/Scott McGehee, co-directed

GERALD K. SIEGEL*
Agent: Barry Perelman Agency - Los Angeles, 310/274-5999

Screenplays:
FUTBOL

RICHARD SIEGEL
STAY TUNED   Warner Bros., 1992, Story w/Jim Jennewein &
    Tom S. Parker

ROBERT J. SIEGEL*
Contact: WGA - New York, 212/245-6180

DESCENDING ANGEL (CTF)   Fredya Rothstein, 1990,
    w/Alan Sharp & Grace Woodard

STEPHEN M. SIEGEL*
Agent: United Talent Agency - Beverly Hills, 310/273-6700

Screenplays:
THE MAN WHO KILLED SHERLOCK HOLMES
THE FAB FOUR
DAY OF RECKONING

STEVEN JAY SIEGEL*
Agent: Original Artists - Santa Monica, 310/394-1067
Contact: 213/558-6360

K-9   Universal, 1989, w/Scott Myers

TAGGART SIEGEL
WILD BLUE MOON   Quetzal Films, 1992,
    w/Francesca Fisher, co-directed

MARC SIEGLER
GALAXY OF TERROR   New World, 1981, w/Bruce Clark

TOM SIERCHIO*
Agent: William Morris Agency - Beverly Hills, 310/274-7451

UNTAMED HEART   MGM, 1993

Screenplays:
ATLANTIC AVENUE
THE BROTHERS

HERBERT SIGUENZA*
(with Richard Montoya & Ric Salinas: Culture Clash)
Agent: William Morris Agency - Beverly Hills, 310/274-7451

A BOWL OF BEINGS (P)   w/Richard Montoya & Ric Salinas
THE MISSION (P)   w/Richard Montoya & Ric Salinas

Screenplays:
*GOMEZ, GOMEZ AND GOMEZ   wRichard Montoya &
    Ric Salinas (UA)*

MIKE SIKOWITZ*
Agent: Paradigm - Los Angeles, 310/277-4400

Screenplays:
THE CRUISE   w/Jeff Astrof

ALAN SILBERBERG*
Contact: WGA - Los Angeles, 310/550-1000

Screenplays:
DADNAPPED

JOEL SILBERG
Agent: The Gersh Agency - Beverly Hills, 310/274-6611

LAMBADA   Warner Bros., 1990, w/Sheldon Renan, directed

BRAD SILBERLING*
Agent: CAA - Beverly Hills, 310/288-4545

Screenplays:
STAY (directing)

JAMES R. SILKE*
Agent: The Morton Agency - Los Angeles, 310/824-4089
Contact: 805/927-4513

REVENGE OF THE NINJA   MGM/UA/Cannon, 1983
SAHARA   MGM/UA, 1984
NINJA III: THE DOMINATION   Cannon, 1984
KING SOLOMON'S MINES   Cannon, 1985, w/Eugene Quintano
THE BARBARIANS   Cannon, 1987

STIRLING SILLIPHANT*
Agent: Kopaloff Company - Los Angeles, 310/203-8430

FIVE AGAINST THE HOUSE   Columbia, 1955, w/John Barnwell
HUK!   United Artists, 1956
NIGHTFALL   Columbia, 1956
THE LINEUP   Columbia, 1958
VILLAGE OF THE DAMNED   MGM, 1960, w/Geoffrey Barclay &
    Wolf Rilla
THE SLENDER THREAD   Paramount, 1966
IN THE HEAT OF THE NIGHT ★★   United Artists, 1967
CHARLY   Cinerama Releasing Corporation, 1968
MARLOWE   MGM, 1969
THE LIBERATION OF L.B. JONES   Columbia, 1970,
    w/Jesse Hill Ford
A WALK IN THE SPRING RAIN   Columbia, 1970
MURPHY'S WAR   Paramount, 1971
THE NEW CENTURIONS   Columbia, 1972
THE POSEIDON ADVENTURE   20th Century-Fox, 1972,
    w/Wendell Mayes
SHAFT IN AFRICA   MGM, 1973
THE TOWERING INFERNO   20th Century-Fox, 1974
THE KILLER EL'TE   United Artists, 1975, w/Marc Norman
THE ENFORCER   Warner Bros., 1976, w/Dean Reisner
TELEFON   MGM/UA, 1977, w/Peter Hyams
THE SWARM   Warner Bros., 1978
THE SILENT FLUTE   Volare, 1978, w/Stanley Mann
CIRCLE OF IRON   Avco Embassy, 1979, w/Stanley Mann
WHEN TIME RAN OUT   Warner Bros., 1980, w/Carl Foreman
OVER THE TOP   Cannon, 1987, w/Sylvester Stallone
CATCH THE HEAT   Trans World Entertainment, 1987

Screenplays:
THE GRASS HARP (Warner Bros.)
FORBIDDEN PLANET (remake)
SOJOURNERS
HIERO'S JOURNEY
PUMA
WEATHER WAR
THE GREAT COLORADO RIVER MARATHON
PUZZLE

ALAN SILLITOE
Contact: British Academy of Film & Television Arts, 195 Piccadilly,
    London W1, England, 071/734-0022

SATURDAY NIGHT AND SUNDAY MORNING   Bryanston, 1960
THE LONELINESS OF THE LONG DISTANCE RUNNER
    British Lion, 1962
THE RAGMAN'S DAUGHTER   Independent, 1974

AMANDA SILVER*
Agent: William Morris Agency - Beverly Hills, 310/274-7451

THE HAND THAT ROCKS THE CRADLE   Buena Vista, 1992

Screenplays:
INTIMATE DISCLOSURES

ARTHUR SILVER*
Agent: Dytman & Schwartz - Beverly Hills, 310/274-8844

MISSING IN ACTION 2: THE BEGINNING   Cannon, 1985,
   w/Larry Levinson & Steve Bing

Screenplays:
THE BUST OUT KING

FRANELLE SILVER*
Agent: The Parness Agency - Los Angeles, 310/273-2233

DOIN' TIME   The Ladd Company/Warner Bros., 1984,
   w/Dee Caruso & Ron Zwang

Screenplays:
SOLDIERS OF MISFORTUNE

JOAN MICKLIN SILVER*
Agent: William Morris Agency - Beverly Hills, 310/274-7451
Business: Midwest Film Productions, 600 Madison Avenue,
   New York, NY 10022, 212/355-0282

LIMBO   Universal, 1972, w/James Bridges
HESTER STREET   Midwest Film Productions, 1975, directed
HEAD OVER HEELS   *CHILLY SCENES OF WINTER*
   United Artists, 1979, directed

Screenplays:
FUN WHILE IT LASTED w/Fred Barron
MEDALLION w/Vicki Polon

MARISA SILVER*
Agent: Richland/Wunsch/Hohman Agency - Los Angeles,
   310/278-1955

OLD ENOUGH   Orion Classics, 1984, directed

STU SILVER*
Agent: CAA - Beverly Hills, 310/288-4545

THROW MOMMA FROM THE TRAIN   Orion, 1987

Screenplays:
THE ACCIDENTAL DON w/David Hurwitz
NIGHT ON THE TOWN
NUTTY PROFESSOR II

DAVID A. SILVERMAN*
Contact: WGA - Los Angeles, 310/550-1000

Screenplays:
STEPPING OUT

JACK SILVERMAN
CRACK HOUSE   Cannon, 1989, Story

PETER SILVERMAN*
Agent: Sanford-Gross & Associates - Los Angeles, 310/208-2100

WHERE THE RIVER RUNS BLACK   MGM/UA, 1986,
   w/Neal Jimenez
AMERICAN HEART   Triton Pictures, 1993

TREVA SILVERMAN*
Agent: Renaissance-H.N. Swanson - Los Angeles, 310/246-6000

Screenplays:
NICE GIRLS

NANCEY SILVERS*
Agent: Innovative Artists - Los Angeles, 310/553-5200

Screenplays:
THE EX-FACTOR

ED SILVERSTEIN*
Agent: The Brandt Company - Sherman Oaks, 818/783-7747

BOCA   Zalman King Collection, 1994

SHEL SILVERSTEIN
THINGS CHANGE   Columbia, 1988, w/David Mamet

LINDA SILVERTHORN
BEVERLY HILLS BRATS   Taurus Entertainment, 1989

HAROLD SILVESTER
Agent: United Talent Agency - Beverly Hills, 310/273-6700

Screenplays:
PASSING GLORY

RANDALL SILVIS
Agent: The Gage Group - Los Angeles, 310/859-8777

Screenplays:
MARGUERITE AND THE MOON MAN

LAWRENCE L. SIMEONE
RAW NERVE   Pyramid Distribution/AIP Studios, 1991,
   w/David A. Prior
BILNDFOLD: ACTS OF OBSESSION (CTF)   Saban Pictures/Libra
   Pictures, 1994, directed

DAVID SIMKINS*
Agent: The Irv Schechter Company - Beverly Hills, 310/278-8070

ADVENTURES IN BABYSITTING   Buena Vista, 1987

Screenplays:
GOOD DOG CARL
THE BIG NASTY
GRAVITY GUY
SUSPECT BEHAVIOR

ANDY SIMMONS*
Agent: The Gage Group - Los Angeles, 310/859-8777

Screenplays:
MY MOTHER THE CROOK
COLLEGE BOUND
BERNIE "X" (shared)

ANTHONY SIMMONS
Business: 50-60 Eastcastle Street, London W1N 7AP, England

FOUR IN THE MORNING   West One, 1965, directed
THE OPTIMISTS   *THE OPTIMISTS OF NINE ELMS*   Paramount,
   1973, directed
BLACK JOY   Hemdale, 1977, w/Jamal Ali, directed

GARNER SIMMONS*
Agent: Wile Enterprises - Santa Monica, 310/828-9768

RARE BREED   New World, 1984

Screenplays:
A WITNESS TO MURDER
STRIKER
THE LAST WESTERN
TITAN
THE ORACLE OF MERMAID AVENUE

REDBEARD SIMMONS
MEET THE APPLEGATES   *THE APPLEGATES*   Triton Pictures,
    1990, w/Michael Lehmann

Screenplays:
LE SURF HOT w/Michael Lehmann
OUT OF THE BOX

ADAM SIMON*
Agent: ICM - Beverly Hills, 310/550-4000

BRAIN DEAD   Concorde, 1989, w/Charles Beaumont,   directed
CARNOSAUR   Concorde Pictures, 1993,   directed

ALEX SIMON
HIT THE DUTCHMAN   21st Century, 1992,   Story
OF UNKNOWN ORIGIN   Concorde, 1994

DAVID S. SIMON*
Agent: Dytman & Schwartz - Los Angeles, 310/274-8844
Business Manager: Melvin J. Kreger, 11424 Burbank Blvd.,
    Hollywood, CA 91601

IN THE MOOD   Lorimar, 1987,   Story w/Bob Kosberg &
    Phil Alden Robinson

ELLEN SIMON*
Agent: Innovative Artists - Los Angeles, 310/553-5200

MOONLIGHT AND VALENTINO   Gramercy, 1995

MAYO SIMON*
Contact: WGA - Los Angeles, 310/550-1000

DOUBLE MURDER AND SUICIDE (P)
THESE MEN (P)
L.A. UNDER SIEGE (P)
WALKING TO WALDHEIM (P)
ELAINE'S DAUGHTER (P)
ANGEL (P)
WALKING TO WALDHEIM (P)
I COULD GO ON SINGING   United Artists, 1963
MAROONED   Columbia, 1969
PHASE IV   Paramount, 1973
FUTUREWORLD   American International, 1976, w/George Schenck

NEIL SIMON*
Agent: CAA - Beverly Hills, 310/288-4545
Personal Manager: Albert DaSilva - New York, 212/752-9323

COME BLOW YOUR HORN (P)
FOOLS (P)
THE STAR SPANGLED GIRL (P)
SWEET CHARITY (P)
LITTLE ME (P)
PROMISES, PROMISES (P)
BROADWAY BOUND (P)   also teleplay
JAKE'S WOMEN (P)
LAUGHTER ON THE 23RD FLOOR (P)
LONDON SUITE (P)
AFTER THE FOX   United Artists, 1966, w/Cesare Zavattini
BAREFOOT IN THE PARK   Paramount, 1967,   from his play
THE ODD COUPLE ★   Paramount, 1968,   from his play

THE OUT-OF-TOWNERS   Paramount, 1970
PLAZA SUITE   Paramount, 1971,   from his play,   also teleplay
LAST OF THE RED HOT LOVERS   Paramount, 1972,   from his play
THE HEARTBREAK KID   20th Century-Fox, 1972
THE PRISONER OF SECOND AVENUE   Warner Bros., 1975,
    from his play
THE SUNSHINE BOYS ★   MGM/UA, 1975,   from his play
MURDER BY DEATH   Columbia, 1976
THE GOODBYE GIRL ★   Warner Bros., 1977,
    (became stageplay in 1992)
CALIFORNIA SUITE ★   Columbia, 1978,   from his play
THE CHEAP DETECTIVE   Columbia, 1978
CHAPTER TWO   Columbia, 1979,   from his play
SEEMS LIKE OLD TIMES   20th Century-Fox, 1980
ONLY WHEN I LAUGH   Columbia, 1981,
    from his play "The Gingerbread Lady"
I OUGHT TO BE IN PICTURES   20th Century-Fox, 1982
MAX DUGAN RETURNS   20th Century-Fox, 1983
THE SLUGGER'S WIFE   Columbia, 1985
BRIGHTON BEACH MEMOIRS   Universal, 1986,   from his play
BILOXI BLUES   Universal, 1988,   from his play
THE MARRYING MAN   Buena Vista, 1991
LOST IN YONKERS   Columbia, 1993,   from his play

Screenplays:
MY SON'S BROTHER
MR. BAD NEWS

PAUL SIMON*
Contact: WGA - New York, 212/245-6180

ONE TRICK PONY   Warner Bros., 1980

RAPHAEL SIMON
Agent: Broder-Kurland-Webb-Uffner - Beverly Hills, 310/281-3400

Screenplays:
THE PINOCCHIO PROGRAM w/Margaret Stohl

ROGER L. SIMON*
Agent: United Talent Agency - Beverly Hills, 310/273-6700

THE BIG FIX   Universal, 1978
BUSTIN' LOOSE   Universal, 1981
MY MAN ADAM   Tri-Star, 1985, w/Renee Missel,   directed
ENEMIES, A LOVE STORY ★   20th Century Fox, 1989,
    w/Paul Mazursky
SCENES FROM A MALL   Buena Vista, 1991, w/Paul Mazursky

Screenplays:
MURDER IN THE SENATE
DEXTER MOST
MY FRIEND THE MESSIAH
TOGETHER AGAIN
THE GARDENER w/Cheech Marin
GOLDEN GATE w/Dyanne Asimow
A WILD SANCTUARY w/Dyanne Asimow
BLOOD TIES
THE RENTAL CASE
BAD DEATH
FINAL ANALYSIS
PICTURES OF FIDELMAN
THE STRAIGHT MAN
JENNIFER ON MY MIND
MOSES WINE
CAFE LUXEMBOURG
VENUS IN FURS

SAM SIMON*
Agent: ICM - Beverly Hills, 310/550-4000

THE SUPER   20th Century-Fox, 1991

Screenplays:
BEETLE BAILEY

P.K. SIMONDS JR.*
Agent: CAA - Beverly Hills, 310/288-4545

Screenplays:
BEVERLY HILLS BODY SNATCHERS
ABSOLUTE ZERO

ROCCO SIMONELLE
ME AND THE MOB   Arrow Releasing, 1994, w/James Lorinz &
   Frank Rainone

DOUG SIMONTON
Agent: Circle of Confusion Ltd. - New York, 212/969-0653

Screenplays:
MAKING TRACKS

A. R. SIMOUN
(See Adam Rodman)

AVRIL SIMPSON
Agent: Shapiro/Lichtman - Los Angeles, 310/859-8877

Screenplays:
NO ACCIDENT w/Tom Simpson
POINT NO POINT w/Tom Simpson
THE BELL RINGER w/Tom Simpson

BYRON SIMPSON*
Agent: United Talent Agency - Beverly Hills, 310/273-6700

THE RESCUERS DOWN UNDER (AF)   Buena Vista, 1990,
   w/Jim Cox, Karvey Kirkpatrick & Joe Ranft

Screenplays:
ONCE UPON A TREE
LOST APRIL

EDWARD SIMPSON
Agent: The Agency - Los Angeles, 310/551-3000

RIVER OF DEATH   Cannon, 1989, w/Andrew Deutsch

GEORGE E. SIMPSON*
Agent: APA - Los Angeles, 310/273-0744

ROADHOUSE 66   Atlantic Releasing Corporation, 1984,
   w/Galen Lee

Screenplays:
UP THE GARDEN PATH w/Neal Burger
GHOSTBOAT w/Neal Burger
DAN HAZARD AND THE LEGEND OF EVIL w/Neal Burger
SPIDER BOY
THE CRIMSON KISS
A TOUCH OF THE COWBOY
NO HIGHWAY ON EARTH

ROGER SIMPSON
SQUIZZY TAYLOR   Satori, 1984
DARLINGS OF THE GODS (CMS)   Simpson LeMesurier Films/
   Australian Broadcasting Corporation/Thames Television, 1991,
   w/Graeme Farmer

TOM SIMPSON
Agent: Shapiro/Lichtman - Los Angeles, 310/859-8877

Screenplays:
NO ACCIDENT w/Avril Simpson
POINT NO POINT w/Avril Simpson
THE BELL RINGER w/Avril Simpson

KELLY B. SIMS
Address: 920 N. Kings Road - #216, Los Angeles, CA 90069,
   213/848-7384

Screenplays:
DEADLY REALITY w/Robert G. Williams
POWER OF ATTORNEY w/Robert G. Williams
GEAR DRIVEN w/Robert G. Williams
MORTAL RELATIONS w/Robert G. Williams
POULTRYGEIST!!! w/Robert G. Williams

ANDREW SINCLAIR
Contact: British Academy of Film & Television Arts, 195 Piccadilly,
   London W1, England, 071/732-0022

BEFORE WINTER COMES   Columbia, 1968
UNDER MILK WOOD   Altura, 1973, directed
BLUE BLOOD   Mallard Productions, 1975, directed

JOSHUA SINCLAIR
JUST A GIGOLO   United Artists Classics, 1981
LILI MARLEEN   United Artists Classics, 1981, w/Manfred Purzer
JUDGMENT IN BERLIN   New Line Cinema, 1988, w/Leo Penn

BRUCE FRANKLIN SINGER*
Agent: Broder-Kurland-Webb-Uffner - Beverly Hills, 310/281-3400

MEATBALLS PART II   Tri-Star, 1984
THE KILLING TIME   New World, 1987, w/Don Bohlinger &
   James Nathan
THE LION OF AFRICA (CTF)   HBO Pictures/Lois Luger
   Productions, 1987

BRYAN SINGER
Agent: ICM - Beverly Hills, 310/550-4000

PUBLIC ACCESS   Cinemabeam, 1993, w/Christopher McQuarrie &
   Michael Feit Dugan, directed

RANDI MAYEM SINGER*
Agent: Broder-Kurland-Webb-Uffner - Beverly Hills, 310/281-3400

MRS. DOUBTFIRE   20th Century Fox, 1993, w/Leslie Dixon

Screenplays:
THE GHOST AND MRS. MUIR
THE SECRET LIFE OF GIRLS
TWO BIT ROMANCE w/June Roberts

JOHN SINGLETON*
Agent: CAA - Beverly Hills, 310/288-4545
Business: New Deal Productions, Columbia Pictures - 310/280-4504

BOYZ N THE HOOD ★   Columbia, 1991, directed
POETIC JUSTICE   Columbia, 1993, directed
HIGHER LEARNING   Columbia, 1995, directed

Screenplays:
TWILIGHT TIME

GARY SINYOR
Agent: William Morris Agency - Beverly Hills, 310/274-7451

LEON THE PIG FARMER   Cinevista/Unapix, 1993,
   w/Michael Normand, co-directed
SOLITAIRE FOR 2   Cavalier Features, 1994, directed

CURT SIODMAK*
Contact: WGA - Los Angeles, 310/550-1000

THE WOLF MAN   Universal, 1940
THE APE   Monogram, 1940, w/Richard Carroll
BLACK FRIDAY   Universal, 1940, w/Eric Taylor
THE CLIMAX   Universal, 1944, w/Lynn Starling
THE BEAST WITH FIVE FINGERS   Warner Bros., 1946

BRIDE OF THE GORILLA   Jack Broder Productions, 1953, directed
RIDERS TO THE STARS   United Artists, 1954
THE CREATURE WITH THE ATOM BRAIN   Columbia, 1955
CURUCU, BEAST OF THE AMAZON   Universal, 1956
EARTH VERSUS THE FLYING SAUCERS   Columbia, 1956, Story

ROSEMARY ANNE SISSON*
Contact: Andrew Mann Ltd. - London, 071/734-4751

ESCAPE FROM THE DARK   Buena Vista, 1976
CANDLESHOE   Buena Vista, 1977, w/David Swift
THE WATCHER IN THE WOODS   Buena Vista, 1980,
    w/Brian Clemens & Harry Spalding

HAL SITOWITZ*
Contact: WGA - Los Angeles, 310/550-1000

Screenplays:
BENNY'S HEIR

BRITTA SJOGREN
JO-JO AT THE GATE OF LIONS   Nana Films, 1992, directed

Screenplays:
CLAIRE'S BONES

PAUL SKEMP
Agent: United Talent Agency - Beverly Hills, 310/273-6700

Screenplays:
FALL TIME w/Steve Alden

JOHN SKIPP
A NIGHTMARE ON ELM STREET, PART V: THE DREAM CHILD
    New Line Cinema, 1989, Story w/Leslie Bohem & Craig Spector

ZACHARY SKLAR*
Contact: WGA - Los Angeles, 310/550-1000

JFK ★   Warner Bros., 1991, w/Oliver Stone

JERZY SKOLIMOWSKI
Agent: ICM - Beverly Hills, 310/550-4000

KNIFE IN THE WATER   Kanuala, 1963, w/Jakub Goldberg &
    Roman Polanski
DEEP END   Paramount, 1971, w/Jerzy Gruza &
    Boleslaw Sulik, directed
THE SHOUT   Films Inc., 1979, w/Michael Austin, directed
MOONLIGHTING   Universal Classics, 1982, directed
MESMERIZED   RKO/Challenge Corp., 1984, Story
SUCCESS IS THE BEST REVENGE   Triumph/Columbia, 1984,
    w/Michael Lyndon, directed
TORRENTS OF SPRING   Millimeter Films, 1990,
    w/Arcangelo Bonaccorso, directed

Screenplays:
FERDYDURKE
ANGEL FACE

ROBERT F. SKOTAK*
Agent: The Gersh Agency - Beverly Hills, 310/274-6611

Screenplays:
THE BRINK w/Nicholas Seldon
RESURRECTUS w/Lynn Barker
CYCLOPS w/Nicholas Seldon

JAN SKRETNY*
Contact: WGA - Los Angeles, 310/550-1000

Screenplays:
POWDERKEG w/Neil Tabachnick
CIGARETTE w/Neil Tabachnick

GEORGE FRANCIS SKROW
BACK TO BACK   Concorde, 1990

BERNARD SLADE*
Contact: 310/274-7271

FATAL ATTRACTION (P)
SPECIAL OCCASIONS (P)
STAND UP AND BE COUNTED   Columbia, 1971
SAME TIME, NEXT YEAR ★   Universal, 1978, from his play
TRIBUTE   20th Century-Fox, 1980, from his play
ROMANTIC COMEDY   MGM/UA, 1983, from his play

PAUL SLANSKY*
Agent: United Talent Agency - Beverly Hills, 310/273-6700

Screenplays:
BEFORE AND AFTER w/Arleen Sorkin
BEDSPREADS w/Arleen Sorkin

PETER SLATE
Agent: Acme Talent & Literary Agency - Los Angeles, 310/550-6808

Screenplays:
RAVE

DAMIAN F. SLATTERY
A DAY IN OCTOBER   Castle Hill Productions, 1992

STEVEN D. SLAVKIN*
Contact: WGA - Los Angeles, 310/550-1000

Screenplays:
CUTTING CLASS
TALKING TO THE MOOSE

TODD SLAVKIN*
Agent: William Morris Agency - Beverly Hills, 310/274-7451

Screenplays:
CHASING GHOSTS w/Darren Swimmer
SUBMERGED w/Darren Swimmer
HEIR MAIL w/Darren Swimmer

EVAN SLAWSON*
Contact: WGA - Los Angeles, 310/550-1000

A HOLLYWOOD STORY   Double Helix Films, 1991,
    w/Tony Zarindast

HENRY SLESAR*
Contact: WGA - New York, 212/245-6180

TWO ON A GUILLOTINE   Warner Bros., 1965
MURDERS IN THE RUE MORGUE   American International, 1971

Screenplays:
THE MADDENING w/Leslie Greif (Trimark)

HOLLY GOLDBERG SLOAN*
Agent: Sanford-Gross & Associates - Los Angeles, 310/208-2100

INDECENCY (CTF)   Point of View Productions/MCA Television
    Entertainment, 1992, w/Amy Jones & Alan Ormsby
MADE IN AMERICA   Warner Bros., 1993
ANGELS IN THE OUTFIELD   Buena Vista, 1994

Screenplays:
THE BIG GREEN (directing)
CHANGE OF HEART
BUMPTIOUS
SWEET TOOTH
HARRIET THE SPY

MICHAEL SLOAN*
Agent: ICM - Beverly Hills, 310/550-4000

THE CALLER   Empire Pictures, 1989

RICK SLOANE
VICE ACADEMY   Rick Sloane Productions, 1989, directed

JAMES SLOCUM
Business: Boss Entertainment Group, 962 North Madison Ave.,
   Pasadena, CA 91104, 818/791-3995

AN AMERICAN SUMMER   Castle Hill, 1991, directed

SHAWN SLOVO*
Agent: United Talent Agency - Beverly Hills, 310/273-6700

A WORLD APART   Atlantic Releasing Corporation, 1988

Screenplays:
VIRGIN OF THE RODEO
DANCIN' CROSS THE RIVER
THE WIDOW
JAMIE
ORPHAN TRAIN
HAND OVER FIST

ADAM SMALL*
Agent: United Talent Agency - Beverly Hills, 310/273-6700

ANOTHER STATE OF MIND   Coastline Films/Magnum
   Entertainment, 1984, directed
SON-IN-LAW   Buena Vista, 1993, w/Fax Bahr & Shawn Schepps
IN THE ARMY NOW   Buena Vista, 1994, w/Fax Bahr,
   Ken Kaufman, Stu Krieger & Daniel Petrie Jr.
JURY DUTY   Buena Vista, 1995, w/Fax Bahr & Neil Tolkin

Screenplays:
SHOCKED w/Fax Bahr (Savoy)
SHACKLED w/Fax Bahr
CRAVINGS w/Fax Bahr
CHAMELEON STREET w/Fax Bahr

ERIC SMALL
Agent: William Morris Agency - Beverly Hills, 310/274-7451

Screenplays:
BLUE BLAZES w/Ace Passmore
RUBICON
HOURGLASS
PURPLE KNIGHT RANGERS
DUAL FORCE

PETER SMALLEY
DEAD END DRIVE-IN   New World, 1986

DAVID H. SMILOW*
Contact: WGA - Los Angeles, 310/550-1000

SPRING BREAK   Columbia, 1983

Screenplays:
DIRTY SECRETS
DREAM TIME
END OF THE LINE
LOST VEGAS
UPWARD BOUND
SMALL WORLD

ANDREW SMITH*
Contact: WGA - Los Angeles, 310/550-1000

ANYTHING, ANYTHING (P)
THE MAIN EVENT   Warner Bros., 1979, w/Gail Parent
WHO'S THAT GIRL   Warner Bros., 1987, w/Ken Finkelman

Screenplays:
40 REGULAR
ACE BANDAGE

APRIL SMITH*
Agent: CAA - Beverly Hills, 310/288-4545

Screenplays:
VIETNAM NURSES

BOBBY SMITH JR.*
Agent: William Morris Agency - Beverly Hills, 310/274-7451

JASON'S LYRIC   Gramercy, 1994

CHRIS SMITH*
Contact: WGA - Los Angeles, 310/550-1000

Screenplays:
FALSE ALARMS

CRAIG SMITH*
Agent: Jon Klane Agency - Beverly Hills, 310/278-0178

SCAM (CTF)   Showtime, 1994

Screenplays:
PERSONS UNKNOWN

DAVID SMITH*
Agent: Peter Turner Agency - Santa Monica, 310/315-4772

Screenplays:
TUXEDO PARK
SAVAGES
AGAINST THE WIND

EBBE ROE SMITH*
Agent: Jon Klane Agency - Beverly Hills, 310/278-0178

HOW MUCH WOULD CHUCK (P)   also screenplay
THE HAND BEHIND THE FACE (P)
THE POLITIC THING (P)
THE SISTERS AND THEIR SORROW (P)
THE OTHER DIMENSION (P)
THE LUCK, THE SHIP AND THE OBJECT (P)
THE PARASITES (P)
FALLING DOWN   Warner Bros., 1993
CAR 54, WHERE ARE YOU?   Orion, 1994, w/Peter Crabbe,
   Peter McCarthy & Erik Tarloff
PARTNERS (Short)   Showtime/Chanticleer, 1994, w/Peter Weller

Screenplays:
NICK OF TIME
SGT. ROCK
MAN PLUS
HIT NUMBER 29
PAYBACK
DREAMING OF BABYLON
THE START OVER
THE MIDDLE PEOPLE

GREG P. SMITH
THE LAST WORD   Samuel Goldwyn Company, 1979,
   w/L.M. Kit Carson & Michael Varhol

HUBERT SMITH
MOONSHINE COUNTY EXPRESS   New World, 1977,
   w/Daniel Ansley
OUT OF THE DARKNESS   *NIGHT CREATURES*
   Dimension, 1978
THE GLOVE   Pro International, 1981, w/Julian Roffman

JOEL T. SMITH*
Agent: Maggie Field Agency - Studio City, 818/980-2001

Screenplays:
BLACK SNOW
THE SPORTING MAN
OUTLAW
MONSTER MAKER
CHAIN OF FIRE
VODOO CHILD
MAYA TRAIL
SCOOP
TONG WAR
BAJA RUN
FREE WOMAN OF COLOR

JOHN N. SMITH
Agent: Great North Artists Management - Toronto, 416/925-2051

THE BOYS OF ST. VINCENT   Alliance Releasing, 1993,
   w/Des Walsh & Sam Grana,   directed

JOSHUA SMITH*
Contact: WGA - Los Angeles, 310/550-1000

Screenplays:
RED SCARE w/Murray Mintz

KAT SMITH*
Agent: Broder-Kurland-Webb-Uffner - Beverly Hills, 310/281-3400

CONSEQUENCE (P)
LADIES IN ERROR (P)

Screenplays:
INTO THE LAND OF NOD
JEAN SEBERG (untitled project)
TIE ME UP, TIE ME DOWN (remake)

KEVIN SMITH
Agent: CAA - Beverly Hills, 310/288-4545

CLERKS   Miramax, 1994,   directed

Screenplays:
BUSING
MALL RATS
DOGMA

LANCE SMITH
MUNCHIES   Concorde, 1987

LINDSAY SMITH
BACK IN THE USSR   20th Century Fox, 1992

MARK ALLEN SMITH*
Agent: William Morris Agency - New York, 212/586-5100

Screenplays:
INFLAMMABLE
THE WITCHING HOUR
GRIFFIN AND SABINE
BLIND MAN'S BLUFF
ROAD SHOW
DATELINE: SALONIKA
COLD AS ICE
ROCK AND A HARD PLACE
BLACK AND WHITE
PLAYIN' IN THE BAND
SLOW BURN

MARTIN J. SMITH*
Contact: 212/534-2664

UNDER THE RAINBOW   Orion/Warner Bros., 1981,
   w/Pat McCormick, Harry Hurwitz, Pat Bradley & Fred Bauer

MEL SMITH
Agent: United Talent Agency - Beverly Hills, 310/273-6700

MORONS FROM OUTER SPACE   Universal, 1985,
   w/Griff Rhys-Jones

MURRAY SMITH
BEAR ISLAND   Taft Inernational, 1980, w/David Butler & Don Sharp

NOELLA SMITH
Agent: Peters, Fraser & Dunlop - London, 071/376-7676

SECRETS   Samuel Goldwyn Company, 1984

RICHARD B. SMITH*
Agent: ICM - Beverly Hills, 310/550-4000

LOCK UP   Tri-Star, 1989, w/Henry Rosenbaum & Jeb Stuart

Screenplays:
THE BEST OF THE FINEST
WILD BLUE

ROBERT D. SMITH*
Agent: Neal Stevens & Associates - Beverly Hills, 310/275-7541

Screenplays:
COOTIES

ROBERT F. SMITH*
Contact: WGA - New York, 212/245-6180

XTRO   New Line Cinema, 1983, w/Iain Cassie

SCOTT SMITH
Agent: Pleshette & Green - Los Angeles, 213/465-0428

Screenplays:
A SIMPLE PLAN

STEVEN PHILIP SMITH*
Agent: ICM - Beverly Hills, 310/550-4000

THE LONG RIDERS   United Artists, 1980, w/Bill Bryden,
   James Keach & Stacy Keach
CHATTANOOGA CHOO CHOO   April Fools, 1984, w/Robert Mundy

SUE SMITH
BRIDES OF CHRIST (CMS)   Roadshow, Coote & Carroll, 1993,
   w/John Alsop

TOM SMITH*
Agent: Neal Stevens & Associates - Beverly Hills, 310/275-7541

Screenplays:
DEVIL KNOWS BEST

WILBUR SMITH
SHOUT AT THE DEVIL   American International, 1976,
   w/Stanley Price & Alistair Reid

STEPHEN SMOKE
LIVING TO DIE   PM Entertainment, 1990
FINAL IMPACT   PM Entertainment, 1990, co-directed
NINJA DRAGONS   PM Entertainment, 1993

Screenplays:
DEAD EVEN
SHADE
DELIVER US FROM EVIL
VOICES IN THE NIGHT

DENNIS SNEE*
Agent: Shapiro/Lichtman - Los Angeles, 310/859-8877

BACK TO SCHOOL   Orion, 1986, Story w/Rodney Dangerfield &
   Greg Fields

JEFFREY M. SNELLER
IN THE SHADOW OF KILIMANJARO   Scotti Bros., 1986,
   w/T. Michael Harry

NORMAN SNIDER*
Manager: Creative Alliance Management - Los Angeles,
   213/962-6090

PARTNERS   Astral Films, 1976, w/Dan Owen
DEAD RINGERS   20th Century Fox, 1989, w/David Cronenberg
BODY PARTS   Paramount, 1991, w/Eric Red

Screenplays:
AMERICAN PSYCHO

SUSAN SNOOKS
THE CARE BEARS ADVENTURE IN WONDERLAND (AF)
   Cineplex Odeon, 1987, w/John DeKlein

MICHAEL ANTHONY SNOWDEN*
Agent: The Rothman Agency - Beverly Hills, 213/655-2020

Screenplays:
SKIN JOB

WILLIAM SNOWDEN
PRIMARY MOTIVE   Fox Video/Blossom Pictures, 1992,
   w/Daniel Adams

BLAKE SNYDER*
Agent: Broder-Kurland-Webb-Uffner - Beverly Hills, 310/281-3400

STOP! OR MY MOM WILL SHOOT   Universal, 1992,
   w/William Davies & Willaim Osborne
BLANK CHECK   Buena Vista, 1994, w/Colby Carr

Screenplays:
THIRD GRADE w/Colby Carr
HERBIE COME HOME w/Colby Carr
NUCLEAR FAMILY w/James Haggin

DEE SNYDER
Agent: Don Buchwald - New York, 212/867-10017

Screenplays:
THE JUNK SQUAD

MIKE SNYDER*
Contact: WGA - Los Angeles, 310/550-1000

RESCUE ME   Cannon, 1993

STEVEN SODERBERGH*
Agent: William Morris Agency - Beverly Hills, 310/274-7451

OCTOBER 16, 1977 (Short)   directed
PASSAGES (Short)   directed
JANITOR (Short)   directed
SKOAL (Short)   directed
RAPID EYE MOVEMENT (Short)   directed
WINSTON (Short)   directed
sex, lies and videotape ★   Miramax, 1989, directed
KING OF THE HILL   Gramercy, 1993, directed

Screenplays:
CRISS CROSS (remake)
DEAD FROM THE NECK UP
THE LAST SHIP

REVOLVER
CROSSTALK
STATE OF MIND
PROOF POSITIVE

GERARD SOETEMAN*
Agent: The Marion Rosenberg Office - Los Angeles, 213/653-7383

MAX HAVELAAR   1976
SOLDIER OF ORANGE   Samuel Goldwyn Company, 1977,
   w/Kees Holierhoek & Paul Verhoeven
SPETTERS   Samuel Goldwyn Company, 1981
THE FOURTH MAN   Spectrafilm, 1984
FLESH + BLOOD   Orion, 1985, w/Paul Verhoeven
THE ASSAULT   Cannon, 1986

Screenplays:
JUDGE DEE

IAIN SOFTLEY
Agent: ICM - Beverly Hills, 310/550-4000

BACKBEAT   Gramercy, 1994, w/Michael Thomas &
   Stephen Ward, directed

JOEL SOISSON*
Business: Neo Motion Pictures, 8315 Beverly Blvd., Los Angeles,
   CA 90048, 213/653-6007

HAMBONE AND HILLIE   New World, 1984, w/Sandra K. Bailey &
   Michael S. Murphey
THE SUPERNATURALS   Republic Entertainment/Sandy Howard
   Productions, 1985, w/Michael S. Murphey
TRICK OR TREAT   DEG, 1986, w/Michael S. Murphey &
   Rhet Topham

Screenplays:
BLUE TIGER (Neo Motion Pictures)

ALEX SOKOLOFF*
Agent: Innovative Artists - Los Angeles, 310/553-5200

Screenplays:
NOCTURNE w/David Arata
DOUBLE FAULT w/David Arata

ALEC SOKOLOW*
Contact: WGA - Los Angeles, 310/550-1000

Screenplays:
MONEY TALKS w/Joel Cohen
FAMILY MAN w/Joel Cohen
TOY STORY (AF) w/Joel Cohen
THE GREAT KIDNAPPING w/Joel Cohen

DIANE SOKOLOW*
Agent: ICM - Beverly Hills, 310/550-4000

Screenplays:
MR. KAUFMAN w/Avery Corman
ENOUGH ROPE w/Susan Rice

REBECCA SOLADAY*
Agent: Richland/Wunsch/Hohman Agency - Los Angeles,
   310/278-1955

SHAME (CTF)   Dalrymple Productions/Steinhardt Baer Pictures/
   Viacom, 1992

Screenplays:
BRUTAL BARGAIN
MARIA'S MISSING

FERNANDO E. SOLANAS
TANGOS: THE EXILE OF GARDEL   New Yorker, 1986, directed

FRANCO SOLINAS
KAPO   Vides, 1960, w/Gillo Pontecorvo
SALVATORE GIULIANO   Lux, 1961, w/others
BURN!   *QUELMADA!*   PEA, 1968, w/Giorgio Arlorio
THE BATTLE OF ALGIERS ★   Allied Artists, 1968,
   w/Gillo Pontecorvo
MR. KLEIN   Quartet, 1977
HANNA K.   Universal, 1983

DAVID SOLMONSON
Agent: Maggie Field Agency - Studio City, 818/980-2001

Screenplays:
LOW AND OUTSIDE
THIS OTHER EDEN

KENNY A. SOLMS*
Agent: Major Clients Agency - Los Angeles, 310/284-6400

SHEILA LEVINE IS DEAD AND LIVING IN NEW YORK   Paramount,
   1975, w/Gail Parent

Screenplays:
RAGS TO RICHES
TEARJERKER
OH SISTER

AUBREY SOLOMON*
Contact: WGA - Los Angeles, 310/550-1000

DEFENSE PLAY   Trans World Entertainment, 1988,
   w/Steven Greenberg

ED SOLOMON*
Agent: CAA - Beverly Hills, 310/288-4545

BILL & TED'S EXCELLENT ADVENTURE   Orion, 1989,
   w/Chris Matheson
BILL & TED'S BOGUS JOURNEY   Orion, 1991, w/Chris Matheson
MOM AND DAD SAVE THE WORLD   Warner Bros., 1992,
   w/Chris Matheson
LEAVING NORMAL   Universal, 1992
SUPER MARIO BROS.   Buena Vista, 1993, w/Parker Bennett &
   Terry Runte

Screenplays:
MEN IN BLACK
THE UNBELIEVABLES

TODD SOLONDZ
Contact: Frankfurt, Garbus, Klein & Selz - New York, 212/980-0120

FEAR, ANXIETY AND DEPRESSION   Samuel Goldwyn Company,
   1989, directed

ANDREW SOLT*
Agent: William Morris Agency - Beverly Hills, 310/274-7451
Business: Andrew Solt Productions, 9121 Sunset Blvd.,
   Los Angeles, CA 90069, 310/276-9522

THIS IS ELVIS (FD)   Warner Bros., 1981,
   w/Malcolm Leo, co-directed
IMAGINE: JOHN LENNON (FD)   Warner Bros., 1988,
   w/Sam Egan, directed

BERNIE SOMERS*
Agent: Broder-Kurland-Webb-Uffner - Beverly Hills, 310/281-3400

COPS AND ROBBERSONS   TriStar, 1994

Screenplays:
HAPPY ENDINGS

ARNOLD SOMKIN
OVER THE BROOKLYN BRIDGE   MGM/UA/Cannon, 1984

SCOTT SOMMER*
Agent: Richland/Wunsch/Hohman Agency - Los Angeles,
   310/278-1955

CRISSCROSS   MGM, 1992

Screenplays:
PITFALL
THE PURSUIT OF HAPPINESS
REFORM SCHOOL
STRANGE DUET
LAST RESORT

STEPHEN SOMMERS*
Agent: William Morris Agency - Beverly Hills, 310/274-7451

CATCH ME IF YOU CAN   MCEG, 1989, directed
THE ADVENTURES OF HUCKLEBERRY FINN   Buena Vista,
   1993, directed
GUNMEN   Dimension, 1994
THE JUNGLE BOOK   Buena Vista, 1994, w/Mark Geldman &
   Ron Yanover, directed

STEPHEN SONDHEIM*
Contact: WGA - New York, 212/245-6180

THE LAST OF SHEILA   Warner Bros., 1973, w/Anthony Perkins

Screenplays:
SWING OUT LOUD w/William Goldman

DAVID SONENBERG
DEAD RINGER   Feature Films, 1991, Story w/Alfred Dellentash,
   filmed in 1981

SHERRIE SONNETT
BELOW THE BELT   Atlantic Releasing Corporation, 1980,
   w/Robert Fowler

MICHAEL D. SONYE
COMMANDO SQUAD   Trans World Entertainment, 1987
BLOOD DINER   Lightning Pictures, 1987
COLD STEEL   CineTel Films, 1987, w/Moe Quigley
OUT ON BAIL   Trans World Entertainment, 1989, w/Jason Booth &
   Tom Badal

TRISH B. SOODIK*
Agent: ICM - Beverly Hills, 310/550-4000

SHAKE, RATTLE AND ROCK (CTF)   Showtime/Drive-In Classic
   Cinema, 1994

Screenplays:
MAMA SAID
THE BLUE PARROT
MARRYING UP
HOME IN ROME (CTF)
CAN'T GET ENOUGH
SHADES

DROR SOREF
Contact: Orbit Entertainment, 5540 Hollywood Blvd. - 2nd Fl,
   Hollywood, CA 90028, 213/993-0199

THE SEVENTH COIN   Hemdale, 1993, w/Michael Lewis, directed

AARON SORKIN*
Agent: CAA - Beverly Hills, 310/288-4545

MAKING MOVIES (P)
HIDDEN IN THE PICTURE (P)
A FEW GOOD MEN   Columbia, 1992, from his play
MALICE   Columbia, 1993, w/Scott Frank

Screenplays:
THE AMERICAN PRESIDENT (Columbia)
BOY WONDER
LIP STATE

ARLEEN SORKIN*
Agent: United Talent Agency - Beverly Hills, 310/273-6700

Screenplays:
BEFORE AND AFTER w/Paul Slansky
BEDSPREADS w/Paul Slansky

MICHAEL SORRENTINO
Agent: Kaplan-Stahler - Beverly Hills, 213/653-4483

Screenplays:
FACE VALUE w/Randy Vampotic
THE WEREWOLF SOCIAL CLUB w/Randy Vampotic

CHRISTOPHER SOTH
Manager: The Anthony Elliot Company - Los Angeles, 310/284-6804

Screenplays:
DAY 5000

MARC D. SOTKIN*
Manager: Brillstein-Grey - Beverly Hills, 310/275-6135

Screenplays:
WITCH DOCTOR

TERRY SOUTHERN*
Contact: WGA - Los Angeles, 310/550-1000

DR. STRANGELOVE OR; HOW I LEARNED TO STOP WORRYING
    AND LOVE THE BOMB ★ Columbia, 1964, w/Peter George &
    Stanley Kubrick
THE CINCINNATI KID   MGM, 1965, w/Ring Lardner, Jr.
THE LOVED ONE   MGM, 1965, w/Christopher Isherwood
BARBARELLA   Paramount, 1968
EASY RIDER ★   Columbia, 1969, w/Peter Fonda & Dennis Hopper
END OF THE ROAD   Allied Artists, 1970, w/Avram Avakian &
    D. MacGuire
THE MAGIC CHRISTIAN   Commonwealth United, 1970,
    w/Joseph McGrath & Peter Sellers
THE TELEPHONE   New World, 1988, w/Harry Nilsson

Screenplays:
OBITS w/Harry Nilsson
EASY RIDER 2 BIKER HEAVEN
BLUE MOVIE
FLOATERS
GROSSING OUT

MICK SOUTHWORTH
TANK MALLING   Pointlane Films, 1989, w/James Marcus

JACK B. SOWARDS*
Agent: The Artists Agency - Los Angeles, 310/277-7779

STAR TREK II: THE WRATH OF KHAN   Paramount, 1982

HARRY SPALDING
HOUSE OF THE DAMNED   20th Century-Fox, 1963
WITCHCRAFT   20th Century-Fox, 1964
ONE LITTLE INDIAN   Buena Vista, 1973
THE WATCHER IN THE WOODS   Buena Vista, 1980,
    w/Brian Clemens & Rosemary Anne Sisson

JAN SPEARS
GAME OF DEATH   Columbia, 1979

KATHERINE SPECKTOR
LOVE CHILD   The Ladd Company/Warner Bros., 1982,
    w/Anne Gerard

CRAIG SPECTOR
Agent: Innovative Artists - Los Angeles, 310/553-5200

A NIGHTMARE ON ELM STREET, PART V: THE DREAM CHILD
    New Line Cinema, 1989, Story w/Leslie Bohem & John Skipp

DAVID SPECTOR
AIRPORT '77   Universal, 1977, w/Michael Scheff

AARON SPEISER
TALKING ABOUT SEX   Curb Entertainment, 1994,
    w/Carl Nelson, directed

AARON SPELLING*
Business: Spelling Entertainment, 5700 Wilshire Blvd. - Suite 575,
    Los Angeles, CA 90036, 213/965-5700

GUNS OF THE TIMBERLAND   Jaguar, 1960, w/Joseph Petracca
ONE FOOT IN HELL   20th Century-Fox, 1960, w/Sydney Boehm

MICHAEL SPENCE
EDGE OF HONOR   Wind River, 1991, w/David O'Malley &
    Mark Rosenbaum, directed

ALAN SPENCER*
Agent: United Talent Agency - Beverly Hills, 310/273-6700
Manager: 3 Arts Entertainment - Los Angeles, 213/851-5700

HEXED   Columbia, 1993, directed

DEREK SPENCER
THE RETURN OF SWAMP THING   Lightyear Entertainment, 1989,
    w/Grant Morris

JANE SPENCER
LITTLE NOISES   Monument Pictures, 1991,
    w/Jon Zeiderman, directed

Screenplays:
THE RED WEATHER

SCOTT SPENCER*
Agent: William Morris Agency - New York, 212/586-5100

SPLIT IMAGE   Orion, 1982, w/Robert Mark Kamen &
    Robert Kaufman
ACT OF VENGEANCE (CTF)   HBO Premiere Films, 1986
FATHER HOOD   Buena Vista, 1993

Screenplays:
JACK OF HEARTS
KINGDOM OF LOVE
ASSASSINATION ON EMBASSY ROW
RAPTIVE
LOVEHUNTER
SWEETZER

PENELOPE SPHEERIS*
Agent: The Gersh Agency - Beverly Hills, 310/274-6611

SUBURBIA *THE WILD SIDE*   New World, 1984, directed
SUMMER CAMP NIGHTMARE *THE BUTTERFLY REVOLUTION*
    Concorde, 1987, w/Bert L. Dragin
THE LITTLE RASCALS   Universal, 1994, w/Paul Guay &
    Stephen Mazur, directed

Screenplays:
BOY CHILD w/Caroline Thompson

LARRY SPIEGEL*
Business Manager: TTA - 310/552-1833

HAIL TO THE CHIEF   20th Century-Fox, 1973, w/others
BOOK OF NUMBERS   Embassy, 1974
SURVIVAL RUN   *SPREE*   Film Ventures, 1978, directed

SCOTT SPIEGEL*
Agent: APA - Los Angeles, 310/273-0744

EVIL DEAD 2   DEG, 1987, w/Sam Raimi
INTRUDER   Phantom Productions, 1989,
   w/Lawrence Bender, directed
THE ROOKIE   Warner Bros., 1990, w/Boaz Yakin

Screenplays:
THE CLUMSY IDIOT   w/Ron Zwang & Bruce Campbell   (directing)
THE NUTTY NUT   w/Sam Raimi & Ron Zwang
WITCHES

ANNE SPIELBERG*
Agent: CAA - Beverly Hills, 310/288-4545

BIG ★   20th Century Fox, 1988, w/Gary Ross

Screenplays:
SEPTEMBER SONG

STEVEN SPIELBERG*
Agent: CAA - Beverly Hills, 310/288-4545
Business: Amblin Entertainment, Universal Studios, 818/777-4600

ACE ELI AND ROGER OF THE SKIES   20th Century-Fox,
   1973, Story
THE SUGARLAND EXPRESS   Universal, 1974,
   w/Matthew Robbins & Hal Barwood, directed
CLOSE ENCOUNTERS OF THE THIRD KIND   Columbia,
   1977, directed
POLTERGEIST   MGM/UA, 1980, w/Michael Grais & Mark Victor
THE GOONIES   Warner Bros., 1985, Story

ED SPIELMAN*
Agent: ICM - Beverly Hills, 310/550-4000

GORDON'S WAR   20th Century Fox, 1973,
   w/Howard Friedlander

AMY SPIES*
Agent: ICM - Beverly Hills, 310/550-4000

GIRLS JUST WANT TO HAVE FUN   New World, 1985

Screenplays:
TOO SMART FOR LOVE
BANDSTAND
WHO'S WHO

JAMES SPILL
Agent: Sanford-Gross & Associates - Los Angeles, 310/208-2100

Screenplays:
THE VELOLCITY OF GARY

TONY SPIRIDAKIS*
Agent: United Talent Agency - Beverly Hills, 310/273-6700

SELF STORAGE (P)   w/Shem Bitterman
QUEENS LOGIC   7 Arts/New Line Cinema, 1990

Screenplays:
THE LAST WORD (Nu-Image, directing)

RICK SPITZNASS
Agent: Susan Smith & Associates - Beverly Hills, 213/852-4777

Screenplays:
GAME OVER w/Cam Jones
INHERIT THE EARTH w/Cam Jones

ROGER SPOTTISWOODE
Agent: William Morris Agency - Beverly Hills, 310/274-7451

48 HRS.   Paramount, 1982, w/Steven E. De Souza, Larry Gross &
   Walter Hill

MARK SPRAGG*
Agent: ICM - Beverly Hills, 310/550-4000

GROSS ANATOMY   Buena Vista, 1989, w/Ron Nyswaner

Screenplays:
THE ASSOCIATE
SOUTH OF PICASSO

MARC SPRINGER
BLACK MAGIC WOMAN   Trimark Pictures, 1991,
   Story w/Gerry Daly & Deryn Warren

NICHOLAS ST. JOHN*
Contact: WGA - Los Angeles, 310/550-1000

MS. 45   Navaron, 1981
FEAR CITY   Chevy Chase Distribution, 1985
CHINA GIRL   Vestron, 1987
KING OF NEW YORK   Miramax, 1990
BODY SNATCHERS   Warner Bros., 1993, w/Stuart Gordon &
   Dennis Paoli
DANGEROUS GAME   MGM, 1993
THE ADDICTION   Fast Films, 1995

Screenplays:
TUMBLIN' DICE
SARAH
UNEMPLOYED

JIM STAAHL*
Agent: ICM - Beverly Hills, 310/550-4000

THE BEVERLY HILLBILLIES   20th Century Fox, 1993,
   w/Jim Fisher, Larry Konner & Mark Rosenthal

Screenplays:
BLOWHARD w/Jim Fisher
CHUMP TOWER w/Jim Fisher
UNDER SURVEILLANCE w/Jim Fisher
DUH BOAT S.O.S. w/Jim Fisher

TIMOTHY STACK*
Agent: CNA & Associates - Los Angeles, 310/556-4343

Screenplays:
ONE NIGHT STAND

WILLIAM STADIEM*
Agent: The Daniel Ostroff Agency - Los Angeles, 310/278-2020

YOUNG TOSCANINI   Motion Picture Corporation, 1988
A BUSINESS AFFAIR   Capella International, 1994

BIMA STAGG*
Agent: CAA - Beverly Hills, 310/288-4545

Screenplays:
STANDER (Cinevisions)

RAMA LAURIE STAGNER*
Agent: Above the Line - West Hollywood, 310/859-6115

OTHER WOMEN'S CHILDREN (CTF)   Crescent
    Entertainment, 1993
BLUE SKY   Orion, 1994, w/Jerry Leichtling & Arlene Sarner
AND THEN THERE WAS ONE (CTF)   Hearst Entertainment, 1994

Screenplays:
CLEAR CUT
A WOMAN'S GUIDE TO ADULTERY
ATOMIC ROMANCE
BUILDERS
SILK SCREEN w/Dan Witt
HOUSE IN THE HAMPTONS

ERIC STEVEN STAHL
Agent: Jon Klane Agency - Beverly Hills, 310/278-0178

FINAL APPROACH   Trimark, 1991, w/Gerald Laurence, directed

Screenplays:
FREE FALL w/Michael Michaud
SHOCK WAVE
VIRUS
BEATING THE ODDS

JOSHUA STALLINGS
THE ICE RUNNER   Borde Film Releasing, 1993,
    w/Clifford Coleman & Joyce Warren

SYLVESTER STALLONE*
Agent: CAA - Beverly Hills, 310/288-4545

ROCKY ★   United Artists, 1976
PARADISE ALLEY   Universal, 1978, directed
F.I.S.T.   United Artists, 1978, w/Joe Eszterhas
ROCKY II   United Artists, 1979, directed
FIRST BLOOD   Orion, 1982, w/Michael Kozoll & William Sackheim
ROCKY III   MGM/UA, 1982, directed
STAYING ALIVE   Paramount, 1983, w/Norman Wexler, directed
RHINESTONE   20th Century-Fox, 1984, w/Phil Alden Robinson
ROCKY IV   MGM/UA, 1985, directed
RAMBO: FIRST BLOOD PART II   Tri-Star, 1985, w/James Cameron
COBRA   Warner Bros., 1986
OVER THE TOP   Cannon, 1987, w/Stirling Silliphant
RAMBO III   Tri-Star, 1988, w/Shelton Lettich
ROCKY V   MGM/UA, 1990
CLIFFHANGER   TriStar, 1993, w/Mike France

LARRY STAMPER
WILD THING   Atlantic Releasing Corporation, 1987,
    Story w/John Sayles

DAVID STANDISH
CLUB PARADISE   Warner Bros., 1986, Story w/Tom Leopold,
    Chris Miller & Ed Roboto

JEFF STANLEY
Agent: Writers & Artists Agency - Los Angeles, 310/824-6300

Screenplays:
THE OBJECTORS

RICHARD STANLEY
Agent: William Morris Agency - Beverly Hills, 310/274-7451 or
    The Casarotto Company - London, 071/287-4450

HARDWARE   Millimeter Films, 1990, directed
DUST DEVIL   Miramax, 1993, directed

Screenplays:
THE ISLAND OF DR. MOREAU (directing)

JEFF STANZLER
Agent: United Talent Agency - Beverly Hills, 310/273-6700

BLAZERMAN TO THE RESCUE (Short)   directed
JUMPIN' AT THE BONEYARD   20th Century Fox, 1992, directed

Screenplays:
SMOKESTACK LIGHTNIN (directing)
THE ATTABOYS
DRY SPELL
LOVE IN FLUSHING
THE CRAIG ROCKELMAN STORY

JAY STAPLETON
Agent: Sanford-Gross & Associates - Los Angeles, 310/208-2100

HEADS (CTF)   Atlantic Films/Evermore/Davis Entertainment, 1994,
    w/Adam Brooks

Screenplays:
ZACH AND REBA

DARREN STAR*
Agent: ICM - Beverly Hills, 310/550-4000

DOIN' TIME ON PLANET EARTH   Cannon, 1989
IF LOOKS COULD KILL   Warner Bros., 1991

JAISON STARKES
J.D.'S REVENGE   American International, 1976
THE FISH THAT SAVED PITTSBURGH   United Artists, 1979,
    w/Edmond Stevens

MANYA STARR*
Agent: Neal Stevens & Associates - Beverly Hills, 310/275-7541

WHITE WATER SUMMER   Columbia, 1987, w/Ernest Kinoy

STEVEN STARR
Agent: William Morris Agency - Beverly Hills, 310/274-7451

JOEY BREAKER   Skouras Pictures, 1993, directed

JEAN STAWARZ
POWWOW HIGHWAY   Warner Bros., 1989, w/Janet Heaney

DOUG STECKLER*
Contact: WGA - Los Angeles, 310/550-1000

Screenplays:
BIG FAT ELVIS w/Doug McIntyre
CON JOB (Shared)

DAVID STEEN*
Contact: WGA - Los Angeles, 310/550-1000

AVENUE A (P)
A GIFT FROM HEAVEN   Hatchwell-Lucarelli, 1994, from his play

FRED STEFAN
SPRING FEVER   Comworld, 1983, w/Stuart Gillard

JOSEPH STEFANO*
Agent: United Talent Agency - Beverly Hills, 310/273-6700

THE BLACK ORCHID   Paramount, 1958
PSYCHO   Paramount, 1960
THE NAKED EDGE   United Artists, 1961
EYE OF THE CAT   Universal, 1969
THE KINDRED   FM Entertainment, 1987, w/others
BLACKOUT   Overseas Film Group, 1989
PSYCHO IV: THE BEGINNING (CTF)   Smart Money/MCA, 1990
TWO BITS   Miramax, 1995

MARK STEILEN
Agent: The Gage Group - Los Angeles, 310/859-8777

THE WHITE APARTMENT (P)

Screenplays:
FRIENDS AND LOVERS
MY BEST MAN
SURF CITY
BRACKEN

HARRY STEIN*
Agent: Lantz-Harris - New York, 212/586-0200

Screenplays:
BLIND MAN'S BLUFF

JOSEPH STEIN*
Contact: WGA - New York, 212/245-6180

RAGS (P)
ENTER LAUGHING   Columbia, 1967, w/Carl Reiner
FIDDLER ON THE ROOF   United Artists, 1971, from his play

MARK STEIN*
Agent: Broder-Kurland-Webb-Uffner - Beverly Hills, 310/281-3400

HOUSESITTER   Universal, 1992

Screenplays:
MURDERING MR. MONTI
DEAD OF SUMMER
MILWAUKEE CONFIDENTIAL

MICHAEL ERIC STEIN*
Contact: WGA - Los Angeles, 310/550-1000

Screenplays:
CAT
BERLIN SHADOW

SEAN STEIN
THE COUCH TRIP   Orion, 1988, w/Steven J. Kampmann &
   Will Aldis

TOM STEINBECK
Agent: The Gersh Agency - Beverly Hills, 310/274-6611

Screenplays:
THE PEARL

DAVID STEINBERG*
Agent: William Morris Agency - Beverly Hills, 310/274-7451
Contact: Highlight Commercials, 1049 N. Las Palmas, Los Angeles,
   CA 90038, 213/871-8488

GOING BERSERK   Universal, 1983, w/Dana Olsen, directed
ALL DOGS GO TO HEAVEN (AF)   MGM/UA, 1989,
   Story w/others

HARRIET STEINBERG
DROP DEAD GORGEOUS (CTF)   Power Pictures Corp.,
   1991, Story

MICHAEL STEINBERG
Agent: United Talent Agency - Beverly Hills, 310/273-6700

NIGHTWATCH (Short)   directed
SLEEP WITH ME   MGM/UA, 1994, w/Duane Dell'Amico,
   Roger Hedden, Neal Jimenez, Joe Keenan & Rory Kelly

NORMAN STEINBERG*
Agent: CAA - Beverly Hills, 310/288-4545

BLAZING SADDLES   Warner Bros., 1973, w/Andrew Bergman,
   Mel Brooks, Richard Pryor & Alan Uger
YES, GIORGIO   MGM/UA, 1982
MY FAVORITE YEAR   MGM/UA, 1982, w/Dennis Palumbo
JOHNNY DANGEROUSLY   20th Century Fox, 1984,
   w/Harry Columby, Jeff Harris & Bernie Kukoff
FUNNY ABOUT LOVE   Paramount, 1990, w/David Frankel

Screenplays:
HOTEL HAWAII   w/Richard Dimitri
MY SUMMER WITH MOM
CHARLES AND LUCY
MURDER AT PREP SCHOOL
SEX IN AMERICA
ATLANTIC CROSSING
HELP, I'M BEING HELD A PRISONER
THE POPCORN CAPER
THE MAN FROM ST. PAUL

ZIGGY STEINBERG*
Contact: WGA - Los Angeles, 310/550-1000

PORKY'S REVENGE   20th Century Fox, 1985
THE BOSS' WIFE   Tri-Star, 1986, directed
ANOTHER YOU   Tri-Star, 1991

REED STEINER*
Agent: Jon Klane Agency - Beverly Hills, 310/278-0178
Business: Bearflag Rebellion Pictures, 110 S. Sweetzer,
   Los Angeles, CA 90048, 213/655-0461

DISCOVERY BAY   Westwind Pictures/Image
   Organization, 1988
THE HIT LIST (CTF)   Westwind Productions, 1993

Screenplays:
TO PROTECT AND SERVE
THINNING THE PREDATORS
WHITE ROSE
OVERKILL
DEAD TIRED
SCARECROW   w/Dan Mazur
STEALING THUNDER
POINT-BLANK
ASSIGNED RISK
MR. MOTO

DANNY STEINMANN
SAVAGE STREETS   Entermark, 1985,
   w/Norman Yonemoto, directed
FRIDAY THE 13TH - A NEW BEGINNING   Paramount, 1985,
   w/Martin Kitrosser, directed

MARTIN STELLMAN
Agent: The Casarotto Company - London, 071/287-4450

QUADROPHENIA   World Northal, 1979, w/Dave Humphries &
   Franc Roddam
DEFENSE OF THE REALM   Hemdale, 1985
FOR QUEEN AND COUNTRY   Atlantic Releasing Corporation,
   1988, w/Trix Worrell, directed

DAVID STENN*
Agent: William Morris Agency - Beverly Hills, 310/274-7451

COOL AS ICE   Universal, 1991

Screenplays:
BAD LITTLE GIRL
DUMB BLONDE
THE IT GIRL

ELLIOT STEPHENS
(See Steven deSouza)

GARY STEPHENS*
Agent: The Gersh Agency - Beverly Hills, 310/274-6611

HUSH LITTLE BABY (CTF)   Power Pictures/Hearst International/
   USA Pictures, 1994, w/Julie Moskowitz

NEAL STEPHENSON
Agent: Pleshette & Green - Los Angeles, 213/465-0428

Screenplays:
SNOUT
MAKING THINGS

JOHN A. STEPPLING*
Agent: William Morris Agency - Beverly Hills, 310/274-7451

PLEDGING MY LOVE (P)
EDDIE COTTREL AT THE PIANO (P)
CHILDREN OF HERAKLES (P)
EXHALING ZERO (P)
TEENAGE WEDDING (P)
MY CRUMMY JOB (P)
THE THRILL (P)
THE SHAPER (P)
THE DREAM COAST (P)
CLOSE (P)
NECK (P)
STANDARD OF THE BREED (P)
A DEEP TROPICAL TAN (P)
SEA OF CORTEZ (P)
POWER TOOLS (P)
52 PICK-UP   Cannon, 1986, w/Elmore Leonard

Screenplays:
IN THE LIFE (Orion)
THE KILLING (Odyssey)
THE ANATOMY LESSON
THE LAST PIMP

ALEX STERN
DEAD AND BURIED   Avco Embassy, 1981, Story w/Jeff Miller

ELLIOT M. STERN*
Contact: WGA - Los Angeles, 310/550-1000

Screenplays:
DOUBLE-CROSS
DAD'S WEEK OFF w/Denise Halma
VALET PARKING
THE APPRENTICE
POT OF GOLD
MURPHY'S LAW
TWO GUYS FROM SPACE
SONNY
MY SECRET IDENTITY

LEONARD B. STERN*
Agent: Sy Fischer Company - Los Angeles, 310/470-0917

THE MILKMAN   Universal-International, 1950, w/Albert Beich,
   James O'Hanlon & Martin Ragaway
THE JAZZ SINGER   Warner Bros., 1953, w/Frank Davis &
   Lewis Meltzer
THREE FOR THE SHOW   Columbia, 1955, w/Edward Hope
JUST YOU AND ME, KID   Columbia, 1979,
   w/Oliver Hailey, directed
THE NUDE BOMB   Universal, 1980, w/Bill Dana & Arne Sultan
TEEN WOLF   Atlantic Releasing Corporation, 1985, Story
TARGET   Warner Bros., 1985, Story
MISSING PIECES   Orion, 1991, directed

NOAH STERN*
Agent: William Morris Agency - Beverly Hills, 310/274-7451

PYRATES   Live America Inc., 1991, directed
THE OPPOSITE SEX and how to live with them   Miramax,
   1993, directed

Screenplays:
VJ

SANDOR STERN*
Agent: Broder-Kurland-Webb-Uffner - Beverly Hills, 310/281-3400

THE AMITYVILLE HORROR   American International, 1979
FAST BREAK   Columbia, 1979
PIN   New World, 1989, directed
WEB OF DECEIT (CTF)   Sankan-Wilshire Court, 1990, directed
DUPLICATES (CTF)   Sankan Productions, 1992,
   w/Andrew Neiderman, directed
JERICHO FEVER (CTF)   Sankan Productions/Wilshire Court, 1993,
   w/I.C. Rappaport, directed

STEVEN HILLIARD STERN*
Agent: The Brandt Company - Sherman Oaks, 818/783-7747

B.S. I LOVE YOU   20th Century-Fox, 1971, directed
NEITHER BY DAY NOR BY NIGHT   Motion Pictures International,
   1972, directed
RUNNING   Universal, 1979, directed
LOVE & MURDER   Norstar Entertainment, 1990, directed

STEWART STERN*
Contact: WGA - Los Angeles, 310/550-1000

TERESA ★ MGM, 1951
REBEL WITHOUT A CAUSE   Warner Bros., 1955
THE RACK   MGM, 1956
THUNDER IN THE SUN   Paramount, 1959
THE OUTSIDER   Universal, 1961
THE UGLY AMERICAN   Universal, 1963
RACHEL, RACHEL ★   Warner Bros., 1968
THE LAST MOVIE   Universal, 1971
SUMMER WISHES, WINTER DREAMS   Columbia, 1973

Screenplays:
AN INFINITY OF MIRRORS w/G. Green
VALDEZ HORSES
THE DEATH OF THE SNOW QUEEN

TOM STERN*
Agent: Sanford-Gross & Associates - Los Angeles, 310/208-2100

SQUEAL OF DEATH (Short)   w/Alex Winter, co-directed
FREAKED   20th Century Fox, 1993, w/Alex Winter &
   Tim Burns, co-directed

Screenplays:
WONDERLAND w/Alex Winter
MILO RIGBY ON WHEELS w/Alex Winter
HOWIE'S REVENGE w/Alex Winter

JEFF STETSON*
Agent: William Morris Agency - Beverly Hills, 213/274-7451

THE MEETING (P)
FRATERNITY (P)
FATHERS-AND OTHER STRANGERS (P)
AND THE MEN SHALL ALSO GATHER (P)
TO FIND A MAN (P)

Screenplays:
CIVIL WARS
THE BUFFALO SOLDIERS
THE GENE ROBERTS STORY (CTF)
DIVIDED SOUL
BIRDIE AFRICA

MONTE STETTIN*
Agent: Preferred Artists - Encino, 818/990-0305

DOUBLE JEOPARDY (CTF) Showtime/CBS Entertainment
   Productions, 1992, w/Craig Tepper

ANDREW STEVENS
Contact: Screen Actors Guild - Los Angeles, 213/954-1600

NIGHT EYES Armitraj-Baldwin Entertainment, 1990, w/Tom Citrano
THE TERROR WITHIN II Concorde, 1991, directed
NIGHT EYES II Prism Pictures, 1993, directed
NIGHT EYES III: ON GUARD Prism Pictures, 1994, directed

DANA STEVENS*
Agent: ICM - Beverly Hills, 310/550-4000

BLINK New Line Cinema, 1994

Screenplays:
THE LION SLEEPS
LOST AT SEA
MAID OF HONOR
EVER AFTER
REAL LIFE

DAVID STEVENS*
Agent: Renaissance-H.N. Swanson - Los Angeles, 310/246-6000

BREAKER MORANT ★ New World/Quartet, 1980,
   w/Bruce Beresford & Jonathan Hardy
THE SUM OF US Samuel Goldwyn Company, 1994, from his play

EDMOND STEVENS*
Agent: Broder-Kurland-Webb-Uffner - Beverly Hills, 310/281-3400

THE FISH THAT SAVED PITTSBURGH United Artists, 1979,
   w/Jaison Starkes

Screenplays:
SEVEN SAMURAI (remake)
NEVERLAND
TELL TCHAIKOVSKY THE NEWS
BABES IN ARMS
BLIND FURY
FINE AND DANDY
SHORT OF MURDER
BRUISERS
TEXAS SWING
ROAD OPRY
KING OF THE MOUNTAIN
REUNION
RUBY RED
CHANNEL CROSSING

JEREMY STEVENS*
Agent: The Irv Schechter Company - Beverly Hills, 310/278-8070

SUMMER RENTAL Paramount, 1985, w/Mark Reisman

Screenplays:
BIG HOSPITAL w/Mark Reisman
NINETY MINUTES w/Mark Reisman

LESLIE C. STEVENS*
Agent: CAA - Beverly Hills, 310/288-4545

THE LEFT HANDED GUN Warner Bros., 1958
THE MARRIAGE GO ROUND 20th Century-Fox, 1961
HERO'S ISLAND United Artists, 1962, directed
BUCK ROGERS Universal, 1979, w/Glen A. Larson
SHEENA Columbia, 1984, Story w/David Newman
THREE KINDS OF HEAT Cannon, 1987, directed
RETURN TO BLUE LAGOON Columbia, 1991
GORDY Miramax, 1994

MARTY STEVENS-HEEBNER
Agent: United Talent Agency - Beverly Hills, 310/273-6700

Screenplays:
BONNIE AND REED
BARRICADES
TRACKSHADOWS
WAY DOWN DEEP

RICK STEVENSON*
Contact: WGA - Los Angeles, 310/550-1000

Screenplays:
ART OF COURTLY LOVE

BILL STEWART
Agent: Cinema Talent International - Los Angeles, 213/656-1937
Business: Stewart Products Co., 2461 Fairbrook Dr., Nashville,
   TN 37214, 615/883-3333

Screenplays:
UNHEARD MELODIES
PAPER DART
WALLS w/Barbara Holder

DONALD STEWART*
Contact: WGA - Los Angeles, 310/550-1000

JACKSON COUNTY JAIL New World, 1976
DEATHSPORT New World, 1978, w/Henry Suso
MISSING ★★ Universal, 1982, w/Costa-Gavras
THE HUNT FOR RED OCTOBER Paramount, 1990,
   w/Larry Ferguson
PATRIOT GAMES Paramount, 1992, w/W. Peter Iliff
CLEAR AND PRESENT DANGER Paramount, 1994,
   w/John Milius & Steven Zaillian

Screenplays:
THE SILVER STRAND
UNDER COVER OF DAYLIGHT
FIRST STRIKE
MRS. REDDEN
FIRE MAN
CABO RIO
KEY WEST
KILLING ZONE
FREEZE OUT
CAPA
DEAD SECTOR

DOUGLAS DAY STEWART*
Agent: William Morris Agency - Beverly Hills, 310/274-7451

WHERE THE RED FERN GROWS 1974, w/E. Lamb
SEVEN ALONE Doty-Dayton, 1975, w/E. Lamb
AGAINST A CROOKED SKY Doty-Dayton, 1975
THE OTHER SIDE OF THE MOUNTAIN - PART 2
   Universal, 1978
BLUE LAGOON Columbia, 1980
AN OFFICER AND A GENTLEMAN ★ Paramount, 1982
THIEF OF HEARTS Paramount, 1984, directed
LISTEN TO ME WEG, 1989, directed
THE SCARLET LETTER Buena Vista, 1995

Screenplays:
ON THE WINGS OF GIANTS KATMANDU
ESCAPE FROM BV-JAY
TOO LATE FOR HEROES

JOHN STEWART
ACTION U.S.A. Stewart & Berger Inc., 1989,
   Story w/David Reskin, directed
CLICK: THE CALENDAR GIRL KILLER Crown International, 1991,
   Story w/Carol Lynn, co-directed

MICHAEL STEWART
EYE OF THE STORM   Odyssey Distributors, 1993,
   w/Yuri Zeltser
MIDNIGHT EDITION   Shapiro Glickenhaus, 1993,
   w/Yuri Zeltser & Howard Libov

R.J. STEWART*
Agent: ICM - Beverly Hills, 310/550-4000

AND GOD CREATED WOMAN   Vestron, 1988
MAJOR LEAGUE II   Warner Bros., 1994, w/David Ward

Screenplays:
THE END OF ETERNITY
FIRE HOUSE
GOOD COMPANY
MAGIC FIVE

ROBERT STIGLIANO
Contact: Angelina Productions, 9005 Cynthia Street - #215,
   West Hollywood, CA 90069

FUN DOWN THERE   Frameline, 1990,
   w/Michael Waite, directed

Screenplays:
BOB, VERUSHKA & THE PURSUIT OF HAPPINESS
   w/Michael Waite (directing)

BEN STILLER*
Agent: CAA - Beverly Hills, 310/288-4545

Screenplays:
TRAITORS, SPIES AND INNKEEPERS w/Jeff Kahn
THE WEATHERMEN
SMOOTH DADDY

WHIT STILLMAN
(J. Whitney Stillman)
Agent: William Morris Agency - Beverly Hills, 310/274-7451

METROPOLITAN ★   New Line Cinema, 1990, directed
BARCELONA   Fine Line Features, 1994, directed

Screenplays:
THE LAST DAYS OF DISCO (directing)

JOSEPH C. STINSON*
Agent: The Coppage Company - North Hollywood, 818/980-1106

SUDDEN IMPACT   Warner Bros., 1983
CITY HEAT   Warner Bros., 1984, w/Blake Edwards
STICK   Universal, 1985, w/Elmore Leonard

Screenplays:
SPIRIT LAKE w/Michael Powell
ON DANGEOUS GROUND w/Michael Powell
WILDERNESS
KIDD
WINNING STREAK
BANDITS
RECOIL

MARC STIRDIVANT*
Agent: The Daniel Ostroff Agency - Los Angeles, 310/278-2020

CONDORMAN   Buena Vista, 1981, w/Glenn Gordon Caron &
   Mickey Rose

JOHN E. STITH
Agent: Berzon Agency - Glendale, 818/548-1560

THE TENDERLOIN   North City Productions, 1994,
   w/Alexandra Tana

Screenplays:
THE WAR OF THE WORLDS w/John Kennedy
USER HOSTILE w/John Kennedy
BRUTE w/Kavin King
NAUGHT FOR HIRE
DAWN QUIXOTE
DEEP QUARRY

MILAN STITT*
Agent: Writers & Artists Agency - New York, 212/947-8765

THE RUNNER STUMBLES   20th Century-Fox, 1979, from his play

ROBERT D. STITZEL*
Agent: Jon Klane Agency - Beverly Hills, 310/278-0178

BRAINSTORM   MGM/UA, 1983, w/Philip Frank Messina
DISTANT THUNDER   Paramount, 1988
THE TENDER *EYES OF AN ANGEL*   Paramount, 1989

Screenplays:
ICARUS
GETTING WANDA MARRIED
MOTORS
DUE DILLIGENCE
UNKNOWN HEROES

OLIVIER STOCKMAN
Contact: Sands Film Studios, 169 Rotherhithe St., London SE16 1QU,
   England, 071/231-2209

THE FOOL   Sands Films, 1991, w/Christine Edzard

JOHN STOCKWELL*
Agent: United Talent Agency - Beverly Hills, 310/273-6700

DANGEROUSLY CLOSE   Cannon, 1986, w/Scott Fields &
   Marty Ross
UNDER COVER   Cannon, 1987, w/Scott Fields, directed

Screenplays:
JUPITER BROWN w/Scott Fields (directing)
DOUBLE CROSS w/Scott Fields
SEE JANE RUN w/Scott Fields
DEAD SLEEP w/Scott Fields
SICILIAN OVERTURE w/Scott Fields
STORK CLUB w/Scott Fields
POINT PANIC w/Scott Fields

HUGH STODDART
Agent: Curtis Brown - London, 071/872-0331

REMEMBRANCE   Channel Four/Film on Four, 1982
WE THINK THE WORLD OF YOU   Cinecom, 1988

Screenplays:
BURMESE DAYS w/Julian Bond

JERRY STOEFFHAAS*
Contact: 716/244-6041

CHEAP SHOTS   Hemdale, 1991, w/Jeff Ureles, co-directed

MARGARET STOHL
Agent: Broder-Kurland-Webb-Uffner - Beverly Hills, 310/281-3400

Screenplays:
THE PINOCCHIO PROGRAM w/Raphael Simon

CHRISTIAN STOIANOVICH*
Agent: Warden, White & Kane - Beverly Hills, 213/852-1028

PERFECT FAMILY (CTF)   O.T.M.L./Wilshire Court, 1992,
  w/Phoebe Dorin

Screenplays:
BULLETPROOF w/Phoebe Dorin
CONDUIT w/Phoebe Dorin
WITHOUT MERCY w/Phoebe Dorin
THE 13TH FLOOR w/Phoebe Dorin
BABY BLUE EYES w/Phoebe Dorin
DEEP SLEEP w/Phoebe Dorin

BRYAN MICHAEL STOLLER
Agent: Cindy Turtle & Associates - Studio City, 818/506-6898
Personal Manager: Russ Blum, The Antares Group, 818/980-8880

UNDERSHORTS: THE MOVIE   Paramount, 1990,
  directed, unreleased

Screenplays:
THE RANDOM FACTOR w/Tristan Russell   (DNA Ent., directing)
LIGHT YEARS AWAY
REX

JEFF STOLZER*
Agent: CAA - Beverly Hills, 310/288-4545

Screenplays:
BACK ON THE MAP w/Roy Sekoff
UNHAPPY RETURNS w/Roy Sekoff

ANDREW L. STONE*
Contact: WGA - Los Angeles, 310/550-1000

STOLEN HEAVEN   Paramount, 1938, w/Eve Greene &
  Frederick Jackson, directed
THERE'S MAGIC IN MUSIC   Paramount, 1941, directed
THE BACHELOR'S DAUGHTER   United Artists, 1946, directed
FUN ON A WEEKEND   United Artists, 1947, directed
HIGHWAY 301   Warner Bros., 1950, directed
CONFIDENCE GIRL   United Artists, 1951, directed
THE STEEL TRAP   20th Century-Fox, 1952, directed
A BLUEPRINT FOR MURDER   20th Century-Fox, 1953, directed
THE NIGHT HOLDS TERROR   Columbia, 1955, directed
JULIE   MGM, 1956, directed
CRY TERROR!   MGM, 1958, directed
THE DECKS RAN RED   MGM, 1958, w/Virginia Stone, directed
THE LAST VOYAGE   MGM, 1960, directed
RING OF FIRE   MGM, 1961, directed
THE PASSWORD IS COURAGE   MGM, 1963, directed
NEVER PUT IT IN WRITING   Allied Artists, 1964, directed
THE SECRET OF MY SUCCESS   MGM, 1965, directed
SONG OF NORWAY   Cinerama Releasing Corporation,
  1970, directed
THE GREAT WALTZ   MGM, 1972, directed

ARNOLD M. STONE
SECRET HONOR   Cinecom International, 1985, w/Donald Freed

JERICO STONE
(See JERICO)

MATTHEW B. STONE*
Agent: Paradigm - Los Angeles, 310/277-4400

Screenplays:
DESTINY TURNS ON THE RADIO w/Rob Ramsey (Savoy)
INTOLERABLE CRUELTY w/Rob Ramsey

MICHAEL STONE
WAITRESS!   Troma, 1982, w/Charles Kaufman

NOREEN STONE*
Contact: WGA - Los Angeles, 310/550-1000

AMY   Buena Vista, 1981
BRENDA STARR   Triumph, 1992, w/James David Buchanan &
  Delia Ephron

OLIVER STONE*
Agent: CAA - Beverly Hills, 310/288-4545
Business: Ixtlan, Inc., 321 Hampton - Suite 105, Venice, CA 90291,
  310/399-2550

SEIZURE   Cinerama Releasing Corporation, 1974,
  w/E. Mann, directed
MIDNIGHT EXPRESS ★★   Columbia, 1978
THE HAND   Orion/Warner Bros., 1981, directed
CONAN THE BARBARIAN   Universal, 1982, w/John Milius
SCARFACE   Universal, 1983
YEAR OF THE DRAGON   MGM/UA, 1985, w/Michael Cimino
8 MILLION WAYS TO DIE   Tri-Star, 1986, w/R. Lance Hill
SALVADOR ★   Hemdale, 1986, w/Richard Boyle, directed
PLATOON ★   Orion, 1986, directed
WALL STREET   20th Century Fox, 1987,
  w/Stanley Weiser, directed
TALK RADIO   Universal, 1988, w/Eric Bogosian, directed
BORN ON THE FOURTH OF JULY ★   Universal, 1989,
  w/Ron Kovic, directed
THE DOORS   Tri-Star, 1991, w/Randy Johnson, directed
JFK ★   Warner Bros., 1991, w/Zachary Sklar, directed
HEAVEN AND EARTH   Warner Bros., 1993, directed
NATURAL BORN KILLERS   Warner Bros., 1994,
  w/Richard Rutowski & David Veloz, directed

Screenplays:
EVITA
NORIEGA w/Lawrence Wright
TOM MIX AND PANCHO VILLA
THE DEMOLISHED MAN w/Brian De Palma
THE BRAZIL RUN w/K. Roberts
THE UNGODLY
WILDERNESS

PETER H. STONE*
Agent: ICM - New York, 212/556-5600

WOMAN OF THE YEAR (P)
SUGAR (P)
MY ONE AND ONLY (P)   w/T. Mayer
THE WILL ROGERS FOLLIES (P)
CHARADE   Universal, 1964
FATHER GOOSE ★★   Universal, 1964, w/Frank Tarloff
MIRAGE   Universal, 1965
ARABESQUE   Universal, 1966
THE SECRET WAR OF HARRY FRIGG   Universal, 1967,
  w/Frank Tarloff
SWEET CHARITY   Universal, 1969
SKIN GAME   Warner Bros., 1971, as "Pierre Marton,"
  w/Richard Alan Simmons
1776   Columbia, 1972, from his play
THE TAKING OF PELHAM 1-2-3   United Artists, 1974
SILVER BEARS   Columbia, 1977
WHO IS KILLING THE GREAT CHEFS OF EUROPE?
  Warner Bros., 1978
WHY WOULD I LIE?   MGM/United Artists, 1980
JUST CAUSE   Warner Bros., 1995, w/Jeb Stuart

Screenplays:
THE FABRICATOR
THE WANTING OF LEVINE   HOLLYWOOD AND LEVINE

ROBERT STONE
Contact: Publisher-Penguin USA - New York, 212/366-2000

WUSA   Paramount, 1970

SHERRI STONER*
Agent: ICM - Beverly Hills, 310/550-4000

CASPER   Universal, 1995, w/Deanna Oliver

TOM STOPPARD*
Agent: Fraser & Dunlop - London, 071/376-7676

TRAVESTIES (P)
JUMPERS (P)
GALILEO (P)
ARTIST DESCENDING A STAIRCASE (P)
EVERY GOOD BOY DESERVES FAVOR (P)
THE REAL INSPECTOR HOUND (P)
THE REAL THING (P)
HAPGOOD (P)
ROUGH CROSSING (P)
ARCADIA (P)
THE ENGAGEMENT   Memorial, 1970
THE ROMANTIC ENGLISHWOMAN   New World, 1975,
    w/Thomas Wiseman
DESPAIR   New Line Cinema, 1978
THE HUMAN FACTOR   MGM/UA, 1979
BRAZIL ★   Universal, 1985, w/Terry Gilliam & Charles McKeown
EMPIRE OF THE SUN   Warner Bros., 1987
THE RUSSIA HOUSE   MGM/Pathe Entertainment, 1990
ROSENCRANTZ & GUILDENSTERN ARE DEAD   Cinecom, 1991,
    from his play, directed
BILLY BATHGATE   Buena Vista, 1991

Screenplays:
CATS (AF)
HOPEFUL MONSTERS
A NOVEL LIFE

ANTHONY STOREY
ZULU DAWN   New World, 1982, w/Cy Endfield

TAD STORIES
THE RETURN OF JAFAR (AHVF)   Buena Vista, 1994,
    Story w/Duane Capizzi, Douglas Langdale, Mark McCorkle &
    Robert Schooley

LISA B. STOTSKY*
Contact: WGA - Los Angeles, 310/550-1000

Screenplays:
LIFESAVERS w/Wendy Graf
ALL MINE w/Wendy Graf
FINAL ARGUMENTS w/Wendy Graf

WILLIAM STOUT*
Business Manager: Cooper, Epstein, Hurewitz - Beverly Hills,
    310/278-1111

THE WARRIOR AND THE SORCERESS   New Horizons, 1984,
    Story w/John Broderick

JIM STRAIN*
Agent: Above the Line - West Hollywood, 310/859-6115

BINGO   Tri-Star, 1991

Screenplays:
BABE AND ME
WINSLOW'S MUSE
THE FLASH
SOLDIERS OF FORTUNE
THE LOVER PRINCE
THE BYTES
JUMANJI w/Greg Taylor

JAN STRAND
THE RETURN OF JAFAR (AHVF)   Buena Vista, 1994,
    w/Kevin Campbell, Mirith J.S. Colao, Bill Motz, Steve Roberts,
    Bob Roth & Brian Swenlin

KEITH W. STRANDBERG
Contact: Seasonal Film Corporation - Pennsylvania, 717/285-3001

NO RETREAT, NO SURRENDER   New World, 1986
NO RETREAT, NO SURRENDER II   Shapiro Glickenhaus, 1989,
    w/Marie Elene Cellino & Roy Horan

Screenplays:
THE HATE STOPS HERE (directing)

BRIAN STRASMANN*
Agent: United Talent Agency - Beverly Hills, 310/273-6700

Screenplays:
FRIAR LEON'S CHRISTMAS SUPPER
FLASHBACK
TOBY
TERMINALS
PRINCIPAL INTENT
DEADHEADS
CYCLONE
THE BUTTONMEN
WARLOCK HOLMES
ABSTRACT ART
MY SOUL TO KEEP
ON MY HONOR

JEAN-MARIE STRAUB
Contact: French Film Office, 745 Fifth Avenue, New York, NY 10151,
    212/832-8860

CLASS RELATIONS   *KLASSENVERHALF-NISSE*   New Yorker,
    1987, directed

JOHN J. STRAUSS*
Agent: Broder-Kurland-Webb-Uffner - Beverly Hills, 310/281-3400

OPTIONS   Vestron, 1989, w/Ed Decter

Screenplays:
FOREVER MURRAY w/Ed Decter
YARD WARS w/Ed Decter
THERE'S SOMETHING ABOUT MARY w/Ed Decter

LARRY STRAWTHER*
Agent: William Morris Agency - Beverly Hills, 310/274-7451

WITHOUT A CLUE   Orion, 1989, w/Gary Murphy

Screenplays:
8:24 TO HEAVEN w/Gary Murphy

BILL STREIB*
Agent: The Agency - Los Angeles, 310/551-3000

Screenplays:
AMERICAN PIE

RUSSELL STREINER
THE RETURN OF THE LIVING DEAD   Orion, 1985,
    Story w/Rudy Ricci & John Russo

BARBRA STREISAND
Agent: CAA - Beverly Hills, 310/288-4545
Business: Barwood Films, 75 Rockefeller Plaza - 18th Floor,
    New York, NY 10019, 212/484-7300

YENTL   MGM/UA, 1983, w/Jack Rosenthal, directed

THOMAS STRELICH*
Contact: WGA - Los Angeles, 310/550-1000

Screenplays:
OUT THERE w/Alison Nigh (I.R.S.)

F
I
L
M

W
R
I
T
E
R
S

WESLEY E. STRICK*
Agent: CAA - Beverly Hills, 310/288-4545

TRUE BELIEVER   Columbia, 1989
ARACHNOPHOBIA   Buena Vista, 1990, w/Don Jakoby
CAPE FEAR   Universal, 1991
FINAL ANALYSIS   Warner Bros., 1992
WOLF   Columbia, 1994, w/Jim Harrison

Screenplays:
PURE HEART
PRACTICAL DEMONKEEPING
BEAUTIFUL NOISE
MADE IN JAPAN

WHITLEY STRIEBER*
Agent: CAA - Beverly Hills, 310/288-4545

COMMUNION   New Line Cinema, 1989

Screenplays:
UNHOLY FIRE

MAX STROM
BEST OF THE BEST 2   The Movie Group, 1993,
   w/John Alan Nelson

Screenplays:
YAKUZA   w/John Alan Nelson   (Neo Motion Pictures)
MIDNIGHT SUN BURNING BRIDGES   w/John Alan Nelson

JOHN STRONG
A SHOW OF FORCE   Paramount, 1990, w/Evan Jones

Screenplays:
NO SECOND CHANCE   (directing)

DANIELE STROPPA
WITCHERY   Filmirage, 1989

WILLIAM STROUM
Agent: CAA - Beverly Hills, 310/288-4545

Screenplays:
CODY AND WHEEZE   w/Raymond Martino

BARRY STRUGATZ*
Agent: Broder-Kurland-Webb-Uffner - Beverly Hills, 310/281-3400

MARRIED TO THE MOB   Orion, 1988, w/Mark Burns
SHE-DEVIL   Orion, 1989, w/Mark Burns

Screenplays:
MY FAVORITE MARTIAN   w/Mark Burns
I OWE YOU MY LIFE   w/Mark Burns
ON THE LAM   w/Mark Burns

JOHN STRYSIK
SAM AND SARAH   Full Circle Films, 1991,
   w/Robert Rothman, directed

ALEXANDER STUART
Agent: Peters, Fraser & Dunlop - London, 071/376-7676

ORDEAL BY INNOCENCE   MGM/UA, 1984

IAN A. STUART
THE PIT   New World, 1984

JEB STUART*
Agent: United Talent Agency - Beverly Hills, 310/273-6700

DIE HARD   20th Century Fox, 1988, w/Steven de Souza
LEVIATHAN   MGM/UA, 1989, w/David Peoples
LOCK UP   Tri-Star, 1989, w/Henry Rosenbaum & Richard Smith

VITAL SIGNS   20th Century Fox, 1990, w/Larry Ketron
ANOTHER 48 HRS.   Paramount, 1990, w/Larry Gross &
   John Fasano
THE FUGITIVE   Warner Bros., 1993, w/David Twohy
JUST CAUSE   Warner Bros., 1995, w/Peter Stone
OUTBREAK   Warner Bros., 1995, w/Ted Tally

Screenplays:
INDIANA JONES PART IV
THE FUGITIVE II
GOING WEST IN AMERICA
FIRE DOWN BELOW
SHOCKWAVE
SHIVA
DISSOCIATED STATES
GIRL'S CLUB
D.C. THRILLER
JURY DUTY
MAXWELL'S TRAIN
PINCUSHION
MIDNIGHT CLUB
IN THE NIGHT
IN EXTREMIS
COUTNERFEIT
ESCAPE

JOHN STUCKMEYER
THE SWORD AND THE SORCERER   Group 1, 1982,
   w/Thomas Karnowski & Albert Pyun

VALERIE STULMAN-BROWN
Agent: The Gage Group - Los Angeles, 310/859-8777

Screenplays:
JUST A PHASE

SCOTT STURGEON*
Agent: CAA - Beverly Hills, 310/288-4545

Screenplays:
HOSTAGES
THE BITTERROOT BURN

PRESTON STURGES*
Manager: Jonathan Baruch/PRO Management - Los Angeles,
   310/478-5159

Screenplays:
SPOOK
TWO GENTLEMEN OF MANHATTAN
THE DARKLING
A JOYFUL NOISE
EDUCATING IGNATIUS

CHARLES STURRIDGE
Agent: United Talent Agency - Beverly Hills, 310/273-6700 or
   Peters, Fraser & Dunlop - London, 071/376-7676

A HANDFUL OF DUST   New Line Cinema, 1988,
   w/Derek Granger & Tim Sullivan, directed
WHERE ANGELS FEAR TO TREAD   Fine Line Features, 1992,
   w/Derek Granger & Tim Sullivan, directed

ELISEO SUBIELA
Agent: ICM - Beverly Hills, 310/550-4000

MAN FACING SOUTHEAST   FilmDallas, 1987, directed

MILTON SUBOTSKY
THE LAST MILE   United Artists, 1959, w/Seton I. Miller
DR. TERROR'S HOUSE OF HORRORS   Amicus, 1965
DR. WHO AND THE DALEKS   British Lion, 1965
THE SKULL   Paramount, 1965
I, MONSTER   Amicus, 1970
TALES FROM THE CRYPT   Metromedia, 1972
VAULT OF HORROR   Metromedia, 1973
AT THE EARTH'S CORE   Amicus, 1976

JOAN SUGERMAN
SLEEPING BEAUTY   Gemini Pictures, 1992, directed

ROBERT A. SUHOVSKY*
Contact: 213/278-1255

THE HOUSE WHERE EVIL DWELLS   MGM/UA, 1982

BETH SULLIVAN*
Agent: ICM - Beverly Hills, 310/550-4000

CIRCLE OF POWER   *MYSTIQUE/BRAINWASH/THE
   NAKED WEEKEND*   Televicine, 1983, w/Stephen Bello

DANIEL G. SULLIVAN*
Agent: William Morris Agency - Beverly Hills, 310/274-7451

WHILE YOU WERE SLEEPING   Buena Vista, 1995, w/Fred Lebow

Screenplays:
NEW YEAR'S EVE w/Fred Lebow
SNOWFLAKES w/Fred Lebow
SANTA'S DAUGHTER w/Fred Lebow
FAMILY BOOK w/Fred Lebow
MOONLESS MIDNIGHT w/Fred Lebow
BAR SONG w/Fred Lebow
TERROR RANCH w/Fred Lebow

FRED G. SULLIVAN
COLD RIVER   Pacific International, 1982, directed
THE BEER DRINKER'S GUIDE TO FITNESS AND FILMMAKING
   SULLIVAN'S PAVILLION   Circle Releasing, 1987, directed

KEVIN SULLIVAN*
Agent: ICM - Beverly Hills, 310/550-4000

Screenplays:
THE GOOD TIMES ARE KILLING ME
RED TAILS
GREEN CARD BLUES
GHETTO BLASTERS

PATTI SULLIVAN*
Agent: Broder-Kurland-Webb-Uffner - Beverly Hills, 310/281-3400

Screenplays:
FOXFIRE
DEAD GIVEAWAY
FAMILY SECRETS
WILD ABOUT HARRY
MEN IN TROUBLE
EMOTIONAL RESCUE

TIM SULLIVAN
Agent: United Talent Agency - Beverly Hills, 310/273-6700 or
   Peters, Fraser & Dunlop - London, 071/376-7676

A HANDFUL OF DUST   New Line Cinema, 1988,
   w/Derek Granger & Charles Sturridge
WHERE ANGELS FEAR TO TREAD   Fine Line Features, 1992,
   w/Derek Granger & Charles Sturridge
JACK AND SARAH   Gramercy, 1994, directed

JARON SUMMERS*
Contact: WGA - Los Angeles, 310/550-1000

KILLER IMAGE   Groundstar Entertainment, 1992,
   w/Stan Edmonds & David Winning

PETER SUMMERS
Business: 3310 Keystone Ave., Los Angeles, CA 90034,
   310/558-4221

THE GAME   Cobra Entertainment Group, 1989

Screenplays:
BRATS w/Gail Willumsen
FILM SCHOOL w/Gail Willumsen
MOUNTAINS OF SPICES
HINDS' FEET ON HIGH PLACES
LITTLE SISTER
DEVIL ON THE RUN

SHIRLEY SUN
Business: Sun Productions, 110 Greene St. - Suite 12G,
   New York, NY 10012

A GREAT WALL   Orion Classics, 1986, w/Peter Wang
IRON AND SILK   Sun Productions, 1990,
   w/Mark Salzman, directed

CEDRIC SUNDSTROM
Agent: Twentieth Century Artists - Los Angeles, 213/850-5516

AMERICAN NINJA 3: BLOOD HUNT   Cannon,
   1989, directed

MADELINE SUNSHINE*
Agent: CAA - Beverly Hills, 310/288-4545

SON OF THE PINK PANTHER   MGM, 1993,
   Story w/Steve Sunshine & Blake Edwards

STEVE SUNSHINE*
Agent: CAA - Beverly Hills, 310/288-4545

SON OF THE PINK PANTHER   MGM, 1993,
   Story w/Madeline Sunshine & Blake Edwards

RONALD A. SUPPA*
Agent: The Kern Agency - 310/276-8080
Business: Suppa Productions, 3737 Ventura Canyon Ave.,
   Sherman Oaks, CA 91423, 818/784-6369

RIDING THE EDGE   Trans World Entertainment, 1989

BARTH JULES SUSSMAN
NIGHT GAMES   Avco Embassy, 1980, Story w/Anton Diether

PETER SUTCLIFFE
DOLLY DEAREST   Trimark, 1992, Story w/Mary Lease &
   Rod Nave

TAYLOR SUTHERLAND
THE LAST CHASE   Crown International, 1981, w/Martyn Burke &
   Christopher Crowe

LISA SUTTON
HOTEL OKLAHOMA   European American Entertainment, 1991,
   w/Bobby Houston

MICHAEL D. SUTTON*
Agent: APA - Los Angeles, 310/273-0744

Screenplays:
VOODOO w/Chris Miller
KEYSTONE COPS w/Chris Miller
THE CO-EDS w/Chris Miller
THE TECHNICOLOR TIME MACHINE w/Chris Miller
ANIMAL HOUSE NOW w/Chris Miller
NO SUCH LUCK w/Chris Miller
WITCHCRAFT w/Chris Miller
JUST LIKE A WOMAN w/Chris Miller
BEL-AIR BUTLER w/Chris Miller

PHOEF SUTTON*
Agent: Broder-Kurland-Webb-Uffner - Beverly Hills, 310/281-3400

BURIAL CUSTOMS (P)

Screenplays:
MRS. WINTERBOURNE (TriStar)
ROPE TRICK

BILL SVANOE*
Agent: The Artists Agency - Los Angeles, 310/277-7779

WALTZ ACROSS TEXAS   Atlantic Releasing Corporation, 1982
FATAL BEAUTY   MGM/UA, 1987, Story
SEDUCED BY EVIL (CTF)   CNM Entertainment/Wilshire Court, 1994

ELIZABETH SWADOS*
Agent: Innovative Artists - Los Angeles, 310/553-5200

RUNAWAYS (P)   also screenplay
THE RED SNEAKS (P)   also screenplay

Screenplays:
HOLLER
INSIDE OUT (AF)
CHEAP THRILLS

BOB SWAIM*
Agent: ICM - Beverly Hills, 310/550-4000

LA BALANCE   Spectrafilm, 1982, w/M. Fabiani, directed
HALF MOON STREET   20th Century Fox, 1986,
    w/Edward Behr, directed

Screenplays:
THE PARIS PROJECT (directing)
L.A. GOLD w/David H. Franzoni

TOM SWALE*
Agent: United Talent Agency - Beverly Hills, 310/273-6700

Screenplays:
THE KOUROS

P. W. SWANN
SURVIVAL GAME   Trans World Entertainment, 1987,
    w/Susannah deNimes & Herb Freed

SCOTT J. SWANTON*
Agent: CAA - Beverly Hills, 310/288-4545

RACE FOR GLORY   New Century/Vista, 1989

MILES HOOD SWARTHOUT*
Agent: The Agency - Los Angeles, 310/551-3000

THE SHOOTIST   Paramount, 1976, w/Scott Hale

Screenplays:
THE TIN LIZZIE TROOP
JOHN WESLEY HARDIN

STEVE SWARTZ
NEVER LEAVE NEVADA   Cabriolet Films, 1989, directed

ALFRED SWEENEY
UP FROM THE DEPTHS   New World, 1979

JULIA SWEENEY
Agent: Above the Line - West Hollywood, 310/859-6115

IT'S PAT, THE MOVIE   Buena Vista, 1994, w/Jim Emerson &
    Steve Hibbert

TERRY SWEENEY*
Agent: Innovative Artists - Los Angeles, 310/553-5200
Business Manager: Hansen, Jacobsen & Teller - Los Angeles,
    310/278-8622

LOVE AT STAKE *BURNIN' LOVE* Tri-Star, 1988, w/Lanier Laney
SHAG: THE MOVIE   Hemdale, 1989, w/Lanier Laney &
    Robin Swicord

BRIAN SWENLIN
THE RETURN OF JAFAR (AHVF)   Buena Vista, 1994,
    w/Kevin Campbell, Mirith J.S. Colao, Bill Motz, Steve Roberts,
    Bob Roth & Jan Strand

EDITHE SWENSEN*
Agent: Innovative Artists - Los Angeles, 310/553-5200

THEY (CTF)   Viacom Productions, 1993

Screenplays:
UNTITLED TANGIERS PROJECT
SAVAGE HEART
TALES OF THE MAGI

CHARLES SWENSON
Business: Marukami/Wolf/Swenson, Inc., 1463 Tamarind Ave.,
    Hollywood, CA 90028, 213/462-6473

DIRTY DUCK (AF)   New World, 1977, Shared, directed
TWICE UPON A TIME (AF)   The Ladd Company/Warner Bros.,
    1983, w/Bill Couterie, Suella Kennedy & John Korty, co-directed
AN AMERICAN TAIL: FEIVEL GOES WEST (AF)   Universal,
    1992, Story

JOHN K. SWENSSON
FIRE BIRDS   Buena Vista, 1990, Story w/Dale Dye & Step Tyner

MICHAEL SWERDLICK*
Agent: William Morris Agency - Beverly Hills, 310/274-7451

CAN'T BUY ME LOVE   Buena Vista, 1987
CLASS ACT   Warner Bros., 1992, Story w/Richard Brenne &
    Wayne Rice

TOMMY SWERDLOW*
Agent: CAA - Beverly Hills, 310/288-4545

COOL RUNNINGS   Buena Vista, 1993, w/Michael Goldberg &
    Lynn Siefert
LITTLE GIANTS   Warner Bros., 1994, w/Michael Goldberg,
    James Ferguson & Tommy Swerdlow

ROBIN SWICORD*
Agent: The Artists Agency - Los Angeles, 310/277-7779

CRIMINAL MINDS (P)
LAST DAYS AT THE DIXIE GIRL CAFE (P)
SHAG: THE MOVIE   Hemdale, 1989, w/Lanier Laney &
    Terry Sweeney
THE RED COAT (Short)   1994, directed
LITTLE WOMEN   Columbia, 1994
THE PEREZ FAMILY   Samuel Goldwyn Company, 1995

Screenplays:
MATILDA w/Nick Kazan (Universal)
THE CURIOUS CASE OF BENJAMIN BUTTON
VOYAGER
NIGHT MAGIC
PIED PIPER
GIRL CRAZY
SEE ROCK CITY
STOCK CARS FOR CHRIST

DAVID SWIFT*
Contact: Bloom, Dekom, Hergott & Cook - Los Angeles,
310/278-8622

POLLYANNA   Buena Vista, 1960, directed
THE PARENT TRAP   Buena Vista, 1961, directed
THE INTERNS   Columbia, 1962, w/Walter Newman, directed
LOVE IS A BALL   United Artists, 1962, w/Frank Waldman &
   Tom Waldman, directed
UNDER THE YUM YUM TREE   Columbia, 1963,
   w/Lawrence Roman, directed
GOOD NEIGHBOR SAM   Columbia, 1964, w/James Fritzell &
   Everett Greenbaum, directed
HOW TO SUCCEED IN BUSINESS WITHOUT REALLY TRYING
   United Artists, 1967, directed
FOOLIN' AROUND   Columbia, 1978, w/Michael Kane

DARREN SWIMMER*
Agent: William Morris Agency - Beverly Hills, 310/274-7451

Screenplays:
CHASING GHOSTS w/Todd Slavkin
SUBMERGED w/Todd Slavkin
HEIR MAIL w/Todd Slavkin

ALAN SWYER*
Agent: Neal Stevens & Associates - Beverly Hills, 310/275-7541

THE BUDDY HOLLY STORY   Columbia, 1978, Story
CRITICAL CONDITION   Paramount, 1987, Story w/Denis Hamill &
   John Hamill

Screenplays:
BAT MASTERSON IN NEW YORK w/Nathan Gottlieb
ANGEL OF HARLEM

MEERA SYAL
Agent: Rochelle Stevens & Co. - London, 071/359-3900

BHAJI ON THE BEACH   First Look Pictures, 1994

PAUL SYLBERT*
Contact: Sydney Cohen, Esq. - New York, 212/757-4000

THE STEAGLE   Avco Embassy, 1971, directed
NIGHT HAWKS   Universal, 1981, Story w/David Shaber

ISTVAN SZABO
MEPHISTO   Analysis, 1980, w/Peter Dobai, directed
COLONEL REDL   Orion Classics, 1985, w/Peter Dobai, directed
HANUSSEN   Hungarofilm, 1988, w/Peter Dobai, directed
MEETING VENUS   Warner Bros., 1992, w/Michael Hirst, directed
SWEET EMMA, DEAR BOBE-SKETCHES, NUDES   Objektiv Film
   Studio, 1992, directed

THOMAS E. SZOLLOSI*
Agent: The Wright Concept - Burbank, 818/954-8943

THREE O'CLOCK HIGH   Universal, 1987,
   w/Richard Christian Matheson
IT TAKES TWO   MGM/UA, 1988, w/Richard Christian Matheson

Screenplays:
SNOW WHITE
BLOOD PRESSURE
HOME PIE
MR. FIXIT
DRIVEN

MICHAEL TAAV*
Agent: ICM - Beverly Hills, 310/550-4000

FRIENDS, LOVERS & LUNATICS   Fries Entertainment, 1989
TOM GOES TO THE BAR (Short)   1991
HOGS HEAVEN (Short)   1992, directed
THE PAINT JOB   Second Son Entertainment, 1992, directed

Screenplays:
MORGAN w/Leslie Ray

MATT TABAK*
Contact: Carlos Goodman, Lichter, Grossman & Nichols -
   Los Angeles, 310/205-6999

THE INVESTIGATOR (Short)   1994, directed

Screenplays:
TRICK
LOVE AND MARRIAGE

JORDAN S. TABAT*
Manager: RKS Entertainment Group - Sherman Oaks, 818/788-3616

Screenplays:
THE BELLHOP'S DAUGHTER

SYLVIO TABET
Business: Films 21, 10845 Sunset Blvd., Los Angeles, CA 90077

BEASTMASTER 2: THROUGH THE PORTAL OF TIME
   New Line Cinema, 1991, w/Ken Hauser, Doug Miles,
   R.J. Robertson & Jim Wynorski, directed

JEAN-CHARLES TACCHELLA
Agent: Jean-Paul Faure, Agence APF, 2 Rue Jules Chaplain, Paris,
   France, tel.: 325-5163

COUSIN,COUSINE   Pomerue, 1975, directed

Screenplays:
SEVEN SUNDAYS (directing)

LINDA TADDEO*
Contact: WGA - Los Angeles, 310/550-1000

Screenplays:
LIGHTNING MANN
SECRETARY'S DAY
HELLION

BRIAN W. TAGGERT*
Agent: The Irv Schechter Company - Beverly Hills, 310/278-8070

VISITING HOURS   20th Century-Fox, 1982
OF UNKNOWN ORIGIN   Warner Bros., 1983
THE NEW KIDS   Columbia, 1985, Story w/Stephen Gyllenhaal
WANTED DEAD OR ALIVE   New World, 1987,
   w/Michael Patrick Goodman & Gary Sherman
POLTERGEIST III   MGM/UA, 1988, w/Gary Sherman
CHILDREN OF DARKNESS, CHILDREN OF LIGHT (CTF)
   G.C. Group/Wilshire Court, 1991
THE COVER GIRL MURDERS (CTF)   River Enterprises/
   Wilshire Court, 1993, Story

Screenplays:
JUNK AND MR. WISCOE

MARTIN TAHSE*
Business: Martin Tahse Productions, 1364 Palisades Beach Rd.,
Santa Monica, CA 90401, 310/451-5164

THE LOOKALIKE (CTF)   Gallo Entertainment Inc., 1990,
w/Linda Bergman
MATTERS OF THE HEART (CTF)   Tahse-Bergman/MCA, 1990,
w/Linda Bergman

DON TAIT*
Contact: WGA - Los Angeles, 310/550-1000

ONE MORE TRAIN TO ROB   Universal, 1971,
w/Donald Nelson
SNOWBALL EXPRESS   Buena Vista, 1972,
w/Arnold Margolin & Jim Parker
THE CASTAWAY COWBOY   Buena Vista, 1974
THE APPLE DUMPLING GANG   Buena Vista, 1974
THE SHAGGY D.A.   Buena Vista, 1976
TREASURE OF MATECUMBE   Buena Vista, 1976
THE NORTH AVENUE IRREGULARS   Buena Vista, 1979
THE APPLE DUMPLING GANG RIDES AGAIN
Buena Vista, 1979
UNIDENTIFIED FLYING ODDBALL   *THE SPACEMAN AND
KING ARTHUR*   Buena Vista, 1979
HERBIE GOES BANANAS   Buena Vista, 1980

RACHEL TALALAY
Agent: ICM - Beverly Hills, 310/550-4000

FREDDY'S DEAD: THE FINAL NIGHTMARE   New Line Cinema,
1991, Story, directed

JULIE TALEN*
Agent: United Talent Agency - Beverly Hills, 310/273-6700
Manager: Melinda Jason - Beverly Hills, 310/289-6134

Screenplays:
A SIMPLE LESBIAN WEDDING   (Story w/Ron Bass)
A TALE OF TWO BRIDES
BECKY RYAN
RESCUE ME
HARRIET THE SPY
MOTHERS DAY

C.M. TALKINGTON
Agent: ICM - Beverly Hills, 310/550-4000

LOVE AND A .45   Trimark, 1994, directed

SHIRLEY TALLMAN
Agent: Favored Artists Agency - Los Angeles, 213/653-3191

Screenplays:
THE ADVENTURES OF JADE STARR   w/Nancy Hersage

TED TALLY*
Agent: ICM - Beverly Hills, 310/550-4000

TERRA NOVA (P)
HOOTERS (P)
WHITE PALACE   Universal, 1990, w/Alvin Sargent
THE SILENCE OF THE LAMBS ★★   Orion, 1991
OUTBREAK   Warner Bros., 1995, w/Jeb Stuart

Screenplays:
BEFORE AND AFTER   (Buena Vista)
ALL THE PRETTY HORSES
THE JUROR
EMERALD CITY
NICE WORK

AMY TAN
Agent: The Gersh Agency - Beverly Hills, 310/274-6611

THE JOY LUCK CLUB   Buena Vista, 1993, w/Ron Bass

Screenplays:
THE KITCHEN GOD'S WIFE   w/Ron Bass

ALEXANDER TANA
Contact: Josh Grode, Christensen, White, Miller, Fink & Jacobs -
Los Angeles, 310/553-3000

Screenplays:
MAD FOR MIMA
EARTHSHAKE
MEMORIES IN DRAG
"AFTER ALL" EXPRESS
UNDER THE SIGN OF CANCER
RATING SCOTT MARRINER   w/R. Rosenberg
THE ZIGZAG MAN
NEW KID IN TOWN
THE MYSTERY OF THE MOSAIC

JOE TANKERSLEY
AFTER SCHOOL   Moviestore Entertainment, 1989, w/John Linde,
Rod McBrien & Hugh Parks

TERRELL M. TANNEN*
Agent: CAA - Beverly Hills, 310/288-4545

Screenplays:
BONES OF CORAL
SUNDOG
A GOOD DAY TO DIE
THE MAN WHO GAVE UP HIS NAME

WILLIAM TANNEN
Agent: Becsey/Wisdom/Kalajian Agency - Los Angeles,
310/550-0535

COVER UP   Live Home Video/Jacob Kotzky/Sharon Harel
Productions, 1991

RICHARD H. TANNENBAUM*
Agent: Jon Klane Agency - Beverly Hills, 310/278-0178

ME AND THE KID   Orion, 1993

Screenplays:
SOUL SURVIVOR
A MAN WITH A PLAN
CONNECTIONS
NIGHTRUNNER

JUSTIN TANNER
Agent: ICM - Beverly Hills, 310/550-4000
Contact: Cast Theatre - Hollywood, 213/462-9872

STILL LIFE WITH VACUUM SALESMAN (P)
ZOMBIE ATTACK! (P)   w/Andy Daley
HAPPYTIME XMAS (P)
PARTY MIX (P)
TEEN GIRL (P)
BITTER WOMEN (P)
POT MOM (P)
THE TENT SHOW (P)

DANIEL B. TAPLITZ*
Agent: CAA - Beverly Hills, 310/288-4545

FIVE OUT OF SIX (Short)   directed
THE SQUEEZE   Tri-Star, 1987
BLACK MAGIC (CTF)   Point of View/MCA Television Entertainment,
1992, directed

Screenplays:
COMMANDMENTS
RANDOM

DANIEL TARADASH*
Contact: WGA - Los Angeles, 310/550-1000

GOLDEN BOY   Columbia, 1939, w/Lewis Meltzer,
   Sarah Y. Mason & Victer Heerman
KNOCK ON ANY DOOR   Columbia, 1949, w/John Monks Jr.
DON'T BOTHER TO KNOCK   20th Century-Fox, 1952
RANCHO NOTORIOUS   RKO, 1952
FROM HERE TO ETERNITY ★★   Columbia, 1953
DESIREE   20th Century-Fox, 1954
PICNIC   Columbia, 1956
STORM CENTER   Columbia, 1956, w/Elick Moll,   directed
BELL, BOOK AND CANDLE   Columbia, 1958
THE SABOTEUR   *CODE NAME MORITURI*
   20th Century-Fox, 1965
HAWAII   United Artists, 1966, w/Dalton Trumbo
CASTLE KEEP   Columbia, 1969, w/David Rayfiel
DOCTOR'S WIVES   Columbia, 1970
THE OTHER SIDE OF MIDNIGHT   20th Century-Fox, 1977,
   w/Herman Raucher

QUENTIN TARANTINO
Agent: William Morris Agency - Beverly Hills, 310/274-7451
Business: A Band Apart Productions, 6525 Sunset Blvd. -
   Garden Suite 12, Los Angeles, CA 90028, 213/468-2555

RESERVOIR DOGS   Miramax, 1992, directed
TRUE ROMANCE   Warner Bros., 1993
NATURAL BORN KILLERS   Warner Bros., 1994, Story
PULP FICTION   Miramax, 1994, directed
FOUR ROOMS   Miramax, 1995, "Thrill of the Bet," directed

Screenplays:
FROM DUST TILL DAWN
MY BEST FRIEND'S BIRTHDAY w/Craig Hamann
THE CRIMINAL MIND w/Craig Hamann

SOONI TARAPOREVELA
Agent: Sanford-Gross & Associates - Los Angeles, 310/208-2100

SALAAM BOMBAY!   Cinecom, 1988
MISSISSIPPI MASALA   Miramax, 1992

ERIK S. TARLOFF*
Agent: Shapiro/Lichtman - Los Angeles, 310/859-8877

CHEETAH   Buena Vista, 1989, w/John Cotter & Griff DuRhone
CAR 54, WHERE ARE YOU?   Orion, 1994, w/Peter Crabbe,
   Peter McCarthy & Ebbe Roe Smith

JAY TARSES*
Agent: ICM - Beverly Hills, 310/550-4000

MAD MAGAZINE PRESENTS UP THE ACADEMY   Warner Bros.,
   1980, w/Tom Patchett
THE GREAT MUPPET CAPER   Universal/AFD, 1981,
   w/Tom Patchett, Jerry Juhl & Jack Rose
THE MUPPETS TAKE MANHATTAN   Tri-Star, 1984,
   w/Tom Patchett & Frank Oz

Screenplays:
THE BRAVE YOUNG MEN OF WEINBERG w/Tom Patchett
CROOKS w/Tom Patchett
THE KID WHO COULD GO TO HIS LEFT w/Tom Patchett
DANCING IN THE DARK
IT LOOKED LIKE FOREVER

MAX TASH*
Agent: Sanford-Gross & Associates - Los Angeles, 310/208-2100

THE RUNNIN' KIND   MGM/UA, 1990,
   w/Pleasant Gehman, directed

PAUL TATARA
Agent: The Tantleff Office - New York, 212/941-3939

Screenplays:
THE ALMOST PERFECT GAME

TOM TATUM
WINNERS TAKE ALL   Apollo Pictures, 1987,
   Story w/Christopher Knight

ALEX TAUB*
Agent: William Morris Agency - Beverly Hills, 310/274-7451

Screenplays:
THE GYM TEACHER
SAVING FACE
HOME GROWN

BILL TAUB*
Agent: Renaissance-H.N. Swanson - Los Angeles, 310/246-6000

Screenplays:
TAKE A CHANCE ON HARRY!

DAVID TAUSIK
Agent: Peter Turner Agency - Santa Monica, 310/315-4772

THINK BIG   Concorde, 1990, w/Edward Kovach & Jon Turtletaub
DRIVING ME CRAZY   Motion Picture Corporation of America, 1991,
   w/Jon Turtletaub & R.M. London
KILLER INSTINCT   Concorde, 1992, directed

Screenplays:
RAND ROBINSON, ROBOT REPAIRMAN w/Dan Mazur
TRAFFIC COP

BERTRAND TAVERNIER
Agent: ICM - Beverly Hills, 310/550-4000

THE CLOCKMAKER OF ST. PAUL   Joseph Green Pictures, 1974,
   w/Jean Aurenche & Pierre Bost,   directed
THE JUDGE AND THE ASSASSIN   Libra, 1976,
   w/Jean Aurenche,   directed
SPOILED CHILDREN   Corinth, 1977, w/Charlotte Dubreuil &
   Christine Pascal,   directed
DEATH WATCH   Quartet, 1980, w/David Rayfiel,   directed
COUP DE TORCHON   *CLEAN SLATE*   Biograph/Quartet/Films Inc./
   The Frank Moreno Company, 1982, w/Jean Aurenche,   directed
A WEEK'S VACATION   *UNE SEMAINE DE VACANCES*   Biograph,
   1982, w/Colo Tavernier & Marie-Francoise Hans,   directed
A SUNDAY IN THE COUNTRY   MGM/UA Classics, 1984,
   w/Colo Tavernier,   directed
ROUND MIDNIGHT   Warner Bros., 1986, w/David Rayfiel,   directed
LIFE AND NOTHING BUT   *LA VIE ET RIEN D'AUTRE*   UGC,
   1989, w/Jean Cosmos,   directed
L.627   AMLF, 1992, w/Michel Alexandre,   directed

PAOLO TAVIANI
Address: via dell'Ongaro 41, Rome, Italy, 06/5817231

PADRE PADRONE   New Yorker, 1977,
   w/Vittorio Taviani,   co-directed
THE MEADOW   New Yorker, 1979, w/Vittorio Taviani,   co-directed
THE NIGHT OF THE SHOOTING STARS   *LA NOTTE DI*
   SANS LORENZO   United Artists Classics, 1981,
   w/Vittorio Taviani,   co-directed
KAOS   MGM/UA Classics, 1985, w/Vittorio Taviani,   co-directed
GOOD MORNING, BABYLON   Vestron, 1987,
   w/Vittorio Taviani,   co-directed
NIGHT SUN   Filmtre/Raiuno/Capoul/Inerpool/Sara Film/Direkt Film,
   1991, w/Vittorio Taviani & Tonino Guerra,   co-directed
FIORILE   Fine Line Features, 1993, w/Vittoria Taviani &
   Sandro Petraglia,   co-directed

VITTORIO TAVIANI
Address: via Orti D'Albert 4, Rome, Italy, 06/6541834

PADRE PADRONE   New Yorker, 1977,
  w/PaoloTaviani, co-directed
THE MEADOW   New Yorker, 1979, w/Paolo Taviania, co-directed
THE NIGHT OF THE SHOOTING STARS   *LA NOTTE DI
  SANS LORENZO*   United Artists Classics, 1981,
  w/Paolo Taviania, co-directed
KAOS   MGM/UA Classics, 1985, w/Paolo Taviani, co-directed
GOOD MORNING, BABYLON   Vestron, 1987,
  w/Paolo Taviani, co-directed
NIGHT SUN   Filmtre/Raiuno/Capoul/Inerpool/Sara Film/Direkt Film,
  1991, w/Paolo Taviani & Tonino Guerra, co-directed
FIORILE   Fine Line Features, 1993, w/Paolo Taviani &
  Sandro Petraglia, co-directed

BRUCE A. TAYLOR*
Contact: WGA - Los Angeles, 310/550-1000

INSTANT KARMA   MGM/UA, 1990, w/Dale Rosenbloom

CHRISTIAN TAYLOR
Agent: United Talent Agency - Beverly Hills, 310/273-6700

THE LADY IN WAITING (Short) ★   1992, directed

DAVID C. TAYLOR*
Contact: WGA - Los Angeles, 310/550-1000

HANKY PANKY   Columbia, 1982, w/Henry Rosenbaum
GET CRAZY   Embassy, 1983, w/Danny Opatoshu &
  Henry Rosenbaum
LASSITER   Warner Bros., 1984
THE LIGHTSHIP   Castle Hill Productions, 1986, w/William Mai
TRAVELING MAN (CTF)   Irvin Kershner Films, 1989
FIRE BIRDS   Buena Vista, 1990, w/Paul Edwards & Nick Thiel
MAJORITY RULE (CTF)   Ultra Entertainment/Citadel Pictures, 1992
DEVLIN (CTF)   Viacom Pictures, 1992
CRACK IN THE KREMLIN WALL (CTF)   Viacom, 1993,
  w/George Lee Marshall
THE DROP SQUAD   Gramercy, 1994, Story

Screenplays:
NIGHT WORK
ANIMAL FACTORY
PRIVATE SCREENING
TICKET TO RIDE
MAN WITH A GUN
MOVING VIOLATIONS

EDWARD TAYLOR*
Contact: WGA - Los Angeles, 310/550-1000

V.I. WARSHAWSKI   Buena Vista, 1991, w/David Aaron Cohen &
  Nick Thiel

FINN TAYLOR*
Agent: Jim Preminger Agency - Los Angeles, 310/475-9491

PONTIAC MOON   Paramount, 1994, w/Jeff Brown

Screenplays:
AVAILABLE LIGHT
BIG BRASS RING
DREAM WITH THE FISHES
THE FOURTH STEP

GREG TAYLOR*
Agent: Above the Line - West Hollywood, 310/859-6115

PRANCER   Orion, 1989

Screenplays:
OCEAN BOULEVARD   w/Rowdy Herrington
HARRIET THE SPY

FAMILY MAN *w/Mike Petzold*
PSYCHICS
HI FI
SWAN LAKE (AF)
JUMANJI w/Jim Strain

JOAN TAYLOR*
Agent: ICM - Beverly Hills, 310/550-4000

Screenplays:
FOOLS RUSH IN
MODERN BRIDE   w/Alice Arlen & Nora Ephron
WOMEN'S WORK
MONEY HONEY
BLACK TIE
NIGHT AND DAY

JOYCE E. TAYLOR*
Contact: Sidewalk Productions - 310/454-7090

BODY PARTS   Paramount, 1991, Story w/Patricia Herskovic

LEVI TAYLOR
Agent: Warden, White & Kane - Beverly Hills, 213/852-1028

Screenplays:
KIDNEYS

PHILIP JOHN TAYLOR*
Business Manager: J. Gunnar Erickson, Armstrong, Hirsch, Jackoway,
  Tyerman & Wertheimer - Los Angeles, 310/553-0305

LUST IN THE DUST   New World, 1984
I'M DANGEROUS TONIGHT (CTF)   MCA TV, 1990,
  w/Bruce Lansbury

RENEE TAYLOR*
Business Manager: Zipperstein & Kantor - Encino, 818/986-4640

LOVERS AND OTHER STRANGERS ★   Cinerama Releasing
  Corporation, 1970, w/Joseph Bologna & David Z. Goodman
MADE FOR EACH OTHER   20th Century-Fox, 1971,
  w/Joseph Bologna
MIXED COMPANY   United Artists, 1974, w/Joseph Bologna
IT HAD TO BE YOU   Limelite Studios, 1989, w/Joseph Bologna,
  from their play
OH NO, NOT HER!   Cinema 7 Productions, 1994,
  w/Joseph Bologna

RICHARD TAYLOR*
Contact: WGA - Los Angeles, 310/550-1000

DECEPTIONS (CTF)   Republic Pictures, 1990

ROBERT TAYLOR
HEIDI'S SONG (AF)   Paramount, 1982, w/Joseph Barbera &
  Jameson Brewer, directed

RODERICK L. TAYLOR*
Agent: Martin Hurwitz Associates - Beverly Hills, 310/274-0240

THE STAR CHAMBER   20th Century-Fox, 1983,
  w/Peter Hyams

Screenplays:
TEEN WOLF 666
EMPIRE MAN

JOHN MICHAEL TEBELAK
GODSPELL   Columbia, 1973, w/David Greene, from his play

ANDRE TECHINE
Contact: French Film Office, 745 Fifth Avenue, New York,
    NY 10151, 212/832-8860

SCENE OF THE CRIME 1986, w/Pascal Bonitzer &
    Olivier Assayas, directed
RENDEZ-VOUS Spectrafilm, 1987, w/Olivier Assayas, directed
MY FAVORITE SEASON AMLF, 1993,
    w/Pascal Bonitzer, directed
WILD REED IMA, 1994, w/Olivier Massart &
    Gilles Taurand, directed

HENRY TEFAY
WEEKEND WITH KATE Phillip Emanuel Productions, 1990,
    w/Kee Young

ROY G. TEICHER*
Contact: Joel Behr - 310/556-9222

INSIDE OUT Hemdale, 1986, w/Kevin Bartelme, directed

Screenplays:
MEN WITHOUT BASES

MIGUEL TEJADA-FLORES*
Agent: Innovative Artists - Los Angeles, 310/553-5200

REVENGE OF THE NERDS 20th Century Fox, 1984,
    Story w/Jeff Buhai, Tim Metcalfe & Steve Zacharias
THREE FOR THE ROAD New Century/Vista, 1987,
    w/Richard Martini & Tim Metcalfe
MILLION DOLLAR MYSTERY DEG, 1987, w/Tim Metcalfe &
    Rudy DeLuca
FRIGHT NIGHT PART 2 New Century/Vista, 1989,
    w/Tim Metcalfe & Tommy Lee Wallace
BLACKMAIL (CTF) Pacific Motion Picture Corporation,
    1991, directed
PSYCHIC (CTF) Trimark, 1992, w/Paul Koval
A HOUSE IN THE HILLS LIVE Entertainment, 1993,
    w/Ken Weiderhorn
RESURRECTION Delta Entertainment, 1993
PAST TENSE (CTF) Showtime Entertainment, 1994,
    w/Scott Frost

Screenplays:
DECEPTIONS III (Saban Entertainment)
FARTMAN
TWISTER
NIGHT PEOPLE
WITH INTENT TO KILL

TORI TELLEM
NATIONAL LAMPOON'S LOADED WEAPON 1 New Line Cinema,
    1993, Story w/Don Holley

TELLER*
Agent: William Morris Agency - Beverly Hills, 310/274-7451

PENN & TELLER GET KILLED Warner Bros., 1989, w/Penn Jilette

GREGG TEMKIN*
Agent: Paradigm - Los Angeles, 310/277-4400

Screenplays:
JUDAS KISS
STRANGE BEDFELLOWS

DURA TEMPLE*
Agent: Solomon Weingarten & Associates - Los Angeles,
    310/479-4706

PHOTOPLAY (P)
TRAILS (P)
SAKUNTALA (P)
GOD'S BLIND EYE (P)

SANCTUARY (P)
SOUTHERN GIRLS (P)
CAT GAME (P)

Screenplays:
THE REHEARSAL CLUB
CARNY MOON
DANCING THROUGH LIMBO
BETWEEN THE SUN & THE MOON

ANDY TENNANT*
Agent: Broder-Kurland-Webb-Uffner - Beverly Hills, 310/281-3400

Screenplays:
CUPID w/Rick Parks (directing)
BLABBERMOUTH (directing)
FRANK
BED & BREAKFAST w/Mike Marvin
HALF BAKED! w/Mike Marvin
CAMP ESCAPE
HALF IN - FULL OUT
DANCIN' MAN
WANDERLUST
FLIPS
BLACK 'N BLUE
LONG WAY HOME
HOME FOR THE HOLIDAYS

WILLIAM TENNANT
Contact: 310/315-7800

THE HOLLYWOOD KNIGHTS Columbia, 1980,
    Story w/Floyd Mutrux & Richard Lederer

KEVIN S. TENNEY
Agent: Above the Line - West Hollywood, 310/859-6115

THE BOOK OF JOE (Short) also screenplay
WITCHBOARD Cinema Group, 1986, directed
PEACEMAKER Fries Entertainment, 1990, directed
WITCHBOARD 2 Republic Pictures, 1993, directed

Screenplays:
BIG GAME
PARDON MY NINJA
TIC TOCK

CRAIG M. TEPPER*
Contact: WGA - Los Angeles, 310/550-1000

DOUBLE JEOPARDY (CTF) Showtime/CBS Entertainment, 1992,
    w/Monte Stettin

Screenplays:
THE LITTLE WIFE
AISHA
PRIVILEGED RELATIONS (CTF) w/Patrick Gilmore
MAN OF STEEL
IN THE DEEP WOODS

WILLIAM TEPPER
Agent: Jon Klane Agency - Beverly Hills, 310/278-0178

MISS RIGHT IAP, 1981

Screenplays:
OUT OF THE WOODS
MONEY TALKS
THE GREAT AND THE NEAR GREAT
PINK & BLUE
MEN WHO DON'T QUIT

GAY PARTINGTON TERRY
Contact: Troma, Inc., 733 Ninth Ave., New York, NY 10019,
212/757-4555

THE TOXIC AVENGER, PART II   Troma, 1988
THE TOXIC AVENGER, PART III: THE LAST TEMPTATION
   OF TOXIE   Troma, 1989, w/Lloyd Kaufman

STEVE TESICH*
Agent: ICM - New York, 212/556-5600

THE CARPENTERS (P)
LAKE OF THE WOODS (P)
GORKY (P)
THE PASSING GAME (P)
TOUCHING BOTTOM (P)
DIVISION STREET (P)
NOURISH THE BEAST (P)
BABA GOYA (P)
KING OF HEARTS (P)
SQUARE ONE (P)
THE SPEED OF DARKNESS (P)
ON THE OPEN ROAD (P)
BREAKING AWAY ★★   20th Century-Fox, 1979
EYEWITNESS   20th Century-Fox, 1981
FOUR FRIENDS   Filmways, 1981
THE WORLD ACCORDING TO GARP   Warner Bros., 1982
AMERICAN FLYERS   Warner Bros., 1985
ELENI   Warner Bros., 1985

Screenplays:
BLOOD MERIDIAN
TRIPHAMMER
WEATHERMAN
LOVE BUSINESS
BROTHERS
CINDERELLA CITY
CANNES GAMES
OFF THE RECORD
ANYWHERE BUT HERE

ABRAHAM TETENBAUM*
Agent: APA - Los Angeles, 310/273-0744

Screenplays:
SH-BOOM

JOAN TEWKESBURY*
Agent: CAA - Beverly Hills, 310/288-4545

THIEVES LIKE US   United Artists, 1974, w/Robert Altman &
   Calder Willingham
NASHVILLE   Paramount, 1976
A NIGHT IN HEAVEN   20th Century-Fox, 1983
COLD SASSY TREE (CTF)   Faye Dunaway/Don Ohlmeyer
   Productions, 1989, directed

Screenplays:
BLUE HIGHWAYS
LADIES NIGHT
INTIMATE RELATIONS

PAUL THEROUX
SAINT JACK   New World, 1979, w/Peter Bogdonavich &
   Howard Sackler

Screenplays:
CHICAGO LOOP
DEAD GIRLS
THE TOM DOOLEY PROJECT

DANIEL THERRIAULT
Agent: Writers & Artists Agency - Los Angeles, 310/824-6300

BATTERY (P)
THE WHITE DEATH (P)
FLOOR ABOVE THE ROOF (P)

Screenplays:
RUTHIE   (Miramax)
OF FLOODS AND FELONS

JACK THIBEAU*
Agent: Jon Klane Agency - Beverly Hills, 310/278-0178

OFF LIMITS   20th Century Fox, 1988, w/Christopher Crowe

Screenplays:
ROUGHSTRING RIDER
OLD MONEY

NICK W. THIEL*
Agent: CAA - Beverly Hills, 310/288-4545

THE EXPERTS   Paramount, .1988, w/Eric Alter & Steven Greene
FIRE BIRDS   Buena Vista, 1990, w/Paul Edwards & David Taylor
WHITE FANG   Buena Vista, 1991, w/David Fallon &
   Jeanne Rosenberg
SHIPWRECKED   Buena Vista, 1991, w/Greg Dinner, Bob Foss &
   Nils Gaup
V.I. WARSHAWSKI   Buena Vista, 1991, w/David Aaron Cohen &
   Edward Taylor

Screenplays:
MR. AND MRS. SEVENTH GRADE
THE MICK
DOGROBBER
HOP
RIDICULOUS MAN
LUCKY STIFF
TRIALS AND TRIBULATIONS OF CHINAMEN
UGLY DUCKLING

MICHAEL THOMA*
Agent: Broder-Kurland-Webb-Uffner - Beverly Hills, 310/281-3400

THE WRONG MAN (CTF)   Polygram/Viacom Pictures, 1993

Screenplays:
LUGENHEIMER

ANNA I. THOMAS*
Agent: ICM - Beverly Hills, 310/550-4000

THE CONFESSIONS OF AMANS   Bauer International, 1977,
   w/Gregory Nava
THE HAUNTING OF M   Independent Productions, 1981, directed
THE END OF AUGUST   Quartet, 1982, w/Gregory Nava,
   Eula Seaton & Leon Heller
EL NORTE ★   Cinecom/Island Alive, 1984, w/Gregory Nava
A TIME OF DESTINY   Columbia, 1988, w/Gregory Nava
MY FAMILY   New Line Cinema, 1995, w/Gregory Nava

DAVE THOMAS*
Agent: CAA - Beverly Hills, 310/288-4545
Manager: Brillstein-Grey - Beverly Hills, 310/275-6135

STRANGE BREW   MGM/UA, 1983, w/Rick Moranis &
   Steve DeJarnatt, directed

Screenplays:
BURY ME IN ST. LOUIS

GUY THOMAS*
Contact: WGA - Los Angeles, 310/550-1000

WHOLLY MOSES!   Columbia, 1980

Screenplays:
FAST TALKERS
THE GHOST GOES WEST
SHIPMATES
JUNGLE BOY

JACK W. THOMAS*
Contact: WGA - Los Angeles, 310/550-1000

FRANCIS OF ASSISI   20th Century-Fox, 1961,
   w/James Forsyth & Eugene Vale
EMBRYO   Cine Artits, 1976, w/Anita Doohan

JIM THOMAS*
Agent: ICM - Beverly Hills, 310/550-4000

PREDATOR   20th Century Fox, 1987, w/John Thomas
THE RESCUE   Buena Vista, 1988, w/John Thomas
PREDATOR 2   20th Century Fox, 1990, w/John Thomas

Screenplays:
THE JERICHO EQUATION w/John Thomas
THE WILD WILD WEST w/John Thomas
THE DOOMSDAY CONSPIRACY w/John Thomas
EXECUTIVE DECISION w/John Thomas
BRANDENBERG w/John Thomas
WORLD WAR w/John Thomas

JOHN THOMAS*
Agent: ICM - Beverly Hills, 310/550-4000

PREDATOR   20th Century Fox, 1987, w/Jim Thomas
THE RESCUE   Buena Vista, 1988, w/Jim Thomas
PREDATOR 2   20th Century Fox, 1990, w/Jim Thomas

Screenplays:
THE JERICHO EQUATION w/Jim Thomas
THE WILD WILD WEST w/JimThomas
THE DOOMSDAY CONSPIRACY w/Jim Thomas
EXECUTIVE DECISION w/Jim Thomas
BRANDENBERG w/Jim Thomas
WORLD WAR w/Jim Thomas

LESLIE E. THOMAS
STAND UP VIRGIN SOLDIERS   Warner Bros., 1977

MICHAEL THOMAS
Agent: United Talent Agency - Beverly Hills, 310/273-6700

THE HUNGER   MGM/UA, 1983, w/Ian Davis
LADYHAWKE   Warner Bros., 1985, w/Edward Khmara &
   Tom Mankiewicz
BURKE AND WILLS   Hemdale, 1987
SCANDAL   Miramax, 1989
DECEPTION   Miramax, 1993, w/Robert Dillon
BACKBEAT   Gramercy, 1993, w/Iain Softley & Stephen Ward

Screenplays:
FLYING DOCTORS
CASTRO
TOM MIX & PANCHO VILLA
WEST WITH THE NIGHT
ISABEL & FIDEL
FIRE ON THE MOUNTAIN
DROP DEAD
QUARTERMAIN
TIL THERE WAS YOU
SUCKERS
THE McGUFFIN
MAN ON FIRE
FIREFALL
GRAVE FOR A DOLPHIN
BROKEN ENGLISH
COMPANY MAN
RUBY KILLS
THE LADY OF SAIGON
OUT OF THE SILENCE
OFFSHORE
CULLA AND RINTHY
DICK TURPIN
HALFWAY TO SHANGHAI
SEVEN YEARS IN TIBET

OH VIENNA
LORD ROCHESTER'S MONKEY
TUPAC AMARU
THE DIVA
HEAVENLY BODIES
INFIDEL
TIGER RAG

P.G. THOMAS
Agent: Epstein-Wyckoff-LaManna - Beverly Hills, 310/278-7222
Manager: The Anthony Elliot Company - Los Angeles, 310/284-6804

Screenplays:
TWO DOGS RUNNING

RAMZI THOMAS
APPOINTMENT WITH FEAR   Galaxy, 1985, directed

RALPH L. THOMAS*
Agent: Camden-ITG - Los Angeles, 310/289-2700

TICKET TO HEAVEN   United Artists Classics, 1981,
   w/Anne Cameron, directed

ROSS THOMAS*
Agent: Roberta Kent - 503/482-7661

HAMMETT   Orion/Warner Bros., 1982, w/Dennis O'Flaherty
BOUND BY HONOR   Buena Vista, 1993, Story
BAD COMPANY   Buena Vista, 1995

ROY THOMAS*
Agent: The Daniel Ostroff Agency - Los Angeles, 310/278-2020

FIRE AND ICE (AF)   20th Century-Fox, 1983, w/Gerry Conway
CONAN THE DESTROYER   Universal, 1984,
   Story w/Gerry Conway

THOM THOMAS*
Contact: WGA - Los Angeles, 310/550-1000

WITHOUT APOLOGY (P)
SET IN MOTION (P)
THE INTERVIEW (P)

Screenplays:
VANISHED

CAMILLE THOMASSON*
Agent: William Morris Agency - Beverly Hills, 310/274-7451

HEROES (Short)   1985, directed
THE BLUE SERGE SUIT (Short)   1986, directed
THE DISAPPEARNCE OF CHRISTINA (CTF)   B.A.L. Productions/
   MCA Television Entertainment, 1993

Screenplays:
TWILIGHT
HARTMAN
SIMPLE GIFTS
AVE MARIA

DAVID THOME
Agent: Writers & Artists Agency - Los Angeles, 310/824-6300

Screenplays:
TERMINAL SEX

CAROLINE W. THOMPSON*
Agent: William Morris Agency - Beverly Hills, 310/274-7451

EDWARD SCISSORHANDS   20th Century Fox, 1990
THE ADDAMS FAMILY   Paramount, 1991, w/Larry Wilson
HOMEWARD BOUND: THE INCREDIBLE JOURNEY   Buena Vista,
   1993, w/Linda Woolverton

THE SECRET GARDEN   Warner Bros., 1993
THE NIGHTMARE BEFORE CHRISTMAS (AF)   Buena Vista, 1993
BLACK BEAUTY   Warner Bros., 1994, directed

Screenplays:
STUART LITTLE
SWEENEY TODD
ONE HAND CLAPPING
MIDKNIGHT w/Larry Wilson
ROUGE w/Larry Wilson
MAI, THE PSYCHIC GIRL w/Larry Wilson
THE GEEK w/Larry Wilson
BOY CHILD w/Penelope Spheeris
DISTANT MUSIC
FIRST BORN

CHRISTOPHER N. THOMPSON*
Agent: ICM - Beverly Hills, 310/550-4000
Business Manager: Kaufman & Bernstein - 310/277-1900

JUMPIN' JACK FLASH   20th Century Fox, 1986,
   w/David H. Franzoni, Patricia Irving & J.W. Melville
BACK TO THE BEACH   Paramount, 1987, w/Peter Krikes &
   Steve Meerson

Screenplays:
RIP VAN HIPPIE
JETSONS

DONALD G. THOMPSON
SIDEKICKS   Triumph Releasing, 1993, w/Sidekicks

EMMA THOMPSON
Agent: William Morris Agency - Beverly Hills, 310/274-7451

Screenplays:
SENSE AND SENSIBILITY

ERNEST THOMPSON*
Agent: Becsey/Wisdom/Kalajian Agency - Los Angeles, 310/550-0535

A SENSE OF HUMOR (P)
WEST SIDE WALTZ (P)   also screenplay
ANSWERS (P)
HUMAN BEINGS (P)
PLAYWRIGHT'S DOG (P)
ON GOLDEN POND ★★   Universal/AFD, 1981, from his play
SWEET HEARTS DANCE   Tri-Star, 1988
1969   Atlantic Releasing Corporation, 1988, directed

Screenplays:
THE LIES BEING TOLD (CTF) (directing)
THE LIFE OF AN HONEST MAN (remake)
THE SAVIOR
CONTACT
KID STUFF
BEAUTY
THE WEST SIDE WALTZ

FRANKLIN THOMPSON*
Contact: 213/935-8325

FORCED VENGEANCE   MGM/UA, 1982

GARY SCOTT THOMPSON*
Agent: Warden, White & Kane - Beverly Hills, 213/852-1028

SPLIT SECOND   InterStar Releasing, 1992

Screenplays:
FATHER'S DAY
THE CHICKEN POX KID
SAFE HOUSE
PUBLIC ENEMY NO. 1
D.C. THRILLER THE INVISIBLE MAN
KOSHER COPS

THE ULTIMATE GAME
SMALL TOWN SYNDROME
MANHUNT
SCARLET RUNNER

J.L. THOMPSON*
Contact: 310/820-7609

FUTURE HUNTERS   Lightning Pictures, 1989

KEITH THOMPSON
Agent: Warden, White & Kane - Beverly Hills, 213/852-1028

Screenplays:
THE DJINN'S EYES
PRAY FOR THE DEAD

RANDY THOMPSON
MONTANA RUN   Greycat Films, 1992, w/Dan Lishner &
   Ron Reid,   directed

ROBERT E. THOMPSON*
Agent: Wile Enterprises - Santa Monica, 310/828-9768

THEY SHOOT HORSES, DON'T THEY? ★   Cinerama Releasing
   Corporation, 1969, w/James Poe

ROBERT F. THOMPSON*
Agent: Broder-Kurland-Webb-Uffner - Beverly Hills, 310/281-3400

HEARTS OF THE WEST   MGM/United Artists, 1975
RATBOY   Warner Bros., 1986
THE COWBOY WAY   Universal, 1994, Story w/Bill Witliff

Screenplays:
WARRIOR
STARS
SWEET PEA
KEN WARD ENTERS THE JUNGLE
KILLERS DON'T KISS
THE LAST AMERICAN COWBOY
PISTOLEERS

SELMA THOMPSON*
Agent: ICM - Beverly Hills, 310/550-4000

Screenplays:
MANIC w/Robert L. Friedman

SHAWN THOMPSON*
Agent: Camden-ITG - Los Angeles, 310/289-2700

Screenplays:
DINNER AT TED'S PARENT'S PLACE

JOHN THOMSON
THE GIRL FROM TOMORROW (CTF)   Film Australia/Nine Network,
   1991, w/Mark Shirrefs

THOMAS THONSON*
Agent: Jim Preminger Agency - Los Angeles, 310/475-9491

CAME TO HERE FROM OVER THERE (Short)   1975
HAPPY ENDINGS (Short)
LANDSCAPE WITH STRANGER (Short)   1987

Screenplays:
ADAM AND EVE OUT WEST
NOTHING BUT THE TRUTH
WHITE COLLAR
HOME FOR THE HOLIDAYS
LIFER SEEKS LADY
HORIZONTAL MEN
SHOOT FRANK MILLER
YOU DON'T DIE OF LOVE

DAVID C. THOREAU*
Agent: Paul Kohner, Inc. - Beverly Hills, 310/550-1060

SIDE OUT   Tri-Star, 1990

STEVEN THORNLEY
HANGAR #18   Sunn Classic, 1980

BILLY BOB THORNTON*
Agent: William Morris Agency - Beverly Hills, 310/274-7451

ONE FALSE MOVE   I.R.S. Releasing, 1992, w/Tom Epperson

Screenplays:
CAMOUFLAGE w/Tom Epperson
THE BOND w/Tom Epperson
THE OTIS REDDING STORY w/Tom Epperson

DEBRA JO THORNTON
Agent: Paradigm - Los Angeles, 310/277-4400

HOT HOUSE (P)
TWO LADDS (P)
BLOOD ON BLOOD (P)
LIFERS (P)
SOLDIERS WITHOUT GUNS (P)

Screenplays:
STILL LIFE
THE LAST KNIGHT
REAL WORLD
CHARGED
GIRLFRIENDS

ROD THORP*
Agent: The Coppage Company - North Hollywood, 818/980-1106

Screenplays:
EAT THIS
SIEGE
KISS OF EVIL
ON THE COCAINE TRAIL

LEE THUNA*
Agent: Gold/Marshak - Burbank, 818/972-4300

FUGUE (P)
SHOW ME WHERE THE GOOD TIMES ARE (P)

Screenplays:
DECOY

ANTONIO TIBALDI*
Agent: Artists Agency - New York, 212/245-6960

ON MY OWN   Alliance Communications Corp., 1992,
   w/Gill Dennis & John Frizzell, directed

GARY TIECHE*
Contact: WGA - Los Angeles, 310/550-1000

Screenplays:
NEVADA
BATTLE OF ONO w/David Henry Hwong

PATRICK TILLEY
WUTHERING HEIGHTS   American International, 1970
THE PEOPLE THAT TIME FORGOT   American International, 1977
THE LEGACY   Columbia, 1978, w/Jimmy Sangster &
   Paul Wheeler

MEG TILLY
Agent: United Talent Agency - Beverly Hills, 310/273-6700

Screenplays:
SINGING SONGS

DEBORAH TILTON
LENA'S HOLIDAY   Prism Entertainment, 1991, w/Michael Keusch

A.J. TIPPING
CAR TROUBLE   Thorn-EMI, 1986, w/James Whaley
ENID IS SLEEPING   Vestron, 1991, w/Maurice Phillips &
   James Whaley

DAVID N. TITCHER*
Agent: William Morris Agency - Beverly Hills, 310/274-7451

MORGAN STEWART'S COMING HOME   New Century/Vista, 1987,
   w/Ken Hixon

Screenplays:
THE ARMY-NAVY GAME
ADAM GETS EVEN
NICK OF TIME
ACTION JUNKIES

STACY TITLE*
Agent: Susan Smith & Associates - Beverly Hills, 213/852-4777

DOWN ON THE WATERFRONT (Short) ★   1993,
   w/Jonathan Penner, directed

Screenplays:
WALL PEOPLE w/Jonathan Penner
DREAD w/Jonathan Penner
PAYBACK w/Jonathan Penner
BE STILL, MY HEART w/Jonathan Penner
KILKRAVEN w/Jonathan Penner
ALL FOR ONE w/Jonathan Penner

JAMES TOBACK*
Agent: ICM - Beverly Hills, 310/550-4000

THE GAMBLER   Parmount, 1974
FINGERS   Brut Productions, 1978, directed
LOVE AND MONEY   Paramount, 1982, directed
EXPOSED   MGM/UA, 1983, directed
THE PICK-UP ARTIST   20th Century Fox, 1987, directed
BUGSY ★   Tri-Star, 1991

Screenplays:
BAD BOYS (Columbia)
VICKY

BRIAN TOBIN
DOUBLE REVENGE   Smart Egg Releasing, 1988, w/John Sharkey

NOREEN V. TOBIN*
Agent: Don Walerstein, Rohner & Walerstein - 310/477-5001

DOWN TWISTED   Cannon, 1987, w/Gene O'Neill

TED TOBIN*
Contact: WGA - Los Angeles, 310/550-1000

Screenplays:
ALONG FOR THE RIDE w/Christopher Leitch

STEPHEN TOBOLOWSKY
Contact: Screen Actors Guild - Los Angeles, 213/954-1600

TRUE STORIES   Warner Bros., 1986, w/David Byrne & Beth Henley
TWO IDIOTS IN HOLLYWOOD   FilmDallas, 1989, directed

Screenplays:
THE FORTUNE TELLER
RULES OF THE ROAD

DONALD TODD*
Agent: The Rothman Agency - Beverly Hills, 213/655-2020

Screenplays:
MANNY
THE ALF MOVIE
I OWE YOU MY LIFE

SERGIO TOLEDO
Contact: National Cinema Council (CONCINE), Rua Mayrink
    Veiga 28, Rio de Janeiro, Brazil, tel.: 2/233-8329

ONE MAN'S WAR (CTF)   TVS Limited, 1991,
    w/Mike Carter, directed

GEORGE TOLES
ARCHANGEL   Zeitgeist Films Ltd., 1991, w/Guy Maddin

JOHN TOLES-BEY*
Agent: Paul Kohner, Inc. - Beverly Hills, 310/550-1060

A RAGE IN HARLEM   Miramax, 1991, w/Bobby Crawford

JONATHAN TOLINS*
Agent: William Morris Agency - Beverly Hills, 310/274-7451

STEWART'S LINE (P)
THE CLIMATE (P)
THE MAN THAT GOT AWAY (P)
THE UNVEILING (P)
THE TWILIGHT OF THE GOLDS (P)   screenplay w/Seth Bass

Screenplays:
THE VESTAL VIRGIN ROOM w/Seth Bass
REDEMPTION w/Seth Bass
KUMBAYA w/Seth Bass
GOING PUBLIC w/Seth Bass

MEL TOLKIN
Agent: Robert Eisenbach Agency - Los Angeles, 310/657-9427

LAST OF THE SECRET AGENTS   Paramount, 1966

MICHAEL L. TOLKIN*
Agent: CAA - Beverly Hills, 310/288-4545
Manager: Addis-Wechsler - Los Angeles, 213/954-9000

GLEAMING THE CUBE   20th Century Fox, 1989
THE RAPTURE   Fine Line Features, 1991, directed
DEEP COVER   New Line Cinema, 1992, w/Henry Bean
THE PLAYER ★   Fine Line Features, 1992, directed
THE BURNING SEASON (CTF)   HBO Pictures, 1994,
    w/Ron Hutchinson & William Mastrosimone
THE NEW AGE   Warner Bros., 1994, directed

Screenplays:
HAROLD AND THE PURPLE CRAYON
TIME BOMB
IT LOOKS ALIVE TO ME
WANTED
COWBOY HEAVEN
POWER OF AN ATTORNEY
IPANEMA (CTF)

NEIL TOLKIN*
Agent: ICM - Beverly Hills, 310/550-4000

LICENSE TO DRIVE   20th Century Fox, 1988
RICHIE RICH   Warner Bros., 1994, Story
JURY DUTY   Buena Vista, 1995, w/Fax Bahr & Adam Small

Screenplays:
CAT AND MOUSE (TriStar)
10 WISHES
LES COMPERES (remake)
BURGERVILLE

STEPHEN M. TOLKIN*
Agent: Richland/Wunsch/Hohman Agency - Los Angeles,
    310/278-1955

12:01 P.M. (Short) ★   1990, w/Jonathan Heap
CAPTAIN AMERICA   21st Century Film Corporation, 1990
THE PRICE OF LIFE (Short)   1991, directed,
    Showtime 30-Minute Film
DAYBREAK (CTF)   HBO Showcase, 1992, directed

Screenplays:
THE SOLOMAN ORGANIZATION
GOLDDIGGERS
THE LAST MARDI GRAS
ASK THE DUST
NOWHERE TO HIDE

JUDY TOLL*
Contact: WGA - Los Angeles, 310/550-1000

CASUAL SEX?   Universal, 1988, w/Wendy Goldman,
    from their play

Screenplays:
THE SECRET LIFE OF GIRLS w/Wendy Goldman

MICHELLE TOMSKI
SAVAGE ISLAND   Empire Pictures, 1985, w/Nicholas Beardsly

DAVID TONEY
HOUSE PARTY 3   New Line Cinema, 1994, Story w/Takashi Buford

WILLIAM TONNER*
Agent: Warden, White & Kane - Beverly Hills, 213/852-1028

Screenplays:
A MATTER OF HEART
WINNING
REAL DANGER
DASVIDANYA JOE
A GREAT AND GOOD FRIEND
MY KNIGHT IN SHINING ARMOR
RENT A FAMILY

RHET E. TOPHAM
TRICK OR TREAT   DEG, 1986, w/Michael S. Murphey &
    Joel Soisson
976-EVIL   New Line Cinema, 1989, w/Brian Helgeland

TOM TOPOR*
Agent: Rosenstone/Wender - New York, 212/832-8330

CHEAP (P)
ROMANCE (P)
BUT NOT FOR ME (P)
NUTS   Warner Bros., 1987, w/Darryl Ponicsan & Alvin Sargent,
    from his play
THE ACCUSED   Paramount, 1988
JUDGMENT (CTF)   Tisch/Wightow/Hershman Productions,
    1990, directed

Screenplays:
SAIGON CODICIL
ALL AROUND THE TOWN
PRIME SUSPECT
HERE TO STAY
BLOOD SPORT
THE LAST HONEYMOON
CRASHING
COURTROOM DRAMA: THE PEOPLE VS. JAMES TRUMAN

TRACY TORMÉ*
Agent: ICM - Beverly Hills, 310/550-4000
Manager: 3 Arts Entertainment - Los Angeles, 213/851-5700

SPELLBINDER   MGM/UA, 1988
FIRE IN THE SKY   Paramount, 1993

GIUSEPPE TORNATORE
Home: via Santamaura 7, Rome, Italy, 06/356-2106

IL CAMORRISTA   Aria Cinematografica/Titanus/Reteitalia,
   1986, directed
CINEMA PARADISO   Miramax, 1990, directed
EVERYBODY'S FINE   Miramax, 1991, w/Tonino Guerra, directed
A PURE FORMALITY   Sony Classics, 1994, directed

PETER J. TOROKVEI*
Agent: William Morris Agency - Beverly Hills, 310/274-7451

REAL GENIUS   Tri-Star, 1985, w/Neal Israel & Pat Proft
ARMED AND DANGEROUS   Columbia, 1986, w/Harold Ramis
BACK TO SCHOOL   Orion, 1986, w/Will Aldis,
   Steven Kampmann & Harold Ramis
CADDYSHACK II   Warner Bros., 1988, w/Harold Ramis
GUARDING TESS   TriStar, 1994, w/Hugh Wilson

Screenplays:
PRIVATE PARTS
CHAMPAGNE NIGHTS   w/Harold Ramis
BEL AIR BUTLER

ROBERT TORRANCE
MUTANT ON THE BOUNTY   Skouras Pictures, 1989,
   Story w/Martin Lopez, directed

GABE TORRES*
Contact: WGA - Los Angeles, 310/550-1000

DECEMBER   I.R.S. Releasing, 1991, directed

JOAN TORRES*
Agent: Sterling Lord Literistic - New York, 212/696-2800

BLACULA   American International, 1972, w/Raymond Koenig

CINZIA TORRINI
Home: via della Biuliana 85, Rome, Italy, tel: 06/356-8976

HOTEL COLONIAL   Columbia, 1987, w/Ira Barmak, Robert Katz &
   Enzo Monteleone, directed

HARRY ALAN TOWERS
(Peter Welbeck)
THE FACE OF FU MANCHU   7 Arts, 1965
FIVE GOLDEN DRAGONS   Towers, 1965
THE BRIDES OF FU MANCHU   Anglo Amalgamated,
   1966, directed
TEN LITTLE INDIANS   Tenlit, 1966, w/Peter Yeldham
THE VENGEANCE OF FU MANCHU   Anglo Amalgamated, 1967
AND THEN THERE WERE NONE   EMI, 1974
CALL OF THE WILD   Constantin, 1975, w/Wyn Wells &
   Peter Yeldham
LIGHTNING: THE WHITE STALLION   Cannon, 1986
POMPEII *WARRIOR QUEEN*   Seymour Borde & Associates,
   1987, Story
OUTLAW OF GOR   Cannon, 1989, w/Rick Marx, directed
MASTER OF DRAGONARD HILL   Cannon, 1990, w/Rick Marx

Screenplays:
THE MANGLER

ROBERT TOWNE*
Agent: CAA - Beverly Hills, 310/288-4545

THE LAST WOMAN ON EARTH   Filmgroup, 1960
THE TOMB OF LIGEIA   American International , 1965
VILLA RIDES   Paramount, 1968, w/Sam Peckinpah
THE LAST DETAIL ★   Columbia, 1973
CHINATOWN ★★   Paramount, 1974
SHAMPOO ★   Columbia, 1975, w/Warren Beatty
THE YAKUZA   Warner Bros., 1975, w/Paul Schrader
PERSONAL BEST   Warner Bros., 1982, directed

TEQUILA SUNRISE   Warner Bros., 1988, directed
DAYS OF THUNDER   Paramount, 1990
THE TWO JAKES   Paramount, 1990
THE FIRM   Paramount, 1993, w/David Rayfiel & David Rabe
LOVE AFFAIR   Warner Bros., 1994, w/Warren Beatty

Screenplays:
THE NIGHT MANAGER
ASK THE DUST (directing)
WITNESS TO THE TRUTH
MERMAID w/A.J. Carothers

ROGER TOWNE*
Agent: ICM - Beverly Hills, 310/550-4000
Business: Rolling Hills Productions, 204 South Beverly Dr. - Suite 166,
   Beverly Hills, CA 90212, 310/275-0872

THE NATURAL   Tri-Star, 1984, w/Phil Dusenberry

Screenplays:
POODLE SPRINGS
BUBBA SKYLAR
FOR LOVE OF THE GAME

BUD TOWNSEND
Home: 5917 Blairstone Drive, Culver City, CA 90230, 310/870-1559

THE HIGH COUNTRY   Crown International, 1981

ROBERT TOWNSEND
Agent: Irvin Arthur Associates - Beverly Hills, 310/278-5934

HOLLYWOOD SHUFFLE   Samuel Goldwyn Company, 1987,
   w/Keenen Ivory Wayans, directed
THE FIVE HEARTBEATS   20th Century Fox, 1991,
   w/Keenen Ivory Wayans, directed
THE METEOR MAN   MGM, 1993, directed

CORT TRAMANTIN
Agent: Writers & Artists Agency - New York, 212/947-8765

Screenplays:
STATIC
TOP OF THE WORLD (directing)

BENNETT TRAMER*
Agent: William Morris Agency - Beverly Hills, 310/274-7451

KIDCO   20th Century-Fox, 1984

Screenplays:
DANGEROUSLY w/Jim Cash & Jack Epps Jr.
TOUR '85
HELLO THERE AMERICA
HOTSHOT

JEAN-CLAUDE TRAMONT*
Agent: ICM - Beverly Hills, 310/550-4000

ASH WEDNESDAY   Paramount, 1973

THOMAS TRAVERS
A TIME TO REMEMBER   FIlmworld Distributors, 1990, directed

MARA TREFFECANTE
Agent: David Shapira & Associates - Sherman Oaks, 818/906-0322

Screenplays:
DOOMED w/Frank Rehwalt

ROB TREGENZA
TALKING TO STRANGERS   The Baltimore Film Factory,
   1988, directed
THE ARC   Film Four International, 1991, directed

**F
I
L
M
W
R
I
T
E
R
S**

DALE TREVILLION*
Contact: 310/455-3476

ONE MAN FORCE   Shapiro Glickenhaus, 1989, directed

Screenplays:
BEYOND DESIRE

NADINE TRINTIGANT
Contact: French Film Office, 745 Fifth Avenue, New York,
   NY 10151, 212/832-8860

NEXT SUMMER   European Classics, 1986, directed

JENNY TRIPP*
Agent: Richland/Wunsch/Hohman Agency - Los Angeles,
   310/278-1955

Screenplays:
RETURN TO MYSTIC PIZZA w/Albert Innaurato
NONNIE
NORTHERN MAN
BABY HUEY
SNOW QUEEN (AF)

DOROTHY TRISTAN*
Contact: WGA - Los Angeles, 310/550-1000

WEEDS   DEG, 1987, w/John Hancock
STEAL THE SKY (CTF)   HBO Pictures/Yoram Ben Ami
   Productions/Paramount TV, 1988, w/Christopher Wood

ROSE TROCHE
GO FISH   Samuel Goldwyn Company, 1994,
   w/Guinevere Turner, directed

MARK M. TROY
Agent: Berzon Agency - Glendale, 818/548-1560

A BAD CORNER (P)
GOING HOME (P)
THE NUDNIKS (P)
MUTILATION (P)

Screenplays:
SWEET TOOTH
MINIMUM SECURITY
DON'T WEAR WHITE
OVER THE LINE

FERNANDO TRUEBA
Agent: ICM - Beverly Hills, 310/550-4000
Contact: Ministry of Culture, Montion Picture Division,
   Avenida de Burgos 5, 28036 Madrid, Spain, 91/202-5351

TWISTED OBSESSION   IVE, 1990,
   w/Manolo Matji, directed

Screenplays:
TWO MUCH w/David Trueba (directing)

GARRY TRUDEAU
Agent: Broder-Kurland-Webb-Uffner - Beverly Hills, 310/281-3400

DOONESBURY, A MUSICAL COMEDY (P)
TANNER '88 (CMS)   Zenith Productions/Darkhorse
   Productions, 1988

Screenplays:
CDC
ZOO PLANE

GUERDON TRUEBLOOD*
Agent: Broder-Kurland-Webb-Uffner - Beverly Hills, 310/281-3400

WELCOME HOME SOLDIER BOYS   20th Century-Fox, 1972
THE LAST HARD MEN   20th Century-Fox, 1976
JAWS 3-D   Universal, 1983, Story

DANIEL TRULY
Agent: Broder-Kurland-Webb-Uffner - Beverly Hills, 310/281-3400

Screenplays:
WARLORD w/Andrew Dettman
JUSTICE RISING w/Andrew Dettman

CHRISTOPHER TRUMBO*
Contact: WGA - Los Angeles, 310/550-1000

THE DON IS DEAD   Universal, 1973, w/Michael Butler
BRANNIGAN   United Artists, 1975, w/Michael Butler,
   William P. McGivern & William Norton

Screenplays:
THE BULL w/Michael Butler

LUCIAN K. TRUSCOTT IV*
Agent: Renaissance-H.N. Swanson - Los Angeles, 310/246-6000

Screenplays:
COMMAND INFLUENCE (CTF)

ALAN R. TRUSTMAN*
Agent: Sterling Lord Literistic - New York, 212/696-2800

BULLITT   Warner Bros., 1968, w/Harry Kleiner
THE THOMAS CROWN AFFAIR   United Artists, 1968
THEY CALL ME MISTER TIBBS!   United Artists, 1970,
   w/James R. Webb
HIT!   Paramount, 1973, w/David M. Wolf
LADY ICE   Tomorrow Entertainment, 1973, w/Harold Clemins
THE NEXT MAN   Artists Entertainment, 1976, w/Michael Chapman,
   Mort Fine & David M. Wolf

Screenplays:
S & L
BOSTON GANG WARS

SLAVA TSUKERMAN
Contact: 212/620-0110

LIQUID SKY   Cinevista, 1983, w/Anne Carlisle &
   Nina V. Kerova, directed

Screenplays:
COSMOLOGICAL CONGRESS (directing)

STANLEY TUCCI
Agent: William Morris Agency - Beverly Hills, 310/274-7451

Screenplays:
PASTA E FASULE (co-directing)

ERIC TUCHMAN*
Agent: William Morris Agency - Beverly Hills, 310/274-7451
Manager: Jonathan Baruch/PRO Management - Los Angeles,
   310/478-5159

Screenplays:
TIMESHARE
ANASTASIA (AF)
THE FAMILY BLOOM
CHANGE OF HEART
ALIAS ALEX

CAMILLE TUCKER
Agent: United Talent Agency - Beverly Hills, 310/273-6700

SWEET POTATO RIDE (Short)   1993,
  w/Kimberly Greene, co-directed

Screenplays:
M'LADY w/Kimberly Greene

RICHARD A. TUGGLE*
Agent: United Talent Agency - Beverly Hills, 310/273-6700

ESCAPE FROM ALCATRAZ   Paramount, 1979
TIGHTROPE   Warner Bros., 1984, directed

Screenplays:
GULF STREAM
IN THE FACE OF EVIL

SANDY TUNG
Agent: Solomon Weingarten & Associates - Los Angeles,
  310/479-4706

BROKEN PROMISE *A MARRIAGE* Cinecom, 1983, directed
ACROSS THE TRACKS   Rosenbloom Entertainment,
  1990, directed

Screenplays:
CONFESSIONS OF A SEXIST PIG (directing)

RON TURBEVILLE
BUSTER & BILLIE   Columbia, 1974

SOPHIA TURKIEWICZ
SILVER CITY   Samuel Goldwyn Company, 1984,
  w/Thomas Keneally, directed

JOHN D. TURMAN*
Agent: ICM - Beverly Hills, 310/550-4000
Manager: Addis-Wechsler - Los Angeles, 213/954-9000

Screenplays:
THE HULK
SILVER SURFER
OUT OF TIME
HYDE
BIG DOGS (Showtime)

ANN TURNER
CELIA   Hoyts, 1989, directed
TURTLE BEACH   Warner Bros., 1992
DALLAS DOLL   ABC International, 1993, directed

BARBARA TURNER*
Agent: Pleshette & Green - Los Angeles, 213/465-0428

LOVE CHILD   Warner Bros., 1982, as "Anne Gerard,"
  w/Katherine Spektor
CUJO   Warner Bros., 1983, as "Lauren Currier,"
  w/Don Carlos Dunaway
GEORGIA   CIBY 2000, 1995

Screenplays:
JACKSON POLLOCK
COLETTE
WAIT TILL THE SUN SHINES, NELLIE
LOVESTORY
A SPOONFUL OF LOVE
#*PETULIA
THE EXHIBITIONIST
JACOB'S LADDER
A SPY IN THE HOUSE OF LOVE
WITH SHUDDERING FALL
AT LAKE LUGANO

BONNIE TURNER*
Agent: CAA - Beverly Hills, 310/288-4545

WAYNE'S WORLD   Paramount, 1992, w/Terry Turner &
  Mike Myers
CONEHEADS   Paramount, 1993, w/Terry Turner, Dan Aykroyd &
  Tom Davis
WAYNE'S WORLD 2   Paramount, 1993, w/Terry Turner &
  Mike Myers
BILLY THE THIRD   Paramount, 1995, w/Terry Turner

Screenplays:
RUDOLPH THE RED-NOSED REINDEER w/Terry Turner

CLIVE TURNER
Contact: British Academy of Film & Television Arts, 195 Piccadilly,
  London W1, England, 071/734-0022

HOWLING IV: THE ORIGINAL NIGHTMARE   Allied Entertainment,
  1988, w/Freddie Rowe

EDWARD S. TURNER, JR. *
Contact: WGA - Los Angeles, 310/550-1000

WINNERS TAKE ALL   Apollo Pictures, 1987
ERNEST SAVES CHRISTMAS   Buena Vista, 1988, w/B. Kline

GUINEVERE TURNER
GO FISH   Samuel Goldwyn Company, 1994, w/Rose Troche

TERRY TURNER*
Agent: CAA - Beverly Hills, 310/288-4545

WAYNE'S WORLD   Paramount, 1992, w/Bonnie Turner &
  Mike Myers
CONEHEADS   Paramount, 1993, w/Bonnie Turner,
  Dan Aykroyd & Tom Davis
WAYNE'S WORLD 2   Paramount, 1993, w/Bonnie Turner &
  Mike Myers
BILLY THE THIRD   Paramount, 1995, w/Bonnie Turner

Screenplays:
RUDOLPH THE RED-NOSED REINDEER w/Bonnie Turner

ROGERS TURRENTINE*
Agent: Pleshette & Green - Los Angeles, 213/465-0428

Screenplays:
ASSIGNED RISK w/John Pleshette

JON TURTLETAUB
Agent: CAA - Beverly Hills, 310/288-4545

THINK BIG   Concorde, 1990, w/Edward Kovach &
  David Tausik
DRIVING ME CRAZY   Motion Picture Corporation of America,
  1991, w/David Tausik & R.M. London, directed

SAUL TURTELTAUB*
Agent: Kaplan-Stahler - Beverly Hills, 213/653-4483

Screenplays:
ROSEANNA'S GRAVE

JOHN TURTURRO
Agent: ICM - Beverly Hills, 310/550-4000

MAC   Samuel Goldwyn Company, 1992,
  w/Brandon Cole, directed

DAVID TWOHY*
(D.T. Twohy)
Agent: William Morris Agency - Beverly Hills, 310/274-7451

CRITTERS 2   New Line Cinema, 1988, w/Mick Garris
WARLOCK   Trimark Pictures, 1991
DISASTER IN TIME   *THE GRAND TOUR* (CTF)
   Wildstreet Productions, 1992, directed
THE FUGITIVE   Warner Bros., 1993, w/Jeb Stuart
TERMINAL VELOCITY   Buena Vista, 1994
WATERWORLD   Universal, 1995, w/Peter Rader

Screenplays:
SHOCKWAVE (Buena Vista, directing)
THE LAST GASP

JONATHAN TYDOR*
Agent: United Talent Agency - Beverly Hills, 310/273-6700

I COME IN PEACE   Triumph, 1990, w/Leonard Maas Jr.
THE HARD TRUTH (CTF)   Promark Entertainment, 1994
FINAL COMBINATION   Rank, 1994, Story

Screenplays:
THE UNINVITED
FROZEN
BODY COUNT
QUIET RAGE

WATT TYLER
ALL'S FAIR   Moviestore Entertainment, 1989,
   Story w/John Finnegan

CORY TYNAN*
Agent: APA - Los Angeles, 310/273-0744
Manager: 3 Arts Entertainment - Los Angeles, 213/851-5700

Screenplays:
GHOSTHUNTER w/John Ries (Cinema Line)
JEEPERS w/John Ries
NIGHTLAND w/John Ries
BORN TO BE WILD w/John Ries
BEAST OF BURDEN

KATHLEEN TYNAN
AGATHA   Warner Bros., 1979, w/Arthur Hopcraft

Screenplays:
LULU IN LOVE

STEP TYNER
FIRE BIRDS   Buena Vista, 1990, Story w/Dale Dye &
   John K. Swensson

BOB TZUDIKER*
Agent: Richland/Wunsch/Hohman Agency - Los Angeles,
   310/278-1955

NEWSIES   Buena Vista, 1992, w/Noni White

Screenplays:
TEMPTED w/Noni White
LUCK w/Noni White
ROGER RABBIT II w/Noni White
THE FROG PRINCE (AF) w/Noni White

YALE M. UDOFF*
Agent: Peter Turner Agency - Santa Monica, 310/315-4772
Contact: Julimar Films - Los Angeles, 213/653-5890

BAD TIMING/A SENSUAL OBSESSION   World Northal, 1980
THIRD DEGREE BURN (CTF)   HBO Pictures, 1989,
   w/Duncan Gibbins
EVE OF DESTRUCTION   Orion, 1991, w/Duncan Gibbins

ALAN UGER*
Agent: Bruce Brown Agency - Los Angeles, 310/208-1835

BLAZING SADDLES   Warner Bros., 1973, w/Andrew Bergman,
   Mel Brooks, Richard Pryor & Norman Steinberg
LEADER OF THE BAND   New Century/Vista, 1988

Screenplays:
FROST BITE

JIM UHLS*
Agent: ICM - Beverly Hills, 310/550-4000

Screenplays:
MACE AND MARDI
DEAD RECKONING
THE HOLLOW MAN

ALFRED F. UHRY*
Agent: Flora Roberts, Inc. - New York, 212/355-4165

THE ROBBER BRIDEGROOM (P)
MYSTIC PIZZA   Samuel Goldwyn Company, 1988, w/Amy Jones,
   Perry Howze & Randy Howze
DRIVING MISS DAISY ★★   Warner Bros., 1989, from his play
RICH IN LOVE   MGM, 1993

Screenplays:
DODSWORTH (remake)
THE BARRYMORES
MRS. SMITH GOES TO WASHINGTON

ROBERT M. ULIN*
Agent: CAA - Beverly Hills, 310/288-4545

Screenplays:
COPY BOYS
CONVENTION
SOUL MATE
C.I.T.
DORIS

FREDERICK R. ULRICH
PHANTOM OF THE MALL: ERIC'S REVENGE   Fries Entertainment,
   1989, Story w/Scott J. Schneid

LEANNE UNGER
TIMES SQUARE   AFD, 1980, Story w/Alan Moyle

MATT UNGER
CLASS OF NUKE 'EM HIGH PART 2: SUBHUMANOID MELTDOWN
   Troma, 1991, w/Lloyd Kaufman, Eric Louzil, Carl Morano,
   Marcus Rolling & Jeffrey W. Sass

ROCCO URBISCI*
Contact: WGA - Los Angeles, 310/550-1000

JO JO DANCER, YOUR LIFE IS CALLING   Columbia, 1986,
    w/Paul Mooney & Richard Pryor

JEFF URELES*
Contact: WGA - Los Angeles, 310/550-1000

CHEAP SHOTS   Hemdale, 1991, w/Jeff Stoeffhaas, co-directed

PETER USTINOV
Home: Rue de Silly, 91200 Boulogne, France, tel.: 1/603-8753

THE WAY AHEAD   *THE IMMORTAL BATTALIO*
    20th Century- Fox, 1944, w/Eric Ambler
SCHOOL FOR SECRETS   General Film Distributors,
    1946, directed
VICE VERSA   GFD, 1948, directed
PRIVATE ANGELO   Pilgrim, 1949, w/Michael Anderson, directed
ROMANOFF AND JULIET   Universal, 1961,
    from his play, directed
BILLY BUDD   Allied Artists, 1962, w/Robert Rossen, directed
LADY L   Concordia, 1965, directed
HOT MILLIONS ★   MGM, 1968, w/Ira Wallach
MEMED, MY HAWK   Filmworld Distribution, 1984, directed

JAMIE UYS
Contact: Showdata, Johan Blignaut, 11 Frost Avenue, Auckland
    Park 2092, Johannesburg, South Africa, tel: 27-11/482-1382

DINGAKA   Embassy, 1965, directed
THE GODS MUST BE CRAZY   TLC Films/20th Century-Fox,
    1979, directed
THE GODS MUST BE CRAZY 2   WEG/Columbia, 1990, directed

V

ROGER VADIM
Contact: Directors Guild of America - Los Angeles, 310/289-2000

BLACKMAILED   Greater Film Distributors, 1950, w/Hugh Mills
AND GOD CREATED WOMAN   Kingsley International,
    1956, directed
THE NIGHT HEAVEN FELL   *LES BIJOUTIERS DU CLAIR DE
    LUNES*   Kingsley International, 1957, Peter Viertel, directed
LES LIAISONS DANGEREUSES   *DANGEROUS LIAISONS 1960*
    Astor, 1959, w/Claude Brule & Roger Vailland, directed
BLOOD AND ROSES   *ET MOURIR DE PLAISIR*   Paramount,
    1960, w/Claude Brule & Claude Martin, directed

STEVEN A. VAIL
SCAVENGER HUNT   20th Century-Fox, 1979, w/Henry Harper

LUIS VALDEZ*
Agent: Writers & Artists Agency - Los Angeles, 310/824-6300

I DON'T HAVE TO SHOW YOU NO STINKING BADGES (P)
CORRIDOS (P)
BERNABE (P)
BANDITO! (P)
ZOOT SUIT   Universal, 1982, directed, from his play
LA BAMBA   Columbia, 1987, directed
THE CISCO KID (CTF)   Esparza-Katz/Goodman-Rosen, 1994,
    w/Michael Kane, directed

Screenplays:
THE TWO FRIDAS w/Lupe Trujillo Valdez
THE CESAR CHAVEZ STORY

MARK VALENTI
Agent: Media Artsts Group - Beverly Hills, 213/658-7434

Screenplays:
THE TIME MACHINE: THE JOURNEY BACK
SCRATCH AND SNIFF (AF)
TYLER MADISON'S COMING TO TOWN
GRADUATION DAY
BOB THE HOUSE

VINCENT VALENTI*
Agent: The Coppage Company - North Hollywood, 818/980-1106

Screenplays:
BUCK
THE CALAMARI BROTHERS
DOUBLE DARE
INDIAN WINTER
THE TENANTS
RAZOR BLUE
MY AUNT FROM BULGARIA

TOR VALENZA*
Agent: The Rothman Agency - Beverly Hills, 213/655-2020

Screenplays:
FREQUENT FLYER
RULES OF THE ROAD
NECROPOLIS
MATZGER'S DOG

NICK VALLELONGA
DEADFALL   Trimark, 1993, w/Christopher Coppola

JEAN VALLELY*
Agent: Broder-Kurland-Webb-Uffner - Beverly Hills, 310/281-3400

Screenplays:
DIVORCED WOMEN
FAIR PLAY
TRAVELING LIGHT

JIM VALLELY*
Contact: WGA - Los Angeles, 310/550-1000

Screenplays:
THE SANDAL BROTHERS w/Jonathan Schmock

RANDY VAMPOTIC
Agent: Kaplan-Stahler - Beverly Hills, 213/653-4483

Screenplays:
FACE VALUE w/Michael Sorrentino
THE WEREWOLF SOCIAL CLUB w/Michael Sorrentino

LEIGH VANCE
Agent: Preferred Artists - Encino, 818/990-0305

THE FLESH IS WEAK   Stross/Eros, 1957
FRIGHTENED CITY   Anglo Amalgamated, 1961
DR. CRIPPEN   ABP, 1962
IT'S ALL HAPPENING   *THE DREAM MAKER*
    British Lion, 1963
CROSSPLOT   United Artists, 1969
THE BLACK WINDMILL   Universal, 1974

SAM VANCE
RIVERBEND   Intercontinental Releasing, 1989

JEAN-CLAUDE VAN DAMME*
Agent: ICM - Beverly Hills, 310/550-4000

KICKBOXER   Pathe Entertainment, 1989, Story w/Mark DiSalle
LIONHEART   Universal, 1991, w/Sheldon Lettich
DOUBLE IMPACT   Columbia, 1991, w/Sheldon Lettich

Screenplays:
THE QUEST (Story)

BRUCE VAN DUSEN
COLD FEET   Cinecom, 1984, directed

NORMAN THADDEUS VANE*
Agent: Epstein-Wyckoff - Beverly Hills, 310/278-7222
Manager: Chris Wyatt, B&W Talent & Management - Hollywood,
   213/957-5110
Business: American New Wave Films, 7441 Sunset Blvd.,
   Sunset Bldg. - Suite 201/202, Hollywood, CA 90046,
   213/851-1987

LOLA *TWINKY*   American International, 1970
SHADOW OF THE HAWK   Columbia, 1976, w/Herbert J. Wright
THE BLACK ROOM   CI Films, 1984, co-directed
FRIGHTMARE   Saturn, 1984, directed
KING OF THE CITY *CLUB LIFE*   MPR/VTC/Prism, 1986, directed
MIDNIGHT   Sony, 1989, directed
TAXI DANCER   Trident, 1993, directed

MARIO VAN PEEBLES
Agent: ICM - Beverly Hills, 310/550-4000

IDENTITY CRISIS   Block & Chip Productions, 1989

Screenplays:
JULIET

MELVIN VAN PEEBLES*
Contact: WGA - New York, 212/245-6180

THE STORY OF A THREE-DAY PASS   Sigma III, 1968, directed
SWEET SWEETBACK'S BAADASSSSSS SONG   Cinemation,
   1971, directed
DON'T PLAY US CHEAP   Movin On Distribution, 1973, directed
GREASED LIGHTNING   Third World, 1977, w/Leon Capetanos,
   Lawrence DuKore & Kenneth Vose
EROTIC TALES   Mercure Distribution, 1994,
   "Vrooom, Vrooom, Vroom," directed
PANTHER   Gramercy, 1995

GUS VAN SANT JR.*
Agent: William Morris Agency - Beverly Hills, 310/274-7451

MALA NOCHE   Frameline, 1987, directed, rereleased 1989
DRUGSTORE COWBOY   Avenue Pictures, 1989,
   w/Daniel Yost, directed
MY OWN PRIVATE IDAHO   Fine Line Features, 1991, directed
EVEN COWGIRLS GET THE BLUES   Fine Line Features,
   1994, directed

CRAIG VAN SICKLE*
Agent: The Wright Concept - Burbank, 818/954-8943

SKI PATROL   Triumph, 1990 w/Steven Long Mitchell

Screenplays:
PUMPKINHEADS II w/Steven Long Mitchell

JOSEPH VAN WINKLE
THE WOMAN INSIDE   20th Century-Fox, 1981, directed

ETHLIE ANN VARE
Agent: Leslie Kallen Agency - Sherman Oaks, 818/906-2785

Screenplays:
CLOSE ENOUGH FOR ROCK'N'ROLL w/Marshall New

MICHAEL C. VARHOL*
Contact: WGA - Los Angeles, 310/550-1000

THE LAST WORD   Samuel Goldwyn Company, 1979,
   w/Greg Smith & Kit Carson
PEE-WEE'S BIG ADVENTURE   Warner Bros., 1985,
   w/Paul Reubens & Phil Hartman
THE BIG PICTURE   Columbia, 1989, w/Christopher Guest &
   Michael McKean

Screenplays:
TWO GUYS IN TUXEDOS

JOHN VARLEY*
Contact: WGA - Los Angeles, 310/550-1000

MILLENNIUM   20th Century Fox, 1989

Screenplays:
GALAXY
HAVE SPACE SUIT WILL TRAVEL

M.C. VARLEY*
Agent: Maggie Field Agency - Studio City, 818/980-2001

BARE RUINED CHOIRS (P)
FIRST SNOW (P)
GHOST DANCE (P)

Screenplays:
A PAIR OF JACKS
LOVE & MARRIAGE

CARLOS VASALLO
FISTFIGHTER   Taurus Entertainment, 1989, Story

JOSEPH P. VASQUEZ
Agent: William Morris Agency - Beverly Hills, 310/274-7451

HANGIN' WITH THE HOMEBOYS   New Line Cinema,
   1991, directed

Screenplays:
HOMEGIRLS

JESSE VAUGHN*
Agent: ICM - Beverly Hills, 310/550-4000

Screenplays:
THE BOB MARLEY STORY

ROGER VAUGHN
WIND   TriStar, 1992, Story w/Jeff Benjamin & Kimball Livingston

GABRIELLA VAZQUEZ
Agent: Jon Klane Agency - Beverly Hills, 310/278-0178

Screenplays:
WHITE COMA

FRANCIS VEBER*
Agent: CAA - Beverly Hills, 310/288-4545

DU COTE DE CHEZ L'AUTRE (P)
THE CONTRACT (P)
THE ABDUCTION (P)
CAUSE TOJOURS (P)
ON AURA TOUT VU (P)

THE TROUBLEMAKER (P)
THE TALL BLOND MAN WITH ONE BLACK SHOE   Cinema 5,
  1972, w/Yves Robert
A PAIN IN THE A   L'EMMERDEUR   Corwin-Mahler, 1973,
  w/Edouard Molinaro
LE MAGNIFIQUE   Cine III, 1973
RETURN OF THE TALL BLOND MAN WITH ONE BLACK SHOE
  Lanir Releasing, 1974
PEUR SUR LA VILLE   Columbia, 1975
LA CAGE AUX FOLLES ★   United Artists, 1979, w/others
COUP D'ETETE   HOTHEAD   Quartet, 1980
SUNDAY LOVERS   MGM/United Artists, 1981,
  w/Leslie Bricusse & Gene Wilder
LE CHEVRE   European International, 1981, directed
LA CAGE AUX FOLLES II   United Artists, 1981, w/others
PARTNERS   Paramount, 1982
LES COMPERES   European International, 1983, directed
LES FUGITIFS   Gaumont, 1986, directed
THE LOVER   Cannon, 1986
THREE FUGITIVES   Buena Vista, 1989, directed
MY FATHER THE HERO   Buena Vista, 1994, w/Charlie Peters

Screenplays:
UNDER MY THUMB
KING FOR A DAY

ADRIAN VELICESCU
THE SECRET LIFE OF HOUSES   Rainbreaker Films, 1994,
  w/Scott Bradfield, directed

DAVID VELOZ
Agent: CAA - Beverly Hills, 310/288-4545

NATURAL BORN KILLERS   Warner Bros., 1994, w/Oliver Stone &
  Richard Rutowski

Screenplays:
THE BATH
SPIDERTOWN
GINGERSNAPS

MARIA VELTRE
Agent: Susan Smith & Associates - Beverly Hills, 213/852-4777

Screenplays:
DREAM MAN w/Jack Sekowski
BIRTHDAY WISHES w/Jack Sekowski
A DOG'S LIFE w/Jack Sekowski
KNOW YOU LIKE A PAPERBACK

DAVID VENABLE*
Agent: William Morris Agency - Beverly Hills, 310/274-7451

FORTRESS   Miramax, 1993, w/Steven Feinberg,
  Troy Neighbors & Terry Curtis Fox

LOUIS VENOSTA*
Agent: United Talent Agency - Beverly Hills, 310/273-6700

BERRY GORDY'S THE LAST DRAGON   Tri-Star, 1985
BIRD ON A WIRE   Universal, 1990, w/Eric Lerner & David Seltzer
THE CORIOLIS EFFECT (Short)   Seventh Art Releasing,
  1994, directed

Screenplays:
COOL AND THE DEAD
THE AMERICAN WAY w/Grant Morris
TOP OF THE WORLD
FORTUNA
THE TOP

JAN F. VENTURA*
Contact: WGA - Los Angeles, 310/550-1000

BREAKIN' 2: ELECTRIC BOOGALOO   Tri-Star, 1984,
  w/Julie Reichert

MICHAEL VENTURA*
Contact: WGA - Los Angeles, 310/550-1000

ROADIE   United Artists, 1981, w/Big Boy Medlin
ECHO PARK   Atlantic Releasing Corporation, 1986

Screenplays:
HOWLING AT THE MOON w/Big Boy Medlin
MEANWHILE BACK AT THE KREMLIN w/Big Boy Medlin
THE GIANT CLAW
HOMAGE TO BARCELONA

SUSAN VERCELLINO
QUIET COOL   New Line Cinema, 1986, w/Clay Borris

MARK D. VERHEIDEN*
Agent: Broder-Kurland-Webb-Uffner - Beverly Hills, 310/281-3400

THE MASK   New Line Cinema, 1994, Story w/Michael Fallon
TIMECOP   Universal, 1994

Screenplays:
AL & JEAN
THE DOOMSDAY CONSPIRACY w/James McQuaide

MICHAEL VERHOEVEN
Contact: German Film & TV Academy, Pommernallee 1, 1 Berlin 19,
  Germany, 0311/302-6096

THE NASTY GIRL   Miramax, 1990, directed

PAUL VERHOEVEN
Agent: The Marion Rosenberg Office - Los Angeles, 213/653-7383

SOLDIER OF ORANGE   Samuel Goldwyn Company, 1977,
  w/Gerard Soeteman & Kees Molierhoek, directed
FLESH + BLOOD   Orion, 1985, w/Gerard Soeteman, directed

CYNTHIA VERLAINE
(See David Goyer)

STEPHEN F. VERONA*
Contact: WGA - Los Angeles, 310/550-1000

PIPE DREAMS   Avco Embassy, 1976, directed
BOARDWALK   Atlantic Releasing Corporation, 1979,
  w/Leigh Chapman, directed

Screenplays:
DECEPTION
PRIMARY COLORS

PATRIC VERRONE*
Agent: United Talent Agency - Beverly Hills, 310/273-6700

THE CIVIL WAR: THE LOST EPISODE (Short)   1991, directed
MEANFELLAS (Short)   1992, directed

LAUREN VERSEL*
Contact: WGA - Los Angeles, 310/550-1000

Screenplays:
CURIOSITY KILLED THE KATZ w/John Arnoldy

CHRISTOPHER VERWIEL
ROCKULA   Cannon, 1989, w/Luca Bercovici & Jefery Levy

RICHARD VETERE
Agent: William Morris Agency - Beverly Hills, 310/274-7451

HAIL THE HERO (P)

MARK VICTOR*
Agent: CAA - Beverly Hills, 310/288-4545

THE THIN LINE   New Yorker, 1980, w/Michael Grais
POLTERGEIST   MGM/UA, 1980, w/Michael Grais &
   Steven Spielberg
DEATH HUNT   20th Century-Fox, 1981, w/Michael Grais
POLTERGEIST II: THE OTHER SIDE   MGM/UA, 1986,
   w/Michael Grais
MARKED FOR DEATH   20th Century Fox, 1990, w/Michael Grais
COOL WORLD   Paramount, 1992, w/Michael Grais

Screenplays:
CAFE BERLIN w/Michael Grais
WARP w/Michael Grais
TRUEST SPORT w/Michael Grais
IN A LONELY PLACE w/Michael Grais & David Z. Goodman
BRAIN w/Michael Grais
TURN LEFT OR DIE w/Michael Grais
OCTOBER CIRCLE w/Michael Grais

PAT A. VICTOR*
Agent: Dytman & Schwartz - Beverly Hills, 310/274-8844

THE KILLING MIND (CTF)   Hearst Entertainment Productions,
   1991, w/William W. Forsythe

GORE VIDAL*
Agent: CAA - Beverly Hills, 310/288-4545

VISIT TO A SMALL PLANET (P)
THE BEST MAN   United Artists, 1946, from his play
THE CATERED AFFAIR   MGM, 1956
I ACCUSE   MGM, 1958
THE SCAPEGOAT   MGM, 1959, w/Robert Hamer
SUDDENLY LAST SUMMER   Columbia, 1960
THE BEST MAN   United Artists, 1964, from his play
IS PARIS BURNING?   Paramount, 1966, w/Francis Ford Coppola
LAST OF THE MOBILE HOT-SHOTS   Warner Bros., 1970
CALIGULA   Analysis Film, 1980

Screenplays:
THEODORA
THE BUCCANEERS
HUEY
ACTING PRESIDENT
THE BEVERLY WILSHIRE
REUNION
KALKI

JACK VIERTEL
DELUSION   New Line Cinema, 1981

PETER VIERTEL*
Agent: ICM - Beverly Hills, 310/550-4000
Business Manager: Jess Morgan & Company - Los Angeles,
   213/937-1552

SABOTEUR   Universal, 1942, w/Joan Harrison & Dorothy Parker
WE WERE STRANGERS   Columbia, 1949, w/John Huston
DECISION BEFORE DAWN   20th Century-Fox, 1951
THE NIGHT HEAVEN FELL   *LES BIJOUTIERS DU CLAIR
   DE LUNES*   Kingsley International, 1957, Roger Vadim
THE SUN ALSO RISES   20th Century-Fox, 1957
FIVE MILES TO MIDNIGHT   United Artists, 1962, w/Hugh Wheeler
WHITE HUNTER, BLACK HEART   Warner Bros., 1990,
   w/James Bridges & Burt Kennedy

DANIEL VIGNE
Agent: CAA - Beverly Hills, 310/288-4545

THE RETURN OF MARTIN GUERRE   European International,
   1983, w/Jean-Claude Carriere, directed
ONE WOMAN OR TWO   Orion Classics, 1985, w/Elisabeth
   Rappeneau, directed

SUMMER INTERLUDE   *COMEDIE D'ETE*   Partners Productions,
   1989, w/Colo Tavernier O'Hagan, directed
THE KING'S WHORE   J & M Entertainment, 1990,
   w/Axel Corti & Frederic Raphael

BRUCE VILANCH*
Agent: William Morris Agency - Beverly Hills, 310/274-7451

DIVINE MADNESS   Warner Bros., 1980, w/Jerry Blatt &
   Bette Midler

Screenplays:
THE DEVIL AND MISS JONES w/Patricia Resnick
MONOPOLY THE MOVIE w/Jeff Silverman
PLATINUM SUNSET
FRUITS AND NUTS
CLARA
BENNY AND THE JETS
SAY GOODNIGHT, LILLIAN
SOUR GRAPES
BLAKE AND BREAK
MY FAT FRIEND
SHEET MUSIC

DIMITRI VILLARD
Business: New Star Entertainment, 260 S. Beverly Dr. - Suite 200,
   Beverly Hills, CA 90212, 310/205-0666

ONCE BITTEN   Samuel Goldwyn Company, 1985, Story

VICTOR E. VILLASENOR*
Contact: WGA - Los Angeles, 310/550-1000

THE BALLAD OF GREGORIO CORTEZ   Embassy, 1983,
   w/Robert M. Young

DAVID VINAS
COCAINE WARS   Concorde, 1986, Story

CHUCK VINCENT
Business: Platinum Pictures, 11-12 44th Avenue, Long Island City,
   NY 11101, 718/766-3701

PREPPIES   Platinum Pictures, 1984, w/Rick Marx, directed
SEX APPEAL   Platinum Pictures, 1986, w/Craig Horrall, directed
WILDEST DREAMS   Platinum Pictures, 1989, Story, directed

LUCIANO VINCENZONI*
Contact: WGA - Los Angeles, 310/550-1000

RAW DEAL   DEG, 1986, Story w/Sergio Donati

DANIEL H. VINING*
Agent: Writers & Artists Agency - Los Angeles, 310/824-6300

PLAIN CLOTHES   Paramount, 1988, Story w/A.Scott Frank

Screenplays:
GOSPEL SINGER
SNAKE EYES
RUBY
DEAD OF NIGHT
IT'S ONLY MONEY
FIRST LOVE
SEMPER FI
BRAWLERS
BLACK DOG
BLACK DRINK SINGER
GRACELAND
UNDERCOVER

RANDAL VISCOVICH
NIGHT VISITOR   MGM/UA, 1988

JEFFREY L. VLAMING*
Agent: Writers & Artists Agency - Los Angeles, 310/824-6300

Screenplays:
THE T-BONE EXPRESS
THE KID FROM OUTER SPACE
DESPERATE BUCK
BOYS FROM MINNESOTA (Shared)

JON VOIGHT
Contact: Screen Actors Guild - Los Angeles, 213/954-1600

LOOKIN' TO GET OUT   Paramount, 1982, w/Al Schwartz
ETERNITY   Paul Entertainment, 1990, w/Steven Paul &
   Dorothy Koster Paul

STEPHEN VOLK*
Agent: Innovative Artists - Los Angeles, 310/553-5200 or
   Seifert Dench Associates - London, 071/437-4551

GOTHIC   Atlantic Releasing Corporation, 1987
THE KISS   Tri-Star, 1988, w/Tom Ropelewski
THE GUARDIAN   Universal, 1990, w/William Friedkin &
   Dan Greenburg

Screenplays:
LOST SOUL w/Jeffrey Bell
LORELEI
SHADES OF GRAY w/Randall Johnson
WHERE THE DARK EYE GLANCES
HORROR MOVIE
TELEPATHY
LAZARUS
NAZARETH NEW YORK
FEAR OF THE DARK
SUPERSTITION
THE NATURE OF ENCHANTMENT

KATJA VON GARNIER
Agent: CAA - Beverly Hills, 310/288-4545

MAKIN' UP!   Seventh Art Releasing, 1994, w/Hannes Jaenicke &
   Benjamin Taylor,   directed

BOBBY VON HAYES
(See Will Aldis & Steven Kampmann)

EHRICH VON LOWE*
Agent: The Gersh Agency - Beverly Hills, 310/274-6611

Screenplays:
HORROR IN THE HOOD

KURT VONNEGUT, JR.*
Contact: WGA - Los Angeles, 310/550-1000

HAPPY BIRTHDAY, WANDA JUNE   Columbia,
   1971,   from his play

LINDA VOORHEES*
Agent: Renaissance-H.N. Swanson - Los Angeles, 310/246-6000

CRAZY FROM THE HEART (CTF)   DeMann
   Entertainment-Papazian/Hirsch Entertainment, 1991

Screenplays:
LION KING SEQUEL (AF)
BRASS BADGES
GUESS WHO'S COMING TO DINNER II
MRS. MIKE (CTF)
END OF THE WORLD IN BEAN BLOSSOM (CTF)

GIGI VORGAN*
Agent: ICM - Beverly Hills, 310/550-4000

CONFESSIONS OF A SORORITY GIRL (CTF)   Showtime/Drive-In
   Classic Cinema, 1994, w/Debra Hill
JAILBREAKERS (CTF)   Showtime/Drive-In Classic Cinema,
   1994,   w/Debra Hill

Screenplays:
HOMETOWN w/Debra Hill

CYRUS VORIS
Agent: United Talent Agency - Beverly Hills, 310/273-6700

DEMON KNIGHT   Universal, 1995, w/Ethan Reiff

Screenplays:
PIECE OF MIND w/Ethan Reiff
SLAYER w/Ethan Reiff
JOSH KIRBY: TIMEMASTER! w/Ethan Reiff
MAN-AT ARMS w/Ethan Reiff

KURT VOSS
BORDER RADIO   International Film Marketing, 1988,
   w/Allison Anders & Dean Lent,   co-directed
THE HORSEPLAYER   Relentless Entertainment, 1989,
   w/Larry Rattner,   directed
GENUINE RISK   I.R.S. Releasing, 1990,   directed
DELUSION   I.R.S. Releasing, 1991, w/Carl Copaert
WHERE THE DAY TAKES YOU   New Line Cinema, 1992,
   w/Michael Hitchcock & Marc Rocco
DANGEROUS TOUCH   Trimark, w/Lou Diamond Phillips

Screenplays:
BAJA (New Line Cinema, directing)
JOURNEY INTO THE HEART OF DARKNESS w/Douchan Gersi
SUICIDE KINGS w/Keoni Waxman
FATAL PUNCH
VIRTUAL REALITY
TWO DICKS

OTAKAR VOTOCEK
WINGS OF FAME   First Floor Productions, 1990,
   w/Herman Koch,   directed

W

ANDY WACHOWSKI
Agent: Circle of Confusion Ltd. - New York, 212/969-0653

Screenplays:
PLASTICMAN w/Larry Wachowski
ASSASSINS w/Larry Wachowski
MATRIX w/Larry Wachowski

LARRY WACHOWSKI
Agent: Circle of Confusion Ltd. - New York, 212/969-0653

Screenplays:
PLASTICMAN w/Andy Wachowski
ASSASSINS w/Andy Wachowski
MATRIX w/Andy Wachowski

ROBERT D. WACHS*
Business: The Robert D. Wachs Company, 345 N. Maple Dr. - Suite
   179, Beverly Hills, CA 90210, 310/276-1123

BEVERLY HILLS COP II   Paramount, 1987, Story w/Eddie Murphy

KEVIN WADE*
Agent: CAA - Beverly Hills, 310/288-4545

KEY EXCHANGE (P)
CRUISE CONTROL (P)
WORKING GIRL   20th Century Fox, 1988
TRUE COLORS   Paramount, 1991
MR. BASEBALL   Universal, 1992, w/Monte Merrick & Gary Ross
JUNIOR   Universal, 1994, w/Chris Conrad

Screenplays:
GOOD BEHAVIOR

ROBERT WADE*
Agent: Lemon Unna & Durbridge - London, 071/727-1346

LET HIM HAVE IT   Fine Line Features, 1991, w/Neal Purvis

Screenplays:
GUILT-EDGED w/Neal Purvis

MICHAEL F. WADLEIGH*
Agent: Innovative Artists - Los Angeles, 310/553-5200

WOLFEN   Orion/Warner Bros., 1981, w/David Eyre, directed

Screenplays:
REVOLUTION

MARK WADLOW
THE SILENT TOUCH   Castle Hill Release, 1993, w/Peter Morgan

JONATHAN BANHART WAESSIL
WOLF RIDGE   Cinetrust Entertainment, 1993, directed

AMY J. WAGNER*
Contact: Colliewood Productions - 310/645-4648

Screenplays:
SHERLOCK SQUIRREL
STRAIGHT AND NARROW
DAKOTA JACK
RAVEN'S COURT

ANDREW WAGNER
Agent: William Morris Agency - Beverly Hills, 310/274-7451

THE LAST DAYS OF HOPE AND TIME (Short)   1992, directed

Screenplays:
THE MAN WHO GAVE UP HIS NAME

BRUCE WAGNER*
Agent: CAA - Beverly Hills, 310/288-4545

YOUNG LUST   RSO Films, 1982, w/Robin Menken
A NIGHTMARE ON ELM STREET 3: DREAM WARRIORS
    New Line Cinema, 1987, w/Wes Craven, Frank Darabont &
    Chuck Russell
SCENES FROM THE CLASS STRUGGLE IN BEVERLY HILLS
    Cinecom, 1989

Screenplays:
MAGNIFICENT OBSESSION
FORCE MAJEURE
THEY SLEEP BY NIGHT
THE GRAVITY OF STARS

HELENE WAGNER
Agent: Leslie Kallen Agency - Sherman Oaks, 818/906-2785

Screenplays:
THE MARRIAGE TALE
SUBSTANTIAL CAPACITY

JANE WAGNER*
Agent: William Morris Agency - Beverly Hills, 310/274-7451

MOMENT BY MOMENT   Universal, 1978, directed
THE INCREDIBLE SHRINKING WOMAN   Universal, 1981
THE SEARCH FOR SIGNS OF INTELLIGENT LIFE IN THE
    UNIVERSE   Orion Classics, 1991, from her play

ELAINE WAISGLASS
THE HOUSEKEEPER   Castle Hill Productions, 1987

MICHAEL WAITE
Contact: Angelina Productions, 9005 Cynthia Street - #215,
    West Hollywood, CA 90069

FUN DOWN THERE   Frameline, 1990, w/Roger Stigliano

Screenplays:
BOB, VERUSHKA & THE PURSUIT OF HAPPINESS
    w/Roger Stigliano

RALPH WAITE
Business Manager: Global Business Management, 15250 Ventura
    Blvd. - Suite 710, Sherman Oaks, CA 91403, 818/385-3100

ON THE NICKEL   Rose's Park, 1980, directed

MARC-HENRI WAJNBERG
JUST FRIENDS   Wajnbrosse Productions, 1993,
    w/Pierre Sterckx & Alexandre Wajnberg, directed

ELLIOT WALD*
Agent: ICM - Beverly Hills, 310/550-4000

SEE NO EVIL, HEAR NO EVIL   Tri-Star, 1989, w/Earl Barret,
    Andrew Kurtzman, Arne Sulton & Gene Wilder
CAMP NOWHERE   Buena Vista, 1994, w/Andrew Kurtzman

Screenplays:
THE WILLIAMS FAMILY w/Andrew Kurtzman
THE SCOUT w/Andrew Kurtzman

MALVIN WALD*
Contact: 818/784-8883

THE DARK PAST   Columbia, 1948, w/Philip Macdonald &
    Oscar Saul
THE NAKED CITY   Universal, 1948, w/Albert Matz
UNDERCOVER MAN   Columbia, 1949, w/Sydney Boehm
BATTLE TAXI   United Artists, 1954
AL CAPONE   Allied Artists, 1959, w/Henry Greenberg
IN SEARCH OF HISTORIC JESUS   Sunn Classic, 1979,
    w/Jack Jacobs

G.A. WALDMAN
(Grant Austin Waldman)
THE CHANNELER   Magnum Entertainment, 1991, Story, directed

WILLIAM WALES
(See David E. Ambrose)

ANDREW KEVIN WALKER*
Agent: United Talent Agency - Beverly Hills, 310/273-6700

BRAINSCAN   Triumph Releasing, 1994
HIDEAWAY   TriStar, 1995, w/Neal Jimenez

Screenplays:
SEVEN
X-MEN
LIE TO ME
SLEEPY HOLLOW

DAVID WALKER
PLATOON LEADER   Cannon, 1988, w/Andrew Deutsch &
   Rick Marx

KEITH A. WALKER*
Contact: 615/665-9845

FREE WILLY   Warner Bros., 1993, w/Corey Blechman

ROB WALKER
Contact: British Academy of Film & Television Arts, 195 Piccadilly,
   London W1, England, 01/734-0022

BEYOND BEDLAM   Feature Film Company, 1994,
   w/Vadim Jean

GARY WALKOW
Contact: Frank Gruber, Gruber, Wender & Levine - Beverly Hills,
   310/553-6900

THE TROUBLE WITH DICK   Fever Dream Production Company,
   1987, directed

Screenplays:
NOTES FROM THE UNDERGROUND (directing)
NOON
THIRTY SIX EXPOSURES

ART WALLACE*
Agent: William Morris Agency - New York, 212/586-5100

Screenplays:
THE TELLTALE HEART

EARL W. WALLACE*
Agent: William Morris Agency - Beverly Hills, 310/274-7451

WITNESS ★★   Paramount, 1985, w/William Kelley
THE BROKEN CHAIN (CTF)   Turner Broadcasting, 1993

Screenplays:
CHOICE OF ARMS
THE RAID ON 330 PARK

JOSEPHINE WALLACE*
Contact: WGA - Los Angeles, 310/550-1000

BAIL JUMPER   Angelika Films, 1990, w/Christian Faber

PAMELA D. WALLACE*
Agent: William Morris Agency - Beverly Hills, 310/274-7451

WITNESS ★★   Paramount, 1985, Story w/William Kelley &
   Earl W. Wallace
STROKE OF MIDNIGHT   Media Home Entertainment, 1991,
   w/Madeline DiMaggio

Screenplays:
FORTUNE'S CHILD
DREAMS LOST, DREAMS FOUND (CTF)
LOVE WITH A PERFECT STRANGER (CTF)

RANDALL WALLACE*
Agent: ICM - Beverly Hills, 310/550-4000

BRAVEHEART   Paramount, 1995

Screenplays:
GROUND BLAST

TOMMY LEE WALLACE*
Agent: Innovative Artists - Los Angeles, 310/553-5200

STARMAN IN NOVEMBER (Short)   directed
AMITYVILLE II: THE POSSESSION   Orion, 1982
HALLOWEEN III: THE SEASON OF THE WITCH   Universal,
   1982, directed
FRIGHT NIGHT PART 2   New Century/Vista, 1989,
   w/Miguel Tejada-Flores & Tim Metcalfe, directed
FAR FROM HOME   Cinecom, 1989
EL DIABLO (CTF)   Wizan/Black Productions, 1990,
   w/John Carpenter & Bill Phillips

Screenplays:
MIDNIGHT
THE NINJA
HOLLYWOOD DELUXE
TEST PATTERN
WHITE RABBIT

IRA WALLACH*
Agent: Earl Graham Agency - New York, 212/489-7730

BOYS' NIGHT OUT   MGM, 1962
DON'T MAKE WAVES   MGM, 1967, w/George Kirgo

TOM WALMSLEY
PARIS, FRANCE   Alliance Communications, 1993

FRANCES WALSH
DEAD/ALIVE   Wingnut Films Ltd./New Zealand Film Commission,
   1993, w/Stephen Sinclair & Peter Jackson
HEAVENLY CREATURES   Miramax, 1994, w/Peter Jackson

Screenplays:
THE FRIGHTENERS w/Peter Jackson (Universal)

JOSEPH WALSH*
Contact: WGA - Los Angeles, 310/550-1000

CALIFORNIA SPLIT   Columbia, 1974

RUPERT WALTERS*
Agent: William Morris Agency - Beverly Hills, 310/274-7451

PRIVILEGED   New Yorker, 1982, w/Michael Hoffman &
   David Woolcambe
SOME GIRLS   MGM/UA, 1989
RESTORATION   Miramax, 1994

Screenplays:
PRIDE AND PREJUDICE
THE DAY OF THE SUNS

FRED WALTON*
Agent: Innovative Artists - Los Angeles, 310/553-5200
Manager: Jon Brown, The Brown Group - Burbank, 818/955-7040

WHEN A STRANGER CALLS   Columbia, 1979,
   w/Stephen Feke, directed
HADLEY'S REBELLION   American Film Distribution, 1984,
   w/Stephen Feke, directed
THE ROSARY MURDERS   New Line Cinema, 1987,
   w/Elmore Leonard, directed
TRAPPED (CTF)   USA/MCA Television, 1989,
   w/Stephen Feke, directed
HOMEWRECKER (CTF)   Joss Communications/Wilshire Court,
   1993, w/Eric Harlacher, directed
WHEN A STRANGER CALLS BACK (CTF)   Krost/Chapin
   Productions/MCA Television Entertainment, 1993, directed

Screenplays:
IN BROAD DAYLIGHT

KENT WALWIN
BIGGLES   New Century/Vista, 1988, w/John P. Groves

JOSEPH WAMBAUGH*
Agent: Martin Hurwitz Associates - Beverly Hills, 310/274-0240

THE ONION FIELD   Avco Embassy, 1979
THE BLACK MARBLE   Avco Embassy, 1980

PETER WANG
Business: Peter Wang Films, Inc., 594 Broadway - Suite 906,
   New York, NY 10012

A GREAT WALL   Orion Classics, 1986, w/Shirley Sun,   directed
THE LASERMAN   Original Cinema, 1990,   directed

WAYNE WANG*
Agent: William Morris Agency - Beverly Hills, 310/274-7451
Business: C.I.M. Productions, 665 Bush Street, San Francisco,
   CA 94108, 415/433-2342

CHAN IS MISSING   New Yorker, 1982, w/Isaac Cronin &
   Terrel Seltzer,   directed
DIM SUM: A LITTLE BIT OF HEART   Orion Classics, 1985,
   Idea w/Lauren Chew & Terrel Seltzer,   directed
LIFE IS CHEAP...BUT TOILET PAPER IS EXPENSIVE
   Silverlight Entertainment, 1990, Story w/Amir M. Mokri &
   Spenser Nakasako,   co-directed

JEFF WANSHEL*
Agent: The Gersh Agency - New York, 212/997-1818
Address: 9009 Wonderland Ave., Los Angeles, CA 90046,
   213/656-7607

Screenplays:
666

DAVID S. WARD*
Agent: CAA - Beverly Hills, 310/288-4545

THE STING ★★   Universal, 1973
CANNERY ROW   MGM/United Artists, 1981,   directed
STEELYARD BLUES   Warner Bros., 1983
THE STING II   Universal, 1983
SAVING GRACE   Embassy, 1986, w/Richard Kramer
THE MILAGRO BEANFIELD WAR   Universal, 1988, w/John Nichols
MAJOR LEAGUE   Paramount, 1989,   directed
KING RALPH   Universal, 1991,   directed
SLEEPLESS IN SEATTLE ★   TriStar, 1993, w/Jeffrey Arch &
   Nora Ephron
THE PROGRAM   Buena Vista/Samuel Goldwyn Company, 1993,
   w/Aaron Latham, directed
MAJOR LEAGUE II   Warner Bros., 1994, w/R.J. Stewart, directed

Screenplays:
DIAL TONE
SAN JOAQUIN
HANDLING SIN

DONAL LARDNER WARD
Agent: CAA - Beverly Hills, 310/288-4545

MY LIFE'S IN TURNAROUND   Arrow Releasing, 1994,
   w/Eric Schaeffer, co-directed

Screenplays:
WHATEVER HAPPENED TO LOVE AT FIRST SIGHT
   w/Eric Schaeffer

EDMUND WARD
THE VIOLENT ENEMY   Trio, 1968
AMSTERDAM AFFAIR   Lippert, 1968
GOODBYE GEMINI   Cinerama Releasing Corporation, 1970
A PRAYER FOR THE DYING   Samuel Goldwyn Company, 1987,
   w/Martin Lynch

KELLY WARD
ONCE UPON A FOREST (AF)   20th Century Fox, 1993,
   w/Mark Young

MORGAN UPTON WARD
Agent: The Gersh Agency - Beverly Hills, 310/274-6611

PYROMANIACS: A LOVE STORY   Buena Vista, 1994

NICK WARD
Contact: British Academy of Film & Television Arts, 195 Piccadilly,
   London W1, England, 01/734-0022

LOOK ME IN THE EYE   Skreba-Creon Films, 1994,   directed

ROBERT JOHN WARD*
Contact: WGA - Los Angeles, 310/550-1000

Screenplays:
THE BLACK ARROW

ROBERT M. WARD*
Contact: WGA - Los Angeles, 310/550-1000

CATTLE ANNIE AND LITTLE BRITCHES   Universal, 1981,
   w/David Eyre

Screenplays:
RED BAKER

STEPHEN WARD
Agent: The Casarotto Company - London, 071/287-4450

BACKBEAT   Gramercy, 1994, w/Iain Softley & Michael Thomas

VINCENT WARD
Agent: CAA - Beverly Hills, 310/288-4545

VIGIL   John Maynard Productions/Film Investment Corporation
   of New Zealand/New Zealand Film Commission, 1984,
   w/Graeme Tetley,   directed
THE NAVIGATOR: AN ODYSSEY ACROSS TIME
   THE NAVIGATOR - A MEDIEVAL ODYSSEY   Circle Releasing,
   1988, w/Geoff Chapple & Kely Lyons,   directed
ALIEN 3   20th Century Fox, 1993, Story
MAP OF THE HUMAN HEART   Miramax, 1993, Story,   directed

BILLY WARDEN
Agent: ICM - Beverly Hills, 310/550-4000
Manager: Ogden House - Los Angeles, 213/851-0458

Screenplays:
ROB ME TENDER

CLYDE WARE*
Agent: Preferred Artists - Encino, 818/990-0305

NO DRUMS, NO BUGLES   Cinerama Releasing Corporation,
   1971,   directed
HUMAN ERROR   Wouk-Ware Productions, 1989,   directed
ANOTHER TIME, ANOTHER PLACE   Transcontinental
   Pictures Industries, 1989,   directed
BAD JIM   21st Century Film Corporation, 1990,   directed

Screenplays:
ROUGH DIAMONDS (directing)
LYDIA w/Jonathan Edwards
THE ANDREW JOHNSON STORY
BOJANGLES: THE BILL ROBINSON STORY

DAVID WARFIELD*
Agent: ICM - Beverly Hills, 310/550-4000

PRIVATE INVESTIGATIONS   MGM/UA, 1987, w/John Dahl
KILL ME AGAIN   MGM/UA, 1990, w/John Dahl

REGIS WARGNIER
INDOCHINE   Sony Classics, 1992, w/Catherine Cohen,
   Louis Gardel & Erik Orsenna, directed

ALLYN WARNER*
Agent: CAA - Beverly Hills, 310/288-4545

HOUSE III: THE HORROR SHOW   MGM/UA, 1989,
   as "Alan Smithee," w/Leslie Bohem

Screenplays:
WHERE THE RAIN IS BORN
RAISING HELL
HAVANA DANCY
RAGGEDY HEARTS CLUB
TRUE CRIME MAGAZINE
GHOST RIDERS IN THE SKY
CURSE OF THE BLACK ROSE
TOP STORY

WANDA WARNER
Agent: Monteiro Rose Agency - Encino, 818/501-1177

Screenplays:
STRAY HEARTS   THE HARD ONES
CHIEF TO CHIEF

DERYN WARREN
BLACK MAGIC WOMAN   Trimark Pictures, 1991,
   Story w/Gerry Daly & Marc Springer, directed

HARVEY WARREN*
Agent: Innovative Artists - Los Angeles, 310/553-5200
Manager: RKS Entertainment Group - Sherman Oaks, 818/788-3616

Screenplays:
ROCKETS RED GLARE w/Joy Warren
PILOT ERROR w/Joy Warren
WILL TO KILL w/Joy Warren
SHOOTERS w/Joy Warren
SHANNA w/Joy Warren
LITTLE EAGLE w/Joy Warren

JOHN WARREN*
Agent: CAA - Beverly Hills, 310/288-4545

GET CHARLIE TULLY   *OOH, YOU ARE AWFUL*   TBS, 1977,
   w/John Singer

Screenplays:
GIRL IN THE CADILLAC CONVERTIBLE
MEN'S CLUB
FLASHFIRE
TRIMMING THE FAMILY TREE
SNEAKY PEOPLE
THE BODY POLITIC
AUGUST FIRE

JOY WARREN*
Agent: Innovative Artists - Los Angeles, 310/553-5200
Manager: RKS Entertainment Group - Sherman Oaks, 818/788-3616

Screenplays:
ROCKETS RED GLARE w/Harvey Warren
PILOT ERROR w/Harvey Warren
WILL TO KILL w/Harvey Warren
SHOOTERS w/Harvey Warren
SHANNA w/Harvey Warren
LITTLE EAGLE w/Harvey Warren

JOYCE WARREN
THE ICE RUNNER   Borde Film Releasing, 1993,
   w/Clifford Coleman & Joshua Stallings

MICHAEL WARREN*
Agent: ICM - Beverly Hills, 310/550-4000
Contact: Ziffren, Brittenham & Branca - Beverly Hills, 310/552-3388

HAWMPS   Mulberry Square, 1976, w/William Bickley

DERIC WASHBURN*
Agent: ICM - Beverly Hills, 310/550-4000

SILENT RUNNING   Universal, 1972, w/Steven Bochco &
   Michael Cimino
THE DEER HUNTER ★   Universal, 1978
THE BORDER   Universal, 1982, w/David Freeman & Walon Green
EXTREME PREJUDICE   Tri-Star, 1987, w/Harry Kleiner

Screenplays:
MURDER OF NAPOLEON
HEAVY DUST
YAMASHITA'S GOLD
TOM MIX & PANCHO VILLA

ART WASHINGTON*
Agent: William Morris Agency - Beverly Hills, 310/274-7451

PERCY AND THUNDER (CTF)   TNT/Amblin TV/Brandman
   Productions, 1993

DALE WASSERMAN*
Manager: Creative Alliance Management - Los Angeles,
   213/962-6090

THE VIKINGS   United Aritsts, 1958, Adaptation
QUICK BEFORE IT MELTS   MGM, 1965
MISTER BUDDWING   MGM, 1966
A WALK WITH LOVE AND DEATH   20th Century-Fox, 1969
MAN OF LA MANCHA   United Artists, 1972

Screenplays:
BABA YAGA

LEE WASSERMAN
RETRIBUTION   Taurus Entertainment, 1988, w/Guy Magar

STEVEN MARK WASSERMAN*
Agent: Broder-Kurland-Webb-Uffner - Beverly Hills, 310/281-3400

Screenplays:
MARK MY WORDS

WENDY J. WASSERSTEIN*
Agent: CAA - Beverly Hills, 310/288-4545

ISN'T IT ROMANTIC? (P)
UNCOMMON WOMEN AND OTHERS (P)
THE SISTERS ROSENSWEIG (P)
THE HEIDI CHRONICLES (CTF)   Turner Network, 1995,
   from her play

Screenplays:
ANTONIA AND JANE (remake)
THE OBJECT OF MY AFFECTION
LOCAL TALENT

DARRELL WASYK
Contact: Academy of Canadian Cinema & Television, 753 Yonge St. -
   2nd Floor, Toronto M4Y 1Z9, Canada, 416/967-0315

MUSTARD BATH   946S Film Production, 1993, directed

DANIEL B. WATERS*
Agent: CAA - Beverly Hills, 310/288-4545

HEATHERS   New World, 1989
THE ADVENTURES OF FORD FAIRLANE   20th Century Fox,
   1990, w/David Arnott & James Cappe

HUDSON HAWKE   Tri-Star, 1991, w/Steven deSouza
BATMAN RETURNS   Warner Bros., 1992
DEMOLITION MAN   Warner Bros., 1993, w/Peter Lenkov &
   Rob Reneau

Screenplays:
MODEL DAUGHTER
STRANGER IN A STRANGE LAND

ED WATERS*
Agent: The Irv Schechter Company - Beverly Hills, 310/278-8070

THE CAPER OF THE GOLDEN BULLS   Embassy, 1966,
   w/William Moessinger
DARKER THAN AMBER   Cinema Center, 1970

JOHN WATERS*
Agent: ICM - Beverly Hills, 310/550-4000

MONDO TRASHO   Film-Makers, 1970, directed
PINK FLAMINGOS   Saliva Films, 1974, directed
FEMALE TROUBLE   New Line Cinema, 1975, directed
DESPERATE LIVING   New Line Cinema, 1977, directed
POLYESTER   New Line Cinema, 1981, directed
HAIRSPRAY   New Line Cinema, 1988, directed
CRY-BABY   Universal, 1990, directed
SERIAL MOM   Savoy Pictures, 1994, directed

Screenplays:
GLAMOURPUSS

ROBERT E. WATERS
ALLEY CAT   Film Ventures International, 1984

ROGER WATERS
PINK FLOYD - THE WALL   MGM/UA, 1982

GREG WATKINS
A LITTLE STIFF   Just Above the Ground Productions, 1991,
   w/Caveh Zahedi, co-directed

CAROL A. WATSON*
Contact: WGA - Los Angeles, 310/550-1000

FRIDAY THE 13TH PART 3   Paramount, 1982, w/Martin Kitrosser
MEATBALLS PART II   Tri-Star, 1984, Story w/Martin Kitrosser

Screenplays:
STRANGE HEARTS
SEE JANE RUN

JOHN WATSON*
Agent: ICM - Beverly Hills, 310/550-4000
Business: Trilogy Entertainment Group, MGM/UA - 310/449-3095

THE ZOO GANG   New World, 1985, w/Pen Densham, co-directed
ROBIN HOOD: PRINCE OF THIEVES   Warner Bros., 1991,
   w/Pen Densham
A GNOME NAMED NORM   7 Arts, 1992, Story w/Pen Densham

Screenplays:
BLIND LUCK w/Pen Densham
FLYING TIGERS w/Pen Densham
UPWORLD

PATRICIA WATSON
WHO HAS SEEN THE WIND?   Astral Bellevue, 1977
THE NUTCRACKER PRINCE (AF)   Warner Bros., 1990

JEREMY WATT
SCRUBBERS   Orion Classics, 1984, w/Roy Minton &
   Mai Zetterling

KEONI WAXMAN
Agent: The Agency - Los Angeles, 310/551-3000

I SHOT A MAN IN RENO   Trans Atlantic Entertainment,
   1994, directed

Screenplays:
ANGEL EYES
ALMOST BLUE
SUICIDE KINGS w/Kurt Voss

RICK WAY*
Manager: Carlyle Management - Los Angeles, 213/469-3086

TRIAL & ERROR (CTF)   Alliance Communications/USA Network,
   1993, w/Jim Lindsay & N.D. Schreiner

Screenplays:
CONVICT COWBOY w/Jim Lindsay
MY MOTHER WEARS ARMY BOOTS w/Jim Lindsay

DAMON WAYANS*
Agent: CAA - Beverly Hills, 310/288-4545

MO' MONEY   Columbia, 1992
BLANKMAN   MGM/UA, 1994, w/J.F. Lawton
MAJOR PAYNE   Universal, 1995, w/Dean Lorey & Gary Rosen

KEENEN IVORY WAYANS*
Agent: CAA - Beverly Hills, 310/288-4545
Contact: Belinkoff-London-Lichtenberg - Los Angeles, 310/470-2484

HOLLYWOOD SHUFFLE   Samuel Goldwyn Company, 1987,
   w/Robert Townsend
EDDIE MURPHY RAW   Paramount, 1987, w/Eddie Murphy
I'M GONNA GIT YOU SUCKA   MGM/UA, 1989, directed
THE FIVE HEARTBEATS   20th Century Fox, 1991,
   w/Robert Townsend
A LOW DOWN DIRTY SHAME   Buena Vista, 1994, directed

MARLON WAYANS
Manager: Gold/Miller - Los Angeles, 310/278-8990

Screenplays:
*DON'T BE MENACE IN SOUTH CENTRAL WHILE DRINKING YOUR
   JUICE IN THE HOOD w/Phil Beauman & Shawn Wayans*

SHAWN WAYANS
Manager: Gold/Miller - Los Angeles, 310/278-8990

Screenplays:
*DON'T BE MENACE IN SOUTH CENTRAL WHILE DRINKING YOUR
   JUICE IN THE HOOD w/Phil Beauman & Marlon Wayans*

MICHAEL WEARING
Contact: British Broadcasting Corp., Woodlands, 80 Wood Lane,
   London W12 7RJ, England, 081/743-8000

BELLMAN AND TRUE   Island Pictures, 1987,
   w/Richard Loncraine & Desmond Lowden

ALISTER WEBB
HEAVEN TONIGHT   Boulevard Films, 1990, w/Frank Howson
MY FORGOTTEN MAN   Boulevard Films, 1993, w/Frank Howson

JAMES WEBB
Agent: ICM - Beverly Hills, 310/550-4000

Screenplays:
RULES OF ENGAGEMENT
MAMA'S BOY
FIELDS OF FIRE

MIKE WEBB
THE HUMAN SHIELD   Cannon, 1992, Story w/Mann Rubin

TOM WEBER
Agent: Writers & Artists Agency - Los Angeles, 310/824-6300

Screenplays:
STRIKE ZONE

LEN WECHSLER*
Contact: WGA - Los Angeles, 310/550-1000

Screenplays:
CALIFORNIA DREAMING w/Jeff Smith

DAVID J. WECHTER*
Agent: William Morris Agency - Beverly Hills, 310/274-7451

MIDNIGHT MADNESS   Buena Vista, 1980,
   w/Michael Nankin, co-directed
MALIBU BIKINI SHOP   *THE BIKINI SHOP*   International Film
   Marketing, 1987, directed

Screenplays:
MURPHY'S LAW OF GOLF (co-directing)
BE TRUE TO YOUR SCHOOL
JUNIOR HIGH SCHOOL

STEPHEN WEEKS
Address: Penhow Castle, Nr. Newport, Gwent., Penhow WP6 3AD,
   England, 0633/400800

GAWAIN AND THE GREEN KNIGHT   United Artists, 1973,
   w/Philip Green, directed
GHOST STORY   Weeks, 1974, w/Rosemary Sutcliff, directed
SWORD OF THE VALIANT   Cannon, 1984, w/Phillip M. Breen &
   Howard C. Pen, directed

HANNA WEG*
Agent: United Talent Agency - Beverly Hills, 310/273-6700

MATCHBOOK (Short)   1993, directed

Screenplays:
THE INTERPRETER
MINOR TRANSGRESSIONS

DEEDEE WEHLE*
Contact: Neal Gantcher, Esq. - 212/983-0400

DISTANT THUNDER   Paramount, 1988, Story w/Robert Stitzel

JOHN WEIDNER
Agent: Jon Klane Agency - Beverly Hills, 310/278-0178

CIA: CODE NAME ALEXA   PM Entertainment, 1993,
   w/Ken Lamplugh, directed

Screenplays:
INDESTRUCTIBLE w/Ken Lamplugh

HERMAN WEIGEL
Business: Neue Constantin Film, GmbH & Co Verleih KG,
   Kaiserstraße 39, D-8000 München 40, West Germany, 38-60-90

CHRISTIANE F.   New World, 1982
THE NEVERENDING STORY   Warner Bros., 1984,
   w/Wolfgang Petersen

YOSSI WEIN
NEVER SAY DIE   Nu-Image, 1994, w/Jeff Albert &
   Danny Lerner, directed

MARC WEINBERG
Agent: The Gersh Agency - Beverly Hills, 310/274-6611

Screenplays:
BLOODLINE w/Victoria Fraser

ED. WEINBERGER*
Agent: ICM - Beverly Hills, 310/550-4000
Manager: Freedman, Kinzelberg, Broder - 310/449-6700

THE LONELY GUY   Universal, 1984, w/Stan Daniels

Screenplays:
SKETCHLIFE
DIRTY SECRETS
THE CASTAWAYS

JAKE WEINBERGER*
Contact: WGA - Los Angeles, 310/550-1000

Screenplays:
COYOTE LOVE w/Mike Weinberger
ESCAPEES w/Mike Weinberger

MICHAEL WEINBERGER*
Contact: WGA - Los Angeles, 310/550-1000

Screenplays:
COYOTE LOVE w/Jake Weinberger
ESCAPEES w/Jake Weinberger

ELLIS WEINER*
Agent: Elliot Hoffman, Beldock, Levine & Hoffman - 212/490-1502

NATIONAL LAMPOON'S MOVIE MADNESS   United Artists, 1982,
   w/Tod Carroll, Shary Flenniken, Pat Mephitis & Gerald Sussman

HAL WEINER
THE IMAGEMAKER   Castle Hill Productios, 1986,
   w/Dick Goldberg, directed

RANDY WEINER
Contact: Project 400 Theater Group - 212/724-5866

PROSPERO'S REVENGE (P)
DOCTOR AMORPHOUS (P)
AL BANGO, FIRST-RATE SLEUTH (P)
CLUB XII (P) w/Rob Hanning, also screenplay
THE GANGS NEW THREADS (P) w/Rob Hanning

Screenplays:
YO' JULIETTE w/Rob Hanning

REX WEINER*
Contact: WGA - Los Angeles, 310/550-1000

BE BOP A LULA (P)
FORGOTTEN PRISONERS: THE AMNESTY FILES (CTF)
   Turner Pictures, 1990, w/Cindy Myers

SOLOMON WEINGARTEN*
Business: Solomon Weingarten & Associates - Los Angeles,
   310/479-4706

BLIND SIDE (CTF)   Chestnut Hill Productions, 1993,
   w/John Carlen & Stewart Lindh
ACTING ON IMPULSE (CTF)   Spectator Films, 1993, Story

HERSCHEL A. WEINGROD*
Agent: CAA - Beverly Hills, 310/288-4545
Business: Myrtos Productions, 20th Century Fox, 310/277-2211

CHEAPER TO KEEP HER   American Cinema, 1980,
   w/Timothy Harris
TRADING PLACES   Paramount, 1983, w/Timothy Harris

BREWSTER'S MILLIONS   Universal, 1985, w/Timothy Harris
MY STEPMOTHER IS AN ALIEN   WEG, 1988, w/Timothy Harris,
    Jonathan Reynolds & Jericho Stone
TWINS   Universal, 1989, w/Timothy Harris, William Davies &
    William Osborne
KINDERGARTEN COP   Universal, 1990, w/Timothy Harris &
    Murray Salem
PURE LUCK   Universal, 1991, w/Timothy Harris

Screenplays:
DUMMIES w/Timothy Harris
SIBERIAN EXPRESS w/Timothy Harris
THE FRENCH KISS w/Timothy Harris
THE PIED PIPER MOTHER'S DAY w/Timothy Harris
THE FUGITIVE PIGEON w/Timothy Harris
BIGFINGER w/Timothy Harris
MICKEY w/Timothy Harris
BEAUTY SCHOOL w/Timothy Harris
DISASTER w/Timothy Harris
THE LITTLE BROTHER w/Timothy Harris

BOB WEINSTEIN*
Business: Miramax Films, Tribeca Film Center, 375 Greenwich St.,
    New York, NY 10013, 212/941-4000

THE BURNING   Filmways/Orion, 1982, w/Peter Lawrence
PLAYING FOR KEEPS   Universal, 1986, w/Harvey Weinstein &
    Jeremy Leven, co-directed

CHARLES WEINSTEIN
UNDER THE BRIDGE   No Distributor, 1994, directed

DAVID Z. WEINSTEIN*
Contact: Marvin Meyer, Rosenfield, Meyer & Susman - 310/246-3218

BIG TROUBLE IN LITTLE CHINA   20th Century Fox, 1986,
    w/Gary Goldman

Screenplays:
RAISING CANE

HARVEY WEINSTEIN*
Business: Miramax Films, Tribeca Film Center, 375 Greenwich St.,
    New York, NY 10013, 212/941-4000

PLAYING FOR KEEPS   Universal, 1986, w/Bob Weinstein &
    Jeremy Leven, co-directed

FRED WEINTRAUB
Business: Fred Weintraub Productions, 1923 1/2 Westwood Blvd. #2,
    Los Angeles, CA 90025, 310/470-8787

THE BIG BRAWL   Warner Bros., 1980, Story w/Robert Clouse

SANDRA WEINTRAUB*
Agent: Amsel, Eisenstadt & Frazier - Los Angeles, 310/939-1188

HIGH ROAD TO CHINA   Warner Bros., 1983, w/S. Lee Pogostin
OUT OF CONTROL   New World, 1985, w/Vicangelo Bullock
THE PRINCESS ACADEMY   Empire Pictures, 1987, directed
THE WOMEN'S CLUB   Lightning Pictures, 1987, directed
CHIPS, THE WAR DOG (CTF)   W.G. Productions, 1990, Story
THE BEST OF THE MARITAL ARTS FILMS (FD)   Miramax,
    1991, directed
CHINA O'BRIEN   Golden Harvest, 1991
CHINA O'BRIEN II   Golden Harvest, 1992

Screenplays:
THE LOST WORLD
ENCORE
CITY
THE BUMBLE BROTHERS
CONFESSIONS OF A BEVERLY HILLS PSYCHIATRIST
THEY ONLY COME OUT AT MIDNIGHT
BIRDS OF A FEATHER
KILLER'S KISS

DAVID WEIR*
Contact: 415/986-5196

ROLLOVER   Orion/Warner Bros., 1981, Story w/Howard Kohn &
    David Shaber

PETER WEIR
Agent: CAA - Beverly Hills, 310/288-4545

THREE TO GO   Commonwealth Film Unit Productions, 1971,
    "Michael," directed
THE CARS THAT ATE PEOPLE   *THE CARS THAT ATE PARIS*
    New Line Cinema, 1974, directed
THE PLUMBER   Barbary Coast, 1978, directed
THE LAST WAVE   World Northal, 1978, w/Tony Morphett &
    Petru Popescu, directed
GALLIPOLI   Paramount, 1981, Story, directed
THE YEAR OF LIVING DANGEROUSLY   MGM/UA, 1983,
    w/David Williamson & C.J. Koch, directed
GREEN CARD ★   Buena Vista, 1990, directed

ALLAN C. WEISBECKER*
Contact: WGA - Los Angeles, 310/550-1000

BEER   Orion, 1985

Screenplays:
GAZER
STOLEN THUNDER
AN ISLAND IN WINTER
FOREIGN POLICY
DRUMS ALONG THE HUDSON

DAVID WEISBERG*
Agent: Writers & Artists Agency - Los Angeles, 310/824-6300
Business: Aurora Productions, 8642 Melrose Ave. - #10, Los Angeles,
    CA 90069, 310/854-6900

PAYOFF (CTF)   Viacom Pictures, 1991, w/Douglas S. Cook
HOLY MATRIMONY   Buena Vista, 1994, w/Douglas S. Cook

Screenplays:
THE ROCK w/Doug Cook

DOUGLAS J. WEISER*
Contact: WGA - New York, 212/245-6180

MIDNIGHT CROSSING   Vestron, 1988, w/Roger Holzberg

MEL WEISER
LOVE YA TOMORROW   Atlas Entertainment, 1991, directed

STANLEY G. WEISER*
Agent: ICM - Beverly Hills, 310/550-4000

COAST TO COAST   Paramount, 1980
PROJECT X   20th Century Fox, 1987
WALL STREET   20th Century Fox, 1987, w/Oliver Stone
FATHERLAND (CTF)   HBO Pictures, 1994, w/Ron Hutchinson

Screenplays:
PATRIMONY
THE THIRD LADY
INDIAN WARS
SERVE AND PROTECT
A HOLE IN THE WORLD w/Richard Rhodes

SUSAN WEISER-FINLEY*
Agent: Becsey/Wisdom/Kalajian Agency - Los Angeles, 310/550-0535

THE FIRST TIME   New Line Cinema, 1982, w/Charlie Loventhal &
    William Finley

MATTHEW WEISMAN*
Agent: CAA - Beverly Hills, 310/288-4545

TEEN WOLF   Atlantic Releasing Corporation, 1985,
   w/Joseph Loeb III
COMMANDO   20th Century Fox, 1985, Story w/Steven de Souza &
   Joseph Loeb III
TEEN WOLF TOO   Atlantic Releasing Corporation, 1987,
   Story w/Joseph Loeb III
BURGLAR   Warner Bros., 1987, w/Joseph Loeb III & Hugh Wilson

Screenplays:
NIGHTTIME GUY w/Joseph Loeb III
SILENT PARTNERS w/Joseph Loeb III
ACCIDENTS WILL HAPPEN w/Joseph Loeb III
INSPECTOR DAD w/Joseph Loeb III

DAVID N. WEISS*
Agent: ICM - Beverly Hills, 310/550-4000

ALL DOGS GO TO HEAVEN (AF)   MGM/UA, 1989
ROCK-A-DOODLE (AF)   Samuel Goldwyn Company, 1992

MARIE WEISS*
Agent: United Talent Agency - Beverly Hills, 310/273-6700

THE REF   Buena Vista, 1994, w/Richard LaGravenese

Screenplays:
FREELOADERS

ROB WEISS
Agent: United Talent Agency - Beverly Hills, 310/273-6700
Manager: Melinda Jason - Beverly Hills, 310/289-6134

AMONGST FRIENDS   Fine Line Features, 1993, directed

Screenplays:
MURDER, INC.

DAVID WEISSMAN
Agent: Original Artists - Santa Monica, 310/394-1067

Screenplays:
WHIZ KID w/David Diamond

CHRIS WEITZ*
Agent: United Talent Agency - Beverly Hills, 310/273-6700

Screenplays:
RHODE ISLAND SMITH AND THE THEME PARK OF DOOM
   w/Paul Weitz
KARMA COPS w/Paul Weitz

PAUL WEITZ*
Agent: United Talent Agency - Beverly Hills, 310/273-6700

ALL FOR ONE (P)

Screenplays:
RHODE ISLAND SMITH AND THE THEME PARK OF DOOM
   w/ChrisWeitz
KARMA COPS w/Chris Weitz

PETER WELBECK
(See Harry Alan Towers)

JULIE WELCH
Agent: Peters, Fraser & Dunlop - London, 071/376-7676

THOSE GLORY, GLORY DAYS   Cinecom, 1983

LES WELDON*
Contact: Zito/Weldon Productions - 310/268-0049

FREE FALL   Nu Image, 1993, w/David Zito
SPANISH ROSE   Nu Image, 1993, w/David Zito

COLIN WELLAND*
Agent: ICM - Beverly Hills, 310/550-4000

YANKS   Universal, 1979, w/Walter Bernstein
CHARIOTS OF FIRE ★★   The Ladd Company/Warner Bros., 1981
TWICE IN A LIFETIME   The Yorkin Company, 1985
A DRY WHITE SEASON   MGM/UA, 1989, w/Euzhan Palcy
THE WAR OF THE BUTTONS   Warner Bros., 1994

Screenplays:
LECH WALESA
YELLOW JERSEY
SHACKLETOWN

MICHAEL WELLER*
Agent: CAA - Beverly Hills, 310/288-4545

MOONCHILDREN (P)
FISHING (P)
LOOSE ENDS (P)   also screenplay
WARFMAN MASTER OF A MILLION SHAPES (P)
THE BALLAD OF SOAPY SMITH (P)
SPOILS OF WAR (P)   also teleplay
HAIR   United Artists, 1979
RAGTIME ★   Paramount, 1981
LOST ANGELS   Orion, 1989

Screenplays:
DEATH OF AN AMERICAN
THE FIFTH HORSEMAN
AND NOW THERE'S JUST THE THREE OF US
BREAKING THROUGH

DAVID WELLINGTON
Contact: Academy of Canadian Cinema & Television, 753 Yonge St. -
   2nd Floor, Toronto M4Y 1Z9, Canada, 416/967-0315

I LOVE A MAN IN UNIFORM   I.R.S. Releasing, 1994, directed

WENDELL E. WELLMAN*
Contact: WGA - Los Angeles, 310/550-1000

FIREFOX   Warner Bros., 1982, w/Alex Lasker

AUDREY WELLS*
Agent: United Talent Agency - Beverly Hills, 310/273-6700

Screenplays:
THE TRUTH ABOUT CATS AND DOGS
RADIO FREE ALASKA
DEMOCRACY

BILL WELLS*
Agent: The Irv Schechter Company - Beverly Hills, 310/278-8070

DROP DEAD GORGEOUS (CTF)   Power Pictures Corp., 1991,
   w/Thomas Baum & Mimi Schapiro

JOHN WELLS*
Agent: CAA - Beverly Hills, 310/288-4545

PRINCESS CARABOO   TriStar, 1994, w/Michael Austin

PETER WELLS
Contact: New Zealand Film Commission, 36 Allen St., Wellington,
   New Zealand, tel.: 4/859-754

DESPERATE REMEDIES   Miramax, 1993,
   wStuart Main, co-directed

TIM WELLS
IRAN: DAYS OF CRISIS (CMS)   Gerald Rafshoon/Consolidated,
   1991, w/Reg Gadney

AMY WELSH
Agent: Writers & Artists Agency - Los Angeles, 310/824-6300

Screenplays:
UPON A TIME
HERO IN YOUR OWN LIFE

WIM WENDERS
Business: Gray City Inc., 853 Broadway, New York, NY 10007,
   212/473-3600

ALICE IN THE CITIES   New Yorker, 1974, directed
KINGS OF THE ROAD   Bauer International, 1976, directed
THE AMERICAN FRIEND   New Yorker, 1977, directed
LIGHTNING OVER WATER   *NICK'S MOVIE*   Pari Films, 1980,
   w/Nicholas Ray, co-directed
TOKYO-GA (FD)   Wim Wenders Produktion/Gray City/Chris
   Sievernich Produktion, 1985, directed
WINGS OF DESIRE   *DER HIMMEL UBER BERLIN*   Orion Classics,
   1987, w/Peter Handke, directed
UNTIL THE END OF THE WORLD   Warner Bros., 1991,
   w/Peter Carey, directed
FARAWAY, SO CLOSE!   Sony Classics, 1993,
   w/Richard Reitinger & Ulrich Zieger, directed

GINA WENDKOS*
Agent: William Morris Agency - Beverly Hills, 310/274-7451
Manager: International Arts Entertainment - Los Angeles,
   310/551-0014

PERSONALITY (P)
BOYS AND GIRLS/MEN AND WOMEN (P)
FOUR CORNERS (P)
SOUTHERN COMFORT (P)
NORTHWEST STORY (P)
DINOSAURS (P)   also screenplay
GINGER ALE AFTERNOON   Skouras Pictures, 1989, from her play
JERSEY GIRL   Columbia, 1993

Screenplays:
QUEEN PINS
MY HUSBAND'S LVOER
I'LL BE SEEING YOU
CARRY ME THROUGH
BEAT OF THE NEW WORLD
WHO IS MRS. MORRISON?

RICHARD WENK
Agent: The Gersh Agency - Beverly Hills, 310/274-6611

VAMP   New World, 1986, directed

Screenplays:
SCALPER

RONNIE WENKER-KONNER*
Contact: Nina Shaw - Los Angeles, 310/552-0700

Screenplays:
THE BIG ROOM

JOHN WENTWORTH
Agent: United Talent Agency - Beverly Hills, 310/273-6700

Screenplays:
SPUD

MIKE WERB*
Agent: William Morris Agency - Beverly Hills, 310/274-7451

THE MASK   Buena Vista, 1994

Screenplays:
HAMLET
STRETCH ARMSTRONG w/Michael Colleary
FACE-OFF w/Michel Colleary
SHERMAN'S SHADOW
MACHINE GUN KELLY
CURIOUS GEORGE

TIMBERLAKE WERTENBAKER*
Contact: Merchant-Ivory - New York, 212/582-8049

OUR COUNTRY'S GOOD (P)
THREE BIRDS ALIGHTING ON A FIELD (P)

Screenplays:
THE PLAYMAKER (Buena Vista)

RICHARD WESLEY*
Agent: The Gersh Agency - Beverly Hills, 310/274-6611

THE MIGHTY GENTS (P)
UPTOWN SATURDAY NIGHT   Warner Bros., 1974
LET'S DO IT AGAIN   Warner Bros., 1975
FAST FORWARD   Columbia, 1985
NATIVE SON   Cinecom International, 1986

Screenplays:
BECKWOURTH (American Cinema Group)
DEAD WOOD DICK

PETER WEST
FISTS OF BLOOD   Virgo Productions/TVM Studios, 1989

VALERIE D. WEST*
Agent: Maggie Field Agency - Studio City, 818/980-2001

Screenplays:
GOOD LUCK TO A SWELL KID
CHOICES
MOTHER'S & SON
MY BROTHER, MY KEEPER

DONALD E. WESTLAKE*
Agent: Paul Kohner, Inc. - Beverly Hills, 310/550-1060

COPS AND ROBBERS   United Artists, 1973
HOT STUFF   Columbia, 1979, w/Michael Kane
THE STEPFATHER   New Century/Vista, 1987
WHY ME?   Triumph, 1990, w/Leonard Maas Jr.
THE GRIFTERS ★   Cineplex Odeon/Miramax, 1990

Screenplays:
LOVE IN THE ATTIC

ELLEN WESTON*
Contact: WGA - Los Angeles, 310/550-1000

Screenplays:
STATE OF THE UNION w/Joyce Brotman

ERIC WESTON
Agent: ICM - Beverly Hills, 310/550-4000

EVILSPEAK   The Frank Moreno Co., 1982,
   w/Joseph Garfalo, directed
MARVIN AND TIGE   *LIKE FATHER AND SON*   20th Century-Fox
   International Classics, 1983, w/Wanda Dell, directed
THE IRON TRIANGLE   Scotti Bros., 1989, w/John Bushelman &
   Larry Hilbrand, directed

Screenplays:
DANGEROUS PLACES

HASKELL WEXLER

Agent: Sanford-Gross & Associates - Los Angeles, 310/208-2100
Business: 1341 Ocean Ave. - Suite 111, Santa Monica, CA 90401,
310/395-0090

MEDIUM COOL   Paramount, 1969, directed
LATINO   Cinecom, 1985, directed

MILTON WEXLER*

Contact: WGA - Los Angeles, 310/550-1000

THE MAN WHO LOVED WOMEN   Columbia, 1983,
w/Blake Edwards & Geoffrey Edwards
THAT'S LIFE!   Columbia, 1986, w/Blake Edwards

NORMAN WEXLER*

Contact: 203/629-2866

PRIVATE OPENING (P)
JOE ★   Cannon, 1970
SERPICO ★   Paramount, 1973, w/Waldo Salt
MANDINGO   Paramount, 1975
DRUM   United Artists, 1976
SATURDAY NIGHT FEVER   Paramount, 1977
STAYING ALIVE   Paramount, 1983, w/Sylvester Stallone
RAW DEAL   DEG, 1986, w/Gary DeVore

Screenplays:
LETHAL GAS
ONE JUST MAN
POWER TRIP
LUNATICS
ANATOMY OF A BURGLARY
GROWING SEASON
BOYD

JAMES WHALEY

Agent: Seifert Dench Associates, 24 D'Arblay St., London W1V 3FH,
071/437-4551, fax 439-1335

CAR TROUBLE   Thorn-EMI, 1986, w/A.J. Tipping
ENID IS SLEEPING   Vestron, 1991, w/A.J. Tipping &
Maurice Phillips

JOSEPH WHALEY

Agent: Warden, White & Kane - Beverly Hills, 213/852-1028

BODILY HARM   Rysher Entertainment, 1994,
w/Ronda Barendse & James Lemmo

Screenplays:
THE PROMISE w/Ronda Barendse

JIM WHEAT*

Agent: The Gersh Agency - Beverly Hills, 310/274-6611

SILENT SCREAM   American Cinema, 1980, w/Ken Wheat &
Wallace Bennett
LIES   International Film Marketing, 1983,
w/Ken Wheat, co-directed
THE FLY II   20th Century Fox, 1989, w/Frank Darabont,
Mick Garris & Ken Wheat
AFTER MIDNIGHT   MGM/UA, 1989,
w/Ken Wheat, co-directed
A NIGHTMARE ON ELM STREET 4: THE DREAM MASTER
New Line Cinema, 1988, w/Ken Wheat as "Scott Pierce" &
Brian Helgeland
THE BIRDS II: LAND'S END (CTF)   Rosemont/MCA Television
Entertainment, w/Ken Wheat & Robert Eisele

Screenplays:
MUTATION w/Ken Wheat

KEN WHEAT*

Agent: The Gersh Agency - Beverly Hills, 310/274-6611

SILENT SCREAM   American Cinema, 1980, w/Jim Wheat &
Wallace Bennett
LIES   International Film Marketing, 1983, w/Jim Wheat, co-directed
THE FLY II   20th Century Fox, 1989, w/Frank Darabont,
Mick Garris & w/Jim Wheat
AFTER MIDNIGHT   MGM/UA, 1989, w/Jim Wheat, co-directed
A NIGHTMARE ON ELM STREET 4: THE DREAM MASTER
New Line Cinema, 1988, w/Jim Wheat as "Scott Pierce" &
Brian Helgeland
THE BIRDS II: LAND'S END (CTF)   Rosemont/MCA Television
Entertainment, w/Jim Wheat & Robert Eisele

Screenplays:
MUTATION w/Jim Wheat

JOSS WHEDON*

Agent: United Talent Agency - Beverly Hills, 310/273-6700

BUFFY THE VAMPIRE SLAYER   20th Century Fox, 1992

Screenplays:
AFTERLIFE
TOY STORY (AF)
ALIENS 4
SUSPENSION
NOBODY MOVE
IN YOUR EYES

ANNE WHEELER

Agent: Writers & Artists Agency - Los Angeles, 310/824-6300
Business: Wheeler Hendren Enterprises Ltd., R.R. 1, 212 Sunset Dr.,
Ganges, British Columbia V0A 1E0, Canada, 604/537-9916

LOYALTIES   Norstar Releasing, 1986, directed
BYE BYE BLUES   Circle Releasing, 1989, directed
ANGEL SQUARE   Miramax, 1991, w/James DeFelice, directed

DOUGLAS N. WHEELER*

Contact: WGA - Los Angeles, 310/550-1000

Screenplays:
TOOTS IN SOLITUDE
ONLY YOU
LONG DAY BEFORE DARK

PAUL WHEELER*

Agent: The Marion Rosenberg Office - Los Angeles, 213/653-7383

PUPPET ON A CHAIN   Cinerama Releasing Corporation, 1972,
w/Alistair MacLean & Don Sharp
CARAVAN TO VACCARES   Crowndale, 1974
RANSOM   *THE TERRORISTS*   Universal-International, 1975
THE LEGACY   Columbia, 1978, w/Jimmy Sangster & Patrick Tilley
A BREED APART   Orion, 1984

GRAEME WHIFLER*

Contact: WGA - Los Angeles, 310/550-1000

SONNY BOY   Triumph, 1990
DR. GIGGLES   Universal, 1992, w/Manny Coto

CYNTHIA WHITCOMB*

Agent: ICM - Beverly Hills, 310/550-4000

MARK TWAIN AND ME (CTF)   Chilmark Productions Inc./Disney
Channel, 1991

DIZ WHITE

BULLSHOT!   Island Alive, 1983, w/Ron House & Alan Shearman

GARRY MICHAEL WHITE*
Agent: Broder-Kurland-Webb-Uffner - Beverly Hills, 310/281-3400

SCARECROW   Warner Bros., 1973
SKY RIDERS   20th Century-Fox, 1976, w/Jack DeWitt &
   Stanley Mann
THE PROMISE   Universal, 1979

J.B. WHITE
Agent: William Morris Agency - Beverly Hills, 310/274-7451

Screenplays:
DOCTOR, LAWYER, INDIAN CHIEF

JIMMY WHITE
Agent: Jon Klane Agency - Beverly Hills, 310/278-0178

Screenplays:
HUNTER'S MOON
'LIL MAN
RED MONEY
THE BETTER HALF
THE BO JACKSON STORY
CRABS IN A BASKET
THE BRAVE AND THE FREE
SUMMER RAIN

KIMBERLY LYNN WHITE
BODY ROCK   New World, 1984,   Story w/Desmond Nakano

NONI WHITE*
Agent: Richland/Wunsch/Hohman Agency - Los Angeles,
   310/278-1955

NEWSIES   Buena Vista, 1992, w/Bob Tzudiker

Screenplays:
TEMPTED w/Bob Tzudiker
LUCK w/Bob Tzudiker
ROGER RABBIT II w/Bob Tzudiker
THE FROG PRINCE (AF) w/Bob Tzudiker

WALLY WHITE
Contact: Grainy Pictures, Miramax

LIE DOWN WITH DOGS   Miramax, 1995, directed

TED WHITEHEAD
Agent: The Casarotto Company - London, 71/287-4450

THE LIFE AND LOVES OF A SHE-DEVIL (CMS) A&E, 1987
THE CLONING OF JOANNA MAY (CTF)   Granada Television/
   A&E, 1992

HUGH J. WHITEMORE*
Agent: Rosenstone/Wender - New York, 212/832-8330

BREAKING THE CODE (P)
PACK OF LIES (P)   also teleplay
THE BEST OF FRIENDS (P)
ALL NEAT IN BLACK STOCKINGS   National General, 1969,
   w/Jane Gaskell
ALL CREATURES GREAT AND SMALL   EMI, 1974
MAN AT THE TOP   Anglo-EMI, 1975
THE BLUE BIRD   20th Century-Fox, 1976, w/Alfred Hayes &
   Alexei Kapler
STEVIE   First Artists, 1978, from his play
THE RETURN OF THE SOLDIER   European Classics, 1985
84 CHARING CROSS ROAD   Columbia, 1987
UTZ   Viva Pictures/BBC Films, 1992
JANE EYRE   Miramax, 1995

RICHARD F. WHITLEY*
Manager: Creative Alliance Management - Los Angeles,
   213/962-6090

ROCK'N'ROLL HIGH SCHOOL   New World, 1979,
   w/Russ Dvonch & Joseph McBride
PANDEMONIUM   MGM/UA, 1982, w/Jaime Klein

Screenplays:
CHARLIE & MORRY
ESKIMO SUMMER
GETTING IT OVER WITH w/Russ Dvonch & Amy Heckerling
UNTITLED A-GO-GO w/Amy Heckerling
ROAD TO RUIN w/Jaime Klein
THE PERFECT MAN
RED HERRING
REGATTA w/Jaime Klein
THE CHICAGO KID
BLUE BLOOD
SOMETHING IN THE PARK
DREAM CHASERS
CAT & MOUSE
PRACTICALLY A JOKE
UNDER THE GUN
LIFE STORY
DEATH OF ME YET
HERO SHOT

JOHN WHITMAN*
Contact: WGA - Los Angeles, 310/550-1000

YOUNGBLOOD   MGM/UA, 1986, Story w/Peter Markle

PRESTON WHITMORE II*
Agent: William Morris Agency - Beverly Hills, 310/274-7451

Screenplays:
BLUELIGHT w/Eddie Griffin
THE NUMBER FOUR
BLACK MARIA
24-7
THE WALKING DEAD
THE SEEKERS

STANFORD C. WHITMORE*
Agent: Paradigm - Los Angeles, 310/277-4400

WAR HUNT   TD Enterprises, 1961
HAMMERSMITH IS OUT   Cinerama, 1972
BABY BLUE MARINE   Columbia, 1976
THE DARK   Film Ventures International, 1979

Screenplays:
ALICIA'S BOOK
FLOWER CHILD

STEVEN WHITNEY*
Agent: Camden-ITG - Los Angeles, 310/289-2700

SURVIVE THE NIGHT (CTF)   Heartstar Productions/
   Once Upon a Time, 1993, directed

JAMES WHITTAKER
MEGAFORCE   20th Century-Fox, 1982, w/Albert S. Ruddy,
   Hal Needham & Andre Morgan

Screenplays:
MUSIC CITY BLUES

STEPHEN WHITTAKER
Agent: Becsey/Wisdom/Kalajian Agency - Los Angeles, 310/550-0535
   or Nigel Britten, Lemon, Unna & Durbridge - London, 071/727-1346

CLOSING NUMBERS   Channel Four, 1994, directed

CORMAC WIBBERLEY
Agent: ICM - Beverly Hills, 310/550-4000

Screenplays:
THE KID WHO STOLE CHRISTMAS w/Marianne Wibberley

MARIANNE WIBBERLEY
Agent: ICM - Beverly Hills, 310/550-4000

Screenplays:
THE KID WHO STOLE CHRISTMAS w/Cormac Wibberley

DAVID WICKES
Agent: William Morris Agency - Beverly Hills, 310/274-7451

SILVER DREAM RACER   Almi Cinema 5, 1980, directed
FRANKENSTEIN (CTF)   TNT/David Wickes Productions,
  1993, directed

W.W. WICKET
(See Clifford & Ellen GREEN)

CHRISTOPHER WICKING
SCREAM AND SCREAM AGAIN   American International, 1969
CRY OF THE BANSHEE   American International, 1970,
  w/Tim Kelly
BLOOD FROM THE MUMMY'S TOMB   Hammer, 1971
TO THE DEVIL A DAUGHTER   EMI, 1976
LADY CHATTERLEY'S LOVER   Cannon, 1982, w/Just Jaeckin
ABSOLUTE BEGINNERS   Orion, 1986, w/Richard Burridge &
  Don MacPherson

HENRY WIDEMAN JR.
DOC'S FULL SERVICE   Brazos Films, 1994, w/Kim Henkel &
  Eagle Pennell

GREGORY C. WIDEN*
Agent: Above the Line - West Hollywood, 310/859-6115

HIGHLANDER   20th Century Fox, 1986, w/Peter Bellwood &
  Larry Ferguson
BACKDRAFT   Universal, 1991
GOD'S ARMY   First Look Pictures, 1994, directed

Screenplays:
*URBAN LEGENDS w/Randy Johnson, William Judkins,
  Donald Knowlton & Ethan Wiley*
SHOOTERS
DELERIUM 237
O.S.S.
CLAN OF ONE
SHADOW WARRIORS

KEN WIEDERHORN*
Agent: The Marion Rosenberg Office - Los Angeles, 213/653-7383

SHOCK WAVES   Joseph Brenner Associates, 1977,
  w/John Harrison, directed
RETURN OF THE LIVING DEAD PART II   Lorimar, 1988, directed
DARK TOWER   Spectrafilm, 1989, w/Robert J.Avrech &
  Ken Blackwell
A HOUSE IN THE HILLS   LIVE Entertainment, 1993,
  w/Miguel Tejada-Flores, directed

CHARLES WIENER
RECRUITS   Concorde, 1986, w/B.K. Roderick

ROBERT WIENER*
Contact: WGA - Los Angeles, 310/550-1000

Screenplays:
LIVE FROM BAGHDAD w/Richard Chapman

JOHN WIERICK*
Agent: The Gersh Agency - Beverly Hills, 310/274-6611

BOPHA!   Paramount, 1993, w/Brian Bird

Screenplays:
MAGNOLIA PASSION w/Brian Bird

JOE WIESENFELD*
Contact: WGA - Los Angeles, 310/550-1000

PRINCES IN EXILE   Cinepix/National Film Board, 1991

STEVEN WILDE*
Manager: 3 Arts Entertainment - Los Angeles, 213/851-5700

SHAKING THE TREE   Miramax, 1992, w/Duane Clark

Screenplays:
PRINCE OF NEW YORK w/Duane Clark
HOOPS w/Duane Clark

BILLY WILDER*
Agent: Paul Kohner, Inc. - Beverly Hills, 310/550-1060

MAUVAISE GRAINE   1933, Shared, directed
MUSIC IN THE AIR   20th Century-Fox, 1934, w/Howard Young
CHAMPAGNE WALTZ   Paramount, 1937, w/Story w/H.S. Kraft &
  Vienna Hall
BLUEBEARD'S EIGHTH WIFE   Paramount, 1938,
  w/Charles Brackett
MIDNIGHT   Paramount, 1939, w/Charles Brackett
NINOTCHKA ★   MGM, 1939, w/Charles Brackett & Walter Reisch
ARISE MY LOVE   Paramount, 1940, w/Charles Brackett
HOLD BACK THE DAWN ★   Paramount, 1941, w/Charles Brackett
THE MAJOR AND THE MINOR   Paramount, 1942,
  w/Charles Brackett
BALL OF FIRE   Goldwyn, 1942, w/Charles Brackett
FIVE GRAVES TO CAIRO   Paramount, 1943,
  w/Charles Brackett, directed
DOUBLE INDEMNITY ★   Paramount, 1944,
  w/Raymond Chandler, directed
THE LOST WEEKEND   Paramount, 1945,
  w/Charles Brackett, directed
THE EMPEROR WALTZ   Paramount, 1948,
  w/Charles Brackett, directed
A FOREIGN AFFAIR ★   Paramount, 1948, w/Charles Brackett &
  Richard Breen, directed
SUNSET BOULEVARD ★★   Paramount, 1950,
  w/Charles Brackett & D.M. Marshman Jr., directed
ACE IN THE HOLE ★★   Paramount, 1951, w/Walter Newman &
  Leslie Samuels, directed
STALAG 17   Paramount, 1953, w/Edwin Blum, directed
SABRINA   Paramount, 1954, w/Ernest Lehman &
  Samuel Taylor, directed
THE SEVEN YEAR ITCH   20th Century-Fox, 1955,
  w/George Axelrod, directed
THE SPIRIT OF ST. LOUIS   Warner Bros., 1957,
  w/Wendell Mayes, directed
LOVE IN THE AFTERNOON   Allied Artists, 1957,
  w/I.A.L. Diamond, directed
WITNESS FOR THE PROSECUTION   United Artists, 1957,
  w/Harry Kurnitz, directed
SOME LIKE IT HOT   United Artists, 1959,
  w/I.A.L. Diamond, directed
THE APARTMENT ★★   United Artists, 1960,
  w/I.A.L. Diamond, directed
ONE, TWO, THREE   United Artists, 1961, w/I.A.L. Diamond, directed
IRMA LA DOUCE   United Artists, 1963, w/I.A.L. Diamond, directed
KISS ME, STUPID   United Artists, 1964, w/I.A.L. Diamond, directed
THE FORTUNE COOKIE ★   United Artists, 1966,
  w/I.A.L. Diamond, directed
THE PRIVATE LIFE OF SHERLOCK HOLMES   United Artists, 1970,
  w/I.A.L. Diamond, directed
AVANTI!   United Artists, 1972, w/I.A.L. Diamond, directed
THE FRONT PAGE   Universal, 1974, w/I.A.L. Diamond, directed
FEDORA   United Artists, 1979, w/I.A.L. Diamond, directed
BUDDY BUDDY   MGM/United Artists, 1981, w/I.A.L. Diamond, directed

DAVID WILDER
KNIGHTS OF THE CITY   New World, 1986,
   Story w/Leon Isaac Kennedy

GENE WILDER*
Agent: CAA - Beverly Hills, 310/288-4545

THE ADVENTURE OF SHERLOCK HOLMES' SMARTER BROTHER
   20th Century-Fox, 1975, directed
YOUNG FRANKENSTEIN ★   20th Century-Fox, 1974,
   w/Mel Brooks
THE WORLD'S GREATEST LOVER   20th Century-Fox,
   1977, directed
SUNDAY LOVERS   MGM/UA, 1981, w/Leslie Bricusse &
   Francis Veber
THE WOMAN IN RED   Orion, 1984, directed
HAUNTED HONEYMOON   Orion, 1986,
   w/Terence Marsh, directed
SEE NO EVIL, HEAR NO EVIL   Tri-Star, 1989, w/Earl Barret,
   Andrew Kurtzman, Arne Sultan & Elliot Wald

JOHN KEITH WILDER*
Agent: CAA - Beverly Hills, 310/288-4545

Screenplays:
THE RIFLEMAN
NEVER SAY DIE
THE LAST OF THE BREED

ETHAN WILEY*
Agent: Above the Line - West Hollywood, 310/859-6115

HOUSE   New World, 1986
HOUSE II: THE SECOND STORY   New World, 1987, directed

Screenplays:
TALL TALES
DETECTIVE POOCH
RED IVORY
JOSH
A STRANGER IN LEADVILLE
DEVIL'S HIGHWAY
URBAN LEGENDS w/Randy Johnson, Gregory Widen,
   William Judkins & Donald Knowlton
SPIDERMAN

RALPH WILEY
Agent: CAA - Beverly Hills, 310/288-4545

Screenplays:
HOOP DREAMS (Fine Line)

JOEL WILF*
Contact: WGA - Los Angeles, 310/550-1000

Screenplays:
THE NEXT BIG THING w/William Schifrin

JEFF WILHELM*
Agent: The Artists Agency - Los Angeles, 310/277-7779

Screenplays:
CAREER MOVES
THE BIG RASCALS
NO PLACE FOR A DAME

KATE WILHELM
THE LOOKALIKE (CTF)   Gallo Entertainment Inc., 1990, Story

DIANE E. WILK*
Agent: William Morris Agency - Beverly Hills, 310/274-7451

Screenplays:
THINGS HAPPEN
TWO LITTLE RICH GIRLS

RICH WILKES*
Agent: ICM - Beverly Hills, 310/550-4000

AIRHEADS   20th Century Fox, 1994
THE STONED AGE   Trimark, 1994, w/Jim Melkonian
THE JERKY BOYS   Buena Vista, 1995, w/Jim Melkonian,
   Kamal Ahmed & John G. Brennan

Screenplays:
BEER MONEY
CRUZ

MIKE WILKINS
Agent: Jon Klane Agency - Beverly Hills, 310/278-0178

Screenplays:
WILD MEN
MORTYVISION

AL WILLIAMS
ARACHNOPHOBIA   Buena Vista, 1990, Story w/Don Jakoby

BRIAN WILLIAMS
SMOKEY BITES THE DUST   New World, 1981, Story

BRUCE WILLIAMS
PRIVATE COLLECTIONS   Red Wing Productions, 1990,
   w/David Heisler, directed

BUCKEYE WILLIAMS
Agent: The Marion Rosenberg Office - Los Angeles, 213/653-7383

Screenplays:
HEARTSTOPPER

CYNTHIA WILLIAMS
Agent: Richland/Wunsch/Hohman Agency - Los Angeles,
   310/278-1955

Screenplays:
SMALL TOWN
HARD BREAKFAST
THERE ARE NO WITCHES

ERIC WILLIAMS
Agent: United Talent Agency - Beverly Hills, 310/273-6700

Screenplays:
MAD CITY (Story w/Tom Matthews)

GARRY WILLIAMS*
Agent: Monteiro Rose Agency - Encino, 818/501-1177

RAIN (P)
REBELS (P)   w/Stephen H. Ridenour
A DEATH IN BETHANY (P)

Screenplays:
BROWN-EYED GIRL
NICKEL AND DIME
TORNADO ALLEY w/Peter Fox

JASON WILLIAMS
DANGER ZONE II: REAPER'S REVENGE   Skouras Pictures, 1989,
   Story w/Tom Friedman
DANGER ZONE III: STEEL HORSE WAR   Dead Zone Company,
   1990, w/Gregory Poirier

LARRY B. WILLIAMS*
Agent: The Gersh Agency - Beverly Hills, 310/274-6611

SPACECAMP   20th Century Fox, 1986, Story w/Patrick Bailey

Screenplays:
ELVES w/Charles Kaufman
WENDELL WILCOX AND THE MONSTER MAKERS
*   w/Charles Kaufman*
THE MAN WHO COULD WORK MIRACLES
GIZMERELDA
PENNY TO THE FERRYMAN
IFFY
ROADS
SPIRIT MOVES
PRESTIDIGITATION
EDISON

LORRAINE WILLIAMS*
Contact: WGA - Los Angeles, 310/550-1000

CARAVANS   Ibex, 1978, w/Nancy Voyles Crawford &
    Thomas A. McMahon

MAIYA WILLIAMS*
Agent: United Talent Agency - Beverly Hills, 310/273-6700

Screenplays:
BUFFALO SOLDIERS

MATT WILLIAMS*
Agent: APA - Los Angeles, 310/273-0744

WILD HEARTS CAN'T BE BROKEN   Buena Vista, 1991,
    w/Oley Sassone

NIGEL WILLIAMS
Agent: Judy Daish Agency - London, 071/486-5405

COUNTRY DANCING (P)

OSCAR WILLIAMS*
Contact: Shelly Surpin, Esq., 213/858-0682

FIVE ON THE BLACK HAND SIDE   United Artists,
    1973, directed
HOT POTATO   Warner Bros., 1976, directed

ROBERT F. WILLIAMS*
Contact: WGA - Los Angeles, 310/550-1000

ESCAPE 2000   New World, 1983, Story w/David Lawrence &
    George Schenck

ROBERT G. WILLIAMS
Address: 920 N. Kings Road - #216, Los Angeles, CA 90069,
    213/848-7384

Screenplays:
DEADLY REALITY w/Kelly B. Sims
POWER OF ATTORNEY w/Kelly B. Sims
GEAR DRIVEN w/Kelly B. Sims
MORTAL RELATIONS w/Kelly B. Sims
POULTRYGEIST!!! w/Kelly B. Sims

SUSAN WILLIAMS*
Contact: WGA - New York, 212/245-6180

AMERICAN ANTHEM   Columbia, 1986, Story w/Evan Archerd &
    Jeff Benjamin

TIMOTHY WILLIAMS*
Agent: The Agency - Los Angeles, 310/551-3000
Contact: Todd Harris, Davis Ent., 310/551-2266

Screenplays:
SPELLS

TYGER WILLIAMS
Agent: ICM - Beverly Hills, 310/550-4000

MENACE II SOCIETY   New Line Cinema, 1993

Screenplays:
FLAVORTALE
TUMBLIN' DOWN

DAVID WILLIAMSON*
Agent: William Morris Agency - Beverly Hills, 310/274-7451

MONEY AND FRIENDS (P)
"JOCK" PETERSEN   Avco Embassy, 1975
ELIZA FRASER   Hexagon, 1976
DON'S PARTY   Satori, 1976, from his play
GALLIPOLI   Paramount, 1981
THE CLUB   Roadshow Distributors, 1982
THE YEAR OF LIVING DANGEROUSLY   MGM/UA, 1983,
    w/Peter Weir & C.J. Koch
PHAR LAP   20th Century-Fox, 1984
TRAVELLING NORTH   Cineplex Odeon, 1987, from his play
A DANGEROUS LIFE (CMS)   HBO/McElroy & McElroy/FilmAccord
    Corp./Australian Broadcasting Corp./Zenith Productions, 1988
EMERALD CITY   Limelight Production Pty Ltd., 1989, from his play

Screenplays:
THE WARRIORS OF THE RAINBOW w/John Briley
*   (Transatlantic Enterprises)*
SELLING THE WAR
MATA HARI
BRADVIK
PAY THE WIDOW

JEFF WILLIAMSON
ONE DOWN TWO TO GO   Almi Pictures, 1982

KEVIN WILLIAMSON
Agent: APA - Los Angeles, 310/273-0744

Screenplays:
KILLING MRS. TINGLE

TONY WILLIAMSON
NIGHT WATCH   Avco Embassy, 1973
SERGEANT STEINER   Palladium, 1979
BREAKTHROUGH   Maverick Pictures International, 1981

CALDER WILLINGHAM*
Agent: United Talent Agency - Beverly Hills, 310/273-6700

PATHS OF GLORY   United Artists, 1957, w/Stanley Kubrick &
    Jim Thompson
THE STRANGE ONE   Columbia, 1957
THE VIKINGS   United Artists, 1958
ONE-EYED JACKS   Paramount, 1961, w/Guy Trosper
THE GRADUATE ★   Avco Embassy, 1967, w/Buck Henry
LITTLE BIG MAN   National General, 1970
THIEVES LIKE US   United Artists, 1974, w/Robert Altman &
    Joan Tewkesbury
RAMBLING ROSE   7 Arts/New Line Cinema, 1991

Screenplays:
GERALDINE BRADSHAW
STILLWELL w/George MacDonald Fraser
THE LUTHER PROJECT
APRIL FOOLS

BRUCE WILLIS
Agent: William Morris Agency - Beverly Hills, 310/274-7451
Business: Flying Heart Films, Columbia Pictures, 310/576-0521

HUDSON HAWK   Tri-Star, 1991, Story w/Robert Kraft &
    Steven de Souza

Wi

**FILM
WRITERS
GUIDE**

**F
I
L
M

W
R
I
T
E
R
S**

BRUCE WILSON
Agent: Solomon Weingarten & Associates - Los Angeles,
310/479-4706
Address: 305 W. Garfield, Seattle, WA 98119, 206/282-9581

DOUBLES   Shapiro Entertainment, 1978, directed
BOMBS AWAY   Shapiro Entertainment, 1985, w/Ed Mast, directed

DAVID CAMPBELL WILSON*
Agent: William Morris Agency - Beverly Hills, 310/274-7451

THE PERFECT WEAPON   Paramount, 1991

Screenplays:
SHANGO

GAHAN WILSON
Agent: APA - Los Angeles, 310/273-0744

THE FREEWAY MANIAC   Cannon, 1989, w/Paul Winters

Screenplays:
TALES FROM THE DARKSIDE: THE MOVIE II w/Michael McDowell

HUGH WILSON*
Agent: William Morris Agency - Beverly Hills, 310/274-7451

STROKER ACE   Universal, 1983, w/Hal Needham
POLICE ACADEMY   The Ladd Company/Warner Bros., 1984,
w/Neal Israel & Pat Proft, directed
RUSTLERS' RHAPSODY   Paramount, 1985, directed
BURGLAR   Warner Bros., 1987, w/Joseph Loeb III &
Matthew Weisman
GUARDING TESS   TriStar, 1994, w/Peter Torokvei, directed

Screenplays:
ARRIVE ALIVE
TEXANS
COLOR MAN
BROTHERS-IN-LAW

JULIA WILSON
THE GAME   Visual Perspectives, 1989, w/Curtis Brown

KENT WILSON
Agent: Neal Stevens & Associates - Beverly Hills, 310/275-7541

Screenplays:
AGAINST THE WIND w/John Scott

KEVIN WILSON
WILD HORSE   Satori, 1984

LANFORD WILSON*
Agent: ICM - New York, 212/556-5600

BURN THIS (P)   also screenplay

Screenplays:
BACK HOME

LARRY WILSON*
Agent: William Morris Agency - Beverly Hills, 310/274-7451

BEETLEJUICE   Warner Bros., 1988, Story w/Michael McDowell
THE ADDAMS FAMILY   Paramount, 1991, w/Caroline Thompson &
Paul Rudnick

Screenplays:
CONCRETE w/Paul Chadwick (directing)
ROUGE w/Caroline Thompson
MAI, THE PSYCHIC GIRL w/Caroline Thompson
THE GEEK w/Caroline Thompson
MIDKNIGHT w/Caroline Thompson
ESCAPE FROM CAMP WANNABARF w/Mike Judge

LEE WILSON
THE ELF AND THE MAGIC KEY (CTF)   USA Network/
Rim of the World Productions, 1993

MICHAEL G. WILSON*
Business Manager: Gregory C. Davis - 310/557-0761

FOR YOUR EYES ONLY   MGM/United Artists, 1981,
w/Richard Maibaum
OCTOPUSSY   MGM/UA, 1983 w/George MacDonald Fraser &
Richard Maibaum
A VIEW TO A KILL   MGM/UA, 1985, w/Richard Maibaum
THE LIVING DAYLIGHTS   MGM/UA, 1987, w/Richard Maibaum
LICENCE TO KILL   MGM/UA, 1989, w/Richard Maibaum

MICHAEL J. WILSON*
Agent: CAA - Beverly Hills, 310/288-4545

Screenplays:
CONRAD JONES
THE MOUTH

OWEN WILSON
Agent: United Talent Agency - Beverly Hills, 310/273-6700

BOTTLE ROCKET   Columbia, 1995, w/Wes Anderson,
from their short film

RALPH GABY WILSON*
Agent: Paradigm - Los Angeles, 310/277-4400

Screenplays:
SUMMER JOB (Sony Pictures)
OUTSIDE CHANCES (Concorde)
INSIDE THE LOVE HOUSE (Concorde)
BITTERSWEET BRONZE
JOE & RONNA
RATTLESNAKE
HARDBALL
SASQUATCH RITES
LEGACY OF EVIL
THE SUMMONING
THE GREED ANTECEDENT
THREE LOST SOULS

ROGER WILSON*
Agent: The Agency - Los Angeles, 310/551-3000

Screenplays:
THROUGH THE TREES
MIA: MISSING IN ACTION
EYE OF THE BEHOLDER

SANDY WILSON
MY AMERICAN COUSIN   Spectrafilm, 1985, directed
AMERICAN BOYFRIENDS   Alliance Entertainment, 1989, directed

SNOO WILSON
Agent: Writers & Artists Agency - Los Angeles, 310/824-6300

THE PLEASURE PRINCIPLE (P)
VAMPIRE (P)
THE NUMBER OF THE BEAST (P)
THE GLAD HAND (P)
THE GRASS WIDOW (P)
MORE LIGHT (P)
80 DAYS (P)
CALLAS (P)
DARWINS FLOOD (P)
HRH (P)
BLUE VIENNA (P)
SHADEY   Skouras Pictures, 1986

Screenplays:
THE GRASS WIDOW
ZODIAC
ORPHEUS IN THE UNDERWORLD

S.S. WILSON*
(Steven S. Wilson)
Manager: The Roberts Company - Los Angeles, 310/552-7800

SHORT CIRCUIT   Tri-Star, 1986, w/Brent Maddock
BATTERIES NOT INCLUDED   Universal, 1987, w/Brad Bird,
   Brent Maddock & Matthew Robbins
SHORT CIRCUIT II   Tri-Star, 1988, w/Brent Maddock
TREMORS   Universal, 1990, w/Brent Maddock
GHOST DAD   Universal, 1990, w/Brent Maddock &
   Chris Reese
HEART AND SOULS   Universal, 1993, w/Brent Maddock,
   Erik Hansen & Greg Hansen

Screenplays:
LINES OF FORCE w/Brent Maddock

DAVID G. WILTSE*
Agent: William Morris Agency - New York, 212/586-5100

HURRY UP OR I'LL BE 30   Avco Embassy, 1973,
   w/Joseph Jacoby
THE ASCENT   RHI Entertainment, 1994

Screenplays:
UNDERGROUND

DARRYL WIMBERLY
Agent: Media Artsts Group - Beverly Hills, 213/658-7434

Screenplays:
SUBTERFUGE
THE LINE
THICKER THAN WATER
DEAD MAN'S BAY
A TINKER'S DAMN
FAIR HAIR
JACK-MAN
LOVE THY FATHER
WHITEWATER

KURT WIMMER
Agent: ICM - Beverly Hills, 310/550-4000

DOUBLE TROUBLE   Motion Picture Corporation of America,
   1992, w/Jeffrey Kerns & Chuck Osbourne
RELATIVE FEAR   Norstar, 1994

Screenplays:
SECOND DEFENSE

CHRIS WINDSOR
BIG MEAT EATER   New Line Cinema, 1984,
   w/Laurence Keane & Phil Savath,   directed

TERRY WINDSOR
FOOL'S GOLD: THE STORY OF THE BRINK'S-MAT ROBBERY
   LWT Production/ITV, 1994, w/Jeff Pope,   directed

MICHAEL WING
THE KISSING PLACE (CTF)   Wilshire Court Productions, 1990,
   w/Richard Altabef & Cynthia A. Cherbak

JENNY WINGFIELD*
Agent: Maggie Field Agency - Studio City, 818/980-2001

THE MAN IN THE MOON   MGM, 1991

Screenplays:
AN INVISIBLE SUMMER

ANTHONY WINKLER*
Manager: Carlyle Management & Productions - Los Angeles,
   213/469-3086

THE LUNATIC   Triton Pictures, 1992

Screenplays:
THE ASSASSINATION OF FISH

CHARLES WINKLER
Agent: The Gersh Agency - Beverly Hills, 310/274-6611

YOU TALKIN' TO ME?   MGM/UA, 1987,   directed
DISTURBED   Odyssey-Cinecom, 1990, w/Emerson Bixby,   directed

DAVID WINKLER*
Agent: Susan Smith & Associates - Beverly Hills, 213/852-4777

Screenplays:
MAN OF THE HOUSE
CAB

IRWIN WINKLER*
Agent: CAA - Beverly Hills, 310/288-4545
Business: Winkler Films, 211 S. Beverly Dr. - Suite 200, Beverly Hills,
   CA 90212, 310/858-5780

GUILTY BY SUSPICION   Warner Bros., 1991,   directed

TERENCE H. WINKLESS
Agent: Peter Turner Agency - Santa Monica, 310/315-4772

THE HOWLING   Avco Embassy, 1981, w/John Sayles
HE'S MY GIRL   Scotti Bros., 1987, Story w/Taylor Ames &
   Peter Bergman
CORPORATE AFFAIRS   Concorde, 1990,
   w/Geoffrey Baere,   directed

Screenplays:
RAGE AND HONOR (directing)
FIVE CAR STUD w/Alec Lorimore
SEQUENCE w/Alec Lorimore
FAST LANE w/Alec Lorimore
OUT OF THE BOX w/Alec Lorimore
TOO GOOD TO BE TRUE w/Alec Lorimore
THE GREAT CAPE GIRARDEAU LEAP w/ Alec Lorimore
WASHINGTON PAGES w/Alec Lorimore
THE JETSONS w/Alec Lorimore
VODONE w/Alec Lorimore
THE RUNNER w/Alec Lorimore
BORN TOO COOL
BLOODFIST

MICHAEL WINNER*
Agent: ICM - Beverly Hills, 310/550-4000
Business: Scimitar Films, Ltd., 6-8 Sackville St., London, W1X 1DD,
   England, 071/734-8385

FIREPOWER   ITC, 1977, Story w/Bill Kerby,   directed
THE SENTINEL   Universal, 1977, w/Jeffrey Konvitz,   directed
THE BIG SLEEP   United Artists, 1978,   directed
THE WICKED LADY   MGM/UA, 1983, w/Leslie Arliss,   directed
APPOINTMENT WITH DEATH   Cannon, 1988, w/Peter Buckman &
   Anthony Shaffer,   directed
A CHORUS OF DISAPPROVAL   South Gate Entertainment, 1989,
   w/Alan Ayckbourn,   directed
BULLSEYE!   21st Century Film Corporation, 1991,
   Story w/Leslie Bricusse & Nick Mead,   directed
DIRTY WEEKEND   UIP, 1993, w/Helen Zahavi,   directed

Screenplays:
PARTING SHOTS w/Nick Mead (directing)

JERRY WINNICK*
Contact: 818/342-0221

Screenplays:
WELCOME TO ZIMM'S

DAVID WINNING
KILLER IMAGE   Groundstar Entertainment, 1992,
   w/Stan Edmonds & Jaron Summers, directed

SETH WINSTON
Agent: Becsey/Wisdom/Kalajian Agency - Los Angeles,
   310/550-0535
Manager: Melinda Jason - Beverly Hills, 310/289-9140

SHE'S OUT OF CONTROL   Columbia, 1989,
   w/Michael J. Nathanson
SESSION MAN (Short) ★★   1991, directed

ALEX WINTER*
Agent: Sanford-Gross & Associates - Los Angeles, 310/208-2100

SQUEAL OF DEATH (Short)   w/Tom Stern, co-directed
FREAKED   20th Century Fox, 1993, w/Tom Stern &
   Tim Burns, co-directed

Screenplays:
WONDERLAND w/Tom Stern
MILO RIGBY ON WHEELS w/Tom Stern
HOWIE'S REVENGE w/Tom Stern

BRADLEY T. WINTER
THE LAST ELEPHANT (CTF)   RHI Entertainment Inc./Quintex
   Entertainment Inc., 1990, Story

PAUL WINTERS
THE FREEWAY MANIAC   Cannon, 1989,
   w/Gahan Wilson, directed

JEANNETTE WINTERSON
Agent: Peters, Fraser & Dunlop - London, 071/376-5999

ORANGES ARE NOT THE ONLY FRUIT   British Broadcasting
   Corp., 1990
GREAT MOMENTS IN AVIATION   Miramax, 1994

TIER WINZE
(Henry Wayne Scheck)
Business: Media Releasing Associates, 300 Leonora St. -
   Suite B356, Seattle, WA 98121, 316/793-9297

Screenplays:
IMPERIAL GREEN-THE FIRST SPACE MOVIE (CMS)
PORT OF EMPIRE (Parts 1-12)

ANTHONY WISDOM
THE RETURN OF SUPERFLY   Triton Pictures, 1990

FOREST WISE
LIFE IS NICE   Freakie Pig Productions, 1990, directed

WILLIAM WISHER*
Agent: The Brandt Company - Sherman Oaks, 818/783-7747

TERMINATOR 2: JUDGMENT DAY   Tri-Star, 1991,
   w/James Cameron

Screenplays:
JUDGE DREDD (Buena Vista)
DAYWORLD
SKIMMER

ELEANOR WITCOMBE*
Contact: Rick Raftos Management, P.O. Box 445, Paddington,
   Sydney, Australia 2021

THE GETTING OF WISDOM   Southern Cross, 1977
MY BRILLIANT CAREER   Analysis, 1980

DAN WITT*
Agent: Above the Line - West Hollywood, 310/859-6115

Screenplays:
DARK AT THE EDGE OF TOWN
BUCKEYE

SUZY WITTEN
Business: Suzy Witten Productions, 855 N. Edinburgh Ave.,
   Los Angeles, CA 90046, 213/651-2467, fax 651-0471

RUNAWAY EDEN   Suzy Witten Productions, 1990, directed

Screenplays:
THE AFFLICTED (THE AFFLICTED GIRLS)
THE ADVENTURES OF PERRINE
THE STAR-SPANGLED GIRL w/Lissa Leff Griffith
10/10THS
MR. WRINKLE AND REX
KAISER MORTUARY w/Gayle Kirschenbaum
THE RAINBOW GYPSIES w/Ricardo & Lothar Delgado

WILLIAM D. WITTLIFF*
Agent: CAA - Beverly Hills, 310/288-4545
Business: 510 Baylor, Austin, TX 78703, 512/476-6821

THE BLACK STALLION   United Artists, 1979,
   w/Melissa Mathison & Jeanne Rosenberg
HONEYSUCKLE ROSE   Warner Bros., 1980, w/John Binder &
   Carol Sobieski
RAGGEDY MAN   Universal, 1981
BARBAROSA   Universal/AFD, 1982
COUNTRY   Buena Vista, 1984
RED HEADED STRANGER   Alive Films, 1987, directed
LONESOME DOVE (TF)   Motown Productions, 1989
THE COWBOY WAY   Universal, 1994
LEGENDS OF THE FALL   TriStar, 1994, w/Susan Shilliday

Screenplays:
WHIRLIGIG
NIGHT IN OLD MEXICO
DEEP ELLUM

STEFAN WODOSLAWSKY
CRAZY MOON   Miramax, 1987, w/Tom Berry

IRA WOHL
BEST BOY (FD)   International Film Exchange, 1980, directed

JOHN WOHLBRUCK*
Contact: WGA - Los Angeles, 310/550-1000

END OF THE LINE   Orion Classics, 1988, w/Jay Russell

PAUL WOLANSKY
DEADLY OBSESSION   Distant Horizon, 1989, w/Brian Cox &
   Jeno Hodi

DAVID M. WOLF*
Contact: WGA - Los Angeles, 310/550-1000

HIT!   Paramount, 1973, w/Alan Trustman

DICK WOLF*
Agent: ICM - Beverly Hills, 310/550-4000
Business: Wolf Films, Universal Studios, 818/777-3131

SKATEBOARD   Universal, 1978, w/George Gage
GAS   Paramount, 1981
NO MAN'S LAND   Orion, 1987
MASQUERADE   MGM/UA, 1988
SCHOOL TIES   Paramount, 1992, w/Darryl Ponicsan

Screenplays:
ACCUSED
THE LAST RIDE

GARY K. WOLF*
Manager: Marty Tudor - 310/247-1660

Screenplays:
TYPHOON LAGOON
FLYING TIGERFISH
GENIE MAN

JAY WOLF*
Agent: Michael Jaffe, The Jaffe Company - 310/319-1617

SILHOUETTE (CTF)   MCA Television Network, 1990,
    w/Victor Buell

Screenplays:
BLUE
NOWHERE FAST w/Vic Buell & Alan Beattie

DIGBY WOLFE*
Contact: Peter Sabiston, 213/826-9732

FIRE AND ICE   Concorde, 1987, w/George Schlatter

GEORGE C. WOLFE*
Agent: ICM - New York, 212/556-5600

QUEENIE PIE (P)
THE COLORED MUSEUM (P)
JELLY'S LAST JAM (P)
SPUNK (P)   also screenplay
BLACKOUT (P)

Screenplays:
FIRE

ANDY WOLFENDON
Agent: Leslie Kallen Agency - Sherman Oaks, 818/906-2785

Screenplays:
SHE'S IN MY CAR

BROOKE WOLFF
Agent: William Morris Agency - Beverly Hills, 310/274-7451

Screenplays:
RENDEZVOUS

JOHN WOLFF
Agent: Above the Line - West Hollywood, 310/859-6115

Screenplays:
VAROOM w/David Engelbach
THE SORCERER'S APPRENTICE w/David Engelbach

MICHELE WOLFF*
Contact: WGA - Los Angeles, 310/550-1000

Screenplays:
THE WHITE HOUSE

PAUL WOLFF*
Agent: The Coppage Company - North Hollywood, 818/980-1106

Screenplays:
MOZZARELLA
ANTHONY AND GINA
OPEN HOUSE

RUTH WOLFF*
Agent: Paul Kohner, Inc. - Beverly Hills, 310/550-1060

THE ABDICATION   Warner Bros., 1974, from her play
THE INCREDIBLE SARAH   Avco Embassy, 1976

JUDITH SHERMAN WOLIN
WELCOME TO 18   American Distribution Group, 1986,
    w/Terry Carr

ANDY WOLK*
Agent: CAA - Beverly Hills, 310/288-4545

WINTER'S TALE (P)
RIBCAGE (P)
QUAIL SOUTHWEST (P)
CRIMINAL JUSTICE (CTF)   Elysian Films, 1990, directed

Screenplays:
CAMPAIGN w/Paul Attansio
HEROIC MEASURE
I MARRIED A DEAD MAN
MEASURE OF DEVOTION
THE 13TH FLOOR   THE LEFT

MICHAEL WOLK*
Agent: William Morris Agency - Beverly Hills, 310/274-7451

HEART STOPPER (P)
FEMME FATALE (P)
INNOCENT BLOOD   Warner Bros., 1992

Screenplays:
ZERO HOUR w/Michael Kassin

JENNY WOLKIND
(See Delia Ephron)

DAVE WOLLERT*
Agent: Broder-Kurland-Webb-Uffner - Beverly Hills, 310/281-3400

QUICKSAND: NO ESCAPE (CTF)   Finnegan Pinchuk/MCA
    Television Entertainment, 1992, w/Peter I. Baloff
NEAR MISSES   Media Home Entertainment, 1992,
    w/Peter I. Baloff

MICHELLE WOLLMERS
Agent: United Talent Agency - Beverly Hills, 310/273-6700

Screenplays:
A WHISPER TO A SCREAM
INFIDELS

J. WALLACE WOLODARSKY*
Agent: United Talent Agency - Beverly Hills, 310/273-6700

COLDBLOODED   Polygram, 1994, directed

Screenplays:
30 WISHES w/Jay Kogen

JAMES WOLPAW
COMPLEX WORLD   Hemdale, 1992, directed

ROBERT WOLTERSTORFF*
Agent: The Irv Schechter Company - Beverly Hills, 310/278-8070

THE LITTLE RASCALS   Universal, 1994, Story w/Mike Scott &
   Penelope Spheeris

JAMES WONG*
Agent: CAA - Beverly Hills, 310/288-4545

THE BOYS NEXT DOOR   New World, 1985, w/Glen Morgan

Screenplays:
HANGMAN w/Glen Morgan

JOHN WOO
Agent: William Morris Agency - Beverly Hills, 310/274-7451
Business: Metropolis Pictures, 20th Century Fox

A BETTER TOMORROW   Film Workshop Company Ltd.,
   1990, directed
THE KILLER   Film Work Shop/Circle Releasing, 1991, directed
A BULLET IN THE HEAD   Film Workshop Company Ltd.,
   1991, directed
HARD-BOILED   Golden Princess, 1992, Story, directed

CHARLES WOOD
Agent: William Morris Agency - Beverly Hills, 310/274-7451

THE KNACK   United Artists, 1965
HELP!   United Artists, 1965, w/Marc Behm
HOW I WON THE WAR   United Artists, 1967
THE CHARGE OF THE LIGHT BRIGADE   United Artists, 1968
THE LONG DAYS DYING   Paramount, 1968
CUBA   United Artists, 1979
RED MONARCH   Enigma Films/Goldcrest Films &
   Television Ltd., 1983
TUMBLEDOWN (CTF)   BBC Lionheart Productions, 1990
AN AWFULLY BIG ADVENTURE   Fine Line Features, 1994

CHRISTOPHER WOOD
Agent: The Gersh Agency - Beverly Hills, 310/274-6611

CONFESSIONS OF A WINDOW CLEANER   Columbia, 1974,
   w/Val Guest
SEVEN NIGHTS IN JAPAN   EMI, 1976
THE SPY WHO LOVED ME   United Artists, 1977,
   w/Richard Maibaum
MOONRAKER   United Artists, 1979
REMO WILLIAMS: THE ADVENTURE BEGINS   Orion, 1985
STEAL THE SKY (CTF)   HBO Pictures/Voram Ben Ami
   Productions/Paramount TV, 1988, w/Dorothy Tristan

DAVID WOOD
BACK HOME (CTF)   TVS Films/Verronmead Productions/Citadel
   Entertainment, 1990

GRACE WOODARD*
Contact: WGA - New York, 212/245-6180

DESCENDING ANGEL (CTF)   Fredya Rothstein, 1990,
   w/Alan Sharp & Robert Siegel

CHRISTOPHER WOODEN
KISS ME A KILLER   Califilm, 1991, w/Marcus DeLeon

Screenplays:
VOICE OF A STRANGER w/Jackson Barr
STEPMONSTER w/Scott McGee

RICHARD WOODS*
Contact: WGA - Los Angeles, 310/550-1000

ENDANGERED SPECIES   MGM/UA, 1982, Story w/Judson Kliner

ABBE WOOL
Agent: Stephanie Mann Agency - Los Angeles, 213/653-7130

SID & NANCY   Samuel Goldwyn Company, 1986, w/Alex Cox
ROADSIDE PROPHETS   Fine Line Features, 1992, directed

Screenplays:
BUFFALO GIRLS w/Chloe Webb
MELMO MEETS ARLO

LINDA WOOLVERTON*
Agent: CAA - Beverly Hills, 310/288-4545

BEAUTY AND THE BEAST (AF)   Buena Vista, 1991, also (P)
HOMEWARD BOUND: THE INCREDIBLE JOURNEY   Buena Vista,
   1993, w/Caroline Thompson
THE LION KING (AF)   Buena Vista, 1994, w/Irene Mecchi &
   Jonathan Roberts

Screenplays:
A WRINKLE IN TIME
DINOTOPIA (AF)

CARL (CHUCK) WORKMAN*
Agent: William Morris Agency - Beverly Hills, 310/274-7451
Business: Calliope Films, 195 S. Beverly Dr., Beverly Hills,
   CA 90212, 310/271-0964

WORDS (Short)   directed
PRECIOUS IMAGES (Short)   directed
THE MONEY   Coliseum, 1977, directed
SWEET DIRTY TONY   Marvin Films, 1981
STOOGEMANIA   Atlantic Releasing Corporation, 1986,
   w/Jim Geoghan, directed
MEATBALLS III   TMS Pictures, 1986, Story
SUPERSTAR (FD)   Aries Film Releasing, 1990, directed

TRIX WORRELL
Agent: ICM - Beverly Hills, 310/550-4000

FOR QUEEN AND COUNTRY   Atlantic Releasing Corporation,
   1988, w/Martin Stellman

MARVIN WORTH*
Contact: Jamner, Pariser & Meschures - Los Angeles, 310/652-0222

THREE ON A COUCH   Columbia, 1966, w/Arne Sultan,
   Bob Ross & Samuel A. Taylor
SEE NO EVIL, HEAR NO EVIL   Tri-Star, 1989,
   Story w/Arne Sultan & Earl Barrett

MICHAEL WORTH
HEART OF THE STAG   New World, 1984, Story

PETER MARTIN WORTMANN*
Agent: ICM - Beverly Hills, 310/550-4000

ODD JOBS   Tri-Star, 1986, w/Robert Conte
WHO'S HARRY CRUMB?   Tri-Star, 1988, w/Robert Conte

Screenplays:
SWEET AUNTIE ROSE w/Robert Conte
WOMEN ON THE VERGE w/Robert Conte
DAYTIME w/Robert Conte
FUGITIVE GUYS w/Robert Conte
THE GREAT PRETENDER w/Robert Conte
HARRY SCARY w/Robert Conte
DOUBLE VISION

KIM WOZENCRAFT
Agent: ICM - Beverly Hills, 310/550-4000

Screenplays:
NOTES FROM THE COUNTRY CLUB
SMACK GODDESS w/Richard Stratton

VICTORIA WOZNIAK-MORRIS*
Agent: The Artists Agency - Los Angeles, 310/277-7779

PURPLE HAZE   Triumph/Columbia, 1983

GEOFFREY WRIGHT
Manager: Addis-Wechsler & Associates - Los Angeles,
   213/954-9000

ROMPER STOMPER   Academy Entertainment, 1993, directed
METAL SKIN   Daniel Scharf Productions, 1994, directed

LAWRENCE WRIGHT*
Agent: Pleshette & Green - Los Angeles, 213/465-0428

Screenplays:
NORIEGA w/Oliver Stone

LENORE A. WRIGHT*
Agent: Shapiro/Lichtman - Los Angeles, 310/859-8877

UNDERGROUND ACES   Filmways, 1981, w/Jim Carabatsos &
   Andrew Peter Marin

THOMAS LEE WRIGHT*
Contact: WGA - Los Angeles, 310/550-1000

THE LAST OF THE FINEST   Orion, 1990, w/George Armitage &
   Jere Cunningham
NEW JACK CITY   Warner Bros., 1991, w/Barry Michael Cooper
EIGHT-TRAY GANGSTER: THE MAKING OF A CRIP (CTD)
   Discovery Channel, 1993, directed

Screenplays:
THE GODFATHER, PART THREE
TRACKER EAST
CHAOS UNDER HEAVEN: THE TIANANMEN SQUARE STORY
MA BARKER AND HER BOYS
THE SIXTH FAMILY
SOUL OF HONOR
DO OR DIE
THE RACE

DONALD WRYE*
Agent: William Morris Agency - Beverly Hills, 310/274-7451

ICE CASTLES   Columbia, 1979, w/Gary L. Baim, directed
THE HOUSE OF GOD   *H.O.G.*   United Artists, 1981, directed

ROBERT WUHL*
Agent: The Gersh Agency - Beverly Hills, 310/274-6611

Screenplays:
BIG TOP
TEENAGE KILLER ZOMBIES
OPEN SEASON (directing)
CHEAPSHOT
S.O.S.

RUDY WURLITZER*
(Rudolf G. Wurlitzer)
Agent: William Morris Agency - Beverly Hills, 310/274-7451

GLEN AND RANDA   UMC, 1971, w/Lorenzo Mars & Jim McBride
TWO LANE BLACKTOP   Universal, 1971, w/Will Corry
PAT GARRETT AND BILLY THE KID   MGM, 1973
WALKER   Universal, 1987
CANDY MOUNTAIN   Metropolis Film, 1987, co-directed
VOYAGER   Castle Hill Productions, 1991, w/Volker Schlondorff
WIND   TriStar, 1992, w/Mac Gudgeon
SHADOW OF THE WOLF   Triumph Releasing, 1993, w/Evan Jones
LITTLE BUDDHA   Miramax, 1994, w/Mark Peploe

Screenplays:
THE BALLAD OF TYPHOID MARY
BEYOND THE MOUNTAIN
ZEBVLON
BAKE AND SHAKE
MAD DOG LAKE
FLATS
MEXICAN JAILBREAK

AMY WYCOFF
WHEN THE PARTY'S OVER   WTPO, 1992, directed

J. DAVID WYLES*
Contact: WGA - Los Angeles, 310/550-1000

Screenplays:
MR. UNCLE ERNIE
MAN WITH A GUN (directing)

NED WYNN*
Contact: WGA - Los Angeles, 310/550-1000

CALIFORNIA DREAMING   American International, 1979

TRACY KEENAN WYNN*
Agent: Renaissance-H.N. Swanson - Los Angeles, 310/246-6000

THE LONGEST YARD   Paramount, 1974
THE DROWNING POOL   Warner Bros., 1975, w/Walter Hill &
   Lorenzo Semple
THE DEEP   Columbia, 1977, w/Peter Benchley

Screenplays:
THE GAME
ENDANGERED
CADILLAC JACK
DEVIL'S ALTERNATIVE
THE INVESTIGATION
PAY DIRT   AMERICAN FLAT

JIM WYNORSKI
Personal Manager: L. Miller Management - Los Angeles,
   310/454-7196

FORBIDDEN WORLD   New World, 1982, Story w/R.J. Robertson
SORCERESS   New World, 1983
SCREWBALLS   New World, 1983, w/Linda Shayne
THE LOST EMPIRE   JGM Enterprises, 1985, directed
CHOPPING MALL   *KILLBOTS*   Concorde, 1986,
   w/Steve Mitchell, directed
DEATHSTALKER II: NECROPOLIS   Concorde, 1986,
   Story, directed
BIG BAD MAMA II   Concorde, 1987, w/R.J. Robertson, directed
NOT OF THIS EARTH   Concorde, 1988, w/R.J. Robertson
THE HAUNTING OF MORELLA   Concore, 1990,
   w/R.J. Robertson, directed
THINK BIG   Concorde, 1990, Story w/R.J. Robertson
BEASTMASTER 2: THROUGH THE PORTAL OF TIME
   New Line Cinema, 1991, w/others
MUNCHIE   Concorde, 1992, w/R.J. Robertson, directed

Screenplays:
MUNCHIE II w/R.J. Robertson
FOUNTAIN OF YOUTH w/R.J. Robertson (directing)
FINAL EMBRACE w/R.J. Robertson

Y

FRANK YABLANS*
Business Manager: Kaufman & Bernstein - Los Angeles, 310/277-1900

NORTH DALLAS FORTY   Paramount, 1979, w/Peter Gent & Ted Kotcheff
MOMMIE DEAREST   Paramount, 1981, w/Frank Perry, Tracey Hotchner & Robert Getchell

YABO YABLONSKY*
Agent: Paul Kohner, Inc. - Beverly Hills, 310/550-1060

JAGUAR LIVES!   American International, 1979
VICTORY   Lorimar/Paramount, 1981, w/Evan Jones
PORTRAIT OF A HITMAN   Wildfire, 1984

JULIETTE YAGER*
Contact: WGA - Los Angeles, 310/550-1000

Screenplays:
MY WAY OR THE HIGHWAY w/Rip Murray

BOAZ I. YAKIN*
Agent: United Talent Agency - Beverly Hills, 310/273-6700

THE PUNISHER   Castle Premier, 1990
THE ROOKIE   Warner Bros., 1990, w/Scott Spiegel
FRESH   Miramax, 1994, directed

Screenplays:
OUTLAWS w/Cassidy Heydt
COLD FIRE
MADELEINE
AFRIKANER
BROTHER DA SILVA
COAST GUARD PROJECT
THE LINE

LEONARD YAKIR
OUT OF THE BLUE   Discovery, 1982, w/Brenda Nielson

RICHARD YALEM*
Contact: Amicus Entertainment - 818/760-3989

DELIRIUM   Odyssey Pictures, 1989

Screenplays:
ALTAR BOUND w/Josephine Cummings

DAVID YALLOP
Agent: The Casarotto Company - London, 071/287-4450

BEYOND REASONABLE DOUBT   Satori Releasing, 1984
CHICAGO JOE AND THE SHOWGIRL   New Line Cinema, 1990

"WEIRD" AL YANKOVIC
Contact: Spotlight Enterprises - Los Angeles, 310/657-8004

U.H.F.   Orion, 1989, w/Jay Levey

RON YANOVER*
Agent: Stone Manners Agency - Los Angeles, 213/654-7575

CYBORG 2: GLASS SHADOW   Trimark, 1993, w/Mark Geldman & Michael Scroeder
THE JUNGLE BOOK   Buena Vista, 1994, w/Mark Geldman & Stephen Sommers

Screenplays:
TOM THUMB w/Mark Geldman (MDP Worldwide)

LOUIS YANSEN
Agent: The Artists Group - Los Angeles, 310/552-1100

MISPLACED   Original Cinema, 1991, w/Thomas DeWolfe, directed

BROCK YATES*
Agent: Camden-ITG - Los Angeles, 310/289-2700

SMOKEY AND THE BANDIT, PART II   Universal, 1980, w/Jerry Belson
THE CANNONBALL RUN   20th Century-Fox, 1981

PETER YELDHAM
Contact: British Academy of Film & Television Arts, 195 Piccadilly, London W1, England, 071/734-0022

THE COMEDY MAN   British Lion, 1964
THE LIQUIDATOR   MGM, 1965
TEN LITTLE INDIANS   Tenlit, 1966, w/Harry Alan Towers
THE LONG DUEL   Rank, 1967
AGE OF CONSENT   Columbia, 1969
CALL OF THE WILD   Constantin, 1975, w/Harry Alan Towers & Wyn Wells
WEEKEND OF SHADOWS   Roadshow Distributors, 1978
TOUCH AND GO   Greater Union Film Distributors, 1980

Screenplays:
OPPY w/David Parker

LINDA YELLEN*
Agent: William Morris Agency - Beverly Hills, 310/274-7451

COME OUT, COME OUT   Beacon Productions, 1969, directed
LOOKING UP   Levitt-Pickman, 1977, directed
CHANTILLY LACE (CTF)   Showtime, 1993, w/Rosanne Ehrlich, directed
PARALLEL LIVES (CTF)   Showtime, 1994, Story, directed

Screenplays:
BURN THIS w/Don Jakoby
A REASONABLE DOUBT
MAYBERRY VICE
THE STEVE DUNLEAVY STORY

BENNETT M. YELLIN*
Contact: WGA - Los Angeles, 310/550-1000

DUMB AND DUMBER   New Line Cinema, 1994, w/Bob Farrelly & Peter Farrelly

Screenplays:
ADULT EDUCATION w/Peter Farrelly
DUST TO DUST w/Peter Farrelly
YOUNG LOVERS w/Peter Farrelly
FREE SPIRITS w/Peter Farrelly
OUR PLANET TONIGHT w/Peter Farrelly
BLACK TIE w/Peter Farrelly
POISON IVY w/Peter Farrelly

ANTHONY H. YERKOVICH*
Agent: CAA - Beverly Hills, 310/288-4545

Screenplays:
SWEETWATER

RAFAEL YGLESIAS*
Agent: Michael Siegel & Associates - Los Angeles, 310/274-5222

FEARLESS Warner Bros., 1993
DEATH AND THE MAIDEN Fine Line Features, 1994,
 w/Ariel Dorfman

Screenplays:
OPENING NIGHT
THE LOBBYIST w/Lewis Cole
THE MURDERER NEXT DOOR
DR. NEMDA'S CURE FOR EVIL

JUSTIN YOFFE
Agent: ICM - Beverly Hills, 310/550-4000

Screenplays:
GRACE
CARD SHARKS

NORMAN YONEMOTO
SAVAGE STREETS Entermark, 1985, w/Danny Steinmann

JEFF YONIS
Contact: Mitchell, Silberberg, Knupp - Los Angeles, 310/312-2000
Business: 310/822-8600

THE LIAR'S CLUB Concorde, 1993
BLACKOUT Concorde, 1993, directed

Screenplays:
PET PEEVES

PHILIP YORDAN*
Contact: WGA - Los Angeles, 310/550-1000

SYNCOPATION RKO, 1942, w/Frank Cavett & Valentine Davies
WHEN STRANGERS MARRY *BETRAYED* Monogram, 1944,
 w/Dennis Cooper
DILLINGER ★ Monogram, 1945
SUSPENSE Monogram, 1946
WHISTLE STOP United Artists, 1946
THE CHASE Nero Pictures, 1947
THE BLACK BOOK Eagle-Lion, 1949, w/Aeneas Mackenzie
HOUSE OF STRANGERS 20th Century-Fox, 1949
ANNA LUCASTA Columbia, 1949, from his play,
 w/Arthur Laurents
BAD MEN OF TOMBSTONE Allied Artists, 1949, w/Arthur Strawn
EDGE OF DOOM Goldwyn, 1950
DRUMS IN THE DEEP SOUTH RKO Radio, 1951
DETECTIVE STORY ★★ Paramount, 1951, w/William Wyler
MARU MARU Warner Bros., 1952, w/others
MUTINY United Artists, 1952, w/Sydney Harmon
BLOWING WILD Warner Bros., 1953
JOHNNY GUITAR Republic, 1953
HOUDINI Paramount, 1953
BROKEN LANCE ★★ 20th Century-Fox, 1954, Story
THE NAKED JUNGLE Paramount, 1954, w/Ranald MacDougall
THE MAN FROM LARAMIE Columbia, 1955, w/Frank Burt
THE BIG COMBO Allied Artists, 1955
JOE MACBETH Columbia, 1955
SAVAGE WILDERNESS Columbia, 1956, w/Russell S. Hughes
THE HARDER THEY FALL Columbia, 1956
NO DOWN PAYMENT 20th Century-Fox, 1957
MEN IN WAR Security, 1957
THE DAY OF THE OUTLAW United Artists, 1958
ANNA LUCASTA United Artists, 1958, black version
THE BRAVADOS 20th Century-Fox, 1958
THE FIEND WHO WALKED THE WEST 20th Century-Fox, 1958,
 w/Harry Brown
GOD'S LITTLE ACRE Security, 1958
STUDS LONIGAN United Artists, 1960
THE BRAMBLE BUSH Warner Bros., 1960, w/Milton Sperling
KING OF KINGS MGM, 1961
EL CID Allied Artists, 1961, w/Ben Barzman
55 DAYS AT PEKING Bronston, 1962, w/Bernard Gordon
THE DAY OF THE TRIFFIDS Allied Artists, 1963

THE FALL OF THE ROMAN EMPIRE Paramount, 1964,
 w/Ben Barzman
BATTLE OF THE BULGE Warner Bros., 1965, w/John Melson &
 Milton Sperling
THE ROYAL HUNT OF THE SUN National General, 1968
CAPTAIN APACHE Scotia International, 1971, w/Milton Sperling
CRY WILDERNESS Visto International, 1971
BAD MAN'S RIVER Zurbano/Apollo/Roitfeld, 1972,
 w/Eugenio Martin
THE UNHOLY Vestron, 1988, w/Fernando Fonseca

DAN YORK
Agent: Renaissance-H.N. Swanson - Los Angeles, 310/246-6000

Screenplays:
AUGUST FIRES

SUSANNAH YORK
Agent: The Casarotto Company - London, 071/287-4450

FALLING IN LOVE AGAIN International Picture Show, 1980,
 Story w/Ted Allan & Steven Paul

DANIEL YOST*
Agent: The Irv Schechter Company - Beverly Hills, 310/278-8070
Contact: Diane Golden, Silverberg, Katz, Thompson & Braun -
 Los Angeles, 310/445-5820

DRUGSTORE COWBOY Avenue Pictures, 1989, w/Gus Van Sant
CRIMINAL ACT Independent Networks Inc./Film Ventures
 International, 1989

Screenplays:
ONE NIGHT STAND (directing)
THE THIEF AND THE STRIPPER
ON THE PROWL
OUR DREAM HOUSE
ESCAPE TO CANADA
STREET WIRED
CRYSTAL CREEK
BOUNTY HUNTER
DOING IT ALL

GRAHAM YOST*
Agent: CAA - Beverly Hills, 310/288-4545

SPEED 20th Century Fox, 1994

Screenplays:
BROKEN ARROW

BURT YOUNG*
Contact: Andrew Giovingo - New York, 212/767-5550

UNCLE JOE SHANNON United Artists, 1978

CATHLEEN YOUNG*
Agent: ICM - Beverly Hills, 310/550-4000

Screenplays:
GETTING RID OF JOEY

DALENE A. YOUNG*
Agent: Kopaloff Company - Los Angeles, 213/203-8430

LITTLE DARLINGS Paramount, 1980, w/Kimi Peck
CROSS CREEK Universal/AFD, 1983

Screenplays:
BABY SITTER'S CLUB
THE BLACK ARROW
PHOTOPLAY w/Martha Coolidge
JASMINE AND THE JELLY THIEF
NIGHTENGALE ON AVENUE B
SARAH WILL
GIOVANNI'S RESTAURANT

JOHN SACRET YOUNG*
Agent: CAA - Beverly Hills, 310/288-4545
Management: George Diskant - Los Angeles, 310/824-3773

CHANDLER   MGM, 1971
TESTAMENT   Paramount, 1983
ROMERO   Four Seasons Entertainment, 1989

Screenplays:
AFTER EDEN
FIRE ON THE MOUNTAIN
UNDERGROUND
SAN JOAQUIN
SIRENS

KEE YOUNG
WEEKEND WITH KATE   Phillip Emanuel Productions, 1990,
   w/Henry Tefay

MARK YOUNG
ONCE UPON A FOREST (AF)   20th Century Fox, 1993,
   w/Kelly Ward

MARLA YOUNG
CHALLENGE THE WIND   Sell Entertainment, 1990,
   w/William Blackburn & Ken Howard

ROBERT M. YOUNG*
Agent: William Morris Agency - Beverly Hills, 310/274-7451

THE BALLAD OF GREGORIO CORTEZ   Embassy, 1983,
   w/Victor Villasenor, directed

ROGER YOUNG
Agent: CAA - Beverly Hills, 310/288-4545

DOUBLECROSSED (CTF)   Green/Epstein Productions/Lorimar TV,
   1991, directed

COREY YUEN
NO RETREAT, NO SURRENDER   New World, 1986,
   Story w/Ng See Yuen, directed

GALEN YUEN
Agent: United Talent Agency - Beverly Hills, 310/273-6700

Screenplays:
SNAKEHEAD
THE KILLER
CRAZY SIX
IT'S ALL IN THE GAME

JOHNNY YUNE
THEY CALL ME BRUCE?   *A FISTFUL OF CHOPSTICKS*
   Artists Releasing Corporation/Film Ventures International, 1982,
   w/Tim Clawson, Elliott Hong & David Randolf
THEY STILL CALL ME BRUCE   Shapiro Entertainment, 1987,
   w/James Orr, co-directed

LARRY YUST
Address: 500 S. Rossmore Ave., Los Angeles, CA 90020,
   213/934-4706

TRICK BABY   Universal, 1973, directed
HOMEBODIES   Avco Embassy, 1974, directed
"SAY YES"   Cinetel, 1986, directed

PETER YUVAL
Business: Action International Pictures, 10726 McCune Avenue,
   Los Angeles, CA 90034, 310/559-8805

DEAD END CITY   Action International Pictures, 1989,
   w/Michael Bogert, directed
FIREHEAD   A.I.P. Studios, 1991, Jeff Mandell, directed

BRIAN YUZNA
FROM BEYOND   Empire Pictures, 1986,
   Adaptation w/Stuart Gordon & Dennis Paoli
HONEY, I SHRUNK THE KIDS   Buena Vista, 1989,
   Story w/Stuart Gordon & Ed Naha
SOCIETY   Wild Street Pictures, 1989, directed
BRIDE OF RE-ANIMATOR   Troma, 1991,
   Story w/Rick Fry, directed

Z

BRYCE ZABEL*
Agent: The Irv Schechter Company - Beverly Hills, 310/278-8070

OFFICIAL DENIAL (CTF)   Wilshire Court, 1993

Screenplays:
LABOR OF LOVE w/Jackie Zabel
TWAS THE NIGHT w/Rex Hauck

JACKIE ZABEL*
Contact: WGA - Los Angeles, 310/550-1000

Screenplays:
LABOR OF LOVE w/Bryce Zabel

MARK ZACHARIA
Agent: Berzon Agency - Glendale, 818/548-1560

Screenplays:
TIL THE END OF TIME

ALFREDO ZACHARIAS
THE BEES   New World, 1978

STEVEN R. ZACHARIAS*
Agent: Broder-Kurland-Webb-Uffner - Beverly Hills, 310/281-3400

THE HARRAD SUMMER   Cinerama Releasing Corporation, 1974
REVENGE OF THE NERDS   20th Century Fox, 1984, w/Jeff Buhai
THE WHOOPEE BOYS   Paramount, 1986, w/Jeff Buhai &
   David Obst
LAST RESORT   Concorde/Cinema Group, 1986, w/Jeff Buhai
JOCKS   Crown International, 1987, w/Jeff Buhai &
   David Obst as "Mike Lanahan & David Oas"
JOHNNY BE GOOD   1988, w/Jeff Buhai & David Obst
IN THE ARMY NOW   Buena Vista, 1994, Story w/Jeff Buhai &
   Robbie Fox

Screenplays:
EDDIE w/Jeff Buhai
NOUVEAU GUINEANS w/Jeff Buhai
BIKERS FROM HELL w/Jeff Buhai
DALLAS DEBS w/Jeff Buhai
GIRLS IN TROUBLE w/Jeff Buhai
DEEP COVER w/Jeff Buhai
HOPELESSNESS AND DESPAIR w/Jeff Buhai
MR. VICE PRESIDENT w/Jeff Buhai & Robert Kears
THE TRUTH ABOUT SWEDES w/Jeff Buhai
LOVELINE w/Jeff Buhai
AFTERGLOW w/Jeff Buhai
HARRAD II w/Jeff Buhai
HOSPITAL w/Jeff Buhai
INSIDE THE INQUIRER w/Jeff Buhai
VULGARIANS w/Jeff Buhai
HEAVY METAL WEEKEND w/Jeff Buhai
REVENGE OF THE NUDES w/Jeff Buhai

JACK ZAFRAN
Agent: Sanford-Gross & Associates - Los Angeles, 310/208-2100

Screenplays:
NEIGHBORHOOD WATCH

MICHAEL ZAGOR*
Agent: Richland/Wunsch/Hohman Agency - Los Angeles, 310/278-1955

THE JOSEPHINE BAKER STORY (CTF)   HBO Pictures/
   RHI Entertainment/Anglia Television Ltd., 1991,
   Story w/Ron Hutchinson

HELEN ZAHAVI
DIRTY WEEKEND   UIP, 1993, w/Michael Winner

CAVEH ZAHEDI
A LITTLE STIFF   Just Above the Ground Productions, 1990,
   w/Greg Watkins, co-directed
I DON'T HATE LAS VEGAS ANYMORE   Complex Corp.,
   1994, directed

STEVEN ZAILLIAN*
Agent: Harold R. Greene Inc. - Marina Del Rey, 310/823-5393

THE FALCON AND THE SNOWMAN   Orion, 1985
AWAKENINGS ★   Columbia, 1990
JACK THE BEAR   20th Century Fox, 1993
SEARCHING FOR BOBBY FISCHER   Paramount, 1993, directed
SCHINDLER'S LIST ★★   Universal, 1993
CLEAR AND PRESENT DANGER   Paramount, 1994,
   w/John Milius & Donald Stewart

Screenplays:
BAD MANNERS
SHOE SHINE

Z. A. K.
(Zak Klobucher)
Agent: CAA - Beverly Hills, 310/288-4545

Screenplays:
MOTHER'S LITTLE HELPER   (New Line Cinema)
NOW I KNOW EVERYTHING

NANCY ZALA
ROUND NUMBERS   Coyote Home Video, 1992, directed

GEORGE ZALOOM
Business: ZM Productions, Universal Studios - 818/777-8870

ENCINO MAN   Buena Vista, 1992, Story w/Shawn Schepps

ALAIN ZALOUM
CANVAS   Optima Productions/ABC Distribution, 1992,
   w/Brenda Newman, directed

JORGE ZAMACONA*
Contact: WGA - Los Angeles, 310/550-1000

WORLD GONE WILD   Lorimar, 1988

Screenplays:
OUTLAWS
BACK IN BLACK
THE MOD SQUAD

ALEX ZAMM*
Agent: William Morris Agency - Beverly Hills, 310/274-7451

BIRTHDAY FISH (Short)   directed
MY FIRST HAIRCUT (Short)   directed
MAESTRO (Short)   directed

Screenplays:
CAMP FANTASY   w/Billy Robertson (directing)
PAWNSHOP KID

TONY ZARINDAST
HARDCASE AND FIST   United Entertainment, 1989,
   w/Bud Fleisher, directed
A HOLLYWOOD STORY   Double Helix Films, 1991,
   w/Evan Slawson, directed

GEORGE T. ZATESLO*
Agent: The Artists Agency - Los Angeles, 310/277-7779

Screenplays:
ALL DAY SUCKER
OUT OF LEFT FIELD
THE GOOD SHIP LOLLIPOP   w/Larry Tucker

YOLANDE ZAUBERMAN
IVAN & ABRAHAM   New Yorker Films, 1994, directed

MICHAEL ZAUSNER*
Contact: WGA - New York, 212/245-6180

LOVE OR MONEY   Hemdale, 1990, w/Bart Davis & Elyse England

Screenplays:
ERNEST SAVES CAMELOT   w/Bart Davis

FRANCO ZEFFIRELLI
Agent: ICM - Beverly Hills, 310/550-4000
Address: via Lucio Volumnio 37, Rome, Italy, 06/799441

THE TAMING OF THE SHREW   Columbia, 1967,
   w/Susi Cecchi d'Amico & Paul Dehn, directed
LA TRAVIATA   Universal Classics, 1982, directed
HAMLET   Warner Bros., 1990, w/Christopher DeVore, directed

PAUL ZEHRER
BLESSING   Starr Valley Films, 1994, directed

JON ZEIDERMAN
LITTLE NOISES   Monument Pictures, 1991, w/Jane Spencer

JIMMY ZEILINGER
Agent: Renaissance-H.N. Swanson - Los Angeles, 310/246-6000

LITTLE SISTER   InterStar Releasing, 1992, directed

Screenplays:
TEMPTED
SPRING BREAK ADVENTURE   w/Scott Posner

BEN ZELIG
TOMBOY   Crown International, 1985

SUSAN ZELOUF
CURSE II: THE BITE   Trans World Entertainment, 1989,
   w/Federico Prosperi

YURI ZELTSER*
Agent: Innovative Artists - Los Angeles, 310/553-5200

BAD DREAMS   20th Century Fox, 1988, Story w/Michael Dick,
   Andrew Fleming & P.J. Pettiette
EYE OF THE STORM   Odyssey Distributors, 1991,
   w/Michael Stewart, directed
MIDNIGHT EDITION   Shapiro Glickenhaus, 1994,
   w/Michael Stewart & Howard Libov

ROBERT ZEMECKIS*
Agent: CAA - Beverly Hills. 310/288-4545

I WANNA HOLD YOUR HAND   Universal, 1977,
   w/Bob Gale, directed
1941   Universal/Columbia, 1979, w/Bob Gale
USED CARS   Columbia, 1980, w/Bob Gale, directed
BACK TO THE FUTURE ★   Universal, 1985,
   w/Bob Gale, directed
BACK TO THE FUTURE II   Universal, 1989,
   Story w/Bob Gale, directed
BACK TO THE FUTURE III   Universal, 1990,
   Story w/Bob Gale, directed
TRESPASS   Universal, 1992, w/Bob Gale

Screenplays:
GANGLAND w/Bob Gale

MICHAEL ZETTLER*
Agent: The Gersh Agency - New York, 212/997-1818

SWEET LORRAINE   Angelika Films, 1987, w/Shelly Altman

HOWARD ZIEHM
FLESH GORDON MEETS THE COSMIC CHEERLEADERS
   Filmvest International, 1991, w/Doug Frisby, directed

RAFAL ZIELINSKI
BREAKING ALL THE RULES   New World, 1985, Story w/Edith Rey

URI ZIGHELBOIM
INSIDE THE GOLDMINE   Cineville, 1994, w/Josh Evans

PAUL ZILLER
DEADLY SURVEILLANCE (CTF)   Westwind Productions, 1991,
   w/Hal Salwen, directed
PROBABLE CAUSE (CTF)   Wilmont Prods./Showtime Ent., 1994,
   Story, directed

HARV ZIMMEL*
Agent: Original Artists - Santa Monica, 310/394-1067

SHOOT TO KILL   Buena Vista, 1988, w/Michael Burton &
   Daniel Petrie Jr.
SNOW KILL (CTF)   Wilshire Court Productions, 1990,
   w/Raymond Hartung

Screenplays:
THE WIZARD FROM FLATBUSH w/Joel Saltzman
DEEP WORK
THE AMATEUR HOUR
SOMETHING IN THE PARK

RON ZIMMERMAN*
Agent: Hilary Wayne - Beverly Hills, 310/289-6186
Manager: 3 Arts Entertainment - Los Angeles, 213/851-5700

Screenplays:
THE BEST MAN w/Marjorie Gross

STAN ZIMMERMAN*
Agent: ICM - Beverly Hills, 310/550-4000

Screenplays:
THE PRITCHARD EXHIBIT w/James Berg
THE RUTHIE RUDDICK STORY

VERNON ZIMMERMAN*
Agent: Wallerstein*Kappelman Agency - Los Angeles, 213/782-0225
Business Manager: Eric Weissmann, Weissmann, Wolff, Bergman,
   Coleman & Schulman - Beverly Hills, 310/858-7888

BOBBIE JO AND THE OUTLAW   American International, 1976
FADE TO BLACK   American Cinema, 1980, directed
TEEN WITCH   Trans World Entertainment, 1989, w/Robin Menken

PAUL ZINDEL*
Agent: William Morris Agency - New York, 212/586-5100

THE EFFECT OF GAMMA RAYS ON MAN-IN-THE-MOON
   MARIGOLDS (P)
LET ME HEAR YOU WHISPER (P)
UP THE SANDBOX   National General, 1972
MAME   Warner Bros., 1974
MARIA'S LOVERS   Cannon, 1984, w/Gerard Brach,
   Marjorie David & Andrei Konchalovsky
RUNAWAY TRAIN   Cannon, 1985, w/Edward Bunker &
   Djordje Milicevic

Screenplays:
*THE AMAZING AND DEATH-DEFYING DIARY OF
   EUGENE DINGMAN*

JOHN ZINMAN
Agent: United Talent Agency - Beverly Hills, 310/273-6700

Screenplays:
ZERO GRAVITY w/Duncan Kenendy

FABRICE ZIOLKOWSKI
Business: Barman/Ziolkowski, 13 Plateau de Rimiez, Nice,
   France 06100; tel/fax: 33/93-53-46-16

CHICAGO BLACK AND WHITE (Short)   1990,
   w/Luli Barzman, co-directed
CACAPHONIE D'AMOUR (Short)   1991,
   w/Luli Barzman, co-directed

Screenplays:
SANDGRASS PEOPLE w/Luli Barzman
CIRCLES IN A FOREST w/Luli Barzman
DOUBLE BIND w/Luli Barzman

WILLIAM ZIPP
FATAL SKIES   AIP, 1990, w/James Eaton

STEVEN ZIRL
Manager: The Anthony Elliot Company - Los Angeles, 310/284-6804

Screenplays:
CHOIR OF BLOOD
COMET QUEEN

JOEL F. ZISKIN
MATA HARI   Cannon, 1985

Screenplays:
DUKE AND THE DIPPER
ECLIPSE

LAURA ZISKIN*
Business: 20th Century Fox - Los Angeles, 310/203-3722

WHAT ABOUT BOB?   Buena Vista, 1991, Story w/Alvin Sargent
HERO   Columbia, 1992, Story w/Alvin Sargent & David Peoples

DAVID ZITO
Contact: Zito/Weldon Productions - 310/268-0049

BREAKIN'   MGM/UA/Cannon, 1984, as "Charles Parker,"
   w/Allen DeBevoise & Gerald Scalfe
FREE FALL   Nu Image, 1993, w/Les Weldon
SPANISH ROSE   Nu Image, 1993, w/Les Weldon

Screenplays:
KID COP

STEPHEN ZITO*
Agent: ICM - Beverly Hills, 310/550-4000

THE ESCAPE ARTIST   Orion/Warner Bros., 1982,
   w/Melissa Mathison

LEE DAVID ZLOTOFF*
Agent: Broder-Kurland-Webb-Uffner - Beverly Hills, 310/281-3400

Screenplays:
CARE OF THE SPITFIRE GRILL   (Mendocino Productions,   directing)

JOSE ANTONIO ZORILLA
THE WINTER IN LISBON   Castle Hill Productions, 1992,
   w/Mason M. Funk

DAVID ZUCKER*
Agent: CAA - Beverly Hills, 310/288-4545

THE KENTUCKY FRIED MOVIE   United Film Distribution, 1977,
   w/Jim Abrahams & Jerry Zucker
AIRPLANE!   Paramount, 1980, w/Jim Abrahams &
   Jerry Zucker, co-directed
TOP SECRET!   Paramount, 1984, w/Martyn Burke,
   Jim Abrahams & Jerry Zucker, co-directed
THE NAKED GUN: FROM THE FILES OF POLICE SQUAD!
   Paramount, 1989, w/Jim Abrahams, Pat Proft &
   Jerry Zucker, directed
THE NAKED GUN 2 1/2: THE SMELL OF FEAR   Paramount, 1991,
   w/Pat Proft, directed
THE NAKED GUN 33 1/3: THE FINAL INSULT   Paramount, 1994,
   w/Pat Proft & Robert LoCash

JERRY ZUCKER*
Agent: CAA - Beverly Hills, 310/288-4545

THE KENTUCKY FRIED MOVIE   United Film Distribution, 1977,
   w/Jim Abrahams & David Zucker
AIRPLANE!   Paramount, 1980, w/Jim Abrahams &
   David Zucker, also co-directed
TOP SECRET!   Paramount, 1984, w/Martyn Burke,
   Jim Abrahams & David Zucker, co-directed
THE NAKED GUN: FROM THE FILES OF POLICE SQUAD!
   Paramount, 1989, w/Jim Abrahams, Pat Proft & David Zucker

ALBERT ZUGSMITH
DONDI   Allied Artists, 1961, w/Gus Edson, directed
MOVIE STAR AMERICAN STYLE OR LSD - I HATE YOU
   Famous Players, 1966, w/Graham Lee Mahn &
   Lulu Talmadge, directed
ON HER BED OF ROSES   Famous Players International,
   1966, directed

MARTIN ZURLA
Agent: Susan Smith & Associates - Beverly Hills, 213/852-4777

Screenplays:
GROUND ZERO w/Sergio Altieri

RON ZWANG*
Agent: APA - Los Angeles, 310/273-0744
Business Manager: The Jaymes Co. - 818/761-7832

DOIN' TIME   The Ladd Company/Warner Bros., 1984,
   w/Dee Caruso & Franelle Silver
FREE RIDE   Galaxy International, 1986, w/Robert Bell &
   Lee Fulkerson

Screenplays:
THE NUTTY NUT w/Scott Spiegel & Sam Raimi
THE CLUMSY IDIOT w/Scott Spiegel & Bruce Campbell

A. MARTIN ZWEIBACH*
Contact: 310/271-5411

ME, NATALIE   Cinema Center, 1969
YOU CAN'T HAVE EVERYTHING   *CACTUS IN THE SNOW*
   General Film Corp., 1971, directed
GORP   Filmways, 1980, Story w/Jeffrey Konvitz
GRACE QUIGLEY   *THE ULTIMATE SOLUTION OF GRACE
   QUIGLEY*   MGM/UA/Cannon, 1984

Screenplays:
MUMMY OF BEVERLY HILLS
SUNLIGHT AND SHADOWS

ALAN ZWEIBEL*
Agent: ICM - Beverly Hills, 310/550-4000

A VISIT TO HOLIDAY PARK (P)
DRAGNET   Universal, 1987, w/Dan Aykroyd & Tom Mankiewicz
NORTH   Columbia, 1993, w/Andrew Scheinman

Screenplays:
THE GOOD HUMOR MAN

EDWARD M. ZWICK*
Agent: ICM - Beverly Hills, 310/550-4000

Screenplays:
BABY GENIUS w/Marshall Herskovitz

★ ★ ★

NOTABLE WRITERS
OF THE PAST

A

IRWIN ALLEN
THE ANIMAL WORLD (FD)   Warner Bros.,
   1956, directed
THE STORY OF MANKIND   Warner Bros.,
   1957, w/Charles Bennett, directed
THE BIG CIRCUS   Allied Artists, 1959,
   w/Charles Bennett & Irving Wallace
THE LOST WORLD   20th Century-Fox, 1960,
   w/Charles Bennett, directed
VOYAGE TO THE BOTTOM OF THE SEA
   20th Century-Fox, 1961,
   w/Charles Bennett, directed
FIVE WEEKS IN A BALLOON
   20th Century-Fox, 1962, w/Charles
   Bennett & Albert Gail, directed

ROBERT ALAN ARTHUR
EDGE OF THE CITY   MGM, 1957,
   from his play
GRAND PRIX   MGM, 1966
FOR LOVE OF IVY   Cinerama
   Releasing, 1968
THE LOST MAN   Universal, 1969, directed
ALL THAT JAZZ ★   20th Century-Fox, 1979,
   w/Bob Fosse

HOWARD ASHMAN
CAUSE MAGGIE'S AFRAID OF THE DARK (P)
THE CONFIRMATION (P)
DREAMSTUFF (P)
GOD BLESS YOU, MR. ROSEWATER (P)
   w/Alan Menken
SMILE (P)
LITTLE SHOP OF HORRORS
   Geffen Company/Warner Bros., 1986,
   from his play (w/Alan Menken)

B

HERBERT BAKER
SO THIS IS NEW YORK   United Artists,
   1948, w/Carl Foreman
JUMPING JACKS   Paramount, 1952,
   w/Robert Lees & Fred Rinaldo
BIG LEAGUER   MGM, 1953
DREAM WIFE   MGM, 1953,
   w/Alfred L. Levitt & Sidney Sheldon
THE GIRL CAN'T HELP IT   20th Century-Fox,
   1953, w/Frank Tashlin
SCARED STIFF   Paramount, 1953
LOVING YOU   Paramount, 1957,
   w/Hal Kanter
KING CREOLE   Paramount, 1958,
   w/Michael V. Gazzo
DON'T GIVE UP THE SHIP   Paramount,
   1959, w/Edmund Beloin & Henry Garson
MURDERER'S ROW   Columbia, 1966
THE AMBUSHERS   Columbia, 1967
HAMMERHEAD   Columbia, 1968,
   w/William Bast
SEXTETTE   Crown International, 1978
THE JAZZ SINGER   EMI, 1980,
   w/Stephen H. Foreman

JAMES LEE BARRETT
ON THE BEACH   United Artists, 1959
THE TRUTH ABOUT SPRING
   Universal, 1965
THE GREATEST STORY EVER TOLD   United
   Artists, 1965, w/George Stevens
SHENENDOAH   Universal, 1965
THE GREEN BERETS   Warner Bros., 1968
BANDOLERO!   20th Century-Fox, 1968
THE UNDEFEATED   20th Century-Fox, 1969
THE CHEYENNE SOCIAL CLUB   National
   General, 1970
FOOLS PARADE   *DYNAMITE MAN FROM
   GLORY JAIL*   Columbia, 1971
SOMETHING BIG   National General, 1971
SMOKEY AND THE BANDIT   Universal, 1977,
   w/Alan Mandel & Charles Shyer
WILD HORSE HANK   Film Consortium of
   Canada, 1979

JOHN BARRY
SATURN 3   AFD, 1980, Story

HALL BARTLETT
NAVAJO (FD) ★   Lippert, 1952, directed
CRAZYLEGS   Republic, 1954, directed
UNCHAINED   Warner Bros., 1955, directed
ZERO HOUR   Paramount, 1957, w/John
   Champion & Arthur Hailey, directed
DRANGO   United Artists, 1957, co-directed
ALL THE YOUNG MEN   Columbia,
   1960, directed
CHANGES   Cinerama Releasing,
   1969, directed
THE CHILDREN OF SANCHEZ   Lone Star,
   1978, w/Cesare Zavattini, directed

JOHN BEAIRD
MY BLOODY VALENTINE   Paramount, 1981
BAKER COUNTY USA   *TRAPPED*
   Jensen Farley Pictures, 1982

RICHARD (DICK) BENNER
OUTRAGEOUS!   Cinema 5, 1977, directed
HAPPY BIRTHDAY GEMINI   United Artists,
   1980, directed
TOO OUTRAGEOUS!   Spectrafilm,
   1987, directed

ROBERT BLOCH
THE CABINET OF CALIGARI
   20th Century-Fox, 1962
THE COUCH   Warner Bros., 1962
STRAIT JACKET   Columbia, 1963
THE NIGHT WALKER   Universal
   International, 1964
THE PSYCHOPATH   Paramount, 1966
THE DEADLY BEES   Paramount, 1967,
   w/Anthony Marriott
TORTURE GARDEN   Columbia, 1968
THE HOUSE THAT DRIPPED BLOOD
   Amicus, 1970
ASYLUM   Amicus, 1972

ALAN BOWNE
THE ABLE-BODIED SEAMAN (P)
THE BEANY AND CECIL SHOW (P)
BEIRUT (P)
FORTY-DEUCE (P)
SHARON AND BILLY (P)
SPIKE OF BENSONHURST   FilmDallas, 1988

LEIGH BRACKETT
GOLD OF THE SEVEN SAINTS   Warner Bros.,
   1961, w/Leonard Freeman
HATARI!   Paramount, 1962
EL DORADO   Paramount, 1966
THE LONG GOODBYE   United Artists, 1973

JON BRADSHAW
THE MODERNS   Alive Films, 1988,
   w/Alan Rudolph

JAMES BRIDGES
THE APPALOOSA   Universal, 1966,
   w/Roland Kibbee
COLOSSOS: THE FORBIN PROJECT
   Universal, 1969
THE BABY MAKER   National General,
   1970, directed
LIMBO   Universal, 1972, w/Joan Micklin Silver
THE PAPER CHASE ★   20th Century-Fox,
   1973, directed
9/30/55 *SEPTEMBER 30, 1955*   Universal,
   1977, directed
THE CHINA SYNDROME ★   Columbia, 1979,
   w/Mike Gray & T.S. Cook, directed
URBAN COWBOY   Paramount, 1980,
   w/Aaron Latham, directed
MIKE'S MURDER   The Ladd Company/
   Warner Bros., 1984, directed
PERFECT   Columbia, 1985,
   w/Aaron Latham, directed
WHITE HUNTER, BLACK HEART   Warner
   Bros., 1990, w/Burt Kennedy & Peter Viertel

HOWARD BROOKNER
BLOODHOUNDS OF BROADWAY   Columbia,
   1989, w/Colman deKay

RICHARD BROOKS
WHITE SAVAGE   Universal, 1943
COBRA WOMAN   Universal International,
   1944, w/Gene Lewis
MY BEST GAL   Republic, 1944
SWELL GUY   Universal-International, 1946
BRUTE FORCE   Universal International, 1947
TO THE VICTOR   Warner Bros., 1948
KEY LARGO   Warner Bros., 1948,
   w/John Huston
ANY NUMBER CAN PLAY   MGM, 1949
CRISIS   MGM, 1950, directed
STORM WARNING   Warner Bros., 1950,
   w/Daniel Fuchs
MYSTERY STREET   MGM, 1950,
   w/Sidney Boehm
THE LIGHT TOUCH   MGM, 1951, directed
BATTLE CIRCUS   MGM, 1952, directed
DEADLINE USA   20th Century-Fox,
   1952, directed
THE LAST TIME I SAW PARIS   MGM,
   1954, w/Philip G. Epstein &
   Julius J. Epstein, directed
THE LAST HUNT   MGM, 1955, directed
THE BLACKBOARD JUNGLE ★   MGM,
   1955, directed
SOMETHING OF VALUE   MGM,
   1957, directed
THE BROTHERS KARAMAZOV   MGM,
   1958, directed
CAT ON A HOT TIN ROOF ★   MGM, 1958,
   w/James Poe, directed
ELMER GANTRY ★★   United Artists,
   1960, directed
SWEET BIRD OF YOUTH   MGM,
   1962, directed
LORD JIM   Columbia, 1964, directed

THE PROFESSIONALS ★   Columbia,
1966, directed
IN COLD BLOOD ★   Columbia,
1967, directed
THE HAPPY ENDING   United Artists,
1969, directed
$ DOLLARS   Columbia, 1971, directed
BITE THE BULLET   Columbia, 1975, directed
LOOKING FOR MR. GOODBAR   Paramount,
1977, directed
WRONG IS RIGHT   Columbia, 1982, directed
FEVER PITCH   MGM/UA, 1985, directed

RONALD L. BUCK
HARRY & SON   Orion, 1984, w/Paul Newman

CHARLES BUKOWSKI
BARFLY   Cannon, 1987

ANTHONY BURGESS
MOSES   Avco Embassy, 1976,
w/Vittorio Bonicelli & Gianfranco de Bosio

C

ANGELA CARTER
THE COMPANY OF WOLVES   Cannon, 1984,
w/Neil Jordan
THE MAGIC TOYSHOP   Skouras
Pictures, 1989

JOHN CASSAVETES
SHADOWS   Lion International, 1961, directed
TOO LATE BLUES   Paramount,
1962, directed
FACES   Continental, 1968, directed
HUSBANDS   Columbia, 1970, directed
MINNIE AND MOSKOWITZ   Universal,
1971, directed
A WOMAN UNDER THE INFLUENCE
Faces Interrntional, 1974, directed
THE KILLING OF A CHINESE BOOKIE
Faces International, 1976, directed
OPENING NIGHT   Faces International,
1979, directed
GLORIA   Columbia, 1980, directed
LOVE STREAMS   Cannon, 1984,
w/Ted Allan, directed
BIG TROUBLE   Columbia, 1986, directed

JOHN CHAMPION
PANHANDLE   Allied Artists, 1948,
w/Blake Edwards
DRAGONFLY SQUADRON
Allied Artists, 1954
SHOTGUN   Allied Artists, 1955
ZERO HOUR   Paramount, 1957,
w/Hall Bartlett & Arthur Hailey
ATTACK ON THE IRON COAST
United Artists, 1968
MUSTANG COUNTRY   Universal,
1976, directed

GRAHAM CHAPMAN
THE RISE AND RISE OF MICHAEL RIMMER
Warner Bros., 1970, w/John Cleese,
Peter Cook & Kevin Billington
RENTADICK   Rank/Paradine/Virgin, 1972,
w/John Cleese

AND NOW FOR SOMETHING COMPLETELY
DIFFERENT   Columbia, 1972,
w/John Cleese, Terry Gilliam, Eric Idle,
Terry Jones & Michael Palin
MONTY PYTHON AND THE HOLY GRAIL
Cinema 5, 1974, w/John Cleese,
Terry Gilliam, Eric Idle, Terry Jones &
Michael Palin
THE ODD JOB   Columbia, 1978,
w/Bernard McKenna
MONTY PYTHON'S LIFE OF BRIAN
Orion/Warner Bros., 1979,
w/Graham Chapman, John Cleese,
Terry Gilliam, Eric Idle & Terry Jones
MONTY PYTHON LIVE AT THE HOLLYWOOD
BOWL   Columbia, 1982, w/John Cleese,
Terry Gilliam, Eric Idle, Terry Jones &
Michael Palin
MONTY PYTHON'S THE MEANING OF LIFE
Universal, 1983, w/John Cleese,
Terry Gilliam, Eric Idle, Terry Jones &
Michael Palin
YELLOWBEARD   Orion, 1983,
w/Peter Cook & Bernard McKenna

PADDY CHAYEVSKY
MARTY ★★   United Artists, 1955
THE GODDESS ★   Columbia, 1958
MIDDLE OF THE NIGHT   Columbia, 1959
THE AMERICANIZATION OF EMILY
MGM, 1964
PAINT YOUR WAGON   Paramount, 1969
THE HOSPITAL ★★   United Artists, 1971
NETWORK ★★   MGM/United Artists, 1976
ALTERED STATES   Warner Bros., 1980

SONIA CHERNUS
THE OUTLAW JOSEY WALES   Warner Bros.,
1976, w/Philip Kaufman

ALICE CHILDRESS
WEDDING BAND (P)
A HERO AIN'T NOTHING BUT A SANDWICH
New World, 1977

JAMES CLAVELL
THE FLY   20th Century-Fox, 1958
WATUSI   MGM, 1959
FIVE GATES TO HELL   20th Century-Fox,
1959, directed
WALK LIKE A DRAGON   Paramount, 1960,
w/Dan Mainwaring, directed
THE GREAT ESCAPE   United Artists, 1963,
w/W.R. Burnett
633 SQUADRON   United Artists, 1964,
w/Howard Koch
THE SATAN BUG   United Artists, 1965,
w/Edward Anhalt
TO SIR, WITH LOVE   Columbia,
1967, directed
THE LAST VALLEY   Cinerama Releasing
Corporation, 1971, directed

JAMES F. COLLIER
THE HIDING PLACE   Evangelistic Association,
1975, directed
JONI   World Wide, 1980, directed
THE PRODIGAL   World Wide, 1984, directed
CAUGHT   World Wide, 1987, directed
CHINA CRY   Penland Inc., 1990, directed

D

ROALD DAHL
YOU ONLY LIVE TWICE   United Artists, 1967
CHITTY CHITTY BANG BANG   United Artists,
1968, w/Ken Hughes
WILLY WONKA AND THE CHOCOLATE
FACTORY   Paramount, 1971

GERRY DAVIS
THE FINAL COUNTDOWN   United Artists,
1980, w/David Ambrose, Thomas Hunter &
Peter Powell

PAUL DEHN
GOLDFINGER   United Artists, 1964,
w/Richard Maibaum
THE DEADLY AFFAIR   Columbia, 1966
BENEATH THE PLANET OF THE APES
20th Century-Fox, 1969, w/Mort Abrahams
FRAGMENT OF FEAR   Columbia, 1970
ESCAPE FROM THE PLANET OF THE APES
20th Century-Fox, 1971

I. A. L. DIAMOND
ALWAYS TOGETHER   Warner Bros., 1947,
w/Henry Ephron & Phoebe Ephron
ROMANCE ON THE HIGH SEAS
Warner Bros., 1948
LET'S MAKE IT LEGAL   20th Century-Fox,
1951, w/F. Hugh Herbert
LOVE NEST   20th Century-Fox, 1951
LOVE IN THE AFTERNOON ★★   Allied Artists,
1957, w/Billy Wilder
SOME LIKE IT HOT   United Artists, 1959,
w/Billy Wilder
THE APARTMENT ★★   United Artists, 1960,
w/Billy Wilder
ONE, TWO, THREE   United Artists, 1961,
w/Billy Wilder
IRMA LA DOUCE   United Artists, 1963,
w/Billy Wilder
KISS ME, STUPID   United Artists, 1964,
w/Billy Wilder
THE FORTUNE COOKIE ★   United Artists,
1966, w/Billy Wilder
CACTUS FLOWER   Columbia, 1969
THE PRIVATE LIFE OF SHERLOCK HOLMES
United Artists, 1970, w/Billy Wilder
AVANTI!   United Artists, 1972, w/Billy Wilder
THE FRONT PAGE   Universal, 1974,
w/Billy Wilder
FEDORA   United Artists, 1979, w/Billy Wilder
BUDDY BUDDY   MGM/United Artists, 1981,
w/Billy Wilder

ANDREA DUNBAR
RITA, SUE AND BOB TOO!   Orion Classics,
1987, from her play

PHILIP DUNNE
THE COUNT OF MONTE CRISTO   Reliance,
1934, w/Roland Lee & Dan Totheroh
LANCER SPY   20th Century-Fox, 1937
SUEZ   20th Century-Fox, 1938,
w/Julien Josephson
STANLEY AND LIVINGSTONE   20th Century-
Fox, 1939, w/Julien Josephson
THE RAINS CAME   20th Century-Fox, 1939,
w/Julien Josephson

HOW GREEN WAS MY VALLEY ★
20th Century-Fox, 1941
THE LATE GEORGE APLEY
20th Century-Fox, 1946
THE GHOST AND MRS. MUIR
20th Century-Fox, 1947
ESCAPE 20th Century-Fox, 1948
PINKY 20th Century-Fox, 1949,
w/Dudley Nichols
DAVID AND BATHSHEBA
20th Century-Fox, 1951
ANNE OF THE INDIES 20th Century-Fox,
1951, w/Arthur Caesar
WAY OF A GAUCHO 20th Century-Fox, 1952
LYDIA BAILEY 20th Century-Fox, 1952,
w/Michael Blankfort
DEMETRIUS AND THE GLADIATORS
20th Century-Fox, 1954
THE EGYPTIAN 20th Century-Fox, 1954,
w/Casey Robinson
THE VIEW FROM POMPEY'S HEAD
20th Century-Fox, 1955, directed
THREE BRAVE MEN 20th Century-Fox,
1956, directed
HILDA CRANE 20th Century-Fox, 1956
TEN NORTH FREDERICK 20th Century-Fox,
1958, directed
BLUE DENIM *BLUE JEANS*
20th Century-Fox, 1959, w/Edith Sommer
BLINDFOLD Universal, 1965,
w/W.H. Menger, directed
THE AGONY AND THE ECSTASY
20th Century-Fox, 1965

E

SPENCER EASTMAN
THE CHAMP MGM/UA, 1979,
w/Walter Newman
HIDE IN PLAIN SIGHT MGM/United
Artists, 1980
KANSAS Trans World Entertainment, 1988
WAR PARTY Hemdale, 1988
NIGHT GAME Trans World
Entertainment, 1989

HENRY EPHRON
MY DAUGHTER, YOUR SON (P)
w/Phoebe Ephron
THREE'S A FAMILY (P) w/Phoebe Ephron
BRIDE BY MISTAKE RKO, 1944,
w/Phoebe Ephron
ALWAYS TOGETHER Warner Bros., 1947,
w/Phoebe Ephron & I.A.L. Diamond
THE JACKPOT 20th Century-Fox, 1950,
w/Phoebe Ephron
BELLES ON THEIR TOES 20th Century-Fox,
1952, w/Phoebe Ephron
WHAT PRICE GLORY? 20th Century-Fox,
1952 w/Phoebe Ephron
THERE'S NO BUSINESS LIKE SHOW
BUSINESS 20th Century-Fox, 1954
w/Phoebe Ephron
DADDY LONGLEGS 20th Century-Fox,
1955, w/Phoebe Ephron
THE GIRL RUSH Paramount, 1955,
w/Phoebe Ephron
CAROUSEL 20th Century-Fox, 1956,
w/Phoebe Ephron
THE DESK SET 20th Century-Fox, 1957,
w/Phoebe Ephron

CAPTAIN NEWMAN MD ★ Universal, 1963,
w/Phoebe Ephron & Richard L. Breen
TAKE HER, SHE'S MINE 20th Century-Fox,
1963, w/Phoebe Ephron,
based on their play

PHOEBE EPHRON
MY DAUGHTER, YOUR SON (P)
w/Henry Ephron
THREE'S A FAMILY (P) w/Henry Ephron
BRIDE BY MISTAKE RKO, 1944,
w/Henry Ephron
ALWAYS TOGETHER Warner Bros., 1947,
w/Henry Ephron & I.A.L. Diamond
THE JACKPOT 20th Century-Fox, 1950,
w/Henry Ephron
BELLES ON THEIR TOES 20th Century-Fox,
1952, w/Henry Ephron
WHAT PRICE GLORY? 20th Century-Fox,
1952 w/Henry Ephron
THERE'S NO BUSINESS LIKE SHOW
BUSINESS 20th Century-Fox, 1954
w/Henry Ephron
DADDY LONGLEGS 20th Century-Fox,
1955, w/Henry Ephron
THE GIRL RUSH Paramount, 1955,
w/Henry Ephron
CAROUSEL 20th Century-Fox, 1956,
w/Henry Ephron
THE DESK SET 20th Century-Fox, 1957,
w/Henry Ephron
CAPTAIN NEWMAN MD ★ Universal, 1963,
w/Henry Ephron & Richard L. Breen
TAKE HER, SHE'S MINE 20th Century-Fox,
1963, w/Henry Ephron, based on their play

LAURA ERNST
TOO MUCH SUN New Line Cinema, 1990,
w/Robert Downey & Al Schwartz

MARTY FELDMAN
EVERY HOME SHOULD HAVE ONE British
Lion, 1970, w/Denis Norden & Barry Took
THE LAST REMAKE OF BEAU GESTE
Universal, 1977, w/Chris Allen
IN GOD WE TRUST Universal, 1980,
w/Chris Allen
THE SECRET POLICEMAN'S OTHER BALL
Miramax, 1982, w/Martin Lewis &
Michael Palin

FEDERICO FELLINI
L'AMORE Tevere Film, 1948,
w/Tullio Pinelli & Roberto Rosselini
IL CAMMINO DELLA SPERANZA Lux,
1950, w/Tullio Pinelli
VARIETY LIGHTS Pathe Contemporary,
1950, w/Tullio Pinelli, Ennio Flaiano &
Alberto Lattuada, co-directed
THE WHITE SHEIK Pathe Contermporary,
1952, w/Tullio Pinelli &
Ennio Flaiano, directed
I VITTELONI API Productions, 1953,
w/Ennio Flaiano, directed
LOVE IN THE CITY Italian Films Export,
1953, Episode IV: "A Matrimonal Agency,"
w/Tullio Pinelli, directed

LA STRADA Trans-Lux, 1954,
w/Tullio Pinelli & Ennio Flaiano, directed
IL BIDONE Astor, 1955, w/Tullio Pinelli &
Ennio Flaiano, directed
NIGHTS OF CABIRIA Lopert, 1957,
w/Tullio Pinelli & Ennio Flaiano
LA DOLCE VITA ★ Astor, 1961,
w/Tullio Pinelli & Ennio Flaiano, directed
BOCCACCIO "70 Embasssy, 1962,
Part II "The Temptations of Doctor Antonio,"
w/Tullio Pinelli & Ennio Flaiano, directed
8-1/2 ★ Embassy, 1963, w/Tullio Pinelli,
Ennio Flaiano & Brunello Rondi, directed
JULIET OF THE SPIRITS Rizzoli, 1965,
w/Tullio Pinelli, Ennio Flaiano &
Brunello Rondi, directed
SPIRITS OF THE DEAD *HISTOIRES
EXTRAORDINAIRES* American
International, 1969, Episode III "Toby
Dammit," w/Bernardino Zapponi, directed
FELLINI SATYRICON United Artists, 1970,
w/Bernardino Zapponi, directed
FELLINI'S ROMA United Artists, 1972,
w/Bernardino Zapponi, directed
AMARCORD ★ New World, 1975,
w/Tonino Guerra, directed
CASANOVA ★ *IL CASANOVA DI FEDERICO
FELLINI* Universal, 1977,
w/Bernardino Zapponi, directed
ORCHESTRA REHEARSAL New Yorker,
1979, w/Bernardino Zapponi, directed
CITY OF WOMEN Gaumont/New Yorker,
1981, w/Bernardino Zapponi &
Brunello Rondi
AND THE SHIP SAILS ON Triumph/
Columbia, 1983, w/Tonino Guerra, directed
GINGER AND FRED MGM/UA, 1986,
w/Tonino Guerra & Tullio Pinelli, directed
THE VOICE OF THE MOON Penta
Distribuzione, 1990, w/Tullio Pinelli &
Ermanno Cavazzoni, directed
INTERVISTA Castle Hill Productions, 1992,
directed, filmed in 1987
DIRECTOR'S NOTEBOOK 1994, directed

MORTON FINE
HOT SUMMER NIGHT MGM, 1957,
w/David Friedkin
HANDLE WITH CARE MGM, 1958,
w/David Friedkin
THE FOOL KILLER Allied Artists, 1965
THE PAWNBROKER ★★ Landau/Allied
Artists, 1965,w/David Friedkin
THE NEXT MAN Allied Artists, 1976,
w/AlanTrustman, Richard C. Sarafian &
David M. Wolf
THE GREEK TYCOON Universal, 1978
CABOBLANCO Avco Embassy, 1981,
w/Milton Gelman

CARL FOREMAN
HIGH NOON United Artitsts, 1952
DAKOTA Republic, 1945, Story
SO THIS IS NEW YORK United Artitsts, 1948,
w/Herbert Baker
CHAMPION ★ Kramer, 1949
THE CLAY PIGEON RKO, 1949
YOUNG MAN WITH A HORN
Warner Bros., 1950
THE SLEEPING TIGER Astor, 1954
THE BRIDGE ON THE RIVER KWAI ★★
Columbia, 1957, w/Michael Wilson
THE KEY Columbia, 1958
THE GUNS OF NAVARONE Columbia, 1961
YOUNG WINSTON Columbia, 1972
WHEN TIME RAN OUT Warner Bros., 1980,
w/Stirling Silliphant

BOB FOSSE
ALL THAT JAZZ ★   20th Century-Fox, 1979,
   w/Robert Alan Arthur, directed
STAR 80   Warner Bros., 1983, directed

CHRISTOPHER FRANK
THE FRENCH WAY   *LOVE AT THE TOP*
   Peppercorn-Wormser, 1975
FEMMES DE PERSONNE   European
   Classics, 1986, directed
L'ANNEE DES MEDUSES   European
   Classics, 1987, directed
MALONE   Orion, 1987

JOHN GAY
SUMMER VIOLENCE (P)
DIVERSIONS AND DELIGHTS (P)
RUN SILENT RUN DEEP   United Artists, 1958
SEPARATE TABLES ★   United Artists,
   1958, w/Terence Rattigan
THE FOUR HORSEMEN OF THE
   APOCALYPSE   MGM, 1961,
   w/Robert Ardrey
THE HAPPY THEIVES   United Artists, 1962
THE COURTSHIP OF EDDIE'S FATHER
   MGM, 1962
THE HALLELUJAH TRAIL
   United Artists, 1965
THE LAST SAFARI   Paramount, 1967
THE POWER   MGM, 1967
NO WAY TO TRAT A LADY   Paramount, 1968
SOLDIER BLUE   Avco Embassy, 1970
SOMETIMES A GREAT NOTION   *NEVER
   GIVE AN INCH*   Universal, 1971
HENNESSY   American International, 1975

MICHAEL V. GAZZO
A HATFUL OF RAINBOWS (P)
A HATFUL OF RAIN   20th Century-Fox,
   1957, from his play
KING CREOLE   Paramount, 1958,
   w/Herbert Baker

THEODORE (TED) GEISEL
(Dr. Suess)
GERALD McBOING BOING (AF)   UPA, 1951
THE FIVE THOUSAND FINGERS OF
   DOCTOR T   Columbia, 1953, w/Allan Scott

MILTON S. GELMAN
CABOBLANCO   Avco Embassy, 1981,
   Story w/James Granby Hunter

DUNCAN GIBBINS
THIRD DEGREE BURN (CTF)   HBO Pictures,
   1989, w/Yale Udoff, directed
EVE OF DESTRUCTION   Orion, 1991,
   w/Yale Udoff, directed
A CASE FOR MURDER (CTF)   Bidega Bay
   Prods./MCA Television Entertainment,
   1993, w/Pablo Fenjves, directed

SHEPARD GOLDMAN
SALSA   Cannon, 1988, w/Tomas Benitez &
   Boaz Davidson

RUTH GORDON
OVER 21 (P)
A DOUBLE LIFE   Universal, 1947,
   w/Garson Kanin
ADAM'S RIB   MGM, 1949, w/Garson Kanin
PAT AND MIKE ★   MGM, 1952,
   w/Ruth Gordon
THE ACTRESS   MGM, 1953
IT SHOULD HAPPEN TO YOU   Columbia,
   1954, w/Garson Kanin

STEVE GORDON
ARTHUR ★   Orion, 1981, directed
THE ONE AND ONLY   Paramount, 1978

CHRISTOPHER GORE
FAME   MGM/United Artists, 1980

BLANCHE HANALIS
THE TROUBLE WITH ANGELS
   Columbia, 1966
WHERE ANGELS GO, TROUBLE FOLLOWS
   Columbia, 1968
FISH HAWK   Avco Embassy, 1981

GUSTAV HASFORD
FULL METAL JACKET ★   Warner Bros.,
   1987, w/Michael Herr & Stanley Kubrick

LUKAS HELLER
WHATEVER HAPPENED TO BABY JANE?
   Warner Bros., 1962
AGENT 8 3/4   *HOT ENOUGH FOR JUNE*
   Continental, 1963
HUSH, HUSH SWEET CHARLOTTE
   20th Century-Fox, 1964, w/Henry Farrell
FLIGHT OF THE PHOENIX
   20th Century Fox, 1965
THE DIRTY DOZEN   MGM, 1967,
   w/Nunally Johnson
THE KILLING OF SISTER GEORGE
   Associates & Aldrich, 1969
MONTE WALSH   National General, 1970,
   w/David Z. Goodman
TOO LATE THE HERO   Cinerama
   Releasing, 1970
THE DEADLY TRACKERS
   Warner Bros., 1973
DAMNATION ALLEY   20th Century Fox, 1977
   w/Alan Sharp
CABO BLANCO   Avco Embassy, 1981,
   w/Mort Fine
BLUE CITY   Paramount, 1986, w/Walter Hill

JIM HENSON
THE DARK CRYSTAL   Universal, 1982,
   Story, co-directed
LABYRINTH   Tri-Star, 1986, Story, directed

DOUGLAS HEYES
DRUMS OF TAHITI   Columbia, 1953,
   w/Robert E. Kent
THE BATTLE OF ROGUE RIVER
   Columbia, 1954
THE IRON GLOVE   Columbia, 1954,
   w/Jesse L. Lasky Jr. & De Vallon Scott

KITTEN WITH A WHIP   Universal,
   1964, directed
BEAU GESTE   Universal, 1966, directed
ICE STATION ZEBRA   MGM, 1968,
   w/Harry Julian Fink
THE GROUNDSTAR CONSPIRACY
   Universal, 1972

COLIN HIGGINS
HAROLD AND MAUDE   Paramount, 1971
SILVER STREAK   20th Century-Fox, 1975
FOUL PLAY   Paramount, 1978, directed
NINE TO FIVE   20th Century Fox, 1980,
   w/Patricia Resnick, directed

JAMES HILL
HIS MAJESTY O'KEEFE   Warner Bros.,
   1954, w/Borden Chase
GIUSEPPINA (Short)   1960, directed
THE BELSTONE FOX   *FREE SPIRIT*
   Cine III, 1973, directed

CY HOWARD
EVERY LITTLE CROOK AND NANNY
   MGM, 1972, w/Jon Axelrod &
   Robert Klane, directed
WON TON TON, THE DOG WHO SAVED
   HOLLYWOOD   Paramount, 1976,
   w/Arnold Schulman

CLAIR HUFFAKER
THE COMANCHEROS   20th Century-Fox,
   1961, w/James Edward Grant
100 RIFLES   20th Century-Fox, 1969
CHINO   DEG, 1973
FLAMING STAR   20th Century-Fox, 1960,
   w/Nunally Johnson
FLAP   Warner Bros., 1970
THE DESERTER   Paramount, 1971,
   w/Burt Kennedy, directed
HELLFIGHTERS   Universal, 1969
RIO CONCHOS   20th Century-Fox, 1964
TARZAN AND THE VALLEY OF GOLD
   American International, 1966
THE WAR WAGON   Universal, 1967

ALEXANDER JACOBS
POINT BLANK   MGM, 1967,
   w/David Newhouse & Rose Newhouse
HELL IN THE PACIFIC   Cinerama Releasing
   Corporation, 1969, w/Eric Bercovici
THE SEVEN-UPS   20th Century-Fox, 1973,
   w/Albert Ruben
FRENCH CONNECTION II   20th Century-Fox,
   1975, w/Laurie Dillon & Robert Dillon
AN ENEMY OF THE PEOPLE
   Warner Bros., 1978

DEREK JARMAN
JUBILEE   Libra, 1979, w/others, directed
THE TEMPEST   World Northal,
   1980, directed
CARAVAGGIO   Cinevista, 1986, directed
WAR REQUIEM   Movie Visions,
   1990, directed
THE GARDEN   Channel Four, 1991, directed

EDWARD II   Fine Line Features, 1992,
    w/Ken Butler & Stephen McBride, directed
WITTGENSTEIN   Zeitgeist Films, 1993,
    w/Ken Butler & Terry Eagleton, directed
BLUE   Channel Four Films, 1993, directed

BILL JESSE
RIFF-RAFF   Parallax Pictures, 1991

K

GARSON KANIN
BORN YESTERDAY (P)
A DOUBLE LIFE   Universal, 1947,
    w/Ruth Gordon
ADAM'S RIB   MGM, 1949, w/Ruth Gordon
PAT AND MIKE ★   MGM, 1952,
    w/Ruth Gordon
IT SHOULD HAPPEN TO YOU   Columbia,
    1954, w/Ruth Gordon

MICHAEL KANIN
RASHOMON (P)   w/Fay Kanin
SEIDMAN AND OSON (P)
HIS AND HERS (P)
THE HIGH LIFE (P)
SUNDAY PUNCH   MGM, 1942
WOMAN OF THE YEAR ★★   MGM, 1942,
    w/Ring Lardner Jr.
THE CROSS OF LORRAINE   MGM, 1944,
    w/Robert Andrews, Alexander Esway &
    Ring Lardner Jr.
CENTENNIAL SUMMER
    20th Century-Fox, 1946
HONEYMOON   RKO Radio, 1947
WHEN I GROW UP   Horizon, 1950, directed
MY PAL GUS   20th Century-Fox, 1952,
    w/Fay Kanin
RHAPSODY   MGM, 1954, w/Fay Kanin
THE OPPOSITE SEX   MGM, 1956,
    w/Fay Kanin
TEACHER'S PET ★   Paramount, 1958,
    w/Fay Kanin
THE RIGHT APPROACH   20th Century-Fox,
    1961, w/Fay Kanin
SWORDMAN OF SIENA   MGM, 1962,
    w/Fay Kanin
THE OUTRAGE   MGM, 1964
HOW TO COMMIT MARRIAGE   Cinerama
    Releasing Corporation, 1969, w/Ben Starr

ROBERT KAUFMAN
DR. GOLDFOOT AND THE BIKINI MACHINE
    American International, 1965,
    w/Elwood Ullman
SKI PARTY   American International, 1965
DR. GOLDFOOT AND THE GIRL BOMBS
    American International, 1966,
    w/Lewis M. Heyward
THE COOL ONES   Warner Bros., 1967
I LOVE MY WIFE   Universal, 1970
GETTING STRAIGHT   Columbia, 1970
FREEBIE AND THE BEAN
    Warner Bros., 1974
HARRY AND WALTER GO TO NEW YORK
    Columbia, 1976, w/John Byrum
THE HAPPY HOOKER GOES TO
    WASHINGTON   Cannon, 1977
LOVE AT FIRST BITE   American
    International, 1979

NOTHING PERSONAL   American
    International, 1980
HOW TO BEAT THE HIGH COST OF LIVING
    American International, 1980
SPLIT IMAGE   Orion, 1982,
    w/Robert Mark Kamen & Scott Spencer
THE CHECK IS IN THE MAIL   Ascot
    Entertainment Group, 1986
SEPARATE VACATIONS
    RSK Entertainment, 1986

DOUGLAS KENNEY
NATIONAL LAMPOON'S ANIMAL HOUSE
    Universal, 1978, w/Chris Miller &
    Harold Ramis
CADDYSHACK   Orion/Warner Bros., 1980,
    w/Brian Doyle Murray & Harold Ramis

ROLAND KIBBEE
ANGEL ON MY SHOULDER   United Artists,
    1946, w/Harry Segall
THE CRIMSON PIRATE   Warner Bros., 1952
THE DESERT SONG   Warner Bros.,
    1953, Adaptation
THE DEVIL'S DISCIPLE   United Artists,
    1959, w/John Dighton
THE AMOROUS ADVENTURES OF MOLL
    FLANDERS   Paramount, 1965,
    w/Dennis Cannan
THE APPALOOSA   Universal, 1966,
    w/James Bridges
VALDEZ IS COMING   United Artists, 1970,
    w/David Rayfiel
THE MIDNIGHT MAN   Universal,
    1974, co-directed

JAMES KIRKWOOD
A CHORUS LINE (P)
EIGHT WOMEN AND A GOAT (P)
HOME FOR STRAY CATS (P)
THERE MUST BE A PONY (P)
UNHEALTHY TO BE PLEASANT (P)
VACANCY IN PARADISE (P)
WITCH STORY (P)
WOMAN AT DEAD OAKS (P)
YOUTH, SPRING, LOVE (P)
SOME KIND OF HERO   Paramount, 1982,
    w/Robert Boris

JERZY KOSINSKY
BEING THERE   United Artists, 1979

MICHAEL KRUEGER
THE AMITYVILLE CURSE   Allegro Films,
    1990, w/Norvell Rose

L

MICHAEL LANDON
SAM'S SON   New World, 1985, directed

WILFORD LEACH
THE PIRATES OF PENZANCE
    Universal, 1983, directed

DAVID LEAN
THIS HAPPY BREED   Universal, 1944,
    w/Anthony Havelock-Allan &
    Ronald Neame, directed
BLITHE SPIRIT   United Artists, 1945,
    Scenario w/Anthony Havelock-Allan &
    Ronald Neame, directed
GREAT EXPECTATIONS ★   Universal, 1947,
    w/Anthony Havelock-Allan, Cecil McGivern,
    Ronald Neame & Kay Walsh, directed
OLIVER TWIST   United Artists, 1948,
    w/Stanley Haynes, directed
SUMMERTIME   SUMMER MADNESS
    United Artists, 1955, w/H.E. Bates, directed
A PASSAGE TO INDIA ★   Columbia,
    1984, directed

ROBERT E. LEE
TOAST OF THE TOWN (P)
    w/Jerome Lawrence
AUNTIE MAME (P)   w/Jerome Lawrence
THE GANG'S ALL HERE (P)
    w/Jerome Lawrence
THE NIGHT THOREAU SPENT IN JAIL (P)
    w/Jerome Lawrence
INHERIT THE WIND (P)   w/Jerome Lawrence
FIRST MONDAY IN OCTOBER   Paramount,
    1981, w/Jerome Lawrence, from their play

RICHARD LEVINSON
ROLLERCOASTER   Universal, 1977,
    w/William Link

ALBERT E. LEWIN
THE MOON AND SIXPENCE   United Artists,
    1943, directed
CALL ME MISTER   20th Century-Fox, 1951,
    w/Burt Styler
DOWN AMONG THE SHELTERING PALMS
    20th Century-Fox, 1952, w/Claude Binyon &
    Burt Styler
THE LIVING IDOL   MGM, 1956, directed
THE NAKED MAJA   MGM, 1959, w/others
BOY, DID I GET A WRONG NUMBER
    United Artists, 1966, w/George Kennett &
    Burt Styler
EIGHT ON THE LAM   United Artists, 1966,
    w/Bob Fisher, Arthur Marx & Burt Styler
I WILL, I WILL...FOR NOW   20th Century-Fox,
    1976, w/Norman Panama

DAVID P. LEWIS
KLUTE ★   Warner Bros., 1971, w/Andy Lewis
CITY ON FIRE   Astral-Bellevue, 1979,
    w/Jack Hill & Celine La Freniere
DEATH SHIP   Avco Embassy, 1980,
    Story w/Jack Hill

EZRA LITWAK
THE BUTCHER'S WIFE   Paramount, 1991,
    w/Marjorie Schwartz

ROY LONDON
TIGER WARSAW   Sony Pictures, 1988

M

RICHARD MAIBAUM
BIRTHRIGHT (P)
THE TREE (P)
TIRADE (P)
BAD MAN OF BRIMSTONE   MGM, 1937,
   w/Cyril Hume
THE AMAZING MR. WILLIAMS   Columbia,
   1939, w/Sy Bartlett & Dwight Taylor
TWENTY- MULE TEAM   MGM, 1940
TEN GENTLEMEN FROM WEST POINT
   20th Century-Fox, 1942
O.S.S.   Paramount, 1946
SONG OF SURRENDER   Paramount, 1949
COCKLESHELL HEROES   Columbia, 1955,
   w/Bryan Forbes
ZARAK   Columbia, 1956
BIGGER THAN LIFE   20th Century-Fox,
   1956, w/Cyril Hume
THE KILLERS OF KILIMANJARO   Columbia,
   1959, w/Cyril Hume
THE DAY THEY ROBBED THE BANK OF
   ENGLAND   MGM, 1960,
   w/Howard Clewes
THE BATTLE AT BLOODY BEACH
   20th Century-Fox, 1961,
   w/Willard Willingham
DR. NO   United Artists, 1962,
   w/Johanna Harwood & Berkeley Mather
FROM RUSSIA WITH LOVE   United Artists,
   1963, w/Johanna Harwood
GOLDFINGER   United Artists, 1964,
   w/Paul Dehn
THUNDERBALL   United Artists, 1964,
   w/John Hopkins
CHITTY CHITTY BANG BANG   United Artists,
   1968, Story
ON HER MAJESTY'S SECRET SERVICE
   United Artists, 1969
DIAMONDS ARE FOREVER   United Artists,
   1971, w/Tom Mankiewicz
THE MAN WITH THE GOLDEN GUN
   United Artists, 1974, w/Tom Mankiewicz
THE SPY WHO LOVED ME   United Artists,
   1977, w/Christopher Wood
FOR YOUR EYES ONLY   MGM/United Artists,
   1981, w/Michael G. Wilson
OCTOPUSSY   MGM/UA, 1983,
   w/George MacDonald Fraser &
   Michael G. Wilson
A VIEW TO A KILL   MGM/UA, 1985,
   w/Michael G. Wilson
THE LIVING DAYLIGHTS   MGM/UA, 1987,
   w/Michael G. Wilson
LICENCE TO KILL   MGM/UA, 1989,
   w/Michael G. Wilson

JOSEPH L. MANKIEWICZ
SKIPPY ★   Paramount, 1931, w/Sam Mintz
DIPLOMANIACS   RKO, 1933,
   w/Henry Meyers
DRAGONWYCK   20th Century-Fox,
   1946, directed
SOMEWHERE IN THE NIGHT
   20th Century-Fox, 1946,
   w/Howard Dimsdale, directed
A LETTER TO THREE WIVES ★★
   20th Century-Fox, 1949
NO WAY OUT   20th Century-Fox, 1950,
   w/Lesser Samuels, directed
ALL ABOUT EVE ★   20th Century-Fox,
   1950, directed
PEOPLE WILL TALK   20th Century-Fox,
   1951, directed
FIVE FINGERS   20th Century-Fox,
   1952, directed
JULIUS CAESAR   MGM, 1953, directed
THE BAREFOOT CONTESSA ★   United
   Artists, 1954, directed
GUYS AND DOLLS   Goldwyn, 1955
THE QUIET AMERICAN   United Artists,
   1957, directed
CLEOPATRA   20th Century-Fox, 1963,
   w/Sidney Buchman & Ranald MacDougall &
   others, directed
THE HONEY POT   United Artists,
   1966, directed

LAURENCE MARKS
BULLSEYE!   21st Century Film, 1991,
   w/Leslie Bricusse & Nick Mead

RICHARD MARQUAND
NOWHERE TO RUN   Columbia, 1993,
   Story w/Joe Eszterhas

WENDELL MAYES
THE WAY TO THE GOLD
   20th Century-Fox, 1957
THE SPIRIT OF ST. LOUIS   Warner Bros.,
   1957, w/Billy Wilder
THE HUNTERS   20th Century-Fox, 1958
FROM HELL TO TEXAS   MANHUNT
   20th Century-Fox, 1958, w/Robert Buckner
THE HANGING TREE   Warner Bros., 1958,
   w/Halstead Welles
ANATOMY OF A MURDER ★
   Columbia, 1959
ADVISE AND CONSENT   Columbia, 1962
IN HARMS WAY   Paramount, 1965
VON RYAN'S EXPRESS   20th Century-Fox,
   1965, w/Joseph Landon
HOTEL   Warner Bros., 1967
THE POSEIDON ADVENTURE   20th
   Century-Fox, 1972, w/Stirling Silliphant
THE REVENGERS   Cinema Center, 1972
THE BANK SHOT   United Artists, 1974
DEATH WISH   Paramount, 1974
THE ENEMY BELOW
   20th Century-Fox, 1976
GO TELL THE SPARTANS
   Avco Embassy, 1978
LOVE AND BULLETS   ITC, 1979,
   w/John Melson
MONSIGNOR   20th Century-Fox, 1982,
   w/Abraham Polonsky

DENNIS MCINTYRE
ESTABLISHED PRICE (P)
MODIGLIANI (P)
NATIONAL ANTHEMS (P)
SPLIT SECOND (P)
STATE OF GRACE   Orion, 1990

NATHAN MONASTER
THE SAD SACK   Paramount, 1957
CALL ME BWANA   Rank, 1962,
   w/Johanna Harwood
A VERY SPECIAL FAVOR   Universal, 1965
HOW TO SAVE A MARRIAGE AND RUIN
   YOUR LIFE   Columbia, 1968,
   w/Stanley Shapiro

RICHARD T. MURPHY
BACK IN THE SADDLE   1941
BOOMERANG! ★   20th Century-Fox, 1947
CRY OF THE CITY   20th Century-Fox, 1948
DEEP WATERS   20th Century-Fox, 1948
SLATTERY'S HURRICANE   20th Century-Fox,
   1949, w/Herman Wouk
PANIC IN THE STREETS ★
   20th Century-Fox, 1950, w/Edna Anhalt &
   Edward Anhalt
YOU'RE IN THE NAVY NOW   USS
   TEAKETTLE   20th Century-Fox, 1951
THE DESERT RATS ★
   20th Century-Fox, 1953
BROKEN LANCE   20th Century-Fox, 1954
THREE STRIPES IN THE SUN   THE GENTLE
   SERGEANT   Columbia, 1955, directed
COMPULSION   20th Century-Fox, 1959
THE LAST ANGRY MAN   Columbia, 1959
THE WACKIEST SHIP IN THE ARMY
   Columbia, 1960, directed
THE KIDNAPPING OF THE PRESIDENT
   Crown, 1980

JOHN MYHERS
THE PRIZE FIGHTER   New World, 1979,
   w/Tim Conway
THE PRIVATE EYES   New World, 1980,
   w/Tim Conway

N

VLADIMAR NABOKOV
LOLITA ★   MGM, 1962

BILL NAUGHTON
ALFIE ★   Paramount, 1966, from his play
THE FAMILY WAY   British Lion, 1966,
   from his play "Honeymoon Deferred"
SPRING AND PORT WINE   1970,
   from his play "Keep It in the Family"

WALTER NEWMAN
ACE IN THE HOLE ★   Paramount, 1951,
   w/Billy Wilder
THE MAN WITH THE GOLDEN ARM   1955,
   w/Lewis Meltzer
UNDERWATER   RKO, 1955,
   w/Robert B. Bailey & Hugh King
THE TRUE STORY OF JESSE JAMES
   Fox, 1956
CRIME AND PUNISHMENT USA
   Allied Artists, 1958
THE MAGNIFICENT SEVEN
   United Artists, 1960
THE INTERNS   Columbia, 1962,
   w/David Swift
THE GREAT ESCAPE   United Artists, 1963
CAT BALLOU ★   Columbia, 1965,
   w/Frank Pierson
BLOODBROTHERS ★   Warner Bros., 1978
THE CHAMP   MGM/UA, 1979,
   w/Spencer Eastman
SAINT JACK   New World, 1979

HARRY NILSSON
THE TELEPHONE   New World, 1988,
   w/Terry Southern

O

MICHAEL O'DONOGHUE
MR. MIKE'S MONDO VIDEO   New Line
    Cinema, 1979, w/Mitch Glazer,
    Emily Prager & Dirk Wittenborn, directed
SCROOGED   Paramount, 1988,
    w/Mitch Glazer

ALUN OWEN
THE CONCRETE JUNGLE   *THE CRIMINAL*
    Merton Park, 1960, w/Jimmy Sangster
A HARD DAY'S NIGHT ★   United Artists, 1964

P

ANTHONY PERKINS
THE LAST OF SHIELA   Warner Bros., 1973,
    w/Stephen Sondheim

ARNOLD PERL
COTTON COMES TO HARLEM
    United Artists, 1970, w/Ossie Davis
MALCOLM X   Warner Bros., 1992,
    w/Spike Lee

ELEANOR PERRY
DAVID AND LISA   Continental, 1962
THE SWIMMER   Columbia, 1968
LAST SUMMER   Allied Artists, 1969
THE LADY IN THE CAR WITH GLASSES AND
    A GUN   Lira Film, 1969, w/Richard Harris
THE DIARY OF A MAD HOUSEWIFE
    Universal, 1970
THE DEADLY TRAP   Corona, 1971,
    w/Sidney Buchman

ROBERT PIROSH
THE WINNING TICKET   MGM, 1935,
    w/others
A DAY AT THE RACES   MGM, 1937,
    w/George Oppenheimer & George Seaton
I MARRIED A WITCH   United Artists, 1942,
    w/Marc Connelly
UP IN ARMS   RKO Radio, 1944
BATTLEGROUND ★★   MGM, 1949
GO FOR BROKE   MGM, 1951, directed
VALLEY OF THE KINGS   MGM, 1954,
    w/Karl Tunberg, directed
SPRING REUNION   United Artists,
    1956, directed
A GATHERING OF EAGLES   Universal
    International, 1962
HELL IS FOR HEROES   Paramount,
    1962, w/Richard Carr
WHAT'S SO BAD ABOUT FEELING GOOD?
    Universal, 1968

DENNIS POTTER
PENNIES FROM HEAVEN ★   MGM/United
    Artists, 1981
BRIMSTONE & TREACLE   United Artists
    Classics, 1982
GORKY PARK   Orion, 1983
DREAMCHILD   Universal, 1985
TENDER IS THE NIGHT (CMS)   Showtime/
    BBC/Seven Network, 1985
THE SINGING DETECTIVE   BBC/ABC
    Australia, 1987
TRACK 29   Island Pictures, 1988
BLACKEYES   BBC/Paravision/Blackeyes Ltd,
    1990, directed
SECRET FRIENDS   Geisler-Roberdeau/Film
    Four International, 1992, directed
MIDNIGHT MOVIE   BBC/Whistling Gypsy
    Productions, 1993
MESMER   Cineplex Odeon Films, 1994

MICHAEL POWELL
HIS LORDSHIP   United Artists, 1932, directed
THE EDGE OF THE WORLD   British
    Independent Exhibitors, 1937, directed
CONTRABAND   *BLACKOUT*   Anglo-American,
    1940, w/Emeric Pressburger & Brock
    Williams, directed
ONE OF OUR AIRCRAFT IS MISSING
    United Artists, 1942, w/Emeric Pressburger,
    co-directed
THE LIFE AND DEATH OF COLONEL BLIMP
    GFO, 1943, w/Emeric Pressburger,
    co-directed
A CANTERBURY TALE   Eagle-Lion, 1944,
    w/Emeric Pressburger, co-directed
I KNOW WHERE I'M GOING   Universal, 1945,
    w/Emeric Pressburger, co-directed
STAIRWAY TO HEAVEN   *A MATTER OF LIFE
    AND DEATH*   Universal, 1946,
    w/Emeric Pressburger, co-directed
BLACK NARCISSUS   Universal, 1947,
    w/Emeric Pressburger, co-directed
THE RED SHOES   Eagle-Lion, 1948,
    w/Emeric Pressburger, co-directed
THE SMALL BACK ROOM   *HOUR OF
    GLORY*   Snader Productions, 1948,
    w/Emeric Pressburger, co-directed
THE WILD HEART   *GONE TO EARTH*
    RKO Radio, 1950, w/Emeric Pressburger,
    co-directed
THE ELUSIVE PIMPERNEL   British Lion,
    1950, w/Emeric Pressburger, co-directed
THE TALES OF HOFFMAN   Lopert, 1951,
    w/Emeric Pressburger, co-directed
OH ROSALINDA!   Associated British
    Picture Corp., 1955, w/Emeric Pressburger,
    co-directed
PURSUIT OF THE GRAF SPEE   *THE BATTLE
    OF THE RIVER PLATE*   Rank, 1956,
    w/Emeric Pressburger, co-directed
NIGHT AMBUSH   *ILL MET BY MOONLIGHT*
    Rank, 1957, w/Emeric Pressburger,
    co-directed
HONEYMOON   *LUNA DE MIEL*   RKO Radio,
    1958, w/Luis Escobar, directed

EMERIC PRESSBURGER
THE CHALLENGE   Korda, 1938,
    w/Patrick Kirwan & Milton Rosmer
CONTRABAND   *BLACKOUT*   Anglo-American,
    1940, w/Michael Powell &
    Brock Williams, directed
ONE OF OUR AIRCRAFT IS MISSING
    United Artists, 1942, w/Michael Powell,
    co-directed
THE LIFE AND DEATH OF COLONEL BLIMP
    GFO, 1943, w/Michael Powell, co-directed

A CANTERBURY TALE   Eagle-Lion, 1944,
    w/Michael Powell, co-directed
I KNOW WHERE I'M GOING   Universal,
    1945, w/Michael Powell, co-directed
STAIRWAY TO HEAVEN   *A MATTER OF
    LIFE AND DEATH*   Universal, 1946,
    w/Michael Powell, co-directed
BLACK NARCISSUS   Universal, 1947,
    w/Michael Powell, co-directed
THE RED SHOES   Eagle-Lion, 1948,
    w/Michael Powell, co-directed
THE SMALL BACK ROOM   *HOUR OF
    GLORY*   Snader Productions, 1948,
    w/Michael Powell, co-directed
THE WILD HEART   *GONE TO EARTH*   RKO
    Radio, 1950, wMichael Powellr, co-directed
THE ELUSIVE PIMPERNEL   British Lion,
    1950, w/Michael Powell, co-directed
THE TALES OF HOFFMAN   Lopert, 1951,
    w/Michael Powell, co-directed
OH ROSALINDA!   Associated British Picture
    Corp., 1955, w/EMichael Powell co-directed
PURSUIT OF THE GRAF SPEE   *THE BATTLE
    OF THE RIVER PLATE*   Rank, 1956,
    w/Michael Powell, co-directed
NIGHT AMBUSH   *ILL MET BY MOONLIGHT*
    Rank, 1957, w/Michael Powell, co-directed

R

CLARK REYNOLDS
GENGHIS KHAN   Columbia, 1965,
    w/Beverly Cross
THE VIKING QUEEN   Warner Bros., 1967
OPERATION THUNDERBOLT ★
    GS Films, 1977

TONY RICHARDSON
A TASTE OF HONEY   Continental, 1962,
    w/Shelagh Delaney, directed
NED KELLY   United Artists, 1970,
    w/Ian Jones, directed
THE HOTEL NEW HAMPSHIRE   Orion,
    1984, directed

MAURICE RICHLIN
OPERATION PETTICOAT ★   Universal, 1959,
    w/Stanley Shapiro
PILLOW TALK ★★   Universal, 1959,
    w/Stanley Shapiro
ALL IN A NIGHT'S WORK   Paramount, 1961,
    w/Edmund Beloin & Sidney Sheldon
COME SEPTEMBER   Universal, 1961,
    w/Stanley Shapiro
SOLDIER IN THE RAIN   Allied Artists, 1963,
    w/Blake Edwards
THE PINK PANTHER   United Artists, 1963,
    w/Blake Edwards
DON'T MAKE WAVES   MGM, 1967
WHAT DID YOU DO IN THE WAR, DADDY?
    United Artists, 1966
FOR PETE'S SAKE   Columbia, 1974,
    w/StanleyShapiro

GARY RIGDON
TRUST ME   Cinecom, 1989,
    w/Bobby Houston

R. J. ROBERTSON
FORBIDDEN WORLD   New World, 1982,
   Story w/Jim Wynorski
BIG MAD MOMA II   Concorde, 1988,
   w/Jim Wynorski
NOT OF THIS EARTH   Concorde, 1988,
   w/Jim Wynorski
THE HAUNTING OF MORELLA   Concorde,
   1990, w/Jim Wynorski
TRANSYLVANIA TWIST   Concorde, 1990
THINK BIG   Concorde, 1990,
   Story w/Jim Wynorski
BEASTMASTER 2: THROUGH THE PORTAL
   OF TIME   New Line Cinema, 1991,
   w/others
MUNCHIE   Concorde, 1992, w/Jim Wynorski

GENE RODDENBERRY
PRETTY MAIDS ALL IN A ROW   MGM, 1971

TERRY RUNTE
MYSTERY DATE   Orion, 1991,
   w/Parker Bennett
SUPER MARIO BROS.   Buena Vista, 1993,
   w/Parker Bennett & Ed Solomon

S

RICHARD SALE
NORTHWEST OUTPOST   Republic, 1947,
   w/Elizabeth Meehan
CALENDAR GIRL   Republic, 1947,
   w/Mary Loos & Lee Loeb
DRIFTWOOD   Republic, 1947, w/Mary Loos
WHEN WILLIE COMES MARCHING HOME
   20th Century-Fox, 1949, w/Mary Loos
MR. BELVEDERE GOES TO COLLEGE
   20th Century-Fox, 1949, w/Mary Loos &
   Mary McCall Jr.
MEET ME AFTER THE SHOW
   20th Century-Fox, 1951, w/Mary Loos
LET'S DO IT AGAIN   Columbia, 1953,
   w/Mary Loos
THE FRENCH LINE   RKO, 1953,
   w/Mary Loos
WOMAN'S WORLD   20th Century-Fox, 1954,
   w/Mary Loos & Claude Binyon
SUDDENLY   United Artists, 1954
GENTLEMEN MARRY BRUNETTES   United
   Artists, 1955, w/Mary Loos, directed
SEVEN WAVES AWAY   ABANDON SHIP
   Columbia, 1956, directed
TORPEDO RUN   MGM, 1958,
   w/William Wister Haines
THE WHITE BUFFALO   United Artists, 1977
ASSASSINATION   Cannon, 1987

WALDO SALT
RACHEL AND THE STRANGER
   RKO Radio, 1948
THE FLAME AND THE ARROW
   Warner Bros., 1950
TARAS BULBA   United Artists, 1962
FLIGHT FROM ASHIYA   United Artists,
   1963, w/Elliot Arnold
CAPTAIN SINBAD   King Brothers, 1963,
   w/Harry Relis, as "Samuel B. West"
WILD AND WONDERFUL   Universal, 1964
MIDNIGHT COWBOY ★★
   United Artists, 1969

THE GANG THAT COULDN'T SHOOT
   STRAIGHT   MGM, 1971
SERPICO ★   Paramount, 1973,
   w/Norman Wexler
THE DAY OF THE LOCUST
   Paramount, 1975
COMING HOME ★★   United Artists, 1978,
   w/Robert C. Jones

OSCAR SAUL
ONCE UPON A TIME   Columbia, 1944,
   w/Lewis Meltzer
THE DARK PAST   Columbia, 1948,
   w/Philip Macdonald & Malvin Wald
ROAD HOUSE   1948
WOMAN IN HIDING
   Universal-International, 1949
THUNDER ON THE HILL   BONAVENTURE
   Universal-International, 1951, w/Andre Solt
AFFAIR IN TRINIDAD   Columbia, 1952,
   w/James Gunn
THE JOKER IS WILD   Paramount, 1957
THE HELEN MORGAN STORY   Warner
   Bros., 1957, w/Nelson Gidding,
   Stephen Longstreet & Dean Reisner
THE NAKED MAJA   MGM, 1959, w/others
THE SECOND TIME AROUND   20th
   Century-Fox, 1961, w/Cecil Van Heusen
MAJOR DUNDEE   Columbia, 1965,
   w/Harry Julian Fink & Sam Peckinpah
THE SILENCERS   Columbia, 1966

JOHN SAXTON
HAPPY BIRTHDAY TO ME   Columbia, 1981,
   w/Timothy Bond & Peter Jobin
CLASS OF '84   United Film Distribution,
   1984, w/Tom Holland and Mark Lester

STANLEY SHAPIRO
THE PERFECT FURLOUGH   Universal
   International, 1958
OPERATION PETTICOAT ★   Universal,
   1959, w/Maurice Richlin
PILLOW TALK ★★   Universal, 1959,
   w/Maurice Richlin
LOVER COME BACK   Universal International,
   1961, w/Paul Henning
COME SEPTEMBER   Universal, 1961,
   w/Maurice Richlin
THAT TOUCH OF MINK ★   Universal
   International, 1962, w/Nate Monaster
BEDTIME STORY   Universal International,
   1964, w/Paul Henning
A VERY SPECIAL FAVOR   Universal, 1965,
   w/Nate Monaster
HOW TO SAVE A MARRIAGE AND RUIN
   YOUR LIFE   Columbia, 1968,
   w/Nate Monaster
CARBON COPY   Avco Embassy, 1981
DIRTY ROTTEN SCOUNDRELS   Orion,
   1989, w/Dale Launer & Paul Henning
RUNNING AGAINST TIME (CTF)
   Finnegan-Pinchuk Productions, 1990,
   w/Robert Glass

BILL SHERWOOD
PARTING GLANCES   1986, directed

WARREN SKAAREN
FIRE WITH FIRE   CAPTIVE HEARTS
   Paramount, 1986, w/Paul Boorstin,
   Sharon Boorstin & Bill Phillips
BEVERLY HILLS COP II   Paramount, 1987,
   w/Larry Ferguson
BEETLEJUICE   Warner Bros., 1988,
   w/Michael McDowell
BATMAN   Warner Bros., 1989, w/Sam Hamm

CAROL SOBIESKI
CASEY'S SHADOW   Columbia, 1978
HONEYSUCKLE ROSE   Warner Bros., 1980,
   w/John Binder & William Wittliff
ANNIE   Columbia, 1982
THE TOY   Columbia, 1982
SYLVESTER   Columbia, 1985
WINTER PEOPLE   Columbia, 1989
FRIED GREEN TOMATOES   Universal, 1991,
   w/Fannie Flagg
MONEY FOR NOTHING   Buena Vista, 1994,
   w/Ramon Menendez & Tom Musca

ARNE SULTAN
THE NUDE BOMB   Universal, 1980,
   w/Bill Dana & Leonard B. Stern
SEE NO EVIL, HEAR NO EVIL   Tri-Star,
   1989, w/Earl Barret, Andrew Kurtzman,
   Elliot Wald & Gene Wilder

GERALD SUSSMAN
NATIONAL LAMPOON'S MOVIE MADNESS
   United Artists, 1982, w/Tod Carroll,
   Shary Flenniken, Pat Mephitis & Ellis Weiner

ROGER SWAYBILL
PORKY'S II: THE NEXT DAY
   20th Century-Fox, 1983, w/Bob Clark &
   Alan Ormsby

T

DIANE THOMAS
ROMANCING THE STONE
   20th Century Fox, 1984

ERNEST TIDYMAN
SHAFT   MGM, 1971, w/John D.F. Black
THE FRENCH CONNECTION ★★
   20th Century-Fox, 1971
HIGH PLAINS DRIFTER   Universal, 1972
SHAFT'S BIG SCORE   MGM, 1972
REPORT TO THE COMMISSIONER
   United Artists, 1974, w/Abby Mann
STREET PEOPLE   American International,
   1976, w/others
A FORCE OF ONE   American Cinema, 1979
LAST PLANE OUT   New World, 1983

FRANCOIS TRUFFAUT
THE 400 BLOWS   Zenith, 1959, directed
SHOOT THE PIANO PLAYER   Astor,
   1960, directed
JULES AND JIM   Janus, 1961,
   w/Jean Gruault, directed
LOVE AT TWENTY   Embassy, 1962,
   co-directed
THE SOFT SKIN   Cinema 5, 1964, directed
FARENHEIT 451   Universal, 1967, directed
THE BRIDE WORE BLACK   Lopert,
   1968, directed
STOLEN KISSES   Lopert, 1969, directed
MISSISSIPPI MERMAID   United Artists,
   1970, directed
THE WILD CHILD   United Artists, 1970,
   w/Jean Gruault, directed
DAY FOR NIGHT ★   Warner Bros. , 1974,
   w/Suzanne Schiffman &
   Jean-Louis Richard, directed

THE STORY OF ADELE H. New World,
1975, w/Jean Gruault &
Suzanne Schiffman, directed
SMALL CHANGE *L'ARGENT DE POCHE*
New World, 1976,
w/Suzanne Schiffman, directed
THE MAN WHO LOVED WOMEN Cinema 5,
1977, w/Michel Fermaud &
Suzanne Schiffman, directed
THE LAST METRO United Artists Classics,
1980, w/Suzanne Schiffman, directed
THE WOMAN NEXT DOOR United Artists
Classics, 1981, directed
VIVEMENT DIMANCHE Spectrafilm, 1983,
w/Jean Aurel & Suzanne Schiffman, directed
CONFIDENTIALLY YOURS Spectrafilm,
1984, w/Jean Aurel &
Suzanne Schiffman, directed
LOVE ON THE RUN Spectrafilm, 1986,
w/others, directed

THOMAS L. TRYON
THE OTHER 20th Century-Fox, 1972

KENNETH TYNAN
MACBETH Columbia, 1971,
w/Roman Polanski

NONA TYSON
HOT SPOT Orion, 1990, w/Charles Williams

FRANK WALDMAN
BATHING BEAUTY MGM, 1944,
w/Alvin Boretz &Luther Davis
OUR HEARTS WERE GROWING UP
Paramount, 1946, Story
HIGH TIME 20th Century-Fox, 1960,
w/Frank Waldman
LOVE IS A BALL United Artists, 1962,
w/David Swift & Tom Waldman
THE PARTY United Artists, 1968,
w/Blake Edwards & Tom Waldman
INSPECTOR CLOUSEAU United Artists,
1968, w/Tom Waldman
DIRTY DINGUS MAGEE MGM, 1970,
w/Joseph Heller & Tom Waldman
THE RETURN OF THE PINK PANTHER
United Artists, 1975, w/Blake Edwards
THE PINK PANTHER STRIKES AGAIN
United Artists, 1976, w/Blake Edwards
REVENGE OF THE PINK PANTHER United
Artists,1978, w/Ron Clark & Blake Edwards
TRAIL OF THE PINK PANTHER MGM/UA,
1982, w/Tom Waldman, Blake Edwards &
Geoffrey Edwards

TOM WALDMAN
HIGH TIME 20th Century-Fox, 1960,
w/Frank Waldman
LOVE IS A BALL United Artists, 1962,
w/David Swift & Frank Waldman
THE PARTY United Artists, 1968,
w/Blake Edwards & Frank Waldman
INSPECTOR CLOUSEAU United Artists,
1968, w/Frank Waldman

DIRTY DINGUS MAGEE MGM, 1970
w/Joseph Heller & Frank Waldman
TRAIL OF THE PINK PANTHER MGM/UA,
1982, w/Frank Waldman, Blake Edwards &
Geoffrey Edwards

IRVING WALLACE
JIVE JUNCTION Producers Releasing
Corp., 1943
THE WEST POINT STORY
Warner Bros., 1948
MEET ME AT THE FAIR Universal, 1953
DESERT LEGION Universal, 1953,
w/Lewis Meltzer
GUN FURY Columbia, 1953,
w/Roy Huggins
SPLIT SECOND RKO Radio, 1953
BAD FOR EACH OTHER Columbia,
1954, w/Horace McCoy
GAMBLER FROM NATCHEZ
20th Century-Fox, 1954,
w/Gerald Drayson Adams
JUMP INTO HELL Warner Bros., 1955
THE BURNING HILLS Warner Bros., 1956
BOMBERS B-52 Warner Bros., 1957
THE BIG CIRCUS Allied Artists, 1959,
w/Irwin Allen &Charles Bennett

HUGH WHEELER
FIVE MILES TO MIDNIGHT United Artists,
1962, w/Peter Viertel
TRAVELS WITH MY AUNT MGM, 1972,
w/Jay Presson Allen
A LITTLE NIGHT MUSIC New World, 1978,
from his play
NIJINSKY Paramount, 1980

CORNEL WILDE
THE DEVIL'S HAIRPIN Paramount, 1957,
w/James Edmiston, directed
THE SWORD OF LANCELOT *LANCELOT
AND GUINEVERE* Universal,
1963, directed
SHARK'S TREASURE United Artists,
1975, directed

CHARLES WILLIAMS
DON'T JUST STAND THERE Universal, 1967
HOT SPOT Orion, 1990, w/Nona Tyson

MICHAEL WILSON
A PLACE IN THE SUN ★★ Paramount, 1951,
w/Harry Brown
FIVE FINGERS ★ 20th Century-Fox, 1952
FRIENDLY PERSUASION Allied Artists, 1956
THE BRIDGE ON THE RIVER KWAI ★★
Columbia, 1957, w/Carl Foreman
THE SANDPIPER MGM, 1965,
w/Dalton Trumbo
PLANET OF THE APES 20th Century-Fox,
1968, w/Rod Serling
CHE! 20th Century-Fox, 1969, w/Sy Bartlett

EDWARD WOOD JR.
GLEN OR GLENDA *I CHANGED MY SEX/I
LED TWO LIVES* Screen Classics,
1953, directed
JAILBAIT Howco, 1955,
w/Alex Gordon, directed
BRIDE OF THE MONSTER *BRIDE OF
THE ATOM* Banner, 1956,
w/Alex Gordon, directed
THE VIOLENT YEARS *FEMALE* Headliner
Productions, 1956

THE BRIDE AND THE BEAST *QUEEN OF
THE GORILLAS* Allied Artists, 1958
PLAN NINE FROM OUTER SPACE
GRAVE ROBBERS FROM OUTER SPACE
DCA, 1959, directed
THE SINISTER URGE Headliner,
1961, directed
THE SHOTGUN WEDDING Arkota, 1963
ORGY OF THE DEAD F.O.G.
Distributors, 1965
1,000,000 AC/DC 1969, as "Akdov Telmig"
TAKE IT OUT IN TRADE 1971, directed
CLASS REUNION 1973
FUGITIVE GIRLS 1974
THE COCKTAIL HOSTESS 1974
NECROMANCY *NECROMANIA*
1975, directed
NIGHT OF THE GHOULS *REVENGE OF THE
DEAD* 1981, directed (filmed in 1951)

BRONTE WOODARD
GREASE Paramount, 1978
CAN'T STOP THE MUSIC AFD, 1980,
w/Allan Carr

Z

MAI ZETTERLING
LOVING COUPLES Prominent, 1964,
w/David Hughes, directed
NIGHT GAMES Mondial, 1966, directed
DOCTOR GLAS 20th Century-Fox,
1968, directed
THE GIRLS New Line Cinema,
1969, directed
VINCENT THE DUTCHMAN 1972, directed
WE HAVE MANY NAMES 1976, directed
SCRUBBERS Orion Classics, 1984,
w/Roy Minton & Jeremy Watt, directed
AMAROSA Sandrews/Swedish Film Institute,
1986, directed

PAUL D. ZIMMERMAN
LOVERS AND LIARS Levitt-Pickman, 1979
THE KING OF COMEDY
20th Century-Fox, 1983
CONSUMING PASSIONS Samuel Goldwyn
Company, 1988, w/Andrew Davies
MR. 247 Tribe Production, 1994

★★★

INDEX BY FILM TITLE

NOTE: This is not a list of every film ever made, only those listed in this directory.

† after a writer's name denotes deceased.

INDEX OF FILM TITLES

BHAJI AT THE BEACH	MEERA SYAL
BICENTENNIAL MAN - S	RICK RAMAGE
BICYCLE DAYS - S	ANTHONY DRAZAN
BICYCLE THIEF, THE	CESARE ZAVATTINI†
BIG	ANNE SPIELBERG
BIG	GARY ROSS
BIG AL (SHORT)	BRYAN GOLUBOFF
BIG AND MEAN (SHORT)	JOHN RAFFO
BIG APPLE, THE - S	JOHN BRILEY
BIG BAD MAMA	WILLIAM W. NORTON SR.
BIG BAD MAMA II	JIM WYNORSKI
BIG BAD MAMA II	R.J. ROBERTSON†
BIG BAND MUSIC - S	MARTYN BURKE
BIG BAND OF BLUES - S	EARL MAC RAUCH
BIG BANG, THE (CTF) - S	TINO INSANA
BIG BLUE, THE	LUC BESSON
BIG BLUE, THE	ROBERT GARLAND
BIG BOODLE, THE	JO EISINGER
BIG BOUNCE, THE	ROBERT DOZIER
BIG BRASS RING - S	FINN TAYLOR
BIG BRASS RING, THE - S	GEORGE HICKENLOOPER
BIG BRASS RING, THE - S	MATT GREENBERG
BIG BRAWL, THE	FRED WEINTRAUB
BIG BRAWL, THE	ROBERT CLOUSE
BIG BREAK, THE - S	SIMON MOORE
BIG BROADCAST - S	JOE FLAHERTY
BIG BROKERS, THE - S	JOEL OLIANSKY
BIG BROTHER - S	ANTHONY DRAZAN
BIG BULLY - S	MARK S. JOHNSON
BIG BUS,THE	FRED FREEMAN
BIG BUS, THE	LAWRENCE J. COHEN
BIG BUSINES (P)	CHARLES BENNETT
BIG BUSINESS	DORI PIERSON
BIG BUSINESS	MARC RUBEL
BIG CHILL, THE	BARBARA BENEDEK
BIG CHILL, THE	LAWRENCE KASDAN
BIG CIRCUS, THE	CHARLES BENNETT
BIG CIRCUS, THE	IRVING WALLACE†
BIG CIRCUS, THE	IRWIN ALLEN†
BIG CITY, BIG SKY - S	JIM BYRNES
BIG COMBO, THE	PHILIP YORDAN
BIG DANCE, THE - S	LARRY GOLIN
BIG DAY, THE (P)	DOUGLAS MCGRATH
BIG DEAL ON MACARTHUR BOULEVARD - S	ALAN MANDEL
BIG DEAL ON MACARTHUR BOULEVARD - S	CHARLES SHYER
BIG DEAL - S	JONATHAN LYNN
BIG DIS, THE	GORDON ERIKSEN
BIG DIS, THE	ROBERT PILOTTE
BIG DOGS - S	JOHN TURMAN
BIG DOLLHOUSE, THE	JACKSON HILL
BIG EASY, THE	DANIEL PETRIE, JR.
BIG FAT ELVIS - S	DOUG MCINTYRE
BIG FAT ELVIS - S	DOUG STECKLER
BIG FIGHT, THE - S	EDWARD KHMARA
BIG FIX, THE	ROGER L. SIMON
BIG FUNK, THE (P)	JOHN P. SHANLEY
BIG GAME - S	KEVIN TENNEY
BIG GIRLS DON'T CRY	FRANK MUGAVERO
BIG GIRLS DON'T CRY	MARK GODDARD
BIG GIRLS DON'T CRY	MELISSA GODDARD
BIG GREEN, THE - S	HOLLY G. SLOAN
BIG GUN DOWN, THE	SERGIO DONATI
BIG GUNS, SMALL MAN - S	GEORGE SAUNDERS
BIG HAIR - S	CHRIS HENDRIKSON
BIG HEAT, THE	SYDNEY BOEHM†
BIG HOSPITAL - S	JEREMY STEVENS
BIG HOSPITAL - S	MARK A. REISMAN
BIG HYPE, THE - S	AVERY KORMAN
BIG KISS, THE - S	JOHN GUARE
BIG LEAGUER	HERBERT BAKER†
BIG LOVE BURNING (P)	MATTHEW CARNAHAN
BIG LOVE, THE (P)	JAY PRESSON ALLEN
BIG MAMOO, THE - S	BUD SHRAKE
BIG MAN EATER	LAURENCE KEANE
BIG MAN ON CAMPUS	ALLAN KATZ
BIG MAN ON CAMPUS - S	PATRICK CLIFTON
BIG MEAT EATER	CHRIS WINDSOR
BIG MEAT EATER	LAURENCE KEANE
BIG MEAT EATER	PHIL SAVATH
BIG MOUTH, THE	BILL RICHMOND
BIG MOUTH, THE	JERRY LEWIS
BIG NASTY, THE - S	DAVID SIMKINS
BIG NOISE, THE - S	STEPHEN METCALFE
BIG NOWHERE, THE - S	CLIVE BARKER
BIG ONE, THE - S	FREDERIC RAPHAEL
BIG ONES, THE - S	LAWRENCE GAY
BIG ONES, THE - S	MICHAEL DIGAETANO
BIG PICTURE, THE	CHRISTOPHER GUEST
BIG PICTURE, THE	MICHAEL MCKEAN
BIG PICTURE, THE	MICHAEL VARHOL
BIG PINK - S	JONATHAN DAY
BIG PLAYER, THE - S	JIMMY HUSTON
BIG PLUNGE, THE	CHRIS NEUFELD
BIG PLUNGE, THE - S	DANNIEL BARRON
BIG PLUNGE, THE - S	CHRIS FABER
BIG PLUNGE, THE - S	E. MAX FRYE
BIG PUNCH, THE	BERNARD GIRARD
BIG QUESTION, THE - S	ISRAEL HOROVITZ
BIG RASCALS, THE	JEFF WILHELM
BIG RED ONE, THE	SAMUEL FULLER
BIG RIVER (P)	WILLIAM HAUPTMAN
BIG ROOM, THE - S	RONNIE WENKER-KONNER
BIG SCORE, THE	GAIL MORGAN HICKMAN
BIG SCORE, THE - S	RONALD SHUSETT
BIG SHOTS	JOE ESZTERHAS
BIG SHOTS - S	DAVID LOUCKA
BIG SHOTS - S	JON CONNOLLY
BIG SKY ROMANCE - S	JULE SELBO
BIG SLEEP, THE	MICHAEL WINNER
BIG STEAL, THE	DAVID PARKER
BIG SUCCESS - S	DENISE DE CLUE
BIG SUCCESS - S	TIM KAZURINSKY
BIG THICKET, THE - S	ADAM RODMAN
BIG TIME RETURN - S	RICHARD MATHESON
BIG TIME - S	MARCEL MONTECINO
BIG TOP PEE WEE	GEORGE MCGRATH
BIG TOP PEE WEE	PAUL REUBENS
BIG TOP - S	RICHARD DIMITRI
BIG TOP - S	ROBERT WUHL
BIG TOWN, THE	ROBERT ROY POOL
BIG TROUBLE	ANDREW BERGMAN
BIG TROUBLE IN LITTLE CHINA	DAVID WEINSTEIN
BIG TROUBLE IN LITTLE CHINA	GARY GOLDMAN
BIG TROUBLE IN LITTLE CHINA	W.D. RICHTER
BIG U, THE - S	HENRY BEAN
BIG WEDNESDAY	JOHN MILIUS
BIGAMIST, THE	FRANCESCO ROSI
BIGAMY - S	DAVID GREENWALT
BIGAMY - S	JIM KOUF
BIGFINGER - S	HERSCHEL WEINGROD
BIGFINGER - S	TIMOTHY HARRIS
BIGGER THAN LIFE	RICHARD MAIBAUM†
BIGGLES	JOHN P. GROVES
BIGGLES	KENT WALWIN
BIGMALEON - S	HARIS ORKIN
BIJOU DREAMS (CTF) - S	DICK BEEBE
BIKER HEAVEN - S	TERRY SOUTHERN
BIKERS FROM HELL - S	JEFF BUHAI
BIKERS FROM HELL - S	STEVE ZACHARIAS
BIKINI BEACH	WILLIAM ASHER
BIKINI BIKER BEACH BABES - S	ROD NAVE
BIKINI ISLAND	EMERSON BIXBY
BIKINI - S	TED MANN
BIKINI SHOP, THE	DAVID WECHTER
BILL & TED'S BOGUS JOURNEY	ED SOLOMON
BILL & TED'S BOGUS JOURNEY	CHRISTIAN L. MATHESON
BILL & TED'S EXCELLENT ADVENTURE	CHRISTIAN L. MATHESON
BILL & TED'S EXCELLENT ADVENTURE	ED SOLOMON
BILLIE BOY (P)	HESPER ANDERSON
BILLION DOLLAR BRAIN	JOHN MCGRATH
BILLIONAIRES - S	ALINE BROSH
BILLY BATHGATE	TOM STOPPARD
BILLY BISHOP GOES TO WAR (P)	JOHN GRAY
BILLY BUDD	PETER USTINOV
BILLY BUDD - S	HESPER ANDERSON
BILLY GALVIN	JOHN GRAY
BILLY HELL - S	MATTHEW MCDUFFIE
BILLY IN THE LOWLANDS	JAN EGLESON
BILLY IRISH (P)	THOMAS BABE
BILLY JACK	TOM LAUGHLIN
BILLY JACK GOES TO WASHINGTON	TOM LAUGHLIN
BILLY MADISON	ADAM SANDLER
BILLY MADISON	TIM HERLIHY
BILLY PHELAN'S GREATEST GAME - S	WILLIAM KENNEDY
BILLY ROSE'S JUMBO	SIDNEY SHELDON
BILLY THE KID AND THE GREEN BAIZE VAMPIRE	TREVOR PRESTON
BILLY THE THIRD	BONNIE TURNER
BILLY THE THIRD	TERRY TURNER
BILLY TURNER'S SECRET (SHORT)	MICHAEL MAYSON
BILLY TWO HATS	ALAN SHARP
BILOXI BLUES	NEIL SIMON
BIMBO - S	MAX EMBER
BIMBO (SHORT)	CARLOS DAVIS
BIMBOS - S	FREDERICA HOBIN
BINARY PROJECT - S	ANDY LEWIS
BINGE, THE - S	STEPHEN PETERS
BINGO	JIM STRAIN
BINGO LONG TRAVELING ALL-STARS & MOTOR KINGS, THE	HAL BARWOOD
BINGO LONG TRAVELING ALL-STARS & MOTOR KINGS, THE	MATTHEW ROBBINS
BIOHAZARD	FRED OLEN RAY
BIOSPHERE - S	ERIC BERGREN
BIPPIDY, BIPPIDY, BOO - S	MAUREEN KELLY
BIRCH INTERVAL	JOANNA CRAWFORD
BIRD	JOEL OLIANSKY
BIRD ARTISTS, THE - S	HOWARD NORMAN
BIRD OF PREY - S	JAMES MELLON
BIRD ON A WIRE	DAVID SELTZER
BIRD ON A WIRE	ERIC LERNER
BIRD ON A WIRE	LOUIS VENOSTA
BIRD WITH THE CRYSTAL PLUMMAGE, THE	DARIO ARGENTO
BIRD'S CHRISMAS CAROL - S	DARREL CAMPBELL
BIRDIE AFRICA - S	JEFF STETSON
BIRDS AND THE BEES, THE	SIDNEY SHELDON
BIRDS DO IT	ARNIE KOGEN
BIRDS II (CTF)	JIM WHEAT
BIRDS II (CTF)	KEN WHEAT
BIRDS II (CTF)	ROBERT EISELE
BIRDS OF A FEATHER - S	ELAINE MAY
BIRDS OF A FEATHER - S	SANDRA WEINTRAUB
BIRDS OF PREY - S	FRANK MILITARY JR.
BIRDS, THE	EVAN HUNTER
BIRDS, THE (P)	STANLEY GREENBERG
BIRDY	JACK BEHR
BIRDY	SANDY KROOPF
BIRTH OF THE BLUES	HARRY TUGEND†
BIRTHDAY FISH (SHORT)	ALEX ZAMM
BIRTHDAY PARTY, THE	HAROLD PINTER
BIRTHDAY - S	ROD MCCALL
BIRTHDAY SUIT (P)	GLEN BERENBEIM
BIRTHDAY WISHES - S	JACK SEKOWSKI
BIRTHDAY WISHES - S	MARIA VELTRE
BIRTHRIGHT (P)	RICHARD MAIBAUM†
BIT OF MAGIC, A - S	LIZ COMICI
BIT OF MAGIC, A - S	LOU COMICI
BITCH, THE	GERRY O'HARA
BITE THE BULLET	RICHARD BROOKS†
BITING RITA - S	FRANK SCHILLING
BITTER MOON	GERARD BRACH
BITTER MOON	JOHN BROWNJOHN
BITTER MOON	ROMAN POLANSKI
BITTER ROOT - S	JOHN MCTIERNAN
BITTER VENGEANCE (CTF)	PABLO FENJVES
BITTER VICTORY	GAVIN LAMBERT
BITTER WOMEN (P)	JUSTIN TANNER
BITTERROOT BURN, THE - S	SCOTT STURGEON
BITTERSWEET BRONZE - S	RALPH G. WILSON
BITTERSWEET LOVE	ADRIAN MORRALL
BITTERSWEET LOVE	D.A. KELLOGG
BIZET'S CARMEN	FRANCESCO ROSI
BLABBERMOUTH -S	ANDY TENNANT
BLACK AND BLUE - S	CAROLYN SHELBY
BLACK AND BLUE - S	CHRISTOPHER AMES
BLACK AND WHITE IN COLOR	GEORGES CONCHON†
BLACK AND WHITE IN COLOR	JEAN-JACQUES ANNAUD
BLACK AND WHITE IN COLOR - S	TAKASHI BUFORD
BLACK AND WHITE - S	LESLIE BOHEM
BLACK AND WHITE - S	MARK ALLEN SMITH
BLACK ANGEL (P)	MICHAEL CRISTOFER
BLACK ANGEL - S	JEAN-CLAUDE CARRIERE
BLACK ANGEL - S	PHILIP KAUFMAN
BLACK ARROW, THE	THOMAS SELLER†
BLACK ARROW, THE - S	DALENE A. YOUNG
BLACK ARROW, THE - S	ROBERT J. WARD
BLACK BEAUTY	CAROLINE THOMPSON
BLACK BEAUTY	WOLF MANKOWITZ
BLACK BIRD, THE	DAVID GILER
BLACK BLOOD - S	DAVID BIRKE
BLACK BOOK, THE	PHILIP YORDAN
BLACK CAT BONE - S	JOHN HUGHES
BLACK CAT, THE	LEWIS COATES
BLACK CAULDRON, THE (AF)	AL WILSON†
BLACK CAULDRON, THE (AF)	RICHARD RICH
BLACK CAULDRON, THE (AF)	TED BERMAN
BLACK CIRCLE BOYS - S	MATT CARNAHAN
BLACK COMEDY (P)	PETER SHAFFER

C

CARIBBEAN WOMAN - S	ANNE BEATTS
CARLA - S	DENNY MARTIN FLINN
CARLESS - S	JOHN LEVENSTEIN
CARLESS - S	MICHAEL A. KAPLAN
CARLITO'S WAY	DAVID KOEPP
CARLTON-BROWNE OF THE F.O.	ROY BOULTING
CARMEN	CARLOS SAURA
CARMEN	FRANCESCO ROSI
CARMEN JONES	HARRY KLEINER
CARNAGE (P)	TIM ROBBINS
CARNAL KNOWLEDGE	JULES FEIFFER
CARNIVAL EARTH - S	NEIL ROMANEK
CARNIVAL - S	MARIO PUZO
CARNIVAL - S	MARK SEVI
CARNIVAL - S	STAN DANIELS
CARNOSAUR - S	ADAM SIMON
CARNOSAUR - S	HENRY DOMONIC
CARNY	PHOEBE KAYLOR
CARNY	ROBBIE ROBERTSON
CARNY	ROBERT KAYLOR
CARNY	THOMAS BAUM
CARNY MOON - S	DURA TEMPLE
CAROUSEL	HENRY EPHRON†
CAROUSEL	PHOEBE EPHRON†
CARPENTERS, THE (P)	STEVE TESICH
CARPETBAGGERS, THE	JOHN MICHAEL HAYES
CARPOOL - S	BOB GALE
CARPOOL - S	DON RHYMER
CARRIE	LAWRENCE D. COHEN
CARRIER, THE - S	AL SEPTIEN
CARRIER, THE - S	TURI MEYER
CARRINGTON	CHRISTOPHER HAMPTON
CARRY ME THROUGH - S	GINA WENDKOS
CARRY ON CRUISING	NORMAN HUDIS
CARRY ON SERGEANT	NORMAN HUDIS
CARS - S	JERRY BELSON
CARS THAT ATE PARIS, THE	PETER WEIR
CARS THAT ATE PEOPLE, THE	PETER WEIR
CARTEL	MOSHE HADAR
CARTOON (P)	MURRAY MEDNICK
CARTOON - S	KEVIN ROONEY
CARTOONED - S	BOB GORDON
CARTOUCHE	PHILLIPE DE BROCA
CARVE HER NAME WITH PRIDE	LEWIS GILBERT
CARVER'S BOX - S	MICHAEL FALLON
CASABLANCA	HOWARD KOCH
CASABLANCA	JULIUS J. EPSTEIN
CASABLANCA	PHILIP G. EPSTEIN†
CASANOVA	FEDERICO FELLINI†
CASANOVA	TONINO GUERRA
CASANOVA SLEPT HERE - S	ROBERT MUNDY
CASANOVA'S BIG NIGHT	HAL KANTER
CASCA - S	DAVID GOYER
CASE CLOSED - S	RANDY FELDMAN
CASE FOR MURDER, A (CTF)	DUNCAN GIBBINS†
CASE FOR MURDER, A (CTF)	PABLO FENJVES
CASE OF THE PURPLE
TERROR, THE - S	PHIL HARTMAN
CASEY JONES - S	SCOTT MORGAN
CASEY SPEAKS - S	ADAM BELANOFF
CASEY SPEAKS - S	P.J. PESCE
CASEY'S SHADOW	CAROL SOBIESKI†
CASHFLOW- S	JOHN HERMAN SHANER
CASINO ROYALE	WOLF MANKOWITZ
CASINO - S	MARTIN SCORSESE
CASINO - S	NICHOLAS PILEGGI
CASKET AND THE
SWORD, THE - S	ANTHONY CLARVOE
CASPER	DEANNA OLIVER
CASPER	SHERRI STONER
CASSANDRA CROSSING, THE	G. COSMATOS
CASSANDRA CROSSING, THE	ROBERT KATZ
CASSANDRA CROSSING, THE	TOM MANKIEWICZ
CAST A DEADLY SPELL	JOSEPH DOUGHERTY
CAST A GIANT SHADOW	MEL SHAVELSON
CAST A LONG SHADOW	JOHN MCGREEVY
CAST OF CHARACTERS - S	LARRY COHEN
CAST OF THOUSANDS, A - S	STEVE SHAGAN
CASTAWAY	ALLAN G. SCOTT
CASTAWAY COWBOY, THE	DON TAIT
CASTAWAYS - S	GORDON GREISMAN
CASTAWAYS, THE - S	ED WEINBERGER
CASTLE FREAK	DENNIS PAOLI
CASTLE FREAK	STUART GORDON
CASTLE KEEP	DANIEL TARADASH
CASTLE KEEP	DAVID RAYFIEL
CASTLE RISING - S	L. VIRGINIA BROWNE
CASTRO - S	MICHAEL THOMAS
CASUAL SEX?	JUDY TOLL
CASUAL SEX?	WENDY GOLDMAN
CASUALTIES OF WAR	DAVID RABE

CAT - S	MICHAEL ERIC STEIN
CAT, THE - S	PAUL D. ZIMMERMAN
CAT AND ALLISON ARE HAVING
A BAD WEEK - S	SHAWN SCHEPPS
CAT AND MOUSE - S	SYRIE JAMES
CAT AND THE CANARY, THE	RADLEY METZGER
CAT BALLOU	FRANK R. PIERSON
CAT BALLOU	WALTER NEWMAN†
CAT CHASER	ALAN SHARP
CAT CHASER	ELMORE LEONARD
CAT CHASER	JIM BORRELLI
CAT FROM OUTER SPACE, THE	TED KEY
CAT GAME (P)	DURA TEMPLE
CAT & MOUSE - S	IAN SEEBERG
CAT & MOUSE - S	NEIL TOLKIN
CAT & MOUSE - S	RICHARD WHITLEY
CAT & MOUSE - S	VALERIE BENNETT
CAT ON A HOT TIN ROOF	RICHARD BROOKS†
CAT O'NINE TAILS	DARIO ARGENTO
CAT PEOPLE	ALAN ORMSBY
CAT'S CLAW - S	TAMAR BROTT
CAT-KILLER (P)	PETER BIEGEN
CATACOMBS	C. COURTNEY JOYNER
CATACOMBS	DAVID SCHMOELLER
CATACOMBS	R. BARKER PRICE
CATCH ME A SPY	DICK CLEMENT
CATCH ME A SPY	IAN LAFRENAIS
CATCH ME IF YOU CAN	STEPHEN SOMMERS
CATCH THE HEAT	STIRLING SILLIPHANT
CATCH, THE -S	LAURA HAYNES
CATCH US IF YOU CAN	PETER NICHOLS
CATCH-22	BUCK HENRY
CATCHING RAYS - S	DAVID CASCI
CATCING CASSANOVA - S	BART JENNETT
CATERED AFFAIR, THE	GORE VIDAL
CATERER, THE - S	BRIAN LANE
CATFISH TANGLE - S	MARK PEPLOE
CATHODE MONSTER, THE - S	DAVID ODELL
CATHOLIC GIRLS (P)	DORIS BAIZLEY
CATHOLIC SCHOOL GIRLS (P)	CASEY KURTTI
CATS (AF)	TOM STOPPARD
CATS	RICHARD LAGRAVENESE
CATS DON'T DANCE (AF) - S	CLIFF RUBY
CATS DON'T DANCE (AF) - S	ELANA LESSER
CATS DON'T
DANCE (AF) - S	ROBERTS GANNAWAY
CATTLE ANNIE AND
LITTLE BRITCHES	DAVID EYRE
CATTLE ANNIE AND
LITTLE BRITCHES	ROBERT M. WARD
CATTLE QUEEN OF MONTANA	ROBERT BLEES
CAT'S CRADLE - S	JORDAN ALAN
CAT'S EYE	STEPHEN KING
CAT'S PAW (P)	WILLIAM MASTROSIMONE
CAUGHT	ARTHUR LAURENTS
CAUGHT	JAMES F. COLLIER†
CAUGHT DEAD	MAGGIE KLEINMAN
CAUGHT IN THE ACT (CTF)	ANDY EVANSON
CAUGHT IN THE ACT (CTF)	KEN HIXON
CAUGHT IN THE DRAFT	HARRY TUGEND†
CAUGHT - S	PHILIP MORTON
CAUSE CELEBRE - S	JOHN MORTIMER
CAUSE TOJOURS (P)	FRANCIS VEBER
CAVEGIRL	DAVID OLIVER
CAVEMAN	CARL GOTTLIEB
CAVEMAN	RUDY DELUCA
CAVERN, THE	JACK DAVIES
CB4	CHRIS ROCK
CB4	NELSON GEORGE
CB4	ROBERT LOCASH
CC PYLE AND THE
BUNION DERBY - S	MICHAEL CRISTOFER
CEASE FIRE	GEORGE FERNANDEZ
CEL 2455 DEATH ROW	JACK DE WITT
CELESTE	PERCY ADLON
CELIA	ANNE TURNER
CELINA'S WORLD - S	JAN ELIASBERG
CELLING OUT - S	JOHN JACOBSEN
CELLS - S	EDWARD ADLER
CELTIC PRIDE - S	JUDD APATOW
CEMENT GARDEN, THE	ANDREW BIRKIN
CEMETARY CLUB, THE	IVAN MENCHELL
CEMETARY HIGH	CARMINE CAPOBIANCO
CEMETARY HIGH	GORMAN BECHARD
CENTENNIAL SUMMER	MICHAEL KANIN†
CENTER OF THE WEB	DAVID A. PRIOR
CENTERFOLD GIRLS, THE	ROBERT L. PEETE
CENTERFOLD - S	LEWIS JOHN CARLINO
CENTERFOLD - S	NANCY DOWD
CENTERFOLD - S	RON SHELTON
CENTERFOLD - S	WALON GREEN

CENTRAL PARK - S	ADAM LEFF
CENTRAL PARK - S	PAUL GUAY
CENTRAL PARK - S	ZAK PENN
CENTRIFUGE	DONALD CAMMELL
CENTURION - S	JERE P. CUNNINGHAM
CENTURIONS - S	PHILIP EISNER
CENTURY	STEPHEN POLIAKOFF
CEREMONIES OF THE
HORSEMEN (P)	PETER BIEGEN
CEREMONY FOR THE MIDGET	JAMES KENNEDY
CERTAIN FURY	MICHAEL JACOBS
CERTAIN SMILE, A	ALBERT HACKETT
CERTAIN SMILE, A	FRANCES GOODRICH
CESAR AND ROSALIE	CLAUDE SAUTET
CESAR CHAVEZ - S	LUIS VALDEZ
CHAFED ELBOWS	ROBERT DOWNEY
CHAIN OF COMMAND (P)	MARK LEE
CHAIN OF DESIRE	TEMISTOCLES LOPEZ
CHAIN OF FIRE - S	JOEL SMITH
CHAIN OF LIFE (P)	LISA LOOMER
CHAIN OF VOICES, A - S	JAY COCKS
CHAIN, THE	JACK ROSENTHAL
CHAINDANCE	ALAN AYLWARD
CHAINDANCE	MICHAEL IRONSIDE
CHAINED HEAT	PAUL NICHOLAS
CHAINED HEAT	VINCENT MONGOL
CHAINLETTER, THE - S	PETER HANKOFF
CHAIRMAN OF THE BOARD - S	AL SEPTIEN
CHAIRMAN OF THE BOARD - S	TURI MEYER
CHALK	ROB NILSSON
CHALK GARDEN, THE	JOHN MICHAEL HAYES
CHALLENGE, THE	JOHN SAYLES
CHALLENGE, THE	RICHARD MAXWELL
CHALLENGE, THE (1938)	EM PRESSBURGER†
CHALLENGE THE WIND	KEN HOWARD
CHALLENGE THE WIND	MARLA YOUNG
CHALLENGE THE WIND	WILLIAM BLACKBURN
CHALLENGER, THE	ALLAN G. SCOTT
CHALLENGER, THE - S	JIM MCBRIDE
CHALLENGER, THE - S	L.M. KIT CARSON
CHAMBER OF HORRORS	STEPHEN KANDEL
CHAMBER, THE - S	WILLIAM GOLDMAN
CHAMELEON STREET	WENDELL B. HARRIS JR.
CHAMELEON STREET - S	ADAM SMALL
CHAMELEON STREET - S	FAX BAHR
CHAMP, THE	SPENCER EASTMAN†
CHAMP, THE	WALTER NEWMAN†
CHAMPAGNE
CHARLIE STAKES (P)	BRUCE GRAHAM
CHAMPAGNE FOR CAESAR - S	DAVID DASHEV
CHAMPAGNE FOR CAESAR - S	STU BIRNBAUM
CHAMPAGNE NIGHTS - S	HAROLD A. RAMIS
CHAMPAGNE NIGHTS - S	PETER TOROKVEI
CHAMPAGNE WALTZ	BILLY WILDER
CHAMPION	CARL FOREMAN†
CHAMPIONS	EVAN JONES
CHAMPIONS FOREVER (FD)	KEN W. GRISWOLD
CHAMPIONS OF HEART - S	SAM KUTE
CHAMPIONS OF THE HEART - S	DAVID ASSAEL
CHAN IS MISSING	ISAAC CRONIN
CHAN IS MISSING	TERREL SELTZER
CHAN IS MISSING	WAYNE WANG
CHANCE OF A LIFETIME - S	DAVID DASHEV
CHANCE OF A LIFETIME - S	STUART BIRNBAUM
CHANCE OF A LIFETIME - S	THOM EBERHARDT
CHANCES ARE	PERRY HOWZE
CHANCES ARE	RANDY HOWZE
CHANDLER	JOHN SACRET YOUNG
CHANEL - S	BENEDICT FITZGERALD
CHANGE OF HABIT	ERIC BERCOVICI
CHANGE OF HEART - S	ERIC TUCHMAN
CHANGE OF HEART - S	GERALD AYRES
CHANGE OF HEART - S	HOLLY G. SLOAN
CHANGE OF HEART - S	LEONARD KASTLE
CHANGE OF HEART - S	LLOYD GARVER
CHANGE OF HEART - S	SCOTT BUSBY
CHANGE OF PACE, A (P)	ED POMERANTZ
CHANGE OF PLANS - S	JEFFREY ALAN FISKIN
CHANGE OF SEASONS, A	ERICH SEGAL
CHANGE OF SEASONS, A	FRED SEGAL
CHANGE OF SEASONS, A	MARTIN RANSOHOFF
CHANGE OF SEASONS, A	RONNI KERN
CHANGELING, THE	DIANA MADDOX
CHANGELING, THE	RUSSELL HUNTER
CHANGELING, THE	WILLIAM GRAY
CHANGELING, THE (CTF)	MICHAEL HASTINGS
CHANGELING, THE (CTF)	THOMAS MIDDLETON
CHANGELING, THE (CTF)	WILLIAM ROWLEY
CHANGING LABELS - S	RICHARD BRENNE
CHANGING SIDES - S	DAVID CHASE
CHANNEL CROSSING - S	EDMOND STEVENS

I N D E X   O F   F I L M   T I T L E S

INDEX OF FILM TITLES

I

467

LONG RIDERS, THE	STEVEN PHILIP SMITH
LONG ROAD WEST, THE - S	BRIAN HELGELAND
LONG ROADS, THE	JOHN McGRATH
LONG SATURDAY NIGHT, THE - S	ROB DUNN
LONG SHADOWS - S	VINCENT ROBERT
LONG SHIPS, THE	BEVERLY CROSS
LONG SHOT	JAMES GRADY
LONG TIME COMING (P)	MICHAEL HACKER
LONG WALK HOME, THE	JOHN CORK
LONG WALK, THE - S	BRIAN COWDEN
LONG WAY HOME - S	ANDY TENNANT
LONG WAY HOME, THE - S	PETER KRIKES
LONG WAY HOME, THE - S	STEVE MEERSON
LONG WEEKED, THE	GREGG ARAKI
LONG WEEKEND, THE	EVERETT DEROCHE
LONGEST DAY, THE	DAVID PURSALL
LONGEST YARD, THE	TRACY KEENAN WYNN
LONGFELLOW BRIDGE -S	JEFFREY ARCH
LONGING TO FALL - S	HOWARD CHESLEY
LONGING TO FALL - S	MICHAEL SCHIFFER
LONGSHOT, THE	TIM CONWAY
LONGTIME COMPANION	CRAIG LUCAS
LOOK BACK IN ANGER	NIGEL KNEALE
LOOK BACK IN ANGER (P)	JOHN OSBORNE
LOOK DOWN AND DIE	LEIGH CHAPMAN
LOOK DOWN AND DIE	PETER S. DAVIS
LOOK DOWN AND DIE	ROB EWING
LOOK DOWN AND DIE	WILLIAM N. PANZER
LOOK HOMEWARD ANGEL - S	STEVEN M. KUNES
LOOK ME IN THE EYE	NICK WARD
LOOK WHO'S TALKING	AMY HECKERLING
LOOK WHO'S TALKING NOW	LESLIE DIXON
LOOK WHO'S TALKING NOW	TOM ROPELEWSKI
LOOK WHO'S TALKING, TOO	AMY HECKERLING
LOOK WHO'S TALKING, TOO	NEAL ISRAEL
LOOKALIKE - S	JON BERNSTEIN
LOOKALIKE, THE (CTF)	KATE WILHELM
LOOKALIKE, THE (CTF)	LINDA BERGMAN
LOOKALIKE, THE (CTF)	MARTIN TAHSE
LOOKALKIES (SHORT)	ELAINE POPE
LOOKER	MICHAEL CRICHTON
LOOKIN' ITALIAN	GUY MAGAR
LOOKIN' TO GET OUT	AL SCHWARTZ
LOOKIN' TO GET OUT	JON VOIGHT
LOOKING FOR ANGELS (P)	LISA LOOMER
LOOKING FOR HARRY - S	EDWARD HUME
LOOKING FOR LOVE - S	SUE JETTE
LOOKING FOR MR. GOODBAR - S	RICHARD BROOKS†
LOOKING FOR WORK - S	NAOMI FONER
LOOKING GLASS WAR, THE	FRANK R. PIERSON
LOOKING OUT - S	WILLIAM GOODHART
LOOKING UP	LINDA YELLEN
LOOPHOLE	JONATHAN HALES
LOOSE CANNON	PAUL F. EDWARDS
LOOSE CANNONS	BOB CLARK
LOOSE CANNONS	RICHARD MATHESON
LOOSE ENDS (P)	MICHAEL WELLER
LOOSE ENDS (SHORT)	DAVID COLEMAN
LOOSE KNIT (P)	THERESA REBECK
LOOSE SCREWS	MICHAEL CORY
LOOSE SHOES - S	MICHAEL DIGAETANO
LOOSE WOMEN - S	BRAD BUCKNER
LOOSE WOMEN - S	BUD SHRAKE
LOOSE WOMEN - S	CAROL DRECHSLER
LOOSE WOMEN - S	DAN JENKINS
LOOSE WOMEN - S	EUGENIE ROSS-LEMING
LOOSE WOMEN - S	JACK BEHR
LOOSE WOMEN - S	PAUL PRICE
LOOSE WOMEN - S	STEVE NATHAN
LOOT - S	OLIVER ROBINS
LORD BUTLER - S	JOE KEENAN
LORD CHARLIE - S	DAVID ROSENFELT
LORD JIM	RICHARD BROOKS†
LORD JIM - S	DANIEL FARRANDS
LORD LOVE A DUCK	GEORGE AXELROD
LORD LOVE A DUCK	LARRY H. JOHNSON
LORD OF ILLUSION - S	CLIVE BARKER
LORD OF THE AMAZON - S	DENNE B. PETITCLERC
LORD OF THE FLIES	PETER BROOK
LORD OF THE MANOR - S	MITCHEL KATLIN
LORD OF THE MANOR - S	NAT BERNSTEIN
LORD OF THE RINGS, THE (AF)	CHRIS CONKLING
LORD OF THE RINGS, THE (AF)	PETER S. BEAGLE
LORD ROCHESTER'S MONKEY - S	MICHAEL THOMAS
LORDS OF DISCIPLINE, THE	LLOYD FONVIELLE
LORDS OF DISCIPLINE, THE	THOMAS POPE

LORDS OF THE DEEP	DARYL HANEY
LORDS OF THE DEEP	HOWARD R. COHEN
LORELEI - S	STEPHEN VOLK
LORENZO DEMICI - S	MENNO MEYJES
LORENZO'S OIL	GEORGE MILLER
LORENZO'S OIL	NICK ENRIGHT
LORNA	RUSS MEYER
LORNA DOON - S	LAURA LAMSON
LOSER	ERIK BURKE
LOSERS - S	IAN MAXTONE-GRAHAM
LOSERS - S	RYAN ROWE
LOSIN' IT	B.W.L NORTON, JR.
LOSIN' IT	BRYAN GINDOFF
LOSING ISIAH	NAOMI FONER
LOSS OF INNOCENCE	HOWARD KOCH
LOST AND FOUND	JACK ROSE
LOST AND FOUND - S	MEREDITH BAER
LOST ANGELS	MICHAEL WELLER
LOST APRIL - S	BYRON SIMPSON
LOST AT SEA - S	DANA STEVENS
LOST BOYS II - S	ERIC RED
LOST BOYS II - S	SCOTT MYERS
LOST BOYS, THE	JAMES JEREMIAS
LOST BOYS, THE	JANICE FISCHER
LOST BOYS, THE	JEFFREY BOAM
LOST CAPONE, THE (CTF)	JOHN GRAY
LOST CITY - S	LEON CAPETANOS
LOST COMMAND, THE	NELSON GIDDING
LOST EMPIRE, THE	JIM WYNORSKI
LOST HIGHWAY, THE - S	ALLISON ANDERS
LOST HORIZON	LARRY KRAMER
LOST IN AFRICA	STEWART RAFFILL
LOST IN AMERICA	ALBERT BROOKS
LOST IN AMERICA	MONICA JOHNSON
LOST IN SPACE - S	AKIVA GOLDSMAN
LOST IN THE CITY OF LIGHTS - S	PETER BARNES
LOST IN YONKERS	NEIL SIMON
LOST LANGUAGE OF CRANES, THE	SEAN MATHIAS
LOST MAN, THE	ROBERT A. ARTHUR†
LOST ONES, THE - S	JOYCE CORRINGTON
LOST PROPHET	DREW MORONE
LOST PROPHET	LARRY O'NEIL
LOST PROPHET	MICHAEL DE AVILA
LOST PROPHET	SHANNON GOLDMAN
LOST - S	GORDON GREISMAN
LOST SOUL - S	JEFFREY BELL
LOST SOUL - S	STEPHEN VOLK
LOST TREASURE OF CAPTAIN CORNELIUS (SHORT)	MICHAEL DIJIACOMO
LOST VEGAS - S	DAVID H. SMILOW
LOST WEEKEND - S	SCOTT RICHARDSON
LOST WEEKEND, THE	BILLY WILDER
LOST WORDS, THE	DAN KEOPPEL
LOST WORDS, THE	MICHAEL KANIECKI
LOST WORDS, THE	SCOTT SAUNDERS
LOST WORLD, THE	CHARLES BENNETT
LOST WORLD, THE	IRWIN ALLEN†
LOST WORLD, THE - S	SANDRA WEINTRAUB
LOTTERY ROSE, THE - S	FRANK MILITARY JR.
LOTTERY, THE - S	TAKASHI BUFFORD
LOTUS MAN, THE - S	BOB HOGE
LOU GEHRIG DID NOT DIE OF CANCER (P)	JASON MILLER
LOUIE, LOUIE - S	DICK BEEBE
LOUIE, LOUIE - S	JOHN NORVILLE
LOUIE, LOUIE - S	THOMAS BAUM
LOUIE - S	ERIC ROTH
LOUIE'S WIDOW - S	LOUIS LA RUSSO
LOUIS QUINZE (P)	SANDRA JENNINGS
LOUISIANA RUN - S	TIM McCANLIES
LOUP-GAROU - S	DAVID DUBOS
LOUSY KILLING, A - S	ERIC HUGHES
LOVE	NANCY DOWD
LOVE 30 - S	SUSAN RICE
LOVE ACT - S	DAVID PIRIE
LOVE AFFAIR	DUSAN MAKAVEJEV
LOVE AFFAIR	WARREN BEATTY
LOVE AFFAIR (1994)	ROBERT TOWNE
LOVE AFFAIR - S	FREDERIC RAPHAEL
LOVE AFTER LOVE	DIANE KURYZ
LOVE AND A .45	C.M. TALKINGTON
LOVE AND ANARCHY	LINA WERTMULLER
LOVE AND BULLETS	WENDELL MAYES†
LOVE AND BULLETS - S	HOWARD KORDER
LOVE AND CHAOS - S	JEAN-YVES PITOUN
LOVE AND DEATH	WOODY ALLEN
LOVE AND MARRIAGE - S	MATT TABAK
LOVE AND MONEY	JAMES TOBACK
LOVE AND MONEY - S	BRUCE FEIRSTEIN

LOVE AND PAIN AND THE WHOLE DAMNED THING	ALVIN SARGENT
LOVE AT FIRST BITE	ROBERT KAUFMAN†
LOVE AT FIRST OVERSIGHT - S	DON HOLLEY
LOVE AT LARGE	ALAN RUDOLPH
LOVE AT STAKE	LANIER LANEY
LOVE AT STAKE	TERRY SWEENEY
LOVE AT THE TOP	CHRISTOPHER FRANK†
LOVE BEHIND BARS - S	DAVID GREENWALT
LOVE BUSINESS - S	STEVE TESICH
LOVE CAGE, THE	RENE CLEMENT
LOVE, CHEAT & STEAL (CTF)	WILL CURRAN
LOVE CHILD	ANNE GERARD
LOVE CHILD	KATHERINE SPECKTOR
LOVE CRAZY - S	CHARLES SHYER
LOVE CRAZY - S	NANCY MEYERS
LOVE CRIMES	ALLAN MOYLE
LOVE CRIMES	LAURIE FRANK
LOVE, FAME AND MONEY - S	LOREN-PAUL CAPLIN
LOVE FIELD	DONALD P. ROOS
LOVE, GRACIE - S	AMY PITTA
LOVE$GREED	BASHAR SHBIB
LOVE, HONOR, THE U.S. ARMY - S	HESPER ANDERSON
LOVE HURTS	RON NYSWANER
LOVE HURTS - S	TED MANN
LOVE IN FLUSHING - S	JEFF STANZLER
LOVE IN GERMANY, A	AGNIESZKA HOLLAND
LOVE IN THE AFTERNOON	BILLY WILDER
LOVE IN THE AFTERNOON	I.A.L. DIAMOND†
LOVE IN THE AFTERNOON - S	TOM BENEDEK
LOVE IN THE ATTIC - S	DONALD E. WESTLAKE
LOVE IN THE CITY	FEDERICO FELLINI†
LOVE IN VAIN - S	ALAN GREENBERG
LOVE IS A BALL	DAVID SWIFT
LOVE IS A BALL	FRANK WALDMAN†
LOVE IS A BALL	TOM WALDMAN†
LOVE IS A DOG FROM HELL	DOMINIQUE DERUDDERE
LOVE IS A GUN	DAVID HARTWELL
LOVE IS A MYSTERY - S	JON EIG
LOVE IS LIKE THAT	GEORGE GARY
LOVE, JANIS - S	ED GRACYZYK
LOVE KILLS (CTF)	COREY MANDELL
LOVE KILLS (CTF)	MARC LIEBERMAN
LOVE KILLS (CTF)	MICHAEL MURRAY
LOVE KILLS -S	DEAN CAIN
LOVE KILLS - S	JEAN-YVES PITOUN
LOVE KILLS - S	RICHARD DAY
LOVE LETTERS	AMY JONES
LOVE LETTERS (P)	A.R. GURNEY
LOVE LUCK - S	JEREMY JOE KRONSBERG
LOVE & MARRIAGE - S	M.C. VARLEY
LOVE MATTERS (CTF)	EB LOTTIMER
LOVE MATTERS (CTF)	EVAN KATZ
LOVE ME TOMORROW - S	ERIC CHAMPNELLA
LOVE ME TOMORROW - S	KEITH MITCHELL
LOVE MINUS (P)	MARY GALLAGHER
LOVE & MURDER	STEVEN HILLIARD STERN
LOVE ON THE RUN	FRANCOIS TRUFFAUT†
LOVE ON THE RUN	SUZANNE SCHIFFMAN
LOVE OR MONEY	BART DAVIS
LOVE OR MONEY	ELYSE ENGLAND
LOVE OR MONEY	MICHAEL ZAUSNER
LOVE POTION #9	DALE LAUNER
LOVE, ROGER - S	GARRY MARSHALL
LOVE, ROGER - S	JERRY BELSON
LOVE, ROGER - S	STEVEN M. KUNES
LOVE SHACK - S	MARK COMBS
LOVE SONG OF RUDY KAZOO, THE - S	ALAN GROSS
LOVE SONGS	ELIE CHOURAQUI
LOVE STORY	ERICH SEGAL
LOVE STORY '78 - S	RONNI KERN
LOVE STREAMS	JOHN CASSAVETES†
LOVE STREAMS	TED ALLAN
LOVE, THE MAGICIAN	CARLOS SAURA
LOVE THY FATHER - S	DARRYL WIMBERLY
LOVE VALOUR COMPASSION (P)	TERRENCE MCNALLY
LOVE WITH A PERFECT STRANGER (CTF) - S	PAMELA WALLACE
LOVE WITH A PERFECT STRANGER - S	LANA FREISTAT-MELMAN
LOVE WITH THE PROPER STRANGER	ARNOLD SCHULMAN
LOVE WITHOUT PITY	ERIC ROCHANT
LOVE YA TOMORROW	MEL WEISER
LOVE YOUR MAMA	RUBY L. OLIVER
LOVED ONE, THE	TERRY SOUTHERN

MAN WITH THE SCREAMING FACE - S ... BRUCE CAMPBELL
MAN WITH TWO BRAINS, THE ... CARL REINER
MAN WITH TWO BRAINS, THE ... GEORGE GIPE
MAN WITH TWO BRAINS, THE ... STEVE MARTIN
MAN WITHOUT A FACE, THE ... MALCOLM MACRURY
MAN WITHOUT WORDS, A - S ... ED KAPLAN
MAN, WOMAN AND CHILD ... DAVID Z. GOODMAN
MAN, WOMAN AND CHILD ... ERICH SEGAL
MAN'S WORLD - S ... GITA ROMANO
MAN-AT-ARMS - S ... CYRUS VORIS
MAN-AT-ARMS - S ... ETHAN REIFF
MAN-EATER - S ... RICK RIDGEWAY
MAN-MOTH - S ... JULIE HICKSON
MANAGER, THE - S ... PAUL CLEMENS
MANAGER, THE - S ... RON MAGID
MANCHESTER ANGEL - S ... JAN EGLESON
MANCHU EAGLE MURDER MYSTERY, THE ... DEAN HARGROVE
MANCHURIAN CANDIDATE, THE ... GEORGE AXELROD
MANDINGO ... NORMAN WEXLER
MANDRAKE - S ... LORENZO SEMPLE
MANDRAKE THE MAGICIAN - S ... MICHAEL ALMEREYDA
MANGLER, THE - S ... HARRY ALAN TOWERS
MANGO - S ... ALFRED GOUGH
MANGO - S ... MILES MILLAR
MANGO TREE, THE ... MICHAEL PATE
MANHATTAN ... MARSHALL BRICKMAN
MANHATTAN ... WOODY ALLEN
MANHATTAN CHARMER - S ... LOUIS LA RUSSO
MANHATTAN GHOST STORY - S ... RONALD BASS
MANHATTAN ISLAND - S ... CHRIS KEYSER
MANHATTAN ISLAND - S ... M.S. FREEMAN
MANHATTAN MURDER MYSTERY ... MARSHALL BRICKMAN
MANHATTAN MURDER MYSTERY ... WOODY ALLEN
MANHATTAN PROJECT, THE ... MARSHALL BRICKMAN
MANHATTAN PROJECT, THE ... THOMAS BAUM
MANHATTAN STAGECOACH - S ... GEORGE GIPE
MANHUNT - S ... DAN BRONSON
MANHUNT - S ... GARY THOMPSON
MANHUNTER ... MICHAEL MANN
MANIAC ... JIMMY SANGSTER
MANIAC COP ... LARRY COHEN
MANIAC COP 2 ... LARRY COHEN
MANIAC SLAYS BLONDE - S ... W.D. RICHTER
MANIC - S ... ROBERT L. FRIEDMAN
MANIC - S ... SELMA THOMPSON
MANIFESTO ... DUSAN MAKAVEJEV
MANITOU, THE ... THOMAS POPE
MANNEQUIN ... ED RUGOFF
MANNEQUIN ... MICHAEL GOTTLIEB
MANNEQUIN TWO ... BETSY ISRAEL
MANNEQUIN TWO ... DAVID A. ISAACS
MANNEQUIN TWO ... ED RUGOFF
MANNEQUIN TWO ... KEN LEVINE
MANNY - S ... DONALD TODD
MANOLETE - S ... MENNO MEYJES
MANON OF THE SPRING ... CLAUDE BERRI
MANON OF THE SPRING ... GERARD BRACH
MANON RHEAUME STORY - S ... JARRE FEES
MANSON IN THE DESERT - S ... DAVID MILES
MANUMIT - S ... HAROLD NEBENZAL
MANUMIT - S ... ROD AMATEAU
MANY ARE CALLED - S ... SHAWN SCHEPPS
MAN'S BEST FRIEND ... JOHN LAFIA
MAN'S BEST FRIEND - S ... RICHARD C. MATHESON
MAN'S BEST FRIEND - S ... TOM FLYNN
MAN'S FATE - S ... DANIEL BARTOLINI
MAN'S FATE - S ... LAWRENCE HAUBEN
MAP OF THE HUMAN HEART ... VINCENT WARD
MAP OF THE WORLD (P) ... DAVID HARE
MAPLE & ELM - S ... STU KRIEGER
MAPS FOR DROWNERS (P) ... NEIL LANDAU
MARATHON MAN ... WILLIAM GOLDMAN
MARATHON MOVIE - S ... GEORGE MCGRATH
MARATHON - S ... MARK KRAM
MARCH OR DIE ... DAVID Z. GOODMAN
MARCH, THE (CTF) ... WILLIAM NICHOLSON
MARCO - S ... ANDY LEWIS
MARCUS TIMBERWOLF - S ... ED BUNKER
MARGARITAVILLE - S ... P.J. O'ROURKE
MARGUERITE & THE MOON MAN - S ... R. SILVIS
MARIANNE AND JULIANE ... M. VON TROTTA
MARIA'S LOVERS ... ANDREI KONCHALOVSKY
MARIA'S LOVERS ... GERARD BRACH
MARIA'S LOVERS ... MARJORIE DAVID
MARIA'S LOVERS ... PAUL ZINDEL
MARIA'S MISSING - S ... REBECCA SOLADAY
MARIE ... JOHN BRILEY
MARIE AND BRUCE (P) ... WALLACE SHAWN
MARIE LAVEAU - S ... DAVID ODELL
MARIGOLDS ... ATHOL FUGARD
MARILYN & BOBBY (CTF) ... GERALD MACDONALD
MARILYN HOTCHKISS BALLROOM DANCING & CHARM SCHOOL (SHORT) ... RANDALL MILLER
MARK MY WORDS - S ... STEVEN WASSERMAN
MARK OF CAIN ... PETER COLLEY
MARK, THE ... STANLEY MANN
MARK TWAIN AND ME (CTF) ... CYNTHIA WHITCOMB
MARKED FOR DEATH ... MARK VICTOR
MARKED FOR DEATH ... MICHAEL GRAIS
MARLOWE ... STIRLING SILLIPHANT
MARLOWE - S ... ALEX AYRES
MARMALADE - S ... GINNY CERRELLA
MARMALADE - S ... MARYEDITH BURRELL
MARNIE ... JAY PRESSON ALLEN
MAROONED ... MAYO SIMON
MARQUIS OF O, THE ... ERIC ROHMER
MARRIAGE, A ... SANDY TUNG
MARRIAGE GO ROUND, THE ... LESLIE STEVENS
MARRIAGE OF A YOUNG STOCKBROKER, THE ... LORENZO SEMPLE
MARRIAGE OF BETTE AND BOO, THE (P) ... CHRISTOPHER DURANG
MARRIAGE OR BUST - S ... JOHN ROMANO
MARRIAGE STORY, THE - S ... BETH GUTCHEON
MARRIAGE TALE, THE - S ... HELENE WAGNER
MARRIAGE THING, THE - S ... ED BURNHAM
MARRIAGE THING, THE - S ... ELAINE NEWMAN
MARRIED LIFE, A - S ... DIANE ENGLISH
MARRIED LIFE - S ... LYNN GROSSMAN
MARRIED TO IT ... JANET KOVALCIK
MARRIED TO THE MOB ... BARRY STRUGATZ
MARRIED TO THE MOB ... MARK BURNS
MARRIED WOMAN, THE ... JEAN-LUC GODARD
MARRY ME A LITTLE (P) ... CRAIG LUCAS
MARRYING MAN, THE ... NEIL SIMON
MARRYING UP - S ... ERIC ALTER
MARRYING UP - S ... STEVEN S. GREENE
MARRYING UP - S ... TRISH SOODIK
MARSABA - S ... LOUIS GARFINKLE
MARSEILLE CONTRACT, THE ... JUDD BERNARD
MARSHAL OF CENTRAL PARK, THE - S ... JOHN SHIRLEY
MARSUPIALS: THE HOWLING III, THE ... PHLILIPPE MORA
MARTHA HONEY- S ... ROY CARLSON
MARTHA MITCHELL - S ... AUDREY SALZBERG
MARTHA MITCHELL - S ... STEVE SALZBERG
MARTIAL LAW ... RICHARD BRANDES
MARTIAL OUTLAW ... GEORGE SAUNDERS
MARTIAL OUTLAW ... JOHN BRYANT
MARTIAL OUTLAW ... THOMAS RITZ
MARTIANS GO HOME ... CHARLIE HAAS
MARTIN ... GEORGE A. ROMERO
MARTIN EDEN - S ... DAVID O'NEILL
MARTINE - S ... RON BASS
MARTIN'S DAY ... ALLAN G. SCOTT
MARTIN'S DAY ... CHRIS BRYANT
MARTY ... PADDY CHAYEVSKY†
MARU MARU ... PHILIP YORDAN
MARVEL OF THE HAUNTED CASTLE, THE - S ... LEM DOBBS
MARVIN AND SARA - S ... GARY DAVID GOLDBERG
MARVIN AND TIGE ... ERIC WESTON
MARVIN AND TIGE ... WANDA DELL
MARY AND RICHARD - S ... DAVID RAYFIEL
MARY BARNES (P) ... DAVID EDGAR
MARY POPPINS II - S ... PERRY HOWZE
MARY POPPINS II - S ... RANDY HOWZE
MARY REILLY ... CHRISTOPHER HAMPTON
MARY SILLIMAN'S WAR (CTF) ... LOUISA B. BISOGNO
MARY SILLIMAN'S WAR (CTF) ... STEVEN SCHECHTER
MARY WANTS TO HAVE AN AFFAIR - S ... BRYAN GORDON
MASK ... ANNA HAMILTON PHELAN
MASK, THE ... MARK VERHEIDEN
MASK, THE ... MICHAEL FALLON
MASK, THE ... MIKE WERB
MASK OF MICHAEL - S ... TOM PAGE
MASK OF MORIARITY (P) ... HUGH LEONARD
MASK OF SARNATH, THE (SHORT) ... NEIL RUTTENBERG
MASK OF THE RED DEATH - S ... MICHAEL J. MURRAY
MASQUE OF THE RED DEATH ... DARYL HANEY
MASQUE OF THE RED DEATH ... LARRY BRAND
MASQUERADE (1965) ... WILLIAM GOLDMAN
MASQUERADE (1988) ... DICK WOLF
MASS APPEAL ... BILL C. DAVIS
MASTER HAROLD AND THE BOYS (P) ... ATHOL FUGARD
MASTER OF DRAGONARD HILL ... HARRY ALAN TOWERS
MASTER OF DRAGONARD HILL ... RICK MARX
MASTER OF LIES - S ... ALAN SACKS
MASTER OF THE LAMP - S ... BRET PLATE
MASTER OF THE WORLD ... RICHARD MATHESON
MASTER, THE - S ... W.D. RICHTER
MASTERGATE (CTF) ... LARRY GELBART
MASTERS OF MENACE ... TINO INSANA
MASTERS OF THE UNIVERSE ... DAVID ODELL
MATA HARI ... JOEL ZISKIN
MATA HARI, AGENT H21 ... FRANCOIS TRUFFAUT†
MATA HARI - S ... DAVID WILLIAMSON
MATADOR ... PEDRO ALMODOVAR
MATARESE CIRCLE - S ... DARRYL PONICSAN
MATCH FACTORY GIRL, THE ... AKI KAURISMAKI
MATCH, THE - S ... JAMES SADWITH
MATCHBOOK (SHORT) ... HANNA WEG
MATES - S ... DANIEL GOLDIN
MATES - S ... JOSHUA GOLDIN
MATEWAN ... JOHN SAYLES
MATILDA ... ALBERT S. RUDDY
MATILDA ... TIMOTHY GALFAS
MATILDA - S ... NICHOLAS KAZAN
MATILDA - S ... ROBIN SWICORD
MATINEE ... JAIME H. HERMOSILLO
MATINEE (1993) ... CHARLIE HAAS
MATINEE (1993) ... JERICHO STONE
MATINEE - S ... BETH GUTCHEON
MATINEE - S ... JACK BEHR
MATINEE - S ... SANDY KROOPF
MATING BIRDS, THE - S ... ALLAN SCOTT
MATING GAME, THE ... WILLIAM ROBERTS
MATING SEASON - S ... NICHOLAS BOGNER
MATRIX - S ... ANDY WACHOWSKI
MATRIX - S ... LARRY WACHOWSKI
MATTER OF DEGREES, A ... JACK MASON
MATTER OF DEGREES, A ... RANDALL POSTER
MATTER OF DEGREES, A ... W.T. MORGAN
MATTER OF DIGNITY, A ... MICHAEL CACOYANNIS
MATTER OF HEART, A - S ... WILLIAM TONNER
MATTER OF HONOR, A - S ... DAN GORDON
MATTER OF LIFE AND DEATH, A ... E. PRESSBURGER†
MATTER OF LIFE AND DEATH, A ... M. POWELL†
MATTERS OF THE HEART (CTF) ... LINDA BERGMAN
MATTERS OF THE HEART (CTF) ... MARTIN TAHSE
MATTIE - S ... HUGH LEONARD
MATZGER'S DOG - S ... TOR VALENZA
MAURICE ... JAMES IVORY
MAURICE ... KIT HESKETH-HARVEY
MAUVAISE GRAINE ... BILLY WILDER
MAVEN, THE - S ... ERIC GETHERS
MAVERICK ... WILLIAM GOLDMAN
MAVIS KEATES - S ... SCOTT DAVIS JONES
MAX AND HELEN (CTF) ... COREY BLECHMAN
MAX DAMAGE - S ... BOB FORWARD
MAX DUGAN RETURNS ... NEIL SIMON
MAX HAVELAAR ... GERARD SOETEMAN
MAX LAKEMAN AND THE BEAUTIFUL STRANGER - S ... GREG BROOKER
MAX Q - S ... MARTY KAPLAN
MAX RENEGADE - S ... DAVID AVALLONE
MAX THE FOX - S ... FLOYD MUTRUX
MAXIE ... PATRICIA RESNICK
MAXIMUM IMPACT ... J.R. BOOKWALTER
MAXIMUM MAX - S ... DAVID DUBOS
MAXIMUM MAXIMUM - S ... CHRIS COSBY
MAXIMUM MAXIMUM - S ... MEL FRIEDMAN
MAXIMUM OVERDRIVE ... STEPHEN KING
MAXWELL (CTF) - S ... ROBERT MUNDY
MAXWELL'S TRAIN - S ... DAVID A. CHAPPE
MAXWELL'S TRAIN - S ... JEB STUART
MAY FOOLS ... JEAN-CLAUDE CARRIERE
MAY FOOLS ... LOUIS MALLE
MAY I SEE YOU AGAIN - S ... ERIC SCHAEFFER
MAYA TRAIL - S ... JOEL SMITH
MAYBE THAT'S YOUR PROBLEM (P) ... LIONEL CHETWYND
MAYBERRY VICE - S ... LINDA YELLEN

Q

I N D E X   O F   F I L M   T I T L E S

INDEX OF FILM TITLES

INDEX OF FILM TITLES

W

YEAR OF THE ZINC
  PENNY, THE - S .... STEVEN BAIGELMAN
YELLOW HANDKERCHIEF, THE - S ...... PETE HAMILL
YELLOW JERSEY - S .... COLIN WELLAND
YELLOW RAFT IN
  BLUE WATER, A - S .... GLORIA KATZ
YELLOW RAFT IN
  BLUE WATER, A - S .... WILL HUYCK
YELLOW SUBMARINE (AF) .... ERICH SEGAL
YELLOWBEARD .... BERNARD MCKENNA
YELLOWBEARD .... GRAHAM CHAPMAN†
YELLOWBEARD .... PETER COOK
YELLOWHAIR AND THE
  FORTRESS OF GOLD .... JOHN KERSHAW
YELLOWHAIR AND THE
  FORTRESS OF GOLD .... MATT CIMBER
YELLOWSTONE KELLY .... BURT KENNEDY
YENTL .... BARBRA STREISAND
YENTL .... JACK ROSENTHAL
YES, GIORGIO .... NORMAN STEINBERG
YES SIR, THAT'S MY BABY .... OSCAR BRODNEY
YESTERDAY - S .... JONATHAN BRETT
YESTERDAY'S HERO .... JACKIE COLLINS
YO' JULIETTE - S .... RANDY WEINER
YO' JULIETTE - S .... ROB HANNING
YO OLIVER - S .... FRANK PUGLIESE
YOJIMBO .... AKIRA KUROSAWA
YOJIMBO - S .... WALTER HILL
YOJUMBO - S .... HENRY BEAN
YONADAB (P) .... PETER SHAFFER
YOR, ... ANTHONY M. DAWSON
YOR .... ROBERT BAILEY
YOSHIKO - S .... MURDO LAIRD
YOU AIN'T KNOWN TRUE
  HATRED TIL YOUR CAR'S
  BEEN TOWED (P) .... ALLISON ROBBINS
YOU BETTER WATCH OUT .... LEWIS JACKSON
YOU CAN'T HAVE
  EVERYTHING .... A. MARTIN ZWEIBACH
YOU CAN'T HURRY LOVE .... RICHARD MARTINI
YOU DON'T DIE OF LOVE - S ..... THOMAS THONSON
YOU FOR ME .... WILLIAM ROBERTS
YOU FOR ME - S .... BO GOLDMAN
YOU LIGHT UP MY LIFE .... JOSEPH BROOKS
YOU ONLY DIE ONCE (CTF) - S .... JIM BYRNES
YOU ONLY DIE ONCE (CTF) - S ..... MATT MCDUFFIE
YOU ONLY LIVE TWICE .... ROALD DAHL†
YOU PLAY THE BLACK - S .... C. CARTWRIGHT
YOU PLAY THE BLACK - S .... TOPPER LILLIEN
YOU SEND ME - S .... RICK CLEVELAND
YOU SHOULD SEE THE CONKLIN'S
  LIVING ROOM - S .... ROBERT NEWCOMBE
YOU SHOULD SEE
  THEM PLAY - S .... KEN RICHARDS
YOU TALKIN' TO ME? .... CHARLES WINKLER
YOUNG AND WILLING .... MORDECAI RICHLER
YOUNG AT HEART .... JULIUS J. EPSTEIN
YOUNG AT HEART - S .... LEWIS KLEINBERG
YOUNG BILLY YOUNG .... BURT KENNEDY
YOUNG BUCKS - S .... ANDY BOROWITZ
YOUNG CATHERINE (CTF) .... CHRIS BRYANT
YOUNG COMMANDOS .... BOAZ DAVIDSON
YOUNG COMMANDOS .... GREG LATTER
YOUNG DOCTORS IN LOVE .... MICHAEL ELIAS
YOUNG DOCTORS IN LOVE .... RICHARD EUSTIS
YOUNG EINSTEIN .... DAVID ROACH
YOUNG EINSTEIN .... YAHOO SERIOUS
YOUNG EVE - S .... CHARLES ROBERT CARNER
YOUNG FRANKENSTEIN .... GENE WILDER
YOUNG FRANKENSTEIN .... MEL BROOKS
YOUNG GIRLS OF
  ROCHEFORT .... JACQUES DEMY†
YOUNG GOODMAN BROWN .... PETER GEORGE
YOUNG GUNS .... JOHN FUSCO
YOUNG GUNS II .... JOHN FUSCO
YOUNG IN HEART, THE, ... CHARLES BENNETT
YOUNG INDIANA JONES
  AND THE HOLLYWOOD
  FOLLIES (CTF) .... JONATHAN HALES
YOUNG INDIANA JONES
  AND THE HOLLYWOOD
  FOLLIES - (CTF) .... MATTHEW JACOBS
YOUNG LILLY - S .... NATALIE COOPER
YOUNG LIONS, THE .... EDWARD ANHALT
YOUNG LOVERS - S .... BENNETT YELLIN
YOUNG LOVERS - S .... PETER FARRELLY
YOUNG LUST .... BRUCE WAGNER
YOUNG LUST .... ROBIN MENKEN
YOUNG MAN WITH A HORN .... CARL FOREMAN†
YOUNG MEN WITH
  UNLIMITED CAPITAL .... WILL ALDIS

○

YOUNG MEN WITH
  UNLIMITED CAPITAL - S .... JOHN BYRUM
YOUNG SAVAGES, THE .... EDWARD ANHALT
YOUNG SHERLOCK HOLMES .... CHRIS COLUMBUS
YOUNG SOUL REBELS .... ISAAC JULIEN
YOUNG TEDDY ROOSEVELT - S .... THOMAS POPE
YOUNG TOSCANINI .... WILLIAM STADIEM
YOUNG WARRIORS .... LAWRENCE D. FOLDES
YOUNG WARRIORS .... RUSSELL W. COLGIN
YOUNG WARRIORS, THE ..... RICHARD MATHESON
YOUNG WINSTON .... CARL FOREMAN†
YOUNGBLOOD .... JOHN WHITMAN
YOUNGBLOOD .... PAUL CARTER HARRISON
YOUNGBLOOD .... PETER MARKLE
YOUNGER AND YOUNGER .... FELIX ADLON
YOUNGER AND YOUNGER .... PERCY ADLON
YOUR BASIC LOUSY
  MARRIAGE - S .... BRUCE JAY FRIEDMAN
YOUR WISH IS MY COMMAND - S .... DANA OLSEN
YOUR WISH IS MY
  COMMAND - S .... ROBERT COLLECTOR
YOURS, MINE AND OURS .... MEL SHAVELSON
YOURS TILL NIAGARA FALLS - S ...... SUSAN BASKIN
YOUTH, SPRING, LOVE (P) .... JAMES KIRKWOOD†
YOU'LL GET USED TO IT! (P) .... PETER COLLEY
YOU'RE A BIG
  BOY NOW .... FRANCIS FORD COPPOLA
YOU'RE IN THE NAVY NOW .... RICHARD T. MURPHY
YOU'RE NEVER TOO YOUNG ...... SIDNEY SHELDON
YUKON KID, THE - S .... D. SHONE KIRKPATRICK
YVONNE'S PERFUME .... PATRICE LECONTE

Z

ZABRISKIE POINT .... CLARE PEPLOE
ZABRISKIE POINT .... MICHELANGELO ANTONIONI
ZABRISKIE POINT .... SAM SHEPARD
ZABRISKIE POINT .... TONINO GUERRA
ZACH AND REBA - S .... JAY STAPLETON
ZACHARY'S TRUTH - S .... MARTIE COOKE
ZADAR! COW FROM HELL .... MERLE KESSLER
ZAJOTA AND THE
  BOOGIE SPIRIT .... AYOKA CHENZIRA
ZANDALEE .... MARI KORNHAUSER
ZANDE - S .... ANDY LEWIS
ZANDY'S BRIDE .... MARC NORMAN
ZAPPED! .... BRUCE RUBIN
ZAPPED! .... ROBERT J. ROSENTHAL
ZARAK .... RICHARD MAIBAUM††
ZARDOZ .... JOHN BOORMAN
ZAZIE .... LOUIS MALLE
ZAZIE DANS LE METRO ..... JEAN-PAUL RAPPENEAU
ZEBRAHEAD .... ANTHONY DRAZAN
ZEBVLON - S .... RUDOLPH G. WURLITZER
ZED AND TWO NOUGHTS, A .... PETER GREENAWAY
ZELDA (CTF) .... ANTHONY IVOR
ZELDA (CTF) .... BENEDICT FITZGERALD
ZELIG .... WOODY ALLEN
ZELLY & ME .... TINA RATHBORNE
ZEPATA M.D. - S .... CARLO ALLEN
ZERO CLUB, THE - S .... AARON LATHAM
ZERO CLUB, THE - S .... MITCH WATSON
ZERO GRAVITY - S .... DUNCAN KENNEDY
ZERO GRAVITY - S .... JOHN ZINMAN
ZERO HOUR .... HALL BARTLETT†
ZERO HOUR .... JOHN CHAMPION†
ZERO HOUR - S .... MICHAEL KASSIN
ZERO HOUR - S .... MICHAEL WOLK
ZERO PATIENCE .... JOHN GREYSON
ZERO VISIBILITY - S .... NICHOLAS BOGNER
ZEUS AND ROXANE - S .... TOM BENEDEK
ZIG-ZAG MAN,THE - S .... THOMAS RICKMAN
ZIGZAG MAN, THE - S .... ALEXANDER TANA
ZINA .... KEN MCMULLEN
ZIPPYVISION - S .... DIANE NOOMIN
ZLATA'S DIARY -S .... PHIL ALDEN ROBINSON
ZODIAC - S .... CHIP PROSER
ZODIAC - S .... KENNETH H. FRIEDMAN
ZODIAC - S .... SNOO WILSON
ZOMBIE ATTACK! (P) .... JUSTIN TANNER
ZOMBIE HIGH - S .... ELIZABETH PASSARELLI
ZONE OF SILENCE - S .... JOAN DIDION
ZONE OF SILENCE - S .... JOHN G. DUNNE
ZONE TROOPERS .... DANNY BILSON
ZONE TROOPERS .... PAUL DE MEO
ZONE TWO - S .... RICHARD HEFT
ZOO - S .... PATRICK O'CONNOR
ZOO GANG, THE .... DAVID DASHEV
ZOO GANG, THE .... JOHN WATSON
ZOO GANG, THE .... PEN DENSHAM

ZOO GANG, THE .... STUART BIRNBAUM
ZOO PLANE - S .... GARRY TRUDEAU
ZOOMAN AND THE SIGN (P) .... CHARLES H. FULLER
ZOOT SUIT .... LUIS VALDEZ
ZORBA THE GREK .... MICHAEL CACOYANNIS
ZORRO - S .... NANCY LARSON
ZORRO - S .... RANDY JOHNSON
ZORRO - S .... TED ELLIOTT
ZORRO - S .... TERRY ROSSIO
ZORRO, THE GAY BLADE .... BOB RANDALL
ZORRO, THE GAY BLADE .... DON MORIARTY
ZORRO, THE GAY BLADE .... GREG ALT
ZORRO, THE GAY BLADE .... HAL DRESNER
ZPG .... FRANK DE FELITTA
ZULU .... CY ENDFIELD
ZULU DAWN .... ANTHONY STOREY
ZULU DAWN .... CY ENDFIELD
ZYZZYX - S .... TRENT HARRIS

★ ★ ★

INDICES

GUILDS · AGENTS & MANAGERS
ACADEMY AWARDS · ADVERTISERS

GUILDS

WRITERS GUILD OF AMERICA-WEST, INC.

8955 Beverly Blvd.

Los Angeles, CA 90048

310/550-1000

310/205-2502 (Agency Information)

WRITERS GUILD OF AMERICA-EAST, INC.

555 West 57th St.

New York, NY 10019

212/245-6180

WRITERS GUILD OF GREAT BRITAIN

430 Edgeware Road

London W21 EH, England

011/071/723-8074

DIRECTORS GUILD OF AMERICA

7920 Sunset Blvd.

Los Angeles, CA 90046

310/289-2000

213/851-3671 (Agency Information)

SCREEN ACTORS GUILD

5757 Wilshire Blvd.

Los Angeles, CA 90036

213/954-1600

213/549-6737 (Agency Information)

*= management company

A

ABOVE THE LINE
9200 Sunset Blvd., Suite 401
West Hollywood, CA 90069
310/859-6115
FAX 310/859-6119

Rima Greer

ABRAMS ARTISTS & ASSOCIATES
9200 Sunset Blvd., Suite 625
Los Angeles, CA 90069
310/859-0625

420 Madison Ave., Suite 1400
New York, NY 10017
212/935-8980

Harry Abrams

**ACME TALENT & LITERARY
AGENCY**
8899 Beverly Blvd., Suite 808
Los Angeles, CA 90048
310/550-6808
FAX 310/550-8220

Lisa Lindo Lieblein
Adam Lieblein

ADDIS-WECHSLER & ASSOCIATES*
955 S. Carrillo Drive, 3rd Floor
Los Angeles, CA 90048
213/954-9000
FAX 213/954-9009

Keith Addis
Nick Wechsler

THE AGENCY
10351 Santa Monica Blvd., Suite 211
Los Angeles, CA 90025
310/551-3000

**AGENCY FOR THE PERFORMING
ARTS, INC. (APA)**
9000 Sunset Blvd., Suite 1200
Los Angeles, CA 90069
310/273-0744
FAX 310/275-9401

888 Seventh Avenue
New York, NY 10106
212/582-1500
FAX 212/245-1647

ALL-STAR TALENT AGENCY
21416 Chase Street, Suite 2
Canoga Park, CA 91304
818/346-4313

Robert Brad Allred

THE ALPERN GROUP
4400 Coldwater Canyon Ave., Suite 125
Studio City, CA 91604
818/752-1877
FAX 818/752-1859

Jeff Alpern

AMBROSIO/MORTIMER
9150 Wilshire Blvd., Suite 135
Beverly Hills, CA 90212
310/274-4274

**AMSEL, EISENSTADT &
FRAZIER, INC.**
6310 San Vicente Blvd., Suite 401
Los Angeles, CA 90048
213/939-1188
FAX 213/939-0630

THE ARTISTS AGENCY
10000 Santa Monica Blvd., Suite 305
Los Angeles, CA 90067
310/277-7779
FAX 310/785-9338

ARTIST'S CREATIVE MANAGEMENT
12001 Ventura Place , 3rd Floor
Studio City, CA 91604
818/769-0469

THE ARTISTS GROUP, LTD.
1930 Century Park West, Suite 403
Los Angeles, CA 90067
310/552-1100
FAX 310/277-9513

ASSOCIATED TALENT AGENCY
9744 Wilshire Blvd., Suite 312
Beverly Hills, CA 90212
310/271-4662

ATLAS ENTERTAINMENT*
7471 Melrose Ave., Suite 11/12
Los Angeles, CA 90046
213/658-9100
FAX 213/658-8115

Cynthia Campos-Greenberg
Christopher E. Henze

B

**BECSEY/WISDOM/KALAJIAN
AGENCY**
9229 Sunset Blvd., Suite 710
Los Angeles, CA 90069
310/550-0535
FAX 310/246-4424

Larry Becsey
Victoria Wisdom
Jerry Kalajian

THE BENNETT AGENCY
150 S. Barrington Ave., Suite 1
Los Angeles, CA 90049
310/471-2251

Carole Bennett

BERZON TALENT AGENCY
1614 Victory Blvd., Suite 110
Glendale, CA 91201
818/548-1560

336 E. 17th St.
Costa Mesa, CA 92627
714/631-5936

Mike Ricciardi

BETWEEN THE LINES AGENCY
1312 Colony Drive
Marietta, GA 30068
404/587-1470
FAX 404/988-8976

Kate Groover

J. MICHAEL BLOOM, LTD.
233 Park Avenue South, 10th Floor
New York, NY 10003
212/529-6500

9255 Sunset Blvd., Suite 710
Los Angeles, CA 90069
310/275-6800
FAX 310/275-6941

**GEORGES BORCHARDT
LITERARY AGENCY**
136 East 57th Street
New York, NY 10022
212/753-5785

**BORINSTEIN, ORECK,
BOGART AGENCY**
8271 Melrose Ave., Suite 110
Los Angeles, CA 90046
213/658-7500

Mark Borinstein
Mary Oreck
Bari Bogart

THE BRANDT COMPANY
15250 Ventura Blvd. , Suite 720
Sherman Oaks, CA 91403
818/783-7747
FAX 818/784-6012

Geoff Brandt

BRESLER-KELLY-KIPPERMAN*
15760 Ventura Blvd., Suite 1730
Encino, CA 91436
818/905-1155

111 West 57th St., Suite 1409
New York, NY 10019
212/265-1980

Sandy Bresler
John S. Kelly
Perri Kipperman (NY)

BRILLSTEIN-GREY*
9150 Sunset Blvd., Suite 350
Beverly Hills, CA 90212
310/275-6135
FAX 310/275-6180

Bernie Brillstein
Brad Grey

**BRODER-KURLAND-WEBB-UFFNER
AGENCY**
9242 Bevery Blvd., Suite 200
Beverly Hills, CA 90210
310/281-3400
FAX 310/276-3207

Bob Broder
Norman Kurland
Elliot Webb
Beth Uffner

THE BROWN GROUP*
3500 W. Olive Avenue, Suite 730
Burbank, CA 91505
818/955-7040

Jon Brown

BRUCE BROWN AGENCY
1033 Gayley Ave., Suite 207
Los Angeles, CA 90024
310/208-1835

CURTIS BROWN, LTD.
606 North Larchmont, Suite 309
Los Angeles, CA 90004
213/461-0148

Ten Astor Place
New York, NY 10003
212/473-5400

162/168 Regent Street
London W1 England
071/872-0331
FAX 071/872-0332

THE BRUSTEIN CO.
2644 30th Street
Santa Monica, CA 90405
310/452-3330

Richard Brustein

DON BUCHWALD & ASSOCIATES
9229 Sunset Blvd., Suite 710
Los Angeles, CA 90069
310/278-3600

10 East 44th St.
New York, NY 10017
212/867-1200

C

LISA CALLAMARO AGENCY
427 N. Canon Drive
Beverly Hills, CA 90210
310/274-6783
FAX 310/274-6536

CAMDEN-ITG
*(In Association with
Candace Lake Agency)*
822 S. Robertson Blvd., Suite 200
Los Angeles, CA 90035
310/289-2700
FAX 310/289-2718

729 Seventh Ave., 16th Floor
New York, NY 10019
212/221-7878

WILLIAM CARROLL AGENCY
120 South Victory Blvd.
Burbank, CA 91502
818/845-3791

CARLYLE MANAGEMENT*
639 N. Larchmont, 2nd Floor
Los Angeles, CA 90038
213/469-3086

Phyllis Carlyle

CASAROTTO RAMSAY
National House
60-66 Wardour Street
London W1V 3HP, England
071/287-4450
FAX 01/287-9128

Jenne Casarotto

THE CHASIN AGENCY
8899 Beverly Blvd.
Beverly Hills, CA 90048
310/278-7505
FAX 310/275-6685

Tom Chasin

CHATTO & LINNIT
Prince of Wales Theatre
Coventry Street
London W1, England

CINEMA TALENT INTERNATIONAL
8033 Sunset Blvd., Suite 808
West Hollywood, CA 90046
213/656-1937

CIRCLE OF CONFUSION LTD.
131 Country Village Lane
New Hyde Park, NY 11040
212/969-0653

2633 Lincoln Blvd., Suite 250
Santa Monica, CA 90405
310/450-0571

THE COOPER AGENCY
10100 Santa Monica Blvd., Suite 310
Los Angeles, CA 90067
310/277-8422
FAX 310/277-8433

Frank Cooper
Jeff Cooper

THE COPPAGE COMPANY
11501 Chandler Blvd.
North Hollywood, CA 91601
818/980-1106
FAX 818/509-1474

Judy Coppage

**CREATIVE ALLIANCE
MANAGEMENT**
1680 N. Vine Street, Suite 1117
Los Angeles, CA 90028
213/962-6090
FAX 213/962-2065

Jeffrey Thal
Judy Friend

CREATIVE ARTISTS AGENCY (CAA)
9830 Wilshire Blvd.
Beverly Hills, CA 90212
310/288-4545
FAX 310/288-4800

PETER CROUCH & ASSOCIATES
59 Frith Street
London W1, England
011/441/734-2167

D

DADE, SCHULTZ ASSOCIATES
11846 Ventura Blvd., Suite 201
Studio City, CA 91604
818/760-3100

Ernie Dade
Kathleen Schultz

JUDY DAISH AGENCY
122 Wigmore Street
London W1H 9FE, England
011/441/486-5405

DISKANT & ASSOCIATES
1033 Gayley Avenue. Suite 202
Los Angeles, CA 90024
310/824-3773

George Diskant

DOUROUX & CO.
445 S. Beverly Drive, Suite 310
Beverly Hills, CA 90210
310/552-0900

Michael Douroux

DYTMAN & SCHWARTZ
9200 Sunset Blvd., Suite 809
Los Angeles, CA 90069
310/274-8844
FAX 310/274-7448

Jack Dytman
Scott Schwartz

E

ROBERT EISENBACH AGENCY
1010 S. Bedford Street, Suite 303
Los Angeles, CA 90035
310/657-9427

THE ANTHONY ELLIOT COMPANY*
1888 Century Park East, Suite 1900
Los Angeles, CA 90067
310/284-6804
FAX 310/284-3290

EPSTEIN-WYCKOFF-LaMANNA
280 S. Beverly Drive, Suite 400
Beverly Hills, CA 90212
310/278-7222
FAX 310/278-4640

Gary Epstein (NY)
Craig Wyckoff
Ross LaManna

F

FAVORED ARTISTS AGENCY
122 S. Robertson Blvd., Suite 202
Los Angeles, CA 90048
310/247-1040
FAX 310/247-1048

230 West 55th St., Suite 29D
New York, NY 10019
212/245-6960
FAX 212/333-7420

MAGGIE FIELD AGENCY
12725 Ventura Blvd., Suite D
Studio City, CA 91604
818/980-2001
FAX 818/980-0754

FILM ARTISTS ASSOCIATES
7080 Hollywood Blvd. , Suite 704
Hollywood, CA 90028
213/463-1010

THE SY FISHER COMPANY
10590 Wilshire Blvd., Suite 1602
Los Angeles, CA 90024
310/470-0917

G

THE GAGE GROUP INC.
9255 Sunset Blvd., Suite 515
Los Angeles, CA 90069
310/859-8777
FAX 310/859-8166

315 W. 57th St., Suite 4H
New York, NY 10019
212/541-5250
FAX 212/956-7466

Martin Gage

HELEN GARRETT AGENCY
P.O. Box 889
Hollywood, CA 90028
213/871-8707

THE GERSH AGENCY
232 N. Cañon Drive
Beverly Hills, CA 90210
310/274-6611
FAX 301/274-4035

130 West 42nd St., Suite 2400
New York, NY 10036
212/997-1818

Bob Gersh
Dave Gersh
Phil Gersh

GOLD/MARSHAK & ASSOCIATES
3500 West Olive Ave.
Burbank, CA 91505
818/972-4300
FAX 818/955-6411

Harry Gold
Darryl Marshak

GOLD/MILLER*
9220 Sunset Blvd., Suite 106
Los Angeles, CA 90069
310/278-8990

Eric Gold
Jim Miller

THE GOLDSTEIN COMPANY*
864 S. Robertson Blvd., Suite 304
Los Angeles, CA 90035
310/659-9511

Gary W. Goldstein

GRAY/GOODMAN, INC.
211 South Beverly Drive, Suite 100
Beverly Hills, CA 90212
310/276-7070
FAX 310/276-6049

Stefan Gray
Mark Goodman

ARTHUR B. GREENE
101 Park Avenue, 43rd Floor
New York, NY 10178
212/661-8200

HAROLD R. GREENE, INC.
13900 Marquesas Way, Bldg. C, #83
Marina del Rey, CA 90292
310/823-5393

LARRY GROSSMAN & ASSOCIATES
211 S. Beverly Drive, Suite 206
Beverly Hills, CA 90212
310/550-8127

H

REECE HALSEY AGENCY
8733 Sunset Blvd., Suite 101
Los Angeles, CA 90069
213/652-2409

A
G
E
N
T
S

&

M
A
N
A
G
E
R
S

531

**THE MITCHELL J. HAMILBURG
AGENCY**
292 S. La Cienega Blvd., Suite 312
Los Angeles, CA 90211
310/657-1501

RICK HASHAGEN & ASSOCIATES
157 West 57th Street
New York, NY 10019
212/315-3130

HATTON & BAKER
18 Jermyn Street
London W1, England
011/441/439-2971

**HEACOCK LITERARY & TALENT
AGENCY**
1523 Sixth Street
Santa Monica, CA 90401
310/393-6227
FAX 310/451-8524

HENDERSON/HOGAN AGENCY, INC.
247 S. Beverly Drive, Suite 102
Beverly Hills, CA 90212
310/274-7815

405 W. 44th Street
New York, NY 10036
212/765-5190

Margaret Henderson
Jerry Hogan (NY)

RICHARD HERMAN AGENCY
124 S. Lasky Drive
Beverly Hills, CA 90212
310/550-8913

MARTIN HURWITZ ASSOCIATES
427 N. Cañon Drive, Suite 215
Beverly Hills, CA 90210
310/274-0240

I

**ICM
(INTERNATIONAL CREATIVE
MANAGEMENT)**
8942 Wilshire Blvd.
Beverly Hills, CA 90211
310/550-4000
FAX 310/550-4108

40 West 57th Street
New York, NY 10019
212/556-5600

76 Oxford House
London, England W1R 1RB
071/636-6565

(TNA, The New Agency)
Viale Paroli, 41
Rome, Italy 00197
011/396-87.87.98

MICHAEL IMISON PLAYWRIGHTS
011/441/354-3274 (London)
212/874-2671 (New York)

INNOVATIVE ARTISTS
1999 Avenue of the Stars, Suite 2850
Los Angeles, CA 90067
310/553-5200
FAX 310/557-2211

130 W. 57th St., Suite 5B
New York, NY 10019-3316
212/315-4455
FAX 212/315-4688

**INTERNATIONAL ARTS
ENTERTAINMENT***
10390 Santa Monica Blvd., Suite 220
Los Angeles, CA 90025
310/551-0014
FAX 310/551-0512

Alan Greenspan

I.R.S./Harris Mangement*
3520 Hayden Avenue
Culver City, CA 90232
310/841-4169

Mark Harris
David McIlvain

J

JANKLOW & ASSOCIATES
5743 Corsa Ave., Suite 201
Westlake Village, CA 91362
818/865-0107

Don Janklow

JANKLOW & NESBITT
598 Madison Avenue
New York, NY 10022
212/421-1700

Morton Janklow
Lynn Nesbit

THE MELINDA JASON COMPANY*
8670 Wilshire Blvd., Suite 231
Beverly Hills, CA 90211
310/289-6134

K

THE LESLIE KALLEN AGENCY
5323 Worster Avenue
Van Nuys, CA 91401
818/906-2785
FAX 818/906-8931

THE KAPLAN-STAHLER AGENCY
8383 Wilshire Blvd.
Beverly Hills, CA 90211
213/653-4483

Mitch Kaplan
Elliot Stahler

PATRICIA KARLAN AGENCY
3575 Cahuenga Blvd. West, Suite 210
Los Angeles, CA 90068
818/752-4800

WILLIAM KERWIN AGENCY
1605 N. Cahuenga Blvd, Suite 202
Los Angeles, CA 90028
213/469-5155

THE JON KLANE AGENCY
120 El Camino Dr., Suite 112
Beverly Hills, CA 90212
310/278-0178
FAX 310/278-0179

PAUL KOHNER, INC.
9300 Wilshire Blvd., Suite 555
Beverly Hills, CA 90212
310/550-1060
FAX 310/276-1083

KOPALOFF COMPANY
1930 Century Park West, Suite 403
Los Angeles, CA 90067
310/203-8430

Don Kopaloff

LUCY KROLL AGENCY
390 West End Avenue
New York, NY 10024
212/877-0627

KROST/CHAPIN MANAGEMENT*
9911 West Pico Blvd., Penthouse I
Los Angeles, CA 90035
310/553-1411

Doug Chapin
Barry Krost

L

THE CANDACE LAKE AGENCY
(In Association with Camden-ITG)
822 S. Robertson Blvd., Suite 200
Los Angeles, CA 90035
310/289-0600
FAX 310/289-0619

LANTZ-HARRIS
888 Seventh Avenue, 25th Floor
New York, NY 10106
212/586-0200

Robert Lantz
Joy Harris

LASHER McMANUS ROBINSON MANAGEMENT*
2372 Veteran Avenue
Los Angeles, CA 90064
310/446-1466
FAX 310/446-1566

Liz Robinson

LEMON UNNA & DURBRIDGE LTD.
24 Pottery Lane
London W11 England
071/727-1346
FAX 071/727-9037

LENHOFF/ROBINSTON TALENT
1728 S. La Cienega Blvd.
Los Angeles, CA 90035
310/558-4700

S. Charles Lenhoff
Lloyd Robinson

LONDON MANAGEMENT
235/241 Regent Street
London W1 2J7, England
011/441/071/493-1610

STERLING LORD LITERISTIC
One Madison Avenue
New York, NY 10010
212/696-2800
FAX 212/686-6976

LYNNE & REILLY
6735 Forest Lawn Drive, Suite 313
Hollywood, CA 90066
213/850-1984

M

MAJOR CLIENTS AGENCY
2121 Avenue of the Stars, Suite 2450
Los Angeles, CA 90067
310/284-6400
FAX 310/284-6499

STEPHANIE MANN AGENCY
8323 Blackburn Avenue, Suite 5
Los Angeles, CA 90048
213/653-7130

ELAINE MARKSON LITERARY AGENCY
44 Greenwich Village
New York, NY 10011
212/243-8480
FAX 212/691-9014

HAROLD MATSON COMPANY, INC.
276 Fifth Avenue
New York, NY 10001
212/679-4490

MEDIA ARTISTS GROUP
8383 Wilshire Blvd., Suite 954
Beverly Hills, CA 90211
213/658-7434
FAX 213/658-7871

HELEN MERRILL
435 West 23rd Street, Suite 1-A
New York, NY 10011
212/691-5326

METROPOLITAN TALENT AGENCY
4526 Wilshire Blvd.
Los Angeles, CA 90010
213/857-4500
FAX 213/857-4599

THE MIRISCH AGENCY
10100 Santa Monica Blvd., Suite 700
Los Angeles, CA 90067
310/282-9940

Lawrence Mirisch

MLR REPRESENTATION
200 Fulham Road
London SW10, England

THE MONTEIRO ROSE AGENCY
17514 Ventura Blvd., Suite 205
Encino, CA 91316
818/501-1177
FAX 818/501-1194

Candy Monteiro
Fredda Rose

MORRA, BREZNER & STEINBERG*
801 Westmount Drive
Los Angeles, CA 90069
213/657-5384

WILLIAM MORRIS AGENCY
151 El Camino Drive
Beverly Hills, CA 90212
310/274-7451
FAX 310/859-4462

1325 Avenue of the Americas
New York, NY 10019
212/586-5100

31-32 Soho Square
London W12 5DG, England
01/434-2191

THE MORTON AGENCY
1650 Westwood Blvd., Suite 201
Los Angeles, CA 90024
310/824-4089

N

CNA & ASSOCIATES
1801 Avenue of the Stars, Suite 1250
Los Angeles, CA 90067
310/556-4343
FAX 310/556-4633

19 West 44th St., Suite 812
New York, NY 10036
212/840-7330
FAX 212/840-7527

Christopher Nassif

O

OGDEN HOUSE*
1511 N. Ogden Drive
Los Angeles, CA 90046
213/851-0458

Warren Zide

OMNI ARTISTS
9107 Wilshire Blvd., Suite 602
Beverly Hills, CA 90210
310/858-0085

ORIGINAL ARTISTS
12301 Wilshire Blvd., Suite 200
Los Angeles, CA 90025
310/394-1067

Jordan Bayer

THE DANIEL OSTROFF AGENCY
9200 Sunset Blvd., Suite 402
Los Angeles, CA 90069
310/278-2020
FAX 310/278-2020

P

PARADIGM
10100 Santa Monica Blvd., 25th Floor
Los Angeles, CA 90067
310/277-4400
FAX 310/277-7820

200 West 57th Street, Suite 900
New York, NY 10019
212/246-1030
FAX 212/246-1521

PARAMUSE ARTISTS ASSOCIATION
1414 Avenue of the Americas
New York, NY 10019
212/758-5055

THE PARKS AGENCY
138 East 16th St., Suite 5B
New York, NY 10003
212/254-9067

Richard Parks

THE PARNESS AGENCY
1424 4th Street, Suite 404
Santa Monica, CA 90401
310/319-1664
FAX 310/319-3743

Leslie Parness

THE PARTOS COMPANY
3630 Barham Blvd., Suite 2108
Los Angeles, CA 90068
213/876-5500

Walter Partos

BARRY PERELMAN AGENCY
9200 Sunset Blvd., Suite 531
Los Angeles, CA 90069
310/274-5999

PETERS, FRASER & DUNLOP
The Chambers, Chelsea Harbour
Lots Road
London, SW10 OXF, England
071/376-7676

PHOENIX LITERARY AGENCY
315 South F Street
Livingston, Montana 59047
406/222-2848

PLESHETTE & GREEN AGENCY
2700 North Beachwood Drive
Los Angeles, CA 90068
213/465-0428
FAX 213/465-6073

Lynn Pleshette
Richard Green

**PMA LITERARY & FILM
MANAGEMENT**
220 West 19th St., Suite 501
New York, NY 10011
212/929-1222

Peter Miller

BARRY POLLACK
9255 Sunset Blvd., Suite 404
Los Angeles, CA 90069
310/550-4525

PREFERRED ARTISTS
16633 Ventura Blvd., Suite 1421
Encino, CA 91436
818/990-0305

PREMIERE ARTISTS AGENCY
8899 Beverly Blvd., Suite 102
Los Angeles, CA 90048
310/271-1414
FAX 310/205-3981

Susan Sussman
John Ufland

JIM PREMINGER AGENCY
1650 Westwood Blvd., Suite 201
Los Angeles, CA 90024
310/475-9491

PRO MANAGEMENT*
11849 West Olympic Blvd., Suite 200
Los Angeles, CA 90064
310/478-5159
FAX 310/479-0617

Jonathan Baruch

R

THE RADMIN COMPANY*
260 S. Beverly Drive, 2nd Floor
Beverly Hills, CA 90212
310/274-9515

Linne Radmin

DOUGLAS RAE MANAGEMENT
28 Charing Cross Road
London, WC2 England
011/441/836-3903

RENAISSANCE-H.N. SWANSON
152 N. La Peer
Los Angeles, CA 90048
310/246-6000
FAX 310/246-1633

Joel Gotler
Irv Schwartz
Mark Jacobson
Alan Nevins

**THE RICHLAND/WUNSCH/HOHMAN
AGENCY**
9220 Sunset Blvd., Suite 311
Los Angeles, CA 90069
310/278-1955
FAX 310/278-1156

Daniel A. Richland
Joseph Richland
Robert J. Wunsch
Robert Hohman

RIX-UBELL MANAGEMENT*
1540 Oriole Lane
Los Angeles, CA 90069
310/859-9733

Brian Rix
Jane Ubell

RKS ENTERTAINMENT GROUP*
4283 Murietta Avenue, Suite 7
Sherman Oaks, CA 91423
818/788-3616

Randall K. Skolnik

THE ROBERTS COMPANY*
10345 W. Olympic Blvd., Penthouse
Los Angeles, CA 90064
310/552-7800
FAX 310/552-9324

Nancy Roberts

FLORA ROBERTS, INC.
157 West 57th Street
New York, NY 10019
212/355-4165

ROGERS & ASSOCIATES
3855 Lankershim Blvd.
North Hollywood, CA 91604
818/509-1010

Stephanie Rogers

THE MARION ROSENBERG OFFICE
8428 Melrose Place, Suite C
Los Angeles, CA 90069
213/653-7383

ROSENSTONE/WENDER
Three East 48th Street
New York, NY 10017
212/832-8330

Howard Rosenstone
Phyllis Wender

THE ROTHMAN AGENCY
8383 Wilshire Blvd., Suite 925
Beverly Hills, CA 90211
310/247-9898

Rob Rothman
Lucy Stutz

S

SANFORD-GROSS & ASSOCIATES
1015 Gayley Avenue, 3rd Floor
Los Angeles, CA 90024
310/208-2100
FAX 310/208-6704

Geoffrey Sanford
Brad Gross

THE SARNOFF COMPANY, INC.
3900 W. Alameda Ave., Suite 700
Burbank, CA 91505
818/972-1779

Jim Sarnoff

JACK SCAGNETTI AGENCY
5330 Lankershim Blvd., Suite 210
North Hollywood, CA 91601
818/762-3871

THE IRV SCHECHTER COMPANY
9300 Wilshire Blvd., Suite 400
Beverly Hills, CA 90212
310/278-8070
FAX 310/278-6058

SCHIOWITZ/CLAY/ROSE, INC.
8228 Sunset Blvd., Suite 212
Los Angeles, CA 90046
213/650-7300

Sheri Mann

**SUSAN SCHULMAN LITERARY
AGENCY, INC.**
454 West 44th Street
New York, NY 10036
212/713-1633
FAX 212/581-8830

THE HAROLD SCHWARTZ CO.
935 N. Croft Ave.
Los Angeles, CA 90069
213/650-8006

SELECT ARTISTS
337 West 43rd St., Suite1B
New York, NY 10036
212/586-4300

DAVID SHAPIRA & ASSOCIATES
15301 Ventura Blvd., Suite 345
Sherman Oaks, CA 91403
818/906-0322
FAX 818/783-2562

THE SHAPIRO/LICHTMAN AGENCY
8827 Beverly Blvd.
Los Angeles, CA 90048
310/859-8877
FAX 310/859-7153

Martin Shapiro
Bob Shapiro
Mark Lichtman

KEN SHERMAN & ASSOCIATES
9507 Santa Monica Blvd., Suite 211
Beverly Hills, CA 90210
310/273-8840

LINDA SIEFERT & ASSOCIATES
8A Brunswick Gardens
London W8 4AJ, England
011/441/229-5163

JEROME SIEGEL ASSOCIATES
7551 Sunset Blvd., Suite 203
Los Angeles, CA 90046
213/850-1275

**MICHAEL SIEGEL &
ASSOCIATES, INC.**
8929 Rosewood Avenue
Los Angeles, CA 90048
310/274-5222
FAX 310/274-4987

Michael Siegel
Judy Clain (NY)

THE SKOURAS AGENCY
725 Arizona Avenue, Suite 406
Santa Monica, CA 90401
310/395-9550

SUSAN SMITH & ASSOCIATES
121 N. San Vicente Blvd.
Beverly Hills, CA 90211
213/852-4777
FAX 213/658-7170

192 Lexington Ave.
New York, NY 10016
212/545-0500
FAX 212/545-7143

**SMITH/GOSNELL/NICHOLSON &
ASSOCIATES**
P.O. Box 1166
1294 Calle de Sevilla
Pacific Palisades, CA 90272
310/459-0307

Creighton Smith
Ray Gosnell
Skip Nicholson

STEVENS & ASSOCIATES
9454 Wilshire Blvd.
Beverly Hills, CA 90212
310/275-7541
FAX 310/275-5929

Neal Stevens

STONE MANNERS AGENCY
8091 Selma Ave.
Los Angeles, CA 90046
213/654-7575

Tim Stone
Scott Manners

T

THE TANTLEFF OFFICE
375 Greenwich St., Suite 700
New York, NY 10013
212/941-3939
FAX 212/941-3997

Jack Tantleff

**ROSLYN TARG LITERARY AGENCY,
INC.**
105 West 13th St.
New York, NY 10011
212/206-9390

3 ARTS ENTERTAINMENT*
7920 Sunset Blvd., Suite 350
Los Angeles, CA 90046
213/851-5700

PETER TURNER AGENCY
3000 Olympic Blvd., Suite 1438
Santa Monica, CA 90404
310/315-4772

CINDY TURTLE & ASSOCIATES
12456 Ventura Blvd., Suite 1
Studio City, CA 91604
818/506-6898
FAX 818/506-1723

TWENTIETH CENTURY ARTISTS
14724 Ventura Blvd., Suite 401
Sherman Oaks, CA 91403
818/788-5516
FAX 818/788-2070

U

UNITED TALENT AGENCY
9560 Wilshire Blvd., 5th Floor
Beverly Hills, CA 90212
310/273-6700
FAX 310/247-1111

V

ANNETTE VAN DUREN AGENCY
925 N. Sweetzer Ave., Suite 12
Los Angeles, CA 90069
213/650-3643
FAX 213/654-3893

W

**WALLERSTEIN-KAPPELMAN
AGENCY**
6399 Wilshire Blvd., Suite 426
Los Angeles, CA 90048
213/782-0225

Michelle Wallerstein
Lee Kappelman

WARDEN, WHITE & KANE, INC.
8444 Wilshire Blvd., 4th Floor
Beverly Hills, CA 90211
213/852-1028
FAX 213/852-0843

David Warden
Steve N. White
Michael Kane

SANDRA WATT & ASSOCIATES
8033 Sunset Blvd., Suite 4053
Los Angeles, CA 90046
213/851-1021

A
G
E
N
T
S

&

M
A
N
A
G
E
R
S

HILARY WAYNE AGENCY
8670 Wilshire Blvd., Suite 233
Beverly Hills, CA 90211
310/289-6186
FAX 310/855-0562

SOLOMON WEINGARTEN & ASSOCIATES
11110 Ohio Ave., Suite 108
Los Angeles, CA 90025
310/479-4706
FAX 310/478-7339

WILE ENTERPRISES
2730 Wilshire Blvd., Suite 500
Santa Monica, CA 90403
213/828-9768

Shelly Wile

THE WILHITE AGENCY
15237 Sunset Blvd., Suite 131
Pacific Palisades, CA 90272
310/459-0627

Patricia Wilhite

WRIGHT CONCEPT TALENT AGENCY
1811 West Burbank Blvd., Suite 201
Burbank, CA 91506
818/954-8943

Marcie Wright

WRITERS & ARTISTS AGENCY
924 Westwood Blvd., Suite 900
Los Angeles, CA 90024
310/824-6300
FAX 310/824-6343

70 West 36th St., Suite 501
New York, NY 10018
212/947-8765

★ ★ ★

ACADEMY AWARDS
1960-1993

★★ = winner in category

1960

Original Screenplay

THE APARTMENT .... Billy Wilder, I.A.L. Diamond ★★
THE ANGRY SILENCE .... Richard Gregson, Michael Craig,
Bryan Forbes
THE FACTS OF LIFE .... Norman Panama, Melvin Frank
HIROSHIMA, MON AMOUR .... Marguerite Duras
NEVER ON SUNDAY ....Jules Dassin

Adaptation

ELMER GANTRY .... Richard Brooks ★★
INHERIT THE WIND .... Nathan E. Douglas,
Harold Jacob Smith
SONS AND LOVERS .... Gavin Lambert, T.E.B. Clarke
THE SUNDOWNERS .... Isobel Lennart
TUNES OF GLORY .... James Kennaway

1961

Original Screenplay

SPLENDOR IN THE GRASS .... William Inge ★★
BALLAD OF A SOLDIER .... Valentin Yoshov,
Grigori Chukhrai
GENERAL DELLA ROVERE ......Sergio Amidei, Diego Fabbri,
Indro Montanelli
LA DOLCI VITA .... Federico Fellini, Tullio Pinelli,
Ennio Flaiano,Brunello Rondi
LOVER COME BACK .... Stanley Shapiro, Paul Henning

Adaptation

JUDGMENT AT NUREMBERG...................... Abby Mann ★★
BREAKFAST AT TIFFANY'S .... George Axelrod
THE GUNS OF NAVARONE .... Carl Foreman
THE HUSTLER .... Sidney Carroll, Robert Rossen
WEST SIDE STORY .... Ernest Lehman

1962

Original Screenplay

DIVORCE—ITALIAN STYLE .... Ennio de Concini,
Alfredo Giannetti, Pietro Germi ★★
FREUD...................... Charles Kaufman, Wolfgang Reinhardt
LAST YEAR AT MARIENBAD .... Alain Robbe-Grillet
THAT TOUCH OF MINK ...... Stanley Shapiro, Nate Monaster
THROUGH A GLASS DARKLY .... Ingmar Bergman

Adaptation

TO KILL A MOCKINGBIRD .... Horton Foote ★★
DAVID AND LISA .... Eleanor Perry
LAWRENCE OF ARABIA .... Robert Bolt
LOLITA... Vladimir Nabokov
THE MIRACLE WORKER .... William Gibson

1963

Original Screenplay

HOW THE WEST WAS WON .... James R. Webb ★★
AMERICA, AMERICA .... Elia Kazan
FEDERICO FELLINI'S 8 1/2 .... Federico Fellini,
Ennio Flaiano,Tullio Pinelli, Brunello Rondi
THE FOUR DAYS OF NAPLES .... Massino Franciosa,
Pasquael Festa Campanile,Nanni Loy,
Vasco Pratolini, Carlo Bernari
LOVE WITH THE PROPER STRANGER .... Arnold Schulman

Adaptation

TOM JONES .... John Osborne ★★
CAPTAIN NEWMAN, M.D. .... Richard L. Breen,
Phoebe and Henry Ephron
HUD ....Irving Ravetch, Harriet Frank Jr.
LILIES OF THE FIELD .... James Poe
SUNDAYS AND CYBELE .... Serge Bourguigon,
Antoine Tudal

1964

Original Screenplay

FATHER GOOSE .... S.H. Barnett, Peter Stone,
Frank Tarloff ★★
A HARD DAY'S NIGHT .... Alun Owen
ONE POTATO, TWO POTATO .... Orville H. Hampton,
Raphael Hayes
THAT MAN FROM RIO .... Jean-Paul Rappeneau,
Ariane Mnouchkine,
Daniel Boulanger, Philippe de Broca

Adaptation

BECKET .... Edward Anhalt ★★
DR. STRANGELOVE OR: HOW I LEARNED
TO STOPWORRYING
AND LOVE THE BOMB ...... Stanley Kubrick, Peter George,
Terry Southern
MARY POPPINS .... Bill Walsh, Don DaGradi
MY FAIR LADY .... Alan Jay Lerner
ZORBA THE GREEK............................... Michael Cacoyannis

1965

Original Screenplay

DARLING .... Frederic Raphael ★★
CASANOVA '70 .... Age Scarpelli, Mario Monicelli,
Tonino Guerra, Giorgio Salvioni,
Susi Cecchi D'Amico
THOSE MAGNIFICENT MEN IN
THEIR FLYING MACHINES ...... Jack Davies, Ken Annakin
THE TRAIN .... Franklin Coen, Frank Davis
THE UMBRELLAS OF CHERBOURG .... Jacques Demy

Adaptation

DOCTOR ZHIVAGO .... Robert Bolt ★★
CAT BALLOU .... Walter Newman, Frank R. Pierson
THE COLLECTOR .... Stanley Mann, John Kohn
SHIP OF FOOLS .... Abby Mann
A THOUSAND CLOWNS .... Herb Gardner

1966

Original Screenplay

A MAN AND A WOMAN .... Claude Lelouch,
Pierre Uytterhoeven ★★
BLOW-UP .... Michelangelo Antonioni, Tonino Guerra,
Edward Bond
THE FORTUNE COOKIE .... Billy Wilder, I.A.L. Diamond
KHARTOUM .... Robert Ardrey
THE NAKED PREY .... Clint Johnston, Don Peters

Adaptation

A MAN FOR ALL SEASONS .... Robert Bolt ★★
ALFIE .... Bill Naughton
THE PROFESSIONALS .... Richard Brooks
THE RUSSIANS ARE COMING THE
RUSSIANS ARE COMING .... William Rose
WHO'S AFRAID OF VIRGINIA WOOLF? .... Ernest Lehman

1967

Original Screenplay

GUESS WHO'S COMING TO DINNER? .... William Rose ★★
BONNIE AND CLYDE .... David Newman, Robert Benton
DIVORCE AMERICAN STYLE .... Norman Lear
LA GUERRE EST FINIE .... Jorge Semprun
TWO FOR THE ROAD .... Frederic Raphael

Adaptation

IN THE HEAT OF THE NIGHT .... Stirling Silliphant ★★
COOL HAND LUKE .... Donn Pearce, Frank R. Pierson
THE GRADUATE .... Calder Willingham, Buck Henry
IN COLD BLOOD .... Richard Brooks
ULYSSES .... Joseph Strick, Fred Haines

1968

Original Screenplay

THE PRODUCERS .... Mel Brooks ★★
THE BATTLE OF ALGIERS .... Franco Solinas,
Gillo Pontecorvo
FACES .... John Cassavetes
HOT MILLIONS .... Ira Wallach, Peter Ustinov
2001: A SPACE ODYSSEY .... Stanley Kubrick,
Arthur C. Clarke

Adaptation

THE LION IN WINTER .... James Goldman ★★
THE ODD COUPLE .... Neil Simon
OLIVER! .... Vernon Harris
RACHEL, RACHEL .... Stewart Stern
ROSEMARY'S BABY .... Roman Polanski

1969

Original Screenplay

BUTCH CASSIDY AND THE
SUNDANCE KID .... William Goldman ★★
BOB & CAROL & TED & ALICE .... Paul Mazursky,
Larry Tucker
THE DAMNED .... Nicola Badalucco, Enrico Medioli,
Luchino Visconti
EASY RIDER .... Peter Fonda, Dennis Hopper,
Terry Southern
THE WILD BUNCH .... Walon Green, Roy N. Sickner,
Sam Peckinpah

Adaptation

MIDNIGHT COWBOY .... Waldo Salt ★★
ANNE OF THE THOUSAND DAYS .... John Hale,
Bridget Boland, Richard Sokolove
GOODBYE COLUMBUS .... Arnold Schulman
THEY SHOOT HORSES, DON'T THEY? .... James Poe,
Robert E. Thompson
Z .... Jorge Semprun, Costa-Gavras

1970

Original Screenplay

PATTON .... Francis Ford Coppola, Edmund H. North ★★
FIVE EASY PIECES .... Bob Rafelson, Adrien Joyce
JOE .... Norman Wexler
LOVE STORY .... Erich Segal
MY NIGHT AT MAUD'S .... Eric Rohmer

Adaptation

M*A*S*H .... Ring Lardner, Jr. ★★
AIRPORT .... George Seaton
I NEVER SANG FOR MY FATHER .... Robert Anderson
LOVERS AND OTHER STRANGERS .... Renee Taylor,
Joseph Bologna,
David Zelag Goodman
WOMEN IN LOVE .... Larry Kramer

1971

Original Screenplay

THE HOSPITAL .... Paddy Chayefsky ★★
INVESTIGATION OF A CITIZEN
ABOVE SUSPICION .... Elio Petri, Ugo Pirro
KLUTE .... Andy and Dave Lewis
SUMMER OF '42 .... Herman Raucher
SUNDAY, BLOODY SUNDAY .... Penelope Gilliatt

Adaptation

THE FRENCH CONNECTION .... Ernest Tidyman ★★
A CLOCKWORK ORANGE .... Stanley Kubrick
THE CONFORMIST .... Bernardo Bertolucci
THE GARDEN OF THE FINZI-CONTINIS .... Ugo Pirro,
Vittorio Bonicelli
THE LAST PICTURE SHOW .... Larry McMurtry,
Peter Bogdanovich

1972

Original Screenplay

THE CANDIDATE .... Jeremy Larner ★★
THE DISCREET CHARM OF THE
    BOURGEOISE.............. Luis Bunuel, Jean-Claude Carriere
LADY SINGS THE BLUES .... Terence McCloy, Chris Clark,
    Suzanne de Passe
MURMUR OF THE HEART .... Louis Malle
YOUNG WINSTON .... Carl Foreman

Adaptation

THE GODFATHER .... Mario Puzo, Francis Ford Coppola ★★
CABARET .... Jay Presson Allen
THE EMIGRANTS .... Jan Troell, Bengt Forslund
PETE'N'TILLIE .... Julis J. Epstein
SOUNDER .... Lonne Elder III

1973

Original Screenplay

THE STING .... David S. Ward ★★
AMERICAN GRAFFITI ....George Lucas, Gloria Katz,
    Willard Huyck
CRIES AND WHISPERS .... Ingmar Bergman
SAVE THE TIGER .... Steve Shagan
A TOUCH OF CLASS .... Melvin Frank, Jack Rose

Adaptation

THE EXORCIST .... William Peter Blatty ★★
THE LAST DETAIL .... Robert Towne
THE PAPER CHASE .... James Bridges
PAPER MOON .... Alvin Sargent
SERPICO .... Waldo Salt, Norman Wexler

1974

Original Screenplay

CHINATOWN .... Robert Towne ★★
ALICE DOESN'T LIVE HERE ANYMORE ..... Robert Getchell
THE CONVERSATION .... Francis Ford Coppola
DAY FOR NIGHT .... Francois Truffaut, Jean-Louis Richard,
    Suzanne Schiffman
HARRY AND TONTO .... Paul Mazursky, Josh Greenfeld

Adaptation

THE GODFATHER PART II .... Francis Ford Coppola,
    Mario Puzo ★★
THE APPRENTICESHIP OF
    DUDDY KRAVITZ .... Mordecai Richler, Lionel Chetwynd
LENNY .... Julian Barry
MURDER ON THE ORIENT EXPRESS .... Paul Dehn
YOUNG FRANKENSTIEN .... Gene Wilder, Mel Brooks

1975

Original Screenplay

DOG DAY AFTERNOON .... Frank R. Pierson ★★
AMARCORD .... Federico Fellini, Tonino Guerra
AND NOW MY LOVE ... Claude Lelouch, Pierre Uytterhoeven
LIES MY FATHER TOLD ME .... Ted Allan
SHAMPOO .... Robert Towne, Warren Beatty

Adaptation

ONE FLEW OVER THE
    CUCKOO'S NEST ..... Lawrence Hauben, Bo Goldman ★★
BARRY LYNDON .... Stanley Kubrick
THE MAN WHO WOULD BE KING .... John Huston,
    Gladys Hill
SCENT OF A WOMAN .... Rugero Maccari, Dino Risi
THE SUNSHINE BOYS .... Neil Simon

1976

Original Screenplay

NETWORK .... Paddy Chayefsky ★★
COUSIN, COUSINE .... Jean-Charles Tachella,
    Daniele Thompson
THE FRONT .... Walter Bernstein
ROCKY .... Sylvester Stallone
SEVEN BEAUTIES .... Lina Wertmuller

Adaptation

ALL THE PRESIDENT'S MEN .... William Goldman ★★
BOUND FOR GLORY .... Robert Getchell
FELLINI'S CASANOVA .... Federico Fellini,
    Bernardino Zapponi
THE SEVEN-PER-CENT SOLUTION .... Nicholas Meyer
VOYAGE OF THE DAMNED .... Steve Shagan, David Butler

1977

Original Screenplay

ANNIE HALL .... Woody Allen, Marshall Brickman ★★
THE GOODBYE GIRL .... Neil Simon
THE LATE SHOW .... Robert Benton
STAR WARS .... George Lucas
THE TURNING POINT .... Arthur Laurents

Adaptation

JULIA .... Alvin Sargent ★★
EQUUS .... Peter Shaffer
I NEVER PROMISED YOU A
    ROSE GARDEN .... Gavin Lambert, Lewis John Carlino
OH, GOD! .... Larry Gelbart
THAT OBSCURE OBJECT OF DESIRE .... Luis Bunuel,
    Jean-Claude Carriere

1978

Original Screenplay

COMING HOME .... Nancy Dowd, Waldo Salt,
    Robert C. Jones ★★
AUTUMN SONATA .... Ingmar Bergman
THE DEER HUNTER ....Michael Cimino, Deric Washburn,
    Louis Garfinkle, Quinn K. Redeker
INTERIORS .... Woody Allen
AN UNMARRIED WOMAN .... Paul Mazursky

Adaptation

MIDNIGHT EXPRESS .... Oliver Stone ★★
BLOODBROTHERS .... Walter Newman
CALIFORNIA SUITE .... Neil Simon
HEAVEN CAN WAIT .... Elaine May, Warren Beatty
SAME TIME, NEXT YEAR .... Bernard Slade

1979

Original Screenplay

BREAKING AWAY .... Steve Tesich ★★
ALL THAT JAZZ .... Robert Alan Arthur, Bob Fosse
....AND JUSTICE FOR ALL ..... Valerie Curtin, Barry Levinson
THE CHINA SYNDROME .... Mike Gray, T.S. Cook,
James Bridges
MANHATTAN .... Woody Allen, Marshall Brickman

Adaptation

KRAMER VS. KRAMER .... Robert Benton ★★
APOCALYPSE NOW .... John Milius, Francis Coppola
LA CAGE AUX FOLLES ..... Francis Veber, Edouard Molinaro,
Marcello Danon, Jean Poiret
A LITTLE ROMANCE .... Allan Burns
NORMA RAE .... Irving Ravetch, Harriet Frank Jr.

1980

Original Screenplay

MELVIN AND HOWARD .... Bo Goldman ★★
BRUBAKER .... W.D. Richter, Arthur Ross
FAME .... Christopher Gore
MON ONCLE D'AMERIQUE .... Jean Gruault
PRIVATE BENJAMIN .... Nancy Meyers, Charles Shyer,
Harvey Miller

Adaptation

ORDINARY PEOPLE .... Alvin Sargent ★★
BREAKER MORANT .... Jonathan Hardy, David Stevens,
Bruce Beresford
COAL MINER'S DAUGHTER .... Tom Rickman
THE ELEPHANT MAN ...... Christopher Devore, Eric Bergren,
David Lynch
THE STUNT MAN .... Lawrence B. Marcus, Richard Rush

1981

Original Screenplay

CHARIOTS OF FIRE .... Colin Welland ★★
ABSENCE OF MALICE .... Kurt Luedtke
ARTHUR .... Steve Gordon
ATLANTIC CITY .... John Guare
REDS .... Warren Beatty, Trevor Griffiths

Adaptation

ON GOLDEN POND .... Ernest Thompson ★★
THE FRENCH LEIUTENANT'S WOMAN .... Harold Pinter
PENNIES FROM HEAVEN .... Dennis Potter
PRINCE OF THE CITY .... Jay Presson Allen, Sidney Lumet
RAGTIME .... Michael Weller

1982

Original Screenplay

GANDHI .... John Briley ★★
DINER .... Barry Levinson
E.T.-THE EXTRATERRESTRIAL .... Melissa Mathison
AN OFFICER AND A GENTLEMAN ..... Douglas Day Stewart
TOOTSIE .... Don McGuire, Larry Gelbart, Murray Schisgal

Adaptation

MISSING .... Donald Stewart, Costa-Gavras ★★
DAS BOOT .... Wolfgang Petersen
SOPHIE'S CHOICE .... Alan J. Pakula
THE VERDICT .... David Mamet
VICTOR/VICTORIA .... Blake Edwards

1983

Original Screenplay

TENDER MERCIES .... Horton Foote ★★
THE BIG CHILL .... Lawrence Kasdan, Barbara Benedek
FANNY & ALEXANDER .... Ingmar Bergman
SILKWOOD .... Nora Ephron, Alice Arlen
WARGAMES .... Lawrence Lasker, Walter F. Parkes

Adaptation

BETRAYAL .... Harold Pinter
THE DRESSER .... Ronald Harwood
EDUCATING RITA .... Willy Russell
REUBEN, REUBEN .... Julius J. Epstein
TERMS OF ENDEARMENT .... James L. Brooks ★★

1984

Original Screenplay

PLACES IN THE HEART .... Robert Benton ★★
BEVERLY HILLS COP .... Daniel Petrie Jr., Danilo Bach
BROADWAY DANNY ROSE .... Woody Allen
EL NORTE .... Gregory Nava, Anna Thomas
SPLASH .... Lowell Ganz, Babaloo Mandel,
Bruce Jay Friedman, Brian Grazer

Adaptation

AMADEUS .... Peter Shaffer ★★
GREYSTOKE: THE LEGEND OF TARZAN,
LORD OF THE APES .... P.H. Vazak, Michael Austin
THE KILLING FIELDS .... Bruce Robinson
A PASSAGE TO INDIA .... David Lean
A SOLDIER'S STORY .... Charles Fuller

1985

Original Screenplay

WITNESS .... Earl W. Wallace, William Kelley,
Pamela Wallace ★★
BACK TO THE FUTURE .... Robert Zemeckis, Bob Gale
BRAZIL .... Terry Gilliam, Tom Stoppard, Charles McKeown
THE OFFICIAL STORY .... Luis Puenzo, Aida Bortnik
THE PURPLE ROSE OF CAIRO .... Woody Allen

Adaptation

OUT OF AFRICA .... Kurt Luedtke ★★
THE COLOR PURPLE .... Menno Meyjes
KISS OF THE SPIDER WOMAN .... Leonard Schrader
PRIZZI'S HONOR .... Richard Condon, Janet Roach
THE TRIP TO BOUNTIFUL .... Horton Foote

1986

Original Screenplay

HANNAH AND HER SISTERS .... Woody Allen ★★
"CROCODILE" DUNDEE .... Paul Hogan, Ken Shadie,
John Cornell
MY BEAUTIFUL LAUNDRETTE .... Hanif Kureishi
PLATOON .... Oliver Stone
SALVADOR .... Oliver Stone, Richard Boyle

Adaptation

A ROOM WITH A VIEW .... Ruth Prawer Jhabvala ★★
CHILDREN OF A LESSER GOD .... Hesper Anderson,
Mark Medoff
THE COLOR OF MONEY .... Richard Price
CRIMES OF THE HEART .... Beth Henley
STAND BY ME .... Raynold Gideon, Bruce A. Evans

1987

Original Screenplay

MOONSTRUCK .... John Patrick Shanley ★★
AU REVOIR, LES ENFANTS .... Louis Malle
BROADCAST NEWS .... James L. Brooks
HOPE AND GLORY ....John Boorman
RADIO DAYS ....Woody Allen

Adaptation

THE LAST EMPEROR .... Bernardo Bertolucci,
Mark Peploe ★★
THE DEAD .... Tony Huston
FATAL ATTRACTION .... James Dearden
FULL METAL JACKET ....Stanley Kubrick, Michael Herr,
Gustav Hasford
MY LIFE AS A DOG .... Lasse Hallstrom, Reidar Jonsson,
Brasse Brannstrom, Per Berglund

1988

Original Screenplay

RAIN MAN .... Ronald Bass, Barry Morrow ★★
BIG .... Gary Ross, Anne Speilberg
BULL DURHAM .... Ron Shelton
A FISH CALLED WANDA .... John Cleese, Charles Crichton
RUNNING ON EMPTY .... Naomi Foner

Adaptation

DANGEROUS LIAISONS .... Christopher Hampton ★★
THE ACCIDENTAL TOURIST .... Frank Galati,
Lawrence Kasdan
GORILLAS IN THE MIST .... Anna Hamilton Phelan,
Tab Murphy
LITTLE DORRIT .... Christine Edzard
THE UNBEARABLE LIGHTNESS
OF BEING............... Jean-Claude Carriere, Philip Kaufman

1989

Original Screenplay

DEAD POETS SOCIETY .... Tom Schulman ★★
CRIMES AND MISDEMEANORS .... Woody Allen
DO THE RIGHT THING... Spike Lee
SEX, LIES AND VIDEOTAPE .... Steven Soderbergh
WHEN HARRY MET SALLY... .... Nora Ephron

Adaptation

DRIVING MISS DAISY .... Alfred Uhry ★★
BORN ON THE FOURTH OF JULY .... Oliver Stone,
Ron Kovic
ENEMIES, A LOVE STORY .... Roger L. Simon,
Paul Mazursky
FIELD OF DREAMS ....Phil Alden Robinson
MY LEFT FOOT .... Jim Sheridan, Shane Connaughton

1990

Original Screenplay

GHOST .... Bruce Joel Rubin ★★
ALICE .... Woody Allen
AVALON .... Barry Levinson
GREEN CARD .... Peter Weir
METROPOLITAN .... Whit Stillman

Adaptation

DANCES WITH WOLVES .... Michael Blake ★★
AWAKENINGS .... Steven Zaillian
GOODFELLAS .... Nicholas Pileggi, Martin Scorcese
THE GRIFTERS .... Donald E. Westlake
REVERSAL OF FORTUNE .... Nicholas Kazan

1991

Original Screenplay

THELMA AND LOUISE .... Callie Khouri ★★
BOYZ N THE HOOD .... John Singleton
BUGSY .... James Toback
THE FISHER KING .... Richard La Gravanese
GRAND CANYON .... Lawrence Kasdan, Meg Kasdan

Adaptation

THE SILENCE OF THE LAMBS .... Ted Tally ★★
EUROPA EUROPA .... Agnieska Holland
FRIED GREEN TOMATOES ..... Fannie Flagg, Carol Sobieski
JFK .... Zachary Sklar, Oliver Stone
THE PRINCE OF TIDES ....Pat Conroy, Becky Johnston

1992

Original Screenplay

THE CRYING GAME .... Neil Jordan ★★
HUSBANDS AND WIVES .... Woody Allen
LORENZO'S OIL .... Nick Enright, George Miller
PASSION FISH .... John Sayles
UNFORGIVEN .... David Webb Peoples

Adaptation

HOWARD'S END ....Ruth Prawer Jhabvala ★★
ENCHANTED APRIL .... Peter Barnes
THE PLAYER .... Michael Tolkin
A RIVER RUNS THROUGH IT .... Richard Friedenberg
SCENT OF A WOMAN .... Bo Goldman

A
C
A
D
E
M
Y

A
W
A
R
D
S

1993

Original Screenplay

THE PIANO .... Jane Campion ★★
DAVE .... Gary Ross
IN THE LINE OF FIRE .... Jeff Maguire
PHILADELPHIA .... Ron Nyswaner
SLEEPLESS IN SEATTLE ...... Nora Ephron, David S. Ward,
Jeff Arch

Adaptation

SCHINDLER'S LIST .... Steven Zaillian★★
THE AGE OF INNOCENCE .... Jay Cocks, Martin Scorcese
IN THE NAME OF THE FATHER .... Terry George,
Jim Sheridan
THE REMAINS OF THE DAY .... Ruth Prawer Jhabvala
SHADOWLANDS .... William Nicholson

★ ★ ★

CALLING ALL CREDITS!

The **Sixth Edition of FILM WRITERS GUIDE** is now in preparation. It will be published in the winter of 1996. We update our records continuously. If you qualify to be listed (please read HOW TO USE THIS BOOK for qualifications), then send us your listing information **ASAP**. All listings are free.
Photocopy the form on the next page.

Our editorial deadline is October 1, 1995
(Please do not wait until then.)

Send all listing information to:

FILM WRITERS GUIDE
Sixth Edition
2337 Roscomare Road, Suite Nine
Los Angeles, CA 90077
310/471-8066 or 1/800-FILMBKS

If you are a director (*film or television*), television writer, film actor or actress, film composer, cinematographer, production designer, costume designer, editor, film producer, agent, casting director, studio personnel, special effects person or stunt coordinator and want to find out about getting listed in our other directories, call **310/471-8066** or write to:

LONE EAGLE PUBLISHING COMPANY
2337 Roscomare Road, Suite Nine
Los Angeles, CA 90077-1851
310/471-8066 • 310/471-4969 (FAX) • 1/800-FILMBKS

• ALL LISTINGS ARE FREE •

Ask for *Lone Eagle* books at these fine bookstores.

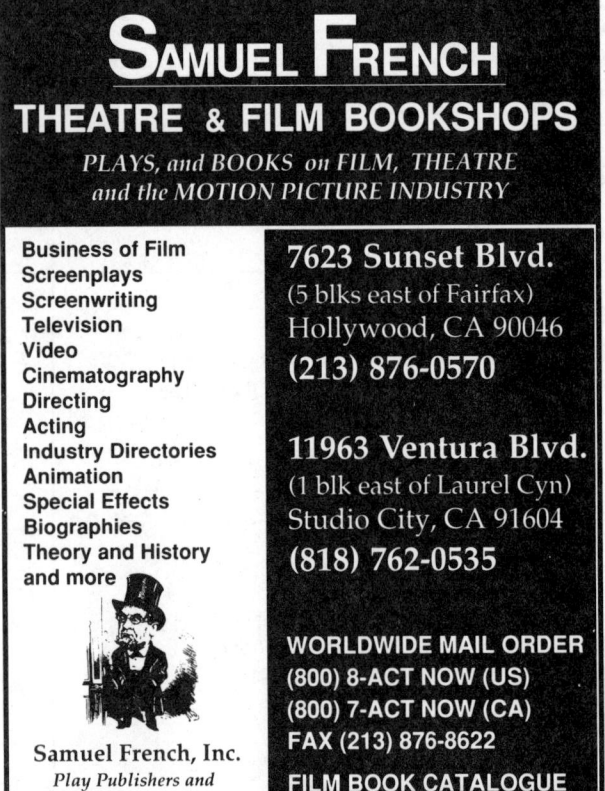

The SIXTH EDITION of

FILM WRITERS
GUIDE

ALL LISTINGS ARE FREE.

DON'T BE LEFT OUT!!! Include your *FREE* listing (read *How To Use This Book* for qualifications) by filling out and returning this form to us *IMMEDIATELY. (Photocopy as many times as necessary).*

Guilds
- ❏ WGA
- ❏ DGA
- ❏ SAG
- ❏ Other

PERSONAL INFORMATION

Name (as you prefer to be listed)

Company

Address

City/State/Zip

Area Code/Telephone

Birth Date & Place
❏ Home   ❏ Business

❏ Please list my home address and phone number in your directory.

REPRESENTATIVE'S INFORMATION

Agent ❏   Personal Manager ❏   Attorney ❏
Business Manager ❏   Other ❏
(List as many representatives as you would like. Continue listing on reverse, if necessary.)

Name (as you prefer to be listed)

Company

Address

City/State/Zip

Area Code/Telephone

CREDITS (*Attach a separate sheet, if necessary*)

List your credits as follows, noting title, type of work, distribution company, year of release, alternate titles in parentheses, Academy nominations/awards for your work, and country of origin.

    JFK (Feature) Warner Bros., 1991, w/Zachary Sklar, directed, Academy Award Nomination
    THE SILENCE OF THE LAMBS (Feature) Orion, 1991, Academy Award Win
    THE NIGHT OF THE SHOOTING STARS (LA NOTTE DI SANS LORENZO) (Feature) United Artists Classics, 1981,
        w/Vittorio Taviani, co-directed
    THE WATER ENGINE (Cable Telefeature) Brandman Productions/Amblin Television, 1992, from his play
    EDMOND (Play)   also screenplay

List your unproduced credits (movies and plays) as follows:
    GREED (screenplay) w/Lowell Ganz

MAIL form IMMEDIATELY to
FILM WRITERS GUIDE   **Sixth Edition**
2337 Roscomare Road, Suite Nine
Los Angeles, CA 90077
310/471-8066 or 310/471-4969 (FAX)

Deadline:
October 1, 1995

Questions ???
Problems ???
Call 310/471-8066

INDEX OF ADVERTISERS

A special thanks to our advertisers whose support makes it possible to bring you the fifth edition of **FILM WRITERS Guide.**

ABOUT THE EDITOR

SUSAN AVALLONE hails from East Brunswick, New Jersey, daughter of novelist Michael and activist Fran, sister of director David. She has a masters in Library Science and was a magazine editor at *Library Journal.*

After working in television and feature development, Susan is now a screenwriter, listed in these very pages (on the advice of her agent!). She resides in lovely Sherman Oaks with her husband Carr D'Angelo and cats Audrey, Zelda and Nathan Junior.